Northern Circuit

Directory 1876 – 2004

Published on behalf of the Northern Circuit by The Bluecoat Press, Liverpool
Book design by MARCH Graphic Design Studio, Liverpool
Printed by Ashford Colour Press Ltd, Gosport, Hampshire

ISBN 1904438 24 5

Acknowledgements I am grateful to the following who arranged for the distribution, completion and collection of over 1000 questionnaires and collected advance orders for the book: Farooq Ahmed, Rob Altham, Steven Ball, Ashley Bames, Karl Berry, Laura Briggs, Peter Buckley, Philip Butler, Philip Cattan, Brendan Carville, Jeffrey Clarke, Yvonne Coppell, Nicola Daley, Alex Frodsham, Suzanne Goddard, Matthew Hall (Smith), David Hernandez, Richard Heap, Peter Horgan, Richard Hunt, Nick Johnson, Jo Kelly, Andrew Loveridge, Joanna Mallon, Richard Oughton, Nigel Power, Damien Sanders, Barrie Searle, Malcolm Sharpe, Sarah Spear, David Temkin and Ian Unsworth.

The Law Lists from 1876 form the basis of the Directory. John Murphy, the Northern Circuit Librarian, Sally Phillips and Nigel Ogilvie and others at the Royal Courts of Justice Library kindly arranged for me to have the Law Lists in batches of five years, so that I could work at home. That made my task much easier. Guy Holborn, the Librarian at Lincoln's Inn has been very supportive. He has sent me much useful material and his, 'Sources of Biographical Information on Past Lawyers' has been invaluable.

My thanks to the Northern Circuit for financing this project and, in particular, to the immediate past Leader, David Steer QC, for enthusiastic support and encouragement throughout his term of office. Susan Chisholme, the Circuit Administrative Secretary, has been a great help.

I hope the Directory has been enhanced by the Grimsdale cartoons and the Burke (senior and junior) sketches and by the many photographs. I have acknowledged the following photographers by initials and they have my thanks: Richard Bingham (RB), Denis Clark (DC), Harold Singer (HS), William George (WG), Terry Mealey (TM), Raymond Farley (RF), Liverpool Daily Post & Echo (LDPE), Lancashire Evening Post (LEP), Universal Pictorial Agency (UPA), Manchester Evening News (MEN) and John Mills Photography (JMP). My photographs are marked (DL). The remainder are without initials because I have been unable to trace the photographer. Sketches: Kenneth Burke (KB), Judge John Burke QC (JB), all other sketches are by Frederick Grimsdale.

Brendan McCormack is first and foremost a classical guitarist, but his computer wizardry and the expertise of my son Christopher enabled me to overcome two badly behaved computers.

Finally, I thank my wife Ann and my sons, Christopher and Peter for tolerating this full blown obsession for the past eight years.

Common Abbreviations

G	Grays Inn
I	Inner Temple
L	Lincolns Inn
M	Middle Temple
AAS	Admitted as a student
ETC	Elected to Circuit
Prop	Proposer
Sec	Seconder. Unless otherwise stated the Seconder is pupil master
WW	Who's Who
DNB	Dictionary of National Biography
Foster	Foster's Men at the Bar
Simpson	Biographical Dictionary of the Common Law
Schofield	Dictionary of Legal Biography

NORTHERN CIRCUIT

DIRECTORY 1876 – 2004

JUDGE DAVID LYNCH

For Brian & Pam Gill
with best wishes
Ann & David Lynch
1st September 2006

The Bluecoat Press

Contents

(RB)

The Rt Hon. Lord Justice Rose in 1988.

Foreword

It is a privilege for me, from the pantheon of well over 4000 men and women catalogued in these pages, to be asked to write this Foreword; and it is flattering to imagine that anyone might recognize me today from the youthful image opposite.

This is a marvellous work, eight years in the making. Every page speaks of the dedication, industry, attention to detail and love of the Northern Circuit which David Lynch and those helping him brought to the task.

The result is a unique, comprehensive and up-to-date work of reference about the people who have underpinned the administration of justice in the North West over a span of almost 130 years. It briefly chronicles the lives of barristers who have given the Circuit its resilient existence to date and its expectation of a vigorous future. Many others who have played important parts in the delivery of justice are listed. Chief Probation Officers, Presidents of Local Law Societies, Prison Governors, Professors of Law, Justices Clerks and barrister's clerks.

The Directory is, however, much more than a reference book. Its pages are enlivened by photographs, sketches and anecdotes which exude an atmosphere of professional commitment, integrity, comradeship and fun which, together, provide the lifeblood of this greatest of Circuits.

I warmly commend this book to all lawyers and non-lawyers who seek a flavour of what it means to belong to and play a part in one of our great national institutions, the Northern Circuit.

The Rt Hon. Lord Justice Rose
The Vice-President, Court of Appeal, Criminal Division

To His Honour Sir Sanderson Temple MBE, QC
Recorder of Liverpool 1978-1991, Northern Circuiteer

Introduction

This Directory had a very modest beginning. Some time ago the Circuit Judges at Liverpool were trying to record the names of the more recent Recorders of the City. We were unable to recall them all so I went to Sandy Temple (to whom the book is dedicated) who, as one would expect, was able to fill in the gaps immediately. I was sufficiently interested to go on to research the Recorders of Manchester and Preston. Matters quickly got out of hand and eight years later we have the Directory of the Northern Circuit, 1876-2004.

I had two reasons for compiling this book. Firstly, it was a way of repaying the kindnesses I have received from countless members of this Circuit over the past 35 years and secondly, I felt it was important to preserve the history of this great Circuit for the new entrants. If information is not recorded in time, it is lost. My researches have produced for the Circuit records, 30 lever arch files of completed questionnaires, letters and photographs.

Essentially the work is in two parts. There are chronological lists of all Northern Circuit office holders with lists of all those who have assisted the administration of justice in the North West. The main section is an A-Z of every judge and barrister on the Circuit commencing with the death, in 1876, of the former Liverpool Stipendiary Magistrate, Thomas James Hall, who was born in 1788 to the 11 elected at Liverpool on 17 December 2004, a total 3417 Circuiteers. Those people marked * are Honorary Members of the Circuit; either members of the Bar who have come to us as a judge from another circuit, or judges appointed to sit on Circuit who were formerly solicitors.

I accept sole responsibility for any errors or omissions. I hope I have kept them to a minimum. I expect to publish a supplement every five years. To enable me to do that, please write to me with any corrections and update me on every aspect of Circuit life.

Judge David Lynch
Queen Elizabeth II Law Courts
Derby Square
Liverpool L2 IX
31st January 2005

1923 Northern Circuit Memorial 'They Shall Shine Like Stars'

1914-1918

Hon E J Kay-Shuttleworth
N Lisbona
H Lumb
H C Maclean
G Parker
H M Robertson
J W Scott
H C Shutt
P Walton
J H Whitworth
F E Bodel
B Bradshaw
T G Brocklebank
H T Cawley
G H Cohen
J L W Collinson
T G R Dehn
Henry, Second Lord Gorell
W H Hall
A Mc W L Johnston
W M Langdon

1939-1945

Patrick Vaughan Anthony
Sydney Edward Ellis
Bernard Patrick H A Goldstone
Brian Kay Heyworth
Arthur Hamilton Lawson
John Mellor Marchington
Michael Law Worthington

Barristers on Circuit 1876-2002

Year	Liverpool	Manchester	Preston	Total
1876	29	32	1	62
1877	33	37	0	70
1878	38	39	1	78
1879	45	38	2	85
1880	45	44	2	91
1881	46	47	2	95
1882	43	44	1	88
1883	47	48	2	97
1884	50	57	2	109
1885	51	54	2	107
1886	53	54	2	109
1887	56	52	2	110
1888	52	52	3	107
1889	59	62	2	123
1890	62	66	3	131
1891	61	63	4	128
1892	58	65	4	127
1893	59	63	5	127
1894	66	65	6	137
1895	65	65	4	134
1896	62	60	3	125
1897	62	57	3	122
1898	60	65	4	129
1899	65	67	3	135
1900	67	70	3	140
1901	65	69	3	137
1902	68	72	2	142
1903	61	66	2	129
1904	64	70	4	138
1905	63	76	4	143
1906	69	86	4	158
1907	65	81	4	150
1908	74	83	5	162
1909	69	93	5	167
1910	70	95	5	170
1911	72	89	6	167
1912	75	92	6	173
1913	77	91	5	173
1914	87	89	7	183
1915	83	81	6	170
1916	66	84	5	155
1917	62	82	5	149

Year	Liverpool	Manchester	Preston	Total
1918	62	85	4	151
1919	62	79	4	145
1920	57	78	6	141
1921	63	85	4	152
1922	63	68	5	136
1923	70	72	7	149
1924	62	72	7	141
1925	64	70	7	141
1926	69	64	6	139
1927	60	70	6	136
1928	58	72	6	136
1929	58	71	6	135
1930	59	71	6	136
1931	61	71	7	139
1932	60	80	7	147
1933	59	81	6	146
1934	61	85	7	153
1935	63	87	7	157
1936	64	88	5	157
1937	72	97	10	179
1938	69	91	9	169
1939	68	84	8	160
1940	71	89	6	166
1941	67	66	5	138
1942	65	64	6	135
1943	65	66	5	136
1944	62	61	5	128
1945	63	62	4	129
1946	63	66	4	133
1947	70	68	5	143
1948	71	73	7	151
1949	71	75	7	153
1950	74	92	10	176
1951	73	88	12	173
1952	88	93	12	193
1953	107	102	12	221
1954	111	107	11	229
1955	114	109	18	241
1956	117	108	8	233
1957	114	119	6	239
1958	113	125	4	242
1959	101	120	3	224
1960	102	122	2	226
1961	98	117	2	217
1962	95	123	2	220
1963	98	125	2	225

Year	Liverpool	Manchester	Preston	Total
1964	94	127	1	222
1965	94	117	1	212
1966	101	122	2	225
1967	107	129	2	238
1968	108	136	2	246
1969	103	144	1	248
1970	108	161	2	271
1971	121	165	1	287
1972	127	174	1	302
1973	139	186	1	326
1974	142	197	1	340
1975	149	214	1	364
1976	162	225	1	388
1977	173	242	1	416
1978	185	250	0	435
1979	184	251	0	435
1980	189	258	0	447
1981	190	266	0	456
1982	197	268	0	465
1983	192	282	0	474
1984	196	297	8	501
1985	202	308	9	519
1986	200	320	9	529
1987	217	333	10	560
1988	212	341	10	563
1989	214	356	12	582
1990	220	365	15	600
1991	214	362	15	591
1992	239	394	14	647
1993	246	411	31	688
1994	260	459	43	762
1995	283	484	44	811
1996	290	506	44	840
1997	299	533	42	874
1998	307	549	46	902
1999	335	576	52	963
2000	349	600	50	999
2001	347	589	51	987
2002	348	635	61	1044

By mid-2004 the total number of the Bar on Circuit had reached 1100. My Preston totals do not include those Manchester and Liverpool chambers with a Preston annexe.

By way of comparison, the figures for the other large cities were:
1931 Birmingham – 40, Leeds – 18 (Liverpool – 61, Manchester – 71)
1948 Birmingham – 49, Leeds – 30 (Liverpool – 71, Manchester – 73)

Lord Chancellor

1886, 1892-1895	Farrer Herschell (Baron Herschell)
1919-1922	Frederick Edwin Smith (Earl of Birkenhead)
1954-1962	David Maxwell Fyfe (Earl of Kilmuir)

Lord Chief Justice

1894-1900	Charles Arthur Russell (Baron Russell of Killowen)
1913-1921	Rufus Daniel Isaacs (Marquess of Reading)
1922-1940	Gordon Hewart (Viscount Hewart of Bury)

Master of the Rolls

1883-1897	William Baliol Brett (Viscount Esher)
1901-1907	Richard Henn Collins (Baron Collins of Kensington)
1919-1923	William Pickford (Baron Sterndale)

President of the Probate, Divorce and Admiralty Division

(now the Family Division)

1891-1892	Sir Charles Parker Butt
1905-1909	John Gorell Barnes (First Baron Gorell of Brampton)
1909-1910	John Charles Bigham (First Viscount Mersey)
1918-1919	William Pickford (Baron Sterndale)
1933-1962	Frank Boyd Merriman (Baron Merriman)

Vice President of the Court of Appeal, Criminal Division

1997-	Sir Christopher Dudley Roger Rose

House of Lords

1876-1886	Colin Blackburn (Baron Blackburn of Killearn)
1894 -	Charles Arthur Russell (Baron Russell of Killowen)
1907-1911	Richard Henn Collins (Baron Collins of Kensington)
1913-1930	John Andrew Hamilton (Viscount Sumner of lbstone)
1960-1975	John William Morris (Baron Morris of Borth-y-Gest)
1998-2004	John Stewart Hobhouse (Baron Hobhouse of Woodborough)
2004-	Brenda Marjorie Hale (Baroness Hale of Richmond)

Farrer Herschell (Baron Herschell).

Frederick Edwin Smith (Earl of Birkenhead).

David Maxwell Fyfe (Earl of Kilmuir).

Rufus Daniel Isaacs (Marquess of Reading).

Gordon Hewart (Viscount Hewart of Bury).

Charles Arthur Russell (Baron Russell of Killowen).

Court of Appeal

1870-1871	Rt Hon Sir George Mellish
1876-1883	Rt Hon Sir William Baliol Brett (Viscount Esher)
1882	Rt Hon Sir John Holker
1897-1901	Rt Hon Sir Richard Henn Collins (Baron Collins)
1907-1915	Rt Hon Sir William Rann Kennedy
1912-1913	Rt Hon Sir John Andrew Hamilton (Viscount Summer)
1914-1918	Rt Hon Sir William Pickford (Baron Sterndale)
1926-1934	Rt Hon Sir Paul Ogden Lawrence
1927-1938	Rt Hon Sir Frederick Arthur Greer (Baron Fairfield)
1935-1948	Rt Hon Sir Leslie Frederic Scott
1948-1957	Rt Hon Sir John Edward Singleton
1951-1960	Rt Hon Sir John William Morris (Baron Morris of Borth-y-Gest)
1957-1968	Rt Hon Sir Frederic Aked Sellers
1957-1963	Rt Hon Sir Benjamin Ormerod
1958-1969	Rt Hon Sir (Henry) Gordon Willmer
1968-1971	Rt Hon Sir Fenton Atkinson
1981-1989	Rt Hon Sir Michael Robert Emanuel Kerr
1985-1995	Rt Hon Sir lain Derek Laing Glidewell
1987-1996	Rt Hon Sir (Thomas) Patrick Russell
1992-	Rt Hon Sir Christopher Dudley Roger Rose
1993-1998	Rt Hon Sir John Stewart Hobhouse
1997-2004	Rt Hon Sir Charles Barrie Knight Mantell
1999-2004	Rt Hon Dame Brenda Marjorie Hale DBE
2000-2004	Rt Hon Sir John William Kay
2002-	Rt Hon Dame Janet Hilary Smith DBE

Justice of the King's Bench

1859-1875	Sir Colin Blackburn (transfer to the Queen's Bench Division of the High Court, 1875-1876)

Justice of Common Pleas

1868-1875	Sir William Baliol Brett (transfer to Common Pleas Division of the High Court, 1875-1876)

Baron of the Exchequer

1868-1875	Sir Anthony Cleasby (transfer to Exchequer Division of the High Court, 1875-1879)

Justice of the High Court

King's/Queen's Bench Division unless otherwise stated

1876-1890 The Hon Sir Henry Manisty
1883-1891 The Hon Sir Charles Parker Butt (Probate, Divorce & Admiralty Division)
1890-1904 The Hon Sir Robert Samuel Wright
1891-1897 The Hon Sir Richard Henn Collins
1892-1905 The Hon Sir John Gorell Barnes (Probate, Divorce & Admiralty Division)
1892-1907 The Hon Sir William Rann Kennedy
1897-1909 The Hon Sir John Charles Bigham
1901-1910 The Hon Sir Joseph Walton
1906-1918 The Hon Sir Ralph Neville
1907-1914 The Hon Sir William Pickford
1909-1912 The Hon Sir John Andrew Hamilton
1910-1937 The Hon Sir Thomas Gardner Horridge
1913-1929 The Hon Sir John Meir Astbury
1917-1930 The Hon Sir Maurice Hill (Probate, Divorce & Admiralty Division)
1918-1926 The Hon Sir Paul Ogden Lawrence (Chancery Division)
1919-1927 The Hon Sir Frederick Arthur Greer
1920-1937 The Hon Sir Rigby Philip Watson Swift
1920-1934 The Hon Sir Edward Acton
1921-1940 The Hon Sir George Arthur Harwin Branson
1924-1927 The Hon Sir Hugh Fraser
1925-1935 The Hon Sir Alexander Dingwall Bateson (Probate Divorce & Admiralty Division)
1933-1948 The Hon Sir Cyril Atkinson
1934-1948 The Hon Sir John Edward Singleton
1935-1940 The Hon Sir Walter Greaves-Lord
1944-1957 The Hon Sir George Justin Lynskey
1945-1958 The Hon Sir (Henry) Gordon Willmer (Probate, Divorce & Admiralty Division)
1945-1951 The Hon Sir John William Morris
1946-1957 The Hon Sir Frederic Aked Sellers
1947-1953 The Hon Sir Fred Eills Pritchard
1948-1957 The Hon Sir Benjamin Ormerod (1948-1950, Probate Divorce & Admiralty Division)
1950-1969 The Hon Sir George Harold Lloyd Jacob (Chancery Division)
1950-1964 The Hon Sir William Gorman
1950-1966 The Hon Sir Patrick Redmond Barry
1953-1956 The Hon Sir (Albert) Denis Gerrard
1954-1975 The Hon Sir John Percy Ashworth
1960-1968 The Hon Sir Fenton Atkinson
1960-1978 The Hon Sir Basil Edward Nield
1961-1982 The Hon Sir John Thompson
1961-1981 The Hon Sir Alan Abraham Mocatta
1962-1975 The Hon Sir Daniel James Brabin
1965-1985 The Hon Sir Joseph Donaldson Cantley
1967-1977 The Hon Sir (John) Robertson (Dunn) Crichton
1969-1973 The Hon Sir George Joseph Bean
1971-1993 The Hon Sir (Alfred) Kenneth Hollings (Family Division)
1971-1982 The Hon Sir (Robert) Hugh Mais
1972-1981 The Hon Sir Michael Robert Emanuel Kerr
1974-1988 The Hon Dame Rose Hellbron DBE (Family Division)

1977-1992	The Hon Sir (Walter) Derek (Thornley) Hodgson
1979-1990	The Hon Sir David Bruce McNeill
1980-1987	The Hon Sir (Thomas) Patrick Russell
1980-1985	The Hon Sir Iain Derek Laing Glidewell
1982-1993	The Hon Sir John Stewart Hobhouse
1985-1992	The Hon Sir Christopher Dudley Roger Rose
1989-2005	The Hon Sir Douglas Dunlop Brown (1989-1996 Family Division)
1989-2004	The Hon Sir Michael Morland
1990-1997	The Hon Sir Charles Barrie Knight Mantell
1990-	The Hon Dame Joyanne Winifred Bracewell DBE (Family Division)
1992-2001	The Hon Dame Ann Marian Ebsworth DBE
1992-2000	The Hon Sir John William Kay
1992-2002	The Hon Dame Janet Hilary Smith DBE
1992-2003	The Hon Sir Michael Alexander Geddes Sachs
1993-2001	The Hon Dame (Anne) Heather Steel DBE
1994-1999	The Hon Dame Brenda Marjorie Hale DBE (Family Division)
1995-	The Hon Sir David Anthony Poole
1998-2001	The Hon Sir Rodney Conrad Klevan
1998-	The Hon Sir Michael John Burton
2000-	The Hon Sir Richard Henry Quixano Henriques
2000-	The Hon Sir Brian Henry Leveson
2002-	The Hon Sir Mark Hedley (Family Division)
2002-	The Hon Sir Peter Winston Smith (Chancery Division)
2003-	The Hon Sir David Clive Clarke
2004-	The Hon Sir Ernest Nigel Ryder (Family Division)

(UPA)

Northern Circuit Judges 1950. Back row: Gorman J, Barry J. Middle row: Sellers J, Pritchard J, Willmer J, Ormerod J, Lloyd Jacob J, Morris J. Front Row: Singleton LJ, Lord Merriman P, Lynskey J.

Presiding Judges

The Hon Mr Justice:

1970-1974	Cantley
1970-1975	Kilner Brown
1975-1978	Hollings
1976-1980	Caulfield
1979-1982	Heilbron (Mrs Justice)
1980-1984	McNeill
1983-1987	Russell
1985-1988	MacPherson of Cluny
1987-1990	Rose
1989-1991	Steyn
1990-1995	Morland
1992-1994	Potter
1994-1997	Kay
1995-1999	Forbes
1998-2001	Douglas Brown
2000-2003	Penry-Davey
2002-	Leveson
2004-	McCombe

Chancery Court of the Duchy and County Palatine of Lancaster

Vice-Chancellor

1871-1881	George Little QC
1881-1893	Henry Fox Bristowe QC
1895-1905	Sir Samuel Hall KC
1905-1912	Octavius Leigh Clare
1912-1919	Dudley Stewart Smith KC
1919-1925	Roger Bernard Lawrence KC
1925-1936	Sir Courthope Wilson KC
1936-1948	Sir John Bennett
1948-1963	Sir Leonard Stone
1963-1973	Sir Thomas Burgess
1973-1987	His Honour Judge James Blackett-Ord
1987-1991	The Hon Sir Richard Rashleigh Folliott Scott
1991-1994	The Hon Sir Robert Andrew Morritt (great-great grandson of John Wickens, Vice-Chancellor 1869-1871)
1994-1999	The Hon Sir Jonathan Frederic Parker
1999-2002	The Hon Sir William Anthony Blackburne
2002-2005	The Hon Sir Timothy Andrew Wigram Lloyd
2005-	The Hon Sir Nicholas John Patten

(UPA)

Northern Circuit Judges 1964. Back row: Mocatta J, Brabin J. Middle row: Barry J, Nield J, Thompson J, Gorman J, Ashworth J, Fenton Atkinson J. Front row: Willmer LJ, Sellers LJ, Lord Morris of Borth-y Gest, Ormerod LJ, Lloyd-Jacob J.

(MEN)

Former Presiding Judges, Hollings J. and Cantley J. Manchester 1982.

Registrars

Liverpool District

1853-1880	James Winckworth Winstanley
1880-1914	Francis Willis Taylor
1914-1919	Roger Bernard Lawrence KC
1919-1942	R W Lowden
1943-1950	Harold Roberts
1951-1955	John M Worthington CVO
1955-1967	W E Helsby JP
1967-1971	William Morris Jones

Manchester District

1857-1883	Henry Wilbraham
1883-1921	Hubert Winstanley
1921-1925	T B Blackburne and A E Steinthal
1925-1951	Harold Roberts
1951-1971	Robert Alexander Forrester

Preston District

1854-1876	Joseph Catterall
1876-1886	William Gilbertson
1886-1914	Alexander Pearce
1914-1921	T B Blackburne
1921-1926	T B Blackburne and A E Steinthal
1926-1955	J M Worthington CVO
1955-1967	W E Helsby JP
1967-1971	William Morris Jones

Further Reading: Bennett's Jurisdiction and Practice of the Chancery, of the County Palatine of Lancaster. 1st edition, John Bennett, 1914; 2nd edition, R A Forrester, 1933.

County Court Judges 1873-1971 Circuit Judges 1972-2004

	His/Her Honour Judge		
1873	Collier	1923	Bairstow
1875	Ffoulkes	1924	Mossop
1882	Thomas Hughes QC		Burgis
1883	Jordan	1925	Leigh
1884	Powell QC	1926	McCleary
1885	Gates QC	1927	Beazley
1886	Coventry	1928	Procter
1888	Edge		Crosthwaite
1889	Shand	1929	Hills
	Edwin Jones		Kennedy QC
1890	Heywood	1931	Longson
1891	Steavenson		Hildesley KC
1892	French QC	1933	Peel
1894	Parry	1934	Allsebrook
1895	Smyly QC		Banks KC
	Addison QC	1935	Galbraith KC
1896	Yate Lee	1936	Gamon
	Bompas QC		Essenhigh
1899	Mulholland QC	1937	Sir Gerald Hurst KC
1900	Gwynne James	1940	Fraser Harrison
	Bradbury	1942	Batt
	Hon Arthur Russell		Rhodes
1903	Scully	1944	Ormerod
1905	Wheeler KC	1947	Clothier KC
	Hamilton		Hamilton
1906	Carver KC	1948	Walmesley KC
1907	Alfred Thomas	1950	Fenwick KC
1909	Graham KC		Emlyn-Jones
1910	Stanger KC		Glazebrook
1911	Mellor KC	1952	Harold Brown
1912	Taylor	1953	Backhouse
1913	Sturgess KC		George Maddocks
	Hogg	1955	Robert Nicklin
1914	Gurner	1958	Edward Steel
1915	Tobin KC		Melville Kennan
	Fox KC		Hugh Mais
1917	Parsons KC	1959	Gerard Lind-Smith
	Acton		Bazil Wingate-Saul
1918	Crawford	1960	John Addleshaw
1919	Elliott		Philip Ingress-Bell QC
1919	Turner	1961	Richard Trotter
1920	Maxwell		William Morris
1921	Dowdall KC	1962	Robert Lambert
	Bradley	1962	Christopher Leigh
	Rees	1963	Thomas Cunliffe
	Hargreaves		James Stansfield
1922	Lias	1964	Glynn Burrell QC

1965	Desmond Bailey	12.02.1979	Henry Lachs
	Gordon Clover	27.04.1979	Roy Ward QC
1966	Edward Youds	11.07.1980	Douglas Brown QC
	Christopher Cunliffe		Norman Lees
	Francis Nance	16.07.1980	Anthony Jolly
	Granville Slack		Gerard Humphries
1967	Joseph Zigmond	16.09.1980	Gerald Crowe QC
1968	Alexander Karmel QC	16.06.1981	Richard Pickering
	Frank Paterson	15.07.1981	Michael Lever QC
	Kenneth Hollings	30.11.1981	Ian Webster
1969	James Booth		Reg Lockett
	John Edward Jones	19.02.1982	Michael O'Donoghue
	Philip Curtis	15.04.1983	Brian Duckworth
1970	Jack Abdela QC		Joyanne Bracewell QC
	John Corcoran		Ann Ebsworth
	John Da Cunha	07.10.1983	John Stannard
	Basil Gerrard	27.01.1984	Donald Forster
	Keith Lawton	23.03.1984	Michael Sachs
	Robert Leech	24.04.1984	Herbert Andrew QC
15.01.1971	Anthony Edmondson	05.11.1984	Harold Singer
13.07.1971	Arthur Prestt QC	03.12.1984	Ian Campbell
30.09.1971	Joseph Davies QC	1984	Thomas Fielding Hatton
25.10.1971	James Blackett-Ord	20.05.1985	Brian Carter QC
1971	Philip Hinchliffe QC	08.07.1985	Keith Naylor
	Philip Kershaw	12.07.1985	Simon Fawcus
	William Openshaw	16.01.1986	Michael Blackburn
01.01.1972	Richard Bingham QC	07.02.1986	Anthony Hammond
	Ralph Wood	30.07.1986	Anne Downey
	Myrella Cohen	21.10.1986	Richard Hamilton
17.03.1972	Keith Dewhurst	03.12.1986	Heather Steel
12.09.1972	Bert Jalland	09.03.1987	David Pirie
	Desmond Franks	17.03.1987	David Marshall Evans QC
1972	Mark Smith	09.09.1987	John Townend
	Leslie Rigg QC		David Hodson
	Thomas Pigot QC	25.05.1988	Robert Brown
	Richard Forrest QC	06.10.1988	Denis Clark
28.06.1974	Norman Sellers	17.10.1988	Sean Duncan
	James Scarlett	21.11.1988	Anthony Procter
03.09.1975	William Wickham	08.05.1989	Charles Mahon
17.10.1975	John Arthur DFC	21.07.1989	Raymond Bennett
13.01.1976	Alan Booth QC	28.11.1989	Donald Hart QC
	Harry Kershaw	31.01.1990	David Lynch
02.07.1976	James Fitzhugh QC	02.05.1990	Michael Kershaw QC
	Ivor Taylor QC	06.06.1990	Rhys Davies QC
06.01.1977	Ifor Morris Jones QC	12.06.1990	Bertram Maddocks
30.09.1977	Mary Holt	15.12.1990	John Morgan
18.11.1977	E Sanderson Temple MBE, QC		Barry Woodward
10.04.1978	John Lord	17.04.1991	Inge Bernstein
	Alistair Bell	14.05.1991	Michael Dean QC
15.01.1979	Robert Hardy	16.05.1991	David Owen TD

07.10.1991	Bruce Caulfield
05.11.1991	Elizabeth Steel DL
19.03.1992	Mark Hedley
	John Appleton
18.05.1992	David Gilliland QC
21.07.1992	Peter Urquhart
22.07.1992	David Mackay
	Bryn Holloway
	Ronald Livesey QC
13.10.1992	David Maddison
14.10.1992	Gerald Clifton
28.10.1992	Christopher Tetlow
02.12.1992	Nigel Howarth
09.12.1992	David Gee
16.03.1993	Ian Trigger
10.05.1993	Gillian Ruaux
12.05.1993	John Roberts
20.10.1993	David Clarke QC
	Bruce MacMillan
16.11.1993	Charles James
23.11.1993	Terence Earnshaw
01.02.1994	Peter Smith
23.03.1994	Jonathan Geake
26.04.1994	Martin Allweis
13.07.1994	Ian Crompton
	Stuart Fish
26.09.1994	Richard Holman
21.02.1995	William Morris
10.05.1995	John Burke QC
15.05.1995	Diana Eaglestone
04.07.1995	Peter Lakin
26.07.1995	Edward Slinger
08.11.1995	William George
13.12.1995	Anthony Ensor
30.04.1996	Kenneth Wilkinson
13.05.1996	Timothy Mort
05.06.1996	Brendan Hegarty QC
26.06.1996	John Phipps
16.12.1996	Adrian Smith
03.02.1997	David Swift
28.07.1997	Brian Lewis
21.10.1997	Charles Bloom QC
05.02.1998	Stuart Baker
24.03.1998	Michael Henshell
06.07.1998	John Phillips
21.07.1999	Andrew Blake
19.06.2000	Adrian Lyon
	Iain Hamilton
26.06.2000	Robert Atherton
10.07.2000	Nigel Gilmour QC
12.07.2000	Lindsey Kushner QC
24.10.2000	Mark Brown
20.12.2000	Barbara Watson
19.03.2001	David Harris QC
01.05.2001	Pamela Badley
09.05.2001	The Hon Bernard Lever
14.05.2001	Philip Raynor QC
	Andrew Lowcock
22.05.2001	David Boulton
30.05.2001	Phillip Sycamore
18.06.2001	Leslie David Hull (to Grimsby)
26.06.2001	Lesley Newton
17.07.2001	Maureen Roddy
23.07.2001	Martin Steiger QC
24.07.2001	John Dowse (to Hull)
08.10.2001	Keith Armitage QC
13.05.2002	Jeffrey Allan Lewis (from North Eastern Circuit)
20.06.2002	Elliot Michael Knopf
24.06.2002	Arthur Anthony Rumbelow QC
	Christopher John Cornwall
25.06.2002	Clement Goldstone QC
03.07.2002	Michael Byrne
25.07.2002	Anthony Derwin Hope (from Western Circuit)
30.07.2002	Martin Rudland (from North Eastern Circuit)
05.09.2002	Barbara Ann Forrester
04.03.2003	Henry Brian Globe QC
06.05.2003	John Montague Appleby (from Midland Circuit)
	Anthony Paul Morris QC (to Central Criminal Court)
21.07.2003	Stephen Stewart QC
07.10.2003	Robert Warnock
11.11.2003	Paul Daniel Batty QC (from North Eastern Circuit)
30.03.2004	Andrew James Gilbart QC
01.04.2004	Jonathan Rowe Foster QC
28.04.2004	Anthony Hall Gee QC
22.07.2004	Margaret Ruth de Haas QC
27.07.2004	Anthony Patrick Russell QC
13.09.2004	Timothy Clayson (from North Eastern Circuit)
25.10.2004	Beverly Anne Lunt
25.10.2004	David Anthony Hernandez
04.11.2004	David Fletcher
24.11.2004	Roger Martin Thomas QC (from North Eastern Circuit)
08.02.2005	Graham Platts

Seniority List of Circuit Judges on the Northern Circuit on 31 December 2004

	Appointed
His Honour Judge David Maddison The Honorary Recorder of Manchester	13.10.1992
His Honour Judge Henry Globe QC The Honorary Recorder of Liverpool	04.03.2003
His Honour Judge Openshaw QC The Honorary Recorder of Preston	16.03.1999
His Honour Judge Hammond	07.02.1986
His Honour Judge Robert Brown	23.05.1988
His Honour Judge Denis Clark	06.10.1988
His Honour Judge Duncan	17.10.1988
His Honour Judge Mahon	08.05.1989
His Honour Judge Lynch	31.01.1990
His Honour Judge Michael Kershaw QC	02.05.1990
His Honour Judge Maddocks	12.06.1990
His Honour Judge Woodward	05.12.1990
His Honour Judge Owen TD	16.05.1991
His Honour Judge Caulfield	17.10.1991
Her Honour Judge Elizabeth Steel DL	05.11.1991
His Honour Judge Appleton	19.03.1992
His Honour Judge Gilliland QC	18.05.1992
His Honour Judge Mackay	22.07.1992
His Honour Judge Holloway	22.07.1992
His Honour Judge Clifton	14.10.1992
His Honour Judge Tetlow	28.10.1992
His Honour Judge Howarth	02.12.1992
His Honour Judge Gee	09.12.1992
His Honour Judge Trigger	16.03.1993
Her Honour Judge Ruaux	10.05.1993
His Honour Judge Roberts	12.05.1993
Ms Honour Judge Macmillan	20.10.1993
His Honour Judge Charles James	16.11.1993
His Honour Judge Earnshaw	23.11.1993
His Honour Judge Peter Smith	01.02.1994
Her Honour Judge Daley	07.02.1994
His Honour Judge Geake	23.03.1994
His Honour Judge Allweis	26.04.1994
His Honour Judge Fish	13.07.1994

His Honour Judge Holman	26.09.1994
His Honour Judge Morris	21.02.1995
His Honour Judge Burke QC	10.05.1995
Her Honour Judge Eaglestone	15.05.1995
His Honour Judge Lakin	04.07.1995
His Honour Judge Slinger	26.07.1995
His Honour Judge George	08.11.1995
His Honour Judge Ensor	13.12.1995
His Honour Judge Kenneth Wilkinson	30.04.1996
His Honour Judge Mort	13.05.1996
His Honour Judge Hegarty QC	05.06.1996
His Honour Judge Phipps	24.06.1996
His Honour Judge Adrian Smith	16.12.1996
His Honour Judge Swift	03.02.1997
His Honour Judge Lewis	28.07.1997
His Honour Judge Charles Bloom QC	21.10.1997
His Honour Judge Baker	05.02.1998
His Honour Judge Henshell	24.03.1998
His Honour Judge Phillips	06.07.1998
His Honour Judge Blake	21.07.1999
His Honour Judge Lyon	19.06.2000
His Honour Judge Hamilton	19.06.2000
His Honour Judge Atherton	20.06.2000
His Honour Judge Gilmour QC	10.07.2000
Her Honour Judge Kushner QC	12.07.2000
His Honour Judge Mark Brown	24.10.2000
Her Honour Judge Watson	20.12.2000
His Honour Judge Harris QC	19.03.2001
Her Honour Judge Badley	01.05.2001
His Honour Judge Lever	09.05.2001
His Honour Judge Raynor QC	14.05.2001
His Honour Judge Lowcock	14.05.2001
His Honour Judge Boulton	22.05.2001
His Honour Judge Sycamore	30.05.2001
Her Honour Judge Newton	26.06.2001
Her Honour Judge Roddy	17.07.2001
His Honour Judge Steiger QC	23.07.2001
His Honour Judge Armitage QC	08.10.2001
His Honour Judge Jeffrey Lewis	08.05.2002
His Honour Judge Knopf	20.06.2002
His Honour Judge Rumbelow QC	24.06.2002
His Honour Judge Cornwall	24.06.2002
His Honour Judge Goldstone QC	25.06.2002

Seniority List of Circuit Judges on the Northern Circuit on 31 December 2004 (continued)

His Honour Judge Byrne	03.07.2002
His Honour Judge Hope	25.07.2002
His Honour Judge Rudland	30.07.2002
Her Honour Judge Barbara Forrester	05.09.2002
His Honour Judge John Appleby	06.05.2003
His Honour Judge Stephen Stewart QC	21.07.2003
His Honour Judge Robert Warnock	07.10.2003
His Honour Judge Paul Batty QC	11.11.2003
His Honour Judge Andrew Gilbart QC	30.03.2004
His Honour Judge Jonathan Foster QC	01.04.2004
His Honour Judge Anthony Gee QC	28.04.2004
Her Honour Judge Margaret de Haas QC	22.07.2004
His Honour Judge Anthony Russell QC	27.07.2004
His Honour Judge Timothy Clayson	13.09.2004
Her Honour Judge Beverly Anne Hunt	25.10.2004
His Honour Judge David Anthony Hernandez	25.10.2004
His Honour Judge David Fletcher	04.11.2004 *
His Honour Judge Roger Martin Thomas QC	24.11.2004

* Judge Fletcher was a District Judge in Sheffield. He is to preside over Liverpool's new Community Court.

(TM)

Lord Chief Justice with Liverpool Circuit Judges and Recorders, 11 August 2002. Standing: George, Recorder Main, Maddison, Recorder Clarke, Lewis, Swift, Roberts, Gilmour QC, Phipps, Brown, James, Holloway, Steel, Lynch, Crompton, Harris QC, Roddy, Mackay, Clifton. Seated: Denis Clark, Leveson J, Samner J, Lady Pilkington (High Sheriff), Lord Woolf, David Clarke QC, Silber J, Marshall Evans QC, Duncan.

Liverpool Court of Passage

The Borough of Liverpool was granted the right to hold a court in 1229. In more recent times the Court was regulated by the Court of Passage Act 1893. It had unlimited jurisdiction in relation to all personal causes within the boundaries of the City of Liverpool and the waters of the Port of Liverpool. Because the Court was speedy and reasonably inexpensive, it was highly regarded by both lawyer and litigant. Despite the fact that it had worked so well for over 700 years, it was abolished by the Courts Act 1971 and the last sitting of the Court at St George's Hall was on the 2 December of that year.

Presiding Judges

1896-1903	Thomas Henry Baylis KC
1903-1948	Sir Francis Kyffin Taylor KC (later Baron Maenan)
1948-1950	Henry Ince Nelson KC
1950-1964	Geoffrey Glynn Blackledge QC
1964-1971	Richard Haddow Forrest QC

Registrars

1877-1884	Joseph Raynor
1885-1886	George James Atkinson
1887-1889	Henry Hodgson Bremner
1890-1893	Harcourt Everard Clare
1894	Edward Ralph Pickmere (Deputy)
1895-1899	Harcourt Everard Clare
1900-1903	Edward Ralph Pickmere
1903-1919	Walter Peel CBE
1920-1940	Reginald Dawbarn Cripps
1941-1949	Roland Marshall JP
1949-1971	Charles J Cocks

Further Reading: The Court of Passage – Rules and Practice, 2nd edition, Walter Peel, Henry Young & Sons, 1934.

(LDPE)

Last sitting of Liverpool Court of Passage at St George's Hall, Liverpool on 2 December 1971. Judge Forrest QC, Lord Mayor (Alderman, Charles Cowlin), Judge Lyons QC, Stan Kirkham, Clerk.

Salford Hundred Court of Record

The Court had its roots in Anglo-Saxon times and served the Hundred of Salford well, until it was abolished on the 31 December 1971. It was regulated by the Salford Hundred Court of Record Act 1868. Speaking for the Bar on the last sitting day, Ben Hytner QC said, "The loss of the Court is to be deplored. It is particularly ironic that Lord Beeching has recommended the abolishing of a court in a centre where there is an efficient rail service." Older members of the Circuit will know that Lord Beeching turned his attention to the courts having recommended to the Government the closure of a good part of the railway branch network. It is a measure of the quality of the presiding judges that the last six went on to the High Court and one to the Court of Appeal.

Presiding Judges

1868-1893	Henry Wyndham West QC
1893-1909	Henry Gordon Shee KC
1909-1937	John Roskill KC
1937-1944	George Justin Lynskey KC
1944-1947	Fred Pritchard KC
1948-1953	(Albert) Denis Gerrard QC
1953-1960	Fenton Atkinson QC
1960-1965	Joseph (Donaldson) Cantley QC
1965-1971	(Walter) Derek (Thornley) Hodgson QC

Registrars

1876-1890	Sir Joseph Heron
1891-1913	Sir William Henry Talbot
1914-1922	Thomas Hudson
1923-1928	P M Heath
1929-1938	F E Warbreck-Howell
1939-1945	R H Adcock CBE
1946-1955	E M Redhead
1956-1970	B Johnson
1971	R Roper

Judges of Appeal – Isle of Man

1918-1921	Sir William Francis Kyffin Taylor KBE, KC
1921-1925	Arthur Jacob Ashton KC
1925-1928	Ernest Wingate Wingate-Saul KC
1928-1933	John Edward Singleton KC
1933-1934	Harold Derbyshire KC
1934-1937	Robert Kingsley Jackson KC
1937-1946	John William Morris KC
1946-1950	Patrick Redmond Joseph Barry KC
1950-1953	Albert Denis Gerrard QC
1953-1956	Neville Jonas Laski QC
1956-1960	John Robertson Dunn Crichton QC
1960-1962	Daniel James Brabin QC
1962-1965	Joseph Donaldson Cantley OBE, QC
1965-1971	Richard Martin Bingham QC
1972-1978	Cecil Montacute Clothier QC
1978-1980	lain Derek Laing Glidewell QC
1980-1997	Benet Alan Hytner QC
1997-	Geoffrey Frank Tattersall QC

Judges of the Court of Appeal of Jersey and Guernsey

1965-1971	H H Judge Richard Haddow Forrest
1984-2000	(John) Martin Collins QC
1991-1999	Lord Carlisle of Bucklow QC
2004-	Dame Heather Steel DBE
2004-	The Rt Hon Sir Charles Mantell

Judges of The Sovereign Base Area, Cyprus

H H Judge Thomas Herbert Pigot QC. Deputy Senior Judge 1971-1984; Senior Judge 1984-1990.

H H Judge Ronald John Deardon Livesey QC. Deputy Senior Judge 1983-1996; Senior Judge 1996-2002.

H H Judge Brian Roy Duckworth. Deputy Senior Judge 1998-

Home Secretary

1874-1880 Richard Assheton Cross (First Viscount Cross) (1823-1914)
1885-1886 " " " "
1951-1954 Sir David Maxwell Fyfe QC (First Earl of Kilmuir) (1900-1967)
1989-1990 David Waddington (Baron Waddington) (1929-)

Attorney General

1875-1880	Sir John Holker QC
1886-1887	Sir Charles Russell QC
1892-1894	" " " "
1910-1913	Sir Rufus Isaacs KC
1915-1919	Sir Frederick Edwin Smith KC
1919-1922	Sir Gordon Hewart KC
1945	Sir David Maxwell Fyfe KC
1945-1951	Sir Hartley William Shawcross KC

Solicitor General

1846-1848	Sir David Dundas QC
1880-1885	Sir Farrer Herschell QC
1885-1886	Sir John Eldon Gorst QC
1910	Sir Rufus Isaacs KC
1915	Sir Frederick Edwin Smith KC
1916-1919	Sir Gordon Hewart KC
1922	Sir Leslie Frederic Scott KC
1928-1929	Sir Frank Boyd Merriman KC
1932-1933	" " " " "
1942-1945	Sir David Maxwell Fyfe KC

Recorders of Cities and Boroughs

Barrow in Furness

1962-1963 Thomas Alfred Cunliffe
1963-1967 James Godby Shorrock
1967-1969 James Booth
1969-1970 Basil Harding Gerrard
1970-1971 (Thomas) Patrick Russell QC

Birkenhead

I have included Birkenhead, part of the Wales and Chester Circuit until 1971, because many Liverpool practitioners appeared there regularly.

1882-1907 Clement Higgins
1907-1912 Rt Hon Sir Ellis Jones Ellis-Griffith
1912-1934 Alexander Merle Latham
1934-1935 Clyde Tabor Wilson
1935-1943 Francis Bertram Reece
1935-1944 John Pascoe Elsden
1950-1958 Francis (John Watkin) Williams QC
1958-1959 Gerard Gustave Lind-Smith
1959-1965 William (Lloyd) Mars-Jones QC
1965-1969 Phillip Solly Wien QC
1969-1971 (William) Thomas Williams QC

Blackburn

Constituted a Quarter Sessions Borough by Warrant under the Queen's Sign Manual dated 27 August 1886. First Quarter Sessions held in Town Hall on Monday 18 October 1886.

1886-1922 Sir Miles Walker Mattison KC
1922-1924 Sir Harold Smith KC
1924 William Madden KC
1925-1944 John Henry Thorpe KC
1944-1947 Wilfred Clothier KC,
1947-1969 Sydney Schofield Allen QC
1969-1971 David Bruce McNeill QC

Assistant Recorders: Desmond Bailey, E Sanderson Temple, John Corcoran and Harry Day (Senior Assistant)

Blackpool

1948-1951 Edmund Rowson KC
1952-1960 (John) Robertson (Dunn) Crichton QC
1960-1961 (Robert) Gordon Glover QC
1961-1965 Joseph Stanley Watson QC
1965-1971 Cecil (Montacute) Clothier QC

Assistant Recorder: Norman Sellers 1962-1971

Bolton

1869-1901 Samuel Pope QC
1901-1903 William Francis Kyffin Taylor KC
1903-1925 Collingwood Hope KC
1925-1938 Joseph Cooksey Jackson KC
1938-1946 Frederick Aked Sellers
1946-1953 Ronw Moelwyn Hughes QC
1953-1962 Daniel James Brabin QC
1962-1968 Alexander David Karmel QC
1968 (Alfred) Kenneth Hollings QC
1968-1971 (Griffith) Winston Guthrie Jones QC
Assistant Recorder: (Thomas) Patrick Russell 1963-1970

Burnley

1893-1907 Henry Gordon Shee QC
1907-1909 John Roskill KC
1909-1915 Adolph Max Lazarus Langdon KC
1915-1921 Samuel Pope
1921-1925 Thomas Bowes Leigh
1925-1929 Alfred Ravenscroft Kennedy
1929-1935 Noel Barré Goldie KC
1935-1956 Neville Jonas Laski QC
1956-1971 Rose Heilbron QC
Assistant Recorder: John Herent Lord 1971.

Honorary Recorders:

1971-1974 Rose Heilbron QC
1991-1995 His Honour Judge Ian Webster
1998-2004 His Honour Judge Raymond Bennett
2004- Her Honour Judge Barbara Watson

Carlisle

1873-1880 Farrer Herschell QC
1881-1891 Leofric Temple QC
1892-1904 Alexander Henry
1904-1929 Ernest Page KC
1929-1963 Edward Wooll KC
1963-1965 Desmond Bailey
1965-1969 George Bean QC
1970-1971 Michael Maguire QC

Honorary Recorder:

1985-1986 H H Judge Robert Leech
1990-1998 H H Judge Alistair Bell

Liverpool

1862-1886	John Bridge Aspinall QC
1886-1904	Charles Henry Hopwood KC
1904-1907	William Pickford KC
1907-1909	Henry Gordon Shee KC
1909-1948	Edward George Hemmerde KC
1948-1950	William Gorman KC
1950-1954	Henry Ince Nelson QC
1954-1956	Graham Rogers QC
1956-1963	Neville Jonas Laski QC
1963-1966	Stephen Chapman QC
1966-1967	William Gerard Morris
1967-1970	Ralph Kilner Brown QC
1970-1971	Rudolph Lyons QC

Honorary Recorders

1972-1977	H H Judge Sir Rudolph Lyons QC
1977-1992	H H Judge Sir (Ernest) Sanderson Temple MBE, QC
1992-1997	H H Judge William Rayley Wickham
1997-2003	H H Judge David Clive Clarke QC
2003-	H H Judge Henry Brian Globe QC.

Manchester

1865-1893	Henry Wyndham West QC
1893-1914	Sir Joseph Francis Leese KC
1914-1925	Arthur Jacob Ashton KC
1925-1935	Sir Walter Greaves-Lord KC
1935-1956	Sir Noel Barré Goldie QC
1956-1960	Sir Basil Nield QC
1960-1967	(John) Robertson Dunn Crichton QC
1967-1971	William Gerard Morris

Honorary Recorders

1971-1977	H H Judge Sir William Gerard Morris
1977-1982	H H Judge Sir Rudolph Lyons QC
1982-1990	H H Judge Arthur Miller Prestt QC
1990-2003	H H Judge Sir Rhys Everson Davies QC
2003-	H H Judge David Maddison

Oldham

1887-1899	James Winterbottom Hamilton QC
1899-1901	George Xavier Segar
1901-1904	William Pickford KC
1904-1914	Allan Gibson Steel KC
1914-1924	George Rhodes KC
1924-1936	Tom Eastham KC
1936-1942	David Maxwell Fyfe KC
1942-1950	Patrick Redmond Barry KC
1950-1959	Bazil Sylvester Wingate-Saul
1959-1960	Joseph Cantley QC
1960-1971	Richard Bingham QC

Preston

1874-1890	John Edmund Wentworth Addison QC
1890-1893	William Housman Higgin QC
1893-1898	Sir Henry Wilson Worsley-Taylor QC
1898-1921	H H Judge Francis Hamilton Mellor KC
1921-1928	Sir Ernest Wingate Wingate-Saul KC
1928-1934	John Edward Singleton KC
1935	Francis Henry Birkett Hodgson
1935-1938	Henry Percy Glover KC
1938-1950	John Catterall Jolly KC
1950-1958	Arthur Edgar Jalland QC
1958-1971	William Harrison Openshaw

Honorary Recorders

1971-1981	H H Judge William Harrison Openshaw
1989-1992	H H Judge Anthony Jolly
1996-1999	H H Judge Reginald Lockett
1999-	H H Judge (Charles) Peter (Lawford) Openshaw QC (The last Honorary Recorder of the Borough of Preston and the first Honorary Recorder of the City of Preston)

Salford Court of Quarter Sessions 1889-1971

By warrant under her Sign Manual, Her Majesty Queen Victoria granted the Borough of Salford a separate Court of Quarter Sessions of the Peace on 7 September 1889.

Recorders

1889-1906	Joseph Maghull Yates, QC
1905-1916	Alfred A Tobin, KC
1916-1939	Adolph Max Langdon, KC.
1941-1945	Hartley William Shawcross. KC
1945-1948	Albert Denis Gerrard, KC
1949-1951	Basil Edward Nield, MBE, KC, MP
* 1951	Francis John Vaudrey Sandbach
1952-1956	Basil Edward Nield, MBE, QC, MP
* 1956	Francis John Vawdrey Sandbach
1957-1964	Richard Haddow Forrest QC
* 1964	James Godby Shorrock
1964-1971	Godfrey Heilpern, QC

* Temporary Recorder appointed pending appointment of permanent Recorder

Deputy Recorders

1922	T S Leigh
1935-1938	Frederick Bancroft Turner
1939	Stephen Lewis Langdon
1940-1941	Percy Butlin
1940	Stephen Lewis Langdon
1942	Albert Denis Gerrard
1943	Percy Butlin
1943	Francis John Vawdrey Sandbach
1944-1945	Percy Butlin
1945	His Honour Judge Francis Raleigh Batt
1948	Joseph Donaldson Cantley
1952	Francis John Vawdrey Sandbach
1953	Neil Ballingall Birrel
1953-1954	Francis John Vawdrey Sandbach
1960-1962	Ernest Sanderson Temple
1963	Basil Harding Gerrard
1964	Ernest Sanderson Temple
1965	James Godby Shorrock
1965-1966	Winston Guthrie Jones
1966	Joseph Zigmond
1967	Basil Harding Gerrard
1968-1969	Desmond Gerald Franks
1969	Basil Harding Gerrard
1969-1970	Ivor Ralph Taylor
1971	Ian S Webster
1971	Desmond Gerald Franks

Assistant Recorders

1956-1957	Francis John Vawdrey Sandbach
1957-1961	William Gerrard Mortis
1957-1962	Desmond Patrick Bailey
1961-1968	Ernest Sanderson Temple
1961-1969	Basil Harding Gerrard
1962-1964	Cecil Montacute Clothier
1964	Arthur Miller Prestt
1965-1966	Joseph Zigmond
1966-1969	Desmond Gerald Franks
1967-1971	Ivor Ralph Taylor
1969-1971	Gerrard W. Humphries
1969-1971	John Michael Lever
1971	Ian S. Webster
1971	Douglas Dunlop Brown
1971	A. Logan Petch

Under Section 3 of the Courts Act, 1971, all Courts of Ouarter Sessions are abolished from 3l December 1971.

Honorary Recorder

On 3 November 1971, the Salford City Council appointed Godfrey Heilpern QC Honorary Recorder

Wigan

1862-1880	Joseph Catterall
1880-1886	John Thompson Fitzadam
1886-1895	William Court Gully QC
1895-1901	Joseph Walton QC
1901-1915	Sir Lancelot Sanderson KC
1915-1920	Rigby Philip Watson Swift KC
1920-1928	Frank Boyd Merriman KC
1928-1934	Reginald Mitchell Banks KC
1934-1948	William Gorman KC
1948-1951	(John) Selwyn (Brooke) Selwyn-Lloyd KC
1952-1962	David Karmel QC
1962-1964	(John) Glyn Burrell QC
1964-1971	(Harry Sibson) Leslie Rigg QC

Chairman of Quarter Sessions

Lancaster

1843-1854	Edward George Hornby
1855-1859	The Rt Hon Talbot Matthew Baines QC, MP
1860-1866	Thomas Green MP
1866-1874	The Rt Hon Richard Assheton Cross GCB
1874-1886	Henry Garnett
1886-1903	John Fell JP, DL
1903-1906	Thomas Fenwick Fenwick
1906-1918	Edward Bousfield Dawson
1918-1926	P J Hibbert
1927-1944	The Rt Hon Sir Lancelot Sanderson PC, KC

Lancashire

(sitting at Preston, Manchester and Liverpool)

1928-1935	Sir James Openshaw
1935-1938	Henry Percy Glover
1938-1950	John Catterall Jolly KC
1950-1958	Arthur Edgar Jalland QC
1958-1971	William Harrison Openshaw

Chairmen of Cumberland Quarter Sessions, 1886-1971

1886-1900	Richard Saul Ferguson
1900-1906	Rt Hon James William Lowther MP (Speaker of the House of Commons, 1905)
1907-1929	George Arthur Rimington
1930-1933	His Honour Judge Eustace Hills
1933-1945	Col Timothy Fetherstonhaugh DSO
1945-1953	His Honour Judge Allesbrook
1953-1963	His Honour Judge Fenwick QC
1963-1970	J M Davies QC (later Recorder of the City or Birmingham and subsequently His Honour Judge Davies QC)
1970-1971	A M Prestt QC (later His Honour Judge Prestt QC)

Deputy Chairman

1900-1905	Samuel Porter Foster
1905-1906	George Arthur Rimington
1907-1928	William Lewthwaite
1928-1933	Col Timothy Fetherstonhaugh
1933-1934	None Appointed
1934-1938	Philip Henry Fox
1938-1949	Charles Henry Roberts
1950-1953	His Honour Judge Fenwick KC
1953-1956	R S Nicklin (later His Honour Judge Nicklin)
1956-1963	J M Davies (and Deputy Chairman, 1971)
1956-1957	I G Sim, Penrith
1956-1957	T Young, Longtown
1958-1960	R D McCowan, Whitehaven
1958-1961	F G Sarsfield-Hall, CMG, DL, Keswick
1960-1971	J Westoll, DL, Longtown
1961-1970	J D Miller, Whitchaven
1962-1971	H R Grice, Bootle
1963-1966	G W Guthrie Jones, QC (later Recorder of Bolton)
1966-1970	A M Presst
1966-1971	R R Leech (later His Honour Judge Leech)
1969-1971	I H Morris Jones, QC
1969-1971	J Martin Collins
1969-1971	C Norman Lees

Chairmen of Westmorland Quarter Sessions

1909-1926	Hugh Cecil Lowther (5th Earl of Lonsdale 1909-1926)
1926-1944	Rt Hon Sir Lancelot Sanderson
1944-1968	Rt Hon Lord Chorley QC
1968-1971	(Ernest) Sanderson Temple MBE, QC

Recorders (COURTS ACT 1971)

Sworn in at:

Liverpool

11.01.1972	William Herbert Wainwright Jalland
	Ian Stephenson Webster
12.01.1972	David Bruce McNeill QC
	Ifor Henry Morris Jones QC
	Alan Shore Booth

Manchester

12.01.1972	Godfrey Heilpern QC
	Ernest Sanderson Temple MBE.,QC
	Thomas Patrick Russell QC
	David Charles Waddington QC
	George Alfred Carman QC
	Keith Ward Dewhurst
	John Michael Lever
	Charles Norman Lees
	John Herent Lord
	Desmond Fergus Franks
	John Martin Collins
	Kenneth James Tetley
	John Woodcock
14.01.1972	Benet Alan Hytner QC
01.03.1972	Robert James Hardy
	James Harvey Anglin Scarlett
	Ivor Ralph Taylor
	Kenneth John Taylor
	John Hugill

Liverpool

01.03.1972	Andrew Rankin QC
	Norman William Malin Sellers
	Roy Livingstone Ward
13.03.1972	Douglas Dunlop Brown

Lancaster

15.03.1972	Brian Roy Duckworth

Manchester

16.03.1972	John Coffey
20.03.1972	Walter Derek Thornley Hodgson QC
04.10.1972	Harry Hague
	Henry Aiden Kershaw

Liverpool

04.10.1972	Max Howard Feeny
15.12.1972	William Geraint Oliver Morgan QC
	Henry Lazarus Lachs
	William Rayley Wickham
19.12.1972	Norman Godfrey Wootton

Lancaster

16.10.1974	Richard Jeffreys Hampton Collinson

Manchester

20.12.1974	Gerard William Humphries

Liverpool

14.01.1975	John Kearns Gore
	Richard Graham Hamilton
11.11.1975	Joyanne Winifred Bracewell
	George Christopher Howsin Spafford
	Joseph Stewart Oakes
	Eric Somerset Jones
	Anthony Charles Jolly
14.11.1975	William James Glover QC
15.10.1976	Gerald Patrick Crowe QC

Manchester

15.10.1976	Iain Derek Laing Glidewell QC
17.01.1977	Mark Carlisle
25.04.1977	Andrew McArthur Gibb
	Richard Edward Ingram Pickering
14.07.1978	Christopher Dudley Roger Rose QC
	Robert Bruce Martin QC
	Frank Donald Hart QC
	Frederick Brian Carter
	Harold Keith Goddard
	John Jermyn Rowe
	Charles Barrie Knight Mantell
	Richard Ninian Barwick Clegg
	Reginald Lockett
	Eric Taylor

Liverpool

17.07.1978	Herbert Henry Andrew
	David Mayer Berkson
	Peter John Briggs
	Ann Marian Ebsworth
	Donald Murray Forster
	Manus Nunan
	Ingeborg Bernstein

(LDPE)

Henry Lachs, Bill Morgan QC, Bill Wickham, December 1972.

Oakes, Spafford, Somerset-Jones, Bracewell, Jolly.

Manchester

23.07.1980	John Kenneth Burke
	Anne Elizabeth Downey
	Simon James David Fawcus
	John Gilchrist
	Philip Michael Kershaw QC
	Rodney Conrad Klevan
	Gordon Keith Naylor
	John Alan Price QC
	Michael Alexander Geddes Sachs
	Leslie Shield
	John Anthony Stannard
05.09.1980	Rhys Everson Davies
30.04.1981	Nigel Ronald Buchanan MacLeod QC
	Ian Stephenson Webster (back from Tribunal Chairmanship)
	Maurice Francis Haigh
	Harold Samuel Singer
	Frank Michael Stanislaus Hudson
	Helen Marjorie Grindrod
	Michael Scott Blackburn

Liverpool

01.05.1981	Ronald John Dearden Livesey QC
	William Derrick Fairclough
	David Anthony Pirie
	David Clive Clarke
	Ian Burns Campbell
	William Henry Waldron

Manchester

28.07.1982	Daniel Joseph Brennan
	Julian Hall
	Charles Edwin Frederic James
	John William Kay
	John Michael Shorrock
	David Moorcroft Sumner
21.04.1983	Charles Bloom
	Philip Charles Clegg
	Thomas David Tattersall Hodson
	Bertram Catterall Maddocks
	David Anthony Poole

(MEN)

Carter, Richard Clegg, Martin QC, Rose QC, Mantell, Hart QC, Rowe, Lockett, Eric Taylor, Goddard.

(MEN)

Daniel Brennan, Michael Shorrock, Charles James, Julian Hall, John Kay.

Preston

25.04.1983	Robert Brown
	Richard Henry Quixano Henriques

Liverpool

26.04.1983	George Anthony Ensor
06.10.1983	John David Newton
08.10.1984	Denis Clark
	Sean Bruce Duncan
	David Marshall Evans QC
	Anne Heather Steel

Manchester

26.09.1985	Charles Joseph Mahon
	John Philip Townend
	Giles Wingate Wingate-Saul QC

Preston

03.10.1985	Anthony James Proctor

Liverpool

07.10.1985	John Fortnam Appleton
	David Leslie Bulmer
	Michael Emanuel Wolff
07.07.1986	Bruce Irvine Caulfield
	Rodney James Scholes

Preston

14.03.1988	Gerald Michael Clifton
	Terence Kay Earnshaw
	Jonathan Rowe Foster
	Jonathan Richard Barr Geake
	Mark Hedley
	Thomas Brendan Hegarty
	Anthony John Christopher Hoggett QC
	John Bruce MacMillan
	John Ambrose Morgan
	Anthony Paul Morris
	John Houghton Roberts
	Arthur Anthony Rumbelow
	Janet Hilary Smith QC

(LDPE)

David Marshall-Evans QC, Denis Clark, Sean Duncan, Heather Steel, 1984.

(LDPE)

Standing: Holloway, Howarth, Hussain, Fordham, Mackay, Tattershall, Armitage, Steiger, Anthony Gee, Gilliland QC, Boulton.
Sitting: Birkett QC, Machell QC, Daley, Steel, Eaglestone, Leeming QC, Grundy.

Liverpool

17.03.1988	David Michael Harris
	Francis David Owen
18.03.1988	Brian Henry Leveson QC
	David Lynch
23.03.1988	Andrew Nicholas Hubert Blake

Manchester

11.11.1988	Raymond Clayton Watson Bennett
	Howard Lownds Bentham
	William Patrick Morris
	Charles Peter Lawford Openshaw
	Leslie Rueben Portnoy
	Barry Woodward

Liverpool

28.07.1989	Ernest Keith Armitage
	Peter Vidler Birkett QC
	David John Boulton
	Judith Mary Philomena Daley
	Diana Barbara Eaglestone
	Robert Allan Fordham
	Anthony Hall Gee
	James Andrew David Gilliland QC
	Martin Anthony Wilson Grundy
	Frederick Reginald Bryn Holloway
	Nigel John Graham Howarth
	Mukhtar Hussein
	Ian Leeming QC
	David Ian Mackay
	Raymond Donatus Machell QC
	Elizabeth Mary Steel
	Martin Thomas Steiger
	Geoffrey Frank Tattersall
05.10.1990	Roderick Carus QC
	Nigel Benjamin Douglas Gilmour QC
	Mark Stephen Eastbum Grime QC
	Martin Peter Allweis
	Charles Francis Chruszcz
	David Simon Gee
	David George Maddison
	Stephen Vaughan Riordan
	Gillian Doreen Ruaux
	Christopher Bruce Tetlow
	Ian James Campbell Trigger
	David Andrew Turner
	Peter William Gordon Urquhart
	Raymond Wigglesworth

Manchester

06.09.1991	David Stephenson Gee
	Henry Brian Globe
	Timothy Roger Alan King QC
	Peter William Smith
	David Steer
	Andrew Thomas Sander

Liverpool

17.10.1991	John Lester Hand QC
17.07.1992	John Martyn Bennett
	Michael David Byrne
	Peter Stuart Fish
	Alastair John Forrest
	Leonard Clement Goldstone
	Gaias Gozem
	Richard Christopher Holman
	Timothy James Mort
	Edward Slinger
	Michael John Williams
24.07.1992	Richard Paul Brittain

Preston

08.07.1993	Christopher David Allen
	William Thomas Scatchard Braithwaite QC
	John Bromley-Davenport
	Roger Boyd Farley QC
	William George
	Raymond Charles Herman
	Leslie David Hull
	Lindsey Joy Kushner QC
	Peter Maurice Lakin
	Brian William Lewis
	Hiranya Garbha Narayan
	John Andrew Phillips
	John Christopher Phipps
	Phillip Ronald Raynor
	Paul Campbell Reid
	Anthony Patrick Russell
	David Andrew Stockdale
	David Rowland Swift
	Richard Kevin Kent Talbot
	Kenneth Henry Pinder Wilkinson
26.10.1994	Christopher John Alldis
	Stuart William Baker
	Christopher John Cornwall
	John Dowse
	David Thomas Fish
	Charles Roger Garside QC
	Michael John Henshell
	Richard Leon Marks
	Robert Platts
	Adrian Charles Smith

(LEP)

Standing, George, Wilkinson, Reid, Herman, Raynor, Allen, Talbot, Bromley-Davenport, Russell, Braithwaite QC, Phillips, Farley QC, Swift, Lakin, Hull, Lewis, Kushner QC, Stockdale, Narayan, Phipps. Sitting, Judge Robert Brown, Judge Lockett, Potter.J, Judge Townend, Judge Livesey QC.

(LEP)

Platts, Smith A, Henshell, Garside QC, Cornwall, Kay J, Fish, Baker, Marks, Dowse, Alldis.

Manchester

06.11.1995	David Stuart Aubrey
	The Hon Bernard Lewis Lever
	Caroline Jane Swift QC

Liverpool

16.01.1996	Anthony Howard Edwards

Manchester

08.10.1996	Philip David Cattan
	Andrew James Gilbart QC
	Iain McCormick Hamilton
	Alistair Stevenson Webster QC
	Pamela Hilary Badley
	Anthony Francis Scott Donovan
	Jonathan Eli Finestein
	Nicholas John Gilchrist
	David Milne Kerr
	Arthur Edwin Randall Noble
	Nicholas John Warren
09.03.1997	Margaret Ruth de Haas QC
	Gerard Francis McDermott
	Phillip Sycamore
02.10.1997	Laurence Frederick Mark Brown
	Alan David Conrad
	James Ross Duggan
	Rowena Margaret Goode
	Timothy Victor Holroyde QC
	Andrew Charles Lowcock
	Adrian Pirrie Lyon
	Andrew Gerard Moran QC
	Graham Eric Morrow QC
	James Kenneth Pickup
	Terence Rigby
	Maureen Bernadette Roddy
	Peter Winston Smith QC
	Barbara Joan Watson
16.03.1999	Peter Atherton
	Robert Kenneth Atherton
	Michael Jonathan Black QC
	Robert Stephen Dodds
	Andrew Jeremy Coulter Edis QC
	Anthony John Elleray
	Roger Hedgeland
	Katherine Lesley Hughes
	Ashley Charles Murray
	Lesley Anne Newton
	Michael Howard Redfern QC
	Stephen Paul Stewart QC
	Norman Alfred Wright

Preston

04.10.1999	Stephen John Bedford
	lain Saville Goldrein QC
	Margaret Wilby

Carlisle

28.07.2000	Barbara Forrester

Liverpool

06.09.2000	Peter Robert Ball
	John Trevor Benson
	Neville Leslie Biddle
	David Mark Brunnen
	Philip Andrew Butler
	Peter Sherwood McCrea Cowan
	Charles Sheridan Feeny
	Benjamin Clive Freedman QC
	Philip Nicholas Hinchliffe QC
	Michael Sloan Johnson
	Heather Claire Lloyd
	Peter Ramsey Main
	John Michael Andrew Murray
	Ernest Nigel Ryder QC
	Warwick Timothy Cresswell Smith
	Alastair Robert Lyon Warnock
11.09.2000	Thomas Patrick Ryan
13.09.2000	Timothy John Horlock QC
	Winston Ronald Hunter QC
	Mark George Turner QC
	Michael Andrew Abelson
	Alan James Booth
	Yvonne Ruth Coppell
	Philip Peter Steven Curran
	Simon Lawrence Earlham
	David Thomas Eccles
	David Anthony Hernandez
	Elliot Michael Knopf
	Eric Alan Lamb
	Mark Dieter Laprell
	Geoffrey James Lowe
	Beverly Anne Lunt
	Christina Margaret Lyon
	David Eric Manley
	Paul O'Brien
	Richard James Pratt
	Campbell Tait
	Bernard Graham Frank Wallwork
	David Henry Williams
20.09.2000	Edward Bartley Jones QC
	Gerard James Martin QC
	Frances Silvia Patterson QC
	Farooq Tahir Ahmed
	Peter Mark Cawson
	Paul Chaisty
	Nicholas Stephen Clarke

	John Vincent Corless
	Robert David Crawford
	Neil Flewitt
	Christopher Edward Freeman
	Sonia Gal
	Alan Kevin Grice
	Philip Michael David Grundy
	Michael Peter George Leeming
	Andrew Peter Long
	Andrew John McLoughlin
	Gail Ann Owen
	Jonathan Parkin
	Theresa Pepper
	Charles Graham Gregory Platts
	Derek Reed
	Margaret Elizabeth Rylands
	Barrie Searle
	Sarah Louise Singleton
	William Francis Waldron
	Graham Nash Wood

Preston

20.10.2000	Tania Veronica Griffiths
	Christopher John Hudson
	John Richard Jones
	Simon Peter Newell
	Timothy Robert Ryder

Manchester

27.03.2001	David Nahum Berkley QC
	Patrick John Field QC
09.05.2001	Nicholas Justin Braslavsky QC
	Angela Mary Nield

Preston

07.06.2001	Nigel Lawrence John Grundy
	Anthony Paul Hayden
	Simon John Killeen
	Jeremy John Bruce Rawkins
	Martin Fraser Walsh
	Peter Duncan Wright QC
	Anthony Patrick Russell QC
02.05.2002	Peter Joseph John Gregory

Liverpool

10.10.2002	Anna Louise Bancroft
	Karen Rachel Brody
	Anthony Francis O'Donohoe
	District Judge Craig Osbome
	Craig Gardener Sephton QC
15.10. 2002	Vincent Fraser QC
	Francis Peter Davies
	Suzanne Hazel Goddard
	Andrew Gwyn Menary
	Ahmed Nadim
	Elizabeth Jane Nicholls
	Jai Penna

Manchester

23.05.2003	Anthony Maurice Cross
	Stephen Richard Davies
	Maurice Alan Greene
	Mark Gareth Halliwell
	Simon Jonathan Hilton
	David Knifton
	Andrew Peter Nuttall
	(Anthony) Dennis Watson
24.06.2003	John Michael Paul Gowran Barratt
	Michael Charles Blakey
	Louis Bartholomew Anthony Browne
	Stuart Frank Driver
	Frances Margaret Heaton
	John James Rowley

Liverpool

27.11.2003	Nigel Garvin Clayton

Preston

30.6.2004	Nicholas Austin Fewtrell
	John Arthur Gibson
	Susan Grocott
	Jeremy Lasker
	Andrew Loveridge

Silks

Year	Name
1840	David Dundas
1855	Percival Andrew Pickering
1857	Henry Manisty
1861	Anthony Cleasby
	George Mellish
1863	John Joseph Powell
1864	John Bridge Aspinall
1865	Clement Milward
1866	Thomas Spinks
	George Little
1868	W Houseman Higgin
	Henry Wyndham West
	John Holker
	Charles Parker Butt
	John Archibald Russell
1869	Joseph Kay
	Thomas Hughes
1872	Leofric Temple
	John Berry Torr
	James Kemplay
	Charles Russell
	Farrer Herschell
	Judah Philip Benjamin
1873	Ralph Daniel Makinson Littler
1874	Charles Henry Hopwood
	William Ambrose
	John Edwards
1875	George Wirgman Hemming
	John Henry Baylis
	John Eldon Gorst
1877	William St James Wheelhouse
1880	James Jones Aston
	Frederick Waymouth Gibbs
	William Potter
	John Addison
	Sir William Thomas Charley
1881	Thomas Hutchinson Tristham
1882	Philip Albert Myburgh
1883	Richard Henn Collins
	John Charles Bigham
1885	Samuel Taylor
	Daniel O'Connell French
1886	Thomas Whittenbury Wheeler
	Lindsey Middleton Aspland
	Seward Brice
1888	Samuel Hall
	Ralph Neville
	John Gorell Bames
1889	(None appointed)
1890	Edmund Macrory
	Albert Venn Dicey
1891	William Cecil Smyly
	Joseph Frances Leese
	Henry Wilson Worsley-Taylor
	Robert Alfred McCall
1892	Henry Gordon Shee
	Alfred Hopkinson
	Joseph Walton
1893	Joseph Maghull Yates
	James Francis Oswald
	Charles James Fleming
	Francis William Raikes
	William Pickford
1894	William Mulholland
1895	Ernest Carpmael
	Edmund Robinson
	James Winterbottom Hamilton
	William Francis Kyffin Taylor
	John Meir Astbury
1896	Miles Walker Mattinson
	Paul Ogden Lawrence
	William Robert McConnell
	Charles Alfred Russell
1897	William Alexander Lindsay
	Charles Benjamin Bright McLaren
	Thomas Gilbert Carver
	Warington Baden-Powell
1898	Ernest Page
	Thomas Raffles Hughes
	Rufus Daniel Isaacs
1899	Butler Cole Aspinall
	Lord Robert Cecil
1900	William Bates Ferguson
1901	Collingwood Hope
	Allan Gibson Steel
	John Andrew Hamilton
	Thomas Gardner Horridge
1902	Ernest Robert Moon
1903	Frank Hamilton Mellor
	Lancelot Sanderson
	John Roskill

Year	Name
1904	Adolph Max Lazarus Langdon
1905	Edward Forbes Lankester
1906	Herbert Addington Rigg
	John Cameron Graham
	Arthur Jacob Ashton
	Arthur James Walter
1908	Sir Thomas Raleigh
	Alexander Grant
	Edward George Hemmerde
	Frederick Edwin Smith
1909	George Rhodes
	Leslie Frederic Scott
1910	Frederick Arthur Greer
	Maurice Hill
	Alexander Dingwall Bateson
	Christopher Clark Hutchinson
1911	(None appointed)
1912	Rigby Philip Watson Swift
	Gordon Hewart
	Joseph Herbert Cunliffe
1913	Sylvain Mayer
	Thomas Arnold Herbert
	Roger Bernard Lawrence
	Walter George Salis Schwabe
	Cyril Atkinson
	Thomas Clarke Pilling Gibbon
1914	William W McKenzie
1915-1916	(None appointed)
1919	Arthur Godfrey Roby
	John Mahan Gover
	Eustace Gilbert Hills
	Sir Claude Schuster
	James Francis Wallace Galbraith
	Ernest Wingate Wingate-Saul
	William Courthope Townsend Wilson
	Walter Greaves Lord
	Alfred Ravenscroft Kennedy
	William Norman Raebum
	Frank Boyd Merriman
	Rt Hon James Ian McPherson
	Alexander Thomas Miller
1920	James William Ross Brown
	Harold Chaloner Dowdall
	Gerald Berkeley Hurst
1921	Henry Straus Quixano Henriques
	John Guy Rutledge
1922	William Madden
	John Henry Layton
	Tom Eastham
	John Edward Singleton
	Sir Edmund Robert Bartley Dennis
1923	Sir Harold Smith
	Reginald Mitchell Banks
1924	Joseph Cooksey Jackson
1925	John Brown Sandbach
1926	Clement Edward Davies
1927	Dennis Nowell Pritt
1928	Noel Barré Goldie
	Harold Derbyshire
1929	Alfred Hildesley
	Robert Kingsley Chappell
	Gerald Rufus, Viscount Erleigh
1930	Neville Laski
	George Justin Lynskey
	James Dickinson
1931	Cyril Fullard Entwistle
1932	Edward Lascelles Fleming
	William Gorman
1933	Wilfred Clothier
1934	David Maxwell Fyfe
1935	John Henry Thorpe
	Frederick Aked Sellers
	Henry Urmston Willink
	John William Morris
1936	Henry Percy Glover
1937	Philip Vos
	Fred Pritchard
	Lionel Frederick Heald
1938	Patrick Redmond Barry
1939	John Catterall Jolly
	Geoffrey Glegg Hutchinson
	Hartley William Shawcross
1940-42	(None appointed)
1943	Edward Wooll
	Geoffrey Clifford Tyndale
	Ronw Moelwyn Hughes
1944	(None appointed)
1945	Christian Bedford Fenwick
	Henry Ince Nelson
	Louis Halle Gluckstein
	Sydney Scholefield Allen
	George Harold Lloyd-Jacob
	Owen Latham Bateson
	Basil Edward Nield
	Albert Denis Gerrard
1946	Sir John Forster
1947	Edmund Rowson
	John Selwyn Brooke Lloyd
1948	Sir Leonard Stone
	Allan Walmstey

Judges Service, Liverpool Cathedral, 1995.

(HS)

Judges at re-opening of Minshull Street, Manchester 1996.

Newsham House, Liverpool 1975. Kilner Brown J, Nield J, Hollings J, Judge Blackett-Ord.

Judges at Manchester 1986. Back Row: Singer, Hardy, Lord, Humphries, O'Donoghue, Sachs, Carter, Lees. Middle: Franks, Da Cunha, Blackett-Ord, Prestt QC, Temple QC, Gerrard, Jalland. Front: Hall, Webster, Fawcus, Jolly, Hammond, Manchester, 16 October 1986.

(DL)

Liverpool Circuit and District Judges, 2001.

Year	Name
1949	Reginald Clark
	Ashton Wentworth Roskill
	Rose Heilbron
1950	Arthur Edgar Jalland
	Geoffrey Glynn Blackledge
	Constantine John Colombos
	David Karmel
1951	David Weitzman
	Alan Abraham Mocatta
	Henry Burton
	John Robertson Dunn Crichton
	Daniel Brabin
1952	Philip Ingress Bell
	Edward Johnson Rimmer
1953	Elliot Marcet Gorst
	Fenton Atkinson
	Jack Messoud Eric Di Victor Nahum
	Richard Haddow Forrest
1954	Alexander Karmel
	John Thompson
	Joseph Donaldson Cantley
1955	John Banks Walmsley
	Joseph Stanley Watson
1958	Robert Gordon Clover
	Richard Martin Gilbert
1960	Leslie Rigg
	Hubert Holmes Munroe
1961	Lord Chorley
	John Glyn Burrell
	Walter Derek Hodgson
	Michael Robert Emanuel Kerr
1962	Godfrey Heilpem
	Joseph Marie Davies
1963	Griffith Winston Guthrie Jones
	George Joseph Bean
1965	Frank Whitworth
	Peter Thomas Sherrington Boydell
	Cecil Montacute Clothier
1966	Jack Samuel Ronald Abdela
	Basil Thomas Wigoder
	Alfred Kenneth Hollings
	David Bruce McNeill
	Richard Buchanan-Dunlop
1967	Thomas Herbert Pigot
	Albert Michael Maguire
1968	Frank Philip Rideal Hinchliffe
	Andrew Rankin
	Richard Frederick Stone
1969	Ernest Sanderson Temple
	Ben Atkinson Wortley
	Ifor Henry Morris Jones
	Iain Glidewell
	William James Glover
1970	Arthur Miller Prestt
	Myrella Cohen
	Benet Alan Hytner
	Stewart Taverner Bates
1971	William Geraint Oliver Morgan
	Thomas Patrick Russell
	David Charles Waddington
	George Alfred Carman
	Mark Carlisle
1972	Roy Livingstone Ward
	John Martin Collins
	John Montague Dovenor
	Michael Morland
1973	James Fitzhugh
	Ivor Ralph Taylor
	Gerald Patrick Crowe
	Gerard Henry Wright
	John Stewart Hobhouse
1974	Norman Alexander Miscampbell
	Reginald Houlker
	Christopher Dudley Roger Rose
1975	Alan Shore Booth
1976	Arnold Justin Price
	Douglas Dunlop Brown
	John Hugill
1977	John Michael Lever
	Bernard Arthur Marder
	Robert Bruce Martin
1978	Eric Somerset Jones
	Arthur Davidson
	Joyanne Bracewell
	Frank Donald Hart
	Derek William Bowett
1979	Harold Keith Goddard
	Charles Barrie Knight Mantell
	Richard Ninian Barwick Clegg
	Nigel Ronald Buchanan MacLeod
	Frederick Harold Dean
	Peter Michael Hall Mottershead
1980	Frederick Brian Carter
	John Alan Price
	Philip Michael Kershaw
	Stephen John Lindsay Oliver

(UPA)

Herbert McMath with his silks, Roy Ward QC and Michael Morland QC, 1972.

(DL)

Judge Henry Globe QC, Leveson J, Rose LJ, Lloyd J, David Clarke J. Judges Service, Liverpool Anglican Cathedral, 17 October 2004.

(WG)

Five Recorders, Bill Wickham, David Maddison, Rhys Davies, Reg Lockett, David Clarke, 16 February 2003.

(DL)

Royal Courts of Justice, October 2001. Standing: Leveson J, Henriques J, Mantell LJ, Lord Hobhouse, Rose LJ, Kay LJ, Smith J, Burton J. Seated: Douglas Brown J, Bracewell J, Hale LJ, Ebsworth J, Morland J, Poole J.

(UPA)

Ten Manchester Silks, 1999. *Marks, Russell, Wright, Wigglesworth, Hincliffe, Booth, Braslavsky, Conrad, Berkley, G McDermott.*

Year	Name
1981	Ronald John Deardon Livesey
	Michael Dean
	Rhys Everson Davies
	David Marshall Evans
1982	Herbert Henry Andrew
	John Jermyn Rowe
	Helen Marjorie Grindrod
	William Henry Waldron
1983	Michael Leon Brent
	David Clive Clarke
	Giles Wingate-Saul
1984	John William Kay
	Rodney Conrad Klevan
	David Anthony Poole
	James Andrew David Gilliland
	Michael John Burton
1985	John Kenneth Burke
	Daniel Joseph Brennan
1986	Richard Henry Quixano Henriques
	Anthony John Christopher Hoggett
	Brian Henry Leveson
	Janet Hilary Smith
1987	Charles Bloom
	Mark Stephen Eastburn Grime
	Rodney James Scholes
	Nicholas James Forwood
1988	John Lester Hand
	Ian Leeming
	Raymond Donatus Machell
	John Michael Shorrock
1989	Peter Vidler Birkett
	Jonathan Rowe Foster
	David Michael Harris
	Brenda Marjorie Hoggett (Hale)
	Anna Maureen Worrall
1990	Roderick Carus
	Anthony Hall Gee
	Nigel Benjamin Douglas Gilmour
	Arthur Anthony Rumbelow
1991	Gerald Edward Barling
	Andrew James Gilbart
	Timothy Roger Alan King
	David Goodwin Lane
	John Vandeleur Martin
	Anthony Paul Morris
	Charles Peter Lawford Openshaw
	David Andrew Turner
1992	William Thomas Scatchard Braithwaite
	Charles Francis Chruszcz
	Thomas Brendan Hegarty
	Mukhtar Hussein
	Lindsey Joy Kushner
	Stephen Vaughan Riordan
	Peter Winston Smith
	Geoffrey Frank Tattersall
1993	Stephen James Allcock
	Anthony John Elleray
	Roger Boyd Farley
	Robert Allan Fordham
	Charles Roger Garside
	Leonard Clement Goldstone
	Michael Howard Redfern
	David Steer
	Caroline Swift
1994	Ernest Keith Armitage
	Henry Brian Globe
	Andrew Gerard Moran
	Philip Ronald Raynor
	Martin Thomas Steiger
1995	Christopher David Allan
	Michael Jonathan Black
	James William Bonney
	Stephen John Sauvain
	David Andrew Stockdale
	Alistair Stephenson Webster
1996	Timothy Victor Holroyde
	Graham Eric Morrow
	Howard Lownds Bentham
	Stephen Paul Stewart
	Ian Hamilton-Douglas Hughes
1997	Gaias Gozem
	Richard Isaacson
	David Thomas Fish
	Iain Saville Goldrein
	Edward Bartley Jones
	Benjamin Clive Freedman
	Andrew Jeremy Coulter Edis
	Timothy John Horlock
	Ernest Nigel Ryder
1998	David Stuart Aubrey
	Margaret Ruth de Haas
	Frances Sylvia Patterson
	Mark George Turner

1999	Raymond Wigglesworth	2001	Paul Campbell Reid
	Anthony Patrick Russell		John Trevor Benson
	Richard Leon Marks		Vincent Fraser
	Alan David Conrad		Craig Gardner Sephton
	Gerard Francis McDermott		Peter Mark Cawson
	David Nahum Berkley		Paul Chaisty
	Philip Nicholas Hinchliffe	2002	John Bromley Davenport
	Peter Duncan Wright		Graham Nash Wood
	Michael John Booth		John Richard Jones
	Nicholas Justin Braslavsky		Anthony Paul Hayden
2000	James Kenneth Pickup	2003	John Raymond Vincent McDermott
	Gerard James Martin		Peter Ramsay Main
	Patrick John Field		David Eric Manley
	Winston Ronald O'Sullivan Hunter		Neil Flewitt
			Andrew Gwyn Menary

Sadly, there were no silks in 2004 as the Government had suspended the selection process. The Bar Council and the Law Society have agreed a scheme for appointing silks. There is to be an independent selection panel of nine including lay members. References will be taken and all those candidates with a realistic prospect of appointment will be interviewed. Any appointments made in 2005 are likely to be late in the year.

(DL)

McDermott, Menary and Flewitt, Maundy Thursday 2003.

County Court Registrars 1876-1991
District Judges 1991-2004

Accrington and Haslington

1876-1896	T Woodcock jnr
1897-1913	J Woodcock
1914	Vacant
1915-1926	W Woodcock (Accrington only from 1921)
1927	R Bremner
1927-1936	R Bremner, W Woodcock
1937-1939	P M C Hayman
1940-1948	Sir James H S Aitken
1949-1961	C Waddington
1962-1978	J Parry
1979	R H Haythornthwaite
1980-1981	J Parry and R H Haythornthwaite
1982-1987	R H Haythornthwaite, W Ashworth
1988-1989	R H Haythornthwaite, W Ashworth, A M Verity, P J L Wolf
1990-1993	R H Haythornthwaite, W Ashworth, A M Verity
1994	I J Belcher, I J Pickup
1995-1998	I J Belcher, I J Pickup, J MGeddes
1999	J D Heyworth, I J Pickup, J M Geddes

Alston (combined with Haltwhistle in Northumberland in 1902)

1876-1895	Joseph Dickinson
1896	Vacant
1897-1901	J Thompson

Altrincham

1876-1888	James Southern
1889	W E Cave
1890-1902	J Lamb
1903-1947	J Bowen-Rowlands
1948-1967	W R Davies
1968-1971	W R Davies and H Kushner
1972-1974	Davies, Kushner, R Lockett
1975	Davies, P F Gavin, Kushner, Lockett
1976-1978	Kushner, Lockett,Gavin, P K M Delroy
1979	P J L Wolf, G P Taylor
1980	Wolf, Taylor, W Ashcroft
1981-1988	Wolf, Taylor
1989-1993	Wolf
1994	Wolf, D J Shannon
1995	Wolf
1996	D E Russell, M J Gregory, Mrs A J C Brazier
1997	Russell, Gregory, Brazier, J R Clegg
1998-1999	Russell, Gregory, Brazier, Clegg, B N Gaunt, C Osbome

Ambleside

1876-1879	John Fisher
1880-1921	George Gatey

Appleby

1876-1909	Edward Heelis jnr
1910-1925	Edward A Heelis
1926-1945	E J Fairer
1946-1947	C Leathes
1948-1957	C Fairer
1958	No entry
1959-1966	J F Beaty

Ashton under Lyne/Tameside

1876-1905	H Hall
1906-1939	H G Hall
1940-1943	H Pownall
1944-1964	John P Peacock
1965-1972	J Irvine Caulfield
1973-1979	Caulfield, F W Smith
1981	Caulfield, Smith, W Ashcroft
1982-1983	Caulfield, Smith
1984-1985	Smith, J L Burton
1986	D Lambert, Burton, Smith
1987-1988	Burton, Smith, D B Chapman and Mrs M J Wilby
1989-1990	Burton, D E Russell and Smith
1991-1993	Burton, Russell, J F Duerden, Smith
1994	Russell, M J Gregory, C R Fairclough, Mrs A J C Brazier, D J Shannon, G A Needham
1995	Russell, Gregory, Brazier, Needham, P S Stockton
1996	Stockton, R R P Ackroyd, J Flanagan, Wilby, B N Gaunt
1998-1999	Stockton, C Osbourne, B N Gaunt

Barrow in Furness

1876-1882	T Postlethwaite
1883-1893	T and W Postlethwaite
1894-1905	W Postlethwaite
1906-1914	C J C Pridham
1915-1918	J F Hodgson
1919-1920	C J C Pridham
1921-1951	J F Hodgson
1952-1970	S J Fisher
1971-1973	A Dunn
1974-1982	Anthony J Proctor
1983	Proctor, J N P White, A N Verity
1984-1985	Proctor, Verity, J Lythgoe
1985-1986	Lythgoe, G C P Walker
1987-1989	Lythgoe, Walker, Proctor, Verity
1990-1993	Lythgoe
1994-1995	Walker
1996-1999	J A James

Reading of the Proclamation

(LDPE)

Liverpool 13 January 1984, Judge Lawton, Judge Nance, Judge Blackett-Ord, McNeill J, Judge Temple MBE QC, Judge Jones, Judge Bingham QC, Judge Pickering, Recorder Price QC.

(TM)

Liverpool 17 January 2001. Judge David Clarke QC, Leveson J, Douglas Brown J, Coleridge J.

Birkenhead

1876-1879	James Watson
1880-1889	J R Williams
1890-1911	W E Cave
1912-1913	W E Cave, J B Ottley
1914-1916	W E Cave
1917-1924	W E Cave, D R White
1925-1928	D R White
1929-1934	E D Symond
1935-1936	T J Benjamin
1937-1940	J K Blackwood
1941-1944	J K Blackwood and T J Benjamin
1945-1952	D H Nield
1953-1961	N G H Atkinson
1962-1965	M Birks
1966-1974	A V Cunliffe
1975	Cunliffe, M A W Grundy, A M Verity
1976-1978	S Prothero
1979-1985	R W Yates
1985	Yates, W A Richardson
1986-1987	Yates, B Wolfson
1988-1990	Yates, Wolfson, R A McCullagh, W A Richardson
1991	S W Travers, McCullagh, Richardson
1992-1993	Richardson, McCullagh
1994	Richardson, McCullagh, Travers
1995	Richardson, McCullagh, Travers, Mrs M A Frost
1996	(as above) and Miss E Johnson
1997-1998	Richardson, McCullagh, Travers, Mrs S Wright
1998-1999	McCullagh, Travers, Mornington, J L Clark, M A Hovington

Blackburn

1876-1899	J Bolton
1900-1920	J N Withers
1921-1927	R Bremner
1928-1939	R Bremner and W Woodcock
1940-1944	R Bremner and W J Plant
1945	Bremner, Plant, A Desquesnes
1946-1947	Plant and Desquesnes
1948-1960	Plant, C R Davies
1961-1978	Davies, G N P White
1979-1982	White, A M Verity
1983-1993	Verity, R H Haythornthwaite, W Ashworth
1993-1994	I J Belcher, I J Pickup
1995-1998	Belcher, Pickup, J T Turner, J M Geddes
1999	Pickup, Turner, Geddes, J D Heyworth

Blackpool

1882-1885	E J Patteson
1886-1887	Patteson, H E J Parry
1888	H E J Parry
1889-1894	H J Parry
1895-1911	H I Parry
1912-1920	H I Parry, Wykeham Parry
1921-1925	H W Clemesha
1926	Vacant
1927-1939	L Matley
1940-1945	R Bremner, W J Plant
1946-1947	Bremner, Plant, A Desquesnes
1947	Plant, Desquesnes
1948-1960	Plant, C R Davies
1961-1978	Davies, G N P White
1979-1983	White, A M Verity
1984	Verity, R H Haythornthwaite, W Ashworth
1985	Verity, F Lythgoe
1986	Verity, Lythgoe, A Proctor
1987	Verity, Proctor, M W Jeffreys, G C P Walker
1988-1993	Jeffreys, Walker
1993	B Woods, G Ashton
1994	Woods, Ashton, J A James
1995-1996	Woods, M E Buckley
1997-1999	Woods, Buckley, R M Forrester

Bolton

1876-1879	T Holden
1880-1887	T Holden, C H Holden
1888-1892	C H Holden
1893-1914	A T Holden
1915-1933	C E Hulton
1934-1947	N Higham
1948-1957	A S Broughton
1958-1960	J A Lloyd Humphreys
1961-1971	D J Macbeth
1972-1975	Macbeth, P J L Wolf
1976-1979	Wolf, G P Taylor
1980-1981	Wolf, Taylor, W Ashworth
1981	Wolf, Taylor, W A Richardson
1983-1985	Wolf, Taylor
1986	Wolf, Taylor, D R Pomfret
1987-1990	Wolf, Taylor, Pomfret, Mrs M J Wilby
1991-1993	Wolf, Taylor, Wilby
1994	Wolf, Wilby, G R Ashton, J F Duerden, D J Shannon
1995	Wilby, Duerden
1996	Wilby, Duerden, B McGrath, Mrs J Shaw
1997-1998	Wilby, Duerden, Shaw
1999	Wilby, Shaw

Brampton

1876-1879	John Lee
1880-1890	John Carrick
1891-1901	J B Lee
1902-1907	A Lee
1908-1942	H S Cartmel

Burnley

1876-1931	W H Hartley
1932-1939	P M C Hayman
1940-1948	Sir J H S Aitken
1949-1961	C Waddington
1962-1975	J Parry
1976-1978	Parry, A M Verity
1979-1981	Parry, R H Haythornthwaite
1982-1987	Haythornthwaite, W Ashworth
1988-1993	Haythornthwaite, Ashworth, A M Verity
1994	I J Belcher, I J Pickup
1995-1998	Belcher, Pickup, J M Geddes
1999	Pickup, Geddes, J D Heyworth

Bury

1876-1882	E A Grundy
1883-1888	T S Grundy
1889-1898	H Brierley
1899-1928	C H Pickstone
1929-1933	F Hall Taylor
1934-1947	N Higham
1948-1957	A S Broughton
1958-1960	J A Lloyd Humphreys
1961-1971	D J Macbeth
1972-1976	Macbeth, P J L Wolf
1976-1979	Wolf, G P Taylor
1980-1981	Wolf, Taylor and W Ashworth
1982-1986	Wolf, Taylor
1986-1987	Wolf, D B Chapman
1988-1993	Taylor, Mrs M J Wilby
1994	Wilby, J F Duerden, D J Shannon
1995	Wilby, Duerden
1996	Wilby, Duerden, B V McGrath, Mrs J Shaw
1996-1998	Wilby, Duerden, Mrs J Shaw
1999	Wilby, Duerden, C M Swintley

Carlisle

1876-1888	H J Halton
1889-1895	Halton, J Hodgson
1896	J Hodgson
1897-1938	J Errington
1939-1945	A M MacPhail
1946-1947	C Leathes
1948-1978	J F Beaty
1979-1999	R J Holloway

Chorley

1876-1883	R Jackson
1884-1917	B A E Jackson
1918-1924	(merged with Preston)
1925-1926	H W Clemesha
1927	W Woodcock
1928-1939	Woodcock, R Bremner
1940-1944	Bremner, W J Plant
1945	Bremner, Plant, A Desquesnes
1946-1947	Plant, Desquesnes
1948-1960	Plant, C R Davies
1961-1978	Davies, G N P White
1979-1982	White, A M Verity
1983-1987	Verity
1988-1991	A J Proctor, J G Turner
1992-1999	Turner, P M Fairclough

Clitheroe

1876-1908	J Eastham
1909	Vacant
1910-1922	T Eastham
1923	Vacant
1924	(merged with Blackburn)

Cockermouth (and Workington from 1884)

1876-1917	Edward L Waugh
1918-1961	J N St George Curwen
1962-1979	J F Beaty
1979-1987	R J Holloway
1988-1992	Holloway, G C P Walker
1993-1994	Holloway
1995	Walker
1996-1999	J A James

Colne/Nelson

1876-1882	W J Carr
1883-1920	J Carr
1921-1932	W A Pilgrim
1933-1939	P M C Hayman
1940-1948	Sir James H S Aitken
1949-1961	C Waddington
1962-1978	J Parry
1979-1981	Parry and Haythornthwaite
1982-1987	Haythornthwaite, W Ashworth
1988-1993	Haythornthwaite, Ashworth, A M Verity
1994	I J Belcher, I J Pickup
1995-1998	Belcher, Pickup, J M Geddes
1999	Pickup, Geddes, J D Heyworth

Garstang

1876-1879	J Stanley
1880-1895	G H Dickson
1896-1913	J B F Whiteside
1914	Vacant
1915-1920	H P Forshaw

Kendal

1876-1908	R F Thompson
1909-1947	G E Cartmel
1948-1958	C Fairer
1959-1961	J F Beaty
1962-1970	S J Fisher
1971-1974	A Dunn
1975-1982	A J Proctor
1983-1986	R J Holloway
1987	F Lythgoe
1988-1994	M W Jeffreys
1994-1996	R H Haythornthwaite
1998-1999	G Nuttall

Keswick

1877-1901	Robert Broatch
1902-1934	J Broatch
1935	(merged with Workington and Cockermouth)

Kirby Lonsdale

1876-1904	A G B Pearson
1905-1945	Alexander Pearson

Kirkham

1876-1899	W J Dickson
1900-1904	R F Addie
1905-1924	W J Read

Lancaster

1876-1895	William T Sharp
1896-1939	L Holden
1940-1944	R Bremner, W J Plant
1945	Bremner, Plant, Desquesnes
1946-1947	Plant, Desquesnes
1948-1960	Plant, C R Davies
1961-1974	Davies, G N P White
1975-1982	A J Proctor
1983	Proctor, White, A M Verity
1984-1986	Proctor, F Lythgoe
1987	Proctor, Lythgoe, Verity, G C P Walker
1988-1993	Lythgoe
1994-1996	R H Haythornthwaite
1997	Haythornthwaite, R M Forrester
1998	Forrester
1999	Forrester, G Nuttall

Leigh

1876-1888	T Holden
1889-1892	A T Holden
1893-1900	H S Ferguson
1901-1929	W W Cannon
1930-1960	D R White
1961-1970	J A Lloyd Humphreys
1971-1974	M A W Grundy
1975	Grundy, A M Verity, A V Cunliffe
1976-1978	Grundy
1979-1986	Grundy, I J Belcher
1987-1993	Belcher
1994	E Donnelly
1995	Donnelly, I Bennett
1996-1998	Donnelly, G J Fitzgerald
1999	Donnelly, N A Law

The Bar

(DC)

Bob Montgomery and Colin Cunningham, Birkenhead 1980s.

(DC)

Bryan Joynes and Michael Montgomery, 1980s.

(DC)

Atherton, McDermott, Edis, Teresa Pepper, Macmillan. Norton Street Robing Room, 1980s.

(DL)

Rod Carus QC, Tony Carus, Cecil Henriques, Richard Henriques QC (60th Anniversary Mess for Tony Caras).

(DC)

Justin Price QC, Gerard Wright QC, Michael Maguire QC.

(DC)

Carville, Simm, Henshell, Riordan, Limont, Pratt, Sessions House Library, 1980s.

(DC)

Michael Montgomery, Stephen Bedford, Richard Brittain, David Aubrey, St George's Hall Library, 1980s.

Liverpool

1876	Henry Hime, J F Watson
1877-1879	J F Watson, Thomas Bellringer
1880-1906	Thomas Bellringer, William Cooper
1907-1916	Thomas Bellringer-Howarth, William Cooper
1917	Bellringer-Howarth, Alleyne Brown
1918-1928	Brown, C E Nield
1929-1934	Nield, E D Symond
1935-1936	Symond, T J Benjamin
1937-1947	Benjamin, J K Blackwood
1948-1956	Benjamin, J G Bryson
1957-1959	J G Bryson, J D Kewish
1960	J G Bryson
1961-1965	Bryson, J Tegid Jones (A V Cunliffe. Assistant)
1966-1971	Bryson, Tegid Jones
1972-1975	Bryson, Tegid Jones, C Winter, W Morris Jones
1976-1978	Bryson, Tegid Jones, Winter,Morris Jones, R Metcalfe, P Berkson
1979	Tegid Jones, Winter, Morris Jones, Metcalfe, Berkson
1980-1981	Tegid Jones, Winter, Morris Jones, Metcalfe, Berkson, K H P Wilkinson
1982	Winter, Morris Jones, Metcalfe, Berkson, Wilkinson
1983-1985	(the above), D L Harris
1986	(the above), W G Harrison
1987-1990	Grundy, Berkson, Wilkinson, Richardson, Harris, D Gee, B Wolfson
1991	(the above), R A McCullagh, B W Travers
1992-1993	Grundy, Berkson, Wilkinson, Richardson, Harris, Gee, Wolfson, McCullagh
1994	(the above), E Knopf
1995	(the above), Miss E Johnson, Miss M Mornington
1996-1998	Grundy, Berkson, Gee, Harris, McCullagh, Wolfson, Travers, I Bennett, Knopf, Johnson, Mornington
1999	Berkson, Harris, Gee, Wolfson, McCullagh, Travers, Bennett, Knopf, Johnson, Mornington, Fitzgerald, Mrs S Wright, J Clark

Manchester

1876	Samuel Kay
1877-1894	Samuel Kay, Charles Lister
1895-1924	A H Atkinson
1925-1934	R F Addie
1935-1948	K T S Dockray
1949-1950	W R Davies
1951-1953	Davies, H Pownall
1954-1955	Davies, Pownall, J E W Booth
1956-1957	Davies, Pownall, J A Lloyd Humphreys
1958-1960	Davies, C N P White (assistant)
1961-1962	Davies, A, H Hibbert (assistant)
1963-1970	Davies, H Kushner (assistant)
1971	Davies, Kushner
1972-1973	Davies, Kushner, R Lockett
1974	Davies, Kushner, Lockett, P F Gavin
1975	Kushner, Lockett, Gavin

1976-1978	(as above), B K M Delroy
1979-1981	(as above), D B Evans
1982	Kushner, Gavin, Delroy, Evans
1983	(as above), P E Keogh
1984	(as above), D S Gee
1985-1987	Kushner, Gavin, Delroy, Evans, Keogh, Gee
1988	(as above), C F Beattie, P S Fish
1989	Kushner, Gavin, Deiroy, Evans, Gee, Beattie and Fish
1990	(as above), C E Freeman
1991-1993	Kushner, Delroy, Evans, Gee, Beattie, Fish
1994	(as above), J M Griffiths, E R Jones, D J Shannon
1995	Beattie, Evans, C E Freeman, Griffiths, C R Fairclough, Jones, Shannon, Mrs V Buckley
1996	(as above) and G A Needham, J J B Rawkins, A J J Harrison, M J Payne
1997-1999	Beattie, Freeman, Griffiths, Fairclough, Jones, Shannon, Needham, Buckley, Rawkins, Harrison, B V McGrath

Oldham

1876-1889	J F Tweedale
1890-1892	C T Tweedale
1893-1906	C T and F N Tweedale
1907-1939	F N Tweedale
1940-1943	H Pownall
1944-1945	N M Higham
1946-1964	John P Peacock
1965-1974	J I Caulfield
1975-1979	Caulfield, F W Smith
1980-1981	Caulfield, Smith, W Ashworth
1982	Caulfield, Smith, W A Richardson
1983	Caulfield, Smith, J L Burton, D E Russell
1984-1986	Smith, Burton and Russell
1987	(as above), Mrs M J Wilby, D B Chapman
1988-1990	Smith, Burton, Russell
1991	(as above), J F Duerden, J M Griffiths
1992-1993	Burton, Russell
1994	Russell, C R Fairclough, M J Gregory, Mrs A J C.Brazier, D J Shannon, G A Needham
1995	Russell, Gregory, Needham, P S Stockton
1996	Stockton, R R P Ackroyd, J Flanagan, P T Wilby
1997-1998	(as above), B N Gaunt
1999	Stockton, Ackroyd, P T Wilby, C R Fox, C Osbome

Penrith

1876-1885	Carleton Varty
1886-1911	C Fairer
1912-1945	E J Fairer
1946-1947	C Leathes
1948-1957	C Fairer
1958-1962	(administered from Kendal)
1963-1978	J F Beaty
1979-1999	R J Holloway

Poulton-le -Fylde

1876-1882	E J Patteson

Preston

1876-1899	F C Hulton
1900-1913	W J Dickson
1914-1925	H W Clemesha
1926	Vacant
1927	W Woodcock
1928-1939	R Bremner, W Woodcock
1940-1944	Bremner, W J Plant
1945	Bremner, Plant, A Desquesnes
1946-1947	Plant, Desquesnes
1948-1960	Plant, C R Davies
1961-1978	Davies, G N P White
1979-1983	White, A M Verity, A J Proctor
1984-1985	Verity, Proctor, F Lythgoe
1986	(as above), G C P Walker
1987	Verity, Proctor, Walker, M W Jeffreys
1988-1989	(as above), J G Turner
1990-1991	Proctor, Tumer
1992-1993	Turner, P M Fairclough
1994	(as above), G R Ashton
1995	(as above), J A James
1996-1999	Tumer, Fairclough, Ashton, R M Forrester

Rawtenstall and Bacup

1876-1891	E M Wright
1892-1925	A Wright
1926	W Woodcock
1927-1928	R Bremner
1929-1932	Bremner, Woodcock
1933-1939	P M C Hayman
1940-1948	Sir J H S Aitken
1949-1961	C Waddington
1962-1979	J Parry
1979-1981	Parry, R H Haythornthwaite
1982-1987	Haythornthwaite, W Ashworth
1988-1993	(as above), A M Verity
1994	I J Belcher
1995-1998	Belcher, I J Pickup, J M Geddes
1999	Pickup, Geddes, J D Heyworth

Rochdale

1876-1891	R Jackson
1892-1910	J T Worth
1911-1933	J A Hudson
1934-1943	Arnold Desquesnes
1944-1947	N M Higham
1948-1957	A S Broughton
1958-1959	J A Lloyd Humphrey
1960-1961	C Waddington
1962-1978	J Parry
1979-1981	Parry, R H Haythornthwaite
1982	Haythornthwaite, W Ashworth
1983 - 1985	J L Burton, D E Russell
1986	Burton, Russell, B A Steinberg, Haythornthwaite
1987	(as above save DB Chapman replaces Burton)
1988-1993	Steinberg Chapman
1994	Steinberg, Chapman, D J Shannon
1995	Chapman
1996	P S Stockton, R R P Ackroyd, J Flanagan, P T Wilby
1997-1999	Stockton, Acroyd, Flanagan, Wilby, B N Grant

St Helens

1876-1882	John Andsell
1883-1884	Andsell, W Tyrer
1885-1911	Tyrer
1912	Vacant
1913-1927	E W Swift
1928	H Brierley
1929-1960	D R White
1961-1970	J A Lloyd Humphreys
1971-1973	M A W Grundy
1974	Grundy, A M Verity
1975	Grundy, Verity, A V Cunliffe
1976-1978	Grundy
1979-1982	Grundy, I J Belcher
1983-1986	Grundy, I J Belcher, R W Yates
1987	(as above), DR Pomfret
1988	(as above), D B Chapman, R A McCullagh
1989-1990	Yates, Pomfret, McCullagh
1991	Pomfret, McCullagh, B W Travers
1992-1993	Pomfret
1994	Pomfret, McCullagh, Travers, I Bennett, E Donnelly, GA Humphreys-Roberts
1995	Pomfret, Bennett, Humphreys-Roberts, Mrs E Johnson
1996	Pomfret, Bennett, Humphreys-Roberts
1997	(as above), Mrs S Wright
1998-1999	Pomfret, Bennett, Humphreys-Roberts, BW Travers

Salford

1876-1886	F C Hulton
1887-1904	F Smith
1905-1924	R Forrester Addie
1925-1933	F Hall Taylor
1934-1943	Arnold Desquesnes
1944-1947	N M Higham
1948	W R Davies
1949-1952	N G H Atkinson
1953-1957	A S Broughton
1958-1960	J A Lloyd Humphreys
1961-1971	D J Macbeth
1972-1975	Macbeth, P J L Wolf
1976-1978	H Kushner, R Lockett, P F Gavin, B K M Delroy
1979	Wolf, G P Taylor
1980-1981	Wolf, Taylor, W Ashworth
1982	Wolf, Taylor, W A Richardson
1983-1985	J L Burton, D E Russell
1986	Burton, Russell, B A Steinberg
1987	(as above), P J L Wolf
1988-1990	Steinberg
1991-1993	Steinberg, D B Chapman

1994	(as above), D J Shannon
1995	Chapman
1996-1998	Chapman, J D Heyworth
1999	Chapman, Miss C E O'Leary

Southport

1876-1881	William Welsby
1882-1891	Wm Welsby, J H Welsby
1892-1898	William Welsby
1899-1907	J Smallshaw
1908-1916	A Brown
1917-1933	F W Brown
1934	Vacant
1935-1960	D R White
1961-1970	J A Lloyd Humphreys
1971-1974	M A W Grundy
1975	Grundy, A M Verity, A V Cunliffe
1976-1978	Grundy
1979-1986	Grundy, I J Belcher
1987	Grundy, Belcher, Pomfret, Wolfson
1988-1990	Pomfret, R A McCullagh
1991-1993	Belcher, Pomfret
1994-1999	Pomfret, G A Humphreys-Roberts

Stockport

1876-1901	W Hyde
1902-1930	L Hyde
1931	Vacant
1932-1941	T Hidderley
1942-1964	John P Peacock
1965-1971	J I Caulfield
1972-1973	Caulfield, J R Scott
1974-1979	Caulfield, F W Smith
1980-1981	Caulfield, Smith, W Ashworth
1982-1983	Caulfield, Smith, W A Richardson
1984-1986	Smith, J L Burton
1987	Smith, Burton, Mrs M J Wilby J Wilkinson
1988-1990	Smith, Burton. D E Russell
1991	Burton, Russell, J F Duerden, J M Griffiths
1992	Russell, Griffiths
1993-1994	Russell, M J Gregory, C R Fairclough, Mrs A J C Brazier, D J Shannon, G A Needham
1995	P S Stockton replaces Fairclough
1996	Russell, Gregory, Brazier
1997-1999	Russell, Gregory, Brazier, J R Clegg

Whitehaven

1876-1900	A B Were
1901-1914	Were, J R Musgrave
1915-1940	G L McKelvie
1941-1961	J N St George Curwen
1962-1970	S J Fisher
1971-1974	A Dunn
1975	A J Proctor
1976-1978	J F Beaty
1979-1985	R J Holloway
1986-1996	No entry
1997-1999	J A James

Wigan

1876-1898	E H Woodcock
1899-1928	H Brierley
1929-1960	D R White
1961-1970	J A Lloyd Humphreys
1971-1974	M A W Grundy
1975	Grundy, A M Verity, A V Cunliffe
1976-1978	Grundy
1979-1986	Grundy, I J Belcher
1987	Belcher
1987-1990	Belcher, Mrs M J Wilby
1991-1993	Belcher, B Woods
1994	E Donnelly, I Bennett, G A Humphreys-Roberts
1995-1998	Donnelly, G J Fitzgerald
1999	Donnelly, N A Law

Wigton

1876-1887	W J Carrick
1888-1934	H A Dudding
1935-1938	J P Errington
1939-1945	A M MacPhail
1946-1947	C Leathes
1948-1968	J F Beaty

Windermere

1922-1947	G E Cartmel
1948-1958	C Fairer
1959-1961	J F Beaty
1962-1969	S J Fisher

(MEN)

HRH Prince Philip, HM the Queen, Lord Parker opening of Crown Square Manchester 1961. Veale J, Nield J, Fenton Atkinson J, Wrangham J, Ashworth J, Gorman J, Lloyd-Jacob J, Ormerod LJ, Sellers LJ.

(MEN)

Opening of Manchester Courts at Crown Square, 24 May 1961. Col. Musgrave-Hoyle, Lord Parker CJ, HM the Queen, HRH Prince Philip, Lord Derby, Lord Goddard, Lord Mayor of Manchester, Lord Meriman.

(LDPE)

HM the Queen Dame Ethel Wormald, Lord Mayor Liverpool. The Recorder HH Judge R KilnerBrown OBE TD QC DL. Speke Airport, June 1966.

(LDPE)

Liverpool 1984. Russell J, Lord Hailshaw, HM the Queen, McNeill J, HRH Prince Philip.

(LDPE)

Raymond Potter, Circuit Administrator, with HM the Queen, 2 May 1984.

HM the Queen and Lord Hailsham, 2 May 1984. Opening of Liverpool Law Courts.

Manchester, HRH Princess Anne with Judge Humphries, Blackburn J.

(DL)

HM the Queen visiting Liverpool 2002, with Lord Lieutenant Alan Waterworth and High Sheriff, Lady Kirsty Pilkington.

Seniority List of District Judges on the Northern Circuit

On 25 May 2004

(L) Liverpool (M) Manchester (P) Preston

L	District Judge PH Berkson	20.08.1978
M	District Judge D E Russell	01.04.1982
P	District Judge G Nuttall	03.06.1985
P	District Judge J G Turner	03.06.1985
M	District Judge M J Wilby	01.11.1985
M	District Judge D B Chapman	02.06.1986
L	District Judge R A McCullagh	05.01.1987
M	District Judge C E Freeman	02.11.1987
L	District Judge B W Travers	17.06.1989
M	District Judge M Griffiths	21.08.1989
M	District Judge J F Duerden	04.09.1989
L	District Judge I Bennett	28.06.1991
M	District Judge M J Gregory	28.06.1991
M	District Judge C R Fairclough	01.10.1991
M	District Judge E Donnelly	01.09.1991
M	District Judge E R Jones	01.01.1992
P	District Judge G R Ashton	07.09.1992
L	District Judge G A Humphreys-Roberts	21.09.1992
M	District Judge A J C Brazier	05.10.1992
P	District Judge I J Pickup	05.10.1992
M	District Judge W H Stansfield	05.07.1993
M	District Judge D J Shannon	04.05.1993
M	District Judge G A Needham	05.07.1993
M	District Judge V Buckley	04.10.1993
L	District Judge E Johnson	01.11.1993
M	District Judge P S Stockton	06.12.1993
P	Disthct Judge J A James	12.01.1994
P	District Judge J M Geddes	14.02.1994
L	District Judge M A Mornington	10.06.1994
M	District Judge J J B Rawkins	01.11.1994
M	District Judge B V McGrath	13.12.1994
M	District Judge R R P Ackroyd	03.01.1995
M	District Judge P T Wilby	16.06.1995
P	District Judge M E Buckley	03.07.1995
L	Disthct Judge Fitzgerald	03.07.1995
P	District Judge J D Heyworth	03.07.1995
M	District Judge J Shaw	31/07.1995
M	District Judge A J J Harrison	07.08.1995
M	District Judge J R Clegg	01.05.1996

Seniority List of District Judges on the Northern Circuit (continued)

M	District Judge B N Gaunt	01.07.1996
L	Dist(ict Judge S Wright	22.07.1996
P	District Judge R M Forrester	29.07.1996
P	Dishict Judge N A Law	16.09.1996
M	District Judge L C Osbome	16.06.1997
L	District Judge J L Clark	01.09.1997
M	District Judge C R Fox	08.09.1997
M	District Judge C M Swindley	29.06.1998
M	District Judge M Gosnell	01.07.1998
	District Judge M A Hovington	06.07.1998
L	District Judge M I Peake	03.09.1998
L	District Judge A Jones	03.09.1998
P	District Judge R Bryce	30.07.1999
M	District Judge S C Jackson	02.09.1999
M	District Judge J Horan	02.09.1999
L	District Judge R Smedley	02.09.1999
P	District Judge R Talbot	02.09.1999
L	District Judge L G Sykes	06.06.2000
L	District Judge N Harrison	02.11.2001
L	District Judge L Henthorn	30.11.2001
M	District Judge A M Saffman	03.12.2001
M	District Judge M J Simpson	03.12.2001
P	District Judge J K Park	16.01.2002
P	District Judge M W Turner	16.01.2002
L	District Judge P St J Dignan	01.05.2002
L	District Judge J F Coffey	25.10.2002
M	District Judge L Stephens	28.10.2002
L	District Judge G D Smith	14.07.2003

(DL)

Lord Chief Justice with Liverpool District Judges, 29 October 2002. Standing: Fitzgerald, Henthorn, Dignan, Smedley, Coffey. Seated: Johnson, Sykes, Leveson J, Lord Woolf, Harrison, Berkson.

Stipendiary Magistrate/District Judge (Magistrates Courts)

Birkenhead

1866-1895 Charles James Preston

Liverpool/Merseyside

1836-1839 Thomas James Hall
1839-1851 Edward Rushton
1851-1860 John Smith Mansfield
1860-1891 Thomas Stamford Raffles
1891-1908 William John Stewart
1908-1910 Thomas Shepherd Little
1910-1946 Stuart Deacon
1946-1947 Geoffrey Glyn Blackledge
1947-1965 Arthur McFarland
1965-1976 Leslie Pugh
1976-1995 Norman Wootton

My thanks to Michael Abelson.

Manchester/Greater Manchester

1839-1860 Daniel Maude
1860-1864 Cuthbert Edward Ellison
1864-1869 Robinson Fowler
1869-1908 Francis John Headlam
1908-1927 Edgar Brierley OBE
1927-1951 John Wellesley Orr
1951-1964 Frederick Bancroft Turner
1964-1976 John Bamber
1976-1981 John Nimmo Coffey
1976-1994 C T Latham OBE
1981-1998 William Derrick Fairclough

My thanks to Derrick Fairclough.

Salford

1813-1818	William David Evans
1818-1845	James Norris
1845-1869	Henry Leigh Trafford
1869-1878	Sir John Iles Mantell
1897-1911	Joseph Makinson
1911-1913	Adam Spencer Hogg
1913-1931	Peter Wilson Atkin OBE
1931-1938	Percy Macbeth
1938-1951	Frederick Bancroft Turner
1951-1975	Leslie Walsh
1975-1976	John Nimmo Coffey
1976-1994	Cecil Thomas Latham OBE

My thanks to T J McNeill, Clerk to the Justices.

1991	Jane Elizabeth Hayward
1992	John Eli Finestein
	David Robert George Tapp
1994	Peter Simms Ward
	Alan Berg
1995	Paul James Firth
	Christopher Richard Darnton
1998	Michael Andrew Abelson
1999	(Elsie) Miriam Shelvey
2001	James Barrington Prowse
	Richard Francis Stephen Clancy
	Trevor Mansel Chatelier
2002	Brigid Agnes Knight
	Ian Stuart Lomax
	Michael Clough Morris
2004	Nicholas Paul Martin Sanders
	Gerald Chalk (Cumbria)

Later appointments to what is now known as the District Judge North West Region.

As from 31 August 2000 all Stipendiary Magistrates are to be known as District Judges (Magistrates Courts).

Diocesan Chancellors and Registrars

Blackburn
Chancellors

1927-1929	Philip Vernon Smith
1929-1935	Wilfrid Hubert Poyer Lewis
1935-1948	Ralph George Scott Bankes
1948-1949	Robert Cecil Mortimer
1949-1976	Robert Alexander Forrester
1977-1990	Quentin Tytler Edwards QC
1990-	John Wallace MacGregor
Bullimore	

Registrars

1927-1965	Reginald Clayton JP
1965-1991	Leslie Ranson
1991-	Thomas A Hoyle

Carlisle
Chancellors

1872-1887	Charles James Burton
1888-1909	Richard Saul Ferguson
1910-1920	John Eustace Prescott
1921-1930	Herbert Ernest Campbell
1931-1934	Harry Bevir Vaisey
1945-1950	Humphrey Hastings-King
1950-1971	Robert Hugh Mais
1971-1991	David John Stinson
1991-2002	Francis John Aglionby
2003-	Geoffrey Frank Tattersall QC

Registrars

1872-1875	George Gill Mounsey
1876-1881	Robert H Mounsey
1882-1890	John G Mounsey
1891-1928	Anthony Nichol Bowman
1929-1964	Gerald Wilberforce Bowman
1964-1991	Ian Sharpe Sutcliffe
1991-	Susan Holmes

Liverpool
Chancellors

1880-1911	Thomas Espinell Espin
1911-1948	Harold Challoner Dowdall KC
1948-1957	Basil Edward Nield KC
1957-1976	Edward Steel
1976-2002	Richard Graham Hamilton
2002-	Sir Mark Hedley

Registrars

1880-?	John Gamon
Prior to	
1911-1948	Richard Farmer
Prior to	
1911-1942	Thomas Hollins Arden
Prior to	
1938-1973	Eric Cuthbert Arden
1968-	Roger Hollins Arden

Manchester
Chancellors

In post in:

1860-1873	Augustus Frederick Bayford
1873-1893	Richard Copley Christie
1894-1929	Peter Vernon Smith
1929-1935	Wilfrid Hubert Poyer Lewis
1935-1948	Ralph George Scott Bankes
1948-1971	Robert Hugh Mais
1971-1976	Edward Steel
1976-1996	George Christopher Howsin
Spafford	
1997-2003	John Leslie Ogilvie Holden
2004-	Geoffrey Frank Tattersall QC

Registrars

In post in

1860-1886	Thomas Dudley Ryder
1886-1926	E P Charlewood
1926-1934	Edward S Cheney
1934-1972	Lewis Edward Orford
1972-1986	John Maloney
1986-	Michael Clifford Darlington

Edward Steel, Chancellor, 1957. Standing: Edmondson, Barter, Hazelwood, Bruce, Feeney, Booth. Seated: Bingham, Steel, Pigot.

Coroners

Cheshire

Birkenhead

1890-1897	H Churton
1898	O W Tibbits
1899-1928	Cecil Holden
1929-1970	J Roberts
1971-1974	R T Humphreys

East Cheshire/Stockport

1876-1890	F W Johnson
1891	T W Johnson (Deputy)
1892-1906	Francis Newton
1907-1928	A E Ferns
1929-1955	J A K Ferns
1956	No entry
1957-1974	Herbert Sidebothan

Wallasey

1932-1945	R T Highet
1946-1969	J S Crook
1970-1971	Vacant
1971-1974	B T Humphreys

West Cheshire

1955-1974	Rex Taylor

Cumberland

Carlisle

1890-1898	John Hewetson Brown
1899-1901	H R Lonsdale
1902-1914	H B Lonsdale
1915-1947	Thomas Slack Strong
1948-1974	Thomas Strong

Cockermouth

1886-1910	J Hayton
1911-1920	E Atter
1921-1948	D J Mason
1949-	No entry

Eastern

1876-1877	W Carrick
1878-1890	J Carrick
1891-1903	James B Lee
1904-1908	Arthur Lee
1909-1963	Frederick William Halton
1963-1974	Peter William Pickles

Egremont

1876-1881	John McKelvie
1882-1902	J Webster
1903-1907	Gordon Falcon
1908-1937	G A L Skerry
1937-1945	Vacant
1946-1948	D J Mason
1949-	No entry

Millom

1876-1878	H M Meakin
1879-1916	P B Stoney
1917-1920	W T Lawrence
1921-1948	D J Mason
1949-	No entry

Western

1876–1889 W W Lumb
1890–1907 Gordon Falcon
1908–1920 E Atter
1921–1948 D J Mason
1949 No entry
1950–1952 E B Mendus
1953–1958 I M Banner-Mendus
1959–1974 H F T Gough

Lancashire

Blackburn District

1876–1881 H Hargreaves
1882–1913 H J Robinson
1914–1928 D N Hazelwood
1929–1951 F Rowland
1952–1960 Henry Backhouse OBE
1961–1974 G Graham

Blackburn Borough

1890–1913 H J Robinson
1914–1921 D N Hazelwood
1922–1928 No entry
1929–1948 T R Thompson
1949–1974 G Wightman

Bolton Borough

1876 J Taylor
1877–1904 R Taylor
1905–1906 J M Rutter
1907–1930 John Fearnley

Bolton District

1876–1890 J B Edge
1891–1920 S F Butcher
1921– No entry

Bolton

1931–1932 John Fearnley
1933–1949 H Fairbrother
1950–1960 K Fairbrother
1961–1974 J Liptrot

Burnley

1894–1913 H J Robinson
1914–1928 A F Sutcliffe
1929–1933 H Procter
1934–1958 Harry Ogden
1959–1974 Henry George Walmsley Cooper

Bury

1922–1932 S F Butcher
1933–1972 R M Barlow MC
1973–1974 R Speakman

Furness

1876–1908 John Poole
1909–1945 Frederick W Poole
1946–1971 John Poole
1972–1974 William Wesley Ellison

Hale

1876–1890 J R Buckton
1891–1893 J Douglas Buckton
1894–1923 Henry Greenall
1924–1942 A P V Pigot
1943–1945 W E V Burgess
1946–1970 A P V Pigot
1971–1974 R A Lloyd

Lancaster

1854–1906 Laurence Holden
1907–1940 Neville Holden
1940–1955 Geoffrey F E Wilson
1955–1974 J Howard Jellyman

Liverpool

1836-1867	Phillip Finch Curry
1867-1891	Clarke Aspinall
1891-1917	Thomas Edward Sampson
1917-1928	Andrew Glover Inglis
1928-1953	George Cecil Mort
1953-1968	John Anthony Blackwood
1968-1974	Stanley Roy Barter MBE

Manchester

1876-1896	E Herford
1897-1903	Sidney Smelt
1904-1915	E A Gibson
1916-1918	W M Sellers
1919-1937	C W W Surridge
1938-1960	George Jessel Rycroft
1961-1974	D Summerfield

Oldham

1899-1906	Dr G Thompson
1907-1916	T J Carson
1917-1926	A E Smith
1927-1959	John L Watson
1960	Vacant
1961-1974	Harry Armistead

Prescot

1876-1914	F Smith
1915-1954	W A Cross
1955-	No entry

Preston

1892-1893	J B Gilbertson
1894-1926	John Parker
1927	Vacant
1928-1939	Harold Parker
1940	Vacant
1941-1967	William Blackhurst OBE
1968-1972	D Fazackerley
1972-1974	Michael Howard McCann

Rochdale

1876-1886	J Molesworth
1887-1920	F N Molesworth
1921-1938	E N Molesworth
1939-1948	S Turner
1949	Vacant
1950-1974	A S Coupe

Salford Borough and District

1876-1896	Frederick Price
1897-1912	John Frederick Price
1913-1916	W Sellers
1917-1922	G S Leresche
1923-1936	R Stuart Rodger
1937	Vacant
1938-1957	F G Ralphs MB, FRCS
1958-1969	J J Rothwell
1970-1974	L M Gorodkin

Salford City

1927-1953	A H Flint
1954	No entry
1955-1974	J B D Haynes

Walton-Le-Dale

1876-1898	W Ashcroft
1899-1917	R W Ashcroft
1918	Vacant
1919-1928	W F Ashcroft
1929-1939	H Parker
1940-1945	No entry
1946-1970	W Blackhurst OBE
1971-1972	D Fazackerley
1973-1974	Michael Howard McCann

West Derby

1876-1882	Charles Edward Driffield
1883	Thomas Wildman Barker
1884-1940	Sir Samuel Brighouse
1941-1967	Cornelius Bolton
1967-1974	Ronald Aldwyn Lloyd

Wigan

1876-1902	L R Rowbottom
1903-1917	H Milligan
1918-1974	J Hopwood Sayer

Westmorland

East and West

1876-1879	J R Thompson
1880-1881	No entry
1882-1892	T Wilson
1893-1925	Wm Hewitson
1926-1940	J Richardson
1941-1951	William Hallam Scorer
1952-1974	William Hallam Scorer (North Westmorland District)

Kendal and Lonsdale

1876-1882	CG Thomson
1883-1907	J B Wilson
1908-1943	George Edward Cartmel
1944-1949	Norman Haygarth Inman
1950-1951	R N Birley (South Westmorland District)
1952-1974	Leslie Gascoigne Powell (South Westmorland District)

Oglebird

1876-1895	T Richardson
1896-1925	E A Heelis
1926-1965	G H Heelis
1966-	No entry

Post 1974 Local Government Reorganisation

Cumbria

North East

1974-1983	Thomas S Strong
1983-	Ian Hugh Morton

Western

1974-1979	H F T Gough
1980-1995	John Adrian Harrison Walker
1996-	John Christopher Taylor

Southern

1974-	Thomas Cyril Prickett

Furness

1974-1990	William Wesley Ellison
1990-	Ian Smith

Greater Manchester

West

1974-1995	David Percival Bailey
1996	Vacant
1997-2001	Martin J Coppel
2001	Aidan J Cotter
2001-	M Jennifer Leeming

North

1974-1978	Leonard Malcolm Gorodkin
1978-1993	John Brian Coulson North
1993-2002	Barrie Williams
2002-	Simon Nelson

South

1974-1995	Peter William Huleatt Revington
1995-	John S Pollard

City

1974-1978	D Summerfield
1979-	L M Gorodkin

Lancashire

North (amalgamated with Preston and Southwest in 2002)

1974-1979 J Howard Jellyman
1979- George Clark Howson

Blackpool and Fylde

1974-1989 John Budd
1989- Samuel George Lee

Preston and South West

1975- Michael Howard McCann

Blackburn, Hyndburn and Ribble Valley

1974-1994 George Graham
1995-1999 Andre J A Rebello
1999- M Singleton

East

1974-1979 Henry George Walmsley Cooper
1979-2001 David Allistair Smith

Merseyside

Knowsley

1974-1983 Ronald Aldwyn Lloyd
1983-1998 Gordon Henry Harper Glasgow
1998- Christopher Kent Sumner

Liverpool

1974-1999 Stanley Roy Barter MBE
1999- Andre J A Rebello

Wirral

1974-1988 Rex Taylor
1988- Christopher William Johnson

Clerks of the Peace

Birkenhead

1883-1916	Alfred Gill
1917-1924	James Fearnley
1925-1928	Cecil Holden
1929-1950	E W Tame
1951-1967	D P Heath
1968-1971	I G Holt

Blackburn

1886-1892	William Edwin Louis Gaine
1892-1904	Sir Robert Fox
1904-1930	Sir Lewis Beard
1930-1935	Briggs Marsden
1935-1956	Charles Stuart Robinson
1956-1971	Frank Squires

Bolton

1876-1879	J Gordon
1879-1928	William Walter Cannon
1929-1934	Samuel Parker
1935-1947	H B Ashford
1948-1965	P S Rennison
1966-1968	G A Harrison
1969-1971	D A Hoggins

Burnley

1876-1893	No entry
1894-1906	William T Fullalove
1907-1930	Arthur F Sutcliffe
1931-1935	Colin Campbell
1936-1946	No entry
1947-1971	C V Thornley

Carlisle

1877-1891	John Nanson
1892-1929	A H Collingwood
1930-1944	F G Webster
1945-1968	H D A Robinson
1969-1971	W Hirst

Cumberland

1876-1891	Thomas Houghton Hodgson
1891-1910	Charles Bernard Hodgson
1910-1927	Charles Courtenay Hodgson
1927-1942	Charles William Allen Hodgson
1942-1946	George Andrew Wheatley
1946-1971	George Norman Cyrus Swift
1970	Thomas John Roland Whitfield

Lancashire

1838-1879	Robert John Harper
1879-1899	Frederick Campbell Hulton
1899-1922	Sir Harcourt E Clare
1922-1944	Sir George Hammond Etherton
O.B.E.	
1944-1960	Sir Robert Adcock
1960-1971	Sir Patrick McCall

Lancaster (County Palatine)

1876-1899	T M Shuttleworth

Liverpool

1876-1877	P Wright
1878-1915	H Gutridge
1916-1928	R D Cripps
1929-1931	Walter Moon
1932-1940	R D Cripps
1941-1943	No entry
1944-1948	L S Holmes
1949-1956	James Michael Marshall
1957-1971	No entry (Crown Court formed)

Manchester

1876-1890	Frederick S Austin
1891-1926	Francis Ogden
1927-1928	E M Redhead
1929-1931	Vacant
1932-1955	E M Redhead
1956	H Binks
1957-1971	No entry (Crown Court formed)

Oldham

1876-1887	No entry
1888-1903	A Nicholson
1904	Vacant
1905-1928	John Armstrong
1929-1931	J J Williams
1932-1938	J Armstrong
1939-1946	No entry
1947-1952	T Alker
1953-1971	E Haines

Salford

1889-1911	Samuel Brown
1911-1926	Arthur Holmes
1926-1935	L C Evans
1935-1936	H H Tomson (Acting)
1936-1954	H H Tomson
1954	L R Martin (Acting)
1954-1966	R Ribblesdale Thornton
1966-1969	R Calderwood
1969-1971	R C Rees.

Westmorland

1876-1888	John Bell
1889-1916	John Bolton
1916-1918	Alexander Milne
1919-1950	Harry Bordley Greenwood
1950-1971	Kenneth Stephenson Himsworth

Wigan

1876-1899	T Heald
1900-1928	Arthur Smith
1929-1930	W H Tyrer
1932-1939	A Smith
1941-1947	W H Tyrer
1948-1969	A Royle
1970-1971	J H Craik

Leaders of the Circuit

1966-1968	Alexander Karmel QC
1968-1971	Richard Forrest QC
1971-1973	Godfrey Heilpern QC
1973-1974	Rose Heilbron QC
1974-1978	David McNeill QC
1978-1980	Patrick Russell QC
1980-1984	Michael Maguire QC
1984-1987	Ben Hytner QC
1988-1991	John Rowe QC
1992-1995	Rodney Klevan QC
1996-1998	Richard Henriques QC
1999-2001	Peter Birkett QC
2002-2004	David Steer QC
2005-	Michael Redfern QC

Juniors of the Circuit

1868	S M Lanigan
	H H Swift
1869	M N Woodward
	R Dunford
1870	J T Goldney
	W C Watson
1871	D N Nichol
	C L Shand
1872	C T Part
	G R Thompson
1873	J W C Carr
	F P Tomlinson
1874	J B Gailie
	C J Rowe
1875	A N Agnew
	R E Melsheimer
1876	S H Woodhouse
	J Williams
1877	F Evans
	J Parsons
1878	J Heywood
	J O Pilkington
1879	A M Cardwell
	C F Wright
1880	H Seton Carr
	A Coysgarve Sim
1881	A Aspinall Tobin
	John Blackburn
1882	J Herbert Williams
	Arthur J Ashton
1883	Collingwood Hope
	Thomas T Greg
1884	Lees Knowles
	P W Atkin
1885	Alfred N Higgins
	William Neill
1886	F G Bames
	S G Lushington
1887	L Sanderson
	H Heape
1888	L W Kershaw
	Arthur S Hargreaves
1889	James A Pixley
	E I Green
1890	A H Maxwell
	G W Wallace
1891	A Davies
	Joseph Fisher
1892	C C Branch
	I W S Kay
1893	Oldshaw Whittaker
	G B Milne-Redhead
1894	George Dodson
	A Spencer Hogg
1895	Fearnley Owen
	Claude Schuster
1896	Harry Collison
	Roscoe Brunner
1897	William Hanbury Aggs
1898	W P Addleshaw
	George A Blair
1899	George A Blair
	A Hildesheimer
1900	Gilbert Jordan
	J Dove
1901	L F C Darry
	W J Dalzell Burnyeat
1902	W J Dalzell Burnyeat
	G H Jager
1903	T S Tomlinson
	H G Smitton

1904	W W Otter-Barry
	John Bridge Aspinall
	A R Kennedy
1905	F Boyd Merriman
	Noel B Goldie
1906	Gerald P Hargreaves
	Norman Kendal
1907	H Gorell Bames
	Robert E Gething
1908	T G Brocklebank
	N H P Whitley
1909	H Hume Barne
	Bartle Bradshaw
1910	Philip M Oliver
	Charles Rae
1911	J R Kenyon
	G C Hans Hamilton
1912	Herbert Lumb
	J H Thorpe
1913	A J Lowther
	H Scott Barrett
1914	Hon E J Kay-Shuttleworth
	E Nuttall
1919	C H Spafford
	B R Rice Jones
1920	Hon O F G Stanley
	F Bancroft Turner
1921	Glynn Blackledge
	W Hinmers
1922	K Rymer Young
	P E Brierley
1923	H I Nelson
	Maxwell Fyfe
1924	F J V Sandbach
	P G R Whalley
1925	P Redmond Barry
	Basil E Nield
1926	George R Younger
	John Addleshaw
1927	R S Nicklin
	Gerald Sparrow
1928	R S Trotter
	Bazil S Wingate-Saul
1929	C T B Leigh
	W G Milne
1930	J S B Lloyd
	J P Ashworth
1931	R H Mais
	Melville Kennan
1932	Desmond Bailey
	W G Morris
1933	Sandy Miller
	G B H Currie
1934	D Cargill Todd
1935	R N Birley
	Hon E B Howard
1936	J R D Crichton
	John Wood
1937	R G Clover
	W H Openshaw
1938	P Anthony
	N B Birrell
1939	R B Verdin
	G W G Jones
1946	R M Bingham
1947	Derek Hodgson
	C J Cunliffe
1948	George Rhodes
	Norman Sellers
1949	F P R Hinchliffe
	Brian Williams
1950	John da Cunha
	A S Booth
1951	W H W Jalland
	J R Arthur
1952	John Lord
	N A Miscampbell
1953	J M Collins
	N H Bruce
1954	M Carlisle
	M Morland
1955	H A Kershaw
	R F Stone
1956	J J Hodgson
	G L Close
1957	A C Jolly
	Max Feeny
1958	Douglas Brown
	B C Maddocks
1959	Alistair Bell
	James Scarlett
1960	Brian Duckworth
	Richard Pickering

1961	J J Rowe
	R G Hamilton
1962	Anthony J M Rubin
	R J D Livesey
1963	Richard N B Clegg
	D A Pirie
1964	Michael Brent
	Michael Dingle
1965	Simon Fawcus
	David Clarke
1966	Charles Mantell
	Charles James
1967	Rhys Davies
	Ian Campbell
1968	Michael Shorrock
	John Kay
1969	David Hodson
	Sean Duncan
1970	G W Wingate-Saul
	John Appleton
1971	Martin Steiger
	B MacMillan
1972	J R B Geake
	David Turner
1973	C P L Openshaw
	M P Burrell
1974	A N H Blake
	H B Globe
1975	T J Mort
	J V Martin
1976	Paul C Reid
	Scott Donovan
1977	Anthony Russell
	Kevin Fletcher
1978	David Stockdale
	Peter Atherton
1979	Timothy Ryder
	Tim Holroyde
1980	John Philips
	Robert Warnock
1981	Alan J Booth
	Ross Duggan
1982	Jonathan Parkin
	Graham N Wood
1983	Robert Elias
	Andrew Edis
1984	Neil Withington
	Peter Cowan
1985	Patrick Field
	Neil Flewitt
1986	Peter Main
	Kevin Reade
1987	Mark Cawson
	Andrew Loveridge
1988	Sarah Singleton
	Dennis Watson
1989	Suzanne Goddard
	William Waldron
1990	Timothy Brennand
	Peter Davies
1991	Anthony Crean
	Keith Sutton
1992	Clare Grundy
	Brian Cummings
1993	Christopher Kennedy
	Richard Crallan
1994	Graham Knowles
	Christine Bispham
1995	Mark Benson
	Jonathan Taylor
1996	Mark Savill
	Rob Altham
1997	Jaime Hamilton
	Felicity Somerset Jones
1998	Annette Gumbs
	Simon Povoas
1999	Benjamin Myers
	Alexander Frodsham
2000	Roderick Priestly
	Steven Ball
2001	Giles Cannock
	Sophie Smith
2002	Katherine Pierpoint
	David Taylor
2003	David Temkin
	Nicola Daley
2004	Lucinda Leeming
	Andrew Howe
2005	Alexander Leach

(RB)

Lord Lane, Lord Chief Justice, 1984.

(MEN)

Lord Lane (Lord Chief Justice) at Crown Square Manchester, winter 1986. The under Sheriff, Andrew Wilson is leading in the Judges (Rose J on left, Russell.J on right. Deputy Chief Constable Stalker follows the Judges.

(LDPE)

Lord Taylor, Lord Chief Justice at Liverpool, January 1993.

(DL)

Court of Appeal Liverpool 2002, Silber J, Lord Woolf (LCJ), Leveson J, with High Sheriff Lady Kirsty Pilkington.

(DL)

Liverpool 15.10.2003, Lady Justice Butler-Sloss DBE, president of the Family Division with the Recorder of Liverpool, Judge Henry Globe QC.

(DL)

Court of Appeal, Douglas Brown J, Rose LJ, Silber J, Liverpool 17.02.2004.

(DL)

Lord Chief Justice, Lord Woolf with Recorder of Liverpool, Judge Henry Globe QC, Liverpool 2004.

Secretary, Circuit Executive Commitee

1965-1970	Douglas Brown
1970-1976	John Rowe
1976-1981	John Appleton
1981-1985	Michael Shorrock
1985-1988	Sean Duncan
1988-1994	Alistair Webster
1994-1997	Andrew Edis
1997-1999	Tim Brennand
1999-2002	Will Waldron
2002-	Mark Savill

Clerk of Assize

1876	Edward Bromley (to Northern Eastern when the 'Old' Circuit divided)
1877-1889	Thomas Moss Shuttleworth
1889-1927	Sir Herbert Stephen
1927-1947	William James Holmes Graham
1947-1970	Ian Anderson Macaulay CBE

Circuit Administrator

1970-1974	Thomas Alan Whittington
1974-1982	Colin Robert Seaton
1982-1986	Raymond Potter
1986-1993	Peter Michael Harris
1993-2001	Robin Anthony Vincent CBE
2001-	Christine Mayer

Clerk to the Justices

Greater Manchester

Bolton

1974-1978	Ronald Kirtley
1978-1998	Peter Dawson MBE
1998-2001	Alex Carlos
2001-	David Greensmith

Bury

1950-1954	George Clough
1954-1981	Charles Fletcher
1981-1988	Ian Webb
1988-1995	Robert Barrett
1996-1998	Steven Platt
1998-	David Greensmith

Leigh

1978-1993	Miles McColl
1994-1995	David Mervyn Speed.
1995-2001	James William Haydock
2001-	David Greensmith

Manchester

1839-1882	Thomas Higson
1882-1887	Samuel Milner Barton
1887-1898	Charles le Court
1887-1893	George Thorpe
1898-1911	Harry Robson
1911-1922	Thomas Bartholomew Wilby
1922-1933	Robert Bell
1934-1945	William Shaw
1945-1952	Walter Lyon
1952-1965	Harold Cooper.
1965-1976	Cecil Thomas Latham
1976-1991	Philip Kevin Dodd
1992-1999	Ian Stuart Lomax
1999-2002	David Edward Scanlan
2002-	David Greensmith

Oldham

1924 (in office)	Herbert Booth
?-1963	Frank Whittaker
1963-1982	Ellis Pollitt
1982-1991	Malcolm Marsh
1991-1996	Stella Roberts
1996-2001	Kathleen Johnson
2001-	David Greensmith

Rochdale

Rochdale PSD

No dates.	Edward Collins
1940s	Joe Freer
Pre 1969-1979	Jack Whitehead
1979-1989	Richard Holland
1990-1992	Philip A Cuddy
1992-1996	David Greensmith

Middleton and Heywood PSA

?-1980	Kenneth W Shaw
1980-1988	Peter J Harling
1988-1992	Philip A Cuddy
1992-1996	David Greensmith

Merger in 1996 to form:

Rochdale, Middleton and Heywood PSA

1996-	David Greensmith

Salford

1960-1968	J W Davies
1968-1992	John William Meredith
1992-1993	Terry J McNeill

Eccles PSD Late

40s or early 50s-1972	George Stanley Green (Manchester County)
1972-1974	Ian William Crompton (Manchester County)
1974-1983	Ian William Crompton
1983-1993	Adrian J Turner

Salford and Eccles merged in 1993 to form:
City of Salford PSA

1993 -2001	Terry J McNeill
2001-	David Greensmith

Stockport

?-1912	Charles Edward Lake
1918-1945	Harry Newton
1945-1957	Joseph Lloyd.
1957-1974	Francis K Newton
1974-1992	Ranson H Lawrence
1992-2002	Philip A Cuddy
2002-	David Greensmith

Tameside

Ashton PSD

1948-1972	Albert Platt
1973-1994	Winston V Gordon

South Tameside PSD

?-1980	K Pickup
1980-1994	Winston V Gordon

Ashton and South Tameside merged in 1994 to become:

Tameside

1994-2001	Winston V Gordon

Trafford

1964-1977	John Reid Newton
1978-1992	Stephen Roy Lomas
1993-2000	John Robinson
2001	David Owen (acting)
2001-	David Greensmith

Wigan

?-1949	R F Jones (Wigan Borough)
1950-1974	J Basil Horsman OBE (Wigan Borough)
1974-1985	J Basil Horsman OBE
1986-1995	David Mervyn Speed
1995-2001	James William Haydock
2001-	David Greensmith

Makerfield PSD

1963-1967	Ronald Kirtley (Wigan County)
1968-1970	D B Isaac (Wigan County)
1970-1974	Tim Francis Moran (Wigan County)
1974-1986	Tim Francis Moran

Makerfield merged with Wigan in 1986 to become Wigan PSD. As from 1 January 2003 Wigan PSA and Leigh PSA were amalgamated to form Wigan and Leigh PSA.

In December 2001 Mr David Greensmith was appointed Director of Legal Services and Justices' Clerk for Greater Manchester. I am grateful to him and his staff for their valuable help in compiling these lists.

Lancashire

On 1 April 2002 John Robinson was appointed Justices' Clerk for Lancashire. The Justices' Chief Executive, Idris Moorby, has informed me that there are no historic records of Justices' Clerks posts available.

Merseyside

Bootle (South Sefton)

1971-1976	F Preston
1977-1991	C Hughes
1992-1998	Dennis Luty

Knowsley/Prescott/Huyton

?-1981	David William Ellis
1984-1991	R Barrett
1992-1993	J Colin Watson
1994-1999	Norman Draper

Liverpool (City)

1833	Benjamin Ellis
	William Shuttleworth, jointly
1841	William Jamieson
	John Wybergh, jointly
1852	John Wybergh
	Philip F Garnett, jointly
1869	Thomas Anderton
	Richard Ellis, jointly
1879	Richard Ellis
1895	Frederick Moss
1902	Sir Edgar Christian Sanders
1918	Charles Thomas Barton
1946	Herbert Allan Guy Langton MBE
1962	George Macavoy
1975	John Edmund Pearson OBE
1991	Malcolm Marsh
1998	Dennis Luty

Liverpool (County) (Islington and Kirby)

?-1972	Robert Trevor Evans (Clerk to Kirkdale bench 1938-)
1972-1975	D H Mason

St Helens

?-1971	J P H Allon
1972-2000	(John) David Green
2000	Norman Draper

Southport (North Sefton)

?-1973	Benjamin James Hartwell OBE
1975-1983	D H Mason
1984-1999	R Hampson

Wirral

Birkenhead

1894-1908 Gerard Copeland
1909-1914 William Saville George
1930s E W Gasking (uncle of H St Clair Gasking)
1950s-1974 John Harker Cullen
1975-1977 R G Melling
1978-1994 Charles J Acred
1995-1999 Robert H Hall

Wallasey

?-1944 J P Wilson
1945-1974 Henry St Clair Glover Gasking.

In 1999 all local Benches joined to form the Merseyside Magistrates Courts Service, with Malcolm Marsh as Chief Executive and Noman Draper as Justices' Clerk. My thanks to Norman Draper and Barbara Foster (Wirral).

Cumbria

The current Clerk to the Justices for the Cumbria Magistrates' Courts Service is C J Armstrong.

Barristers Clerks c1957. Standing: Godfrey Whitehead, Ronnie Lynch, Bob Butler, Kenneth Nugent, Bill Robertson, Roy Tully, Eric Johnson, Joe Patterson, Walter Berry, Tom Rothwell. Seated: Judges Clerk (unknown), Robert Isaac, Silks Clerk (unknown), Edward Burns, Tommy Hughes, Teddy Love, Jimmy McMillan, Herbert McMath (inset).

Barrister's Clerks (By Chambers)

These lists are not as extensive as I would wish because the Law Lists did not give clerks' names until 1967. I have been able to go back further with the help of circuiteers and clerks. Where I am able, I have given the name of the person I believe founded chambers, or who was an early head of chambers.

Liverpool

Melville Kennan's Chambers
34 Castle Street (1939-)
54 Castle Street (1973-)
14 Castle Street (1988-)
Atlantic Chambers, 4-6 Cook Street (2003-)

1939-1947	Kenneth Nugent
1947-1971	Roy Tully
1971-1982	Doris M Jones
1982-2003	Stuart Jones (son of Doris)
2004-	Lee Cadwallader

Present Clerks: Lee Cadwallader, Gary Quinn, Neil Grisdale. David Blunsden,
Administrator: Susan Henhaw.

Edward Steel's Chambers
14 Cook Street
Ground floor, Peel House, Harrington Street (1973-1999)

1935-1973	Robert Isaac
1973-1999	Michael Gray (now with Oriel Chambers)

Harold Brown's Chambers
9 Cook Street
20 Hackins Hey
2nd floor 14 Cook Street
7 Queen Avenue (1985-1996) when merged with 14 Castle Street

1965-1981	Miss E S Swainson
1981-1996	Gary Quinn (now with Atlantic Chambers)

Colin Cunningham's Chambers
41 North John Street
3rd floor, 15 Victoria Street
3rd floor, 46 Stanley Street
25 Victoria Street
19 Castle Street
2nd floor 10 James Street
24 Fenwick Street
14 Cook Street
(Merged with New Bailey Chambers, Liverpool 16.8.2004)
Clerks have included: Peter Taplin, Neil Spracklin, Thomas Morrison, Beverley Jones, Mark Morley, Mark Wearsden, Jenny Connor, Savannah Biswas, Mark Wainwright, Mark Bloor, Gillian Webb, Helen Davies, Louise Atherton.

Fred Pritchard's Chambers
25 Castle Street (1934-)
27 Lord Street (1945-)
49 Castle Street (1947-)
The Corn Exchange, Fenwick Street (1966-)
1 Exchange Flags, Dale Street (1983)
Exchange Chambers, Pearl Assurance House, Derby Square (1994-). Also at 7 Ralli Court, West Riverside, Manchester.

1913-1963	Edward Burns
1963-1992	Maureen McCann
1992-1994	Anne Astle
1994-	Tom Handley (Chambers Director)

Practice Manager: Roy Finney. Clerks: Barbara Jones, Ainsley Pritchard, Kate Masher. Client Liason Manager: Margaret McFarlane.

(RB)

Maureen and her Judges. Inset left: Hamilton. Inset right: Clark. Arthur DFC, Campbell, Naylor, Nance, Maureen McCann, Morris-Jones QC.

Iain Goldrein's Chambers
5 Castle Street (1981-)
48-50 Castle Street (1987-) merged with Corn Exchange in 1989 which in 1999 joined Martins Building to form 7 Harrington Street.
Clerks: Gillian D Hyde followed by Bernard Carroll.

Charles Feeney's Chambers
42 Castle Street (1998-)
Clerks: Andrew Heap, Louise Wynn Jones, Nathan Oliver.

Linda Brown's Chambers
Westminster Chambers, 3 Crosshall Street (1989-)
Clerk: Mrs Jenny Brown

Edward Youd's Chambers
North House, 17 North John Street (1951-)
Martins Building, Water Street (1971-)
7 Harrington Street (6.9.99-) (merger with Corn Exchange)

1951-1961	Thomas Hughes
1961-1976	Eric Johnson (who had been a junior clerk at the opening of chambers in 1951 and also clerked Rose Heilbron in Silk and on the High Court Bench)
1976-1983	Yvonne Heighway
1983-	John Kilgallon (Senior Clerk/Practice Manager) (formerly junior to Nick Parry at Melbourne Buildings)

Assistant Practice Manager: Nick Roberts. Criminal Clerks: Rachel Kehoe (Senior), Sarah Harrison (Assistant), Claire Smith (Junior). Civil Clerks: Sarah Gleaves, Kate Groom. Family Clerks: Carolyn Cregeen, Marna Jones. Admin and Fees Clerks: Pauline Haines, Andrea Gear, Jennifer Jones, Elaine Baker, Denise Skerritt.
Times have changed. When I joined these chambers in 1969 we had a clerk and two typists. However, we were only seven strong. Now they are eighty-two. The remarkable achievement of Thomas Hughes must be recorded. He was a barristers' clerk for sixty years, having joined F Cuthbert Smith's chambers as a junior clerk on 16 January 1901.

Chambers of Henry Lachs
27 Dale Street (1956-)
Melbourne Buildings, 21 North John Street (1977-)
3rd floor, Peel House, Harrington Street (1989-)
7th floor, India Buildings, Water Street (1998-)

1962-1977	John Parry
1977-1991	Nick Parry (son of John)
1991-1993	Michelle Cochrane
1993-2004	Robert Moss
2004-	Stuart Jones (Senior Clerk/Practice Manager)

Clerks: Mark Shannon, Alastair Webster, Greg Brooker, Claire Labio, Gail Curran. Fees and Admin: Helen Southworth.

Chambers of William Geddes
20 North John Street (1953-)
(Merged with 14 Castle Street, now Atlantic Chambers, in 1997)

?-1965	Miss Wishart
1965-1980	Margaret Donnelly
1980-1982	William Brown
1982-1997	Neil Grisdale.

Chambers of Eric Somerset Jones
Oriel Chambers, 14 Water Street (1965-)
The chambers moved within the same building and at one time had the address: 5 Covent Garden)

1965-1980	Leslie Biggs
1980	Peter Taplin
1981-1982	Richard Moore
1982-1998	John Laking
1999-	Sarah Cavanagh (Chambers Director)

Clerk/Manager: Paul Thompson. Civil Clerk: Michael Gray. Family Clerk: Andrew Hampton. Criminal Clerk: Ian Pitt.

Chambers of Justin Price
7 Rumford Street (1969-)
34 Castle Street (1970-)
Queen Avenue, Castle Street (1974-)
2nd floor, Peel House, Harrington Street (1983-)
25-27 Castle Street (1994-)

1967-1969	Miss D McFadyen
1969-1991	Malcolm Ostrin
1991-	Joanne Stapley

Practice Manager: Carol Mooney. Junior Clerks: Maureen Kemp and Sarah Curran. Assistant Clerk (Fees): Chris Jones.

Chambers of John Gore
9 Rumford Street (1961-)
1st floor, Fruit Exchange Buildings, Victoria Street (1974-)
Chavasse Court, 24 Lord Street (1992-)

1958-1973	Tom Rothwell
1973-	Colin Cubley

Chambers of George England
The Temple, Dale Street (1959-)
3rd floor, 27 Dale Street (1970-)
5th floor, Corn Exchange, Fenwick Street (1989-1999) (merger with Martins Building to form 7 Harrington Street on 6.9.99)

pre1967-1989	Jean Hibbert
1989-1993	David Jackson
1993-1999	Alex Keith

Chambers of Bob Nicklin
27 Lord Street (1939-)
10 Water Street (1959-)
2nd floor, 14 Water Street (1969-)
Refuge Assurance House (re-named Merchants Court in 1997), Derby Square (1982-2003). When chambers closed on 31 December 2003 many in chambers moved to Oriel Chambers and some went to Atlantic Chambers.

1939-1981	Herbert McMath
1981-2003	Allan Weston

I am very grateful to my former clerk Eric Johnson and to Michael Gray for helping me to fill in many gaps.

New Bailey Chambers (see Preston)

Manchester

Chambers of James Fowler
9 Albert Square
Deans Court Chambers, Cumberland House, Crown Square
24 St John Street

1967-1980	J Pattison
1981-1994	Trevor Doyle
2001	Matthew Gibbons (Acting)
2002-	Clive Witcomb

2004 Clerking Team: Senior Clerk: Matthew Gibbons. Principal Civil and Family Clerk: Paul Laverty. Principal Criminal Clerk: Leigh Royall.

Chambers of C Q Henriques
2 Booth Street
13 Police Street
6th Floor, Arkwright House, Parsonage Gardens,
Parsonage Chambers, 20 St Mary's Parsonage
Kingsgate Chambers, 51-53 South King Street

1967-1971	W Blood
1972-1978	J Pickles
1979-1998	Catherine M Thomas
1999-	Frederick Greene

Chambers of C N Glidewell
28 Kennedy Street (1946-)
25 Bow Lane (1957-)
Room 460, Royal Exchange (1976-)
Kings Chambers, 40 King Street (1987-)

1949-1950	Arthur Morello
1951-1988	Albert Shuttleworth
1988-	William Brown

Current Clerks: William Brown and Colin Griffin. Practice Manager: Deborah André. Chief Executive Louise Dixon.

Chambers of Benet Hytner QC
Byrom House (1975-) – Silks' Chambers
25 Byrom Street (1980-)
12 Byrom Street (1999-) also at 22 Old Buildings, Lincoln's Inn.
Senior Clerk: Peter Collison. Peter joined Byrom Street as Junior Clerk in 1975, succeeding Ronnie Lynch in 1981. Assistant Clerk: Steven Price. Administration Clerks: Jennifer Mumford-Lloyd and Michelle Seaton.

Chambers of James Fitzhugh
4 Clarence Street (1952-)
72 Bridge Street (1983-)
(Merged with Hollins Chambers in May 1997 which became Cobden House Chambers in 1997)

1967-1971	L M Dagger
1972-1984	Mrs V C Grimshaw
1985-1988	Mrs Sandra Tysall
1989-1993	Mrs Margaret A Perkins
1994-1997	Miss N Cross

Chambers of Peter Ferns
196 Deansgate (1959-)

1967-1968	C Poynton
1969-1980	T S Tysall
1981-1989	C R Taylor

Chambers of Harold Rhodes
43 King Street (1935-)
Queen's Chambers, 5 John Dalton Street (1989-)

1967	J Wheatley
1968-1982	Vincent Hemmingway (Mayor of Salford)
1983-	Terry Mylchreest

Chambers of Kenneth Chambers
60 King Street (Pre 1967-1972)
Pre 1967-1972 Edith Taylor (Kenneth's sister)

Chambers of E S Temple
60 King Street (1961-)
Crown Square Chambers, 1 Deans Court (1983-)
9 St John Street (1994-)

1961-1973	John Mellor (formerly clerk to 26 King Street)
1974-1975	A Edwards
1976-1979	E M Brayshaw
1980-1987	Graham Rogers and Graham Livesey
1988-2001	Graham Rogers

Current Team: Senior Criminal Clerk: Graham Livesey. Senior Civil Clerk and Clerk to Silks: Tony Morrisey. Director of Finance and Administrator: Jo Kelly.

In 1961, 26 King Street split up. Desmond Bailey took over as Head of Chambers and Sandy Temple led a group from 26 King Street to join with C T B Leigh's existing set at 60 King Street, renting that part of the premises vacated by Godfrey Heilpern's set when they moved to 47 Peter Street. So there were three sets of chambers in 60 King Street at the same time. I am relieved that Leslie Portnoy was able to explain all this to me.

Chambers of Henry Burton
60 King Street (1930-)
47 Peter Street (1961-)
12th floor, Sunlight House, Quay Street
28 St John Street (later adding number 26)
St Johns Building Chambers (merger with 24a St John Street on 1.10.02).
Merchants Court Chambers joined St Johns in 2004.
Ronnie Lynch was Henry Burton's first clerk and only clerk.

1967-1974	F Turner
1975-1988	D W Underwood
1989-1991	Anita Mosesson
1992-	Christopher Ronan.

Chambers of Denis Gerrard
3rd floor, 3 St James's Square (1928-1941)
4 Chapel Walks (1945-)
601 Royal Exchange (1964-)
8 King Street (1989-)

1930-1945	Godfrey Whitehurst son of John Whitehurst, who was clerking for Neville Laski on the same floor of 3 St James's Square. There had been no room for Denis Gerrard when he completed his pupillage so he opened up on his own with Laski's approval)
1945-1967	Vicar Johnson
1968-1984	N A Ashton
1985-1988	William Brown
1989-1991	Chris Slater
1992-	Peter Whitman

Chambers of James Booth
36 St Ann Street
27 Byrom Street (1980-)
26 Cross Street (1983-)
83 Bridge Street (1988-) – Kenworthy's Chambers

1967-1981	C S Simpson
1982-1997	Stuart A Johnson
1998-	John Walter

Current Clerking team: Maria Rushworth, Paul Mander, Sue Barlow, Wilma Frangenheim, Sam Kilroy.

Chambers of Neville Laski
3 St James's Square (1917-)
St James Chambers, 68 Quay Street (1985-)
John Whitehurst was Laski's Clerk.

1967-1970	R C Randall
1971-	Stephen Diggles

Current Clerking Team. Senior Clerk: Stephen Diggles. First Junior: Jennifer Pleavin. Juniors: Paula Garlick and John Blain.

Chambers of Arthur Jalland
40 Kennedy Street (1935-)
Ship Canal House, King Street (1966-)
2 Old Bank Street (1981-)
Peel Court Chambers, 45 Hardman Street (1992-)

1967-1985	W A Peace
1986	B C S O'Neill
1987-1998	Donald Waller
1999-	Shell Edmonds

Current Clerking Team: Senior Clerks: Shell Edmonds and David Haley. Administrator: Lynsey Dronsfield.

Chambers of Victor Williamson
Northern Assurance Building, Albert Square (1968)
Post Office Chambers, 26 Brown Street (1970-)
4 th floor, Sunlight House, Quay Street (1977-)
1 Central Street (1984-)
33 King Street West (1988-)
Old Colony House, 6 South King Street (1995-2001)

1968	P Guerin
1969-1971	William Sheldon
1972-1978	J B McGarty
1979-2001	Leslie F Dooley

Chambers of Frank Hudson
67 Princess Street (1972-)
Hollins Chambers, 64a Bridge Street (1988-)
Cobden House Chambers, 19 Quay Street (01.12.97-)
(merger with 72 Bridge Street)

1972-1984	William Sheldon
1985-1997	Robert Davis
1998-	Trevor Doyle

Current Clerking Team: Senior Clerk/Practice Manager: Trevor Doyle. Assistant Clerk: David Hewitt. Junior Clerks: Daniel Monaghan and Gary Douglas. Chambers Administrator: Mrs Jackie Morton.

Chambers of Philip Bagley

21 Spring Gardens
4th Floor, Sunlight House, Quay Street
121 Princess Street
3 Peter Street
211 Deansgate
3 The Parsonage

1973	Mrs R Colllins
1974	Mrs M Eggleton
1975	W Emmerson
1976-1978	Miss S Godfrey
1979-1980	W Sheldon
1981-1985	A F Kettle
1986	Francis Burke
1987-1988	Miss E D Stokes
1989-1999	Miss K L Cuttle

Chambers of Kenneth Taylor

4 th floor, Astley House, Quay Street (1973-)
18 St John Street (1977-)

1973-1991	James Haley
1992-1999	Michael Farrell
2000	Dominic Longhurst
2000-	William Sheldon

Current Clerking Team: Senior Civil Clerk: John Hammond. Senior Criminal Clerk: William Sheldon. Chambers Administrator: Jane Ginnever.

Chambers of Peter Crichton-Gold

6th-9th floor, Sunlight House, Quay Street (1976-)
Young Street Chambers, 38 Young Street (1993-)
Young Street Chambers, 76 Quay Street (2004-)

1976-1996	Valerie Willeringhouse
1996-1997	Nicholas Geary (Acting)
1997-	Peter Wright

Current Clerking Team: Senior Clerk: Peter Wright. Criminal Clerks: Nicholas Geary and Peter Kelly. Family/Civil Clerks: Paul Reeves and Rachel Campbell.

Chambers of Ian Mclvor

Lawrence Buildings, 2 Mount Street (1976-)
3 St James's Square (1985-)
38 King Street West (1990-)
24a St John Street (1996-)
On 23.9.2002 chambers merged with 28 St John Street to form St John's Buildings Chambers.

1976-1980	Lynn Wallwork
1981-1983	B Hindle
1984-2000	Lynn Wallwork
2001-2002	Gail McDermott.

Chambers of Ian Mclvor
334 Deansgate (1993-)
Brooklands Chambers (2001-)

Chambers of David Sumner
Rational House Chambers, 64 Bridge Street (1978)
Lincoln House Chambers, 1 Brazennose Street (1995-)

1978-1993	Jack Prickles
1994	T Hevicon
1995-2001	Andrew Weaver
2001-	Nick Buckley

2004 David Gibbons joining Clerking Team. Junior Clerks: David Wright and Mandy Greenroyd.

Chambers of R J D Lewis
1st Floor, 26 Brown Street

1984-1985	S Parkinson

Chambers of John Wishart
Conavon Court Chambers, 12-13 Blackfairs Street (1974-)
Manchester House Chambers, 18-22 Bridge Street (1990-)

1984-1988	T Mills and Miss S Mercer
1989	Miss S Mercer and Miss L Judge
1990-1997	Miss Susan Mercer
1998-1999	Teresa Thiele

Chambers of Ian MacDonald QC
Garden Court North (1996)
1 Booth Street, then, 5 Cooper Street and now 22 Oxford Court.
Clerks: David Skinner, Jane Lever, Neil Vickers.
Current Clerking Team: Senior Clerk: David Skinner. First Junior Clerk: Sarah Wright. Junior Clerk: Annmarie Tetlow.

Chambers of Paul Marshall
3 Peter Street (1990-)
18 Lloyd Street (1992-)
2 St John Street (2000-)

1990-1995	Barbara L Boulton
1996-1999	Hilary Smith
2000-	Lee Grindley

Chambers of David Berkeley QC
Merchant Chambers, I North Parade,
Parsonage Gardens (1996-2004)
Chambers merged with St John's Building Chambers in 2004.

1996-2003	Alastair Campbell
2003-	Paul Moorcroft.

Assistant Clerk: Joe Gibson. Accounts Clerk: Kate Thomas.

Preston

I have not included 'branch chambers' of Liverpool and Manchester.

Chambers of Mary Holt

1a Chapel Street (1967-1977)

1967-1968	Susan Boddy
1969-1972	Susan Procter
1973-1974	Miss J Allanson
1975	Miss Denise Hamlin
1976-1977	Miss E Ingham

Chambers of Keith Thomas

14 Winckley Square (1983-)
15 Winckley Square (1994-)

1983-1991	Peter Whitman
1992-	Michael Jones

Current Clerking Team: Senior Clerk: Michael Jones. Junior Clerk: Nicholas Haley. Clerks: Jon Borrow, Chris Foweraker, Mikael Welsh. Practice Manager: John Schofield. Accounts Clerk: David Usherwood.

Chambers of Patricia Bailey

New Bailey Chambers (1992-)
10 Lawson Street and later at 9-11 Ormskirk Road
also at Corn Exchange, Fenwick Street, Liverpool

1992-1998	Alastair G R Campbell
1998-	Savannah Biswas

Current Clerking Team: Senior Clerk: Savannah Biswas. Junior Clerks: John Stewart, David Ellis, Claire Sharples.

St Georges Hall, Liverpool 1893.

(RB)

St Georges Hall, Liverpool, 1983.

(RB)

Sessions House, Liverpool 1983.

(JMP)

Queen Elizabeth II Law Courts, Liverpool 1984.

(JMP)

Large Court Queen Elizabeth II Law Court, Liverpool 1984.

Shire Hall, Lancaster, 1985, Judge Lockett.

Shire Hall, Lancaster 1985, The Bar.

Manchester Minshull Street Courts.

Manchester Minshall Street, Atrium.

Minshull Street, Court.

Barrister's Clerks to Circuit Silks in London and/or High Court Judges

Bob Butler	Clerk to Hollings J
John Butler	(Bob's Son) Clerk to Michael Maguire QC
Donald Donkin	Clerk to Oliver J
Archibald Evans	Clerk to Thomas Swift between 1888-1899 and then clerked Thomas's son Rigby Swift at the Bar and on the Bench from 1899-1937.
Ronnie Goldsmith	Clerk to Bean J
George Hopgood	Clerk to Fenton Atkinson J
Eric Johnson	Clerk to Rose Heilbron in Silk and on the Bench
Ronnie Lynch	Clerk to Henry Burton KC and later to Ben Hytner QC
Kate McCall	Clerk to Heilbron J
Dick Newman	Clerk to Harry Nelson QC
Ken Nugent	Clerk to Brabin J
Terry Phipps (uncle of His Honour Judge Phipps)	Clerk to Michael Maguire QC
John Pickford	Clerk to Lynskey J
William Robertson	Clerk to Glyn Blackledge QC
George Shannon	Clerk to Edward Wooll QC
Roy Tully	Clerk to Boreham J
Godfrey Whitehurst	Clerk to Gerrard J and later Cantley J.
Eric Willoughby	Clerk to Gorman J

Liverpool Court Reporters

(DL)

Ray Holmes is a remarkable man. In 1940 he was flying a Hurricane over London. He saw a Dornier bomber heading for Buckingham Palace. Having run out of ammunition, he rammed the Dornier bringing it down. He was made a Freeman of the Borough of Wirral an 24 January 2005.

Lynda Roughley.

Prosecution Service

Carlisle

1979-1986	Duncan Sharp (Chief Prosecuting Solicitor)

Cumbria

In October 1986 the Crown Prosecution Service began nationally. Cumbria was part of the Lancashire/Cumbria Area. The Chief Crown Prosecutor (based in Preston) was John Bates, with Cumbria operating as a branch office. In April 1993 the Crown Prosecution Service reorganised in 13 Areas and Cumbria became part of the CPS North which included Northumbria, Durham and Cleveland. The first Chief Crown Prosecutor (1993-1995) was Dickie Dickinson and the Assistant Chief Prosecutors were David Farmer and Mike Graham. Mike Graham became the second Chief Prosecutor (1995-1999). All were based in Newcastle-upon-Tyne and again Cumbria was a branch office.

In April 1999 the Crown Prosecutions Service reorganised into 42 Areas and Cumbria became a separate CPS Area. The first and continuing Chief Prosecutor is David Farmer. The head office is in Carlisle with branch offices in Workington, Kendal and Barrow.

My thanks to David Farmer.

Greater Manchester

1974-1986	David Gandy
1986-1987	Brian Crebbin
1987-2004	Tony Taylor
2004-	John Holt

My thanks to John Holt.

Lancashire

1980-1993	John Bates
1994-1999	Graham Brown
1999-2004	Dickie Dickinson
2004	Ian Rushton (Acting)
2004-	Robert Marshall

Merseyside Crown Prosecution Service

1974-1981	Richard Hornby Nicholson (formerly Prosecuting Solicitor of Liverpool City Council)
1981-1986	Brian Holt Crebbin
1986-1996	Evan Clive Woodcock
1996-1999	Graham Brown
1999-2004	John Holt
2004	Norman Larkin (Acting)
2004-	Paul Whittaker

Probation Service

Cumbria

	George Hilton
	Alan Scott
?-2001	Ian White
2001-	Michael Maiden

Greater Manchester

1969-1974	Hugh Crudge
1974-1982	Jack W Marsh
1982-1998	Cedric Fulwood
1998-2004	Christine Knott
2004-	Bob Mathers (Acting)

Lancashire

?-1969	Geoff Lampard
1970-1983	Robert Lee
1984-1993	Harry Rooney
1994-	John Crawforth

Merseyside

1974-1981	Dennis Hall
1981-1999	David Mathieson
1999-	John Stafford

Liverpool University Faculty of Law

Chair of Law (1892-1994)

Queen Victoria Chair of Law from 1894

1892-1996	Edward Jenks
1896-1916	George Henry Emmott
1919-1949	Walter Lyon Blease
1949-1954	Joseph Turner
1955-1965	Denis Browne
1970-1987	David Berkeley Parker
1998-	Christina Margaret Lyon

Chair of Commercial Law (1903-1946) thereafter Chair of Common Law

1903-1907	Alfred Patten Thomas
1907-1914	William John Sparrow
1919-1942	Francis Raleigh Batt
1946-1971	David Richard Seaborne Davies
1971-1977	Frederick James Odgers
1977-1992	Anthony Hugh Hudson
1993-1998	Christina Margaret Lyon
1998-	Michael Anthony Jones

Chair of European Law

1995-	Nanette Alice Emma Marianne Neuwahl

Chairs of Law (Second Chairs)

1964-1971	Frederick James Odgers
1971-1977	Anthony Hugh Hudson
1977-	John Keith Macleod

Chair of Law (Third Chair)

1995-2000	Brian John Doyle

Alsop Wilkinson Chair of Law

1991-1995	Avrom Hirsh Sherr

Deans of Faculty of Law

1904-1916	George Emmott
1916-1919	John Findlay
1919-1925	Professor Walter Lyon Blease
1925-1942	Professor Francis Raleigh Batt
1942-1945	Professor Walter Lyon Blease
1945-1946	Joseph Turner
1946-1953	Professor David Richard Seaborne Davies
1953-1954	Professor Joseph Turner
1954-1956	Professor David Richard Seaborne Davies
1956-1960	Professor Denis Browne
1960-1963	Professor David Richard Seaborne Davies
1963-1964	Professor Denis Browne
1964-1971	Professor David Richard Seaborne Davies
1971-1978	Professor Anthony Hugh Hudson
1978-1984	Professor David Berkeley Parker
1984-1991	Professor Anthony Hugh Hudson
1991-1994	Professor Michael Anthony Jones
1994-1997	Professor Christina Margaret Lyon
1997-1999	Professor Michael Anthony Jones
1999-2000	Professor Brian John Doyle
2000-	Professor Anu Arora

My thanks to His Honour Frank Paterson for the Liverpool University lists.

Liverpool John Moores University Professors of Law

1993-	Professor Roger Evans (Criminal Justice)
1995-	Professor George Mair (Criminal Justice)
2004-	Professor John Cooke
2004-	Professor Peter de Cruz

My thanks to Huw Thomas for this list.

(RF)

Opening of LJMU Moot Hall, 14 January 2005 by the Chancellor of the University, Cherie Booth QC.

Liverpool Law Review Lecture

Speakers

1991 Hon. Judge Gordon Slynn (Judge, European Court of Justice)
1992 Rt. Hon. Lord Justice Glidewell
1993 Rt. Hon. Lord Justice Stephen Brown (President of Family Division)
1994 The Hon. Mr Justice Morland
1995 Hon. Judge Christopher Bellamy (Judge, Court of First Instance, EC)
1996 Sir Nicholas Lyell QC., MP. (Attorney General)
1997 The Hon. Mrs Justice Arden
1998 Lord Falconer of Thoroton QC (Minister of State, Cabinet Office)
1999 The Hon. Mr Justice Hooper
2000 Rt. Hon. The Lord Slynn of Hadley (return visit)
2001 Hon. Judge Nicholas Forwood (Judge, Court of First Instance, EC)
2002 Sir David Calvert-Smith QC (Director of Public Prosecutions)
2003 (No lecture)
2004 His Honour Judge David Lynch

(RF)

Lord Falconer's Law Review Lecture, 1998.

(RF)

Lord Slynn's Law Review Lecture, 2000.

(RF)

DPP and Lynch, 2002.

(RF)

Law Review Lecture, 2004.

(RF)

Haw Thomas, Senior Lecturer LJMU, Stuart Christie, High Sheriff, Commodore Roderick Walker (Pro Chancellor LJMU), Judge David Lynch, Liason Judge, LJMU, Judge Nicholas Forwood, Alan Waterworth, Lord Lieutenant.

(RF)

Ann Lynch and David Lynch, Liverpool Law Review Lecture, 2004.

Presidents of Local Law Socities

Blackburn (Incorporated 1882)

1882-83	Thomas Ainsworth
1883	John Bolton
1885	William Pickup
1886-87	William Wheeler
1888	R C Radcliffe
1889	John Wilding
1890	H J Robinson
1891	W King-Wilkinson
1892	W E L Gaine
1893	O Polding
1893-94	R C Needham
1895	Malam Brothers
1896	C A Sanderson
1897	Bancroft Haworth
1898	R E Fox
1899	D J Preston
1900	J N Withers
1901	E Cooper
1902-03	J W Carter
1904	J Higginson
1905	R B Cliff
1906	S Crossley
1907	Alfred Read
1908	J R Reddish
1909	S Sanderman
1910-12	Sir Lewis Beard
1913-14	J W Marsden
1915-21	L King Wilkinson
1922-23	E Rennison
1924-26	W S Weeks
1927	R Wilding
1928	H A Smitton
1929	R Bremner
1930	Sir John Taylor
1931	Henry Schofield
1932	T R Thompson
1933	Sir Frederick Hindle
1934	P Haworth
1935	F G Haworth
1936	G N Robinson
1937	R K Whittaker
1938	T J Blackhouse
1939	J H Ramsbottom
1940	A B Roebuck
1941	H S Haworth
1942	H D Holland
1943	J E Chadwick
1944	F Britcliffe
1945	J Hargreaves
1946	H Weeks
1947	J W Hollows
1948	L C King-Wilkinson
1949	C S Robinson
1950	A Carter
1951	F A Heys
1952	H Backhouse
1953	G F Nuttal
1954	R H G Horne
1955	C B G Blanthorne
1956	N Lees
1957	G Haworth
1958	G Wightman
1959	L Ranson
1960	W E S Weeks
1961	R H Wilson
1962	E Yates
1963	R Arkwright
1964	J Yates
1965	E C Marsden
1966	F S Squires
1967	J D Forbes
1968	D Johnson
1969	J E Hargreaves
1970	J F Nuttall
1971	A M Verity
1972	A Hardman
1973	W Isherwood
1974	W E T Walsh
1975	D G Watson
1976	J L Lumley
1977	Ian F Warburton
1978	John A Backhouse
1979	A G Britcliffe
1980	T W Ibbotson
1981	J B Haworth
1982	W D Greenwood
1983	P A Scholes
1984	J Whittaker
1985	W R King-Wilkinson
1986	E Slinger
1987	J O Sharples
1988	R S H Brunt
1989	J T Dewhurst
1990	P B Turner
1991	M S Clay
1992	Mrs Catherine Hooper
1993	J B S McDonald
1994	D I Forbes
1995	J C Barker
1996	Miss K L Hughes
1997	M J Hardman
1998	M J H Singleton
1999	C R J Bury
2000-02	Mrs Ann Bamford
2002-04	T A Hoyle

Blackpool and Fylde

1892-94	Alfred Ashcroft
1894-95	Richard Banks
1895-96	R Forrester Addie
1896-97	John J Johnson
1897-98	W J Dickinson
1898-99	I N Parry
1899-00	
1909-10	
1900-01	Frank Anderson
1901-02	Will J Read
1921-24	
1902-03	S Sharpe Waterhouse
1931-32	
1903-04	J H Kean
1910-11	
1924-27	
1904-05	Sir Harry Cartmell
1917-21	
1905 07	T E Topping
1907-09	T Reveley
1911-12	Wylieham Parry
1913-14	J R Johnson
1927-28	
1914-15	R K Singleton
1915-17	W Lockwood
1928-29	W Wilkins
1929-30	J E Harper
1930-31	C M Phillips
1931-35	Eric Read
1935-36	S O Taylor
1936-38	G E M Woosnam
1938-45	G H Walker
1945-48	Alec Barker
1948-49	Eric Read
1949-50	J K Lawson
1951-53	Luke Matley
1953-54	T Underwood
1954-55	T Carter
1955-56	J Addishead JP
1956-57	R M Bland
1957-58	H S Ellis
1958-59	John Budd
1959-60	Norman Lees
1960-61	V Waring JP
1961-62	B K Leathley MA
1962-63	F J Hall JP
1963-64	B M Woosnam
1964-65	E Read TD, MA
1965-66	H A Yates
1966-67	H I Cartmell
1967-68	A Warham
1968-69	G M Whiteside
1969-70	M Wren-Hilton
1970-71	B V Woods
1971-72	C J Waring MA
1972-73	D Eastwood
1973-74	V Collinson
1974-75	R O Sutton
1975-76	C Collins
1976-77	Mrs C W Shaw
1977-78	K Chadwick LLB
1978-79	G O Barton
1979-80	Samuel G Lee
1980-81	H C Pond
1981-82	M E Buckley
1982-83	R W Darbyshire
1983-84	A M MacPherson
1984-85	M Wren-Hilton
1985-86	J K Walmsley
1986-87	Miss B J Lester LLB
1987-88	Raymond Green
1988-89	N Law LLB
1989-90	J Brewer LLB
1990-91	T Colebourne
1991-92	C J Waring MA
1992-93	P J Lawson
1993-94	His Honour Judge P Sycamore Past President of the Law Society
1994-95	C J Beverley LLB
1995-96	D Cameron LLB
1996-97	J Brown LLB
1997-98	S Coupe LLB
1998-99	A MacPhie LLB
1999-00	S Turner LLB
2001-01	G Stuart
2001-02	A Greensmith BA
2002-03	Miss C Bridson BA
2003-04	M Bland

Liverpool

1827-28	Joshua Lace
1828-29	George Ashby Pritt
1829-30	John Eden
1830-31	Richard Radcliffe
1831-32	M D Lowndes
1832-33	Ambrose Lace
1833-34	G J Duncan
1834-35	Richard Finlow
1835-36	Thomas Harvey
1836-37	E G Deane
1837-38	James Robinson
1838-39	Thomas Carson
1839-40	John Eden
1840-41	Joachim Andrade
1841-42	R A Payne
1842-43	Thomas Fisher
1843-44	John Peacock
1844-45	Thomas Avison
1845-46	H H Statham
1846-47	J B Lloyd
1847-48	Charles Falcon
1848-49	Robert Norris
1849-50	Robert Norris
1850-51	Peter Wright
1851-52	G B Carter
1852-53	W Wareing
1853-54	John Fletcher
1854-55	John Whitley
1855-56	Edward Banner
1856-57	Ambrose Lace
1857-58	Henry Jenkins
1858-59	Henry Bell
1859-60	Thomas Dodge
1860-61	Thomas Dodge
1861-62	William Radcliffe
1862-63	F S Hull
1863-64	W A Jevons
1864-65	W Shuttleworth
1865-66	A T Squarey
1866-67	W G Bateson
1867-68	J Thornely
1868-69	John Yates
1869-70	M J Hore
1870-71	I H E Gill
1871-72	F D Lowndes
1872-73	John Atkinson
1873-74	T E Paget
1874-75	P F Garnett
1875-76	E W Bird
1876-77	H C Duncan
1877-78	Edward Whitley
1878-79	William Barlett
1879-80	William Stone
1880-81	A T Squarey
1881-82	Enoch Harvey
1882-83	H W Collins
1883-84	John Hughes
1884-85	J E Gray Hill
1885-86	T Bellringer
1886-87	J H Kenion
1887-88	A Bright
1888-89	R S Cleaver
1889-90	F J Hawkins
1890-91	F Archer
1891-92	A F Warr
1892-93	J W Alsop
1893-94	J Dickinson
1894-95	C H Morton
1895-96	J Lawrence
1896-97	F Gregory
1897-98	H H Gibbons
1898-99	C E Steve
1899-00	W A Weightman
1900-01	Arthur S Mather
1901-02	Harold D Bateson
1902-03	Septimus Castle
1903-04	F Marton Hull
1904-05	Arnold J Cleaver
1905-06	John Cameron
1906-07	George Dickinson
1907-08	B Arkle
1908-09	W C Thorne
1909-10	Charles Collins
1910-11	Godfrey A Solly
1911-12	Robert Norris
1913-14	W Forshaw Wilson
1914-15	Edward V Crooks
1915-16	Morris P Jones
1916-17	F Russell Roberts

1917-18	C E Nield
1918-19	Finlay Dun
1919-20	Sir Norman Hill, Bart
1920-21	John L Williams
1921-22	Hadden Todd
1922-23	F H Edwards
1923-24	David McIver
1924-25	Francus Weld
1925-26	Edgar L Billson
1926-27	J Graham Kenion
1927-28	W H T Brown
1928-29	A E Chevalier
1929-30	Park N Stone
1930-31	L S Holmes
1931-32	R D Cripps
1932-33	C W Wright
1933-34	W Glasgow
1934-35	F C Gregory
1935-36	J W Cocks
1936-37	A E Frankland
1937-38	G E Castle
1938-39	V D Heyne
1939-40	S R Dodds
1940-41	J B McKaig
1941-42	Benjamin Arkle
1942-43	Roland Marshall
1943-44	J Roberts
1944-45	W L Bateson
1945-46	H M Alderson-Smith
1946-47	J C Bryson
1947-48	Alfred W Brown
1948-49	M Cory Dixon
1949-50	D H Mace
1950-51	J W T Holland
1951-52	L E Rutherford
1952-53	H R Pruddah
1953-54	T W Harley
1955-56	Charles J Cocks
1954-55	R W Abercromby
1956-57	J D Kewish
1957-58	E Holland-Hughes
1958-59	James E Hadfield
1959-60	George H Twyford
1960-61	W R Cafferata
1961-62	J S Crook
1962-63	E S Russell
1963-64	G Percival Harris
1964-65	T B Roberts
1965-66	M O Morris
1966-67	A Lewis-Jones
1967-68	G N Booth
1968-69	J Norton
1969-70	J H C Byrne
1970-71	J G Bryson
1971-72	J W Bateson
1972-73	W Morris-Jones
1973-74	J M Marshall
1974-75	A Cohen
1975-76	C R Hewetson
1976-77	Rex Taylor
1977-78	Sir Stanley Holmes
1978-79	G Barrie Marsh
1979-80	G C Lindsay
1980-81	P Howell Williams
1981-82	G A Ensor
1982-83	B B Wright
1983-84	K M Tamlin
1984-85	J W H Tournafond
1985-86	R A McCullagh
1986-87	Derek H Morris
1987-88	David Thomas
1988-89	Roger H Arden
1989-90	Elizabeth M Steel
1990-91	Lawrence Holden
1991-92	Richard Bark-Jones
1992-93	Michael H Hill
1993-94	Andrew Holroyd
1994-95	W A Twemlow
1995-96	D R Swift
1996-97	T J Marshall
1997-98	N J Fagan
1998-99	P W Rhodes
1999-00	D R Swaffield
2000-01	E R Goldsmith
2001-02	J D A Leith
2002-03	M R Feeny
2003-04	J Benson
2004-	P McCarthy

Manchester

1840	James Crossley
1841	Oswald Milne
1842	Samuel Kay
1843	Stephen Heelis
1844	John Taylor
1845	Robert H Wilson
1846	John Bagshaw
1847	John Owen
1848	Joseph Grave
1849	R M Whitlow
1850	Thomas Taylor
1851	J F Beever
1852	George Healey
1853	John Barlow
1854	John Vaughan
1855	T L Rushton
1856	William Beaumont
1857	James Crossley
1858	William Slater
1859	T P Bunting
1860	R R B Cobbett
1861	James Street
1862	Richard Radford
1863	Christopher Briggs
1864	John Grundy
1865	Thomas Baker
1866	John Summerscales
1867	Stephen Heelis
1868	G G Withington
1869	George Taylor
1870	M Bateson Wood
1871	John Cooper
1872	Thomas Holden
1873	Thomas Jepson
1874	W H Guest
1875	John Ponsonby
1876	Thomas Claye
1877	Thomas Diggles
1878	M Bateson Wood
1879	William Harper
1880	Isaac Hall
1881	George Hadfeild
1882	Alfred Leaf
1883	J F Milne
1884	W L Welsh
1885	Henry Wood
1886	P Watson
1887	W S Boddington
1888	James Heelis
1889	James Heelis
1890	J F Milne
1891	W Cobbett
1892	J A Foyster
1893	John Cooper
1894	G P Allen
1895	Leonard Tatham
1896	G W Fox
1897	W C Lord
1898	R A Edgar
1899	C L Samson
1900	J B Parkinson
1901	J T Doyle
1902	R W Williamson
1903	C J E Crosse
1904	W H Norton
1905	E J Carlisle
1906	W Cabbott
1907	W S Boddington
1908	Elkanah Hewitt
1909	S F Butcher
1910	G H Charlsworth
1911	W H Foyster
1912	A Tarbolton
1913	J McDonald
1914	A F Maclure
	J Marriott
1915	R S Milford
1916	F A Padmore
1917	A Hosegood
1918	S H Seville
1919	A F Maclure
1920	D F Heart
1921	T H Davies-Colley
1922	F R Osbome
1923	R W Rylands

1924	G W Charlsworth
1925	H D Simpson
1926	Adam Fox
1927	P J Skelton
1928	W E M Mainprice
1929	K H Atkison
1930	F S Stancliffe
1931	A R Moon
1932	J W Robinson
1933	K T S Dockray
1934	J W B Hodgeson
1935	W Paterson
1936	T A Higson
1937	C F Morgan
1938	F A Padmore
1939	W E M Mainprice
1940	Paul Archer
1941	A E Hanson
1942	H L Haddleshaw
1943	J H Lawton
1944	G F Strange
1945	R J Walker
1946	A H Goughly
1947	Ernest Farrington
1948	J A Hancock
1949	N C O'Brien
1950	J F Bentley
1951	W G F Ballantyne
1952	S C Breakell
1953	A J Moon
1954	R M Greenhalgh
1955	N G C Pearson
1956	D J Macbeth
1957	D P Hilton
1958	G Davies
1959	J Eva
1960	W G Haig
1961	G W W Bunting
1962	A. E McKenna
1963	E J N Harris
1964	V Steinart
1965	R V B Webb
1966	R A Davies
1967	J G Smith
1968	F W Towns
1969	W Bolton
1970	W G Beckett
1971	C J Mettcalfe
1974	G F L Royle
1976	M Hurst
1978	M A G Sachs
1979	M S Blackburn
1980	D S Gandy
1981	J C F Pickford
1982	J C K Elliot
1983	N Marks
1984	D J Tully
1985	J D Sands
1986	A T Parkinson
1987	P K Dodd
1988	P Hodson
1989	K M Mellor
1990	M G Green
1991	G K Jump
1992	M R Mattison
1993	G R G Robson
1994	J Wilner
1995	A Kershaw
1996	R J C Potter
1997	R J C Ince
1998	N G S Day
1999	D A Healey
2000	A Obodai
2001	Michael Clavell-Bate
2002	G McCool
2003	Paul Boucher
2004	Franklin Sinclair

Rochdale

1952-53	G G Collins
1954-55	C M Hudson
1956-57	C H Thomas
1958-59	J A Milns
1960-61	J S Stoney
1962-63	R S Clegg
1964-65	A Littlewood
1966	F W Kay
1967-69	B E L Taylor
1969-71	A H Sutcliffe
1971-73	A Wright
1973-75	H M Ledger
1975-77	W B Tomlinson
1977-79	J L Taylor
1979-80	A S Coupe
1980-81	K J Freer
1981-82	R Halstead
1982-83	E G L Collins OBE
1983-84	R S Greenwood MBE
1984-85	C Ashworth
1985-86	B Atherton
1986-87	D Everett
1987-Jan 1988	S J Greenwood
1988-89	D C H Owen
1989-90	J F Kay
1990-91	Miss V Buckley
1991-92	K Walker
1992-93	I Hampson
1993-94	P Rhodes
1994-95	C J Healy
1995-96	P R Miller
1996-97	G Haigh
1997-98	R G Addington
1998-99	E Taylor
1999-2000	P A Riley
2000-2001	P L Taylor
2001-2002	D Morrell
2002-2003	P J Watson

Southport and Ormskirk

1922	Sir S Brighouse
1923	Sir S Brighouse
1924	Sir S Brighouse
1925	J J Cockshott
1926	J J Cockshott
1927	W E Mawdsley
1928	W E Mawdsley
1929	F A Jones
1930	F A Jones
1931	W J Worden
1932	W H Watson
1933	W A Cook
1934	F W Brown
1935	Wilmot Hodge
	R W Brighouse
1936	Geo Cockshott
1937	Sir Ernest Hadfield
1938	Reginald Hodge
1939	T Goffey
1940	A Quayle
1941	J T Rigby
1942	W D Briscombe
1943	A E Grundy
1944	J Peatfield
1945	E W Mawdsley
1946	A F Worden
1947	J Yates
1948	K Peck
1949	R W Sumner
1950	C D Watson
1951	W D Briscombe
1952	E W Mawdsley
1953	A V Cunliffe
1954	J W Cook
1955	F H Duncan
1956	W A Raynor, MBE
1957	I G W Newington
1958	B J Hartwell
1959	R E Perrins
1960	W H Bellis, CBE
1961	R A Lloyd
1962	A R Lewis
1963	G H Newton
1964	G L Belshaw

1965	P P Bayley-Brown
1966	J E D P A Loy
1967	L Duckworth
1968	G A Batty
1969	K G Hickson
1970	C Rawstron
1971	J T Wright
1972	S A Brighouse
1973	F W Cartwright
1974	N Adler
1975	N Adler
1976	A F Russell
1977	G H H Glasgow
1978	P St J Haslam-Fox
1979	B G Cox
1980	R B Farley
1981	G K Watson
1982	G K Hurtley
1983	E Barton
1984	P J Carter
1985	J A Walsh
1986	J D R Lloyd
1987	A L Blackhurst
1988	G Hough
1989	C J Byron
1990	T J Mills
1991	A H A Cook
1992	L J L Gallaway
1993	S P Holmes
1994	C K Sumner
1995	M J Yates
1996	A J G Cottrell
1997	M L Cook
1998	L D Grant
1999	G Hatton
2000	R J Fletcher
2001	D T Bushell
2002	R A Barnett
2003	M P Braham
2004	Gail Peterson

West Cumberland

1993-1994	John Taylor
1994-1995	Christine McKay
1995-1996	Brian Kyle
1997-1998	Graham Quigley
1998-1999	Joe Kelly
1999-2000	Stephen Moore
2000-2001	Simon Smith
2001-2002	Peter James
2002-2003	Claire Madden
2003-2004	Richard Taylor

Westmorland

Mr E Moser	'A considerable number of years'
Mr J F Hopkinson	1970-1973
Mr L Powell	1976-1979
Mr R Sykes	1979-1982
Mr G Moser	1982-1985
Mr L Hayton	1985-1988
Mr M Hopkinson	1988-1991
Mr M Winckley	1991-1993
Mr R Broady	1993-1995
Mr J Chapman	1995-1997
Mr N Longworth	1997-1999
Mr M Crompton	1999-2001
Mrs J Robinson	2001-2003
Mr T Fitch	2003-

Lord – Lieutenants

Lancashire

1858-1897	William Philip, 4th Earl of Sefton KG
1897-1908	Frederick Arthur, 16th Earl of Derby
1908-1928	Ughtred James, 1st Baron Shuttleworth
1928-1948	Edward George Villiers, 17th Earl of Derby KG
1948-1950	Arthur William Ashton, 2nd Earl Peel
1951-1968	Edward John, 18th Earl of Derby MC
1968-1971	Baron Rhodes of Saddleworth
1971-1976	Ralph Assheton, 1st Baron Clitheroe of Downham
1976-1996	Sir Simon Towneley KCVO
1997-	Charles Geoffrey Nicholas, 5th Baron Shuttleworth

Greater Manchester

1974-1987	Alderman Sir William Downward
1987-	Colonel Sir John B Timmins KCVO, OBE

Merseyside

1974-1979	Brigadier Sir Douglas Crawford CB, DSO
1979-1989	Wing Commander Sir Kenneth Stoddart KCVO
1989-1993	Henry Cotton
1993-	Alan W Waterworth

Lord Lieutenants of Cumberland and Westmorland, 1660-1974

Cumberland and Westmorland

1661-1685	Charles Howard	1st Earl of Carlisle (of Westmorland from 1660)
1685-1687	Thomas Tufton	6th Earl of Thanet
1687-1688	Richard Graham	1st Viscount Preston
1689-1694	John Lowther	1st Viscount Lonsdale
1694-1712	Charles Howard	3rd Earl of Carlisle
1712-1714	Thomas Tufton	6th Earl of Thanet
1714-1738	Charles Howard	3rd Earl of Carlisle
1738-1751	Henry Lowther	3rd Viscount Lonsdale

Cumberland

1751-1759	Charles Wyndham	2nd Earl of Egremont
1759-1602	Sir James Lowther	From 1784 Earl of Lonsdale

Westmorland

1751-1753	Sir John Pennington	3rd Baronet, Muncaster
1753-1756	Sir William Lowther	3rd Baronet, Marske and Holker
1756-1763	Sir John Pennington	3rd Baronet. Muncaster
1763-1802	Sir James Lowther	From 1784 Earl of Lonsdale

Cumberland and Westmorland

1602-1844	William Lowther	1st Earl of Lonsdale
1844-1872	William Lowther	2nd Earl of Lonsdale
1872-1876	Henry Lowther	3rd Earl of Lonsdale

Cumberland

1876-1917	Sir Josslyn Francis Pennington	9th Bart, 5th Baron Muncaster
1918-1944	Hugh Cecil Lowther	5th Earl of Lonsdale
1944-1949	Col F H Ballantyne Dykes	
1950-1959	Lt Col Sir Robert Chance	
1960-1968	Lt Col Sir Fergus Graham	
1968-1974	John Wade	

Westmorland

1876-1881	Sir Richard Musgrave	10th Baronet, Edenhall
1881-1926	Henry Tulton	1st Lord Hothfield
1926-1931	Lord Henry Cavendish Bentinck	
1931-1939	Captain Stanley Hughes le Fleming	
1939-1945	Captain Anthony Lowther	Viscount Lowther 1944
1945-1957	Major James Winstanley Cropper	
1957-1965	Henry Hornyold Strickland	
1965-1974	Lt Cmdr. Paul Norman Wilson, from 1976 Lord Wilson of High Wray	

(List compiled by C Bruce Jones, County Archivist)

Lord Lieutenants

Cumbria

1974-1983	John Wade
1983-1994	Sir Charles Graham
1994-	Sir James Anthony Cropper

High Sheriffs

Lancashire

1875	John Pearson	Golborne Park
1876	Oliver Ormerod Walker	Chesham, Bury
1877	George Blucher Hinsage Marton	Capernuray
1878	Nathaniel Eckersley	Standish Hall
1879	William Garnett	Quernmore Park
1880	Ralph John Aspinall	Standon Hall
1881	William Poster	Hornby Castle
1882	George McCorquodale	The Willows, Newton-le-Willows
1883	Thomas Ashton	Ford Bank, Didsbury
1884	Thomas Brooks	Crawshaw Hall, Rawtenstall
1885	James Williamson	Ryelands, Lancaster
1886	Sir Andrew Barclay Walker, Bart	Gateacre Grange, Liverpool
1887	John Hardy Thursby	Omerod House and Bank Hall, Burnley
1888	Oliver Heywood	Claremont, Manchester
1889	Clement Monyeux Royds	Greenhill, Rochdale
1890	Charles Henry Bird	Crookhey Hall, Garstang
1891	George Theophilus Robert Preston	Ellel Grange
1891	William Henry Foster	Hornby Castle
1892	John Knowles	Westwood, Pendlebury
1893	Sir Thomas Storey Kt	Westfield House, Lancaster
1894	Joshua Walmsley Radcliffe	Werneth Park, Oldham
1895	Frank Hardcastle	Firwood, Bolton
1896	Sir Peter Carlaw Walker Bt	Bewsby New Hall and Osmastin Manor, Derbyshire
1897	Samuel Radcliffe Platt	Werneth Park, Oldahm
1898	William Balle Huntington	The Woodlands, Darwen
1899	William Charles Jones	The Oaklands, Preston Brook and Bold Old Hall, Warrington
1900	Frederick Baynes	Salmesbury Old Hall, nr Preston
1901	Charles Hesketh Bibby Hesketh	The Rookery, Southport
1902	Arthur Knowles	Westwood, Pendlebury and Alvaston Hall, Nantwich
1903	Henry Whitehead	Haslem Hey, Bury
1904	Herbert Lushington Storey	Bailrigg, Lancaster
1905	Sir John Ormerod Scarlett Thursby Bt	Ormerord House, Burnley
1906	Edward Tootal Broadhurst	Manchester
1907	Sir William Henry Yates, Bart	Highfield, Woolton, Liverpool
1908	Sir Thomas Brocklebank, Bart	The Hollies, Woolton, Liverpool
1909	Sir William Bower Forwood Kt	Liverpool
1910	Reginal Arthur Tatton	Cuerdon Hall, nr Preston
1911	George Augustas Pilkington	Knight of Belle Vue, Southport
1912	John Stone	Blacklow, Roby
1913	John William Makant	Gillow Lodge, Bolton
1914	John Henry Maden	Rockliffe House, Bacup
1915	Edward Graham Wood	Cambridge Road, Southport

1916	Percy John Hibbert	Hampsfield, Grange over Sands
1917	Sir William Hesketh Lever	Rivington, near Horwich and Thornton Manor, Cheshire
1918	Col George Hesketh, VD	Linwood, Astley Bridge, nr Bolton
1919	Ralph Cockayne Assheton	Downham Hall, Clitheroe
1920	Edward Deakin	Egerton Hall, nr Bolton
1921	George Hildyard Banks	Winstanley Hall, nr Wigan
1922	Myles Kennedy	Stone Cross, Ulverston
1923	Sir Benjamin Sands Johnson	Abbot's Lea, Woolton, Liverpool
1924	Arthur Moore Lamb	Eskdale, Birkdale
1925	George Owen Sandys	Graythwaite Hall, Ulverston
1926	John Percy Taylor	Woodside, Heaton, Bolton
1927	Sir James Philip Reynolds Bart	Levens Hall, Westmorland
1928	Sir Arthur Meyrick Hollins, Bart	The Coppice, Cromwell Road, Ribbleton, Preston
1929	Charles Sydney Jones	Eastbourne, Princes Park, Liverpool
1930	Samuel Turner	Springbank, Bamford, Rochdale
1931	Sir Frederick Charles Bowring	Sefton Park, Liverpool
1932	Lt Col Austin Townsend Porritt	Yewbarrow Lodge, Grange over Sands
1933	Arthur Samuel Mitchell	Manor Drive, West Didsbury
1934	Sir Thomas Edward Higham	Bank House, Accrington
1935	Myles Noel Kenyon DL	Manchester Road, Bury
1936	Thomas Stone	Yew Tree, Roby
1937	William James Garnett	Quernmore Park, Lancaster
1938	Charles Eastwood	Moss House, Leyland
1939	Col Alan Cecil Tod	Allerton, Liverpool
1940	Major Edmund Barwick Clegg	Shore, Littleborough
1941	William James Garnett	Quernmore Park, Lancaster
1942	Francis Joseph Weld	Liverpool
1943	Sir William Fawell Ascroft	Preston
1944	Edwin Thompson	Liverpool
1945	Sir Henry Clayton Darlington	Melling Hall, Carnforth
1946	Sir Percy MacDonald	Manchester
1947	Col Roger Fleetwood Hesketh	Meols Hall, Southport
1948	Sir Robert Rankin, Bart	Broughton Tower, Lancashire and Iver Lodge Buckinghamshire
1949	Col Wilfred Hugh Burton	Fair View, Ulverston Rowley Kennedy
1950	Sir Harold Parkinson	Burnley and Hornby Castle, nr Lancaster
1951	Francis Grundy	Prestwich, nr Manchester
1952	Sir John Francis Roskell Reynolds, Bart	Liverpool
1953	Major Mervyn Edwyn Myles Sandys	Graythwaite Hall, nr Ulverston
1954	Col Leonard Green	The Manor House, Whalley
1955	Sir Cuthbert Barwick Clegg	Higher Shore House, Littleborough
1956	Col Vere Egerton Cotton	Langdale, Grassendale Park, Liverpool
1957	Alan Thomas Trevor Storey	Lancaster
1958	Col Robert Goulborne Parker	Browsholm Hall, Clitheroe
1959	Sir Eric Ashton Carpenter	Manchester
1960	Peter Fleetwood Hesketh	The Manor House, Hale, Liverpool
1961	Col Walter Musgrave Musgrave-Hoyle	Caton, Lancaster

1962	Col Geoffrey George Hargreaves Bolton	Littlemoor House, Clitheroe
1963	Sir Frank Lord	Werneth, Oldham
1964	Brigadier Philip John Denton Toosey	Liverpool
1965	Col Henry Cary Owtram	Lancaster
1966	Col Frederick William Jones	Lytham
1967	Col Robert Ward	Greenhalgh, Bolton
1968	Albert Wild	Preston
1969	Sir Douglas Inglis Crawford	Liverpool
1970	Col Henry John Darlington	Halton, Lancaster
1971	Simon Peter Edmond Cosmo, William Townley	Burnley
1972	Lt Col Joshua Geoffrey Barber-Lomax	Bromley Cross, Bolton
1973	Sir Henry Lumby	Ormskirk
1974	Col Denis Arthur Sydenham Houghton	Broughton, Preston
1975	Major Basil Greenwood	Whalley
1976	Captain Geoffrey Price Bowring	Halton Park, Lancaster
1977	Stanley Hyde Riddiough	Colne
1978	Col Michael Albert Astley Birwistle	Tunstall
1979	Cyril Joseph Ainscough	Dalton, Parbold
1980	Edward Anthony Nickson	Lytham
1981	Captain Sidney Roy Fisher	Whittle-le-Woods, Chorley
1982	Lt Col Alastair Fordyce	Cherry Tree, Blackburn
1983	Leonard Broughton	Cleveleys, Blackpool
1984	Surgeon Lt Commander Peter John James Wren	Whittle-le-Woods, Chorley
1985	Edmund Christopher Parker	Clitheroe
1986	Edward Chambre Dickson	Goosnargh, nr Preston
1987	Robert Priestley Shepherd	Horncliffe, Rossendale
1988	Col John Frederick Greenhough	Lytham
1989	Charles Joseph Weld-Blundel	Chipping
1990	Patrick William Townsend	Gisburn, Lancashire
1991	John Renshaw Holt	Lower Tatham, Lancaster
1992	Kenneth Ainsworth Gledhill	Blackpool
1993	Col Robert Rainey Craik	Mawdesley
1994	Mrs Judith Josa Duckworth	Garstang
1995	Ralph William Goodall	Hoghton
1996	Timothy Roy Henry Kimber	Carnforth
1997	Sir David Trippier	Rossendale
1998	Charles Anthony Beresford Brennan	Hoghton
1999	The Lady Shuttleworth	By Carnforth
2000	Rodney Newman Swarbrick CBE	Preston
2001	Gloria Oates OBE	Ramsbottom
2002	Thomas Geoffrey Bowring	Lancaster
2003	Bryan Gray	Parbold
2004	Gail Simpson Stanley	Ormskirk
2005	J C Armfield OBE., DL	

Greater Manchester

1974	Sir Neville Butterworth	Knutsford
1975	Douglas John Edwards	Juniper Hill, Cheshire
1976	Col Richard Downay Martin-Bird	Stockinwood, Macclesfield
1977	Vernon Stott	Greenfield, Oldham
1978	Col Robert George Watson Ollerenshaw	Didsbury
1979	Major Leslie Stamford Raffles	Didsbury
1980	David Israel Goldstone	Didsbury
1981	Col Donald Edwin Gibbs	Middleton, Manchester
1982	John Nightingale	Manchester
1983	Mrs Avril Fishwick	Wigan
1984	Bartle Hodgkiss	Bolton
1985	Col Thomas Sherman	Wilmslow
1986	Col John Bradford Timmins	Warburton
1987	Col Arthur Axford	Ashton-under-Lyne
1988	Alan William Guest	Alderley Edge
1989	Col William Marriott Elder	Lymm
1990	Norman Quick	Altrincham
1991	Major David Geoffrey Wilson	Wilmslow
1992	Samuel Jack Victor Arditti	Bowdon
1993	Lawrence Duncan Lawton	Oldham
1994	John Basil Zochonis	Warburton
1995	Major Edmund Travis Gartside	Rochdale
1996	Mrs Mary Flora MacKinnon Firth OBE	Oldham
1997	Warren James Smith	Fallowfield
1998	John Robert Louis Lee	Altrincham
1999	Norman Kelvin Stoller OBE	Bolton
2000	Major John Noel Abbott	Alderley Edge
2001	Lady Montgomery,	Altrincham
2002	Professor Sir Netar Mallick	Manchester
2003	Susan Katrian Hodgkiss	West Didsbury
2004	Robert Hough	Bowden
2005	Sir David Wilmott QPM., DL.	

Merseyside

1974	Sir Kenneth Maxwell Stoddart KCVO	Willaston
1975	Lt Col Frank Vernon Denton OBE	Freshfield, Formby
1976	Stephen Minion OBE	Liverpool
1977	Lt Col George Fortnam Appleton OBE	Ainsdale
1978	Major Henry Bertram Chrimes	Heswall
1979	Joseph Alexander Duncan	Landican, Birkenhead
1980	Col Sir Gerard Thomas McClellan CBE	Hightown, Liverpool
1981	Major Philip Johnson	St Helens
1982	Derek Isaac Heys CBE	Liverpool
1983	Henry Brussel Bicket	Liverpool
1984	Lt Col Charles Henry Elston	West Kirby
1985	Col Dudley Frank Moore	Birkdale
1986	Henry Egerton Cotton	Liverpool
1987	Col Mary Creagh OBE	Formby
1988	Col Francis J K Williams CBE	Wirral
1989	Col David Richard Morgan OBE	Birkdale
1990	Commander Edward John Billington CBE	Heswall
1991	Mrs Jean Wotherspoon OBE	St Helens
1992	Alan William Waterworth	Frodsham
1993	Commodore Roderick H Walker	Heswall
1994	Mrs Anita Samuels OBE	Liverpool
1995	Anthony Wilson Shone	West Kirby
1996	Mrs Jennifer Anne Grundy	Roby, Liverpool
1997	Brian Thaxter OBE	Mollington
1998	Sir Christopher Raynor Hewetson	Birkdale
1999	Derek Hazlitt Morris	Lydiate
2000	William D Fulton	Puddington
2001	Professor Peter Toyne	Caldy
2002	Lady Kirsty Pilkington	Kingsley
2003	Dr Robert David Atlay	Blundellsands
2004	Stuart Christie	Liverpool
2005	Mrs R H Hawley DL	

I am grateful to Under Sheriff Andrew Wilson and to Nicolas Davies, formerly of the Duchy of Lancaster Office, for their help with the Lancashire, Greater Manchester and Merseyside lists.

Cumbria

1972	Major Frank Gordon Wilson	Millom
1973	Nicholas Austhwaite Stanley DSO, OBE	Eskdale
1974	George Nigel Fancourt Wingate OBE	Cockermouth
1975	Michael Charles Stanley MBE	Grange over Sands
1976	Joseph Hugh Harris	Penrith
1977	Edward Hubert Fleming-Smith TD	Carlisle
1978	Richard Hugh Cavendish	Grange over Sands
1979	Stafford Vaughan Stepney Howard	Penrith
1980	Charles Henry Bagot	Kendal
1981	Timothy Ross Fetherstonhaugh	Penrith
1982	William John Montague Chaplin	Near Ulverston
1983	Peter Eric Fryers Crewdson	Kendal
1984	Edward Peter Ecroyd	Carlisle
1985	Major Antony James Robinson Harrison	Carlisle
1986	Major Nigel James Clarkson Webb	Burton in Kendal
1987	William Victor Gubbins	Penrith
1988	Roger Brockbank	Kendal
1989	Major Timothy Richard Riley	Penrith
1990	Thomas Peter Naylor	Ambleside
1991	Ian Cufaude Caff	Brampton
1992	Myles Christopher Ross Sandys	Ulverston
1993	Margaret Helen Armstrong	Nr Penrith
1994	Martin Brodrick	Carlisle
1995	Hugh William Lawson	Carlisle
1996	Henry Charles Fraser Bowring	Kirkby Lonsdale
1997	John Henry Fryer Spedding OBE	Keswick
1998	Simon Philip Pease	Kirkby Lonsdale
1999	Arthur Ian Bullough	Brampton
2000	The Lady Hothfield.	Appleby in Westmorland
2001	Robert Bryce Hazell-McCosh	Penrith
2002	David Trimble	Carlisle
2003	Anthony Leeming	Penrith
2004	Frederick Markham	
2005	Dr A C I Naylor	

Chief Constables

Birkenhead Borough

1844-1855 McHarg
1855-1863 James Birnie
1863-1869 F Benswick
1869-1875 R H Kinchant
1876-1898 J B Barker
1898-1912 Walter S Davies
1913-1923 Edward Parker
1923-1942 A C Dawson
1942-1958 Henry J Vann
1958-1967 Sydney J Harvey

Merged with Cheshire Police on 01.07.1967 and later with Merseyside Police on 01.04.1974.

Bolton

1839-? Superintendent Hyram Simpson
1842-? Superintendent John Boyd
?-1867 James Harris
1867-1877 Thomas Beech
1877-1911 John Holgate
1911-? Fred Mullineaux
1930-? W J Howard
1957-1964 Edward Barker
1964-1969 John William Moody

In 1969 amalgamated with Lancashire Constabulary and in 1974 became K Division of Greater Manchester Police.

Bootle

1887-1888 James P Arrowsmith
1888-1890 Adrien D'Espiney
1891-1905 James T Cumming
1906-1919 John Stewart
1919-1920 William D Allan
1920-1926 Phillip T B Browne
1926-1949 T Bell
1949-1953 William E Pitts
1953-1967 Harold E Legg

On 01.04.1967 amalgamated with Liverpool City Police to form Liverpool and Bootle Constabulary, which on 01.04.1974 became part of Merseyside Police.

Burnley

1887-1901 J Harrop
1901-1905 H C Rawle
1905-1924 W H Smith
1924-1937 W Fairclough
1937-1939 A Edwards
1939-1942 H Bames
1942-1948 W Green
1948-1960 R A Noble GM
1960-1962 L Massey MBE
1962-1968 J H Thompson
1968-1969 Superintendent N Greenwood (Acting)

Amalgamated with Lancashire Constabulary in 1969.

Lancashire

1839-1856 Captain John Woodford
1856-1859 Thomas Walker Sheppard
1859-1868 William Percival Elgee
1868-1876 Robert Bruce
1877-1880 Charles Gouter Legge
1880-1909 Henry Martin Moorsom
1909-1912 Charles Villiers Ibbetson
1912-1927 Sir Harry Philip Parnell Lane (Kt 1925)
1927-1935 Wilfred Trubshaw
1935-1950 Sir Archibald Frederick Hodern (Kt 1948)
1950-1967 Sir Eric St Johnston (Kt 1968)
1967-1972 William John Henry Palfrey
1972-1977 Stanley Parr
1977-1978 John William Moody
1978-1983 Albert Laugharne
1983-1995 Robert Brian Johnson CBE
1995-2002 Pauline Ann Clare CBE
2002- Paul Stephenson

Suggested reading: Policing in Lancashire 1839-1989. Bob Dobson, Landy Publishing, 1989.

Liverpool

(Before 1920 the Chief Constable was called Head Constable)

1836-1844 Michael James Whitty
1844 Henry Miller
1845-1852 Matthew Maurice George Dowling
1852-1881 John James Greig
1881-1902 Sir John William Nott-Bower
1902-1912 Sir Leonard Dunning
1912-1923 Francis Caldwell
1925-1931 Lionel Decimus Longcroft Everett
1932-1940 Archibald Kennedy Wilson
1940-1948 Herbert Winstanley CBE
1948-1958 Sir Charles Carnegie Martin CBE
1958-1964 Joseph Wright Teasdale Smith
1965-1967 Sir James Haughton

Merseyside

1974-1975 Sir James Houghton
1976-1989 Sir Kenneth Gordon Oxford
1989-1998 Sir James Sharples
1998-2004. Norman Bettison
2004- Bernard Hogan-Howe

Suggested reading: From Cutlasses to Computers: Police Force in Liverpool 1836-1989, W R Cockcroft, S B Publications, 1991. On the Mersey Beat, Mike Brogden, Oxford University Press, 1991. Spike Island, James McClure, MacMillan London Ltd, 1980.

Manchester

1842-1857 Captain Edward Willis
1857-1880 Captain William Henry Palin
1881-1896 Charles Malcolm Wood
1897-1898 W Fell-Smith (Acting)
1898-1926 Robert Peacock
1927-1943 John Maxwell
1943-1958 Joseph Bell
1958-1965 John Andrew McKay
1966-1974 William James Richards (Manchester and Salford from 1968)

Greater Manchester

1974-1976 William James Richards
1976-1991 Sir (Cyril) James Anderton
1991-2002 David Wilmot
2002- Michael J Todd

Suggested reading: A History of Policing in Manchester, Eric J Hewitt, E J Morten Publishers, 1979. The Police: 150 years of Policing in the Manchester Area, Archive Publications, 1989.

Oldham

1849-1858 John Jackson CB
1858-1859 Abraham Augustus Hunter
1859-1861 Edward Lees
1861-1866 James Wetherell
1866-1892 Charles Hodgkinson
1892-1898 Sir Robert Peacock MVO
1898-1917 David Henry Turner
1917-1942 Arthur Killick Mayall OBE
1942-1958 Walter Edward Schofield OBE
1958-1966 Fred Berry
1967-1969 Leslie Palmer (Acting)

Amalgamated with Lancashire Constabulary on 01.04.1969 and became 'Q' Division of Greater Manchester Police on 01.04.1974.

Suggested reading: 999 And All That, Denis Taylor, Oldham Corporation, 1968.

Rochdale

1829-1837	Charles Johnson
1837	Samuel Milnes
1837-1844	James Butterworth
1857-1863	John Henry Callender
1863-1866	Lieutenant William Charles Sylvester
1867-1869	Captain Roland Davies
1869-1881	Samuel Stephens
1882-1893	Joseph Wilkinson
1893-1898	Charles Buck
1898-1917	Leonard Campbell Barry
1917-1945	Henry Howarth
1946-1958	Major Sydney Joseph Harvey
1958-1964	Frank Stanley Gale
1964-1969	Patrick Ross

In 1969 amalgamated with Lancashire Constabulary and in 1974 became 'P' Division of Greater Manchester Police.

Suggested reading: Story of Rochdale Police, 1252-1957, Stanley Waller, Rochdale Watch Committee, 1957.

St Helens

1887-1905	James Wood
1905-1935	A R Ellerington
1939-1947	A Cust
1947-1964	William G Symmons
1964-1969	A Atherton

Merged with Lancashire Constabulary on 01.04.1969 and with Merseyside Police on 01.04.1974.

Salford

1844-1845	John Diggles
1845-1848	Captain Edwin Sheppard
1848-1852	Stephen Neale
1852-1866	James Taylor
1866-1868	William C Sylvester
1868-1869	Edward Hibbert
1869-1880	Captain R W Torrens
1880-1889	William L Marshall
1889-1898	Commander C T Scott
1898-1908	John W Hallam
1908-1946	Major C V Godfrey OBE

In 1968 Salford amalgamated with Manchester City Police and became 'F' Division of Greater Manchester Police in 1974.

Southport

1887-1896	Samuel Kershaw
1896-1906	William Elliott
1907-1919	Charles L Armitage
1919-1920	Frank Brook
1920-1942	Michael J Egan
1942-1946	Charles Carnegie Martin
1946-1960	Harold Mighall
1961-1964	Joseph Pessell
1964-1969	James G C Longhurst

Southport merged with Lancashire in 1969 and with Merseyside in 1974.

Wallasey

1913-1930	Percy Linnel Barry
1931-1959	John Omerod
1959-1967	Walter Marshall

Merged with Cheshire in 1967 and with Merseyside in 1974.

Wigan

1836-1840	John Whittle
1840-1852	Thomas Latham
1852-1875	William Simm
1875-1879	George Williams
1879-1880	Charles Alison
1880-1883	Robert Kennion
1883-1890	F Tobias Webb
1890-1899	Alexander Bell
1899-1914	George Hardy
1914-1921	John Percival
1921-1946	Thomas Joseph Pey
1946-1957	Paul Foster
1957-1968	David Aitkin
1968-1969	William Henry Taylor (Acting)

Amalgamated with Lancashire 1969 and became 'L' Division of Greater Manchester Police in 1974.

Suggested reading: Wigan Borough Police Force 1836-1969, James Fairhurst, Landy Publishing, 1996.

Carlisle City

1827-1831	Benjamin Batty
1831-1839	Robert Brown
1839-1844	John Graham
1844-1857	John Sabbage
1857-1873	George Edward Bent
1873-1876	Walter Hemingway
1876-1904	George MacKay
1904-1913	George Hill
1913-1928	Eric Herbert de Schmid (later called Spence)
1928-1929	Archibald Kennedy Wilson
1929-1938	Andrew Alexander Johnston
1938-1961	William Henry Lakeman
1961-1967	Frank Edgar Williamson

City and County Forces amalgamated to form Cumbria Constabulary. My thanks to Bob Lowther, late of the Carlisle City Force.

Cumberland/Westmorland/Cumbria

1857-1902	Sir John Dunne
1902-1920	Charles de Courcey Parry
1920-1925	Lt Col H S Turnbull
1926-1954	P T B Brown
1954-1959	J S H Gaskain
1959-1963	H Watson
1963-1967	F E Williamson
1968-1980	William J Cavey OBE
1980-1987	Barry David Keith Price
1988-1991	Leslie Sharp
1991-1997	A G Elliot
1997-2001	Colin Phillips
2001-	Michael Baxter

My thanks to Susan George, Business Support Manager at Cumbria Constabulary.

H M Prison Service

Altcourse

Opened in December 1997. Operational capacity 1010.

Directors

1997-2004	Walter MacGowan
2004-	John McLoughlin

Buckley Hall

Operational capacity 326.

Governor – Susan Morrison

Garth

Opened October 1988. Operational capacity 667.

Governors

1988-1989	T Bone
1989-1991	D Curtis
1991-1992	A J Fitzpatrick
1992-2000	W Rose-Quire OBE
2000-2003	J R Illingsworth
2003-	R McColm

Haverigg

Opened 1967. Operational capacity 564.

Governors

1967-1971	D W Fisher
1971-1981	W E Cowper-Johnson
1981-1985	P Buxton
1985-1987	B McLuckie
1988-1990	D I Lockwood
1990-1997	B A Wilson
1997-2003	G Brunskill
2003-	Miss S McCullagh

Hindley

Opened as a Borstal in 1961. Reclassified as a Young Offender Institution in 1983. Since 1997 it has housed both adult prisoners and young offenders. Operational capacity 539.

	Governors
1961-1962	P C Jones
1962-1966	A C Miller MBE
1966-1972	M H P Coombs
1972-1979	F S Richardson
1979-1983	A J Webley
1983-1986	G Shore
1986-1989	J H M Anderton
1989-1991	A F Jennings
1991-1994	D Roberts
1994-1995	R J Crouch
1995-1997	L Lavender
1997-1999	C P Sheffield
1999-2002	J M Heavens
2002-	Jayne G Blake

Kirkham

Opened 1962. Operational capacity 590.

	Governors
1962-1965	N Clay
1965-1968	R A B A Howden
1968-1969	F Satchwell
1969-1975	N Clay
1975-1982	J K Beaumont
1982-1984	J L Rham
1984-1986	K L Taylor
1986-1988	F V Weigh
1988-1998	R B Coombs
1998-2001	A F Jennings OBE
2001-2004	D Thomas
2004-	S Lawrence

Lancaster Castle

Operational Capacity 232.

	Keepers
1199	Worinus Jointor (alias Janitor)
1208	Henry de Lea
1216	Adam de Jeland
1247	Earl Ferrers
1265	William Boteler
1342	John Travers

From 1585 The Castle served as a gaol, hence it is the oldest prison building in use in England.

1591	Thomas Covell
1639	Symon Arrowsmith

1643 Captain Shuttleworth
1644 Colonel George Dodding
1644 James Hunter
1647 William Ripon

From 1648 the Castle became a full time Gaol, therefore all the following persons were Governors:

1648 William Ripon
1710 E North
1714-15 John Beardsworth (of the Horse and Farrier Inn; Farmer of the Vicarage Lands. He signed his name Birdsworth on 09.02.1716 and was Governor for four years.
1726 Anthony Helme
1747 Dr Henry Bracken, (son-in-law of James Beardsworth and Mayor from 1747-1757)
1758 James Jackson
1764 Edmund Styth
1767 James Styth, son of above. After inheriting a large property he changed his name to Greenhalgh. His descendents lived at Myerscough.
1769 John Dane, who, during a fit of insanity, hanged himself in the Judges' Lodgings.
1770 Mr Cowburn, former keeper of the House of Correction, Preston.
1779 John Higgin, ex-master of a vessel which he built in America. He died 1783 of jail fever aged 48.
1782 John Higgin, son of the above.
1833 Captain James Hansbrow – Adjutant, ex 3rd Lancashire Militia. Born in Dublin in 1790.
1862 Arthur Hansbrow, son of the above. Born in Preston in 1822.
1867 Harrington Welford Parr, son of Canon Owen Parr, Vicar of Preston. He was paid a, salary of £325 per annum, with house, coal and gas free.
1884 William Repulse Shenton, former Chief Warder.

The Castle closed as a prison in 1915 due to the need for manpower in the First World War.

Governors after reopening of the Castle in 1955 were:

1955 Major G F Bride
1959 Capt L R Ogier, who was the last Governor to live at the Castle.
1964 J M Crawford, who resided at the Governor's house on Derwent Road.
1969 A W Driscoll
1971 A Fall
1978 G Walker. The Derwent Road property was sold after Mr Walker left.
1981 C B Scott
1985 B A Wilson
1987 W J Ginn
1990 D G McNaughton
1999 J R Illingsworth
2001 Mrs T Williams – the first female Governor
2003 D Harrison

I am grateful to Jim Capstick, an officer at HMP Lancaster Castle, for researching and producing this delightful list.

Lancaster Farms

Opened in March 1992 as a remand centre and now comprises several Juvenile Units. Operational capacity 532.

	Governors
1992-1997	David Waplington
1997-2001	David Thomas
2001-2003	Robert McColm
2003-	Mrs Terry Williams

Liverpool (Walton)

Opened in 1855 to replace the 'New Gaol' in Great Howard Street. Operational capacity 1476.

	Governors
1855-1865	W Jameson
1867-1876	Captain J Veitch
1877-1885	C Concannon
1885-1890	J M Anderson
1890-1893	J Haverfield
1894-1899	J M Walker
1899-1901	Captain F G Frith
1901-1904	Captain H T Price RN
1904-1907	Captain W M T Synge
1908-1917	J Dillon
1917-1921	J H Hellier
1921-1923	Major H G MacTier
1923-1930	Lt Col C E F Rich DSO
1930-1939	Major A C H Benke DSO, MC
1939-1943	J Holt OBE
1947	Captain F A P Foster RN
1948-1952	A C W Richards
1952-1959	S T E P Ennion
1959-1964	S G Clarke
1964-1967	A D W Sanderson
1967	J H Waylen MBE
1967-1972	Major G F McBride
1972-1976	D T Cross
1976-1981	A W Driscoll
1981-1982	C J Jones
1982-1987	J H Richardson OBE
1987-1991	A N Joseph OBE
1991-1992	R D Dixon
1992-1995	R H Jaques
1995-1997	R S Duncan
1997-1999	W J Abbott
1999-2003	C P Sheffield
2003	J B Smith
2003-	Mrs C James

ARMITAGE, Vernon Kirk
Born 20 October 1842. Youngest son of late Sir Elkaneh Armitage. Kt. of Hope Hall, Eccles. Married 3.2.1870 Emily daughter of late John Fenton MP for Rochdale. Trinity College, Cambridge, BA 1865; MA 1868. AAS. I. 27 January 1863. Call 6 June 1966. Special Pleader. Lancs. Sessions & Salford Hundred Court. No address, 1876-1934. Not in 1935 Law List. Foster.

ARMITSTEAD, Francis Edward
Born 1849. 2nd Son of Robert Armistead of Bolton-le-Moors, Lancs. Exeter College, Oxford, MA. AAS L. 4 November 1871. Call 6 June 1874. ETC. 16 March 1875. Prop. Edwards QC. Sec. Baylis. Equity draftsman & conveyancer. Lancs. Chancery Court. 9 New Square, 1876-1879; 12 Old Square, 1880-1885; 11 Stone Buildings, 1886-1890; 3 Stone Buildings, 1891-1906. No address 1907. Not in 1908 Law List. Foster.

ARMSTRONG, Francis Charles
Born 1826. 5th Son of late Captain Matthew Armstrong. Co. Wexford 9th Regiment. Married 2 March 1871 Julia Augusta Vaughan of Hampton Wick. AAS. M. 12 November 1859. Call 11 June 1862. Special pleader, Liverpool Sessions. 2 Brick Court, 1876. No address, 1877-1933. Not in 1934 Law List. Foster.

ARNAUD, Henry Bruce
Born 1828. Only son of Elias Arnaud of Abercromby Square, Liverpool. Christchurch, Oxford, MA 1855. AAS. I. 11 November 1851. Call 17 November 1854. Liverpool Sessions. Law List gives no address, 1876-1899. However he has signed the Liverpool Prosecutions Book giving 8 Kings Bench Walk as Chambers. Not in 1900 Law List. Foster.

ARNOLD, Sir Alfred MP
Born 18 November 1835. Died 31 October 1908 age 72. 3rd Son of late Rev. Frederick Arnold, Rector of Brimington, Derby. Chesterfield Grammar School, Sidney Sussex College, Cambridge. AAS. I. 6 November 1875. Call 3 July 1878. ETC. 7 February 1881. Prop. Temple QC. Sec. Pope. Liverpool & Manchester Sessions. 4 Hare Court, 1881-1890; 10 Kings Bench Walk, 1891-1893; 1 Stone Building, 1894-1897. No address, 1898-1908. MP (C) Halifax, 1895-1900. JP. for West Riding. Kt. 1903. WW. Foster.

ARNOLD, Frederick Octavius
I. 20 April 1910. ETC. 15 June 1910. Prop. Mellor QC. Sec. Dehn. Acting Junior, 1914-1918. Palatine Bank Buildings, Norfolk Street, Manchester, 1910-1914. No address, 1915-1916. 60 King Street, Manchester, 1917-1920. Not in 1921 Law List.

ARNOLD, Herbert Derek
Born 1913. Only son of Herbert William Arnold of Hale, Cheshire, stockbroker. Trinity College, Cambridge. AAS. M. 5 March 1934. Call 26 January 1937. ETC. 24 February 1937. Prop. Gorman QC. Sec. Jolly. 60 King Street, Manchester, 1937-1940. No address, 1941-1963. Not in 1964 Law List.

ARTHUR, John Rhys DFC (His Honour John Arthur DFC)

(RB)

Born 29 April 1923. Married 1951, Joan Tremearne Pickering qv (died 1995). Mill Hill School, Christ's College, Cambridge, MA. Navigator, RAF, 1943-1946. DFC 1944. I. November 1949. ETC. January 1950. Pupilmaster, James Crossley Vaines. Circuit Junior, 1951. Liverpool Chambers; 3 Cook Street, 1949-1958; The Temple, Dale Street, 1959-1966; 606 The Corn Exchange, Fenwick Street, 1967-1975. Assistant Recorder, Blackburn QS, 1970. Deputy Chairmanm Lancs. County QS, 1970-1971. JP. 1970. Recorder 1972. Circuit Judge, 1975-1993. Retirement Speeches, Liverpool Crown Court (Judge Wickham/ Rodney Klevan QC) Transcript in Circuit Records, WW.

ASHFORD-THOM, Ian
Exeter University, LLB. G. July 1977. Northern Circuit, 1980-1981. South East Circuit, 1982. 1 Temple Gardens.

ASHTON, Arthur Jacob KC

Born 4 February 1855. Died 23 March 1925 aged 80. Manchester Grammar School, Balliol College, Oxford, BA, 1878. AAS. I. 4 November 1876. Call 26 January 1881; Bencher 1914. ETC. 23 January 1882. Prop. Crompton QC. Sec. E Robertson. Circuit Junior 1882. 7 Fig Tree Court, 1882-1889; 3 Temple Gardens, 1890-1894; 2 Paper Buildings, 1895-1905; 2 Mitre Court Buildings, 1906-1925. Silk 1906. Recorder of Manchester, 1914-1925. Judge of Appeal, Isle of Man, 1921-1925. Publication:- "As I Went On My Way" Nisbet & Co, London, 1924. WW. Foster.

ASHWORTH, Fiona Katherine Anne
Born 2 August 1966 Derby. Bolton School (Girls Division). University of Leeds, LLB. L. July 1988. ETC. December 1988. Prop. John Hoggett QC. Sec. Philip Raynor. 40 King Street, Manchester, 1988. Member, Legal Aid Appeals Committee now Legal Services Commission Appeal Board, 1993.

ASHWORTH, Janet Elizabeth
London University LLB. L. November 1976. ETC. 26 October 1978. Rational House, 64 Bridge Street, Manchesterm 1978-1989. No address, 1990-1996. Not in Bar Directory 1997.

ASHWORTH, John Nigel Laurence
London University, LLB. I. July 1973. Directorate of Legal Sevices, Ministry of Defence (RAF) rising to Wing Commander, 1976-1990. Not in 1991-1992 Bar Directory. Senior Crown Prosecutor, Cambridgeshire, 1994. Legal Advisor, External Affairs Division, British Forces, Germany, 1997.

ASHWORTH, John Percy (The Hon. Mr Justice Ashworth)
Born 3 February 1906. Died 26 September 1975 aged 69. Winchester; Christ Church, Oxford. I. 14 May 1930. ETC. 9 July 1930. Prop. Jackson KC. Sec. Rhodes. Circuit Junior, 1930. 3 Hare Court, 1930-1954. Junior Counsel: to the Post Office, 1936; to the Treasury (Common Law), 1950-1954. Chairman Staffs. QS, 1963-1971 (Deputy, 1951-1963). Chancellor of the Diocese: of Rochester, 1943-1954; of London, 1944-1954. High Court Judge (QBD), 1954-1975. Presiding Judge, Midland & Oxford Circuit, 1970-1974. Intelligence Corps, 1940-1945. MBE 1944. Kt. 1954. WW.

ASKEY, Robert John
Born 10 August 1964 Stoke on Trent. Westwood High School, University of Wales, Aberystwyth, LLB; The College of Law. Solicitor, 1988-1995. L. 23 July 1998. ETC. December 1998. Prop. Nigel Gilmour QC. Sec. Ben Morris. Pupilmaster, Nadine Hope. Victoria Chambers later New Bailey Chambers, 19 Castle Street, Liverpool, 1998.

ASPINALL, Sir Algernon Edward KCMG
Born 1871. Died 6 May 1952 aged 81. Eton, Magdalen College, Oxford, BA, 1894. I. 30 June 1897. 2 Hare Court, 1905-1908. No address, 1909-1952. Life in commerce. Cotton, Cocoa & Shipping. CBE 1926. Kt. 1928. KCMG 1939. Publications: Pocket Guide to the West Indies; West Indian Tales of Old; Wayfarer in the West Indies. WW.

ASPINALL, Butler Cole KC
Born 1861. Died 15 November 1935 age 74. Son of Butler Cole Aspinall (Attorney General of Victoria) and nephew of John Bridge Aspinall qv., (Recorder of Liverpool) AAS. M. 12 November 1879. Call 17 November 1884; Bencher 1907; Reader Autumn 1919; Treasurer 1929. ETC. 9 February 1885. Prop. Aspinall QC. Sec. Samuell. 2 Paper Buildings, 1884-1935. Expert in Shipping Law as Arbitrator and Wreck Commissioner. Counsel for the Board of Trade in the Titanic Inquiry and for Cunard in the Lusitania Inquiry. WW.

ASPINALL, GEOFFREY
I. 17 November 1909. 4 New Square, 1910-1914. No address, 1915-1953. Not in 1954 Law List.

ASPINALL, John Bridge QC
Born 12 December 1818. Died 5 February 1886 aged 67. Grandson of John B Aspinall (Mayor of Liverpool, 1813). Brother of Clarke Aspinall (Liverpool Coroner). Brother of Butler Cole Aspinall (Attorney General of

Victoria). Uncle of Butler Cole Aspinall QC qv., Rugby School. AAS. M. 6 January 1838. Call 19 November 1841; Bencher 1864; Reader, Autumn 1868; Treasurer 1877. 1 Paper Buildings, 1846. East Riding Yorkshire, Hull & Liverpool Sessions. Goldsmith Building, 1876-1886. Silk 1864. Recorder of Liverpool, 1862-1886. Attorney General, County Palatine of Durham, 1872. Obituary, Liverpool Courier, 8 February 1886. His portrait hangs in the corridor outside the chambers of the present Recorder of Liverpool. Foster.

ASPINALL, John Bridge
Born 1877. Died 21 June 1932 aged 55. Only son of John Audley Frederick Aspinall of Bolton, Chief Mechanical Engineer of the Lancashire & Yorkshire Railway. Stonyhurst; Christ Church, Oxford. AAS. M. 18 November 1895. Call 6 May 1903. ETC. 17 February 1904. Prop. Pickford KC. Sec. Stewart Brown. Circuit Junior, 1904. 2 Paper Buildings, 1903-1927. City Remembrancer, Guildhall, London, 1927-1932. WW.

ASPLAND, Lindsey Middleton QC

Born 9 April 1843. Died 6 May 1891 aged 48. 2nd son of Rev. Robert Brook Aspland, Dissenting Minister of Hackney, Middlesex. London University, MA, 1863; LLD, 1867. AAS. M. 11 September 1863. Call 27 January 1868. ETC. 12 March 1868. Prop. Aspinall QC. Sec. Russell QC. Special pleader. 4 Lamb Building, 1876-1881. 4 Elm Court, 1882-1891. Silk 1886. Foster.

ASSHETON, Ralph (Baron Clitheroe)
Born 24 February 1901. Died 18 September 1984 aged 83. Only son of Sir Ralph Assheton, 1st Bt. Eton; Christ Church, Oxford, MA. I. 26 January 1925. ETC. 17 February 1926. Prop. Greaves Lord KC. Sec. Fyfe. 1 Paper Buildings, 1925-1934. MP (Nat U) for Rushcliffe, City of London & Blackburn West, 1934-1955. Financial Secretary to the Treasury, 1943-1944. Chairman: Conservative Party Organisation, 1944-1946; Public Accounts Committee, 1948-1950. Chairman/Director of many City Companies. JP., Lancs., 1934. WW.

ASTBURY, John Meir QC., MP. (Rt. Hon. Sir John Meir Astbury)
Born 14 June 1860 Manchester. Died 21 August 1939 aged 79. Manchester Grammar School; Trinity College, Oxford, BA 1882. BCL, 1883; Hon. Fellow, 1923. Vinerian Law Scholar, 1884. Assistant Lecturer, Owens College, Manchester. AAS. M. 24 April 1880. Call 25 June 1884. ETC. 18 July 1884. 60 King Street, Manchester, 1886-1888; 78, King Street, 1889-1895. Silk 1895. 5 New Court, 1895-1913. High Court Judge (Chancery Division), 1913-1929. PC 1929. Kt 1913. MP (L) Southport, 1906-1910. WW. DNB. Foster. Simpson's Biographical Dictionary of the Common Law.

ASTBURY, Philip Ian
Born 13 September 1967 Liverpool. Quarry Bank Comprehensive School; Liverpool John Moores University, LLB. G. October 1999. ETC. December 2000. Prop. David Harris QC. Sec. John Gibson. 7th floor, India Buildings, Water Street, Liverpool, 1.11.2000. Criminal Cases Review Commission, 1999-2000.

ASTLEY, Brian Martin
Born 16 May 1954. Doncaster Grammar School; Peterhouse, Cambridge, BA. AAS. M. 8 December 1975. Call November 1977. In Northern Circuit Bar List in Law Lists, 1978-1979 but no address. Not in 1980 Law List.

ASTLEY, Peter Campbell
Born 1920. Only son of James Campbell Astley of Heaton Moor, Stockport, wine merchant. AAS. 8 July 1946. Call 26 January 1949. Manchester Chambers: 1 b Cooper Street, 1949-1953; 24 Brazennose Street, 1954-1956; 2 Booth Street, 1957-1960, No chambers address, 1961-1963. Not in 1964 Law List.

ASTON, James Jones QC
Born 12 December 1822. Died 17 January 1885 aged 62. 2nd Son of Benjamin Richard Aston of Pentonville, coal merchant. AAS. M. 31 May 1843. Call 6 November 1846. 5 Pump Court, 1846. 4 Middle Temple Lane, 1876-1885. QC in the County Palatine of Lancaster, 1867 and Assessor to the Sheriff of Lancashire. Silk 1880. Publication: "Chancery Practice of the County Palatine of Lancaster".

ASTON, Theodore QC
Born 1827. Died 24 October 1910 aged 83. Eldest son of Thomas Aston of Handsworth, Stafford. St Johns College, Cambridge, MA, 1850. AAS. L. 14 November 1850. Call 17 November 1853. Silk 1872. Bencher, 8 May 1872. 4 Elm Court, 1876-1878; 11 New Square, 1879-1895. No address, 1896-1910. WW. Foster.

ATHERTON, Peter
Born 8 November 1952 Wigan. Mount St Mary's College, Birmingham; Birmingham University, LLB. G. July 1975. ETC. 1975. Prop. Andrew Rankin QC. Sec. John Stannard. Circuit Junior, 1978. 1st floor, Oriel Chambers, Water Street, Liverpool, 1975-1985; Deans Court Chambers: at (1) Crown Square, Manchester, 1985-1999 and (2) 24 St John Street, Manchester, 1999. Assistant Recorder 1995. Recorder 1999. Member of the American Bar Association. Accredited Mediator (trained at Harvard University). Circuit Executive Committee, 1981-1984. Chairman, Young Barristers Committee of Bar Council, 1982-1983.

ATHERTON, Robert Kenneth (His Honour Judge Atherton)
Born 22 June 1947 Warrington. Boteler Grammar School; Liverpool University, LLB. G. July 1970. Liverpool Chambers: 27 Dale Street, 1970-1976; Melbourne Building, 21 North John Street, 1977-1988; 3rd Floor, Peel House, Harrington Street, 1989-1997; 7th floor, India Buildings, Water Street, 1998-2000. Legal Member, Mental Health Review Tribunal, 1989-2000. Assistant Parliamentary Boundary Commissioner, 1992-2000. Assistant Recorder, 1994-1999. Recorder, 1999-2000. Circuit Judge, June 2000. WW.

ATKIN, Peter Wilson OBE
Born 4 February 1859 Rock Ferry. Died 27 February 1931 aged 72. 2nd Son of George Atkin of Egerton Park, Rock Ferry. Royal Institution School, Liverpool; Mill Hill School; Jesus College, Cambridge, MA., LLM. Rowed for Cambridge. AAS. 12 November 1879. Call I. 17 November 1883. ETC. 6 February 1884. Prop. Crompton QC. Sec. Samuell. Circuit Junior, 1884. 6 Pump Court, 1886-1888. Liverpool Chambers: 15 Lord Street, 1889-1890; 25 Lord Street, 1891-1913. Contested Everton, 1892. Deputy Recorder of Liverpool. Chairman Manchester Munitions Court, 1915-1916. Arbitrator, Manchester Ship Canal Dock Strike, 1916. Chairman, Salford Tribunal. Stipendiary Magistrate at Salford 1913-1931. WW. Foster.

ATKINSON, Cyril KC., MP (The Hon. Mr Justice Atkinson)
Born 9 May 1874. Died 29 January 1967 aged 92. (Father of Lord Justice Fenton Atkinson qv) L. 30 June 1897; Bencher, 1920; Treasurer, 1942. London University, LLD. ETC. 27 July 1897. Prop. Leese QC. Sec. Sutton. Manchester Chambers: 78 King Street, 1897-1901; 5 St James's Street, 1902-1913. Silk 1913. 12 Kings Bench Walk, 1913-1933. MP (C) Altrincham, 1924-1933. High Court Judge (QBD), 15.5.1933-1948. Kt. 1913. Member of Church Assembly, 1950-1955. Lay Reader, Dioceses of St Edmundsbury, Ipswich & Southwark. Past President, Churches' Fellowship for Psychic Study. WW.

ATKINSON, Fenton QC (Rt. Hon Sir Fenton Atkinson)
Born 6 January 1906. Died 28 March 1980 aged 74. Son of Mr Justice Cyril Atkinson qv. Winchester; New College, Oxford, MA. L. 2 May 1928. ETC. 4 July 1928. Proposed by his father. Sec. Laski. Manchester Chambers: 3 St James's Square, 1928-1940; 4 Chapel Walks, 1945-1953. Served in India, 1940-1944. Pres. Military Government Court Germany 1945 as a Colonel. Silk, 1953. 2 Pump Court, 1953-1956; 1 Hare Court, 1954-1960. Judge of Salford Hundred Court of Record, 1953-1960. High Court Judge (QBD) 1960-1968. Tried Brady & Hindley (Moors Murder Case) at Chester Castle April-May 1966. Lord Justice of Appeal, 1968-1971. WW.

ATTKINS, Edgar
Born 1856. Younger son of the late Ambrose Attkins of Broughton, Manchester, wire merchant. AAS. M. 2 August 1894. Call 19 November 1894. ETC July 1895. Prop. Ambrose QC. Sec. Sutton. Formerly a solicitor. Equity draftsman & conveyancer. Manchester Chambers: Aldine Chambers, 57 Princess Street, 1894-1909; 42 Spring Gardens, 1910-1930; 69 Burton Rd, Manchester, 1931-1948. Not in 1949 Law List

AUBREY, David Stuart QC
Born 26 February 1962 Barnet, Herts. Married to Gail Owen qv. Queen Elizabeth Boys' Grammar School, Barnet; Liverpool University, LLB. G. July 1974. ETC. 1975. Prop. Michael Maguire QC. Sec. Manus Nunan. Liverpool Chambers: 1st floor, Oriel Chambers, Water Street, 1975-1981; 3rd floor, 27 Dale Street, 1982-1989; Corn Exchange, Fenwick Street, 1989-1999; 7 Harrington Street (merger of Corn Exchange with Martins Bank), 6.9.1999. Assistant Recorder 1991. Recorder 1995. Silk 1998.

AUSTIN, Alfred
Born 30 May 1835 Headingley. Second son of Joseph Austin, wool stapler and JP. Died 2 June 1913 aged 78. Stonyhurst College; Oscott College (graduating at London University, BA.) AAS. I. 23 January 1854. Call 17 November 1857. No address in Law Lists. He abandoned law for literature very soon after call and seems to have made the right choice. After a prolific output of poetry and prose he was appointed Poet Laureate in 1896 and remained in post until his death. Publications: Autobiography, 2 vols, 1911. WW. DNB.

B

BACKHOUSE, Kenneth
G. June 1945. Manchester Chambers: 78 King Street, 1945-1958. 196 Deansgate, 1959-1964. Not in 1965 Law List.

BACKHOUSE, Marguerite Elizabeth
BL. I. November 1947. 60 King Street, 1953-1956. No address, 1957-1963. Not in 1964 Law List.

BACKHOUSE, Thomas Mercer (His Honour Judge Backhouse)
Born 2 October 1903. Died 16 September 1955 aged 51. Denstone; Selwyn College, Cambridge, BA 1925. G. 16 June 1926. ETC. 13 July 1926. Prop. Atkinson KC. Sec. Rhodes. Manchester Chambers: 60 King Street, 1926-1939. 43 King Street, 1945-1953. Judge Advocate General's Branch, 1939-1945. TD 1943. OBE 1945. Colonel and officer in charge, War Crimes Section, BAOR, Chief Prosecutor, Belsen Trial. County Court Judge, Circuit 18 (Notts. & Yorks.) 1953-1955. WW.

BACON, Sir Roger (Sewell) MBE
Born 23 January 1895. Died 17 February 1962 aged 67. Rugby; Balliol College, Oxford. AAS. M. 23 March 1922. Call 13 June 1923. ETC. 28 January 1925. Prop. Greaves-Lord KC. Sec. Hughes. 10 Kings Bench Walk, 1925-1933. 3 Paper Buildings, 1934-1939. Deputy Judge Advocate, 1940-1943. Legal Advisor later Chief Legal Advisor to various Military Bodies, 1944-1946. MBE 1943. Chief Justice Gibraltar, 1946-1955. Justice of Appeal, East Africa, 1955-1957. Kt. 1958. Publications: Commercial Arbitration, 1925. WW.

BACON, Stephen Francis Theodore AKC
Born 3 September 1945 Oldham. The Perse School, Cambridge. London University, LLB. G. & ETC. July 1969. Pupilmaster, John Coffey. 36 St Ann Street, Manchester, 1969-1980. Express Newspapers: Deputy Legal Manager/Legal Advisor, 1980.

BADEN-POWELL, (Henry) Warington (Smyth) QC
Born 3 February 1847 son of Rev. Baden Powell FRS., sometime Vicar of Plumstead and Savilian Professor of Geometry at Oxford. Died 24 April 1921 aged 74. Seafarer, 1860-1873. AAS I. 26 April 1872. Call 28 June 1876. ETC. 12 February 1880. Prop. Myburgh. Sec. Raikes. 3 Paper Buildings, 1880-1914. Silk 1897. Admiralty & Wreck Courts. By Royal Licence in 1902 he assumed his fathers first name as an additional surname. WW. Foster.

BADLEY, Pamela Hilary (Her Honour Judge Badley)
Married to His Honour Judge Henschell qv. Warwick University, LLB. Leicester University, LLM. L. November 1974. Same Liverpool Chambers: Queen Avenue, Castle Street, 1974-1983. 2nd Floor Peel House, Harington Street, 1983-1994. 25-27 Castle Street, 1995-2001. Recorder 1996. Circuit Judge, 2001.

BAERLEIN, Arthur Adolphe
Born February 1887 son of Max Baerlein of the Grange, Withington, Manchester, engineer. AAS. M. 6 June 1910. Call 16 April 1913. 1 Paper Buildings, 1914-1925. 5 Pump Court, 1926-1927. No address, 1928-1938. PO Box 21, Jinja, Uganda, 1939-1940. Not in 1941 Law List.

BAGLEY, Michael Wallace Welsby
Born 17 October 1958 Thurso, Caithness. Thurso High School, 1970-1974. Manchester Grammar School, 1974-1976. Bristol University BSc(Civil Engineering) G. November 1984. ETC. 16 December 1986. Prop. William Waldron QC. Sec. Tony Carus. Liverpool Chambers: Fruit Exchange, Victoria Street. 1986-1991; Chavasse Court, 24 Lord Street 1992. Civil Engineer, 1980-1982. Founder member of "Prestons" qv.

BAGLEY, Philip William
MA.,ACII. L. November 1955. ETC. 1957. Pupilmaster, James FitzHugh. Manchester Chambers : 4 Clarence Street, 1957-1958. Left Circuit to join an Insurance Company. Rejoined Circuit in 1965. Law Lecturer, Manchester College of Commerce, 1966-1967. Northern Assurance Building, Albert Square, 1968-1969; Post Office Chambers, 26 Brown Street, 1971-1972; 21 Spring Gardens, 1973-1975; 4th Floor, Sunlight House, Quay Street, 1976-1985; 121 Princess Street, 1986. Non practising 3 Peter Street. Not in 1989 Law List.

BAGNALL-WILD, Ralph Bagnall
Born 23 March 1845. 2nd son of William Kirby of Waterloo, Liverpool. Died 11 October 1925 aged 80. Assumed the surnames of Bagnall-Wild by Royal Licence in 1868 when he succeeded to the estates of Samuel Bagnall-Wild. Ruabon School; Gonville & Caius College, Cambridge. Rowed in college boat; BA 1868; MA 1871. AAS. I. 10 November 1866. Call 17 November 1870. ETC. 9 March 1871. Prop. Holker QC. Sec. Hosack. Goldsmith Building, 1870-1882. Liverpool & Kirkdale Sessions. According to the Liverpool Prosecutions Book, he left the Bar in June 1882. WW.

BAILEY, Desmond Patrick (His Honour Desmond Bailey)
Born 6 May 1907. Died 29 January 1996 aged 88. Brighton College; Queens College, Cambridge, BA., LLB. I. 17 June 1931. ETC. 2 July 1931. Prop. Lynskey KC. Sec. Ormerod. Circuit Junior, 1932. Manchester Chambers : 6 St Ann's Passage, 1931-1935; 43 King Street, 1936-1939. War of 1939-1945; Rifle Brigade, Lancashire Fusiliers; Special Operations Executive, North Africa, Italy. Major. 26 King Street, 1945-1965. Recorder of Carlisle, 1963-1965. County Court/Circuit Judge, 1965-1979.

BAILEY, Eric Alfred George Shackleton
I. 19 November 1928. No address, 1929-1935. 26 King Street, 1936; 6 St Ann's Passage 1937-1940. No address, 1941-1954. Not in 1955 Law List.

BAILEY, Graham Robert
Born 11 March 1968. Walkden High School, Brunei University, LLB. I. February 1993. ETC. 1993. Prop. Roger Farley QC. Sec. John Wishart. Manchester Chambers : Manchester House, 18-22 Bridge Street, 1993-1999; 8 King Street, 1999-.

BAILEY, John Charles Williams
Born 11 March 1932 Staffordshire. Wolstanton School, Exeter College, Oxford, MA. G. November 1966. ETC. 1967. Prop. J M Davies QC. Sec. H Day. Manchester Chambers: 43 King Street, 1966-1988; Queens Chambers, 5 John Dalton Street, 1989. Assistant Recorder, 1977-1886.

BAILEY, Patricia Lucy
Born 24 September 1940 Cleveleys. Arnold High School; Sheffield University, LLB. Manchester University, Postgraduate Diploma in Advanced Studies (Economics). Manchester Metropolitan University, Postgraduate Diplomas in Family Law and Personal Injury. AAS. M. 6 February 1962. Call 25 November 1969. ETC. 1969. Manchester Chambers: Post Office Chambers, 26 Brown Street, 1969-1971; 67 Princess Street, 1972-1987; Hollins Chambers, 63 Bridge Street, 1988-1992; New Bailey Chambers, Preston 1992. Industrial Tribunal Member, 1974-1992.

BAISDEN, Howard Ralph
Born 24 January 1948 Caterham, Surrey. Queen Elizabeth's Grammar School, Barnet, Herts; Hull & London Universities, LLM. Law Lecturer, Trent Polytechnic, Nottingham. AAS. M. 20 January 1971. Call 20 July 1972. Manchester Chambers; 67, Princess Street, 1972-1987; Hollins Chambers, 1988-1997. Cobden House Chambers, 19 Quay Street, 1998.

BAKER, Clive Adrian
Born 7 January 1972 Bristol. Rushmoor School, Bedford; Wrenn School, Wellingborough; Birmingham University, LLB (Law with Politics) G. October 1995. ETC. 19 December 1995. Prop. David Steer QC. Sec. Richard Pratt (for Kevin Grice, pupilmaster) Liverpool Chambers; Corn Exchange, Fenwick Street, 1995-1999; 7 Harrington Street (merger of Corn Exchange with Martins Bank), 6.9.1999. Research Assistant to Shadow Local Government Minister, David Blunkett, 1990-1991.

BAKER, Stephen George
University of York, BA. M. February 1994. 40 King Street, Manchester, 1994-1999. Harris, Fowler, Solicitors, Taunton Somerset, 2000.

BAKER, Stephen Randle
Born 1915. Only son of Stephen Baker of St Annes-on-the-Sea, Secretary. Maternal uncle of Mr Justice Henriques. qv. King Edward VII School, Lytham; Queens College, Cambridge, BA. AAS. M. 6 October 1933. Call 9 June 1937. ETC. 14 July 1937. Prop. Gorman KC. Sec. Jolly. Circuit Junior, 1943. Manchester Chambers. 2 Booth Street, Manchester, 1940-1975. 13, Police Street, 1976-1978. 64 Bridge Street, 1979-1984. Not in 1985 Law List.

BAKER, Stuart William (His Honour Judge Baker)
Born 1 June 1952. University of Newcastle upon Tyne, LLB, 1973. I. 1974. ETC 17 June 1975. Prop. Gerald Crowe QC. Sec. Vincent Saunders. Pupilmasters, John Leslie, 1 Garden Court & Vincent Saunders. Martins Bank Building, Water Street, Liverpool, 1975-1998. Assistant Recorder 1991. Member, Legal Aid Area Appeals Committee, 1991-1998. Recorder 1994. Legal Member, Mental Health Review Tribunal, 1996-1998. Circuit Judge, 5.2.1998.

BAKER, William Arthur
Born 12 November 1967 Manchester. City of London Freemens School. Lancaster University LLB. M. 15 October 1991. ETC 1991. Prop Michael Shorrock. Sec Richard Marks. Peel Court Chambers 45 Hardman Street, Manchester 1991.

BALDWIN, Edward Thomas
Born 31 May 1846. 2nd Son of Rev. John Baldwin late of Dalton-in-Furness. Trinity College, Oxford, MA. AAS I. 5 June 1867. Call 30 April 1870. ETC. 3 March 1871. Prop. Quain QC. Sec. Mellor. Special pleader & conveyancer. 5 Essex Court, 1870-1877. 13 Kings Bench Walk, 1878-1939. Not in 1940 Law List. Publication: Concise Law of Bankruptcy. Foster.

BALDWIN, John Grant
Born 5 March 1968 Southport. Merchant Taylors School, Crosby. King George VI 6th Form College, Southport. St John's College, Cambridge, MA. G. October 1990. ETC. 1990. Prop. Eric Somerset Jones QC. Sec. B S Joynes. Pupilmaster, William Rankin. Oriel Chambers, 5 Covent Garden / 14 Water Street, Liverpool, 1990. Member: Hoghton Players Gilbert & Sullivan Society; Southport Dramatic Club; Southport Bach Choir.

BALDWIN, Roger Miles
Born 11 March 1946 Blackburn. St Mary's College, Blackburn. Kings College University of London, LLB. G. July 1969. ETC. 1970. Pupilmaster, Robert Hardy. Manchester Chambers; 3 St James's Square, 1970-1986. St James's Chambers, 68 Quay Street, 1986-1993. 15 Winckley Square, Preston, 1993.

BALL, Steven James
Born 7 February 1974 Chester. Whitby High School, Cheshire. University of Hull, LLB. I. October 1996. ETC. 1999. Prop. Peter Birkett QC. Sec. Pepper. Pupilmaster, Timothy Bubb. Circuit Junior 2000. 39 Park Square, Leeds, 1996-1998. Earl Street Chambers, Maidstone, 1998-1999. Chavasse Court, 24 Lord Street, Liverpool, 1999.

BALLOCH, Robert Hugh
I. 28 January 1889. ETC. 20 March 1890. Prop. Barnes QC. Sec. A Russell. 4 Paper Buildings, 1891-1892; 8 Fig Tree Court, 1893-1919. 12 Kings Bench Walk, 1920-1935. Not in 1936 Law List.

BALMER, Arnold Whatley
G. 16 June 1926. ETC. 5 July 1933. Prop. Lynskey KC. Sec. Broadbent. No address, 1926-1930. Bank of England Chambers, Tib Lane, Manchester, 1934-1940. No address, 1941-1953. Not in 1954 Law List.

BALMER, Joseph Eduard
I. 18 November 1907. No address to 1920. 60 King Street, Manchester, 1921-1929. Not in 1930 Law List.

BAMBER, John
Born 10 August 1915.Died 27 April 1976 aged 60. Manchester Grammar School. Wadham College, Oxford. G. 17 November 1938. ETC. 1 Mar 1939. Prop. Gorman KC. Sec. Rhodes. 43 King Street, Manchester, 1938-1939 & 1946-1965. Manchester Regiment in England and South East Asia, 1940-1946. Stipendiary Magistrate, City of Manchester/ Greater Manchester, 1965-1976. WW.

BANCROFT, (Anna) Louise
Born 15 March 1961 Blackburn. Married to S H M Denney qv. Casterton School, Kirkby Lonsdale, 1971-1979; St Anne's College, Oxford, MA (Modern History), 1980-1983. University of Westminste,. Diploma in Law, 1983-1984. I. July 1985. ETC. Dec 1985. Prop. Keith Goddard QC. Sec. A J Hammond. Manchester Chambers: Deans Court, Crown Square, 1985-1999; Deans Court, 24 St John Street, 1999. Qualified Family Mediator, 1999. Recorder 2002.

BANKS, (Francis) Andrew
Born 15 November 1955. Uncle of Rachael Banks qv. Preston Catholic College; Wolverhampton Polytechnic, BA. G. July 1995. ETC. 19 December 1995. Prop. Benet Hytner QC. Sec. Adrian Lyon. 14 Castle Street, Liverpool 1995. (now Atlantic Chambers). Formerly admitted as a solicitor in 1984 (with Peter Rickson & Partners of Preston).

BANKS, Rachael (Eda)
Born 20 September 1969. Married to David Watson (14 Castle Street) qv & niece of F. Andrew Banks qv. Bolton School; Perse School for Girls, Cambridge; Manchester University, LLB. I. October 1993. ETC. 18 December 1997. Prop. Andrew Edis QC. Sec. Adrian Lyon. London pupillage at 3 Temple Gardens & Phoenix Chambers, 47a Bedford Row; 14 Castle Street, Liverpool, 1997. (since 2003, Atlantic Chambers, 4/6 Cook Street, Liverpool)

BANKS, Reginald Mitchell KC, MP (His Honour Judge Sir Reginald Banks KC)
Born 1880. Son of Sir William Banks MD.,LLD.,FRCS. of Liverpool. Died 9 July 1940 aged 60. Rugby; Christ Church, Oxford, BA. I. 5 July 1905. ETC. 16 February 1906. Prop. Tobin KC. Sec, F E Smith. 4 Elm Court, 1905-1914. East Surrey Regiment 1914. 5th Gurkha Rifles. Served in India & Mesopotania. 1 Temple Gardens, 1919-1933; 3 Temple Gardens, 1933-1934. Silk 1923. Kt. 1928. MP (C) Swindon, 1922-1929 & 1931-1934. Recorder of Wigan, 1928-1934. Bencher 1930. County Court Judge, 1934-1940 (Circuit 16 –Yorks.) Publication; The Conservative Outlook, 1929. WW.

BANKS, Thomas Mercer
L. 24 June 1936. ETC. 1 July 1936. Prop. Gorman KC. Sec. Jalland. 25 Castle Street, Liverpool, 1936-1939; 13 Harrington Street, Liverpool 1940-1949. No address, 1950-1963. Not in 1964 Law List.

BANNON, Tammi Elizabeth
University of Sheffield, LLB. L. November 1994. ETC. 20 December 1994. Prop. David Steer QC. Sec. Grant Lazarus. Corn Exchange, Fenwick Street, Liverpool, 1997-1999. Not in 2000 Bar Directory.

BARBER, (Dorothy) Muriel. (Mrs Bush)
LLB. I. February 1965. 25 Bow Lane, Manchester, 1960. Joined Midland & Oxford Circuit. Nottingham Chambers at Wheelergate-12 High Pavement & 17 College Street, 1961-1984. Not in 1985 Bar Directory.

BARBOUR, George
Born 1841. Only son of Robert Barbour of Bolesworth Castle, Chester. Died 3 November 1919 aged 78. Harrow; Trinity College, Cambridge, MA 1871. AAS. I. 30 October 1862. Call 17 November 1865. No chambers address. Said to be attending Manchester & Salford Sessions, 1876-1919. JP., DL. High Sheriff, Cheshire, 1890. Hon Major, Earl of Chester's Yeomanry Cavalry. WW. Foster.

BARKER, Algernon Prest Bird
I. 8 May 1895. ETC. 29 July 1895. Prop. Shee QC. Sec. Steel. Stevenson's Chambers, 25 Lord Street, Liverpool, 1896-1897. Left Circuit to practice in Newcastle upon Tyne. Various Newcastle addresses. Practising at Durham Palatine Court, 1898-1906. No address, 1907-1949. Not in 1950 Law List.

BARKER, Henry Sandys
L. 5 July 1905. Equity draftsman & conveyancer. Manchester Chambers; 35, Brown Street, 1911-1914; 37, Brown Street, 1915-1918; 78 King Street, 1919-1948. No address, 1949-1953. Not in 1954 Law List.

BARKER, (John) Stephen (Roy)
Died 16 October 2000 aged 43. Tributes, Manchester Crown Court on 24 October 2000 by HH Judge Sir Rhys Davies QC & Keith Goddard QC. Transcript in Circuit Records. Obituary "In Brief", January 2001. MA (English Literature), Cambridge University. MA (American Literature), Cornell University. Met his wife Kathy at Cornell. L. July 1983. ETC. 1983. Pupilmaster, J C W Bailey. Civil Practitioner. 43 King Street, Manchester, 1983-1988; Queen's Chambers, 5 John Dalton Street, Manchester, 1989-2000.

BARLING, Gerald Edward QC
Born 18 September 1949 Preston. St Mary's College, Blackburn; New College, Oxford, MA. AAS. M. 19 January 1971. Call 22 November 1972. ETC. 1973. 601, Royal Exchange, Manchester, 1973-1981; Brick Court Chambers, London, 1981. EC Law practice in London & Brussels. Assistant Recorder 1990. Silk 1991. Recorder 1993.

BARLOW, Mark David
Born 23 January 1962 Kenya. University of Central Lancashire, LLB. M. October 1992. Manchester Chambers: 211, Deansgate, 1994-1996; 1 Booth Street, 1997-1998; Waldorf House, 5 Cooper Street, 1999.

BARLOW, Richard Leonard
Born 14 March 1948 Lancaster. Kendal Grammar School; Moseley Hall Grammar School; London School of Economics, LLB. AAS. M. 29 October 1968. Call 16 July 1970. Post Office Chambers, 26 Brown Street, Manchester, 1970-1973. Legal Assistant rising to Assistant Solicitor with Customs & Excise, 1974-1988. Thereafter practice in Leeds and at 11 Kings Bench Walk. Part time Chairman, Social Security & Disability Appeals Tribunals since 1998.

BARLOW, William Wycliffe
Born 18 March 1854. Eldest son of William Barlow of Wilmslow. Married 23 April 1884, Emily, 2nd daughter James Jardine JP., of Alderley Edge. St John's College, Cambridge, MA. AAS. L. 24 July 1875. Call 6 June 1883. ETC. 24 July 1883. Prop. Ambrose QC. Sec. Gouldthorp. No address, 1883-1913. Not in 1914 Law List. Foster.

BARNE, Henry Hume

I. 18 November 1907. ETC. 6 March 1908. Prop. Tobin KC. Sec. Maxwell. Circuit Junior, 1909. 25 Lord Street, Liverpool, 1908-1924; 6 Crown Office Row, 1925-1930; 4 Paper Buildings, 1930-1935. No address, 1936-1953. Not in 1954 Law List.

BARNES, Ashley James

Born 27 July 1968 Leigh. Wirral Grammar School for Boys; Huddersfield Polytechnic, LLB. I. October 1990. ETC. 25 March 1993. Prop. Nigel Gilmour QC. Sec. John Leech. Pupilmaster, Roger Booth. Liverpool Chambers: 2nd Floor, 24, Fenwick Street, 1993-2000; 2nd Floor, 14 Cook Street, 2000. New Bailey Chambers, Liverpool, 2004.

BARNES, Christopher Paul

Born 13 March 1973. Son of Timothy Paul Barnes QC of 7 Bedford Row. Winchester College; University of Nottingham, BA. G. 28 July 2000. ETC. November 2001. Prop. David Harris QC. Sec. Graham Wood. 7th floor, India Buildings, Water Street, Liverpool, 2001. Solicitor, 1997-2000.

BARNES, Sir Frederic Gorell MP

Born 1857. Son of Charles Barnes JP. of Mossley Hill, Liverpool. Died 17 March 1939 aged 82. Royal Institution, Liverpool; Jesus College, Cambridge, MA. AAS. I. 8 May 1882. Call 26 January 1885. ETC. 31 July 1885. Prop. Kennedy QC. Sec. J Gorell Barnes. Circuit Junior, 1886. 1 Garden Court, 1885-1887; 3 Dr Johnson's Building, 1888-1893. No chambers address, 1894-1939. MP (C) Faversham, 1895-1900. Member of numerous Government Bodies and Trade Organisations. JP., DL. Kt. 1916. WW. Foster.

BARNES, Hon Henry Gorell DSO (Second Baron Gorell)

Born 21 January 1882. Eldest son of John Gorell Barnes qv. Died 16 January 1917 aged 34. Winchester; Trinity College, Oxford, MA. Harvard Law School. Call 27 June 1906. ETC. 19 February 1907. Prop. Pickford KC. Sec. Maurice Hill. Circuit Junior, 1907. 2 Pump Court, 1907-1910; 2 Kings Bench Walk, 1911-1915. Private Secretary to his father. Secretary to the Royal Commission on Divorce & Matrimonial Causes, 1909-1912. Member of TA. See "Life of First Lord Gorell" by J E E Montmorency. John Murray, 1920. He was a Major in ALIAS regiment when killed in action at Ypres on 16 January 1917. According to "Officers Who Died" he had originally served in Royal Horse Artillery and later with 19th (London) Battery, 47th Division of RHA. Robert O'Hara tells me that he and other WW1 advisors to the Public Records Office believe ALIAS to be Airborne Liason Artillery Spotter. Buried. Lijssenthoek Cemetery, Poperinge, West-Vlaanderen, Belgium. WW.

BARNES, John Gorell QC (First Baron Gorell)

Born 16 May 1848, Walton on the Hill, Liverpool. Son of Henry Barnes, Liverpool shipowner. Died 22 April 1913 aged 64. Peterhouse, Cambridge, MA, 1871; Hon LLD, 1898; Hon Fellow, 1899. After two years articles with a firm of Liverpool Solicitors, he switched to the Bar. AAS. I. 19 April 1873. Call 26 January 1876; Bencher, 1896. ETC. 27 March 1876. Prop. Judah Benjamin QC. Sec. Myburgh. Special pleader & Admiralty Court. 2 Dr Johnson's Building, 1876-1879; Lamb Building, 1880-1888; 2 Paper Buildings, 1889-1892. Silk 1888. High Court Judge (PDA), 30 May 1892. President, PDA Division, 1905-1909. PC 1905. Peerage 1909. The following account is taken from De Montmorency's "Life of Lord Gorell": "On Circuit I had some little work. I never attempted the criminal work except for a few "soup" prosecutions, and I only went to the Liverpool Sessions (once I got as far as Kirkdale) I had a certain amount of mercantile work, and, of course I got to know nearly everyone who went to the Liverpool Assizes. The Leaders about this time were Charles Russell, the most famous advocate of my day, who was leading the Circuit, and Farrer Herschell. These two became respectively Attorney General and Solicitor General when Gladstone came in. Later the former was a Law Lord for a short time and Chief Justice, and the latter Lord Chancellor. Jack Holker, who became a Lord Justice, Sam Pope, the great railway counsel, J B Aspinall, Recorder of Liverpool, and others, and later we had Gully, Bigham, Myburgh, Kennedy, before I came out of touch with the circuit. I suppose no practical legal school ever equalled that when Russell and Herschell were opposed to each other. I was once with one or other of them in two or three cases. At the Assizes, I think in 1879, where eleven special jury cases were tried in the day. This was done by each discarding all superfluity and merely reducing the case to its real point, which was generally capable of statement very shortly. It was a school for anyone to be proud to learn in, and the (Great) Northern Circuit never shone more brilliantly than when I first saw it from behind such advocates as I have spoken of." WW. DNB. Foster. Simpson.

BARR, Finola Katherine Franklin

Born 2 May 1968. Loreto Grammar School; University of Nottingham, LLB. G. November 1994. ETC. 16 December 1994. Prop. Rodney Klevan QC. Sec. Paul Chambers. Manchester Chambers: 38 King Street West, 1994-1995; 24a St John Street, 1997-2000. No address 2001.

BARRACLOUGH, Anthony Roger
Born 19 October 1947 Bradford. St Bede's Grammar School, Bradford; Durham University, 1967-1970, BA., BL (St Cuthbert Society). I. November 1978. ETC. February 1980. Prop. Justin Price QC. Sec. Locke. Call to Irish Bar, Trinity 1991. Member of Kings Inns. Pupilmaster, Paul Kennedy (Temple). 11 Kings Bench Walk, 1970-1971. Marshal to McKenna J on Midland Circuit, 1971. Same Liverpool Chambers: 16 Queen Avenue, 1980-1984; Peel House, 1984-1994; 25-27 Castle Street, 1994.

BARRANS, Basil Victor
G. November 1947. Manchester Chambers: lb Cooper Street, 1949-1952; Halifax House, 134 Deansgate, 1953-1955. Not in 1956 Law List.

BARRETT, Rev. Hugh Scott CB., CBE.
Born 3 March 1887. Died 30 July 1958 aged 71. Youngest son of Sir William Scott Barrett. Aldenham School; St John's College, Cambridge. I. 28 June 1911. ETC. 7 February 1912. Prop. Sanderson KC. Sec. Miller. Circuit Junior, 1913. 25 Lord Street, Liverpool, 1912-1915. Served in First World War, 1915-1918. OBE. Office of Judge Advocate General, 1919-1949 serving in Germany, Palestine & France. Deputy Judge Advocate General retiring as a Brigadier in 1949. Chairman, Pensions Appeal Tribunal, 1949-1950. Ordained as a Priest, 1952. CBE 1937. CB 1946. WW.

BARRATT, John Michael Paul Gowran
Born 18 April 1959 Chadderton. Our Lady's Roman Catholic School, Royton; Manchester Polytechnic, BA. G. May 1982. ETC. 1983. Prop. Christopher Rose QC. Sec. Andrew Gilbart. Manchester Chambers: 460 Royal Exchange, 1983-1987. 40 King Street, 1999. Assistant Editor, Sweet & Maxwell's Encyclopaedia of Environmental Health. Recorder 2003.

BARRETT-LENNARD, Sir Fiennes Cecil Arthur
Died 26 January 1963. University of Bonn. Severely wounded in the Boer War. L. 5 July 1905. Chambers addresses; 5 New Square; 19 Old Square; 2 Mitre Court Buildings; 4 Harcourt Buildings & 3 Kings Bench Walk. Puisne Judge; Gold Coast (Ghana) & Uganda, 1914-15; Straits Settlements, 1920-1926. Chief Justice of Jamaica, 1926-1932. Kt. 1926. WW.

BARRIE, Michael Lyn
L. November 1973. 3 St James's Square, Manchester, 1975-1983. Not in 1984 Bar Directory.

BARRON-EAVES, Emma Lorraine
Born 23 July 1967, Stourport-on-Severn, Worcs. St Benedict's Roman Catholic School, Colchester; University of Central Lancashire, LLB. Solicitor, 1993-1998. L. 23 July 1998. ETC. 28 July 1998. Prop. David Harris QC. Sec. Ross Duggan. 7th Floor, India Buildings, Water Street, Liverpool March, 1998, now at 15 Winckley Square, Preston.

BARRY, Kirsten Lesley
Born 17 August 1971, Manchester. Fallibroome High School, Macclesfield; University of Sheffield, LLB. L. November 1993. ETC. 7 December 1993. Prop. Brendan Hegarty QC. Sec. Elizabeth Rylands. Pupilmasters; Tim Mort, Gerard McDermott & Elizabeth Rylands. 8 King Street, Manchester, 1993.

BARRY, Patrick (Redmond) MC, KC. (The Hon. Sir Patrick Barry)
Born 4 September 1898. Only son of Rt. Hon. Redmond Barry PC., Lord Chancellor of Ireland. Died 6 May 1972 aged 73. Downside; Sandhurst; Balliol College, Oxford, BA. 1st Battalion, Irish Guards. Served in France & Germany, 1918-1919. MC. I. 28 June 1922; Bencher 1946. ETC. 20 February 1924. Prop. Eastham KC. Sec. Laski. Circuit Junior, 1925. 3 St James's Square, 1928-1939. Contested (L) Bolton, 1928. Silk 1938. 12 Kings Bench Walk, 1938-1941. Recalled to Irish Guards 1939. Captain & Adjutant, 1939-1940. General Staff, 1940. Lt. Col., 1942. 3 South Kings Bench Walk, 1942-1949; 6 Kings Bench Walk, 1950. Recorder of Oldham, 1942-1950. Judge of Appeal, Isle of Man, 1946-1950. High Court Judge (QBD), 1950-1966. Chairman of Advisory Committee on the Treatment of Offenders, 1958-1966. WW.

BARTER, (Stanley) Roy MBE.
Born 3 August 1927 Liverpool. Liverpool Institute; School of Oriental & African Studies, London (Studying Cantonese in Intelligence Corps, 1945-1947). Trinity Hall, Cambridge, 1948-1951, MA., LLM. G. June 1953. ETC. 4 February 1954. Prop. Forrest QC. Sec. Booth (pp Edward Steel, pupilmaster). 14 Cook Street, Liverpool, 1953-1957. Resident Magistrate, Uganda Protectorate, 1957- remaining after independence. Acted as Judge Advocate & Legal Adviser to the Ministry of Defence when Brigadier Idi Amin was Army Commander. MBE 1964. HM Coroner for City of Liverpool/Merseyside, 1968-1999.

BARUCHSON, Arnold de Beer
Born 1844. Only son of Arnold Baruchson of the Downs, Blundellsands, merchant. AAS. M. 11 January 1868. Call 17 November 1870. ETC. 24 March 1871. Prop. Aspinall QC. Sec. R G Williams. Goldsmith Buildings, 1876-1877. Kirkdale Sessions. No address, 1878-1934. Not in 1935 Law List.

BASSANO, Alaric Julian
Born 17 October 1968 Halifax. Shelley High School, Huddersfield; Merton College, Oxford, BA. English Teacher in Colombia, June-October 1990. G. 22 November 1993. ETC. 1993. Prop. Roger Farley QC. Sec. Barry Grennan. Manchester Chambers; Kenworthy's Chambers, 64 Bridge Street, 1993-1998; 9 St John Street, 1998.

BATES, Stewart Taverner QC (His Honour Stewart Bates QC)
Born 17 December 1927. Universities of Glasgow and of St Andrews, MA; Corpus Christi College, Oxford. AAS. M. 14 September 1951. Call 6 July 1964; Bencher, 1975; Lent Reader, 1992. London Chambers; 1 Essex Court; 4 Pump Court. Manchester Chambers: 4 Chapel Walks, 1961-1964; 601 Royal Exchange, 1965-1989. Silk 1970. Recorder 1981. Circuit Judge, 1989-1995. WW.

BATESON, Alexander Dingwall KC (The Hon. Mr Justice Bateson)
Born 30 April 1866 Allerton, Liverpool. Youngest son of William Gandy Bateson, a Liverpool shipping solicitor. Father of Owen Latham Bateson KC qv. and Sir Dingwall Latham Bateson (President of The Law Society) Died (while sitting on the bench in London) on 11 January 1935 aged 68. Rugby; Trinity College, Oxford. I. 26 January 1891; Bencher 1920. ETC. 29 July 1891. Prop. Barnes QC. Sec. McConnell. 1 Garden Court, 1891-1892; 2 Kings Bench Walk, 1893-1917; 4 Kings Bench Walk, 1918-1925. Junior Counsel to the Admiralty, 1909-1910. Silk 1910. High Court Judge (PDA), 1925-1935. Kt 1925. WW. DNB. Times Obituary, 12 January 1935.

BATESON, Owen Latham KC
Born 24 July 1900. Son of Mr Justice Bateson qv. and brother of Sir Dingwall Latham Bateson (President of the Law Society). Died 24 March 1947 aged 46. Rugby; Wadham College, Oxford. I. 6 May 1925. ETC. 15 July 1925. Prop. Wingate-Saul KC. Sec. McCleary. 1 Brick Court, 1925-1930; 1 Essex Court, 1931-1942. Junior Counsel to the Admiralty, 1936. 2 Essex Court, 1943-1945. Silk 1945.

BATHER, Edward William
Born 1854. Eldest son of John Bather of Meole Brace, Salop. Christ's College, Cambridge, BA. AAS. L. 25 January 1879. Call 17 November ETC. 18 July 1892. Prop. Cottingham. Sec. Byrne, equity draftsman & conveyancer. Lancs. Chancery Court. 19 Old Buildings, 8 St James's Square, Manchester, 1883-1908; 40 Brazennose Street, Manchester, 1909-1927. No address, 1928-1940. Not in 1941 Law List. Foster.

BATRA, Bunty Lalit
Born 5 October 1963, New Delhi, India. Fernwood Comprehensive School; Leeds Metropolitan University, LLB. G. February 1988. ETC. 1989. London pupillage. 1 Hare Court, 1988. 50 High Pavement, Nottingham, 1989. Manchester Chambers: 20 St Mary's Parsonage, 1989-1993; 58 King Street Chambers, 51/53 King Street South, 1994-1999; 28 St John Street, 1999. (now St John's Buildings).

BATT, Francis Raleigh (His Honour Francis Raleigh Batt)
Born 9 June 1890. Died 25 March 1961 aged 70. Mount Radford School, Exeter; Law Society School of Law. LLM. Solicitor 1911. Academic at Aberystwyth, Sheffield & Liverpool. Professor of Commercial Law; Dean of the Law Faculty and Honorary Professor of Common Law at Liverpool University between 1919 and 1945. G. 26 January 1917. ETC. 1920. Liverpool Chambers: 25 Lord Street, 1920-1927; 15 Union Court, 1928-1933; 3 Cook Street, 1934-1942. Assistant Recorder of Liverpool, 1940-1942. Deputy Chairman of Lancashire Quarter Sessions. County Court Judge: Circuit 10 (Cheshire, Lancashire & Yorkshire), 1942-1958; Circuit 8 (Manchester & Leigh), 1958-1961. Publications: Law of Master & Servant, 1928 (4th Edition); Law of Negotiable Instruments, 1931; Editor of Chalmer's Bills of Exchange, 1946. WW. Obituary, Liverpool Echo, 28 March 1961.

*** BATTY, Paul Daniel QC (His Honour Judge Batty QC)**
Born 13 June 1953. St Aiden's Grammar School, Sunderland; Newcastle-upon-Tyne University, LLB. L. 1975. North Eastern Circuit; Bar Mess Junior, 1982-1984; Circuit Junior, 1985. Assistant Recorder, 1994. Recorder, 1994. Silk, 1995. Circuit Judge, Carlisle, 11 November 2003.

BAUCHER, Albert Edward
G. 17 November 1926. Liverpool Chambers: 15 Lord Street, 1926-1930; 43 Castle Street, 1931-1934; 5 Harrington Street, 1935-1941; 27 Dale Street, 1942-1945; 3 Cook Street, 1946-1958; The Temple, Dale Street, 1959-1963. No chambers address 1964-1965 (living in Southport) Not in 1966 Law List.

BAXTER, Arthur Yates
I. 25 April 1888. ETC. 27 July 1888. Prop. Gibbs QC. Sec. C A Russell. 7 Crown Office Row, 1888-1893. 8 Harrington Street, 1894-1905. No address, 1906-1940. Not in 1941 Law List.

BAXTER, Bernadette
Born 25 April 1965 Kingston-upon-Hull. St Mary's High School, Hull; London School of Economics, LLB. AAS. M. 6 February 1986. Call 23 July 1987. Manchester Chambers: 1st floor. Central Buildings, 3 Peter Street, 1989-1991; 211 Deansgate, 1992-1993; Rational House Chambers, 64 Bridge Street, 1994-1995; Lincoln House Chambers, 1 Brazennose Street, 1999.

BAXTER, Gerald Pearson
Born 27 July 1949 Leigh. Bolton School. Sheffield University, LLB., LLM. L. July 1971. ETC. June 1974. Prop. W G O. Morgan QC. Sec. Justin Price. Same Liverpool Chambers: Queen Avenue, 1974-1984; 2nd floor, Peel House, Harrington Street, 1984-1994; 25-27 Castle Street, 1994. Winner of Bar Point to Point on "Carhoo Hope" owned by Keith Thomas, 1990. Winning Rider and Owner – "Printer" in 1991. Has ridden in a foxhunter chase at Aintree over Grand National fences.

BAXTER, Richard Walter
L. 26 January 1904. Liverpool Chambers: 4 Harrington Street, 1910-1913; 8 Harrington Street, 1914-1931. No address, 1932-1953. Not in 1954 Law List.

BAYLEY, Christopher Robert Stewart
Born 18 December 1951, Newmarket. Died 24 November 2002 aged 50. Cranbrook School. Worked for Leeds City Council then to Bristol University, LLB. I. October 1998. Legal Advisor at RAC. Assistant Secretary at Bar Council. ETC March 2001. Prop. Keith Goddard QC. Sec. J O'Shea for Beverly Lunt. Kingsgate Chambers, Manchester, Nov. 2001-2002. Obituary 'In Brief', March 2003 (Beverly Lunt). Talented potter.

BAYLIS, Thomas Henry QC

His Honour Judge Baylis
Liverpool Court of Passage

Born 22 June 1817 London. Died 4 October 1908 aged 91. Harrow; Brasenose College, Oxford, MA. AAS. I. 9 June 1834. Call 26 January 1856; Bencher, 1877; Lector, 1898; Treasurer, 1899. 2 Paper Buildings, 1876-1908. Presiding Judge of the Liverpool Court of Passage, 1876-1903. Lt. Col, late 18th Rifle Volunteers. Publications: The Temple Church and Chapel of St Ann; Domestic Servants; Fire Hints; Treasure Trove & Lost Property; Nelson's Famous Signal. WW. DNB.

BEAN, George Joseph QC (The Hon. Mr Justice Bean)
Born 19 September 1915. Son of George & Phoebe Bean. Married 1953, Zdenka White, father of David Bean QC (Chairman of the Bar Council, 2002 and High Court Judge, Queen's Bench Division, July 2004). Died 19 November 1973 aged 58. Liverpool Institute; Liverpool University. AAS. M. 9 November 1934. Call 26 January 1940; Bencher 1969. Served in Army, 1939-1946, Lt. Col., RASC. OBE 1945. 49 Castle Street, Liverpool, 1946-1963. Silk 1963. 1 Temple Gardens, 1963-1970. Recorder of Carlisle, 1965-1969. High Court Judge (QBD), 1970-1973. Member of the Parole Board, 1972-1973. He gave permission for a photograph to be taken of the last Assize sitting in Carlisle in 1971. When his son David visited the Liverpool Bar in December 2002, I gave him the Carlisle newspaper recording the event. WW.

BEARD, Sir Lewis

Born 12 April 1858. Only son of Rev Charles Beard, LLD of Liverpool. Died 17 March 1933 aged 74. Royal Institution School, Liverpool; Trinity College, Cambridge, BA. AAS. I. 7 November 1879. Call 21 June 1882. ETC. 29 July 1882. Prop. Gully QC. Sec. Aspland. Liverpool Chambers; 11 Lord Street, 1882-1884; Commerce Chambers, 15 Lord Street, 1885-1889; Stephensons Chambers, 25 Lord Street, 1890-1891. Liverpool Prosecutions Book records:- "2/1891 (Coventry)". Deputy Town Clerk, Coventry, 1891-1893; Town Clerk, 1893-1904. Town Clerk, Blackburn, 1904-1930. Kt. 1919. Member of Royal Commission on Local Government. WW. Foster

BEATTIE, Ann Louise
Born 12 December 1964 Carlisle. Newman School; Durham University (Van Mildert College), BSc. University of Westminster, Diploma in Law. Cartmel Shepherd, Solicitors, 1988-1989. AAS. M. 15 July 1987. Call 27 July 1989. ETC. December 1989. Prop, Tim King QC. Sec. John Roberts. Derby Square Chambers, Merchants Court, Derby Square, Liverpool 1989-31 December 1993; Atlantic Chambers, 4-6 Cook Street, Liverpool, 1 January 2004.

BEAUFORT, Sir Leicester Paul
Born 1850 Warburton, Cheshire. Died 12 August 1926 aged 76. Westminster School; Queens College, Oxford, MA., BCL. AAS. I. 30 June 1876. Call 7 May 1879. ETC. 6 July 1880. Prop. Temple QC. Sec. Gibbs QC. 4 Paper Buildings, 1879-1886; 3 Paper Buildings, 1887; 7 Kings Bench Walk, 1888-1889. Judicial Commissioner, British North Borneo, 1889. Governor and Commander in Chief, Labuan & North Borneo, 1895-1900. Chief Justice, Northern Rhodesia, 1901-1918. Kt. 1919. WW. Foster.

BEAUMONT, John Richard
Oxford University, MA. I. November 1976. Manchester Chambers: 43 King Street, 1976-1988; 5 John Dalton Street, 1989-1994; 4 Camden Street, Preston 1995. Not in 1996 Bar Directory.

BEAZLEY, His Honour Sir Hugh Loveday
Born 16 October 1880. Died 17 July 1964 aged 83. Cheltenham College; Oriel College, Oxford, MA. I. 5 July 1905; Bencher 1941. ETC. 31 July 1905. Prop. Horridge KC. Sec. Leslie Scott. Goldsmith Building, 1905-1927. Served in France, 1917-1919 with Kings Liverpool Regiment and later on Headquarters Staff of First Army (despatches). Member of the Bar Council, 1924-1927. County Court Judge; Circuit 16 (Hull & East Riding), 1927-1934; Circuit 38 (Middlesex, Essex & Herts.), 1934-1937. Judge of the Mayor's and City of London Court, 1937-1942. Common Serjeant of the City of London, 1942-1953. Kt. 1953. WW.

BECKER, Paul Anthony
Born 7 April 1968 Crosby. Kingswood School; Leeds University, LLB. G. 27 November 1990. CPS, Prosecutor /Senior Prosecutor, Crosby, 1990-1998. ETC. 2 April 1998. Prop. Nigel Gilmour QC. Sec. Simon Christie. Liverpool Chambers: Ground floor, Peel House, Harrington Street, 1998-1999; Chavasse Court, 24 Lord Street, 1999.

BEDFORD, Stephen John
Born 25 April 1952 Liverpool. Liverpool Institute High School for Boys; St Edmund Hall, Oxford, BA. G. July 1974. ETC. 1975. Sec. Henry Lachs. Pupilmasters:- Anthony Temple (4 Pump Court) & C S Rawlins (Albion Chambers, Bristol) Addresses of same Liverpool Chambers; 27 Dale Street, 1975-1977; Melbourne Buildings, 1977-1988; 3rd floor, Peel House, Harrington Street, 1988-1998; 7th floor, India Buildings, Water Street, 1998. Assistant Recorder 1995. Recorder 1999.

BEEBY, Francis
Born 1855. Only son of Rev William Beeby of Birkby House, Maryport. AAS. 29 January 1881. Call M. 26 January 1888. ETC. 24 February 1888. Prop. Hopwood QC. Sec. Williams. No Chambers address, 1888-1899. Not in 1900 Law List.

BEESLEY, Mark
Born 30 June 1967 Doncaster. Doncaster Grammar School; Hull University, LLB. Chartered Accountant (Insolvency Practitioner), 1989-1997. L. November 1998. ETC. 1998. Prop. David Steer QC. Sec. Andrew MacDonald. Liverpool Chambers: Martins Building, Water Street, 1998-1999; 7 Harrington Street (merger of Martins Bank & Corn Exchange), 6.9.1999.

BEESON, Nigel Adrian Laurence

Born 26 March 1958 Cambridge. Lancaster Royal Grammar School; Wolverhampton University, LLB. L July 1983. ETC. December 1984. Prop. Eric Somerset Jones QC. Sec. A H Edwards. Liverpool Chambers: Oriel Chambers, 5 Covent Garden, 1984-1985.; 2nd Floor, Fruit Exchange, Victoria Street, 1986-1989; 3rd floor, 46 Stanley Street, 1990-1994; 2nd floor, 24 Fenwick Street, 1995-2000; 3rd floor, 14 Cook Street, 2000. New Bailey Chambers, Liverpool, 2004.

BEEVER, Prudence

Born 26 June 1957 Huddersfield. Hulme Grammar School for Girls, Oldham; Manchester Metropolitan University, BA. Solicitor, 1985-2000. M. July 2000. ETC. November 2000. Prop. Peter Birkett QC. Sec. Christine Riley. Pupilmaster, Stephen Dodds. 9 St John Street, Manchester, April -November 2000; 15 Winckley Square, Preston, November 2000. New Bailey Chambes, Liverpool, 2004.

BELBIN, Heather Patricia

Born 18 September 1966 West Midlands. Sheffield Girls High School; Sheffield University, LLB. L. October 1992. ETC. 15 December 1992. Prop. David Turner QC. Sec. Norman Wright. Oriel Chambers, 5 Covent Garden/ 14 Water Street, Liverpool, October 1992.

BELL, Alistair Watson (His Honour Alistair Bell)

Born 31 March 1930 Edinburgh. Lanark Grammar School; George Watson's College; University of Edinburgh, MA; Wadham College, Oxford, MA., BCL. AAS. M. 16 November 1951. Call 28 June 1955. 2nd Lieutenant, Royal Army Service Corps, 1955. ETC. June 1957. Prop. W G Morris. Sec. Desmond Bailey. Circuit Junior, 1959. Manchester Chambers: 26 King Street, 1957-1963; 60 King Street, 1964-1978. Recorder 1972-1978. Circuit Judge, 1978-1997. Honorary Recorder of Carlisle, 1990-1997. The following extract from Dick Hamilton's excellent "Foul Bills & Dagger Money" reflects well upon Alistair: "James Parke used to spend three days riding from Newcastle to Carlisle; now it takes less than three hours. Barristers dart up and down the motorways, and Circuit life is very different. Yet something of the old spirit lingers on. Only a few years ago at Lancaster Assizes, the Judge came into Court to find one of the Counsel missing:

MR JUSTICE HINCHCLIFFE: Mr Bell. I have been waiting to try this case since 10.30. It is now 11.00 am. Where is Mr Lord?

ALISTAIR BELL: My Lord, I very much regret that my learned friend must have been delayed by the inclement weather.

JUDGE: That is no excuse, When I was a young man at the Bar I was invariably at Court one full hour before my case was due to be heard.

MR BELL: Perhaps the weather has worsened since your Lordship was a young man.

JUDGE: Where precisely is Mr Lord coming from?

MR BELL; My Lord, the BBC newcasters announced this morning that blizzards have cut off all roads leading from both sides of the Pennines. My learned friend is struggling from some obscure place in the middle.

JUDGE: It is sheer nonsense to try to motor in this weather.

MR BELL: My Lord, determination sometimes overcomes madness. My learned friend is a very determined motorist. I feel sure that at this very moment he is bowling along the motorway to this Court.

JUDGE: You're doing very well Mr Bell. You have been talking for a quarter of an hour and he still has not come.

MR BELL: May I respectfully suggest that your Lordship retire for a short time?

JUDGE; I don't want to retire. This is the warmest room in the building."

BELL, Rt. Hon. Sir Francis Henry Dillon KC

Born 31 March 1851 Nelson, New Zealand. Died 13 March 1936 aged 84. AAS. M. 8 November 1871. Call 6 June 1874. ETC. 30 July 1874. Prop. Temple QC. Sec. Torr QC. Address:- Wellington NZ but shown as practising at Preston & Liverpool Sessions, 1876-1877. Notary Public & Solicitor of the Supreme Court at Wellington where he was: Crown Solicitor, 1885-1911; MP, 1893-1897; Mayor, 1892, 1893 & 1897. Attorney General, 1918-1926. Prime Minister of New Zealand, 1926. KC 1907. KCMG 1915. GCMB 1923. PC 1926. WW. Foster. Simpson.

BELL, P(hilip) Ingress Bell QC (His Honour P. Ingress Bell QC)
Born 10 January 1900. Died 12 September 1986 aged 86. Stonyhurst, Blackburn; Royal Naval College, Keyham. RN; Cadet, RN 1918; Midshipman, 1918-1920. Queens College, Oxford (BA Jurisprudence, BCL) I. 17 November 1925. ETC. 17 February 1926. Prop. Atkinson KC. Sec. Abbott. Equity draftsman & conveyancer. Lancs. Chancery Court. Manchester Chambers: 78 King Street, 1925-1948; 4 Clarence Street, 1949-1952. J A G Dept, 1941. Temporary Major, 1944. TD 1950. MP (C) Bolton East, 1951-1960. Silk 1952. 11 New Square, 1952-1960. County Court later Circuit Judge, 1960-1975. (Circuit 40, Middlesex 1960-1962; Circuit 4, North Lancashire, 1962-1975) WW.

BELL-COX, Leslie Colville
I. 5 July 1905. ETC. 31 July 1905. Prop. Tobin KC. Sec. Stewart Brown. Liverpool Chambers: 13 Harrington Street, 1905-1908; 8 Cook Street, 1909-1913. No address, 1914-1953. Not in 1954 Law List.

BELLIS, (William) Gordon
I. July 1972. ETC. 7 December 1972. Pupilmaster, A D Pappworth. Same Liverpool Chambers: 27 Dale Street, 1972-1989; 5th floor Corn Exchange, Fenwick Street, 1989-1999; 7 Harrington Street (merger of Corn Exchange with Martins Bank)6.9.1999.

BENAS, Bertram Benjamin Baron CBE

Above: Benas and the Judges, 1963. Back row, Addleshaw, Leigh. Middle row, Fraser Hamson, Edward Steele, Trotter. Front row, Burgess, Laski, Harold Brown, Crichton and Benas, front centre.

Born 26 July 1880 Toxteth, Liverpool. Died 8 December 1968 aged 88. LLM, Liverpool. AAS. M. 19 November 1903. Call 19 November 1906; Bencher 1853; Autumn Reader 1968. ETC. 20 February 1907. Prop. Taylor KC. Sec. Thomas. Pupilmaster, John Rutherford. Equity draftsman & conveyancer. Lancs. Chancery Court. Liverpool Chambers: 4 Harrington Street, 1906-1922; 43 Castle Street, 1923-1925; 8 Harrington Street, 1926-1935; 13 Harrington Street, 1936-1941; 14 Cook Street, 1942-1968. Also at 8 Old Square. He was involved fully in the affairs of the City of Liverpool as a magistrate and university lecturer. He was chairman or president of numerous committees, clubs and bodies advancing music, literature and history in the City. His huge contribution to British Jewry was recognised in 1954 with a CBE. I knew none of this when in the early 1950s I often saw a very small man walk along Princes Boulevard in Liverpool dressed in black jacket and pin stripes with wing collar and bowler hat. He also carried a rolled umbrella whatever the weather. All was revealed years later when he proposed me for admission to Middle Temple and when as Autumn Reader he congratulated me on my Call in November 1968. Sadly he died a few weeks later.
On the 7 June 1978 Professor Sefton D Temkin, Professor of Jewish History at the State of New York University at Albany, gave a memorial lecture entitled "The Life and Times of a Jewish Victorian, Bertram B. Benas." Judge Henry Globe QC has handed me a copy of the published lecture which I have placed in the Circuit Records. Publications: Precedents of Pleading (with Judge Essenhigh); The New Law of Property Explained (with Lord Justice Scott). Contributed to Halsbury's Laws of England on property and conveyancing matters. WW. Times Obituary, December 1968. Portrait, Liverpool Athenaeum.

BENHAM, Charles Daniel
I. 26 January 1893. ETC. 12 July 1894. Prop. Pickford QC. Sec. Bateson. Kings Bench Walk, 1893-1894; 1 Crown Office Row, 1895-1896; 1 Dr Johnson's Buildings, 1897-1904; 7 Fig Tree Court, 1905-1919; 6 Crown Office Row, 1920-1923; 1 Kings Bench Walk, 1924-1941. Not in 1942 Law List.

BENJAMIN, Judah Philip QC

(US Army Signals Corps)

Benjamin was born at St Croix in the British Virgin Islands on 11 August 1811. He died in Paris on 8 May 1884 aged 72. Although he achieved great fame at the English Bar, he is best remembered as a Cabinet Minister in the Confederate Government led by Jefferson Davies during the American Civil War. His family had left St Croix for North Carolina in 1818. After attending Yale, Benjamin moved to New Orleans where in 1832 he was called to the Bar. He prospered both as an attorney and politician having been elected a senator for Louisiana in 1852 and in 1857. His reputation grew to such an extent that President Franklin Pierce offered him a seat in the United States Supreme Court. Benjamin refused this great honour preferring a life at the Bar and in politics. He was a firm supporter of the South and when Jefferson Davies formed his Provisional Government in 1861, Benjamin became Attorney General and eventually Secretary of War. Paul Johnson in his "History of the American People" (Weidenfeld & Nicolson, 1997) describes Benjamin as "by far the ablest member of the Confederate Government". When General Lee surrendered at Appomattox Court House, Benjamin fled Richmond with a very large price on his head. After an adventurous journey he arrived almost penniless in Liverpool in 1885. Benjamin later wrote to his law partner in New Orleans that "when called to the Bar I shall take the Northern Circuit which includes Liverpool where I hope to get my first start with the aid of some of our old clients there". In his excellent biography "Judah P Benjamin–The Jewish Confederate", Eli Evans states, "Liverpool was home to the largest number of Confederate Sympathizers–shipping firms and mercantile bodies whose owners had supported the South during the war and, having known Benjamin as the South's reigning international lawyer, would welcome his services once again." Because of his standing and experience Benjamin was not required to wait the normal three years of studentship. Having been pupilled to Charles Pollock in Lamb Building, he was called to the Bar at Lincolns Inn on 13 January 1866 within five months of having been admitted as a student. He was elected to the Northern Circuit some weeks later. Despite being befriended by Quain and Holker, the then Leaders of the Circuit, Benjamin made a slow start. He put all of his efforts into a text book on the sale of goods. It achieved immediate, widespread success and is a fitting memorial to him having achieved a 6th edition in 2002. When he first arrived in England Lord Chelmsford refused him Silk for fear of causing offence to the United States Government. However, Benjamin was appointed Queen's Counsel of the Court of the County of Lancaster (See Bennett's Chancery Practice and "Life in the Law" J G Witt KC) He did take Silk in 1872 and his performance in Court so impressed Lord Hatherley that he granted Benjamin a Patent of Precedence. It has been suggested that Lord Coleridge wished to make Benjamin a High Court Judge but Lord Cairns refused because he was not British born (Victorian Bar–J R Lewis). Despite that Benjamin pronounced Cairns the greatest lawyer before whom he had argued a case (The Victorian Chancellors. Vol II. J B Atlay, 1908). In "Bench and Bar" (Hurst & Blackett, 1889) Serjeant Robinson described Benjamin thus:

> I am bound also to mention that Benjamin's appearance was far from prepossessing; he was short and stout – in fact what the irreverent might call stumpy, and his voice had about it what we are in the habit of deeming the very worst of American twangs. There was nothing in his gait or bearing that could compare with the dignity of aspect which characterised Sir William Follett, for instance, and many other leaders. If I refer to these difficulties and defects, it is only for the purpose of suggesting how powerful must have been the energy and the intellect that could defy and surmount them all.

This description accords with that given by Sir John Hollam when he deals with Benjamin's unorthodox approach to advocacy. It comes from Judge Parry's "Seven Lamps of Advocacy" under the chapter "the Lamp of Courage"

> It was in a case which came on for hearing before Lord Justice James, then Vice-Chancellor, and " it appeared to be generally thought that, as usual at the time, a decree would be made directing inquiries in chambers. The matter was being so

dealt with when Mr Benjamin, then unknown to any one in Court, rose from the back seat in the Court. He had not a commanding presence, and at that time had rather an uncouth appearance. He, in a stentorian voice, not in accord with the quiet tone usually prevailing in the Court of Chancery, startled the Court by saying, "Sir, notwithstanding the somewhat off-hand and supercilious manner in which this case has been dealt with by my learned friend Sir Roundell Palmer, and to some extent acquiesced in by my learned leader Mr Kay, if, sir, you will only listen to me – if, sir, you will only listen to me" (repeating the same words three times, and on each occasion raising his voice), " I pledge myself you will dismiss this suit with costs." The Vice-Chancellor and Sir Roundell Palmer, and indeed all the Court, looked at him with a kind of astonishment, but he went on without drawing rein for between two and three hours. The Court became crowded, for it soon became known that there was a very unusual scene going on. In the end the Vice-Chancellor did dismiss the suit with costs, and his decision was confirmed on appeal."

Benjamin's courage was further demonstrated when arguing a case in the House of Lords with Lord Selbourne presiding. Benjamin stated the propositions of law for which he was about to contend. One drew from Lord Selbourne the comment "Nonsense". Benjamin stopped short, slowly put his papers together; tied the tape around them; made a low bow and left the Bar of the House. His able junior stepped into the breach but before long the Lord Chancellor said that he was sorry that Mr Benjamin had left the House and that he was afraid that he was the cause of it by saying that which he ought not to have said. Before long Benjamin took only appeals to the House of Lords or Privvy Council. He is reputed to have earned more than any member of the Bar of his time – having received £480,000 in his sixteen years of practice. In 1883 the year in which Benjamin retired Lord Chief Justice Coleridge in an address to the New York State Bar Association put Benjamin's achievements into perspective when he said: "It is delightful to find that as we familiarly quote your great men, Kent, Story, Parsons, Duer, Philips and Greenleaf – so you on your side are familiar not only with our old great men, with Sir William Blackstone and with Lord Hale and Lord Coke but with our modern men, with Lindley, with Pollock with Benjamin, the common honour of both Bars of England and America". (The Life and Correspondence of Lord Coleridge Vol II. D Appleton & Co., New York, 1904) Upon his retirement, Benjamin was given a farewell dinner in Inner Temple Hall on the 30 June 1883. He thanked his many friends on the Bench and at the Bar for "the kindness and generosity with which they had received a destitute fugitive from another land" He died at his home in Paris the following year. DNB; Times Obituary, 9 May 1884; Simpson; Biography – "Judah P Benjamin – The Jewish Confederate," Eli N Evans, The Free Press. New York 1988; "Judah P Benjamin. Confederate Statesman," Robert Douthat Meade, Oxford University Press, New York, 1943.

BENNETT, David Laurence

Born 12 November 1954 Liverpool. Liverpool College; Coventry University, BA(Business Law). AAS. M. 7 January 1976. Call 22 November 1977. ETC. July 1978. Prop. Michael Maguire QC. Sec. Tony Carus. Liverpool Chambers: Fruit Exchange, Victoria Street, January 1978-April 1991; Chavasse Court, 24 Lord Street, April 1991-August 1999; 42 Castle Street, September 1999.

BENNETT, Sir John

Born 28 October 1876. Died 30 August 1948 aged 71. Clifton College; New College, Oxford, MA. L. 27 June 1900; Bencher 1935. ETC. 4 February 1901. Prop. Ferguson QC. Sec. Acton. Practiced at the Lancashire Palatine Bar. Served in France, 1914-1918 with 21st Battalion of the Manchester Regiment. Manchester Chambers; 5 St James's Square, 1900-1902; 78 King Street, 1903-1936. London Chambers at 18 later 15 Old Square. Vice Chancellor of the County Palatine of Lancaster, 1936-1948. Kt 1937. Publication:- Practice of the Chancery of the County Palatine of Lancaster, 1914. WW.

BENNETT, (John) Martyn

Born 14 February 1946 Crosby. Rydal; Liverpool University, LLB. Law Lecturer, 1967-1968. G. July 1969. ETC. 1970. Pupilmaster, Alan Shore Booth. Liverpool Chambers: 14 Cook Street, 1970-1973; ground floor, Peel House, Harrington Street, 1973-1999; Oriel Chambers, 14, Water Street 1999. Assistant Recorder 1988-1992. Recorder 1992-1995. Member of Legal Services Review Panel.

BENNETT, Philip Ridgeway

Born 1875. Son of Thomas Bennett of Birch Vale, Stockport, calico printer and JP. London University. AAS. M. 13 June 1893. Withdrew 1899. Readmitted 6 May 1912. Call 26 January 1914. Bank of England Chambers, Tib Lane, Manchester, 1919-1932. No address, 1933-1948. Not in 1949 Law List.

BENNETT, Raymond Clayton Watson (His Honour Raymond Bennett)
Born 20 June 1939, Clayton-le-Moors. Brother of Richard John Bennett qv. Bury Grammar School; Manchester University, LLB. Articled to John Backhouse of Backhouse, Dunkerly & Isherwood of Blackburn. Solicitor 1964-1972. AAS. M. 5 June 1972. Call 22 November 1972. Manchester Chambers; 3 St James's Square, 1972-1985; St James's Chambers, 68 Quay Street, 1986-1989. Assistant Recorder 1984. Recorder 1988. Circuit Judge, 21 July 1989-23 July 2004. Resident Judge, Burnley 2 June 1995-2004. Honorary Recorder of Burnley, 1998-2004. WW.

BENNETT, Richard John
Born 8 May 1954 Bury. Brother of His Honour Judge Bennett qv. Queen Elizabeth's Grammar School, Blackburn; Preston Polytechnic, LLB. AAS. M. 23 July 1985. Call 24 July 1986. ETC. Aug 1986. Prop J J Rowe QC. Sec. A R D Stuttard. Manchester Chambers: St James's Chambers, 1986-1989; 38 King Street West, 1989-1992; 15 Winckley Square, Preston, 1992.

BENNETT, John Alexander
Born 1849. Eldest son of Isaac Bennett of Manchester. Corpus Christi, Cambridge, MA. AAS. I. 18 November 1881. Call 25 June 1884. Prop. Addison. Sec. McKeand. 1 St James's Square, Manchester, 1884-1894. No address, 1895-1900. Not in 1901 Law List. Foster.

BENSON, James D'Arcy
Born 10 November 1971 London. Magdalen College School; St Catherine's, Oxford, BA. G. November 1975. ETC. March 1997. Prop. Graham Morrow QC. Sec. Graham Wells. Derby Square Chambers, Merchants Court, Derby Square, Liverpool, 1996-31 December 2003; Oriel Chambers, 14 Water Street, Liverpool, 1 January 2004.

BENSON, John Trevor QC
Born 22 January 1955 Oxford. Helsby County Grammar School for Boys; Liverpool University, LLB. AAS. M. 3 November 1976. Call 27 July 1978. ETC. 1979. Prop. Michael Maguire. Sec. Ingeborg Bernstein. Liverpool Chambers: 54 Castle Street 1979-1987 – relocating to 14 Castle Street, 1988-2002 and then to Atlantic Chambers, 4-6 Cook Street, Liverpool, 2003. Part time Chairman, Industrial Tribunals, 1995. Assistant Recorder 1998. Recorder 2000. Silk 2001.

BENSON, Mark Gilpin
BA, Birmingham, MA. M. October 1992. ETC. 17 December 1992. Prop. Rodney Klevan QC. Sec. William Morris. Circuit Junior 1995. 18 St John Street, Manchester, 1992.

BENTHAM, Howard Lownds QC
Born 26 February 1948, Chester. The Grange School, Hartford, Northwich; The Ryleys School, Alderley Edge; Malvern College, Worcester; Liverpool University, LLB. G. 24 November 1970; Bencher, December 2003. ETC. November 1970. Prop. George Carman QC. Sec, J Stewart Oakes. Manchester Chambers; 47 Peter Street, 1970-1975. Relocated to Sunlight House, 1975-1980. Relocated to 28 St John Street, 1980-1990. Changed chambers to Old Bank Street, St Anne's Square, relocated to Peel Court Chambers, 45 Hardman Street, 1990. Assistant Recorder 1985. Recorder 1988. Silk 1996. WW.

BENTLEY, David Paul
Born 12 October 1973 Manchester. The Hulme Grammar School for Boys, Oldham; Nottingham Trent University, LLB. L. 8 October 1998. ETC. February 1999. Prop. Rodney Scholes QC. Sec. Julian Holt. Manchester Chambers: Parsonage Chambers, 3 The Parsonage, 1998-2000; 24a St John Street, 2000 (now St Johns Buildings).

BERKLEY, David Nahum QC
Born 3 December 1955, Haifa. Manchester Jewish Grammar School; Gateshead Yeshiva; Manchester University, LLB. Litigation Assistant with Haliwell, Landau Solicitors, 1978-1979. AAS. M. 17 January 1976. Call 15 May 1979. ETC. August 1979. Pupilmaster, F M S Hudson. Manchester Chambers: 67 Princess Street, 1979-1991; Hollins Chambers, 64a Bridge Street, 1991-1996; Founding Head of Merchant Chambers, 1 North Parade, Parsonage Gardens, November 1996-2004. Merger with St Johns Buildings, 2004. Deputy District Judge, 1998-2001. Silk 1999. Recorder 2001. Interests; early printed books. WW.

BERKSON, David Mayer
Born 8 September 1934. Brother of District Judge P H Berkson (Liverpool), uncle of His Honour Judge Henry Globe QC qv., and of Simon Berkson qv. Birkenhead School. G. July 1957. ETC. 1957. Pupilmaster, George Bean. Same Liverpool Chambers; 47-49 Castle Street, 1957-1967; 606 The Corn Exchange, Fenwick Street, 1968-1982; 1 Exchange Flags, 1983-1984. Recorder 1978-1999. Legal Member, Mental Heath Review Tribunal, 1982-1984. Deputy Judge Advocate. 1984-1987. Assistant Judge Advocate General. 1988-1999.

Deputy Judge Advocate General, Germany, 1994-1999. Magistrate of the Standing Civil Courts, 1991-1999. Part time Special Adjudicator, Immigration Appeal Authority. 1998. A man with a wonderful sense of humour and an excellent storyteller. I have always thought of him as the Peter Ustinov of the Northern Circuit. WW.

BERKSON, Simon Nathaniel
Born 19 August 1964, Birkenhead. Son of District Judge P H Berkson. Nephew of David Berkson qv. Brother of Jonathan Berkson (Liverpool Solicitor). Calday Grange Grammar School, West Kirby; Bristol Polytechnic, LLB. G. July 1986. ETC. 16 December 1986. Prop. John Kay QC. Sec. David Berkson. Liverpool Chambers: 1 Exchange Flags, 1986-1991; relocated to Exchange Chambers, Pearl Assurance House, Derby Square, 1992.

BERNSTEIN, Ingeborg (Her Honour Inge Bernstein)
Born 24 February 1931. Married to Eric Goldrein qv. Peterborough County School; St Edmund's College, Liverpool; Liverpool University. I. November 1952. Liverpool Chambers (all relocations) 34 Castle Street, 1952-1972; 54 Castle Street, 1973-1988; 14 Castle Street, 1988-1991. Head of Chambers. Recorder, 1978-1991. Member of Mental Health Act Commission, 1984-1986. President, Mental Health Review Tribunal. Circuit Judge, 1991-2001. Retirement tributes at Liverpool Crown Court on 30 April 2001. (HH Judge David Clarke QC/ John Benson QC) Transcript in Circuit Records. WW.

BERRAGAN, (Howard) Neil
Born 1 March 1959 York. Pocklington School, York; Pembroke College, Oxford, MA. G. July 1982. L. ad eundem. Elected North East Circuit 1982. Pupilmaster, Alastair McCallum. ETC, Northern Circuit, 1992. 23 Park Square South, Leeds, 1982-1987; 22 Old Buildings, Lincolns Inn, 1988-1999; Manchester Chambers; Merchant Chambers, 1 North Parade, Parsonage Gardens, 1999-2001; 40 King Street, 2001.

BERRIDGE, Elizabeth Rose
Born 22 March 1972, Oakham, Rutland. Vale of Catmose College; Rutland 6th Form College; Emmanuel College, Cambridge, MA. I. November 1996. ETC. November 1996. Prop. Roger Farley QC. Sec. Fiona Ashworth. 40 King Street, Manchester, 1996.

BEST, James George
Born 1846. Only son of Thomas Best of Eltville, Didsbury, Manchester, merchant. MA, Trinity College, Cambridge, 1871. AAS. I. 15 January 1868. Call 17 November 1870. ETC. 10 March 1871. Prop. Higgin QC. Sec. Leresche. In Law List 1876-1911 without an address – merely Salford & Manchester Sessions. Foster's "Men at the Bar" in 1885 has him at 57 Princess Street, Manchester. Not in 1912 Law List.

BHADRESA, Magenlal Nanji
Born 1940. 4th son of Nanji Meghji Bhadresa of Nyeri, Kenya. Liverpool University, LLB. AAS. M. 7 June 1961. Call 23 June 1964. 606 The Corn Exchange, Fenwick Street, Liverpool, 1965-1971. Left the Liverpool Bar. Not in 1972 Law List.

BHAT, Saima
Born 31 July 1976 Blackpool. Westholme School; Queen Elizabeth's Grammar School; Bristol University, LLB., LLM. M. July 1999. ETC. December 1999. Prop. Keith Goddard QC. Sec. Simon Newell.
15 Winckley Square, Preston, 1999.

BIBBY-TREVOR, Robert Nicholas
MA, Oxford. I. 29 April 1931. ETC. 1 February 1933. Prop. Derbyshire KC. Sec. Pereira. 2 Dr Johnson's Buildings, 1933-1956. Transferred to South Eastern Circuit in 1949. Cloisters, 1957-1985. Same address but non practising, 1986-1988. Not in 1989 Bar Directory.

BIDDLE, Neville Leslie
Born 24 April 1951 West Kirby. Wrekin College, Shropshire; University College of Wales (Aberystwyth), BSc(Economics). G. November 1974. ETC. 1975. Prop. Ifor Morris Jones QC. Sec. Max Feeny. Liverpool Chambers: Ground Floor, Peel House, Harrington Street, 1975-1998; 25 Castle Street, 1998. Assistant Recorder 1996. Recorder 2000. Director of R S Clare & Co. Liverpool's oldest manufacturing company – founded in 1746.

BIGGS, Arthur Holland
I. 26 June 1895. ETC. 15 July 1896. Prop. McCall QC. Sec. Byrne. 2 Kings Bench Walk, 1895-1903. Liverpool City Sessions. 3 Paper Buildings, 1904-1908. No address, 1909-1949. Not in 1950 Law List.

BIGHAM, Hon. Sir (Frank) Trevor Roger
Born 1876. 2nd son of First Viscount Mersey qv. Died 23 November 1954 aged 78. Eton; Magdalen College, Oxford. AAS. M. 19 June 1896. Call 28 January 1901. ETC. 31 July 1901. Prop. Pickford KC. Sec. Dove. 2 Garden Court, 1901; 2 Kings Bench Walk, 1903; Goldsmiths Building, 1904-1909. Chief Constable, Metropolitan Police, 1909; Assistant Commissioner, 1914; Deputy Commissioner, 1931-1934. CB 1919. KBE 1929. WW.

BIGHAM, Sir John Charles QC., MP. (First Viscount Mersey of Toxteth)

Born 3 August 1840. 2nd son of John Bigham, Liverpool merchant. Father of Sir Trevor Bigham qv. Died 3 September 1929 aged 89. Liverpool Institute; Further education in Paris, Berlin & University of London (matriculated 1861) AAS. M. 14 November 1867. Call 10 June 1870; Bencher 1886; Autumn Reader 1896; Treasurer 1906. ETC. 19 August 1870. Prop. Manisty QC. Sec. Torr. Goldsmith Building, 1870-1897. Silk 1883. Contested (Liberal) Liverpool Toxteth, 1895. Contested Liverpool Exchange, 1892. MP (Liberal Unionist) Liverpool Exchange, 1895-1897. High Court Judge, Queens Bench Division, 1897-1909. President of the Railway & Canal Commission, 1904-1909. President of the Probate, Divorce and Admiralty Division, 1909-1910. Kt 1897. PC 1909. Baron 1910. Viscount 1916, He retired as a Judge in March 1910 due to ill health. Viscount Mersey is best known for chairing the inquiries into the wreck of the SS Titanic in 1912 and the sinking of SS Lusitania by a German submarine in 1915. Leslie Harrisons "A Titanic Myth" Parts 1 & 2. (1992-1996) although written with a view to exonerating Captain Stanley Lord of the "Californian", contains much of Lord Mersey's conduct of the Inquiry. Similarly Colin Simpson's "Lusitania" (with a forward written by Lord Mersey's great grandson in 1993) has a full account of the proceedings before the Tribunal. Two days after submitting his "Lusitania" report, and unhappy with political interference, Lord Mersey wrote to Prime Minister Asquith waiving his fee and asking to be excused from all future judicial duties. WW. DNB. Simpson. Times Obituary, 4 September 1929.

BILL, Charles

Born 8 January 1843. Died 9 December 1915 aged 72. Eton; University College, Oxford, MA (Law & History) 1869. AAS. L. 31 October 1864. Call 16 November 1868. ETC. 26 July 1869. Prop. Manisty QC. Sec. Herschell. No address, 1876-1882. Not in 1883 Law List. Served on General Stewart's Staff in Ruby Mines Expedition, Upper Burma in 1886; medal with clasp; MP (C) Leek Division of Staffs, 1892-1906. JP. WW. Foster.

BILSLAND, Alisan

Born 24 September 1975, Newcastle-upon-Tyne. King Edward VI Grammar School; University of Durham (Collingwood College), BA(Law & Sociology). L. November 2000. ETC. 2001. Prop. Ian Leeming QC. Sec. Michael Mulholland. St James's Chambers, 68 Quay Street, Manchester, 2000.

BINGHAM, Richard Martin QC., MP. (His Honour Richard Bingham QC)

Born 26 October 1915, Liverpool. Died 26 July 1992 aged 76. Harrow; Clare College, Cambridge. I. November 1940; Bencher 1964. Royal Artillery, Dunkirk and NW Europe. Major 1945. TD. 1949. ETC. 1946. Pupilmaster, Selwyn Lloyd. Liverpool Chambers: 34 Castle Street, 1946-1949; 14 Cook Street, 1950-1958. Silk 1958. 2 Pump Court, 1958-1972. Liverpool City Councillor, 1946-1949. MP (C) Liverpool, Garston, 1957-1966. Recorder of Oldham, 1960-1971. Judge of Appeal, Isle of Man, 1965-1972. Member of Home Office Committee on Coroners, 1965. Member of Royal Commission on Assizes and Quarter Sessions (Beeching Commission), 1966. Circuit Judge, 1972-1988. Publications: Cases on Negligence, 1961; Cases and Statutes on Crime, 1980; Crown Court Practice, 1987. Retirement Speeches, Liverpool Crown Court 7

September 1988 (Judge Paterson/JJ Rowe QC). Tributes, Liverpool Crown Court, 30 July 1992 (Judge Wickham/Rodney Klevan QC) WW. Times Obituary, 28 August 1992.

BINNEY, James
Born 14 August 1868. Youngest son of Edward William Binney, FRS & Manchester solicitor. Died 3 September 1935 aged 67. Rugby; Trinity Hall, Cambridge, MA. AAS. M. 19 November 1889. Call 6 June 1894. ETC. 27 February 1895. Prop. C A Russell. Sec. Acton. No Address given in Law Lists. Soldier; Captain, 3rd battalion Kings Regiment. Landowner in Lancashire & Cambridgeshire. Conservative candidate for Crewe, 1908 & 1909. DL., JP. Publication: Nineteenth Century Geologist. WW.

BINNS, David Andrew
Born 26 June 1961, Manchester. St Ambrose College, Cheshire. Liverpool University, LLB. AAS. M. 6 May 1982. Call 28 July 1983. ETC. 1884. Pupilmaster, Arthur Stuttard. St James's Chambers, 68 Quay Street, Manchester, 1984. Legal Aid Appeal Committee, 1994. NPAS Adjudicator, 2000.

BIRD, Arthur Hatfield Sumner
Born 1857. 3rd son of Major Robert Wilberforce Bird of Barton House, Shipston-on-Stow, Warwick. Trinity College, Cambridge, BA. AAS. I. 4 July 1878. Call 11 May 1881. ETC. 13 February 1886. Prop. Kennedy QC. Sec. Pickford. Chambers address; Bank Chambers, Cook Street, Liverpool. In Law Lists from 1887-1921 shown as advocate practising before the High Court in Allahbad, India. Not in 1922 Law List. Foster.

BIRD, Charles Henry
Born 1840. 2nd son of William Smith Bird of Aigburth, Liverpool. Trinity College, Oxford, BA. St John's College, Oxford, MA. AAS. I. 26 January 1860. Call 17 November 1863. No address, 1876-1909. JP. Not in 1910 Law List. WW.

BIRD, Nigel David
Bury Grammar School; Selwyn College, Cambridge, MA. I. November 1991. Pupilmaster, Michael Johnson. Manchester Chambers; Crown Square Chambers, 1 Deans Court, 1991-1993; 9 St John Street, 1994.

BIRKENHEAD, First Earl of (See Smith, Frederick Edwin)

BIRKETT, Peter Vidler QC.

Born 13 July 1948 Kendal. Sedbergh School; Leicester University, LLB 1971. I. July 1972; Bencher 1996. One year working in the Steel Industry in Hamilton, Ontario. South Eastern Circuit, 1973-1977. 8 New Square, 1973-1974; Old Square Chambers, 1974-1977. Pupilmasters, Anthony Hidden /Anthony Scrivener. Northern Circuit, 1977. 18 St John Street, Manchester, 1977. Head of Chambers, 2004. Assistant Recorder, 1986. Silk & Recorder, 1989. Leader of the Northern Circuit, 1999-2001. Acting Deemster, Isle of Man, 1999. Keyboard player in 'Prestons' qv. WW.

BIRLEY, Francis Hornby
Born 14 March 1850. Only surviving son of Thomas Hornby Birley, late of Pendleton, Lancs. University College, Oxford, BA. AAS. I. 27 January 1873. Call 26 January 1876. 2 Mitre Court Buildings, 1866-1882. No address, 1883-1910. Not in 1911 Law List. Foster.

BIRLEY, Robert Neville
G. 17 November 1933. ETC. 28 February 1934. Prop. Gorman KC. Sec. Rycroft. Circuit Junior 1935. 26 King Street, Manchester, 1934-1938; Liverpool Chambers; 32 Castle Street, 1939-1940; 34 Castle Street, 1941-1949. No address, 1950-1963. Not in 1964 Law List.

BIRLEY, William Hornby
Born 22 December 1834. 4th son of Hugh Hornby Birley of Manchester. Balliol College, Oxford, MA. AAS. 4 March 1856. Call 26 January 1860. 13 Old Square, 1876-1921. Equity practitioner & conveyancer. Lancs. Chancery Court. Publication: Parliamentary Elections Act 1868. Not in 1922 Law List. Foster.

BIRON, Sir (Mosche Chaim Ephraim) Philip
Born 20 August 1909. Died 31 December 1981 aged 72. Manchester Talmudical College; Yeshiv (Rabbi); Manchester University, LLB. G. May 1941. Royal Air Force, 1941-1946. (AC2 to Flight Lieutenant) 8 Kennedy Street, Manchester, 1946-1949. Resident Magistrate, Tanganyika, 1949-1955; Senior Resident Magistrate, 1955-1956; Acting Judge, 1956-1961; Substantive Judge, 1961-1965; Senior Puisne Judge, 1965-1981. Kt. 1980. WW.

BIRRELL, Neil Ballinghall
G. 11 May 1938. ETC. 6 July 1938. Prop. Gorman KC. Sec. Leigh. Circuit Junior 1938. 60 King Street, Manchester, 1938-1953. Deputy Judge Advocate General, 1954-1963. Not in 1964 Law List.

BIRTLES, Samantha Jane
Born 4 April 1967, Manchester. Married to Richard Simons qv. Manchester High School for Girls; Birmingham University, LLB. L. July 1989. ETC. December 1989. Prop. Rhys Davies QC. Sec. Paul Dockery. 18 St John Street, Manchester, 1989.

BISAYRA, Neil
Born 15 February 1974 London. Merchant Taylors' School, Crosby; Queens College, Cambridge, BA. L. November 1998. ETC. Easter 1999. Prop. David Steer QC. Sec. Tim Kenward. Pupilmaster, David Owen. 25-27 Castle Street, Liverpool, 1998.

BISPHAM, Christine
Born 28 June 1969, Whiston. St Ann's Infant & Junior Schools; Rainhill High School; Leicester University, LLB. L. October 1991. ETC. December 1991. Prop. Rodney Klevan QC. Pupilmaster, Iain Goldrein. Corn Exchange, Fenwick Street, Liverpool, 1991-1999; 7 Harrington Street (Merger of Corn Exchange with Martins Bank), 6.9.1999. Circuit Junior 1994. Elected Circuit Representative on Bar Council 1997-1999 & 2000-2002. Publications: Case Digest Editor, Butterworths Personal Injury Litigation Service (Iain Goldrein QC & Margaret De Haas QC); Domestic Injunctions 2nd edition, Sweet & Maxwell (with Margaret De Haas QC).

BISWAS, Nisha Sujata
Born 23 October 1971 Ormskirk. Scarisbrick Hall School; Liverpool John Moores University, LLB. L. 10 October 1996. ETC. December 1996. Prop. David Turner QC. Sec. Eric Lamb. Liverpool Chambers; Exchange Chambers, 1996; Chavasse Court, 24 Lord Street, 1996. Married to Zoltan Katona. Zoltan & Peter Katona are the "Katona Twins" a classical guitar duo of high international repute.

BLACK, Charles Augustus Harold
Born November 1847. Eldest son of Cornelius Black. MD., physician of Chesterfield. Exeter College, Oxford, BA. AAS. I. 16 August 1866. Call 30 April 1870. ETC. 4 August 1870. Prop. Baylis. Sec. Greenhow. 3 Dr Johnson's Building, 1876; 4 Harcourt Buildings, 1877-1889; 4 Plowden Buildings, 1890-1931. Special pleader. Manchester, Salford & Bolton Sessions. Not in 1932 Law List.

*** BLACK, Jill (Margaret) Hon Mrs Justice Black DBE**

(DL)

Born 1 June 1954. Penthos College, Colwyn Bay; Durham University BA (Law). I. 1976. Silk 1994. Recorder 1999. High Court Judge, Family Division, 1999-. Liason Judge, Northern Circuit 2001- 2005. WW.

BLACK, Michael Jonathan QC
Born 31 March 1954 Hope Hospital. Stand Grammar School; University College, London, LLB. AAS. M. 8 September 1976. Call 7 February 1978. ETC. 1978. Prop. George Carman QC. Sec. Michael Kershaw. Manchester Chambers; Deans Court, Crown Square, 1978-1995. Fellow Chartered Institute of Arbitrators, 1993. Silk & Assistant Recorder, 1995. Byrom Street Chambers, 1995-2000. Recorder 1999. 2 Temple Gardens, 2000. Visiting Research Fellow, UMIST, 1995. Deputy Judge, Technology & Construction Court, 1999. Civil Procedure Rules Committee 2000. Assistant Commissioner, Boundary Commission, 2000. Court of Appeal, Panel of Mediators, 2001. Deputy Judge, Grand Court of the Cayman Islands, 2001. Freeman of the City of London, 2002. WW.

BLACKBURN, Colin (Baron Blackburn of Killearn, Stirlingshire)
Born 18 May 1813. Died 8 January 1896 aged 82. Eton; Trinity College, Cambridge, BA., MA, 1838. AAS. L. 20 April 1835 but called I. 23 November 1838; Bencher I. 1877. According to James McMullen Rigg's entry in DNB, Blackburn "went to the Northern Circuit in a briefless or almost briefless condition and was better known in the Courts as a reporter than as a pleader Lord Campbell startled the profession by appointing him to fill a vacant puisne judgeship. He proved to be an excellent judge and when in 1876 the first two Lords of Appeal in Ordinary were appointed, there was universal approbation when he was one of the two." He sat in the House of Lords for ten years. In 1845 he wrote what was to become the standard textbook on the Sale of Goods until displaced in 1868 by that of Judah Philip Benjamin qv. Serjeant & Kt 1859. PC 1876. DNB. Foster. Simpson.

BLACKBURN, John
Born 24 August 1854. Eldest son of Andrew Blackburn of Edinburgh. Exeter College, Oxford, MA. AAS. I. 5 November 1875. Call 26 January 1880. ETC. 7 February 1881. Prop. Gully QC. Sec. C F Wright. Circuit Junior 1881. 12 Kings Bench Walk, 1885-1890. No address 1891-1940. Not in 1941 Law List.

*** BLACKBURN, Michael Scott (His Honour Judge Blackburn)**
Born 16 January 1936. Died 9 August 2000 aged 64. Dame Allan's School, Newcastle-upon-Tyne; William Hulme's Grammar School, Manchester; Keble College, Oxford, MA. Articled to Jack Goldberg of Conn, Goldberg & Co of Deansgate, Manchester. Remained with same firm (which later became Pannone Blackburn) until his appointment. President, Manchester Law Society, 1979-1980. Recorder, 1981-1986. Parole Board, 1985-1988. Circuit Judge, 1986-2000. President, Mental Heath Review Tribunal. Tributes Manchester Crown Court, 11 August 2000 (Judge Sir Rhys Davies QC/Martin Steiger QC) Transcript in Circuit Records. On the 13 March 2002, the Senior Presiding Judge of England & Wales, Lord Justice Judge, opened at Manchester Crown Square the Michael Blackburn Suite for Child & Vulnerable Witnesses. WW.

BLACKBURN, William
Born 1920. Elder son of the Rev. W Erskine Blackburn of Aberdeen. Edinburgh University, MA. AAS. M. 8 October 1946. Call 17 November 1948. 9 Rumford Street, Liverpool, 1949-1963. Not in 1964 Law List.

*** BLACKBURNE, William (Anthony). The Hon. Mr Justice Blackburne**

(DL)

Born 24 February 1944. High Court Judge, Chancery Division, 1993-. Vice Chancellor of the County Palatine of Lancaster 1998-2002. WW.

BLACKETT-ORD, (Andrew) James (His Honour James Blackett-Ord)

(RB)

Born 21 August 1921. Eton; New College, Oxford, MA. Scots Guards, 1943-1946. I. January 1947; Bencher 1985. 2 New Square, 1947-1971. County Court Judge, 1971. Circuit Judge, 1972-1987. Vice Chancellor, County Palatine of Lancaster, 1973-1987. Chancellor, Diocese of Newcastle-upon-Tyne, 1971-1998. WW.

BLACKLEDGE, (Geoffrey) Glynn MC., QC.
Born 11 July 1894. Died 25 June 1964 aged 69. Only son of William Thomas Blackledge, a Liverpool Surgeon. Shrewsbury School; St John's College, Oxford, MA. Served in the 1914-1918 War in 6th Battalion, The Kings Regiment. AAS. M. 29 January 1919. Call 17 November 1920. Pupilmaster, Singleton. Liverpool Chambers; 5 Harrington Street, 1920-1928; 3 Cook Street, 1929-1930; 34 Castle Street, 1931-1946. Stipendiary Magistrate for Liverpool, 1946-1947. Returned to practise at the Liverpool Bar in 1947. 15 Victoria Street, 1947-1950. Silk 1950. 10 Kings Bench Walk. Presiding Judge, Liverpool Court of Passage, 1950-1964. Collected with Sir Fred Pritchard "The Sayings in Court of Sir Noel Goldie KC., MP" commonly called "Goldiana" The collection is in the Circuit Records but many stories appear in Dick Hamilton's "Foul Bills & Dagger Money" Tony Edmondson says "My pupilmaster was Glynn Blackledge (MC and Bar). Sellers L. J. (MC and two Bars) told me that during heavy shelling in the Battle of the Somme he entered a dugout to find Blackledge calmly reading Salmond on Torts." WW.

BLACKSHAW, Henry William Randle
Born 1 January 1966 Birmingham. Cheadle Hulme School; Durham University, BA (Archeology), Dip Law. St Cuthbert's Society. M. 8 October 1993. ETC. 7 December 1993. Prop. Anthony Morris QC. Sec. Stephen Meadowcroft. Peel Court Chambers, 45 Hardman Street, Manchester. 3.10.1993.

BLACKWELL, Sir (Cecil) Patrick (the Hon Mr Justice Blackwell)
Born 8 November 1881. Only son of Patrick Thomas Blackwell, Barrister of Inner Temple. Blackheath Proprietary School; City of London School; University College, London; Wadham College, Oxford, BA, 1905. I. 28 January 1907. ETC. 6 March 1908. Prop. Sanderson KC. Sec. J W Mansfield. 1 Crown Office Row. Liverpool & Preston Sessions. 1908-1919; 6 Crown Office Row, 1920-1922; Farrars Building, 1923-1926. High Court Judge, Bombay, 1926-1944. MBE 1919. WW.

BLACKWELL, Katherine Elizabeth
Born 5 October 1969 Manchester. Loreto Convent Grammar School. Bowden; Birmingham University, LLB. L. 1 November 1992. ETC. 7 December 1993. Prop. Hussain QC. Sec. Nuttall. Lincoln House Chambers, 5th floor, 1 Brazennose Street, Manchester, 1993.

BLACKWELL, Louise Mary
Born 24 December 1961, Salford. Married to Winston Hunter QC qv. Mount Carmel School, Alderley Edge; Leeds University, LLB. L. 15 July 1985. ETC. 1985. Pupilmaster, Jonathan Foster. Manchester Chambers: 18 St John Street, 1985-1986; Hollins Chambers, 64a Bridge Street, 1986-1997; Cobden House Chambers, 19 Quay Street, 1997.

BLAIR, George Alexander
Born 1865. Eldest son of Alexander Blair of Bradford. St John's College, Cambridge. AAS. M. 2 November 1893. Call 17 November 1896. ETC. 4 February 1898. Prop. Pickford QC. Sec. Scott. Circuit Junior, 1898 & 1899. 25 Lord Street, Liverpool 1898-1923. No address 1924-1949. Not in 1950 Law List.

BLAIR, Harrison Falkner
Born 1839. Eldest son of Harrison Blair of Manchester. Matriculated London University, 1856. Corpus Christi, Oxford, BA. AAS. I. 1 May 1861. Call 6 June 1864. 4 St James's Square, Manchester, 1876-1891. Puisne Judge, Allahbad, India, 1892-1905. No address 1906-1907. Not in 1908 Law List. Foster.

BLAKE, Andrew Nicholas Hubert (His Honour Judge Blake)
Born 18 August 1946 Devon (but brought within the boundaries of Preston by 6 months of age) Ampleforth College; Hertford College, Oxford, MA (History). I. November 1971. ETC. December 1971. Prop. Patrick Russell QC. Sec. F Donald Hart. Same chambers in Manchester at; 43 King Street, 1971-1973; 4th floor, Astley House, Quay Street, 1973-1977; 18 St John Street, 1977-1999. Recorder 1988-1999. Circuit Judge based at Preston, 1999. Speeches of welcome at Preston Courts, 22 July 1999 (Judge Peter Openshaw QC/Stephen Riordan QC) Transcript in Circuit Records. WW.

BLAKE, Maurice Bernal
I. 9 May 1906. ETC. 21 January 1932. Prop. Hemmerde KC. Sec. Fyfe. 1 Hare Court, 1932-1939. Not in 1940 Law List

BLAKEY, David Percival
Born 1925. Only son of Alfred Blakey of Bolton. Wadham College, Oxford, BA. AAS. M. 30 October 1950. ETC. 4 March 1954. Prop. Crichton. Sec. Morris. 26 King Street, Manchester, 1953-1958. Legal Assistant Ministry of Agriculture & Fisheries, 1959-1963. Disbarred at his own request on 18.12.1961 in order to become a solicitor. Admitted as a Solicitor in October 1962. Solicitor with Manchester City Council, 1966-75.

BLAKEY, Lee
Born 5 August 1972 Burnley. Haberrgham High School; University of Central Lancashire, LLB. L. October 1995. ETC. 2 April 1996. Prop. Klevan QC. Sec. A M Cross. 15 Winckley Square, Preston, 2.10.1995.

BLAKEY, Michael Charles
Born 4 August 1956 Hull. Birley High School, Manchester; Army, 1973-1980; Manchester Polytechnic, LLB. AAS. M. 30 September 1986. Call 21 November 1989. ETC. April 1990. Prop. Anthony Gee QC. Sec. Roderick Carus. Manchester Chambers; 6th floor, Sunlight House, Quay Street, 1990-1994; Young Street Chambers, 1995. Recorder 2003.

BLAND, Carolyn
Born 9 September 1967 North Shields. Married to Darren Preston qv. Dr Challoner's High School for Girls; Reading University, LLB. Solicitor, 1991-1995. I. July 1995. ETC. 21 December 1995. Prop. Henriques QC. Sec. Standsby. Manchester Chambers: Kenworthy's Chambers, 83 Bridge Street, 1995-1998; Young Street Chambers, 1998.

BLAND, Edna Phyllis
G. 29 June 1927. 15 Union Court, Liverpool, 1927-1930. No address 1931-1936. Not in 1937 Law List.

BLEASE, Professor (Walter) Lyon

Born 1884 Liverpool. Died 12 April 1963 aged 79. Parkfield School, Liverpool: Shrewsbury; Liverpool University, LLM. L. 27 June 1906; (Studentship). ETC. 25 February 1907. Prop. Mellor KC. Sec. Thomas. Liverpool Chambers: 13 Harrington Street, 1906-1911; 2 Harrington Street, 1912-1925; 26 North John Street, 1925-1928; 3 Cook Street, 1929-1958; 14 Water Street, 1959-1963. Served with hospital units in Serbia (1915) and in Russia and Roumania, 1916-1918. Contested: Chorley (L) 1910; East Toxteth (L) 1945; Garston (L) 1950. Assistant Editor, The New East, Tokyo 1918. Liverpool University: Lecturer in Constitutional Law, 1910; Queen Victoria Professor of Law, 1919-1949; Public Orator, 1931-1949. Governor of the British Film Institute, 1936. Chairman, Liverpool Philharmonic Society, 1950-1951. Chairman, Executive Council for Liverpool under the National Health Service Acts, 1952-1960. Publications: Emancipation of English Women, 1910; Short History of English Liberalism, 1913; A Red Cross Unit in Serbia, 1916; General Suvorof, 1921. See the charming profile by his nephew, His Honour James Scarlett in "A Century of Liverpool Lawyers", (Fagan, Bryson & Elston. Bluecoat Press, 2002.) WW.

BLEASEDALE, Marie-Claire
Born 21 October 1967 London. Ursuline Convent, Wimbledon; University of Cambridge, MA; Dip Law, Westminster. L. October 1993. ETC. 13 December 1994. Prop. Leeming QC. Sec. Adrian Kirsten. Manchester House Chambers, 18-22 Bridge Street, Manchester, 1994. Ground floor, 11 New Square, Lincolns Inn, 1995.

BLOOM, Charles QC (His Honour Judge Bloom QC)

Born 6 November 1940. Manchester Central Grammar School; Manchester University, LLB 1962. G. November 1963. ETC. 1963. Pupilmaster, Arthur Logan Petch. Manchester Chambers; 47 Peter Street, 1963-1974; 12th floor, Sunlight House, Quay Street, 1975-1979; 28 St John Street, 1980-1997. Chairman, Medical Appeals Tribunal, 1979-1997. Recorder 1983. Silk 1987. Circuit Judge 1997.

BLOOMER, Charles Howard

Born 24 September 1961, Cleethorpes. Son of a Grimsby solicitor. Shrewsbury School; Nottingham University, LLB. L. July 1985. ETC. March 1986. Pupilmaster, Alistair Webster. Same Manchester Chambers; Rational House, 64 Bridge Street, 1986-1995; Lincoln House Chambers, 1 Brazennose Street, 1996. Wildlife Photographer.

BODDINGTON, Frank Hubert

G. 19 June 1901. ETC. 10 February 1902. Prop. Russell KC. Sec. Sanderson. Preston & Wigan Sessions. 2 Kings Bench Walk, 1903; 2 Pump Court, 1904-1915; 2 Mitre Court Buildings, 1916-1921. No address, 1922-1954. Not in 1955 Law List

BODEL, Frederick Ernest MC

Born 2 August 1881 at 29 Stanley Road, Bootle. Son of Rev. James & Cassie Bodel. Liverpool University College & Liverpool University, LLB. G. 27 January 1908. ETC. 29 July 1908. Prop. Sanderson KC. Sec. Whiteley. 25 Lord Street, Liverpool, 1908-1914. Commissioned 2nd Lt, 8th Kings Own Liverpool Regiment. Promoted to Captain and seconded to Trench Mortar Battery, 164th infantry Brigade, 55 Division. He was killed in action on 31 July 1917 at Ypres aged 36. The memorial at Ypres (Menin Gate) Panels 4 & 6 bear the names of men who were lost without trace during the defence of the Ypres Salient. I obtained this information from the Public Record Office & Commonwealth War Graves Commission. E S Fay in his 'Life of Mr Justice Swift' Methuen & Co, 1939, says that "Swift's junior at the inquiry into the Whitehaven mine disaster of 1910 in which 132 miners perished was F E Bodel a former pupil. Bodel was a young Irishman whose slight stature and mild appearance concealed a valiant and tenacious spirit. Swift had a great affection for 'Beetle' as he always called him, and carefully preserved his young friend's regimental badges and medals when they were sent back from France. His Honour Edgar Fay QC (now in his 96th year) kindly sent me the photograph of Bodel & Swift at the Whitehaven Colliery which appears in his book and which has been reproduced in "A Century of Liverpool Lawyers", Fagan, Bryson & Elston, 2002.

BOLTON, Hubert Ernest Langtree

I. 22 June 1898. ETC. 13 July 1899. Prop. Pickford. Sec. Wingate-Saul. 3 Kings Bench Walk, 1901-1914. No address, 1916-1949. Not in 1950 Law List.

BOLTON, Sproule

G. February 1952. Barrister, Supreme Court of New Zealand. 14 Cook Street, Liverpool, 1952-1954; 34 Castle Street, Liverpool & 2 Pump Court, 1955-1957. Assistant Secretary to the Bar Council, 1957-1967. Country Landowners Association, 1968-1971. Not in 1972 Law List.

BOLTON, William Henry

Born 1853. Eldest son of Joseph Cheney Bolton, MP., of Stirling. Trinity College, Oxford, BA. AAS. I. 14 November 1873. Call 26 January 1878. ETC. 23 March 1878. Prop. Gully QC. Sec. Dickinson. 4 Crown Office Row, 1880; 3 Temple Gardens, 1881-1890. No chambers address, 1891-1896. Not in 1897 Law List.

*** BOMPAS, Henry Mason QC (His Honour Judge Bompas QC)**

Bom 6 April 1836 London. Youngest son of Serjeant Charles Carpenter Bompas (said to be the inspiration for Charles Dickens' Serjeant Buzfuz in Pickwick Papers). Brother of William Carpenter Bompas, Bishop of Selkirk. Died 5 March 1909 aged 72. I. 26 January 1863; Bencher 1881; Treasurer 1905. Practised on the Western Circuit from 3 Harcourt Buildings. Recorder of Poole, 1882-1885. Recorder of Plymouth & Davenport, 1885. County Court Judge, Circuit 11 (Burnley & Colne) November, 1896-1909. WW.

BONNER, Lee

Born 12 January 1977, Birkenhead. Wirral Grammar School for Boys; Sheffield University, LLB. L. 22 November 2000. ETC. 14 December 2000. Prop. Andrew Edis QC. Sec. Stuart Driver. 14 Castle Street, Liverpool, 2000.

BONNEY, James William QC

Born 6 September 1948 Lytham. Died July 2003 aged 54. King Edward VII School, Lytham; Keble College, Oxford, BCL., MA. Solicitor, 1970-1975. L. November 1975. Manchester Chambers; 196 Deangate, 1975-1989; 18 St John Street, 1990-1998; 15 Winckley Square, Preston, 1998. London Chambers; 10 Old Square. Silk 1995. Deputy High Court Judge, Chancery Division, 1996. Reader, St Cuthbert's Parish Church, Lytham. WW.

BONNEY, John David

LLB. G February 1971. ETC. 1971. Pupilmaster, John Coffey. Manchester Chambers; 36 St Ann Street, 1971-1980; 27 Byrom Street, 1981-1983; 26 Cross Street, 1984; Sunlight House, Quay Street, 1985-1994; 38 Young Street, 1995-1996. Retired from practice, 1995.

BONNEY, (John) Dennis
L. February 1956. 9 Rumford Street, Liverpool, 1958-1959. No address, 1960-1963. Not in 1964 Law List.

BOOCOCK, Lisa Jane.
Born 20 December 1975 Keighley. Temple Bank School, Bradford; Robinson College, Cambridge, BA(Law). G. 8 October 1998. Research Assistant, Law Commission (Property & Trusts Team), 1998-1999. ETC. 14 December 1999. Prop. Roger Farley QC. Sec. A Longworth. Manchester Chambers; Old Colony House, 1999-2001; Queens Chambers, 5 John Dalton Street, 2001.

BOOKER, John Lee
Eldest son of Septimus Booker of Swarthdale House, Carnforth. Hertford College, Oxford. AAS. I. 12 November 1880. Call 17 November 1884. ETC. 30 January 1885. Prop. Ambrose QC. Sec. French. No address, 1886-1940. Not in 1941 Law List. Foster.

BOORA, Jinder Singh
Born 29 April 1966 Warwickshire. Warwick University, LLB. G. October 1990. ETC. 17 December 1992. 334 Deansgate, Manchester, 1992-1993. Joined Midland & Oxford Circuit, 1994. Regent Chambers, 29 Regent Street, Stoke-on-Trent, 1994-1999; 24 The Ropewalk, Nottingham, 1999.

BOOTH, Alan James
Born 18 January 1955, Stockport. Son of His Honour James Booth qv, brother of Joy Booth qv, married to Anne Booth qv. Bolton School; Selwyn College, Cambridge, MA. G. July 1978. ETC. 26 October 1978. Circuit Junior, 1981. Pupilmaster, Michael Kershaw. Manchester Chambers; 1 Deans Court, 1978-1983; at Cumberland House, Crown Square, 1983-1999 and at 24 St John Street, 4.5.1999. Assistant Recorder 1996. Recorder 2000.

BOOTH, Alan Shore QC (His Honour Alan Booth QC)

(RB)

Born 1 August 1922. Shrewsbury School; Served Second World War. RNVR, Fleet Air Arm. 1833 Squadron (Despatches, 1944) Sub-Lt. 1942; HMS Illustrious, Eastern & Pacific Fleets, 1943-1945; Lt, 1945. Liverpool University, LLB. G. November 1949. ETC. January 1950. Circuit Junior 1950. Liverpool Chambers; 14 Cook Street, 1949-1972; ground floor, Peel House, Harrington Street, 1973-1976. Recorder, 1972-1976. Circuit Judge based in Liverpool, 1976-1992. Retirement Tributes at Liverpool Law Courts, 22 May 1992 (Judge Wickham/ Ronnie Livesey QC) Transcript in Circuit Records. Former Captain, Royal Liverpool Golf Club. WW.

BOOTH, Anne Lesley
Married to Alan James Booth qv. Sheffield University, LLB. G. 26 November 1998. ETC. 14 December 1999. Ribchester House, Lancaster Rd, Preston, 1999.

BOOTH, James (His Honour Judge James Booth)
Born 3 May 1914. Died 31 August 2000 aged 86. Father of Alan & Joy Booth qv. Bolton School; Manchester University. G. 27 January 1936. ETC. 26 February 1936. Prop. Lynskey KC. Sec. Birley. Pupilmaster, Joseph Lustgarten. Town Clerk, Ossett, Yorks., 1939-1941. RAFVR, 1941-1946 (Flt. Lt.). Contested (L); West Leeds, 1945; Darwen, 1950. Manchester Chambers: 60 King Street, 1946-1955; 36 St Ann Street, 1956-1969. Recorder of Barrow-in-Furness, 1967-1969. County Court Judge, Circuit 12, 1969-1972. Circuit Judge, 1972-1984. Tributes: Preston Law Courts, 5 September 2000 (Judge Lockett/ Richard Heap); Manchester Law Courts, 8 September 2000 (Judge Sir Rhys Davies QC /Peter Birkett QC) Transcripts in Circuit Records. WW.

BOOTH, Michael John QC
Born 24 May 1958, Salford. Manchester Grammar School; Trinity College, Cambridge, MA. President, Cambridge Union Society, 1979. L. November 1981. ETC. 1983. Pupilmaster, Roderick Cams. Manchester Chambers; Crown Square Chambers, 1 Deans Court, 1983-1992; 40 King Street, 1992. Silk 1999.

BOOTH, Simon Mark
Born 9 March 1962, Liverpool. Bluecoat School, Liverpool; Liverpool University, LLB. L. November 1985. ETC. 16 December 1986. Pupilmaster, N F Riddle. Liverpool Chambers; 7 Queen Avenue, 1986-1996; merger with and move to 14 Castle Street, 1996-; Atlantic Chambers, 4-6 Cook Street, Liverpool, 2003.

BOOTH, (Sylvia) Joy
daughter of His Honour James Booth & sister of Alan James Booth qv. Sheffield University, LLB. G. October 1992. 18 St John Street, Manchester, 1992-2000.

BOOTHMAN, Charles James
Born 1843. Eldest son of Thomas Boothman of Manchester. Stonyhurst; Matriculated London University, 1861. AAS. 20 November 1865. Call 6 June 1868. ETC. 10 March 1870. Prop. Holker QC. Sec. Baylis. 6 Crown Office Row, 1876-1882. No address 1883-1915. Not in 1916 Law List. Foster

BOR, Ellis
L. January 1951. ETC. 5 July 1951. Prop. Burton KC. Sec. Ingress Bell. 4 Clarence Street, Manchester, 1951-1953. No address, 1954-1963. Not in 1964 Law List.

BORRAJO, Jose Carlos Pedro
G. 18 November 1907. ETC. 4 March 1908. Prop. Langdon KC. Sec. Cockshutt. 1 Garden Court, 1907-1908, Probate & Divorce Courts. No address, 1909-1913. Not in 1914 Law List.

BORROWS, Kenneth Ambrose
LLB. G. February 1953. 9 Rumford Street, Liverpool, 1953-1957. Joined National Coal Board, 1958. Not in Law List after 1963.

BOULTON, David John (His Honour Judge Boulton)
Born 2 July 1945 Liverpool. Quarry Bank High School, Liverpool; Liverpool University, LLB. AAS. M. 28 September 1967. Call 16 July 1970. 5 Essex Court, 1970, pupilmaster, Frederick Reynold. Liverpool Chambers; North House, 17 North John Street, 1970-1972. Pupilmaster, Gerald Crowe. Chambers relocated to Martins Building, Water Street, 1972-1999; merger with Corn Exchange to form 7 Harrington Street, 6.9.1999-2001. Standing Counsel; DTI., 1989-1999; Customs & Excise, 1993-1999; Inland Revenue, 1997-1999. Recorder, 1989-2001. Elected Member, Bar Council, 1995-2001. Circuit Judge, 22.5.2001. Liason Judge, St Helens Magistrates, 2005-. WW.

BOURCHIER, Amaury Robert MacNamara
Born 1850. Only son of James McNamara Bourchier of Rathglass, Galway. Christ Church, Oxford, MA. AAS. 24 January 1876. Call 9 June 1880. 1 St James's Square, Manchester, 1883. Equity draftsman and conveyancer. Assistant Registrar, Lancs. Chancery Court, 1884-1916. Not in 1917 Law List.

BOURKE, Southwell George Theobald
Born 1852. Eldest son of Richard Bourke of Dublin, barrister. AAS. M. 7 January 1885 (whilst Lt. in Royal Navy). Call 17 November 1887. ETC. 20 February 1888. Prop. French QC. Sec. Walton. 12 Kings Bench Walk, 1890. In British Guiana, 1891-1938. Not in 1939 Law List.

BOWCOCK, Samantha Jane
Born 29 November 1967 Manchester. St Peter's High School, Prestwich; Holy Cross College, Bury; Manchester University, LLB. M. 16 October 1990. ETC. February 1991. Prop. JJ Rowe QC. Sec. Stephen Dodds. 15 Winckley Square, Preston, 1.8.1990.

BOWDLER, Richard Hope
BCL.,MA. I. 26 January 1925. ETC. 15 July 1925. Prop. Singleton KC. Sec. Graham. 3 Temple Gardens, 1928-1934. No address, 1935-1944. Not in 1945 Law List.

BOWER, Alastair Ross
Born 2 December 1963 Bradford. Ermysteds Grammar School, Skipton; Leeds University, LLB. I. July 1986. ETC. 1987. Prop. Jack Price QC. Sec. Keith Thomas. 14 Winckley Square, Preston, 1987-1991; 5 John Dalton Street, Manchester, 1991-1995; Barrister & Solicitor, New Zealand High Court, 1995-1997; Forbes & Partners, Solicitors, Blackburn, 1998-2000; 8 King Street, Manchester, 2000.

BOWETT, Professor Derek William CBE., QC
Born 20 April 1927. William Hulme School, Manchester; Downing College, Cambridge, MA., LLB., LLD; PhD (Manchester). Academic Lawyer. AAS. M. 29 June 1950. Call 24 November 1953. Re admitted M. 9 May 1974 as Honorary Master of the Bench. 4 Chapel Walks, 1956-1963. 3 Essex Court, 1965-1990. Lecturer in Law,

Manchester University, 1951-1959; Cambridge University, 1960-1976; Reader, 1976-1981; Fellow Queens College, 1960-1969, President, 1969-1982. Whewell Professor of International Law, Cambridge, 1981-1991. Professorial Fellow of Queens College, 1982-1991 (Hon Fellow 1991). CBE 1983. Silk 1978. Publications:- 7 Books on International Law. WW.

BOWLER, Christopher Fairfax
LLB, Liverpool. G. July 1978. ETC. 30 November 1978. Sec. Colin Cunningham. Room 22, 15 Victoria Street, Liverpool, 1978-1981 since which time he has been a clerk in the magistrates courts and presently Justices Clerk at Bury St Edmunds.

BOWLEY, Ivan Richard
Born 12 May 1964, Rustington, Sussex. Shebbear College; Newcastle-upon-Tyne University, BSc. Central London Polytechnic, Dip Law. M. November 1990. ETC. April 1992. Pupilmaster, Neil Block (Temple) 3 Pump Court, 1990-1992. Manchester Chambers; Rational House, 64 Bridge Street, 1992-1995 relocated to Lincoln House Chambers, 1 Brazennose Street, 1996.

BOWMAN, Sir (Edwin) Geoffrey. KCB
Born 27 January 1946, Blackpool. Roundhay School; Trinity College, Cambridge, Senior Scholar, MA., LLM. L. November 1968. 14 Cook Street, Liverpool, Chancery Bar, 1969-1971. Parliamentary Counsel Office, 1971. Deputy, 1981-1984. Parliamentary Counsel, 1984. Seconded to Law Commission, 1996. First Parliamentary Counsel, 2002. CB 1991. KCB, 2004. Publication:- Elements of Conveyancing (with E L G Tyler qv) WW.

BOYD, James Andrew Donaldson
Born 16 December 1969 Cardiff. Leeds Grammar School; Manchester University, LLB; University of Indiana, LLM. I. November 1994. ETC. 13 December 1994. Prop. Clegg QC. Sec. P J Holmes. 8 King Street, Manchester, 1994. Part time lecturer in Law at Manchester Metropolitan University.

BOYD, (Philip) Joseph (George)
Born 2 July 1953 Belfast. Loretto School, Musselburgh; St John's College, Cambridge, MA. G. November 1993. ETC. 7 December 1993. Prop. Hussain QC. Sec. P P Curran. Lincoln House Chambers, 1 Brazennose Street, Manchester, 1993. Formerly solicitor in Bristol. Lecturer College of Law in Chester. CPS Manchester-Branch Crown Prosecutor, Rochdale & Bury, 1981-1993.

BOYDELL, (The Worshipful Chancellor) Peter Thomas Sherrington QC
Born 20 September 1920. Died 23 February 2001 aged 80. Arnold School Blackpool; Manchester University, LLB, 1940. Served in Royal Artillery in various Divisions – finally Brigade Major, 10th Indian Division in Italy. Admitted as a solicitor, 1947. AAS M. 25 January 1946. Call 26 January 1948; Bencher 1970; Treasurer 1989. 4 Paper Buildings, 1948-1952. Joined South Eastern Circuit, 1950. 2 Harcourt Buildings, 1953-1997. Leader of Parliamentary Bar, 1975. Chancellor of Dioceses of Truro, 1957.; Oxford, 1958.; Worcester, 1959. Silk 1965. Member, Legal Board of Church Assembly. 1958-1971. Contested Carlisle (C). 1964. WW. Times Obituary. 7 March 2001.

BOYLE, David Stuart
Born 5 November 1971 Manchester. Manchester Grammar School; Churchill College, Cambridge. MA. G. March 1996. ETC. 2 April 1996. Prop. Goddard QC. Sec. Craig Sephton. Deans Court Manchester Chambers at Cumberland House, Crown Square. 1996-1999 and at 24 St John Street. 4.5.1999.

BOYLE, Karen
Born 20 May 1978 Glasgow. Huntcliffe Comprehensive; John Leggott 6th form College; Warwick University. LLB. L. July 2000. ETC. 12 December 2001. Prop. Alan Conrad QC. Sec. Hugh Davies. Lincoln House Chambers, 1 Brazennose Street, Manchester. 2000.

BRABIN. Daniel James QC (The Hon Mr Justice Brabin)
Born 14 August 1913. Died 22 September 1975 aged 62. Douai School; Trinity Hall, Cambridge, BA., LLM. I. 27 January 1936. ETC. 2 February 1938. Prop. Lynskey KC. Sec. Hartley Shawcross. Liverpool Chambers; 32 Castle Street, Liverpool, 1937-1939; 34 Castle Street, 1939-1951. Served in Royal Artillery in 1939-1945 War. MC 1945. Silk 1951. Recorder of Bolton, 1953-1962. Judge of Appeal, Isle of Man, 1960-1962. High Court Judge, QBD, 1962-1975. Kt 1962. In 1965 conducted the Inquiry into the cases of Christie & Evans (murders at 10 Rillington Place) His report is in the Circuit Records. WW. & see biographical sketch of 'Danny' Brabin by His Honour Richard Pickering in 'A Century of Liverpool Lawyers'.

BRACEWELL, Joyanne (Winifred). (The Hon. Mrs Justice Bracewell DBE)
Born 5 July 1934. Manchester University, LLB., LLM. G. November 1955. ETC. 1956. Pupilmaster, Godfrey Heilpern. Manchester Chambers; 60 King Street, 1955-1960; 47 Peter Street, 1961-1974; 12th floor, Sunlight House, Quay Street, 1975-1979; 28 St John Street, 1980-1983. Recorder, 1975-1983. Circuit Judge, 1983-1990. High Court Judge, Family Division, 1990. DBE 1990. Family Liason Judge, London, 1990-1997. Hon LLD, Manchester 1991. Consulting Editor; Butterworths Family Law Service, 1989-; Family Practice, 1993. FRSA 1994. WW.

BRADBURN, John Maddock
Born 1861. Eldest son John Bradburn of Brierfield House, Little Sutton. Formerly a solicitor. AAS. M. 29 September 1893. Call 17 November 1893. ETC. 14 March 1894. Prop. Bigham QC. Sec. McConnell. 2 Pump Court, 1897. No address, 1898-1949. Not in 1950 Law List.

BRADBURY, James Kinder (His Honour Judge Bradbury)
Born 5 November 1847. Died in France 1 February 1913 aged 65. 2nd son of George Thomas Bradbury of Liverpool. Liverpool College; Caius College, Cambridge, MA & Fellow. AAS I. 24 April 1872. Call 26 January 1865. ETC. 16 March 1875. Prop. Torr QC. Sec. Smyly. 9 St James's Square, Manchester, 1875-1900. County Court Judge, (Circuit 5), March 1900-1913. Foster.

BRADBURY, Sara Patricia
Born 12 January 1948 Monton, Eccles. Wardley Grammar School, Swinton; Director of own business, 1988-1996. Manchester Metropolitan University, LLB, 1997. G. October 1998. ETC. November 2000. Prop. Keith Armitage QC. Sec. Andrew Clark. Pupilmaster, Glyn Williams. 15, Winckley Square, Preston, 2000; 8 King Street, Manchester, 2000-2001; New Bailey Chambers, 9-11 Ormskirk Rd, Preston, 2001.

BRADLEY, Francis Ernest (His Honour Judge Bradley)
Born 16 April 1862. Died 3 September 1933 aged 71. Manchester Grammar School; Manchester University (MA., MCom., LLB.) London University, LLD. Started a scientific career following in father's footsteps but switched to Law. Studentship in Bar Finals. Barstow & Arden Scholar. G. 28 January 1889. ETC. 6 March 1889. Prop. Henn Collins QC. Sec. C A Russell. 2 Harcourt Buildings, 1889. Manchester Chambers; 2 St James's Square, 1890-1914; Bank of England Chambers, Tib Lane, 1915-1921. Practised in the Lancs. Chancery Court. Law Lecturer, Liverpool University, 1892-1893. Law Tutor, Owens College, Manchester University, 1892-1899. Examiner, Council of Legal Education. County Court Judge, Circuit 4 (North West Lancs.), October 1921-1933. Publications:- 4 books on Company Law. WW.

BRADLEY, Frederic Charles
Born 1849. Only son of Charles Rathbone Bradley of Greenbank, Manchester. Christ's College, Cambridge, MA 1873. AAS. I. 23 April 1870. Call 7 June 1873. ETC. 2 August 1873. Prop. Edwards. Sec. Gouldthorp. 1 Harcourt Buildings, 1876-1885. Special pleader. South Lancs. Sessions. No address, 1886-1935. Not in 1936 Law List. Foster.

BRADLEY, John
Born 1815. Only son of Robert Bradley of Kirkby Lonsdale. AAS. 13 November 1847. Call 22 November 1850. 5 Brick Court, 1876-1881. 1 New Court, 1882-1898. Special pleader & conveyancer. Lancs. & Westmorland Sessions. Not in 1899 Law List. Foster

BRADLEY, Lionel James Herbert
G. 28 January 1924. ETC. 21 June 1924. Prop. Ross Brown KC. Sec. Jalland. Bank of England Chambers, Tib Lane, Manchester, 1924-1928. No address, 1929-1953. Not in 1954 Law List.

BRADLEY, Nigel Frank
Sheffield University, LLB. L. July 1981. 196 Deansgate, Manchester, 1981-1987. Commercial Lawyer, Costain Petrocarbon, Manchester, 1988-1989. Senior Legal Advisor, Kellogg & Co, Manchester, 1990-1991. Divisional Secretary later Legal Division of British Aerospace Defence Ltd, near Preston, 1993.

BRADLEY, Richard
Born 22 September 1955 Southport. King George V Grammar School, Southport; Reading University, LLB. AAS. M. 6 November 1975. Call July 1978. ETC. February 1980. Prop. Eric Somerset Jones QC. Sec. John Stannard. Oriel Chambers, Covent Garden/14 Water Street, Liverpool, January 1980.

BRADSHAW, BartIe
L. 24 April 1907. Son of Mr & Mrs R B D Bradshaw of Barrow-in-Furness. ETC. 11 March 1909. Prop. Tobin KC. Sec. Leslie Scott. Circuit Junior 1909. 1 Pump Court, 1909-1914. Carlisle, Kendal, Lancaster & Preston Sessions. He enlisted as a private in the Middlesex Regiment and on 6 March 1915 was commissioned 2nd Lt in the Border Regiment. He was killed in action on the 11 June 1915 in the Dardenelles aged 33. He is

buried in Twelve Tree Copse Cemetery, Turkey. Grave Reference/Panel Number X1.D.21. The Cemetery is in the Helles area about 1 km south west of the village of Krithia. Details from the Public Record Office and the Commonwealth War Graves Commission.

BRADSHAW, Francis Thomas
Born 1862. Eldest son of Sandys Yuyr Burges Bradshaw of South Shore Vicarage, Lancs., Clerk in Holy Orders. Wadham College, Oxford. AAS. M. 23 November 1883. Call 22 June 1887. ETC. 5 February 1888. Prop. Gully QC. Sec. Yates. Preston Chambers; 33 Guildhall Street, 1890-1891; 2 Chapel Street, 1892-1896. Manchester Chambers; Temple Chambers, Brazennose Street, 1894-1896; 78 King Street, 1897-1916. No address, 1917-1940. Not in 1941 Law List.

BRADSHAW, Howard Sydney
Born 30 March 1953 Urmston, Manchester. William Hulmes Grammar School, Manchester; Queens College, Cambridge, MA. AAS. M. 29 April 1975. Call July 1977. Manchester Chambers; 43 King Street, 1980-1988; Queens Chambers, 5 John Dalton Street, 1989.

BRADSHAWE, George Paris
Born 9 July 1853. Only son of late Major-General George Paris Bradshawe. Eton; Christ Church, Oxford, MA. AAS. M. 15 April 1872. Call 26 January 1881. ETC. 23 January 1882. Prop. Russell QC. Sec. Blair. 1 Mitre Court Buildings, 1883-1889. Not in 1890 Law List. Foster.

BRADY, Michael Antony
Born 24 January 1966 Folkstone, Kent. Prior Park School; Manchester Polytechnic, LLB. G. October 1992. ETC. October 1993. Prop. Rod Carus QC. Sec Beverly Lunt. Kingsgate Chambers, 51-53 South King Street, Manchester, 1993.

BRAITHWAITE, William Thomas Scatchard QC
Born 20 January 1948 Liverpool. Gordonstoun School; Liverpool University, LLB. G. November 1970. ETC 1970. Pupilmaster, John Arthur. Same Liverpool Chambers; 606 The Corn Exchange, Fenwick Street, 1970-1982; 1 Exchange Flags, 1983-1991; Exchange Chambers, Pearl Assurance House, Derby Square, 1992. Consultant Editor, Kemp & Kemp- Quantum of Damages, 1994. Brain & Spinal Injuries – The Fight for Justice, 2001. Joint Editor, Medical Aspects of Personal Injury Litigation, 1997. Assistant Recorder 1990-1993. Silk 1992. Recorder 1993-1999. Bill Braithwaite decided not to continue as a Recorder wishing to concentrate fully on his claimants' brain & spinal injury practice. WW.

BRAITHWAITE-WILSON, Christopher Wilson
Born 25 February 1853. 2nd son of Garnett Braithwaite, late of Heversham, Westmorland. AAS. I. 16 November 1863. Call 18 November 1867. ETC. 29 July 1868. Prop. Pickering QC. Sec. Jones QC. No address, 1876-1916. Not in 1917 Law List. JP., Westmorland. Major, 4th Battalion Border Regiment, 1883. Foster

BRANCH, Charles Churchill
I. 22 April 1891. ETC. 20 July 1891. Prop. Smyly QC. Sec. Shee. Circuit Junior, 1892. 3 Temple Gardens, 1892-1894. No address, 1895-1930. Not in 1931 Law List.

BRANDON, Helen Elizabeth
Born 23 December 1970 Bebington. Birkenhead High School; Lancaster University (Furness College), LLB. M. October 1993. ETC. 21 December 1993. Prop. Eric Somerset Jones QC. Sec. Richard Bradley. Oriel Chambers, 5 Covent Garden/14 Water Street, Liverpool, 1993.

BRANDRETH, Benjamin
I. 18 November 1907. ETC. 4 March 1908. Prop. Taylor KC. Sec. Layton. Liverpool Chambers; 11 Harrington Street, 1907-1909; 8 Harrington Street, 1910-1918; 2 Harcourt Buildings, 1919-1921. Not in 1922 Law List.

BRANSON, Rt. Hon. George Arthur Harwin (Mr Justice Branson)
Born 11 July 1871 Great Yarmouth. Died 23 April 1951 aged 79. Eldest son of James Branson, Barrister. Bedford School; Trinity College, Cambridge, BA, 1893. Bow of University Boat, 1893. Articled to Markby, Stewart & Co, London, Solicitors, 1894. I. 26 April 1899. ETC. 16 February 1901. Prop. Isaacs QC. Sec. Sanderson. 1 Garden Court, 1901-1906; 2 Garden Court, 1907-1913; 5 Essex Court, 1914-1921. Junior Counsel to the Treasury, 1912-1921. High Court Judge, KBD, 1921-1939. Kt. 1921. PC. 1940. Publication:- Schwabe & Branson on the Law of the Stock Exchange. His son Edward was appointed a metropolitan magistrate in 1971. WW.

BRANT, Paul David
Born 28 October 1969 London. Trinity School; Liverpool University, LLB. L. October 1993. ETC. 21 December 1993. Prop. Eric Somerset Jones QC. Sec. Ashley Murray. Oriel Chambers, Covent Garden/14 Water Street, Liverpool, 1993. Liverpool City Councillor.

BRASLAVSKY, Nicholas Justin QC
Born 9 February 1959 Blackpool. Blackpool Grammar School; High Pavement Grammar School, Nottingham; Birmingham University, LLB., MJur., PhD. I. July 1983. ETC. December 1983. Prop. Christopher Rose QC. Sec. Roger Farley. Pupilmasters, Andrew Gilbart & Roger Farley. Manchester Chambers; 460 Royal Exchange, 1983-1987; chambers move to 40 King Street, 1987. Silk 1999. Recorder 2000. WW.

BRASSEY-EDWARDS, Stanley
G. 19 November 1923. ETC. 30 January 1924. Prop. Kennedy KC. Sec. Rimmer. No address in Law List, 1924-1953 but in Liverpool Prosecutions Book addresses given are:-10 Cook Street & Farrars Buildings. Not in 1954 Law List.

BREACH, Sarah Louise
Sheffield University, LLB. G. July 1969. Manchester Chambers; Central Street Chambers, 1 Central Street, 1985-1987; 33 King Street West, 1988-1994; Old Colony House, 6 South King Street, 1995-1996. Not in 1997 Bar Directory.

BREEN, Carlo Enrico
Born 21 April 1966 Rome. Essex University, LLB; MA Queensland. Queensland Bar, 1991. AAS. M 26 July 1986. Call 24 November 1987. Manchester Chambers; Crown Square Chambers, 1 Deans Court, 1988-1993; chambers move to 9 St John Street, 1994.

BREHENY, Mark Patrick
Born 5 October 1961 Dublin. University of Kent, BA. L. 1986. Liverpool Chambers; 1st floor, Peel House, Harrington Street, 1989-1994; Ground floor, 1995-1999; Oriel Chambers, 14 Water Street, 1.3.1999-2001; 22 Nicholas Street, Chester, 2001. (Wales & Chester Circuit)

BREMNER, Henry Hodgson

Born 4 May 1842. 2nd son of Henry Bremner of Liverpool, attorney. Matriculated London University; Clare College, Cambridge, BA 1867. AAS. I. 28 January 1867. Call 17 November 1869. ETC. 24 March 1870. Prop. Leofric Temple. Sec. Gainsford Bruce. 15 Lord Street, Liverpool, 1876-1884. Deputy Registrar, Liverpool Court of Passage, 1.10.1884-1887; Registrar, 1887-1890. Foster.

BRENNAN, Daniel Joseph QC (Baron Brennan of Bilbury in the County of Gloucester)
Born 19 March 1942. St Bede's Grammar School, Bradford; Manchester University, LLB. G. July 1967; Bencher 1993. ETC. 2 May 1968. Manchester Chambers; 2 Booth Street, 1968-1973; 4th floor, Astley House, Quay Street, 1974-1977; 18 St John Street, 1978. London Chambers; 5 Essex Court; 39 Essex Street; Matrix Chambers. Recorder 1982. Silk 1985. Kings Inns, Dublin 1990. Member, Criminal Injuries Compensation Board, 1989-1997. Chairman of Bar Council, 1999. Hon. LLD; Nottingham Trent 1999; Manchester 2000. Publications: Provisional Damages, 1986; Contrib. to Bullen & Leake – Precedents of Pleadings; General Editor, Personal Injury Manual, 1997. Baron, 2000. WW.

BRENNAN, Elizabeth Gail
Born 17 November 1974 Clatterbridge, Wirral. Wirral County Grammar School for Girls; Newcastle University, LLB. L. 26 November 1998. ETC. December 1998. Prop. Nigel Gilmour QC. Sec. Barnes. Pupilmaster Nigel Beeson. 2nd floor, 14 Cook Street, Liverpool, 1998-2002; 7 Harrington Street, Liverpool, 2003.

BRENNAN, Patrick James
Born 1900. 4th son of Joseph Brennan, HM Inspector of Taxes. University College, London, LLB. London School of Economics, BSc(Econ). AAS. M. 22 April 1947. Call 29 June 1949. ETC. 5 July 1951. Prop. Laski KC. Sec. Curtis. Irish Bar 1953. 11 New Court, 1950-1951; 3 Temple Gardens, 1952-1954; 1 Harcourt Building, 1955-1962; 78, King Street, Manchester, 1953-1959; 27 Dale Street, Liverpool, 1960-1962. No address, 1963-1967. Not in 1968 Law List.

BRENNAND, Timothy William
Born 23 January 1964, Kendal. Heversham Grammar School, Milnthorpe; Manchester Polytechnic (now Manchester Metropolitan University), LLB. G. November 1987. ETC. March 1988. Prop. John Burke QC. Sec. John Wishart. Circuit Junior, 1990. Elected Member of Bar Council, 1993-1996. Hon. Sec. of Northern Circuit, 1996-1999. Manchester Chambers; Conavon Chambers, 12 Blackfriars Street, 1987-1989; chambers moved to Manchester House Chambers, 18-22 Bridge Street, 1989-1999; 24a St John Street, 1999-2001; 28 St John Street, 2001. On 23 September 2002 28 St John Street merged with 24a St John Street to form St John's Building Chambers.

BRENT, Michael Leon QC
Born 8 June 1936. Manchester Grammar School; Manchester University LLB. G. May 1961. ETC. 1961. Prop. Watson QC. Sec. Heilpern. Circuit Junior, 1964. Northern Circuit, 1961-1967 (47 Peter Street, Manchester); Midland & Oxford Circuit, 1967-2000. 2 Dr Johnson's Buildings, 1967-1994; 9 Gough Square, 1994. Silk 1983. Recorder, 1990-2000. Deputy High Court Judge, 1994-2000. Member, Criminal Injuries Compensation Appeals Panel, 1999. WW.

BRERETON, Fiorella
Born 21 January 1957 Macclesfield. St Hilary's School, Alderley Edge; North London University, BA (Law). G. November 1979. South Eastern Circuit, 1980-1985. Pupilmaster, John Foy (Temple). Mitre Court Buildings, 1980-1985. ETC. 1985. Peel Court Chambers, 45 Hardman Street, Manchester, 1985. Qualified Family Law Mediator, July 1999.

BRESNAHAN, Jane
Born 24 June 1976 Stockport. Marple Hill School; Marple Ridge 6th Form College; Birmingham University, LLB. G. 23 July 1998. ETC. 14 December 1999. Prop. J J Rowe QC. Sec. Rachel Hamilton-Hague. Pupil Masters, Kim Foudy & Simon Vaughan. 8 King Street, Manchester, 1990.

BRETT, Michael
Born 1871. Eldest son of John Brett, ARA, artist of Putney. AAS. M. 27 January 1891. Call 17 November 1896. ETC. 23 February 1898. Prop. Carver QC. Sec. Llewellyn Davies. 2 Garden Court, 1897-1902. No address, 1903-1943. Not in 1944 Law List.

BRETT, Sir William Baliol QC (First Viscount Esher)
Born 13 August 1815. Died 24 May 1899 aged 83. Westminster School; Caius College, Cambridge, MA. Rowed in University Eight, 1837. AAS. L. 30 April 1839. Call 29 January 1846; Bencher 1860. Silk 1860. MP (C) for Helston, Cornwall, 1866-1868. Solicitor General, 1868. Justice of the Common Pleas, 1868-1875. High Court Judge (Common Pleas Division), 1875-1876. Lord Justice of Appeal, 1876-1883. Master of the Rolls, 1883-1897. Kt 1868. PC 1876. Baron 1885. Viscount 1897. WW. DNB. Foster. Simpson. Foss "English Judges."

BREWER, Peter
July 1952. ETC. 4 February 1954. Prop. Brabin QC. Sec. Rankin. 7 Rumford Street, Liverpool, 1954-1960. Not in 1961 Law List.

BRICE, Seward William KC
Born 1846. Died 18 December 1914 aged 68. University College, London, BA, 1866, MA, 1869, LLB, 1871, LLD, 1873. AAS. I. 28 May 1869. Call 17 November 1871; Bencher 1894. ETC. 26 March 1872. Prop. Pope QC. Sec. Crompton. 7 New Square, 1882-1883; 5 New Court, 1884-1898; 22 Old Buildings, 1899-1907; 14 Old Buildings, 1908-1914. Silk 1886. Practised in South Africa. Publications:- Law of Public Worship, 1876; Law of Patents, Designs & Trade Marks, 1884; Doctrine of Ultra Vires, 1893; Law of Tramways & Light Railways, 1902. WW. Foster.

BRIDGE, Arthur Liddall
L. 27 June 1906. ETC. 24 February 1909. Prop. Langdon KC. Sec. Cockshutt. 5 Pump Court, 1910. No address, 1911-1913. 16 Dalton Chambers, 41 John Dalton Street, Manchester, 1914-1932. Not in 1933 Law List.

BRIDGMAN, Andrew Michael
Born 11 May 1958, South Wales. Newbridge Grammar School; Manchester & Manchester Metropolitan Universities, BDS., LLB., MA. dentist, 1981-1995 & Clinical Lecturer, Manchester University, 1990-2000. G. 1.10.2001. ETC. 12.12.2001. Prop. Peter Birkett QC. Sec. MacNeill. 24a St John Street, Manchester (now St John's Buildings), 11.9.2001.

BRIERLEY, Edgar OBE
Born 1858. Died 25 January 1927, aged 68. 5th son of James Brierley of Rochdale. Rugby School; University College, Oxford, BA. AAS. I. 5 November 1878. Call 3 May 1882. ETC. 15 July 1882. Prop. Gully QC. Sec. Potter QC. 1 Dr Johnson's Buildings, 1883-1884. Manchester Chambers; 2 St James's Square, 18854887; 60 King Street, 1888-1903. Stipendiary Magistrate for the City of Manchester, 1903-1927. Member, Royal Commission on Divorce, 1909-1912. Chairman, Manchester Tribunal, 1915-1918. OBE 1918. WW. Foster

BRIERLEY, Philip Edgar
G. 17 November 1921. ETC. 1 February 1922. Prop. Miller KC. Sec. Pratt. Manchester Chambers: Bank of England Chambers, Tib Lane, 1925-1940; 3 St James's Square, 1941-1948. No address, 1949-1963. Not in 1964 Law List.

BRIGGS, Laura Judith
Born 8 February 1979. Edgbarrow Comprehensive, Crowthorne, Berkshire; Manchester University, LLB. Chair of University Law Society & Member of Debating Society, 1998-1999. Involved in providing legal assistance to US death row prisoners, 1998-2000. I. 27 July 2001. ETC. 12 December 2001. Prop. Jonathan Foster QC. Sec. Yvonne Healing. 18 St John Street, Manchester, 1.10.2001.

BRIGGS, (Peter) John
Born 15 May 1928 London. King's School, Peterborough; Balliol College, Oxford, MA., BCL. I. June 1953. ETC. 4 February 1954. Prop. Brabin QC. Sec. Alan Booth for Edward Steel. Liverpool Chambers; 14 Cook Street, 1954; The Temple, Dale Street, 1955-1956; 27 Dale Street, 1957-1976. Chambers then moved to Melbourne Buildings, 1976-1988 and to 3rd floor, Peel House, Harrington Street, 1988-1998; and finally to India Buildings, Water Street, 1998 until John's retirement in May 2000. Recorder 1978-1998. Legal Member; Mersey Mental Health Review Tribunal, 1969 (Deputy Chairman,1971, Chairman, 1981-1994) North West Mental Health Review Tribunal, 1994-1998. President, Merseyside Medico-Legal Society, 1982-1984. Chairman, Merseyside Opera, 1996. When I mentioned to John that I proposed to start work on this Directory, he was enthusiastic and gave me a great deal of support and information, for which I am very grateful. WW.

BRIGGS, William Edward
I. 19 November 1888. ETC. 28 February 1889. Prop. Hopwood QC. Sec. Smyley. York Chambers, Brazennose Street, Manchester, 1890-1891. No address, 1892-1903. Not in 1904 Law List.

BRINDLE, Elaine
Birmingham University, LLB. ETC. 3 April 1979. Prop. Carman QC. Sec. Duckworth. Office of Chief Prosecuting Solicitor, Chester House, Boyer Street, Manchester, 1980-1985. Not in 1986 Bar List.

BRISCOE, Sir Alfred Leigh Bt.
Born 26 April 1870. Died 13 May 1921 aged 51. Corpus Christi College, Oxford. L. 14 June 1893. ETC. 29 July 1893. Prop. Pickford KC. Sec. Sanderson. 2 Harrington Street, Liverpool, 1893-1921, also at 8 Old Square. JP. succeeded his father, the 1st Bt, in 1919. WW.

⋆ BRISTOWE, Sir Henry Fox QC
Born 8 May 1824. Died 20 February 1893 aged 69. 2nd son of Samuel Ellis Bristowe of Beesthorpe, Newark, Notts. Married 2 April 1850, Selina, daughter of Hon. Orlando Henry Bridgeman. Trinity Hall, Cambridge. AAS. M. 15 April 1842. Call 11 June 1847; Bencher 1870; Autumn Reader 1875; Treasurer 1885. 16 Carey Street, 1848; 21 Old Buildings, 1881-1882; 25 Old Buildings, 1883-1893. Vice Chancellor, County Palatine of Lancaster, 1881-1893. Kt. 1887. Foster.

BRITTAIN, Richard Paul
Born 1 April 1948, Dublin. Died 3 February 2004 aged 55. Liverpool College; Liverpool University, LLB; Keele University, MA; Strasbourg University, Dip. de droit compare. I. November 1971. ETC. 7 December 1972. Prop. Michael Maguire QC. Sec. Collinson. Liverpool Chambers; Oriel Chambers, 14 Water Street, 1972-1980; Melbourne Buildings, 21 North John Street, 1980-1988; chambers moved to 3rd floor, Peel House, Harrington Street, 1989-1998 and then to India Buildings, Water Street, 1998-2001; Derby Square Chambers, Merchants Court, January 2001. Assistant Recorder 1988. Recorder 1992. Special Adjudicator, Asylum Appeals, 1998. Member, Legal Services Commission, 2001. Tributes, Liverpool Law Courts, 10 February 2004. (Judge Henry Globe QC. /David Steer QC. Transcript in Circuit Records.

BROADBENT, Harold
Oxford University, MA. G. 17 November 1920. Manchester Chambers: 44 King Street, 1925-1929; Bank of England Chambers, Tib Lane, 1930-1940; 3 St James's Square, 1941-1963. Not in 1963 Law List.

BROADBRIDGE, Frederick
L. 22 April 1891. ETC. 3 August 1891. Prop. French QC. Sec. Segar. 25 Lord Street, 1891-1898. Lancs. Chancery Court. 1 New Court, Carey Street, 1899-1900; 8 New Court, Carey Street, 1901. Not in 1902 Law List.

BROADHURST, Simon Thomas
Oxford University, BA. I. November 1994. ETC. December 1994. Prop. Rodney Klevan QC. Sec. Paul Dockery. 18 St John Street, Manchester, 1994-2000. In 2001 Bar Directory but no address.

BROADLEY, John
Born 23 June 1951 Oldham. St Ambrose College, Altrincham; Bristol University, LLB. AAS. M. 5 April 1972. Call 19 July 1973. ETC. November 1973. Prop. Benet Hytner QC. Sec. Frank Hudson. Manchester Chambers; 67 Princess Street, 1973-1987; Hollins Chambers, 64a Bridge Street, 1987-1998; Cobden House Chambers, 19 Quay Street, 1998-

BROCHWICZ-LEWINSKI, Stefan Andrew
Born 11 August 1971 Stockport. Stockport Grammar School; Bristol University, LLB; Université de Caen (Euro Demi Licence). G. November ETC. 1 March 1997. Prop. Richard Henriques QC. Sec. David Berkley. Pupilmaster, Shaun Ferris (Temple), 1 Paper Buildings, 1995- Merchant Chambers, 1 North Parade, Parsonage Gardens, Manchester, 1997. Junior Counsel to the Crown (Provincial Panel), 2000.

BROCKBANK, Barbara Anne
LLB. G November 1969. Oriel Chambers 14, Water Street, Liverpool, 1969-1982 when she ceased practice. Married to Roy Ward QC.qv. in 1972. Marriage dissolved.

BROCKLEBANK, Thomas Geoffrey
Born 3 November 1882 at 4 Fulwood Park, Liverpool. Elder son of Harold Brocklebank of Grizedale Hall, Hawkshead. Eton & Trinity College, Oxford. I. 18 November 1907. ETC. 4 February 1908. Prop. Sanderson KC. Sec. Leslie Scott. Circuit Junior, 1908. Goldsmith Building, 1908-1913. Commissioned 2nd Lt. 8th Battery, 7th London Brigade. Promoted Captain, D Battery, 277 (West Lanes) Brigade RFA. Killed in action 5 August 1916, aged 33. Dive Copse British Cemetery, Somme, France. Grave Reference II.E.28. The cemetery is about 1.5 km. north east of Sailly-le-Sec Church which is 20 Kms east of Amiens. Information provided by Public Record Office & Commonwealth War Graves Commission.

BROCKLEHURST, Frederick
MA. L. 6 May 1903. ETC. 14 July 1903. Prop. Pickford KC. Sec. Rycroft. Manchester Chambers; 5 St James's Square, 1903-1908; 33 King Street, 1909-1917; 2 Booth Street, 1918-1926. Chairman, Court of Quarter Sessions for the Salford Hundred of Lancaster, 1923-1926. Not in 1927 Law List.

BRODRICK-SMITH-BRODRICK, Harold Gilbert
G. 26 January 1897. ETC. 4 August 1897. Prop. Taylor QC. Sec. Walter Russell. No Address, 1894-1910. Liverpool Chambers; 25 Lord Street, 1911-1926. No address, 1927-1935. 5 Cook Street, 1936-1939; 8 Cook Street, 1940-1949. Not in 1950 Law List.

BRODY, Karen Rachel
Born 11 August 1964, Stockport. Daughter of Louis Brody, Rochdale, solicitor, sister of Saul Amos Brody qv. Bury Grammar School, 1974-1982; Nottingham University, LLB, 1982-1985; Inns of Court School of Law, 1985-1986. Research Assistant, Law Commission (Family Law Team) 1986-1987. G. November 1986. ETC. 1987. Prop. Keith Goddard QC. Sec. Diana Eaglestone. Deans Court Chambers, Crown Square, Manchester, 1987-4.5.1999 when chambers moved to 24 St John Street. Recorder.

BRODY, Saul Amos
Born 18 January 1966, Manchester. Son of Louis Brody, Rochdale, solicitor. Brother of Karen Rachel Brody qv. Bury Grammar School; Leeds University, LLB. I. October 1996. ETC. 1996. Pupilmaster, Raymond Wigglesworth. 18 St John Street, Manchester, 1996.

BROGAN, Michael Shaun
Born 26 May 1967, Andover, Hants. Whitley High School, Wigan; Huddersfield Polytechnic, LLB. I. October 1990. ETC. 17 December 1992. Prop. David Poole QC. Sec. John Wishart. 8 Kings Bench Walk, 1990-1992. Pupilmaster, Alan Williams. Manchester House Chambers, 18-22 Bridge Street, Manchester, 1992-1999; 25-27 Castle Street, Liverpool, 1999.

BROMLEY, Edward
Born 1 March 1831. Youngest son of Sir Robert Howe Bromley Bt. of Stoke Hall, Notts. Merton College, Oxford, BA. I. 17 November 1866. 1 Paper Buildings, 1876. Clerk of Assize of the Northern Circuit, 1872-76. When the "old" Northern Circuit divided in 1876. Bromley went off to clerk the "new" North Eastern Circuit until 1900 and was replaced here by Thomas Moss Shuttleworth. Bromley's last Law List entry is 1908.

BROMLEY, Professor Peter Mann
Born 20 November 1922. Ealing Grammar School; The Queen's College, Oxford, MA, 1948. Academic. Moving from Assistant Law Lecturer in 1947 to Professor of English Law at Manchester University, 1985-1986. Editor of Butterworths Family Law Service, 1983-1996. Textbook; Bromley's Family Law. M. 1951. Pupilmaster, Desmond Franks. 601 Royal Exchange, Manchester, 1976-1982. On the 18 July 2001 at Manchester University, Lady Justice Hale gave a lecture in honour of Professor Bromley. WW.

BROMLEY-DAVENPORT, John QC
Born 13 March 1947 Singapore. Eton; London Academy of Music & Dramatic Arts; College of Law, London. Articled to Peat, Marwick, Chartered Accountants, 1968-1969. G. February 1972. ETC. 1972. Pupilmaster, Norman Lees. Manchester Chambers; Albert Square, 1972; Deans Court Chambers, Crown Square, 1972-1999; 24 St John Street 1999. (same Chambers- different addresses) Assistant Recorder 1989. Recorder 1992. Silk 2002.

BROOKE, Thomas
AAS. M. 14 January 1851. Call 17 November 1853. Eldest son of Samuel Brooke of Druisdale, Isle of Man. 6 Pump Court, 1876-1877. Not in 1878 Law List.

BROUN, James
Only son of Neil Broun of Greenock, Scotland. AAS. M. 2 November 1844. Call 19 November 1847. 4 Kings Bench Walk, 1848. Special pleader, Liverpool Sessions. No address, 1876-1915. Not in 1916 Law List. NB. The anglicized "Brown" appears in the Middle Temple Admissions Register. Foster.

BROWN, Alexander Theodore
L. 18 November 1918. Liverpool Chambers; 25 Lord Street, 1919-1930; 5 Cook Street, 1931-1939; 8 Cook Street, 1940-1941. No address, 1942-1944. Not in 1945 Law List.

BROWN, (Andrew) Charles
Born 29 February 1956 Radcliffe, Lancs. Bury Grammar School; University College, London, BSc(Zoology), 1974-1977. Westminster University, Dip Law. G. November 1982. ETC. 1983. Prop. John Hugill QC. Sec. Robert Brown. Manchester Chambers: 2 Old Bank Street, 1983-1985; Old Colony House, 1985-1995; Queens Chambers, 5 John Dalton Street, 1995-2002; 15 Winckley Square, Preston.

BROWN, Anne Margaret
Born 1977 Newcastle upon Tyne. Christleton High School, Chester; St Hilda's College, Oxford, BA. M. 27 July 2001. ETC. 18 December 2001. Prop. Peter Birkett QC. Sec. Geoffrey Lowe. India Buildings, Water Street, Liverpool, 2001.

BROWN, Archibald
Born 8 May 1881. Eldest son of James Brown of Galashiels, Scotland, factory manager. Christ Church, Oxford, MA., BCL; Edinburgh University, MA. AAS. M. 2 January 1868. Call 17 November 1870. Certificate of Honour, 1870. ETC. 7 August 1875. Prop, Russell QC. Sec. Hardy. 89 Chancery Lane, 1876-1881. Lancs. Chancery Court. 8 New Square, 1882-1901; 3 Stone Buildings, 1902-1916. Not in 1917 Law List. Editor, Snells Principles of Equity 7th edition and books on Mines, Copyholds & Boundaries. Foster.

BROWN, Catherine Joanne
Born 15 December 1972 Manchester. St Monica's RC High School; Loreto VI Form College; Leeds University, BA (Russian & Spanish) I. 25 November 1999. ETC. 14 December 1999. Prop. David Stockdale QC. Sec. Harold Halliday. Pupilmasters, Harold Halliday & Lucy Powis. Kings Chambers, 40 King Street, Manchester, 1999.

BROWN, Charles Metcalfe
G. 26 January 1934. MD., DPH. Medical Officer for Health, Manchester. He led the campaign to have fluoride put in drinking water and was instrumental in alleviating air pollution in Manchester. G. 26 January 1934. ETC. 2 May 1968. Pupilmaster, J Stewart Oakes. 47 Peter Street, Manchester, 1968-1974. Non practising, 1975-1987. Not in 1988 Law List.

BROWN, Claude Anstice
MA(Oxon); LLB(New Zealand) I. 17 November 1920. ETC. 31 January 1923. Prop. Miller KC. Sec. Thorpe. 3 Dr Johnson's Buildings, 1923-1934. No address, 1935-1953. Not in 1954 Law List.

BROWN, Douglas Dunlop QC (The Hon. Mr Justice Douglas Brown)

(DL)

Born 22 December 1931 Manchester. Ryleys School, Alderley Edge; Manchester Grammar School; Manchester University, LLB. Royal Navy, 1953-1955. Lieut., Royal Naval Reserve. G. November 1953. ETC. March 1956. Prop. Fenton Atkinson QC. Pupilmaster, C N Glidewell. Circuit Junior, 1958. Circuit Secretary, 1966-1970. Manchester Chambers (same chambers at different addresses) 28 Kennedy Street, 1955-1957;
25 Bow Lane, 1957-1976; 460 Royal Exchange (now Kings Chambers 40 King Street), 1976-1980. London Chambers; 5 Essex Court and later 2 Pump Court.

Member, General Council of the Bar, 1967-1971. Assistant Recorder, Salford City Quarter Sessions, 1971. Crown Court Recorder, 1972-1980. Silk 1976. Circuit Judge, 1980-1988. Member, Parole Board, 1985-1987. High Court Judge (Family Division), 1989-1996; (Queen's Bench Division), 1996-2005. Bencher & Kt. 1989. Northern Circuit Family Liason Judge, 1990-1995. Presiding Judge, Northern Circuit, 1998-2001. WW.

BROWN, His Honour Harold

Born 18 June 1895. Died 26 January 1969 aged 73. Father of Roger Brown, one time senior partner of Bremner, Sons & Corlett, solicitors of Liverpool. Liverpool University, LLB; Merton College, Oxford, MA. Served in France & Belgium, 1915-1919. G. 26 January 1921. Bacon, Holt & Arden Scholar. ETC. 15 June 1921. Prop. Greaves-Lord QC. Sec. Sellers. Chancery Practitioner. Liverpool Chambers; 9 Cook Street, 1921-1946; 20 Hackins Hey, 1946-1952. Lecturer & Tutor in Law at Liverpool University, 1926-1938. Served 1939-1945 War in Royal Artillery & in Army Legal Service reaching rank of Lt. Col., County Court Judge, (Circuit 6, Liverpool), 1952-1963. West Kirby man. WW.

BROWN, (Laurence) (Frederick) Mark. (His Honour Judge Mark Brown).

Born 16 March 1953 Preston. Son of Rt. Rev. Ronald Brown (Bishop Suffragan of Birkenhead, 1974-1992). Bolton School; St John's College, Durham University, BA (Law & Economics) I. July 1975. London pupillage; Joe Harper (2 Paper Buildings) & Alistair Hill (5 Essex Court). ETC. February 1977. Prop. Benet Hytner QC. Sec. Ann Ebsworth. Liverpool Chambers; 3rd floor, 27 Dale Street, 1977-1989; relocating to Corn Exchange, 1989-1999 and then merging with Martins Bank to form 7 Harrington Street, 6.9.1999-2000. Assistant Recorder, 1993-1997. Recorder, 1997-2000. Assistant Boundary Commissioner, 2000. Member, Disciplinary Tribunal of the Council of the Inns of Court, 1994-2000. Circuit Judge, 2000. Member, Parole Board, 2003. WW.

BROWN, Linda JP

Born 26 July 1945. LLB (London), ACIArb. AAS. M 13 October 1982. Call 22 November 1983. Liverpool Chambers; Scottish Life House, 2nd floor, 10 James Street, 1983-1988; Westminster Chambers, 3 Crosshall Street, 1988.

BROWN, Mandy Joanne

Born 17 April 1963. Lancaster University, LLB. AAS. M. 24 August 1984. Call 10 February 1987. 18 St John Street, Manchester, 1988-1999. Wansbroughs, Willey, Hargrave, Solicitors, 13 Police Street, Manchester, 2000.

BROWN, Matthew James

LLB. Call M. 1994. Lloyds House Chambers, 18 Lloyd Street, Manchester, 1995-1998.

BROWN, Nicola Helen

Born 25 October 1974 Bellshill, Scotland. Married to Mark Stephen Ford qv. Loreto Grammar School; Leeds University, LLB; Manchester University, LLM. M. July 1998. ETC. December 1998. Prop. Rodney Scholes QC. Sec. Christopher Limb. Young Street Chambers, Manchester, 1998.

*** BROWN, Hon. Sir Ralph Kilner**

Born 28 August 1909. Died 15 June 2003 aged 93. Trinity Hall, Cambridge, MA. Call M. 26 January 1934; Bencher 1964; Reader 1982. Midland Circuiteer. Distinguished war record (planning operations) 1939-1946. Brigadier. OBE (Mil). Silk 1958. Recorder of Lincoln & Birmingham. Judge of the Central Criminal Court, 1965-1967. Recorder of Liverpool, 1967-1969. High Court Judge, Queen's Bench Division, 1970-1984. Presiding Judge, Northern Circuit, 1970-1975. Member of Northern Circuit, 1975. Judge of the Employment Appeal Tribunal, 1976-1984. Represented Cambridge & Great Britain in athletics. British AAA Champion, 440yards hurdles, 1934. Publications; The Office of Reader in the Middle Temple, 1982; Top Brass & No Brass, 1991.1 have obtained copies of both for the Circuit records. Top Brass is a fascinating and, as one would expect, impartial account by one who was there of the involvement of Churchill, Eisenhower, Montgomery, Patton and many others in the invasion of mainland Europe and the defeat of Nazi Germany. WW. Times Obituary (David Lynch).

*** BROWN, His Honour Reginald KC**

Born 1846. Died 18 September 1936 aged 90. 2nd son of Joseph Brown QC of London. AAS. M. 13 June 1865. Call 30 April 1870. Silk 1898. Practised from Lamb Building. County Court Judge (Circuit 9, Stockport & Ashton-under-Lyne), June 1901-1919. WW.

BROWN, Robert (His Honour Judge Robert Brown)

Born 21 June 1943. Arnold School, Blackpool; Downing College, Cambridge, BA., LLB. I. July 1968. ETC. July 1968. Pupilmaster, T P Russell. Manchester Chambers; Ship Canal House, King Street, 1968-1980; 2 Old Bank Street, 1981-1988. Recorder, 1983-1988. Circuit Judge, 1988. WW.

BROWN, Roger Charles Arthur
Born 4 May 1951 Lydney, Glos. Sir William Borlase School; Leeds University, LLB. EMI, Hayes, 1974-1976. I. November 1976. ETC. 26 October 1978. Pupilmaster, Phillip Valance. Manchester Chambers; 1 Central Street, 1983-1987; 33 King Street West, 1988-1994; Old Colony House, 6 South King Street, 1995-2001;Young Street Chambers, 28.6.2001.

BROWN, Roger William
Born 10 September 1951. Lancaster Royal Grammar School; Manchester University, LLB. AAS. M. 13 May 1974. Call 25 November 1975. 4th floor, Sunlight House, Quay Street, Manchester, 1978-1983. Not in Bar Directory, 1984-1993. Deputy Clerk to the Justices, Bishopgate, Norwich 1994. Head of Legal Services, Norwich Magistrates Court, 1997.

BROWN, William Frederick Wyndham
Born 1884, 1 Pengwern Terrace, New Brighton. Only son of William Henry Brown of Fairfield, Liverpool. AAS. M. 8 June 1910. ETC. 16 April 1913. Prop. Swift KC. Sec. Kennedy. 25 Lord Street, Liverpool, 1913-1923. No address, 1924-1953. Not in 1954 Law List.

BROWN-WESTHEAD, George Montague
Born February 1881. Only son of Marcus Brown-Westhead of Altrincham. Trinity College, Cambridge, LLB, 1881. AAS. I. 26 January 1881. Call 26 January 1884. ETC. 18 July 1884. Prop. Ambrose QC. Sec. J H Hamilton. 40 South King Street, Manchester, 1886-1894. No address, 1895-1937. Not in 1938 Law List.

BROWNE, Professor Denis.
Born 25 December 1903. Died 8 May 1965 aged 61. Winchester; New College, Oxford, MA. L. 2 May 1928. 9 Old Square, 1928-1935; 4 Stone Buildings, 1936-1940; 14 Cook Street, Liverpool, 1956-1965. Professor of Law, 1936-1955; Pro Chancellor, 1950-1954: Sheffield University; Queen Victoria Professor of Law, Liverpool University, 1955-1965. Publication; (with author), McGillivray on Insurance, (1937 & 1947 eds).

BROWNE, John Henry Valentine
Born 1844. Eldest son of Henry Browne of Banner, Ardfleet, Kerry. Trinity College, Dublin, BA. AAS. M. 6 June 1871. Irish Bar, Hilary 1874. Call M. 17 November 1875. ETC. 13 March 1876. Prop. Russell QC. Sec. Smyly. 42 John Dalton Street, Manchester, 1876-1878; 4 Brick Court, 1879; Selbourne Chambers, Chancery Lane, 1880-1882. No address 1881-1920. Not in 1921 Law List. Foster.

BROWNE, Louis Bartholomew Anthony
Born 9 August 1963 Birkenhead. St Hugh's College, Birkenhead; St Anselm's College, Birkenhead; Liverpool Polytechnic, LLB; Balliol College, Oxford, BCL. L. November 1988. London pupillage. ETC. November 1992. Prop. David Harris QC. Sec. Michael Wolff. Liverpool Chambers; 3rd floor, Peel House, Harrington Street, September 1992-January 1998. Chambers relocated to India Buildings, Water Street, 1998-2000; Exchange Chambers, Derby Square, January 2000. Junior Counsel to the Crown (Provincial Panel, Civil) 2000. Recorder 2003.

BROWNE, Roland Jay
L. 20 November 1845. 3 Hare Court, 1848-1882. Not in 1883 Law List.

BROWNE, Valentine Somers
Born 1851. 5th son of John Browne late of Liverpool, timber merchant. London University, MA 1874. AAS. L. 23 April 1875. Call 26 January 1878. ETC. 5 August 1885. Prop. French QC. Sec. Walton. Equity draftsman & conveyancer. Lancaster Chancery Court. Liverpool Chambers; 4 Harrington Street, 1879-1883; Equity Chambers, 9 Cook Street, 1884-1915. Not in 1916 Law List.

BROWNE, Vincent Robert Ramsay Balfour
Born 1881. Died 9 April 1963 aged 82. 2nd son of J H Balfour KC of Kirkcudbright. Radley; Magdalen College, Oxford. AAS. M. 16 January 1900. Call 24 June 1903. No address on Law List. JP. and Hon. Sheriff Substitute, Dumfries & Galloway. Publications; A Day's Stalking. The Story of a Stag. WW.

BRUCE, David Livingstone
Born 20 August 1955. Queen Mary Westfield College, London University, LLB. AAS. 10 November 1980. Call 29 July 1982. Manchester Chambers; 26 Cross Street, 1983-1987; Kenworthy's Buildings, 83 Bridge Street, 1988-1998; 24a St John Street, 1999. (now St Johns Buildings).

BRUCE, John.
Born 1862. 2nd son of James Bruce of Aberdeen, banker. University of Aberdeen. AAS. M. 3 May 1886. Call 15 May 1889. ETC. 16 March 1892. Prop. Wheeler QC. Sec. Parry. 3 Pump Court, 1891-1892; 4 Pump Court, 1893; 4 Middle Temple Lane, 1894; 5 Essex Court, 1895; Various other addresses. No address, 1902-1940. Not in 1941 Law List.

BRUCE, Nigel Howard
G. June 1953. Circuit Junior 1953. 14 Cook Street, Liverpool, 1953-1958. Left Bar. Not in 1964 Law List.

BRUNNEN, David Mark
Born 13 August 1953 Bad Lippspringe, Germany. Son of L J Brunnen of Caldy, retired Army Major & Insurance Broker. Rossall School; Christ Church, Oxford, MA. AAS. M. 16 April 1975. Call 29 June 1976. ETC. Autumn 1976. Pupilmaster, Michael Dingle. Liverpool Chambers; 2nd floor, Oriel Chambers, 14 Water Street, 1976-1982; Chambers moved to Refuge Assurance House (later renamed Merchants Court) Derby Square 1982. Assistant Recorder, 1996. Recorder 6.9.2000. Part time Immigration Adjudicator, 2001. Full time as from 5 May 2003.

BRUNNER, (Harold) Roscoe
Born 22 January 1871. Died 3 November 1926 aged 55. 3rd son of late Rt. Hon. Sir John Tomlinson Brunner, 1st Bt. Cheltenham; Cambridge University, BA. I. 18 November 1895. ETC. 13 March 1896. Prop. Mulholland QC. Sec. C A Russell. Circuit Junior, Summer 1896. 2 Harcourt Buildings, 1898-1903. No address, 1904-1926. DL & JP. Director of Brunner, Mond & Co Ltd. WW.

BRYCE, James (First Viscount Bryce)
Born 10 May 1838 Belfast. Died 22 January 1922 aged 83. Belfast Academy; Glasgow University; Trinity College, Oxford, BA 1862., DCL 1870; Hon Fellow. AAS. L. 28 January 1862. Call 11 June 1867. 7 Stone Building, 1867-1882. Regius Professor of Civil Law at Oxford. Professor of Roman Law & Jurisprudence to the Council of Legal Education, 1878. MP for Tower Hamlets, 1880. MP (L) Aberdeen South, 1885-1903. Chancellor of the Duchy of Lancaster, 1892. President of the Board of Trade, 1894. Chief Secretary for Ireland, 1905-1907. Ambassador to Washington, 1907-1913. A British Member of the International Tribunal at the Hague. Accomplished mountaineer and President of the Alpine Club, 1899-1901. OM 1907, GCVO 1917, PC 1892, FRS 1893, FBA 1902. Numerous publications including The Holy Roman Empire, 1863. Impressions of South Africa, 1897. Studies in History & Jurisprudence, 1901. Modern Democracies, 1912. WW. DNB.

BUCHAN, Sir John (First Baron Tweedsmuir)
Born 26 August 1875 Perth, Scotland. Died 11 February 1940 Montreal Canada aged 64. Glasgow University; Brasenose College, Oxford, MA; Hon Fellow. President of the Union, 1899. AAS. M. 20 March 1897. Call 19 June 1901; Hon Bencher 9.5.1935. ETC. February 1904. Prop. Tobin KC. Sec. F E Smith. Chambers; 3 Temple Gardens, 1901-1905; 2 Harcourt Buildings, 1906-1907; 3 Temple Gardens, 1908-1921. Buchan practiced at the Bar for only a few months before going to South Africa as Private Secretary to Lord Milner, the High Commissioner. He returned to the Bar in 1903 but his future lay in literature and politics. He served on Headquarters Staff in France, 1916-1917 and came home to be Director of Information for the Prime Minister, 1917-1918. High Office followed. After 8 years as Conservative Member of Parliament for the Scottish Universities, he was appointed Governor General of Canada in 1935 and Chancellor of Edinburgh University in 1937. He published many histories, biographies and novels. The one for which he is best remembered is the fine thriller "The 39 Steps" which has been filmed three times (Robert Donat, 1935. Kenneth More, 1959 & Robert Powell, 1978). Autobiography "Memory Hold the Door", 1940. Biography "The Presbyterian Cavalier," Andrew Lownie, 1997. WW. DNB.

BUCHAN, Jonathan Maxfield
Born 12 May 1969 Leeds. Allerton High School, Leeds; Churchill College, Cambridge, MA. Research Assistant to Derek Fatchett MP, 1990-1992. M. October 1994. ETC. 20 December 1994. Prop. David Harris QC. Sec. Paul Hart. 15 Winckley Square, Preston, 1994.

BUCHANAN-DUNLOP, Richard QC
Born 19 April 1919. Marlborough College; Magdalen College, served in Royal Corps of Signals, 1939-1946 (Hon Major). Cambridge, BA. AAS. M. 10 December 1948; Harmsworth Scholar. Call 18 April 1951. ETC. 30 June 1958. Prop. Nelson QC (for Cantley QC). Sec. Shorrock. 9 Old Square, 1951-1953; 4 Pump Court, 1954-1966. 4 Chapel Walks & 606 Royal Exchange, Manchester, 1958-1966. Silk 1966. Went to live in Greece to write and paint. Publications; Skiathos and other poems, 1984; Old Olive Men, 1986; Paeeon: songs from the Greek Isles, 1989.

BUCKLEY, Christopher John
BA, Liverpool. G March 1997. 24 Fenwick Street, Liverpool, 1998-1999. No address 2000. Not in 2001 Bar Directory.

BUCKLEY, David Esmond
G. November 1966. 60 King Street, Manchester, 1966-1968; 1 Temple Gardens & Northern Assurance Building, Albert Square, Manchester 1969. Then to the Office of the National Insurance Commissioners, London and later to the Western Circuit.

BUCKLEY, Patrick James

Born 10 June 1970 Royton, Lancs. Ratcliffe College, Leicester; Keele University, BA. Formerly a solicitor with solicitors; Alsop, Wilkinson, 1994-1997; Sutcliffe Speakman, 1997-1998; Norcross Lees & Co, 1998-1999; Kemps, 1999-2000. G. 23 July 1998. ETC 2000. Prop Peter Birkett QC. Sec John McNeill. Pupilmaster Hugh McKee. 24a St John Street, Manchester (now St John's Buildings), 2000.

BUCKLEY, Peter Evered

Born 18 February 1948, Blackpool. Brother of District Judge Buckley. Arnold School, Blackpool; University College, Oxford, BA. Teacher in Greece, 1969-1970. G. July 1972. ETC 13 February 1973. Sec, Henriques. Manchester Chambers; 2 Booth Street, 1972-1975; 13 Police Street, 1976-1978; 43 King Street, 1979-1988; 5 John Dalton Street, 1989.

BUCKLEY, Sophie Florence

BA(Cantab). M. 25 November 1999. ETC. 14 December 1999. Prop. Leeming QC. Sec. Nigel Grundy. 9 St John Street, Manchester, 2001.

BUESNEL, Clement

Born 1849. Only surviving son of Clement Buesnel of St Martins, Jersey. Matriculated London University, 1869. AAS. M. 19 April 1869. AAS. I. 1 June 1871. Call I. 18 November 1872. L.ad eundem, 4 November 1873. ETC. 20 July 1878. Prop. Temple QC. Sec. Hopkinson. 19 Old Buildings, 1877-1881; 15 Old Buildings, 1882-1897. No address, 1898-1922. Not in 1923 Law List. Foster.

BULMER, David Leslie

BA.,LLB. G. July 1952. ETC 1952. Pupilmaster, George England. Liverpool Chambers; 3 Cook Street, 1952-1958; 3rd floor, 27 Dale Street, 1959-1989; 5th floor, Corn Exchange, Fenwick Street, 1989-1996. Law Lecturer, Liverpool University, 1952-1988. Recorder, 1985-1996.

BUNDRED, Gillian Sarah

Born 14 March 1960 Sunderland. Sunderland Church High School. University College, London, LLB. G. July 1982. ETC. 1983. Pupilmaster, Ian Trigger. Oriel Chambers, Water Street, Liverpool, March 1984.

BURDER, John Winsland

Born 1846. Eldest son of John Burder of Manchester, solicitor. AAS. I. 18 November 1867. Call 10 June 1870. ETC. 10 March 1871. Prop. Quain QC. Sec. Herschell. 1 Harcourt Buildings, 1876-1915. Manchester & Salford Sessions. No address, 1916-1935. Not in 1936 Law List. Foster.

BURGESS, Roy Anthony

LLB (Bristol); Mphil (London). L. November 1970. ETC. 13 February 1973. Sec. Henriques. Manchester Chambers; 2 Booth Street, 1973-1975; 13 Police Street, 1976-1978; 1 Dean's Court, 1979-1984; 14 Winckley Square, Preston, 1986-1991; 38 King Street West, 1992; 334 Deansgate, 1993; 25 Victoria Street, Liverpool & 16 Winckley Square, Preston, 1994-1995. London Chambers, 1996.

BURGESS, His Honour Sir Thomas (Arthur Collier)

Born 14 April 1906. Died 19 June 1977 aged 71. Charterhouse; Lincoln College, Oxford, MA. I. 20 June 1928; Bencher 1957. ETC. 3 July 1930. 78 King Street, Manchester, 1930; 6 New Court, 1931-1963, RAFVR, 1940-1945. Bar Council, 1953-1957. Member Council, Duchy of Lancaster, 1966-1973. DL., Lancs 1974. Legion of Merit (Officer), 1946. Vice Chancellor, County Palatine of Lancaster, 1963-1973. Kt 1972. WW.

BURGIS, His Honour Sir Edwin Cooper

Born 1878. Died 4 February 1966 aged 88. Lincoln College, Oxford MA.,BCL. Victoria University, Manchester, LLB. G. 15 June 1904; Certificate of Honour. ETC. February 1905. 60 King Street, Manchester, 1905-1924. County Court Judge, (Lancs., Yorks., Cheshire & Shropshire, Circuits 10 & 7), February 1924-1950. Kt 1948. Lecturer in Law at Manchester University, 1906-1914. WW.

BURKE, Brendan Edward

Born 9 December 1969 Shotley Bridge, Co Durham. St Leonard's RC School, Durham City; King's College, Cambridge, BA. I. October 1995. ETC. 19 December 1995. Prop. Timothy King QC. Sec. Nadine Hope. Liverpool Chambers; Victoria Chambers, 25 Victoria Street, 1995-1995; relocated to 19 Castle Street, 1998-1999; Martin's Buildings, Water Street 1999 (merger with Corn Exchange to form 7 Harrington Street), 1999.

BURKE, John Kenneth QC (His Honour Judge Burke QC)
Born 4 August 1939. Son of Kenneth Burke qv. Stockport Grammar School. Cheshire Regiment, 1958-1960. TA., Parachute Regiment, 1962-1967. AAS. M. 15 November 1961. Call 9 February 1965: Bencher 1992. ETC. Spring 1965. Pupilmaster, John Bamber. Manchester Chambers; 43 King Street, 1965-1973; 4th floor Astley House, Quay Street, 1974-1977; 18 St John Street, 1978-1995. Recorder, 1980-1995. Silk 1985. Circuit Judge, 1995. Caricaturist of Circuit personalities (as was his father). His drawing of the late Bert Jalland, which appears in this directory, raised over £1000 for the Barristers' Benevolent Association. WW.

BURKE, Kenneth

(KB)

The Silk who interupted. The Silk who objected to being interupted.

Born 1899 Dundee. Died 1960. Father of His Honour Judge Burke QC qv. Served in Great War in Royal Marine Light Infantry. AAS. M. 12 April 1920 (then described as a journalist as was his father) Call 19 November 1923. ETC. 20 February 1924. Prop. Wingate-Saul KC. Sec. McCleary. Manchester Chambers; 1b Cooper Street, 1924-1955; 78 King Street, 1955-1958; 19 Brazennose Street, 1959; 60 King Street, 1959-1960. He was an extremely able and persuasive advocate appearing for the defence without a Leader in about 50 murder cases. The most famous was that of R-v- Walter Rowland which is reported in great detail in Henry Cecil's 1975 book in the Celebrated Trials Series. Kenneth's caricature of J B Sandbach qv appears in this directory and some of his other works are in Crown Square.

BURKE, Maisie
Born 26 May 1975 Bath. Falmouth Comprehensive; Sussex University LLB. With Donne, Mileham & Haddock, solicitors, Brighton 1995 and Wilson, Howard, solicitors, Islington, London, 1997-1998. L. 14 October 1999. ETC. 14 December 1999. Prop. Shorrock QC. Sec. Andrew O'Byrne. Peel Court Chambers, 45 Hardman Street, Manchester, 1999.

BURKE, Peter S.L.
Born 7 May 1811 London. Died South Kensington 26 March 1881 aged 69. Son of John Burke (1787-1848) genealogical and heraldic writer. Brother of Sir John Bernard Burke (1814-1892) Ulster King of Arms. College of Caen, Normandy. I. 7 June 1839. Manchester & Lancs. Sessions. Parliamentary Bar. QC of Lancs County Palatine, 1858. Serjeant-at-Law, 1859. 2 Churchyard Court, Temple. Publications; The Wisdom and genius of Edmund Burke, 1845; Celebrated Trials in connection with the Aristocracy, 1049-1851; The Romance of the Forum, 4 vols, 1854; Public and Domestic Life of Edmund Burke, 1853; Celebrated Naval & Military Trials, 1866. DNB.

BURMAN, Jeanette Rozella (Mrs Goodman)
I. November 1952. ETC. 1952. Pupilmaster, George Boyle Hanna Currie. Liverpool Chambers; 34 Castle Street, 1952-1955; relocated to Corn Exchange, Fenwick Street, 1956-1957; 27 Dale Street, Liverpool, 1958-1976. Chambers relocated to Melbourne House, 21 North John Street 1977. Retired from practice 1978. Legal Member, Mental Health Review Tribunal to May 2000. JP.

BURN, Richard
Born 16 November 1811. Only son of Joseph Burn of Orton Hall, Westmorland. AAS. M. 21 January 1837. Call 24 April 1840. JP., DL. High Sheriff, Westmorland, 1852. Lieut. Col., Westmorland & Cumberland Yeomanry, 1876. No chambers address. Last entry in Law List 1899. Foster.

BURNELL, Kate (Katherine)
Born 10 October 1975 Liverpool. Lymm High School; Liverpool University, LLB. with Fiona Bruce & Co, solicitors, 1996-1998. M. 8 October 1998. ETC. December 1998. Prop. David Harris QC. Sec. Michael Kennedy. 8th floor, India Buildings, Water Street, Liverpool, 7.9.1998.

BURNS, Francis Joseph
Born 23 April 1941 Northumberland. St Aiden's Grammar School, Sunderland; Durham University, LLB. Lecturer, Manchester Metropolitan University, 1967-1971. G. May 1971. ETC. 1971. Prop. George Carman QC. Sec. John Coffey. Manchester Chambers; 36 St Ann Street, 1971-1980; 27 Byrom Street, 1981-1983; 26 Cross Street, 1984-1987; Kenworthy's Building, 83 Bridge Street, 1988. Deputy District Judge, 1993.

BURNS, Paul Andrew
Born 4 October 1975 Liverpool. St Mary's College, Crosby; Liverpool University, LLB. L. 8 October 1998. Sir Thomas More & Hardwick Scholarships. ETC. December 1998. Prop. David Turner QC. Sec. Gerard Martin. Exchange Chambers, Derby Square, Liverpool, 1999.

BURNS, Peter Richard
Born 1970. North Cestrian Grammar School; Manchester Grammar School; Merton College, Oxford, BA. G. October 1993. ETC. 7 December 1993. Manchester Chambers; Dean's Court, Crown Square, 1993-1999; 24 St John Street, 1999.

BURNYEAT, William John Dalzell MP
Born 13 March 1874. Died 8 May 1916 aged 42. Rugby: Corpus Christi, Oxford, MA. I. 14 June 1899. ETC. 30 June 1900. Prop. Henry. Sec. Lumb. Circuit Junior, Summer 1901 & Winter 1902. Goldsmith Building, 1902-1910. No address, 1911-1916. MP (L) Whitehaven, 1906-1910. JP.

BURRELL, John Glyn QC (His Honour Judge Burrell QC)
Born 10 October 1912. Died 6 March 1984 aged 71. Friars School, Bangor; University College of Wales, LLB. I. 6 May 1936. ETC. 10 June 1936. Prop. Goldie KC. Sec. F E Pritchard. Liverpool Chambers; 25 Castle Street, 1936-1939. Army service, 1940-1945 (notional chambers 27 Lord Street); 49 Castle Street, 1947-1961.Silk 1961. London Chambers; 1 Hare Court; 1 Paper Buildings & 2 Essex Court. Recorder of Wigan, 1962-1964. Chairman, Radnorshire Quarter Sessions, 1964-1971. County Court, later Circuit Judge, 1964-1980. Publication:- Epitome on Salmond on Torts. WW.

BURRELL, Michael Peter (The Hon. Mr Justice Burrell)
Born 18 July 1948. Birkenhead School; Magdalene College, Cambridge, MA. I. July 1971. ETC. 1972. Pupilmaster, A S Booth. Circuit Junior, Summer 1973. Northern Circuit, 1972-1986. Ground floor, Peel House, Harrington Street, Liverpool. Hong Kong; Permanent Magistrate, 1986-1990: Principal Magistrate, 1990-1991: District Court Judge, 1991-1995: Judge of the Court of First Instance of the High Court (formerly Judge, Supreme Court), 1995. Member, Hong Kong Judicial Studies Board, 1992-1995. Chairman, Insider Dealing Tribunal, 1996-1998. WW.

BURROWS, Charles Lionel
L. 19 November 1902. ETC 5 February 1904. Prop. Sanderson KC. Sec. Wingate-Saul. 78 King Street, Manchester, 1905-1928. Lancs. Chancery Court. No address, 1929-1933. Not in 1934 Law List.

BURROWS, Simon Paul
Born 23 January 1967 Plymouth. Tarring High School; Worthing 6th Form College; Durham University, BA; City University, Dip Law. Married to Emma Cornish qv. I. 27 November 1990. ETC. July 1992. Prop. Keith Goddard QC. Sec. White. Pupilmaster, Jane McNeill (daughter of McNeill. J.), 14 Winckley Square, Preston, 1992-1993; 15 Winckley Square, 1994-1999; Peel Court Chambers, 45 Hardman Street, Manchester, 1999. Under 18 Cricket for Sussex and University. Plays double bass. Involved in Meningitis Research Foundation having survived the infection in 1999.

BURTON, Henry KC

With Clerk Ronnie Lynch, 1951.
Born 18 July 1907. Died 8 October 1952 aged 45. Father of Mr Justice Michael Burton qv. Manchester Grammar School; Merton College, Oxford, BA. G. 2 July 1930. ETC. 9 July 1930. Prop. Jackson KC. Sec. Jolly. 60 King Street, Manchester, 1930-1951. 1 Brick Court, 1951-52. Henry was one of 112 people killed in a three train collision at Harrow and Weald just 18 months after taking Silk in 1951. WW.

BURTON, Michael John QC (The Hon Mr Justice Burton)
Born 12 November 1946. Son of Henry Burton KC qv. Eton College; Balliol College, Oxford, MA. G. November 1970; Bencher 1993. 2 Crown Office Row, 1970-1994; 3 Kings Bench Walk North, 1995-1998. Silk 1984. Recorder, 1989-1998. High Court Judge, Queens Bench Division, 1998. President, Employment Appeal Tribunal, 2002. Circuit Congratulatory Dinner, Middle Temple Hall, 14 October 2000. WW.

BURTON, Raymond
G. November 1968. ETC 10 June 1969. Prop. Pigot QC. Sec. John Gore. Liverpool Chambers; 9 Rumford Street, 1969; 27 Dale Street, 1970-1973. Australia, 1974-1976 (Barrister & Solicitor of the Supreme Court of Victoria & the High Court of Australia) He joined the Department of Trade in 1976 as a legal assistant rising to Assistant Solicitor & Head of Solicitors A2 Prosecutions Branch.

BUSHELL, Frederick Edwin
Born 1859. 7th son of Christopher Bushell of Hinderton, Neston, JP. Admitted as a solicitor. AAS. M. 5 May 1890. Call 22 April 1891. ETC. 4 August 1891. Prop. C A Russell. Sec. Walton. 3 Harcourt Buildings, 1892; 2 Kings Bench Walk, 1893; 3 Elm Court, 1894-1907. No address, 1908-1928. Not in 1929 Law List.

BUTLER, Jonathan Charles
Born 28 May 1959 Oxford. Abingdon School; Leicester University, BA., MA; Manchester University, MEd. British Council Teacher, 1983-1985. Lecturer, Manchester University, 1986-1987. Lecturer, Liverpool University, 1987-1990. Hon Lecturer, Dept of Clinical Psychology, 1992-1999. G. October 1992. ETC. 1993. Prop. David Harris QC. Sec. Graham Wood. 3rd floor, Peel House, Harrington Street, Liverpool, 1993-1998; chambers moved to India Buildings, Water Street, 1998. Legal Member, Mental Health Review Tribunal, 2001.

BUTLER, Philip Andrew
Born 13 April 1957, Manchester. St Peter's Grammar School; Manchester University, LLB., LLM. AAS. M. 10 November 1977; Harmsworth Scholar. Call 26 July 1979. ETC. December 1979. Prop. Hytner QC. Sec. Gerard Humphries. Dean's Court Chambers at Crown Square & 24 St John Street, Manchester, 1979. Assistant Recorder 1998. KHS. 1999. Recorder 2000. Legal Assessor, General Medical Council, 2002.

BUTLER, William Henry
Born 1832. Eldest son of John Butler of Dublin. Trinity College, Dublin, MA, 1860. AAS. I. 30 May 1853. Call 7 June 1858. Revising Barrister. 1 Tanfield Chambers, Temple, 1876-1878; 1 King's Bench Walk, 1879-1912. Not in 1913 Law List. Foster.

BUTLIN, Percy
G. January 1921. 48 King Street, Manchester, 1921-1936; 60 King Street, 1937-1945. Not in 1946 Law List.

BUTT, The Hon Sir Charles Parker QC., MP.
Born 24 June 1830. Died 25 May 1892 aged 61. AAS. L. 22 January 1849. Call 17 November 1854; Bencher 1869. Practised in the Consular Courts at Constantinople whilst acting as correspondent for "The Times". London Chambers; 4 Crown Office Row. MP (L) Southampton, 1880-1883. High Court Judge, Probate, Divorce & Admiralty Division, 1883. President of Division, 1891-1892. Member, Royal Commission on Merchant Shipping, 1884. DNB. Foster.

BUTTERFIELD, John Riley
BA., LLB. I. 26 January 1926. ETC. 2 March 1926. Prop. Jackson KC. Sec. Jolly. Bank Chambers, Fishergate, Preston, 1931-1938. Not in 1939 Law List.

BUTTERFIELD, Marlene Leslie (nee Greenwood)
Born 25 February 1945 Bolton. London Polytechnic, LLB. AAS. M. 5 September 1974. Call 25 November 1975. Sunlight House, Quay Street, Manchester, 1977-1983; 2 Plowden Buildings, 1984-1989. Not in 1990 Bar Directory.

BUTTERWORTH, James Hartley
MA. I. 19 November 1888. ETC. 13 July 1894. Prop. C A Russell. Sec. Hamilton. Equity draftsman. & conveyancer. Lancs. Chancery Court. No address, 1888-1896. 2 Paper Buildings, 1897-1899. No address, 1900-1906. 3 (N) King's Bench Walk, 1907. No address, 1908-1910. 78 King Street, Manchester, 1911-1925. No address, 1926-1940. Not in 1941 Law List.

BYRNE, James Patrick
Born 26 January 1961. Stonyhurst College; Liverpool University, LLB. G. July 1983. ETC. 1983. Prop. Michael Maguire QC. Sec. John Roberts. Derby Square Chambers, Merchants Court, 1983.

BYRNE, Michael David (His Honour Judge Byrne)
Born 7 December 1945, Newcastle upon Tyne. St Edward's College, Liverpool; Liverpool University, BA, 1967, LLB, 1970. G. July 1971. ETC. September 1971. Prop. David McNeill QC. Sec. Gerard Wright. Same Liverpool Chambers; 27 Dale Street, 1971-1976; Melbourne Buildings, 21 North John Street, 1977-1988; 3rd floor, Peel House, Harrington Street, 1989-1998; India Buildings, Water Street, 1999-2002. Assistant Recorder 1989. Recorder 1992. Vice Chairman, Ashworth Special Hospital Authority, 1997-1998. Chairman of Governors, St Edwards College, 1995. Circuit Judge, 3 July 2002.

BYRNE, Thomas Francis
Born 1856. Eldest son of Patrick Byrne of Drogheda. Trinity College, Dublin, BA. AAS. M. 4 May 1875. Call 3 July 1878. ETC. 27 January 1879. Prop. S Taylor. Sec. Crompton. 2 Elm Court, Temple, 1879; 60 King Street, Manchester, 1880-1909. Not in 1910 Law List.

BYRTH, William Stewart

Born 1837. Youngest son of Rev Thomas Byrth, D.D., late Rector of Wallasey. AAS. M. 31 December 1863. Call 17 November 1866. Special pleader. Kirkdale & Liverpool Sessions. Liverpool Court of Passage. London Chambers; 3 Elm Court, 1866-1879. St George's Chambers, 10, St George's Crescent, Liverpool, 1877-1880. No address, 1881-1911. Not in 1912 Law List.

C

CADWALLADER, Neil Anthony
Born 14 September 1959 Hampstead, London. Downside School, Pembroke College, Cambridge, MA, Dip Law. I. July 1984. ETC. 22 May 1986. Prop. Michael Maguire. Sec. William George. Liverpool Chambers; 20 North John Street, 1985-1997; Exchange Chambers, Derby Square, 1997. Accredited Mediator.

CADWALLADER, Peter
LLB. G. July 1973. Manchester Chambers: Post Office Chambers, 26 Brown Street, 1973-1976; 60 King Street, 1977-1983; 1 Deans Court, 1984-1993; 9 St John Street, 1994.

CAINE, William
Born 1874. Elder son of William Sproston Caine, MP., of London. Balliol College, Oxford. AAS. M. 17 April 1894. Call 17 November 1897. ETC. 13 July 1899. Prop. Pope QC. Sec. Hartley. 3 Hare Court, 1900-1901; 6 Stone Buildings, 1902-1907. No address 1908-1949. Not in 1950 Law List. Foster.

CAIRNS, Alexander
Born 1868. Eldest son of Alexander Cairns of Middlesex. AAS. M. 13 June 1896. Call 26 April 1899. ETC. 1 August 1899. Prop. Pickford QC. Sec. Horridge. Shorthand Writer & Reporter. Carlisle, Cumberland & Westmorland Sessions. 2 Harcourt Buildings, 1900-1901; 2 Brick Court, 1902-1905; 5 Pump Court, 1906-1913; 3 Paper Buildings, 1914; 1 Elm Court, 1915; 1 Garden Court, 1916-1922; 2 Hare Court, 1923-1934; 3 Paper Buildings, 1938-1939; 5 St James's Square, Manchester, 1913-1915. Not in 1940 Law List.

CAIRNS, Walter Talbot
Born 1852. 2nd son of Charles Cairns of Darlington. AAS. M. 18 November 1873. Call 17 November 1876. Equity draftsman & conveyancer. Bolton, Manchester & Preston Sessions. Manchester Chambers: 1 St James's Square, 1876-1881; 2 South King Street, 1882. Not in 1883 Law List.

CALDWELL, Jennifer Joan
Born 5 February 1946, Abingdon. Manchester University, LLB. M. November 1973. ETC. 1973. Pupilmaster, Charles Mantell. Manchester Chambers: Astley House, Quay Street, 1973-1978; Crown Prosecution Service, 1986-1996. 18 St John Street, 1996. (formerly Astley House)

CALLAN, Philip MP
Born 27 May 1837. Only son of Owen Callan of Cookstown, Co. Louth. AAS. I. 28 May 1861. Call 30 April 1864. No chambers address. MP; Dundalk, 1868-1880; Louth, 1880. Not in 1903 Law List. Foster.

CALLAND, Thomas Bullough
Born 1874. 1st son of Peter Calland of Astley, Lancs. AAS. M. 5 November 1919 (then a 45 year old medical practitioner). Call 2 July 1924. ETC. 15 June 1927. Prop. Singleton KC. Sec. Laski. No chambers address. Addresses in the Scarisbrick/Southport area. Not in 1964 Law List.

CALLERY, Martin
LLB (Wales). M. March 1997. Formerly a solicitor & Principal Crown Prosecutor. Cobden House Chambers, 19 Quay Street, Manchester, 1999.

CALVERT, David Edward
Born 9 December 1971, Carlisle. St Catherine's, Oxford, BA. I. November 1995. ETC. 2 April 1996. Prop. Elleray QC. Sec. Searle. St James's Chambers, 68 Quay Street, Manchester, 1996.

CAMERON, Geoffrey Valentine
L. 20 June 1928. ETC on a date not recorded but between 5.7.1933 and 20.1.1934. Prop. Fyfe QC. Sec. Nield. 3 Dr Johnson's Buildings, 1936-1937. Legal Adviser, Aden, 1938-1940. Legal Secretary, Malta, 1941. Not in 1942 Law List. The Liverpool Prosecutions book (which I have found to be very reliable) lists him as Attorney General of St Lucia but no date is given.

CAMPBELL, Hon. Charles Henry Gordon
G. 28 June 1911. (Certificate of Honour). ETC. 7 July 1914. Prop. Ashton KC. Sec. Thorpe. 3 Dr Johnson's Buildings, 1914-1936. Parliamentary Draftsman & Railway Commission Court. No address, 1937-1940. Not in 1941 Law List.

CAMPBELL, Graham John
Born 2 April 1958 Cheadle Hulme. Hazel Grove High School; North East London Polytechnic, BA (Law). AAS. M. 27 February 1980. Call 23 November 1982. ETC. 1984. Pupilmasters, Stephen Hockman & Robert Kirk (Temple). Pupillage in London at 6 Pump Court & 3 Paper Building. Manchester Chambers: 27 Byrom Street/26 Cross Street, 1983-1984; Arkwright House, 1984; Sunlight House, 1985; 121 Princess Street, 1985-1987; 3 Peter Street, 1987-1990; Deansgate, 1990-1993; 38 King Street West, 1993-1995; 24a St John Street, 1995. (now St John's Buildings after merger with 28 St John Street on 23.9.2002) Part Time Immigration Adjudicator, August 2001.

CAMPBELL, Ian Burns (His Honour Ian Campbell. CMG)
Born 7 July 1938. Tiffin Boys' School; Cambridge University, MA., LLM., PhD; Higher Diploma in Comparative Law (Strasbourg). Assistant Law Lecturer progressing to Visiting Professor at Liverpool University; Hon. LLD, 2004. AAS. M. 17 January 1956. Call 22 November 1966. ETC. 1966. Circuit Junior, 1968. Pupilmaster, Ifor Morris Jones. Liverpool Chambers: 606 The Corn Exchange, Fenwick Street, 1966-1982; Chambers then moved to Exchange Chambers, Exchange Flags, 1982-1984. Recorder, 1981-1984. Circuit Judge, 1984-2003. Liason Judge, North & South Sefton Justices, 1988-2000. Sitting as a judge at Liverpool, 1984-1999. Seconded to Legal Department, Office of the High Representative, Sarajevo, 1999-2000. Deputy High Representative for Legal Affairs & Head of Legal Affairs Department, Sarajevo, 2000-2003. CMG. 2003. Member, Judicial Studies Board, 1996-2000. Member, Editorial Board, Liverpool Law Review, 1996. Publication; Legal Visions of the New Europe, 1993. WW.

CAMPBELL, Thomas
G. 17 November 1920. ETC. 2 March 1922. Prop. Greaves-Lord KC. Sec. Leigh. 3 Brick Court, 1922-1936; 2 Harcourt Buildings, 1937- 1941. No address 1942. Not in 1943 Law List.

CANNELL, Alfred Edward
LLB., ACIS., FIArb. G. July 1968. 3 St James's Square, Manchester, 1970-1978. Left the Bar to become a Company Lawyer with British American Tobacco in London.

CANNOCK, Giles Michael Morgan
Born 24 February 1974 Liverpool. Merchant Taylors' School, Crosby; Emmanuel College, Cambridge, MA., LLM. G. 8 October 1998. ETC. December 1998. Prop. Keith Goddard QC. Sec. Simon Hilton. Circuit Junior, 2001. 40 King Street, Manchester (now called Kings Chambers) 12.10.1998.

CANNON, Sophia Rebecca
Born 31 December 1975. Keveston & Grantham Girls School; Queen Mary's College, London, LLB; Brunel, LLM (Child Law & Policy) Teacher, 1997-2001. M. October 2001. ETC. 2001. Prop. Foster QC. Sec. Samantha Birtles. 18 St John Street, Manchester 2001.

CANTLEY, The Hon. Sir Joseph (Donaldson)
Born 8 August 1910. Died 6 January 1993 aged 82. Manchester Grammar School; Manchester University. AAS. M. 26 April 1930. Certificate of Honour. Call 28 June 1983; Bencher 22.1.1963; Treasurer 1981. ETC. 5 July 1933. Prop. Gorman KC. Sec. Denis Gerrard. (in 1966 he married Lady Gerrard, the widow of his pupilmaster). 3 St James's Square, Manchester, 1933-1939. Royal Artillery, 1939-1945 (2nd Lt to Lt Col) Served in North Africa & Italy (despatches twice), OBE 1945. 4 Chapel Walks, Manchester, 1945-1954. Silk 1954. 1 Brick Court, 1954-1956; 1 Hare Court, 1956-1965. Recorder of Oldham, 1959-1960. Judge of Salford Hundred Court, 1960-1965. Judge of Appeal, Isle of Man, 1962-1965. High Court Judge, Queen's Bench Division, 1965-1985. Presiding Judge; Northern Circuit, 1970-1974; South Eastern Circuit, 1980. Hon. LLD, Manchester University. He headed the Public Inquiry into the "Summerland Disaster" arising from a fire in 1973 in Douglas, Isle of Man in which 50 people perished and many more were seriously injured. He also tried Jeremy Thorpe, a former leader of the Liberal Party who was acquitted of conspiracy to murder. WW.

CAPLAN, Leonie Susan
Born 5 May 1957, Salford. Bury Grammar School; Keele University, BA (Law & Psychology). Solicitor, 1982 in Liverpool, Manchester & Bolton. I. March 2001. ETC. April 2001. Prop. Peter Birkett QC. Sec. Yvonne Healing. 18 St John Street, Manchester, 2001.

CAPP, Jonathan Charles
LLB (London); LLM (Paris). L. October 1990. 5 John Dalton Street, Manchester, 1992-1994. Went to practice overseas. He is a member of the Bars of New York & California.

CAPSTIK, William
Oxford University, MA. I. 29 June 1927. ETC. 30 January 1929. Prop. Singleton KC. Sec. Gething. 10 Dale Street, Liverpool, 1931. No address, 1932-1953. Not in 1954 Law List.

CARDWELL, Arthur McKenzie
Born 19 November 1852. 3rd son of Thomas Cardwell of London. Brother of Thomas Holme Cardwell. qv. Christ Church, Oxford, MA. AAS. I. 10 October 1873. Call 17 November 1877. ETC. 10 July 1878. Prop. Temple QC. Sec. Crompton. Circuit Junior, 1879. 8 King's Bench Walk, 1880-1882; 3 Paper Buildings, 1883-1888. No address, 1889-1935. Not in 1936 Law List. Foster

CARDWELL, Reginald
Born 14 July 1834. 2nd son of Rev. Edward Cardwell DD, Principal of St Alban Hall, Oxford. Christ Church, Oxford, BA. AAS. L. 15 April 1858. Call 26 January 1863. 2 Dr Johnson's Building, 1876-1888. Liverpool & Kirkdale Sessions. No address, 1889-1929. Not in 1930 Law List. Foster.

CARDWELL, Thomas Holme
Born 22 October 1845. Eldest son of Thomas Cardwell of London. Brother of Arthur McKenzie Cardwell. qv. Christ Church, Oxford, BA. AAS. I. 25 April 1867. Call 26 January 1872. ETC. 31 July 1872. Prop. Torr QC. Sec. R G Williams. 7 Fig Tree Court, 1876-1883; 3 Paper Buildings, 1884-1917. Not in 1918 Law List.

CAREY, Edward
I. 29 April 1896. ETC. 4 August 1897. Prop Taylor QC. Sec Baxter. Liverpool Chambers: Equity Court, 9 Cook Street, 1899-1908; 2 Harrington Street, 1909-1915. Equity draftsman & conveyancer. No address, 1916-1949. Not in 1950 Law List.

CAREY, John
BA. G. 26 January 1910. ETC. 20 July 1910. Prop. Stephen KC. Sec. Webster. 11 Lord Street, Liverpool, 1913-1915. No address, 1916-1920. 3 Essex Court, 1921-1923; 1 Pump Court, 1924-1928. Not in 1929 Law List.

CARLETON, Erica Jayne
Born 17 February 1967, Liverpool. Liverpool Girls' College; Liverpool Polytechnic, LLB. Solicitor, November 1992-November 1999. M. 9 March 2000. ETC. 6 April 2000. Prop. Webster QC. Sec. Barry Grennan. Pupilmaster, Deborah Lambert. Kenworthy's Buildings, 83 Bridge Street, Manchester, November 1999.

CARLISLE, Mark QC. (Rt. Hon. Baron Carlisle of Bucklow)
Born 7 July 1929 Montevideo. Radley College; Manchester University, LLB, 1952. G. February 1954; Bencher 1980. ETC. 4 March 1954. Prop. Daniel Brabin QC. Sec. Hugh Mais. Manchester Chambers; 43 King Street, 1954-1982; 18 St John Street, 1982. Silk 1971. London Chambers; 3 Kings Bench Walk; Queen Elizabeth Building. MP (C) Runcorn, 1964-1983; Warrington South, 1983-1987. PC 1979. Various Government posts including:- Minister of State, Home Office, 1972-1974; Secretary of State for Education & Science, 1979-1981. Chairman; Parole Review Committee, 1987-1988; Criminal Injuries Compensation Board, 1989-2000. Judge of Appeal, Jersey & Guernsey, 1990-1999. Crown Court Recorder, 1976-1979 & 1981-1998. Baron 1987. WW.

CARMAN, George Alfred QC
Born 6 October 1929 Blackpool. Died 2 January 2001 aged 71. St Joseph's College, Blackpool; Balliol College, Oxford, BA. L. June 1953; Bencher 1978. ETC. 1953. Manchester Chambers; 60 King Street, 1953-1960; 47 Peter Street, 1960-1971. Silk 1971. London Chambers; 5 Essex Court; New Court; New Court Chambers, 5 Verulam Buildings, Grays Inn; 4-5 Grays Inn Square. Recorder, 1972-1984. Retired from practice due to ill health in August 2000. Obituaries:- Times & Daily Telegraph, 3 January 2001. WW.
The Lord Chancellor, Lord Irvine said "He was an outstanding trial lawyer of the old school, a gifted and deadly cross examiner. These skills, honed in the criminal courts, were turned to devastating account in all the major libel trials that marked the climax of his long career". According to Frances Gibb, the Legal Editor of the Times, "He was the ultimate jury advocate with an ear for the telling soundbite that would turn a case to his advantage his second stock in trade was the dramatic mid trial white

rabbit from a hat whether by chance or design"
His most famous results were the acquittals of Jeremy Thorpe, the former leader of the Liberal Party on charges of conspiracy to murder and the Liverpool comedian, Ken Dodd on income tax evasion. His son Dominic wote a biography of his father. "No Ordinary Man – A Life of George Carman", Hodder & Stoughton. 2002. The book contains all of his father's important cases as well as an attack on him as husband and father. Carman's final companion, barrister Karen Phillipps, is said to be writing her biography of George Carman.

CARNELLEY, William
I. 27 January 1890. ETC. 17 March 1892. Prop. Bigham QC. Sec. C A Russell. 6 Pump Court, 1892-1902; 1 Kings Bench Walk, 1903-1916; 2 Temple Gardens, 1917-1923; 11 Kings Bench Walk, 1924-1934. Not in 1935 Law List.

CARNEY, Andrew Patrick
Born 30 April 1966 Blackpool. St Benedict's School, Ealing, London; College of St Hild & St Bede, Durham University, BA(Geography); London School of Economics, MSc(International Relations). British Army 1989-1993. Married to Helen Wrenn qv. I. October 1995. ETC. 19 December 1995. Prop. Robert Fordham QC. Sec. Stephen Knapp. Liverpool Chambers; Martins Buildings, Water Street, 1995-1999; 7 Harrington Street, 6.9.1999. (merger with Corn Exchange).

CARPMAEL, Ernest QC
Born 1844. Died 4 December 1921 aged 77. 7th son of William Carpmael of Streatham, civil engineer & member of Lincoln's Inn. St John's College, Oxford, BA 1867; MA (Fellow) 1870. Married in 1876, Matilda, daughter of James Butler FRCS., Deputy Inspector General of Hospitals, Bengal Army. AAS. M. 8 November 1866. Call 17 November 1869. ETC. 12 July 1871. Prop. Quain QC. Sec. Thompson. 3 Harcourt Buildings, 1876-1898; 7 Fig Tree Court, 1899-1910. Patent practice. No address, 1911-1921. Foster.

CARR, Joseph William Comyns
Born 1849. 3rd son of Jonathan Carr of Lavender Hill, Surrey. Matriculated London University, 1870. AAS. 4 June 1869. Call 30 April 1872. ETC. 16 July 1872. Prop. C Russell QC. Sec. RG Williams. Circuit Junior, Spring 1873. 4 Garden Court, 1876-1879. No address, 1880-1916. Not in 1917 Law List.

CARROLL, Jonathan Neil
BA., AKC. G. October 1994. ETC. 20 December 1994. Prop. David Turner QC. Sec. David Bennett. Chavasse Court Chambers, 24 Lord Street, Liverpool, 1994-98. Left Circuit to practice in Middlesborough and later in Leeds.

CARROTHERS, Mildred Frances
Born 1901. 2nd daughter of Edward Carrothers of 10 Linnet Lane, Liverpool, produce merchant. Oxford University. AAS. M. 13 January 1921. Call 2 July 1924. ETC. 29 January 1925. Prop. Jackson KC. Sec. Sellers. 10 Cook Street, Liverpool, 1924-1928. No address, 1929-1963. Not in 1964 Law List.

CARTER, (Frederick) Brian QC (His Honour Brian Carter QC)
Born 11 May 1933. Son of Arthur Carter, Solicitors' Managing Clerk. Stretford Grammar School; King's College, London, LLB. G. February 1955. ETC. 1957. Pupilmaster, Godfrey Heilpern. Manchester Chambers; 60 King Street, 1957-1972; 47 Peter Street, 1973-1975; Chambers relocated to 12th floor, Sunlight House, Quay Street, 1975-1979 and to 28 St John Street, 1979-1985. London Chambers; 5 Essex Court. Prosecuting Counsel for Inland Revenue on Northern Circuit, 1973-1980. Recorder, 1978-1985. Silk 1980. Circuit Judge, (Circuit G), 1985-2001. Acting Deemster, Isle of Man, 2001. WW.

CARTER, Lesley Ann
Born 28 May 1967 Liverpool. Deyes High School, Maghull; Sheffield University, BA. G. October 1990. ETC. 1990. Prop. Rodney Klevan QC. Sec. Brian Lewis. Liverpool Chambers: 2nd floor, Peel House, Harrington Street, 1990-1994. Chambers relocated to 25-27 Castle Street, 1994.

CARTER, Martin Richard
Born 16 September 1969 Bromsgrove, Worcs. King Charles I School, Kidderminster; New College, Oxford, MA. M. 24 November 1992. ETC. December 1992. Prop. Andrew Gilbart QC. Sec. John Barrett. 40 King Street, Manchester (now Kings Chambers), September 1992.

CARTER, Richard Charles
Born 25 July 1968 Braintree, Essex. Felstead School; Manchester University, LLB. I. November 1990. 3 Pump Court, September, 1990-October 1991. Pupilmaster, Adam Pearson. ETC. 1992. Prop. Anthony Rumbelow QC. Sec. Beverly Lunt. Manchester Chambers; 58 King Street Chambers, 51-53 South King Street, Manchester, 1992-2001; Merchant Chambers, Parsonage Gardens, September 2001.

CARTWRIGHT, Ivan Matthew
Born 18 October 1969 Dublin. Wimbledon College, London; Manchester Metropolitan University,LLB. G. 25 November 1993. CPS, Manchester, Law Clerk, 1994. ETC. July 1995. Prop. Nigel Gilmour QC. Sec. Charles Feeny. Liverpool Chambers; Peel House. Harrington Street, May 1995-October 1996; Derby Square Chambers, Merchant Court, October 1996-2003. Travel & Work (Sabbatical) in Australia May 2000- December 2001.Oriel Chambers, 14 Water Street, Liverpool, 1 January 2004.

CARTWRIGHT, Nathaniel
Born 1847. Eldest son of Nathaniel Milnes Cartwright of Manchester. AAS. 17 November 1874. Call 13 June 1877. ETC. 15 July 1878. Prop. Hopwood QC. Sec. Collins. 51 King Street, Manchester, 1880-1881; 2 Harcourt Buildings, 1882. No address, 1883-1930. Not in 1931 Law List.

CARTWRIGHT, Sophie Pamela
Born 8 May 1976 Oldham. St Augustine's RC School, Billington; Blackburn College, Warwick University, LLB. I. October 1998. ETC. December 1998. Prop. Keith Goddard QC. Sec. Stuart Denney. Deans Court Chambers, 24 St John Street, Manchester, 1998.

CARTY, Hazel Frances
Born 22 December 1954 Liverpool. Married to His Honour Judge Graham Platts qv. Lasagesse, Liverpool; St Anne's College, Oxford, MA. AAS. M. 11 April 1975. Call July 1977. ETC. December 1977. Sec. David Berkson. Pupilmaster. P G Smith. 606 Corn Exchange, Fenwick Street, Liverpool, 1977-1978. Into further education. Senior Lecturer, Manchester University. Co editor, Clerk & Lindsell on Torts.

CARUS, Anthony
Born 22 May 1913 Hoddleston Lancs. Died 14 March 2005 aged 91. Ampleforth College. Father of Christopher Carus qv. & Roderick Carus QC. qv. G. 26 January 1938. ETC. 7 March 1938. Prop. Pritchard KC. Sec. Glyn Blackledge. Pilot in Royal Air Force/Fleet Air Arm during Second World War. Liverpool Chambers: 34 Castle Street, 1946-1955; Corn Exchange, Fenwick Street, 1956-1957; 9 Rumford Street, 1957-1974; Fruit Exchange Buildings, Victoria Street, 1974-1991; Chavasse Court, 24 Lord Street, 1991-2000. Mess at Adelphi Hotel, Liverpool in 1998 to mark 60 years in practice at the Bar.

CARUS, Christopher

Born 29 January 1940, Windermere. Died 1 December 1978, aged 38. Son of Anthony Carus qv. brother of Roderick Carus QC qv. Wirral Grammar School; Kings College, Durham, LLB. G. February 1963. ETC. 1963. Pupilmaster, Frank Nance. 606 The Corn Exchange, Fenwick Street, Liverpool, 1963-1978.

CARUS, Roderick QC
Born 4 June 1944, Windermere. Son of Anthony Carus qv. brother of Christopher Carus qv. Wirral Grammar School; University College, Oxford, BA (Law). Manchester Business School (Postgraduate Diploma in Advanced Business Studies). Merchant Bank, investments 1966-1970. G. November 1971. ETC. 1972. Pupilmaster, Jack Price. Manchester Chambers: (same chambers at different locations) 60 King Street, 1972-1983; 1 Deans Court, Crown Square, 1984-1993; 9 St John Street, 1994. Assistant Recorder 1987. Recorder & Silk 1990. WW.

CARVER, Thomas Gilbert KC (His Honour Judge Carver QC)
Born 14 November 1848 Gibraltar. Died 12 May 1906 aged 57. Forest School, Snaresbrook. St John's College, Cambridge, MA 1874. AAS. L. 7 April 1870. Call 7 June 1873; Bencher 1904. ETC. 28 March 1874. Prop. Williams QC. Sec. Collins. Liverpool Chambers; 22 North John Street, 1876. Kirkdale & Liverpool Sessions; 15 Lord Street, 1877-1887; Stephenson's Chambers, 25 Lord Street, 1888-1890; 1 Brick Court, 1891-1892; 2 Garden Court, 1893-1906. Silk 1897. Admitted M. 1891. County Court Judge, Circuit 12. (Yorks., West Riding), March 1906. Died two months after appointment. Publication; Law relating to the Carriage of Goods by Sea, 1885, 4th edition, 1905. WW. Foster.

CARVILL, Henry John
Irish Bar 1914. G. 17 November 1922. ETC. 15 June 1923. Prop. Madden KC. Sec. Chappell. No address, 1923-1953. Not in 1954 Law List.

CARVILL, Patrick George Hamilton MP
Born 1839. 4th son of Francis Carvill of Newry, merchant. London University. JP., of the Counties of Down & Armagh. Sheriff, County of Armagh, 1878. AAS. M. 22 January 1884. Call 26 January 1888. ETC. 4 March 1889. Prop. Gully QC. Sec. Briggs. MP (N) Newry, 1892-1906. 2 Garden Court, 1890-1899; 2 Pump Court, 1900-1903. No address, 1904-1907. 5 King's Bench Walk, 1908-1924. Member of the Court of Referees in the House of Commons. WW.

CARVILLE, (Owen) Brendan (Neville)
Born 19 October 1956 Liverpool. Liverpool Blue Coat School; Liverpool Polytechnic, BA. Office of County Prosecuting Solicitor, 1978-1979. I. July 1980. ETC. December 1980. Prop. Justin Price QC. Sec. David Maddison. Same Liverpool Chambers (different locations) 16 Queen Avenue, 1980-1983; 2nd floor, Peel House, Harrington Street, 1983-1994; 25-27 Castle Street, 1994.

CASE, Julie
Born 10 July 1968. Leicester University, LLB. M. October 1990. ETC. 1991. Liverpool Chambers: 7 Queen Avenue, 1991-1995; Exchange Chambers, Pearl Assurance House, Derby Square, 1995.

CASE, Magdalen Mary Claire
Born 9 December 1966 Wigan. Bolton School (Girls Division); Pembroke College, Oxford, MA; Dip Law. BP Oil International, 1988-1990. M. October 1992. ETC. 17 December 1992. Prop. Charles Bloom QC. Sec. Andrew Lowcock. 28 St John Street, Manchester, September 1992.

CASEMENT, David John
Born 19 November 1969 Belfast. Methodist College, Belfast; St Hugh's College, Oxford, BA. President, Oxford University Law Society. Editor, "Verdict" & Oxbridge Legal Review. Member, Kings Inns, Dublin. M. 13 October 1992. ETC. 1992. Prop. William Waldron QC. Sec. Henry Globe. Pupilmaster, Simon Earlam. Exchange Chambers, Pearl Assurance House, Derby Square, 1992.

CASSIDY, Patrick Stephen
Born 23 March 1960, Newcastle-upon- Tyne. St Cuthbert's Grammar School, Newcastle-upon-Tyne; Leicester Polytechnic, BA. L. July 1982. Law Centre & Young Peoples Advice Centre, 1983-1984. ETC. 23 May 1985. Pupilmaster, Maurice Haigh. Manchester Chambers: 26 Cross Street, 1984-1987; Kenworthy's Building, 83 Bridge Street, 1987.

CATTAN, Philip David
Born 8 December 1948 Manchester. Wilbraham High; Manchester University, LLB. G. November 1970. ETC. April 1971. Prop. E S Temple QC. Sec. C D R Rose. Circuit, Solicitor General. Manchester Chambers; 60 King Street, 1970-1978; 12th floor, Sunlight House, Quay Street, 1979; Chambers moved to 28 St John Street, 1980. Assistant Recorder 1992. Recorder 1996.

CATTERALL, Joseph
Youngest son of Paul Catterall, late of Lytham deceased. AAS. M. 23 May 1842. Call 23 May 1845. Sydney, New South Wales, 1848. Registrar, Preston District, Lancs. Chancery Court, 1854-1876. Recorder of Wigan, 1862-1880. Not in 1883 Law List.

*** CAULFIELD, The Hon Sir Bernard**

(DC)

Born 24 April 1914 St Helens. Died 17 October 1994 aged 80. St Francis Xavier College, Liverpool; Liverpool University, LLB, 1938; LLM 1940; Hon LLD, 1980. Solicitor 1940. Army Service, 1940-1946; RAOC. L. January 1947; Bencher 1968. Joined Midland Circuit, 1949; Leader, 1965-1968. Silk 1961. Recorder of Coventry, 1963-1968. High Court Judge, Queen's Bench Division, 1968-1989. Presiding Judge, Northern Circuit, 1976-1980. Hon. Member, Northern Circuit 1979. Retirement speeches at Liverpool Law Courts on 21 March 1989 (His Honour Judge Sir Sanderson Temple MBE., QC / J J Rowe QC) Transcript in Circuit Records. WW. Obituary, Times 21 October 1994.

CAULFIELD, Bruce Irvine (His Honour Judge Caulfield)
Born 1945. 3rd son of James Irvine Caulfield, Registrar of County Courts & District Registrar of the High Court. Haileybury School; Trinity Hall, Cambridge, BA. AAS. M. 1 December 1964. Call 26 November 1968. ETC.1968. Pupilmaster, Arthur Prestt. Manchester Chambers; 601 Royal Exchange, 1968-1988. Chambers then moved to 8 King Street, 1989-1991. Standing Prosecuting Counsel to Inland Revenue on Northern Circuit. Recorder, 1986-1991. Circuit Judge 1991.

CAVANAGH, Christopher
Born 1849. 4th son of Charles Cavanagh of Dublin. Ushaw College; BA 1872; LLB 1875 (London University). AAS. M. 4 April 1870. Call 26 January 1874. ETC. 12 July 1880. Prop. Temple QC. Sec. Henry. 5 Essex Court, 1881-1882. Special pleader & conveyancer; 3 Paper Buildings, 1883-1887; 5 Elm Court, 1888-1915. Not in 1916 Law List. Publications on Conveyancing; Money Securities; Parliamentary Costs. Foster.

CAVANAGH, Lorraine
Born 11 March 1976 Whiston. St Gregory's RC High School, Warrington. Manchester University, LLB. G. 27 July 2000. ETC. December 2000. Prop. Clement Goldstone QC. Sec. Sarah Singleton. 28 St John Street, Manchester (now St Johns Buildings), 4.3.2000.

CAVAN-IRVING, Herbert
Born 1855. 3rd son of John Irving of London. Trinity College, Cambridge MA., LLM, 1880. AAS. I. 28 January 1876. Call 26 January 1880. ETC. 6 February 1883. Prop. Crompton QC. Sec. Lowther. 3 Harcourt Buildings, 1884; 1 King's Bench Walk, 1885-1889. No address, 1890-1930. Not in 1931 Law List.

CAWLEY, Harold Thomas MP
Born 12 June 1878. Died 23 September 1915 aged 37. Second son of Sir Frederick (later Lord Cawley) and Lady Cawley of Berrington Hall. Leominster. Rugby; New College, Oxford MA. I. 11 June 1902. ETC 1 August 1902. Prop. Shee KC. Sec. Langdon. 78 King Street, Manchester 1909-1914. MP (L) for Heywood Division of Lancs. 1914-1915. Harold Cawley was commissioned Lt. in the 2nd Volunteer Btn. of the Manchester Regt and promoted Captain in the 6th Btn. Whilst acting as Aide de Camp to GOC East Lancashire Division, he was killed in action on 23 September 1915 at Gallipoli. He is buried in the Lancashire Landing Cemetery, Turkey. Grave reference A.76. The Cemetery is 1 km west of Sedd El Bahr village on a small ridge named Oghul Tepe, 110 metres above the sea and overlooking "W" Beach which became known as Lancashire Landing. His brothers John and Oswald were also killed in this War. WW. Public Record Office. Commonwealth War Graves Commission.

CAWSON, (Peter) Mark QC
Born 4 June 1959 Crosby. Wrekin College; Liverpool University, LLB. L. 29 July 1982. ETC. July 1983. Pupilmaster, Bertram Maddocks. Manchester Chambers; St James's Chambers, 68 Quay Street, 1983-2001; Exchange Chambers, Manchester & Liverpool, 5.3.2001. Junior Counsel to the Treasury (Charity matters in Manchester), 1992-2001. Assistant Recorder 1998. Recorder 2000. Silk 2001. His father was a solicitor partner in Hill., Dickinson & Co. WW.

CECIL, Edgar Algernon Robert QC., MP (Viscount Cecil of Chelwood)
Born 14 September 1864. Died 24 November 1958 aged 94. Third son of the 3rd Marquess of Salisbury (Prime Minister, 1886-1892 & 1895-1902). Eton; University College, Oxford, MA. I. 17 November 1887; Bencher 1910. ETC. 28 July 1888. Prop. Bigham QC. Sec. McKeand. Pupilmaster, John Gorell Barnes. Practised at first from Fountains Court attending Kirkdale and Liverpool Sessions. In 1882 he joined the South Eastern Circuit and concentrated on parliamentary work. Silk 1899. MP (C) East Marylebone, 1906-1910. MP (Ind.C) Hitchin, 1911-1923. Junior Minister, Foreign Office, 1915-1918. Minister of Blockade, 1916-1918. Lord Privy Seal, 1923-1924. Chancellor of the Duchy of Lancaster, 1924-1927. Chairman, Herts., Quarter Sessions, 1911-1920. Chancellor of Birmingham University, 1918-1944. Rector, Aberdeen University, 1924-1927. A founder of the League of Nations. President of League of Nations Union, 1923-1945. Hon. Life President, United Nations Association. Nobel Peace Prize for 1937. PC. CH. Publications; Principles of Commercial Law; The Way to Peace, 1928; A Great Experiment- an autobiography, 1941; A Real Peace, 1941; An Emergency Policy, 1948; All the Way, 1949. WW. DNB.

CHADWICK, John
I. 26 January 1904. ETC. February 1905. Prop C A Russell. Sec Kennedy. Certificate of Honour H.1904. Equity draftsman & conveyancer. 4 New Square, 1907-1918; 11 Old Square, 1919-1920; 2 Stone Buildings, 1921-1930. Not in 1931 Law List.

CHADWICK, John Moor Knighton
Born 1881. Eldest son of Richard Michael Chadwick of Estcourt, Natal, solicitor. AAS. M. 9 April 1902. Call 26 January 1905. No address, 1910-1953. Not in 1954. Law List.

CHADWICK, Neville

Born 1 January 1948 Manchester. Queen Mary College, London University, BA., LLM. AAS. M. 12 March 1970. Call 20 July 1972. Manchester Chambers; 2 Booth Street, 1974-1975; 13 Police Street, 1976-1978. Non Practising, 1979-1988. Principal State Counsel, Attorney General's Chambers, Francistown, Botswana. Advocate of High Court of Botswana, 1989-2000.

CHAISTY, Paul QC

Born 12 March 1958 Manchester. Parrswood High School, Manchester; Nottingham University, LLB; Exeter College, Oxford, BCL. L. July 1982. Hardwicke & Cassell Scholar. ETC. 1984. Pupilmasters; Nicholas Le Poidevin, William George & David Gilliland. 20 North John Street, 1984-1985; 460 Royal Exchange, Manchester, 1986-1987; 40 King Street, 1988. Assistant Recorder 1999. Recorder 2000. Silk 2001. WW.

CHAMBERS, Kenneth William Glyndwr

Formerly a solicitor. G. 17 November 1920. Manchester Chambers; 3 St James's Square, 1921-1948; 60 King Street, 1949-1978. Not in 1979 Law List.

CHAMBERS, Paul Victor St John

BA. G. November 1973. Manchester Chambers; 67 Princess Street, Manchester, 1975-1977; Lawrence Buildings, 2 Mount Street, 1978-1984; 3 St James's Square, 1985-1989; 38 King Street West, 1990-1995; 24a St John Street (now St Johns Building), 1996.

CHAPLIN, John Lawton

Born 25 May 1960. Rugby; Exeter University, BA (Latin). English Teacher, 1982-1984. I. November 1986. ETC. 1989. Prop. Rodney Scholes QC. Sec. Paul Chambers. London pupillage with Jeremy Carter-Manning. Manchester Chambers; 38 King Street West, 1989-1995; 24a St John Street, 1996-2002. (merger with 28 St John Street to form St Johns Building, 2002).

CHAPMAN, Rennick Andrew

LLB. M. March 1997. Lloyds House Chambers, 18 Lloyds House, Lloyd Street, Manchester, 1999-2000; 2 St John Street, Manchester, 2001.

CHAPMAN, Richard Harold

Born 29 October 1975 Manchester. The Manchester Grammar School; Brasenose College, Oxford, BA. G. October 1998. ETC. December 1998. Prop. Foster QC. Sec. Andrew Blake. Pupilmaster, Malcolm McEwan. 18 St John Street, Manchester, October 1998.

CHAPMAN, Selkirk

G. 27 January 1930. No address, 1930-1963. Not in 1964 Law List.

*** CHAPMAN, Stephen QC (The Hon Sir Stephen Chapman)**

Born 5 June 1907. Died 23 March 1991 aged 83. Westminster; Trinity College, Cambridge. Certificate of Honour, Bar Finals. I. 17 November 1931. South Eastern Circuit. Silk 1955. Recorder of Rochester, 1959-1961. Recorder of Cambridge, 1961-1963. Judge of the Crown Court and Recorder of Liverpool, 1963-1966. High Court Judge, Queen's Bench Division, 1966-1981. WW.

CHAPPELL, Robert Kingsley KC

Born 29 November 1884. Died 11 August 1937 aged 52. Leeds Grammar School; Merchant Taylors School, Crosby; Liverpool University, LLB. I. 17 November 1909; Bencher 1937. Served in European War, 1915-1919 (despatches, twice). 13 Harrington Street, Liverpool, 1909-1924; 10 Cook Street, Liverpool, 1925-1929. Silk 1929. 4 Temple Gardens, 1929. 12 King' Bench Walk, 1930-1937. Judge of Appeal, Isle of Man, 1934-1937. WW.

CHARLEY, Sir William Thomas QC., MP.

Born 5 March 1833 Woodbourne, County Antrim. Died 8 July 1904 aged 71. Elstree Hill House, Kent; St John's College, Oxford. AAS. I. 3 June 1857. Call 9 June 1865. 4 Crown Office Row & 4 St James's Square Manchester. MP (C) Salford, 1868-1880. Common Serjeant in the City of London, 1878-1892.Silk 1880. Kt. 1880. Publications; The Real Property Acts 1874-1877; The Judicature Acts 1873-1875; The Crusade against the Constitution; The Holy City, Athens & Greece. President of Pickwick Bicycle Club. WW. DNB.

CHATTERTON, Mark

Liverpool University LLB. G. July 1983. 10-11 Gray's Inn Square, 1985-1986. Liverpool Chambers; Martins Building, Water Street, Liverpool, 1987-1999; 7 Harrington Street, 1999. (merger with Corn Exchange).

CHAUDHRY, Zia Uddin

Born 20 May 1969 Burnley. Liverpool Bluecoat School; Manchester University, LLB. I. 26 November 1991. ETC. December 1991. Prop. David Harris QC. Sec. Robert Atherton. Liverpool Chambers; 3rd floor, Peel House, Harrington Street, 1991-1997. Chambers moved to India Buildings, Water Street, 1998.

CHEETHAM, Julia Ann
Born 21 September 1967 Niagara Falls, Canada. Married to Marc Willems qv. Wilmslow High School; Nottingham University, LLB. L. October 1990. ETC. 1991. Prop. Keith Goddard QC. Sec. Howard Baisden. Pupilmaster, Martine Kushner. Manchester Chambers; Hollins Chambers 64a Bridge Street, 1991-1997; Cobden House Chambers, 19 Quay Street, 1998-2001; Deans Court Chambers, 24 St John Street, 2001.

CHIBBETT, Ernest James
Born 1888. Elder son of James Chibbett of Canonbury, London. AAS. M. 15 October 1912. Call 16 June 1915. Formerly a Surveyor of Taxes. ETC. c1952. 20 Hackins Hey, 1953-1957. No address, 1958-1962. Not in 1963 Law List.

CHORLEY, Robert Samuel Theodore QC (First Baron Chorley)
Born 1895 Kendal. Died 27 January 1978. Kendal School; Queen's College, Oxford, MA. Certificate of Honour in Bar Finals. I. 26 January 1920. Professor of Commercial & Industrial Law, London University, 1930-1949. Chairman, Westmorland Quarter Sessions, 1944-1968. Lord in Waiting to HM King George VI, 1946-1950. QC 1961. Publications;- Case Books on Shipping, Banking & Mercantile Law. Arnoulds Law of Marine Insurance, 13th, 14th, 15th editions. Editor, Modern Law Review, 1937-1971. WW.

CHORLTON, James Dewsbury
Born 1873. Second son of James Chorlton of Didsbury Priory, Manchester. AAS. M. 29 April 1895. Call 4 May 1898. Prop. Russell QC. Sec. Woodruffe- Fletcher. 2 Garden Court, 1902-1909; 3 Plowden Buildings, 1910-1911. No address, 1912-1949. Not in 1950 Law List.

CHORLTON, (Margaret) Denise
Oxford University, MA. I. 18 November 1935. ETC. 26 February 1936. Prop. Gorman QC. Sec. Jalland. Manchester Chambers; 40 Kennedy Street, 1935-1944; 1b Cooper Street, 1945-1949; No address, 1950-1955; 26 King Street, 1956-1958; 9 Albert Square, 1959-1972; Deans Court Chambers, 1973. All England Law Reporter.

CHRISTIE, Simon Paul William
Born 19 July 1963 Hackney, London. Hey Comprehensive, Knowsley; Liverpool University, LLB. AAS. M. 23 August 1984. Call 9 February 1988. ETC. July 1988. Prop. Somerset Jones QC. Sec. John Leach. Liverpool Chambers; 24 Fenwick Street, 1988-1996; Ground floor, Peel House, Harrington Street, 1996-1999; Chavasse Court, Lord Street, 1999.

CHRUSZCZ, Charles Francis QC
Born 19 November 1950. Queen Mary College, London, LLB. AAS. M. 16 March 1971. Call July 1973. Manchester Chambers; 47 Peter Street, 1973-1976; 12th floor, Sunlight House, Quay Street, 1976-1979; 28 St John Street, 1979-2001; Exchange Chambers, Liverpool & Manchester 2001. Assistant Recorder 1986. Recorder 1999. Silk 1992. WW.

CHUKWUEMEKA, John Okechukwu
Born 24 November 1969 Liverpool. Liverpool College; King's College, London, BSc(Biochemistry). L. 24 November 1993. ETC. December 1996. Prop. Tim King QC. Sec. Geoffrey Lowe. Liverpool Chambers; 3rd floor, Peel House, Harrington Street, 1993-1996; Chambers moved to India Buildings, Water Street, 1996.

CLARE, Octavius Leigh
Born 1841. 8th son of William Clare of Liverpool, broker. Died 16 July 1912, aged 71. Rossall; St John's College, Cambridge, BA 1864. AAS. I. 4 November 1862. Call 26 January 1866; Bencher 1900. MP (C) Eccles, 1895-1906. Vice Chancellor, County Palatine of Lancaster, 1905-1912. London Chambers; 21 Old Square & 11 New Court, Carey Street. WW.

CLARE, (Reginald) Stuart
Born 25 October 1945 Kidsgrove, Staffs. Married to Pauline Clare, Chief Constable of Lancashire. The High School, Newcastle-under-Lyme; Solicitor, 1977-1997. Private Practice, 1977-1980. Crown Prosecution Service, Merseyside, 1980-1997. M. 22 May 1997. ETC. 18 December 1997. Prop. David Steer QC. Sec. Richard Pratt. Liverpool Chambers; Corn Exchange, Fenwick Street, 1997-1999; 7 Harrington Street 1999. (merger with Martins Bank).

CLARK, Andrew Richard
Born 3 September 1964 Birmingham. Dyson Perrins C of E High School; New College, Oxford, MA. Trainee Solicitor, Mills & Reeve, 1986-1988; Solicitor, Evershed, Wells & Hind, 1988-1994. I. 28 July 1994. ETC. 4 April 1995. Prop. Wingate-Saul QC. Sec. Paul Sheridan. Manchester Chambers; Manchester House Cambers, 6th floor, 18-22 Bridge Street, 1994-1999; 8 King Street, 1999.

CLARK, Denis (His Honour Judge Denis Clark)
Born 2 August 1943. Father of Rebecca Jane Clark qv. St Anne's RC Primary School, Rock Ferry; St Anselm's College, Birkenhead; Sheffield University, LLB. I. July 1966. ETC. 1966. Pupilmaster, Ifor Morris Jones. Liverpool Chambers; 606 The Corn Exchange, Fenwick Street 1966-1982; Chambers moved to 1 Exchange Flags, 1983-1988. Recorder 1984. Circuit Judge, 1988. WW.

CLARK, Paul Robert
Born 7 May 1953 Liverpool. St Mary's College, Crosby; Liverpool University, LLB. Formerly a solicitor, 1977-1994. Liverpool City Councillor, 1976. Leader of Opposition (Liberals), Liverpool City Councilm 1988-1991. Chairman, Social Services Committeem 1980-1983. Chairman, Standards Committeem 1999. Contested, Cheadle 1983; Liverpool Walton, 1987 & 1991. European Parliamentary Candidate for West Merseyside, 1985. AAS. M. 23 May 1994. ETC. 16 December 1994. Prop. David Turner QC. Sec. Richard Isaacson. Exchange Chambers, Pearl Assurance House, Derby Square, Liverpool 1994.

CLARK, Rebecca Jane
Born 19 August 1967, Birkenhead. Daughter of His Honour Judge Clark qv. Upton Hall Convent School; Sheffield University, LLB. I. July 1989. ETC. December 1989. Pupilmaster, Christopher Cornwall. Exchange Chambers, Derby Square, Liverpool, 1989.

CLARK, His Honour Judge Reginald QC
Born 18 March 1895. Died 15 January 1981 aged 85. Trinity Hall, Cambridge. L. 16 June 1920. ETC. 7 July 1920. Prop. Greaves-Lord QC. Sec. Jordon. Manchester Chambers; Bank of England Chambers, Tib Lane, 1920-1921; 60 King Street, 1921-1924. Rangoon Bar, 1924-1941. Judge of High Court of Madras, 1944-1948. Silk 1949. Commissioner of Assize, 1949. County Court Judge, Ilford, 1950-1955; Clerkenwell, 1955-1966. Served in 1914-1918 War in Gallipoli & France and in Burma & India, 1942-1944. WW.

CLARKE, David Clive QC (The Hon. Mr Justice Clarke)

(LDPE)

Born 16 July 1942. Father of Jonathan Clive Clarke qv. Winchester College; Magdalen College, Cambridge, MA. I. May 1965; Bencher, 1992. ETC. 27 May 1965. Circuit Junior, 1965. Circuit Treasurer, 1988-1992. Pupilmaster, Michael Maguire. Liverpool Chambers; 10 Water Street, 1965-1969; relocated to 14 Water Street, 1970-1982 and to Refuge Assurance House, Derby Square, 1983. Silk 1983. 5 Essex Court & 25 Byrom Street, Manchester. Recorder, 1981-1993. Circuit Judge, 1993-1997. Senior Circuit Judge and Honorary Recorder of Liverpool, 1997-2003. High Court Judge, Queen's Bench Division, 2003. Kt. 2003. Hon. LLD., Liverpool University, 9 July 2004. WW.

CLARKE, Humphrey Francis Norbury
I. 18 November 1929. 48 King Street, Manchester, 1932; Bank of England Chambers, Tib Lane, Manchester, 1933-1934; 1 Garden Court, 1935-1938; No address, 1939-1963. Not in 1964 Law List.

CLARKE, John Joseph
Born 2 April 1879. Died 1 October 1969 aged 90. Liverpool University, MA. G. 29 June 1927. Liverpool Chambers; 10 Dale Street, 1931-1935; 31 Dale Street, 1936-1940; 27 Lord Street, 1941-1959; 10 Water Street, 1960-1969. Lecturer in Housing & Planning Law at Liverpool & London Universities. Numerous books on Housing, Planning & Public Health & Local Government. WW.

CLARKE, Jonathan Clive
Born 28 August 1972 Liverpool. Son of Mr Justice Clarke. qv. Birkenhead School; Loughborough University, BSc. Britannia Royal Naval College, 1996-1997; Chester College of Law. I. 14 October 1999. ETC. 16 December 1999. Prop. Graham Morrow QC. Sec. William F Waldron. Exchange Chambers, Derby Square, Liverpool, 1999.

CLARKE, Lindsay Jane
Born 17 May 1976 Wrexham. The Maelor School, Whitchurch; Newcastle upon Tyne University, BA (Law & French). G. 22 July 1999. ETC. 16 December 1999. Prop. Nigel Gilmour QC. Sec. Richard Bradley. Oriel Chambers, Water Street, Liverpool, 1999.

CLARKE, Nicholas Stephen
Born 30 December 1959 Rochdale. Xaverian College, Manchester. Sheffield University, LLB. AAS. M. 18 March 1980. Call 23 July 1981. ETC. 1982. Prop. Benet Hytner QC. Sec. Howard Baisden. Manchester Chambers; 67 Princess Street, 1982-1988; Hollins Chambers, 64a Bridge Street, 1988-1991; Crown Square Chambers, 1 Deans Court, 1992-1993; 9 St John Street, 1994. Assistant Recorder 1999. Recorder 2000.

CLARKE, Susan Lesley
Born 21 November 1966 Liverpool. Stanley Park School, Liverpool; Liverpool University, LLB., LLM(International Law). Liverpool City Council, 1986-1991. M. October 1996. ETC. December 1996. Prop. Nigel Gilmour QC. Sec. Neville Biddle. Liverpool Chambers; ground floor, Peel House Harrington Street, 1996-1999; merger with Oriel Chambers, 28 February 1999.

CLARKSON, Eugene C
L. 26 January 1854. ETC. 1 August 1877. Prop. Temple QC. Sec. Foard. 3 Paper Buildings, 1876-1881. Equity draftsman & conveyancer and Admiralty Courts. Not in 1882 Law List.

CLARKSON, Thomas
Born 1849. Eldest son of Rev. Thomas Clarkson of Wyvreston, Suffolk. Kings College, Cambridge, MA & Fellow. Formerly assistant master at Tonbridge School. AAS. L. 14 November 1874. Call 17 November 1877. ETC. 3 February 1886. Prop. Gully QC. Sec. Yates. Chancery practitioner. Manchester Chambers; 78 Cross Street, 1886-1890; 6 St James's Square, 1891-1896; 9 St James's Square, 1897; 6 St James's Square, 1898-1905; 78 King Street, 1906-1918. Not in 1919 Law List. Joint author of Conveyancing & the Law of Property Act 1881, Foster.

CLAY, Peter William John
G. June 1955. 60 King Street, Manchester, 1958-1962. No address, 1963-1967. Not in 1968 Law List. Leslie Portnoy tells me that Peter Clay left chambers to join RADA later appearing on the stage and television.

CLAYTON, Nigel Garvin
Born 14 February 1964 Worksop, Notts. Ilkley Grammar School; Nottingham Trent University, LLB. I. July 1987. ETC. 1987. Prop. Rodney Scholes QC. Sec. Peter Keenan. Manchester Chambers; 72 Bridge Street, 1987-1994; 28 St John Street, 1994-2001; 40 King Street, 2002. Junior Counsel to the Crown (Provincial Panel), 2000. Publications; Mortgage Possession Actions, Sweet & Maxwell. Recorder, 27 November 2003.

CLEASBY, Hon. Sir Anthony
Son of Stephen Cleasby of Cragg House, Westmorland, Russian Broker. Born 27 August 1804. Died 6 October 1879 aged 75. Eton; Trinity College, Cambridge, BA 1827; Fellow 1828. I. 10 June 1831. Commercial practice on Northern Circuit. Silk 1861. Exchequer Baron, 1868-1879.

CLEAVER, Arnold Jeffries
Born 1851. 4th son of William Cleaver of Sandfield Park, West Derby, Liverpool, Superintendent Registrar of the District of West Derby & Toxteth Park. Liverpool College (Matric London University) AAS. M. 13 November 1869. Call 17 November 1874. ETC. 29 March 1875. Prop. Pope QC. Sec. Bigham. 1 Cook Street, Liverpool, 1876-1900. Liverpool & Kirkdale Sessions & Liverpool Court of Passage. Not in 1901 Law List.

CLEAVER, William Edward
L. 18 November 1895. ETC. 22 March 1897. Prop. Pickford QC. Sec. Collingwood-Hope. No address, 1898-1907. Penang, Straits Settlements, 1908-1940. No address, 1941-1949. Not in 1950 Law List.

CLEGG, Philip Charles (His Honour Judge Clegg)
Born 17 October 1942. Rossall; Bristol University, LLB. AAS. M. 1 February 1962. Call 19 July 1966. Manchester Chambers; 2 Booth Street, 1966-1975; 13 Police Street, 1976-1978; Rational House, 1979-1987. Assistant Recorder 1980. Recorder 1983. Circuit Judge, 1987. Resident Judge, Basildon Combined Court Centre, 1996. WW.

CLEGG, Richard Ninian Barwick QC
Born 28 June 1938. Only son of Sir Cuthbert Clegg, TD. Aysgarth; Charterhouse; Trinity College, Oxford, MA. Captain of Oxford Pentathlon Team, 1959. I. July 1960; Bencher 1985. Manchester Chambers; 4 Chapel Walks, 1960-1964; 601 Royal Exchange, 1965-1979; Byrom Street Chambers, 1979-1993. Silk 1979. Recorder, 1978-1993. London Chambers; 5 Essex Court & 61 Fleet Street. Active in local & national politics (Bow Group & Winston Circle). WW.

CLEGG, Sebastian James Barwick
Born 30 August 1969 Wythenshawe. Son Richard Clegg QC qv and cousin of Martin Collins QC qv. Eton College; Bristol University, BA (Maths & Philosophy) I. 26 May 1994. ETC. December 1994. Prop. Richard Clegg QC. Sec. Patrick Field. Deans Court Chambers, Manchester at Crown Square, 1.4.1995 and at 24 St John Street, 2000.

CLIFF, Elizabeth Dunbar
Born 20 January 1954 Hastings. Married to His Honour Judge Cornwall qv. St Mary's, Baldslow, Essex. AAS. M. I May 1972. Call 17 July 1975. ETC. 1976. Prop. Douglas Brown QC. Sec. John Gore. Liverpool Chambers; Fruit Exchange, Victoria Street, 1975-1991 and chambers moved to Chavasse Court, 24 Lord Street, 1991.

CLIFTON, Charles Darnley
G. 18 November 1907. Bristowe Chambers, 8 Harrington Street, Liverpool & 13 Kings Bench Walk, 1914-1916; 4 Paper Buildings, 1917-1919; 11 King's Bench Walk, 1920-1925; 2 Brick Court, 1926. District Probate Registrar, Bodmin, 1927-1947.11 Seymour House WC1, 1948-1955. Not in 1956 Law List.

CLIFTON, Gerald Michael (His Honour Judge Clifton)
Born 3 July 1947 Eccleston, St Helens. Liverpool College; Brasenose College, Oxford (Open Classical Scholar), MA. AAS. M. 9 May 1968. Call July 1970. ETC. 1970. Pupilmaster, Alan Booth. Liverpool Chambers; 14 Cook Street, 1970-1972; chambers moved to ground floor Peel House, Harrington Street, 1973-1989 and to the 1st floor, 1989-1992. Assistant Recorder 1982. Recorder 1988. Member, Manx Bar, 1992. Life Governor, Liverpool College, 1992. Circuit Judge, 1992. President, Mental Health Review Tribunal, 1997-2004. First sittings at Central Criminal Court, 2003. Member, Parole Board, 2004. WW.

CLOSE, George Leonard
Born 1935. Son of Lt. Col. Close of Blundellsands. Liverpool University, MA. AAS. M. 26 January 1951. Call 9 February 1954. 49 Castle Street, Liverpool, 1954-1960. Circuit Junior, 1956. Left the Bar to join the Civil Service. 1961-1973 rising to Assistant Solicitor in the Department of the Environment (Transport Branch). Not in 1974 Law List.

CLOSE, Jon Richard
Born 4 November 1974 Billinge, Wigan. Deanery High School; Warwick University, LLB. L. 9 October 1997. ETC. 2 April 1998. Prop. Nigel Gilmour QC. Sec. Simon Christie. Liverpool Chambers; Peel House, Harrington Street, February/March 1999; Oriel Chambers, 14 Water Street, 1999.

CLOTHIER, Sir Cecil Montacute KCB., QC. ("Spike" Clothier)

Born 28 August 1919. Stonyhurst College; Lincoln College, Oxford, BCL., MA; Hon Fellow 1984. Served, 1939-1945 War (51 Highland Div. & British Army Staff, Washington, DC. Hon. Lt. Col. Royal Signals.)
I. January 1950; Bencher 1973. ETC. 1950. Prop. Basil Neild QC. Sec. Richard Forrest. Liverpool Chambers; 3 Cook Street, 1950-1957; 14 Cook Street, 1958-1965. Silk 1965. Goldsmith Building, Temple, 1965. Recorder of Blackpool, 1965-1971. Crown Court Recorder, 1972-1978. Judge of Appeal, Isle of Man, 1972-1978.He has held many important public offices including Chairman, Police Complaints Authority, Parliamentary Commissioner for Administration and Health Service Commissioner for England, Wales & Scotland and Chairman, Council on Tribunals. Knight Commander of the Order of the Bath, 1982. WW.

CLOTHIER, Wilfrid QC. (His Honour Judge Clothier QC)
Born 19 February 1887. Died 9 February 1967 aged 79. Liverpool University, LLB., LLM. Solicitor, 1909. Served, 1914-1918 War (Hon. Artillery Company & Legal Assistant to the Director General of Recruiting) I. 26 January 1920; Bencher 1941; Treasurer 1965. Liverpool Chambers: 25 Lord Street, 1920-1929; 5 Cook Street, 1930-1933. Silk 1933. 5 Paper Buildings, 1933-1934; Paper Buildings, 1934-1947. County Court Judge, Circuit 48 (Lambeth, Surrey/Sussex) 1947-1959. Recorder of Blackburn, 1944-1947. Contested (C) Liverpool, Edge Hill, 1945. WW.

CLOVER, (Robert) Gordon QC. (His Honour Judge Clover QC)
Born 14 November 1911. Died 25 July 1993 aged 81. Lancing College; Exeter College, Oxford MA., BCL. L. 28 January 1935. ETC 16 January 1936. Prop Lynskey KC. Sec Blackledge. Liverpool Chambers; 10 Cook Street 1936. 25 Castle Street 1937-1939. Royal Artillery 1939-1945 (Despatches 1944). 49 Castle Street 1946-1958. Junior Defence Counsel in Liverpool Cameo Murder Case. Silk 1958. 2 Harcourt Buildings 1958-1965.Recorder of Blackpool 1960-1961. Deputy Commissioner for National Insurance Acts 1961-1965. County Court later Circuit Judge (Circuit 40) 1965-1982. WW.

CLUCAS, John Donald
Born 1869 of Cambridge University & Ramsey, Isle of Man. Eldest son of John Thomas C. Advocate deceased. AAS. M. 15 November 1889. Call 17 November 1892. ETC 17 July 1893. Prop Gully QC. Sec C A Russell. In Law List 1893-1939 but no chambers address.

COBBETT, J. P.
L. 18 November 1831. St James Square, Manchester 1831-1881. Special Pleader Bolton, Kirkdale, Lancs, Manchester, Preston, Salford, Wigan Sessions. Not in 1882 Law List.

COBDEN-SANDERSON, Thomas James
Born 1841.Died 7 September 1922 aged 81. Clare College, Cambridge MA & Fellow. Married in 1882. Anne, daughter of the late Richard Cobden MP. He prefixed her surname to his own. AAS. I. 17 February 1868. Call 26 January 1871. ETC 27 July 1884. Prop Hopwood QC. Sec Kay QC. London Chambers: 2 Brick Court 1876-1878; 3 Paper Buildings 1879-1884. Parliamentary Dr. & Committees. He left the Bar shortly after his marriage and decided to learn bookbinding. He became the pupil of the famous Roger de Coverly and in June 1884 he opened his own bindery at Maiden Lane in the Strand. Many regard him as the finest designer bookbinder of his generation. In March 1893 he opened the, now world famous, Doves Bindery in Hammersmith which he ran until the year before he died. DNB.

COCHRAN, William Harmood
Born 1849. Only son of William Cochran, late of Liverpool, deceased. Exeter College, Oxford, BA, 1871. AAS. M. 24 May 1869. Call 26 January 1874. ETC. 4 August 1876. Prop. Gully QC. Sec. Pickford. Liverpool Chambers; Commerce Chambers, Harrington Street, 1886-1888; 5 Cook Street, 1889-1991; 9 Cook Street, 1892-1923. 7 New Square, Lincoln's Inn, 1924-1931. No address, 1932-1933. Not in 1934 Law List.

COCKERELL, Robert Rennie Pepys
Born 1870. Eldest son of Frederick Pepys Cockerell, architect, deceased. New College, Oxford. AAS. M. 28 January 1888. Call 17November 1892.ETC. July 1900. Prop. Ferguson QC. Sec. Maurice Hill. No address, 1902-1907. Not in 1908 Law List. Harold Jager in "Brief Life" p.164-165 writes "Cockerell was the grandson of the architect of the Bank of England in Castle Street, Liverpool. He joined the Circuit in the same year that I did. He was extraordinarily handsome and a conspicuously able man. FE (Smith) held him in high regard. Cockerell had practised in India and had amassed a sufficient sum to enable him to burn his boats and try his fortunes at the Bar of England. But for his untimely death a few months after joining the Circuit, he would have risen to great heights".

COCKIN, John Garforth
Born 1847, Pembleton, Manchester. Died 27 July 1900 aged 53. Eldest son of James Cockin of Halifax. Completed his articles with Wavell & Co, Solicitors of Halifax before reading for the Bar. AAS. L. 27 May 1868. Call 17 November 1870. ETC. 13 March 1876. Prop. Russell QC. Sec. Hopwood QC. Studentship 1870 (First in Bar Finals) of 50 guineas a year for 3 years. He never put his talents to use at the Bar. Although he had Liverpool chambers addresses at 10 St George's Crescent and Duchy Chambers,Victoria Street, he never practised. His niece wrote in 1948;"He spent his time walking the Dales and climbing the Pennines, studying Latin & Russian in his spare time." His great passion was climbing mountains. He did some very impressive first ascents in the Caucasus between 1880 and 1890 including Janga, Ushba and Shkhara. He was buried at the English Church in Zermatt, Switzerland in 1900 following an accident on the Weisshorn. Information from Mr John Gaukroger of Halifax and Guy Holborn, Lincoln's Inn Librarian. Foster.

COCKSHUTT, Nicholas
I. 17 November 1905. ETC. 4 August 1906. Prop. Tobin KC. Sec. Lias. 13 Harrington Street, Liverpool, 1906-1913; 18 Tib Lane, Manchester, 1914-1921; 4 Harcourt Buildings, 1922; 1 Crown Office Row, 1923-1926. Not in 1927 Law List.

COFFEY, John Nimmo
Born 20 February 1929. Died 26 June 1981 aged 52. Stockport Grammar School; Manchester University, LLB. G. June 1951. ETC. 7 June 1951. Prop. Gerrard QC. Sec. Cunliffe. Manchester Chambers; 60 King Street, 1951-1955; 36 St Ann Street, 1956-1975. Crown Court Recorder, 1972-1981. Stipendiary Magistrate, Greater Manchester, 1975-1981. WW.

COGLEY, Stephen William
Born 13 August 1961 Winchester. Spalding Grammar School; Ripon Grammar School; Newcastle University, LLB. G. November 1984. Pupilmaster, P Towler (Midland & Oxford) ETC. 1988. Manchester Chambers; Hollins Chambers, 64a Bridge Street, 1988-1996; Merchant Chambers, 1 North Parade, Parsonage Gardens, 1997-2003; 4 Essex Court, Temple, 2003.

COHEN, George Hubert
Son of Louis & May Cohen of Liverpool. I. 17 November 1902. ETC. 19 February 1903. Prop. Taylor KC. Sec. Cuthbert Smith. Liverpool Chambers; 43 Castle Street, 1907; 10 Cook Street, 1908-1914. Lt., 5th Btn, Liverpool Regt. Killed in action 16 May 1915 at Richebourg-L'Avoue, France aged 36. Cemetery; Guards Cemetery, Windy Corner, Cuinchy, Pas de Calais. Grave reference VIII.B.34. Information supplied by Commonweath War Graves Commission.

COHEN, Howard Jonathon
Born 4 September 1975, Harrow. City of London Boys' School; St Catherine's College, Oxford BA; Trinity Hall, Cambridge, M.Phil. G. 1999. ETC. December 2000. Prop. Grime QC. Pupilmaster Jonathan Grace. 1 Temple Gardens, 1999-2000. Deans Court Chambers, 24 St John Street, Manchester, December 2000.

COHEN, (Joseph) Michael
Born 19 May 1947. Manchester Central Grammar School. Lancaster University (Lonsdale College), BA. Road Transport Training Board, 1969-1982; own Computer Software Company, 1982-1990. G. October 1992. ETC. 17 December 1992. Prop. Gee QC. Sec. P. McDonald. Manchester Chambers; 33 King Street West, 1992-2000; 5 John Dalton Street, 2000. Qualified Accountant. Diploma in Management Studies, 1974.

COHEN, Lionel Arthur
MA., LLB (Cantab) I. June 1948. Manchester Chambers; 2 Booth Street, 1952-1975; 13 Police Street, 1976-1979. No Chambers address, 1980-1984; 11 Old Square, Lincoln's Inn, 1985; 1 Central Street, 1986-1987; 33 King Street West (not practising), 1988. Not in 1989 Law List.

COHEN, Myrella QC (Her Honour Judge Cohen QC)
Born 16 December 1927. Died 25 October 2002 aged 74. Manchester High School for Girls; Colwyn Bay Grammar School; Manchester University, LLB (1948). G. January 1950. ETC. 1950. 26 King Street, Manchester, 1950-1953; 51 Westgate Rd, Newcastle-on- Tyne, 1954-1972. & North Eastern Circuit. Silk 1970. Recorder of Hull, 1971. Circuit Judge, 1972-1995. Resident Judge, Harrow from 1993. Parole Board, 1983-1986. Hon. LLD, Sunderland,; 1992. Obituary The Times, 6 November 2002. WW.

COKE, Reginald Henry
I. 17 November 1885. Call 7 February 1887. Prop. Hopwood QC. Sec. McConnell. 4 Hare Court, Temple, 1887-1890. No address, 1891-1897. Not in 1898 Law List.

COLE, Gordon Stewart
Born 25 March 1956 Liverpool. Wirral Grammar School; Liverpool Polytecnic, BA. I. July 1979. ETC. 1979. Pupilmaster, Anthony Carus. Fruit Exchange, Victoria Street, Liverpool, 1979-1988; 40 King Street, Chester, 1989-1997; 38 Young Street, Manchester, 1998-1999; Exchange Chambers, Liverpool, 1998.

COLE, Richard John
BSc (Eng), ACGL, LLB (London), CEng., MIEE., MBCS. G. July 1988. 1st Floor, New Court, Temple, 1992. 77, Deansgate, Manchester, 1999-

COLEMAN, Charles James
2nd son of Joseph Coleman of Turnham Green, Middlesex. Died 14 January 1908. AAS. G. 7 June 1849. Call 7 June 1852. 4 Pump Court, Temple. Stipendiary Magistrate for Middlesborough, 1875-1908.
Foster. WW.

COLES, Francis Eagland
A.I.B. I. June 1951. c/o C P Harvey QC, 1 Temple Gardens, 1952. PO Box 176, Dar es Salam, 1953-1957; Glebe House, Dumfries, 1958-1967; Manchester Chambers; Northern Assurance Building, Albert Square, 1968-1969; Post Office Chambers, 26 Brown Street, 1970-1976; 4th floor, Sunlight House, Quay Street, 1977-1983; 1 Central Street, 1984; Room 624, Sunlight House, 1985; 121 Princess Street, 1986. Not in 1987 Law List.

COLE-WILSON, Yatoni Iyamide Elizabeth
BA. L. November 1980. Not in Law Lists, 1980-1998. 77 Deansgate, Manchester, 1999.

★ COLLIER, John Francis (His Honour Judge Collier)

Born 19 June 1829, Plymouth. Died 10 December 1913 aged 84. Winchester. AAS. I. 11 January 1855. Call 10 June 1859. Recorder of Poole, 1870-1873. Judge of the Liverpool County Court, 1873-1907. Joint author of the Manual of Military Law. JP., Lancs. Foster. WW.

COLLINGE, Ronald Ashton Hilton

MA. I. June 1950. ETC. 7 February 1952. Prop. Crichton QC. Sec. George Bean. 9 Rumford Street, Liverpool, 1953-1957. No address, 1958-1963. Not in 1964 Law List.

COLLINS, (John) Martin QC

Born 24 January 1929. Uppingham School; Manchester University, LLB. G. 31 July 1952; Bencher 1984; Treasurer 1999. ETC. 1952. Prop. Fenton Atkinson QC. Sec. Joseph Cantley. Circuit Junior, Winter 1953. Manchester Chambers; 4 Chapel Walks, 1952-1964; 601 Royal Exchange, 1965-1972. Silk 1972. 2 Pump Court, 1972-1986; 10 Essex Street, 1987. Deputy Chairman, Cumberland Quarter Sessions, 1969-1972. Recorder, 1972-1988. Judge of the Court of Appeal of Jersey, 1984-1999. Commissioner, Royal Court of Jersey, 2000. Gibraltar Bar, 1990. WW.

COLLINS, Richard Henn QC (Baron Collins of Kensington)

Born 1842. Died 3 January 1911 aged 68. Son of Stephen Collins QC (Dublin). Trinity College, Dublin; Downing College, Cambridge, MA; Fellow 1865; Hon Fellow 1885. AAS.M. 8 May 1862. Call 18 November 1867; Bencher 1886; Autumn Reader 1895; Treasurer 1905. ETC. 29 July 1868. Prop. Quain QC. Sec. RG Williams. Liverpool Court of Passage & Sessions. 4 Garden Court, 1876-1883; 4 Brick Court, 1884-1891. Atlay writes: "He did not possess either in voice or manner the external graces of an advocate, but he scarcely had a rival at the Bar of presenting his cases or framing his arguments." He was joint editor of "Smith's Leading Cases" 8th & 9th editions- a task normally carried out by High Court Judges. Judge of the High Court, Queen's Bench Division, 1891. Lord Justice of Appeal, 1897. Master of the Rolls, 1901. Lord of Appeal in Ordinary, 1907-1910. Atlay:- "When at the Bar his contributions in prose and verse to the Grand Court of the Northern Circuit won him the honorary title of poet laureate" WW. DNB.

COLLINSON, Francis John

Born 1854. 3rd son of late Rev. George John Collinson of Clapham, Surrey. Married in 1882, Alice Elizabeth Sedgewich who died 18 months later in India. AAS. I. 18 November 1875. Call 3 July 1878. ETC. 20 July 1885. Prop. Taylor QC. Sec. Smyly. He practised before the High Court in Calcutta until 1886 when he returned home. In 1887 he appeared in the Lancs. Chancery Court in Manchester but the following year he moved to Kimberley, Cape of Good Hope. 3 Essex Court, 1902. 2 Brick Court, 1915-1928. Not in 1929 Law List.

COLLINSON, Jeffreys Lewis William

(uncle of His Honour Judge Collinson qv) Born 12 October 1884, bachelor, son of George Frederick Hampson Collinson, solicitor of 20 Castle Street, Liverpool. Home address, 12 Gambier Terrace, Hope Street, Liverpool. MA., BCL. L. 8 June 1910. ETC. 20 July 1910. Prop. Stephen. Sec. Cavanagh. Wason Chambers, 4 Harrington Street, Liverpool, 1910-1915. Lancs. Chancery Court. 2nd Lt. 3rd Btn., South Lancs Regt. Killed in action on 15 July 1916 at Mash Valley, Ovillers-Le Boisselle aged 31. Memorial 33, Ovillers Military Cemetery, Somme. Information from Commonwealth War Graves Commission.

COLLINSON, Richard Jeffreys Hampson (His Honour Judge Collinson)

(Nephew of Jeffreys Lewis Hampson Collinson qv.) Born 7 April 1924 Halifax. Died 9 April 1983 Wallasey aged 59. Heath Grammar School, Halifax; Wadham College, Oxford, BCL., MA. Sub Lt., RNVR 1944-1946. AAS. M. 30 October 1946. Call 26 January 1950. ETC. 1950. Pupilmasters, Glyn Blackledge, Leo Gradwell & Robertson Crichton. Liverpool Chambers; 9 Rumford Street, 1950-1957; 27 Lord Street, 1958-1959; 10 Water Street, 1960-1969; 2nd floor, Oriel Chambers, Water Street, 1970-1975. Second Junior to William Gorman KC & Glynn Blackledge in the Liverpool Cameo murder case in 1950. He was an Admiralty specialist and junior to J V Naisby QC for Canadian Pacific Steamship Company at the Inquiry into the loss of the Empress of

Canada which caught fire and sank in Gladstone Dock in January 1953. His daughter Alicia followed her father to Middle Temple. She was the Harmsworth Scholar in 1982 and joined Midland & Oxford. Her mother Gwen told me that Alicia designed the logo for Wirral Borough Magistrates Court. WW.

COLLISON, Harry
I. 19 November 1894. ETC. 2 July 1895. Prop. Hopwood QC. Sec. Sanderson. Circuit Junior, Winter 1896. 2 Dr Johnson's Buildings, 1896. 6 Pump Court, 1897. 4 Harcourt Buildings, 1898. 1 Temple Gardens, 1899-1940. No address, 1941-1949. Not in 1950 Law List.

COLOMBUS, Constantine John QC
Born 1886 Malta. Died 18 April 1968 aged 82. AAS. M. 3 June 1921. Call 26 January 1923; Bencher 1963. ETC. 18 February 1925. Prop. Jackson KC. Sec. Sellers. International Law specialist as a practitioner and academic. Professor of the Hague Academy of International Law. Silk 1950. WW.

COMMINS, Andrew MP
Born 1829. 2nd son of John Commins of Ballybeg. Co.Carlow. Died 7 January 1916 aged 86. Queen's University, Cork, MA; London University, LLD 1859. AAS. L. 19 November 1855. Call 26 January 1860. Eldon Chambers, Liverpool, 1876-1909; 20 South John Street, Liverpool, 1910-1916. MP (N) Roscommon, 1880-1885; South Division, 1885-1892; MP (N) Co. Cork SE, 1892-1900. His entries in the Law Lists demonstrate how on occasions people appear long after they have died. Commins appears in the Law Lists until 1928! WW. Foster

COMPTON-RICKETT, Mary Anne
Born St Albans. St Albans High School; Bristol University, LLB. G. 1972. ETC. 1974. Pupilmaster, Beryl Cooper (London). Liverpool Chambers; Martins Building, Water Street, 1974-1999; 7 Harrington Street, 6.9.1999. (Merger of Martins Building with Corn Exchange).

COMPTON-SMITH, William
Born 1859 only son of William Compton-Smith, solicitor of London. Trinity College, Cambridge, BA., LLB. 1882. AAS. I. 10 November 1879. Call 21 June 1882. ETC. 22 February 1889. Prop. Bigham QC. Sec. Byrne. Formerly of the Midland Circuit. Various London Chambers & at 1 Paper Buildings, 1903-1935. Not in 1936 Law List.

CONNELL, Anthony Edward
Birmingham University, LLB. G. July 1982. Scottish Life House, 10 James Street, Liverpool, 1986. Crown Prosecutions Service in London rising to Branch Crown Prosecutor, 1987.

CONNOLLY, Joanne Marie
Born 14 February 1970, Belfast. St Louis Grammar School, Ballymena; Nottingham University, LLB. M. 13 October 1992. ETC. 17 December 1992. Prop. Brendan Hegarty QC. Sec. McDermott. Pupilmasters, Gerard McDermott & Peter Main. 8 King Street, Manchester, 7.9.1992.

CONNOLLY, Michael
Born 19 April 1955 Birkenhead. St Hugh's, Birkenhead; Staffordshire University, BA (Law). G. July 1985. Pupilmaster, John Mockett. Liverpool Chambers; 2nd floor, Fruit Exchange, 1985-1992. Australia, 1992-1997; Peel House Chambers, 1997-1999; Chavasse Court, 1999-2001; Crown Prosecutor, Queensland, Australia 2001.

CONNOR, Laurence Joseph
Born 29 December 1949. Manchester University, LLB., MA. AAS. M. 17 April 1970. Call 27 November 1973. Queen's Insurance Building, Queen Avenue, 13 Castle Street, Liverpool, 1973-1979. Left Liverpool to become a magistrates clerk. Principal Clerk, Coventry Magistrates Court, 1997.

CONRAD, Alan David QC
Born 10 December 1953 Manchester. Bury Grammar School; Brasenose College, Oxford, BA. AAS. M. 9 January 1975. M. July 1976. ETC. December 1976. Prop. Waddington QC. Sec. Philip Clegg. Manchester Chambers; 13 Police Street, 1976-1978; Rational House, 64 Bridge Street, 1978-1994; Lincoln House Chambers, 5th floor, 1 Brazennose Street, 1994. Assistant Recorder 1993. Recorder 1997. Silk 2001. WW.

CONWAY, Helen Lois
Born 3 August 1970 St Helens. Cowley High School; Hull University, LLB; Trinity Hall, Cambridge, MPhil. Mace & Jones, Solicitors, 1993-1995 & 1996-1999; J Keith Park & Co, Solicitors, 1995-1996. L. July 1999. ETC. 1999. Prop. David Harris QC. Sec. Ross Duggan. India Buildings, Water Street, February 1999. Publications; Domestic Violence: Picking up the Pieces (Lion) & Domestic Violence & the Church (Paternoster).

COOK, Christopher Graham
Born 7 April 1963 Nottingham. Nottingham High School; Birmingham University, BSc, BCom; City University, Dip Law. I. 16 October 1990. ETC. 16 December 1997. Prop. Anthony Elleray QC. Sec. Mark Cawson. Pupilmaster, John Baldwin. Francis Taylor Building, Temple (pupillage). Manchester Chambers; St James's Chambers, 68 Quay Street, 1991-2001; Exchange Chambers, 4 Ralli Courts, West Riverside, 5.3.2001.

COOKE, Roger Arnold (His Honour Judge Roger Cooke)
Born 30 November 1939. Repton; Magdalene College, BA 1961; MA 1966. AAS. M. 4 December 1958. Call 17 July 1962. L. 1967 (Bencher 1994). Chancery Practitioner from 11 New Square, Lincoln's Inn & 4 Clarence Street, Manchester & 72, Bridge Street, Manchester. Recorder 1987. Circuit Judge 1989. Sits in Central London County Court and occasionally in Liverpool. WW.

COOKSAMMY, Natalie Camille
Leeds University, LLB. L. October 1995. Victoria Chambers, 19 Castle Street, Liverpool, 1999; Pannone & Partners, Solicitors, 123 Deansgate, Manchester, 1999.

COOPER, George
Born 1851. Eldest son of John Cooper, JP., of the Oaks, Preston. St John's College, Cambridge, MA. AAS. I. 9 November 1872. Call 10 May 1876. ETC. 12 July 1876. Prop. Temple QC. Sec. Addison. 3 New Inn, Strand, 1878; 6 Winckley Square, Preston, 1879-1891. Died December 1891 aged 40 (Liverpool Prosecutions Book).

COOPER, George Henry
Born 1822. Eldest son of George Edward Cooper of London. Trinity College, Cambridge, BA 1844. AAS. I. 30 April 1844. Call 5 May 1848. 5 Pump Court, 1876-1890. Associate of Western Circuit, 1885-1890. Not in 1891 Law List. Foster.

COOPER. John
Born 14 August 1960, Newcastle-upon-Tyne. Mount St Mary's College; Reading University, LLB. I. 1985. 11 King's Bench Walk, 1985-1999. Pupilmasters, Jeffrey Pegden & Nicholas Campbell. North Eastern Circuit, 1986-1999. King's Chambers, 40 King Street, Manchester, 1999-2004. ETC. 2001. Prop. Philip Raynor QC. brother of Roger Cooper of 1 Plowden Buildings (Co author of Charlesworth & Percy on Negligence). Publication: 4 part series on the prosecution of regulatory offences in Solicitors Journal Vol. 145. Nos. 22-25. Crown Office Chambers, 2004.

COOPER, Professor Sir William Mansfield
Born 20 February 1903 Manchester. Died 19 November 1992 aged 89. Ruskin College, Oxford; Manchester University, LLB., LLM. G. November 1940. Academic rising to Professor of Industrial Law, Manchester University, 1949-1970; Professor Emeritus; Vice Chancellor, 1956-1970. Publication; Outlines of Industrial Law, 1947. 6th edition by John C Wood, 1972. Kt. 1963. WW.

COPINGER, Harold Bernard
Born 1881. 3rd son of Walter Arthur Copinger qv. AAS. M. 25 April 1899. Call 12 June 1907. ETC. 15 February 1908. Prop. Tobin KC. Sec. Smith-Carington. 40 South King Street, Manchester, 1910-1921. No chambers address, 1922-1932. Cloisters, Temple, 1933-1934. No address, 1935-1953. Not in 1954 Law List.

COPINGER, Walter Arthur
Born 14 April 1847. Died 13 March 1910 aged 62. Father of Harold Bernard Copinger qv & father in law of James Marshall Eason qv. MA., LLD. AAS. M. 12 April 1866. Call 26 January 1869. ETC. 1908. 3 Elm Court, Temple, 1876-1880; South King Street, Manchester, 1881-1910. Many publications, mainly historical & Copinger on Copyright, 1904. Professor & Dean of the Faculty of Laws, Manchester University. WW.

COPELAND, Matthew Scott
Born 17 March 1976. University of Edinburgh, BSc (Environment Geoscience). G. 27 July 2000. Pupillage, Mitre Court Buildings. ETC. 31 July 2001. Prop. Andrew Gilbart QC. Sec. Matthew Smith. King's Chambers, 40 King Street, Manchester, 2001. England Squad, international hockey player.

COPPELL, Yvonne Ruth
Born 24 July 1954 Salford. North Manchester High School for Girls; Birmingham University, LLB. I. July 1976. ETC. 1976. Sec. Mclvor. Pupilmaster, Harry Turcan. Manchester Chambers; Lawrence Building, 2 Mount Street, 1976-1984; 3 St James Square, 1985-1989; 38 King Street West, 1990-1995; 24a St John Street 1996. (now St Johns Buildings) Assistant Recorder 1996. Recorder 2000. Married to Bradley Feld, solicitor.

COPPOCK, Theodore
Born 9 May 1858. 5th son of late Henry Coppock of Stockport, solicitor. Owens College, Manchester, BA 1877; St John's College, Cambridge, LLB 1882; MA 1884. AAS. I. 16 May 1881. Call 26 January 1884. ETC. 18 July 1886. 8 King's Bench Walk, 1887-1890. Salford Sessions. Not in 1891 Law List.

CORCORAN, Percy John (His Honour Judge Corcoran)
Born 26 November 1920. Died 5 October 1984 aged 63. Christian Brothers College, Adelaide, Australia; Royal Australian Air Force, 1941-1947. G. January 1948. Pupilmasters, William Rees Davies, London & Jack Nahum, Manchester. 26 King Street, Manchester, 1949-1953 & 1957-1961. Deputy Judge Advocate, Nicosia, Cyprus, 1953-1957. 60 King Street, Manchester, 1962-1970. Assistant Recorder, Blackpool, 1959-1970; Assistant Recorder; Blackburn, 1962-1970. Chairman, N W Mental Health Review Tribunal, 1962-1970. County Court Judge, 1970-1971. Circuit Judge, 1972-1984. He sat for 6 months in Liverpool and for 2 years at the Old Bailey. In the main he was the senior civil judge at West London County Court. Circuit records; Photograph on call in 1948 and swearing in with Mrs Corcoran in 1970. WW, and information from his wife Jean Corcoran who was a magistrate in the Fyde and sat occasionally at Preston Sessions.

CORDEROY, George
I. 17 November 1926. ETC. 18 February 1931. Prop. Goldie KC. Sec. Gething. 5 Crown Office Row, 1931-1934. He then entered the Office of the Treasury Solicitor, retiring in 1964 as Senior Legal Assistant. Not in 1991 Law List.

CORKHILL, Sylvia Margaret
Born 1934. University College London. AAS. M. 22 March 1954. Call 21 May 1957. Liverpool Chambers; 27 Dale Street, 1964-1976; Melbourne Building, 21 North John Street, 1977-1984. Subsequently a Recorder on the Midland & Oxford Circuit.

CORLESS, John Vincent
Born 6 January 1952. St Andrew's University, MA. AAS. M. 17 May 1984. Call 27 November 1984. Liverpool Chambers; 54 Castle Street, 1985-1987; Chambers moved to 14 Castle Street (now Atlantic Chambers, Cook Street), 1987.

CORNAH, Emma Louise
Married to Simon Burrows qv. LLB. I. November 1992. ETC. 30 March 1993. Prop. Klevan QC. Sec. Timothy White. 15 Winckley Square, Preston, 1994-2000. Not in 2001 Bar Directory.

CORNWALL, Christopher John (His Honour Judge Cornwall)
Born 20 December 1950 Liverpool. Married to Elizabeth Dunbar Cliff qv. Shrewsbury School; St Catherine's College, Oxford, BA (English Literature). L. July 1975. ETC. 1975. Prop. Morris Jones QC. Sec. David Berkson. Liverpool Chambers; (same chambers at different locations) 606 The Corn Exchange, Fenwick Street, 1975-1982; 1 Exchange Flags, 1983-1991; Exchange Chambers, Derby Square, 1992-2002. Assistant Recorder 1990. Recorder 1994. Circuit Judge 24 June 2002. WW.

CORTA, Jerzy Antoni
L. January 1948. 1 Chapel Street, Preston, 1949-1962. No address, 1963-1967. Not in 1968 Law List.

COSTELLOE, Benjamin Francis Conn
Born 1854. Only son of Martin Richard Costelloe of Glasgow, Surveyor to the Board of Trade. Balliol College, Oxford, MA. Eglinton Fellow, Glasgow University. AAS. L. 19 November 1875. Call 26 January 1881. ETC. 1 February 1881. Prop. Russell QC. Sec. Crompton. 33 Chancery Lane WC2, 1881-1899. Not in 1900 Law List. Equity draftsman & conveyancer. Liverpool, Preston & Kirkdale Sessions. Sometimes on editorial staff of Shipping & Mercantile Gazette. Foster.

COTTINGHAM, James
Born 1821. Eldest son of James Courtney Cottingham of Dublin. Matriculated, Trinity College, Dublin. AAS. L. 24 January 1848. Call 17 November 1854. Manchester Chambers; 4 St James's Square, 1876-1893; 8 St James's Square, 1894-1905. No address 1906. Not in 1907 Law List. Foster.

COTTON, Wilfred Stapleton
Born 1885. 2nd son of William Cotton of Manchester. University of London, LLB. AAS. M. 2 November 1907. Call 17 November 1910. ETC. 25 July 1911. Prop. Ashton KC. Sec. Atkinson. Manchester Chambers; 33 King Street, 1914-1921; 22 Tib Lane, 1922-1928. No address, 1929-1953. Not in 1954 Law List.

COTTRELL, Matthew Robert
Born 10 June 1971 Heswall. Son of Patricia Cottrell, Solicitor, Cuff Roberts & Co, Liverpool. Birkenhead School; Sheffield University, LLB. G. 16 October 1996. ETC. December 1996. Prop. Eric Somerset Jones QC. Sec. Richard Bradley. Oriel Chambers, 14 Water Street, Liverpool, September 1996.

COULSON, Alice Monica (Nee Pullen)
G. January 1950. Pupilmaster, Glyn Blackledge. 34 Castle Street, Liverpool, 1952-1963. No address, 1964-1967. Not in 1968 Law List.

COVENEY, Christopher James
LLB. I. July 1976. 192 Manor Street, Fenton, Stoke on Trent, 1979-1981. Midland & Oxford Circuit. 9th floor, Sunlight House, Quay Street, Manchester, 1982-1985; 6th floor, 1986-1988. Sun Alliance Group WC2, 1990. Not in Law List 1991-1993. Sunlight House, 1994; 38 Young Street, Manchester, 1995-1999. Admitted as a solicitor June 1999. Corbett & Co, Teddington, Middlesex, 2001.

COVENTRY, Millis Jnr. (His Honour Judge Coventry)
Born 1838. Died 5 November 1930 aged 92. 4th son of Millis Coventry of Wandsworth Common, Surrey. King's College School; King's College, London; Trinity Hall, Cambridge, BA, 1862. Rowed against Oxford at Putney in 1860 & 1861. AAS. I. 18 January 1861. Call 26 January 1864. 64 Cross Street, Manchester to 1886. County Court Judge at Preston, March 1886-1905. WW. Foster.

COWAN, Jack
Born 7 January 1949 Glasgow. Wallasey Grammar School; Leicester University, LLB. I. 23 November 1971. ETC. 1972. Pupilmaster, Justin Price. Liverpool Chambers; Queen Insurance Building "D", 13 Castle Street, 1972-1979; 16 Queen Avenue, 1980-1983; 2nd floor, Peel House, Harrington Street, 1984-1992. Moved chambers to Martins Bank Building, 1992-1999; 7 Harrington Street (Merger of Martins Bank with Corn Exchange, 6.9.1999.

COWAN, Peter Sherwood McCrea
Born 24 September 1958 Ottawa, Canada. Rugby School; Oriel College, Oxford, MA. AAS. M. 19 January 1978. Call 24 July 1980. ETC. Autumn 1980. Prop, Somerset Jones QC. Sec. Andrew Sander. Circuit Junior, Summer 1984. Oriel Chambers, 14 Water Street, Liverpool, 1980. Recorder July 1999.

COWARD, Edward Maurice
Born 1869. Cotton spinner & bleacher of Bowden, Cheshire. Only son of Edward Coward of Bowden, same occupation. AAS. M. 6 May 1895. Call 26 April 1899. ETC. 3 February 1900. Prop. Russell QC. Sec. Hildesheimer. No address, 1902-1910. Not in 1911 Law List.

COX, Ralph Bouverie
G. 17 November 1913. ETC. 4 February 1914. Prop. Hewart KC. Sec. Miller. No address, 1914-1953. Not in 1954 Law List.

CRABTREE, Simon Jeremy Gerhard
Born September 1963 Rochdale. Bacup & Rawtenstall Grammar School; Leeds University, LLB. L. November 1988. ETC. Dec 1988. Prop. Rodney Scholes QC. Sec. Keith Thomas. 14 Winckley Square, Preston, 1988-1990; 38 King Street West, Manchester, 1990-1995; 24a St John Street, Manchester, 1996.(now St Johns Buildings).

CRAIG, Frederick William Cotter
G. April 1923. ETC. 5 July 1923. Prop. Madden KC. Sec. Hooper. Liverpool Chambers; 25 Lord Street, 1923-1926. No address, 1927-1942. 27 Lord Street & 31 Market Square, Northampton, 1943-1949. No address, 1950-1951. 58, Derngate, Northampton, 1952-1963. Not in 1964 Law List.

CRAIG, Norman Vincent
I. 2 July 1930. ETC. 27 January 1932. Prop. Goldie KC. Sec. Blackledge. 1 Essex Court, Temple, 1932-1949. No address, 1950-1963. Not in 1964 Law List.

CRAINE, George Victor
MB., ChB. G. 26 January 1938. ETC. 10 June 1938. Prop. Goldie KC. Sec. Blackledge. Liverpool Chambers; 13 Harrington Street, 1941-1946; 27 Lord Street, 1947-1954. He drowned in June 1954 aged 42 when his dinghy capsized in the River Alt.

CRALLAN, Richard Wharton
Born 21 August 1968 Chester. Upton by Chester County High School; Liverpool University, LLB. I. 16 October 1990. ETC. July 1991. Prop. John Rowe QC. Sec. G. Pickavance. Circuit Junior, Summer 1993. Chavasse Court, 24 Lord Street, Liverpool, July 1992-September 1999; 10 King's Bench Walk, September 1999-August 2002; Solicitor advocate specialising in ancillary relief cases with Sears, Tooth of Mayfair, 1 February 2002.

CRANE, Richard Steven
Born 2 October 1971 Cambridge. Jack Hunt Comprehensive School, Peterborough; Universities of Keele; Cambridge; Nottingham & London (BSc., P.G.C.E., PgDL) Teacher of Mathematics at Rugby School, 1994-1999. G. 26 July 2001. ETC. 18 December 2001. Prop. David Steer QC. Sec. Neil Flewitt. 7 Harrington Street, Liverpool, 2001.

CRANGLE, Charlotte Mary
Born 14 February 1973 Manchester. Daughter of G P Crangle, solicitor of Stretford, Sale & Stockport. Stockport Grammar School; Sheffield University, LLB. G. 12 October 1995. ETC. 1996. Prop. Howard Bentham

QC. Sec. John Marsh. Pupilmaster, Julian Holt. Manchester Chambers; 211 Deansgate/ Parsonage Chambers, October 1995-June 2000; Old Colony House, June 2000- June 2001; 24a St John Street, June 2001.(now St Johns Buildings).

CRAWFORD, Colin
Born 22 April 1953 Glasgow. Married to Lesley Anderson qv. University of Edinburgh LLB., LLM. M. 24 July 1997. ETC. 16 December 1997. Prop. Andrew Gilbart QC. Sec. Vincent Fraser. University Lecturer; Edinburgh, 1975-1999; Reading, 1977-85; Manchester, 1985-1989. Senior Lecturer, Birmingham, 1989-2001. King's Chambers, 40 King Street, Manchester, September 1998. Editor of numerous volumes of Planning & Local Government Law including Financial Editor of Sweet & Maxwell's Encyclopaedia of Local Government Law and editor of the Journal of Local Government Law.

CRAWFORD, John Dawson (His Honour Judge Crawford)

Born 4 August 1861. Died 28 June 1946 aged 84. Son of Joseph Dawson Crawford, surgeon, of 40 Rodney Liverpool. Trinity College, Cambridge. AAS. I. 14 May 1881. Call 26 January 1884. ETC. 2 August 1884. Prop. Addison. Sec. McKeand. 9 New Square, 1885-1887; 3 King's Bench Walk, 1888-1918. County Court Judge March, 1918-1934. Circuit 38 (Essex, Herts. & Middlesex) Publications; Ministry of Justice; Reflections & Recollections, 1936.

CRAWFORD, Robert David
Born 4 February 1953, Droylesden, Manchester. De la Salle College, Salford; Pembroke College, Cambridge, MA. L. July 1976. ETC. 1976. Prop. Benet Hytner QC. Sec. Anthony Jolly. Manchester Chambers; 36 St Ann Street, 1976-1980; 27 Byrom Street, 1981-1983; 26 Cross Street, 1984-1987; 83 Bridge Street, 1988-1991; 15 Winckley Square, Preston, 1991. Assistant Recorder 1998. Recorder 2000. Breeder of Hereford cattle.

CRAWSHAW, Richard M.P. (Baron Crawford of Aintree)
Born 25 September 1917. Died 16 July 1986 aged 68. Pendleton Grammar School; Tatterford School; Pembroke College, Oxford, MA., University of London, LLB. Clerk, 1929-1931. Engineer, 1933-1936. Theological Student, 1936-1939. Royal Artillery & Parachute Regt, 1939-1945. I. November 1948. Liverpool Chambers; 24 Dale Street, 1949-1954; 14 Cook Street, 1955; 36 Dale Street, 1956-1960; 9 Rumford Street, 1962-1973; Fruit Exchange, Victoria Street, 1974-1986. Liverpool City Council, 1948-1965. M.P. for Liverpool, Toxteth, 1964-1983. (Lab. 1964-1981; SDP 1981-1983) Deputy Speaker, House of Commons, 1979-1981. Contested (SDP) Liverpool Broadgreen, 1983. TD. 1958. DL., Merseyside 1970. Life Peer 1985. (First Social Democrat nominee in the House of Lords) Set world non stop walking record of 231 miles at Aintree in 1974. WW. Times Obituary 17 July 1986.

CREAN, Anthony
Born 9 June 1962. Essex University, BA. Manchester University, MPhil. G. July 1987. ETC. December 1987. Prop. John Hoggett QC. Sec. Halliday. Circuit Junior, Winter 1991. 40 King Street, Manchester, 1987-1999. 5 Fountain Court, Steelhouse Lane, Birmingham, 2000.

CREAN, Mary Angela
Born 17 May 1966 Zimbabwe. Sacred Heart High School, Crosby; Liverpool John Moores University, LLB. Stewardess with Dan Air, 1988-1991. G. October 1996. 9 Baker Street, Middlesbrough, December 1997-December 1998. ETC. December 1998. Prop. Nigel Gilmour QC. Sec. Ashley Barnes. Liverpool Chambers; 24 Fenwick Street /14 Cook Street, 1998. New Bailey Chambers, Liverpool, 2004.

CREMIN, James Augustine
G. 17 November 1937. No chambers address, 1937-1963. Not in 1964 Law List.

CREMLYN, John Williams Jones.
G. 28 January 1901. ETC. 24 February 1903. Prop. Hope KC. Sec. Lord. 2 Middle Temple Lane, 1901. No address, 1902-1903. 3 Essex Court, 1904. No address, 1905-1909. Manchester Chambers; 78 King Street, 1910. No address, 1911-1922; 4 Chapel Walks, 1923-24. Thereafter various London addresses. Not in 1964 Law List.

CRICHTON, (John) Robertson Dunn QC. (The Hon Mr Justice Crichton)
Born 2 November 1912. Son of a Wallasey stockbroker. Died 12 July 1985 aged 72. Sedbergh School; Balliol College, Oxford. AAS. M. 5 November 1932. Call 27 January 1936. ETC. 29 January 1936. Prop. Maxwell Fyfe KC. Sec. Hartley Shawcross. Circuit Junior, Summer 1936. Liverpool Chambers; 43 Castle Street, 1936-1939. Royal Artillery, 1939-1945. 34 Castle Street, 1945-1949; 9 Rumford Street, 1950-1951. Silk 1951. Plowden Buildings, 1951-1952; 2 Harcourt Buildings, 1953-1960. Recorder of Blackpool, 1952-1960. Judge of Appeal, Isle of Man, 1956-1960. Recorder of Manchester & Judge of the Manchester Crown Court, 1960-1967. High Court Judge (Queen's Bench Division), 1967-1977. WW.

CRICHTON-GOLD, Peter Leonard
LLB (London). FCIArb. G. July 1972. Manchester Chambers; 26 Brown Street, 1973-1975; 1 Deans Court Crown Square, 1976; Sunlight House, Quay Street, 1977-1992. Stoke on Trent chambers, 1994-1998. 40a Young Street, Manchester, 1999. Not in 2000 Bar Directory.

CRILLEY, Darrel
Born 1 August 1967 Oldham. Roch Valley High School, Rochdale; Mansfield College, Oxford, BA (Geography); University of London, LLB., PhD. I. 18 March 1996. ETC. 2 April 1996. Prop. Clement Goldstone QC. Sec. John Phillips. 28 St John Street, 1996-2002. (23.9.2002 Merger with 24a to form St John's Chambers.)

CRITCHLEY, Walter Asheton Paget
I. 18 November 1907. ETC. 23 June 1908. Prop. Sanderson KC. Sec. Sharpe. No address, 1908-1953. Not in 1954 Law List.

CROASDELL, William Carlyle
G. 20 April 1910. ETC. 7 February 1912. Prop. Langdon KC. London Chambers; 4 Pump Court; 3 Elm Court; 2 Brick Court, 1912-1925. Not in 1926 Law List.

CROFTON, Richard Ffolliot
Born 29 September 1849. 3rd son of General John Ffolliot Crofton of London. Worcester College, Oxford, MA. AAS. I. 31 May 1871. Call 7 June 1875. ETC. 2 March 1877. Prop. Pope QC. Sec. Addison. 19 Cooper Street, Manchester, 1877-1901. Lancs. Chancery Court. Not in 1902 Law List. Foster.

CROMPTON, Abraham
Born 1848. Eldest son of Abraham Crompton of Oldham. Matriculated London University, 1876 from Owens College. AAS. L. 30 April 1878. Call 21 June 1882. ETC. 20 July 1885. Prop. Ambrose QC. Sec. Edwin Jones. Manchester Chambers; 42 John Dalton Street, 1885-1893; 5 St James Square, 1894-1895. Lancs. Chancery Court. No address, 1896-1940. Not in 1941 Law List. Foster.

CROMPTON, Charles QC., M.P
Born 4 February 1833. Died 25 June 1890 aged 57. Eldest son of Sir Charles John Crompton, Assessor of the Liverpool Court of Passage and later Queen's Bench Judge. Trinity College, Cambridge, MA, 1858. AAS. I. 15 April 1852. Call 6 June 1864; Bencher 1887. Silk 1882. 3 Harcourt Buildings, 1876-1890. MP, Staffordshire (Leek), 1885-1886. Foster.

*** CROMPTON. His Honour Ian William**
Born 28 June 1936. Manchester Grammar School; University of Manchester, LLB. National Service (Army), 1954-1956. Articled to George Stanley Green, Clerk to the Manchester County Justices. Admitted as a solicitor, November 1962. Solicitor in private practice, 1962-1972. Clerk to the Justices; Manchester County, 1972-1974; Eccles, 1974-1983. Stipendiary Magistrate, South Yorks., 1983-1994. Assistant Recorder 1984. Recorder 1989. Circuit Judge at Liverpool, 13.7.1994-6.8.2004. WW.

CROOK, Peter Rothwell
Born 1833. Son of Richard Smethurst Crook. qv. Matric. London University, 1850. AAS. I. 2 May 1851. Call 6 June 1855. No chambers address. Lancs. Chancery Court. Not in 1888 Law List. Foster.

CROOK, Richard Smethurst
Father of Peter Rothwell Crook. qv. I. 26 November 1830. No address. Liverpool Probate Registrar, 1876-1882. Not in 1883 Law List.

CROSHAW, Frank
I. 1 July 1908. ETC. 15 June 1910. Prop. Sanderson KC. Sec. Hewart. 2 Cloisters, 1910; 5 Paper Buildings, 1911; 3 Temple Gardens, 1912-1913; 9 King's Bench Walk, 1914; 3 King's Bench Walk, 1915-1938. No address, 1939-1953. Not in 1954 Law List.

CROSS, Anthony Maurice
Born 16 June 1958 Accrington. St Mary's College, Blackburn; Manchester University, LLB. AAS. 26 September 1980. Prop. Michael Maguire QC. Sec. John Ward. Manchester Chambers; 6th floor, Arkwright House, Parsonage Gardens, 1982-1985; 26 Cross Street, 1986-1987; Kenworthy's Buildings, 83 Bridge Street, 1988-1992; 15 Winckley Square, Preston, 1992. Recorder 2003.

CROSS, Charles Albert
G. June 1949. Town Clerk, Town Hall, Prestwich, 1972-1974; Town Clerk, 25 Bow Street, 1975-1976. Room 460, Royal Exchange, Manchester, 1977-1988; 40 King Street, 1988-1993. No address, 1994.

CROSS, Jane Elizabeth
Born 13 November 1958. Liverpool University, LLB. AAS. M. 27 April 1981. Call 29 July 1982. Preston Chambers; 14 Winckley Square, 1984-1993; 15 Winckley Square, 1994.

CROSS, Richard Assheton (First Viscount Cross)
Born 30 May 1823, Preston. Died 8 January 1914 aged 90. Father of William Henry Cross qv. Rugby; Trinity College, Cambridge, BA., 1846. AAS. I. 14 November 1844. Call 8 June 1849; Bencher 2 May 1876; Treasurer 1895. Preston & Salford Sessions. Chairman Lancs. Quarter Sessions, 1866-1874. MP.(C) Preston, 1857-1862; South West Lancs, 1868-1885; (beating Gladstone); Lancs, (Newton), 1885-1886. Home Secretary, 1874-1880. Secretary for India, 1886-1892. Lord Privy Seal, 1895-1900. GCB 1880. Viscount 1886. GCSI., 1892. JP., Cheshire; JP., & DL., Lancs. WW. DNB. Foster.

CROSS, Hon. William Henry MP
Born 22 August 1856. Eldest son of First Viscount Cross qv. University College, Oxford, BA. AAS. I. 22 November 1878. Call 26 January 1882. ETC. 25 January 1853. Prop. Gibb QC. Sec. Collins. 2 Harcourt Buildings, 1883. 3 Dr Johnson's Building, 1884-1892. Not in 1893 Law List.

CROSTHWAITE, Arthur Tinsley OBE (His Honour Judge Crosthwaite)
Born 6 May 1880. Son of late Alderman Arthur Crosthwaite, JP., Liverpool. Died 28 November 1951 aged 71. Winchester College, New College, Oxford, BA. I. 19 November 1906. ETC. 20 February 1907. Prop. Tobin KC. Sec. F E Smith. Liverpool Chambers 25 Lord Street, 1907-1914 & 1919-1926. Army Service, 1914-1919. Temp. Major BAOR. (Despatches twice, OBE) Deputy Recorder of Liverpool, 1926-1928. 21 Harrington Street, 1927-1928. County Court Judge, Circuit 5 (Salford & Bolton), 1928-1940; Circuit 6 (Liverpool), 1940-1951. JP. WW.

CROWDER, William Irwin Robert
I. 17 November 1909. ETC. 20 July 1910. Prop. Stephen KC. Sec. Sharpe. 2 Plowden Buildings, 1912-1921. No address, 1922-1953. Not in 1954 Law List.

CROWE, His Honour Gerald Patrick QC

(RB)

Born 3 April 1930. St Francis Xavier's College, Liverpool; Liverpool University, LLB. G. November 1952, ETC. 1952. Prop. Brabin QC. Sec. John Edward Jones. Liverpool Chambers; North House, 17 North John Street, 1952-1971; Martins Building, Water Street, 1972-1973. Silk 1973. Goldsmith Building, 1973-1980. Recorder, 1976-1980. Circuit Judge, 1980-1995. Lord Chancellor's Committee on Legal Aid, 1984-1991. Retirement Speeches Liverpool, 29 September 1995.(Judge Wickham / Rodney Klevan QC.) WW.

CRUTTENDEN, Frank
G. 10 May 1922. Liverpool Chambers; 20 Hackins Hey, 1948-1964; 14 Cook Street, 1965-1968. Lancs. Chancery Court. No address, 1968-1970. Not in 1971 Law List.

CSOKA, Simon
Born 12 April 1968 Blackburn. Stonyhurst College; Fitzwillian College, Cambridge, MA. G. November 1991. Weinstock Senior Award. ETC. 30 March 1993. Prop. David Poole QC. Sec. Marshall. Pupilmaster, Peter Finnegan. Manchester Chambers. Lloyd's House, Lloyd Street, 1993-1999; 3rd floor, 2 St John Street, 2000-2001; 18 St John Street, 2001.

CUMELLA, Mary Agnes ("Molly") MBE., JP
L. November 1951. Liverpool Chambers; 34 Castle Street, 1953-1955; Corn Exchange, 1956; 36 Dale Street, 1957-1960; 9 Rumford Street, 1961-1973; Fruit Exchange, Victoria Street, 1974. Not in 1975 Law List.

CUMMINGS, Brian
Born 10 April 1965 Belfast. Christ's Hospital, Horsham; Trinity College, Cambridge, MA. L. November 1988. ETC. Dec 1989. Prop. John Kay QC. Sec. David Turner. Pupilmasters; Colin McKay/David Turner. Circuit Junior, 1992/3. 2 Garden Court October, 1988-September 1989. Exchange Chambers, Liverpool; 1 Exchange Flags/Derby Square, 1989.

CUNINGHAM, Henry
L. November 1885. Liverpool Chambers; 9 Cook Street, 1888-1910; 5 Harrington Street, 1911-1923; 10 Dale Street, 1924-1940. Lancs. Chancery Court. Not in 1941 Law List.

CUNLIFFE, Christopher Joseph (His Honour Judge Christopher Cunliffe)
Born 28 February 1916. Died 23 September 1995 aged 79. Rugby School; Trinity Hall, Cambridge, BA. L. 19 November 1938. Legal Cadet, British North Borneo Civil Service, 1938-1939. RAFVR, 1941-46 in Intelligence & with Judge Advocate General's Dept. Liverpool Chambers; 27 Lord Street, 1946-1952; 34 Castle Street, 1953-1966, Deputy Coroner, Liverpool, 1953-1966. Chairman: National Insurance Tribunal, Bootle, 1956-1966: Mental Health Review Tribunal, 1961-1966. County Court, later, Circuit Judge, 1966-1982. WW.

CUNLIFFE, Sir (Joseph) Herbert KBE., QC., MP.
Born 1 July 1867. Died 9 April 1963 aged 95. AAS. M. 7 June 1893. Call 29 April 1896. Bencher, L. 1919; Treasurer 1941. ETC. 15 July 1896. Prop. McCall QC. Sec. Byrne. Manchester Chambers; 77 King Street, 1897-1898; 78 King Street, 1899-1912. 6 New Court, Carey Street, 1913-1921; 15 Old Square, 1922-1963. Silk 1912. Attorney General of the Duchy of Lancaster, 1921-1946. MP (U) Bolton, 1923-1929. Chairman, Essex Quarter Sessions, 1937-1946. Chairman, General Council of the Bar, 1942-1948. WW.

CUNLIFFE, Karen
LLB. G. November 1977. Fruit Exchange, Victoria Street, Liverpool, 1978-1985. Not in 1986 Law List.

CUNLIFFE, Thomas Alfred (His Honour Judge Cunliffe)
Born 9 March 1905. Died 11 April 1993 aged 88. Lancaster Royal GS; Sidney Sussex College, Cambridge. I. 26 January 1927. Manchester Chambers; 6 St Ann's Passage, 1927-1940. Squadron Leader, RAFVR 1940-1945. 60 King Street, 1946-1955; 36 St Ann Street, 1956-1963. Dep. Chairman, Lancs. County Quarter Sessions, 1961-1963. Recorder, Barrow in Furness, 1962-1963. County Court, later, Circuit Judge, 1963-1975. Sat in the Birkenhead County Court. WW. Obituary, Methodist Recorder, 6 May 1993.

CUNNINGHAM, Colin Jonathan Irving DSC.
G. June 1947. Died 12 December 1985 aged 69. Liverpool Chambers; 9 Rumford Street, 1949-1955. Resident Magistrate, Northern Rhodesia, 1956-1957. No address, 1958-1968 (In Africa). 4 Brick Court, South Eastern Circuit, 1969. No address, 1970-1972. Liverpool Chambers; Queen Insurance Building, 13 Castle Street, 1973; 41 North John Street, 1974-1978; 15 Victoria Street, 1979-1985.

CURRAN, Philip Peter
Born 13 October 1952 Belfast. St Malachy's College, Belfast; Manchester University, BA (English & History). L. May 1979. ETC. 28 June 1979. Prop. Chrisropher Rose QC. Sec. Ward. Manchester Chambers; 6th floor, Arkwright House, Parsonage Gardens, Deansgate, 1979-1984; 26 Cross Street, 1985-1987; Kenworthy's Buildings / Lincoln House Chambers, 1988. Recorder 1998.

CURRIE, George Boyle Hanna MBE., MP.
Born 19 December 1905. Died 20 January 1978 aged 72. Campbell College, Belfast; Trinity College, Dublin, BA., MA., LLB. AAS. 4 November 1929. Call 8 June 1932. ETC. 14 June 1933. Prop. Goldie KC. Sec. Maxwell Fyfe. Circuit Junior, Winter 1933. Liverpool Chambers; 45 Castle Street, 1933-1935; 43 Castle Street, 1936; 5 Harrington Street, 1937-1939. Squadron Leader, RAFVR, 1939-1946 (MBE 1946). 3, Cook Street, 1946-1948; 34 Castle Street, 1949-1972; Queen Insurance Building, 13 Castle Street, 1973-1978. Councillor, Wirral UDC, 1934-1950 (Chairman 1938). Contested (C) East Flintshire, 1950 & 1951; MP (UU) North Down 1955-1970. WW.

CURRIE, Piers Alexander OBE
I. 27 January 1908. 2 King's Bench Walk, 1910-1914. No address, 1915-1937. Assistant Solicitor, Ministry of Health, Whitehall SW1., 1938-1949. No address, 1950-1953. Not in 1954 Law List.

CURTIS, Charles Nelson
1.28 January 1901. ETC. 29 July 1901. Prop. Russell KC. Sec Mansfield. 2 Harcourt Buildings, 1902-1921. No address, 1922-1953. Not in 1954 Law List.

CURTIS, His Honour Philip
Born 29 April 1908, Gorton, Manchester. Died 9 May 1998, aged 90. Manchester Grammar School; Brasenose College, Oxford. Admitted as a solicitor. Prosecuting Solicitor, Halifax, 1939. G. June 1944. Manchester Chambers; 60 King Street, 1944-1960; 47 Peter Street, 1961-1969. Breathalyser specialist; Manchester United Supporter (Sir Bobby Charlton read the lesson at Curtis's funeral) and junior defence counsel for Myra Hindley in the 'Moors Murders' trial at Chester Assizes in 1966. County Court, later, Circuit Judge, 1969-1980. WW. Obituaries; Telegraph, 22 May 1998; Times, 9 June 1998; Graya, Vol. 108.

CUTTER, Roy Carnegie
G. 20 April 1910. ETC. 11 July 1912. Prop. McCall KC. Sec. Hamilton. 2 Harcourt Buildings, 1911-1921. No address, 1922-1953. Not in 1954 Law List.

D

DABLE, Jeremy Richard
Born 6 September 1961 Nottingham. King's School, Grantham; Leeds University, LLB. 2 years in commercial litigation with Dibb, Lupton in Leeds & Sheffield. G. November 1987. ETC. 17 December 1992. Prop. Klevan QC. Sec. Webster. Pupilmaster Phillip Walter. New Bailey Chambers, 10 Lawson Street/ 9-11 Ormskirk Rd, Preston, 1992.

DACRE, Ian Thomas
Barrow in Furness Grammar School; Sheffield Polytechnic, BA(English); MA(English Literature) London. Formerly a secondary school teacher. M. November 1991. New Bailey Chambers, 10 Lawson Street/9-11 Ormskirk Road, Preston, 1993.

da CUNHA, John Wilfred (His Honour John da Cunha)
Born 6 September 1922. Stonyhurst College; St John's College, Cambridge, MA, 1954. Served, 1942-1947. 23rd Hussars (RAC). Wounded, Normandy 1944. Judge Advocate General (War Crimes); Hon Major. AAS. M. 6 November 1944. Call 17 November 1948. ETC. February 1949. Prop. William Gorman KC. Sec. Tommy Backhouse. Circuit Junior, 1950. 43 King Street, Manchester, 1948-1970. Assistant Recorder, Oldham, 1966-1970. Chairman, Industrial Tribunals, 1966-1970. Deputy Chairman, Lancs. County Quarter Sessions, 1968-1971. County Court, later, Circuit Judge, 1970-1992. Parole Board, 1976-1978. Criminal Injuries Compensation Board, 1992-1997. JP., Lancs. 1968. WW.

DAICHES, Samuel
L. 17 November 1920. ETC. 20 June 1922. Prop. Wingate-Saul KC. Sec. Gething. 8 King's Bench Walk, 1922-1927; 2 Hare Court, 1928-1934. No chambers address, 1935-1949. Not in 1950 Law List.

DALAL, Rajen Charles James
Born 30 July 1968 Littleborough. Bury Grammar School; Manchester University, LLB. L. October 1991. ETC. 1992. Prop. Anthony Gee QC. Sec. S. Neale. Manchester Chambers; Hollins Chambers, 64a Bridge Street, 1992-1998; Cobden House Chambers, 19 Quay Street, 1998.

DALE, Jonathan Paul
Born 4 June 1968 Keighley, West Yorks. Hume Grammar School for Boys, Oldham; Oriel College, Oxford, MA. G. October 1991. Pupilmasters; John Sabido, Nigel Tozzi & John Ticciati. 1 Dr Johnson's Building (pupil, 1991-1992); 4 Pump Court (pupil 1992); 10 King's Bench Walk, 1992-1996. ETC. December 1996. Prop. Fordham QC. Sec. David Boulton. Martins Bank/ 7 Harrington Street, Liverpool, 1996.

DALEY, Eunice Catherine
G. November 1950. ETC. 14 February 1952. Prop. Rose Heilbron QC. Sec. Anthony Carus. 34 Castle Street, Liverpool, 1952-1955. No address, 1953-1963. Not in 1964 Law List.

DALEY, Judith Mary Philomena (Her Honour Judge Daley)
Born 12 August 1948. Seafield Convent Grammar School, Crosby; King's College, London, LLB. G. 1970. ETC. 1970. Pupilmasters; Justin Price & Michael Morland. Liverpool Chambers; 34 Castle Street, 1971; 38 Park Square, Leeds, 1972; 27 Dale Street, 1973-1976; Melbourne Buildings, 21 North John Street, 1977-1988; 3rd floor, Peel House, Harrington Street, 1989-1994. Assistant Recorder, 1984. Recorder, 1989. Circuit Judge, 1994, on Wales & Chester Circuit and later in Liverpool. WW.

DALEY, Nicola Elizabeth
Born 12 June 1978 Liverpool. Belvedere GPDST; Leeds University, LLB. G. 27 July 2000. ETC. 26 July 2001. Prop. David Turner QC. Sec. William Waldron. Exchange Chambers, Derby Square, Liverpool, 2000. Circuit Junior, 2003.

DANIEL, William Atkinson
Born 1856. 3rd son of Samuel Daniel of Timperley, Cheshire. Trinity Hall, Cambridge, BA. AAS. M. 27 January 1876. Call 19 November 1879. ETC. 27 January 1880. Prop. Leofric Temple QC. Sec. Smelt. Goldsmith Building, 1880-1882. No address, 1883-1935. Not in 1936 Law List.

*** DANIEL, William Thomas Shave QC. (His Honour Judge Daniel QC)**
Born 17 March 1806. Eldest son of William Daniel of Derbys. AAS. L. 27 January 1825. Call 8 February 1830. Silk & Bencher, 1851. 41 Chancery Lane. Equity draftsman & conveyancer. Midland Circuit & Warwicks. Sessions. Recorder of Ipswich, 1867-1884. County Court Judge, Circuit 11, (Burnley & Colne), 1967-1884. Foster.

DARBY, Lionel Frank Christopher
I. 4 May 1898. ETC. 1 August 1899. Prop. Pickford QC. Sec. Maurice Hill. Circuit Junior, Winter 1901. 2 King's Bench Walk, 1899-1907; Goldsmith Building, 1908-1932. Registrar, Admiralty Division, Royal Courts of Justice, WC2., 1933-1948. Assistant Registrar, 1949-1960. Not in 1961 Law List.

DARBYSHIRE, (William) Robert
Born 18 January 1972, Blackpool. Rossall School, Blackpool; Christ Church, Oxford, BA (Law); King's College, London, LLM. L. November 1995. ETC. 21 December 1995. Prop. Leeming QC. Sec. M. Johnson. Pupilmasters; Michael Johnson & Neil Berragan. 9 St John Street, Manchester, 1996.

D'ARCY, Martin Valentine
Born 1845. Died November 1917 aged 72. 3rd son of Nicholas D'Arcy of Ballyforan, Roscommon, Ireland. Brother in law of Joseph Waton, qv. After leaving school he worked as a clerk for 6 years. In 1869 he returned to Dublin to study law at Kings Inns. AAS. M. 1 November 1870. Call 26 January 1878. ETC. 6 April 1878. Prop. Russell QC. Sec. Mulholland. 2 Middle Temple Lane, 1879; 1 Elm Court, 1880-1890; 25a Winckley Square, Preston, 1893-1894; 2 Victoria Street, Blackburn, 1895-1899; 8 Harrington Street, Liverpool, 1900; 25 Lord Street, Liverpool, 1901-1917. In 1880 he received an appointment as a parliamentary draftsman. Three years later he became the electoral agent to Lord Weymouth, the heir to the Marquess of Bath. They fell out because he let it be known that he wished to succeed to the constituency when Lord Weymouth went to the Lords. In 1904 he accepted the post of Revising Barrister with the task of revising electoral rolls in the Liverpool area. Information from 'Father Martin D'Arcy' (his son) by H J A Sire. Gracewing Press.

DAVEY, Michelle Maria
Born 26 March 1971 Whiston. Tower College; Liverpool University, LLB. L. November 1993. ETC. December 1993. Pupilmaster Vincent Deane. Liverpool Chambers; Stanley Street Chambers, 1993-1994; Victoria Street Chambers, 1994-1996; 14 Castle Street, 1996. (now Atlantic Chambers).

DAVIDSON, Arthur QC., MP.
Born 7 November 1928. Liverpool College; King George V School, Southport; Trinity College, Cambridge, BA. Served in the Merchant Navy. AAS. M. 19 October 1949. Call 10 February 1953. Pupilmaster, Edward Youds. Liverpool Chambers; North House, 17 North John Street, 1954-1958; 9 Rumford Street, 1959-1960. Thereafter London chambers & member of the South Eastern Circuit. MP (Lab) Accrington, 1966-1983. PPS to the Solicitor General, 1968-1970. Parliamentary Secretary, Law Officers Dept., 1974-1979. Opposition spokesman on legal affairs, 1981-1983. Shadow-Attorney General, 1982-1984. Chairman, House of Commons Jazz Club. Legal Director, Associated Newspapers Holdings, 1987-1990; Mirror Group, 1991-1993. WW.

DAVIDSON, Henry
Born 1837, eldest son of Henry Marshall Davidson of Holme House, Haddington. Trinity Hall, Cambridge, LLB 1860. MA, 1862.; late fellow & bursar. AAS. I. 5 November 1859. Call 17 November 1862. Examiner in Civil Law to Cambridge University, 1871-1872. Sheriff Clerk, East Lothian. 4 Crown Office Row, 1876-1883; 3 Paper Buildings, 1884-1896. Not in 1897 Law List. Foster.

DAVIES, Arthur Leslie Llewelyn
I. 3 July 1889. ETC. 30 July 1890. Prop. Gibbs QC. Sec. Walton. Circuit Junior, Winter 1891. 2 Garden Court, 1893-1907. Not in 1908 Law List.

DAVIES, Rt. Hon. Clement Edward KC., MP.
Born 19 February 1884. Died 23 March 1962 aged 78. Llanfyllin County School; Trinity Hall, Cambridge, BA., LLB. 1907; Hon Fellow, 1950. Law Lecturer, University College, Wales, Aberystwyth, 1908-1909. L. 5 May 1909. (Certificate of Honour); Bencher, 1953. ETC. 14 June 1912. Prop. Greer KC. Sec. Rigby Swift. 2 Pump Court, 1911-1915; 2 Mitre Court Buildings, 1916-1940. Secretary to: President Probate, Divorce & Admiralty Division, 1918-1919; Master of the Rolls, 1919-1923. Junior Counsel to the Treasury, 1919-1925. Silk 1926. MP (L) Montgomeryshire, 1923-1962. Leader of the Liberal Parliamentary Party, 1945-1956. PC 1947. Numerous government committees. Chairman, Montgomeryshire Quarter Sessions, 1935-1962. Publications on Agricultural & Auction Law and Finance matters. WW.

DAVIES, Clive Robin Michael
LLB London. G. July 1962. Liverpool Chambers; 7 Rumford Street, 1965; The Temple, Dale Street, 1967-1970. Not in 1971 Law List.

DAVIES, David Gareth Griffiths
BA (Cantab) I. July 1975. 1 Dean's Court Chambers, Manchester, 1977-1983. Not in 1984 Law List.

DAVIES, (Francis) Peter
Born 29 January 1961 Prescot. Son of His Honour Joseph Davies QC. qv. Liverpool College; Liverpool Polytechnic, BA 1982. G. 24 July 1986. ETC. 16 December 1986. Prop. Michael Maguire QC. Sec. Michael Wolff. Liverpool Chambers; Melbourne Building, 21 North John Street, 1986-1988; 3rd floor, Peel House, Harrington Street, 1989-1993; Corn Exchange, Fenwick Street, 1993-1999; 7 Harrington Street, 6.9.1999. (merger with Martins Bank). Recorder 2002.

DAVIES, Frederick
L. November 1952. Manchester chambers; 4 Clarence Street, 1957-1960; 42 Kennedy Street, 1961-1963; No address, 1964-1969; 26 Brown Street, 1970; 67 Princess Street, 1971-1978. Not in 1979 Law List.

DAVIES, Hugh Michael
Born 9 November 1958 Coventry. Cheltenham Grammar School; Lincoln College, Oxford, MA. AAS. 11 February 1981. Call 29 July 1982. ETC. 1984. Prop. Keith Goddard QC. Sec. Mark Lamberty. Manchester Chambers; 43 King Street, 1984-1988; 5 John Dalton Street, 1988-1995; Lincoln House Chambers, 5th floor, 1 Brazennose Street, 1995.

DAVIES, John Verdin
Born 23 April 1932 Worsley. Manchester Grammar School; Manchester University, LLB. FCIA. G. February 1955. Iron & Steel Board, 1966-1968; Contractors Plant Association, 1969-1973; Federation of Bakers, 1974-1975; 12 South Square L.I., 1976-1979; 11 Old Square, 1980-1981; Brussels, 1982-1986; British Medical Association, 1988-1990; 6 Pump Court, 1997. Chairman; Social Security Appeals Tribunal, 1991-; Medical Appeals Tribunal 1993. Publication; Encyclopaedia of Health Services & Medical Law. Sweet & Maxwell, 1987.

DAVIES, Joseph Marie QC (His Honour Joseph Davies QC)

(RB)

Born 13 January 1916 St Helens. Father of (Francis) Peter Davies qv. Stonyhurst College; Liverpool University. G. 17 November 1938. ETC. 1 February 1939. Prop. Sellers KC. Sec. Trotter. Pupilmasters, Hartley Shawcross/ Richard Trotter. Liverpool Chambers; 43 Castle Street, 1939. Served, 1939-1946, The King's Regiment, 1939-1941; RIASC & Staff Allied Landing Forces, SE Asia, 1942-1946. Colonel, JAG Staff, prosecuting Japanese war criminals in Singapore. 34 Castle Street, 1946; 24 Dale Street, 1947-1955; 27 Lord Street, 1956-1959; 10 Water Street, 1960-1962. Silk 1962. 2 Pump Court, 1962-1971. Chairman, Cumberland County Quarter Sessions, 1963-1970 (Deputy, 1956-1963). Recorder of Birmingham, 1970-1971. County Court, later, Circuit Judge, 1971-1991. Retirement Speeches, Liverpool Law Courts, 11 January 1991 (Judge Paterson/John Rowe QC). WW.

DAVIES, Kenneth Boyd
G. 13 June 1934. ETC. 10 July 1935. Prop. Gorman KC. Sec. Ormerod. 6 St Ann's Passage, Manchester, 1937-1940. Not in 1941 Law List.

DAVIES, Martin John
G. July 1975. Oriel Chambers, 14 Water Street, Liverpool, 1978-1982; Refuge Assurance House, Derby Square, Liverpool, 1983-1985. Senior Assistant Prosecuting Solicitor, South Yorks; CPS, London; Southern Water Authority; National Rivers Authority.

DAVIES, Michael Iwan
Born 28 June 1956 Liverpool. Son of John Davies, Headmaster. Holt Comprehensive School; Liverpool University, LLB. AAS. M. 11 December 1975. Call July 1979. ETC. 1979. Pupilmaster, David Lynch. Martins Building, Water Street, Liverpool, October 1978-September 1999; 7 Harrington Street, 6.9.1999. (merger with Corn Exchange).

DAVIES, Rhys Everson QC (His Honour Sir Rhys Davies QC)

(HS)

Born 13 January 1941. Cowbridge Grammar School; Neath Grammar School; Manchester University, LLB. G. June 1964; Bencher 1993. ETC. 1964. Prop. Heilpern QC. Sec. da Cunha. Circuit Junior, 1967. Manchester Chambers; 43 King Street, 1964-1973; 4th floor, Astley House, Quay Street, 1974-1977; 18 St John Street, 1978-1990. Silk 1981. London Chambers; 5 Essex Court. Recorder 1980. Senior Circuit Judge & Honorary Recorder of Manchester, 1990- 2003. Member, Sentencing Advisory Panel, 2000. Kt. 2000. Retirement speeches Crown Square, Manchester, 20 December 2002. (Penry-Davey J & Judge Humphries) WW.

DAVIES, Richard David Trevor

G June 1949. 24 Dale Street, Liverpool, 1951-1957; 4 Brick Court, 1958-1963. Not in 1964 Law List.

DAVIES, Russell Dewi Thomas

Born 13 April 1960, Gorseinon, South Wales. Married to Clare Davies, Senior Crown Prosecutor. Penvrheol School; Liverpool University, LLB. AAS. M. 9 March 1982. Call 22 November 1983. Pupilmaster, John Wishart. Manchester Chambers; Conavon Court Chambers, 12 Blackfriar Street, 1985-1989; Manchester House Chambers, 18-20 Bridge Street, 1990-1992; Dean's Court Chambers, Cumberland House, Crown Square, Manchester, 1992-1999; 24 St John Street, 4.5.1999.

DAVIES, Stephen Richard

Born 7 February 1963 Bexley, Kent. Baines School, Poulton-le-Fylde; Downing College, Cambridge, MA. AAS. M. 27 January 1984. Call 25 July 1985. ETC. December 1986. Prop. John Rowe QC. Sec. Brendan Hegarty. 601, Royal Exchange/8 King Street, Manchester, 1986. Recorder 2003.

DAVIS, Paul John

I. November 1996. 15 Winckley Square, Preston, 1998-2001.

DAVIS, Richard Cecil

I. 22 June 1898. ETC. 30 July 1898. Prop. Shee QC. Sec. Horridge. No address, 1899-1949. Not in 1950 Law List.

DAVISON, Charles Frederic

I. 26 January 1872. ETC. 7 March 1873. Prop. Herschell QC. Sec. Crompton. 1 Elm Court, 1876-1878; 1 Dr Johnson Building, 1882-1884. SE Circuit, 1882. Not in 1885 Law List.

DAVITT, Paula

LLB. G. November 1988. Manchester Chambers; 38 King Street West, 1990-1995; 24a St John Street, 1996.

DAW, Christopher

LLB, Manchester. G. November 1993. Manchester Chambers; 211 Deansgate & Parsonge Chambers, 1995.

DAWBARN, Climenson Yelverton Charles

Brother of Joseph Yelverton Dawbarn. qv. I. 30 April 1890. ETC. 6 August 1890. Prop. French QC. Sec. Segar. Equity draftsman & conveyancer. London Chambers; 11 King's Bench Walk & 5 KBW. Liverpool Chambers; Wason chambers, Harrington Street, 1899-1926. No address, 1927-1949. Not in 1950 Law List.

DAWBARN, Joseph Yelverton

Born 24 October 1857. 3rd son of late William Dawbarn of Liverpool, merchant, brother of Climenson Dawbarn qv. Queen's College, Cambridge, MA., LLM. AAS. I. 20 May 1878. Call 3 May 1882. Lancs. Chancery Court. Liverpool Chambers; 21 Harrington Street, 1883-1886; 7 Orange Court, 1887-1888; 34 South John Street, 1889-1898; 37 Moorfields, 1899-1924. No chambers address, 1925-1949 (living in Waterloo). Not in 1950 Law List. Foster.

DAWES, Simon Robert

Born 12 November 1965 Farnborough. Backwell School; Liverpool University, LLB. I. October 1990. ETC. December 1990. Prop Maguire QC. Sec. Simon Newton. Derby Square Chambers, Refuge House/Merchants Court 1990.

DAWSON, Edward Bousfield

Born 16 August 1830. Eldest son of Edward Dawson of Aldcliffe Hall, Lancs. London University, BA 1849. LLB 1852. AAS. I. 29 October 1849. Call 17 November 1852. No chambers address, 1876-1916. Chairman Quarter Sessions, Lancaster, 1916. JP., Lancs. Not in 1917 Law List. Foster.

DAWSON, James Robert
Born 30 August 1972 Ashby de la Zouch. Ashby Grammar School; Southampton University, LLB. I. November 1994. ETC. 20 December 1994. Prop. Somerset Jones QC. Sec. Richard Bradley. Oriel Chambers, 5 Covent Garden/14 Water Street, Liverpool, 1994.

DAY, George Harold
I 26 April 1899. ETC. 16 February 1901. Prop. Steel KC. Sec. Tobin. Kuala Lumpar, Federated Malay States, 1904-1940. No address, 1941-1949. Not in 1950 Law List.

DAY, Harold ("Harry")
G. June 1948. 43 King Street, 1948-1976. Chairman of Industrial Tribunals, 1977-1986. Examiner, Ecclesiastical Jurisdiction Measure, 1963. (1997-1998.) Died 1998 aged 83.

DEACON, Stuart
Born 29 May 1868 Widnes. Died 29 November 1947 aged 79. Rugby; Trinity College, Cambridge, BA., LLB. 1890. I. 17 November 1892. ETC. 22 March 1893. Prop. Addison QC. Sec. Wannop. Equity Chambers, 9 Cook Street, Liverpool, 1893-1910. Stipendiary Magistrate for Liverpool, 1910-1946. JP.; Liverpool; Cheshire & Wallasey Borough. Captain, Wallasey Golf Club, 1910. WW & Liverpool & Birkenhead in 20th Century-Biographies. Edited by W T Pyke, 1911.

DEAKIN, Joseph
Born 1835. 2nd son of late William Deakin of Manchester, merchant. AAS. M. 7 November 1857. Call 6 June 1860. Auburn Lodge, Urmston, 1876-1892. Not in 1893 Law List.

DEAN, (Frederick) Harold CB., QC
Born 5 November 1908. Died 29 October 1994 aged 85. Manchester Grammar School; Manchester University, LLB (1930), LLM (1932). AAS. M. 5 July 1930. Call 17 November 1933. Prop. Goldie KC. Sec. Barry. 3 St James's Square, Manchester, 1935-1939 & 1945-1950. Served in RAFVR, 1939-1945 in UK, Iraq, Egypt & East Africa. Squadron Leader. Assistant Judge Advocate General, 1950. Deputy JAG; Far East, 1954-1957 & 1962-1965; Middle East, 1958-1961; Germany, 1967-1968. Vice, JAG, 1968-1972; Judge Advocate General, 1972-1979. CB 1976. Silk 1979. Publications on Military Law & History. WW.

DEAN, Michael QC (His Honour Judge Dean QC)
Born 2 February 1938. Altrincham County Grammar School; Nottingham University, LLB. G. July 1962. 43 King Street, Manchester, 1962-1965. Lecturer in Law, London School of Economics, 1966-1967. 7 King's Bench Walk, 1968. Silk 1981. Assistant Recorder 1986. Recorder 1989. Circuit Judge 1991. WW.

DEANE, Charlotte Barbara
Daughter of Vincent Deane qv. L. 28 November 2002. ETC. 19 December 2002. Prop. John Benson QC. Sec Nick Riddell. 14 Castle Street/Atlantic Chambers, Cook Street, Liverpool, 2002.

DEANE, Vincent
Born 13 February 1954, Liverpool. Father of Charlotte Deane qv. Lancaster Royal Grammar School; Liverpool University, LLB. L. July 1976. ETC. 1977. Prop. David McNeill QC. Sec. Edward Tyler. Liverpool Chambers; 14 Cook Street, 1976-1977; 41 North John Street, 1977-1979; 15 Victoria Street, 1979-1984; Fruit Exchange, 1984-1989; 46 Stanley Street, 1989-1994; 25 Victoria Street, 1994-1998; 19 Castle Street, 1998-1999; Central Chambers, Princess Street, Manchester, 1999.

DEANS, Jaqueline Elaine
Born 9 March 1970, Bradford. St Joseph's College; Liverpool John Moores University, LLB. L. 25 July 1997. ETC. 8 December 1998. Prop. Richard Henriques QC. Sec. Andrew Mattison. Chavasse Court, 24 Lord Street, Liverpool, October 1999.

DE BONO, John Hugh
Born 6 November 1972, Cambridge. Downside; Oriel College, Oxford, MA (Philosophy & Theology). G. 12 October 1995. ETC. 19 December 1995. Prop. David Harris QC. Sec. Scott Donovan. Derby Square Chambers, Refuge Assurance House/ Merchants Court, Liverpool October 1995.

DEARDEN-GRIFFITH, James
Born 23 August 1839. Only son of James Dearden-Griffith of Lincoln's Inn, barrister. Trinity Hall Cambridge. AAS. L. 27 January 1857. Call 27 January 1862. Rochdale Manor, Lancs., 1876-1912. Not in 1913 Law List. Foster

de HAAS, Margaret Ruth QC. (Her Honour Judge de Haas QC)
Born 21 May 1954, Zimbabwe. Married to Iain Goldrein QC. qv; neice of Her Honour Inge Bernstein qv & Eric Goldrein qv; cousin of Clive Freedman QC qv. Townsend High School, Zimbabwe; Bristol University, LLB. AAS. 4 March 1978. Call July 1977. ETC. 1980. Pupilmasters; Tim Stow & A Kenny. 12 King's Bench Walk, 1977-1980; 460 Royal Exchange, Manchester, 1980-1981; Liverpool Chambers; 5 Castle Street, 1981-1984; 48 Castle Street, 1984-1989; Corn Exchange, 1989-1999; 7 Harrington Street, 6.9.1999-2004. (merger with Martins Building). Assistant Recorder 1995. Recorder 1998. Deputy High Court Judge, 1999-2004. Member CICB. 1999. Joint Publications; Butterworths Personal Injury Litigation Service, 1988.; Property Distribution on Divorce, 1989; Domestic Injunctions, 1997; Medical Negligence-Cost Effective Management, 1997; Structured Settlements, 1997. Co Editor; Civil Court Practice (Green Book); Personal Injury Major Claims Handling; Genetics Law Monitor. Circuit Judge, Liverpool, 22 July 2004. WW.

DEHN, Thomas George Rudolph
Born 20 July 1884, Manchester. Son of Rudolph & Meta Dehn of Withington. His father was born in Hamburg in 1850 of Danish parents. Manchester Grammar School; Balliol College, Oxford. Married Margaret Schuster 29 May 1914. Son, Roy Arthur born 2 July 1915. I. 18 November 1907. ETC. 24 February 1908. Prop. Langdon KC. Sec. Atkinson. 5 St James's Square, Manchester, 1908-1915. Commission; 2nd Lt. 3rd battalion, Wiltshire Regt., 31 May 1916. Died of wounds 19 April 1917 aged 32. Cemetery; Manchester Crematoium, Barlow Moor Road, West Didsdbury. Casualties of the 1914-1918 War are commemorated on a stone near the entrance to the grounds. Information from the Public Record Office & Commonwealth War Graves Commission.

DELANEY, Kenneth Joseph
Born 6 June 1967 Liverpool. Range School, Formby; Darwin College, Cambridge, LLB., MPhil. S.G. Warburg, 1990-1992. I. October 1996. ETC. May 1997. Prop. William Waldron QC. Sec. Simon Newton. Pupilmaster James Byrne. Liverpool Chambers; Derby Square Chambers, Merchants Court, 1997-2003; 7 Harrington Street, 2003.

DELANEY, Royston ("Rory") Harlow
MA (Cantab) L. November 1996. Formerly a solicitor. 38 Young Street, Manchester, 1999.

DEMPSEY, Brian Paul
BCL., LLB. (Dublin). L. May 1972. 77 Deansgate, Manchester, 2000; 6 Gate Street, Lincoln's Inn Fields, 2001.

DENMAN, Hon. Richard (later 3rd Baron Denman)
Born 13 January 1814. Died 19 March 1887 aged 73. 3rd son of Thomas, Lord Denman, then Chief Justice, King's Bench, father of Thomas Hugh Anderson Denman qv. Eton; Trinity College, Cambridge, MA 1835. AAS. L. 13 April 1835. Call 8 May 1838. 3 Paper Buildings. Clerk of Assize, Home Circuit, 1840-1876. Foster, Debrett.

DENMAN, Hon. Thomas Hugh Anderson
Born 16 January 1855. Died 9 December 1918 aged 63. 2nd son of 3rd Baron Denman. qv. Trinity College, Cambridge, BA. AAS. L. 19 April 1876. Call 17 November 1881. ETC. 6 February 1882. Prop. Gully QC. Sec. Elliot. 4 Paper Buildings, 1882; 1 King's Bench Walk, 1883-1885. No address, 1886-1918. Foster.

DENNETT, Angelina Brunhilde
Born 11 June 1956. BA., LLM.(London). AAS. M. 21 August 1979. Call 25 November 1980. ETC. 27 May 1982. Manchester Chambers; Conavon Court Chambers, 12 Blackfriars Street, 1982-1989; Manchester House Chambers, 18-22 Bridge Street, 1990-1997; 24a St John Street 1998-30.11.2001. Angelina has ceased practice to spend more time with her family.

DENNEY, Stuart Henry MacDonald
Born 15 June 1959 Welwyn. Married to Louise Bancroft. qv. St John's School, Leatherhead; Gonville & Caius College, Cambridge, MA. Teacher, Rossall Junior School, Fleetwood, 1981-1982. I. July 1982. ETC. December 1982. Pupilmaster, Tony Hammond. Deans Court Chambers, Cumberland House, Crown Square/24 St John Street, Manchester, 1982.

DENNIS, David Edward
Hull University, LLB. I. July 1979. Liverpool Chambers; 20 North John Street, 1979-1998; 14 Castle Street, 1999-2002.

DENNISS, Sir Edmund Robert Bartley KC, MP.
Born 9 April 1854. Died 20 March 1931 aged 76. Eldest son of Edmund Pinnock Denniss of London. Christ's Hospital; Hertford College, Oxford, 1874; Sidney Sussex College, Cambridge. Legacy Duty Office, Somerset House prior to admission to Middle Temple on 16 January 1877. Call 17 November 1879. ETC. 27 January 1880. Prop. Gully QC. Sec. Foard. 11 King's Bench Walk,

1880-1881; 1 Essex Court 1882-193l. MP (C) Oldham, 1911-1922. Silk 1922. Kt. 1922. Freeman of the City of London. WW.

DE PINNA, Louis Alfred
MA., LLB (Cantab) L. 9 June 1937. Equity draftsman & conveyancer. 5 New Square, 1938; 8 Old Square, 1939-1949; 5 New Square, 1950-1976; 9 Stone Buildings, 1977-1982; 76b Chancery Lane, 1983-1989. Liverpool Chambers; 34 Castle Street, 1971-1975; Queen's Insurance Building, 13 Castle Street, 1976-1983; 2nd floor, Peel House, Harrington Street, 1984-1989. Not in 1990 Law List.

DERBYSHIRE, Sir Harold MC, KC.
Born 1886. Died 14 September 1972 aged 86. Son of James Derbyshire of Blackburn. Queen Elizabeth's Grammar School, Blackburn; Sidney Sussex College, Cambridge, MA., LLB. G. 17 November 1911; Bencher 1931; Treasurer 1948. Certificate of Honour, 1911. ETC. 29 February 1912. Prop. Tobin KC. Sec. Atkinson. Served 1914-1918 War. M.C.; Liason Officer between Royal Artillery & Royal Air Force. Commanding a battery and later a brigade of artillery. Manchester Chambers; 5 St James's Square, 1912-1920; 75 Princess Street, 1921-1925; 6 St Anne's Passage, 1926-1928. Silk 1928. 2 Hare Court, 1928-1934. Judge of Appeal, Isle of Man, 1933-1944. Chief Justice, High Court, Calcutta, 1934-1946. Contested (L) Clitheroe, 1923; Royton, 1929. Fruit farmer in Suffolk, 1950-1972. WW.

DE SOBERON, Henry
G. 17 November 1897. ETC. 2 February 1898. Prop. Taylor QC. Sec. Ambrose Jones. 2 St James's Square, Manchester & 7 Stephensons Chambers, 25 Lord Street, Liverpool, 1899-1908. No address, 1909-1949. Not in 1950 Law List.

DEVEY, Joseph
2nd son of Thomas Devey of Manchester. St John's College, Cambridge, MA, 1867. AAS. I. 23 October 1858. Call 17 November 1865. No chambers address, 1876-1897. Liverpool & Kirkdale Sessions. Not in 1898 Law List.

DEVINE, Francesca Maria (later DEVINE-BAILLIE)
BA. G. February 1884. 2nd floor, Scottish Life House, 10 James Street, Liverpool, 1986-1989. Crown Prosecutor, Bootle 1994-1995; Senior Crown Prosecutor, 1997.

DEWHURST, Keith Ward (His Honour Judge Dewhurst)
Born 11 March 1924. Died 4 March 1984 aged 59. Son of James Dewhurs, solicitor. Shrewsbury School; Trinity College, Oxford, BA. I. June 1947. Manchester Chambers; 26 King Street, 1948-1958; 9 Albert Square, 1959-1972. Preston Chambers; 10a Winckley Street, 1954-1957; 38 Fishergate, 1958-1959; 1a Chapel Street, 1959-1972. Recorder 1972. Circuit Judge in Preston, 1972-1984. WW.

DIAMOND, Christopher Leslie William
Born 11 January 1952 Nicosia, Cyprus. North Cestrian Grammar School, Altrincham; Sheffield University, LLB. G. 25 November 1975. ETC. 1976. Pupilmaster, Donald Hart. Manchester Chambers; Astley House, 1976-1977; 18 St John Street, 1977. Qualified to fly light aircraft 1983.

DIAMOND, Hyman
G. 24 June 1936. ETC. 27 January 1937. Prop. Sellers KC. Sec. Macaulay. 34 Castle Street, Liverpool, 1940-1963. Not in 1964 Law List.

DIAMOND, Morris
G. 18 November 1929. ETC. 9 July 1930. Prop. Eastham KC. Sec. Allan. 1 Cooper Street, Manchester, 1933-1935. No address, 1936-1957. PO Box 166 Lusaka, Northern Rhodesia, 1958-1963. QC (N Rhodesia), 1956. Not in 1964 Law List.

DICEY, Albert Venn QC
Born 4 February 1835. Died 7 April 1922 aged 87. King's College, School, London; Balliol College, Oxford, BA, 1858; MA, 1861; BCL, 1877. Fellow; Balliol 1886; Trinity College, 1860-1873; All Souls, 1882-1909. AAS. I. 19 November 1858. Call 26 January 1863. 2 Brick Court 1876-1922. Junior Counsel to the Commissioners of Inland Revenue, 1876-1890. Silk 1890. Vinerian Professor of Common Law, Oxford University, 1882-1909. Publications include; Law of Domicil, 1879; Law of the Constitution, 1885; Conflict of Laws, 1896; WW. DNB. Foster.

DICK, John Staveley Graham
G. 26 January 1931. ETC. 18 February 1931. Prop. Goldie KC. Sec. Broadbent. Bank of England Chambers, Tib Lane Manchester, 1932-1935. Not in 1936 Law List.

DICKINS, Frederick Victor CB

Born 24 May 1838. Died 16 August 1915 aged 77. Eldest son of late Thomas Dickins, JP., Manchester. Rossall School; University of London, M.B., BSc. Served as medical officer in Royal Navy in China & Japan. AAS. M. 21 November 1867. Call 10 June 1870. ETC. 26 January 1880. Prop. Hopwood QC. Sec. Jordan. 2 Temple Gardens, 1880-1882. London University; Assistant Registrar, 1882; Registrar, 1896-1901. Reader in Japanese, Bristol University. CB 1901. WW. Foster.

DICKINSON, George Fryer

I. 10 May 1911. ETC. 7 July 1911. Prop. Greer KC. Sec. Barnes. No chambers address, 1911-1953. Not in 1954 Law List.

DICKINSON, James KC

Born 1885. Died 4 October 1933 aged 48. Son of James Dickinson, solicitor, of Liverpool. I. 28 April 1920. ETC. 8 March 1922. Admitted M. 19 November 1925. Prop. Kennedy KC. Sec. Pritt. 1 Brick Court, 1920-1925; 3 Essex Court, 1926-1933. Silk 1930. WW.

DICKINSON, Sir John

Born 17 November 1848. Died 29 October 1933 aged 84. Liverpool Collegiate School; Cheltenham College; Trinity College, Cambridge. AAS. I. 11 November 1868. Call 17 November 1871. ETC. 7 March 1872. Prop. Temple QC. Sec. Hills. 6 Crown Office Row, 1872-1890 Deputy Stipendiary Magistrate, Liverpool, 1880-1889. Metropolitan Magistrate, 1890-1920. Chief Magistrate, 1913-1920. Kt. 1913. WW. Foster.

DICKINSON, Jonathan David

Born 13 November 1963 Blackburn. Queen Elizabeth Grammar School, Blackburn; Bristol University, LLB. I. November 1986. ETC. December 1986. Prop. Donald Hart QC. Sec. Cynthia Pilling. Manchester Chambers; Parsonage Chambers, 2nd floor, 20 St Mary's Parsonage, 1986-1993; Kingsgate Chambers, 51-53 South King Street, 1994.

DICKSON, George Cyril

L. 27 January 1913. No address, 1913-1925. ETC. 28 January 1925. Prop. Singleton KC. Sec. Graham. 10a Winckley Street, Preston, 1926-1939. Lancs. Chancery Court. No address, 1940-1942. Not in 1943 Law List.

DICKSON, Ian

I. November 1978. ETC. 28 June 1979. Prop. Russell QC. Sec. Mclvor. Lawrence Buildings, 2 Mount Street, Manchester, 1979-1983. Law Dept, Digital Equipment Co Ltd, Reading, 1986-1988; Senior Legal Advisor, NCR Ltd, WC2, 1989; Company Secretary, C'mage Corp, Bracknell, 1990-1996; Creative Labs. UK Ltd, Ruscombe, Berks, 1997.

DINAN, Paul Joseph

G. November 1975. Manchester Chambers; 36 St Ann Street, 1977-1980; 27 Byrom Street, 1981-1982; 603 Hang Chong Building, Hong Kong, 1985.

DINGLE, Michael Burrington

Born 17 October 1939. Died 27 June 1985 aged 45. Son of Sir Phillip Dingle, Town Clerk of Manchester. Leas, Hoylake; Uppingham; Oriel College, Oxford, BA. I. February 1963. ETC. 1963. Pupilmaster, Michael Maguire. Circuit Junior, 1964. Same Liverpool Chambers at; 10 Water Street, 1963-1969; 2nd floor, Oriel Chambers, 14 Water Street, 1970-1982; Derby Square Chambers, Refuge Assurance House, 1983-1985 (Head of Chambers, 1974-1985). Boundary Commissioner, 1975. Deputy Circuit Judge. Assistant Recorder, 1977. Tributes, Liverpool Law Courts, 28 June 1985. Waterhouse J/ Judge Wickham/ Michael Morland QC.

DIXON, Hugh

Born 26 February 1976 Billinge, Wigan. Bolton School, 1982-1994; University of Birmingham, BA (History), 1994-1997; University of Manchester, LLM, 1999-2000. L. 23 November 1999. ETC. December 2000. Prop. Gerard McDermott QC. Sec. Paul Creaner. Pupilmasters; David Kenny & Paul Creaner. 15 Winckley Square, Preston, 2000.

DIXON, John

Born 13 February 1972, North Shields. Whitley Bay High School; Essex University, LLB. G. 23 November 1995. ETC. 19 December 1995. Prop. David Harris QC. Sec. Robert Atherton. Liverpool Chambers; 3rd floor, Peel House, Harrington Street, 4.9.1995-1999; 8th floor, India Buildings, Water Street, 1999.

DOBSON, (Patricia) Louise

Born 8 May 1965, Kendal. Kendal High School; City of London Polytechnic (Silversmithing); Jeweller / Silversmith, 1990-1994. Liverpool John Moores University, LLB. L. 12 October 2000. ETC. 31 July 2001. Prop. Peter Birkett QC. Sec. Gillian Irving. 9 St John Street, Manchester, 2001.

DOCKERY, Paul
Born 17 May 1949, Crewe. St Joseph's College, Stoke-on- Trent; Ealing Technical College (External LLB (London)). G. July 1973. ETC. December 1973. Prop. Patrick Russell QC. Sec. Rhys Davies. Manchester Chambers; 4th floor, Astley House, Quay Street, 1973-1977 which became, 18 St John Street, 1978.

DODD, Frank
Son of John Dodd of Rock Ferry, glass merchant. AAS. G. 16 January 1877. Call 9 June 1880. ETC. 27 July 1880. Prop. Temple QC. 18 Stephenson's Chambers, Harrington Street, Liverpool, 1881-1891; 4 Brick Court, 1892; 6 Crown Office Row, 1893-1895; 2 Harcourt Buildings, 1896-1902; 2 Pump Court, 1903-1916. Not in 1917 Law List.

DODD, Sarah
Born 19 November 1964, Burnley. St Hilda's RC Girls High School, Burnley; St Theodore's RC 6th Form, Burnley; Birmingham Polytechnic, LLB. L. July 1987. ETC. 1989. Prop. John Rowe QC. Sec. Beverly Lunt. 10-11 Gray's Inn Square, September 1987-March 1988; 4 Brick Court, March 1988-March 1989; Kingsgate Chambers, 20 St Mary's Parsonage/51-53 South King Street, Manchester, 1988.

DODSON, George
I. 10 June 1891. ETC. 6 March 1893. Prop. Addison QC. Sec. McNab. Circuit Junior with Milne Redhead, Winter 1894. Temple Chambers, 6 St James's Square, Manchester, 1898-1907. Not in 1908 Law List.

DODDS, (Robert) Stephen
Born 6 November 1952, Blackburn. Queen Elizabeth Grammar School, Blackburn. Leeds Polytechnic, LLB. G. July 1976. ETC. 1976. Pupilmaster, Keith Thomas. Manchester Chambers; 36 St Ann Street, 1976-1980; 27 Byrom Street, 1981-1983; 15 Winckley Square, Preston, 1983. Assistant Recorder 1995. Recorder 1999.

DONALD, Keith Malcolm Hamilton
Sheffield University, LLB. G. July 1978. ETC. 26 October 1978. National Farmers Union, 1981-1983; Legal Advisor, J H Minet & Co., E1, 1884- 1988; Legal Advisor, AMI Healthcare Group NW1, 1989-1990; Senior Legal Advisor, Mercury Communications WC1, 1994-1995; Senior Solicitor, BTR PLC SW1, 1997-1998; General Counsel, International Water Ltd, 1999.

DONNELLY, Kevin Gerard Eastwood
Born 10 October 1968, Newry, Co Down. St Coleman's College, Newry; Trinity Hall, Cambridge, BA. L. 9 October 1991. ETC. 1991. Prop. Henriques QC. Sec. Webster. Manchester Chambers; Rational House, 64 Bridge Street, 1991-1994; Lincoln House Chambers, 5th floor, 1 Brazennose Street, 1994.

DONOVAN, (Anthony Francis) Scott
Born 10 January 1948, Waterloo. St Mary's College, Crosby; New College, Oxford, BA (PPE); American University, Washington, DC., MA (Politics & Communications). Liverpool Council of Voluntary Service 1974-1975. G. 17 June 1975. ETC. 1975. Prop. Michael Maguire QC. Sec. David Clarke. Circuit Junior 1976. Derby Square Chambers, Liverpool at; 2nd floor, Oriel Chambers, 14 Water Street, 1975-1982 and Refuge Assurance House/Merchants Court 1982. Moved to 14 Castle Street/ Atlantic Chambers. Assistant Recorder 1992. Recorder 1996.

DOOHER, Nancy Helen
Born 4 February 1974, Leicester. New Parks High School, Leicester; King's College, London, LLB. L. 27 November 1997. ETC. 16 December 1997. Prop. Elleray QC. Sec. Cawson. Manchester Chambers; St James Chambers, 68 Quay Street, 1997-2001; Exchange Chambers, 4 Ralli Courts, West Riverside, 5.3.2001.

DOUGLAS, Stephen John
Born 2 January 1955 Crewe. Crewe County Grammar School for Boys; Manchester University, LLB. Cheshire Constabulary, 1977-1990. I. November 1994. ETC. 2 April 1996. Prop. Keith Goddard QC. Sec. Longworth. Manchester Chambers; Old Colony House, 6 South King Street, April 1995-November 1996; 24a St John Street November, 1996. (now St Johns Buildings).

DOVE, John
I. 17 November 1898. ETC. 16 February 1900. Prop. Carver QC. Sec. Maurice Hill. Circuit Junior, Summer 1900.Goldsmith Building, 1902-1907. No address, 1908-1934. Not in 1935 Law List.

DOVENOR, John Montague QC. "Monty"
Born 7 December 1923. Died 4 August 1981 aged 57. Shrewsbury School. Pilot, RAF, 1941-1947. Later, Captain, Territorials (RA). AAS. M. 16 January 1950. Call 23 June 1953.Liverpool Chambers; 47-49 Castle Street, 1953-1958; 36 Dale Street, 1959-1960; 9 Rumford Street, 1961-1973; Fruit Exchange, Victoria Street, 1974-1981. Silk 1972. 2 Pump Court. Publications; fiction (as Montague Jon) The Wallington Case; A Question of Law. WW.

DOWDALL, Harold Chaloner KC (His Honour Judge Dowdall KC)
Born 1868. Died 8 April 1955 aged 87. Rugby; Trinity College, Oxford MA., BCL. I. 26 January 1893. ETC. 22 March 1893. Prop. Smyly QC. Sec. Hill. Liverpool Chambers; 8 Harrington Street, 1894-1908; 10 Cook Street, 1909-1915; 25 Lord Street, 1916-1917. 2 Mitre Court Buildings, 1918-1921. Silk 1920. Lord Mayor of Liverpool, 1908-1909. First Chairman of Liverpool Council of Social Service, 1909-1917. Chancellor of the Diocese; of Liverpool, 1913-1948; of Bristol, 1919-1948. County Court Judge, Circuit 6, (Lancs.) 1921-1940. First Chairman of the Legal Board of the National Assembly of the Church of England, 1923-1928. Draftsman of the York-Antwerp Rules. President of the Society of Public Teachers of Law, 1947. WW.

DOWDALL, James Borthwick
G. 24 April 1934. ETC. 26 May 1934. Prop Maxwell Fyfe KC. Sec. Graham. No address, 1934-1963. Not in 1964 Law List.

DOWNEY, Anne Elisabeth (Her Honour Judge Downey)

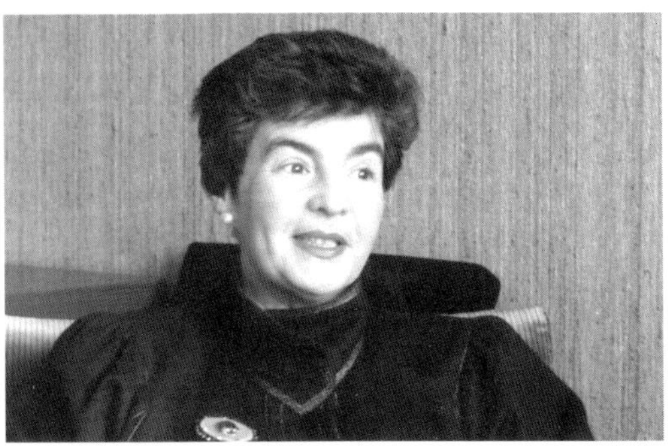

(RB)

Born 22 August 1936. Died 24 June 2002 aged 65. Notre Dame Convent, Liverpool; Liverpool University, LLB. G. February 1958, ETC (in the Library of St George's Hall, Liverpool). Prop. Brabin QC. Sec. Melville Kennan. Pupilmasters; Melville Kennan & Christopher Cunliffe. Same Liverpool Chambers; 34 Castle Street, 1958-1972; 54 Castle Street, 1973-1986. Recorder 1980. Circuit Judge, Liverpool, 1986-2002. Designated Family Judge, Merseyside, 1998-2002. Tributes at Liverpool Law Courts, 28 June 2002 (Leveson J; Judge David Clarke QC; David Steer QC. WW.

DOWNEY, Neil James
Born 19 December 1973 Liverpool. St Edward's College, Liverpool; Wadham College, Oxford, BA. M. 13 March 1997. ETC. 18 December 1998. Prop. Andrew Edis QC. Sec. Adrian Lyon. 14 Castle Street/ Atlantic Chambers, Cook Street, Liverpool, September 1998.

DOWNIE, Andrew James
Born 8 June 1959, Crosby. St Bede's. Crosby; Hugh Baird College, Bootle; Keele University, BA., MA. Teacher; Gothenburg University, Sweden, 1981-1983; British Council, Malaysia, 1984-1988. G. November 1990. ETC. 1991. Pupilmaster, Andrew Moran. Liverpool Chambers; Martins Building, Water Street, 1991-1999; 7 Harrington Street, 6.9.1999 (merger with Corn Exchange).

DOWSE, John (His Honour Judge Dowse)
Born 12 November 1946 Crayford, Kent. University of Leeds, LLB., 1972; University of Wales, Cardiff, LLM., 1996. L. July 1973. ETC. 1973. Member of American Bar Association. Manchester Chambers; 26 Brown Street, 1973-1976; 60 King Street, 1977-1983; Crown Square Chambers, 1 Dean's Court, 1984-1993; 9 St John Street, 1994-2001. Assistant Recorder, 1990. Recorder, 1994. Circuit Judge (Hull), 24 July 2001. Magistrates' Liason Judge, N. Bank of Humberside, 2002. WW.

DOYLE, Kathleen Margaret
G. July 1973. 43 King Street, Manchester, 1976-1980. Not in 1981 Bar Directory.

DRISCOLL, Christopher William
LLB. G. November 1974. 43 King Street, Manchester, 1976-1980. Not in 1981 Bar Directory.

DRIVER, Simon Gregory
Born 5 January 1965 Liverpool. Brother of Stuart Frank Driver qv. New Heys Comprehensive School, Liverpool; University of Reading, BA. I. November 1991. ETC 1991. Prop. Rodney Klevan QC. Sec. Gerald Baxter. Liverpool Chambers; 2nd floor, Peel House, Harrington, Street, 1991-1994; 25-27 Castle Street, 1995.

DRIVER, Stuart Frank
Born 1 October 1962. Brother of Simon Gregory Driver qv. New Heys Comprehensive School; St John's College, Oxford, BA (English). G. 22 November 1988. ETC 1988. Pupilmasters; Adrian Smith & Adrian Lyon. 14 Castle Street/ Atlantic Chambers, Cook Street, Liverpool, September 1988. Recorder 2003.

DRUMMOND, William Herbert
I. 26 January 1905. ETC. 21 February 1906. Prop. Pickford KC. Sec. Sutton. 3 Pump Court, 1907-1913. No address, 1914-1921. Straits Settlements, Singapore, 1922-1927. No address, 1928-1953. Not in 1954 Law List.

DUCKWORTH, Brian Roy (His Honour Judge Duckworth DL)
Born 26 July 1934. Sedbergh School; Worcester College, Oxford, MA. L. February 1958. ETC. February 1959. Prop. Brabin QC. Sec. Charles Elliott. Circuit Junior 1960. Manchester Chambers; 9 Albert Square, 1958-1972; 1 Dean's Court, Crown Square, 1973-1983. Councillor, Blackburn RDC, 1960-1974 (Chairman, 1970-1972). Recorder 1972. Member, Bar Council, 1979-1982. Circuit Judge, 1983-2004. Magistrates' Liason Judge; South Cumbria, 1987-1992; SW Lancs., 1993-2004. Committee Member, Council of Circuit Judges, 1995-2004. DL. Lancs., 1995.
In recent times the former Home Secretary, David Blunkett, when decisions have gone against him or his Department, has complained that "judges are out of touch with the real world." I liked Brian's response, published by the Times on 8 March 2004.
JUDGES IN TOUCH WITH 'REAL WORLD'
From His Honour Judge Brian Duckworth
Sir, David Blunkett cannot be allowed to get away with his contention that judges are out of touch with the real world (report, March 3).
Like most judges I was in practice at the Bar for 25 years dealing with a wide spectrum of clients. Now on the Circuit Bench I deal with all kinds of cases and personalities.
At home I talk to people in the pub, shop at Tesco and Sainsbury's, play golf, tinker with my car, dig my garden, watch TV, had my heart by-pass on the NHS, and occasionally go to shout abuse at Blackburn Rovers. Any shortcomings in my understanding are quickly pointed out by my wife and four children.
I know what makes people tick just as well as an MP or minister who shelters his life in the corridors of power, and I can well "respond to the real challenges" – even though it becomes increasingly difficult to make sense of the legislation with which Mr Blunkett's Government burdens the Statute Book.
Yours,
BRIAN DUCKWORTH (Circuit Judge), Preston Crown Court, Ringway, Preston PR1 2LL.

DUDLEY, Robert Michael
Born 28 December 1968 West Bromwich. King Edward's School, Birmingham; Britannia Royal Naval College, Dartmouth; Jesus College, Cambridge, MA. Half blue, (Rugby League). Royal Navy Officer, 1987-1992. G. 14 October 1993. ETC. 21 December 1993. Prop. William Waldron QC. Sec. Tim Holroyde. Exchange Chambers, Pearl Assurance House, Derby Square, Liverpool, 1993. Father at Bar in Birmingham.

DUDLEY-JONES, Elizabeth Sarah
Born 21 May 1973 Munster, W. Germany. Cowbridge School, South Glamorgan; The King's School, Macclesfield; Hull University, LLB. I. 9 October 1997. ETC. 12 December 2001. Prop. Keith Goddard QC. Sec. Denney. Pupilmaster, Richard Roberts. New Court Chambers, Temple, 1998-2001; 24 St John Street, Manchester, 2001.

DUGDALE, John Appleyard
I. 17 November 1891. ETC. 15 March 1894. 3 Paper Buildings, 1898-1909. No address, 1910-1949. Not in 1950 Law List.

DUGDALE, John Marshall
Born 1851. Rugby; Brasenose College, Oxford, BA. JP., Montgomeryshire. Captain Montg. Yeomanry. AAS. I. 18 January 1871. Call 26 January 1875. ETC. 22 February 1875. Prop. RG Williams QC. Sec. Elliott. 1 Brick Court, 1876-1878; 1 Paper Buildings, 1879-1882. No address, 1883-1935. Not in 1936 Law List. Foster.

DUGDALE, Norbury
Born 11 August 1920 Bootle. Linacre School, Bootle. FCOM.A. FRSA. LLB. Spitfire Pilot. Estate Agent, G. May 1965. ETC. 27 May 1965. Pupilmaster, Andrew Rankin. Liverpool Chambers; 7 Rumford Street, 1965-1968. The Temple, Dale Street, 1969; 27 Dale Street, 1969-1977. Kenya; Magistrate, 1977-1980; High Court Judge, 1980-1989.

DUGGAN, (James) Ross
Born 14 July 1956 Ormskirk. Merchant Taylors' School, Crosby. Liverpool University, LLB. AAS. M. 18 November 1975. Call July 1978. ETC. 26 October 1978. Prop. David McNeill QC. Sec. Mark Hedley. Circuit Junior, 1981. Liverpool Chambers; 3rd floor, 27 Dale Street, 1978-1989; 3rd floor, Peel House, Harrington Street, 1989-1998; India Buildings, Water Street, 1998. Assistant Recorder 1993. Recorder 1997. Director of Local Solutions (Formerly Merseyside Council for Voluntary Services).

DUGGINS, Francis "Frank"
L. November 1957. ETC. 27 May 1965. Liverpool Chambers; 9 Rumford Street, 1965-1973; Fruit Exchange Buildings, Victoria Street, 1974-1976; 41 North John Street, 1977-1978; room 22, 3rd floor, 15, Victoria Street, 1979-1981. Not in 1982 Bar Directory.

DUKE, (Paul) Stewart
G. November 1989. Crown Prosecution Service, Salford, 1994-1997. ETC. 1 November 1996. Old Colony House, 6 South King Street, Manchester, 1997.

DUNBAR, Eric
Born 1878. 3rd son of James Dunbar of Glasgow, solicitor. AAS. M. 25 April 1901. Call 26 January 1904. ETC. 3 February 1906. Prop. Shee QC. Sec. Roe Rycroft. 1 Pump Court, 1907; 2 Brick Court, 1908-1911; 2 Pump Court, 1912-1933. Not in 1934 Law List.

DUNCAN, George William
Born 6 September 1864. Only son of William Henry Duncan M.D. of Liverpool. Christchurch, Oxford, BA. AAS. I. 6 April 1875. Call 26 January 1878. ETC. 29 July 1878. Prop. Gully QC. Sec. Kennedy. Commerce Chambers, Lord Street, Liverpool, 1880-1883; 2 Harcourt Buildings, 1884-1885; 2 Garden Court, 1886-1893; Lamb Building, 1894-1922. No address, 1923-1930. Not in 1930 Law List. Foster.

DUNCAN, James Archibald MP
Born 1858. Died 13 February 1911 aged 52. Eldest son of David Duncan MP., of Gayton Hall, Cheshire, merchant. Amersham Hall School; Trinity College, Cambridge, BA., LLB. AAS. I. 18 January 1881. Call 17 November 1883. ETC. 31 July 1885. Prop. Kennedy QC. Sec. Lankester. 1 Crown Office Row, 1885; 2 Garden Court, 1886-1908; 2 Brick Court, 1909-1911.WW. Foster.

DUNCAN, John Christopher
Born 1942 Dunoon. Royal Hospital School; University College, London, BSc; University of Sussex, BA. I. July 1971. ETC. December 1985. Bristol Chambers; Guildhall Chambers, 23 Broad Street, 1973-1978; St John's Chambers, 28 Broad Street, 1979-1981. Not in, 1982-1985. Ground floor, Peel House, Harrington Street, Liverpool, 1985-1990; Manchester Chambers; Dean's Court Chambers, Cumberland House, Crown Square, 1990-2000.

DUNCAN, Sean Bruce (His Honour Judge Duncan)
Born 21 December 1942. Son of Joseph Alexander Duncan, High Sheriff of Merseyside, 1979. Shrewsbury School; St Edmund Hall, Oxford, MA. I. 1966. ETC. July 1967. Prop. David McNeill QC. Sec. Frank Paterson. Northern Circuit; Junior, 1969-1970; Secretary, 1985-1988. Same Liverpool Chambers; 34 Castle Street, 1966-1972; 54 Castle Street, 1973-1987; 14 Castle Street, 1988. Recorder 1984. Circuit Judge, Liverpool, 1988-. Council of HM Judges ; Hon. Sec., 1996- 1999; President, 2002. Captain, Royal Liverpool Golf Club, 2003. WW.

DUNDAS, Sir David QC.,MP.
Born 1799. Died 30 March 1877 aged 78.Christ Church, Oxford, MA. I. 7 February 1823. Northern Circuit and Scottish Bar. 13 King's Bench Walk in 1848. Silk 1840. MP Sutherlandshire, 1840-1842 & 1861-1867. Solicitor General, 1846-1848. Kt.1847. Judge Advocate General, 1849-1852. PC 1849. He retired in 1852 devoting himself to bringing together a fine library at 13 King's Bench Walk. DNB.

DUNDAS, Hon. John Charles MP
Born 21 September 1845. Died 13 September 1892 aged 46. 2nd son of Hon. John Charles Dundas late of Woodhall, Yorks., MP., deceased. Harrow; Trinity College, Cambridge, BA. 1868. AAS. L. 23 November 1866. Call 7 June 1869. ETC. 26 February 1870. Prop. Quain QC. Sec. Williamson. 7 New Square, 1876. Equity draftsman & conveyancer. No address, 1877-1892. MP., Richmond, Yorks., 1873-1885. Lord Lieutenant, Orkney & Zetland, 1872-1892. JP. & DL., North Riding of Yorkshire & Chairman of Quarter Sessions, 1881-1892. Warrant of precedency to rank as son of an earl, 1873. Foster. Burkes Peerage.

DUNN, Alfred Willan
I. 17 June 1896. ETC. 15 July 1898. Prop. Pickford QC. Sec. Sanderson. 1 Essex Court, 1897-1909. No address, 1910-1932. Not in 1933 Law List.

DUNN, Darren William
Born 5 January 1976. Methodist College, Belfast; University of Leicester, LLB, 1995-1998. I. 25 November 1999. ETC. 14 December 1999. Prop. Peter Birkett QC. Sec. Paul Dockery. 18 St John Street, Manchester, September 1999.

DUNN, Katherine Elspeth
Born 21 October 1963, Dunfermline, Fife. St George's School for Girls, Edinburgh; Clare College, Cambridge, MA. AAS. M. 26 April 1985. Call 24 November 1987. ETC. 1988. Pupilmaster, Peter Winston Smith. King's Chambers, 40 King Street, Manchester, 1988-.

DUNNETT, Thomas
Eldest son of Thomas Dunnett of Liverpool. Trinity College, Dublin, BA 1849. AAS. M. 6 November 1849. Call 17 November 1852. of Mount Road, New Brighton. 5 Harrington Street, Liverpool, 1876-1902, conveyancer. No address, 1903-1915. Not in 1916 Law List.

DURANDU, Arthur
Born 1861. 3rd son of Henry Durandu of Liverpool, merchant. Trinity College, Cambridge, BA. AAS. L. 26 April 1881. Call 26 January 1884. Prop. Aspinall QC. Sec. Woodburne. Equity draftsman & conveyancer. Bristowe Chambers, 8 Harrington Street, Liverpool, 1889-1908. No address, 1909-1931. Not in 1933 Law List.

DURRANT, Jennifer Joan
LLB. M. November 1973. Manchester Chambers; 4th floor, Astley House, Quay Street, 1975-1978; 18 St John Street, 1979-1983. Not in 1984 Bar Directory.

DUTCHMAN-SMITH, Malcolm Charles
Born 24 July 1947, Bolton. Rivington & Blackrod Grammar School; University of Hull, LLB. Solicitor, 1973-1995. G. February 1995. ETC. 1995. Pupilmaster, Walter Heap. Kenworthy's Chambers, 83 Bridge Street, Manchester, 1995-1997; Martins Bank, Water Street, Liverpool, 1997-1999; 7 Harrington Street, Liverpool (merger with Corn Exchange), 6.9.1999.

DWYER, Joseph Matthew Francis
MA. G. May 1958. ETC. 8 June 1969. Prop. Hinchliffe QC. Sec. F. Coles. 6 Park Square, Leeds, 1967-1968; Manchester Chambers; Northern Assurance Buildings, Albert Square, 1969; Post Office Chambers; 26 Brown Street, 1970-1971; 67 Princess Street, 1972-1976. Not in 1977-1978; 2 Mount Street, 1980-1981. Not in 1982 Law List.

DYER, Jacob Jackson
Born 22 April 1971, Barrow-in- Furness. Sedbergh School; St Catherine's, Cambridge, MA. L. November 1995. ETC. 1 November 1996. Prop. Roger Farley QC. Sec. Richard Howarth. 15 Winckley Square, Preston, September 1996.

DYKES, Lamplugh Brougham
3rd son Joseph Ballantine Dykes of Dovenby Hall, near Cockermouth. St Peter's College, Cambridge, MA; Fellow, 1832. AAS. M. 6 February 1828. Call 31 January 1834. 1 Elm Court, 1848. Cumberland. & Westmorland Sessions, 1876-1886. Not in 1887 Law List.

DYKES, Philip John
BA (Oxon). L. July 1977. Deans Court Chambers, Manchester, 1977-1986. Went to Hong Kong in May 1985 to work in Attorney General's Chambers. QC (Hong Kong) 1997.

E

EAGLESTONE, Diana Barbara (Her Honour Judge Eaglestone)
Born 24 May 1949. Married to Michael Howard Redfern QC. qv. University of Manchester, LLB. G. July 1971. ETC. 1971. Prop. George Carman QC. Sec. Keith Goddard. Manchester Chambers; 9 Albert Square, 1971-1972; Dean's Court Chambers, Crown Square, 1973-1995. Recorder 1989. Circuit Judge, Manchester, 1995. WW.

EARLAM, Simon Lawrence
Born 21 July 1950 Frodsham. Stowe School; Mansfield College, Oxford MA., BCL.(3 golf blues) G. February 1975. ETC. 27 November 1975. Pupilmaster, Dick Hamilton. Same Liverpool Chambers at different locations; 606 The Corn Exchange, Fenwick Street, 1975-1982; 1 Exchange Flags, 1983-1991; Exchange Chambers, Derby Square, 1992. Assistant Recorder 1999. Recorder 2000.

EARLES, Charles Graham
MA (Cantab) L. October 1990. 40 King Street, Manchester, 1990-1992. Admitted solicitor, 1992, with Slaughter & May E.C.2., 1997.

EARNSHAW, Terence Kay (His Honour Judge Earnshaw)
Father of Zoe Katherine Earnshaw qv. LLB (London), LLM, (Manchester) L. November 1970. Manchester Chambers; 601 Royal Exchange, 1973-1988; 8 King Street, 1989-1993. Recorder 1988. Circuit Judge 1993.

EARNSHAW, Zoe Katherine
Born 11 May 1979 Manchester. Daughter of His Honour Judge Earnshaw qv. Manchester High School for Girls; King's College, London, LLB. L. 22 November 2001. ETC. 12 December 2001. Prop. Gerard McDermott QC. Sec. Michael Smith. 8 King Street Chambers, Manchester, 8.10.2001. Richard Isaacson Memorial Scholar, October 2001.

EASON, His Honour Robert Kinley
Born 12 April 1908. Died 28 August 1991 aged 83. Douglas High School; King William's College, Isle of Man; University College, London, LLB. G. 12 June 1929. ETC. 18 February 1931. Prop. Ross Brown KC. Sec. Ormerod. Advocate, Manx Bar 1930. Atholl Chambers, Atholl Street, Isle of Man. High Bailiff and Chief Magistrate, Isle of Man, 1961-1969. HM's Second Deemster, 1969-1974. HM's First Deemster, Clerk of the Rolls and Deputy Governor, Isle of Man, 1974-1980. WW.

EASTHAM, His Honour Sir Tom KC
Born 22 February 1879. Died 11 April 1967 aged 88. Father of Eastham J (Family Division). Manchester Grammar School; Owens College, Manchester; University of Manchester; St Bart's Hospital MB., ChB. Resident Medical Officer, Royal Boscombe Hospital, West Hants, 1902. L. 26 January 1904; Bencher, 1927; Treasurer, 1948. ETC. 27 July 1905. Prop. Langdon KC. Sec. Rhodes. Manchester Chambers; 78 King Street, 1905-1918; Bank of England Chambers, Tib Lane, 1919-1922. Silk 1922. 2 Harcourt Buildings, 1922-1936. Recorder of Oldham, 1924-1936. Official Referee, Supreme Court, 1936-1944. Senior Official Referee, 1944-1954, Kt., 1948. DL., Surrey 1953. WW.

EASTON, Humphrey Copinger
son of James Marshall Easton qv. BA (Oxon); Manchester University, LLB. L. 29 June 1927. 3 St James Square, Manchester, 1928-1967. Lancs. Chancery Court. Full Time Chairman, Industrial Tribunals, Manchester. Publications; Rentcharge Conveyancing, 1960; 2nd edition of his father's Law of Rentcharges. Died c1995, aged 90.

EASTON, James Marshall
Father of Humphrey Copinger Easton qv, son in law of Walter Arthur Copinger qv. I. 17 November 1891. ETC. 17 February 1899. Prop. Taylor QC. Sec. Horridge. 7 Stone Building, 1892-1895; 5 Stone Building, 1896-1901; 43 Castle Street, Liverpool, 1902-1904; Manchester Chambers; 40 South King Street, 1905-1917; 3 St James Square, 1918-1943. Lancs. Chancery Court. Not in 1944 Law List. Publications; Law of Rentcharges, 1st edition; Appointment of Trustees; Editor of Copinger on Copywright.

EASTWOOD, Charles Peter
BA (Oxon). L. July 1988. 28 St John Street, Manchester, 1988.

EASTWOOD, Professor Reginald Allen OBE
Born 3 April 1893. Died 22 June 1964 aged 71. Central High School & Victoria University, LLB, 1914. LLD, 1918. G. 2 July 1919. Manchester Chambers; 60 King Street, 1935-1940; 43 King Street, 1949-1964. Manchester University; Lecturer in Law, 1924 to Professor of English Law, 1946-1960. Publications; Introduction to Austin's Jurisprudence; Williams on Real Property, (24th ed.); The Contract of Sale of Goods; Williams & Eastwood on Real Property; Strahan, Equity, (6th ed.). WW.

EASTWOOD, Thomas Crossley
G. 19 May 1886. ETC. 18 July 1886. Prop. Henn Collins. Sec. Hopkinson. 2 St James's Square, Manchester, 1889-1937. Conveyancer. Not in 1938 Law List.

EATON, Thomas Edward David
Born 15 February 1954 Wallasey. Repton School; Queen Mary College, London, LLB. AAS. M. 1 November 1973. Call November 1976. Pupillage at 5 Essex Court; pupilmaster, Alastair Hill. ETC. 1979. Same Liverpool Chambers at; 54 Castle Street, 1979-1986; 14 Castle Street, 1987-2003; Atlantic Chambers, Cook Street, 2003.

EBSWORTH, Ann Marian (The Hon Mrs. Justice Ebsworth DBE)

(LDPE)

Born 19 May 1937. Died 4 April 2002 aged 64. Notre Dame Convent, Worth, Sussex; Portsmouth High School GPDST; University of London, BA (History). G. July 1962; Bencher 1992. ETC. 1962. Pupilmaster, George England. 3rd floor, 27 Dale Street, Liverpool, 1962-1983. Chairman of Housing & Childrens' Committees of Wallasey Council. Mental Health Review Tribunal, 1975-1990. Recorder, 1978-1983. Circuit Judge, 1983-1992. Parole Board, 1989-1992. Civil & Family Committee, Judicial Studies Board, 1991-1992. Judge of the High Court of Justice, Queen's Bench Division, 1992-2001. The first woman ever to go directly to QBD. Tributes upon retirement, Liverpool Law Courts, 31 July 2001 (Sachs J, Judge David Clarke QC, Henry Globe QC); Further tributes on her death at Liverpool Law Courts on 8 April 2002 (Judge David Clarke QC and David Steer QC). Obituaries; Times, 8 April 2002; Daily Telegraph, 9 April 2002; "In Brief" June 2002. WW.

ECCLES, David Thomas
Born 22 March 1953 Manchester. Wilmslow Grammar School; Clare College, Cambridge, MA. AAS. M. 14 November 1974. Call July 1976. ETC. December 1976. Prop. Patrick Russell QC. Sec. Robert Newton. Manchester Chambers; 601 Royal Exchange, 1976-1988; 8 King Street, 1989. Assistant Recorder 1999. Recorder 2000.

EDE, Harry Penwarne
Born 1869. Son of late John Ede of Kersall, Manchester, merchant. Pembroke College, Oxford, BA 1882. AAS. I. 17 November 1879. Call 6 June 1883. ETC. 24 July 1883. Prop. Crompton QC. Sec. Collins. 10 St James's Square, Manchester, 1888-1905. Special pleader and equity draftsman. Lancs. Chancery Court. No address, 1906-1934. Not in 1935 Law List.

EDGE, Harry Broughton
Born 1866. Son of His Honour Judge James Broughton Edge qv. University of London, LLB. AAS. M. 18 November 1885. Call 30 April 1890. ETC. 17 March 1892. Prop. Ambrose QC. Sec. Goldthorpe. 1 Garden Court, 1891-1892; 5 New Square, 1893-1938. Not in 1939 Law List.

EDGE, Henry William
Born 1834. Youngest son of late John Edge of Rusholme Lodge, Manchester. University College, Durham, MA. AAS. I. 10 May 1859. Call 27 January 1862. 5 King's Bench Walk, 1866-1900; 9 King's Bench Walk, 1901-1906. Liverpool Court of Passage. Not in 1907 Law List.

EDGE, His Honour James Broughton
Born 3 November 1836. Died 23 October 1926 aged 89. Father of Harry Broughton Edge qv. Admitted, solicitor, 1858 (Certificate of Honour) AAS. M. 7 November 1868. Call 6 June 1871 (Certificate of Honour). ETC. 28 July 1871. Prop. Pope QC. Sec. Ambrose. 5 St James's Square, Manchester, 1871-1888. Coroner for Lancashire, 1869-1888. Chairman, Devon Quarter Sessions, 1895-1898. County Court Judge, 1888-1911 in Devon & London. WW. Foster.

EDGE, Timothy Richard
Born 23 April 1967 Manchester. William Hulme School; St Hugh's, Oxford, MA. G. October 1992. ETC. 17 December 1992. Prop. Armitage QC. Sec. Eccles. Pupilmasters; David Eccles & Ernest Ryder. Manchester Chambers; 8 King Street, 1992-1999; Dean's Court Chambers, 24 St John Street, 1999.

EDIS, Andrew Jeremy Coulter QC
Born 9 June 1957, Liverpool. Brother of William Edis of 1 Crown Office Row. Liverpool College; University College, Oxford, MA. AAS. M. 26 September 1979. Call 24 July 1980; Bencher 2004. Pupilmasters; Lynton Tucker, Charles Puree & Richard Fernyhough (all London). ETC. 1981. Northern Circuit; Junior, 1983-1984; Hon. Secretary, 1994-1997. Member of Bar Council, 1989-1990. Same Liverpool Chambers at; 54 Castle Street, 1981-1986; 14 Castle Street, 1986-2003; Atlantic Chambers, Cook Street, 2003. Assistant Recorder 1994. Silk 1997. Recorder 1999. Deputy High Court Judge 2001. WW.

EDMONDSON, His Honour Anthony Arnold

Born 6 July 1920. Liverpool University, LLB; Lincoln College, Oxford, BCL. Royal Artillery, 1940-1944; RAF Pilot, 1944-1946. G. June 1947. ETC. 29 January 1948. Prop. H.I. Nelson QC. Sec. Melville Kennan. Pupilmaster, Glynn Blackledge. 14 Cook Street, Liverpool, 1948-1971. Deputy Chairman, Lancashire Quarter Sessions, 1970-1971. County Court Judge, 1971. Circuit Judge, 1972-1991 sitting in Cumbria. WW.

EDMONDSON, Russell
Born 11 March 1972 Morecambe. Sedbergh School; University of Central Lancashire, BA. G. November 1999. ETC. June 2000. Prop. Keith Goddard QC. Sec. Keith Thomas. New Bailey Chambers, Preston, September 1999.

EDWARDS, Anthony Howard
Born 19 June 1950 Scarborough. Died March 2004 aged 53. Colwyn Bay Grammar School; Liverpool University, LLB. I. November 1972. ETC. 20 March 1973. Prop. David McNeill QC. Sec. Manus Nunan. Pupilmaster, Eric Somerset Jones. Oriel Chambers, 14 Water Street, Liverpool, 1972-2004. Recorder 1996. Deputy Chairman, Appeals Tribunals 1997.

EDWARDS, David Gareth
Born 31 November 1970, Chester, son of His Honour Judge Gareth Edwards QC. King's, Chester; Warwick University, LLB. G. October 1994. ETC. 20 December 1994. Pupilmaster, Michael Davies. Liverpool Chambers; Martins Building, Water Street, 1994-1999; 7 Harrington Street, 6.9.1999. (merger with Corn Exchange).

EDWARDS, Ernest Eric
MA., LLB (Cantab). I. 17 November 1922. ETC. 31 January 1923. Prop. Kennedy KC. Sec. Chappell. Liverpool Chambers; 10 Cook Street, 1922-1930; No address, 1931-1936; 9 Cook Street, 1937-1939; 34 Castle Street, 1940-1946. 28.8.1956 Deputy Clerk of the Crown, Manchester Crown Court and Assistant Clerk of Assize. Not in 1971. Law List.

EDWARDS, George
2nd son of John Edwards QC. qv. Owens College, Manchester. AAS. G. 21 November 1886. Call 17 November 1870. ETC. 25 March 1878. Prop. Higgin QC. Sec. Edwards QC. Manchester Chambers; St James's Chambers, South King Street; 9 St James's Square; 39 Princess Street; 9 Albert Square, 1877-1906. Equity draftsman & conveyancer. No address, 1907-1935. Not in 1936 Law List.

EDWARDS, John QC
Born 1836. Died 15 September 1885, aged 49. Father of George Edwards qv, and eldest son of John Edwards of Lower Broughton, Salford. Owen's College, Salford. AAS. G. 3 November 1850. Call 26 January 1860; Bencher 7 July 1874. 1 Harcourt Building, 1876-1885. Silk 6 July 1874. Foster.

EDWARDS, Kendrick Buckley
G. June 1931. No address, 1931-1941. Town Clerk, Crewe, 1942-1952. Liverpool Chambers; 14 Cook Street, 1953-1955; 7 Rumford Street, 1956; 3 Cook Street, 1957-1961; 27 Dale Street, 1962-1974. Note in Liverpool prosecutions book "Died December 1974".

EDWARDS, Nigel David Harrington
Born 18 January 1970, Sri-Lanka. Kingston Grammar School; St John's College, Cambridge, MA. Lieutenant, Royal Navy. L. March 1999. ETC. 1999. Prop. Keith Armitage QC. Sec. Stephen Davies. 8 King Street, Manchester, September 1998.

EDWARDS, Susan Ann
Born 30 October 1959, Cheshire. Wirral County Grammar School for Girls; Merseyside Police, 1979-1987. Liverpool John Moores University, LLB. L. November 1998. Pupilmaster, Simon Ward. 1 Fountain Court, Steelhouse Lane, Birmingham, 1998-2000; ETC. December 2000. Derby Square Chambers, Merchants Court 2000.

EDWARDS, Tenison
Born 23 December 1815. 6th son of James Edwards, late of Friars Hill, Wicklow deceased. Matriculated, Trinity College, Dublin. AAS. I. 17 November 1835. Call 25 January 1839. 4 Stone Buildings, 1846. Equity draftsman & conveyancer. No address, 1876-1899. Not in 1900 Law List. Foster.

EELEY, Rebecca Elizabeth Antonia
Born 19 December 1977, Manchester. Parrs Wood High School; St Hugh's College, Oxford, BA (Juris.), BCL. M. 11 October 2001. ETC. 12 December 2001. Prop. Charles Garside QC. Sec. Terence Rigby. 9 St John Street, Manchester, 2001.

ELGEE, Percival Charles
I. 17 June 1896. ETC. 27 July 1898. Prop. William Pickford QC. Sec. Rufus Isaacs QC. 6 Crown Office Row, 1897-1914. No address, 1915-1949. Not in 1950 Law List.

ELIAS, Robert Willoughby
Born 24 November 1955 Cardiff. Alleynes Grammar School; Sheffield University, LLB. AAS. M. 12 July 1977. Call 26 July 1979. ETC. December 1979. Prop. John Hugill QC. Sec. Christopher Sumner. Circuit Junior, 1983. Manchester Chambers; Rational House, 64 Bridge Street, 1979-1995; Lincoln House Chambers, 1 Brazennose Street, 1996.

ELIAS, William Alfred
LLB. G. 15 June 1904. ETC. 17 February 1905. Prop. Shee QC. Sec. Jellicoe. 25 Lord Street, Liverpool, 1905-1914. No address, 1915-1941. Not in 1942 Law List.

ELLENBOGEN, Gershon
MA (Cantab). FCIArb. G. January 1948. ETC, 1951. London Chambers. 3 Essex Court; 4 Essex Court; 10 King's Bench Walk; 1 Mitre Court Building; Goldsmith Building; 4 Kings Bench Walk; 3 Kings Bench Walk; 2 Gray's Inn Square, 1948-1988. Not in 1989 Law List.

ELLERAY, Anthony John QC
Born 19 August 1954, Northampton. Bishop's Stortford College; Trinity College, Cambridge, MA. I. July 1977. Pupilmasters; Charles Aldous & E W H Christie. ETC. 1979. Manchester Chambers; Duchy Chambers, Clarence Street, 1979-1983; 72 Bridge Street, 1984-1987; St James's Chambers, 68 Quay Street, 1988-2001; Exchange Chambers, 4 Ralli Courts, West Riverside, 5.3.2001. Silk 1993. Assistant Recorder 1994. Recorder 1999. Deputy High Court Judge.

ELLETSON, Daniel Hope
Born 1908. St John's College, Oxford, MA. 1st son of H C Elletson of Panox Hall, Fleetwood, barrister & JP., deceased. AAS. M. 17 November 1929. Call 17 November 1931. ETC. 6 July 1932. Prop. Lynskey KC. Sec. Edgar Lustgarten. 3 St James's Square, Manchester, 1932-1948; 38 Fishergate, Preston, 1949-1956. No address, 1957-1963. Not in 1964 Law List.

ELLIOT, Hon. Arthur Ralph Douglas MP
Born 17 December 1846. Died 12 February 1923 aged 76. 2nd son of Rt. Hon. William Hugh, 3rd Earl of Minto. Edinburgh University; Trinity College, Cambridge, MA, 1873. AAS. I. 27 January 1868. Call 17 November 1870. ETC. 21 February 1871. Prop. Leofric Temple. Sec. Herschell. 7 King's Bench Walk, 1876-1906. No address, 1907-1923. MP; Roxburghshire, 1880 & 1886-1892; Durham, 1898-1906. Financial Secretary to the Treasury, 1903. Editor, Edinburgh Review, 1895-1912. WW. Foster. Burkes Peerage.

ELLIOTT, Adshead (His Honour Judge Elliott)
Born 1869. Died 7 September 1922 aged 53. Manchester Grammar School; Oriel College, Oxford. I. 19 November 1894. ETC. 28 February 1895. Prop. Gully QC. Sec. Byrne. Manchester Chambers; 60 King Street, 1895-1898; 7 Brazennose Street, 1899-1901; 15 Brazennose Street, 1902-1918. County Court Judge, March 1918-1922, Circuit 13 (Derbys. & WR Yorks.) President of Pension Appeals Tribunal, 1918-1919. JP. Publication; Treatise on Workmens' Compensation Acts (7. editions) WW.

ELLIOTT, Charles Morris William
Born 1898. Only son of Charles Herbert Elliott of Chorlton-cum-Hardy, manufacturer. Lincoln College, Oxford. AAS. M. 17 November 1919. Call 10 May 1922. Manchester Chambers; 78 King Street, 1929-1941; 26 King Street, 1942-1958; 9 Albert Square, 1959-1968. Not in 1969 Law List.

ELLIOTT, Christopher David
Born 22 July 1950 Brecon. Cardiff High School; Manchester University, BA. G. July 1974. ETC. 1975. Pupilmaster, Adrian Kirsten. Manchester Chambers; 37 Princess Street, 1974-1975; Sunlight House, Quay Street, 1976-1993; Young Street Chambers, 1993.

ELLIS, Catherine Anne
Born 29 August 1965 Bolton. Canon Slade; Lancaster University, LLB. L. July 1987. ETC. March 1988. Pupilmaster, Charles James. Derby Square Chambers, Refuge Assurance House/ Merchants Court, 1987-31 December 2003; Oriel Chambers, 14 Water Street, 1 January 2004.

ELLIS, Charles Gregson
Born 1857. 2nd son of Richard Gregson Ellis of Plas Newydd. Denbighshire, gent. Exeter College, Oxford, BA. AAS. L. 28 May 1878. Call 29 June 1881. ETC. 29 January 1886. Prop. Collins QC. Sec. Aspland. 6 King's Bench Walk, 1886-1887; 1 Paper Buildings, 1888-1890; 11 King's Bench Walk, 1891-1899. Not in 1900 Law List. Foster.

ELLIS, Sydney Edward MC
Born 17 May 1908. Died 15 March 1945 aged 36. Son of Arthur & Elizabeth Ellis of Hoylake. BA. I. 26 January 1933. ETC. 26 February 1934. Prop. Lynskey KC. Sec. Hartley Shawcross. 43 Castle Street, Liverpool, 1933-1937. Crown Counsel, Gold Coast, 1938-1940. Commissioned, 31 December 1938 in the Gold Coast Regt. Promoted Lt., 26 February 1941. Acting Captain, 12 January 1943. Attached HQ., 2nd West African Infantry Brigade. Killed in action 15 March 1945. His name appears on Face 19 and is one of 27,000 names on the Rangoon Memorial, Myanmar in the Taukkyan Cemetery about 35 km north of Rangoon. Information from Commonwealth War Graves Commission.

ELLIS, Sylvia Mary
Birmingham University, LLB. G. November 1969. Pupilmaster Arthur Prestt. 601 Royal Exchange, Manchester, 1970-1973. Left to join Civil Service.

EMLYN-JONES, Hugh (His Honour Judge Emlyn Jones)
Born 1902. Son of Evan Jones of Newton-le-Willows, wagonbuilder. Died 9 June 1970 aged 68. Manchester Grammar School; Manchester University, LLB. Solicitor. AAS. M. 22 November 1929. Call 2 July 1930. ETC. 9 June 1930. Prop. Jackson KC. Sec. Turner. 6 St Ann's Passage, 1931-1932. Farrar's Building, 1933-1939. North Wales Circuit from 1937. War 1939-1945; Intelligence Officer with 604 Squadron and later on Staff (Acting Wing Commander). 3 Hare Court, 1945-1950. Contested (L) Chorley. County Court Judge, Circuit 7, (Birkenhead & Chester), 1950-1965. JP. WW.

EMMOTT, George Henry
Born 28 September 1855. Eldest son of Thomas E of Oldham, cotton manufacturer. Owen's College, Manchester; Trinity Hall, Cambridge, MA., LLM. Reader & Law Lecturer, Birmingham Law Society. AAS. I. 3 November 1876. Call 25 June 1879. Temple Chambers, 4 St James Square, Manchester, 1881-1892; John Hopkins University, Maryland, USA, 1893. 13 Union Court, Liverpool, 1898-1900; 10 Cook Street, Liverpool, 1901-1916. Equity draftsman & conveyancer. Lancs. Chancery Court. Not in 1917 Law List. Foster.

ENGLAND, George Nicholas
G. 2 July 1930. ETC. 9 July 1930. Prop. Jackson KC. Sec. Gorman. Liverpool Chambers; 15 Union Court, Cook Street, 1930-1933; 3 Cook Street, 1934-1958; The Temple, Dale Street, 1959-1968. Not in 1969 Law List.

ENNESS, Frank George
Born 1874. 2nd son of George Ambrose Enness of Braintree, Kent, building contractor. Former science lecturer. AAS. M. 30 April 1907. Call 26 January 1910. ETC. 23 February 1911. Prop. Leslie Scott KC. Sec. Raeburn. 5 Paper Buildings, 1910-1913; 2 Harcourt Buildings, 1914-1941. No address, 1942-1963. Not in 1964 Law List.

*** ENSOR, (George) Anthony (His Honour Judge Ensor)**

(HS)

Born 4 November 1936. Malvern College; Liverpool University, LLB. Articled to Laurence Edgar Rutherford, 1956-1961. Admitted as a solicitor, 1961. Atkinson Conveyancing Medal 1962. Rupert Bremner Medal 1962. Rutherfords (later Weightman Rutherfords); Partner, 1962-1992; Senior Partner, 1992-1995. Deputy Coroner, Liverpool, 1966-1995. Part time Chairman, Industrial Tribunals, 1975-1995. President, Liverpool Law Society, 1982. Recorder, 1983-1995. Member, Judicial Studies Board, 1987-1989. Trustee, Empire Theatre, Liverpool, 1986. Director, Liverpool Football Club, 1985-1993. Assistant Parliamentary Boundary Commissioner, 1992-1995. Circuit Judge, December 1995. WW.

ENTWISTLE, Sir Cyril Fullard MC, QC, MP.
Born 23 December 1887. Died 9 July 1974 aged 86. Bolton School; Manchester University, LLB. Served 1914-1918 War. Commanded, 235 Siege Battery, RGA. Major. I. 17 November 1919. 3 Elm Court, 1919-1938; 1 Temple Gardens, 1939-1940; 3 Temple Gardens, 1941-1963. MP (L) South West Hull, 1918-1924. MP (U) Bolton, 1931-1945. Silk 1931. Kt. 1937. Introduced as a Private Member's Bill, Matrimonial Causes Act 1923. WW.

ERLEIGH, Viscount
See Gerald Rufus Isaacs.

ERRINGTON, Sir Eric, Bart.
Born 17 March 1900. Died 3 June 1973 aged 73. Mill Hill School; Liverpool College; Trinity College, Oxford, MA. I. 25 April 1923. ETC. 14 June 1923. Prop. Singleton KC. Sec. Chappell. Liverpool Chambers; 13 Harrington Street, 1923-1930; 34 Castle Street, 1931-1946; 24 Dale Street, 1947-1955; 27 Dale Street, 1956-1970; Lombard Chambers, Bixteth Street, 1971-1973. 2nd Lt., Gordon Highlanders, 1918. Pilot Officer, AAF (Balloon Barrage) 1939. Wing Commander, 1944. Liverpool City Council, 1934-1935. MP (U) Bootle, 1935-1945. MP (C) Aldershot, 1954-1970. Kt. 1952. WW.

ESHER, Viscount (See William Baliol Brett)

ESSENHIGH, Reginald Clare MP (His Honour Judge Essenhigh)
Born 7 September 1890, Warrington. Died 1 November 1955 aged 65. Warrington Secondary School; Manchester School of Art; Royal College of Art; London University, School of Architecture. 1914-1918 War, with 3rd later 2nd batn, Manchester Rgt., Captain. Severely wounded in Flanders in 1917. G. 26 January 1922. ETC. 1 February 1922. Prop. Greaves Lord KC. Sec. Howard Jones. Liverpool Chambers; 25 Lord Street, 1922-1927; 15 Union Court, Cook Street, 1928-1934. 2 Harcourt Buildings, 1935-1936. MP (U) Newton, 1931-1935. Circuit Judge, October 1936-1955, Circuit 13 (Sheffield). WW.

ETHERTON, Ralph (Humphrey) MP
Born 11 February 1904. Died 10 December 1987 aged 83. Charterhouse; Trinity Hall, Cambridge, MA. I. 16 June 1926. ETC. 7 July 1926. Prop. Singleton KC. Sec. Griffith. 1 Brick Court, 1926-1936; 1 Harcourt Buildings, 1936-1939; Flt. Lt. RAFVR, 1940-1942. Goldsmith Building, 1943-1963. MP (Nat.C) Stretford, 1939-1945. WW.

EVANS, Alan
Born 8 May 1955 Dumfries. Morecambe Grammar School; Downing College, Cambridge, MA., LLB. L. July 1978. Lecturer in Law, Manchester University, 1978-1985. ETC. 1985. Prop. Jack Price QC. Sec. Philip Raynor. Manchester Chambers; 460 Royal Exchange, 1985-1987; King's Chambers, 40 King Street 1987. Junior Counsel to the Crown, Provincial Panel, 2000. Legal Assessor, General Medical Council, 2002.

EVANS, Anthony David
BA (Cantab). L. November 1968. Goldsmith Building, 1970. 47 Peter Street, Manchester, 1971-1973. Non practising, 1974-1976. Not in 1977 Law List.

EVANS, Claire Louise
Born 14 September 1971, Blackpool, married to Graham Knowles qv. St Mary's RC High School, Blackpool; Newman College, Preston; Manchester University, BSc. (Maths.) M. 13 October 1994. ETC. 13 December 1994. Prop. Michael Shorrock QC. Sec. Christopher Melton. Peel Court Chambers, 45 Hardman Street, Manchester, 1994.

EVANS, His Honour David Marshall QC
Born 21 July 1937. Son of Robert Trevor Evans, Clerk to the Lancashire County Justices. Liverpool College; Trinity Hall, Cambridge, MA., LLM; Law School, University of Chicago, JD. Teaching Fellow, Stanford University, Law School, 1961-1962. Assistant Professor, University of Chicago Law School, 1962-1963. Lecturer in Law, University College of Wales, Aberystwyth, 1963-1965. G. November 1964. ETC. 1965. Pupilmasters, David McNeill, Christopher Cunliffe & Frank Paterson. Same Liverpool Chambers at; 34 Castle Street, 1965-1972; 54 Castle Street, 1973-1981. Silk 1981. Byrom Street Chambers, Manchester & 5 Essex Court, 1981-1987. Recorder 1984. Circuit Judge, 1987-2003. Designated Civil Judge for Merseyside, 1998. Senior Circuit Judge, 2002-2003. Retirement Speeches, Liverpool Law Courts, 28 April 2003 (Judge David Clarke QC/ David Steer QC) WW.

EVANS, Frank
Born 11 December 1850. 4th son of Henry Edwin Evans of Oldham, merchant. AAS. L. 25 January 1873. Call 28 June 1876. ETC. 12 July 1876. Prop. Temple QC. Sec. Hamilton. Circuit Junior, Spring 1877. 19 Old Square, 1877; 21 Old Buildings, 1878-1888; 15 Old Square, 1889-1896; 5 New Square, 1897-1921. Equity draftsman & conveyancer, Lancs. Chancery Court. Not in 1922 Law List.

EVANS, John Findley Melville
MA (Cantab) G. November 1984. Manchester Chambers; 33 King Street West, 1988-1992; Lloyds House Chambers, 18 Lloyd Street, 1994-1996. Not in Bar Directory 1997.

EVANS, John Overend
Born 1845. Only surviving son of David Owen Evans of Moor Side, Kersall. Owen's College, Manchester. AAS. I. 13 January 1879. Call 26 January 1882. Manchester Chambers; 60 King Street, 1883-1887; 40 King Street, 1888-1912. Not in 1913 Law List.

EVANS, (Paul) Timothy
Born 17 December 1962, Liverpool. St Francis Xaviers College; St Edmund Hall, Oxford, MA; University College, London, LLM.; University of East Anglia, Norwich, LLM. Investment Manager, Robert Fleming, 1984-1986; Part time Lecturer, UEA, 1986-1987. Law Lecturer, Liverpool University, 1987-1991. G. November 1992. ETC. 1992. Prop. Brian Leveson QC. Sec. Henry Globe. Exchange Chambers, Derby Square, Liverpool, 1992.

EVANS, Simeon Vaughan
Born 22 June 1967 Truro. Richard Lander School, Truro; Manchester Metropolitan University, BA. L. 17 November 1997. ETC. 30 July 1998. Prop. Roger Farley QC. Sec. Russell. Pupilmaster F Khan. Manchester Chambers; 89 Princess Street, 1998-2000; 38 Young Street, 2000.

EVANS, Suzanne Marie
Born 6 May 1962, Colwyn Bay. Fairholme / Lowther College / Wrexham Technical College; St Anne's College, Oxford, MA. AAS. M. 10 May 1984. Call 26 November 1985. ETC. 1986. Prop. Eric Somerset Jones QC. Sec. William Rankin. Oriel Chambers, 5 Covent Garden / 14 Water Street, Liverpool, 1985.

EYERS, Anthony Edward
Born 28 January 1968, Andover, Hants. Coopers School, Chislehurst, Kent; St Peter's College, Oxford, BA. I. November 1994. ETC. 21 December 1995. Prop. Jonathan Foster QC. Sec. Roger Stout. Manchester Chambers; 18 St John Street, 1995-1996; 24a St John Street, 1996-2002; St John's Building Chambers (merger with 28 St John Street), 23.9.2002.

F

FAIRCLOUGH, Matthew Hayes

Born 1900. Eldest son of Matthew Hayes of Liverpool, wine merchant. Resident Secretary of Manchester University. AAS. M. 14 October 1940. Call November 1943. 27 Lord Street, Liverpool, 1947-1956. Not in 1957 Law List.

FAIRCLOUGH, (William) Derrick

Born 5 March 1929. Died 11 April 2005 aged 76. G. November 1950. ETC. 6 March 1952. Prop. Wooll QC. Sec. Backhouse. Manchester Chambers; 26 King Street, 1952-1958; 9 Albert Square, 1959-1972; Dean's Court, Crown Square, 1973-1982. Practised in Preston. Recorder, 1981-1998. Stipendiary Magistrate for Greater Manchester, 1982-31.1.1998.

FAIRFIELD, Baron (See Frederick Arthur Greer)

FALCON, Charles Henry

I. 18 April 1894. ETC. 2 July 1894. Prop. Gully QC. Sec. Mattinson. Commerce Court B, 11 Lord Street, Liverpool, 1896. 4 Harcourt Buildings, 1897. 4 Pump Court, 1899-1901. No address, 1902-1916. Not in 1917 Law List.

FALCON, Ralph

I. 5 July 1905. ETC. 31 July 1905. Prop. Pickford QC. Sec. Burnyeat. No address, 1906-1953. Not in 1954 Law List.

FALLOWS, (Mary) Paula

Born 20 April 1959 Widnes. Notre Dame High School, St Helens; Liverpool Polytechnic (now Liverpool John Moores University), BA. L. July 1981. ETC. 1981. Pupilmaster, Frank Hudson. Manchester Chambers; 67 Princess Street, 1981-1987; Hollins Chambers, 64a Bridge Street, 1988-1998; Cobden House Chambers, 19 Quay Street, 1998. (Same Chambers at different locations).

FARADAY, Wilfred Barnard

Born 14 March 1874. Died 15 June 1953 aged 79. Son of F J Faraday, Commercial Manager of Manchester Guardian. Grammar School; Manchester College of Technology & University, LLB 1897. G. 26 January 1900. ETC. 4 February 1901. Prop. Shee QC. Sec. Roe Rycroft. Manchester Chambers; 19 Brazennose Street, 1902-1906; 78 King Street, 1909. Equity draftsman & conveyancer. Lancs. Chancery Court. 6 Figtree Court, 1910-1914. Lieut., 5th Batt, York & Lancaster Regt., 1914-1916. Secretary, Royal Aeronautical Society & Editor, Aeronautical Journal, 1917-1919. Joined Western Circuit, 1920 practising from 2 Middle Temple Lane. Contested (C); Combined Universities, 1922; Sheffield, Attercliffe, 1924 & 1929. Recorder of Barnstable and Bideford, 1932-1953. Publications on economic and aeronautical matters. WW.

FARLEIGH, Edward Austin

G. 26 January 1897. Certificate of Honour. ETC. 15 February 1899. Prop. Russell QC. Sec Fraser. Various London Chambers and finally at 2 Dr Johnson's Building, 1913-1949. No address, 1950-1961. Not in 1962 Law List.

FARLEY, Roger Boyd QC

Born 24 April 1944, Blackburn. Son of Frank Farley, founder of Farley, Parker & Pickles, Solicitors of Blackburn, father of David Dunbar Farley qv. Liverpool University, LLB. Admitted as a Solicitor, January 1969. Joined his father's firm. AAS. M. 27 March 1974. Call 14 May 1974; Bencher 2003. ETC. 1974. Pupilmaster, Jack Price. Manchester Chambers; 25 Bow Lane, 1974-1976; Room 460, Royal Exchange, 1977-1987; 40 King Street, 1988-2000; Cobden House Chambers, 19 Quay Street, 2000. Recorder 1993. Silk 1993.

FARROW, Adrian John

Born 19 July 1960 Stockport. Stockport School (Mile End); Leicester University, LLB. Formerly a solicitor. Brian Taylor & Co, Stockport, 1983-1988. Crown Prosecutions Service, 1988-1997 (Principal Crown Prosecutor). M. 24 July 1997. ETC. 16 December 1997. Prop. Roger Farley QC. Sec. J. Jackson. Manchester Chambers; 40 King Street, 1997-1999; Cobden House Chambers, 19 Quay Street, 1999-.

FAUX, Rachael Elizabeth

Born 20 May 1974 Chester. Cousin of Andrew Faux (Midland & Oxford). Casterton School; Nottingham Trent University, LLB. L. 9 October 1997. ETC. 16 December 1997. Prop. Foster QC. Sec. Anastasia Ioannou. Pupilmasters Anastasia Ioannou & David Heaton. 18 St John Street 1.10.1997-.

FAWCETT, John

Eldest son of Rev. John Fawcett of Carlisle. AAS. M. 9 November 1822. Call 9 November 1827. Address Carlisle. Cumberland Sessions. Conveyancer. Last entry in Law List 1883.

FAWCETT, Sir (John) Henry KCMG
Born 11 December 1831. Died 22 August 1898 aged 66. Rugby; Trinity Hall, Cambridge, LLB 1854. AAS. M. 6 June 1853. Call 6 June 1857. Revising Barrister 1868. 5 Pump Court . Cumb. Westm. & Liverpool Sessions. Contested Cockermouth, February 1874. Judge, Supreme Court, Constantinople, 1875. Chief Judge and Consul General for Turkey, 1877. KCMG 1887. Publications; A Treatise on Referees in Parliament. WW. Foster.

FAWCUS, His Honour Simon James David

(HS)

Born 12 July 1938. Aldenham School; Trinity Hall, Cambridge, MA. G. November 1961. ETC. 1971. Pupilmaster, Ken Hollings. Circuit Junior, 1965. Manchester Chambers; 4 Chapel Walks, 1961-1964; 601 Royal Exchange, 1965-1985. Recorder, 1980-1985. Circuit Judge, 1985-12.7.2003. President, Council of Circuit Judges, 1996. WW.

FEENY, Charles Sheridan
Born 3 August 1954 Redditch. Son of Max Howard Feeny. qv. Birkenhead School; Corpus Christi, Cambridge, BA. I. November 1977. ETC. April 1978. Prop. Michael Maguire QC. Sec. Bert Andrew. Liverpool Chambers; Peel House, Harrington Street, 1978-1998; 42 Castle Street, 1998. Recorder 2001.

FEENY, Max Howard
Born 5 November 1928. Died 24 March 1995 aged 66. Father of Charles Sheridan Feeny, qv., Stonyhurst College, Oratory School; Birmingham University, LLB. I. November 1953. Circuit Junior, 1957. Liverpool Chambers; 14 Cook Street, 1956-1972; Ground floor, Peel House, Harrington Street, 1973-1978. Recorder, 1972-1978. Senior Law Lecturer, Queen's University of Belfast, 1982-1991. Part Time Chairman, Med. Appeals Tribunals, 1987-1991. Member, Council of Legal Education (N. Ireland), 1983-1987. WW.

FEETHAM, Daniel Anthony
Reading University, BA; Manchester University, LLB. G. February 1994. ETC. 13 December 1994. Prop. Rodney Scholes QC., Sec. Cogley. Manchester Chambers; Hollins Chambers, 64a Bridge Street, 1994-1997; Merchant Chambers, 1 North Parade, Parsonage Gardens, 1998-2000.

FELL, Henry Walter
Born 12 July 1852. Eldest son of Rev. James Alexander Fell, MA. Maryborough College; Trinity College, Cambridge, MA. AAS. L. 22 April 1873. Call 10 May 1876. ETC. 23 February 1877. Prop. Temple QC. Sec Crompton. London Chambers, 1877-1886. Liverpool Chambers; Bank Chambers, Cook Street, 1886-1888; 9 Commerce Chambers, 1889-1905. No address, 1906-1930. Not in 1931 Law List.

FELL, John
Born 1 November 1826. Eldest son of John Fell of Ulverstone. Wadham College, Oxford. AAS. I. 17 November 1848. Call 9 June 1854. No chambers addresses. Private addresses; Stock Park, Windermere; Dane Ghyll, Furness Abbey via Carnforth. JP., DL. Vice Chairman, Lancs Quarter Sessions. Chairman, Petty Sessions for Barrow-in- Furness. Foster.

FELL, Richard Irton
Born 27 September 1852. 3rd surviving son of late Rev. Samuel Irton Fell of Ambleside. Trinity Hall, Cambridge, BA. AAS. I. 29 January 1874. Call 26 January 1878. Manchester Chambers; 60 King Street, 1878-1882; 4 St James Square, 1883-1896. Equity draftsman & conveyancer. Lancs. Chancery Court. Not in 1897 Law List. Foster

FENTON, Frank John
Eldest son of John Fenton of Liverpool, physician. Sidney Sussex College, Cambridge, BA 1869. AAS. I. 29 January 1867. Call 17 November 1870. ETC. 23 March 1871. Prop. Aspinall QC. Sec. Temple. Unity Buildings, 22 Lord Street, Liverpool, 1876-1896. No address, 1897-1935. Not in 1936 Law List. Foster

★ FENWICK, His Honour Christian Bedford QC
Born 15 September 1888 London. Died 5 October 1969 aged 81. Eton; Magdalen College, Oxford, MA. I. 26 January 1911. 3 Paper Buildings, 1911-1914. Enlisted TA, 1914; Captain, Northern Cyclists' Battn., BEF, France, 1916-1917. North Eastern Circuit. 46 Grainger Street, Newcastle upon Tyne, 1920-1945. Silk 1945. 7 King's Bench Walk, 1945-1950. Recorder; Doncaster, 1933-1946; Halifax, 1946-1947; Kingston upon Hull, 1947-50. County Palatine of Durham (Solicitor General, 1946. Attorney General, 1947-1950). County Court Judge, Circuit 3, (Cumberland, Westmorland, Northumberland & Lancashire), 1950-1961. Chairman, Cumberland Quarter Sessions, 1953-1963. WW.

FENWICK, Edward Matthew
2nd son of Edward James Reid Fenwick of Salt Ponds in the island of Jamaica. Father of Thomas Fenwick Fenwick qv. Address; Burrow Hall, Kirkby Longsdale, Lancs. No chambers address, 1876-1877. Not in 1878 Law List. Foster.

FENWICK, Thomas Fenwick
Born 1 August 1842. Eldest son of Edward Mather Fenwick. qv. Eton; Christ Church, Oxford, MA. AAS. I. 23 November 1866. Call 7 June 1869. ETC. 26 July 1869. Prop Jones QC. Sec. Quain QC. 3 Hare Court, 1876-1878. Lancs, Carlisle & Liverpool Sessions. No address, 1879-1907. Not in 1908 Law List. DL. & JP., Westmorland, West Riding of Yorkshire & Lancs. Foster.

FERGUS, James Alfonso
G. 18 November 1935. ETC. 1 July 1936. Prop. Lynskey KC. Sec. Newman. 14 Cook Street, Liverpool, 1942-1949. No address, 1950-1963. Not in 1964 Law List.

FERGUSON, Richard Saul
Born 28 July 1837, Carlisle. Died 3 March 1900 aged 62. Shrewsbury; St John's College, Oxford, MA., LLM. AAS. L. 13 October 1858. Call 11 June 1862. Practised as equity draftsman and conveyancer, 1862-1872. Thereafter prominent in Carlisle public life. Chairman, Cumberland Quarter Sessions, Chancellor of Diocese of Carlisle, Alderman of Carlisle (Mayor twice). Numerous local history publications. WW. DNB.

FERGUSON, William Bates KC
Born 1853. Died 7 October 1937. Manchester Grammar School; Merton College, Oxford; Christ Church, Oxford, MA. AAS. L. 20 January 1874. Call 21 June 1882. ETC. 15 January 1883. Prop. Ambrose QC. Sec. Lowther. 33 Chancery Lane, 1883-1884. 3 Plowden Buildings, 1885-1937. Lancs. Chancery Court. Silk 1900. Fellow Institute of Chemistry. Medalist of Royal Photographic Society and inventor of Ferguson Method of Copper Toning. Publications on scientific and photographic matters; joint author of Ambrose & Ferguson's Land Transfer Acts. WW.

FERNLEY, Joseph Holdsworth
Born 1829. 2nd son of James Fernley of Plymouth. AAS. I. 26 May 1849. I. 7 June 1852. Lancs, Manchester & Salford Sessions. No address, 1876-1928. Not in 1929 Law List.

FERNS, Peter Astley
MA (Cantab). I. 3 July 1935. ETC. 10 July 1935. Prop. Gorman KC. Sec. Green. Manchester Chambers; 78 King Street, 1935-1958; 196 Deansgate, 1959-1972. Value Added Tax Tribunals, Manchester, 1973-1986. Not in 1987 Bar Directory.

FEWTRELL, Nicholas Austin
Born 1 July 1955 Bridge, Kent. Bramcote Hills Grammar School; Queen Mary College, London, LLB. I. November 1977. ETC. 3 April 1979. Prop. George Carman QC. Sec. Hodgson. London pupillage. Manchester Chambers; 43 King Street November, 1978-1988; 5 John Dalton Street, 1989-1995; 18 St John Street, October 1995. Recorder 2004.

★ FFOULKES, His Honour William Wynne
Born 14 July 1821. Died 27 June 1903 aged 81. 4th son of John Powell Ffoulkes of Erivat Hall, Denbighs. Shrewsbury School; Jesus College, Oxford, MA. AAS. 2 November 1844. Call 23 November 1947. 4 Middle Temple Lane, 1848. North Wales Circuit. County Court Judge, Circuit 7, (Altrincham, Birkenhead, Leigh, Warrington & Wigan.), 1875-1899. WW. Foster.

FIELD, Patrick John QC
Born 19 March 1959, Bromsgrove. Bishop Wordsworth GS, Salisbury; Wilmslow County GS; King's College, London, LLB. G. November 1981. ETC 1982. Circuit Junior, 1985. Pupilmaster, David Poole. Assistant Recorder, 1998. Silk & Recorder, 2000. Manchester Chambers; Deans Court Chambers at Crown Square, 1982-1999 and at 24 St John Street, 4.5.1999. WW.

FIELDHOUSE, Nigel Richard Arnold
LLB. G. July 1976. Manchester Chambers; 67 Princess Street 1976-1987; Hollins Chambers, 64a Bridge Street, 1988-1997; Cobden House Chambers, 19 Quay Street, 1998.

FIELDING, William Thomas
G. 13 June 1923. ETC. 29 January 1930. 3 Plowden Buildings, 1924-1928. 1 Elm Court, 1929. Liverpool Chambers; 8 Harrington Street, 1930-1935; 5 Cook Street, 1936-1939; 8 Cook Street, 1940-1949. No address, 1950-1963. Not in 1964 Law List.

FINIGAN, James Lysaght
L. 26 January 1880. ETC. 3 August 1883. Prop. Russell QC. Sec. Commins. 1 Cloisters, 1886. No address, 1888-1940. Not in 1941 Law List.

FIREMAN, Mark Phillip
Born 17 January 1962 Manchester. Manchester Grammar School; University College, London, LLB. G. February 1986. ETC. Summer 1987. Prop. Mark Carlisle QC. Sec. Roger Brown. Manchester Chambers; Old Colony House, 1987-1994; Manchester House Chambers, 18-22 Bridge Street, 1994-2000; 24a St John Street 2001. (now St Johns Buildings)

FIRTH, Cecil Mallaby
I. 26 January 1904. No address, 1910-1925. Assize Office, 1 Chapel Street, Preston, 1926-1940. No address, 1941-1950. Not in 1951 Law List.

FIRTH, Ernest Cecil
Born 1886. Eldest son of Rev. Raywood Firth of Preston, Clerk in Holy Orders. Lincoln College, Oxford, MA., BCL. AAS. M. 2 November 1887. Call 18 June 1890. ETC. 27 February 1891. Prop. Bigham QC. Sec. McCall QC. Chapel Street, Preston, 1892-1915. Lancs. Chancery Court. No address, 1916-1949. Not in 1950 Law List.

FISH, David Thomas QC
Born 23 July 1949 Ashton under Lyne. Married to Angelina Dennett qv. Ashton under Lyne Grammar School; London School of Economics, LLB. I. July 1973. Western Circuit, 1975. Pupilmaster, Patrick Whelan. 2 Mitre Court Buildings, 1975-1983. ETC 1983. Prop. Goddard QC. Manchester Chambers; Deans Court; at Crown Square, 1983-1999 and at 24 St John Street, 4.5.1999. Assistant Recorder 1989. Recorder 1994. Silk 1997. WW.

*** FISH, (Peter) Stuart (His Honour Judge Fish)**
Born 18 December 1938. Rydal School: Trinity Hall, Cambridge, MA. Admitted solicitor 1963 having served articles with Oakey Charnhill & Thurnhill of Preston. Brighouses, Solicitors, Southport, 1963-1987. Registrar later District Judge, Manchester, 1987-1994. Recorder 1991-1994. Circuit Judge, Manchester 1994. WW.

FISHER, Catherine Jane
Born 20 October 1966, Woking. Guilford High School; London School of Economics, LLB. Hertford College, Oxford, BCL. G. October 1990. (Entrance & Macaskie Scholar & Holker award). Research Assistant (Property) at Law Commission, 1991-1992. Pupillage at 2 Hare Court & 8 New Square. Ropewalk Chambers, Nottingham, 1992-1997. Midland & Oxford Circuit. ETC 1997. Merchant Chambers, 1 North Parade, Parsonage Gardens, Manchester December 1997-2004; merger with St Johns Buildings 2004. Member, American Bar Association & New York State Bar.

FISHER, George Gregory
G. 26 January 1897. ETC. 31 July 1897. Prop. Taylor QC. Sec. Greer. Various London Chambers and finally at 3 Paper Buildings, 1930-1935. Liverpool Sessions & Central Criminal Court. Not in 1936 Law List.

FISHER, Joseph Robert
Born 1855. Died 26 October 1939 aged 84. 3rd son of Ringland Fisher of Raffrey, Down, Ireland, presbyterian minister. Royal Academical Institution, Belfast; Queen's College, Galway, BA 1876. AAS. M. 1 May 1876. Call 19 November 1888. ETC. 27 February 1891. Prop. Bigham QC. Sec. McCall QC. Circuit Junior, Summer 1891. Various London chambers and finally at 3 Essex Court, 1914-1939. Foreign Editor of the Daily Chronicle. Assistant Editor of the Standard. Editor & Managing Director of Belfast Northern Whig. Member of Irish Boundary Commission, 1924-1925. Various historical & political publications and Fisher & Strahan's Law of the Press. WW.

FISHER, Richard
L. 17 November 1885. ETC. 7 February 1887. Prop. Addison QC. Sec. McKeand. Liverpool Chambers; 9 Orange Court, Castle Street, 1888; Marldon Chambers, 30 North John Street, 1889-1893; 7 Cook Street, 1894-1899. No address, 1900-1930. Not in 1931 Law List.

FITZHUGH, His Honour James
Born 2 April 1917. Died 27 February 1989 aged 71. St Bede's College, Manchester; Manchester University, BA(Admin); London University, LLB. Captain, War of 1939-1945. G. January 1948. Manchester Chambers; 78 King Street, 1948-1951; 4 Clarence Street, 1952-1976. Circuit Judge, 1976-1988.

FITZPATRICK, Thomas Andrew Michael
Born 17 April 1953, Croydon. St Mary's School, Croydon; Manchester University, LLB. Police Officer, Lancashire, 1971-1986. L. 22 November 1988. ETC. 15 December 1988. Prop. John Kay QC. Sec. Kevin Grice. Pupilmaster, Mark Hedley. 27 Dale Street/ Corn Exchange, 1988-1992. Manchester Chambers; 83 Bridge Street, 1992-1995; Kingsgate Chambers, 1995-1999; 9 St John Street, 1999.

FITZPATRICK, William Henry Mulleneux
Born 1887. Only son of William John Fitzpatrick of Stoneycroft, Liverpool. AAS. M. 3 November 1910. Call 4 June 1913. ETC. 15 June 1913. Prop. Hewart QC. Sec. Riley. Liverpool Chambers; Commerce Court, 14 Harrington Street, 1913-1914. No address, 1915-1921. 10 Dale Street, 1922. 13 Harrington Street, 1923-1928; 25 Lord Street, 1929-1930; Commerce Court, 11 Lord Street, 1931-1940. No chambers address, 1941-1946; 27 Lord Street, 1947-1959; 10 Water Street, 1960-1969; 2nd floor, Oriel Chambers, 14 Water Street, 1970-1973. Not in 1974 Law List.

FLEETWOOD-HESKETH, Charles Hesketh
Son of late John Bibby and of Anna Fleetwood of Allerton, Liverpool. Died 13 April 1947. He took the surname and Arms of Hesketh (his maternal grandfather's name) by Royal Licence in 1899 and by a subsequent Royal Licence, in 1907, the surname and arms of Fleetwood-Hesketh. Eton; Trinity College, Cambridge, BA 1893; MA, 1897. I. 18 November 1895. ETC. 2 February 1898. Prop. J Walton QC. Sec. Moon. Served; South African War, 1900; Major, 1914-1917. 2 Garden Court, 1896-1902. No address, 1903-1947. High Sheriff of Lancashire, 1901. Lord of the Manor of North Meols (Southport) & of Holcombe Court. (Taunton). WW.

FLEMING, Charles James QC., MP.
Born 26 November 1839, Sheffield. Died 25 December 1904 aged 65. AAS. G. 18 November 1869. Call 6 June 1872; Bencher 1893. ETC. 10 March 1873. Prop. Holker QC. Sec. Temple QC. 4 St James's Square, Manchester, 1876-1898. No address, 1899-1904. Chief Assistant to Accountant General, Bombay, 1865-1871. Silk 1893. Contested (L) Pontefract, 1886 and Dudley, 1895. MP for Doncaster, 1892. WW.

FLEMING, Edward Lascelles KC., MP.
Born 1892. Son of Thomas Fleming of Blackburn. Died 17 February 1950 aged 58. London University, Lieut., 4th Battn. East Lancashire Regt. & attached to Royal Flying Corp. G. 26 January 1921. Manchester Chambers; 60 King Street, 1924-1925; 48 King Street, 1926-1930; Bank of England Chambers, Tib Lane, 1931-1932. Silk 1932. MP (U) Manchester, Withington, 1931-1950. Squadron Leader, World War II. Publications; Sheba's Ring, 1933. WW.

FLETCHER, Alfred Woodroofe
Born 1870. 2nd son of Alfred James Fletcher of Manchester, banker. Victoria University, Manchester, LLB. AAS. M. 1 November 1889. Call 26 April 1893. ETC. 17 July 1893. Prop. Ambrose QC. Sec. Sutton. Manchester Chambers; 78 Cross Street, 1894-1897; St Ann's Passage, 1898-1908. No address, 1909-1949. Not in 1950 Law List. Foster.

FLETCHER, Charles
Born 1849. Eldest son of late Charles Jack of Liverpool, merchant. Assumed the name Fletcher, 14 December 1882. Christ Church, Oxford, BA., SCL. 1872. AAS. I. 2 November 1871. Call 7 June 1875. 2 Pump Court, 1883-1887; 6 Crown Office Row, 1888-1890; 9 Stone Buildings, 1891-1897. No address, 1898-1935.

FLETCHER, Charles Melbourne
Born 1850. 2nd son of William Fletcher of Cheltenham. Jesus College, Cambridge, BA 1872. AAS. I. 29 December 1871. Call 7 June 1875. ETC. 6 March 1877. Prop. Bayliss QC. Sec. Collins. Commerce Court, Harrington Street, 1878-1895. No address, 1896-1935. Not in 1936 Law List. Foster.

FLETCHER, John Devonald
I. 22 June 1898. ETC. 2 February 1889. Prop. Pickford QC. Sec. Foard. 1 Garden Court, 1900-1901; 5 Essex Court, 1902-1906; 78 King Street, Manchester, 1907-1922. Not in 1923 Law List.

FLETCHER, John Dunnington
Born 1820. Eldest son of John Fletcher of St Michael's Mount, Liverpool. Christ College, Cambridge, MA 1843. AAS. I. 22 January 1838. Call 2 May 1845. 3 Tanfield Court, 1848. Assistant barrister at Liverpool Sessions, 1876-1879. 1 Essex Court, 1876-1886. Chairman (2nd Court) Middlesex Sessions, Clerkenwell, 1879. Not in 1890 Law List.

FLETCHER, John Henry
Born 1860. 2nd son of John Fletcher of Ashton under Lyne, cotton spinner. Rugby; University of London. AAS. M. 9 November 1881. Call 17 November 1884. ETC. 2 February 1885. Prop. Gully QC. Sec. French. No address, 1885-1940. Not in 1941 Law List.

FLETCHER, Kevin Francis
G. November 1974. Liverpool Chambers; 14 Water Street, 1974-1982; Refuge Assurance House, Derby Square, 1983-1988. Admitted solicitor, May 1988. Weightmans, Solicitors, Liverpool, 1988.

FLEWITT, Neil QC
Born 3 July 1959, Liverpool. St Edward's College, Liverpool; Liverpool University, LLB. AAS. M. 15 January 1980. Call July 1981. ETC. 1981. Prop. Michael Maguire QC. Sec. Mark Hedley. Circuit Junior, 1985. Liverpool Chambers; Same chambers at; 27 Dale Street, 1981-1989; Corn Exchange, 1989-1999; 7 Harrington Street (merger with Martin's Bank Building) 6.9.1999. Assistant Recorder 1998. Recorder 2000. Silk 2003.

FLINTOFF, Albert Nevins
Born 1833. 2nd son of John Flintoff of Witton-le-Wear, Co. Durham. Trinity College, Oxford, MA. AAS. L. 3 April 1856. Call 6 June 1860. No address, 1877-1895. Not in 1896 Law List.

FLOOD, David Edward
Born 2 September 1968, Stockport. St Peter's RC Comprehensive School, Orrell, Wigan; University College Wales, Aberystwyth, LLB. M. 9 February 1993. ETC. December 1993. Prop. Nigel Gilmour QC. Pupilmasters; Peter Wain (Ipswich), John Mockett, Robert Atherton. Liverpool Chambers; Stanley Street, 1993-1994; 3rd floor, Peel House, Harrington Street/ India Buildings, 1994.

FLOOD, Diarmuid Brendan Martin
Born 29 July 1963, Sheffield. College St Michel, Belgium, 1975-1977; Stonyhurst College, 1978-1981; King's College, London, LLB. Maitrise en Droit Prive, Sorbonne- Pantheon, Paris. L. April 1989. Department of Trade & Industry, 1990-1992. Yamaichi (Europe) Ltd, 1992-1993. Smiths Industries, 1993-1994. ETC. 20 December 1994. Prop. Tim King QC. Sec. Vincent Deane. Pupilmaster, Stephen Furst. 58 King Street, Manchester, 1994; Victoria Chambers at; 25 Victoria Street, 19 Castle Street & 2nd floor, 14 Cook Street, 1995.

FOARD, James Thomas

Born 1831. Eldest son of James Foard of Brighton. AAS. I. 23 April 1860. Call 26 January 1863. 5 Essex Court, 1876-1879; 3 Harcourt Buildings, 1880. Manchester Chambers; 4 St James's Square, 1881-1889 & 1896; 42 John Dalton Street, 1890-1895; Atlantic Chambers, 7 Brazennose Street, 1897-1903; 15 Brazennose Street, 1904-1906. Not in 1907 Law List. Publication; Law of Merchant Shipping. Foster.

FOGARTY, Peter Dominic
Born 2 January 1959. Died 15 June 2002 aged 43. Deyes High, Maghull; Downing College, Cambridge, MA. L. July 1982. ETC. 1983. Prop. Eric Somerset Jones QC. Sec. Ian Trigger. Oriel Chambers, CoventGarden/Water Street, Liverpool, 1982-2002. Accomplished cellist & horseman. Captain in Territorial Army. Family law specialist. Tributes at Liverpool Law Courts on 19 June 2002 (Judge David Clarke QC/ David Steer QC.) Transcript in Circuit Records.

FOLEY, Frank Settle
LLB. G. 9 May 1906. ETC. 5 February 1907. Prop. Shee KC. Sec. Sutton. Manchester Chambers; 78 King Street, 1909-1910. No address, 1911-1921. 7 Kennedy Street, 1922-1932. No chambers address, 1933-1937. Not in 1938 Law List.

FOLEY, John Maurice
G. 17 November 1937. Lord Justice Holker Senior Scholar, 1937. ETC. 15 June 1938. Prop. David Maxwell Fyfe QC. Sec. Hartley Shawcross. 27 Lord Street, 1939-1948. Not in 1949 Law List.

FONG, Jane
LLB, London ETC. Autumn 1980. Sec. Andrew Mattison. Fruit Exchange, Victoria Street, Liverpool, 1980-1982. "Went to Hong Kong in 1982 " is the note in the Liverpool Prosecutions book.

*** FORBES, Thayne (The Hon. Mr Justice Forbes)**

(DL)

Born 28 June 1938. Winchester College; Wolverton Grammar School; University College, London, LLB., LLM. Lieut. Instructor, Royal Navy, 1963-1966. I. 1966; Bencher 1991. Silk 1984. Recorder 1986. Circuit Judge (Official Referee), 1990-1993. High Court Judge, Queen's Bench Division, 1993. Presiding Judge of the Northern Circuit, 1995-1999. He tried Harold Shipman, a doctor from Hyde who was convicted of murdering 15 of his patients. (See also The Rt. Hon. Lady Justice Smith who chaired the subsequent public inquiry) WW.

FORD, John Buchan
MA., LLB. I. 17 November 1919. 6 Fig Tree Court, 1920; 5 Pump Court, 1921; 1 Garden Court, 1922-1923; 1 Paper Buildings, 1924-1930; 3 Plowden Buildings, 1931-1935; 1 Tanfield Court, 1936-1943; 5 King's Bench Walk, 1944-1945; 2 Dr Johnson's Building, 1946-1949. No address, 1950-1961. Not in 1962 Law List.

FORD, Mark Steven
Born 11 June 1961 Bowden, Cheshire. Married to Nicola Brown qv. Cheadle Moseley Grammar School; Birmingham University LLB. Solicitors; Brian Koffman & Co., 1986-1987; Cohens, 1987-1988; Glaisters, 1988-1991. G. 21 November 1991. ETC. December 1991. Prop. David Poole QC. Sec. Philip Andrews. Pupilmaster, John Bonney. Manchester Chambers; 6th floor, Sunlight House, Quay Street, August 1991-November 1993; Young Street Chambers, November 1993.

FORD, His Honour Peter
Born 30 September 1930. Died 9 March 2003 aged 72. Ellesmere College; Manchester University, LLB. G November 1952. ETC. 1952. 60 King Street, Manchester, 1952-1955. He then became a patent law specialist joining Queen Elizabeth Building Chambers and moving to South Square in 1976. Member, Board of Appeal, European Patents Office, Munich, 1979-1990. Chairman, Legal Board of Appeal, 1979-1990. Circuit Judge and first Judge of the Patents Court, 1990-2000. WW. Obituary, Times, 20 March 2003.

FORDHAM, Judith
Born 19 September 1950 London. Widow of Robert Allan Fordham QC. qv. St David's School, Ashford, Middlesex. Admitted as a solicitor, 1975 after articles with Maxwell, Entwistle & Byrne. Louis Berkson & Globe, Solicitors, Liverpool, 1975-1991. (Senior Partner). I. July 1991. ETC. December 1991. Prop. William Waldron QC. Sec. Bill Braithwaite. Exchange Chambers, Derby Square, Liverpool, 1991. Deputy District Judge 1989.

FORDHAM, Robert Allan QC
Born 21 December 1936. Died 8 December 2002 aged 65. Married to Judith Fordham. qv. London Grammar School; Nottingham University, LLB. I. November 1967. ETC. June 1968. Pupilmaster, John Edward Jones. Same Liverpool Chambers; North House, 17 North John Street, 1968-1971; Martins Building, Water Street, 1972-1999 (Head of Chambers); 7 Harrington Street (merger with Corn Exchange) 6.9.1999-2002. Recorder. Assistant Boundary Commissioner. Senior Law Lecturer, Liverpool John Moores University. Silk 1993. I shared a room in chambers with Bob for almost 20 years. My abiding memory of him is his humour. I am grateful to David Watson for letting me have Bob's particulars of cruelty in a petition filed in the Liverpool County Court 20 years ago. It reads:
"The general nature of the case
Is that the Respondent set his face
Against the Petitioner and saw her less than he
In intelligence and worth;
But thought himself the earth.
Imposed on her a strict regime
In which he was both King and Queen
Controlled finance and taste and her own ornament
Kept for himself the greater aliment
Pursued affairs with others sub. nom. Jennie and Suzanne
And offered nothing but abuse to Jan
But what is worse
Both courted and abused in verse."
Tributes at Liverpool Law Courts 11 December 2002 (Judge David Clarke QC/ David Steer QC/ Mark Feeney. Transcript in Circuit Records. WW.

FORMBY, Jonathan

Born 1854. Eldest son of Richard Formby. qv. AAS. I. 17 April 1874. Call 15 May 1878. ETC. 29 July 1878. Prop. Aspinall QC. Sec. Butler. 6 Crown Office Row, 1879-1881; 1 Dr Johnson's Building, 1882-1886; Liverpool Chambers; 7 Commerce Court, 15 Lord Street, 1887-1891; 25 Lord Street, 1909-1920. No address, 1921-1944. Not in 1945 Law List.

FORMBY, Richard
Born 1815. Eldest son of Henry Greenhalgh Formby, father of Jonathan Formby. qv. Brasenose College, Oxford, BA 1836. AAS. I. 7 November 1849. Call 17 November 1852. Eldon Chambers, South John Street, Liverpool, 1876-1895. No address, 1896-1897. Not in 1898 Law List. Conveyancer. Lancs. Chancery Court.

FORMBY, Richard
Born 3 July 1828. Only son of Richard Formby of Liverpool, M.D. Trinity College, Cambridge, LLB 1852. AAS. I. 30 May 1850. Call 6 June 1853. No address, 1876-1915. Not in 1916 Law List.

FORREST, Alastair John
Born 1 September 1950 Glasgow. Glasgow Academy; The Queen's College, Oxford, MA. G. July 1972. Lecturer, University of Manchester, 1972-1974. ETC. 1974. Prop. Benet Hytner QC. Sec. Donald Hart. Same Manchester Chambers at; Astley House, Quay Street, 1974-1978 and 18 St John Street, 1978. Assistant Recorder 1990. Recorder 1996. Legal Assessor, General Medical Council, 2002.

FORREST, His Honour Judge Richard Haddow QC
Born 13 September 1908. Died 29 October 1977 aged 69. Merchant Taylors' School, Crosby; Pembroke College, Oxford, MA. King's Regiment, 1930-1945 (SR 1930-1939) G. 8 June 1932; Bencher 1960. ETC. 1 February 1933. Prop. Lynskey KC. Sec. Sellers. Liverpool Chambers; 10 Cook Street, 1933-1939; 3 Cook Street, 1946-1953. Silk 1953. Goldsmith Building, 1953-1970. Recorder of Salford, 1956-1964. Presiding Judge, Liverpool Court of Passage, 1964-1971. Judge of Courts of Appeal, Jersey & Guernsey, 1965-1971. Leader, Northern Circuit, 1968 1971. Lieutenant Bailiff of Jersey, 1970-1977. Circuit Judge, 1970-1977. WW.

*** FORRESTER, Her Honour Judge Barbara Ann**
Solicitor, June 1976. Assistant Recorder, September 1995. Recorder, July 2000. Circuit Judge, 5 September 2002.

FORRESTER, Robert Alexander
Died 13 November 1976. G. 16 June 1926. ETC. 13 July 1926. Prop. Atkinson KC. Sec. Abbott. Equity draftsman & conveyancer. Lancs. Chancery Court. 78 King Street, Manchester, 1926-1951. Registrar, Manchester District of Lancs. Chancery Court based at 4 Clarence Street, Manchester, 1951-1971. Chancellor, Diocese of Blackburn, 1949-1976. Publications; Bennett's Chancery of Lancashire Practice.

FORSTER, His Honour Donald Murray
Born 18 June 1929. Died 12 October 2000 aged 71. Hollylea School, Liverpool; Merton House School, Penmaenmawr; Wrekin College, Wellington; St Edmund Hall, Oxford, BA. G. November 1953. ETC. 4 February 1954. Prop. Brabin QC. Sec. Kennan. Same Liverpool Chambers at; 34 Castle Street, 1953-1972; 54 Castle Street, 1973-1984 (Head). Recorder, 1978-1984. Circuit Judge, 1984-1990. Retired due to ill health. Enthusiastic footballer and tennis player. Liverpool Ramblers AFC/ Mersey Bowmen. Tributes at Liverpool Law Courts, 17 October 2000 (Judge David Clarke QC/ Andrew Edis QC). Transcript in Circuit Records. WW.

FORSTER, John (First Baron Forster of Harraby)
Born 15 September 1888, Carlisle. Died 24 July 1972 aged 83. Sedburgh. Served in RA in 1914-1918 War. G. 14 May 1919. ETC 1919. 2 Mitre Court, 1919-1822; 1 Brick Court, 1923-1957. South Eastern Circuit. Kt. 1939. Silk 1946. KBE 1948. Presided over Trinidad Labour Riots Commission in 1937 and the Court of Inquiry into the London Bus Dispute. President of the Industrial Court, 1946-1960. Judge, Administrative Tribunal, International Labour Organisation, 1957-1960. Baron 1959. WW.

FORSTER, Michael Williams
LLB London. G. February 1984. 9th & 6th floor, Sunlight House, Quay Street, Manchester 1984-1989. 17 Carlton Crescent, Southampton 1990.

FORSTER, Ralph (William Elliot)
Born 1862. Eldest son of James Forster of Berwick-upon-Tweed. Caius College, Cambridge, MA 1861. AAS. L. 19 January 1860. Call 26 January 1863. 2 Harcourt Buildings, 1876-1880. No address, 1881-1921. Not in 1922 Law List. Publications; Copyright & Customary Tenure. Foster.

FORSYTH, Julie Patricia
Born 17 June 1961, Liverpool. Evered Avenue Comprehensive School; Liverpool University, LLB. G. July 1983. ETC. October 1983. Prop. Justin Price QC. Sec. Andrew Mattison, same Liverpool Chambers at; Fruit Exchange, Victoria Street, 1983-1990; and at Chavasse Court, 24 Lord Street, 1990.

FORT, Sir Hugh
Born 14 May 1862. Died 28 May 1919 aged 57. 4th son of Richard Fort, MP for Clitheroe. Winchester; New College, Oxford. I. 17 November 1887. ETC. 5 February 1888. Prop. Hopwood QC. Sec. Shee. 2 Harcourt Buildings, 1888; 11 King's Bench Walk, 1889-1890; 12 King's Bench Walk, 1891-1892; New Court, Carey Street, 1893-1903. No address, 1904-1919. Advocate & Solicitor, Straits Settlements, 1893. Unofficial Member of the Legislative Council of the Straits Settlements, 1905-1908 and 1909-1911. WW.

FORTE, Mark Julian Carmino
Born 14 October 1965 Lisburn, Northern Ireland. Belfast Royal Academy; Manchester Polytechnic, LLB. I. November 1989. ETC. 1991. Pupilmaster, Bruce Caulfield. 8 King Street, Manchester, 1991. Northern Ireland Bar, 1996.

FORWOOD, Hon. Judge Nicholas James QC
Born 22 June 1948 Scarborough. Son-in-law of His Honour Basil Gerrard qv. Stowe School; St John's College, Cambridge, BA (Mechanical Sciences) 1968. MA (Law), 1973. AAS. M. 12 November 1968. Call 16 July 1970. ETC. 6 May 1971. Pupilmaster, John Rowe. Moved in 1971 to 4 Pump Court and specialised in European Law practising from London and Brussels culminating in his appointment on 15 December 1999 as Judge of the Court of First Instance, European Community. Silk 1987. WW.

FOSTER, Arthur La Trobe
Born 12 January 1861. 2nd son of Thomas Barham Foster of Manchester, civil engineer. Haileybury College; Jesus College, Cambridge, BA 1883. AAS. M. 19 April 1882. Call 26 January 1885. ETC. 30 January 1886. Prop. Hopwood QC. Sec. Aspland. 3 Dr Johnson's Building, 1886-1887; 1 Hare Court, 1888-1889; Queen's Chambers, 5 John Dalton Street, 1890-1899; 3 Plowden Buildings, 1900-1901. No address, 1902-1921. Not in 1922 Law List. Foster.

FOSTER, (Brian) Ian
Born 9 July 1965, Lincoln. Mirfield High School; Newcastle University, LLB. L. July 1988. ETC 1989. Pupilmaster, Nigel Howarth. Manchester Chambers; St James's Chambers, 68 Quay Street January, 1989-March 2001: Exchange Chambers, 4 Ralli Courts, West Riverside, 5 March 2001.

FOSTER, John Porter
I. 14 June 1899. ETC. 21 January 1900. Prop. Pickford QC. Sec. Sanderson. 2 Paper Buildings, 1902; 11 King's Bench Walk, 1903-1907. Cumberland Sessions. Cairo, Egypt, 1908-1919. Advocat Pres La Cour D'Appel Mixte D'Alexandrie. Not in 1920 Law List.

FOSTER, Jonathan Rowe QC (His Honour Judge Foster QC)
Born 20 July 1947, Bowden, Cheshire. Oundle School; Keble College, Oxford, MA. G. July 1970; Bencher 1998. ETC. March 1971. Prop. Bingham QC. Sec. John Lord. Pupilmasters; Hubert Picarda, John Lord. Manchester Chambers; 43 King Street, 1971-1978; 18 St John Street, 1978-2004 (Head). Recorder 1988. Silk 1989. Deputy High Court Judge, (Family) 1994. Member; CICB, 1994; CICAP, 1996. Treasurer Northern Circuit, 1993-1997. Circuit Judge, 1 April 2004. WW.

FOSTER, Peter William
30 March 1969, Billinge, Wigan. St Peter's School, Orrell; Owens University, Manchester, LLB. M. 15 November 1992. ETC. 25 March 1993. Prop. Nigel Gilmour QC. Sec. John Leach. Liverpool Chambers; First National Building, 24 Fenwick Street, 1992-1997; Peel House, Harrington Street, 1998-1999; Oriel Chambers, 14 Water Street, 1999.

FOSTER, Samuel Porter
Born 1845. Only son of John Porter Foster of Cumberland. Trinity College, Cambridge, MA, 1871. AAS. I. 13 November 1866. Call 17 November 1869. ETC. 10 February 1870. Prop. Campbell Foster. Sec. J H Fawcett. 3 Plowden Buildings, 1876; 12 King's Bench Walk, 1877-1885. No address, 1886-1909. Not in 1910 Law List. High Sheriff Cumberland, 1881. JP., DL. Foster.

FOUDY, Kim Frances
Born 16 March 1959 Lancashire. Mount St Joseph School, Bolton; Manchester Metropolitan University, LLB. G. July 1982. ETC. 1983. Prop. Tattersall QC. Sec. Earnshaw. 601 Royal Exchange/ 8 King Street, Manchester, 1982. Legal Member, Mental Health Review Tribunal, 1996.

FOWLER, James Edward
MA., LLB (Cantab). I. 28 January 1935. ETC. 26 February 1936. Prop. Lynskey KC. Sec. Rycroft. Manchester Chambers; 26 King Street, 1935-1958; 9 Albert Square, 1959-1972; 1 Deans Court, Crown Square, 1973-1977. Deputy Coroner, Manchester. Chairman, Medical Appeals Tribunal & Mental Health Review Tribunal. Not in 1997 Bar Directory. Sandy Temple gave me an advice of James Fowler's in matrimonial proceedings which begins: " I am developing a somewhat gloomy view of the quality of Instructing Solicitor's clientele, from the cross section, whose almost insoluble matrimonial difficulties have been submitted to me for my anxious consideration and febrile pleading. It is a popular aphorism, unsupported by any scientific evidence, that a worm will turn, and I have hesitated to comply with my instructions in this case, since I hold the view that it could only succeed before an absent minded or senile judge who, even then, was thinking of something else, on the evidence before me" In 1990 Fowler wrote a letter to Sandy congratulating him on his Knighthood. In it he says "You, of course, look splendid on a horse. Indeed I can, in some respects, claim the gift of prophesy. I recall some 30 years ago, when it was reported to me that at some Bar point to point, you had fallen from your horse at the feet of Pilcher J, remarking to Henry Gore "There's a lad who's going somewhere" Henry agreed, save that he remarked that he personally would have selected some less painful way of attracting attention" Later in the letter when reminding Sandy of two County Court Judges sitting on undefended divorce cases. "One Allsebrook insisted on Counsel asking leading questions of the Petitioner to save time whereas the other, Fenwick would not tolerate such questions but had difficulty understanding the case without them. So, ingenious counsel like yourself developed the art of doing both in the same question. You will remember that immortal question of yours, Sandy, at Preston, which so impressed me that I took it down in writing and had Arthur Prestt who was sitting next to me to certify. Question "What was it he poured over your head from out of a tea pot?" Answer, which surprised none of us but which seemed to satisfy Fenwick 'tea'.

FOWLER, John Anderson
I. 28 January 1907. ETC. 20 February 1907. Prop. Horridge KC. Sec. Thomas. 10 Cook Street, Liverpool, 1909-1923. No address, 1921-1925. 6 Crown Office Row, 1926-1934. No address, 1935-1953. Not in 1954 Law List.

FOX, Andrew Patrick
Born 13 December 1966 Manchester. William Hulme's Grammar School; Buckingham University, LLB. L. 16 October 1990. ETC. December 1990. Prop. Lyndsey Kushner QC. Sec. Lesley Newton. Pupilmaster, John Bonney. Manchester Chambers; 6th floor, Sunlight House, Quay Street, 1990-1994; 38 Young Street, 1995-2001; 28 St John Street, 2001-2002; St John's Chambers (merger with 24a St John Street) 23 September 2002.

FOX, Anna Katherine Helen
Born 20 August 1961 Liverpool. Merchant Taylors' School for Girls, Crosby; Courtauld Institute of Art; Liverpool University, LLB. AAS. M. 8 February 1985. ETC. 16 December 1986. Prop. Eric Somerset Jones QC. Sec. Anthony Edwards. Oriel Chambers, 5 Covent Garden/ 14 Water Street, 1986.

*** FOX, His Honour Judge John Scott KC.**
Born 17 January 1852 Selby, Yorks. Died 3 March 1918 aged 66. North Eastern Circuit. QC 1898. County Court Judge, Birkenhead, 1915-1916. WW.

FOX, Roland
BA, (Cantab) I. July 1975. 460 Royal Exchange, Manchester, 1977-1980. Ass. Legal Advisor, UAC Ltd., Blackfriars Rd., SE1, 1981-1983; Legal Advisor, Tri Central Oil Company, New Broad Street EC2., 1984-1988. Not in 1989 Bar Directory.

FOX, Simon James
Born 17 June 1967 Cardiff. Cheltenham College; Charing Cross & Westminster Medical School; MB., B.S. Hospital Doctor, 1990-1994. I. November 1994. ETC. 20 December 1994. Prop. Bill Braithwaite QC. Sec. Gerard Martin. Exchange Chambers, Derby Square, Liverpool, 1994-1999. St Philip's Chambers, Steelhouse Lane, Birmingham, 2000.

FRANCE-HAYHURST, Jean Gaynor
Born 20 January 1950 Chester. Towyn Grammar; University of Wales, Aberystwyth LLB. G. 1972 & 1990. 32 Park Place, Cardiff, 1974-1979. Wales and Chester Circuit. Pupilmaster, Christopher Compston. Solicitor, 1980-1990, with Wayman Hales, Chester, 1980-1987. ETC. 1992. Liverpool Chambers; Corn Exchange, 1992-1995; India Buildings, Water Street, 1995. Cheshire County Councillor, 2002

FRANKLIN, Sir Leonard Benjamin OBE
Born 1862. Died 11 December 1944. King's College, London; Athenee Royale, Bruxelles. I. 6 June 1894. ETC. 12 July 1894. Prop. Gully QC. Sec. McConnell. 3 New Square, 1898-1906. Senior partner, A Keyser & Co, bankers, 31 Throgmorton Street. MP (L) Central Hackney, 1923-1924. Received OBE for dealing with Belgian Refugees during war. Kt. 1932. Advocate and inventor of Percentage Proportional Representation having written a book on the topic in 1922. WW.

FRANKS, His Honour Desmond Gerald Fergus

(HS)

Born 24 January 1928. Cathedral Choir School, Canterbury; Manchester Grammar School; University College, London LLB. AAS. M. 8 October 1946. Call 5 February 1952. ETC. 6 March 1952. Prop. Wooll QC. Sec. Atkinson. Manchester Chambers 4 Chapel Walks/601 Royal Exchange 1952-1972. Circuit Judge, Manchester 1972-1993. WW.

FRASER, Sir Hugh (The Hon. Mr Justice Fraser)
Born 26 April 1860. Died 8 July 1927 aged 67. Charterhouse; Trinity Hall, Cambridge MA., LLD. Hon Fellow. Examiner in Law for Inns of Court and Universities of Oxford, Cambridge & London. I. 17 November 1886. Certificate of Honour in Bar Finals. Bencher 1918. ETC. 20 July 1888. Prop. Ambrose QC. Sec. Cross. 2 Cloisters, 1887-1890; 1 Cloisters, 1891; 4 Elm Court, 1892-1915; 1 Brick Court, 1916-1924. High Court Judge, Queen's Bench Division, 1924-1927. JP Ross & Cromarty. Publications; Law of Torts 11th ed; Law of Libel & Slander 6th ed; Law of Parliamentary Elections 3rd ed; Representation of the People Act 1918 2nd ed; Amid the High Hills 1923. WW.

FRASER, Vincent QC
Born 18 October 1958, Crosby. St Mary's College, Crosby; University College, Oxford MA. G. July 1981. ETC. 1981. Pupilmaster, Andrew Gilbart. Manchester Chambers; 460 Royal Exchange, 1981-1987; 40 King Street, 1987. Silk 2001. Recorder 2002. Publications; Planning Decisions Digest 1st & 2nd editions.

FREEDMAN, Benjamin Clive QC
Born 16 November 1955 Manchester. Son of Lionel Freedman, formerly senior partner of Eversheds, Solicitors. Cousin of Iain Goldrein QC qv. The Manchester Grammar School; Pembroke College, Cambridge, MA. M. 1978. ETC. 1 July 1980. Pupilmaster, Julian Hall. 601 Royal Exchange, Manchester, 1980-1988. 2 Crown Office Row, 1989-1994; Littleton Chambers, 3 King's Bench Walk, 1995. Also at 28 St John Street, Manchester. Assistant Recorder 1997. Silk 1997. Recorder 2000. WW.

FREEMANTLE, Clive James
BA. I. July 1982. Room 22, 3rd floor, 15 Victoria Street, Liverpool 1985. Crown Prosecutions Service; Merseyside, 1988-1989; Newcastle, 1990. Senior Crown Prosecutor.

FRENCH, His Honour Daniel O'Connell KC
Born 1843. Died 4 August 1902. 3rd son of Bartholemew French of Maghull, shipowner. Jesuit College, Tournai, Belgium. Formerly a solicitor. AAS. M. 22 January 1870. Certificate of Honour 1871. Call 30 April 1872; Bencher 1888, Autumn Reader 1899. ETC. 31 July 1872. Prop. Russell QC. Sec. Goldney. 1 Pump Court, 1876-1882; Goldsmith Building, 1883-1892. Silk 1885. County Court Judge, Circuit 20, (Leicester), 1892-1894; Circuit 40, (Bow & Shoreditch), 1894-1902. WW.

FRIESNER, David Jonathan
Born 13 December 1965, Manchester. Bury Grammar School; Manchester University, LLB. G. November 1988. Manchester Chambers; Kenworthy's Buildings, 83 Bridge Street, 1994-1998; 9 St John's Street, 1999.

FRIEZE, Daniel Isaac
Born 8 August 1971, Manchester. Stockport Grammar School; Manchester University, BA (Theology). G. October 1994. Fruhman Davies, Solicitors, 1994-1996. ETC. December 1996. Prop. Tim King QC. Sec. Nadine Hope. Victoria Chambers, Liverpool, 1996-1998; Manchester Chambers; Manchester House, 1998-1999; 24a St John Street 1999.(now St Johns Buildings).

FRITH, Heather Vivien
Born 23 January 1966. Bristol University, LLB. AAS. M. 15 March 1988. Call 27 July 1989. ETC. 21 December 1995. Prop. Farley QC. Sec. Standsby. Devon Chambers, 3 St Andrew Street, Plymouth, 1992-1995. Kenworthy's Buildings, 83 Bridge Street, Manchester, 1997-2000.

FRODSHAM, Alexander Miles
Born 20 September 1973, London. St John's College, Johannesburg; Liverpool University, LLB. L. 10 October 1996. ETC. December 1996. Prop. Eric Somerset Jones QC. Sec. Peter Goodbody. Circuit Junior, 1999/2000. Oriel Chambers, 14 Water Street, Liverpool, 30 September 1996. Great nephew of Leo Frodsham and nephew of Aiden Frodsham both of Byrne Frodsham, Solicitors. Member, Selden Society.

FROST, Robert
L. 7 July 1886. ETC. 2 March 1889. Prop. Henn Collins QC. Sec. Carver. 8 King's Bench Walk, 1890-1895; 5 New Court, Carey Street, 1896-1936. No address, 1937-1940. Not in 1941 Law List.

FRYER-SPEDDING, James Walter
Born 8 June 1970, Carlisle. Keswick School; Atlantic College, South Glamorgan; King's College, London, LLB; New College, Oxford, BCL. G. 17 February 1994. Research Assistant, Law Commission, 1994-1995. ETC. 16 December 1997. Pupilmasters Robert Sterling & Mark Cawson. Manchester Chambers; St James's Chambers, 68 Quay Street, 1996-2002; 9 St John Street March, 2002.

FRYMAN, Neil
Born 28 May 1966 Manchester. William Hulme Grammar School, Manchester; Leicester University, LLB. AAS. M. 14 December 1987. Call 27 July 1989. ETC. 1990. Pupilmaster A P Morris. Peel Court Chambers, 45 Hardman Street, Manchester, 1990.

FULLERTON, T. Grey
I. 30 April 1857. No address, 1876-1923. Not in 1924 Law List.

FULTON, David
Born 1855. Eldest son Rev. John Morris Fulton, clergyman of the Church of Scotland. Manchester civil engineer when admitted to M. on 10 January 1889. Call 17 November 1891. ETC. 13 February 1902. Prop. Pickford KC. Sec. Maberley. London Chambers; 3 Essex Court & 2, later, 1 Garden Court, 1892-1915.Manchester Chambers; 1 St James's Square. Not in 1916 Law List.

FYFE, Rt. Hon. Sir David Patrick Maxwell KC., MP (Earl of Kilmuir)
Born 29 May 1900 Edinburgh. Died 17 January 1967 aged 66. George Watson's College, Edinburgh; Balliol College, Oxford MA; Hon. Fellow, 1954. Married 1925 Sylvia (DBE 1957) sister of the actor Rex Harrison. Served Scots Guards, 1918-1919. G. 28 June 1922; Bencher 1936; Treasurer 1949. ETC. 31 January 1933. Prop. Singleton KC. Sec. Howard Jones. Circuit Junior, Winter 1923. Liverpool Chambers; 25 Lord Street, 1923-1925; 13 Harrington Street, 1926-1928; 5 Harrington Street, 1929-1934. Silk 1934. 1 Harcourt Buildings, 1934-1945; 1 Paper Buildings, 1946; 1 Temple Gardens, 1947-1952 & 1954; 2 Raymond Building, 1953. MP(C) Liverpool West Derby, 1935-1954. Recorder of Oldham, 1936-1942. Solicitor General, 1942-1945. Attorney General, 1945. Deputy Chief Prosecutor at Nurenburg. Home Secretary, 1951-1954. Lord Chancellor, 1954-1962. Kt. 1962. PC. 1945. GCVO. 1953 (for coronation duties) Viscount Kilmuir 1954. Baron Fyfe of Dornoch 1962. First Earl of Kilmuir 1962. WW. DNB.
Recommended Reading;
Autobiography "Political Adventure – Memoirs of the Earl of Kilmuir." 1964. Weidenfeld & Nicholson. Lives of the Lord Chancellors, 1940-1970. Professor Heuston. 1987, Clarendon Press, Oxford p161-180. Life Sentence. Lord Shawcross QC. 1995. Constable. The MacMillan Years 1957-1963. Richard Lamb 1995. John Murray (Publishers) Ltd. Fyfe appeared in many of the Circuits famous cases including Dr Buck Ruxton reported in Notable British Trials (See Singleton LJ. for details) He also defended Haigh, the 'Acid Bath' murderer (Notable British Trials). He said that Sir Herbert Stephen, the Clerk of Assize, told him that "in 1876 we retained the name 'Northern' because we were the circuit which went to Appleby." He had tremendous energy which was essential to combine a busy legal practice with his political career. In his book he says "during the Assizes I was constantly conferring from 9.00am until 10.30, in Court until 5.15pm, then on the 5.25 from Liverpool or 5.45 from Manchester reaching London at 9.00pm. Then in the House of Commons until the 11.00pm division, then back on the midnight train to the North."
Professor Heuston says of Fyfe, "His personal popularity at the Bar and at Westminster was great; his simple integrity was manifest." Fyfe was proud to be a Northern Circuiteer and was deeply touched when the Circuit gave him a dinner upon his appointment as Lord Chancellor. He said, "The Dinner was for me and Jack Ashworth, my first judicial appointment. Nearly 170 turned up at Gray's Inn Hall and it was a great experience to see so many old friends."
Although Sir Hartley Shawcross gave the opening and closing speeches at the Nurenburg War Crimes Trials, it is generally accepted that Fyfe played a more important role. He effectively led the British team throughout and his cross examination of Goering was brilliant.
As Home Secretary he is remembered for refusing to reprieve Derek Bentley, convicted of murdering a police officer.
He was the backbone of the Conservative Party, intensely loyal to his colleagues and a very popular and effective Government Minister. It was Fyfe who after Suez made sure that The Queen understood that the Cabinet wished Harold MacMillan to succeed Anthony Eden. It was a great surprise when on 12 July 1962 ("The Night of the Long Knives." "RAB" Butler described it as "The Massacre at Glencoe.") he was one of seven ministers (another was Selwyn Lloyd qv) dismissed by MacMillan upon seven hours notice. The Prime Minister was worried about the Government's standing in the country and claimed that new blood was needed. Fyfe, who had every right to feel angry, later wrote; "I got the impression that he was extremely alarmed about his own position and was determined to eliminate any risk for himself by a massive change of Government. It astonished me that a man who had kept his head under the most severe stresses and strains should lose both nerve and judgment in this way." Fyfe complained that his cook would have been given more notice of dismissal than he had. When MacMillan heard this he observed that it was easier to get Lord Chancellors than cooks. Jeremy Thorpe, the Leader of the Liberal Party, said of the Prime Minister, "Greater love hath no man that he lay down his friends for his life." MacMillan's fears were not realised until October 1964 when Labour, led by Harold Wilson, gained power with an overall majority of five seats. After his dismissal Fyfe refused to take part in legal or political life. He would not accept the pension due to him as a former Lord Chancellor and went off to the City to become Chairman of the Plessy Company.

G

GAL, Sonia
Born 19 October 1945, Cluj, Rumania. Educated in Rumania & Norway. Open University, BA. I. November 1982. ETC. March 1983. Pupilmaster, Philip Raynor. Manchester Chambers; 460 Royal Exchange/ 40 King Street, 1982-1999; 28 St John Street, 1999. (now St Johns Buildings). Assistant Recorder 1996. Recorder 2000.

GALBRAITH, James Francis Wallace KC, MP (His Honour Judge Galbraith KC)
Born 1872. Died 29 January 1945. Blackheath Proprietary School; Oriel College, Oxford. L. 16 June 1895. Certificate of Honour. Bencher 1922. ETC. 14 March 1896. Prop. Walton QC. Sec. Greer. 19 Old Square, 1897-1900; 2 New Square, 1901-1913; 3 New Square, 1914-1935. 25 Lord Street, Liverpool, 1901-1908. Lancs. Chancery Court. Silk 1919. County Court Judge, Circuit 20, (Beds., Leicester, Lincs & North Rutland), November 1935-1945. WW.

GALLIE, James Butler
Born 1848. Only son of John Gallie, late of Dublin, merchant. Matriculated, Trinity College, Dublin. AAS. I. 3 May 1870. Call 30 April 1873. ETC. 11 July 1873. Prop. Kay QC. Sec. Campbell Foster. Circuit Junior, Spring 1874. 1 Hare Court, 1876-1879; 6 Pump Court, 1880-1884; 3 Hare Court, 1885-1893; No address, 1894-1896; 7 Fig Tree Court, 1897-1907. Not in 1908 Law List. Foster.

GALLOWAY, John
I. 27 June 1906. 78 King Street, Manchester, 1916-1920. Not in 1921 Law List.

GAMON, His Honour Judge Hugh Reece Percival
Born 9 January 1880. Died 26 January 1953 aged 73. 5th son of John Gamon of Chester, solicitor. Harrow; Exeter College, Oxford, BCL. AAS. M. 15 November 1902. Call 27 June 1906. ETC. 6 March 1908. Prop. Sanderson KC. Sec. Rigby Swift. Liverpool Chambers; 2 Harrington Street, 1910-1918; 26 North John Street, 1919-1928; 5 Cook Street, 1929; 3 Cook Street, 1930-1936. Chancery Practitioner. County Court Judge, Circuit 15, (Yorks. & Durham), 1936-1937; Circuit 2, 1937-1953. Publications; The London Police Court Today & Tomorrow, 1907. WW.

GANDY, Charles
Born 1886. 2nd son of Charles Gandy of Newcastle-upon-Tyne. AAS. M. 25 January 1911. Call 26 January 1914. 3 St James's Square, Manchester, 1922-1950. Not in 1951 Law List.

GANNER, Joseph Michael
Born 9 January 1961 London. Southampton University, LLB. I. July 1983. Oriel Chambers, 5 Covent Garden, Liverpool, 1987-1991; Kenworthy's Buildings, 83 Bridge Street, Manchester, 1995-1999; 22 Nicholas Street, Chester, 2000.

GARDEN, Ian Harrison
Born 18 June 1961, Liverpool. Sedburgh School; University College Wales, Aberystwyth, LLB. L. July 1989. ETC. 1989. Prop. Michael Maguire QC. Sec. David Owen. Derby Square Chambers, Refuge Assurance House/Merchants Court, Liverpool, 1989-2003. Door tenant, Oriel Chambers, 14 Water Street, 2004. Deputy Chancellor, Diocese of Sheffield, 1997. Member, General Synod for Diocese of Blackburn, 1995. Member of Crown Appointments Commission, 1997. Member, Archbishops Council, 2001.

GARDNER, Harold Ennis
Born 1869, New York. Died 20 April 1946, Bradford on Avon. Son of William Robert Gardner, Liverpool timber exporter and his American wife, Louise. Lived in Blundellsands, Aigburth & Willaston before retiring to Wiltshire. Married in 1897, Edith Amelia Allen, daughter of Rev. William Allen, Vicar of Eccleshall, Staffordshire and the wedding took place in his church. 3 daughters. MA. I. 26 April 1893. ETC. 19 July 1907. Prop. Horridge KC. Sec. Greer. Liverpool Chambers; 4 Harrington Street, 1902-1911; 9 Cook Street, 1912-1940. Equity draftsman & conveyancer. No chambers address, 1941-1946. Information provided by Rt. Hon. Lord Justice Kay.

GARDNER, Ralph Rodman
G. July 1946. ETC. 1946. Pupilmaster, Glyn Blackledge. Liverpool Chambers; 34 Castle Street, 1946-1949; 9 Rumford Street, 1950-1951; 7 Rumford Street, 1952-1954. 10 King's Bench Walk, 1952-1953. Fairfield, Tattenhall, Cheshire, 1955-1963. Not in 1964 Law List.

GARLICK, Pamela Ann
London University, LLB. G. November 1985. Manchester Chambers; Conavon Court Chambers, 12 Blackfriars Street, 1988-1989; Manchester House Chambers, 18-22 Bridge Street, 1990-1995. Not in 1996 Bar Directory.

GARRATT, Basil Saunders
Born 13 July 1930 Didsbury. Gatley High School; Cheadle Hulme Schools; Leeds University, LLB 1952. National Service, 2nd Lieut., Royal Artillery. Employed as underwriter with Royal Insurance and merchandising representative with Nestle Ltd. G. February 1971. ETC. 1972. Prop. Glidewell QC. Sec. Nowell. Manchester Chambers; 25 Bow Lane, 1972-1977; 460 Royal Exchange, 1978-1987; 40 King Street, 1988-1989. Retired from practice in 1989 to join magistrates courts service (Eccles & Salford) finally retiring in 1995.

GARSIDE, Charles Roger QC
Born 13 August 1948, Hamilton, Bermuda. Tonbridges School. G. November 1971. ETC. 1972. Prop. E S Temple QC. Sec. A W Bell. Manchester Chambers; 60 King Street / 9 St John Street 1972. Assistant Recorder 1989. Silk & Recorder 1993. WW.

GARTSIDE, John Gibson
Born 1856. Only son of James Hampson Gartside of Victoria Park, Manchester. St John's College, Cambridge, BA. AAS. M. 21 November 1878. Call 17 November 1881. ETC. 22 July 1887. Prop. Ambrose QC. Sec. Yates. 25 Old Square, 1886-1887; 4 St James's Square, Manchester, 1888-1901. No address, 1902-1949. Not in 1950 Law List. Foster.

GAVIN, Michael
Born 27 October 1970, Wigan. Bolton School; University College, Oxford, BA. I. November 1994. ETC. December 1994. Prop. Rodney Klevan QC. Sec. James Bonney. 18 St John Street, Manchester 1994.

GATENBY, James Michael
Born 3 February 1953. St Mary's Crosby. Liverpool Polytechnic/ John Moores University, LLB. M. October 1994. ETC. December 1994. Prop. David Harris QC. Sec. Leach. Liverpool Chambers; 24 Fenwick Street, September 1994-1999; Chavasse Court, 24 Lord Street, 1999.

*** GATES, His Honour Philip Chasemore**
Born 19 August 1824. Died 25 February 1914 aged 89. Caius College, Cambridge, BA 1847. I. 22 November 1850; Bencher 1887; Treasurer 1897. South Eastern Circuit. Silk 1874. Recorder of Brighton, 1879. County Court Judge, Circuit 11, (Burnley, Colne & part of West Riding) 1885-1896. Foster.

GAULTER, Derek Vivien CBE.
Born 10 December 1924. Denstone College; Peterhouse, Cambridge, MA. RNVR, Sub. Lt. in MTB's & Minesweepers, 1943-1946. G. January 1949. 26 King Street, Manchester, 1950-1955. Federation of Civil Engineering Contractors, 1955-1986 rising from Legal Secretary to Director General. CBE 1978. Chairman, Construction Industry Training Board, 1985-1990. WW.

GEAKE. Jonathan Richard Barr (His Honour Judge Geake)
Born 27 May 1946. Sherborne School; Fitzwilliam College, Cambridge, BA. I. November 1969. ETC. 1969. Pupilmasters; John Da Cunha & John Lord. Manchester Chambers; 43 King Street, 1969-1973; 4th floor Astley House, Quay Street, 1974-1977; 18 St John Street, 1978-1994. Standing Counsel for Customs & Excise, 1989. Recorder 1989. Circuit Judge 1994. WW.

GEBOLYS, Julian Christopher
BA, (Cantab). I. July 1971. Ship Canal House, Manchester, 1971-1975. Died 1975 aged 28.

GEDDES, William
MA., LLB. L. 2 July 1924. Certificate of Honour & Studentship, T 1924. ETC. 4 March 1925. Prop. Eastham KC. Sec. Jordan. Equity draftsman & conveyancer. Lancs. Chancery Court. Liverpool Chambers; 9 Cook Street, 1925-1926; 8 Harrington Street, 1927-1941; 15 Union Court, 1942-1952; 20 North John Street, 1953-1970. London Chambers, 15 Old Square. Lecturer, Liverpool University (Warr Memorial Lecturer). Died August 1970.

GEE, Anthony Hall QC (His Honour Judge Gee QC)
Born 4 November 1948. Cousin of His Honour Judge David Gee qv. Cambridge High School for Boys; Chester City Grammar School. Inns of Court, School of Law. G. July 1972. ETC. December 1972. Prop George Carman QC. Sec. J Stuart Oakes. Manchester Chambers; 47 Peter Street, 1972-1974; 12th floor, Sunlight House, Quay Street, 1977-1982; 28 St John Street, 1983-2004. Recorder 1989. Silk 1990. Circuit Judge, 28 April 2004. WW.

*** GEE, David Stephenson (His Honour Judge Gee)**

(HS)

Born 16 December 1944. Cousin of Judge Gee QC. qv. William Hulme's Grammar School; Leeds University, LLB. Admitted solicitor, 1970. Articled to Kenneth J. Statham of Thomas R. Dootson & Co., of Leigh where he remained until appointed Registrar at Manchester on 31 August 1982. District Judge, 1991-1992. Recorder 1991. Circuit Judge 1992. Adv. Editor, Atkin's Court Forms, 1989. Editor, Butterworths Family Law Service, 1990. WW.

GEE, Richard Simon
MA (Oxon). L. October 1993. ETC. 7 December 1993. Manchester Chambers; Hollins Chambers, 64a Bridge Street, 1996-1997; Cobden House Chambers, 19 Quay Street, 1998-2000.

GEEY, David Simon
Born 11 January 1946 Liverpool. Liverpool Collegiate School; University College, London, LLB. I. July 1970. ETC. July 1970. Prop. Richard Bingham QC. Sec Donald Forster. Liverpool Chambers; 34 Castle Street, 1970-1972; 54 Castle Street, 1973-1986; 14 Castle Street, 1987-1996; Martins Building, Water Street, 1996-1999; 7 Harrington Street (merger with Corn Exchange) 6.9.1999. Recorder 1990.

GEORGE, William (His Honour Judge George)

(DL)

Born 28 September 1944. Son of Elizabeth George and of William Henry George, teacher and documentary film maker. Herbert Strutt Grammar School; Victoria University of Manchester, LLB., LLM. L. July 1968; Bencher 2003. Mansfield Scholar, 1968. ETC. 1968. Pupilmaster, Joseph Turner. 20 North John Street, Liverpool, 1968-1995. Head of Chambers, 1986-1995.Assistant Recorder, 1990. Chairman, Northern Circuit Chancery Bar Association, 1992-1994. Recorder, 1993. Circuit Judge, Manchester 1995-1998; Liverpool, 1998. WW.

GEORGES, Antonis
Born 22 January 1949, London. Wandsworth Compehensive; Trent Polytechnic (external London LLB) I. July 1972. ETC. 7 December 1972. Pupilmaster, Justin Price. Liverpool Chambers; Queen Insurance Building D, 13 Castle Street, 1972-1979; 16 Queen Avenue, 1980-1983. 2nd floor, Peel House, Harrington Street, 1984-1992; Martins Building, Water Street, 1993-1999; 7 Harrington Street (merger with Corn Exchange) 6.9.1999. Publication; Industrial Disease Litigation – Practice & Procedure, Sweet & Maxwell, 1998. 2nd ed., 2002, entitled "Occupational Illness Litigation". Chairman, Pensions Appeals Tribunal, 2001.

GERRARD, Albert Denis KC (The Hon. Mr Justice Gerrard)
Born 27 May 1903. Died 23 January 1965 aged 61. Uncle of His Honour Basil Harding Gerrard qv. Merchant Taylors' School, Crosby; Gonville & Caius College, Cambridge, MA., LLB. G. 11 May 1927; Bencher 1948; Treasurer, 1964. ETC. 6 July 1927. Prop. Eastham KC. Sec. Laski. 3 St James's Square, Manchester, 1927-1941. No chambers address, 1942-1945. Silk 1945. New Court, 1945-1948; 1 Plowden Buildings, 1949-1953. Recorder of Salford, 1945-1948. Judge of the Salford Hundred Court of Record, 1948-1953. Judge of Appeal, Isle of Man, 1950-1953. High Court Judge, Queen's Bench Division, 1953-1956; retired 1956. WW.

GERRARD, His Honour Basil Harding
Born 10 July 1919. Died 29 June 1994 aged 74. Nephew of Mr Justice Gerrard. qv. Bryanston School; Caius College, Cambridge, BA. Royal Navy, 1940-1946. G. November 1947. Pupilmaster, Fenton Atkinson. Manchester Chambers; 4 Chapel Walks, 1947-1964; 601 Royal Exchange, 1965-1970. Recorder of Barrow in Furness, 1969-1970. Circuit Judge, (formerly County Court Judge) 1970-1982. Member, Parole Board, 1974-1976. Chairman, Selcare Trust, 1971-1978. Chairman, Residential Homes Tribunal, 1985. WW.

GERRARD, Suzanne Lynne
Married to Nicholas Simmonds. qv. BA., LLB. I. July 1972. ETC. 13 February 1973. Pupilmaster, Douglas Brown. Manchester Chambers; 25 Bow Lane, 1973-1976; 460 Royal Exchange, 1977-1985.

GETHING, Robert Eills
Born 1880. Died 14 March 1951. 3rd son of Constantine Gething of Liverpool, shipowner. MA., BCL. AAS. M. 19 November 1904. Call 28 January 1907. Certificate of Honour, T. 1906. Bencher 1946. ETC. 20 February 1907. Prop. Horridge KC. Sec. Leslie Scott. Circuit Junior, Winter 1907. Liverpool Chambers; 25 Lord Street, 1907-1929; 3 Cook Street, 1930; 5 Crown Office Row, 1931-1938; 2 Paper Buildings, 1939-1951.

GIBB, Andrew (McArthur)
Born 8 September 1927. Died 6 July 1992 aged 64. Sedbergh; Queen's College, Cambridge, MA. AAS. M. 1 November 1949. Call 1 July 1952. ETC 1952. Manchester Chambers; 4 Chapel Walks, 1952-1964; 601 Royal Exchange, 1965-1982. Recorder 1977-1982.

GIBBONS, Sir Thomas Clarke Pilling KC
Born 2 August 1868. Died 2 June 1934 aged 65. 2nd son of Benjamin Gibbons of Oxton, Cheshire, JP., St Peter's College, Radley. Admitted, solicitor, 1891. I. 17 November 1897. ETC. 2 February 1898. St Ann's Passage, King Street, Manchester, 1900-1907; 6 King's Bench Walk, 1908-1915; 2 Mitre Court, 1916-1917. Advocate General, Bengal, 1917-1922; member of the Racial Distinctions Committee. Silk 1913. Kt. 1923. 4 Paper Buildings, 1923-1934. WW.

GIBBONS-TURNER, Dilys Margaret
I. June 1961. Manchester Chambers; 196 Deansgate, 1963-1989; 72 Bridge Street, 1990-1996. Not in 1997 Bar Directory.

GIBBS, Frederick Waymouth CB., QC

Born 1821. Died 18 February 1898. Only son of Samuel Newcomen Gibbs of Plymouth. King's College, London; Trinity College, Cambridge, BA 1843; MA, 1846; Fellow, 1845-1853. Fellow, Kings, 1849. AAS. L. 12 November 1844. Call 28 January 1848; Bencher 1882. 3 Brick Court, 1848. 2 Harcourt Buildings, 1876-1898. Tutor to the Prince of Wales, 1852-1858. CB 1858. Silk 1880. Publications; Hospices de Paris et Londres; English Law & Irish Tenure, 1870.

GIBSON, Arthur George Adrian
Born 31 October 1957 Blackpool. Wellingborough School; University College, London, LLB. L. July 1980. ETC. December 1982. Pupilmaster, Donald Forster. Liverpool Chambers; 54 Castle Street/14 Castle Street/ Atlantic Chambers, Cook Street, October 1982.

GIBSON, Ernest Augustine
Born 1862. 3rd son of Thomas Gibson of Liverpool, accountant. Trinity College, Cambridge, BA., LLB. 1884. AAS. I. 25 April 1882. Call. 17 June 1885. ETC. 31 July 1885. Prop. Kennedy QC. Sec. Mansfield. Home address; 1 East Rd, Albert Park, Liverpool. Chambers; 4 Harrington Street, 1887-1908. No address, 1909-1915. Not in 1916 Law List.

GIBSON, John Arthur
Born 26 May 1950. Liverpool College, Birmingham University, LLB. Solicitor, 1975-1993. L. November 1993. ETC. 21 December 1993. Prop. Stephen Riordan QC. Sec. Geoffrey Lowe. 3rd floor, Peel House, Harrington Street / India Buildings, Water Street, Liverpool, 1993. Recorder 2004.

GIBSON, Robert Mark Timothy (aka "Titus")
Born 21 February 1956 Eastbourne. Stowe School; Balliol College, Oxford, MA. AAS. M. 26 October 1979. Call 24 November 1981. ETC. 1984. Prop. Ronnie Livesey QC. Sec. John Morgan. Liverpool Chambers; Peel House, Harrington Street, 1984-1999; Oriel Chambers, 14 Water Street, 1.3.1999. Accomplished organist having played at memorial services of Dick Bingham & Colin Cunningham and a number of weddings of Circuiteers. Very reasonable rates!

GIBSON, William George
MA. G. 26 January 1912. Irish Bar T. 1897. KC, Ireland. ETC. 15 June 1923. Prop. Ashton KC. Sec. Hodgson. Liverpool Chambers; 15 Lord Street, 1923-1925; 13 Harrington Street, 1926. No address, 1927-1949. Not in 1950 Law List.

GILBART, Andrew James QC (His Honour Judge Gilbart QC)
Born 13 February 1950 Hastings, East Sussex. Westminster School; Trinity Hall Cambridge, MA. AAS. 18 May 1971. Call 22 November 1972; Bencher 2000. ETC. 1973. Prop. Iain Glidewell QC. Sec. Nigel MacLeod. Member, American Bar Association. Planning Specialist. Same Manchester set of chambers at; 25 Bow Lane, 1973-1976; 460 Royal Exchange, 1976-1987; 40 King Street, 1987-2004.(Head). Silk 1991. Assistant Recorder 1992. Recorder 1996. President, Mental Health Review Tribunals, 2000. Circuit Judge, 30 March 2004.

GILBERT, Sir William Scwenck
Born 18 November 1836 Southampton Street, Strand. Died 29 May 1911 aged 74. Great Ealing School; King's College, London, BA. 1857. Clerk in the Privvy Council Office, 1857-1862. AAS. I. 11 October 1855. Call 1863. ETC. 15

March 1866. Prop. John Holker. He set up chambers in Clement Inn and practised at the Bar for four years at Liverpool Sessions and Court of Passage. Business was slow. He averaged five clients a year and earned £75 in all. It was as a dramatist he made his mark. His collaboration with the composer Arthur Sullivan led to a memorable series of operas including; Trial by Jury (1875); The Pirates of Penzance (1879); Iolanthe (1882); and The Mikado (1885). JP., DL., Middlesex. Kt. 1907. WW. DNB, Foster.

GILCHRIST, David Somerled
Born 6 April 1964, London. St Chad's College, Durham University, BA. I. November 1987. Western Circuit, 1988. Pupilmaster, Martin Steen. Albion Chambers, Broad Street, Bristol, May 1988- May 1996 but worked in 1989 with Chapman Tripp of Wellington, New Zealand having been awarded an Inner Temple Scholarship. ETC. 1999. Prop. Ian Leeming QC. Sec. Jaime Hamilton. 9 St John Street, Manchester, May 1996.

GILCHRIST, John
Born 28 November 1929. Died 12 June 1982 aged 52. Father of Nicholas John Gilchrist qv. Schoolmaster, 1958-1964. G. November 1967. ETC. 1967. 606 The Corn Exchange, Fenwick Street, 1967-1982. Recorder, 1980-1982. WW.

GILCHRIST, Nicholas John
Died 26 April 2001 aged 49. Son of John Gilchrist. qv. Ruthin School; University of Wales, Aberystwyth, LLB. G. July 1975. ETC. 1975. Pupilmaster, John Arthur. Same Liverpool Chambers at; 3rd floor, 27 Dale Street, 1975-1989; Corn Exchange, Fenwick Street, 1989-1999; 7 Harrington Street, 6.9.1999-2001. (merger with Martins Building). Recorder 1996. Had been placed on the reserve list for appointment to Circuit Judge shortly before his death. Tributes Liverpool Law Courts 2 May 2001. (Judge David Clarke QC/ David Steer QC). Transcript in Circuit Records.

GILLBANKS, Cecil Owtram
L. 17 November 1887. ETC. 2 March 1889. Prop. Bigham QC. Sec. Leresche. 4 St James Square, Manchester, 1889-1895. No address, 1896-1928. Not in 1929 Law List.

GILLBANKS, Jonathan Cremer
Born 1843. Eldest son of Jonathan Gillbanks of London, merchant. Trinity Hall, Cambridge, BA 1866. AAS. I. 22 January 1864. Call 18 November 1867. Prop. Aspinall QC. Sec. Payne. 3 Dr Johnson's Building, 1876; 4 Harcourt Buildings, 1877-1881. No address, 1882-1884. Rangoon, British Burma, 1885-1893. Not in 1894 Law List.

GILLILAND, (James Andrew) David QC (His Honour Judge Gilliland QC)

(DL)

Born 29 December 1937. Campbell College, Queen's University, Belfast, LLB. Holt, Atkin & Macaskie Scholar, 1964. Law Lecturer, Manchester University, 1960-1972. G. 1964. ETC. 27 May 1965. Pupilmaster, Joseph Turner. 20 North John Street, Liverpool, 1965-1992. Silk 1984. Recorder 1989. Circuit Judge (Official Referee) 1992. WW.

GILLOTT, Alan Ashley
Born 28 December 1971, Enfield. St Edward's School, Oxford; St Peter's College, Oxford, BA. M. October 1996. ETC. 1996. Prop. Roger Farley QC. Sec. David Kenny. 15 Winckley Square, Preston, 1996. Counsel & Legal Advisor to Wycombe Wanderers Football Club.

GILLOW, George William
Born 1851. 3rd son of Richard Thomas Gillow of Leighton Hall, Carnforth JP. AAS. M. 6 December 1872. Call 17 November 1875. ETC. 13 March 1876. Prop. Russell QC. Sec. Edwards QC. 2 Cloisters, 1876-1878; 3 Elm Court, 1879; 1 Cloisters, 1880-1881; 3 Garden Court, 1882-1883; 4 Brick Court, 1884-1909. No address, 1910-1918. Not in 1919 Law List.

GILMORE, Dennis Gelston
MA (Oxon). L. 27 January 1902. ETC. 1 July 1936. Prop. Lynskey KC. Sec. Wood. Private address in Glasgow, 1910-1940. 43 King Street, Manchester, 1941-1954. Not in 1955 Law List.

GILMORE, Randolph Orme
Born 1854. Eldest son of William Gilmore of Stockport. LLB. AAS. M. 30 October 1879. Call. 21 June 1882. ETC. 25 January 1883. Prop. Hopwood QC. Sec. Wharton. 78 Cross Street, Manchester. A solicitor 1889-1897. Readmitted M. 8 April 1897. Call 30 June 1897. ETC (again) 5 February 1898. Prop. Shee QC. Sec. McKeand. 47 Moseley Street, Manchester, 1898-1901; 26 King Street, Manchester, 1902-1908. No address, 1909-1940. Not in 1941 Law List.

GILMOUR, John
Eldest son of Andrew Gilmour late of Glasgow, merchant, deceased. AAS. 13 November 1846. Call 23 November 1849. 1 Elm Court, 1876-1878. No address, 1879-1880. Not in 1881 Law List.

GILMOUR, Nigel Benjamin Douglas QC (His Honour Judge Gilmour QC)
Born 21 November 1947, Birmingham. Tettenhall College, Staffs.; Liverpool University, LLB. I. July 1970. ETC. December 1970. Pupilmaster, Anthony Edmondson. Liverpool Chambers; 14 Cook Street, 1970-1972; Peel House, Harrington Street, 1973-1999; Oriel Chambers, 14 Water Street, 1.3.1999-2000. Silk and Recorder 1990. Circuit Judge, Liverpool 2000. Liason Judge: Liverpool University; North & South Sefton Magistrates, 2003. WW.

GILMOUR, Susan Evelyn Mary
Sussex University, LLB. I. November 1994. Cobden House Chambers, 19 Quay Street, Manchester, 1999.

GILPIN. Roma Elizabeth
BA (Oxon). M. November 1993. Ground floor, Peel House, Harrington Street, Liverpool, 1994-1999. Scotland 2001.

GILROY, Paul
Born 1 May 1962, Newcastle-upon-Tyne. Hutcheson Grammar School, Glasgow; Dundee University, LLB. G. 25 November 1985. ETC. 1986. Prop. John Hand QC. 1 Deans Court/ 9 St John Street, Manchester, 1986. Part time Chairman, Employment Tribunals August 2000.

GINNIFF, Nigel Thomas
Born 23 January 1956, Bristol. Lancaster Royal Grammar School; Hull University, LLB. I. July 1978. Inspector of Taxes, Inland Revenue 1978-1984, thereafter tax manager / director of several large companies. ETC. 1996. Pupilmaster, Pat Bailey. New Bailey Chambers at Preston, 1996 and at Liverpool, 1996.

GINSBURG, Benedict William
Born 1 October 1859 Liverpool. Died 1 September 1933 aged 73. Son of Christian David Ginsburg, LLD. Charterhouse; St Catherine's College, Cambridge, BA 1880; MA., LLM, 1885; LLD. 1894. AAS. I. 16 April 1880. Call 26 January 1883. ETC. 2 February 1883. Prop. Gully QC. Sec. Aspland. Liverpool Chambers; 11 Lord Street, 1884; Commerce Chambers, 15 Lord Street, 1995-1886. 12 King's Bench Walk, 1887-1933. He was an admiralty court specialist appearing in Board of Trade Wreck Enquiries. Secretary of Royal Statistical Society and editor of its journal. Numerous books, articles and contributions to the DNB on shipping and legal subjects. WW.

GINSBURG, Israel
G. 26 January 1909. ETC. 15 February 1911. Prop. Leslie Scott KC. Sec. Beazley. 3 King's Bench Walk, 1911-1914. No address, 1915. Not in 1916 Law List.

GIRVAN, Robert James
Born 7 January 1968, Liverpool. Salesian High School, Netherton, Liverpool; Wolverhampton University, LLB. G. November 1990. ETC. 1990. Pupilmaster, John Leach. Liverpool Chambers; 24 Fenwick Street, 1990-1996. Called to United States Federal & Tennessee State Bars In November 1996. Practised as an attorney in USA until his return to UK in 2000. Presently door tenant at 14 Cook Street, Liverpool. New Bailey Chambers, Liverpool, 2004.

GLADWELL, James William
MA (Oxon). I. January 1949. Pupillage in London and then pupil of Glyn Blackledge. 15 Victoria Street, Liverpool, 1949-1952. 1 Essex Court, 1953-1976. Not in 1977 Law List.

GLAZEBROOK, His Honour Francis Kirkland
Born 18 February 1903. Died 7 March 1988 aged 85. Marlborough College; Trinity College, Cambridge; Harvard University. I. 20 June 1928. ETC. 30 January 1929. Prop. Singleton KC. Sec. Blackledge. 7 Fig Tree Court, 1929-1939. Served in Army, 1939-1945. Croix de guerre (France), Bronze Star (USA). 3 Temple Court, 1945-1950. Circuit Judge, (formerly County Court Judge), 1950-1972. Circuits, 58, 56 & 63 (Essex, Kent, Surrey & Sussex). WW.

GLEAVE, Edward Ernest James
B.Com. L. July 1968. ETC. 1968. Pupilmaster, AA Edmondson. Liverpool Chambers; 14 Cook Street 1968; 34 Castle Street, 1969-1972; Queen Insurance Building D, 13 Castle Street, 1973-1976; 41 North John Street, 1977; Third floor, 15 Victoria Street. He went to Fiji as a prosecutor and later to Hong Kong as a magistrate.

GLEDHILL, James Grierson
Born 1857. 2nd son of William Gledhill of Preston. Glasgow University (Bachelor of Medicine & Master of Surgery). AAS. M. 7 May 1889. Call 26 January 1892. Prop. Ambrose QC. Sec. Hughes. Address, Hollingwood, Oldham. No chambers address, 1892-1949. Not in 1950 Law List.

GLIDEWELL, Charles Norman
Father of Rt. Hon Sir Iain Glidewell qv. G. 17 November 1939. ETC. 1939. Pupilmaster, Arthur Jalland. War Service. Manchester Chambers; 40 Kennedy Street / 28 Kennedy Street / 25 Bow Lane, 1939-1972. Not in 1973 Law List.

GLIDEWELL, Rt. Hon. Sir Iain Derek Laing
Born 8 June 1924. Son of Charles Norman Glidewell qv. Bromsgrove School; Served RAFVR (pilot), 1942-1946. Worcester College, Oxford, BA; Hon. Fellow, 1986. G. June 1949; Bencher 1977; Treasurer 1995. ETC. 1949. Pupilmaster, Thomas Cunliffe. Manchester Chambers; 60 King Street, 1949-1951; 28 Kennedy Street, 1952-1956; 25 Bow Lane, 1957-1969. Silk 1969. 2 Paper Buildings, 1969-1980. Recorder, 1976-1980. Conducted Heathrow Fourth Terminal Inquiry, 1978. Judge of Appeal, Isle of Man, 1979-1980. High Court Judge, Queen's Bench Division, 1980-1985. Presiding Judge, North Eastern Circuit, 1982-1985. Lord Justice of Appeal, 1985-1995. Kt. 1980. PC. 1985. Hon. RICS., 1982. Chairman, Judicial Studies Board, 1989-1982. Conducted Review of the Crown Prosecutions Service, 1997-1998. Judge of Appeal, Gibraltar 1998. WW.

GLOBE, Henry Brian QC (His Honour Judge Globe QC)
Born 18 June 1949 Liverpool. Liverpool College; Birmingham University, LLB. AAS. M. 26 August 1968. Bencher 2005. Call 20 July 1972. ETC. 7 December 1972. Prop. Ifor Morris Jones QC. Sec. David Berkson. Circuit; Junior, 1974/1975; Treasurer, 2001-2003. Exchange Chambers, Liverpool at 606 Corn Exchange, 1972-1982; 1 Exchange Flags, 1983-1991; Pearl Assurance House, Derby Square, 1992-2003. Standing Counsel; DSS, 1985-1994; Customs & Excise, 1992-1994. Assistant Recorder 1987. Recorder 1991. Silk 1994. Chairman, Board of Governors, King David School, 1990-2000. Member, Bar Council, 2001-2003. Member, Judicial Studies Board, Criminal Committee, 2001. Circuit Judge, 4 March 2003. Senior Circuit Judge, 1 September 2003. Senior Circuit Judge (Crime), Resident Judge, Liverpool & Honorary Recorder of Liverpool, 1 October 2003. WW.

GLOVER, Henry Percy KC
Born 1877, St Helens. Died 29 April 1938. Son of William James Glover and father of William James Glover QC qv. Cowley School, St Helens. L. 18 November 1907. ETC. 7 March 1908. Prop. Sanderson KC. Sec. Merriman. Equity draftsman & conveyancer. Lancs. Chancery Court. Preston Chambers; 9 Winckley Square, 1908-1916; 10a Winckley Square, 1916-1932. Liverpool Chambers; 5 Harrington Street, 1920-1921; 10 Dale Street, 1923-1936. Silk 1936. Goldsmith Building, 1936-1938. Recorder of Preston & Chairman of Lancashire Quarter Sessions at Preston, Liverpool & Manchester, 1935-1938. WW.

GLOVER, William James QC
Born 8 May 1924. Son of Henry Percy Glover KC qv. Harrow; Pembroke College, Cambridge. Served with Royal West African Frontier Force in West Africa & Burma, 1944-1947. I. January 1950; Bencher 1977. Second Junior Counsel to Inland Revenue (Rating & Valuation), 1963-1969. Silk 1969. Recorder 1975-1991. 2 Mitre Court Buildings, 1950-1996. Now living in France.

GLUCKSTEIN, Sir Louis Halle QC., MP.
Born 23 February 1897. Died 27 October 1979 aged 82. St Paul's School; Lincoln College, Oxford, MA; Fellow 1968. Served, 1915-1918 as Lt., Suffolk Regiment (wounded, despatches) and 1939-1945; France 1940 (despatches) and Italy 1944. TD 1950. L. 28 June 1922; Bencher 1952; Treasurer 1970. ETC. 15 July 1924. Prop. Jackson KC. Sec. Gorman. London Chambers; 2 Mitre Court & 14 Old Square. MP (U) East Nottingham, 1931-1945. Silk 1945. DL., 1952-1977. Member London County Council (St Marylebone), 1955-1964; GLC (Westminster), 1964-1967. Alderman, 1967-1973. President, Royal Albert Hall, 1965. CBE. 1964. GBE 1969. Kt. 1953. WW.

GLYDE-COLEMAN, (Kenneth) Shane
Manchester University, LLB. G. July 1970. ETC. 1970. Oriel Chambers, 14 Water Street, Liverpool, 1970-1977. Admitted as a solicitor, December 1977. Senior Prosecuting Solicitor with Sussex Police Authority and later with CPS in Brighton.

GLYNN, Walter Samuel
I. 22 April 1891. ETC. 1 April 1892. Prop. French QC. Sec. Walton. 3 Elm Court, 1892-1905; 2 Cloisters, 1906-1924. No address, 1925-1933. Not in 1934 Law List.

GODDARD, (Harold) Keith QC
Born 9 July 1936 Stockport. Father of Richard Andrew Keith Goddard qv. Manchester Grammar School; Corpus Christi College, Cambridge, MA., LLM. G. June 1959 (Bacon Scholar). ETC. 1959. Prop. Daniel Brabin QC. Sec. Charles Elliott. Circuit Attorney General, 2000. Deans Court Chambers, 9 Albert Square, 1959-1972/ Crown Square, 1973-1999/ 24 St John Street, 4 May 1999. Head of Chambers, 1983. Recorder 1978. Silk 1979. Member, CICB, 1993. Deputy High Court Judge, 1993. WW.

GODDARD, Richard Andrew Keith
Born 14 December 1966, Macclesfield. Son of (Harold) Keith Goddard QC qv. Manchester Grammar School; Lancs. Polytechnic, BA (Law). Solicitor, 1992-1999. G. March 1999. ETC 1999. Prop. Keith Goddard QC. Sec. Marc Willems. Cobden House Chambers, 19 Quay Street, Manchester, 1999.

GODDARD, Suzanne Hazel
Born 26 September 1963, Manchester. Wrekin College, Wellington; Manchester University, LLB. G. November 1986. ETC. December 1986. Pupilmaster, Alan Conrad. Circuit Junior, 1989. Rational House Chambers/ Lincoln House Chambers, Manchester, 1986. Recorder 2002.

GODFREY, Christopher Nicholas
Born 22 December 1968, Christchurch. Strabane Grammar School; Trinity Hall, Cambridge, BA. L. February 1993. ETC. 30 March 1993. Prop. David Poole QC. Sec. Lamberty. Queens Chambers, 5 John Dalton Street, Manchester, 1993.

GOFF, Anthony Thomas
Born 10 October 1955 Bishop's Stortford, Herts. 3rd son of Thomas Henry Goff, Research Officer. Mark Hall Comprehensive, Harlow, Essex; University College, Oxford, BA. AAS. M. 21 November 1975. Call July 1978. Lecturer, Inns of Court School of Law, 1980-1983. ETC. 1983. Prop. Justin Price QC. Sec. David Maddison. Pupilmasters, John Uff, Derrick Turriff. 2nd floor, Peel House, Harrington Street/ 25-27 Castle Street, Liverpool, 1983.

GOLDBERG, Jonathan Jacob QC
Born 13 November 1947 Manchester. Manchester Grammar School; Trinity Hall, Cambridge, MA., LLM. AAS. M. 4 March 1969. Call 9 February 1971. ETC. 1971. Post Office Chambers, 26 Brown Street, Manchester, 1971-1973. South Eastern Circuit, 1973-2003. Re elected to Northern Circuit, 15 April 2003. Prop. Roger Farley QC. Sec. Hilary Manley. London Chambers; 2 Harcourt Buildings, 1974-1978; 9 King's Bench Walk, 1979-1981; 3 Temple Gardens, 1982. Member, New York State Bar 1985. QC 1989. Recorder 1993. Cobden House Chambers, 19 Quay Street, Manchester, 2003. WW.

GOLDIE, Sir Noel Barre KC., MP
Born 26 December 1882. Died 4 June 1964 aged 81. Rugby; Trinity College, Cambridge BA., LLB I. 5 July 1905. Bencher 1935. Reader 1958. ETC. 31 July 1905. Prop. Tobin KC. Sec. FE Smith. Circuit Junior Winter 1905. Liverpool Chambers; Stephenson's Chambers, 25 Lord Street 1905-1906; 8 Cook Street 1907-1910; 16 Harrington Street 1911-1914. Staff Captain, Royal Artillery, 57th West Lancs. in France & Belgium 1914-1918. 5 Harrington Street 1918-1928. Silk. 1928. 8 King's Bench Walk 1928-1940; Farrar's Building 1941-1945; 3 Dr Johnson's Building 1946-1964. MP (C) Warrington 1913-1945. Recorder of Burnley 1929-1935. Recorder of Manchester 1935-1956. WW.
There are many humorous stories of Goldie's performances in court, collected and preserved in the Circuit Records under the title 'Goldiana'. Dick Hamilton in his 'Foul Bills and Dagger Money' devoted a chapter to Goldie, suggesting that he would have made an excellent Lord Chancellor of Mirth.
Mr Justice Douglas Brown has related the following stories which are not in 'Goldiana' but which give the flavour of the man:
In 1956, Basil Nield succeeded Goldie as a Recorder of Manchester. As Goldie put it, "it took an act of Parliament to get rid of me". One of the new Recorder's first cases had Goldie leading for the prosecution. As the jury were leaving court to consider their verdict, Goldie turned to his Junior and in a stage whisper, said "Well, for a chap from Harrow and Magdelene, that wasn't a bad summing up".
Within weeks of the implementation of the Homicide Act 1957, Goldie was prosecuting a murder at Lancaster Assizes. On the way up the hill to the castle, Goldie said to the Junior (Douglas Brown), "Do you know Junior, this is the clearest case of diminished responsibility I've seen in all of my career. I'll be on the 12 o'clock train back to London". And he was.
At the Lancaster Summer Assizes of 1958, the

commission was read before Mr Justice Pilcher, and the Bar crowded into the semi circular seats. The Judge was about to turn to leave court to replace his full bottom wig with his bench wig and begin the business of the day, when Goldie rose and made a flowery speech of welcome which included the following: "My Lord, I first came to Lancaster in nineteen hundred and five. The Bar stayed in the Constitutional Club but the Bar Mess was held in the King's Arms and I had to stay there as Junior, my job being to see that they did not put sheep's hearts on the menu." At that, the bemused Judge and High Sheriff left the court.

My favourite is: Goldie's client had been injured when a falling bale knocked him off his cart.

GOLDIE KC: Were the bales at the back of the lorry standing on end, and the bales in the middle lying down?

MR JUSTICE WILLMER: What size are these bales, Sir Noel?

GOLDIE: Four feet by four feet by four feet, My Lord.

JUDGE: Sir Noel, if they are four feet square, what is the difference between standing up and lying down?

GOLDIE: My Lord, I'll leave that to my expert.

GOLDNEY, Sir John Tankerville

Born 15 June 1846. Died 11 April 1920 aged 73. 3rd son of Sir Gabriel Goldney of Beechfield House, Wiltshire, 1st Bt. Harrow; Trinity College, Cambridge, BA 1868; LLB 1869. AAS. I. 22 October 1864. Call 30 April 1869. ETC. 14 July 1869. Prop. Quain QC. Sec. Herschell. Circuit Junior, Spring 1870. 13 Harrington Street, Liverpool, 1869-1880. Attorney General later Acting Chief Justice, Leeward Islands, 1881. Puisne Judge; British Guiana, 1883; Straits Settlements, 1887. Chief Justice, Trinidad, 1892-1900. Kt. 1893. High Sheriff for Wiltshire, 1910-1911. Lay Rector of Corsham. WW.

GOLDREIN, Eric Geoffrey

Born 29 May 1921, London. Married to Her Honour Inge Berstein qv, brother of Neville Goldrein solicitor, uncle of Iain Goldrein QC qv and Her Honour Judge Margaret de Haas QC qv. Hymers College, Hull. Served Royal Artillery during 1939-1945 War. Territorial Army, 1953-1960. Pembroke College, Cambridge, MA. Admitted as a solicitor, October 1949. Articled to Harry Livermore of Silverman, Livermore of Liverpool. AAS. M. 23 November 1960. Call 27 June 1961. ETC. 1962. Pupilmaster David McNeill. Liverpool Chambers; 34/54/14 Castle Street 1961-2001.

GOLDREIN, Iain Saville QC

Born 10 August 1952, Waterloo, Liverpool. Son of Neville Clive Goldrein CBE., solicitor, married to Her Honour Judge de Haas QC qv, nephew of Eric Goldrein qv and Her Honour Inge Bernstein qv. Merchant Taylors' School, Crosby; Hebrew University, Jerusalem; Pembroke College, Cambridge, MA. I. 17 July 1975. M. 6 March 1981. ETC. December 1975. Pupilmaster, David Harris. Liverpool Chambers; Chambers of Henry Lachs; 27 Dale Street, 1975-1977 & 21 North John Street, 1977-1981. Chambers of Iain Goldrein; 5 Castle Street, 1981-1987 & 48 Castle Street, 1987-1989. Chambers of Mark Hedley (David Steer from 1992) & Iain Goldrein at 5th floor, The Corn Exchange, 1989-1999. Chambers of David Steer QC, Robert Fordham QC & Ian Goldrein QC at 7 Harrington Street, 6.9.1999. Also at 3 Serjeant's Inn. Assistant Recorder 1995. Silk 1997. Recorder 1999. Visiting Professor, Nottingham University, 1991. Member, Mental Health Review Tribunal, 1999. Publications; 15 books on subjects relating to personal injury litigation, commercial actions, pleadings, distribution of matrimonial property, sale of ships & human rights. WW.

GOLDSTEIN, Wayne Nathan

Born 17 January 1963 Sydney, Australia. Hewington Preparatory School, Sydney; Sydney Boys High School; Sydney University, LLB. New South Wales Bar, February 1992- April 1998. L. November 1999. ETC. 2002. Central Chambers, 89 Princess Street, Manchester, 1999-2004. 15 Winckley Square, Preston, 12 July 2004.

GOLDSTONE, Bernard Patrick Horace Anthony

Born 17 March 1909. G. 17 November 1931. ETC. 17 February 1932. Prop. Hemmerde KC. Sec. Gorman. Manchester Chambers; 60 King Street, 1932-1933; 28 King Street, 1934-1939. Commissioned 27.9.1940 in Manchester Regt. Personal No P/149498. Acting Captain, 25.6.1941. War subst. Lt. 25.9.1941. Acting Major 10.5.1943. War subst. Captain 10.8.1943. Killed in action 25 October 1944 aged 35. Cemetery; Ghent City Cemetery, Oost-Vlaanderen, Belgium. Plot 18. Row B. Grave 7. Information from Commonwealth War Graves Commission.

GOLDSTONE, Heather Gillian

L. November 1954. 60 King Street, Manchester, 1954-1957. No address, 1958-1963. Not in 1964 Law List.

GOLDSTONE, (Leonard) Clement QC (His Honour Judge Goldstone QC)

(HS)

Born 20 April 1949, Manchester. Cousin of His Honour Judge Peter Goldstone. Manchester Grammar School; Churchill College, Cambridge, BA. AAS. M. 30 October 1968. Call 22 July 1971; Bencher 2004. ETC. December 1971. Prop. Godfrey Heilpern QC. Sec. Ivor Taylor. Circuit Treasurer, 1998-2001. Same Manchester Chambers at; 47 Peter Street, 1971-1974; 12th floor, Sunlight House, Quay Street, 1975-1979; 28 St John Street, 1980-2001.Head of Chambers, 1999-2002. Assistant Recorder 1988. Recorder 1992. Silk 1993. President, Mental Health Review Tribunal, 1999. Circuit Judge, Manchester, 25 June 2002. WW.

GOLDTHORPE, William

Only son of John Goldthorpe of Chorley. AAS. G. 4 June 1864. Call 30 April 1867. Manchester Chambers; 37 Cross Street, 1877-1882; 4 St James Square, 1883-1900; 4 Clarence Street, 1901-1904. Not in 1905 Law List. Chairman, Salford Hundred Quarter Sessions for County of Lancaster. Foster.

GOLDWATER, Michael Philip

Born 24 March 1954 Manchester. Bury Grammar School; Brasenose College, Oxford, MA. AAS. M. 11 November 1975. Call 14 July 1977. ETC. April 1978. Prop. Douglas Brown QC. Sec. Frank Hudson. Manchester Chambers; 67 Princess Street, 1977-1985; Hollins Chambers, 64a Bridge Street, 1985-1997 now Cobden House Chambers, 19 Quay Street, 1998.

GOLINSKI, Robert Felix

Born 6 October 1959, London. Maidstone Grammar School; Sussex University & City of London Polytechnic, BA. M. October 1990. ETC. 1990. Pupilmaster, John Benson. 14 Castle Street/ Atlantic Chambers, Cook Street, Liverpool, 1990.

GOLLAN, Sir Henry Cowper

Born 8 January 1868, Coquimbo, Chile. Died 5 August 1949 aged 81. Eldest son of late Sir Alexander Gollan KCMG., British Consul at Manilla. Charterhouse, Edinburgh University. AAS. M. 27 April 1888. Call 26 January 1891. ETC. 29 July 1892. Prop. McCall QC. Sec. Foard. 1 New Court, 1891-1899. Private Secretary to Brig. Gen. Lugard CB., High Commissioner of Northern Nigeria. Att. Gen. & Chief Justice of N. Nigeria, 1901. Chief Justice, Bermuda 1904-1911. Att. Gen., Trinidad, 1911-1918. Att. Gen., Ceylon, 1918-1924. Chief Justice, Hong Kong, 1924-1930. KBE 1918. Kt 1921. WW.

GOODBODY, Peter James

Born 26 May 1964 Liverpool. Birkenhead School; Manchester University, LLB. L. July 1986. ETC. 16 December 1986. Prop. Eric Somerset Jones QC. Sec. Ian Trigger. Oriel Chambers, 5 Covent Garden/ 14 Water Street, Liverpool, 1986.

GOODE, Rowena Margaret

Born 17 June 1952, Shrewsbury. Shrewsbury High School; Liverpool University, LLB. G. July 1974. Wales & Chester Circuit, 1974. Sedan House, Stanley Place, Chester, 1974-1990. ETC. April 1991. 28 St John Street, Manchester, 1990-2002. Exchange Chambers, Liverpool, 2002. Recorder 1997.

GOOLDEN, Charles Edward

MA (Cantab). I. 28 April 1920. Manchester Chambers; 60 King Street, 1923-1937; 2 Booth Street, 1938-1941; 26 King Street, 1942-1964. Living in Oswestry, 1965-1967. Not in 1968 Law List.

GOODMAN, Bernadette Tracy

Born 3 May 1958. Married to Timothy King QC qv. Queen Elizabeth's School, Devon; Keele University, BA (Law & Music). I. November 1983. ETC. 1983. Pupilmaster, David Mackay. Derby Square Chambers, Merchants Court, Liverpool, 1983-2003; St Johns Buildings, Manchester 2003.

GOODWIN, Nell Eleanor Catherine

Born 14 August 1976, Birmingham. Bingley & Ilkley Grammar Schools; Manchester University, BA (Law & Accounting). L. October 2000. ETC. December 2000. Prop. Peter Birkett QC. Sec. Elizabeth Tythcott. 18 St John Street, Manchester, 2000.

GORDON, Charles Gordon Snowden

LLB. L. 17 November 1922. ETC. 31 January 1923. Prop. Kennedy KC. Sec. Chappell. 10 Cook Street, Liverpool, 1923-1940. No address, 1941-1962. Not in 1963 Law List.

GORDON, James Charles
G. 7 July 1886. ETC. 16 July 1889. Prop. French QC. Sec. C A Russell. 4 Harcourt Buildings, 1890-1891; 4 King's Bench Walk, 1892-1895; 1 Mitre Court Building, 1896-1899; 2 Garden Court, 1900-1901; 8 New Square, 1902-1906; 16 Old Buildings, 1907-1910; 22 Old Buildings, 1911-1912. No address, 1913-1940. Not in 1941 Law List.

GORE, Henry
Formerly a police sergeant. G. November 1942. Manchester Chambers; 26 King Street, 1950; 3 St James's Square, 1951-1971. Chairman; Industrial Tribunals; Medical Appeal Tribunals. Deputy Coroner SE Lancashire. Not in 1983 Law List. Henry Gore sustained a fractured femur when a car mounted the pavement and pinned him to a shop front. Months later he recounted the incident to the Mess in Manchester thus; "Mr Junior, the moment the car hit me I said to myself, bloody hell, res ipsa loquitor!"

GORE, John Kearns
Born 3 August 1924. Died 18 February 1980 aged 55. Served with RAFVR, 1943-1945, wounded NW Europe, 1944. Worcester College, Oxford, BA, 1948. G. June 1949. ETC 1949. Liverpool Chambers; 14 Cook Street, 1949-1956; 36 Dale Street, 1957- 1960; 9 Rumford Street, 1961-1973; Fruit Exchange Buildings, Victoria Street, 1974-1980.(Head of Chambers). Chairman, National Insurance Tribunal, 1972-1978. Recorder 1974-1980. WW.

GORELL, First Baron (See Barnes, John Gorell)

GORELL, Second Baron (See Barnes, Henry Gorell)

GORMAN, William KC (The Hon. Mr Justice Gorman)
Born 1897. Died 21 December 1964 aged 67. Son of William Gorman, ironmonger. Wigan Grammar School. Served in Royal Artillery in France, Belgium & Italy, 1914-1918 War. AAS. M. 21 June 1919. Call 8 June 1921; Bencher 1938; Autumn Reader, 1950; Treasurer 1959. ETC. 22 February 1922. Prop. Greaves Lord KC. Sec. Jackson. 60 King Street, Manchester, 1921-1932. Silk 1932. 2 Mitre Court Buildings, 1932; 3 Pump Court, 1933-1939. 1 Brick Court, 1945-1950. MP (L) Royton, 1923-1924. Recorder of Wigan, 1934-1948. RAFVR, 1940-1945; Wing Commander. Assistant Judge Advocate General, 1942-1944. Recorder of Liverpool, 1948-1950. High Court Judge, Queen's Bench Division, 1950-1964. Hon. Freeman of Wigan, 1954. Hon LLD., Manchester 1957. WW.

GORNA, Anne Christina
Born 1937. Daughter of John Gorna of Hale, solicitor. Manchester University, LLB. AAS. M. 9 November 1955. Call 12 July 1960. ETC. 1960. Prop. Forrest QC. Sec. Da Cunha. 4 Paper Buildings, 1963. Midland & Oxford Circuit.

GORNALL, Mark Andrew
LLB (Lancs.) M. July 1987. New Bailey Chambers, Preston, 1994-1998. Crown Prosecutor, Blackpool 1999.

GORST, Elliot Marcet QC
Born 18 November 1885. Died 28 November 1973 aged 88. Temple Grove; Harrow; Jena; Sorbonne; Florence. I. 19 June 1912. ETC. 15 June 1913. Prop. Swift KC. Sec. Stewart Brown. Served in War (1915-1919). 2 Elm Court, 1921-1924; 6 Pump Court, 1925-1965. Admitted M. 20 January 1932. Silk 1953. Sheep & cattle farmer in Kent. Publications; Guide to Railway Rates Tribunal; Titles in Halsbury's Statutes on Railways & Canals. WW.

GORST, Rt. Hon. Sir John Eldon KC, MP.
Born 24 May 1835, Preston. Died 4 April 1916 aged 80. Preston Grammar School; St John's College, Cambridge, MA; Fellow & Hon. Fellow 1890. AAS. I. 18 April 1857. Call 1 May 1865. Civil Commissioner for Waikato district of New Zealand. 6 Crown Office Row, 1876-1893. Silk 1875. Solicitor General, 1885-1886. Under Secretary for India, 1886-1891. Kt. 1885. PC. 1890. Financial Secretary to the Treasury, 1891-1892. MP (C); Chatham, 1875-1892; Cambridge University, 1892-1906. Contested Preston, 1910. Publications; Children of the Nation, 1907; New Zealand Revisited, 1908. WW. DNB.

GORTON, Simon Anthony
Born 16 March 1966, Liverpool. Married to Anne Whyte qv. Brother Carl is at King Street Chambers, Manchester. Cardinal Godfrey/De La Salle; Queen Mary College, London, LLB. I. July 1988. ETC. December 1990. Prop. Brian Leveson QC. Sec. Bruce Macmillan. 14 Castle Street / Atlantic Chambers, Cook Street, Liverpool, 1990.

GOULD, Deborah Samantha
Born 28 March 1964, Teddington Lock, Middlesex. Pates Grammar School, Cheltenham; Warwick University, LLB. I. February 1990. ETC 1990. Pupilmaster, Martyn Bennett. Liverpool Chambers; Peel House, Harrington Street, 1990-1997; India Buildings, Water Street, 12.1.1998.

GOURLEY, Claire Roberta Jean
Born 14 December 1973 Belfast. Belfast Royal Academy; Magdelene College, Cambridge, MA. M. October 1996. 3 Paper Buildings & Bournemouth annexe, 1996-1998. Western Circuit. Pupilmasters; Richard Tyson, Nicholas Leviseur & Michael Norman. ETC. 1998. Prop. David Turner QC. Sec. Judith Fordham. Exchange Chambers, Derby Square, Liverpool, 1998.

GOVER, John Mahan KC
Born 1867. Died 18 April 1947. London University, LLD. AAS. M. 5 March 1886. Call 28 January 1889; Bencher 1925; Lent Reader 1935; Treasurer 1943. ETC. 27 February 1891. Prop. Kennedy QC. Sec. Cavanagh. 1 Garden Court, 1889-1892; 5 New Square, 1893-1947. Silk 1919. WW.

GOW, Henry
Born 26 January 1953, Glasgow. St Augustine's Secondary School. British Army (12 years); Royal Ulster Constabulary (6 Years). Leeds Metropolitan University, LLB; University of East Anglia, MA (International Relations). G. October 1995. Pupilmaster, Orlando Pownall. 1 Crown Office Row. Liverpool Chambers; Victoria Chambers, 25 Victoria Street/19 Castle Street, 1996-2000; New Bailey Chambers, 19 Castle Street, 2000.

GOZEM, Gaias QC
Born 15 February 1950, Stockport. William Hulme Grammar School; Mid Essex Technical College (London University External, LLB). AAS. M. 25 August 1971. Call 22 November 1972. ETC 1972. Pupilmaster, Ian Webster. Manchester Chambers; 2 Booth Street, 1972-1975; 13 Police Street, 1975-1978; 64 Bridge Street, 1979-1995; Lincoln House Chambers, 1 Brazennose Street, 1996. Recorder 1992. Silk 1997. Member New South Wales Bar. Guitarist with Prestons qv.

GRACE, Jonathan Robert
Born 28 July 1965, Liverpool. St Edwards College, Liverpool; Oriel College, Oxford, BA (English); Central London Polytechnic, Dip. Law. AAS. M. 11 February 1987. Call 7 February 1989. ETC. 1990. Prop. Keith Goddard QC. Sec. David Stockdale. Dean's Court Chambers, Crown Square/ 24 St John Street, Manchester, 1989.

GRACE, Timothy Michael
Born 20 May 1971, Liverpool. St Edward's College, Liverpool; Lincoln College, Oxford, BA (Jurisprudence). M. November 1993. ETC. 21 December 1993. Prop. Brian Leveson QC. Sec. Adrian Lyon. 14 Castle Street/ Atlantic Chambers, Cook Street, Liverpool, 1993.

GRADWELL, Joseph Leo Anthony DSC.
Born 28 July 1899. Died 9 November 1969 aged 70. Son of Joseph Gradwell, solicitor. Stonyhurst College, Balliol College, Oxford, MA. Served 1917-1918 as midshipman, RNVR. I. 17 November 1925. ETC. 27 January 1926. Prop. Singleton. Sec. Lynskey. Liverpool Chambers; 13 Harrington Street, 1925-1930; 43 Castle Street, 1931-1934; 10 Cook Street, 1934-1939. Served 1939-1945, RNVR; served at sea in command of HMS Ayshire and other anti submarine vessels in Western Approaches (DSC). 34 Castle Street, 1946-1950. Metropolitan Stipendiary Magistrate; Thames 1950-1961; Gt. Marlborough Street, 1961-1967. WW.
Leo Gradwell was a guest during Manchester Assizes at one of Mr Justice Rigby Swift's lunch parties held in the rooms behind his court. The High Sheriffs chaplain misjudging the suitability of the occasion tried to embark upon a religious discussion. Rigby's response was prompt and typical. "Chaplain", he said, "I think there is a proper time and place for a religious discussion. You know when Gradwell and I are conducting a little criminal business in my court it would be a dreadful thing if we were saying our prayers all the time, wouldn't it Gradwell?" "One of us is" said Gradwell. (Oxford Book of Legal Anecdotes. edited by Michael Gilbert 1986)
In June 1940 Gradwell commanded HMS Ayshire which was part of Convoy PQ 17 en route from Iceland to Archangel. The convoy was ordered to scatter because it was thought, wrongly, that the German battleship, Tirpitz, was about to attack. Only 11 out of 35 ships survived. Gradwell led 5 merchant ships into the northern ice fields. Discovering a large quantity of white paint on board one of the merchantmen, Gradwell ordered that the decks and the starboard sides (facing Norway) of all the ships be painted white. This was so effective that German reconnaissance planes flying within 20 miles failed to spot them. Several days later Gradwell led them safely to Russia. For his bravery and initiative he was awarded the DSC. Gradwell's First Lieutenant was also a lawyer. This prompted the Senior British Naval Officer, North Russia to say "The more law that comes to sea the better and let litigation look after itself.
Further reading: Convoy. Paul Kemp. Brockhampton Press 1993. Convoy is to Scatter. Captain Jack Broome. William Kimber 1972.
In 1963 Gradwell presided over the committal proceedings in the case of Stephen Ward in what was later to be known as the "Profumo affair".

GRAHAM, George Boughen QC
Born 17 July 1920. Died 28 February 1994 aged 74. Keswick School. Royal Signals, 1940-1946. LLB. L. November 1950; Bencher 1972. Manchester Chambers;

78 King Street, 1951; 3 St James's Square, 1955-1971. London Chambers; 8 New Square, 1951-1953; 5 Paper Buildings, 1954-1971; 24 Old Buildings, 1972-1980. Chancellor, Diocese of; Wakefield, 1959-1992; Sheffield, 1971-1992, Member of Lloyds, 1968. Commander, Order of Merit (West Germany); Order of the Aztec Eagle (Mexico). Publications; Covenants, Settlements & Trusts, 1953; Estate Duty Handbook, 1954. WW.

GRAHAM, His Honour John Cameron KC
Born 1847. Died 6 August 1929. Only son of John Graham of the Royal Mint, engineer. University College, London, BSc (Engineering) 1871. AAS. M. 22 June 1876. Call 7 May 1879. ETC. 30 July 1880. Prop. Macrory. Sec. McConnell. various London Chambers and finally at 2 Garden Court, 1896-1909. Silk 1906. County Court Judge, Circuits 11, (Burnley, Colne & Nelson) & 14, (Bradford), January 1909-1915; Circuit 40, (Bow), 1915-1922. JP for Stirlingshire. Publications; edited Blackburn on Sales. Joint editor, Hindemarsh on Law of Patents. WW. Foster.

GRAHAM, Reginald Stuart
Born 1882. 2nd son of Philip Graham of Twincroft, Darwen, Lancs., Clerk in Holy Orders. Pembroke College, Oxford. AAS. M. 16 October 1903. Call 10 May 1911. ETC. 27 February 1912. Prop. Sanderson KC. Sec. Lumb. 1 Harcourt Buildings, 1911-1914. No address, 1915-1953. Not in 1954 Law List.

GRAHAM, William James Holmes
I. 17 November 1896. Clayton Chambers, Westgate Road, Newcastle-upon-Tyne, 1897-1900. North Eastern Circuit. ETC. 3 February 1900. Prop. Russell QC. Sec. Mellor. Manchester Chambers; 78 King Street, 1900-1917; Bank of England Chambers, Tib Lane, 1918-1926. Associate, Northern Circuit, 1927-1928. Clerk of Assize, Northern Circuit, 1 Chapel Street, Preston, 1929-1948. Not in 1950 Law List.

GRAHAM, William Woodman
Born 1859. 3rd son of William Frederick Graham of Wallington, Surrey. New College, Oxford, BA 1880. AAS. M. 13 August 1878. Call 26 January 1883. ETC. 29 July 1884. Prop. Collins QC. Sec. Lees Knowles. 4 Elm Court, 1886-1891. No address, 1892-1940. Not in 1941 Law List.

GRANET, Sir (William) Guy GBE
Born 13 October 1867. Genoa. Died 11 October 1943 aged 75. Married to daughter of First Viscount Selby. Rugby, Balliol College, Oxford. L. 14 June 1893. ETC. 4 July 1893. Prop. Gully QC. Sec. Henry. 2 Harcourt Buildings, 1894; 1 Kings Bench Walk, 1895-1902. General Manager, Midland Railway, 1906. Kt. 1911. Member, Royal Commission on the Civil Service, 1911-1914. Director General of Movements & Railways, and member of Army Council, 1917. GBE 1923. Chairman of London, Midland & Scottish Railway, 1924-1927. WW. DNB.

GRANT, Alexander KC
Born 5 September 1866, Bolton. Died 21 March 1941 aged 74. Bank Street British Schools, Bolton, 1870-1878; Manchester Grammar School; Merton College, Oxford (Postmaster) MA., BCL. Fellow, All Souls College, 1890-1897. Eldon Law Scholar; Lecturer in Roman Law & Jurisprudence, Victoria University, Manchester, 1892. I. 6 June 1894; Bencher 1918; Treasurer 1940. ETC. 3 February 1900. Prop. Pickford QC. Sec. Sutton. 78 King Street, Manchester, 1896-1908. Equity draftsman & conveyancer. Lancs. Chancery Court. Silk 1908. 11 New Court, Carey Street, 1908-1906; 11 New Court, 1907-1926; 1 New Square, 1927-1941. WW. His Honour Judge Sir Gerald Hurst KC in "Closed Chapters" Manchester University Press, 1942 says of Grant at p 43 "Grant was the cleverest of all the local Bar. I thought him a marvel. He claimed that at the age of 11 (1877) he was a half timer in a Bolton cotton mill. At 24 he was a fellow of All Souls and Eldon Scholar, with three firsts and a second in BCL to his credit. Unlike the typical Chancery man, he was both terse and spirited in argument. He was a stout fighter all of his life".

GRANT, Julie
BSc (Manchester) MA., Dip Law. M. July 1991. Manchester Chambers; 6th floor, Sunlight House, Quay Street, 1993-1994; 38 Young Street, 1995-1998. Now at Westgate Chambers, 144 High Street, Lewes.

GRANT, Kenneth John
Born 11 September 1953 Liverpool. De La Salle School, Liverpool. University of York, BA (Social Sciences). Solicitor in private practice, 1980-1997. I. 12 March 1998. ETC. 2 April 1998. Prop. Stephen Riordan QC. Sec. Gerald Baxter. 25-27 Castle Street, Liverpool, 1998.

GRANT, Veronica
BA., Dip Law. G. November 1984. Manchester Chambers; 121 Princess Street, 1986-1987; Central Buildings, 3 Peter Street, 1988. British Coal Corporation, Doncaster, 1989.

GRANTHAM, Andrew Timothy
Born 19 November 1966, Liverpool. Son of David Grantham of Gregson Ashton, solicitors, Liverpool. King David High School; St Catherine's College, Oxford, MA., BCL. Lecturer in Law; Wadham College, Oxford, 1989-1990; part time, King's College, London, 1990-1991. FCIArb. AAS. M. 15 October 1991. Call March 1992. Prop. Keith Goddard QC. Sec. Michael Black. Manchester Chambers; Dean's Court Chambers, Crown Square/ 24 St John Street, 1.9.1991-27.8.2001; King's Chambers, 40 King Street, 28.8.2001.

GRAVES, Samuel Haughton
Born 1853. 2nd son of Anthony Elly Graves of Rosbercon Castle, Co Kilkenny. Trinity College, Cambridge, MA. AAS. I. 20 January 1872. Call 26 January 1875. ETC. 3 August 1875. Prop. Russell QC. Sec. Gully, lla Commerce Chambers, Harrington Street, 1880-1895. Liverpool & Kirkdale Sessions, Liverpool Court of Passage. No address, 1896-1935. Not in 1936 Law List. Foster.

GRAY, Mark Julian
Born 26 April 1967, Aldershot. Rydal School, Colwyn Bay; Liverpool John Moores University (Degree in Mechanical Engineering). Qualified Chartered Engineer and a Project Engineer. G. November 1996. ETC. July 1997. Pupilage at 14 Castle Street, Liverpool, March-September 1997. Pupilmaster Robert Warnock. Army Prosecuting Service, September 1997-April 1998. Liverpool Chambers; 25 Fenwick Street/ 3rd floor, 14 Cook Street, May 1998.

GRAY, Richard
Born 19 October 1958. Liverpool Polytecnic (now John Moores University), LLB. AAS. M. 10 July 1984. Call 25 November 1986. ETC. 1986. Liverpool Chambers; 2nd floor, Fruit Exchange, Victoria Street/ 3rd floor, 46 Stanley Street, 1988-1991; Manchester Chambers; 211 Deansgate, 1992-1993; 38 King Street West, 1994-1995; 24a St John Street (now St John's Buildings), 1996.

GREAVES, John Hall
L. 3 July 1889. ETC. 20 July 1889. Prop. Addison QC. Sec. J W Hamilton. No address, 1890-1894. 19 Old Square, 1895. 2 Garden Court, 1896-1897. Not in 1898 Law List.

GREAVES-LORD, Walter KC, MP. (The Hon. Mr Justice Greaves-Lord)
Born 1 September 1878. Died 18 June 1942 aged 63. Assumed additional surname of Greaves in 1910. Wigan Grammar School; Victoria University of Manchester, LLB. AAS. G. 15 November 1897. Call 27 June 1900 (Arden Scholar); Bencher 1920; Treasurer 1933. Admitted M. 22 April 1918. ETC. July 1900. Prop. Ferguson QC. Sec. Rigby Swift. Liverpool Chambers; 8 Harrington Street, 1900-1906; 5 Harrington Street, 1907-1918. Silk 1919. 1 Brick Court, 1919-1920; 1 Garden Court, 1921-1935. Member, Council of Legal Education, 1924. Recorder of Manchester, 1925-1935. Chairman, Primrose League, 1926-1927. High Court Judge, Queen's Bench Division, 1935-1940. Freeman of the City of London. Contested (C) Ince, Lancs., January and December 1910. MP (C) Lambeth (Norwood), 1922-1935. WW.

GREEN, Alan Laurence
Born 2 February 1946, Manchester. Carmel College; Altrincham Grammar School; University of Sussex, BA. G. February 1973. Pupillage 2 Crown Office Row. ETC. 1973. Manchester pupilmaster, Arthur Logan Petch. Ship Canal House, King Street, Manchester, 1973-1979. 50 Essex Street, 1985-1987; 1 Verulam Buildings, 1987-1990; 199 Strand, 1990 to retirement in 2001.

GREEN, Colin Richard
Born 27 August 1958, Portsmouth. School of Art, Birmingham. Leeds University, BA; City University, London Dip. Law. L. July 1982. ETC. 1983. Liverpool Chambers; 14 Cook Street, 1983-1985; 7 Queen Avenue, 1986-1996. 72 Bridge Street/ Cobden House Chambers, Manchester, 1996.

GREEN, David Cameron
Born 13 June 1971, Leicester. Beauchamp School Leicester; Lancaster University (Pendle College), LLB. L. October 1993. ETC. 1994. Pupilmaster, Nicholas Riddle. Liverpool Chambers; 7 Queen Avenue, 1993-1996; merger with 14 Castle Street, 1996. (now Atlantic Chambers, Cook Street).

GREEN, Edmund Ironsides
Born 1863. 2nd son of Samuel Richard Green of Folkstone, engineer. London University. AAS. M. 23 October 1884. Call 13 June 1888. ETC. 28 February 1889. Prop. Ambrose QC. Sec. Fort. Circuit Junior, Summer 1889. 4 Essex Court, 1890; 3 Elm Court, 1891-1900. Manchester & Salford Sessions. Not in 1901 Law List.

GREEN, Henry Rupert CBE
Born 29 December 1900. Died 28 December 1988 aged 87. Only son of Henry Green JP., solicitor. Father of Roger John Bailey Green qv. Charterhouse; Hertford College, Oxford, MA. L. 28 April 1926. ETC. 13 July 1926. Prop. Jackson KC. Sec. Sec. Gorman. 60 King Street, Manchester, 1926-1939. Commissioned RAF, served as Operations Staff Officer, Malta, 1941-1943. Commissioner, Board of Control (Lunacy & Deficiency), 1943-1953; Legal Senior Commissioner, Ministry of Health 1953 until retirement in 1971. CBE 1960. Publications; Chapters on Persons Mentally Disordered/ of Unsound Mind In Halsbury's Laws, Halsbury's Statutes & Encyclopaedia of Court Forms. WW.

GREEN, Max James Dalton Sullivan
Dublin University, BA. Eire Bar. L. April 1947. ETC. 1947. No address, 1947-1949. 20 Hackins Hey, Liverpool, 1950-1958. No address, 1959-1963. Not in 1964 Law List. There is a Max Sullivan Green JP. (1864-1922) listed in WW. He was an engineer and Chairman of the Irish Prison Board. Sounds like a relative.

GREEN, Roger John Bailey
Born 10 August 1949 Gerrards Cross, Bucks. Son of Henry Rupert Green CBE qv. Bedford School; College of Law, (LLB London). L. July 1972. London pupillage. ETC. November 1973. Prop. Ivor Taylor QC. Sec. J C W Bailey. Manchester Chambers; 43 King Street, 1973-1989; 5 John Dalton Street, 1989.

GREENE, Maurice Alan
Born 19 April 1960 Salford. Stand Grammar School; Liverpool John Moores University, LLB. I. November 1982. 19 Figtree Lane, Sheffield, 1982-1991.North Eastern Circuit. Pupilmaster, David Gothorp. ETC. 1991. Manchester Chambers; Kenworthy's Buildings, 1991-1994; 38 Young Street, 1994-1999; 28 St John Street, 1999. Acting Stipendiary Magistrate, 1999. Deputy District Judge (Magistrates Courts), October 1999. Recorder 2003.

GREENFIELD, (Alex) Jeremy
Born 6 July 1957, Manchester. Stockport Grammar School; Liverpool University, BCom. Formerly an Insurance Manager at Standard Life Assurance Co. dealing with investments and occupational pensions. I. October 1995. ETC. 19 December 1995. Prop. David Turner QC. Sec. Stephen Knapp. Pupilmaster, Graham Morris. Liverpool Chambers; Martins Building, Water Street, 1995-1999; 7 Harrington Street, 6.9.1999. (merger with the Corn Exchange)

GREENWOOD, Celestine Lesley
Born 25 July 1969. Haslingden High School; Liverpool University, LLB. L. October 1991. ETC. December 1991. Prop. Timothy King QC. Sec. Scott Donovan. Liverpool Chambers; Derby Square Chambers, Refuge Assurance House, September 1991-September 1997; Chavasse Court, 24 Lord Street, September 1997.

GREENWOOD, John
MA (Cantab) I. 26 January 1912. ETC. 3 July 1913. Prop. Tobin KC. Sec. Brown. 2 Elm Court, 1916. No address, 1917-1953. Not in 1954 Law List.

GREER, Frederick Arthur KC (Baron Fairfield of Caldy)
Born 6 October 1863. Died 4 February 1945 aged 81. Eldest son (of fourteen children) of Arthur Greer of Liverpool and Isle of Man, metal merchant; father-in-law of Ronw Moelwyn Hughes KC. Ormskirk Grammar School; Old Aberdeen Grammar School; Aberdeen University, MA (Philosophy) and Fullerton Scholarship, 1883. G. 17 November 1889; Bacon & Arden Scholarships; Bencher 1910; Treasurer 1921. ETC. 7 February 1887. Prop Collins QC. Sec. Mansfield. Liverpool Chambers; Commerce Court, 11a Lord Street, 1887-1890; 2 Harrington Street, 1891-1896; 7 Cook Street, 1897-1900; 13 Harrington Street, 1901-1910. During his early years at the Liverpool Bar, Greer supplemented his earnings by writing for the Liverpool Daily Post & Liverpool Courier. He decided to quit the Bar and applied to Sir Edward Ritchie Russell (Later Lord Russell) for a full time job on the Post. Sir Edward advised him to persevere in practice. Greer did and never looked back. He took silk in 1910 and, practising from 2 Pump Court & later 2 Mitre Court Buildings, he built up a considerable practice in the Commercial and Prize Courts. High Court Judge, King's Bench Division, 1919-1927. Kt. 1919. Lord Justice of Appeal, 1927-1938. PC 1927. Chairman, Council of Legal Education, 1934-1936. Hon. LLD; Aberdeen 1926; Liverpool 1930. Address; Fairfield House, Caldy, Cheshire. WW. DNB.

GREG, Thomas Tylston
Born 1859. Eldest son of Edward Hyde Greg of Quarry Bank, Handforth, Cheshire. Oriel College, Oxford, BA. AAS. I. 9 May 1879. Call 17 November 1882. ETC. 25 January 1883. Prop. Crompton QC. Sec. Smyley. 15 Cliffords Inn, 1883. & 1885-1888; 3 Harcourt Buildings, 1884. Not in 1889 Law List.

GREGG, (William) Jonathan
Born 7 March 1968, Belfast. Belfast Royal Academy; Newcastle-upon-Tyne University, LLB. G. 1 October 1990. 6 Pump Court, October 1990-September 1991. ETC. December 1991. Pupilmaster, Howard Baisden. Manchester Chambers; Hollins Chambers, 64a Bridge Street / Cobden House Chambers, 19 Quay Street, September 1991.

GREGORY, James Han
Born 6 June 1944, Halifax. University College, London, BA. G. February 1970. ETC 1970. Manchester Chambers; 2 Booth Street, 1970-1975; 13 Police Street, 1976-1978; Rational House, 64 Bridge Street, 1979-1995; Lincoln House Chambers, 1 Brazennose Street, 1996.

GREGORY, John Raymond
Born 18 April 1949, Waterloo, Liverpool. St Ambrose College; Stretford Grammar School; Hull University, LLB. AAS. M. 26 August 1968. Lecturer, 1970-1973. Call 20 July 1972. ETC. 13 February 1973. Prop. Godfrey Heilpern QC. Sec. Reg Houlker. Dean's Court Chambers, Crown Square/ 24 St John Street, 1973. Contested (C) Stretford & Urmston, 1997.

GREGORY, Karen Ann
Born 26 October 1960, Liverpool. St Albans RC Comprehensive; Liverpool University, BA (Psychology) 1982; Trainee Costs Management Accountant, British Leyland, Cowley, 1982-1983. Central London Polytechnic, Dip. Law, 1984. AAS. M. 8 February 1984. Call 25 July1985. ETC. December 1986. Pupilmasters; Denis Clark & Bill Braithwaite. Exchange Chambers at 1 Exchange Flags and Derby Square, Liverpool, 1985.

GREGORY, Norman Hector
G. November 1942. No address, 1944-1955. Not in 1956 Law List.

GREGORY, Peter Joseph
Born 18 September 1958 Belfast. St Macnissi's College, Co. Antrim; Manchester University, LLB. G. July 1982. ETC. December 1982. Prop. Bert Andrew QC. Sec. Iain Goldrein. Liverpool Chambers; 5 Castle Street, 1982-1986; 48/50 Castle Street, 1987-1988; merger with Corn Exchange, Fenwick Street, 1989-1990; Peel House, Harrington Street, 1990-1999; Martins Building, 1999; 7 Harrington Street, 6.9.1999. (merger with Corn Exchange) Recorder (Civil) 2001.

GRENNAN, Barry Edward
Born 15 June 1952 Salford. De La Salle, Salford; Nottingham University, BA. L. July 1977. Pupilmaster Inigo Bing. ETC. 3 April 1979. Prop. Douglas Brown QC. Sec J Ward. Manchester Chambers; 6th floor, Arkwright House, Parsonage Gardens, 1979-1984; 26 Cross Street, 1985-1987; Kenworthy's Building, 83 Bridge Street, 1988.

GRIBBIN, Henry Thomas
Born 1875. Eldest son of Henry Gribbin of Southport. Journalist when AAS. M. 22 January 1919. Call 26 January 1922. ETC. 1 February 1922. Prop. Greaves-Lord KC. Sec. Peace. 25 Lord Street, Liverpool, 1923-1926. No address, 1927-1953. Not in 1954 Law List.

GRICE, (Alan) Kevin
Born 24 October 1955 Bromsgrove, Worcs. King Edward's School, Birmingham; Liverpool University, LLB. Lecturer in Law, Liverpool University, 1977-1979. G. July 1977. ETC. 1979. Prop. Bruce Martin QC. Sec. Ann Ebsworth. Pupilmaster, Mark Hedley. Liverpool Chambers; 27 Dale Street, 1979-1987; relocated to 5th floor, Corn Exchange, Fenwick Street, 1989-1999; 7 Harrington Street, 6.9.1999. (merger with Martins Bank). Member, Legal Aid Committee. Assistant Recorder 1996. Recorder 2000.

GRIERSON, Nigel Jonathan
Born 16 October 1961, Stockton on Tees. The Grange School, Stockton on Tees. Hull University, LLB. a solicitor, October 1986-November 1999. M. 25 November 1999. ETC. 14 December 1999. Prop. Jonathan Foster QC. Sec. Yvonne Healing. Pupilmaster, Mark Laprell. 18 St John Street, Manchester September, 1999.

GRIFFITH, Arthur Ernest
I. 19 November 1888. ETC. 22 March 1897. Prop. Bigham QC. Sec. T R Hughes. 4 Paper Buildings, 1897. Liverpool Chambers; 11 Lord Street, 1898-1908; 5 Harrington Street, 1909-1928; 3 Cook Street, 1929. Not in 1930 Law List.

GRIFFITH, Eric William
BCL., MA. G. 28 January 1935. ETC. 30 January 1935, Prop. Maxwell Fyfe KC. Sec. Dowdall. Liverpool Chambers; 31 Dale Street, 1935-1941; 15 Union Court, 1942-1952; 20 North John Street, 1953-1961. 4 Stone Buildings, Lincoln's Inn, 1962-1974. Not in 1975 Law List.

GRIFFITH, Rodney Owen
MA (Oxon) I. July 1969. 14 Cook Street, Liverpool, 1972-1973. Went to Hong Kong. Not in 1976 Law List.

GRIFFITHS, John Owen Pugh
I. 17 November 1936. ETC. 27 January 1937. Prop. Sellers KC. Sec. Pritchard. Liverpool Chambers; 25 Castle Street, 1937; 13 Harrington Street, 1938-1949. No address 1950-1963. Non practising, CARTREF, Saughall, Chester, 1964. Not in 1965 Law List.

GRIFFITHS, Tania Veronica
Born 7 December 1959 Southport. Christ the King RC Comprehensive, Southport. Liverpool Polytechnic (now John Moores University), BA. G. 29 July 1982. ETC. December 1982. Prop. Benet Hytner QC. Sec. John Kay. Exchange Chambers, 1 Exchange Flags/ Derby Square, Liverpool, 1982. Assistant Recorder 1999. Recorder 2001.

GRIME, (Mark) Stephen (Eastburn) QC
Born 16 March 1948 Manchester. Wrekin College, Trinity College, Oxford, MA. AAS. M. 27 July 1967. Call 10 February 1970; Bencher 1997. ETC. Summer 1970. Prop. Derek Hodgson QC. Sec. Keith Goddard. Dean's Court Chambers at; 9 Albert Square/ Crown Square/ 24 St John Street, Manchester, 1970. (Head of Chambers 2000.) Silk 1987. Assistant Recorder 1988. Recorder 1990 (Technology & Consruction Court). FCIArb, 1997. Chairman, Northern Circuit Medical Law Association. WW.

GRIMSDALE, Frederick
Born 1861. 2nd son of Thomas Frederick Grimsdale, MD., of 29 Rodney Street, Liverpool. AAS. M. 13 January 1883. Call 17 November 1885. ETC. 13 February 1886. Prop. Gully QC. Sec. Gorell Barnes. 9 Commerce Chambers, Liverpool, 1889-1895. No address, 1896-1940. Not in 1941 Law List. The sketches he made in late 1880's of Judges & Barristers at St George's Hall, Liverpool are in the Circuit Records. Many of the drawings are in this Directory.

GRIMSHAW, David
BA (Cantab), MA (Commercial Law) MBA. AAS. M. 25 January 1974. Call November 1975. Oriel Chambers, 14 Water Street, Liverpool 1977-1978. Note in Liverpool Prosecutions Book "Left September 1978". No address, 1979-1986. In house lawyer, Conoco (UK) Ltd 1987 rising to Senior Legal Advisor, 1994.

GRIMSHAW, Joseph Stanfield
Born 1837. 2nd son of John Grimshaw of Manchester. London University, BA 1855. Member of Convocation. AAS. I. 19 January 1856. Call 26 January 1859. 1 Tanfield Court, 1876-1885. No chambers address, 1886-1929. Not in 1930.

GRIMSHAW, Nicholas Edward
Born 1963. Keble College, Oxford, MA. I. November 1988. ETC. 1988. Dean's Court Chambers at Crown Square/ 24 St John Street, Manchester, 1988.

GRINDROD, Helen Marjorie QC
Born 28 February 1936, Aigburth, Liverpool. Died 11 July 2002 aged 66. Liverpool Institute High School for Girls at Blackburne House; St Hilda's College, Oxford, MA (English); Hon. Fellow. Teacher, 1956-1959 in Bristol. Read for the Bar at home. L. July 1966; Bencher 1990. ETC. 1966 pupilmaster, Arthur Logan Petch. Manchester Chambers; Ship Canal House, King Street, 1966-1980; 2 Old Bank Street, 1981-1983; 18 St John Street, 1984-2000. London Chambers; 5 Essex Court; 95a Chancery Lane; 15-19 Devereux Court (Head of Chambers). Recorder 1981-1995. Silk 1982. Obituaries; The Guardian, 17 July 2002 (His Honour Judge Sir Rhys Davies QC); The Times, 9 August 2002. WW.

GRITTEN, William George Howard MP
Died 5 April 1943. Brasenose College, Oxford, MA. I. 14 June 1899. ETC. 18 July 1901. Prop. Shee KC. Sec. Langdon. 9 King's Bench Walk, 1900-1901; No address, 1902-1903; 3 Paper Buildings, 1904; 12 King's Bench Walk, 1905-1909; 11 King's Bench Walk, 1910-1934. No address, 1935-1943. MP (C) The Hartlepools, 1918-1922 & 1929-1943. Freeman, City of London. WW.

GROCOTT, Susan
Born 30 March 1963 Rochdale. Oulder Hill Community School, Rochdale; Exeter College, Oxford, BA. AAS. M. 31 July 1985. Call 24 November 1986. ETC. April 1988. Prop. Keith Goddard QC. Sec. Eric Shannon. Fountains Court, September 1986- April 1987; 5 Pump Court, April 1987- January 1988; 5 John Dalton Street, Manchester, January 1988. Recorder 2004.

GROSJEAN, James Keith
Born 1840. Eldest son of Pierre Frederic Grosjean of Kensington, Middlesex, merchant. MD., FRCS when AAS. M. 20 October 1871. Call 7 June 1873. ETC. 26 July 1877. Prop. Russell. Sec. French. Alexandria, 1878-1883. Not in 1884 Law List.

GROSSMAN, Gustav
I. 10 May 1911. ETC. 30 January 1913. Prop. Sanderson KC. Sec. Gorell Barnes. No chambers address, 1912-1945. Not in 1946 Law List.

GROUT-SMITH, Jeremy Gaywood
Born 30 May 1958 Aldwick, West Sussex. Cranleigh School; Chichester C of E School; Bristol Polytechnic, LLB; Bristol University, LLM. Akroyd & Smithers Ltd, 1979-1981. I. July 1986. 8 New Court September, 1986-April 1988. Pupilmasters; John Haines, Mark Lowe & Richard Rundell. ETC. 1988. Prop. John Hugill QC. Sec. Michael Shorrock. 2 Old Bank Street/ 45 Hardman Street, Manchester, 1988.

GROVER, Timothy Russell
Born 3 March 1968 Sheffield. Queen Park High School, Chester; Essex University, LLB. I. November 1991. ETC. December 1991. Prop. John Rowe QC. Sec. Graham Morris. Liverpool Chambers; Martins Building, Water Street, 1991-1999; 7 Harrington Street (merger with Corn Exchange), 6.9.1999.

GROVES, Keith Grimble
Born 1888. 5th son of James Grimble Groves of Chapel en le Frith, brewer. Trinity College, Cambridge. AAS. M. 9 May 1908. Call 18 November 1912. ETC. 19 February 1913. Prop. Tobin KC. Sec. Hans Hamilton. Various London Chambers and 1 Essex Court, 1921-1963. Non practising, 1964-1979 with an address in the Isle of Man. Not in 1980 Law List.

GRUFFYDD, John
Born 1 June 1949. Cardiff. Whitchurch Grammar School, Cardiff. External LLB of London University. A solicitor, 1975-1991. G. February 1992. ETC. 1992. Prop. David Clarke QC. Sec. Ian Trigger. Oriel Chambers, 5 Covent Garden/ 14 Water Street, Liverpool, 1992.

GRUNDY, Clare
Born 18 November 1966. Leeds. Manchester High School for Girls; Birmingham University, LLB. G. July 1989. ETC. December 1989. Prop. Charles Bloom QC. Sec. Clement Goldstone. Circuit Junior, Winter 1992. 28 St John Street, Manchester, 1989. (now St. Johns Buildings Chambers).

GRUNDY, Liam
Born 6 February 1972. Liverpool. Bootle High School; University of Hull, LLB; Jesus College, Cambridge, LLM. I. July 1995. ETC. 1996. Sec. Nicholas Riddle. 14 Castle Street/ Atlantic Chambers, Cook Street, Liverpool, 1996.

GRUNDY, Nigel Lawrence John
Born 9 January 1960, Bolton. Brother of Philip Michael David Grundy qv. Bolton School; Pembroke College, Oxford, BA (Jurisprudence). AAS. M. 27 April 1981. Call 28 July 1982. ETC. December 1983. Prop. John Hugill QC. Sec. Peter Openshaw. Manchester Chambers; 2 Old Bank Street, 1983-1985; Crown Square Chambers/ 9 St John Street, 1984. Recorder 2001.

GRUNDY, Philip Michael David
Born 1 October 1956, Bolton. Brother of Nigel Lawrence John Grundy qv. Bolton School; University College, Cardiff, LLB. AAS. M. November 1977. Call July 1980. ETC. 19 May 1981. Sec. Barry Woodward. Manchester Chambers; 67 Princess Street/ Hollins Chambers, 1980-1987; 28 St John Street, 1988. Assistant Recorder 1996. Recorder 2000. On Treasury Counsel Civil List. Winner of Bar Golf 1996.

GRUNDY, Samuel Percy
I. 17 May 1905. ETC. 20 July 1905. Prop. Shee KC. Sec. Sellers. 78 King Street, Manchester, 1909-1910. No address, 1911-1948. Not in 1949 Law List.

GRUNDY, Sydney
Born 23 March 1848, Manchester. Died 4 July 1914 aged 66. Only son of Alderman Charles Sydney Grundy, ex Mayor of Manchester. Owen's College, Manchester. AAS. M. 17 November 1869. ETC. 10 March 1870. Prop. Holker QC. Sec. Hopwood. He practised in Manchester until 1876 and then had chambers at 2 Cloisters, 1876-1879 and 13 King's Bench Walk, 1880-1882. In fact between 1872 and 1908 he was a "dramatic author" writing 38 plays/comic operas. His "Vicar of Bray" was first produced at the Globe Theatre on the 22 July 1882. A revised version was produced at the Savoy Theatre in 1892 under the management of Mr. Richard D'Oyly Carte. The same year Grundy's light opera "Haddon Hall" with music by Sir Arthur Sullivan was a great success at the Savoy. George Bernard Shaw thought it was the best of the Savoy operas and for a while it beat even "The Mikado" in box office receipts. Grundy came in as librettist because Sullivan and W S Gilbert qv, were hardly on speaking terms at that time. WW.

GUERIN, Thomas Austin
Born 1854. Only son of John Guerin of Failsworth Hall nr. Manchester, merchant. AAS. M. 30 January 1872. Call 26 January 1877. ETC. 25 March 1878. Prop. Temple QC. Sec. Hamilton. 4 St James's Square, Manchester, 1878-1892. Equity draftsman & conveyancer. Kimberley, Cape of Good Hope, 1893-1911. No address, 1912-1935. Not in 1936 Law List.

GULLY, James William Herschell (Second Viscount Selby)
Born 4 October 1867. Died 2 February 1923 aged 55. Eldest son of William Court Gully (First Viscount Selby) qv. Winchester; Balliol College, Oxford. I. 11 May 1892. ETC. 3 July 1895. Prop. Bigham QC. Sec. Sanderson. Farrar's Building, 1896-1898; Palace Chambers, 9 Bridge Street, Westminster, 1899-1910. Parliamentary draftsman. WW.

GULLY, John
Born 1835. 2nd son of John Gully of Maswell Hall, Hants. Wadham College, Oxford, MA. AAS. I. 15 May 1857. Call 30 April 1860. 5 Crown Office Row, 1877-1894. No address, 1895-1907. Not in 1908 Law List.

GULLY, William Court QC, MP. (First Viscount Selby)
Born 29 August 1835 London. Died 6 November 1909 aged 74. 2nd son of James Manby Gully MD of Great Malvern. Went aged 16 to Trinity College, Cambridge. President of Cambridge Union. MA 1859. Hon. LLD, 1900. Hon DCL, Oxford, 1904. AAS. I. 5 November 1853. Call 26 January 1860; Bencher 1879. ETC. 1860. 13 King's Bench Walk to 1876; Farrar's Building, 1877-1895. Silk 1877. Recorder of Wigan, 1886-1895. Contested Whitehaven, 1880 & 1885. MP (GL) Carlisle, 1886-1905. Speaker of House of Commons, 1895-1905. PC. Viscount 1905. Chairman, Royal Commission; on motor cars and on vaccination. Freeman of the City of London. WW. DNB.
Courtney Peregrine Ilbert, in DNB, records: "He joined the Northern Circuit and shared the usual struggles of a junior barrister. There is a well authenticated story of a meeting between three members of the circuit who, despairing of their prospects at home, agreed to try their fortunes in India or the colonies. But they reconsidered their determination, and all of them rose to eminence in their own country. The three were Charles Russell, afterwards Lord Chief Justice of England, Farrer Herschell, afterwards Lord Chancellor of Great Britain, and Gully." Sir Edward Parry in "Seven Lamps of Advocacy" speaks of Lord Chief Justice Coleridge writing from the Northern Circuit; "Gully was excellent. His phrase, when he asked for a stay of execution " in order to consider more at leisure some of your lordship's observations," tickled my fancy very much. Misdirection was never more courteously described."

GUMBS, Annette Patricia
Born 16 February 1971, Manchester. Trinity C of E High School; Leeds Metropolitan University, LLB. G. 13 October 1994. ETC. 13 December 1994. Prop. Anthony Rumbelow QC. Sec. Graham Platts. Pupilmaster, Philip Grundy. Circuit Junior, 1998. 28 St John Street, Manchester, 1994. Member; Bar Council, 1998-2001; Bar Council Equal Opportunities Committee, 1997-2001.

GUNNING, Alastair John Alan Bond
Harrow. Lifeguards. MA (Oxon). L. November 1961. Originally Midland Circuit. 47 Peter Street, Manchester, 1966-1972 & 5 Essex Court. Not in 1974 Law List. Ivor Taylor told me that Gunning was appointed Crown Counsel in Bermuda.

*** GURNER, Henry Edward (His Honour Judge Gurner)**
Born 29 July 1853. Died 21 July 1915 aged 61. Eldest son of Henry Field Gurner, for 40 years Crown Solicitor for Victoria, Australia. Trinity College, Cambridge, MA. 3 Dr Johnson's Buildings. North Eastern Circuit. County Court Judge, Circuit 7, (Birkenhead, Salford, Wigan & Leigh), July 1914. WW.

GUTHRIE, Hugh Miller
Born 1863. 5th son of Charles Guthrie of Renfrews. Glasgow University. AAS. M. 20 January 1885. Call 28 January 1889. ETC. 9 March 1891. Prop. Aspland QC. Sec. Green. 5 Pump Court, 1891-1893; 3 Plowden Buildings, 1894; 3 Dr Johnson's Buildings, 1895-1901. No address, 1902-1940. Not in 1941 Law List.

GWINNER, Herman George
I. 7 July 1886. ETC. 24 January 1887. Prop. Bigham QC. Sec. Smyly. 3 Temple Gardens 1888; 2 Plowden Buildings, 1889-1894. No address, 1895-1910. Not in 1911 Law List.

*** GWYNNE-JAMES, His Honour Sir Arthur Gwynne**
Born 10 April 1855. Died 17 March 1936 aged 80. Son of J Gwynne James of Hereford, solicitor. Cheltenham College; Trinity College, Cambridge, LLB, 1878. AAS. M. 15 January 1878. Studentship 1879. Call 26 January 1881. 2 Temple Gardens. Oxford Circuit. Recorder of Hereford, 1894-1935. County Court Judge; Circuit 7, (Altrincham, Birkenhead, Leigh, Warrington & Wigan, January 1900; Circuit 52 (Glos., Somerset & Wiltshire), 1901-1935. JP. Kt. 1935. WW.

H

HACKETT, Martin John
Born 22 October 1970, Easington, Co. Durham. Benard Gilpin Comprehensive; Royal Grammar School, Newcastle; University of Wales at Aberystwyth, LLB. M. February 1995. ETC February 1995. Prop. Roger Farley QC. Sec. Nick Kennedy. 15 Winckley Square, Preston, 1996. Member of MCC.

HACKING, Gilbert
Born 1924. Only son of Frank Hacking of Bolton, farmer. Trinity Hall, Cambridge. AAS. M. 1 November 1943. Call 3 July 1946. 40 Kennedy Street, Manchester, 1947-1950. No address, 1951-1963. Not in 1964 Law List.

HAGUE, Harry
Born 9 April 1922, Blackpool. Died February 1985 aged 62. Arnold School, Blackpool; Manchester University. External LLB (London). Served in Army, 1941-1944. AAS. M. 5 June 1944. Call 18 November 1946. ETC. 1946. Manchester Chambers; 26 King Street, 1946-1961; 60 King Street, 1962-1980. Assistant Recorder, Burnley, 1969-1971. Crown Court Recorder, 1972-1979. Member, National Executive of the Liberal Party, 1956-1959 & 1962-1964. Contested; Blackburn East, 1950; Blackpool North, 1959, 1962 & 1964. WW.

HAGUE, Paul
Born 28 June 1949, Sale. Ashton on Mersey Secondary Modern. Great Universal Stores, Manchester, 1969-1982. Manchester Polytechnic, BA (Law). L. July 1983. ETC. 1983. Prop. Rhys Davies QC. Sec. David Hodson. St James's Chambers at 3 St James's Square/ 68 Quay Street, 1983-1995; 15 Winckley Square, Preston, 1996. Immigration Adjudicator, 2001.

HAHLO, Herman Barker
I. 12 May 1897. ETC. 2 February 1898. Prop. Leese QC. Sec. McKeand. 2 King's Bench Walk, 1899-1900. No address, 1901-1934. Not in 1935 Law List.

HAIGH, John
BA. L. November 1976. Manchester Chambers; 4th floor, Sunlight House, Quay Street, 1982-1985; 121 Princess Street, 1986. Later Group Corporate Lawyer, Kalon Group PLC, Batley, W. Yorks.

HAIGH, Maurice Francis
Born 6 September 1929. Repton School. Assistant cameraman in film Production, 1946-1949 working for; Leslie Lawrence Productions Ltd, London; Manchester Film Studios; Anglo Scottish Pictures Ltd at London Film Studios, Shepperton. In commerce, 1950-1952. G. June 1955. ETC. 1955. Manchester Chambers; 36 St Ann Street, 1955-1980; 27 Byrom Street, 1981-1983; 26 Cross Street, 1984-1987; Kenworthy's Buildings, 83 Bridge Street, 1988. Recorder, 1981-1996. Chairman of Tribunals, 1984-2001. WW.
Take 1. A late arrival in court.
Haigh: "Your Honour, a thousand apologies."
His Honour Judge Ralph Wood; "One will suffice."
Haigh: "Please may I have leave to withdraw the other 999?"

HAISLEY, Matthew John
Born 6 April 1976 Billinge. Bolton School; Birmingham University, LLB. L. 14 October 1999. ETC. 14 December 1999. Prop. John Rowe QC. Sec. John Parr. 8 King Street Chambers, Manchester, 1999.

HALE, Brenda Marjorie QC (The Rt Hon. The Baroness Hale of Richmond)
Born 31 January 1945. Richmond High School for Girls, Yorks.; Girton College, Cambridge, MA & Hon. Fellow, 1996. G. July 1969. ETC. 1969. Pupilmaster, John da Cunha. Manchester Chambers; 43 King Street/ 5 John Dalton Street, 1969-1972. Manchester University; Assistant Lecturer 1966; Lecturer 1968; Senior Lecturer 1976; Reader 1981; Professor, 1986-1989. Visiting Professor; Kings College London, 1990. Visiting Fellow, Nuffield College, Oxford, 1997. Law Commissioner, 1984-1993. Silk 1989. Recorder, 1989-1994. Legal Member, Mental Health Review Tribunal, 1979-1980. High Court Judge, Family Division, 1994-1999. DBE, 1994. Family Division Liason Judge for London, 1997-1999. Civil & Family Committee, Judicial Studies Board, 1990-1994. Hon LLD; Sheffield 1989; London Guildhall,1996; Manchester, 1997; Bristol, 2002. The first woman from the Northern Circuit to go to the Court of Appeal, 1999-2004. (PC 1999) and the first woman to go to the House of Lords, 2004. (Baroness 2004). Publications; include; Mental Health Law, 1976 (4th ed. 1996); Parents & Children, 1977 (4th ed. 1993); From the Test Tube to the Coffin, (Hamlyn Lecture, 1996). WW.

HALHEAD, Thomas Edmund
L. November 1960. 36 St Ann Street, Manchester, 1964-1975. No address (non practising), 1976.

HALL, Arthur Eric
4th floor, Sunlight House, Quay Street, Manchester, 1978. No chambers address, 1979-1982. Not in 1983 Bar Directory.

HALL, Edward Allecock
Born 1852. Eldest son of Isaac Hall of Manchester, solicitor. AAS. I. 22 November 1872. Call 17 November 1875. ETC. 13 March 1876. Prop. Edwards QC. Sec. Gully. 6 Crown Office Row, 1877-1886. Manchester & Salford Sessions. No address, 1887-1915. Not in 1916 Law List. Foster.

HALL, Gwynne
G. 19 November 1894. ETC. 27 July 1895. Prop. Bigham QC. Sec. Carver. 3 Pump Court, 1896-1903; 3 Tanfield Court, 1904-1912; 3 Paper Buildings, 1913. No chambers address, 1914-1949. Not in 1950 Law List.

HALL, His Honour Judge Julian
Born 13 January 1939. Eton (Scholar); Christ Church, Oxford (Scholar & MA); Trinity College, Dublin, LLB., ARCM (flute). Industrial Chemist, Shell International Chemical Co, 1961-1963. G. July 1966; Bencher 2002. ETC. 1966. 601 Royal Exchange, Manchester, 1966-1986. Standing Counsel to Inland Revenue on Northern Circuit, 1985-1986. Recorder 1982-1986. Circuit Judge, 1986. Resident Judge, Northampton, 2000-2002. Resident Judge & Honorary Recorder of Oxford, 2002. Tutor Judge, Judicial Studies Board, 1989-1993. Chairman, Mental Health Review Tribunal, 1997. WW.

HALL, Matthew (See Matthew Hall Smith)

HALL, Philip John
Born 21 March 1951, Liverpool. St Edward's College, Liverpool; King's College, London, LLB. G. November 1973. ETC. 1974. Prop. Ifor Morris Jones QC. Sec. Alan Booth. Liverpool Chambers; First & Ground Floors, Peel House, Harrington Street, 1974-1999; Chavasse Court Chambers, 24 Lord Street, 1999. Impersonator of His Honour Richard Pickering qv.

HALL, Richard Arthur
Born 21 January 1966 Carlisle. Stonyhurst College; Merton College, Oxford, MA. Trainee Chartered Accountant, 1988. L. November 1991. ETC. 25 March 1993. Prop. David Harris QC. Sec. William George. Liverpool Chambers; 20 North John Street, 1993-1998; 14 Castle Street / Atlantic Chambers, Cook Street, 1999.

HALL, Sam
Born 1863. Son of Samuel Hall of Bradford. Solicitor of Southport until AAS. M. 24 March 1905. Call 19 November 1905. ETC. 9 July 1907. Prop. Mellor KC. Sec. Roe Rycroft. 7 Kennedy Street, Manchester, 1907-1934. Equity draftsman & conveyancer. No chambers address, 1935-1953. Not in 1954 Law List.

HALL, Sir Samuel QC
Born 1841. Died 6 April 1907. Son of Samuel Hall of Leftwich, Cheshire, farmer. Trinity College, Dublin, MA. AAS. M. 25 April 1868. Call 10 June 1870; Bencher 1893; Lent Reader 1905. ETC. 4 August 1870. Prop. Higgins QC. Sec. Ambrose. 54 John Dalton Street, Manchester, 1877-1878. Equity draftsman & conveyancer. 3 Old Buildings, 1879-1882; 6 New Court, 1883-1895. Silk 1888. Attorney General, Duchy of Lancaster, 1893-1895. Vice-Chancellor, County Palatine of Lancaster, 1895-1905. Kt. 1902. WW. Foster.

HALL, Thomas James
Born 5 December 1788 Jamaica. Died 20 March 1876 aged 87. 4th son of Crossley Hall. Harrow, Trinity College, Cambridge, BA 1811; MA 1815. AAS. M. 30 April 1811. Call February 1815. Judge Advocate & Advocate General, Jamaica, 1819 and member, House of Assembly. ETC 1824. Commissioner in Bankruptcy, Liverpool. Stipendiary Magistrate, Liverpool, 1836-1839. Chief Magistrate, Bow Street, 1839-1864. Refused knighthood & baronetcy. Schofield.

HALL, William Holden
Born 21 April 1889 Royton. Died 26 September 1917 aged 28. Son of Annie Hall & of William Hall, veterinary surgeon. Hulme Grammar School, Oldham; Keble College, Oxford, BA 1911. AAS. M. 20 March 1911. Call 26 January 1914. ETC. 20 February 1914. Prop. Stewart KC. Sec. Thorpe. 37 Brown Street, Manchester, 1914-1916. Equity draftsman & conveyancer. Private, Inns of Court OTC, 7 February 1916. Commissioned 2nd Lt, D Battery, 51st Brigade, RFA, 19 April 1916. Killed in action, 26 September 1917, Belgium. Cemetery Vlamertinghe New Military Cemetery, Ieper, West Vlaanderen, Belgium. Grave Reference XI.G.14. Information from Public Records Office & Commonwealth War Graves Commission.

HALLIDAY, Harold David
Born 15 November 1948, Belfast. Trinity College, Glenalmond, Perthsire; Christ Church, Oxford, MA. G. July 1972. ETC. 1973. Sec. John Coffey. Pupilmaster, Jeremy Roberts, Temple. 2 Dr Johnson's Building, 1972-1973; Manchester Chambers; 36 St Ann Street, 1974-1980; 27 Byrom Street, 1981-1983; 460 Royal Exchange, 1984-1987; 40 King Street, 1988.

HALLIGAN, Rodney Lewton
Born 27 October 1948, Maghull. Married to Theresa Pepper qv. Waterloo Grammar School; Liverpool University, LLB. G. July 1972. ETC. 1973. Prop. Michael Maguire QC. Sec. Vincent Albert Saunders. Liverpool Chambers; Martins Building, Water Street, 1973-1999; 7 Harrington Street (merger with Corn Exchange), 6.9.1999.

HALLIWELL, Mark Gareth
Born 26 November 1960. Queen's College, Taunton, Somerset; London School Of Economics, BSc. (Econ.); Dip. Law. L. June 1985. ETC. 1987. Prop. John Hugill QC. Sec. Peter Winston Smith. Manchester Chambers; 460 Royal Exchange, September 1986- August 1987; chambers relocated to 40 King Street, August 1987. Junior Counsel to the Treasury in Charity Matters, 1992. DTI Panel for Company Disqualification Cases. Publication; Distribution on Intestacy (FT Law & Tax, 1996, now Sweet & Maxwell). Recorder 2003.

HALSALL, Edward Francis
Born 1822. Eldest son of Richard John Halsall of Joy House, Middleton, Lancs. St Cuthbert's College, Ushaw, Durham. AAS. I. 25 September 1839. Call. 20 November 1846. 18 Devereux Court, 1846; 3 Middle Temple Lane, 1876-1883. No address 1884. Not in 1885 Law List.

HAMILTON, His Honour Allister McNicholl
Born 23 January 1895. Died 8 February 1973 aged 78. Father of His Honour Judge Donald Hamilton, Designated Family Judge, Birmingham. Liverpool University, LLB. Served War, 1914-1918 as officer with Infantry & Trench Mortar Battery (wounded). G. 2 July 1919. ETC. 15 June 1921. Prop. Greaves-Lord QC. Sec. Procter. Liverpool Chambers; 25 Lord Street, 1922-1924; 13 Harrington Street, 1925-1942; 27 Lord Street, 1942-1945; 49 Castle Street, 1946-1947. County Court Judge, Circuit 23, (Coventry, Northampton), 1947-1966.

HAMILTON, Archibald Henry
Born 22 December 1847. Eldest son of James Hamilton of Ballymacoll, Co. Meath. Christ College, Cambridge, LLB 1874. AAS. I. 24 April 1869. Call 26 January 1876. ETC. 27 January 1881. Prop. Hopwood QC. Sec. Leresche. 8 St James's Square, Manchester, 1881-1895. No address, 1896-1900. Not in 1901 Law List. Nominated Puisne Judge, Gold Coast Colony, July 1883. Foster.

HAMILTON, Elaine Vera
M. June 1950. ETC 1950. 60 King Street, Manchester, 1953-1958. No address, 1959-1963. Not in 1964 Law List.

HAMILTON, George Cecil Hans
Born 1888. 2nd son of His Honour Henry Best Hans Hamilton qv of Chorley., Lancs., County Court Judge. King's College, Cambridge, LLB., BA. AAS. M. 9 January 1907. Call 8 June 1910. ETC. 7 July 1910. Prop. Tobin KC. Sec. Cavanagh. Circuit Junior, Winter 1911. Bank of England Chambers, Tib Lane, Manchester, 1910-1921. 3 Paper Buildings, 1910-1914; 2 Dr Johnson's Building, 1915-1921. No address, 1922-1953. Not in 1954 List.

HAMILTON, His Honour Henry Best Hans
Born 14 October 1850. Died 5 August 1935 aged 84. Father of George Cecil Hans Hamilton qv. Second son of Venerable George Hans Hamilton, Archdeacon of Northumberland. Durham School. AAS. I. 12 November 1872. Call 30 April 1873. Admitted M. 30 October 1890. Elected to Old Northern Circuit 11 July 1873. Prop Herschell QC. Sec. Bruce. Joined North Eastern Circuit in 1876. Practising from 1 Brick Court and Palace Chambers, 9 Bridge Street, Westminster. Parliamentary draftsman & committees. Recorder of Berwick on Tweed, 1899-1905. County Court Judge, Circuit 4, (North Lancashire), 1905-1913. Distinguished military career which included Commanding the guard on the Manchester Ship Canal and of the Guard of prisoners of war at Queensferry during the First World War. He was also Commandant of "J" area, Somme, 1917 and Town Major, Meaulte, Somme. (despatches). WW. Foster.

HAMILTON, His Honour Judge Hugh Montgomerie
Born 26 June 1854 Parramatta, New South Wales. Died 11 August 1930 Strathfield, N.S.W aged 76. Eldest son of Hugh Hamilton, a sheep farmer, who emigrated to Australia from Ayrshire. Marlborough College, 1868-1872; Universities of London & Heidelberg. AAS. I. 22 May 1975. Call 15 May 1878. ETC. 15 July 1878. Prop. Gully QC. Sec. McConnell. 7 King's Bench Walk, 1878-1881; 10 KBW, 1882-1883; 3 Harcourt Buildings, 1884; 2 Harcourt Buildings, 1885-1889.
He returned to New South Wales in 1889 and joined the local bar. On the 15 May 1914 he was appointed a District Court Judge and Chairman of Quarter Sessions, serving in the Northern District of New South Wales to 1918 and thereafter in the Southern & Hunter Districts

until retirement in 1922.
He was a remarkable sportsman. He played rugby for Scotland in 1874 and 1875 and was an excellent golfer being a founder of the (now Royal) Sydney Golf Club. As far as I know he is the only Northern Circuiteer to have a mountain named after him. Mount Hamilton is 3023 metres high in the Malte Brun Range of New Zealand's Southern Alps. He received this honour to mark his outstanding mountaineering skills. He was a lifelong Freemason, joining the Northern Bar Lodge in 1883 and becoming Grand Master of the United Grand Lodge of New South Wales in 1909. I am grateful to Richard Heap for giving me much of this information. NB. The final year of entry in the Law List does not always indicate retirement or death. This is another example of a person appearing in the Law Lists for a number of years after he died. He died in 1930 but continued to appear in the book until 1935.

*** HAMILTON, His Honour Judge Iain McCormick**
Born 11 November 1948 Penrith. Heversham Grammar School; Manchester Poytechnic, BA. Admitted as a solicitor, 14 June 1974. Walls, Johnston & Co, Solicitors, Stockport, 1971-1994 (articled clerk to partner); Jones Maidment Wilson, Solicitors, Manchester, 1994-2000 (salaried partner). President Stockport Law Society, 1990-1991. Assistant Recorder, 1992-1996. Recorder, 1996-2000. Circuit Judge, 19 June 2000. Chairman, Child Concern, 1992-1993 & 1996-1999. WW.

HAMILTON, Jaime Richard
LLB (Wales). G. October 1993. ETC. October 1993. ETC. 23 March 1994. Pupilmaster, Michael Murray. Circuit Junior, Winter 1997. 9 St John Street, Manchester, 1994.

HAMILTON, James Winterbottom QC
Born 8 December 1849 Oldham. Died 18 October 1899 aged 49. London University, LLB. AAS. I. 16 November 1870. Call 7 June 1873. ETC. 4 August 1873. Prop. Holker QC. Sec. Baylis. Manchester Chambers; 4 St James's Square, 1876-1885 & 1894-1895; 48 King Street, 1886-1893. Silk 1895. Recorder of Oldham, 1887-1899. 1 Dr Johnson Buildings, 1895-1899. WW. Foster.

HAMILTON, John Andrew QC (First Viscount Sumner of Ibstone)
Born 3 February 1859 Manchester. Died 24 May 1934 aged 75. Son of Andrew Hamilton of Manchester, iron merchant. Manchester Grammar School; Balliol College, Oxford, (Scholar) Fellow of Magdalen College, 1882-1889; Hon Fellow 1909. AAS. I. 6 November 1880. Call 17 November 1883; Bencher 1909; Treasurer 1930. ETC. 26 January 1864. Prop. Gully QC. Sec. Bigham. Goldsmith Building, 1884-1909. Silk 1901. High Court Judge, King's Bench Division, 1909-1912. Lord Justice of Appeal, 1912-1913. Lord of Appeal in Ordinary, 1913-1930. Kt 1909. PC 1912. Baron 1913. GCB 1920. Viscount 1927. Hon LLD; Edinburgh, Manchester & Cambridge. Hon DCL Oxford. He was one of the most voluminous contributors to the Dictionary of National Biography, his name appearing in 58 of the original 65 volumes. Lord Justice MacKinnon who wrote Hamilton's DNB entry believed Hamilton to be one of the greatest judges of his time. He says "in the three and a half years in the King's Bench Division, he never once reserved judgment; but what he said at the conclusion of every case, whether complicated or difficult, when taken down in shorthand was better than the laboured writings of other judges, while it scintillated with phrases that none of them could rival by the consumption of midnight oil." WW. DNB. Obituary Times, 26 May 1934.

HAMILTON, Patrick Swinglehurst
L. 17 November 1911. ETC. 3 July 1912. Prop. Sanderson KC. Sec. Rankin. No chambers address, 1912-1953. Not in 1954 Law List.

HAMILTON, His Honour Richard Graham
Born 26 August 1932. Charterhouse; University College, Oxford, MA. AAS. M. 5 October 1953. Call 27 November 1956. ETC 1957. Circuit Junior, 1961. Pupilmasters, Roger Fray Ormrod (Temple) and Frank Nance. Same Liverpool Chambers at; 606 The Corn Exchange, 1966-1982; Exchange Chambers, 1 Exchange Flags, 1982-1986. Head of Chambers. Chancellor of the Diocese of Liverpool, 1976-2002. Recorder, 1974-1986. Circuit Judge at Liverpool, 1986-1997. After retirement he enrolled at Liverpool John Moores University and achieved an MA in Screenwriting in 1999. He has broadcasted regularly on Radio Merseyside and produced at Liverpool "The Maybrick Case" in 1989 and "The Veronica Mutiny" in 1990. Publications; "Foul Bills & Dagger Money" (800 years of Lawyers & Lawbreakers), 1979 and "All Jangle & Riot" (A Barrister's History of The Bar), 1986; "A Good Wigging," 1988-illustrated by Hugh Dodd. Retirement Tributes at Liverpool Law Courts, 19 December 1997 (Judge David Clarke QC/ William Waldron QC). Transcript in Circuit Records. WW.

HAMILTON-HAGUE, Rachael Elizabeth
Born 7 September 1969 Odense, Denmark. King David School, Liverpool; Liverpool College; Keele University, BA (Law & American Studies). G. October 1993. ETC. 21 December 1993. Prop. David Steer QC. Sec. Neil Flewitt. Corn Exchange, Fenwick Street, Liverpool, 1993-1998; 8 King Street Chambers, Manchester, 1998.

HAMLYN, Clarence Adolphus
Born 1862. 3rd son of Lesoufe Hamlyn of Richmond, Surrey. Edinburgh University. AAS. M. 24 January 1884. Call 4 May 1887. ETC. 7 March 1889. Prop. Gully QC. Sec. Parry. 3 Essex Court, 1890-1893; 4 Essex Court, 1894-1897. Rangoon, Burma, 1898-1928. Private London Address, 1929-1949. Not in 1950 Law List.

HAMMOND, (James) Anthony (His Honour Judge Hammond)

(RB)

Born 25 July 1936. Wigan Grammar School; St Catherine's College, Oxford, MA. L. April 1959. National Service, 1959-1961. Pupilmaster, Robert Lambert. Manchester Chambers; 9 Albert Square, 1961-1972; Dean's Court, Crown Square, 1973-1986. Recorder, 1980-1986. Circuit Judge, Manchester, 1986. Local Councillor, 1962-1972. WW.

HAMMOND, Reginald Francis
I. 22 June 1898. ETC. 3 August 1898. Prop. Taylor QC. Sec. Mellor. 3 Elm Court, 1899. No address, 1900-1949. Not in 1950 Law List.

HAMOND, Sir Charles Fred MP
Born 1817 Newcastle upon Tyne. Eldest son of Fred George Hamond of Surrey. Merchant & JP when AAS. M. 26 May 1862. Call 1 May 1865. 58 Grey Street, Newcastle upon Tyne, 1877-1897. No address, 1898-1905. Not in 1906 Law List.

HAMPSON, Robert Hamer
Born 1872. 3rd son of John Hampson of Summerseat, Lancs. Trinity Hall, Cambridge. AAS. M. 8 November 1893. Call 17 June 1896. ETC. 19 February 1898. Prop. Carver QC. Sec. Crawford. 4 Essex Court, 1899-1907; Lamb Building, 1908-1923. Not in 1924 Law List.

HAMWEE, David
I. 17 November 1932. ETC. 15 March 1933. Prop. Gorman QC. Sec. Arthur Jalland. Manchester Chambers; 2 Booth Street, 1933-1935; 40 Kennedy Street, 1936-1948. No address, 1949-1963. According to Denise Chorlton, he went to the Far East. Not in 1964 Law List.

HANCE, Edward Walker Brandard Malkin
Born 20 May 1844. 3rd son of John William Hance of Liverpool, architect. London University, LLB, 1870. Clerk to the Liverpool School Board, 1871. AAS. M. 29 January 1868. Call 17 November 1870. ETC. 15 August 1871. Prop. Higgin QC. Sec. Bremner. No address, 1876-1893. Municipal Offices, Liverpool, 1894-1908. No address, 1909-1917. Not in 1918 Law List.

HANCOCK, Henry Hilton
L. 29 June 1927. ETC. 6 July 1927. Prop. Wingate-Saul KC. Sec. Blackledge. No address, 1927-1933. 2 Dr. Johnson's Building, 1934; 1 King's Bench Walk, 1937-1938. No address, 1939-1953. Not in 1954 Law List.

HAND, John Lester QC
Born 16 July 1947, Huddersfield. Huddersfield New College; Nottingham University, LLB. Lecturer in Law, Manchester Polytechnic, 1970-1972. G. July 1972; Bencher 1996. ETC. 2 November 1972. Prop. E S Temple QC. Sec. Jack Price. Manchester Chambers; 60 King Street, 1972-1984; 1 Deans Court, Crown Square, 1984-1993; 9 St John Street, 1993. Head of Chambers. Silk 1988. Assistant Recorder 1988. Recorder 1991. Legal Assessor since 1990; General Medical Council; General Dental Council. Part time Judge, Employment Appeal Tribunal, 2002. Publication; Editor, UK & EU Employee Consultation- Sweet & Maxwell. WW.

HARDING, Harry Harcourt
G. 24 June 1903. ETC 22 February 1904. Prop. Tobin KC. Sec. Greer. 8 Cook Street, Liverpool, 1908-1924. 6 Pump Court, 1925-1933. Associate, Northern Circuit. Not in 1934 Law List.

HARDING, Jonathan Patrick
I. July 1975. Manchester Chambers; 60 King Street, 1977-1983; Crown Square Chambers, 1984-1993; 9 St John Street, 1994-1995. Not in 1996 Bar Directory.

HARDY, Oswald Henry

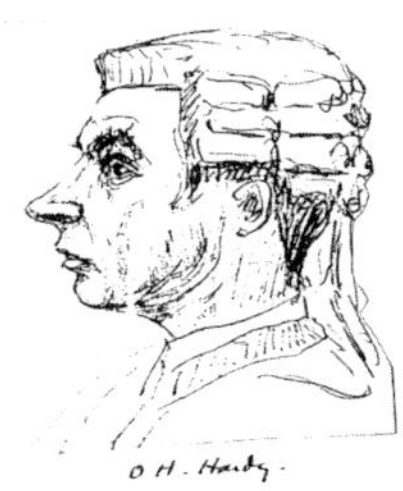

Born 28 May 1853. Died 31 March 1940 aged 86. 2nd son of George Hardy, Chief Clerk to the Secretary of the Post Office. Highgate School; Queen's College, Oxford, MA., BCL 1870. AAS. L. 14 January 1876. Call 26

January 1880. ETC. 12 July 1880. Prop. Russell QC. Sec. Crompton. 6 Crown Office Row, 1881-1882. Liverpool Chambers; Commerce Chambers, Lord Street, 1883-1885; 13 Harrington Street, 1886-1889; Bristowe Chambers, 8 Harrington Street, 1890-1894. Counsel to the Post Office, 1887-1894. District Registrar, Manchester, 1895-1899. Registrar of Probate & Divorce Court, Somerset House, 1906-1915. District Probate Registrar, Exeter 1916-1931. No address, 1932-1940. Publication; Joint Author of the Law Affecting the Contract of Affreightment. WW. Foster.

HARDY, His Honour Robert James

(HS)

Born 12 July 1924. Mostyn House School; Wrekin College; University College, London, LLB. Served, 1942-1946, Royal Navy, Fleet Air Arm Pilot. G. June 1950. ETC 1950. 3 St James Square, 1950-1979. Recorder 1972-1979. Circuit Judge, Manchester, 1979-1994. WW.

HARDY, William

Born 1849. 2nd son of John Pimperly Hardy of Dunham Massey, Cheshire, Land Agent. AAS. M. 5 May 1870. Call 27 January 1873. ETC. 19 March 1873. Prop. Holker QC. Sec. Charley. 27 King Street, Wigan, 1879-1882. 5 St James's Square, 1883-1894. No address, 1895-1935. Not in 1936 Law List.

HARGREAVES, Arthur Shepherd
I. 17 November 1886. ETC. 4 February 1888. Prop. Henn Collins QC. Sec. J W Hamilton. Circuit Junior, Summer 1888. 3 Pump Court, 1888; 9 King's Bench Walk, 1889-1896. No address, 1897-1928. Not in 1929 Law List.

HARGREAVES, His Honour Sir Gerald De La Pryne
Born 1881. Died 29 April 1972. Son of Thomas Hargreaves of Birkdale. Eton; Magdalen College, Oxford, BA 1903. I. 5 July 1905. ETC. 3 February 1906. Prop. Ferguson KC. Sec. Openshaw. Circuit Junior, Summer 1906. Bedfordshire Yeomanry, 1914-1917. Court-Martial Officer, Xth Army Corps, 1917-1918 (Despatches & Belgian Croix de Guerre). 4 Elm Court, 1906-1914 & 1918-1922. County Court Judge, March 1922-1955; Circuit 18 (Nottingham & West Riding of Yorkshire). 1922-1923; Circuit 48 (Middlesex & Sussex), 1923-1928; Circuit 37 (West London), 1928-1955. Kt. 1944. Home Guard, 1942-1945. Chairman, London Tribunal for Conscientious Objectors, 1939-1945. Publication; Deeds of Arrangement. WW.

HARGREAVES, Herbert Frank
I. 27 January 1902. ETC. 20 February 1902. Prop. Shee KC. Sec. Mellor. 5 Paper Buildings, 1904-1906. No address, 1907-1953. Not in 1954 Law List.

HARGREAVES, Walter Yeates
Born 5 July 1856. 3rd son of Charles Hargreaves of Ridgmont, Lancs. Trinity Hall, Cambridge, BA. AAS. I. 9 April 1879. Call 3 May 1882. ETC. 24 July 1883. Prop. Crompton QC. Sec. Lowther. 1 Temple Gardens, 1883-1893. No address, 1894-1940. Not in 1941 Law List. Foster.

HARLAND, William Dugdale
Born 16 December 1846. Youngest son of Thomas Harland of Manchester, MD. Owens College, Manchester. AAS. I. 9 November 1878. Call 29 June 1881. ETC. 23 January 1882. Prop. West QC. Sec. Sington. Manchester Chambers; 18 South King Street, 1885-1908; 48 King Street, 1909-1925. Not in 1926 Law List.

HARLOW, Irma Sylvia
BA., Dip Ed (Leeds). L. November 1971. Manchester Chambers; 2 Booth Street, 1975; 13 Police Street, 1976-1979. 6th floor, Arkwright House, Parsonage Gardens, 1980-1986; 20 St Mary's Parsonage, 1987-1991.

HARLOW, Stephen Donald
L. July 1977. ETC. 26 October 1978. Manchester Chambers; 13 Police Street, 1979; 6th floor, Arkwright House, Parsonage Gardens, 1980-1986. No address, 1987-1988. Not in 1989 Bar Directory.

HARPER, Catherine Mary Elizabeth
Born 19 February 1960 Preston. Married to Ian Haselhurst qv. Notre Dame, Woolton, Liverpool; University of Hull, LLB. I. July 1982. ETC. 1982. Prop. David Marshall Evans QC. Sec. Inge Bernstein. Same Liverpool Chambers at 54 Castle Street, 1982-1986; 14 Castle Street 1986-1990.

HARPER, Mark Eliot George
Born 16 May 1970 Nottingham. Arnold Hill Comprehensive School; Downing College, Cambridge, BA (Law). L. October 1993. ETC. 7 December 1993. Prop. Peter Winston Smith. Sec. M J Booth. King's Chambers, 40 King Street, Manchester, 1993.

HARRINGTON, Joseph Miller
Born 1840. Youngest son of James Harrington of Carlisle, calico printer. AAS. 7 February 1863. Call 26 January 1866. Cumberland & Westmorland Sessions but no chambers address, 1876-1919. Not in 1920 Law List.

HARRIS, David Michael QC (His Honour Judge Harris QC)
Born 7 February 1943. Liverpool Institute for Boys; Lincoln College, Oxford, BA 1964: MA 1967; Trinity Hall, Cambridge, PhD, 1969. Assistant Lecturer in Law, Manchester University, 1967-1969. AAS. M. 10 May 1962. Call 25 November 1969; Bencher 1997. ETC. 1969. Pupilmaster, Henry Lachs. Same Liverpool Chambers at; 27 Dale Street, 1969-1976; Melbourne Buildings, 1977-1988; 3rd floor, Peel House, Harrington Street, 1989-1997; India Buildings, Water Street, 1998-2001.(Head). Assistant Recorder 1984. Recorder 1988. Silk 1989. Deputy High Court Judge, 1993. Circuit Judge at Liverpool, March 2001. Liason Judge, Liverpool John Moores University 2005-. Publications; Winfield on Tort, 9th edition, 1971; Supplement to Bingham's Modern Cases on Negligence, 3rd edition, 1985.

HARRIS, Ian Robert
Born 28 August 1954. Admitted as a solicitor November 1979. I. November 1990. Liverpool Chambers; 2nd floor, Peel House, Harrington Street, 1990-1994; 25-27 Castle Street, 1995-2001; Exchange Chambers, Derby Square, 2002.

HARRIS, Rev. Seymour Frederick
Born 18 April 1851. 2nd son of Rev. James Harris, Wesleyan Minister. Worcester College, Oxford, MA., BCL, 1875. AAS. I. 15 November 1872. Call 7 June 1875. ETC. 27 March 1876. Prop. Temple QC. Sec. Little. No chambers address, 1876-1920. Liverpool, Kirkdale & Preston Sessions. Vicar of St Michael & All Hallows, Blackburn, 1884. Publications; Elements of Roman Law; Principles of Criminal Law. Foster.

HARRISON, Sir Archibald Frederick CBE
Born 1894. Died 18 November 1976. Appleby, Westmorland; Queen's College, Oxford. Served War, 1914-1918 in Border Regiment, NW Frontier, India. I. 17 November 1919. Assistant Solicitor rising to the Solicitor to the Ministry of Labour & National Service, 1939-1959. CBE. 1947. Kt. 1955.

HARRISON, Harrop William Abel
L. 30 April 1890. ETC. 16 March 1892. Prop. Bigham QC. Sec. Walton. 1 Brick Court, 1892-1907; 4 Harcourt Buildings, 1908-1921. Not in 1922 Law List.

HARRISON, His Honour James Fraser

Born 7 May 1890. Died 16 January 1971 aged 81. Liverpool College; Sedbergh; Liverpool University, LLM. I. 19 June 1912. ETC. 4 July 1912. Prop. Tobin KC. Sec. Millar. Army, 1914-1918. Liverpool Chambers; 5 Harrington Street, 1913-1914 & 1918-1922; 25 Lord Street, 1923-1927; 15 Union Court, Cook Street, 1928-1933; 3 Cook Street, 1934-1940. Assistant Recorder of Liverpool, 1929-1940. Deputy Chairman, Preston, Manchester & Liverpool County Quarter Sessions, 1938-1940. County Court Judge, Liverpool, 1940-1962. Commissioner of Assize, Northern Circuit, 1946. WW.

HARRISON, (John) Keith
Born 16 May 1960, Hexham. Queen Elizabeth Grammar School, Hexham; Newcastle University, LLB. L. November 1983. ETC. December 1983. Prop. Keith Goddard QC. Sec. Beverly Lunt. Pupilmasters; Ivan Krolick & Justin Phillips (Temple); John Ward. Manchester Chambers; 6th floor, Arkwright House, 1983-1986; 20 St Mary's Parsonage, 1987-1989; 3 Peter Street, 1990-1991; 211 Deansgate, 1992-1993; 38 King Street West, 1994-1995; 24a St John Street, 1996. (now St Johns Buildings).

HARRISON, Leona Melanie
Born 3 August 1968 London. Married to Toby Sasse qv. Leeds Girls High School; Manchester University, BA (Law & Accountancy). M. 14 October 1993. ETC. 21

December 1993. Prop. Robert Fordham QC. Sec. Graham Morris. Liverpool Chambers; Martins Bank, Water Street, 1993-1995; India Buildings, Water Street, 1996.

HARRISON, Peter John
Born 10 December 1960, Manchester. Rydal School, Colwyn Bay; Liverpool University, LLB. AAS. M. 3 February 1982. Call 28 July 1983. Manchester Chambers; 3 St James's Square, 1984-1989; 38 King Street West, 1990-1996; 24a St John Street 1996. (now St Johns Buildings).

HARRISON, Reginald
I. 17 November 1891. ETC. 5 April 1892. Prop. Bigham QC. Sec. McConnell. 2 Garden Court, 1893-1895. Liverpool Chambers; 25 Lord Street, 1896-1902; 8 Cook Street, 1903. Clerk of Indictments, Preston, 1904-1911. 22 Old Bank Buildings, Chester, 1912-1924. North Wales & Chester Circuit. No address, 1925-1933. 4 Pump Court, 1934-1940. No address, 1941-1949. Not in 1950 Law List.

HARRISON,Sally
Born 4 November 1968, Cheshire. Married to Richard Norton qv. Daughter of District Judge George Harrison. Howell's School, Denbigh; Reading University (BSc Pathobiology) Dip. Law (City University). G. October 1992. ETC 1992. Prop. John Hoggett QC. Sec. Roger Farley. Manchester Chambers; 40 King Street, 1992-1999; 28 St John Street 1999. (now St Johns Building).

HARRISON, Sarah Louise
L. November 1989. Manchester Chambers; 72 Bridge Street, 1992-1997; Cobden House Chambers, 19 Quay Street, 1998.

HARRISON, Susan Kathryn
Born 26 November 1970 Blackburn. Married to Ian Ponter qv. Cheadle Hulme School, Stockport; Bristol University, LLB. M. 14 October 1993. ETC. 7 December 1993. Prop. Jonathan Foster QC. Sec.Andrew Blake. 18 St John Street, Manchester, 1993.

HART, His Honour (Frank) Donald QC
Born 6 January 1933. Married to Joan Turton (Member of Mental Health Review Tribunal). Altrincham Grammar School; Magdalen College, Oxford, MA. G. June 1956 (Macaskie Scholar; Arden & Atkin Prize; Lee Essay Prize). ETC. 1956. Prop. Fenton Atkinson QC. Sec. Hugh Mais. Manchester Chambers; 43 King Street, 1956-1973; 4th floor, Astley House, Quay Street, 1974-1977; chambers relocated to 18 St John Street, 1978-1989. Recorder 1978-1989. President, Mental Health Review Tribunal (Restricted Patients), 1983-2000. Circuit Judge, 1989-1998. Designated Family Judge, Merseyside, 1992-1998. Retirement Tributes at Liverpool Law Courts on 30 June 1998. (Judge David Clarke QC/ Jonathan Foster QC). Transcript in Circuit Records. WW.

HART, Joseph William
Born 5 February 1977, Blackburn. Queen Elizabeth's Grammar School; Corpus Christi College, Oxford, MA. I. 2000. ETC. 2000. Prop. Keith Goddard QC. Sec. Russell Davies. Dean's Court Chambers, Manchester, 2000.

HART, Paul
Born 10 May 1959, Warrington. Boteler Grammar School, Warrington; Newcastle University, LLB. G. July 1982. ETC. 1982. Prop. Michael Kershaw QC. Sec. T S Whittingham. Manchester Chambers; 3 St James's Square, 1982-1984; relocated to St James's Chambers, 68 Quay Street, 1985-1992; 15 Winckley Square, Preston, 1992.

HARTLEY, Arthur Addleshaw
Born 1857. Only son of Richard Hartley of Barnsley. Trinity Hall, Cambridge, BA. AAS. I. 17 November 1877. Call 11 May 1881. ETC. 25 January 1883. Prop. Higgins QC. Sec. Blair. Dalton Chambers, John Dalton Street, Manchester, 1884-1896. No address, 1897-1940. Not in 1941 Law List. Foster.

HARTLEY, Edwin Leach
I. 30 April 1890. ETC. 13 July 1898. Prop. Russell QC. Sec. Mellor. No address, 1890-1898. 1 Essex Court, 1899-1900; 4 Paper Buildings, 1901-1902; 1 Paper Buildings, 1903-1936. No address, 1937-1949. Not in 1950 Law List.

HARTLEY, Henry
I. 17 November 1936. ETC. 24 February 1937. Prop. Gorman KC. Sec. Gerrard. 78 King Street, Manchester, 1938-1947. Not in 1949 Law List.

HARTLEY, Ivor
G. July 1952. 243 Brazennose Street, Manchester, 1956-1958. No address, 1959-1963. Not in 1964 Law List.

HARTLEY, James Walker
Born 16 November 1852. Eldest son of John Bernard Hartley of Dumbarton. Trinity College, Cambridge, MA. AAS. I. 30 April 1872. Call 27 January 1879. ETC. 31 July 1879. Prop. Temple QC. Sec. Shand. Library Chambers, Middle Temple Lane, 1879; 5 King's Bench Walk, 1880-1881; 6 Pump Court, 1882-1886. No address, 1888-1935. Not in 1936 Law List.

HARTLEY, Richard Anthony
Born 7 November 1962 Crewe. Sandbach School; Liverpool University, LLB. AAS. M. 13 January 1984, Call 25 July 1985. ETC. 1985. Prop. Keith Goddard QC, Sec. John Ward. Manchester Chambers; 20 St Mary's Parsonage, 1985-1989; Hollins Chambers, 64a Bridge Street, 1989-1998 relocating to Cobden House Chambers, Quay Street, 1999. Recorder 2002.

HAWORTH, Kate Jessica
BA (Liverpool). M.St. (Oxon). Dip. Law (College of Law, Chester). M. October 1999. ETC. 16 December 1999. Prop. Nigel Gilmour QC. Sec. Peter Goodbody. Oriel Chambers, 14 Water Street, Liverpool, 1999-2001. Left Liverpool Bar to become Assistant Parliamentary Counsel at 36 Whitehall, SW1.

HAWORTH, Richard Anthony
Born 3 September 1955, Manchester. Oundle School; Leeds University LLB. I. November 1978. ETC. 1979. Prop. Patrick Russell QC. Sec. K S Thomas. Manchester Chambers; 36 St Ann Street, 1978-1980; 27 Byrom Street, 1981; 15 Winckley Square, Preston, 1981.

HAYCOCK, Alexander Wilkinson Frederick MP
Born 1882, Cataraqui, Ontario, Canada. Died 15 December 1970. Cataraqui School; Kingston Collegiate Institute; Queen's University. Organising Secretary, Norman Angell League; Foreign Policy Committee before the War; Ex President, Manchester & Salford Independent Labour Party Federation. Contested Winchester 1922. MP (Lab) West Salford, 1923-1924 & 1929-1931. G. June 1939. ETC. 19 July 1939. Prop. Gorman KC. Sec. Jalland. 1b Cooper Street, Manchester, 1942-1952. WW.

HAYDEN, Anthony Paul QC
Born 24 June 1961, Salford. De La Salle College; Cardinal Langley Grammar School; Manchester University, BA., Dip. Law (City University, London). AAS. M. 1 November 1983. Call 24 November 1987. ETC. 1987. Prop. John Burke QC. Sec. J D S Wishart. Manchester Chambers; Conavon Court Chambers, 12 Blackfriars Street, 1987-1989; Manchester House Chambers, 18-22 Bridge Street, 1990-1995; 28 St John Street, 1995. (now St Johns Buildings). Recorder 2000. Silk 2002. WW.

HAYES, Lomond Anne
G. November 1970. 2 Booth Street, Manchester, 1973-1974. Not in 1975 Law List.

HAYGARTH, Edmund Bruce
Born 1 April 1965 Oundle, Northants. Married to Janet Reaney qv. Seltus Grammar School, Bermuda, 1969-1978; Liverpool College, 1979-1983; University College, London, LLB. Rice Lane Community Association, 1986-1987. G. November 1988. ETC. 1988. Pupilmaster, Michael Henshell. Same Liverpool Chambers; 2nd floor, Peel House, Harrington Street, 1988-1995; 25-27 Castle Street, 1995.

HAYHOE, Justin Oliver
Born 26 February 1972 Bury. Bury C of E High School; De Monfort University, BA. G. 13 October 1994. CPS, Manchester, April 1995-April 1996. ETC. December 1996. Seconder John Marsh. Manchester Chambers; Parsonage Chambers, 3 The Parsonage, July 1996-October 2000; Queen's Chambers, 5 John Dalton Street, November 2000.

HAYMAN, Perceval Mills Cobham
Born 31 October 1883. Died 9 January 1974 aged 90. Eastbourne School. I. 27 January 1913. ETC. 15 June 1913. Prop. Swift QC. Sec. Kennedy. 13 Harrington Street, Liverpool, 1913-1914. Served European War, 1914-1919; with East Lancs Regt. (wounded 1918); District Courts Martial Officer, 1919 (Captain). Admitted as a solicitor, 1919. Registrar of County Courts, 1932-1956. Re admitted I. Hon. Member of Oxford Circuit. Home Guard, 1940-1944. Deputy Chairman, Gloucester Quarter Sessions, 1947-1958. Scout Medal of Merit & Hon. Commissioner, 1939. Coronation Medal, 1953. Publication; Some Elementary Notes on Military Law & Procedure (4 editions, 1941). WW.

HAYTON, Michael Pearson
Born 3 November 1970, Preston. Brother of Virginia Hayton (Wales & Chester Circuit). Queen Elizabeth's Grammar School, Blackburn; St Anne's College, Oxford, MA (Jurisprudence). Inns of Court, School of Law (Sir Thomas More Scholar; Sir Louis Gluckstein Prize for Advocacy). L. 14 October 1993. ETC. 16 December 1993. Prop. Roger Farley QC. Sec. K S Thomas. Manchester Chambers; Queen's Chambers, 5 John Dalton Street, 1993-1998; Dean's Court Chambers, 24 St John Street, Manchester, 1998.

HAYWARD, Philip George
BA (Oxon). G. January 1949. Liverpool Chambers; 47-49 Castle Street, 1949-1960; 606 The Corn Exchange, 1967-1975. Chairman, Industrial Tribunals, Liverpool, 1975. Not in 1989 Bar Directory.

HAZELWOOD, Maurice Charles
BSc. G. February 1952. ETC. 7 February 1952. Prop. Brabin QC. Sec. Richard Bingham. 14 Cook Street, Liverpool 1952-1958. Left the Bar in 1959 and went to Shell International Chemical Co. in London. 2 Temple Gardens, 1981-1985. No address, 1983-1990. Not in 1991 Bar Directory.

HEADLAM, Francis John
Born 9 June 1829. Died 29 March 1908 aged 78. Eton; University College, Oxford; MA, 1852; Fellow, 1854; Bursar, 1863-1871. Assistant Master, Westminster School, 1855-1856. AAS. I. 4 February 1855. Call 17 November 1858. ETC 1858. Durham & Northumberland Sessions. Stipendiary Magistrate for Manchester, 30 April 1869-1908. WW. Foster.

HEALD, Rt. Hon. Sir Lionel Frederick QC., MP.
Born 7 August 1897. Died 7 November 1981 aged 84. Second son of James Heald, solicitor of Parrs Wood, Lancs. Charterhouse. Served Royal Engineers, 1915-1919 (Italian Bronze Medal). RAFVR, 1939-1945 (Air Commodore). Christ Church, Oxford, BA, 1920. AAS. M. 3 November 1921. Call 19 November 1923; Bencher 1946; Reader Lent 1958; Master Emeritus, April 1976. ETC. 28 January 1925, Prop. Singleton KC. Sec. Stewart Brown. 1 Essex Court, 1924-1927 & 1941-1945; 3 Elm Court, 1928-1940; 3 Essex Court, 1946-1957; Queen Elizabeth Building, 1958-1975. Junior Counsel to the Board of Trade in technical matters. Silk 1937. Contested (Nat. C) SW St Pancras Division 1945. MP (C) Chertsey, 1950-1970. Attorney General, 1951-1954. Kt. 1951. PC 1954. WW.

HEALING, Yvonne Mary
Born 19 December 1959, Whiston. Prescot Girls Grammar School; Liverpool University, LLB. Laboratory Assistant, C C Spice (UK) Ltd., 1976-1977. I. May 1987. ETC. 1987. Prop. David Poole QC. Sec. Stephen Redmond. Manchester Chambers; 6th floor, Sunlight House, Quay Street, 1987-1994; 38 Young Street, 1995-1998; 18 St John Street, 1998.

HEAP, Ralph
Born 1841. Only son of Ralph Heap of Southport. Wadham College, Oxford. AAS. M. 10 November 1863. Call 6 June 1866. ETC. 3 August 1868. Prop. Russell QC. Sec. Bruce, G. No address, 1876-1886. 1 Brick Court, 1887-1901. Not in 1902 Law List. Foster.

HEAP, (Walter) Richard (Cartwright)
Born 30 March 1940, Littleborough. Stowe; Manchester University, LLB. I. 26 November 1963. ETC. 2 days later. Prop. Cantley QC. Sec. Desmond Bailey. Manchester Chambers; 26 King Street, 1963-1965; 36 St Ann Street, 1966-1980; 27 Byrom Street, 1981-1983; 26 Cross Street, 1984-1987; Kenworthy's Buildings, 83 Bridge Street, 1988. Assistant Recorder, 1978-1990.

HEAPE, Herbert
I. 17 November 1886. ETC. 24 January 1887. Prop. Gully QC. Sec. Leese. Circuit Junior, Summer 1887. 60 King Street, Manchester, 1889-1902. No address, 1903-1940. Not in 1941 Law List.

HEATH, Arthur Raymond MP
Born 1855. Died 8 June 1943. Son of Admiral Leopold George Heath. Marlborough; Trinity College, Cambridge, LLB 1877. AAS. I. 6 November 1874. Call 7 May 1879. ETC. 19 July 1879. Prop. Russell QC. Sec. Gully QC. 6 Pump Court, 1880-1889. No address, 1890-1935. Not in 1936 Law List. MP (C) Lincolnshire, Louth Division, 1886-1892. JP. WW. Foster.

HEATHCOTE, John Moyer Jnr.
Born 12 July 1834 London. Died 5 October 1912 aged 78. Eton; Trinity College, Cambridge. AAS. L. 27 March 1856. Call 17 November 1859. No chambers address. His claim to fame is that in about 1869 he was regarded as the equal of any tennis player in the world. It was he who first suggested and tried the experiment of covering the ball with flannel. Publications; Tennis, 1890; Speed Skating, 1891. DNB. Foster.

HEATON, David Michael
Born 26 October 1960, Sale. William Hulme's Grammar School; Corpus Christi, Cambridge, MA. AAS. M. 4 February 1982. Call 28 July 1983. ETC. December 1983. Prop. Donald Hart QC. Sec. Daniel Brennan. 18 St John Street, Manchester, 1983-1994; 22 Old Buildings, 2004.

HEATON, Frances Margaret
Born 9 December 1961, Wigan. Bolton Girls School; Sheffield University, LLB. G. November 1985. South Eastern Circuit, 1985. Cloisters, Temple. Pupilmaster, Witold Pawlak. 4 Brick Court to 1992. ETC 1992. Prop. Jonathan Foster QC. Sec. John Wishart. Manchester Chambers; Manchester House Chambers; 1992-1996; Deans Court Chambers, Crown Square/ 24 St John Street, 1996. Recorder 2003.

HEDGELAND, Roger

Born 16 December 1948 ,Burnley. Baines Grammar School, Poulton-le-Fylde; Downing College, Cambridge, MA. G. November 1972. ETC. 1973. Prop. Patrick Russell QC. Sec. Kenneth Taylor. Manchester Chambers; Astley House, Quay Street/18 St John Street from 1973 until retirement from practice in May 2002. Assistant Recorder 1992. Recorder 1998. Legal Chairman, Pensions Appeals Tribunal, 1998.

HEDGES, Robert Yorke

Born 6 August 1903. Died 29 May 1963 aged 59. Central High School;Victoria University, Manchester, LLM., LLD. Dip. International Law, Geneva. Lecturer/ Senior Lecturer in Law, Manchester University, 1925-1936. Professor of Law & Dean of Law School, Queensland University, 1936-1945. Chief Justice of Sarawak & Judge of Appeal, Brunei, 1946-1951. Puisne Judge, Supreme Court of Nigeria, 1952-1955. High Court Judge, Western Nigeria, 1955-1959. Chief Justice, Western Nigeria, 1959-1960. Legal Assistant, Lord Chancellor's Office (Council on Tribunals), 1961-1963. Publications; Legal History of Trade Unionism, 1930; Law relating to Restraint of Trade, 1932; Laws of Sarawak (6 vols); Laws of Brunei; Introduction to Nigerian Criminal Law, 1962. WW.

HEDLEY, Mark (The Hon. Mr Justice Hedley)

(DL)

Born 23 August 1946. Framlingham College; University of Liverpool, LLB; Hon. LLD, 2003. G. 1969; Bencher 2002.Voluntary Service Overseas, Sudan, 1969-1970. ETC. 1971. Pupilmaster, Abram David Pappworth. 27 Dale Street/ 5th floor, Corn Exchange, Fenwick Street, 1971-1992. Head of Chambers, 1983-1992. Recorder 1988-1992. Circuit Judge, Liverpool 1992-2002. High Court Judge, Family Division, 11 January 2002. Kt. 2002. Chancellor, Diocese of Liverpool, 2002. Family Division Liason Judge, Wales and Chester Circuit. WW.

HEGARTY, Kevin John

Born 9 January 1960. Newcastle University, LLB. AAS. M. 22 July 1981. Call 23 November 1982. Manchester Chambers; 67 Princess Street, 1985-1987; Hollins Chambers; 64a Bridge Street, 1988-1991; 7 Fountains Court, Birmingham, 1992-2000; St Philip's Chambers, Fountains Court, Birmingham, 2001.

HEGARTY, (Thomas) Brendan QC (His Honour Judge Hegarty QC)

(DL)

Born 6 June 1943. St Joseph's College, Dumfries; St John's College, Cambridge, MA., LLB. AAS. M. 25 November 1963. Call 16 July 1970. ETC. 2 November 1972. Prop. Patrick Russell QC. Sec. J J Rowe. Manchester Chambers; 601 Royal Exchange, 1972-1988; 8 King Street, 1989-1996. Recorder 1988. Silk 1992. Circuit Judge, 5 June 1996. WW.

HEILBRON, Rose QC (The Hon. Mrs Justice Heilbron DBE)

(RB)

The following is my contribution to 'A Century of Liverpool Lawyers', 2002. The photograph was taken by Judge Richard Bingham QC in 1984.
Rose Heilbron was born in Liverpool on the 19th August 1914, the daughter of Max and Nellie Heilbron. Educated at Belvedere School and at Liverpool University, in 1935 she achieved a first class honours degree in law with an LLM two years later. Her outstanding performance in Bar Finals earned her the prestigious Lord Justice Holker Scholarship. She was called to the Bar at Gray's Inn on the 3rd May 1939. Her many years devoted service to her Inn were recognised

when she became a Bencher in 1968 and Treasurer in 1985. She joined chambers at 43 Castle Street as the pupil of Richard Trotter (later a County Court Judge). She had one pupil, the late Judge John Edward Jones (father of local solicitor Glenys Arden and barrister Michael Jones), Her election to the Northern Circuit on the 2nd February 1940 was proposed by the Recorder of Liverpool, Edward Hemmerde KC. She soon built up a substantial Criminal and Personal Injury practice because she was a persuasive advocate who gave her all in the preparation of a case and the mastery of detail. Whilst still a junior and without a silk she argued before the House of Lords and against two King's Counsel, one of whom was the Attorney General, Sir Hartley Shawcross KC, the case of Adam-v-Naylor (1946. 2 All ER 241) In 1945, Rose married Dr Nathaniel Burstein and in 1949 their daughter Hilary was born. Hilary followed in her mother's footsteps and took silk in 1987. Rose Heilbron's practice was such that in 1949, after onlv ten years' Call, she was included in Lord Jowitt's list of Silks. For the next 25 years she was in constant demand appearing in many important cases at Assize in St George's Hall and on appeal in London. The criminal case for which she is best remembered is her defence of George Kelly who was convicted in 1950 of the murder of the manager and assistant manager of the Cameo Cinema in Webster Road, The first trial of Kelly and another man took 13 days. At that time it was the longest ever murder case. The jury disagreed. Kelly was subsequently tried on his own, convicted and hanged. The Court of Criminal Appeal rejected her efforts to have the conviction quashed on the ground that a juror was a convicted felon and was disqualified from sitting. The case was referred to the Court of Appeal by the Criminal Cases Review Commission and in 2003 the convictions were quashed for non disclosure. This was just one of the countless murder trials in which she appeared. It was also one of the many firsts she achieved during her career:

(a) Rose Heilbron was the first woman: to take a first class honours degree at Liverpool University;
(b) with Helena Normanton to take Silk in 1949;
(c) to lead in a murder trial;
(d) to plead a case before the House of Lords;
(e) to be appointed a Recorder. In 1956 she replaced Neville Laski as Recorder of Burnley; she held the appointment until it was abolished by the Courts Act 1971. Thereafter she was the Honorary Recorder until 1974.
(f) To sit as a Commissioner of Assize;
(g) to sit at the Central Criminal Court;
(h) to be elected Leader of a Circuit (Northern Circuit 1973/74);
(i) to be a Treasurer of an Inn;
(j) to be appointed Presiding Judge of a Circuit (Northern Circuit 1979/82). The first woman High Court Judge was not Rose Heilbron! It was Dame Elizabeth Lane. Rose was the second. She was appointed to the Family Division in August 1974. She seems to have started a trend as five Northern Circuit women High Court Judges have followed her example – Mrs Justice Bracewell (Family Division 1990): Mrs Justice Ebsworth (the first woman to go directly to the Queen's Bench Division – in 1992); Mrs Justice Smith (QBD 1992) and subsequently to the Court of Appeal: Mrs Justice Steel (QBD 1993); and Mrs Justice Hale (Family Division 1994). Mrs Justice Hale was appointed to the Court of Appeal in October 1999 the first ever woman from the Northern Circuit to be so honoured and, now in 2004, is the first woman to go to the House of Lords. Dame Rose sat with distinction in the Family Division (with a period in Queen's Bench whilst Presiding Judge) until her retirement on the 1st November 1988. Her remarkable achievements were marked by the award of an honorary LLD from the Universities of Liverpool, Manchester and Warwick.

HEILPERN, Godfrey QC

Born 29 October 1911. Died 3 May 1973 aged 61. Manchester Grammar School; Hertford College, Oxford, MA. AAS. M. 20 June 1935. Call 11 May 1938; Bencher, 7 February 1968. Harmsworth Scholar. ETC. 13 July 1938. Prop. Pritchard KC. Sec. Henry Burton. Manchester Chambers; 60 King Street, 1938-1960; 47 Peter Street, 1961-1962. Silk 1962. 5 Essex Court, 1962-1973. Recorder of Salford, 1964-1971 and thereafter Honorary Recorder. Crown Court Recorder, 1972-1973. Leader of the Northern Circuit, 1971-1973. He assisted the Attorney General in the prosecution of Frederick Sewell for the murder of Police Superintendent Gerald Richardson after a jewellery store robbery in Blackpool and led for the defence of Myra Hindley in the Moors Murder trial at Chester Assizes in 1966. WW. Times Obituary, 5 May 1973.

HELM, James Howard

I. 26 January 1904. ETC. 7 February 1906. Prop. Tobin KC. Sec. Roby. 77 King Street. Manchester, 1909-1913. No address, 1914-1953. Not in 1954 Law List.

HELME, James Miner

I. 26 January 1912. ETC. 29 February 1912. Prop. Sanderson KC. Sec. Rankin. 2 Mitre Court Buildings 1912-1913; 1 Garden Court 1914-1965. Coroner; West Ham 1935-1939; City of London 1940-1963. Not in 1966 Law List.

HELSBY, William Ernest

LLM. G. July 1946. Liverpool Chambers; 15 Union Court, 1950-1952; 20 North John Street, 1953-1956. Registrar, Liverpool & Preston Districts of the Chancery Court of the Duchy & County Palatine of Lancaster, 1955-1967. JP.

HEMELRYK, Charles Joseph

MA. I. 19 November 1917. No address, 1917-1936. 10a Winckley Street, Preston, 1937-1958. No address, 1959-1962. Not in 1963 Law List.

HEMMERDE, Edward George KC., MP.

Born 13 November 1871 London. Died 24 May 1948 aged 76. Winchester (Cricket XI); University College, Oxford, MA. Diamond Sculls, 1900. I. 26 January 1897. ETC. 18 February 1900. Prop. Butler. Sec. Leslie Scott. 25 Lord Street, Liverpool, 1903-1906. 4 Temple Gardens, 1897-1899; 1 Hare Court, 1904-1948. Silk 1908. Recorder of Liverpool, 1909-1948. Contested Winchester, 1900; Shrewsbury, 1906; and Portsmouth, 1910. MP (L) East Denbigh, 1906-1910; N W Norfolk, 1912-1918; (Lab) Crewe, 1922-1924. Playwright. WW. "A Century of Liverpool Lawyers" 2002. (William Lister pp 69-77).

In 1931 Hemmerde prosecuted William Wallace for the murder of his wife. Wallace was convicted at Liverpool Assizes and sentenced to death. The Court of Appeal quashed the conviction stating that that the jury's verdict could not be supported having regard to the evidence. It was the first time an appeal had been allowed on this ground. The mystery was so intriguing it features in over 30 books. My favourites are: The Wallace Case. John Rowland. (Carroll & Nicolson, 1949); The Killing of Julia Wallace. Jonathan Goodman. (Charles Scribner's Sons, 1969); The Murder of Julia Wallace. James Murphy. (The Bluecoat Press. 2001.) Edgar Lustgarten, qv., attended the trial at St George's Hall. He says: "You are for Wallace. Or against him. You are certain he was innocent. Or certain he was guilty. That, I think, reflects ninety-nine per cent of the views about the most contentious murder trials this century. I belong to the residual one per cent. The public opinion polls would put me down as a don't know. For I have never been able to make up my mind. The Wallace debate will go on for ever." Hemmerde was a man of much ability and charm. He was expected to achieve the highest offices in the Law. His failure to achieve his full potential was due in the main to his desperate financial situation having sustained heavy losses speculating on the stock market. He failed to repay a loan of £1000 and when sued, pleaded the Statute of Limitations. He fought the case all the way to the House of Lords in 1921 and lost. He was most unfortunate in that the Liverpool City Council during his time as Recorder was Conservative controlled and two successive Leaders of Council disliked Hemmerde, a Liberal and later a Labour supporter. The fact that he did not pay his debts would not endear him to them. In any event the Town Clerk was instructed not to brief him. This was a great slight as the Recorder traditionally conducted all of the important City prosecutions. Hemmerde was not invited to ceremonial functions and in particular to the opening by the King in 1934 of the first Mersey Tunnel. Hemmerde rightly regarded his treatment as a "calculated impertinence." So he said in open court on 2 August 1934. Sadly the dispute was fully aired in the pages of the Liverpool Daily Post and Mercury and the story ran into the following year. Hemmerde was treated shabbily by the City Council. However in 1936 with a change in City Council Leader the differences were put to one side and Hemmerde was able to exercise fully the office of Recorder and put his undoubted ability to good use, serving the City well until his death in 1948. He had been Recorder of Liverpool for 39 years.

HEMMING, George Wirgman QC
Born 19 August 1821. Died 6 January 1905 aged 83. Clapham Grammar School; St John's College, Cambridge, BA; Senior Wrangler & Fellow, 1844; MA 1847. AAS. L. 15 November 1844. Call 3 May 1850; Bencher 1876; Treasurer 1897. 15 Old Buildings, 1876-1884; 13 New Square, 1885-1905. Standing Counsel to Cambridge University, 1875-1879. Junior Counsel to the Treasury, 1871-1875. Silk 1875. Editor of Equity Cases & Chancery Appeals which subsequently merged with the Law Reports of the Chancery Division. Official Referee of the Supreme Court, 1877-1905. Publications; Differential & Integral Calculus, 1848, 2nd ed., 1852; Billiards Mathematically Treated, 1893, 2nd ed., 1904. WW. DNB. Foster. Times Obituary, 7 January 1905.

HENDRICKSON, Christine
University College, London, LLB. I. November 1982. Manchester Chambers; 211 Deansgate, 1994-1996; Parsonage Chambers, 5th floor, 3 The Parsonage, 1997; Trinity Chambers, 88 Fishergate Hill, Preston, 1998. No address, 1999-2000. Solicitor 2001.

HENLEY, Raymond Francis
Liverpool University, BSc. L. July 1998. 77 Deansgate, Manchester, 2000-.

HENNELL, (Peter) Gordon
Born 12 April 1959, Birkenhead. Burnage High School, Manchester; Trinity College, Cambridge, MA. AAS. M. 3 March 1981. Call 29 July 1982. ETC 1982. Pupilmaster, John Bailey. Manchester Chambers; 43 King Street, 1982-1988; Queen's Chambers, 5 John Dalton Street, 1989-2001; 22 Nicholas Street, Chester, 2001. Wales & Chester Circuit.

HENNESSY, Shirley Jane
Born 21 September 1972 Clatterbridge, Wirral. Birkenhead High School GDST; University College, Oxford, BA. L. 9 October 1997. ETC. 18 December 1997. Prop. William Waldron QC. Sec. Graham Wells. Derby Square Chambers, Merchants Court, Liverpool, 1997.

HENRIQUES, Cecil Quixano
Born 6 February 1914. Died 28 July 2001 aged 87. Father of Henriques J. qv. Bradfield College, Berkshire; Worcester College, Oxford, MA., BCL. I. 24 June 1936. ETC. 1 July 1936. Prop. Gorman QC. Sec. Arthur Jalland. Manchester Chambers; 40 Kennedy Street, 1936-1939; 2 Booth Street, 1940-1975; 13 Police Street, 1976-1978; Deans Court Chambers, 1979. Northern Circuit, Solicitor General & Attorney General. Mess at Ramada Hotel, Manchester on 27 June 1996 to mark the 60th anniversary of his Call to the Bar.

HENRIQUES, Henry Straus Quixano KC
Born 8 November 1866. Died 12 November 1925 aged 59. Uncle of Cecil Henriques qv. Manchester Grammar School; Worcester College, Oxford, MA. (Senior Classical Scholar) First in Greats followed by top first in BCL. Vinerian Law Scholar, 1891. Examiner for BCL, 1897. I. 11 May 1892. 4 King's Bench Walk, 1892-1915; 4 Harcourt Buildings, 1916-1925. Silk 1921. President of the Jewish Board of Deputies. President; Jewish Historical Society of England; St George's in the East Jewish Settlement; West London Synagogue of British Jews. Executive Committee Member of; Grotius Society; International Law Association. Publications; The Law of Aliens & Naturalisation; The Jews & The English Law; The Return of the Jews to England; Jewish Marriages & The English Law. WW.

HENRIQUES, Richard Henry Quixano QC (The Hon. Mr Justice Henriques)
Born 27 October 1943 Lytham St Annes. Son of Cecil Henriques qv. Bradfield College, Berkshire; Worcester College, Oxford, BA. I. November 1967; Bencher 1994. ETC. November 1967. Prop. Godfrey Heilpern QC. Sec. Ian Webster. Manchester Chambers; 2 Booth Street, 1967-1975; 13 Police Street, 1976-1978; Dean's Court Chambers, 1979-2000. Recorder, 1983-2000. Silk 1986. Member; General Council of the Bar, 1993-1998; Criminal Justice Liason Committee, 1993-1995. Member, Northern Circuit Executive Committee, 1993-1998. Council Member, Rossall School, 1985-1995. Leader of the Northern Circuit, 1995-1998. High Court Judge, Queen's Bench Division, 2000. Congratulatory Dinner at Middle Temple on 14 October 2000. Presiding Judge, North Eastern Circuit 2001. Prosecuting Counsel in the cases of; Thompson & Venables (young boys convicted of the murder of the child Jamie Bulger); and Harold Shipman, (the Hyde GP, convicted of murdering 15 of his patients). WW.

HENRY, Alexander
Born 1837. Died 18 November 1904. Eldest son of Rev. Alexander Henry of Kingsmith, Armagh, Ireland. Queen's University, Ireland, MA; London University, LLB. AAS. M. 26 January 1860. Call 17 November 1865. Certificate of Honour. 6 Pump Court, 1876-1904. Reader & Examiner in Evidence and Procedure to the Council of Legal Education, 1892-1898. Emeritus Professor of Jurisprudence, University College, London. Recorder of Carlisle, 1892-1904. Publications; Jurisprudence, or the Science of Law. WW. Foster.

HENRY, (Philip) Bruce
Born 19 February 1965, Preston. Bedford School; King's College, London, LLB. AAS. M. 13 November 1986. Call 22 November 1988. ETC. 1989. Pupilmaster, John Appleton. 15 Winkley Square, Preston, 1989. Publication; The English Legal System, 1988.

HENSHELL, Michael John (His Honour Judge Henshell)
Born 19 October 1946, Liverpool. Married to HH Judge Badley qv. St Francis Xavier, Liverpool; Hull University, LLB. Police Inspector in Hong Kong for 3 years. I. July 1975. Pupillage at 6 King's Bench Walk (Rosamund Blundell-Jones). ETC. 1976. Prop. Justin Price QC. Same Liverpool Chambers; Queen Insurance Building "D", Queen Avenue, 1976-1979; Queen Avenue, 16, Castle Street, 1980-1983; 2nd floor, Peel House, Harrington Street, 1984-1994; 25-27 Castle Street, 1995-1998. Circuit Judge, 24 March 1998.

HENSTOCK, Francis William
Born 1846. Only son of Jesse Henstock of Bonsall, Derbys. Downing College, Cambridge, MA. AAS. L. 18 November 1875. Call 26 January 1880. ETC. 12 July 1880. Prop. Gully QC. Sec. Potter QC. 7 New Court, 1882-1885. Equity draftsman & conveyancer. Lancs. Chancery Court. No address, 1886-1940. Not in 1941 Law List.

HEPPENSTALL, Rachel Elizabeth
Born 24 May 1974, Sheffield. Oakwood Comprehensive, Rotherham. Surrey University, BSc (Law & German). M. 9 October 1997. Pupilmasters; Pamela Radclife & Marilyn Fricke. 25 Park Square, Leeds. ETC. 31 July 2001. Prop. Peter Birkett QC. Sec. Jaime Hamilton. 9 St John Street, Manchester, 2001.

HERBERT, (Thomas) Arnold KC, MP
Born 1 September 1863. Died 22 November 1940 aged 77. Son of Thomas Herbert, Professor of Philosophy and Church History at the Lancashire Independent College. Mill Hill School; Owen's College, Manchester; St John's College, Cambridge, BA., LLB. I. 15 May 1889. ETC. 18 July 1889. Prop. Aspland QC. Sec. Scott. 7 New Square, 1890-1895; 5 New Court, Carey Street, 1896-1933. MP (L) South Bucks, 1906-1910. Silk 1913. JP., Bucks. Chancery practitioner. Publication; The Law of Prescription. WW.

HERFORD, Harry Francis
Born 1863. 4th son of Edward Herford of West Bank, Macclesfield, Coroner. AAS. M. 6 March 1883. Call 17 November 1897. ETC. 19 February 1903. Prop. Shee KC. Sec. Mellor. 9 King's Bench Walk, 1903-1911. No address, 1912-1928. Not in 1929 Law List.

HERIOT-HILL, Eric Douglas Mackay
G. 28 April 1926. ETC. 26 May 1934. Prop. Jackson KC. Sec. Newman. Liverpool Chambers; 34 Castle Street, 1934-1936; 8 Cook Street, 1937-1938. 4 Paper Buildings, 1939-1940. No address, 1941-1949. 30 High Street, Newport, I.O.W; 14 Hampshire Terrace, Portsmouth & 1 Temple Gardens, 1950-1952; 4 Paper Buildings, 1953. Not in 1954 Law List.

HERMAN, Raymond Charles
Born 1 January 1949 Harrogate. Ashville College; Liverpool University, LLB. I. February 1972. ETC. March 1972. Prop. Michael Maguire QC. Sec. John Briggs. Same Liverpool Chambers; 27 Dale Street, 1972-1977; Melbourne Building, 21 North John Street, 1977-1988; 3rd floor, Peel House, Harrington Street, 1989-1998; India Buildings, Water Street 1998. (Head of Chambers). Assistant Recorder 1989. Recorder 1993. Vice Chairman, Ashworth Special Hospital Authority, 1996. Immigration Adjudicator, 2001.

HERNANDEZ, David Anthony (His Honour Judge Hernandez)
Born 15 September 1953 Trinidad. Married to HH Judge Newton qv. Bury Grammar School; St Catherine's College, Oxford, MA. L. November 1976. ETC. December 1976. Prop. Benet Hytner QC. Sec. Philip Bagley. Manchester Chambers; 4th, 9th & 6th floors, Sunlight House, Quay Street, 1976-1994. Young Street Chambers, 1995. Recorder 2000. Circuit Judge, 2004.

HERON, Robert Matthews
Born 1823. 3rd son of John Heron of Belfast. Matriculated Trinity College, Dublin. AAS. I. 11 January 1841. Call 1 May 1846. 4 Inner Temple Lane, 1848. No address, 1877-1892. Not in 1893 Law List.

HERSCHELL, Rt. Hon. Sir Farrer QC, MP (First Baron Herschell of the City of Durham)

Born 2 November 1837 Brampton, Hants. Died 2 March 1899 aged 61 in Washington DC of injuries received as the result of a fall. He was there as a member of the Anglo-American Arbitration Commission. University College, London, BA (Classics). AAS. L. 12 January 1858. Call 17 November 1860; Bencher 1872. Pupilmaster, Thomas Chitty. Silk 1872. 3 Harcourt Buildings, 1878-1881; 11 New Court, Carey Street, 1881. Recorder of Carlisle, 1873-1880; MP (L) City of Durham, 1874-1885. Solicitor General, 1880-1885. Lord High Chancellor, 1886 and 1892-1895. Captain of Deal Castle, 1890-1899. Chancellor of London University, 1893-1899. Biographies; Victorian Chancellors. J B Atlay, 1908; Some Eminent Victorians, J Comyns Carr, 1914; Lives of the Lord Chancellors, 1885-1940, R F V Heuston, 1964; Biographical Dictionary of the Common Law. Simpson. Times Obituary 2 March 1899. WWW. DNB. PC 1880. GCB 1893. Kt 1880. After the division of the Circuit in 1876 he remained a member of the Northern & North Eastern. As well as being a very able lawyer, he loved fine music. I like the reference in DNB which reads "he was not without skill as an executant on the violoncello."

HERTZ, Gerald Berkley

MA., BCL. L. 23 April 1902. ETC. 16 July 1902. Prop. Shee KC. Sec. Radford. Manchester Chambers; Duchy Chambers, 4 Clarence Street, 1903-1904; 28 John Dalton Street, 1905-1916. Lancs. Chancery Court. Equity draftsman & conveyancer. Not in 1917 Law List.

HESFORD, Stephen MP

Born 27 May 1957. Bradford University, BSc Sociology (Economics & Politics) 1978; Central London Polytechnic, Dip Law, 1980. G. November 1981. Manchester Chambers; 6th floor, Sunlight House, Quay Street, 1988-1994; Young Street Chambers, 1995. MP (Lab) Wirral West, 1997.

HESKETH, Edward Fleetwood

Born 1834. Eldest son of Charles Hesketh of North Meols, Lancs. Cheltenham College; New College, Oxford. AAS. I. 6 May 1854. Call 17 November 1857. No address, 1876-1887. Not in 1888 Law List. Hon. Col. Southport Rifle Volunteers, 1881. Late Captain 6th Royal Lancashire Militia.

HESLING, Edith OBE (Mrs Bradbury)

She was the first woman student admitted to Gray's Inn and the first woman elected to the Northern Circuit. Born 1899. Died 22 June 1971 aged 72. G. 13 June 1923. ETC. 9 July 1923. Prop. Ashton KC. Sec. Jolly. Manchester Chambers; 23 King Street, 1924-1928; 2 Booth Street, 1929-1963. Lecturer in Law. Victoria University of Manchester. Member, Unemployment Appeal Tribunal.

HEWART, Rt. Hon. Sir Gordon KC, MP. (First Viscount Hewart of Bury in the County of Lancaster)

Born 7 January 1870, Bury. Died 5 May 1943 aged 73. Son of Giles Hewart, draper. Manchester Grammar School; University College, Oxford, BA 1891; MA 1893; Hon. Fellow 1922. Hon. LLD Manchester, 1922. Journalist writing for Bury Guardian, Bury Times, Manchester Guardian, The Star & The Morning Leader. I. 11 June 1902; Bencher 1917; Treasurer 1938. ETC. 26 July 1902. Pupilmaster, Edmund Sutton. Prop. Taylor QC. Sec. Hemmerde. Manchester Chambers; Bank of England Chambers, Tib Lane, 1902-1911; Palatine Bank Buildings, Norfolk Street, 1912-1922. Silk 1912. MP (CL) East Leicester, 1913-1922. Solicitor General, 1916-1919. Attorney General, 1919-1922. A British Signatory of the Irish Peace Treaty, 1921. Freedom of Bury, 1922. Lord Chief Justice of England, 1922-1940. Kt 1916. PC 1918. Baron 1922. Viscount 1940. Publications; The New Despotism; Essays & Observations, 1930; Not without Prejudice, 1937. WW. DNB. Biography. The Chief. Robert Jackson (Harrop & Co Ltd., 1959).

HEWITT, Penelope Ann CBE

Born 4 May 1932. Howell's School, Denbigh; Open University, BA. G. 1978. ETC. 30 November 1978. Liverpool Chambers; Queen Avenue, 16 Castle Street, 1978-1983; 2nd floor, Peel House, Harrington Street, 1984-1990. JP., Bolton, 1968-1990. Stipendiary Magistrate (later District Judge), Leeds 1990-2000. Senior District Judge (Chief Magistrate), 2000-March 2003. Lay Chairman, Bolton Deanery Synod, 1984-1990. CBE 2003.

HEY, Peter Michael Ignatius Wilson
MA., LLB, Cantab. I. June 1948. 3 St James Square, Manchester, 1950-1956. 105 Onslow Square, SW7, 1957-1963. Not in 1964 Law List.

HEYWOOD, George Washington (His Honour Judge Heywood)
Born 6 January 1842. Died 17 January 1896 aged 54. 2nd son of Abel Heywood, paper manufacturer and publisher of Manchester. AAS. M. 12 January 1866. Call 6 June 1868. Certificate of Honour, 1868. ETC. 4 August 1868. Prop. J J Aston. Sec. Herschell. 3 Elm Court & 2 St James's Square, Manchester, 1876-1890. County Court Judge, Circuit 8, 1890-1894. JP., Lancs. Editor, County Court Practice, 1890-1895.

HEYWOOD, George William
I. 17 November 1897. ETC. 2 February 1898. Manchester chambers; 7 Brazennose Street, 1900-1908; 15 Brazennose Street, 1909-1921. No address, 1922-1928. Not in 1929 Law List.

HEYWOOD, John
Born 1850. Eldest son of Robert Heywood of the Pike, Bolton, JP. St John's College, Oxford, MA. AAS. I. 16 April 1873. Call 26 January 1877. ETC. 12 July 1877. Prop. Temple QC. Sec. Hopwood QC. Circuit Junior, Spring 1878. 1 Hare Court, 1879. 1 King's Bench Walk, 1880. Manchester Chambers; 4 St James Square, 1881-1884; 64 Cross Street, 1885-1887. No chambers address, 1888-1910. Not in 1911 Law List.

HEYWOOD, Thomas
Born 1893. Eldest son of Matthew Heywood of Rochdale. Journalist aged 42 when AAS. M. 22 August 1935. Call 29 June 1938. ETC. 20 July 1938. Prop. Gorman KC. Sec. Leech. 2 Booth Street, Manchester, 1938-1948. Not in 1949 Law List.

HEYWORTH, Alison
Born 29 October 1964 Macclesfield. Withington Girls School; Warwick University, BA. University Lecturer, Paris, 1989-1996. French Tutor, Cheshire, 1996-1999. I. 11 October 2001. ETC. 12 December 2001. Prop. Charles Garside QC. Sec. Nick Clarke. 9 St John Street, Manchester, 2001.

HEYWORTH, Brian Kay
Born 26 March 1907. Died 28 May 1940 aged 33. Only son of Lawrence and Elizabeth Heyworth of Whinfield, Preston New Road, Blackburn. BA (Oxon). AAS. M. 14 October 1926. Call 12 June 1929. ETC. 1929. 6 St Ann's Passage, Manchester, 1930-1937. Treasury Solicitor's Dept, SW1, 1938-1939. Husband of Elizabeth Heyworth of Formby, Lancs. Commissioned in TA (4/5 Batn, East Lancs. Regt) on 18 December 1925. Promoted Lt., 18 December 1928; Captain, 31 July 1929. Transferred to Reserve, 22 April 1936. Transferred to active service and to 1st Bucks Batn., Oxford & Bucks Light Infantry on 16 April 1939. Temporary Major (Substantive Captain) Personal Number P/34001. Killed in action 28 May 1940 during the fighting covering the retreat of the British Expeditionary Force to Dunkirk. Cemetery, Hazebrouck, Nord, France. Grave; Plot 4, Row B, Grave 20. Hazebrouck is 56 kms south of Calais. Information provided by Public Records Office & Commonwealth War Graves Commission.

HIBBERT, Luke Taylor
MA (Oxon). L. 1 July 1908. ETC. 9 July 1908. Prop. Tobin KC. Sec. Hewart. Manchester Chambers; 16 John Dalton Street, 1908-1910; 6 St Ann's Passage, 1911-1913; 78 King Street, 1914-1940. No chambers address, 1941-1963. Not in 1964 Law List.

HIBBERT, Thomas Dorning
Only son of Thomas Hibbert of Everton, Lancs. AAS. M. 16 April 1844. Call 16 April 1847. 2 Serjeants Inn, 1848. Kirkdale, Liverpool & North Lancs. Sessions. No address, 1876-1880. Not in 1881 Law List.

HIBBERT-WARE, Titus
Eldest son of Samuel Hibbert-Ware of Edinburgh, doctor of medicine. AAS. M. 12 June 1841. Call 11 June 1844. Manchester, conveyancer, 1848; Southport, conveyancer, 1876-1890. Not in 1891 Law List. Foster.

HICKLAND, Margaret
Born 13 September 1964 Ballinderry, County Antrim. St Michael's High School, Lurgan; University College of Wales, Aberystwyth, LLB. G. July 1988. ETC. December 1988. Prop. Ronnie Livesey QC. Sec. Nigel Gilmour. Peel House, Harrington Street, Liverpool, 1988-1999; Young Street Chambers, Manchester, 1999.

HICKS, Pascale Anne
Born 18 March 1976 Liverpool. Ormskirk Grammar School; King George V College; Liverpool University, LLB (English & French Law); Université de Montesquieu, Licence en Droit. Stage, European Commission. L. 4 October 1999. 9 Stone Building, 1999-2000. ETC. 12 December 2000. Prop. Stephen Grime QC. Sec. Nicholas Grimshaw. Deans Court Chambers, Manchester, 2000.

HICKS, William Arthur
Born 1841. Only son of John Hicks of Liverpool. Trinity College, Oxford. AAS. L. 25 April 1861. Call 17 November 1864. Private address, Tangley House, Felixstowe. No chambers address, 1876-1934. Not in 1934 Law List. Foster.

HIGGIN, William Housman QC.
Born 1820. Died 30 January 1893. Only son of John Higgin of Greenfield, Lancaster. AAS. M. 23 December 1842. Call 28 January 1848; Bencher 1868; Autumn Reader 1874; Treasurer 1884. Grecian Chambers, Devereux Court, 1848; 1 Essex Court, 1876-1879; 2 Plowden Buildings, 1880-1893. Manchester Chambers; 4 St James Square, 1880-1889; 32 St Ann Street, 1890-1893. Silk 1868. QC, County Palatine of Lancaster. JP; Lancs. & Cheshire. Chairman; Preston Quarter Sessions and Salford Hundred Quarter Sessions. Recorder of Preston, 1890-1893. Foster.

HIGGINS, Alfred
I. 26 January 1886. ETC. 27 January 1887. Prop. Collins QC. Sec. Blair. No address, 1886-1940. Not in 1941 Law List.

HIGGINS, Alfred Herbert

Born 1847. 4th son of James Higgins of Stocks House, Cheetham, Manchester, engineer. Trinity College, Cambridge, BA 1872. AAS. I. 26 April 1870. Call 26 January 1884. ETC. 29 July 1884. Prop. Bigham QC. Sec. French. Circuit Junior, Winter 1885. 10 Commerce Chambers, 15 Lord Street, Liverpool, 1886-1899. No address, 1900-1938. Not in 1939 Law List. Foster.

HIGGINS, Paul Andrew
Born 8 July 1969 Manchester. Manchester Grammar School; Trinity College, Oxford, BA (Physics); BA (Jurisprudence). L. March 1996. ETC. 2 April 1996. Prop. Keith Goddard QC. Sec. Brown. Manchester Chambers; Old Colony House, 6 South King Street, 1996-2000; 8 King Street, 2000.

HIGSON, Peter
L. 27 January 1913. ETC. 20 February 1913. Prop. Tobin KC. Sec. Thorpe. No address, 1914-1921. 2 Booth Street, Manchester, 1922-1927. Not in 1928 Law List.

HILDESLEY, Alfred QC (His Honour Judge Hildesley QC)
Born 5 September 1873 Manchester. Died 31 May 1958 aged 84. Son of Albert Hildesheimer of Chorlton up Medlock, Manchester. Pembroke College, Oxford, BA 1896; MA 1899. I. 22 June 1898. ETC. 2 February 1899. Prop. Russell QC. Sec. Mansfield. Circuit Junior, Summer 1899. 2 Harcourt Buildings, 1898-1909; 1 Temple Gardens, 1910-1916; 3 Paper Buildings, 1917-1921; 2 Mitre Court Buildings, 1922-1929; 5 Crown Office Row, 1930-1931. Silk 1929. County Court Judge, Circuit 33, (Essex, Suffolk & Ipswich), May 1931-1947. Chairman, East Suffolk Quarter Sessions, 1932-1947. WW. Foster.

HILDITCH, John Edgerley
Born 1867. 3rd son of Thomas Hilditch of Middletown, Montgomerys. AAS. M. 23 January 1896. Call 26 January 1899. ETC. 20 July 1903. Prop. Shee KC. Sec. Byrne. Manchester Chambers; 78 King Street, 1904-1908; 60 King Street, 1909-1911. Equity draftsman & conveyancer. Lancs. Chancery Court. No address, 1912-1921. Not in 1922 Law List.

HILDITCH, Richard
Eldest son of Richard Hilditch of Shrewsbury, Salop. St John's College, Cambridge, BA 1836. AAS. M. 18 October 1833. Call 24 November 1837. 30 Cross Street, Manchester, 1876-1891. Conveyancer. Not in 1892 Law List. Foster.

HILL, Arthur Maurice
I. 26 January 1927. 13 Harrington Street, Liverpool, 1930. Not in 1931 Law List.

HILL, (Edward) Maurice KC (The Hon. Mr Justice Hill)
Born 8 January 1862. Died 6 June 1934 aged 72. Haleybury; Balliol College, Oxford. I. 26 January 1888; Bencher 1917. Admiralty Specialist. He represented the White Star Line in the Board of Trade investigation into the sinking of the "Titanic". Temporary Chairman, Licensing Committee of the Board of Trade, 1915-1917. ETC. 20 February 1888. Prop. French QC. Sec. Walton. 5 Crown Office Row, 1889-1892; 2 King's Bench Walk, 1893-1917. Silk 1910. High Court Judge, Probate, Divorce and Admiralty Division, 18 January 1917-12 October 1930. He dealt almost exclusively with shipping cases. He found divorce work distasteful. Kt. 1917. WW. DNB.

HILL, William Ellis
I. 17 November 1885. ETC. 7 February 1887. Prop. Collins QC. Sec. Mansfield. 13 Old Square, 1886; 1 Dr Johnson's Building, 1887-1896; 3 Paper Buildings, 1897-1910; 1 Harcourt Buildings, 1911-1936. No address, 1937-1938. Not in 1939 Law List.

HILL, William Sephton
Born 24 July 1926. Died 8 December 1993 aged 67. Cowley School, St Helens: BA., LLB., (Cantab). Served RAF, 1944-1948 as Japanese interpreter. G. June 1951. ETC 1951. 24 Dale Street, Liverpool, 1951-1954. Solicitor's Office, HM Customs & Excise in 1954 rising to Principal Assistant Solicitor, 1980-1985. European Affairs Advisor to BAT, 1985-1989. Development Director, International Duty Free Federation, Brussels, 1989-1993. WW.

HILLMAN, Roger John
Born 10 November 1960 Heswall, Wirral. Son of Brian Hillman, solicitor who was formerly with Gair Roberts of Liverpool. Monkton Combe School, near Bath; Liverpool University, LLB. G. July 1983. ETC. December 1983. Prop. David Clarke QC. Sec. Ian Campbell. Liverpool Chambers; Exchange Chambers at 1 Exchange Flags, September 1983-1991; and at Derby Square, 1992.

HILLS, Eustace Gilbert KC (His Honour Judge Hills KC)
Born 26 July 1868. Died 17 October 1934 aged 66. Youngest son of Herbert Augustus Hills of Highhead Castle, Cumberland, Judge of Appeal, International Courts, Alexandria, Egypt. Eton; Balliol College, Oxford, BA 1891. I. 19 November 1894; Bencher 1924. ETC. 15 February 1897. Prop. Bigham QC. Sec. Granet. 2 Pump Court, 1896; Library Chambers 1897-1920; 2 Garden Court 1921-1929. Silk 1919. County Court Judge, Circuit 3, (Cumberland) 1929-1934. Chairman of Cumberland Quarter Sessions, 1930-1933. Member of Council of Legal Education, 1926-1929. Married 1st, 1899, Louisa, daughter of 1st Baron Phillimore (died 1904); 2nd, 1910, Nina, daughter of 1st Baron Shuttleworth. WW.

HILSDON, James Spencer
L. November 1993. ETC. December 1994. Prop. Robert Fordham QC. Sec. Oughton. Manchester Chambers; 72 Bridge Street, 1994-1997; Cobden House Chambers, 19 Quay Street, 1998-2000.

HILTON, Simon Jonathan
Born 25 February 1963 Manchester. Cousin of Richard Marks QC qv. Manchester Grammar School; Clifton College; Worcester College, Oxford BA (English). G. November 1987. ETC. 1988. Prop. Philip Raynor QC. Sec. Harold Halliday. Pupilmaster Christopher Purchas. King's Chambers, 40 King Street, Manchester June 1989. Junior Counsel to the Crown (Provincial Panel) February 2000. Recorder 2003.

HINCHCLIFFE, Thomas Edward
Born 1897. 2nd son of Thomas Henry Hinchcliffe of 40 Brazennose Street, Manchester, solicitor. AAS. M. 19 March 1919. Call 2 July 1930. ETC. 9 July 1930. Prop. Jackson KC. Sec. Milne. Manchester Chambers; 4 Clarence Street, 1932-1934; 26 King Street, 1935-1936; 40 Kennedy Street, 1937-1940. 38 Fishergate, Preston, 1941-1959. Not in 1960 Law List.

HINCHLIFFE, (Frank) Philip (Rideal) QC (His Honour Judge Hinchliffe QC)
Born 13 January 1923. Died 18 October 1976 aged 53. Father of (Philip) Nicholas Hinchliffe QC qv. Worksop College; New College, Oxford MA. President, Oxford Union Society, Trinity Term, 1942. War Service, RA, 1942-1946 (despatches 1945). Captain. I. November 1947. ETC. 1947. 60 King Street, Manchester, 1947-1968. Silk 1968. 5 Essex Court, 1968-1971. County Court/ Circuit Judge, 1971-1976. Deputy Chairman, Westmorland Quarter Sessions, 1969-1971. President, SW Pennines Magistrates Association, 1974-1976. WW.

HINCHLIFFE, (Philip) Nicholas QC
Born 23 September 1957, Wilmslow. Son of His Honour Judge Philip Hinchliffe QC qv. Uppingham School; Manchester University, LLB. AAS. M. 30 March 1979. Call 25 November 1980. ETC. 1980. Prop. Jack Price QC. Sec. John Hand. Manchester Chambers; 60 King Street, 1980-1983; Deans Court & 9 St John Street, 1984. Assistant Recorder 1998. Silk 1999. Recorder 2001. Represented Great Britain and England in target rifle shooting. Captain of both teams in major international matches.

HINDLE, Edward Bruce
Born 30 March 1851. Eldest son of John Hindle of Stockport, stationer. AAS. M. 13 November 1875. Call 25 June 1879. ETC. 19 July 1879. Prop. Hopwood QC. Sec. Edge. No address, 1879-1884. Queen's Chambers, Ridgefield, Manchester, 1885-1889. Queen's Advocate, Gold Coast Colony, 1890-1895. Chief Justice, Sierra Leone, 1896-1897. Not in 1898 Law List.

HINMERS, William
I. 8 June 1921. ETC. 6 July 1921. Prop. Langdon KC. Sec. Burgis. Circuit Junior, Winter 1921. 78 King Street, Manchester, 1924-1928. No address, 1929-1932. Not in 1933 Law List.

HIRST, Henry Edward
Born 13 January 1849. Only son of Charles Hirst, MD., of Morley, Yorks. Queen's College, Oxford, MA., BCL. AAS. L. 27 January 1870. Call 17 November 1874. ETC. 16 March 1875. Prop. Torr QC. Sec. Wheeler. 4 Crown Office Row, 1877-1879; 1 Essex Court, 1880-1889; Goldsmith Building, 1890-1895; 2 Hare Court, 1896-1902. No address, 1903-1922. Not in 1923 Law List. Publication; Editor, Chitty's Equity Index to Reported Cases, 4th edition. Foster.

HOARE, Gregory Blake
Born 7 September 1950, Rawtenstall. St Theodore's School, Burnley. University of Central Lancashire, LLB. Solicitor, 1979-1992. G. November 1992. ETC. 17 December 1992. Prop. Rodney Scholes QC. Sec. Nigel Beeson. Pupilmaster, Ian McIvor. Kenworthy's Chambers, 83 Bridge Street, Manchester, 1992-1996; Martin's Building, Water Street, Liverpool, 1996-1999; 7 Harrington Street, Liverpool, 6.9.1999. (merger with Corn Exchange).

HOBHOUSE, John Stewart QC (The Rt. Hon. The Lord Hobhouse of Woodborough in the County of Wiltshire)
Born 31 January 1932, Liverpool. Died 15 March 2004 aged 72. Eton; Christ Church, Oxford, BCL., MA 1958. I. November 1955. Pupilmasters, Tony Cripps and Michael Kerr. ETC. Prop. Harry Nelson QC. Sec. Michael Morland. 3 Essex Court, 1955-1959; 7 King's Bench Walk, 1960-1982. Silk 1973. High Court Judge, Queen's Bench Division, 1982-1993. Kt. 1982. Lord Justice of Appeal, 1993-1998. PC 1993. Lord of Appeal in Ordinary, 1998-2004. Baron (Life Peer) 1998. WW.

HOBLEY, John William Dixon CMG
Born 11 June 1929. Died 4 March 1993 aged 64. University School, Southport; Liverpool University, LLB. G. November 1950. ETC. 1950. 9 Rumford Street, Liverpool, 1950-1953. Hong Kong: Crown Counsel, 1953-1962; Senior Crown Counsel, 1962-1965; Principal Crown Counsel, 1965-1972; QC (Hong Kong); Attorney General, Bermuda, 1972. Hong Kong: Solicitor General, 1973; Attorney General, 1973-1979. CMG 1976. Principal Legal Advisor, Wigan Borough Council, 1985-1991. WW.

HOBSON, Heather Fiona
LLB, London. L. November 1987. Manchester Chambers; 20 St Mary's Parsonage, 1989; 5 John Dalton Street, 1990.

HODGE, James Philip MP
Born 1879. Died 12 July 1946. 2nd son of Archibald Hodge of Hoole Park, Chester, formerly a Fifeshire miner. Chester Cathedral Choir School. Chartered Accountant in Chester, 1900-1914. Commissioned and served in France, Salonica & Egypt, 1914-1918. Lt. Col. & Inspector of Pay Offices. I. 19 November 1917. ETC 1917. 5 Paper Buildings, 1919-1930; 4 Crown Office Row, 1931-1934. No address, 1935-1946. MP (L) Preston, 1922-1924. WW.

HODGSON, Arthur John
MA., LLB. I. 27 January 1913. ETC. 30 January 1913. Prop. Ashton KC. Sec. Kennedy. Liverpool Chambers; 13 Harrington Street, 1913-1918 & 1928-1935; 9 Commerce Chambers, 15 Lord Street, 1919-1927. Goldsmith Building, 1936-1940; Lamb Building, 1941; 3 Hare Court, 1942-1943; 1 Paper Building, 1944-1950. Not in 1951 Law List.

HODGSON, Francis Henry Birkett
Born 3 July 1879. Died 8 August 1935 aged 56. Preston Grammar School; Hertford College, Oxford, MA. I. 19 June 1901. ETC. 28 July 1903. Prop. Tobin KC. Sec. Sharpe. Preston Chambers; 13 Winckley Square, 1903-1910; 14 Chapel Street, 1911-1935. Lancs. Chancery Court. Commission in Loyal North Lancs (TF) in European War. Recorder of the Borough of Preston & Judge & Assessor of the Borough Court of Pleas, 1935. WW.

HODGSON, James
G. 19 November 1894. ETC. 1 August 1895. Prop. Shee QC. Sec. Knowles. 78 King Street, Manchester, 1899-1925. Private Blackpool address, 1926-1934. Not in 1935 Law List.

HODGSON, John Hargrave
Eldest son of Richard Hodgson of Salisbury Street, Strand. AAS. M. 14 April 1845. Call 8 November 1850. 3 Brick Court, 1876-1905. No address, 1906-1913. Not in 1914 Law List.

HODGSON, John James
MA. G. June 1955. 43 King Street, Manchester, 1955-1982. Not in 1983 Law List.

HODGSON, Timothy Paul
Born 25 May 1957 Shipley, West Yorks. Salt Grammar School; Wellington High School; Victoria University (NZ), BA; Corpus Christi College, Oxford, BA., D.Phil.; City University, Dip. Law. Tutor, Oxford, 1985-1986. Lecturer in Law, Manchester University, 1986-1988. I. November 1991. ETC. 1991. Prop. Richard Clegg QC. Sec Brendan Hegarty. Pupilmaster, Tim Mort. 8 King Street, Manchester, 1991. Part time Lecturer in Law, Manchester Metropolitan University, 1992.

HODGSON, (Walter) Derek (Thornley) QC (The Hon. Mr Justice Hodgson)
Born 24 May 1917 Manchester. Died 10 October 2002 aged 85. Malvern College; Trinity Hall, Cambridge, MA., LLB. AAS. M. 2 July 1936. Harmsworth Scholar. Captain, Royal Artillery in Burma, 1942-1945. Call 18 November 1946; Bencher 1967; Reader 1985. ETC. 1946. Pupilmaster, Joseph Cantley. 4 Chapel Walks, Manchester, 1946-1961. Silk 1961. 1 Hare Court, 1961-1965; 2 Pump Court, 1966-1971. Judge, Salford Hundred Court, 1965-1971. Law Commissioner, 1971-1977. Recorder, 1972-1977. High Court Judge, Queen's Bench Division, 1977-1992. Parole Board, 1981-1983. Obituary, Daily Telegraph, 21 October 2002.

HODSON, John
G. 17 November 1919. 3 Harcourt Buildings, 1921-1937. Not in 1938 Law List.

HODSON, (Thomas) David (Tattersall) (His Honour Judge Hodson)
Born 24 September 1942. Sedbergh School; Manchester University, LLB. Leader Writer, Yorkshire Post, 1964-1965. I. November 1966; Bencher 2001. ETC. 1967. Sec. David Waddington. Circuit Junior, 1969. Manchester Chambers; 3 St James Square, 1966-1984; St James Chambers, 68 Quay Street, 1984-1987. Recorder, 1983-1987. Circuit Judge, 1987. Parole Board, 1996-1997. Senior Circuit Judge & Honorary Recorder of Newcastle upon Tyne, 1997. Publication; "One week in August: the Kaiser at Lowther Castle, August 1895" (1995). WW.

HOFFMAN, David Alexander
Born 30 December 1971 Manchester. Son of Colin Hoffman, solicitor and grandson of HH Judge H J Hoffman (Rhodesia). Manchester Grammar School; University College, Oxford, MA., BCL. Lecturer, Somerville College, Oxford, 1994-1995. L. 9 October 1997. ETC. 16 December 1997. Prop. Keith Armitage QC. Sec Digby Jess. 8 King Street, Manchester, 1997. Publication; Co Author, Current Law Annotations on the Anti Terrorism, Crime & Security Act 2001.

HOGG, Adam Spencer (His Honour Judge Hogg)
3rd son of Adam Hogg of Bowden. Died 19 September 1937. Uppingham School; Trinity College, Oxford, BA. I. 26 April 1893. ETC. 26 July 1893. Prop. Wheeler QC. Sec A G Sparrow. Circuit Junior, Summer 1894. Manchester Chambers; 41 John Dalton Street, 1893-1908; 49 Princess Street, 1909-1911. Stipendiary Magistrate, Salford, 1911-1913. County Court Judge, Circuit 5 (Lancs.), 1913-1928 and Circuit 48, (Lambeth, Epsom & Guilford), 1928-1937.

HOGG, James Seddon
Born 1888. Only son of John Hogg of Glasgow, wholesale fruit broker. Universities of Glasgow & South Africa. AAS. M. 3 June 1939. Call 21 June 1939. ETC. 12 July 1939. Prop. Gorman KC. Sec. Lambert. 26 King Street, Manchester, 1939-1949. Not in 1950 Law List.

HOGGETT, (Anthony) John (Christopher) QC
Born 20 August 1940, Leeds. Married, Brenda Hale qv (marr. diss. 1992) Leeds Grammar School; Hymers College, Hull; Clare College, Cambridge, MA., LLB; Manchester University, PhD. Lecturer in Law, Manchester University, 1963-1969. G. July 1969. ETC. 1970. Prop. Benet Hytner QC. Sec. Douglas Brown. Manchester Chambers; 25 Bow Lane, 1970-1976; 460 Royal Exchange, 1977-1987; Kings Chambers, 40 King Street, 1988. Head of Chambers, 1985-1996. Silk 1986. Recorder 1988. WW.

HOLDEN, John Leslie Ogilvie
LLM (Cantab); M.Litt. G. July 1981. Bridge Street Chambers, 72 Bridge Street, Manchester, 1985-1995. Not in 1996 Bar Directory.

HOLDEN, Philip Anthony
Born 24 April 1972, Preston. Bury Grammar School; University of Northumbria, LLB. Formerly a solicitor. L. October 1994. ETC. 1999. Prop. Keith Goddard QC. Sec. Peter Buckley. Queen's Chambers, 5 John Dalton Street, Manchester, 1999.

HOLDER, Simon Michael
Born 5 December 1963, Widnes. St Margaret's C of E High School; Queen Mary College, London, LLB; London School of Economics, LLM. I. July 1989. ETC December 1991. Prop. David Harris QC. Sec. Graham Wood. Liverpool Chambers; 3rd floor, Peel House, Harrington Street, 1991-1999; 8th floor, India Buildings, Water Street, 1999. Assistant Deputy Coroner 1999.

HOLGATE, Maurice Wilcock
Born 1912. 2nd son of James Wilcock Holgate of Blackburn. Christ's College, Cambridge, BA. AAS. M. 16 January 1931. Call 19 November 1934. ETC. 1 July 1936. Prop. Lynskey KC. Sec. Burton. 1 Essex Court, 1936-1956. No address, 1957-1963. Not in 1964 Law List.

HOLLAND, Charlotte Kate
Born 11 January 1973 Manchester. Sale Girls Grammar School; Birmingham University, BA 1994. (East Mediterranean History). L. October 1996. ETC. December 1996. Prop. Howard Bentham QC. Sec. P McDonald. Manchester Chambers; Old Colony House, 6 South King Street, 1996-2001; Lincoln House Chambers, 1 Brazennose Street, 2001.

HOLLAND, Franklin
I. 19 November 1906. ETC. 25 February 1907. Prop. Tobin KC. Sec. Greer. 25 Lord Street, Liverpool, 1908-1923. No address, 1924-1953. Not in 1954 Law List.

HOLLAND, Ricky John
Born 18 June 1959 Coventry. Son-in-law of David Gandy former Deputy Director of Public Prosecutions. Fulford School, York; University of East Anglia, LLB 1981; Darwin College, Cambridge, LLM 1982. Chester College of Law, 1982-1983. Solicitor with CPS, 1984-1994. G. 27 November 1994. ETC. 13 December 1994. Prop. Rodney Klevan QC. Sec. Alan Conrad. Manchester Chambers; 64 Bridge Street, 1994-1995; Lincoln House Chambers, 1 Brazennose Street, 1996.

HOLLINGS, (Alfred) Kenneth MC., QC (The Hon. Mr Justice Hollings)
Born 12 June 1918. Youngest son of Alfred Holdsworth Hollings of Southport. Leys School, Cambridge; Clare College, Cambridge, 1936-1939, MA. Served Shropshire Yeomanry, 1939-1946. MC 1944. AAS. M. 22 October 1945; Call 18 June 1947; Harmsworth Scholar; Bencher 1971. ETC. 1947. Pupilmaster, Joseph Cantley. Manchester Chambers; 4 Chapel Walks June, 1947-1964; 601 Royal Exchange, 1965-1966. Silk 1966. 2 Pump Court, 1966-1968. Recorder of Bolton, 1968. County Court Judge, Circuit 5 (East Lancs.), 1968-1971. High Court Judge, Family Division, 1971-1993. Presiding Judge, Northern Circuit, 1975-1978. WW.

HOLLORAN, Fiona Anne
Born 8 July 1965.Helensburgh, Scotland. Our Lady's Convent, Stamford Hill, London; Warwick University, LLB. G. November 1989. ETC. November 1990. Sec. Cynthia Pilling. Pupilmasters, Richard McGregor-Johnson & Cynthia Pilling. Manchester Chambers; 20 St Mary's Parsonage, 1990-1993; 58 King Street Chambers, 51/53 King Street South, 1994.

HOLLOWAY (Frederick) (Reginald) Bryn (His Honour Judge Holloway)
Born 9 January 1947. Mill Mead, Shrewsbury; Wrekin College, Wellington, Salop; College of Law. L. July 1971. ETC. 1972. Prop. Michael Maguire. Sec. Henry Lachs. Same Liverpool Chambers at; 27 Dale Street, 1972-1976; Melbourne Building, 21 North John Street, 1977-1988; 3rd floor, Peel House, Harrington Street, 1988-1992. Assistant Recorder 1984. Recorder 1989. Circuit Judge, Liverpool, 22 July 1992. WW.

HOLLOWAY, Timothy Richard
Born 24 May 1969, Sheffield. Silverdale Comprehensive, Sheffield; St Johns, Cambridge, MA. I. November 1991. ETC. December 1991. Puilmaster, Charles James. Merchants Court, Derby Square, Liverpool 1991-31 December 2003; Oriel Chambers, 14 Water Street, 1 January 2004. Junior Counsel to the Crown (Provincial Panel) 2000.

HOLLYOAK, Kate Elaine
Manchester High School for Girls; Manchester University, LLB. G. 27 November 1997. ETC. 16 December 1997. Prop. Roderick Carus QC. Sec. Christine Riley. 9 St John Street, Manchester, 1997.

HOLMAN, Richard Christopher (His Honour Judge Holman)
Born 16 June 1946. Watford Grammar School for Boys; Eton College; Gonville & Caius College, Cambridge, MA 1968. Admitted as a solicitor, 1971. Partner, Foysters, later Davies Wallis Foysters, 1973-1994; Managing Partner, 1988-1989. Deputy District Registrar, 1982-1988. Assistant Recorder, 1988-1992. Recorder, 1992-1994. Circuit Judge, 1994. Designated Civil Judge, Manchester, 1998. Senior Circuit Judge, 2002. Captain, Wilmslow Golf Club, 1999. WW.

HOLMES, Paul Cyril
MA (Cantab) G. July 1979. ETC. December 1979. Manchester Chambers; 43 King Street, 1982-1988; Queen's Chambers, 5 John Dalton Street, 1989-2000. Part time Chairman of Industrial Tribunals. Perkins & Co, Solicitors. 1 King Street, Manchester, 2001.

HOLMES, Philip John
Born 1 December 1956 Salford. Stockport Grammar School; Queen's College, Cambridge, BA 1979; MA 1983. L. July 1980. ETC 1982. Prop. Christopher Rose QC. Sec. Keith Armitage. Manchester Chambers; 601 Royal Exchange, 1982-1989; 8 King Street, 1989.

HOLROYDE, Timothy Victor QC
Born 18 August 1955 Liverpool. Bristol Grammar School; Wadham College, Oxford, BA (Jurisprudence) M. November 1977. Bencher 2005. Astbury Scholarship. 2 Harcourt Buildings, 1977-1978. Pupilmasters, Colin Milner-Smith & Geoffrey Grigson. ETC. 30 November 1978. Sec. John Kay. Circuit Junior, Summer 1979. Same Liverpool Chambers at; 606 The Corn Exchange, Fenwick Street, 1978-1982; 1 Exchange Flags, 1983-1991; Exchange Chambers, Derby Square, 1992. Assistant Recorder 1994. Silk 1996. Recorder 1997. WW.

HOLT, Abigail Claire
Born 13 February 1967, Bolton. Married to Simon Nichol qv. Bury Grammar School; Chef at "Kosmos Taverna" in Fallowfield, 1988-1989. Regents Park College, Oxford, 1989-1992, MA (Jurisprudence). L. 14 October 1993. ETC. 7 December 1993. Pupilmaster, John McNeill. Manchester Chambers; 38 King Street, 1993-1995; 24a St John Street, 1996-2000; Lincoln House Chambers, 1 Brazennose Street, 2000. Part time consultant on the Bar Vocational Course at Manchester Metropolitan University, 1993.

HOLT, Charles Louis John OBE
MA., LLB. G. 18 November 1912. Certificate of Honour M. 1912. ETC. 20 February 1913. Prop. Tobin KC. Sec. Thorpe. Bank Chambers, 38 Fishergate, Preston, 1912-1953. Not in 1954 Law List. OBE 1940.

HOLT, Frederick Appleby OBE
Certificate of Honour H. 1912. I. May 1912. ETC. 18 February 1914. Prop. Langdon KC. Sec. Jolly. 4 Essex Court, 1914; 3 Harcourt Buildings, 1915-1922; 7 King's Bench Walk, 1923-1934. No address, 1935-1948. Not in 1949 Law List.

HOLT, James Richard Trist
LLB (London), MA (Oxon) G. November 1973. Manchester Chambers; 3 St James Square, 1975-1984; St James Chambers, 68 Quay Street, 1985-1986. No address, 1987-1988. Not in 1989 Bar Directory.

HOLT, Margaret Evelyn
Born 18 May 1944 Liverpool. Cheltenham Ladies College; Manchester University, BA; London University, External LLB. L. February 1978. Legal Trainee, Sefton MBC, 1981-1983. Assistant Solicitor, Co-operative Wholesale Society, Manchester, 1984-1985; Knowsley MBC; Conveyancing Solicitor, 1986-1987; Deputy Chief Solicitor, 1988-1990. ETC. 25 March 1993. Prop. Nigel Gilmour QC. Sec. Leach. Pupilmaster, Nick Riddle. Liverpool Chambers; 24 Fenwick Street, 1993-1999; 14 Cook Street, 2000.

HOLT, Mary MP (Her Honour Mary Holt)
Daughter of Henry James Holt, solicitor. Park School, Preston; Girton College, Cambridge, MA., LLB. G. January 1949. ETC. 1949. Pupilmaster, Bertram Benas. Preston Chambers; 38 Fishergate, 1950-1960; 10 Lune Street, 1961-1964; 1a Chapel Street, 1965-1977. Chancery Practitioner. MP(C) Preston North, 1970-1974. Circuit Judge, 1977-1995. Freedom of the Cities of Dallas & Denton, Texas, 1987. Publication; 2nd edition of Benas & Essenhigh's Precedents of Pleadings, 1956. WW.

HOLT, (Michael) Julian
Born 21 January 1949. Manchester Polytechnic, BA. AAS. M. 28 September 1981. Call 9 February 1982. Manchester Chambers; 121 Princess Street, 1986-1987; 3 Peter Street, 1988-1991; 211 Deansgate, 1992-1996; 3 The Parsonage, 1997.

HOLT, Sarah Louise
Born 23 September 1975 Manchester. Two Trees High School, Denton, Manchester; University of Central England, LLB. M. October 1999. Wigan Family Welfare, August 1999-July 2001. ETC. 26 March 2002. Prop. David Steer QC. Sec. Gerald Baxter. 25 Castle Street, Liverpool, July 2001.

HOLT, Philip Durning
L. 24 June 1903. No address, 1903-1953. Not in 1954 Law List.

HOME, Noel Charles Minchin
I. 17 June 1896. ETC. 24 February 1909. Prop. Sanderson KC. Sec. Gibbons. 6 King's Bench Walk, 1911-1915; 2 Mitre Court Buildings, 1916-1925. No address, 1926-1949. Not in 1950 Law List.

HOOPER, Oswald Stokes
L. 18 November 1918. Liverpool Chambers; 26 Lord Street, 1923-1926; 25 Lord Street, 1927-1934; 13 Harrington Street, 1935-1936. Not in 1937 Law List.

*** HOPE, Antony Derwin (His Honour Judge Hope)**
Born 22 August 1944, Wellington, Somerset. Leighton Park School, Reading; London College of Estate Management, BSc.; College of Law, London. M. November 1970. Elected to Western Circuit, 1970. 3 Paper Buildings and 4 St Peter Street, Winchester, 1970-2002. Assistant Recorder 1992. Recorder 1996. Circuit Judge, Bolton 2002. Publications; 1990-1991-Town and Country Planning Acts. (RIBA Publications.)

HOPE, Collingwood CBE., KC

Born 10 November 1858. Died 5 May 1949 aged 90. 5th son of Thomas Arthur Hope, JP, of Bebington. Rugby; Pembroke College, Oxford. AAS. I. 7 November 1878. Call 21 June 1882. ETC. 14 July 1882. Prop. Gully QC. Sec. Collins. 5 Pump Court, 1883-1885. Liverpool Chambers; Commerce Chambers, 15 Lord Street, 1886-1890; Stephenson's Chambers, 25 Lord Street, 1891-1901. Silk 1901. Goldsmith Buildings, 1901-1912. Revising Barrister for Lancs., 1892-1897. County Councillor for Cheshire, 1898-1901. Recorder of Bolton, 1903-1925. Chairman, Essex Quarter Sessions, 1921-1935. High Steward, Borough of Southwold, Suffolk, 1905-1945. CBE, 1918 for wartime work with Essex Territorial Association. WW. Foster.

HOPE, Jacques Derek
LLB Manchester. G. November 1952. Manchester Chambers; 196 Deansgate, 1966-1989; Bridge Street Chambers, 72 Bridge Street, 1990-1993; Manchester House Chambers, 18-22 Bridge Street, 1994-1995. No address 1996.

HOPE, Nadine Samantha
Born 7 January 1963, Liverpool. St Edmund's College, Liverpool; Liverpool University, LLB. MA(Cantab) Music; ARCO; FRCO; LRAM. L. February 1988. ETC. 1988. Prop. Michael Maguire QC. Sec. John Mockett. Pupilmaster, Vincent Deane. Liverpool Chambers; 46 Stanley Street, 1988-1993; 25 Victoria Street, 1994-1999; 19 Castle Street, 1999.

HOPKINSON, Sir Alfred KC., MP
Born 28 June 1851, Manchester. Died 11 November 1939 aged 88. Owens College, Manchester; Lincoln College, Oxford (Scholar), MA., BCL; Hon. Fellow 1903. Vinerian Scholar; Stowell Fellow of University College, Oxford, 1873. AAS. L. 22 October 1870. Call 7 June 1873; Bencher 1896; Treasurer 1921. ETC. 2 August 1873. Prop. Herschell QC. Sec. Crompton. Manchester Chambers; 8 St James's Square, 1876-1877; 2 St James's Square, 1878-1889. 3 Harcourt Buildings, 1876-1888; 2 Mitre Court Buildings, 1890-1891; 12 New Court, Carey Street, 1892-1899. Silk 1892. Owens College (First constituent college of Victoria University, Manchester); Professor of Law, subsequently Principal. Vice Chancellor Victoria University of Manchester, 1900-1913. MP (U) Wilts, 1895-1898; Combined English Universities, 1926-1929. Publications; Rebuilding Britain, 1918; Penultima-Life and thought in Mid Victorian Days, 1930. Kt 1910. WW. DNB.

HOPKINSON, Martin
L. 17 November 1909. Goldsmith Building, 1910-1921. No chambers address, 1922-1953. Not in 1954 Law List.

HOPPER, Alvin William Laurie
Born 28 October 1945. Only son of Garnet Alvin Hopper of Dartford, Kent, engineer. LLB (Wales); LLM (London & Melbourne). AAS. M. 14 October 1969, Call February 1972. 41 North John Street, Liverpool, 1975-1976. Owen Dixon Chambers, William Street, Melbourne, Australia, 1977. Not in 1978 Bar Directory.

HOPWOOD, Charles Henry QC., MP

Born 20 July 1829 at 47 Chancery Lane. 5th son of John Stephen Spindler Hopwood, solicitor. Died 14 October 1904 aged 75. King's College School; King's College, Cambridge. AAS. M. 2 November 1850. Call 6 June 1853; Bencher 1876; Reader Lent 1886; Treasurer 1895. 3 Paper Buildings, 1876-1877; 1 Essex Court, 1878-1904. Silk 1874. MP (L) Stockport, 1874-1885; Middleton, 1892-1895. Recorder of Liverpool, 1886-1904. Founder, Romilly Society, 1897 " to reform the criminal law and prison administration." Member of the Council of Legal Education. Publications; Registration Cases, 1863-1872; Middle Temple Records, 1904. DNB. Hopwood was a lenient Judge. The Humanitarian League dubbed him "Hopwood the Good" because of his merciful sentences. William Stewart, Liverpool's Stipendiary Magistrate regarded Hopwood as "lenient to the point of absurdity", and refused to commit for sentence to the Quarter Sessions. He either sentenced himself or committed to the Assizes. One Chairman of Quarter Sessions believed Hopwood's approach to be wrong and believed that, "all the rascality of the country will flock to Liverpool." This was not born out by the statistics produced by Liverpool's Chief Constable which showed a reduction in crime. Hopwood's philosophy is best demonstrated by the address he gave to a Grand Jury at Quarter Sessions in 1889. Commenting on the savage sentences then prevalent he said, "A woman pleaded guilty before me of stealing some articles of little value. I looked at the record of her history. She had just come out after three served sentences of penal servitude a poor, broken down miserable being. She had served twenty one years for stealing food worth ten shillings. I gave her a slight punishment and have never seen her since." Sir Louis Blom-Cooper QC kindly invited me as his guest at Middle Temple Hall on 9 March 1998 on his Reader's Reading "Hopwood, the Good: A Study in a Rational Sentencing Policy and Practice." At my request he repeated the talk to the Bench & Bar in Liverpool on 1 October 1998 in the court room of the Recorder of Liverpool and a transcript is in Circuit Records.

HOPWOOD, Julia Elizabeth
LLB, Sheffield. L. July 1984. 67 Princess Street, Manchester, 1986. CPS, Macclesfield 1989-1990. Not in 1991 Bar Directory.

HORGAN, Peter Thomas
Born 14 April 1968, Birkenhead. St Anselm's College, Birkenhead; Manchester University, BA(Econ); Dip Law (City). M. October 1993. ETC. 1994. Pupilmaster, Paul Marshall. Manchester Chambers; 18 Lloyd's House, September 1993-June 1997; Queen's Chambers, 5 John Dalton Street, June 1997.

HORLOCK, Timothy John QC
Born 4 January 1958, Cambridge. Son of Sir John Horlock, engineer & Vice Chancellor of the Open University, 1981-1990. Manchester Grammar School; St John's College, Cambridge, MA. AAS. M. 30 January 1980. Call 23 July 1981. ETC. January 1982. Prop. Jack Price QC. Sec. John Hand. Manchester Chambers; 60 King Street/ Deans Court Chambers at Crown Square & 9 St John Street, 1981. Silk & Assistant Recorder 1997. Recorder 2000. WW.

HORNBY, James Angus
BA., LLB (Cantab). L. April 1947. Cassell Scholar. No address, 1947-1963. Not in 1964 Law List.

HORNBY, John
Born 2 December 1832. Eldest son of William Henry Hornby of Blackburn. Trinity College, Cambridge, MA 1859. Liverpool, Preston & Salford Sessions. No address, 1876-1923. Not in 1924 Law List.

HORNE, (Charles) (Hugh) Wilson
Born 25 October 1969, Glasgow. Royal Grammar School, Newcastle-upon-Tyne; Leeds University, LLB. L. October 1992. ETC. December 1993. Prop. Peter Winston Smith QC. Sec. Paul Chaisty. Pupilmasters, Michael Booth & Paul Chaisty. 40 King Street, Manchester, October 1992.

HORNE, Kenderik Thomas Clarke
Born 13 April 1972 Lancaster. Lancaster Royal Grammar School; Emmanuel College, Cambridge, BA (Law). L. March 1996. ETC. December 1996. Prop. Nigel Gilmour QC. Sec. John Benson. 14 Castle Street, Liverpool (now Atlantic Chambers, Cook Street), 1996.

HOROWITZ, Solomon
I. 28 January 1907. ETC. 2 February 1907. Prop. Langdon KC. Sec. Ambrose Jones. Manchester Chambers; 32 Kennedy Street, 1909-1916; 40 Kennedy Street, 1917; 10 St James's Square, 1918-1921; 78 King Street, 1922-1924. No address, 1925-1930. PO Box 393 Jerusalem, 1931-1963. Not in 1964 Law List.

HORRIDGE, Thomas Gardner QC, MP (The Rt. Hon. Mr Justice Horridge)

Born 12 October 1857, Bolton. Died 25 July 1938 aged 80. Only son of John Horridge of Bolton, bleacher. Nassau School, Barnes. Practised as a solicitor in Southport, 1879-1884. AAS. M. 7 November 1881. Call 25 June 1884; Bencher 1909; Reader Autumn 1921; Treasurer 1929. ETC. 30 July 1884. Prop Crompton QC. Sec. Kennedy. Liverpool Chambers; 5 Cook Street, 1884-1887; 8 Harrington Street, 1888-1897. 2 Mitre Court Buildings, 1895-1897; 2 Pump Court, 1898-1901; Silk 1901. 1 Garden Court, 1902-1910. MP (L) Manchester East, 1906-1910. He defeated Arthur Balfour who had been Conservative Prime Minister until one month before the General Election. High Court Judge, King's Bench Division, 1910-1937. Judge in Bankruptcy, 1913-1921. PC 1937. WW. DNB. Foster. Obituary Times, 26 July 1938. Horridge decided in 1919 the case of Phillips- v- Brooks. The contract case well known to all first year students as to whether title in goods passes from the jeweller to the fraudster. With Lord Reading and Avory J in 1916 he tried Sir Roger Casement for treason. In January 1911 he presided over the first mixed jury to sit in the Divorce Court, consisting of six men and six women. Evelyn Graham in "Fifty Years of Famous Judges" describes Horridge as "A big burly Lancastrian – a man of action; economical of every minute, a man before whom Counsel do well not to drone on or ramble too far afield. His average speed with undefended divorces is reputed to be 25 a day."

HORROCKS, Gilbert
Born 1917. 2nd son of John May Horrocks of Wilmslow, manufacturing chemist. Manchester University, LLB. AAS. M. 9 November 1927. Call 2 July 1930. ETC. 9 July 1930. Prop. Jackson KC. Sec. Jalland. 2 Booth Street, Manchester, 1932-1935. No address, 1936-1963. Not in 1964 Law List.

HORROCKS, Thomas
Born 1825. Only son of James Horrocks of Orrell Lodge, Lancs. AAS. I. 14 January 1845. Call 8 June 1849. Address; Brisco Hill, Cumberland, 1876-1904. JP., Cumberland. Not in 1905 Law List. Foster.

HORSFALL, William Hodgson
Born 7 August 1856. Son of George Henry Hodgson of Liverpool, merchant. Trinity Hall, Cambridge, MA. AAS. I. 13 April 1877. Call 9 June 1880. ETC. 18 July 1881. Prop. Russell QC. Sec. Crompton. 2 Harcourt Buildings, 1882-1912. No address, 1913-1940. Not in 1941 Law List. Private address in 1885; Larkfield, Toxteth Park, Liverpool. Foster.

HORSFIELD, Joseph
Born 1864. 2nd surviving son of Ralph Horsfield of Slack House, Hyde. Christ's College, Cambridge. AAS. M. 8 October 1885. Call 28 January 1889. ETC. 6 March 1890. Prop. Aspland QC. Sec. Yates. 6 King's Bench Walk, 1891-1900; Lamb Building, 1901-1908. No address, 1909-1940. Not in 1941 Law List.

HORWOOD, Anya Louise
Born 9 November 1967 Cardiff. Married to Stephen Swift qv. Cowley High School; Lancaster University, LLB. I. November 1991. ETC. December 1991. Prop. John Rowe QC. Sec. Pamela Badley. Liverpool Chambers; 2nd floor, Peel House Harrington Street/ 25-27 Castle Street, September 1991- August 2001.

HOSACK, John

Born 1809. Died 3 November 1887. 3rd son of John Hosack of Glengaber, Dumfries. AAS. M. 26 January 1838. Call 29 January 1841; Bencher 1875; Reader Lent 1884. 6 King's Bench Walk, 1848; 3 Pump Court, 1876-1877. Police Magistrate, Clerkenwell, 5 June 1877-1887. Middle Temple Examiner in International & Constitutional Law. Publications; Treatise on Conflict of English & Scottish Law, 1847; Mary Queen of Scots and her Accusers, 1869. DNB. Foster.

HOUGHTON, Lisa Jane

Born 3 September 1970 Lancs. Turton High School; Lancaster University, BA. Formerly a solicitors' clerk. G. October 1994. ETC. 4 April 1995. Prop. John Rowe QC. Sec. Beverly Lunt. 58 King Street Chambers, 51/53 South King Street, Manchester, 1995.

HOUGHTON-GRAY, Tredwell John

I. 18 April 1894. ETC. 30 July 1895. Prop. Pickford QC. Sec. Horridge. 8 Harrington Street, Liverpool, 1896-1902. No address, 1903-1907. Grahamstown, South Africa, 1908-1949. Not in 1940 Law List.

HOULDING, William

Born 1862. Only son of John Houlding of Liverpool, brewer. Edinburgh University. AAS. M. 5 May 1897. Call 18 November 1901. ETC. 20 February 1902. Prop. Taylor KC. Sec. F E Smith. No address, 1903-1953. Not in 1954 Law List.

HOULKER, Reginald QC

G. February 1955. ETC 1955. Manchester Chambers; 26 King Street, 1958; 9 Albert Square, 1959-1972; 1 Dean's Court, Crown Square, 1973-1981. Silk 1974. Goldsmiths Building, 1982-1993. Recorder 1974-1995.

HOWARD, Amanda Jayne

Born 5 March 1967 Birkenhead. The Ridgeway High School, Noctorum, Birkenhead; Huddersfield Polytechnic, LLB(Business Law). Articled Clerk with Phillip Con & Co, Manchester 1989-1991. Solicitor with Pannone & Partners, Manchester, 1991-1994. I. November 1994. ETC. 6 April 1995. Prop. Nigel Gilmore QC. Sec. David Brunnen. Derby Square Chambers, Merchants Court, Liverpool 1995-1999 & 2003. 37 Park Square, Leeds 1999-2003. Atlantic Chambers, Cook Street, Liverpool, 2004.

HOWARD, Anthony John

Born 5 July 1969, Nuneaton. St John Payne RC School, Chelmsford; Pendle College, Lancaster University, LLB. I. October 1992. ETC. 17 December 1992. Roderick Cams QC. Sec. Tim Horlock. 9 St John Street, September 1992. On secondment to John Stokes & Mester, Hong Kong September 1999-May 2000.

HOWARD, Hon Edmund Bernard Carlo

Born 8 September 1909. 4th son of Sir Esme Howard, First Baron Howarth of Penrith. Downside, New College, Oxford, BA. AAS. M. 20 June 1928. Call 26 January 1934. ETC. 27 February 1935. Prop. Goldie KC. Sec. Karmel. Circuit Junior, Winter 1935. 11 King's Bench Walk, 1935-1936. 2 Harcourt Buildings, 1937-1939. Served King's Royal Rifle Corps, 1939-1945. Joined Diplomatic Service in 1947. Italy, Spain, South America & Foreign Office, 1947-1969. CMG 1969. LVO 1961. Consul General, Genoa, 1965-1969. Commander, Order of Merit, Italy, 1973. Publications; Genoa, History & Art in an old seaport, 1971. WW. Burke's Peerage.

HOWARD, William Reginald

Born 10 June 1879. Died 17 February 1966 aged 86. Son of Alderman John Howard of Bootle and Hoylake. Bootle College; King's School Chester. In commerce. AAS. M. 15 April 1907. Call 26 January 1911. ETC. 6 February 1911. Prop. Tobin KC. Sec. Miller. Liverpool Chambers; 25 Lord Street, 1912; 16 Harrington Street, 1913-1914. War Service in King's 6th Liverpool Regiment, 1914. Captain 1916. Seconded to War Office. Joined South Eastern Circuit 1916 and practised in London until appointed; Stipendiary Magistrate, East Ham, 1935; Greenwich & Woolwich, 1939-1949. WW.

HOWARD-JONES, Glynn Howard OBE

LLB. I. 1 May 1912. Certificate of Honour E. 1912. ETC. 14 June 1912. Prop. Taylor KC. Sec. Layton. Liverpool Chambers; 8 Cook Street, 1919; 25 Lord Street, 1920-1930; 5 Cook Street, 1931-1939. 8 Cook Street, 1940-1941; 27 Lord Street, 1942-1946; 24 Dale Street, 1947-1956. No address 1957. Not in 1958 Law List.

HOWARTH, Christopher

I. 19 November 1894. No address, 1896-1949. Not in 1950 LL.

HOWARTH, Nigel John Graham (His Honour Judge Howarth)

Born 12 December 1936. Manchester Grammar School; Manchester University, LLB., LLM. G. November 1960. Studentship & Certificate of Honour. Atkin & Macaskie Scholar. ETC. 1961. Pupilmaster, Humphrey Copinger Easton. Manchester Chambers; 3 St James's Square, 1960-1984; St. James's Chambers, 68 Quay Street, 1985-1992. Acting Deemster, Isle of Man, 1985 & 1989. Recorder, 1989-1992. Chairman, Northern Circuit Chancery Bar Association, 1990-1992. Circuit Judge, 1992. WW.

HOWARTH, Richard Anthony

ETC 1979. Prop. Russell QC. Sec. Thomas. Not in 1984. Bar Directory.

HOWE, Bernard Robert

Born 10 December 1926. Died 18 January 1984 aged 57. Father of Ruth Alyson Howe qv. SFX, Liverpool (Head Boy). LLB (London), MA (Cantab), ACIS. Formerly an accountant & lecturer. L. July 1970. ETC 1972. Pupilmaster, David Morgan Hughes (Wales & Chester). Liverpool Chambers; 34 Castle Street, 1971-1972; Queen Insurance Building 'D', 13 Castle Street, 1973-1980; 16 Queen Avenue, Castle Street, 1981-1984.

HOWE, Ruth Alyson

Born Birkenhead. Daughter of Bernard Robert Howe qv. Queen's, Chester; Deeside Grammar School; Liverpool Polytechnic (now Liverpool John Moore's University), BA. Inland Revenue, 1975-1980. L. July 1983. ETC. 1983. Pupilmasters; Colin Cunningham & John Mockett. Liverpool Chambers; 2nd floor, Fruit Exchange, Victoria Street, 1986-1989; 46 Stanley Street, 1990-1993; 24 Fenwick Street, 1993-1997; Derby Square Chambers, Merchants Court 1997-31 December 2003; Atlantic Chambers, 4-6 Cook Street, 1 January 2004-.

HOWELLS, Catherine Jane

Born 13 January 1967 Kilgetty, Pembrokeshire. Greenhill School, Tenby; Liverpool University, LLB. G. 29 July 1989. Goldie Award. ETC. December 1989. Prop. John Kay QC. Sec. Bill Braithwaite. Exchange Chambers, Derby Square, Liverpool, 4 September 1989-.

HOWORTH, Sir Henry Hoyle MP

Born 1 July 1842 Lisbon. Died 15 July 1923 aged 81. Rossall School. AAS. I. 18 April 1864. Call 11 June 1867. 2 St James's Square, Manchester, 1876-1895. Special pleader. Manchester, Salford & Lancs. Sessions. No address, 1896-1923. MP (C) South Salford, 1886-1900. KCIE 1892. DCL. FRS. Trustee & Hon. Librarian, Cheltenham College. Trustee of British Museum. Publications include; A History of the Mongols; St Gregory the Great; Golden Days of the Early English Church, 1916. WW.

HUDSON, Christopher John

Born 6 December 1950, Bournemouth. Shaftesbury Grammar School; Christ Church, Oxford, MA (Modern History). Woollcombe Walls, Solicitors, 1976-1979. CPS, 1979-1987. L. May 1987. ETC. 1987. Prop. Jack Price QC. Sec. Roger Farley. Pupilmaster, Paul Reid. Manchester Chambers; Rational House, 64 Bridge Street, 1987-1992; Dean's Court Chambers, Crown Square and at 24 St John Street, 1992-, Recorder 2000,

HUDSON, Frank Michael Stanislaus

Born 1917. Died 14 April 2001 aged 84. 3rd son of Frederick Francis Hudson of Wimbledon, Surrey. BA (London). Formerly a local government officer. AAS. M. 10 March 1955. Call 27 June 1961. ETC. 1969. Prop. Hinchliffe QC. Sec. V. Williamson. Manchester Chambers; Post Office Chambers, 26 Brown Street, 1970-1971; 67 Princess Street, 1972-1986. Recorder, 1981-1983.

HUDSON, John Taylor

Lieutenant Commander, RN (Rtd). G. February 1961. ETC. 1961. Pupilmaster, E S Temple. 60 King Street / 1 Dean's Court, Manchester, 1961-1987. Retired to Bordeaux.

HUFFER, (Thomas) Ian

Born 7 March 1957, Ludlow. Ludlow Grammar School; Christ Church, Oxford, MA. G. November 1979. ETC. 1981. Pupilmaster, Alan Ward (Temple). Manchester Chambers; 9th & 6th floors, Sunlight House, Quay Street, 1981-1994; Young Street Chambers, 1995.

HUGHES, Archibald Owen
LLM. G. November 1940. Liverpool Chambers; 20 Hackins Hey, 1947-1958; 27 Dale Street, 1959-1966. Not in 1967-1977 Law Lists. 41 North John Street, 1978; 15 Victoria Street, 1979-1983; 10 St James Street, 1984-1989; 24 Fenwick Street, 1990-1999. Not practising, 2000-2001. Not in 2002 Bar Directory.

HUGHES, Iain Hamilton-Douglas QC (His Honour Judge Hughes QC)
Born 7 December 1950, London. Married to Claudia Ackner, daughter of Baron Ackner. Moseley Hall Grammar School, Cheadle; Bristol University, LLB. I. July 1974; Bencher 2001. ETC. 1977. Pupilmaster, Brian Carter. Sunlight House, Quay Street, Manchester, 1974-1977. 2 Crown Office Row, 1977-1999; 4 New Square, 1999-2002. Silk 1996. Assistant Recorder 1997. Recorder 2000. Circuit Judge, Portsmouth, 2002. Publication; (ed) Jackson & Powell on Professional Negligence, 1992 & 1997 and supplements. WW.

HUGHES, Kathryn Lesley
BA. L. July 1977. 3 St James Square, Manchester, 1979-1984. Solicitor, January 1985. Partner, Farleys, Solicitors, Blackburn, 1988.

HUGHES, Paul
St Catherines College, Oxford, BA (Jurisprudence). Call 2001. ETC. 12 December 2001. Prop. Peter Birkett QC. Sec. Lucy Davis. King's Chambers, 40 King Street, Manchester, 2001.

HUGHES, Rachel
Born 16 January 1973. Married to W K Rankin qv. Crosshall School, Ormskirk; New College, Oxford, LLB. G. November 1995. ETC. 19 December 1995. Prop. Nigel Gilmour QC. Sec. Charles Feeny. Pupilmaster, Heather Lloyd. Liverpool Chambers; Ground floor. Peel House, 5 Harrington Street, October 1995-February 1999; Oriel Chambers, 14 Water Street, Liverpool, 1 March 1999.

HUGHES, Ronw Moelwyn QC., MP.
Born 1 October 1897 Cardigan. Died 1 November 1955 aged 58. University College of Wales, Aberystwyth, BA; Downing College, Cambridge, BA., LLB. I. 10 May 1922. Yarborough Anderson Scholar. Bencher 1950. ETC. 31 January 1923. Prop. Layton KC. Sec. Stewart-Brown. 8 Cook Street, Liverpool, 1923-1926; 6 Crown Office Row, 1927-1929; 3 (N) King's Bench Walk, 1930; 2 Paper Buildings, 1931-1952. Lecturer in International Law, LSE; Examiner for Council of Legal Education & Law Society. Councillor for; Birkenhead; Ealing. Silk 1943. MP (Lab) Carmarthen, 1941-1945; Islington North, 1950-1951. Retired from practice 1952. Active service W.Yorks. Regt, 1916 & RFC & RAF, 1917-1919. Publications; 7th ed. Lord Birkenhead's International Law, 1928; Road & Rail Traffic Act 1933 (with Dingle Foot). WW.

*** HUGHES, Thomas QC (His Honour Judge Hughes QC)**
Born 20 October 1822 Uffington, Berkshire. Died 22 March 1896 Brighton aged 73. Rugby; Oriel College, Oxford, BA 1845. I. 28 January 1848; Bencher 1870. Joined the Western Circuit and practised from 7 Old Square & 3 Old Building. Silk 1869. County Court Judge, July 1882-1896. He went to live in Chester and sat on Circuit 9 which included Stockport and Ashton-under-Lyne (now Tameside). He wrote "Tom Brown's Schooldays." There is a statue of Hughes at Rugby School. DNB. Foster.

HUGHES, Sir Thomas Raffles KC
Born 28 January 1856. Died 24 October 1938 aged 82. Birkenhead School; Trinity College, Cambridge, MA. 1881. AAS. L. 26 April 1876. Call 9 June 1880; Bencher 1905; Treasurer 1928. ETC. 12 July 1880. Prop. Temple QC. Sec. Collins. 3 New Square, 1882-1885; 9 Stone Buildings, 1886. Liverpool Chambers; 9 Cook Street, 1886-1888; 8 Harrington Street, 1889. 11 Stone Buildings, 1890-1899; 8 Old Square, 1900-1938. Silk 1898. Chairman, Bar Council, 1920-1931. Kt. 1926. WW.

HUGHES, Walter
Born 1855. 2nd son of William Hughes of Manchester. University of London. Cotton spinner. AAS. M. 5 November 1887. Call 18 June 1890. ETC. 9 March 1891. Prop. Leese QC. Sec. (not recorded). No address, 1891-1899. St James Street, Manchester, 1899-1901. No address, 1902-1949. Not in 1950 Law List.

HUGILL, John QC
Born 11 August 1930. Sydney C of E Grammar School, New South Wales; Fettes College; Trinity Hall, Cambridge, MA. AAS. 17 April 1951. Call 9 February 1954; Bencher 1984. ETC. May 1954. Prop. Laski QC. Sec. A M Knight. Manchester Chambers; 40 Kennedy Street, 1954-1965; Ship Canal House, King Street, 1966-1980; 2 Old Bank Street, 1981-1991; Peel Court Chambers, 45 Hardman Street, 1992-1996. Silk 1976. London Chambers 5 Essex Court. Assistant Recorder, Bolton, 1971. Crown Court Recorder, 1972-1996. Deputy High Court Judge, 1993-1995. Chairman of the Committee of Inquiry relating to Darren James Clarke. (Report November 1979. HMSO. Cmnd. 7730.)

Chairman, Stanley Royd Inquiry, 1985. Member; Senate of the Inns of Court and the Bar, 1984-1986; General Council of the Bar, 1987-1989. Retired from practice 1996. WW.

HULL, Sir Hubert
Born 10 September 1887. Died 24 March 1976 aged 88. Stonyhurst. I. 8 June 1910; Bencher 1945. ETC. 3 July 1913. Temporary civil servant, 1914-1919 & 1939-1948. 3 Hare Court, 1912-1913; 1 Brick Court, 1914-1922; 4 Paper Buildings, 1923-1949. Junior Counsel, Ministry of Agriculture & Fisheries and Commissioners of Common Land. Assistant Procurator General. Official Referee, Supreme Court, 1949-1950. Member, Royal Commission on the Press, 1947. President of the Transport Tribunal, 1951-1962. CBE 1945. Kt. 1959. WW.

HULL, Leslie David (His Honour Judge Hull)
Born 7 January 1950, St Helens. Brasenose College, Oxford MA. AAS. M. 29 July 1971. Call 22 November 1972. ETC. 13 February 1973. Pupilmaster, H A Kershaw. Manchester Chambers; 60 King Street, 1973-1983; 1 Dean's Court, 1984-1993; 9 St John Street, 1994-2001. Recorder 1993. Circuit Judge, Grimsby, 18 June 2001.

HULME, Thomas Allen
Born 17 March 1842. Eldest son of Rev. Samuel Hulme, Wesleyan Minister of Altrincham. Trinity College, Dublin, LLB. Captain, 11 Lancs. Rifle Volunteers. AAS. L. 18 November 1868. Call 26 January 1872. ETC. 4 August 1873. Prop. Pope QC. Sec. Blair. 57 Princess Street, Manchester, 1876-1888. Equity draftsman & conveyancer. Not in 1889 Law List. Foster.

HULTON, Arthur Hyde
Trinity College, Cambridge, LLB. I. 12 May 1897. ETC. 27 July 1897. Prop. Leese QC. Sec. Sutton. 41 John Dalton Street, Manchester, 1899-1921. No address, 1922-1949. Not in 1950 Law List.

HULTON, Harrington Arthur Harrop
Born 9 November 1846. Eldest son of Rev. Arthur Hyde Hulton of Bardsley House, Lancs. BA, Downing College, Cambridge, 1873, from Trinity Hall, Cambridge. AAS. L. 4 November 1869. Call 27 January 1873. ETC. 12 March 1873. Prop. Herschell QC. Sec. Bruce. Library Chambers, Middle Temple, 1876-1879; 3 Plowden Buildings, 1880-1892. No address, 1893-1923. Not in 1924 Law List. Foster.

HULTON, Samuel Fletcher
I. 19 November 1888. ETC. 4 March 1889. Prop. Aspland QC. Sec. Moon. 12 King's Bench Walk, 1891-1892; 10 King's Bench Walk, 1893-1930. Not in 1931 Law List.

HULTON, William Adam (His Honour Judge Hulton)
Born 18 October 1802 Preston. Died 3 March 1887 Penwortham aged 84. Manchester Grammar School. AAS. I. 6 June 1822. Call 29 June 1827. Treasurer of County of Lancaster, 1831-1849. Assessor, Lancs. Sheriffs Court to 1847. County Court Judge, Circuit 4, (Lancs.) 13 March 1847-1886. JP., DL., Lancs. Publications include; Treatise on the Law of Convictions, 1835. Documents relating to the Priory of Penwortham, 1853. DNB.

HUMBER, Thomas
Born 1827. Eldest son of William Humber of Preston. St John's College, Cambridge, MA 1852. AAS. I. 29 May 1849. Call 17 November 1853. Preston Chambers; 6 Chapel Walks, 1876; 2 Chapel Street, 1877-1900. Equity draftsman & conveyancer, Lancs. Chancery Court. London chambers; 77 Chancery Lane and 3 Brick Court from 1884. Not in 1901 Law List.

HUMPHREYS, Michael
Born 28 September 1954, Cardiff. Married to Caroline Humphreys, solicitor. St Illtyd's College, Cardiff; Hull University, LLB. Solicitor, 1980-2001 with; Thompsons; John Pickering & Partners; Silverbeck Rymer; Christopher Thomas & Co; Edwards Goldard. L. 8 March 2001. ETC. 18 December 2001. Prop. Peter Birkett QC. Sec. Graham Wood. India Buildings, Water Street, Liverpool, October 2001. Part time Chairman, Employment Tribunals, 2001.

HUMPHRIES, David John
Born 3 February 1966. Son of His Honour Gerard Humphries qv, brother of Paul Humphries qv. Lancashire Polytechnic, LLB. AAS. M. 20 July 1987. Call 28 July 1988. 28 St John Street, Manchester, 1990-2000. Now at the Irish Bar.

HUMPHRIES, His Honour Gerard William
Born 13 December 1928. Father of David & Paul Humphries qv, and of Bernard Humphries, solicitor in the South of France. St Bede's College, Manchester; Manchester University, LLB. Flying Officer, RAF, 1951-AAS. M. 14 November 1949. Call 1 July 1952. ETC. 4 March Prop. Brabin QC. Sec. Lambert. Manchester Chambers; 26 King Street, 1954-1958; 9 Albert Square, 1959-1972; 1 Dean's Court, Crown Square, 1973-1980. Assistant Recorder of Salford, 1969-1971. Crown Court Recorder, 1974-1980. Chairman; Medical Appeals Tribunal, 1976-1980; Vaccine Damage Tribunals, 1979-1980. Circuit Judge, Manchester, 1980-2003. Foundn. Governor, St Bede's College, 1978. KHS 1986. KCHS 1996. Publication; Stations of the Cross: stations for vocation, 1995. Retirement tributes at Manchester Law Courts, 11 July 2003. (His Honour Judge David Maddison/ David Steer QC). Transcript in Circuit Records. WW.

HUMPHRIES, Paul Benedict
Born 22 November 1962, Gatley, Cheadle. Son of His Honour Gerard Humphries qv, brother of David Humphries qv and of Bernard Humphries, solicitor. St Augustine's Grammar School; Loreto 6th form College; St Anne's College, Oxford, MA. AAS. M. 9 May 1985. Call 25 November 1986. ETC. 1986. Pupilmaster, Raymond Machell. Dean's Court Chambers, Crown Square & 24 St John Street, Manchester, 1986.

HUMPHRY, Richard Michael
Born 5 April 1949, Bristol. High Storrs Grammar School, Sheffield; Fitzwilliam College, Cambridge, MA., LLB. G. July 1972. ETC. 2 November 1972. Prop. Godfrey Heilpern QC. Sec. F Brian Carter. Same Manchester Chambers at; 47 Peter Street, 1972-1974; 12th floor, Sunlight House, Quay Street, 1974-1980; 28 St John Street, 1980.(now St Johns Buildings Chambers).

HUNT, Richard Mark
Born 1 July 1959, Preston. Repton School, Derbys. Liverpool University, LLB. with Weightmans, solicitors, Liverpool 1981-1984. L. July 1985. ETC. December 1985. Prop. R J D Livesey QC. Sec. John Appleton. Ground & first floor, Peel House, Harrington Street, Liverpool, 1985-1989. Preston Chambers; 14 Winckley Square, 1989-1991; 15 Winckley Square, 1991.

HUNTER, Robert
G. November 1999. ETC. 12 December 2001. Prop. Keith Goddard QC. Sec. Tim Ryder. Pupilmaster, Julian Holt. Queen's Chambers, 5 John Dalton Street, Manchester, 2001.

HUNTER, Winston Ronald O'Sullivan QC
Born 7 September 1960, St James, Jamaica. Married to Louise Blackwell qv. Stretford Grammar School for Boys; Leeds University, LLB. L. July 1985. ETC. November 1985. Pupilmaster, John Townend. Manchester Chambers; 28 St John Street, 1985-2000. Silk 2000. 12 Byrom Street, 2000. Assistant Recorder 1999. Recorder 2000.

HURD, James Robert
Born 25 May 1971, Bromsgrove, Worcs. Married to Joanna Hurd, solicitor advocate with Eversheds, Birmingham. Cheadle Hulme High School; Birmingham University, LLB (Law & Politics). G. October 1994. ETC. 4 April 1995. Prop. Elleray QC. Sec. Searle. St James's Chambers, 68 Quay Street, Manchester, 1994.

HURST, Alfred Stone
Born 1881. Younger son of Tom Hurst of Stockport, gentleman farmer. AAS. M. 4 November 1903 when a shorthand writer of 61 Chancery Lane. ETC. 27 June 1906. Prop. Sanderson KC. Sec. Hewart. Fountain Court 1910; 2 Brick Court 1911-1920; 1 Garden Court 1921-1931. Not in 1932 Law List.

HURST, His Honour Sir Gerald Berkeley QC., MP.
Born 4 December 1877 Bradford. Died 27 October 1957 aged 79. Bradford Grammar School; Lincoln College, Oxford, MA., BCL. L. 23 April 1902; Bencher 1924; Treasurer 1944. ETC. 16 June 1902. Prop. Shee KC. Sec. Radford. Manchester Chambers; 78 King Street, 1902-1914. Served in Sudan, Gallipoli, Egypt, Sinai & Flanders, 1914-1918. Late Lt. Col. Commanding 7th Btn. Manchester Regiment. 28 John Dalton Street, 1918; 15 Brazennose Street, 1919-1920. Silk 1920. 8 Old Square, 1920-1937. Chancery Practitioner. MP (C) Manchester (Moss Side), 1918-1923 & 1924-1935. Kt. 1929. County Court Judge, Circuit 56, (Croydon & West Kent), 1938-1952. Chairman, Home Office Committee on Adoptions, 1953. Publications Autobiography "Closed Chapters," 1942; Short History of Lincoln's Inn, 1946; Lincoln's Inn Essays, 1949. WW.

HURST, Joseph
I. 26 January 1887. ETC. 28 July 1888. Prop. Aspland QC. Sec. H Swift. 3 Plowden Buildings, 1887-1888; 2 Paper Buildings, 1889-1924. No address, 1925-1940. Not in 1941 Law List.

HUSBAND, John
Very little information save that he signed the Liverpool Prosecutions Book some date between 1952 & 1956 from 7 Rumford Street, Liverpool. The entry is marked "Returned to British West Indies" but no date is given. Never appeared in the Law Lists.

HUSSAIN, Mukhtar QC
Born 22 March 1950 Geelan, Mirpur, Pakistan. Came to live in the United Kingdom in 1964. William Temple Secondary School, Preston; Blackburn College of Technology & Design. AAS. M. 24 October 1968. Call 22 July 1971; Bencher 2001. ETC. 1973. Prop. Benet Hytner QC. Sec. John Hodgson. Manchester Chambers; 4th floor, Sunlight House, Quay Street, 1973-1976; 43 King Street, 1977-1978; Rational House, 64 Bridge Street, 1979-1997; Lincoln House Chambers, 1 Brazennose Street, 1997. (Head of Chambers 1992-). Immigration Counsellor, 1971-1973. Presenter, Granada Television, 1982-1987. Assistant Recorder 1986. Recorder 1989. Silk 1992. Chairman; Police Disciplinary Tribunal, 1997; Mental Health Review Tribunal, 1998. Formerly a member of Criminal Injuries Compensation Board. WW.

HUTCHINSON, Christopher Clark KC
Born 1854. Died 7 March 1914. Royal College of Science, Dublin. MInstCE., FIC, FCS. Consulting engineer and chemical engineer in UK & USA before AAS. M. 29 April 1893, aged 38. Call 27 January 1896. ETC. 26 February 1897. Prop. Bigham QC. Sec. Moon. 3 Harcourt Buildings, 1897-1914 and at Palace Chambers, 9 Bridge Street, Westminster. Parliamentary Draftsman. Silk 1910. WW.

HUTCHINSON, Godfrey Cresswell
LLB. I. 28 January 1907. Parliamentary Draftsman. 3 Harcourt Buildings & Palace Chambers, 9 Bridge Street, Westminster, 1910-1940. No address, 1941-1953. Not in 1954 Law List. Joined the Midland Circuit on Call but transferred to the Northern Circuit in 1934.

HUTCHINSON, Sir Geoffrey Clegg MC, QC, MP. (Baron Ilford of Bury)
Born 14 October 1893. Died 20 August 1974 aged 80. Cheltenham College; Clare College, Cambridge, MA 1919. Joined the Lancashire Fusiliers, 1914; served BEF, 1915-1916 & 1918-1919. Wounded. MC, 1916. Deputy Assistant Military Secretary, War Office, 1941-1942. Hon. Col. 5th Btn., the Lancs. Fusiliers, 1948-1954. I. 17 November 1920; Bencher 1946. 2 Paper Buildings, 1922-1974. MP (C); Ilford, 1937-1945; Ilford North, 1950-1954. Chaired many central and local government committees. Chairman, National Assistance Board, 1954-1964. Hon. Freeman of Borough of Ilford and of the London Borough of Camden. Kt. 1952. Life Peer 1962. WW.

HUTTON, His Honour Crompton
Born 5 December 1822. Died 5 January 1910 aged 87. Eldest son of Robert Hutton MP of Roehampton. Rugby; Trinity College, Cambridge, BA, 1846. AAS. I. 13 June 1843. Call 6 June 1853. Junior Counsel to Inland Revenue. County Court Judge, Circuit 5, (Lancs.), 27 December 1872-1889. JP; Lancs. & Glos. Foster.

HYMANSON, Deanna Susan
LLB (London). AAS. M. 18 February 1986. Call February 1988. Manchester Chambers; Hollins Chambers, 64a Bridge Street, 1990-1997; Cobden House Chambers, 19 Quay Street, 1998-2001. Not in 2002 Bar Directory.

HYTNER, Benet Alan QC

Born 29 December 1927. Manchester Grammar School; Trinity Hall, Cambridge, MA. AAS. M. 5 September 1946. National Service, RASC., 1949-1951 (commnd). Call 5 February 1952; Bencher 1977; Reader 1995. ETC. 6 March 1952. Prop. Wooll QC. Sec. Heilpern. Manchester Chambers; 60 King Street, 1952-1960; 47 Peter Street, 1961-1970. Silk 1970. 5 Essex Court, 1970-1992; 61 Fleet Street, 1993-1996; 25 later 12 Byrom Street, Manchester & 22 Old Buildings. Judge of Appeal, Isle of Man, 1980-1997. Deputy High Court Judge, 1975-1997. Crown Court Recorder, 1972-1997. Leader of the Northern Circuit, 1984-1988. Member; General Council of the Bar, 1969-1973 & 1986-1988; Senate of the Inns of Court and Bar, 1977-1981 & 1984-1986. WW.

I

ILFORD, Baron (See Sir Geoffrey Hutchinson)

INGHAM, Charles Neil
BA (London). Also member of Hong Kong Bar. I. November 1972. ETC. 13 February 1973. Pupilmaster, John Coffey. 36 St Ann Street, Manchester, 1973-1974. Police Prosecutions Unit, Manchester, 1975-1977. Legal Dept, Central Government Offices, Hong Kong, 1978-1981. Legal Officer, China Light & Power Co, Hong Kong, 1982-1983. Not in Bar Directory, 1984-1993. Assistant Chief later Chief Crown Prosecutor, St Albans, 1994. Part time Chairman, Industrial Tribunals (London Area).

INGHAM, His Honour Theophilus Hastings
Born 15 July 1808. Died 5 January 1900 aged 91. Only son of Ignatius Ingham of Skipton. AAS. I. 8 February 1828. Call 2 May 1834. Commissioner in Bankruptcy. Judge of Burnley Court of Requests, 1842-1846. Recorder of Clitheroe, 1859-1891. County Court Judge, Circuit 3, (Cumberland, Westmorland & Northumberland), 1847-1891. Chairman, Yorks. West Riding Quarter Sessions. WW. Foster.

IOANNOU, Anastasia (Mrs Raleigh McKenzie)
LLB., BA(Sheffield) I. July 1982. Pupilmaster, Dan Brennan. 18 St John Street, Manchester, 1984-1998. On the 18 March 1998 Anastasia attended the Lord Chancellor's Department for interview for Assistant Recorder. Whilst at the Department, sadly, she collapsed and died. On 23 March 1998 at the Manchester Law Courts the Recorder of Manchester, His Honour Judge Sir Rhys Davies QC paid tribute to Anastasia. A transcript is in Circuit Records.

IRELAND, John Hilton
Born 1857. 4th son of Rev. Thomas Ireland of Werneth, Lancs. St John's College, Cambridge, MA. AAS. I. 19 January 1876. Call 27 January 1879. ETC. 1 February 1879. Prop. Collins. Sec. Leese. No address, 1881-1935. Not in 1936 Law List. Foster.

IRO, Augustine Okevurumba
Born 12 December 1963, Nigeria. St Francis Xaviers Grammar School, Woolton, Liverpool; North Staffs University, LLB. Solicitor with; Jackson & Canter, Liverpool, 1986-1992; Linskills, Liverpool, 1992-1995. G. 25 May 1995. ETC Easter 1995. Prop. David Harris QC. Sec. Nigel Beeson. Liverpool Chambers; 24 Fenwick Street, 1995-2000; 14 Cook Street, 2000. New Bailey Chambers, Liverpool, 2004.

IRONFIELD, Janet Ruth
Born 8 February 1964, Bury. Bolton School; St Hilda's College, Oxford, BA. G. October 1992. ETC. 17 December 1992. Prop. Keith Goddard QC. Sec. Mark Turner. Dean's Court Chambers at; Crown Square & 24 St John Street, 1992.

IRVINE, Francis Hugh
Born 18 November 1880. Only son of Alexander Forbes Irvine, advocate of Drum Castle, Aberdeen. New College, Oxford, MA 1883. AAS. I. 20 January 1876. Call 26 January 1880. ETC. 12 July 1880. Prop. Gully QC. Sec. Collins. 1 Dr. Johnson's Buildings, 1882; 3 Harcourt Buildings, 1883-1884; 1 Mitre Court Buildings, 1885-1893. No address 1894. Not in 1895 Law List. Foster

IRVINE, Pearson Robert
Born 1846. 4th son of James Pearson Irvine, physician of Lancaster. Corpus Christi, Cambridge. AAS. I. 25 May 1869. Call 18 November 1872. ETC. 28 March 1873. Prop. Watson. Sec. Commins. No address, 1877-1935. Not in 1936 Law List. Foster.

IRVING, Gillian
Born 1 November 1958 Carlisle. Married to P. Cadwallader qv. Caldew School. Dalston; Nottingham Trent Polytechnic, BA. I. July 1984. ETC. 1985. Prop. Christopher Rose QC. Sec. Janet Smith. Manchester Chambers; Crown Square Chambers/ 9 St John Street, 1984. Chairman, Care Standards Tribunal, 1998. Legal Member, Mental Health Review Tribunal, 1999.

ISAACS, Dennys Godfrey
Born 1896. Younger son of Godfrey Isaacs, deputy chairman & managing director of Marconi Wireless Telegraph Co., nephew of Rufus Daniel Isaacs qv. Exeter College, Oxford. AAS. M. 24 March 1919. Call 10 May 1922. ETC. 4 July 1923. Prop. Ashton KC. Sec. Helme. 3 Dr Johnson's Building, 1924-1934. No address, 1935-1953. Not in 1954 Law List.

ISAACS, Gerald Rufus MC., KC (Second Marquess of Reading)
Born 10 January 1889. Died 19 September 1960 aged 71. Only son of Rufus Daniel Isaacs, First Marquess of Reading. Rugby; Balliol College, Oxford. AAS. M. 7 October 1908. Call 19 June 1912; Bencher 1936; Reader Lent 1947; Treasurer 1958. ETC. 28 January 1914. Prop. Tobin KC. Sec. Lowther. 2 Garden Court, 1912-1960. Served War, 1914-1918, Royal Fusiliers (MC. Croix de Guerre). Silk 1929. Served on many government committees and boards. Training & Staff appointments during War 1939-1945 rising to Hon. Brigadier. TD

1945. CBE 1945. Minister of State for Foreign Affairs, 1953-1957. Baron 1914. Viscount Reading 1916. Viscount Erleigh 1917. Earl 1917. Marquess 1926. Publications. South Sea Bubble, 1933; Rufus Isaacs, First Marquess of Reading Vol 1 (1943) Vol 2 (1945). WW.

ISAACS, Sir Rufus Daniel Isaacs QC., MP (First Marquess of Reading)
Born 10 October 1860 London. Died 30 December 1935 aged 75. Son of a London fruit merchant. Father of Gerald Rufus Isaacs qv. Anglo-Jewish Academy, Regents Park; University College School and abroad. Worked in family fruit business and then at the Stock Exchange as a jobber on the foreign market. AAS. M. 10 January 1885. Pupil to Joseph Walton qv. Call November 1887; Bencher 1905; Reader Autumn 1917; Treasurer 1927. ETC. 20 March 1890. Prop. Bigham QC. Sec. Walton. Set up his own chambers at 1 Garden Court, specialising in commercial and trade union cases. Silk 1898. MP (L) Reading, 1904-1913. Solicitor General, 1910. Attorney General, 1910-1913. Lord Chief Justice of England, 1913-1921. In 1915 he led an Anglo-French mission to the USA and obtained a loan of 500 million dollars for war supplies. High Commissioner and Special Ambassador to USA, 1918. Viceroy & Governor General of India, 1921-1926. Secretary of State for Foreign Affairs, 1931. First Attorney General to become a member of the Cabinet. Captain of Deal Castle, 1926-1934. Lord Warden of the Cinque Ports, 1934-1935. Kt. 1910. KCVO & PC 1911. GCB 1915. GCSI & GCIE 1921. GCVO 1922. Baron 1913. First Viscount, Reading 1916. Viscount Earleigh 1917. Earl 1917. First Marquess of Reading 1926. WW. DNB.
As Attorney he prosecuted the poisoner Frederick Seddon; and Mrs. Emmeline Pankhurst for conspiring to commit injury and damage.
In 1916 as Lord Chief Justice with Horridge & Avory JJ's, he tried Sir Roger Casement for treason. F E Smith prosecuted as Attorney General. In 1918 Lloyd George wrote to him as follows " When the time comes....the leading part which you played in co-ordinating the war effort of the United States and the other Allies, and, above all, in helping to bring about that dramatic movement of the American Army in Europe in the spring and summer of 1918, which contributed so strikingly to the Allied victory in the autumn, will be understood in its true perspective."
Biographies; Rufus Isaacs. by his son, 2 vols. Hutchinson, 1943 & 1945. Lord Reading and his Cases. Derek Walker Smith. Chapman & Hall, 1934. Lord Reading. H Montgomery Hyde. Heineman, 1967. Lord Reading. Denis Judd. Weidenfeld & Nicholson, 1982. Earl of Reading. Syed Sirdar Ali Khan, 1924. Lord Reading. Cecil J C Stokes, 1928. Rufus Isaacs. Stanley Jackson, 1935. Advocates of the Golden Age. Charlie Broad, 1958. Five Jewish Lawyers of the Common Law. Arthur Goodhart, 1949.

ISAACSON, Richard QC
Born 7 September 1950. Died 18 April 1998 aged 47. Son of (Soloman) Herbert Isaacson, Liverpool pharmaceutical chemist, nephew of the late Lord Cohen of Birkenhead, uncle of Charles Lander qv. Liverpool College, Liverpool University, LLB. 1971. President of Law Faculty, 1970-1971. AAS. 31 December 1968. Call 22 November 1972. ETC. 7 December 1972. Pupilmaster, Henry Lachs. Liverpool Chambers; 27 Dale Street, 1972-1976; Melbourne Buildings, 21 North John Street, 1977-1988; 3rd floor, Peel House, Harrington Street, 1989-1991; Exchange Chambers, Derby Square, 1992-1998. Standing Counsel to HM Customs & Excise (Northern Circuit), 1994-1997. Assistant Recorder 1995. Silk 1997. He was junior defence counsel to Brian Walsh QC in the Jamie Bulger murder trial. Elected to Liverpool City Council (SDP) for Dingle Ward, 1986-1990. Contested Liverpool, Garston, 1987. Tributes at Liverpool Law Courts 22 April 1998 (Judge David Clarke QC/ Richard Henriques QC) & Jewish Chronicle, May 1998 (Henry Globe QC) WW.

ISHERWOOD, Thomas
MA., LLD., DCL. I. 27 January 1896. 1 Cambridge Rd, Southport, 1898-1926. No address, 1927-1949. Liverpool Sessions. Not in 1950 Law List.

ISMAY, Thomas Bruce
I. 17 November 1920. ETC. 30 January 1924. Prop. Greaves-Lord QC. Sec. Blackledge. 3 King's Bench Walk, 1925-1940. No address, 1941-1953. Not in 1954 Law List.

J

JACK, Charles
I. 7 June 1875. ETC. 13 July 1876. Prop. Torr QC. Sec. Crompton. 7 King's Bench Walk, 1877-1878; 7 Crown Office Row, 1879-1881; 2 Pump Court, 1882. Not in 1883 Law List.

JACKSON, John Edgar
Born 11 December 1939, Burnley. Son of Wilfred Jackson, JP., electro chemical engineer & company director. Burnley Grammar; Central Kansas City, USA. Marks & Spencer PLC, 1960-1962. R Clegg & Co, 1962-1968. AAS. M. 16 January 1968. Call 16 July 1970. ETC. 1970. Pupilmaster, Robert Hardy. Manchester Chambers; 3 St James's Square, 1970-1984; 40 King Street, 1984-1999; Young Street Chambers, 1999. Chairman, Burnley Football Club, 1981-1983.

JACKSON, Joseph Cooksey KC, MP.
Born 1879. Died 26 April 1938. Royal Grammar School, Lancaster; Clare College, Cambridge, BA, 1900. M. 5 May 1909. ETC. 4 July 1909. Prop. Tobin KC. Sec. Roe Ryecroft. 60 King Street, Manchester, 1918-1924. Silk 1924. 2 Mitre Court Buildings, 1925-1935; 4 Brick Court, 1936-1938. Recorder of Bolton, 1925-1938. MP (U) Heywood & Radcliff, Lancs., 1931-1935. Defended Chung Yi Miao for murder in 1928. For further details see Cumbria Murder Casebook. Paul Harris, 1995 and see Singleton LJ. Prosecuted Buck Ruxton for murder in 1936. See Notable British Trials, "Dr Buck Ruxton," 1937. See also entry for Singleton LJ. WW.

JACKSON, Lowry (Stephen) Hart
Born 13 March 1913. Died May 2002 aged 89. G. 3 July 1935. ETC. 26 February 1936. Prop Gorman KC. Sec. Jolly. Manchester Chambers; 60 King Street, 1937-1983; Crown Square Chambers, 1983-1986. Retired from practice in 1986. Lived in Arnside.

JACKSON, Nicholas David Kingsley
Born 29 April 1969. Krönberg, West Germany. King William's College, Isle of Man; Newcastle University, LLB. L. November 1992. ETC. March 1994. Sec. Nicholas Riddle. Pupilmaster David Elvin (London). Liverpool Chambers; 7 Queen Avenue, 1994-1996; merged with 14 Castle Street, 1996-2003; chambers moved to Atlantic Chambers, Cook Street, 2003.

JACKSON, Richard England
I. 11 May 1892. ETC. 25 February 1896. Prop. McCall QC. Sec. Howarth. 4 Harcourt Buildings, 1896-1913. No address, 1914-1949. Not in 1950 Law List.

JACKSON, Thomas Hughes
L. 29 April 1896. 2 Harrington Street, Liverpool, 1897-1912. No address, 1913-1949. Not in 1950.

JACKSON, Wayne Thomas
Born 8 February 1961, Sheffield. Stand Grammar School, Whitefield, Manchester; Sheffield University, LLB. AAS. M. 14 April 1983. Call 27 November 1984. ETC 1984. Manchester Chambers; Conavon Court Chambers, 13 Blackfriars Street, 1986-1989; Manchester House Chambers, 18-22 Bridge Street, 1990-1999; Young Street Chambers, 38 Young Street, 2000-2001; 24 St John Street, 2001.

JACKSON, William
Born 1858. Glasgow University. M.D., DPH., LRCP. 2nd son of Robert Jackson of Swinden, Nelson, farmer. AAS. M. 10 March 1891. Call 18 April 1894. Coley Hall, Nelson, 1895-1936. Preston & Burnley Sessions. Not in 1937 Law List.

JACKSON-LIPKIN, Miles Henry (The Hon. Mr Justice Jackson-Lipkin)
Born 24 May 1924, Liverpool. Only son of Isaac Jackson-Lipkin, consultant physician of Liverpool. Harrow; Trinity College, Oxford. AAS. M. 19 October 1948. Call 6 June 1951. Liverpool Chambers; 9 Rumford Street, 1954; 49 Castle Street, 1955; 34 Castle Street, 1956-1970. Hong Kong Bar, 1963. New South Wales Bar, 1980. QC (Hong Kong) 1974. High Court Judge, Hong Kong, 1981-1987. FCIArb, 1986. Chartered Arbitrator, Canada, 1995. Publications; Beaufort Legitimation, 1957; Scales of Justice, 1958; Israel Naval Forces, 1959. WW.

JACONELLI, Joseph
MA., LLB (Cantab); PhD (Manchester) St James's Chambers, 68 Quay Street, Manchester, 1996-2001 & Manchester University.

JAFFE, Jacob
LLB. G. July 1957. 2 Booth Street, Manchester, 1958-1974. Not in 1975 Law List.

JAGER, (George) Harold
Born 9 January 1877. Died 9 February 1954 aged 77. I. 27 January 1902. ETC. 14 February 1902. Prop Shee KC. Sec. Leslie Scott. Circuit Junior, Summer 1902. Liverpool Chambers; 10 Cook Street, 1902; Stephenson's Chambers, 25 Lord Street, 1903-1911. He married Dorothy Maclver in 1908 and they had 6 children. Not being able to support his wife in the standard of living to be expected by the daughter of a wealthy shipowner, MP and director of the Great Western Railway, he went into paint manufacture at Greenford in Middlesex. When his wife died in 1924 he sold the business. He was worried about the dangers of lead in paint. He returned to Wirral and joined his brother in the family firm of George Jager, sugar refiners which was sold to Tate & Lyle in the 1940's. He was an active member of Royal Liverpool Golf Club. Autobiography; "Brief Life," Henry Young & Sons Ltd, Liverpool, 1934. An interesting account of circuit life in the early 1900's and of F E Smith's early days in Liverpool. Information supplied by his sons Hamish and Giles and His Honour Alan Booth QC.

JALLAND, Arthur Edgar QC
Born 1889. Died 21 January 1958. Father of His Honour William Herbert Wainwright Jalland qv and Marjorie Wainwright Jalland qv. Manchester Grammar School; Manchester University, LLB 1910. G. 28 June 1911. ETC. 20 July 1911. Prop. Langdon KC. Sec. Gordon Hewart. Manchester Chambers; Duchy Chambers, Clarence Street, 1911-1921; 2 Booth Street, 1922-1935; 40 Kennedy Street, 1936-1952. Served, 1915-1919, Lt., in European War. Contested (L) Knutsford, 1929. Silk 1950. Chairman, Lancs. Quarter Sessions and Recorder of Preston and Judge of Preston Borough Court of Pleas, 1950-1958. WW.

JALLAND, Marjorie Wainwright (Mrs Fell)
Daughter of Arthur Edgar Jalland QC qv and sister of His Honour "Bert" Jalland qv. LLB. G. 9 June 1937. ETC. 1 July 1937. Prop. Gorman KC. Sec. Jolly. Manchester Chambers; 40 Kennedy Street, 1941-1965; Ship Canal House, King Street, 1966-1978. Sat as a Deputy County Court Judge on family cases. Retired from practice 1979. Not in 1988 Law List.

JALLAND, William Herbert Wainwright (His Honour Judge Jalland)

(JB)

Born 1922. Died August 2000 aged 78. Only son of Arthur Edgar Jalland QC qv and brother of Marjorie Wainwright Jalland qv. Manchester Grammar School. Served HM Forces at home and abroad, 1941-1946; Captain, King's Own Royal Regiment attached to 8th Btn., Durham Light Infantry. Manchester University, LLB 1949. G. January 1950. ETC 1950. Pupilmaster, Albert Mayne Knight. Circuit Junior, 1952. Manchester Chambers; 40 Kennedy Street, 1950-1965; Ship Canal House, King Street, 1966-1972. Part time Deputy Coroner, Salford, 1955-1965. Deputy Recorder, Burnley, 1962-1970. Deputy Chairman, Lancs. County Sessions, 1970-1971. Crown Court Recorder 1972. Bert was proud of the fact that he was the first Recorder to be sworn in on Circuit following the Courts Act 1971. Circuit Judge, 1972-1988. (Liverpool, 1972-1975; Manchester & Salford, 1975-1988) At the tributes at Crown Square on the 11 August 2000, the Recorder of Manchester, His Honour Judge Sir Rhys Davies QC said " I found him to be a jovial and somewhat patriarchal figure who treated young members of the Bar with enormous kindness and to whom he dispensed so much good advice" Martin Steiger QC replying captured the essence of Bert Jalland with the following anecdote " I recall on one occasion going into court with a young defendant who asked me who the judge was. When I said it was His Honour Judge Jalland, my client was taken with a sudden urge to visit the lavatory. He was on the run for six months.
In that six month period I had occasion to make a speech at a Law Society dinner and retailed this account thinking it might amuse the assembled solicitors. When my client eventually appeared before Judge Jalland, the judge, demonstrating his complete grasp of everything that happened in the legal scene at Manchester said "Mr Steiger, Is this the case that was discussed at the recent Law Society dinner?" WW.

JAMES, Charles (His Honour Judge Charles James)
Born 17 April 1943. Trent College, Long Eaton, Derbys; Selwyn College, Cambridge, MA 1968. Marshal to Mr Justice Nield. I. July 1965. ETC. October 1965. Sec. Michael Maguire. Circuit Junior, 1966. Same Liverpool Chambers at 10 Water Street, 1965-1969; 2nd floor. Oriel Chambers, 14 Water Street, 1970-1982; Refuge Assurance House (now Merchants Court), Derby Square, 1983-1993. Head of Chambers, 1985-1993. Recorder, 1982-1993. Circuit Judge, 16 November 1993. WW.

JAMES, David John
Born 14 February 1970 Edgeware, London. Nower Hill High School, Harrow; Brighton Polytechnic, BSc; Nottingham Trent University, LLB. Court Clerk, Hillingdon Magistrates Courts Committee, 1992-1998. I. October 1998. ETC. December 1998. Pupilmaster, Ahmed Nadim. Young Street Chambers, Manchester, 1998.

JAMES, Simon John
Born 24 January 1966 Plymouth. Brookfield Comprehensive; Leeds University, LLB. L. November 1988. ETC. 1988. Prop. Helen Grindrod QC. Sec. Christopher Limb. Manchester Chambers; 6th floor, Sunlight House, Quay Street, 1998-1992; Crown Square Chambers/ 9 St John Street, 1992.

JAMES, Thomas Henry
L. 11 June 1862. Law Association Building, 13 Harrington Street, Liverpool, 1876-1883. Special pleader, Liverpool, Kirkdale & Preston Sessions. Not in 1884. Law List.

JAMIESON, Anthony George
Born 9 May 1947 Wallasey. Marlborough Grammar School; University College, Wales at Aberystwyth, BA (English Language & Literature); LLB. G. July 1974. 54 Castle Street, Liverpool, 1975-1981. 21 Whitefriars, Chester, 1982. Now Wales & Chester Circuit.

JANION, Richard Garnett
Born 1853. 2nd son of Joseph Janion, solicitor, of Manchester. New College, Oxford, MA. AAS. L. 19 November 1873. Call 13 June 1877. ETC. 11 July 1877. Prop. Hopwood QC. Sec. Burder. Various London Chambers and eventually at 4 New Square. 51 King Street, Manchester, 1889-1991. No address, 1892-1935. Not in 1936 Law List.

JARVIS, Oliver Martin
LLB. I. November 1992. ETC. 30 March 1993. Prop. David Poole QC. Sec. Marshall. 18 Lloyds House, Lloyd Street, Manchester, 1994-1999; Nicholas Street Chambers, 22 Nicholas Street, Chester, 2000-2001.

JAY, Grenville Richard
Born 15 February 1953 Rochdale. Shrewsbury School; Christ's College, Cambridge, MA. I. November 1975. ETC 1976. Pupilmaster, John Lord. Manchester Chambers; 6th floor, Sunlight House, Quay Street, 1976-1994; Young Street Chambers, 1999.

JEFFERY, Dorothy OBE
G. 17 November 1924. ETC. 19 February 1925. Prop. Wingate-Saul KC. Sec. J B Sandbach. 6 St Ann's Passage, Manchester, 1925-1940. OBE for services to WVS, North West Administration during the War and later at the Ministry of Labour.

JELLICOE, Edwin George
Admitted as a solicitor 1878. G. 17 November 1904. ETC. February 1905. Prop. Horridge KC. Sec. Ross Brown. 2 Elm Court, 1906; 1 Mitre Court, 1907-1914; 2 Pump Court, 1913. League of Nations, Geneva, 1925-1935. Counsel of Bars of New Zealand, Tasmania & Queensland (1884), and High Court of Australia. Advocate, Natal. Parliamentary draftsman & committees. Equity draftsman & conveyancer. Not in 1936 Law List.

JENKINS, Kenneth Thomas
I. January 1939. ETC. 6 March 1940. Prop. Lynskey KC. Sec. Millers. No address, 1941-1963. Not in 1964 Law List.

JENKINSON, Lee David
Born 18 March 1969 Liverpool. Bluecoat School, Liverpool; Liverpool University, LLB. Trainee solicitor with Lace Mawer, Liverpool, 1991-1993; Solicitor with Hill Dickinson, 1993-1999 (Partner 1998). G. March 2001. ETC. 2001. Prop. Iain Goldrein QC. Sec. Peter Gregory. 7 Harrington Street, Liverpool, 2001.

JENKYNS-JONES, Toby Richard Wyndham
Born 10 July 1957. Manchester Polytechnic, BA. AAS. M. 10 July 1978. Call 26 July 1979. Room 22, 15 Victoria Street, Liverpool, 1981-1982. Went to Hong Kong.

JESS, Digby Charles
Born 14 November 1953, Plymouth. Plymouth College; Aston University, BSc; Manchester University, LLM., PhD. G. July 1978. ETC. November 1981. Pupilmaster, Ian McIvor. Manchester Chambers; Lawrence Buildings, 2 Mount Street, 1981-1984; 3 St James's Square, 1985-1988; 8 King Street, 1989. Treasury Counsel (Region 1), 1990. Publications; Insurance of Commercial Risks: Law and Practice, 2001 (3rd ed); Insurance of Professional Negligence Risks: Law & Practice, 1993 (2nd Ed); Vol 20 (Insurance) Encyclopaedia of Forms & Precedents, 1988 (5th ed); Consultant Editor, Butterworth's Insurance Handbook, 1992 (3rd ed.) Legal Assessor, General Medical Council, 2002.

JEVONS, Thomas Seton
I. 24 June 1903. ETC. 20 February 1904. Prop. Hope KC. Sec. Greer. New York State Bar, 1907. 66 Broadway, New York, 1910-1940. No address, 1941-1953. Not in 1954 Law List.

JOHNSON, Albert
G. 26 January 1934. ETC. 1 July 1936. Prop. Gorman KC. Sec. Turner. No address, 1935-1963. Not in 1964 Law List.

JOHNSON, Amanda
Born 25 November 1968, Oldham. Arnold School. Blackpool; University of Wales, Cardiff, LLB. Wales & Chester Circuit, 1992. 9 Park Place, Cardiff, 1993-1998. ETC. 2000. Manchester Chambers; 40 King Street, May 1998-June 1999; Young Street Chambers, Manchester, June 1999.

JOHNSON, Arthur
G. 28 January 1935. No address, 1935-1949. 2 Stone Buildings, 1950-1952; 11 New Square, 1953-1963. Not in 1964 Law List.

JOHNSON, Arthur Russell
Born 1855. 2nd son of Thomas Johnson of Manchester. Christ Church, Oxford, BA. AAS. I. 8 June 1875. Call 7 May 1879. ETC. 18 July 1879. Prop. Edwards QC. Sec. Collins. 1 Dr Johnson's Buildings, 1881-1883; 4 Brick Court, 1884-1895. No address, 1896-1935. Not in 1936 Law List. Foster.

JOHNSON, Carolyn Ann
Born 15 May 1952, Blackpool. Elmslie Girls School, Blackpool; Manchester University, LLB. G. 26 November 1974. ETC. 31 March 1998. Prop. David Allan QC. Sec. Keith Thomas. Pupilmaster, Pat Bailey. Chairman, Preston Area Hospitals NHS Trust, 1993-1997. New Bailey Chambers, 10 Lawson Street, Preston, 1997-2001; Cobden House Chambers, Quay Street, Manchester, May 2001.

JOHNSON, Christine Margaret
Born 13 October 1961 Liverpool. Liverpool Girls' College; North East London Polytechnic, LLB. AAS. M. November 1991. ETC. 1991. Prop. Rodney Klevan QC. Sec. David Geey. 14 Castle Street/ Atlantic Chambers, Cook Street, Liverpool, 1991. Non executive Director, North Mersey Community Trust, 1994. Appeal Manager for mental health within the Trust, 1995. Qualified registered nurse; paediatric nurse and midwife.

JOHNSON, Eric Townend
Born 13 November 1875. Died 17 June 1942 aged 66. Sedbergh; Trinity Hall, Cambridge, BA., LLB. I. 17 November 1902. ETC. 19 February 1903. Prop. Taylor KC. Sec. Sutton. Bank of England Chambers, Tib Lane, Manchester, 1902-1915. Resident Magistrate, Kenya, 1915-1929 (Acting Judge, 1924-1925 & 1928-1929); HBM Court for Zanzibar, 1929-1934; Member, Court of Appeal for Eastern Africa; Judge of High Court, Nyasaland, 1934 until retirement in 1937. WW.

JOHNSON, Ian Frederick
Born 10 March 1960, Wolverhampton. Son of Alan Johnson, solicitor of Oswestry. Oswestry Boys' High School; Reading University, LLB. G. July 1982. ETC. 1982. Pupilmaster, John Newton. Liverpool Chambers; 20 North John Street, 1982-1998; 14 Castle Street/ Atlantic Chambers, Cook Street, Liverpool, 1999. Senior Lecturer in Law, Manchester Metropolitan University, 1998.

JOHNSON, John Hernaman
Born 1848. Only son of John Smallshaw Johnson of Great Crosby, Lancs. Sidney Sussex College, Cambridge, BA 1871. AAS. I. 28 January 1868. Call 17 November 1875. ETC. 27 July 1876. Prop. Hopwood QC. Sec. James. No address, 1875-1882. 3 Garden Court, 1883-1885. Liverpool & Manchester Sessions; Liverpool Court of Passage. No address, 1886-1900. Not in 1901 Law List. Foster.

JOHNSON, Kathryn Margaret
Born 21 May 1967, Blackburn. Notre Dame High School & St Mary's 6th Form College, Blackburn; Sheffield University, LLB. G. July 1989. ETC. 1990. Prop. Richard Henriques QC. Sec. Arthur Stuttard. St James's Chambers, 68 Quay Street, Manchester, 1989-1992; 15 Winckley Square, Preston, 1992.

JOHNSON, Michael Sloan
Born 3 June 1947, London. Upper Canada College, Toronto; St Andrew's Scots School, Buenos Aires; Trinity College, Cambridge, BA 1969; MA, 1973; LLM, 1970. President, Cambridge University Law Society, 1969. L. November 1971. ETC. 1971. Pupilmaster, Derek Mallard. Manchester Chambers; 196 Deansgate, 1971-1989; Crown Square Chambers, 1 Dean's Court, 1990-1993; 9 St John Street, 1994. Assistant Recorder 1994. Recorder 2000. Chairman, VAT Tribunals & Special Commissioner of Income Tax, 1992. Reader, Church of England.

JOHNSON, Nicholas Robert
Born 28 August 1964, Leigh. Manchester Grammar School; Leeds University, BA., Dip. Law. I. July 1987. ETC. December 1987. Pupilmaster, David Maddison. Same Liverpool Chambers at; 1st floor, Peel House, Harrington Street, 1987-1994; 25-27 Castle Street, 1994. Chorister, St Paul's Cathedral, 1973-1978. Played rugby league for British Students, 1985. Played rugby union, cricket & football for Northern Circuit.

JOHNSON, Steven
Born 4 March 1961, Burnley. Bilston Grammar School; Great Whirley High School; King's College, London, LLB. AAS. M. 11 November 1981. Call 26 July 1984. ETC. December 1984. Pupilmasters, Roger Farley & Harold Halliday. Manchester Chambers; 460 Royal Exchange, 1984-1985; Arkwright House, 1985-1989; Kenworthy's Building, 1989-1991; 9 St John Street, 1991-1999; Peel Court Chambers, 45 Hardman Street, 1999.

JOHNSTON, Arthur McWilliam Lawson MC
Born 1 May 1884. Son of John & Elizabeth Elliot Lawson Johnston of Marble Arch, London. Eton; Trinity College, Cambridge, BA. I. 10 May 1911. ETC. 20 February 1912. Prop. Tobin KC. Sec. Otter-Barry. 2 Plowden Buildings, 1911-1914. Lt. Bucks Yeomanry, 1 February 1911. Transferred to 2nd Grenadier Guards. Died of wounds at 2/2nd London Casualty Clearing Station on 22 February 1917 aged 32. Cemetery, Grove Town, Meaulte, Somme, France. Grave III A.6. Information supplied by Public Record Office & Commonwealth War Graves Commission.

JOHNSTONE, Roy Harvey OBE
Liverpool University, LLB. G. January 1949. 24 Dale Street, Liverpool, 1949-1956. Legal Assistant, Solicitors Office, Inland Revenue, Somerset House in 1960's. Criminal Injuries Compensation Board WC1, 1965-1987 (Secretary & Solicitor, 1971-1987). Panel of Chairmen, Medical Appeals Tribunal, 1988-1994. Not in 2000 Bar Directory.

JOLLY, Anthony Charles (His Honour Judge Jolly)
Born 25 May 1932. Died 26 September 1992 aged 60. Royal Naval College, Dartmouth; Balliol College, Oxford, MA (History). I. November 1954. ETC. 1954. Pupilmaster, Philip Kershaw. Circuit Junior, 1957. 36 St Ann Street, Manchester, 1954-1980. Recorder, 1975-1980. Circuit Judge, 1980-1992. Hon. Recorder of Preston, 1989-1992. Tributes, 28 September 1992; Preston (Judge Lockett/ Richard Henriques QC); Bolton (Judge Hodson/ Raymond Wigglesworth). Transcripts in Circuit Records. WW.

JOLLY, John Catterall KC
Born 1887. Died 11 January 1950. Son of Thomas Jolly, JP., and cotton manufacturer of Preston. Aldenham; King's College, Cambridge, BA 1909. I. 28 June 1911. Certificate of Honour, T. 1911. Bencher 1946. ETC. 20 July 1911. Prop. Langdon KC. Sec. Gordon Hewart. Manchester Chambers; Palatine Bank Buildings, 10 Norfolk Street, 1911-1919; 60 King Street, 1920-1939. Silk 1939. 5 Essex Court, 1939-1940; 1 Essex Court, 1941-1950. Chairman, Preston, Liverpool & Manchester County Quarter Sessions & Recorder of Preston, 1938-1950. WW.

JONES, Allen Glynne
L. 30 June 1897. ETC. 31 July 1897. Prop. Pickford QC. Sec. Henry. 14 Old Square, 1898-1903. No address 1904. Not in 1905 Law List.

JONES, Sir Arthur Probyn (2nd Bt)
Born 28 July 1892. Died 17 October 1951 aged 59. Son of Sir Robert Jones. Clifton; King's College, Cambridge, BA., LLB, 1913; MA, 1918. Served, 1914-1919. Captain, King's Liverpool Regt. I. 2 July 1919. 2 Mitre Court, 1921-1922. ETC. 1922. Liverpool Chambers; 25 Lord Street, 1922-1929; 3 Cook Street, 1930-1931. 5 Elm Court, 1935-1941. With Ministry of Food until 1945. Chairman, Medical Appeals Tribunal (North Midland Region); Dep. Chairman, National Health Service Tribunal. JP., Sussex. Contested (L) Liverpool, West Derby, 1929. WW.

JONES, (John) Benedict

Born 1855 Rock Ferry, Birkenhead. Only son of Rev. Charles Jones, BA of Higher Bebington, Cheshire. St John's College, Cambridge, MA, 1884. AAS. L. 11 November 1876. Call 21 June 1882. ETC. 21 July 1882. Prop. Ambrose QC. Sec. Collins. Liverpool Chambers; 13 Harrington Street, 1885-1894; 25 Lord Street, 1895-1914. No address, 1915-1928. Chilcompton, The Long Road, Cambridge, 1929-1940. Not in 1941 Law List. Foster.

JONES, Benjamin William
Born 21 July 1970 Sheffield. Liverpool College; Liverpool University, LLB. M. February 1993. ETC. 25 March 1993. Prop. Eric Somerset Jones QC. Sec. Herman. Same Liverpool Chambers at; 3rd floor, Peel House, Harrington Street, 1993-1997; India Buildings, Water Street, 1998.

JONES, Brian Edward
Born 1 November 1953 Liverpool. Liverpool Collegiate School; Merseyside Police, 1972-1992. Liverpool John Moores University, LLB. M. 13 October 1994. ETC. 20 December 1994. Prop. Tim King QC. Sec. Vincent Deane. Victoria Chambers, 25 Victoria Street, Liverpool, 1994-1997; Manchester Chambers; Manchester House Chambers, 18-22 Bridge Street, 1997-1999; Queen's Chambers, 5 John Dalton Street, 1999-2001; Ribchester House, Lancaster Road, Preston 2002.

JONES, Claire-Louise
Born 10 March 1977 Wrexham. Castell Alun High School & Sixth Form College; Liverpool University, LLB. L. 14 October 1999. ETC. 2001. Prop. Keith Goddard QC. Sec. Theresa Pepper. Pupilmaster, Simon Christie. Chavasse Court Chambers, Lord Street, Liverpool, 2001. Previously a solicitors' clerk with Edwards, Abram & Doherty.

JONES, David Prys
Born 7 May 1913. Died 6 February 1982 aged 68. Wigan Grammar School; Manchester University, LLB. G. 3 July 1935. ETC. 26 February 1936. Prop. Gorman KC. Sec. Gerrard. Command, Manchester Regt (TA), 1939. JAG's Staff as Captain; Major, Deputy Judge Advocate General, 1944-1945. Joined the staff of DPP in 1946 as temporary Legal Assistant rising to Assistant Director of Public Prosecutions in 1966. Metropolitan Stipendiary Magistrate, 1969-1981. WW.

JONES, Edward Bartley QC
Born 24 December 1952, Oswestry. Cardiff High School; Balliol College, Oxford, BA (Modern History). L. July 1975. ETC. 1976. Liverpool Chambers; 14 Cook Street, 1976-1985; 7 Queen Avenue, 1986-1994; Exchange Chambers, Derby Square, 1995. Assistant Recorder 1996. Silk 1997. Recorder 2000. WW.

JONES, Edwin (His Honour Judge Edwin Jones)
Born 21 June 1841, Wales. Died 18 February 1900 aged 58. Father of William Ambrose Jones qv. Owens College, Manchester. AAS. M. 16 November 1872. Call 7 June 1875. ETC. 2 August 1875. Prop. Ambrose QC. Sec. Gouldthorp. Manchester Chambers; 7 St James's Square, 1876-1879; 62 King Street, 1880; 4 St James's Square, 1881-1889. County Court Judge, Circuit 5, July 1889-1900. JP., Lancs., & Isle of Man. WW.

JONES, Elaine Thomson
Ludlow Grammar School; Liverpool Polytechnic, BA (Law). L. July 1984. Liverpool Chambers; 3rd floor, 27 Dale Street, 1984-1988; Corn Exchange, Fenwick Street, 1989-1999; 7 Harrington Street (merger with Martins Bank Building), 6.9.1999.

JONES, Gareth Daryl
Born 24 November 1961 Swansea. Ysgul Gyfan Ystalyfera; University College of Wales, Aberystwyth, LLB. G. 27 November 1984. Wales & Chester Circuit. Sedan House, Stanley Place, Chester, 1984-1998. ETC. 28 July 1998. Prop. David Harris QC. Sec. Robert Atherton. India Buildings, Water Street, Liverpool, 1998.

JONES, Gareth Edward
University College of Wales, Aberystwyth, LLB. Certificates in Roman Law and the History of Spanish Law from the University of Salamanca. M. 10 October 2002. ETC. 17 December 2002. Prop. Webster QC. Sec. Boyd. Lincoln House Chambers, 1 Brazennose Street, Manchester, 2002.

JONES, Gerald William
Born 7 February 1953 Liverpool. Liverpool Collegiate School; Sheffield University, LLB. Solicitor in private practice, 1978-1981. County Prosecuting Solicitor's Office (later CPS), 1981-1995. G. 21 July 1995. ETC. 19 December 1995. Prop. David Turner QC. Sec. Richard Isaacson. Liverpool Chambers; Exchange Chambers, Derby Square, 1995-2000; 25-27 Castle Street, 2000.

JONES, Gladys Forshaw (Mrs Rathbone)
G. 26 January 1934. 3 St James's Square, Manchester, 1936-1960. Left the Bar to live in Arnside and later in Milnthorpe. Not in 1987 Bar Directory.

JONES, (Griffith) Winston Guthrie QC
Born 24 September 1914. Died 4 August 1996 aged 81. Bootham School, York; University of Wales, LLB; St John's College, Cambridge, MA. G. 26 January 1939. ETC. 1 February 1939. Prop. Fred Pritchard KC. Sec. Selwyn Lloyd. Circuit Junior, Winter 1939. Royal Artillery, 1940-1946. Liverpool Chambers; 27 Lord Street, 1939-1946; 49 Castle Street, 1947-1963. Silk 1963. 2 Pump Court, 1963-1984. Deputy Chairman, Westmorland Quarter Sessions, 1963-1971. Recorder of Bolton, 1968-1971. Crown Court Recorder, 1972-1974. Retired to Sligo in 1985. Publication; The Wynnes of Sligo & Leitrim, 1995. WW.

JONES, Hannah Louise
Born 7 June 1977 Manchester. Cheadle Hulme School; Hull University, LLB. L. 25 November 1999. ETC. July 2000. Prop. Keith Goddard. Sec. Keith Thomas. Pupilmaster, Patricia Bailey. New Bailey Chambers, Preston, October 1999.

JONES, Harold Emyr
Born 1913. 2nd son of Cyril Jones, solicitor of Gresford, Wrexham. London School of Economics. AAS. M. 7 November 1930. Call 25 April 1934. ETC. 26 February 1936. Prop. Lynskey KC. Sec. Birley. 5 Harrington Street, Liverpool, 1936-1940. No address, 1941-1963. Not in 1964 Law List.

JONES, Hilary Jean
Born 1928. Daughter of Iolo Jones of Silwood House, Gateacre, Liverpool, building contractor. University College of Wales, Aberystwyth, LLB. AAS. M. 15 November 1948. Call 6 June 1951. ETC. 14 February 1952. Prop. Basil Nield QC. Sec. Hughes. 20 Hackins Hey, Liverpool, 1952-1953. No chambers address 1954.

JONES, Ifor Henry Morris QC (His Honour Ifor Morris Jones QC)

(RB)

Born 5 March 1922. Died 23 October 1999 aged 77. Son of Rev. Professor Morris Jones. Taunton School. Sidney Sussex College, Cambridge, BA. L. June 1947. ETC. 1947. Pupilmaster, Glyn Burrell. Liverpool Chambers; 49 Castle Street, 1947-1965; 606 The Corn Exchange, Fenwick Street, 1966-1969. Silk 1969. 5 Essex Court, 1969-1977. Assistant Recorder, Carlisle, 1962. Deputy Chairman, Cumberland Quarter Sessions, 1969-1972. Crown Court Recorder, 1972-1976. Member of Bar Council, 1972. Circuit Judge, 1977-1992 sitting initially at Manchester and then at Preston where he became Resident Judge and finally at Liverpool. His and Sandy Temple's retirement speeches, Liverpool Law Courts, 20 December 1991. (Judge Frank Paterson/ J J Rowe QC); Tributes at Liverpool Law Courts, 26 October 1999 (Judge Anne Downey /William Waldron QC) and further tributes by his former pupil, Mr Justice Kay and by Keith Goddard QC. Transcripts in Circuit Records. WW.

JONES, (John) Edward (His Honour John Edward Jones)

(RB)

Born 23 December 1914. Died 28 June 1998 aged 83. Father of Michael Wyn Jones qv and Glenys Arden, solicitor. Sefton Park Council School; Liverpool Institute. British Engine Insurance Company, Manchester for 12 years. ACIS. London external; BCom (1942); LLB (1945) G. November 1945. ETC 1945. Pupilmasters; Glyn Blackledge & Rose Heilbron. Liverpool Chambers; 34 Castle Street, 1945-1949; 15 Victoria Street, 1950; North House, 17 North John Street, 1951-1969. Deputy Chairman, Lancs. Quarter Sessions, 1966-1969. Circuit Judge (formerly County Court Judge), 1969-1984. President; Liverpool Welsh Choral Union, 1987.; Merseyside Branch, British Red Cross Society, 1980-1988; Liverpool Free Church Federal Council, 1988. Deacon, Welsh Presbyterian Church, 1947. Liverpool Presbytery Moderator, 1971,1997. Life Member, Welsh National Eisteddford Court; Gorsedd of Bards (Ioan Maesgrug), 1987. JP., Lancs 1966. Retirement tribute at Liverpool Law Courts, 21 December 1984 (Judge Temple QC); Tributes; at Liverpool Law Courts 2 July 1998 (Judge David Clarke QC/ Robert Fordham QC); Bethel Welsh Presbyterian Church 3 July 1998 (Judge David Lynch). Obituaries; Independent, 9 July 1998 (Rev. D. Ben Rees); Graya, Vol 108 p92 (Judge David Lynch) All transcripts are in Circuit Records.

JONES, John Richard QC
Born 8 February 1959, Billinge. Shevington High School; Upholland Grammar School; Liverpool University, LLB. AAS. M. 5 November 1979. Call 23 July 1981. ETC. March 1982. Prop. Benet Hytner QC. Sec. Lindsey Platt. Manchester Chambers; Central Street Chambers, 1982-1987; Hollins Chambers, 64a Bridge Street, 1987-1988; 28 St John Street, 1988-2002; Exchange Chambers, Liverpool & Manchester, 2002. Assistant Recorder, 1998. Recorder 2000. Silk 2002, Carlisle Cup Winner (Golf). WW.

JONES, John Walter
Born 21 July 1892. Died 18 December 1973 aged 81. Merthyr County School; University College of Wales, Aberystwyth; Emmanuel College, Cambridge (First Class, Law Tripos Parts 1 & 2); Hon Fellow, 1949. I. 28 January 1918. Certificate of Honour, M. 1917. Barstow Scholar, H 1918. ETC. 1918. 25 Lord Street, Liverpool, 1921-1931. Lecturer and Tutor in Law, Liverpool University, 1920-1926. Fellow, Tutor & Praelector in Law, Queen's College, Oxford, 1927-1948. Junior Proctor, 1942-1943. Provost of the Queen's College, Oxford, 1948-1962. Publications; Bona Fide Purchase of Goods, 1918; Historical Introduction to the Theory of Law, 1940; The Law and Legal Theory of the Greeks, 1956. WW.

JONES, Joseph Alun
Born 22 December 1842 Liverpool. Liverpool College; Queen's College, Liverpool. AAS. M. 11 November 1867. Call 10 June 1870. ETC. 19 August 1870. Prop. Aspinall QC. Sec. Lewis William. 40 Castle Street, Liverpool, 1883-1896. Practised before Superior Courts of Cape Colony. Defended Tini Maccomo and other Chiefs when tried for high treason in 1878. Sole acting judge for Griqualand West in 1880 and standing counsel to the municipality of Kimberley. Not in 1897 Law List. Foster.

JONES, Joseph Birdsall
Born 4 November 1845. Son of William Roscoe Jones, Master of the Liverpool Athenaeum. London University, BA 1881, LLB 1882. FRMS. Late of Madras Civil Service. AAS. L. 3 November 1874. Call 13 June 1877. ETC. 6 April 1878. Prop. Temple QC. Sec. Butler. 11 St George's Chambers, St George's Crescent, Liverpool, 1879-1899. Liverpool & Kirkdale Sessions & Liverpool Court of Passage. No address, 1900-1935. Not in 1936 Law List. Foster.

JONES, Lewis Rouse
BA., BCL (Oxon). I. 8 June 1932. ETC. 15 March 1933. Prop. Goldie KC. Sec. Shackleton Bailey. 60 King Street, Manchester, 1934-1959. Senior Legal Assistant; Board of Trade (Export Credits Guarantee Branch, 1959-1967; Prosecutions Branch, 1967-1975) Not in 1976 Law List.

JONES, Michael
Born 27 September 1975, Vienna. Birmingham University, LLB. L. October 1998. ETC. December 1999. Prop. Keith Goddard QC. Sec. John Broadley. Pupilmaster, Richard Hartley. Cobden House Chambers, 19 Quay Street, Manchester, October 1998.

JONES, Michael Wyn
Born 15 June 1951 Liverpool. Son of His Honour (John) Edward Jones qv and brother of Glenys Arden, solicitor. Liverpool College. Articled clerk, assistant solicitor & partner with Maxwell Entwistle & Byrne, February 1974-December 1998. G. 11 March 1999. ETC. 1999. Prop. Andrew Edis QC. Sec. Gerald Baxter. 25-27 Castle Street, Liverpool, January 1999.

JONES, Phillipa Nancy Hudson
LLB. G. October 1992. Derby Square Chambers, Merchant's Court 1994-1998. Went to live in Tasmania.

JONES, Reginald
Born 1858. 2nd son of Thomas, 7th Viscount Ranelagh. Jesus College, Cambridge, BA, 1881. AAS. I. 13 January 1877. Call 17 November 1880. 3 Pump Court, 1882-1885. No address, 1886-1940. Not in 1941 Law List. Foster

JONES, Robert Albert
Born 16 September 1851. 2nd surviving son of Rev. John Jones of Wrexham. Corpus Christi College, Oxford, BA. AAS. L. 24 April 1875. Call 7 May 1879. ETC. 30 July 1880. Prop. Temple QC. Sec. J William. Liverpool Chambers; 13 Union Court, 1881-1884; 5 Harrington Street, 1885-1892. Equity draftsman & conveyancer. Lancs. Chancery Court. Not in 1893 Law List. Foster.

JONES, Siân Scott
Born 4 October 1974, Bath. Bath High School; St John's College, Cambridge, BA. L. 8 October 1998. ETC. December 1998. Prop. Anthony Rumbelow QC. Sec. Winston Hunter. 28 St John Street, Manchester, September 1998. (now St Johns Buildings Chambers).

JONES, William Ambrose
Born 1867. Elder son of His Honour Judge Edwin Jones qv. London University. AAS. M. 13 November 1886. Call 27 January 1890. ETC. 10 March 1890. Prop. Ambrose QC. Sec. Yates. Manchester Chambers; 4 St James's Square, 1891-1896; 2 Clarence Buildings, Booth Street, 1897-1900; 34 Kennedy Street, 1901-1908. Not in 1909 Law List.

JONES, William Kenneth Howcroft
Liverpool University, LLB. G. November 1948. 20 Hackins Hey, Liverpool, 1949-1958. No address, 1959-1963. Not in 1964 Law List.

JORDAN, Ernest William
G. 17 November 1885. ETC. 1 February 1886. Prop. Gibbs QC. Sec. Heywood. No address, 1887-1895. Manchester Chambers; 78 Cross Street, 1896-1899; St Ann's Passage, King Street, 1900. Not in 1901 Law List.

JORDAN, Fiona Claire
London University, LLB. G. October 1991. Liverpool Chambers; Corn Exchange, Fenwick Street, 1994-1999; 7 Harrington Street (merger with Martins Bank Building). 6.9.1999-2000.

JORDAN, Gilbert
I. 22 June 1898. ETC. 2 February 1899. Prop. Russell QC. Sec. McKeand. Circuit Junior, Winter 1900. Acting Junior, 1914-1918. St Ann's Passage, Manchester, 1906-1925. Not in 1926 Law List. Harold Roberts qv says Jordan was a famous Oxford miler.

JORDAN, Thomas Hudson (His Honour Judge Jordan)
Born 1828. Died 3 November 1899. 3rd son of William Jordan of Manchester. Journalist on staff of Manchester Courier and reporter in London for the Manchester Examiner, 1859-1862. AAS. G. 7 November 1859. Call 11 June 1862. Cross Street, Manchester, 1876-1883. County Court Judge, Circuit 26, 1883-1899. JP., Lancs. & Staffs. Foster.

JOYNES, Bryan Stanley
Born 7 March 1931 Harrow. Harrow County School; Trinity College, Cambridge, MA. L. February 1957. Journalism in Cambridge, Manchester & Fleet Street, 1954-1967. ETC. 1967. Prop. Michael Maguire QC. Sec. John Stannard. Oriel Chambers, Covent Garden/14 Water Street, Liverpool, 1967. Chairman; Medical Appeal Tribunals; Social Security Tribunals.

JUDGE, Lisa Jane
Born 10 May 1968, Worsley. St Ambrose Barlow School; Barristers' Clerk, 1987-1989. Sheffield Hallam, LLB. G. October 1993. ETC. 13 December 1994. Prop. Rodney Klevan QC. Sec. John Wishart. Manchester Chambers; Manchester House Chambers, 18-22 Bridge Street, September 1993-14 September 1998; Dean's Court Chambers, 24 St John Street, 14 September 1998.

JULIAN, Adrian Leslie
Born 1921. Elder son of Dr F B Julian of Liverpool, Consulting Physician. Lincoln College, Oxford, MA. AAS. M. 6 April 1948. Call 26 January 1951. ETC 1951. Liverpool Chambers; 3 Cook Street, 1951-1958; 3rd floor, 27 Dale Street, 1959-1986. Not in 1987 Bar Directory.

K

KANDEL, Philip Albert
LLB. G. November 1974. 60 King Street, Manchester, 1976-1979. No address, 1980-1994. Not in 1995 Bar Directory.

KARMEL, Alexander David QC. (His Honour Alexander Karmel QC)
Born 16 May 1904. Died 27 September 1998 aged 94. First cousin of David Karmel QC qv. Newcastle upon Tyne Royal Grammar School. AAS. M. 16 September 1929. Call 8 June 1932; Bencher 1962; Reader Lent 1980. ETC. 5 July 1933. Prop. Lynskey KC. Sec. Jolly. 3 Elm Court, 1932-1940; 4 Paper Buildings, 1941-1952; 2 Harcourt Buildings, 1953-1963. Silk 1954. 5 Essex Court, 1964-1968. Member of Bar Council, 1950-1953 & 1961-1964. Recorder of Bolton, 1962-1968. Leader of the Northern Circuit, 1966-1968 (first elected Leader). Commissioner of Assize, Stafford, summer 1967. Circuit Judge (formerly County Court Judge) and additional Judge at the Old Bailey, 1968-1979. Ignoring the rule which excluded women barristers from Mess, Karmel, as Leader, insisted that Rose Heilbron QC dine with the men at Lancaster. Played wing three quarter for Northumberland. Obituaries; Daily Telegraph, 10 September 1998; Times, 27 October 1998. WW.

KARMEL, David CBE., QC.
Born 1907. Died 31 May 1982. First cousin of His Honour Alexander Karmel QC. qv. St Andrew's College; Trinity College, Dublin, BA., LLB. G. 2 May 1928; Bencher 1954; Treasurer 1970. ETC. 13 June 1928. Prop. Eastham QC. Sec. Benas. Liverpool Chambers; 8 Harrington Street, 1928-1931; 13 Harrington Street, 1932-1939. War of 1939-1945. Major, active service in North Africa, Italy & Jugoslavia. 3 Paper Buildings, 1946-1951. Silk 1950. 1 Brick Court, 1952-1982. Recorder of Wigan, 1952-1962. Deputy Chairman, Glos. Quarter Sessions, 1970-1971. Crown Court Recorder, 1972-1979. Sat on numerous government tribunals & committees. CBE 1967. WW.

KARR, Henry Seton
Born 1853. Eldest son of George Berkeley Seton Karr, late Bombay Civil Service. Corpus Christi College, Oxford, BA 1876. AAS. L. 31 March 1874. Call. 25 June 1879. Circuit Junior, Winter 1880. 3 Paper Buildings, 1880; 7 Crown Office Row, 1881-1884, 2 Pump Court, 1885.

KAUR, Rani
Born 30 July 1968. Died May 2003 aged 34. West Midlands/Hull University, LLB. G. 25 November 1993. ETC. 15 April 2003. Prop. David Steer QC. Sec. Mark George. Garden Court North Chambers, Manchester, 1998-2003. Tribute, "In Brief", June/July 2003. (David Steer QC.)

KAY, Andrew Cassels OBE
OBE 1918. I. 26 January 1887. ETC. 20 February 1888. Prop. Bigham QC. Sec. Hamilton. 1 Dr Johnson Building, 1891-1894. Charity Commission, 1895-1928. Retired 1928. Not in 1938 Law List.

KAY, John Lawrence
Born 2 April 1950. Only son of Thomas V Kay of Chadderton, industrial valuer. Moseley Grammar School; Sheffield University, LLB; London University, LLB. AAS. M. 11 May 1971. Call 19 July 1973. 43 King Street, Manchester, 1974-1977. Legal Services Manager, ICI Chemicals, Middlesborough, 1989.

KAY, John Walters Sellers
Born 1866. 1st son of Thomas Kay of Burnley, cotton spinner. Trinity Hall, Cambridge. AAS. M. 4 November 1885. Call. 27 January 1890. ETC. 17 March 1892. Prop. Wheeler QC. Sec. C A Russell. Circuit Junior, Summer 1892. 3 King's Bench Walk (North), 1892-1901; 2 Garden Court, 1902-1942. No address, 1943-1949. Not in 1950 Law List.

KAY, John (William) QC. (The Rt. Hon. Lord Justice Kay)

(DL)

Born 13 September 1943. Died 2 July 2004 aged 60. Denstone; Christ's College, Cambridge, MA. G. 1968; Bencher 1992. ETC. 1968. Pupilmaster, Ifor Morris Jones. Circuit Junior, 1968. Tutor in Law, Liverpool University, 1968-1969. Same Liverpool Chambers at; 606 The Corn Exchange, Fenwick Street, 1968-1982; Exchange Chambers at 1 Exchange Flags, Dale Street and at Pearl Assurance House, Derby Square, 1983-1992. (Head of Chambers). Recorder, 1982-1992. Silk 1984. Member, General Council of the Bar, 1988-1992. High Court Judge, Queen's Bench Division, 1992-2000. Kt. 1992. Presiding Judge of the Northern Circuit, 1994-1997. Member; Crown Court Rules Committee, 1995-; Judicial Studies Board, 1998-2001; (Chairman, Criminal Committee). Lord Justice of Appeal, 2000-2004. PC 2000. Chairman, Criminal Justice Consultation Council, 2001. Husband of Jeffa; father of; Amanda Yip qv. Ben (England rugby international) and Tiffany. WW. Tributes, Liverpool Law Courts, 7 July 2004 (Leveson J./ David Steer QC. / James Benson / Amanda Yip) Transcript in Circuit Records. Funeral service, Liverpool Cathedral, 9 July 2004. Obituaries. Daily Telegraph 7 July 2004; Independent, 22 July 2004 (Lord Justice Rose); Times, 2 August 2004.

KAY, Joseph QC
Born 27 February 1821. Died 9 October 1878 aged 57. Brother of Lord Justice Edward Ebeneezer Kay. Patricroft School; Trinity College, Cambridge, BA 1845; MA 1849. I. 5 May 1848; Bencher 1870. 9 King's Bench Walk, 1876-1878. Judge, Salford Hundred Court, 1862-1878. Solicitor General, County Palatine of Durham, 1872-1878. Publications; Free Trade in Land, 1879; Law Relating to Shipmasters & Seamen, 1875.

KAY, Sam Sidley
L. 17 November 1899. ETC. 16 July 1902. Prop. Shee KC. Sec Roby. 11 Old Square, 1902; 78 King Street, Manchester, 1903-1911. Equity draftsman & conveyancer. No address, 1912-1949. Not in 1950 Law List.

KAY-SHUTTLEWORTH, Hon. Edward James
Youngest son of 1st Baron Shuttleworth. Eton & Balliol, BA. I. 16 April 1913. ETC. 5 June 1913. Prop. Sanderson KC. Sec. Hills. Circuit Junior, summer 1914. Library Chambers, Middle Temple, 1913-1914. Lt., 7th Btn. Rifle Brigade. Served in France, 19 May 1915-4 March 1916 when invalided home. Later Staff Captain, 218 Infantry Brigade. Died on 10 July 1917 aged 27 in a road traffic accident riding his motorcycle from home leave back to Brigade. Buried north east corner Barbon (St Bartholemew) Churchyard, Westmorland. His family presented to the Circuit the memorial, upon which are inscribed the names of all Circuiteers who died in both World Wars. WW.

KEAN, Donald Anthony
LLB. G. November 1971. 41 North John Street, Liverpool, 1978; 4th floor, Sunlight House, Quay Street, Manchester, 1982-1983. Not in 1984 Bar Directory.

KEARNEY, Robert Michael
Born 9 March 1971, Uppermill, Saddleworth. Saddleworth School; Huddersfield University, LLB. I. 28 November 1996. ETC. 27 July 2000. Prop. Fish QC. Sec. McKee. Pupilmaster, Mario Addezio (Gray's Inn Square). 6 Gray's Inn Square, October 1996-December 1998; Manchester Chambers; Central Chambers, December 1998-June 1999; 24a St John Street, 2000- (now St Johns Buildings).

KEAVENY, John Anthony
G. June 1948. No address, 1948-1968. Northern Assurance Building, Albert Square, Manchester, 1969-1970. Not in 1971 Law List.

KEENAN, Peter Bernard
Born 23 January 1935 Salford. De La Salle College, Salford; Manchester University, LLB; Magdalen College, Oxford, BLitt. Lecturer in Law, London School of Economics, 1959-1962. G. November 1962. ETC. 1964. Prop. Joseph Cantley QC. Sec. James Fitzhugh. Manchester Chambers; 4 Clarence Street, 1964-1984; 72 Bridge Street, 1984-1998; Cobden House Chambers, 19 Quay Street, 1999-. Contributed (with co-editors) sections on carriage by air & surface damage to 3rd edition of Shawcross & Beaumont "Air Law".

KELLY, John Nixon
Born 24 January 1977, Manchester. St Thomas Moore/Xaverian College; University of East Anglia, Norwich, LLB; Sidney Sussex College, Cambridge, LLM. L. 11 October 2001. Prop. Clement Goldstone QC. Sec. Maurice Greene. 28 St John Street, Manchester, 3 September 2001.

KELLY, Louis Sullivan
Irish Bar 1903. G. 17 November 1914. No address, 1914-1924. Not in 1925 Law List.

KELLY, Mary Josephine
BSc., Dip. Law. G. November 1986. Kenworthy's Buildings, 83 Bridge Street, Manchester, 1988-1991. Crown, later Senior Crown Prosecutor, Wakefield, 1994.

KELLY, Sean
Born 26 January 1966 Nottingham. Trent College; Selwyn College, Cambridge, MA. G. October 1990. Manchester Chambers; 72 Bridge Street, 1993-1997; Cobden House Chambers, 19 Quay Street, 1998.

KELLY, Thomas Joseph DSO., MC.
I. 14 May 1924. 4 Harcourt Buildings, 1924-1934 Oxford Circuit. ETC. 25 June 1934. Prop. Hemmerde KC. Sec. Saul. 1 Hare Court, 1934-1952; 3 Pump Court, 1953-1963. Not in 1964 Law List.

KEMP, Stephen Richard
Born 23 March 1963 Belfast. Thurston Upper School, Suffolk; York University, BA; Birmingham University, Dip Law. Teacher, 1988-1992. L. 12 October 1995. ETC. 18 December 1997. Prop. Nigel Gilmour QC. Sec. Philip Hall. Pupilmasters, David Mayell & Simon Christie. Liverpool Chambers; ground floor, Peel House, Harrington Street, September 1997-1999; Oriel Chambers, 14 Water Street, 1 March 1999-2002; 7 Harrington Street, 2002.

KEMPLAY, James QC
Born 1810. Died 4 June 1882. Second son of Richard Kemplay of Leeds. Leeds Grammar School; Trinity College, Cambridge, BA 1833; MA 1836. AAS. M. 1 June 1833. Call 30 January 1852; Bencher 1874. 1 King's Bench Walk, 1876-1880. Silk 1872.

KENDALL, Sir Norman CBE
Born 1880. Died 8 March 1966. Rossall; Oriel College, Oxford, BA. I. 9 May 1906. ETC. 17 July 1906. Prop. Langdon KC. Sec. Acton. Circuit Junior, Winter 1906. 41 John Dalton Street, Manchester, 1906-1914. Served European War, 1914-1918, 5th Cheshire Regt (wounded 1916); attached to Ministry of National Service, 1917. Deputy Assistant Commissioner, CID, New Scotland Yard, 1918-1928; CBE 1927. Assistant Commissioner, 1928-1945. Kt 1937. Chairman, Bucks. Quarter Sessions Appeals Committee, 1950-1955. WW.

KENNAN, John Melville (His Honour Judge Kennan)
Born 9 August 1904. Died 21 April 1960 aged 55. Liverpool Institute; Keble College, Oxford, BA. I. 2 July 1930. ETC. 9 July 1930. Prop. Eastham KC. Sec. Jalland. Pupilmasters, Harold Mather & David Maxwell Fyfe. Circuit Junior, Winter 1931. Liverpool Chambers; 5 Harrington Street, 1930-1932; 43 Castle Street, 1933-1938; 32 Castle Street, 1938-1940. Royal Corps of Signals, 1941. Captain, Military Dept, JAG's Office, 1942; Major, Deputy Judge Advocate, Palestine & Transjordan, 1945. 34 Castle Street, 1946-1958. County Court Judge, Circuit 12, (Bradford & Huddersfield), 1958-1960. Captain, Childwall Golf Club, 1949. WW.

KENNEDY, Alexander Dunkeld
Served in 1939-1945 European War in Royal Artillery. LLB (London). AMBIM., FRSA. Teacher/Lecturer. G. February 1965. ETC. 27 May 1965. Pupilmaster, Keith Lawton. Same Liverpool Chambers at; North House, 17 North John Street, 1965-1971; Martin's Building, Water Street, 1972-1989. Died 9 March 1989 aged 67. Tributes at Liverpool Law Courts 9 March 1989 (Judge Sir Sanderson Temple MBE., QC/ Michael Maguire QC.) Transcript in Circuit Records.

KENNEDY, Alfred Ravenscroft KC., MP. (His Honour Judge Kennedy)
Born 15 February 1879. Died 10 February 1943 aged 63. Son of Lord Justice Kennedy qv. Eton; King's College, Cambridge, BA. L. 6 May 1903; Bencher 1922. ETC. 20 February 1904. Prop. Sanderson KC. Sec. Mansfield. Circuit Junior, Winter 1904. 25 Lord Street, Liverpool, 1903-1908; 13 Harrington Street, 1909-1919; Goldsmiths Building, 1909-1916; 2 Harcourt Buildings, 1917-1918. Legal Advisor at the Foreign Office during 1914-1918 War. Silk 1919. 3 Brick Court, 1919-1929. Recorder of Burnley, 1924-1929. MP (U) Preston, 1924-1929. Commissioner of Assize, 1933 & 1934. County Court Judge, 1929-1943; Circuit 49 (Kent), 1929-1930; Circuit 53 (Glos., Herefordshire, Warwickshire & Worcs.), 1930-1943. Publications; Contracts of Sale CIF; editor, Kennedy's Law of Civil Salvage; editor of Benjamin on Sale. WW.

KENNEDY, Christopher Lawrence Paul
Born 10 August 1966, Sheffield. Son of Lord Justice Kennedy and grandson of Lord Diplock. Ampleforth College; Gonville & Caius College, Cambridge, LLB. G. July 1989. ETC. December 1989. Prop. John Hand QC. Sec. Charles Garside. Same Manchester Chambers at 1 Dean's Court & 9 St John Street, 1990.

KENNEDY, John Lawson
Born 1816. Only son of John Kennedy of Ardwick House near Manchester. Trinity College, Cambridge, BA 1837; MA 1860. JP., Lancs; JP & DL Kirkudbright. No chambers address, 1876-1899. Not in 1900 Law List. Foster.

KENNEDY, Michael John
Born 15 March 1962 Preston. Preston Catholic College; Bristol University, LLB. AAS. M. 30 March 1983. Call 6 May 1985. ETC. December 1985. Prop. Gerard Wright QC. Sec Michael Byrne. Same Liverpool Chambers at; Melbourne Buildings, 21 North John Street, 1985-1988; 3rd floor, Peel House, Harrington Street, 1989-1997; India Buildings, Water Street, 12 January 1998. Member of Northern Circuit "Three Tenors" with Simon Killeen and Jonathan Taylor.

KENNEDY, (Peter) Nicholas (Dodgson)
Born 24 November 1954, Crosby, Liverpool, married to Heather Claire Lloyd qv. Malvern College; Liverpool Polytechnic (now John Moores University) external London LLB. L. July 1977. ETC July 1978. Pupilmaster, R J D Livesey. Ground floor, Peel House, Harrington Street, Liverpool, 1978-1989; 15 Winckley Square, Preston, 1989.

KENNEDY, Sir William Rann QC (The Rt. Hon. Lord Justice Kennedy)

Born 11 March 1846. Died 17 January 1915 aged 68. Father of His Honour Judge Alfred Kennedy qv. Eton; King's College, Cambridge, BA 1868; MA 1871. President, Cambridge Union Society. Fellow, Pembroke College, 1868-1874; Hon Fellow 1893. Assistant Master at Harrow. AAS. L. 12 July 1867. Call 26 January 1871. Bencher 1888; Treasurer 1914. M. (ad eundem), 4 April 1882. ETC. 25 February 1873. Prop. Aspinall QC. Sec. Crompton. 12 Commerce Chambers, Harrington Street, Liverpool, 1873-1872, practising mainly in commercial and shipping cases; 4 Essex Court, 1873-1878; Farrar's Building 1879-1881; 3 Garden Court, 1882; 2 King's Bench Walk, 1884-1885; Silk 1885. 2 Garden Court, 1886-1892. Contested (L); Birkenhead, 1885, 1886; St Helens, 1892. High Court Judge, King's Bench Division, 1892-1907. Kt. 1892. Lord Justice of Appeal, 1907-1915. PC. 1907. FBA 1909. Publications; Law of Salvage, 1891. WW. DNB. Obituary, Times, 18 January 1915.

KENNEY, Frank Bryant
MA., LLB (Cantab) FCII. I. January 1946. No address, 1946-1953. 1 North John Street, Liverpool, 1954-1963. Not in 1964 Law List. (This was the address of the Royal Insurance Co Ltd. 1 suspect he was an in house lawyer for the Royal)

KENNY, Charlotte
Born 9 August 1968 Bootle, Liverpool. Warwick Bolam High School; Hull University, BA (Philosophy) 1990. Dip. Law (City), 1992. G. November 1993. ETC. 21 December 1993. Prop. William Waldron QC. Sec. Richard Isaacson. Exchange Chambers, Pearl Assurance House, Derby Square, Liverpool, 1993.

KENNY, David Joseph
Born 5 April 1958, London. Gillingham Technical High School; Nottingham University, BA (Law), MPhil. AAS. M. 19 August 1981. Call 23 November 1982. ETC. 1983. Prop. Roger Farley QC. Sec. Stephen Dodds. Pupilmaster, Tom Saunt. Preston Chambers; 14 Winckley Square, 1983-1993; 15 Winckley Square, 1993.

KENWARD, Timothy David Nelson
Born 4 November 1963 Paddington, London. Marlborough College; St Anne's College, Oxford, MA. G. November 1987. ETC. 1989. Prop. Michael Maguire QC. Sec. David Maddison. Pupilmasters, Huw Lloyd & John Grace (3 Sergeants Inn). Same Liverpool Chambers at; 2nd floor, Peel House, Harrington Street, 1 May 1989-3 July 1994; 25-27 Castle Street, 4 July 1994.

KENYON, Hon. Edward Frederick
Born 27 August 1842. Died 4 January 1892 aged 49. 3rd son of Lloyd, 3rd Lord Kenyon of Whitchurch, Salop. Trinity College, Cambridge, MA. AAS. M. 17 April 1863. Call 11 June 1867. 7 New Square, 1876-1892. Equity draftsman and conveyancer. JP., Flintshire. Foster. Debrett.

KENYON, Joseph Robert
I. 18 November 1907. ETC. 18 July 1908. Prop. Horridge KC. Sec. Sharpe. Circuit Junior, Summer 1911. 1 Garden Court, 1910-1911; 8 Harrington Street, Liverpool, 1913-1922; 8 Cook Street, Liverpool, 1923-1926; 6 Crown Office Row, 1924-1936. No address, 1937-1954. Not in 1955 Law List.

KEOGH, George Darell
Born 1860. 2nd son of George Keogh of Geevagh, Sligo DL., JP. Irish Bar E. 1884. G. 26 January 1897. ETC. 31 July 1897. Prop. Shee KC. Sec. Horridge. Admitted M. 2 August 1910. Liverpool Chambers; 24 Lord Street, 1897-1900; 5 Harrington Street, 1901-1910. 3 Brick Court, 1912-1936. Not in 1937 Law List.

KERR, David Milne
Born 29 July 1947 Manchester. Burnage Grammar School, Manchester; Kingston College of Technology, (LLB London). I. November 1971. ETC. 7 December 1972. Pupilmaster, Gerald Crowe. Same Liverpool Chambers at; Martins Building, Water Street, 1972-1999; 7 Harrington Street (merger with Corn Exchange), 6.9.1999. Assistant Recorder 1992. Recorder 1996. Legal Member, Mental Health Review Tribunal.

KERR, Francis James
L. 18 November 1901. ETC. 5 February 1903. Prop. Horridge KC. Sec. Acton. Manchester Chambers; Economic Buildings, 21 Spring Gardens, 1903-1910; 42 Spring Gardens, 1911-1937. No address 1938. Not in 1939 Law List.

KERR, Michael (Robert Emanuel) QC (The Rt. Hon. Lord Justice Kerr)
Born 1 March 1921, Berlin. Died 14 April 2002, London aged 81. Father of Tim Kerr QC and son of Alfred Kerr, Jewish-German writer, poet, drama critic and opponent of Adolph Hitler. The family escaped from Germany in 1933, eventually arriving in England in 1935. At the outbreak of war, Kerr was interned as an enemy alien but secured his release after four months and went on to fly Wellingtons in Coastal Command with the rank of Flt. Lt. at the end of the war. His autobiography "As Far as I Remember," published in 2002, tells the full story. Aldenham School; Clare College Cambridge; BA, 1947; MA 1952; Hon Fellow 1982. L. June 1948; Cassell Scholar; Bencher 1968; Treasurer 1989. 3 Essex Court, 1948-1961. Pupilmasters, Eustace Roskill and John Megaw. Silk 1961. 4 Essex Court, 1961-1972. ETC. 5 July 1951. Prop. Neville Laski KC. Sec. Bertram Benas. Member, Bar Council, 1968-1972. Deputy Chairman, Hants. Quarter Sessions, 1961-1971. High Court Judge, Queen's Bench Division and of the Commercial and Admiralty Courts, 1972-1978. Kt. 1972. Chairman, Law Commission, 1978-1981. Lord Justice of Appeal, 1981-1989. PC 1981. Thereafter he was a much sought after International Arbitrator. WW. Obituary; Daily Telegraph, 23 April 2002; Times, 25 April 2002.

KERR, Samuel Parnell
G. 26 January 1900. ETC. 19 February 1903. Prop. Taylor KC. Sec. Morris. 3 Pump Court, 1903-1905; 3 Essex Court, 1906-1914 & 1917-1927; 1 Dr Johnson's Building, 1915-1916; 4 Brick Court, 1928-1932; 1 Brick Court, 1933-1934; 2 Garden Court, 1935-1952; 1 Essex Court, 1953-1955. No address, 1956-1963. Not in 1964 Law List.

KERSHAW, Frank
I. 27 April 1904. ETC. 3 February 1906. Prop. Langdon KC. Sec. Maurice Hill. Manchester Chambers; 2 Booth Street, 1906-1915; 78 King Street, 1916-1919. Not in 1920 Law List.

KERSHAW, Henry Aidan (His Honour "Harry" Kershaw)

(HS)

Born 11 May 1927. Died 29 October 1995 aged 68. St John's School, Leatherhead. Served, Royal Navy, 1946-1948. Brasenose College, Oxford, BA. I. November 1953. ETC. 4 May 1954. Prop. Robertson Crichton QC. Sec. Christopher Leigh. Circuit Junior, 1955. 60 King Street, Manchester, 1954-1976. Assistant Recorder of Oldham, 1970-1971. Crown Court Recorder, 1972-1976. Deputy Chairman, Agricultural Land Tribunal, 1972-1976. Chairman, Lancs. Schools Golf Association, 1981-1984. Vice President, English Schools Golf association, 1984. Circuit Judge, 1976-1992. Senior Judge at Bolton, 1984-1992. Commodore, Bolton Sailing Club. Captain, Bolton Golf Club. Honorary Fellow, Bolton Institute. Michael Lever described Harry Kershaw as "one of those sportsmen of effortless brilliance to whichever sport he turned his hand". Harry was a fine golfer, skier, sailor and scrum half. He was my tutor judge and when we finished early, he would take me to John Spencer's hall in Bolton and demonstrate the finer points of snooker. Tributes at Bolton Crown Court, 30 October 1995 (Judge Michael Lever QC / Michael Maguire QC) Transcript in Circuit Records.

KERSHAW, Sir Leonard William
Born 18 November 1864. Died 9 February 1949 aged 84. Only surviving son of Rev. J C Kershaw, Vicar of Walton-le-Dale. Rossall; Queen's College, Oxford, BA. I. 26 January 1886. ETC. 20 July 1887. Prop. Addison QC. Sec. Sharpe. Circuit Junior, Winter 1888. 14 Outer Temple, 1888-1893; 3 Elm Court, 1894-1906; 4 Brick Court, 1906. 1 Essex Court, 1907. Assistant Registrar, Court of Criminal Appeal, 1908; King's Coroner and Attorney; Master of the Crown Office, King's Bench Division and Registrar of the Court of Criminal Appeal, 1912-1933. Kt. 1921. Publications; Joint editor, 7th ed., Russell on Crimes; 4th edition of Wise on Riots; 7th & 8th editions of Wigram's Justices Note Book. WW.

KERSHAW, (Philip) Michael QC (His Honour Judge Kershaw QC)
Born 23 April 1941. Son of His Honour Philip Kershaw qv. Ampleforth College; St John's College, Oxford, MA. FCIArb, 1991. G. 1963. ETC. 1963. Manchester Chambers; 9 Albert Square, 1963-1972; 1 Dean's Court, Crown Square, 1973-1980. Silk 1980. 5 Essex Court & 25 Byrom Street, Manchester. Recorder, 1980-1990. Mercantile Judge (formerly Circuit Commercial Judge), 1990. Publications; Fraud and Misrepresentations, Injunctions and Banking and Bills of Exchange in Atkin's Court Forms; Contrib., Interests in Goods, 1993. WW.

KERSHAW, Philip Charles Stones (His Honour Philip Kershaw)

Born 9 April 1910. Died 1 July 1986 aged 76. Stonyhurst College; Merton College, Oxford, BA. G. 28 June 1933. ETC. 5 July 1933. Prop. Goldie KC. Sec. John Catterall Jolly. Major, 1939-1945. Manchester Chambers; 60 King Street, 1933-1939 & 1945-1955; 36 St Ann Street, 1956-1961. Circuit Judge (formerly Full Time Deputy Chairman, Lancs. Quarter Sessions), 1961-1983. He was junior to Norman Birkett KC in the defence of Dr Buck Ruxton at Lancaster Assizes before Singleton J in March 1936. This very complicated murder case is in Notable British Trials. WW.

KEWISH, Michael John
Born 13 October 1949, Kendal. Only son of John Douglas Kewish, Head of County Court Branch of the Lord Chancellor's Department. Rydal School. AAS. M. 10 October 1967. Call 23 November 1971. Oriel Chambers, 14 Water Street, Liverpool, 1972-1977. Admitted as a solicitor June 1977. Partner with Cartmel Mawson & Main of Carlisle.

KEY, Richard William
Born Christmas Day 1847. Only son of Richard Charles Key of Suffolk Lodge, Stamford Hill, London. AAS. I. 4 November 1868. Call 6 June 1871. ETC. 12 July 1871. Prop. Quain QC. Sec. Bruce. 3 Hare Court, 1876. 3 King's Bench Walk, 1877-1881; 2 Hare Court, 1882-1893; 9 King's Bench Walk, 1894-1896; 4 Harcourt Buildings, 1897-1901. Not in 1902 Law List.

KHAN, Aaminah
Born 19 May 1979, Preston. Brownedge St Mary's, Preston; Brunel University, LLB. M. 11 October 2001. ETC. 26 March 2002. Prop. David Turner QC. Sec. Keith Thomas. New Bailey Chambers, Preston, 4 September 2001.

KHAN, Abdul
L. 26 January 1899. ETC. 30 July 1898. Prop. Mulholland QC. Sec. Ross Brown. No address, 1902-1919. Not in 1920 Law List.

KHAN, (Basharat) Jamil
LLB. L. July 1986. ETC 1986. Liverpool Chambers; 3rd floor, 27 Dale Street, 1986-1989; Corn Exchange, Fenwick Street, 1989-1999; 7 Harrington Street (merger with Martins Building), 6.9.1999.

KHAN, Ghulam Sabir
Advocate, Higher Courts of Pakistan. BA (Pujab); LLB (Karachi); PhD (Manchester). I. July 1966. ETC. 11 July 1968. Pupilmaster, Desmond Franks. 601 Royal Exchange, Manchester, 1968-1975. University Lecturer and Diplomat.

KHAN, Hassan
Born 3 April 1976, Rochdale. Balderstone School; Liverpool University, LLB. L. 15 November 1999, with Louis Berkson & Globe, Solicitors, 1999-2001. ETC. 18 December 2001. Prop. Margaret de Haas QC. Sec. Michael Kennedy. India Buildings, Water Street, Liverpool, 2001.

KHAN, Shokat
Born 18 May 1956, Kotli, Pakistan. Ashmeadow High School, Bury; Warwick University, LLB; London School of Economics, LLM. AAS. M. 10 July 1978. Call 27 November 1979. ETC 1980. Pupilmaster, Daniel Brennan. 40 King Street, Manchester, 1981.

KHAWAR, Aftab
Born 18 December 1959. Greenhill Senior School, Rochdale; Lancaster University, LLB. G. July 1983. Manchester Chambers; 3 St James's Square, 1986-1989; 38 King Street West, 1990-1995; 24a St John Street, 1996 (now St Johns Buildings Chambers).

KIDD, Peter William
Born 19 January 1965, Belfast. Royal Belfast Academical Institution; Liverpool University, LLB. I. July 1987. ETC. December 1987. Pupilmaster, Graham Morris. Liverpool Chambers; Martins Building, Water Street, 1987-1999; 7 Harrington Street (merger with Corn Exchange), 6.9.1999-.

KILLEEN, Simon John
Born 22 August 1960, Bolton. Derby Grammar School; Leicester Polytechnic, BA (Law). I. July 1984. ETC. October 1984. Pupilmaster, Robert Atherton. Liverpool Chambers; Melbourne Buildings, 21 North John Street, 1984-1988; 3rd floor. Peel House, Harrington Street, 1988-1996; Corn Exchange, Fenwick Street, 1996-1999; 7 Harrington Street, (merger with Martins Building), 6.9.1999. Recorder, May 2001.

KILMUIR, The Earl of (See David Maxwell Fyfe)

KILVINGTON, Sarah Elizabeth
Born 9 October 1973 Whitehaven, Cumbria. Sister of Simon Kilvington qv. Wyndham Comprehensive, Egremont; Hertford College, Oxford, BA (English). M. 14 October 1999. ETC. 14 December 1999. Prop. Lindsey Kushner QC. Sec. Lesley Newton. Young Street Chambers, Manchester, September 1999.

KILVINGTON, Simon Charles
Born 8 October 1970, Whitehaven, Cumbria. Brother of Sarah Kilvington qv. Wyndham Secondary School, Cumbria; Hertford College, Oxford, BA. L. November 1995. ETC. 21 December 1995. Prop. Jonathan Foster QC. Sec. Andrew Blake. 18 St John Street, Manchester, 1995.

KING, Alexandra Margaret
Born 20 May 1953, Chesterfield. Married to Kevin Talbot qv. St Elphin's School; Liverpool University, LLB. G. July 1975. ETC. 1975. Prop. Gerald Crowe QC. Sec. Eric Somerset Jones. Oriel Chambers, 14 Water Street, Liverpool, 1975-1981 when retired from practice.

KING, Timothy Roger Alan QC
Born 5 April 1949. Married Bernadette Goodman (qv.) in 1986. Booker Avenue County Primary School; Liverpool Institute; Lincoln College, Oxford, MA., BCL. Assistant Professor, University of Connecticut Law School, 1970-1971. L. November 1973; Bencher 2000. ETC. 1974. Prop. Gerald Crowe QC. Sec. Henry Lachs. Same Liverpool Chambers at; 27 Dale Street, 1973-1976; Melbourne Buildings, 21 North John Street, 1977-1988; 3rd floor, Peel House, Harrington Street, 1989-1991. Silk 1991. Byrom Street Chambers (25, later 12 Byrom Street) Manchester 1991. Assistant Recorder, 1988. Recorder, 1991. Acting Deemster, Isle of Man, 1998. Deputy High Court Judge, 2001.

KINGHORN, John

Born 1839. Only son of William Kinghorn of Dunse, Berwick, merchant. Matric., Edinburgh University. AAS. L. 25 October 1859. Call 11 June 1862. 1 Brick Court, 1876-1908; 2 Elm Court, 1909-1927. Not in 1928 Law List. Practised at Liverpool & Bolton Sessions. Lived at 221 Upper Parliament Street, Liverpool 8.

KINGSBURY, Carol Jayne
Born 3 January 1961. MA (Cantab). AAS. M. 10 January 1983. Call 26 July 1984. 196 Deansgate, Manchester, 1986-1988. Legal Advisor, NatWest Bank EC2, 1990-1994. With solicitors; Cameron Markby Hewitt EC3, 1997-1998; Allen & Overy, EC4, 1999.

KINGSBURY, George Chadwick
Born 1859. 2nd son of Andrew Kingsbury of Dublin. Dublin University MA., MD. AAS. M. 2 November 1896. Call 17 November 1902. ETC. January 1903. Prop. McCall KC. Sec. Wingate Saul. 1 Elm Court, 1906-1933; 2 Brick Court, 1934-1936. No address 1937. Not in 1938 Law List. Preston Sessions & Parliamentary Committees.

KINGSLEY, Hyman Herbert (Hon. Mr Justice Kingsley)
Born 28 October 1897, Manchester. Died 29 November 1956 aged 58. Manchester Grammar School; Manchester University. Served, First World War, King's Own Regt (Lt., despatches. Afghan War, 1919) G. 27 January 1936. ETC. 26 February 1936. Prop. Gorman KC. Sec. Gerrard. 26 King Street, Manchester, 1936-1940. War 1939-1945, served as Paymaster Lt. in Tanganyika Naval Volunteer Force. Crown Counsel, Tanganyika Territory, August 1940-1947. Puisne Judge, Sierra Leone, 1947-1956. WW.

KINGSTON, Sarah Jane
Born 7 June 1968 Ormskirk. Ormskirk Grammar School; Crown Prosecutions Service, August 1987-September 1995. University of Central Lancs., LLB. I. 14 October 1999. ETC. December 1999. Prop. Dan Brennan QC. Sec. John Wishart. Young Street Chambers, Manchester, January 2001.

KINIPPLE, Walter Robert
Born 1861. 2nd son of Walter Robert Kinipple of Greenock, civil engineer. St John's College, Cambridge, BA, 1884. AAS. M. 6 April 1882. Call 17 June 1885. ETC. 31 July 1885. Prop. Samuell. Sec. Welsby., 9 New Square, 1886-1887; 3 King's Bench Walk, 1888-1896; 2 Cloisters, 1897-1901; 3 Plowden Buildings, 1902-1921. No address, 1922-1925. Not in 1926 Law List. Foster.

KIRBY, Lawrence Daniel
I. 6 June 1868. ETC. 18 August 1868. Prop. West QC. Sec. C Russell. 40 Castle Street, Liverpool, 1876. Alexandria, Egypt, 1877-1880. Not in 1881 Law List.

KIRKHAM, Arthur MacDonald
Born 1851. Only son of Arthur Leeche Kirkham of Berehurst, Surrey. Trinity College, Cambridge, BA 1875; LLM 1879. AAS. L. 3 July 1878. Call 11 May 1881. ETC. 18 July 1881. Prop. Russell QC. Sec. Bigham. 6 King's Bench Walk, 1882-1883; 1 Harcourt Buildings, 1884-1887; 12 King's Bench Walk, 1888-1892. No address, 1893-1940. Not in 1941 Law List. Foster.

KIRSTEN, Adrian Richard Calthorpe

LLB., LLM (London) G. November 1962. ETC. 1969. Prop. Hinchliffe QC. Sec. Morgan. Manchester Chambers; Post Office Chambers, 26 Brown Street, 1969-1971; 67 Princess Street, 1972-1977; 4 Clarence Street, 1978-1983; 72 Bridge Street, 1984-1993; Manchester House Chambers, 18-22 Bridge Street, 1994-2000. Not in 2001 Bar Directory. Publications; Kirsten & Harrison on Property Notices, Sweet & Maxwell, 1994.

KITCHIN, Louise Jane

Born 21 May 1970, Stockport. St Anne's RC High School, Stockport; Leeds University (Bretton Hall), BA. Law Clerk with Trantors, Solicitors, 1991-1995. M. 8 October 1998. ETC. December 1998. Prop. Peter Birkett QC. Sec. W R Heap. Pupilmaster, B E Grennan. Manchester Chambers; Kenworthy's Chambers, 83 Bridge Street, October 1998-April 2002; Cobden House Chambers, 19 Quay Street, April 2002.

KITCHING, Robin Miles

Born 23 August 1964, Stockton-on-Tees. Grange School, Stockton; Manchester University, BA. AAS. M. 10 February 1988. Call 21 November 1989. Pupilmaster, Anthony Leonard. ETC. 17 December 1992. Prop. Rodney Klevan QC. Sec. Webster. Manchester Chambers; Hollins Chambers, 64a Bridge Street, 1992-1997; Cobden House Chambers, 19 Quay Street, 1998.

KLEVAN, Rodney Conrad QC (The Hon. Mr Justice Klevan)

Born 23 May 1940. Died 26 December 2001 aged 61. Temple Primary School; Manchester Central Grammar School; Birmingham University, LLB; President, Guild of Undergraduates. G. May 1966; Bencher 1992. ETC. 1966. Prop. Godfrey Heilpern QC. Sec. Philip Hinchliffe. Manchester Chambers; 60 King Street, Manchester, 1966-1978; 18 St John Street, 1979-1998. Deputy Circuit Judge, 1977. Silk 1984. Recorder, 1984-1998. Leader of the Northern Circuit, 1992-1995. High Court Judge, Queens Bench Division, 1998-2001. Circuit Congratulatory Dinner (with Lord Hobhouse) at Midland Hotel, Manchester on 5 December 1998. Tributes; Manchester Law Courts, 7 January 2002 (Judge Sir Rhys Davies QC/ David Steer QC); Liverpool Law Courts 9 January 2002 (Judge Anne Downey/ David Steer QC). Transcripts in Circuit Records. WW. Obituaries; Daily Telegraph, 31 December 2001; Liverpool Daily Post, 10 January 2002.

Rodney Klevan was the supreme jury advocate, best known for his successful defences of Derek Hatton on fraud charges in 1993 and footballer Bruce Grobbelaar on bribery allegations in 1997. His reputation was such that he was retained to defend the serial killer Frederick West who committed suicide in prison shortly before his trial. Lord Woolf, Lord Chief Justice said "what a tremendous loss it has been for the judiciary to be deprived of the immense contribution he would have made. I have no doubt that the success he achieved at the Bar would have been repeated on the Bench if his time as a judge had not been cut short."

KLONIN, Susan Jane

Born Philadelpia, USA. King Edwards, Camp Hill, Birmingham; Birmingham University, LLB. G. November 1970. ETC. 1971. Pupilmaster, Joyanne Bracewell. Manchester Chambers; Peter Street, 1970-1971; Post Office Chambers, 26 Brown Street, 1971-1976; 4th floor, Sunlight House, Quay Street, 1977-1983; Central Street Chambers, 1984-1987; 33 King Street West, 1988-1994; Old Colony House, 6 South King Street, 1995-2001; Kingsgate Chambers, 51-53 South King Street, 2001.

KLOSS, Alexander Wolfgang

Born 11 November 1967, Manchester. Son of Diana Mary Kloss qv. William Hulme's Grammar School. Manchester; Bristol University, BA. Dip. Law. G. 14 October 1993. ETC. 7 December 1993. Prop. Charles Bloom QC. Sec. Bernard Wallwork. 28 St John Street, 1993.(now St Johns Buildings).

KLOSS, Diana Mary

Born 2 September 1938 Hornchurch, Essex. Mother of Alexander Wolfgang Kloss qv. Ursuline High School, Brentwood; King's College, London, LLB; LLM (Tulane). Hon. Fellow of the Faculty of Occupational Medicine, Royal College of Physicians. G. 24 July 1986. ETC 1992. Prop. Charles Bloom QC. Sec. John Philips. 28 St John Street, Manchester, 1992. (now St Johns Buildings). Senior Lecturer in Law, Manchester University, 1980. Part time Chairman, Employment Tribunals, 1995. ACAS Arbitrator. Expert Advisory Group on AIDS. UK Panel on Health Care Workers with Bloodborne Viruses. Publications; Occupational Health, 3rd ed; Chapter in Hunter's Diseases of Occupation and in Textbook of Medical Law (OUP).

KNAPP, Stephen John
Born 29 October 1953 Dunstable. Dunstable Grammar School; University College, London, LLB. Solicitor, 1978-1986. G. July 1986. ETC. 1986. Sec. David Boulton. Liverpool Chambers; Martin's Building, 1986-1999; 7 Harrington Street (merger with Corn Exchange) 6.9.1999. NPAS Adjudicator, 1999. Publications; Rowe & Knapp Evidence & Procedure in the Magistrates Court, Longman Press.

KNIFTON, David
Born 4 February 1964 Waterloo, Liverpool. Brother of Ian Knifton, solicitor. Married to sister of Donal & Deidre Maguire. Merchant Taylors' School, Crosby; Nottingham University, LLB. I. 25 July 1986. ETC. 16 December 1986. Prop. Michael Maguire QC. Pupilmaster, Eryl Lloyd Parry. Liverpool Chambers; Fruit Exchange, 1st floor, Victoria Street, 1986-1991 when chambers moved to Chavasse Court, 24 Lord Street, 1991-1998; Corn Exchange, Fenwick Street, 1998-1999; 7 Harrington Street (merger with Martins Building), 6.9.1999. Recorder 2003.

KNIGHT, Albert Mayne ("Bert")
Born 1906. Died 1970. 4th son of Albert Knight of Wigan, music teacher. BSc, (Manchester). Schoolteacher. AAS. M. 29 April 1933. Call 27 January 1936. ETC. 26 February 1936. Prop. Gorman KC. Sec. Jalland. Manchester Chambers; 40 Kennedy Street, 1936-1964; Ship Canal House, King Street, 1965-1966. Full Time Deputy Chairman of Lancashire Quarter Sessions in Preston, 1966-1970. Would have been "translated" to Circuit Judge had he survived.

KNIGHT, Christopher Michael St John
Born 1944. Only son of Eric Gordon Knight of Poulton-le-Fylde, solicitor. BA (Cantab). AAS. 5 October 1962. Call 22 November 1966. Manchester Chambers; 60 King Street, 1966-1983; 1 Dean's Court, 1984-1993; 9 St John Street, 1994-2000. Not in 2001 Bar Directory.

KNIGHT, Martin Andrew
Born 10 January 1976 Leicester. Lutterworth Grammar School; Liverpool University, LLB. G. November 1998. ETC. 1998. Prop. David Steer QC. Sec. Kevin Grice. Liverpool Chambers; Corn Exchange, Fenwick Street, 1998-1999; 7 Harrington Street (merger with Martin's Building), 6.9.1999.

*** KNOPF, Elliot Michael (His Honour Judge Knopf)**
Born 23 December 1950. Bury Grammar School; University College, London, LLB; College of Law, Chester. Admitted solicitor, 1976. Partner, Pannone & Partners, Manchester, 1979-1991. Deputy District Judge, April 1987. District Judge, Liverpool, October 1991-2002. Assistant Recorder, March 1996-2000. Recorder, July 2000-2002. Circuit Judge, Bolton 20 July 2002. WW.

KNOWLES, Graham Roy
Born 20 February 1968 Manchester. Married to Claire Evans qv. Queen Elizabeth II High School, Peel, Isle of Man: King's College, Cambridge, MA. M. 10 October 1990. ETC. December 1990. Prop. John Hugill QC. Sec. Anthony Russell. Circuit Junior, Winter 1994. Bar Council, 1995-1997. Manchester Chambers; 2 Old Bank Street, 1990-1992 when chambers moved to Peel House, 45 Hardman Street, 1992.

KNOWLES, Gwyneth
Born 11 July 1962. Loreto Grammar School, Altrincham; St Peter's School, Solihull; Lady Margaret Hall/Green College, Oxford, BA (Modern History), 1981-1984., MSc.(Applied Social Studies), 1986-1988. Social Worker; Royal Borough of Kensington & Chelsea, 1988-1991; NSPCC, 1991-1993. Dip. Law, University of Westminster, 1991-1992. Bar Vocational Course at Inns of Court School of Law, 1992-1993. G. October 1993. 4 Brick Court, October 1994-September 2001. ETC. 18 December 2001. Prop. John Benson QC. Sec. Malcolm Sharpe. 14 Castle Street/Atlantic Chambers, Cook Street, 2001.

KNOWLES, Henry Joseph
I. 26 January 1887. ETC. 7 February 1887. Prop. Hopwood QC. Sec. White. No address, 1887-1904. Not in 1905 Law List.

KNOWLES, John
Born 1852. Son of John Knowles of Burnley & Todmorden, surgeon. Formerly a solicitor. AAS. M. 5 November 1885. Call 26 January 1887. ETC. 14 February 1887. Prop. Collins QC. Sec. Shee. 12 King's Bench Walk, 1889-1890; 9 King's Bench Walk, 1891-1912. Not in 1913 Law List.

KNOWLES, Sir Lees MP., First Bt.
Born 16 February 1857. Died 7 October 1928 aged 71. Rugby; Trinity College, Cambridge, MA., LLM, 1882. Amateur Champion Athlete and President, Cambridge University Athletic Club. AAS. L. 6 November 1879. Call. 17 November 1882. ETC. 18 July 1883. Prop. Gully QC. Sec. Leese. Circuit Junior, Autumn 1883 & Winter 1884. 4 New Square, 1886-1922. Contested (C) Leigh, 1885. MP., Salford West, 1886-1906. Member of many public committees & boards. CVO 1909. OBE 1920. DL. TD. Publications; mainly historical including, War in the Peninsula, the British in Capri. WW.

KNOWLES, Leonard Joseph
LLB (London). G. 26 January 1939. (Certificate of Honour, M. 1938). ETC. 14 June 1939. Prop. Lynskey KC. Sec. Benas. Liverpool Chambers; 5 Harrington Street, 1941. 27 Dale Street, 1942-1946. 3 Cook Street, 1947-1953. Nassau, Bahamas, 1954-1963. Not in 1964 Law List.

KNOWLES, Mark

Born 26 September 1834. Youngest son of Mark Knowles of Blackburn. St John's National School, Blackburn. Ironfounder and engineer, 1856-1876. Inventor of patent expanding comb, patent centre point and patent centre warping machine. AAS. M. 17 January 1866. Call 17 November 1879. 18 Adam Street, Adelphi WC., 1888-1890; 1 Elm Court, 1891-1902. Vice Chairman, Blackburn School Board, 1875. Not in 1903 Law List. Biography " From the Loom to the Lawyers Gown" by Harriet S Carson, 1884. The book has little to say about his practice of the law and concentrates on his prowess as an inventor and his work for the Temperance Cause.

KNOWLES, Michael John
Born 13 July 1952. Xaverian College, Victoria Park, Manchester; Manchester University, LLB. Formerly solicitor & Principal Crown Prosecutor. M. 12 October 2000. ETC. 8 July 2003. Prop. Keith Goddard QC. Sec. Adrian Farrow. Cobden House Chambers; 19 Quay Street, Manchester, 2000.

KNOWLES, Townley Rigby
Born 1811. Eldest son of Lt. Col. Joseph Knowles, late, Madras Army. AAS. I. 23 April 1833. Call 10 June 1836. 3 Raymond Buildings, 1846-1882. No address, 1883-1886. Not in 1887 Law List. Equity draftsman & conveyancer. Foster.

KNOX-MAWER, Ronald
Born 2 August 1925. Grove Park School, Denbighs.; Emmanuel College, Cambridge, MA. Royal Artillery, 1943-1945. AAS. 23 January 1948. Call 3 May 1950. Wales & Chester Circuit, 1950-1952. 20 Hackins Hey, Liverpool, 1952. Chief Magistrate & Acting Chief Justice, Aden, 1952-1958. Senior Magistrate, Puisne Judge, Justice of Appeal, Acting Chief Justice of Fijii and conjointly Chief Justice, Nauru & Tonga, 1958-1971. ETC. 1971. Oriel Chambers, 14 Water Street, Liverpool, 1971-1975. Metropolitan Stipendiary Magistrate, Marylebone & Tower Bridge, 1975-1984. Deputy Circuit Judge, London, 1979-1984. Publications include; Tales From a Palm Court, 1986; Tales of a Man called Father, 1989; A Case of Bananas and other South Sea Trials, 1992; Land of My Father, 1994. WW.

KOPPEL, Percy Augustus CMC., CBE
Born 3 November 1876. Died 31 October 1932 aged 53. Bradfield College; Magdalen College, Cambridge, MA. I. 26 January 1900. ETC. 17 February 1903. Prop. Carver QC. Sec. G W. Duncan. 2 Garden Court, 1903-1921. No address, 1922-1932. Board of Education, 1903-1905. Law Clerk, National Health Insurance Commission, 1912. News Department, Department of Information, 1917-1918. Political Intelligence Department, Foreign Office, 1918-1920. Counsellor in Diplomatic Service & Foreign Office. CBE 1920. CMG 1928.

KOROL, Kathryn Margaret
Born 5 October 1958 Manchester. Bury Convent Grammar School; University of Central Lancs., LLB. Social Worker in Child Protection for 10 years prior to Call (CQSW). M. 18 March 1996. ETC 1996. Prop. Roger Farley. Sec. Barry Grennan. Kenworthy's Buildings, 83 Bridge Street, Manchester, 1996.

KRAYCZYK, Monica Ursula
LLB. M. July 1998. ETC. 27 July 2000. Prop. Peter Birkett QC. Sec. Beverlet A Lunt. Kingsgate Chambers, 51-53 South King Street, Manchester, 2000.

KUSHNER, Lindsey Joy QC (Her Honour Judge Kushner QC)
Born 16 April 1952 Birmingham. Daughter of District Judge Harry Kushner. Manchester High School for Girls; Liverpool University, LLB. AAS. M. 16 March 1972. Call 18 July 1974. ETC. 1974. Manchester Chambers; 12 floor, Sunlight House, Quay Street, 1974-1979; 28 St John Street, 1980-2000. Assistant Recorder, 1989-1993. Silk 1992. Recorder, 1993-2000. Part time Chairman; Medical Appeal Tribunal, 1989; Disablement Appeal Tribunal, 1992. Member, Ethnic Advisory Committee, LCD 1994. Circuit Judge 2000.

KYDD, Samuel
2nd son of James Kydd of Arbroath, Forfar. AAS. G. 13 October 1858. Call 6 June 1861. 5 Mitre Court Chambers, 1876-1889. West Riding, Yorks. Sessions. No address, 1890-1892. Not in 1893 Law List. Foster.

KYFFIN, Sidney Alton
LLB. L. 1 May 1901. ETC. 29 July 1903. Prop. Isaacs KC. Sec. Sander. 4 Pump Court, 1904-1907; 2 Paper Buildings, 1908-1954. No address, 1955-1962. Not in 1963 Law List.

L

LACHS, Henry Lazarus (His Honour Henry Lachs)
Born 31 December 1927. Died New Year's Day 2000 aged 72 (the day following his retirement). Younger son of Samuel Lachs, supervising shocket. Liverpool Institute High School; Pembroke College, Cambridge, MA., LLB. AAS. M. 20 October 1948. Call 6 June 1951. ETC. 6 June 1951. Prop. Neville Laski QC. Sec. Bertram Benas. Same Liverpool Chambers at; 24 Dale Street, 1951-1956; 27 Dale Street, 1956-1976; Melbourne Buildings, 21 North John Street, 1977-1979. Head of Chambers, 1961-1979. Recorder, 1972-1979. Chairman, Mental Health Review Tribunal, 1968-1999. Circuit Judge, Liverpool, 1979-1999. Tributes; Liverpool Law Courts, 10 January 2000 (Judge David Clarke QC/ David Harris QC); David Harris QC, "In Brief" May 2000; Ray Herman, Liverpool University Chanukah Lecture, 14 December 2000. Transcripts in Circuit Records. WW.

LAHIRI, Indrajit
BA (Oxon). L. November 1978. ETC. 3 April 1979. Prop. Douglas Brown QC. Sec. Harold Singer. 25 Bow Lane, Manchester, 1978-1979. Attorney in Bakersfield, California, 1980-1994. Not in 1995 Bar Directory.

LAING, Hugh Charles Desmond
I. November 1976. Manchester Chambers; 60 King Street/ Crown Square Chambers, 1978-1991. No chambers address, 1992.

LAING, Paula Ulander
MA (London). I. October 1991. 5 John Dalton Street, Manchester, 1991-1997. Now Sister Paula (Carmalite Monastry).

*** LAKIN, Peter Maurice (His Honour Judge Lakin)**
Born 21 October 1949. King Henry VIII School, Coventry; Manchester University, LLB. Solicitor. Articled to Michael Blackburn qv at Conn, Goldberg, 1971-1974. Assistant Solicitor with Goldberg & Blackburn (later Pannone & Partners) Partner, 1976-1995. Assistant Recorder, 1989-1993. Recorder, 1993-1995. Circuit Judge, 1995. WW.

LALENG, Per Christian
Born Norway. Monmouth School, Kent; Kent University, BA; Bordeaux, DE. UG; Fitzwilliam, Cambridge, M. Phil. Lecturer in Law, University of Kent, 1994-1997. G. May 1997. Pupilmasters, Derek Sweeting & Tim Spencer, 9 Bedford Row, September 1997-September 1998; 42 Castle Street, Liverpool, October 1998.

LAMB, Charles Astley
BA. I. 7 July 1886. ETC. 17 February 1906. Prop. Steel KC. Sec. Greer. 5 Harrington Street, Liverpool, 1908-1926. No address, 1927-1931. Not in 1932 Law List.

LAMB, Eric Alan
Born 3 March 1953, Wallasey. Park High School, Birkenhead; Liverpool University, LLB. L. July 1975. ETC 1975. Pupilmaster, Christopher Carus. Same Liverpool Chambers; 606 The Corn Exchange, Fenwick Street, 1975-1981; Exchange Chambers at: 1 Exchange Flags, 1982-1991; Derby Square, 1992. Assistant Recorder 1999. Recorder 2000. Attorney & Counsellor at Law, Texas.

LAMBERT, Deborah Mary
Born 2 April 1954, Preston. Daughter of His Honour Judge Robert Lambert qv. St Anne's School, Windermere; Lady Margaret Hall, Oxford, BA (Jurisprudence). L. May 1977. ETC. 1980. Pupilmaster, Anthony Jolly. Manchester Chambers; 27 Byrom Street, 1979-1983; 26 Cross Street, 1984-1987; Kenworthy's Buildings, 83 Bridge Street, 1988. Equal Opportunities Commission, 1976-1979. Deputy District Judge, 2000. Publications; "Equality at Work" – A Guide to the Sex Discrimination Act 1981.

LAMBERT, John
MA., FCIArb. L. July 1977. Manchester Chambers; Bridge Street Chambers, 72 Bridge Street, 1986-1995; 77 Deansgate, 1999-2001; Old Colony House, 6 South King Street, 2001.

LAMBERT, Robert (His Honour Robert Lambert)
Born 28 May 1908. Died 21 November 1971 aged 63. Father of Deborah Mary Lambert qv. Preston Grammar School; London University, LLB. L. 16 June 1931. ETC. 2 July 1931. Prop. Goldie KC. Sec. Rowson. Manchester Chambers; 26 King Street, 1931-1939. Squadron Leader, RAFVR, 1939-1945 in UK, Iceland & NW Europe, Coastal Command and JAG's Staff. 26 King Street, 1945-1958; 9 Albert Square, 1958-1962. Deputy Chairman, Lancashire County Quarter Sessions, 1961-1962. Chairman, Agricultural Land Tribunal (Lancs. & Yorks.) 1962. Deputy Chairman, Manchester Mental Health Review Tribunal, 1960-1962. JP. County Court Judge, Circuit 3, (Cumberland), 1968-1970. Publications; Ebb Tide (play), 1930. WW.

LAMBERTY, Mark Julian Barker
Born 17 August 1947 Burnley. Rugby School; Keble College, Oxford, BCL., MA. G. November 1970. ETC. 1971. Prop. Patrick Russell QC. Sec. Ian Webster. Manchester Chambers; 2 Booth Street, 1971-1975; 13 Police Street, 1976-1978; 43 King Street, 1979-1988; Queen's Chambers, 5 John Dalton Street, 1989.

LANDALE, Tina Jeanette
Born 25 November 1965 Hebden, West Yorks. Wolverhampton, LLB. AAS. M. 16 July 1987. Call 28 July 1988. ETC 1989. Pupilmaster, Roger Brown. Manchester Chambers; 33 King Street West, 1989-1994; Old Colony House, 6 South King Street, 1995-2000; Peel Court Chambers, 45 Hardman Street, 2000.

LANDER, Charles Gideon
Born 27 June 1971 Liverpool. Nephew of Richard Isaacson QC qv. King David High School, Liverpool; Leeds University, LLB. L. 25 November 1993. ETC. 1994. Prop. Stephen Riordan QC. Sec. Gerald Baxter. 25-27 Castle Street, Liverpool, 1994.

LANDER, Richard Mark
Born 30 June 1971 Leicester. Loughborough Grammar School; Downing College, Cambridge, MA. L. October 1993. Research Assistant, Law Commission, October 1993-September 1994. ETC. 13 December 1994. Prop. Peter Smith QC. Sec. Katherine Dunn. King's Chambers, 40 King Street, Manchester, October 1994.

LANE, David Goodwin QC.
Born 8 October 1945 Gloucester. Crypt School, Gloucester; King's College, London, LLB. AKC. G. 26 November 1968. Western Circuit with chambers in London & Bristol, 1968-2000. ETC 27 July 2000. Prop. Howard Bentham QC. Sec. O'Byrne. Peel Court Chambers, 45 Hardman Street, Manchester, 2000. Assistant Recorder, 1981. Recorder, 1987. Silk 1991. Freeman, City of London. WW.

LANGDON, Adolph Max Lazarus KC
Born 10 March 1861. Died 1 March 1949 aged 87. Assumed name Langdon in 1892. Manchester Grammar School; Pembroke College, Oxford, MA., BCL. I. 19 May 1886; Bencher 1913; Treasurer 1934. ETC. 28 July 1886. Prop. Gully QC. Sec. Smyly. 3 Temple Gardens, 1887-1890. 2 St James's Square, Manchester, 1891-1892; 40 Kennedy Street, Manchester, 1893-1904. Silk 1904. 12 King's Bench Walk, 1904-1909; 11 King's Bench Walk, 1910-1927; 15 Old Square, 1928-1940. Recorder; Burnley, 1909-1915; Salford, 1915-1941. Commissioner of Assize, 1923 & 1924. Head of the Inns of Court School of Law and Director of Legal Studies, 1925-1935. Member of Bar Council. WW.

LANGDON, Wilfred Max
Born 14 February 1889 Manchester. Son of Edward Henry & Ada Langdon. Rugby (Whitelaw's); New College, Oxford. Address Silver-lands, Altrincham. I. 27 January 1913. ETC. 20 February 1914. Prop. Langdon KC. Sec. Acton. Commissioned Lt, 10 Btn., Cheshire Regiment on 26 September 1914. Promoted Captain. Killed in action 21 May 1916 aged 27. Buried in Ecoivres Military Cemetery, Mont-St Eloy, Pas de Calais. Grave II. B. 6. Information from Public Records Office & Commonwealth War Graves Commission.

LANGDON, William Charles Alfred
G. 28 January 1901. ETC. 1 August 1902. Prop. Pickford KC. Sec. Sanderson. No address, 1902-1953. Not in 1954 Law List.

LANIGAN, Stephen Charles Martin
Born 1841. Eldest son of John Lanigan, JP., of Glenagrule, Templemore, Tipperary. Trinity College, Dublin, BA 1865. Kings Inns, Dublin, 1865. AAS. I. 4 May 1859. Call 11 June 1867. Circuit Junior, 1868. He began the Northern Circuit Proposition Book on 9 March 1868. It records the name of every person elected to the Circuit with date of election, proposer and seconder. 3 Stone Buildings, conveyancer & equity draftsman, 1883-1897. No address, 1898-1914. Not in 1915 Law List.

LANKESTER, Edward Forbes KC
Born 31 January 1855. Died 20 April 1934 aged 79. Son of Dr. Edwin Lankester, Coroner, Central Middlesex, nephew of Samuel Pope QC. St Paul's School; Lincoln College, Oxford, BA 1877. AAS. M. 12 January 1874. Call 3 July 1878; Bencher 1915; Reader Lent 1926. ETC. 29 July 1878. Prop. Temple QC. Sec. McConnell. Practised in Liverpool 1878-1882. He then moved to London to the Parliamentary Bar, took Silk in 1905 and was a Metropolitan Stipendiary Magistrate from 1919-1925. WW.

LAPRELL, Mark Dieter
Born 10 July 1956 Halifax. Bradford Grammar School; Magdalen College, Oxford, BA. G. November 1979. 18 St John Street, Manchester, 1981. Recorder 2000.

LASCELLES, Rev. John
Born 13 May 1841. Only son of Robert Morley Lascelles, surgeon of Slingsby, Yorks. Clare College, Cambridge, BA 1863; MA 1877. AAS. 20 November 1862. Call 30 April 1866. 2 St James's Square, Manchester, 1876-1877. No address, 1878-1899. Not in 1900 Law List. Curate of Slingsby, 1879-1880. Vicar of Sheriff Hutton, Yorks., 1880. Publications; Local Government and Sanitary Law Reform. Foster.

LASKER, Jeremy Stewart
Born 18 March 1954 Manchester. Rugby School; Birmingham University, LLB. I. July 1976. ETC. 1977. Pupilmaster, Harry Day. Manchester Chambers; 43 King Street, 1976-1988; 5 John Dalton Street, 1989-1996. Lincoln House Chambers, 1 Brazennose Street, 1997. Serious Fraud Office Panel, 2001. Recorder 2004.

LASKI, Neville Jonas QC
Born 18 December 1890. Died 24 March 1969 aged 78. Manchester Grammar School; Clifton College; Corpus Christi College, Oxford, MA. I. 17 November 1913; Bencher 1938. ETC. 20 February 1914. Prop. Atkinson KC. Sec Dehn. Captain, 1914-1918 War, 6th Lancashire Fusiliers. Served in Gallipoli, Sinai & France. Manchester Chambers; 5 St James's Square, 1918-1919; 3 St James's Square, 1919-1930. Silk 1930. 5 Crown Office Row, 1930-1936. 2 Mitre Court Buildings, 1937-1940. 2 Paper Buildings, 1941-1943. 1 Hare Court, 1944-1956. Recorder of Burnley, 1935-1956. Judge of Appeal, Isle of Man, 1953-1956. Judge of the Crown Court & Recorder of Liverpool, 1956-1963. Hon. LLD. Liverpool 1957. Publications; Jewish Rights & Wrongs, 1939. WW.

LATIMER, Andrew Gerard
Born 9 November 1971, Wallsend, Northumberland. St Mary's RC School, Newcastle-upon-Tyne; Hertford College, Oxford, BA., BCL. G. November 1995. ETC. 21 December 1995. Prop. Peter Smith QC. Sec. Lesley Anderson. Pupilmasters, Katherine Dunn & Michael Booth. King's Chambers, 40 King Street, Manchester, 1995. Attorney General's Panel for Civil Litigation (Provincial), February 2000.

LAU, Wei Shieong
Born 23 September 1977 Singapore. Sunway College, Malaysia; Leicester University, LLB., LLM. L. 8 October 1998. ETC. 6 April 2000. Prop. Keith Goddard QC. Sec. Peter Buckley. Queen's Chambers, 5 John Dalton Street, Manchester, 2000.

LAUGHARNE, Roland Hugh Polden
I. 17 November 1922. ETC. 31 January 1923. Prop. Singleton KC. Sec. Blackledge. No address, 1922-1931. 5 Crown Office Row, 1932-1936. No address, 1937-1963. Not in 1964 Law List.

LAVERY, Michael James
Born 20 February 1966, Manchester. Urmston Boys Grammar School; LLB. G. February 1990. ETC. December 1990. Prop. Janet Smith QC. Sec. Ian McIvor. Manchester Chambers; 38 King Street West, 1990-1995; 24a St John Street, 1996-2001; Peel Court Chambers, 45 Hardman Street, 2001.

LAWN, Edgar
G. 26 January 1916. Northern Circuiteer but election not recorded probably due to world events. No address, 1921-1923. Not in 1924 Law List.

LAWRENCE, Edwin Joseph Bell
Born 1864. Eldest son of Joseph Lawrence, journalist of Croydon. London University. AAS. M. 4 November 1882. Call 7 July 1886. ETC. 27 January 1887. Prop. Addison QC. Sec. Slater. 3 Plowden Buildings, 1888; 5 Pump Court, 1889-1895; 6 Plowden Buildings, 1896-1906; 2 Hare Court, 1907-1910. No address, 1911-1940. Not in 1941 Law List.

LAWRENCE, Nigel Stuart
Born 4 November 1965 Heswall, Wirral. Kingsmead School, Hoylake; Rydal School, Colwyn Bay; Leicester University, LLB. L. 28 June 1988. ETC. 1988. Prop. Brian Leveson QC. Sec. David Kerr. Liverpool Chambers; Martins Building, Water Street, 1988-1999; 7 Harrington Street (merger with Corn Exchange), 6.9.1999.

LAWRENCE, Paul Ogden QC (Rt. Hon. Lord Justice Lawrence)
Born 8 September 1861 Wimbledon where he died on 26 December 1952 aged 91. 2nd son of Philip Henry Lawrence, barrister of Lincoln's Inn. Brother of Roger Bernard Lawrence KC qv. Malvern College. AAS. L. 22 June 1878. Call 17 November 1882; Bencher 1900; Treasurer 1925. ETC. 22 June 1878. Prop. Gully QC. Sec. Kennedy. Chancery Practitioner. Lancs. Chancery Court. Liverpool Chambers; 25 Lord Street, 1883-1887; 8 Harrington Street, 1888-1896. Silk 1896. 4 New Court, 1897-1904; 6 New Court, 1905-1918. Chairman; General Council of the Bar, 1913-1918; Incorporated Council of Law Reporting, 1917-1918. High Court Judge, Chancery Division, 1918-1926. Kt. 1919. Lord Justice of Appeal, 1926-1933. PC. 1926. WW. DNB.

LAWRENCE, Roger Bernard KC
Born 2 January 1869, London. Died 8 December 1925 aged 56. Son of Philip Henry Lawrence, barrister, of Lincolns Inn and brother of Lord Justice Lawrence qv. London University, LLB. L. 26 January 1891. ETC. 21 March 1893. Prop. Shee QC. Sec. by his brother. Chancery Practitioner. Liverpool Chambers; 7 Harrington Street, 1892-1913. Silk 1913. 6 New Court, 1913. Registrar, Liverpool District Registry of Lancs. Chancery Court, 1914-1919. Vice Chancellor of the County Palatine of Lancaster, 1919-1925. WW.

LAWRENCE, William Frederick MP
Born 29 December 1844. Died 15 January 1935 aged 90. Son of Rev. Charles Washington Lawrence, Vicar of St Luke's, Liverpool. Eton; Christ Church, Oxford, MA. AAS. L. 26 April 1867. Call 1 May 1871. 1 Quality Court, Chancery Lane, 1876; 40 Chancery Lane, 1877-1882. Conveyancer. No address, 1883-1935. MP (C) Liverpool, Abercromby, 1885-1906. JP. WW.

LAWRIE, Richard Henegan
Born 1815. Eldest son of Archibald Lawrie of Carlisle. Pembroke College, Cambridge, BA 1838. AAS. L. 27 May 1835. Call 16 June 1840. 10 Farrar's Building, 1876; 3 Pump Court, 1877-1886. No address, 1887-1891. Not in 1892 Law List. He was one of a small number who, after the North Eastern Circuit was formed in 1876, was a member of both Circuits. Foster.

LAWSON, Andrew Charles
Born 4 March 1971, Lytham St Annes. Charterhouse, Godalming, Surrey; Leeds University, BA (English) Dip Law. I. October 1995. ETC. December 1996. Prop. Jonathan Foster QC. Sec. P Harrison. 24a St John Street, Manchester 1996. (now St Johns Buildings).

LAWSON, Arthur Hamilton
Born 19 September 1915. 2nd son of Arthur Lawson, solicitor, of Bolton. Trinity Hall, Cambridge. AAS. M. 23 November 1933. Call 26 January 1937. ETC. 24 February 1937. Prop. William Gorman QC. Sec. Gerrard. 3 St James's Square, 1937. Commissioned, 8 June 1938. Reconnaissance Corps. Lt., 1 January 1941. Promoted Captain. Killed in Action in Malaya on 5 February 1942 aged 26. He is one of 24,000 names recorded on the walls of the Singapore Memorial in Kranji War Cemetery who have no known grave. (Column 95). Information supplied by the Ministry of Defence & Commonwealth War Graves Commission.

LAWTON, Arthur
L. 17 November 1902. Palace Chambers, Bridge Street, Westminster, 1904-1915; 4 Pump Court, 1904-1909; 3 Plowden Buildings, 1910-1911; 6 Pump Court, 1912-1921. He left the Circuit in 1916 to join Midland Circuit. Not in 1922 Law List.

LAWTON, (Kenneth) Keith (Fullerton) (His Honour Judge Lawton)

(RB)

(DC)

Judge Lawton at Sessions House, Liverpool 1983.

Born 6 August 1924. Died 28 March 1985 aged 60. Only son of John William Lawton, MA., BSc., Schoolmaster & Educational Administrator. Barrow Grammar School: Trinity Hall, Cambridge, MA. Fleet Air Arm, 1943-1945. AAS. M. 4 May 1945. Call 17 November 1947. ETC 1948. Liverpool Chambers; 27 Lord Street, 1948-1950; North House, 17 North John Street, 1950-1970. Contested (C) Barrow, 1951. Part time Deputy Chairman, Lancs. Quarter Sessions, 1969 (full time 1970). Circuit Judge, 1972-1985. Parole Board, 1981-1983. Liason Judge, St Helens Magistrates. WW.

Keith Lawton was my pupilmaster. He was one of the few people who could do a number of things at the same time and perform them well. My earliest recollections of him are sitting at his desk discussing a case with a solicitor over the telephone, signing pleadings, giving me my instructions for the day and solving the Times crossword. He got through a huge amount of work at the Bar and on the Bench. He often found a short but just solution to a criminal case. When this was impossible, he despatched the trial speedily and expertly.

LAWTON, Paul Anthony

Born 12 July 1964, Stoke on Trent. Alsager School, Stoke on Trent; Manchester Metropolitan University, LLB. L. November 1987. Pupilmaster Rock Tansey, (London). ETC. July 1989. Manchester Chambers; Central Buildings, 3 Peter Street, 1988-1991; 211 Deansgate, 1992-1993; 6th floor, Sunlight House, Quay Street, 1994; 38 Young Street, 1995-1999; Lincoln House Chambers, 1 Brazennose Street, 2000.

LAYCOCK, Ann

Liverpool University, LLB. G. July 1980. ETC. Autumn 1980. Pupilmaster, Mark Hedley. Same Liverpool Chambers at; 3rd floor, 27 Dale Street, 1980-1989; 5th floor, Com Exchange, Fenwick Street, 1989-1994.

LAYTON, John Henry QC

Born 19 September 1876. Died 29 January 1952 aged 75. Son of George Layton of Liverpool. Charterhouse. I. 4 May 1898. ETC. 3 August 1898. Prop. Taylor QC. Sec. Mellor. Liverpool Chambers; 25 Lord Street, 1898-1900; 11 Lord Street, 1901-1903; 10 Cook Street, 1903-1914. Major, Royal Field Artillery, 1914-1918. 10 Cook Street, 1918-1922. Silk 1922. 1 Tanfield Court, Temple, 1922-1923. Silk revoked at his own request on 23 April 1923. Not in 1924 Law List.

LAZARUS, Grant Philip

Born 6 May 1959 Woolwich. Brentwood School; University College, Cardiff, LLB. G. November 1981. 3 Dr Johnson's Buildings, October 1981-May 1982; 2 Gray's Inn Square, May 1982-November 1982; 3 Old Square, November 1982-November 1983. Pupilmasters, J Howard Shaw & Leonard Sieve. ETC. December 1983. Prop. Bert Andrew QC. Sec. Richard Pratt. Liverpool Chambers; 5 Castle Street, November 1983-May 1987; chambers relocated to 48 Castle Street, May 1987-September 1989; Corn Exchange, Fenwick Street (merger), September 1989-September 1999; 7 Harrington Street (merger with Martins Building), 6.9.1999.

LEACH, Alexander

Born 22 July 1979 Epping. Birkdale School, Sheffield. Manchester University, LLB. I. 11 October 2001. ETC. 12 December 2001. Prop. Alan Conrad QC. Sec. Elizabeth Nichols. Lincoln House Chambers, 1 Brazennose Street, Manchester, 22 October 2001.

LEACH, John

Born 15 April 1926. Ellergreen School, Liverpool; Royal Navy, March 1944 – January 1946. Liverpool City / Merseyside Police, 27 December 1946-1975. Detective Inspector and Chief Antecedents Officer, St George's Hall, Liverpool. External LLB, London University. G. 3 November 1974. ETC. 1975. Pupilmaster, Colin Cunningham. Liverpool Chambers; 15 Victoria Street, 1975-1984; 10 James Street, 1984-1989; 24 Fenwick Street 1989 to retirement in November 1997.

LEACH, Robert Webber

G. 19 November 1917. Manchester Chambers; Bank of England Chambers, Tib Lane, 1919-1923; 8 Booth Street, 1924-1929; 2 Booth Street, 1930-1960. Not in 1961 Law List.

LEADLEY-BROWN, Cicely

L. 2 July 1924. ETC. 17 July 1924. Prop. Singleton KC. Sec. Stewart-Brown. 8 Cook Street, Liverpool, 1924 – 1949. No address, 1950-1963. Not in 1964 Law List.

LECK, David Henry MC

Born 1894. 2nd son of David Calder Leek KC (North Eastern Circuit). Trinity College, Oxford, MA. AAS. M. 7 April 1913. Call 16 June 1920. ETC. 20 June 1922. Prop. Greaves Lord KC. Sec. Thorpe. 3 Essex Court, 1920 – 1923; 5 Paper Buildings, 1924-1940. No address, 1941 – 1953. Not in 1954 Law List.

LEDWIDGE, Francis Andrew

MA (Oxon). G. October 1990. Derby Square Chambers, Merchants Court, Liverpool, 1992-1998.

LEE, Daniel William Cartan
I. 25 April 1888. ETC. 27 July 1888. Prop. Henn Collins QC. Sec. Heywood. 12 King's Bench Walk, 1893-1903; 4 Paper Buildings, 1906-1913; 1 Dr Johnson's Building, 1914-1922. Not in 1923 Law List.

LEE, Helen Frances
Sheffield University, LLB. G. October 1992. ETC. 17 December 1992. Prop. Rodney Scholes QC. Sec. Paul Chambers.

LEECH, Robert (Radcliffe) (His Honour Robert Leech)
Born 5 December 1919. Died 30 April 2004 aged 84. Monmouth School; Worcester College, Oxford. Served War, 1940-1944, Border Regiment (despatches twice). AAS. M. 29 April 1946. Call 17 November 1949. Harmsworth Scholar. ETC. 1951. Pupilmaster, R S Nicklin. Liverpool Chambers 27 Lord Street, 1951-1959; relocated to 10 Water Street, 1960-1970. Deputy Chairman, Cumberland Quarter Sessions, 1966-1971. Circuit Judge (formerly County Court Judge), 1970-1986. Hon. Recorder of Carlisle, 1985-1986. WW.

LEEMING, Ian QC
Born 10 April 1948, Preston. Father of Lucinda Leeming qv. Catholic College, Preston; Manchester University, LLB. G. November 1970. L. 1981. ETC. 1971. Prop. Arthur Prestt QC. Sec. A W Simpson. Manchester Chambers; 196 Deansgate, 1971-1978; 9 St John Street, 1988-2001; St James's Chambers, 68 Quay Street 2001. Part time Lecturer in Law, Manchester University, 1971-1975. Silk 1988. Recorder, 1989. Deputy Deemster, Manx High Court & Member of Court of Appeal, Isle of Man 1998. Publications; (with James Bonney) Observations on the Insolvency Bill. 1985; (ed) Equity & Trusts Section of Butterworth's Law of Limitation. WW.

LEEMING, Lucinda Clare
Daughter of Ian Leeming QC qv. LLB. M. 1999. ETC. 27 July 2000. Prop. Leeming QC. Sec. James. 9 St John Street, Manchester, 2000. Circuit Junior, 2004.

LEEMING, Michael Peter George
Born 16 April 1961, Salford. Thornleigh Salesian College, Bolton; Leeds University, LLB. I. July 1983. ETC. 1983. Prop. John Hugill QC. Sec. Michael Shorrock. Manchester Chambers; 2 Old Bank Street, 1983-1984; 6th floor, Arkwright House, Parsonage Gardens, 1984-1988; Kenworthy's Buildings, 1988-1991; Crown Square Chambers/9 St John Street, 1991. Assistant Recorder, 1999. Recorder, 2000.

LEEMING, Richard Brettargh
Eldest son of Richard Leeming, merchant. AAS. M. 7 January 1882. AAS. I. 20 October 1884. Call. I. 17 November 1884. ETC. 27 January 1885. Prop. Bigham QC. Sec. Synnott. Goldsmith Buildings, 1885-1886; 3 Plowden Buildings, 1887; 2 Temple Gardens, 1888-1889. No address, 1890-1940. Not in 1941 Law List.

LEES, C(harles) Norman (His Honour Norman Lees)

(HS)

Born 4 October 1929. Stockport School; Leeds University, LLB, 1950. L. June 1951. ETC. 6 March 1952. Prop. Wooll QC. Sec. Backhouse. Pupilmaster, Charles Elliott. Manchester Chambers; 26 King Street, September 1951-1958; 9 Albert Square, 1959-1972; 1 Dean's Court, Crown Square, 1973-1980. Deputy Chairman, Cumberland County Quarter Sessions, 1969-1971. Crown Court Recorder, 1972-1980. Member, Mental Health Review Tribunal, 1971-1998 (President, Restricted Patients, 1983-1998); Chairman, Manchester Region, 1977-1980. Circuit Judge, 1980-1996. Designated Family Judge, Greater Manchester, 1991-1996. WW.

LEESE, Sir Joseph Francis Bt., QC., MP.
Born 28 February 1845. Died 29 July 1914 aged 69. 2nd son of Joseph Leese of Altrincham, cotton spinner. Regents Park College; London University, BA 1863; St Johns College, Cambridge. AAS. I. 11 November 1864. Call 30 April 1868; Bencher 1899. ETC. 4 March 1877. Prop. Edwards QC. Sec. Coventry. 2 Mitre Court Buildings, 1880-1888; 5 Crown Office Row, 1889-1892; 2 King's Bench Walk, 1893-1914. Silk 1891. Contested; Preston, 1868; Accrington, 1886. MP (L) Accrington, 1892-1909. Recorder of Manchester, 1893-1914. Kt. 1895. 1st Bt. 1908. WW. Foster.

LEES-JONES, John OBE., MP
Born 1887. Died 13 January 1966. Son of John William Jones, surgeon, of Manchester. Lymm Grammar School; Wrekin College, Shropshire, brewers apprentice when AAS. M on 25 January 1910. Served, 1914-1918 War. Call 26 January 1916. ETC. 9 July 1920. Prop. Mayer QC. Sec. Macbeth. No chambers address. MP (U) Manchester, Blackley, 1931-1945. Member, Advisory Council on Treatment of Offenders. OBE 1953. WW.

LEIGH, Christopher Thomas Bowes OBE (His Honour Judge Leigh OBE)
Born 3 January 1905. Died 21 May 1971 aged 66. Son of His Honour Thomas Bowes Leigh qv. Cheltenham College; Queen's College, Oxford, BA., LLB. G. 26 January 1928. Circuit Junior, Summer 1929. 60 King Street, Manchester, 1928-1962. Commissioned 7th Btn., Lancashire Fusiliers (TA) 1926; Major 1935. Served North Africa & Italy, 1939-1945 War. OBE 1944. Chairman, Agricultural Land Tribunal, Yorks. & Lancs., 1947-1962. County Court Judge, Circuit 8, 1962-1970. WW.

LEIGH, His Honour Thomas Bowes
Born 22 May 1867. Died 29 July 1947 aged 80. Son of William Leigh of Stockport JP., & cotton Spinner. Father of His Honour Judge Leigh qv. Manchester Grammar School; University of Manchester, BSc, 1885. Cotton industry until AAS. M. 17 October 1898. Call 18 November 1901. ETC. 13 February 1902. Prop. Shee KC. Sec. Acton. Manchester Chambers; 40 Kennedy Street, 1902-1917; 10 St James's Square, 1918-1921; 46 Crown Street, 1922-1924; 44 King Street, 1925. Recorder of Burnley, 1921-1925. County Court Judge, Circuit 8, May 1925-1942. JP. Hon. LLD., Manchester

LEIGH, William Gerald
G. 2 July 1924. ETC. 11 July 1924. Prop. Greaves-Lord KC. Sec. Leigh. 26 King Street, Manchester, 1929-1938. Not in 1939 Law List.

LE MESURIER, Cecil John Reginald
L. 27 January 1902. ETC. 29 July 1902. Prop. Pickford KC. Sec. Maxwell. 8 Stone Buildings, 1903-1904. Perth, Australia, 1905-1940. No address, 1941-1953. Not in 1954 Law List.

LEMMY, Michael David
Born 23 February 1970, England. Married to Stephanie Lemmy, solicitor. Cleeve School, Cheltenham; Queen Mary College, University of London, LLB. M. November 1994. ETC. 2 April 1996. Prop. J J Rowe QC. Sec. Tim Brennand. Pupilmaster, Paul Sheridan. Manchester Chambers; Manchester House Chambers, September 1995-October 1996; Old Colony House, 6 South King Street, October 1996-2001; 9 St John Street, July 2001.

LENNON, Desmond Joseph
Born 20 May 1956, Liverpool. St Mary's College, Crosby; Liverpool Polytechnic (now Liverpool John Moores University), BA (Law). Researcher, Liverpool Museum, 1981-1985. Office Manager, 1982-1985. G. November 1986. ETC. 16 December 1986. Prop. William Waldron QC. Sec. Vincent Deane. Liverpool Chambers; 2nd floor, Fruit Exchange, Victoria Street, 1986-1989; 46 Stanley Street, 1990-1994; 25-27 Castle Street, 1994.

LEON, Marc Edward
Born 20 June 1965. Huddersfield Polytechnic, LLB. AAS. M. 24 July 1986. ETC. 1991. Prop. Rodney Klevan QC. Sec. Paul Marshall. Pupilmasters, David Altaras, John Bowen & Peter Kyte. Manchester Chambers; 18 Lloyds House, 1991-1999; 2 St John Street, 2000.

LEONG, Simon George
Born 27 August 1978, Liverpool. St Edward's College, Liverpool; University of Newcastle-upon-Tyne, LLB. M. 11 October 2001. ETC. 26 March 2002. Prop. David Turner QC. Sec. Keith Thomas. Pupilmaster, Jeffrey Clarke. New Bailey Chambers, Liverpool, September 2000.

LERESCHE, Gerard Sunderland
Born 1859. Eldest son of John Henry Proctor Leresche qv. St John's College, Cambridge, BA. AAS. M. 13 November 1880. Call 6 June 1883. ETC. 1 February 1886. Prop. Gully QC. Sec. Hardy. Manchester Chambers; 60 King Street, 1885-1892; 40 Kennedy Street, 1893-1917; 78 King Street, 1918-1922. Not in 1923 Law List. Coroner, Salford District, 1917.

LERESCHE, John Henry Proctor
Eldest son of Samuel Leresche of Manchester. Father of Gerard Sunderland Leresche qv. AAS. M. 26 January 1844. Call 29 January 1847. 60 King Street, Manchester, 1880-1894. Deputy Recorder of Manchester. Stipendiary Magistrate, Manchester, 30 December 1885-1894.

LESLIE, Alan
Born 1890. Eldest son of Frank John Leslie, solicitor of Knowsley. AAS. M. 6 December 1909. Call 18 November 1912. ETC. 30 January 1913. Prop. McCall KC. Sec. Scott Barrett. Goldsmith Building, 1914-1927; 3 Essex Court, 1928. Chancellor of the Diocese of Lichfield, 1924-1928. Not in 1929 Law List.

LEVER, Hon. Bernard Lewis (His Honour Judge Lever)
Born 1 February 1951, Manchester. Son of Baron Lever of Ardwick in the City of Manchester (Leslie Maurice Lever), solicitor, MP & Lord Mayor of Manchester 1957-1958, nephew of Dorothy Rae Lever qv, and Baron Lever of Cheetham in the City of Manchester. (Norman Harold Lever) qv. Clifton College, Queen's College, Oxford, MA. AAS. M. 2 October 1972. Call 17 July 1975. ETC. 1975. Pupilmaster, J Stewart Oakes. Manchester Chambers; 12th floor, Sunlight House, Quay Street, 1975-1979; 28 St John Street, 1980-1988; 2 Old Bank Street, 1989-1991; Peel Court Chambers, 45 Hardman Street, 1992-2001. Standing Counsel to Inland Revenue, 1997-2001. Co founder SDP in North West, 1981. Contested (SDP) Manchester, Withington, 1983. Recorder, 1995-2001. Circuit Judge, May 2001. WW.

LEVER, Dorothy Rae (Mrs Stone)
Born 9 October 1908. Died 10 March 1995 aged 86. Daughter of Bernard Lever of Manchester. Sister of Baron Lever of Ardwick and of Baron Lever of Cheetham. Her four siblings became lawyers and her nephew, Bernard, a Circuit Judge. Manchester High School for Girls; Manchester University, LLB. AAS. 11 January 1927. Call 18 November 1929. She passed her Bar Finals aged 20 and had to wait a year before call to the Bar. When she became Neville Laski's pupil in St James's Square, she was the youngest member of the Bar in Manchester. In 1931 she married Hyman Stone a Sheffield solicitor and law don. Later they moved to London where she sat frequently as a magistrate. She sat on Government Committees for Consumer Protection and on the Age of Consent and was active on hospital boards. She had the distinction of being the first woman president of the Jewish Historical Society of England, 1982-1984. Times Obituary, 1995 and information provided by Bernard Lever.

LEVER, His Honour (John) Michael QC
Born 12 August 1928. Bolton School; Gonville and Caius College, Cambridge, BA 1949. Flying Officer, Royal Air Force, 1950-1952. M. April 1951. ETC. July 1952. Pupilmaster, A M (Bert) Knight. Manchester Chambers; 40 Kennedy Street, 1952-1965; Ship Canal House, King Street, 1966-1980. Silk 1977. 2 Old Bank Street, 1981. London Chambers, 5 Essex Court. Assistant Recorder, Salford, 1969-1971. Crown Court Recorder, 1972-1981. Vice Chairman, Governors, Bolton School. Circuit Judge, 1981-1997. Resident Judge, Bolton, 1992-1997. WW.
Retirement tributes at Bolton Law Courts, 14 July 1997. (His Honour Judge Sir Rhys Davies QC/ Michael Shorrock QC) Transcript in Circuit Records. Upon retirement Michael stressed the importance of humour in the often very serious practice of law and has reminded me of the following:
In a murder before Kerr J. (Michael was Pat's junior) **Russell QC** having established that a certain degree of consensual force in passionate sexual intercourse is not unknown, put it to the pathologist that the victim's death in this case might have been accidental.
Dr Benstead "In theory, Mr Russell, the proposition may be valid but in my experience the lady usually survives."

2. Examination in chief of the Defendant concludes at 4.30 pm. **Baldwin** rises to cross examine.
Judge Lever QC "Cross Examination tomorrow, Mr Baldwin." **Baldwin,** smartly, "Yes, Your Honour, and I may have some questions too."

3. Defence Counsel, mitigating, asks for a suspended prison sentence.
Judge Lever QC "but your client is only twenty years of age." (A Defendant had to have reached 21 years of age before a sentence of imprisonment, even suspended, could be imposed).
Counsel "Yes, I know, Your Honour, and he does look a lot older."

4. In the first case I did at Bolton, the clerk addressing the Defendants in the dock said "John Smith" and the chap on the right said "Yes" and "Jim Jones" and the fellow on the left said "Yes". I said "the other way around" and they both obediently turned and faced the wall.

LEVER, (Norman) Harold MP (Baron Lever of Cheetham in the City of Manchester)
Born 15 January 1914. Died 6 August 1995 aged 81. 3rd son of Bernard Lever of Manchester, brother of Dorothy Rae Lever qv and of Baron Lever of Ardwick, uncle of His Honour Judge Bernard Lever qv. Manchester Grammar School; Manchester University. AAS. M. 26 January 1932. Call 28 January 1935. ETC. 13 March 1935. Prop. Hemmerde QC. Sec Jolly. 60 King Street, Manchester, 1935-1939. Flying Officer, RAF Regiment, 1939-1945. MP (Lab) Manchester; Exchange, 1945-1950; Cheetham, 1950-1974; Central, 1974-1979. PC. 1969. Baron 1979. He held many Government posts including, Financial Secretary to the Treasury, 1967-1969, Paymaster General, 1969-1970; Chancellor of the Duchy of Lancaster and Chief Economic Advisor to the Prime Minister, 1974-1979. Had it not been for a stroke in 1972 it is likely that he would have been Chancellor of the Exchequer. He was a financial wizard and a bridge

player of international class. Promoted Defamation Act 1952. Director; Guardian & Manchester Evening News. Publication; (jointly) Debt & Danger, 1985. WW. Obituaries; Times; Telegraph; Independent & Guardian.

LEVESON, Brian Henry QC (The Hon. Mr Justice Leveson)

(DL)

Born 22 June 1949 Liverpool. Liverpool College; Merton College, Oxford, MA; Hon. Fellow, 2001. AAS. M. 28 May 1968. Harmsworth Scholar. Call. 24 November 1970; Bencher 1995. 11 New Square, Lincoln's Inn, January-June 1971. Pupilmaster, Roger Cooke. ETC. 1971. Prop. David McNeill QC. Sec. Eric Goldrein. Pupilmaster, Eric Goldrein, September-December 1970 & July-September 1971. Lecturer in Law, Liverpool University, 1971-1981. Same Liverpool Chambers; 34 Castle Street, 1970-1972; 54 Castle Street, 1973-1986. Silk 1986. 25 later 12 Byrom Street, Manchester. London Chambers at, 5 Essex Court, 61 Fleet Street & 22 Old Buildings. Recorder, 1988-2000. Parole Board, 1992-1995. High Court Judge, Queen's Bench Division, May 2000-. Presiding Judge, Northern Circuit, 2002-. WW.
In October 1995, before Mantell J, he prosecuted to conviction Rosemary West for ten murders. Her husband Fred escaped justice by hanging himself in Winston Green prison on New Years Day 1995.

LEVINE, Steven Adrian
Born 1963, Manchester. Manchester Polytechnic, LLB. King's College, London, LLM. L. November 1989. 1 Harcourt Buildings, 1995-1997. Manchester Chambers; Parsonage Chambers, 3 The Parsonage, 1998-1999; St John's Chambers, 2 St John Street, 2000-2001. LEVY, Raina Joy LLB. G. June 1959. 27 Dale Street, Liverpool, 1963-1965. Non practising, 1966-1968. Law Reporter. Not in 1969 Law List.

LEVY, Raina Joy
LLB. G. June 1959, 27 Dale Street, Liverpool 1963-1965. Non practising 1966-1968. Law Reporter. Not in 1969 Law List.

LEWIS, Brian William (His Honour Judge Lewis)
Born 23 July 1949. Sale County Grammar School for Boys, 1960-1968; Hull University, LLB 1968-1971. Lecturer, Barnet College, 1972-1974. I. July 1973. 55 Park Place, Cardiff, August 1974-January 1976. Pupilmaster David Morris. ETC. 1976. Same Liverpool Chambers at; Queen Avenue, April 1976-1983; 2nd floor, Peel House, Harrington Street, 1984-1994; 25-27 Castle Street, 1995-1998. Assistant Recorder 1989. Recorder 1993. Circuit Judge, 1997-.

*** LEWIS, Jeffrey Allan (His Honour Judge Jeffrey Lewis)**
Born 25 May 1949 Johannesburg. Educated in Johannesburg. National Service, Witwatersrand Rifles, 2nd South African Infantry Battalion. University of the Witwaterrand, BA, 1971. Scholarship to Stratford High School, Connecticut, USA. University College, Cardiff, PGCE. Teacher, 1973-1975. Leeds University, LLB, 1977. M. 27 July 1978. North Eastern Circuit. Leeds Chambers, 1978-2002. Part time Chairman of Industrial Tribunals, 1991-1995. Assistant Recorder 1993. Recorder 1997. Circuit Judge, Manchester 8 May 2002.

LEWIS, (Henry Roger) Justin CBE
LLB. G. February 1952. ETC. 1952. 27 Lord Street, 1952-1955. Fiji Bar, 1955. Fiji; Crown Counsel, 1955-1958; Solicitor General, 1959-1963; Attorney General, 1964-1970. QC (Fiji). Goldsmith Building & South Eastern Circuit, 1972-1994. Not in 1995 Bar Directory.

LEWIS, Joseph
G. 14 May 1930. ETC. 9 July 1930. Prop. Derbyshire KC. Sec. Rhodes. Bank of England Chambers, Tib Lane, Manchester, 1930-1940. No address, 1941-1963. Not in 1964 Law List.

LEWIS, Lawrence Frederick
G. July 1954. 20 Hackins Hey, Liverpool, 1954-1958. Lancs. Chancery Court. No address, 1959-1963. Not in 1964 Law List.

LEWIS, Roy John David
LLB (London). I. July 1968. ETC. 24 April 1969. Prop. Hinchliffe. Sec. Victor Williamson. Manchester Chambers; Northern Assurance Buildings, Albert Square, 1969; Post Office Chambers, 26 Brown Street, 1970-1971 & 1982-1985; 67 Princes Street, 1972-1981. Not in 1986 Bar Directory.

LEWIS, Sir Walter Llewellyn
Born 13 November 1849 Banbury. Died 26 September 1930 aged 80. Queen's College, Galway, MA; Gold Medallist in Experimental Science 1869 & 1871. AAS. M. 6 June 1872. Call 26 January 1876. ETC. 4 August 1876. Prop. Herschell QC. Sec. Gully. 9 King's Bench Walk, 1876; Lincoln Chambers, South King Street, Manchester, 1877-1878. Wales and Chester Circuit, 1879-1930. 1 Hare Court, 1879-1880; 8 King's Bench Walk, 1881-1885. Trinidad; Stipendiary Magistrate, 1885; Puisne Judge, 1893. Chief Justice, British Honduras, 1900-retirement in 1906. Coronation Medal, 1902. Kt. 1904.

LEWTHWAITE, Joanne Elizabeth
Born 23 April 1968 Hereford. Married to John Binks, Solicitor, Manager of Criminal Defence Service, Merseyside. John Wilmott School, Sutton Coldfield; Liverpool University, LLB. I. October 1990. ETC. December 1990. Prop. Nigel Gilmour QC. Sec. Martyn Bennett. Liverpool Chambers; Peel House, Harrington Street, 1990-1999; Oriel Chambers, 14 Water Street, 1.3.1999. Senior Lecturer, Manchester Metropolitan University & Advocacy Trainer.

LEY, Nigel Joseph
LLM (Manchester). G. November 1969. ETC. 1969. Manchester Chambers; Post Office Chambers, 26 Brown Street, 1969-1973; 21 Spring Gardens, 1974-1975; 4th floor, Sunlight House, Quay Street, 1976-1985; 121 Princess Street, 1986-1987; 3 Peter Street, 1988. 1 Brick Court, 1980-1981; 10 King's Bench Walk, 1982; 2 Temple Gardens, 1983-1994; 1 Harcourt Buildings, 1995-1997; 2nd floor south, Gray's Inn Chambers, 1998. Publication; Breathalyser Law & Practice.

LEYS, John Kirkwood
Born 1847. Died 10 November 1909. Eldest son of Rev. Peter Leys of Lanark, Minister of the Gospel. Glasgow University, MA. AAS. M. 10 June 1871. Call 30 April 1874. ETC. 2 August 1874. Prop. Temple QC. Sec. J B Gaillie. 4 Harrington Street, Liverpool, 1874-1876. Joined North Eastern Circuit 1876 and practised from 21 West Grainger Street, Newcastle-upon-Tyne, 1876-1884. 1 New Court, 1884-1886. He then devoted his time to writing novels which included; The Lindsays; The Lawyer's Secret; The Black Terror; The Houseboat Mystery; A Wolf in Sheep's Clothing & The Broken Fetter. WW.

LIAS, His Honour William John
Born 13 March 1868. Died 20 July 1941 aged 73. Son of Rev. John James Lias, Chancellor of Llandaff Cathedral. Haileybury College; Jesus College, Cambridge, BA 1889; MA. 1898. Editor, Cambridge Review, 1890-1891. Headmaster, Downs School, Clifton, Bristol, 1894-1899. L. May 1901. ETC. 31 July 1901. Prop. Horridge KC. Sec. Scott. Liverpool Chambers; 10 Cook Street, 1901-1908; 25 Lord Street, 1909-1913; 8 Harrington Street, 1914-1920; 25 Lord Street, 1921-1922. Sub Lt/Lt., RNVR, 1904-1912; Capt in Lancashire Fusiliers, 1915; Transferred to RE, 1917; served in France, 1916-1919; Officer Commanding, Gas School. Rouen (Despatches). Contested (L) Liverpool, West Derby, January & December 1910. County Court Judge, 1922-1940; Circuit 13 (Sheffield), October 1922-1929; Circuit 59 (Plymouth), 1930-1940. WW.

LIGHT, Enoch
G. November 1948. Magistrate, Fiji, 1953-1959; Magistrate, Aden, 1960-1963. Chief Magistrate, Aden 1964-1967. Not in 1968 Law List.

LIMB, Christopher
Born 12 March 1953, Grappenhall, Cheshire. Lymm Grammar School; Liverpool University, LLB. G. July 1975; ETC. 1975; pupilmaster, Michael Kershaw. Manchester Chambers; 1 Dean's Court, Crown Square, 1975-1976; 6th floor, Sunlight House, Quay Street, 1977-1978; 9th floor, 1979-1985; 6th floor, 1986-1994; 38 Young Street, 1995. Part time Chairman, Family Health Service Appeal Authority, 2002. Chairman, Salford Choral Society. Governor, Lymm High School.

LIMONT, (William) Anthony
Born 4 February 1942, Southport. Married to Valerie Anne Limont, Liverpool solicitor. Fettes College, Edinburgh; Liverpool University, LLB. G. November 1964. ETC 1964. Pupilmaster, Ifor Morris Jones. Liverpool Chambers; 49 Castle Street/606 The Corn Exchange, Fenwick Street, 1964-1967; First floor, Oriel Chambers, Water Street, 1968-1994; Chavasse Court Chambers, Lord Street, 1994.

LINDSAY, Rev., Hon. Edward Reginald MM
Born 15 March 1876. Died 17 June 1951 aged 75. 4th son of 26th Earl of Crawford & 9th Earl of Balcarres. Magdalen College, Oxford, MA. I. 19 November 1900. ETC. 16 February 1901. Prop. Pickford QC. Sec. Sanderson. No chambers address. Served WW1, MM. RC Parish Priest of Stone. Burke's Peerage.

LINDSAY, Joseph Rutherford
B.Com., LLB. G. 11 May 1927. ETC. 15 June 1927. Prop. Hemmerde KC. Sec. Fraser Harrison. Liverpool Chambers; 15 Lord Street, 1928-1930; 43 Castle Street, 1931 -1939. Not in 1940 Law List.

LINDSAY, William Alexander CVO., QC
Born 8 June 1846. Died 13 September 1926 aged 80. Eton; Trinity College, Cambridge, BA, 1868; MA 1872. Member of Lloyds's, 1868. AAS. M. 21 December 1869. Call 30 April 1873; Bencher 1906; Reader Lent 1919. ETC. 16 August 1873. Prop. Herschell QC. Sec. Elliot. 1 Pump Court, 1876-1882; Goldsmith Building, 1883-1926., Silk 1897. CVO 1924. Peerage-Counsel; Windsor Herald, 1894; Norroy King of Arms, 1919; Clarenceux, 1922-1926. Contested; Burnley, 1874,1876,1894, 1896; Huddersfield, 1880; Forfarshire, 1885. WW. Foster.

LIND-SMITH, His Honour Gerard Gustave
Born 1903. Died 3 February 1982. Son of C F Lind-Smith of Liverpool. Wellington College; University College, Oxford. I. 2 May 1928. ETC. 13 June 1928. Prop. Jackson KC. Sec. Sellers. 10 Cook Street, Liverpool, 1928-1934. Wales & Chester Circuit, 1935-. 1 Hunter Street, Chester, 1935-1959. JP & Deputy Chairman, Cheshire Quarter Sessions, 1957; Chairman, 1961-1968. Recorder of Birkenhead, 1958-1959. Circuit Judge, (formerly County Court Judge), 1959-1975, Circuits 21 & 23. WW.

LISBONA, Nissim
Born 1882 Manchester. Son of Moses & Mazal Lisbona. G. 13 May 1908. ETC. 26 February 1909. Prop. Tobin KC. Sec. Pope. Manchester Chambers; 32 Kennedy Street, 1909-1911; 15 Brazennose Street, 1912-1914. Private (PS 5212) 20th Btn., Royal Fusiliers 13 January 1915. Killed in action, 20 July 1916 aged 34. Buried Caterpillar Valley Cemetery, Longueval, Somme, France (13km east of Albert). Information provided by Public Record Office & Commonwealth War Graves Commission.

LISTER, Stephen William
Born 16 September 1955. MA (Oxon). AAS. 2 February 1978. Call 26 July 1979. 6 floor, Arkwright House, Parsonage Gardens, Manchester, 1982-1986.

LITTLE, George QC
Born 1815. Died 27 January 1881. 3rd son of George Little of Blackburn. Articled to a Manchester solicitor. AAS. M. 21 January 1837. Call 8 May 1840; Bencher 30 January 1867; Reader Lent 1873. 11 New Square, 1848. 6 Stone Buildings, 1876-1881. Vice Chancellor, County Palatine of Lancaster, 22 April 1871-1881.

LITTLE, Ian
Born 7 September 1961, Colne. Kirkham Grammar School; Mansfield College, Oxford, BA (History); City University, (Dip. Law). AAS. M. 22 July 1987. Call 7 February 1989. ETC 1990. Prop. John Hand QC. Sec. Terence Rigby. Manchester Chambers; Crown Square Chambers, 1 Dean's Court/ 9 St John Street, 1990-. Formerly Greater London Council, Administrative Officer.

LITTLE, James Hayward
L. 15 May 1935. ETC. 10 June 1936. Prop. Lynskey KC. Sec. Pritchard. 8 Harrington Street, 1936-1938. 13 Old Square, 1939-1941; 5 New Square, 1942-1946. Not in 1947 Law List.

LITTLE, Thomas Shepherd MP

Born 1846. 3rd son of Thomas Little of Liverpool. Trinity College, Cambridge, BA. AAS. I. 21 April 1871. Call 6 June 1874. ETC. 29 March 1875. Prop. Pope QC. Sec. Swift. 14 Cook Street, 1876-1880; 13 Union Court, 1881-1890. 5 Paper Buildings, 1879-1882; 3 Harcourt Buildings, 1891-1893; 3 King's Bench Walk, 1894-1900; 1 Harcourt Building, 1901-1908. Stipendiary Magistrate, Liverpool, 1909-1910. Foster.

LITTLER, Martin Gordon
Brother of Richard Mark Littler qv. LLB. G. November 1989. ETC 1989. Manchester Chambers; 38 King Street West, 1992-1993; Kenworthy's Buildings, 83 Bridge Street, 1993-1997; Cobden House Chambers, 19 Quay Street, 1998.

LITTLER, Sir Ralph Daniel Makinson CB., QC
Born 2 October 1835. Died 23 November 1908 aged 73. University College School; University College, London, BA, 1854. AAS. I. 14 November 1854. Call. 6 June 1857. Call M. 28 April 1870; Bencher 1882; Reader Autumn 1892; Treasurer 1900. Member of Northern & North Eastern Circuits. 1 Plowden Buildings, 1876-1881; 4 Temple Gardens, 1882-1893; 6 Pump Court, 1894-1906; 2 Plowden Buildings, 1907-1908. Silk 1873. CB 1890. Kt 1902. Lieutenant, City of London. Chairman, Middlesex Sessions, 1889-1908. WW. DNB. Foster.

LITTLER, Richard Mark
Born 13 August 1970 Preston. Brother of Martin Gordon Littler qv. Queen Elizabeth Grammar School, Blackburn; Manchester University, LLB. G. October 1994. ETC 1996. Prop. Roger Farley QC. Sec. Richard Heap. Manchester Chambers; Kenworthy's Buildings, 83 Bridge Street, 1996-1999; Cobden House Chambers, 19 Quay Street, 2000.

LIVESEY, (Michael) Fraser (Stanier)
Born 9 September 1969, Rochdale. Bolton School; Newcastle-upon-Tyne University, LLB. L. October 1992. ETC. June 1993. Pupilmaster, Richard Haworth. 15 Winckley Square, Preston, January 1993.

LIVESEY, Ronald John Dearden QC (His Honour Judge Livesey QC)
Born 11 September 1935. Died 17 January 2002 aged 66. Son of John William Livesey, solicitor of Liverpool. Ronnie's son John is on the Western Circuit at Bristol. Terra Nova; Malvern College; Lincoln College, Oxford, MA. National Service, commission in Royal Marines. Teacher, Dragon School, Oxford. L. February 1962; Bencher 1989. ETC. February 1962. Prop. Richard Forrest QC. Sec. Cecil Clothier. Circuit Junior, 1962. Same Liverpool Chambers; 14 Cook Street, 1962-1972; Peel House, Harrington Street, 1973-1992. (Head of Chambers). Silk 1981. Goldsmith Building, 1981-1992. Deputy Senior Judge, Sovereign Base Area, Cyprus, 1983; Senior Judge, 1996. Recorder, 1981-1992. Circuit Judge, Preston, 1992-2002. Captain, Royal Birkdale Golf Club, 1978. Captain, Bar Golfing Society. Played scrum half for Waterloo first XV and for Oxfordshire. Tributes; Liverpool Law Courts, 22 January 2002 (Judge David Clarke QC/ David Steer QC); Preston Law Courts, 23 January 2002 (Judge Peter Openshaw QC/ David Steer QC) Transcripts in Circuit Records. WW.

LIVESLEY, Rhian Danielle
Born 24 August 1978 Taunton, Somerset. Castell Alun High School; Warwick University, LLB. G. 27 July 2000. Legal Services Commission, May 2000-September 2001. ETC. 18 December 2001. Prop. John Benson QC. Sec. Robert Warnock. 14 Castle Street/Atlantic Chambers, Cook Street, Liverpool, 1 October 2001.

LLOYD, Heather Claire
Born 16 May 1957, Bebington. Married to Nick Kennedy qv, sister of Wendy Lloyd qv. Sister in law of Michael Sellars qv. St Edmund's College, Liverpool; Liverpool University, LLB. G. July 1979. ETC. December 1979. Prop. Michael Maguire QC. Sec. Bert Andrew. Liverpool Chambers; Peel House, Harrington Street, 1979-1999; Chavasse Court, 24 Lord Street, 1999. Assistant Recorder 1998. Recorder 2000.

LLOYD, Rt Hon, (John) Selwyn (Brooke) CBE., QC., MP (Baron Selwyn Lloyd of Wirral, Merseyside)

Born 28 July 1904. Died 17 May 1978 aged 73. Fettes; Magdelene College, Cambridge. President, Cambridge Union, 1927. G. 27 January 1930; Bencher 1951. ETC. 29 January 1930. Prop. Goldie KC. Sec. Lind-Smith. Circuit Junior, Summer 1930. Liverpool Chambers; 3 Cook Street, 1930-1933; 25 Castle Street, 1934-1939. Served WWII from 2nd Lt. to Brigadier, General Staff Officer on HQ Second Army. 27 Lord Street, 1945-1947. Silk 1947. 1 Temple Gardens, 1947. Recorder of Wigan, 1948-1951. MP (C) Wirral, 1945-1970. Minister of Supply, 1954-1955. Minister of Defence, 1955; Foreign Secretary, 1955-1960; Chancellor of the Exchequer, 1960-1962. Lord Privy Seal and Leader of the House of Commons, 1963-1964. Speaker of the House of Commons, 1971-1976. Hon. LLD., Liverpool 1957. OBE 1943. CBE 1945. PC. 1951. Baron 1976. Publications; Mr Speaker, Sir, 1976; Suez, 1956: A Personal View, 1978. Biography; Selwyn Lloyd, D R Thorpe, Jonathan Cape, 1989. WW.

★ LLOYD, Timothy (Andrew Wigram) QC. The Rt. Hon. Lord Justice Lloyd

Born 30 November 1946. Winchester College; Lincoln College, Oxford MA M. 1970; Bencher 1994. Silk 1986. Also a member of Lincoln's Inn. Attorney-General, Duchy of Lancaster 1993-1996. High Court Judge, Chancery Division, 1996-. Vice Chancellor, County Palatine of Lancaster, 2002-2005. Lord Justice of Appeal, 2005.

LLOYD, Wendy Jane
Born 31 October 1960 Liverpool. Married to Michael Sellars qv, sister of Heather Lloyd qv, sister in law of Nick Kennedy qv. St Edmund's College, Liverpool; Liverpool University, LLB. AAS. M. 5 March 1982. Call 28 July 1983. ETC. 1983. Prop. Justin Price QC. Sec. Antonis Georges. Same Liverpool Chambers at; 2nd floor, Peel House, Harrington Street, 1983-1994; 25-27 Castle Street, 1995.

LLOYD-GEAME, Rt. Hon. Sir Philip KBE
I. 27 January 1908. ETC. 10 March 1909. Prop. C A Russell QC. Sec. Leslie Scott. 7 Stone Buildings, 1916-1922. No address, 1923-1924. Not in 1925 Law List.

LLOYD-JACOB, George Harold KC (The Hon. Mr Justice Lloyd-Jacob)
Born 1 October 1897. Died 3 December 1969 aged 72. Southgate Grammar School; King's College, London; Lt., Royal Flying Corps, 1916-1918. Christ Church, Oxford, BA, 1921, BCL., MA 1923. AAS. M. 11 November 1921. Call. 26 January 1923; Bencher 1950; Reader Lent 1963. 4 Brick Court, 1923-1930; New Court, 1931-1949. Junior Counsel to Board of Trade in Patent Matters, 1937-1945. Silk 1945. Lay Reader, Diocese of Guildford. Judge of the High Court, Chancery Division, 1950-1969. Kt 1950. Chairman, Council of Legal Education, 1964-1967. WW.

LLOYD-JONES, His Honour David Trevor VRD
Died April 1998 aged 81. Holywell Grammar School. G. January 1951. ETC. 1951. Pupilmaster, Daniel Brabin. 14 Cook Street, Liverpool, 1951-1953. Wales & Chester Circuit, 1953. 39 Whitefriars, Chester, 1953-1972. Served War, 1939-1945, RNVR, in Atlantic, Mediterranean & Pacific. Lt. Commander, RNR, 1952-1960. VRD 1958. Deputy Recorder, Chester & Birkenhead, 1964-1970. Legal Member, Mental Health Review Tribunal, 1960-1972. Circuit Judge, 1972-1988. WW. Obituary, Graya, vol 108 (Lord Emlyn Hooson QC) He was junior defence counsel (led by Emlyn Hooson) for Ian Brady in the Moors Murder case tried by Fenton Atkinson J at Chester Assizes in 1966.

LLOYD-JONES, William Peter
LLB (Liverpool). G. November 1969. 2 Booth Street, Manchester, 1969-1973. Not in 1974 Law List.

LLOYD-SMITH, Rebecca Jane
Born 1 March 1971 Leamington Spa. Married to Mark Rhiad qv. Bluecoat Cof E School; Leicester University, BA. L. October 1994. ETC. 13 December 1994. Prop. Anthony Morris QC. Sec. Andrew O'Byrne. Peel Court Chambers, 45 Hardman Street, Manchester, 1994.

LOCHEE, Baron (See Edmund Robertson)

LOCHTENBERG, Abigail
LLB (Liverpool). I. July 1984. 3 St James's Square, Manchester, 1985-1986. Not in 1987 Bar Directory.

LOCKE, Geoffrey Norman Wanstall
Army Major. G. November 1970. Same Liverpool Chambers at; Queen Avenue, 1970-1983; 2nd floor Peel House, Harrington Street, 1984-retirement in 1989. Head of Chambers. Deputy Stipendiary Magistrate.

LOCKETT, His Honour Reginald
Born 24 June 1933. Ashton in Makerfield Grammar School; Manchester University; London University, LLB 1954. Articled to James William Francis of Walkden, 1950-1955. Solicitor, 1955. National Service, RASC, 1955-1957. Vincent & Co (later Vincent, Hilton & Lockett), 1957-1965; Partner, Edward Alker & Ball, 1965-1970. Assistant Coroner, Wigan, 1963-1970. Part time Chairman, Industrial Tribunals, 1967-1970. District Registrar & County Court Registrar, Manchester, 1970-1981. Recorder, 1978-1981. Circuit Judge, 1981-1999. Senior Circuit Judge, 1997-1999. Hon. Recorder of Preston, 1996-1999. Acting Deemster, Isle of Man to 2003. Vice President, The Boys' Brigade. Reader, Anglican Church. Editor, Butterworths Family Law Service, 1983-1990. Consultant Editor, Sweet & Maxwell's High Court Litigation Manual, 1990. Retirement Tributes at Preston Law Courts, 26 February 1999 (Forbes J/ Richard Henriques QC) Transcript in Circuit Records. WW.

LODGE, Adam Robert
Born 8 December 1971 Derby. William Hulme's Grammar School, Manchester; University of West of England, Bristol, LLB. G. 10 October 1996. ETC. 16 December 1997. Prop. Martin Steiger QC. Sec. Beverly Lunt. Kingsgate Chambers, 51-53 South King Street, Manchester, July 1997.

LODGE, Oliver
Born 1841. 2nd son of Robert John Lodge of London. Scholar, Pembroke College, Oxford. AAS. M. 29 April 1861. AAS. I. 19 April 1865. Call
1 May 1865. ETC. 23 July 1868. Prop. Udall. Sec. Kay. 5 Brick Court, 1878-1882. No address, 1883-1914. Not in 1915 Law List.

LOFTUS, Teresa Anne Martine
Born 12 September 1970. Convent of Mercy Grammar School, West Derby, Liverpool; Hull University, LLB. L. February 1995. ETC. 6 April 1995. Prop. Stephen Riordan QC. Sec. Brian Lewis. 25-27 Castle Street, Liverpool, 1995.

LOGAN, John
LLB. I. July 1960. Pupilmaster Iain Glidewell. 25 Bow Lane, Manchester, 1960-1970. Not in 1971 Law List.

LOGAN, Maura
LLB. I. July 1971. Manchester Chambers; 3 St James's Square, 1971-1984; St James's Chambers, 68 Quay Street, 1985-1997. St John's Chambers, Hale Barns, Cheshire, 1998.

LOMAS, Herbert Harold
MA (Oxon). L. November 1953. Manchester Chambers; 78 King Street, 1956-1958; 196 Deansgate, 1959-1985. Chancellor of the Diocese of Chester. Not in 1986 Law List.

LONG, Andrew Peter
Born 12 April 1959 Darwen, Lancs. Cheadle Hulme School; Sheffield University, LLB. I. July 1981. ETC. 1981. Prop. John Hugill QC. Sec. Michael Shorrock. Same Manchester Chambers at; 2 Old Bank Street, 1981-1992; Peel Court Chambers, 45 Hardman Street, 1992. Assistant Recorder 1999. Recorder 2000.

LONGSON, Edward Harold (His Honour Judge Longson)
Born 1872. Died 21 March 1941. New College, Oxford. I. 18 November 1895. ETC. 26 February 1896. Prop. Taylor QC. Sec. Bradshaw. Manchester Chambers; 78 King Street, 1896-1906; 2 Booth Street, 1907-1931. Lancs. Chancery Court. County Court Judge, 1931-1941, Circuit 19, (Derbys. & Staffs). WW.

LONGWORTH, Antony Stephen
Born 6 November 1955 Warrington. Buteler Grammar School, Warrington; Hertford College, Oxford, BA. AAS. M. 2 September 1976. Call 27 July 1978. ETC. 1980. Prop. Keith Goddard QC. Sec. J V Williamson. Manchester Chambers; 4th Floor, Sunlight House, Quay Street, 1979-1983; 1 Central Street, 1984-1987; 33 King Street West, 1988-1994; Old Colony House, 6 South King Street, 1995-1999; 24a St John Street 2000. (now St Johns Buildings Chambers)

LONSDALE, Arthur Pemberton
Born 1835. 2nd son of Rev. Henry Lonsdale, late Vicar of St Mary's, Lichfield. Balliol College, Oxford, BA. AAS. L. 5 July 1856. Call 27 January 1862. No address, 1876-1934. Not in 1935 Law List. Foster.

LORAINE, Wilfred Howard
Born 1865. 2nd son of Nevison Loraine, Vicar of Grove Park West, Middlesex. Brasenose College, Oxford. AAS M. 19 November 1885. Call. 3 July 1889. ETC. 30 July 1890. Prop. Gully QC. Sec. Page. 1 Brick Court, 1890-1895. 15 Lord Street, Liverpool, 1896-1913. No address, 1914-1940. Not in 1941 Law List.

LORD, His Honour John Herent

(HS)

Born 5 November 1928. Died 20 December 1994 aged 66. Son of Sir Frank Lord, KBE., JP., DL. Manchester Grammar School; Merton College, Oxford, BA (Jurisprudence). Half Blue, Oxford University Lacrosse II, 1948 & 1949; represented Middlesex, 1950. I. June 1951. ETC. 7 June 1951. Prop. Neville Laskie QC. Sec.

Hugh Mais. Circuit Junior, 1952. 43 King Street, Manchester, 1951-1977. Assistant Recorder of Burnley, 1971. Crown Court Recorder, 1972-1978. Trustee, Frank Lord Postgraduate Medical Centre. Circuit Judge, 1978-1993. WW.

When first appointed I was sent to sit, mainly in Oldham Crown Court for best part of a year. John sat on the ground floor and I was upstairs in Oldham Town Hall. I have every reason to be grateful to him for his kindness to the new boy and for his generous hospitality at his home on Saddleworth Moor. See entry under Alistair Bell.

LOUGHREY, James Terence John
LLB (Hull). I. July 1979. Manchester Chambers; 2 Mount Street, 1981-1984; 3 St James's Square, 1985-1986. Ferranti International PLC, 1994. Legal Advisor, Siemans Group Services, Bracknell, Berks, 1997.

LOUGHREY, William John
Born 1880. 3rd son of Patrick Joseph Loughrey of Liverpool. When AAS. M. on 26 June 1911 aged 31, he was a journalist and organising secretary of the United Irish League of Great Britain. Call. 16 June 1915. Liverpool Chambers; 25 Lord Street, 1930-1935; 21 Harrington Street, 1936-1940; 14 Cook Street, 1941-1949; 15 Sweeting Street, 1950-retirement in 1953.

LOVERIDGE, Andrew Robert
Born 31 August 1960. Dulwich College; King Edward VII School, Sheffield; Newcastle-upon-Tyne University, LLB. L. 27 July 1983. ETC. December 1984. Prop. Michael Maguire QC. Sec. Mark Hedley. Circuit Junior, 1987. Same Liverpool Chambers at; 3rd floor, 27 Dale Street, November 1984-September 1989; Corn Exchange, Fenwick Street, September 1989-September 1999; 7 Harrington Street (merger with Martins Building), 6.9.1999. Recorder 2004.

LOVETT, Adrian Thomas
BA., Dip. Law. M. October 1991. ETC 17 December 1992. 334 Deansgate, Manchester, 1993-1994. Not in 1995 Bar Directory.

LOWCOCK, Andrew Charles (His Honour Judge Lowcock)
Born 22 November 1949, Cheadle Hulme. Malvern College; New College, Oxford, MA. AAS. M. 10 June 1970. Call 19 July 1973. ETC. 1974. same Manchester Chambers at; 12th floor, Sunlight House, Quay Street, 1974-1979; 28 St John Street, 1989-2001. Assistant Recorder 1993. Recorder 1997. Circuit Judge, Manchester, 2001. Governor, The Ryley's School, 1996. WW.

LOWE, Charles James Blackburn
Born 1858. Eldest son of James Lowe of Manchester, merchant. Magdalen College, Cambridge, LLB, 1879; MA 1882. AAS. L. 16 June 1877. Call 9 June 1880. ETC. 30 January 1885. Prop. Ambrose QC. Sec. French. Manchester Chambers; 5 St James's Square, 1885-1911; 8 Southgate, 1912-1921. No address, 1922-1927. Not in 1928 Law List.

LOWE, Geoffrey James
Born 13 March 1953 St Helens. Prescot Grammar School; King's College, London, LLB. G. July 1975. ETC 1975. Pupilmaster, Colin Cunningham. Same Liverpool Chambers at; Melbourne Building, 21 North John Street, 1975-1988; 3rd floor, Peel House, Harrington Street, 1989-11.1.1998; India Buildings, Water Street, 12.1.1998. Assistant Recorder 1999; Recorder 2000.

LOWE, Henry Parker
Born 1867. 2nd son of Henry William Lowe of South Kensington, Shipowner. Christ Church, Oxford. AAS. M. 27 January 1888. Call 17 November 1890. ETC. 27 July 1893. Prop. Walton QC. Sec. Sharpe. 1 Essex Court, 1892; 3 Temple Gardens, 1893-1910. No address, 1911-1940. Not in 1941 Law List.

LOWE, James Walter
Born 1836. Eldest son of James Lowe of Salford, merchant. St John's College, Cambridge. AAS. M. 21 March 1857. Call 30 April 1860. In practice before High Court of Calcutta. ETC. 8 March 1869. Prop. Holker QC. Sec. C Russell. Lancs. Chancery Court. 2 Plowden Buildings, 1876-1885. 1 Dr Johnson's Building, 1891-1892; 12 King's Bench Walk, 1893-1901. Manchester Chambers; 32 South King Street, 1877; 9 St James's Square, 1878-1890. No address, 1902-1918. Not in 1919 Law List. Foster.

LOWE, Roger
LLB (Sheffield). I. July 1984. 14 Winckley Square, Preston, 1988-1993; 15 Winckley Square, 1994-1996. Not in 1997 Bar Directory.

LOWNDES, John James
Born 1814. Eldest son of John Lowndes of Arthurlie House, Renfrewshire, North Britain. AAS. I. 22 November 1833. Call 30 April 1841. Admitted M. 23 April 1849. 5 Hare Court, 1848. Special pleader, Lancs. & Liverpool Sessions. No address, 1876-1899. Not in 1900 Law List. Foster.

LOWSON, Norman Laurence
Born 29 June 1959, Durham City. St Michael's, Houghton-le-Spring. Polytechnic of Central London, Dip.Law. L. July 1989. New Bailey Chambers, Preston, 1993. Publications; Mission in Avignon- Book 1, The Chessboard.

LOWTHER, Arthur James Beresford
I. 26 January 1912. ETC. 17 January 1913. Prop. Sanderson KC. Sec. Lumb. Circuit Junior, Summer 1913. 2 Garden Court, 1913-1914; 2 Plowden Buildings, 1915-1917. No address, 1918-1953. Not in 1954 Law List.

LOWTHER, James William MP (First Viscount Ullswater)
Born 1 April 1855. Died 27 March 1949 aged 93. Eldest son of Hon. William Lowther, MP for Westmorland. Eton; Associate, King's College, London; Trinity College, Cambridge, LLM. AAS. I. 26 January 1875. Call. 7 May 1879. ETC. 17 January 1880. Prop. Edwards QC. Sec. Elliot. 4 Paper Buildings, 1881; 3 Temple Gardens, 1882-1893. MP (C) Rutland, 1883; Penrith, 1886-1921. Chairman, Cumberland Quarter Sessions, 1886-1900. Served on numerous Government boards & committees. Speaker of the House of Commons, 1906-1921. PC 1898. Viscount & GCB 1921. Publications; A Speaker's Commentaries, 1925. WW. DNB.

LOYD, Edward Noel Farnham
I. 27 June 1906. ETC. 26 February 1909. Prop. Tobin KC. Sec. Pope. 6 King's Bench Walk, 1911-1915; 2 Mitre Court Buildings, 1916-1921. No address, 1922-1953. Not in 1954.

LUCAS, Edwin
Born 1847. 3rd son of Samuel Lucas, brewer. AAS. M. 15 January 1856. Call 17 November 1868. ETC. 28 February 1871. Prop. Pope QC. Sec. Littler. No chambers address, 1876-1893. Not in 1894 Law List.

LUMB, Sir Charles Frederick
Born 19 September 1846. Died 23 February 1911 aged 64. Eldest son of Richard Lumb of Liverpool. Downing College, Cambridge, Scholar, MA. AAS. L. 31 May 1870. Call 26 January 1874. ETC. 28 March 1874. Prop. Herschell QC. Sec Kinghorn. 11 Commerce Chambers, Harrington Street, Liverpool, 1876-1887. Junior Counsel to the Treasury, 1886. Puisne Judge; Trinidad, 1887-1892; Supreme Court of Jamaica, 1893-1909. Kt. 1909. WW. Foster.

LUMB, Herbert
I. 17 November 1910. ETC. 26 January 1911. Prop. Tobin KC (Langdon KC acted). Sec. Eustace Hill (Barnes acted). Circuit Junior, Summer 1912. 5 Paper Buildings 1912; 6 King's Bench Walk 1913-1914. Private, 28th City of London, 5.8.1914-12.9.1914. In October 1914 he was commissioned 2nd Lt., A Battery, 66 Brigade, RFA. He died at sea of peritonitis on the 8 October 1915, the day on which his troopship arrived at Suvla Bay, Gallipoli. Buried at sea. His name is recorded on the Helles Memorial, Turkey (Panels 21 & 22). Information supplied by Public Records Office & Commonwealth War Graves Commission.

LUMB, James
Born 1852. 3rd son of William Lumb of Whitehaven, solicitor. Clare College, Cambridge, MA. AAS. I. 17 November 1877. Call 9 June 1880. ETC. 15 July 1881. Prop. Gully QC. Sec. Dickinson. 5 Crown Office Row, 1883-1887; 6 Crown Office Row, 1888-1890; 3 Harcourt Buildings, 1891-1893. 3 King's Bench Walk, 1894-1900; 5 Paper Buildings, 1901-1936. Not in 1937 Law List.

LUND, Celia
Born 12 November 1954 Chester. The Queen's School, Chester; Liverpool University; The Drama Studio, London; Liverpool Polytechnic, LLB. L. November 1988. ETC. 1989. Pupilmasters, William George & Nicholas Orr. Liverpool Chambers; 20 North John Street, 1988-1997; merger with, 14 Castle Street/ Atlantic Chambers, Cook Street, 1997.

LUNT, Beverly Anne (Her Honour Judge Lunt)
Born 8 March 1954 Rochester, Kent. Oswestry Girls High School; Shrewsbury Priory; Chester City High School; BA, (London). G. 28 July 1977. ETC. December 1980. Prop. Benet Hytner QC. Sec. John Ward. Pupilmasters, Paul Focke & John Collins. 1 Mitre Court, May 1977-October 1977; 3rd floor, Francis Taylor Building, November 1977- May 1980. Manchester Chambers; Kingsgate Chambers, June 1980. Assistant Recorder 1999. Recorder 2000. Circuit Judge, 2004.

LUPTON, William
I. 26 January 1864. Oxford Chambers, Lord Street, Liverpool, 1876. Not in 1877 Law List.

LUPTON, William Holland

Born 1870. Only son of William Lupton of Trafalgar House, Burnley, waste cotton dealer. King's College, Cambridge. AAS. M. 28 April 1892. Call. 29 April 1896. ETC. 5 August 1898. Prop Shee QC. Sec. Gregson Ellis. 5 King's Bench Walk, 1900; 4 Pump Court, 1901-1902; 3 Middle Temple Lane, 1903. No address, 1904-1949. Not in 1950 Law List.

LUSHINGTON, Sydney George

Born 6 April 1859. Died 18 August 1909 aged 50. Eton; University College, Oxford, BCL; MA. AAS. I. 12 November 1880. Call. 7 May 1884. ETC. 13 February 1886. Prop. Gully QC. Sec. C Arnold White. 3 Temple Gardens, 1887-1894; 4 Temple Gardens, 1895-1909. Standing Counsel to Board of Trade in Bankruptcy and to General Medical Council. Editor; Justice of the Peace; Lumley's Public Health; Archbold's Lunacy. WW.

LUSTGARTEN, Edgar Marcus

Born 3 May 1907. Died 15 December 1978 aged 71. Son of Joseph Lustgarten qv and uncle of His Honour Judge Clement Goldstone QC qv. Manchester Grammar School; St John's College, Oxford BA. President, Oxford Union, 1930. G. 2 July 1930. ETC. 9 July 1930. Prop. Eastham KC. Sec. Jalland. 48 King Street, Manchester, 1930-1940. He then went into radio, television & films. Circuiteers of my generation and older will recall his cinema presentations in the 1950's when he introduced 40 half hour episodes of "Scotland Yard". They were all true murder cases and each episode began with a police car speeding through London streets with its bell ringing. In the early 1960's he appeared in a dozen short films entitled "Scales of Justice". He was regularly on BBC Radio & Television and ATV. He wrote five novels and studies in true crime including; Verdict in Dispute 1949; Defender's Triumph 1951; The Chalk Pit Murder 1975 and a Century of Murderers 1975. WW.

LUSTGARTEN, Joseph

Born 1879. Eldest son of Jacob Lustgarten of Salford, merchant. Father of Edgar Lustgarten qv. He was a 38 year old solicitor when AAS. M. 14 May 1917. Call 19 November 1917. 48 King Street, Manchester, 1919-1937. Not in 1938 Law List.

LYNCH, David (His Honour Judge Lynch)

With past and present St Helens Bench Chairmen 2004. Michael McManus, Jean Wotherspoon OBE, Ann Snowling and Margaret Henley.

Born 23 August 1939. Son of Harry Lynch, motor mechanic. Granby Street School, Liverpool 8, 1945-1950; Liverpool Collegiate Grammar School, 1950-1955. Sharman & Son, Solicitors, Liverpool, 1955-1958. Served, Royal Air Force, (Signals Intelligence) in Germany, 1958-1961. Bremner Sons & Corlett, Solicitors, Liverpool, 1961-1965. External London LLB, 1965. Schoolmaster, 1965-1968. AAS. M. 28 March 1966. Call 26 November 1968. ETC. 15 June 1969. Prop. Griffith Winston Guthrie Jones QC. Sec. Keith Lawton. Same Liverpool Chambers at; North House, 17 North John Street, 1969-1971; Martins Building, Water Street, 1971-1990. Member, North West Legal Aid Area Appeals Committee, 1980-1990. Assistant Recorder, 1983. Recorder, 1988. President, Mental Health Review Tribunal, 1988-2001 (restricted patients 1991-2001). Circuit Judge, 31 January 1990-2005. Liason Judge; St Helens Magistrates, 1991-2004; Liverpool John Moores University, 1994-2004; (Hon. Fellow, July 2003). Liverpool Law Review Lecture, 2004. Publications; Northern Circuit Directory, 1876-2004; Contributed to "A Century Of Liverpool Lawyers." Fagan, Bryson & Elston, Liverpool Law Society, 2002. WW.
I recall clearly the first trial I had in the old Town Hall at Oldham in 1990. John Lord sat on the ground floor. I was upstairs beneath a leaking roof. Shortly after the trial commenced I received a note from the usher. I have kept it. On the note is written, "Your Honour. It is raining on the juror on the back row, second from the left." What to do? As Bert Jalland often said to his trainee Assistant Recorders, "You won't find the answer to that in Archbold." I told the juror that the situation was intolerable. He, with typical Oldham fortitude, said he could manage if he moved his head a little to the right. The problem was solved during our discussion. The rain stopped.

LYNSKEY, George Justin KC (The Hon. Mr Justice Lynskey)
Born 5 February 1888, Knotty Ash, Liverpool. Son of George Jeremy Lynskey, solicitor. Died 21 December 1957 aged 69. St Francis Xavier's College, Liverpool; Liverpool University; LLB, 1907; LLM, 1908; Hon LLD, 1951. Admitted a solicitor, 1910. I. 26 January 1920; Bencher 1938. ETC 1920. Liverpool Chambers; 25 Lord Street, 1920-1925; 13 Harrington Street, 1926-1930. Silk 1930. Lamb Building, 1930-1941; New Court, 1942-1944. Judge, Salford Hundred Court of Record, 1937-1944. High Court Judge, King's Bench Division, 1944-1957. Kt. 1944. WW. DNB (Fred E Pritchard).

LYON, Adrian Pirrie (His Honour Judge Lyon)
Born 18 October 1952. Married to Christina Margaret Lyon, Recorder and Queen Victoria Professor of Law at Liverpool University. Leeds Grammar School; Hampton Grammar School; University College, London, LLB. G. July 1975. ETC 1975. Same Liverpool Chambers at; 54 Castle Street, 1975-1986; 14 Castle Street, 1987-2000. Head of Chambers, 1997-2000. Assistant Recorder, 1993. Member, General Council of the Bar, 1995. Recorder, 1997. Circuit Judge, Manchester, 19 June 2000. Temporary Assistant Judge of Employment Appeals Tribunal, 2002. WW.

LYONS, John Edward Patrick
LLB (Birmingham). Call M. November 1980. 601 Royal Exchange, Manchester, 1983-1988. Not in 1989 Bar Directory.

*** LYONS, His Honour Sir Rudolph QC**
Born 5 January 1912. Died 25 January 1991 aged 79. Leeds Grammar School; Leeds University, LLB. G. June 1934; Bencher 1961. North Eastern Circuit. Leeds Chambers; 47 Park Square, 1934-1940; 28 Park Square West, 1941; 38 Park Square, 1942-1953. Silk 1953. 1 Dr Johnson's Buildings, 1953-1959; 11 King's Bench Walk, 1960-1970. Recorder; Sunderland, 1955-1956; Newcastle-upon-Tyne, 1956-1961; Sheffield, 1961-1965; Leeds, 1965-1970; Liverpool, 1970-1977; Manchester, 1977-1982. Circuit Judge, 1972-1982. Kt. 1976. Leader of North Eastern Circuit, 1961-1970. Honorary Member of Northern Circuit, 1979. Solicitor General, later Attorney General of County Palatine of Durham, 1961-1970. Joint President, Council of HM Circuit Judges, 1974. Tributes at Liverpool Law Courts, 29 January 1991 (His Honour Judge Sir Sanderson Temple MBE., QC/ Eric Somerset Jones QC) WW. Times Obituary, 26 February 1991.

M

MABERLY, Alexander Cahill
Born 1843. Youngest son of Rev. Charles Maberly, incumbent of Owlesbury, Hants. Queen's College, Oxford, MA. AAS. L. 12 November 1868. Call 6 June 1871. ETC. 13 July 1877. Prop. Higgin QC. Sec. Smyly. Manchester Chambers; Temple Chambers, 1 St James's Square, 1876-1895; Westminster Buildings, Brown Street, 1896-1908; 37 Brown Street, 1909-1919. Lancs. Chancery Court. Not in 1920 Law List.

MACAULAY, Ian Anderson CBE
Liverpool Collegiate Grammar School; Christ College, Cambridge. I. 26 January 1933. ETC. 1 February 1933. Prop. Lynskey KC. Sec. Sellers. Liverpool Chambers; 34 Castle Street, 1933-1938; 27 Lord Street, 1939-1948. Clerk of Assize, Northern Circuit, St George's Hall, Liverpool, 1948-1971. Clerk of the Crown Courts at Liverpool & Manchester, 1956-1971. CBE, 1 January 1961.

MACBETH, Percy
Born 23 December 1877 Manchester. Died 14 January 1938 aged 60. Merton College, Oxford. M. 19 November 1906. ETC. 9 July 1907. Prop. Taylor KC. Sec. Atkinson. Manchester Chambers; 5 St James's Square, 1907-1914. Served in 1914-1918 War in 6th & 4th Rifle Brigades. 3 St James's Square, 1919-1931. Stipendiary Magistrate for Salford, 1931-1938. WW.

McBRIDE, Gavin John
Born 30 November 1971 Chester. Manchester Grammar School; Pembroke College, Cambridge, MA. Call. M. October 1996. ETC. December 1996. Prop. Michael Shorrock QC. Sec. Fiorella Brereton. Peel Court Chambers, 45 Hardman Street, Manchester, 1996.

McCALL, Sir Robert Alfred KCVO., QC.
Born 9 July 1849 Lisburn, Ireland. Died 6 April 1934 aged 84. 3rd son of Hugh McCall, newspaper editor. Queen's College, Belfast, MA; Queen's College, Galway. AAS. M. 7 November 1867. Call. 6 June 1871; Bencher 1894; Reader Autumn 1906; Treasurer 1917. ETC. 22 March 1873. Prop. Herschell. Sec. McConnell. 3 Harcourt Buildings, 1873-1880; 1 Temple Gardens, 1881-1921. Silk 1891. Senator, London University. Vice Chairman, Council of Legal Education, 1917. Commissioner of Assize, Wales & Chester Circuit, 1919. Registrar of the Railway & Canal Commission, 1921-1934. KCVO, 1921. Attorney General & Queen's Serjeant of the Duchy of Lancaster, 1899-1921. WW.

McCALL, Robert Forster
Born 28 February 1882. Died 11 September 1942 aged 60. 2nd son of Sir Robert Alfred McCall KC qv. Charterhouse, 1895-1901; Oriel College, Oxford, LLB. AAS. M. 15 November 1902. Call. 12 June 1907. ETC. 9 March 1908. Prop. Mellor KC. Sec. J W Mansfield. 1 Temple Gardens, 1919-1942. He worked in the Ministry of Munitions during the War of 1914-1918. After the War he went to South Africa. The Old Carthusian records have him down as a member of the East African Circuit but it is not known if he practised. He returned to England in 1934 and joined the Home Office. Information supplied by Robert's son, Hilary F. McCall.

McCANN, Simon Howard
Born 9 February 1970, Preston. Son of M H McCann, solicitor & Coroner for Preston. St Cuthbert Mayne RC High School, Preston; Leeds University, BA. G. November 1996. ETC 1996. Prop. Keith Goddard QC. Sec. John Bromley-Davenport. Dean's Court Chambers, Crown Square/ 24 St John Street, Manchester, 1996. Member, General Council of the Bar, 2000.

McCARROLL, John Johnson
Born 16 November 1964 Enniskillen. Married to Jane Rachel Andrews qv. Portora Royal School, Enniskillen; Trinity College, Dublin, LLB. I. 22 November 1988. ETC. 1990. Prop. William Waldron QC. Sec. Edward Bartley Jones. Member, Bar of the Republic of Ireland, 1994. Liverpool Chambers; 7 Queen Ave, 1990-1995; Exchange Chambers, Derby Square November, 1995. In April 2002 moved to Ireland to practise at the Irish Bar.

MCCARTHY, William
LLB (Leeds). M. November 1996. New Bailey Chambers, Preston, 1999.

McCLEARY, Robert (His Honour Judge McCleary)
Born 2 December 1869. Died 27 September 1936 aged 66. Youngest son of George McCleary of Manchester, wine importer. Trinity Hall, Cambridge, BA 1891. AAS. M. 24 May 1889. Call. 8 May 1895. ETC. 4 February 1901. Prop. Shee QC. Sec. McKeand. Manchester Chambers; 17 Brazennose Street, 1901-1905; 16 John Dalton Street, 1906-1925. County Court Judge, Circuit 12, (Bradford, Halifax, Huddersfield), 1926-1936. Publications; McCleary's County Court Precedents. WW.

McCLUGGAGE, Brian Thomas
Born 1 June 1972, Co. Down. Regent House Grammar School, Northern Ireland; Emmanuel College, Cambridge, MA; University of Toronto, LLM. M. October 1995. Pupillage 2 Crown Office Row. ETC. 1997. Prop. Charles Garside QC. Sec. Tim Horlock. 9 St John Street, Manchester, 1997.

McCLURE, John Patrick
Born 1 March 1952 Salford. 2nd son of Thomas McClure, production services engineer. Kings College, London, LLB. AAS. M. 16 November 1973. Call 25 November 1975. Manchester Chambers; Lawrence Buildings, 2 Mount Street, 1979-1984; 3 St James's Square, 1985-1989; 38 King Street West, 1990-1995; 24a St John Street, 1996 (now St John's Building).

• McCOMBE, Richard (George Bramwell) QC. (The Hon. Mr Justice McCombe)

Born 23 September 1952. Sedbergh School; Downing College Cambridge, MA. L. 1975; Bencher. First Junior Counsel to the Director of Fair Trading, 1987-1989. Silk 1989. Member of the Bar Council & Chairman of Committees. Assistant Recorder 1993. Recorder 1996. Attorney General, Duchy of Lancaster, 1996-2001. High Court Judge, Queen's Bench Division, 2001. Presiding Judge, Northern Circuit, 2004. WW.

MacCONKEY, William Dixon
Born 17 February 1855. Eldest son of late Rev. Andrew MacConkey. Scholar, Trinity College, Cambridge, BA, 1876. AAS. I. 8 November 1873. Call 27 January 1878. ETC. 13 February 1879. Prop. Russell QC. Sec. Bigham. Liverpool Chambers; 12 Commerce Chambers, Harrington Street, 1880; 7 Commerce Chambers, 15 Lord Street, 1881-1926. Not in 1927 Law List. Foster.

McCONNELL, William Robert KC

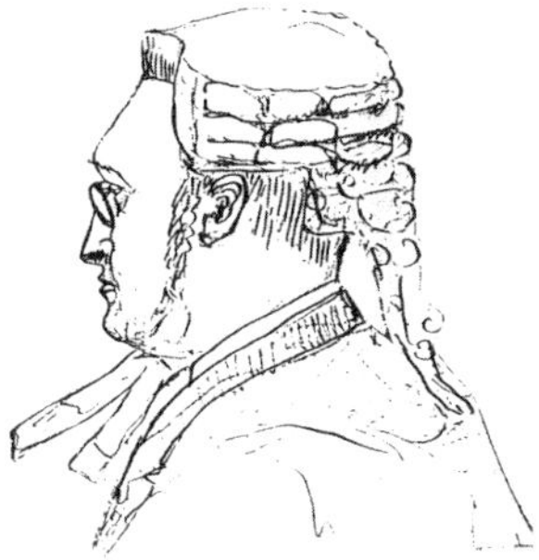

Born 2 July 1837 Ireland. Died 21 December 1906 aged 69. Royal Academical Institution, Belfast; London University, BA. AAS. I. 30 May 1859. Call 30 April 1862. ETC 1862. 12 Kings Bench Walk, 1862-1896. Revising Barrister for Liverpool 1868. Junior Counsel to; Board of Trade, 1875; Board of Customs, 1876. Royal Commissioner to inquire into corrupt practices at elections in the City of Gloucester. Silk 1896. Prosecuted Mrs Maybrick. Chairman, County of London Sessions, 1896-1906. WW. Foster.

McCULLOUGH, Judith Ann
Born 17 November 1966 Bangor, Northern Ireland. Methodist College, Belfast; University College, Wales at Aberystwyth, LLB. M. April 1991. 10 Lawson Street, Preston, 1995; 5 John Dalton Street, Manchester, 1999.

McDERMOTT, Gerard Francis QC
Born 21 April 1956 Ashton under Lyne. De La Salle College, Salford; Manchester University, LLB. AAS. 26 October 1976. Call 27 July 1978. ETC. 1979. Prop. Clegg QC. Sec. Wingate-Saul. Same Manchester Chambers; 601 Royal Exchange, 1979-1988; 8 King Street, 1989. Member, General Council of the Bar, 1983-1988, 1990-1996, 1998. Member, New York State Bar, 1990. Recorder & Silk 1999. Treasurer, Northern Circuit. WW.

McDERMOTT, John Raymund QC
Born 12 July 1954, Waterloo, Liverpool. St Mary's College, Crosby; Liverpool University, LLB. G. November 1976. ETC. October 1977. Pupilmaster, Eryl Lloyd-Parry. Same Liverpool Chambers; Fruit Exchange Buildings, Victoria Street, 1977-1991; Chavasse Court, 24 Lord Street 1991. Silk 2003.

MACDONA, Egerton Milne Cumming
Born 1868. Died 1948. Only son of John Cumming Milne, (1826-1907), barrister of West Kirby, MP for Rotherhide & breeder of champion St Bernard dogs. New College, Oxford. AAS. M. 20 January 1888. Call 10 June 1891. Prop. Addison QC. Sec. Parry. No chambers address. Egerton's wife died in 1969 aged 104. She had been the driving force behind Wirral Conservatives for over 50 years. She bequeathed her home, Hilbre House, West Kirby to the MP for Wirral, Selwyn Lloyd qv as she wanted the house to retain it's links with Wirral Conservatism. See "Selwyn Lloyd" by D R Thorpe; Jonathan Cape 1989.

McDONALD, Andrew
Born 27 February 1949 Wirral. Calday Grammar School, West Kirby; Liverpool University, LLB. G. July 1971. ETC. December 1971. Prop. David McNeill QC. Sec. Anthony Carus. Liverpool Chambers; 9 Rumford Street, 1971-1973; Fruit Exchange Building, Victoria Street, 1974-1991; Martin's Building, Water Street, 1992-1999; 7 Harrington Street (merger with Corn Exchange), 6.9.1999. Publications; Industrial Diseases Litigation, 1998; Occupational Diseases Law & Practice, 2002.

MacDONALD, Eileen Agnes
Born 1905. Only daughter of Percy MacDonald of Chorlton-cum-Hardy, dentist. AAS. M. 21 March 1923. Call 17 November 1926. Pupilmaster, Neville Laski. Manchester Chambers; 3 St James's Square, 1930-1948; 60 King Street, 1949-1955. No address, 1956-1963. Not in 1964 Law List. According to Joseph Cantley's short history of 3 St James's Square which he wrote in 1986, she was a very capable barrister who only came to the Bar to please her father. When father died she left the Bar to become a greatly respected JP, widely regarded as an unpaid Stipendiary Magistrate.

McDONALD, Paul
Born 15 May 1953, Chorley. Park High School, Birkenhead; Liverpool University, LLB. L. July 1975. ETC 1976. Prop. Douglas Brown QC. Sec J V Williamson. Manchester Chambers; Post Office Chambers, Brown Street, 1976; 4th floor, Sunlight House, Quay Street, 1977-1983; Central Street Chambers, 1984-1987; 33 King Street West, 1987-1994; Old Colony House, 6 South King Street, 1994-2001; 9 St John Street, 2001.

MacDONALD, William Patrick
Born 1837. Eldest son of Simon MacDonald of Inverness. AAS. M. 25 January 1862. Call 17 November 1864. 2 Middle Temple Lane, 1876-1877 Liverpool Sessions; 4 Plowden Buildings, 1878-1879. North Eastern Circuit. Not in 1880 Law List.

McDOUGALL, Archibald
Born 5 August 1903 Hobart. Died 14 January 1984 aged 80. Hutchins School, Hobart; University of Tasmania, BA; Balliol College Oxford; MA., BCL. Columbia University. US Senate Legislative Counsel's Office, Washington DC., 1928. AAS. M. 30 July 1929. Harmsworth Scholar. Call 8 June 1932. ETC. 15 March 1933. Prop. Gorman KC. Sec. Jolly. 78 King Street, Manchester, 1931-1935. Lancs. Chancery Court. Lecturer in Law, Manchester University, 1931-1935. Thereafter travelled the world as notable international lawyer, economist and diplomat. WW.

McENERY, Patrick Joseph
Irish Bar; M. 1925; QC. G. April 1940. 38 Fishergate, Preston, 1950-1956; 3 King's Bench Walk, 1957-1967; 2 Pump Court, 1968-1979. Chairman, Rent Assessment Committees. Not in 1980 Law List.

McEWAN, Malcolm Charles
Born 31 May 1953 Burton upon Trent. 3rd son of R K McEwan, Headmaster. Hertford College, Oxford, MA. AAS. M. 15 January 1974. Call July 1976. Manchester Chambers; 196 Deansgate, 1978-1989; 18 St John Street, 1990.

McFARLAND, Arthur
Born 25 January 1893. Died 9 May 1966 aged 73. St Luke's, Tranmere. Captain with Cheshire Regt., 1914-1918 War. Lt., Paymaster, RAPC 1940-1941. Liverpool University, LLB. G. 14 May 1930. ETC. 18 June 1930. Prop. Goldie KC. Sec. Fraser Harrison. Liverpool Chambers; 15 Union Court, 1930-1933; 3 Cook Street 1934-1947. Assistant Recorder, Liverpool, 1942-1947. Stipendiary Magistrate for Liverpool, 1947-1965. WW.

MACGILL, John Bardsley
Born 1932. 1st son of John Macgill of Denton, medical practitioner. Trinity College, Cambridge. AAS. 9 March 1951. Call 10 May 1955. 4 Chapel Walks, Manchester, 1957-1960. No address, 1958-1963. Not in 1964 Law List. According to Desmond Franks, Macgill joined Minnesota Mining Company and ended up as European customer and staff relations manager/ troubleshooter.

MCGINTY, Robert Fraser
BA (Oxon). I. November 1994. New Bailey Chambers, Preston, 1996.

MACGOWAN, Edward Turner
Born 21 December 1860. Rugby; Trinity College, Cambridge, BA., LLB. AAS. 20 March 1880. I. 26 January 1884. ETC. 18 July 1884. Prop. French QC. Sec. Nash. 13 King's Bench Walk, 1885. Goldsmith Building, 1886-1894; 10 King's Bench Walk, 1895-1906. No address, 1907-1934. Not in 1935 Law List. Foster.

MacGREGOR, John
Born 24 January 1825. Eldest son of Col. Sir Duncan MacGregor, KCB. Trinity College, Cambridge, MA, 1850. AAS. I. 7 November 1846. Call 31 January 1851. No chambers address, 1876-1892. Not in 1893 Law List. Captain, Royal Canoe Club and author of several books on the "Rob Roy" canoe. Foster.

McGRAIL, Elizabeth Caroline
LLB (Leeds). L. July 1986. Manchester Chambers; Central Street Chambers, 1987; 33 King Street West, 1988. Donald Race & Newton, Solicitors, Burnley, 1989-1990. Not in 1991 Bar Directory.

McGUCKIN, John
Born 1883. Eldest son of Peter McGuckin of Dundee, wine & spirit merchant. AAS. M. 17 January 1931. Call 28 June 1933. ETC. 31 January 1934. Prop. Lynskey KC. Sec. Fyfe. 2 Dr Johnson's Building, 1934-1937; 2 Brick Court, 1938-1940; 1 Tanfield Court, 1941-1943; 2 Hare Court, 1944-1949; 3 Middle Temple Lane, 1952-1953. No address, 1954-1963. Not in 1964 Law List.

McGUIRE, Deirdre Maria
Born 13 February 1961, St Helens. Sister of Donal Patrick McGuire qv. Notre Dame High School, St Helens; Leeds University, LLB. Bury Magistrates Court, 1982. I. November 1983. Manchester City Council, 1985. ETC. February 1987. Prop. Michael Maguire QC. Sec. Stuart Baker. Member of the Irish Bar. Liverpool Chambers; Martin's Building, Water Street, 1987-1999; 7 Harrington Street 6.9.1999.(merger with Corn Exchange).

McGUIRE, Donal Patrick
Born 21 June 1959, St Helens. Brother of Deidre McGuire qv. St Edwards College, Liverpool; Liverpool University, LLB. G. 28 July 1983. ETC. 1985. Prop. Michael Maguire QC. Sec. Iain Goldrein. Pupilmaster, Ian James Crofton Peddie. Member of Irish Bar (Kings Inns, Dublin) July 1991. Liverpool Chambers; 5 Castle Street, February 1985-March 1987; chambers relocated to 48 Castle Street, March 1987-September 1989; merger with Corn Exchange, September 1989-September 1999; 7 Harrington Street (merger with Martins Building), 6.9.1999.

MACHELL, Raymond (Donatus) QC
Born 8 April 1949, Manchester. St Bede's College, Manchester; Christ's College, Cambridge, MA., LLB. G. July 1973. ETC. 1973. Prop. Benet Hytner QC. Sec. Gerard Humphries. Manchester Chambers; 1 Dean's Court, Crown Square/ 24 St John Street, 1973-2001; 12 Byrom Street 2001. Silk 1988. Recorder 1989. Deputy High Court Judge.

MACHIN, Charles Kim
Born 29 November 1950 Blackheath, London. Maryhill Comprehensive School, Stoke-on-Trent; University College, Oxford, MA. L. November 1973. ETC. November 1974. Prop. James Fitzhugh QC. Sec. Peter Keenan. Pupilmasters, John Morcon & Robert Reid. Manchester Chambers; 4 Clarence Street, 1974-1985; Bridge Street Chambers, 72 Bridge Street, 1985-1998; Cobden House Chambers, 19 Quay Street, 1998.

McHUGH, Pauline Mary
Born 5 July 1972, Manchester. Hollies RC High School; Queen's College, Cambridge, MA. G. 12 October 1995. Pupillage at 1 Garden Court, Temple. Family Department, Jones Maidment Wilson, Solicitors, 1996-1997. ETC. December 1997. Prop. Anthony Rumbelow QC. Sec. Bernard Wallwork. 28 St John Street, Manchester, September 1997 (now St Johns Buildings Chambers).

McILRAITH, John Robert
Born 1862. Eldest son of John McIlraith of Erskine, Renfrews., clergyman. Glasgow University, MA. AAS. M. 4 November 1884. Call 22 June 1887. ETC. 30 July 1890. Prop. Ambrose QC. Sec. Gully QC. 4 Harcourt Buildings, 1891-1927. Not in 1928 Law List.

McINTYRE, Angus George Milward
Born 1856. Eldest son of Aeneas John Mclntyre QC. London University, LLB. AAS. M. 11 January 1873. Call 10 May 1876. ETC. 12 July 1876. Prop. Pope QC. Sec. Temple QC. 1 Brick Court, 1877-1904. Joined South Eastern Circuit in 1879. Not in 1905 Law List.

McIVER, Alan Squarey
I. 10 May 1922. ETC. 13 January 1923. Prop. Singleton KC. Sec. Blackledge. 3 Dr. Johnson's Building, 1923-1935. No address, 1936-1953. Not in 1954 Law List.

McIVOR, Helen Susannah
Born 16 January 1970 Bristol. Daughter of Ian Walker Mclvor qv. Prospect Vale Primary School; Loreto Convent Grammar School; Leicester University, LLB. G. 13 October 1992. ETC. 1992. Prop. Anthony Gee QC. Sec. Christopher Limb. Manchester Chambers; 6th floor, Sunlight House, 1992-1995; relocated to Young Street Chambers, 1995.

McIVOR, Ian Walker
Born 19 January 1944 Worsley. Father of Helen Susannah Mclvor qv. Worsley High School; Bolton Institute; London University, LLB. I. July 1973. Manchester Chambers; 67 Princes Street, 1973-1975; Lawrence Buildings, 2 Mount Street, 1976-1984; 3 St James's Square, 1985-1989; 38 King Street West, 1990-1992; 334 Deansgate, 1993-2000; Brooklands Chambers, Manchester, 2001.

MACKAY, David Ian (His Honour Judge Mackay)
Born 11 November 1945. Birkenhead School; Brasenose College, Oxford, BA (Jurisprudence), 1968; MA 1992. I. November 1969. ETC. 1970. Pupilmaster, Robert Leech. Same Liverpool Chambers at; 2nd floor, Oriel Chambers, 14 Water Street, 1970-1982; Refuge Assurance House, Derby Square, 1983-1992. Assistant Recorder 1986. Recorder 1988. Legal Member, Mental Health Review Tribunal, 1988-1992. Governor, Birkenhead School, 1979.; Chairman, 1991. Circuit Judge, 1992. (Official Referee's Business, 1993-1998; Provincial Judge, Technology & Construction Court, 1998.) WW.

McKEAND, Charles Pilling

Born 29 October 1854. Eldest son of Joseph McKeand of Manchester, surgeon. AAS. I. 20 January 1873. Call 13 June 1877. ETC. 11 July 1877. Prop. Higgin QC. Sec. Addison. 1 Temple Gardens, 1880. Hong Kong, 1881. 1 St James's Square, Manchester, 1883-1896; 8 St James's Square, 1897-1901. Not in 1902 Law List. Foster.

McKEE, Hugh Anthony
Born 16 November 1959 Ballymena, Northern Ireland. Rainey Endowed School, NI; Wolverhampton Polytechnic, BA (Law). AAS. M. 30 July 1981. Call. 22 November 1983. ETC. 1983. Prop. Rhys Davies QC. Sec. John Wishart. Manchester Chambers; Conavon

Court Chambers, 13 Blackfriars Street, 1983-1991; Manchester House Chambers, 18-22 Bridge Street, 1991-1999; 24a St John Street, February 1999.; merger with No 28 to form St John's Chambers, 23.9.2002.

McKEEVER, John
Born 1856. Only surviving son of James McKeever of Wigton, solicitor. Formerly a solicitor when AAS. M. 30 November 1892. Call 26 January 1893. ETC. 21 February 1893. Prop. Shee QC. Sec. Henry. 12 King's Bench Walk, 1893-1896; Manchester Chambers; 33 Princess Street, 1895-1908; Canada Chambers, Spring Gardens, 1909-1914. No address, 1915-1917. 22 Tib Lane, 1918-1929. No address, 1930-1936. Not in 1937 Law List.

McKENNA, Brian Malachy
Born 16 December 1960, Northern Ireland. Married to Karen Gregory qv. St MacNissi's College, NI; Liverpool University, LLB. AAS. M. 5 March 1982. Call 28 July 1983. ETC 1986. Prop. David Poole QC. Sec. John Wishart. Manchester Chambers; Conavon Court Chambers, 12 Blackfriars Street, 1986-1989; Manchester House Chambers, 18-22 Bridge Street, 1990-1999; 24a St John Street, 1999. Merged with no. 28 to form St John's Chambers, 23.9.2002.

McKENZIE, Sir William Warrender GBE., KC. (First Baron Amulree)
Born 1860. Died 5 May 1942. Perth Academy; Edinburgh University, MA 1885; University College, London. L. 19 May 1886. ETC. 18 July 1886. Prop. Ambrose QC. Sec. Ferguson. Lamb Building, 1887; Goldsmith Buildings, 1888-1890; 9 King's Bench Walk, 1891-1919; 3 Paper Buildings, 1920-1926. Served on numerous Government Boards and Inquiries and on several Royal Commissions. President, Industrial Court 1919-1926. Silk 1914. CBE 1917. KBE 1918. GBE 1926. Baron 1929. PC. 1930. He was a prolific editor and his works included Halsbury's Laws of England; Pratt's Highways & Paterson's Licencing Acts. He was, for a very brief period, Secretary of State for Air in Ramsay MacDonald's Government. WW.DNB.

McKEON, James Patrick
Born 12 October 1959, Birmingham. St Philip's Grammar School, Birmingham; Liverpool University, LLB. G. November 1982. Pupilmaster, John Hodgson. 3 Dr. Johnson's Building's, 1982-1989. South Eastern Circuit. ETC. 1989. Prop. R J D Livesey QC. Sec. Nigel Gilmour. Peel House, Harrington Street, 1989-1999; Martins Building, Water Street, February, 1999. Merger with Corn Exchange to form 7 Harrington Street, 6.9.1999.

MACKIE, Alice Josephine
I. 29 June 1927.15 Union Court, 1928-1930. No address, 1931-1937. Not in 1938 Law List.

McKISACK, Henry Charles
I. 17 November 1924.2 Cloisters, 1927-1934. No address, 1935-1953. Not in 1954 Law List.

MacLACHLAN, David
Youngest son of James MacLachlan of Dundee. AAS. M. 5 November 1849. Call 7 June 1852. MA. Author of Law of Merchant Shipping. 11 King's Bench Walk, 1876-1893. No address, 1894-1900. Not in 1901 Law List.

McLACHLAN, David Robert
Born 15 July 1971 Liverpool. De La Salle School, Liverpool; Essex University, LLB; LLM. Teacher of English as a foreign language in Japan, July 1994-1995. Law Tutor, 1995-1997. I. 10 October 1996. ETC. 18 December 1997. Prop. Stephen Riordan QC. Sec. Michael Henshell. 25-27 Castle Street, Liverpool, 1997. Captain Liverpool Bar Cricket Team, 2001-2002.

McLAREN, The Rt. Hon. Sir Charles Benjamin Bright Bt., QC, MP (First Baron Aberconway)
Born 12 May 1850, Edinburgh. Died 23 January 1934 aged 83. Edinburgh University, MA; Universities of Bonn & Heidelberg. AAS. L. 21 May 1870. Call. 17 November 1874. ETC. 13 March 1876. Prop. Torr QC. Sec. A Robertson. 22 Chancery Lane, 1877; 3 New Square, 1878-1885; 3 New Court, Carey Street, 1886-1911. Silk 1897. Parliamentary draftsman & conveyancer. Lancs. Chancery Court. MP (L); Stafford, 1880-1886; Bosworth, 1892-1910. His wife inherited a considerable fortune and McLaren gave up the Bar upon taking silk in order to manage her very substantial business interests. He became Chairman of; John Brown, the Clydeside Shipbuilders; the Metropolitan Railway Company; the Tredegar and the Sheepbridge Iron & Coal Companies and was director of a number of collieries in the Midlands. He was eminently qualified to write, in 1927 "The Basic Industries of Great Britain." The family gardens at Bodnant, Tal-y-Cafn near Conway were given to the National Trust by his son in 1949. Well worth a visit at any time but particularly in spring. Baronet 1902; PC 1908; Baron 1911. WW. DNB. Obituary, The Times, 24 January 1934.

MacLEAN, Henry Chevers

Born 31 October 1884. 2nd son Henry MacLean of "The Laurels," Newton by Chester. AAS. M.5 November 1907. Call. 8 June 1910. ETC. 13 February 1911. Prop. Taylor KC. Sec. Cuthbert Smith. 8 Harrington Street, Liverpool, 1911-1914. Commissioned Lt., 13 September 1914, 9th Btn, Royal Inniskilling Fusiliers. He went to France on 15 October 1915, was promoted to Captain and was killed in action on 1 July 1916 aged 31. Thiepval Memorial, Somme, France. Pier & Face 4D & 5B. The memorial is on the D73 off the main Bapaume to Albert road (D929). Information supplied by Public Records Office & Commonwealth War Graves Commission.

MACLEOD, Nigel Ronald Buchanan QC

Born 7 February 1936. Wigan Grammar School; Christ Church, Oxford MA., BCL. Served RAF, 1954-1956. G. February 1961; Bencher 1993. I. 1984. ETC 1962. Pupilmaster Iain Glidewell. Manchester Chambers; 25 Bow Lane, 1962-1976; 460 Royal Exchange, 1977-1983; 40 King Street, 1984. Silk 1979. Assistant Boundary Commissioner for England, 1981- Recorder, 1981. Chairman; Planning & Environmental Bar Association, 1998-2000 (Hon Member 2002); Hon. Member, Parliamentary Bar Association, 2001. Member, Bar Council, 1998-2000. President, Mental Health Review Tribunals, 2000. Deputy High Court Judge, 1992-2001. WW.

McLOUGHLIN, James

LLB., LLM. G. February 1966. ETC. 2 May 1968. 25 Bow Lane, 1967-1970. Not in 1971 Law List.

McMAHON, Sir Lionel 4th Bt

Born 30 June 1856. Died 20 February 1926 aged 69. Youngest son of Sir Beresford Burston McMahon, 2nd Bt. Rugby. Late, Lt., 58th Regt. of Foot. AAS. I. 10 March 1880. Call 26 January 1883. ETC. 6 February 1883. Prop. Potter QC. Sec. Collins. 3 Dr Johnson's Buildings, 1887-1888. No address, 1889-1926. Succeeded brother, 1905. DL.& High Sheriff, Co Tyrone. WW. Foster.

McMASTER, Henderson

L. 3 July 1889. Equity draftsman & conveyancer. Lancs. Chancery Court. Liverpool Chambers; 4 Harrington Street, 1893-1920; 5 Harrington Street, 1921; 10 Dale Street, 1922-1935; 31 Dale Street, 1936-1941; 15 Union Court, 1942-1949. Not in 1950 Law List.

McMEEKIN, Ian

Born 9 September 1962 Barrow-in-Furness. Ulverston School; Leeds University, BA. City of London University, Dip. Law. AAS. M. 30 November 1984. Call 23 July 1987. ETC. 1987. Prop. Donald Hart QC. Sec. Beverly Lunt. Manchester Chambers; 2nd floor, St Mary's Parsonage, 1987-1992; 58 King Street Chambers, 51-53 South King Street, 1992.

MACMILLAN, (John) Bruce (His Honour Judge Macmillan)

Born 17 March 1946. Uppingham; Sheffield University, BJur, L. June 1969. ETC 1970. Prop. David McNeill QC. Sec Donald Forster. Same Liverpool Chambers at 34/54/14 Castle Street, Liverpool, 1970-1993. Recorder 1988-1993. Circuit Judge 1993.

McMILLAN, Robert James

G. July 1974. 41 North John Street, Liverpool, 1976-1977. 15 Old Square, 1981-1984. Not in 1985 Law List.

MacMULLEN, Edmund Ronalds

Born 1885. 2nd son of William Francis MacMullen of Cork. Trinity College, Cambridge. AAS. M. 15 March 1904. Call 1 July 1908. ETC. 10 March 1909. Prop. Tobin KC. Sec. Maurice Hills. No address, 1916-1919. Not in 1920 Law List.

McNAB, Robert Allan

I. 4 May 1887. ETC. 20 July 1887. Prop. Aspland QC. Sec. Blair. 4 Plowden Buildings, 1888-1890; 3 Temple Gardens, 1891-1895. Preston Chambers; 2 Chapel Street, 1891-1900; Bank Chambers, Fishergate, 1901-1908; 8a Winckley Square, 1909-1914; 14 Winckley Square, 1920-1925. No address, 1926-1931. Not in 1932 Law List.

McNEILE, (Watson) Hugh

Born 24 May 1903. Died 1 June 1998 aged 95. Harrow; Emmanuel College, Cambridge, MA. G. 26 January 1931. ETC. 27 January 1932. Prop. Goldie KC. Sec. Pritchard. Liverpool Chambers; 3 Cook Street, 1932-1933; 25 Castle Street, 1934-1939; 27 Lord Street, 1940. During War years he was a Flying Officer (Intelligence) at Air Ministry. Clerk of Indictments, Northern Circuit, 1945-1947; Associate, 1947-1962; Assistant Clerk of Assize, 1962- retirement in 1966. His main hobby was building and running large scale model working steam trains. Information from Mrs McNeile.

McNEILL, David Bruce QC (The Hon. Mr Justice McNeill)

(RB)

Born 6 June 1922. Died 26 February 1990 aged 67. Rydal School; Commissioned into Reconnaissance Corps, 1943; served in North Africa, Sicily, Italy & Germany. Merton College, Oxford, BCL., MA., 1947. L. November 1947; Bencher 1974. ETC. 29 January 1948. Prop. Nelson KC. Sec. Melville Kennan. Lecturer in Law, Liverpool University, 1948-1958. 34 Castle Street, 1948-1966. Silk 1966. 5 Essex Court, 1966-1979. Recorder of Blackburn, 1969-1971. Crown Court Recorder, 1972-1978. Chairman of the Bar, 1977-1978. Leader of the Northern Circuit, 1974-1978. High Court Judge, Queen's Bench Division, 1979-1990. Kt. 1979. Presiding Judge, Northern Circuit, 1980-1984. Member, Parole Board, 1986-1988. Hon. LLD., Liverpool, 1982. WW. Times Obituary, 27 February 1990. Memorial Service, Lincoln's Inn Chapel, 16 May 1990 (Judge Frank Paterson) Transcript in Circuit Records.

McNEILL, Fiona Kirsty

Born 26 July 1970, Edinburgh, Bradford Girls Grammar School; Nottingham University, LLB. L. October 1992. ETC. 15 December 1992. Prop. Nigel Gilmour QC. Sec. Alldis. Liverpool Chambers; Ground floor, 5 Harrington Street, October 1992-March 1999;Chavasse Court, 24 Lord Street, March 1999.

McNEILL, John Seddon

Born 5 June 1950, Blackburn. St Bees, Cumberland; Bradford University, BA. G. July 1974. ETC. 1974. Pupilmaster, Frank Hudson. Manchester Chambers; 67 Princes Street, 1975-1977; 2 Mount Street, 1977-1983; 3 St James's Square, 1983-1989; 38 King Street West, 1989-1995; 24a St John Street. 1995.; merger with 28 to form St John's Chambers on 23.9.2002.

MACOUBRY, John

Born 1811. Youngest son of John Macoubry of Downpatrick. Trinity College, Dublin, BA. AAS. L. 7 May 1835. AAS. M. 23 January 1839. Call M. 20 November 1940. 20 Cable Street, Liverpool, 1876-1878. No address, 1879-1887. Liverpool Prosecutions Book records, "Died 1/1887." Foster.

MACPHERSON, Rt. Hon. Sir (James) Ian KBE., KC, MP (First Baron Strathcarron)

Born 14 May 1880 Newtonmore, Inverness. Died 14 August 1937 aged 57. 2nd son of James Macpherson, JP, corn factor & contractor. George Watson's College, Edinburgh; Edinburgh University, MA., LLB. AAS. M. 14 November 1903. Call 27 June 1906; Bencher 1930. Fountains Court, 1910-1937. South East Circuit but Northern Circuit in 1926. MP, Ross & Cromarty; (Co. L), 1911-1931; (L. Nat.), 1931-1935. Under Secretary of State for War, 1916-1919. Chief Secretary for Ireland, 1918-1920. Minister of Pensions, 1920-1922. Recorder of Southend, 1931-1937. PC, 1918. Silk 1919. 1st Baronet 1933. Baron 1936. WW. DNB.

★ MACPHERSON OF CLUNY and BLAIRGOWRIE, Sir William (Alan)

(RB)

Born 1 April 1926. Wellington College, Berkshire; Served in Scots Guards (Captain), 1944-1947. Commanded (Lt. Col.) 21st Special Air Service Regt. (TA), 1962-1965. TD 1966. Trinity College, Oxford, MA; Hon. Fellow, 1991. I. February 1952; Bencher 1978. 2 Garden Court, 1952-1983. South Eastern Circuit. Silk 1971. Recorder 1972-1983. High Court Judge, Queen's Bench Division, 1983-1996. Kt 1983. Presiding Judge, Northern Circuit, 1985-1988.Honorary Member, Northern Circuit 1987. Member, Queen's Bodyguard for Scotland, Royal Company of Archers, 1977-.; Brigadier 1989. Chairman of Inquiry into the Death of Stephen Lawrence, 1998. WW.

MacQUITTY, James Lloyd OBE

Born 2 November 1912. Campbell College & Methodist College, Belfast; St Catherine's College, Oxford, MA; Trinity Hall, Cambridge, MA., LLM. I. June 1938. ETC. 1 February 1940. Prop. Shawcross KC. Sec. Nield. No Chambers address. Northern Ireland Bar, 1941. Home Guard Instructor, 1940-1943; Heavy Anti-Aircraft Duties, 1943-1944. QC (NI) 1960. OBE 1983. Member of many Tribunals & Government Committees. Chairman, Ulster TV Ltd, 1977-1983. WW.

MACRORY, Edmund QC

Born 1831. Died 18 April 1904. 2nd son of Adam J Macrory of Belfast, advocate. Trinity College, Dublin, BA, 1850, MA, 1857. AAS. M. 17 November 1849. Call. 26 January 1853; Bencher 1878; Reader Autumn 1888; Treasurer 1897. Irish Bar H. 1852. 7 Fig Tree Court, 1876-1903. Silk 1890. Chairman, Board of Examiners, Inns of Court, 1891. Publications; joint author, Hindmarsh on Law of Patents. WW. Foster.

MACVEAGH, Jeremiah MP

Born 1870 Belfast. Died 17 April 1922. St Malachy's College, Belfast. G. 28 January 1918. 2 Mitre Court Buildings, 1919-1921; 5 Essex Court, 1922-1932. MP (N) South Down, 1902-1922. Director; Alliance Gas Company, Dublin; East Kent Railway; Devon & Cornwall Railway; North Shropshire Railway. WW.

MADDEN, William QC

Born 1853. Died 10 August 1925. Son of William Madden of Liverpool. St Francis Xavier College, Liverpool; Stonyhurst. Liverpool solicitor, 1879-1888. G. 19 November 1888. ETC. 23 February 1907. Prop. Mellor KC. Sec. Greer. Liverpool Chambers; 25 Lord Street, 1907-1908; 14 Harrington Street, 1909-1914. No address, 1915-1925. Silk 1922. Recorder of Blackburn, 1924-1925. Criminal Specialist. He successfully defended, in 1902, John McKeever charged with murder of Protestant Leader John Kensit.

MADDISON, David George (His Honour Judge Maddison)

(DL)

Born 22 January 1947. King's School, Chester; University of Durham (Grey College), BA, 1968. I. February 1970. ETC. 7 December 1972. Prop. Justin Price QC. Sec. Geoffrey Locke. Pupilmaster, David Kemp, Gray's Inn. Same Liverpool Chambers; Queen Avenue, Castle Street, 1972-1983; 2nd floor, Peel House, Harrington Street, 1984-1992. Recorder 1990. Circuit Judge, 1992-. Member, Parole Board & Judicial Studies Board. Senior Circuit Judge & Hon. Recorder of Manchester, 13 January 2003-. First sitting in Court of Appeal, December 2000. WW.

MADDISON, David Thomas James

Born 7 August 1972 Manchester. Stockport Grammar School; Birmingham University, LLB. G. 12 October 1995. ETC. 14 December 1999. Prop. J J Rowe QC. Sec. Howard Baisden. 22 Old Buildings, February 1997-August 1998; 1st & 4th floor, 4 Brick Court August, 1998-June 1999; Cobden House Chambers, 19 Quay Street July, 1999-.

MADDOCKS, Bertram Catterall (His Honour Judge Maddocks)

(DL)

Born 7 July 1932. Son of His Honour George Maddocks qv. Malsis Hall, nr Keighley; Rugby; 2nd Lt., Royal Artillery, 1951. Trinity Hall, Cambridge, MA. AAS. M. 16 November 1953. Harmsworth Scholar. Call June 1956. ETC. 1956. Pupilmaster, Humphrey Copinger Easton. Circuit Junior, 1959. 3 St James's Square, Manchester, 1956-1984; relocated to; St James's Chambers, 68 Quay Street, 1985-1990. Chancery Practitioner. Member, Lincoln's Inn. Recorder 1983. Part time Chairman, VAT Tribunals. Circuit Judge, 1990-. WW.

MADDOCKS, His Honour George
Born 5 April 1896. Died 3 April 1980 aged 83. Father of His Honour Judge Bertram Maddocks qv. Christ Church Hall, Southport; Manchester University. Civil servant when AAS. M. 5 November 1920. Call 13 June 1923. ETC. 17 February 1926. Prop. Jackson KC. Sec. Abbott. 78 King Street, Manchester, 1926-1953. County Court Judge, Circuit 3, 1953-1968. WW.

MADEN, Henry MP
Born 31 March 1892. Died 17 November 1960 aged 68. Son of late Sir (John) Henry Maden of Bacup, cotton manufacturer. Exeter College, Oxford, BA. AAS. M. 8 July 1912. Call 5 July 1916. No chambers address. MP (L) for Lonsdale, 1923-1924. WW.

MAENAN, Lord (See Sir William Francis Kyffin Taylor)

MAGILL, John
Pupillage with Kenneth Hollins. Left to go into business as soon as pupillage ended. Did not get into Bar Directory.

MAGUIRE, (Albert) Michael MC., MM., QC

Born 30 December 1922. Died 13 December 2001 aged 78. Eldest son of Richard Maguire of Preston, printer. Hutton Grammar School. Served War of 1939-1945, North Irish Horse in North Africa (MM, 1943); Italy (MC, 1945) Captain, Inns of Court Regiment, 1946. War Crimes Investigation Unit, 1946. AAS. M. 20 February 1947. Harmsworth Scholar. Trinity Hall, Cambridge, BA, 1948. Call 26 January 1947; Bencher 1973. Pupilmasters, Cyril Pearce Harvey (Temple) & Robert Shenstone Nicklin. ETC. 1949. Liverpool Chambers; 27 Lord Street, 1949-1959; 10 Water Street, 1960-1967(Head of Chambers). Preston Chambers; 38 Fishergate; 10 Lune Street; 18a Winckley Street; la Chapel Street. Silk 1967. Goldsmith Buildings, 1966 to retirement in 2000. (Head of Chambers). Leader of the Northern Circuit, 1980-1984. "Last Recorder of Carlisle," 1970-1971. He showed no interest in sitting as a Recorder of Crown Courts. Mick was a famous son of the Northern Circuit. David Steer QC described him as "one of the all time great jury advocates. Fearless, straight talking ... and a truly formidable opponent." Many will recall the six months in 1981 when, leading Charles Mantell & Rhys Davies, he prosecuted the 'Handless Corpse' murder before Heilbron J. at Lancaster. Marty Johnson, a New Zealand drugs dealer, was murdered by his associates and his remains were thrown into a flooded quarry. During the trial, which resulted in nine convictions, Counsel for all Defendants requested that the trial be moved to the Old Bailey claiming that the cells at Lancaster Castle were inhumanely cold. The judge turned to the prosecution – "Mr Maguire, what do you say?" Mick replied "None of them are so cold as Mr Johnson." The trial proceeded. Retirement Dinner at Manchester for Mick and Eric Somerset Jones QC on 15 February 2001. WW.
Daily Telegraph, 28 December 2001. Tributes at Preston, Liverpool & Manchester Law Courts (Transcripts in Circuit Records) Memorial Service, St Ann's Church, Manchester (Judge David Clarke QC).

MAHMOOD, Ghazan

Born 24 May 1974 Bury. Broad Oak High School; Brunel University, LLB; Visiting Fellow, 1996. I. 9 October 1997. Pupillage at 1 Hare Court. ETC. 14 December 1999. Prop. David Berkley QC. Sec. Neil Berragan. Pupilmasters, Stephen Cogley & Neil Berragan. Merchants Chambers, 1 North Parade, Parsonage Gardens, Manchester, 1999. (Merger with St Johns Buildings Chambers, 2004.)

MAHON, Charles Joseph (His Honour Judge Mahon)

Born 16 August 1939. Cheetham's Hospital; Gonville & Caius College, Cambridge, BA., LLB. G. February 1962. ETC. 1962. Pupilmaster, Desmond Bailey. Manchester Chambers; 26 King Street, 1962-1969; 3 St James's Square, 1970-1984; St James's Chambers. 68 Quay Street, 1985-1989. Recorder 1985; Circuit Judge, 1989. Parachute Regt (TA), 1966-1972. WW.

MAIN, Peter Ramsay QC

Born 17 May 1958 Stonehaven, Scotland. Repton School; London School of Economics, LLB; Centre for Petroleum Studies, Dundee (Dip, Petroleum Law). Mediator (Academy of Experts). I. July 1981. ETC. December 1982. Prop. J J Rowe QC. Sec. Simon Fawcus. Circuit Junior, 1986. Manchester Chambers; 601 Royal Exchange, 1982-1988; 8 King Street, 1989-1999; Deans Court Chambers, 24 St John Street, 2000. Assistant Recorder 1999. Recorder 2000. Silk 2003.

MAINS, Archibald

I. 26 January 1911. ETC. 7 July 1911. Prop. Greer KC. Sec. Beezley. Goldsmith Buildings, 1911-1920; Farrar's Building, 1921-1930; 11 King's Bench Walk, 1931-1936. No address, 1937-1947. Not in 1948 Law List.

MAIRS, Robin Gordon James

LLB (Manchester), LLM (Cantab) G. October 1992. Victoria Chambers, 19 Castle Street, Liverpool, 1999. St Paul's Chambers, 23 Park Square, Leeds, 2000.

MAIS, (Robert) Hugh (The Hon. Mr Justice Mais)

Born 14 September 1907. Died 14 February 1996 aged 88. Shrewsbury School; Wadham College, Oxford, MA (Hon Fellow 1971). I. 27 January 1930; Bencher 1971. ETC. 9 July 1930. Prop. Derbyshire KC. Sec. Rhodes. Manchester Chambers; 60 King Street, 1930-1935; 43 King Street, 1936-1958. Wing Commander, RAF, 1940-1944. Chancellor of the Diocese of; Manchester, 1948-1971; Carlisle, 1950-1971; Sheffield, 1950-1971. County Court Judge, Circuits, 37 & 42 (London), 1958-1971. High Court Judge, Queen's Bench Division, 1971-1982. Kt. 1971. He presided over the trial of the "Flying Pickets" at Shrewsbury Crown Court in 1973 for conspiracy to intimidate workers to abstain from work, sentencing six Defendants to periods of imprisonment up to three years. In the same year he ordered the arrest of a man who had made a reverse V sign as he passed in his car on the way to court in Newcastle. The man spent two hours in the cells before the judge accepted his apology and his explanation that he had mistaken the judge for the mayor. Just try that today! WW. Obituary Daily Telegraph, 25 March 1996.

MAKIN, Thomas

Born 1831. Died 25 April 1881 according to Liverpool prosecutions book. Eldest son of Thomas Makin of Walnut Bank, Stodday, Lancs. AAS. M. 26 April 1861. Call 26 January 1864. Law Association Buildings, Harrington Street, Liverpool, 1876-1881.

MAKINSON, Joseph

Born 25 August 1836. Died 14 March 1914 aged 77. 6th son of John Makinson of Manchester, solicitor. Owen's College, Manchester; Huddersfield College; Clare College, Cambridge, BA. AAS. L. 13 November 1861. Call 6 June 1864. 2 St James's Square, Manchester, 1876-1878. Stipendiary Magistrate for the Borough of Salford, 5 July 1878- 1 March 1911. Cricket; Cambridge Eleven (Captain in his 3rd year); Lancashire County Eleven. WW. Foster.

MALLARD, Derek Blaise

Born 10 May 1925. Died 11 July 1997 aged 72. His son Nicholas is a solicitor. Wallasey Grammar School; Evacuated to Cheltenham at beginning of 1939-1945 War. Thereafter trained as an RAF Pilot in Arizona. Played tennis for RAF National team and at Wimbledon. Corpus Christi College, Oxford, MA. L. November 1950. ETC. 7 June 1951. Prop. Laski KC. Sec. George Maddocks. Manchester Chambers; 78 King Street, 1951-1958; 196 Deansgate, 1959-1989 (Head of Chambers); 72 Bridge Street, 1990. Retired 1990. Member of Wallasey and later Caldy Golf Club. Information provided by Mrs Sheila Mallard.

MALLON, Joanna

Born 9 January 1967, Liverpool. St Edward's College, Liverpool; Asahi Sankyo, Shinbuku, Tokyo, 1989-1994. Durham University (Trevelyan College), BA (History); Dip. Law (Chester). L. October 1996. ETC. December 1996. Prop. Timothy King QC. Sec. Bernadette Goodman. Liverpool Chambers; Derby Square Chambers, Merchants Court, 1996-2002; 7 Harrington Street, 2003.

MALLORY, Katherine Lucy
Born 10 May 1974, Kingston-upon-Hull. Hull High School for Girls; Trinity & All Saints College, University of Leeds, BA. I. October 1998. ETC. 12 December 2001. Prop. Charles Garside QC. Sec. Charles Kennedy. Pupilmaster, Nigel Grundy. 9 St John Street, Manchester, 2001.

MALONE, George
I. 10 May 1922. ETC. 12 July 1923. Prop. Wingate Saul KC. Sec. Burgis. 78 King Street, Manchester, 1929-1938. No address, 1939-1953. Not in 1954 Law List.

MANASSE, Paul Reuben
Born 29 August 1966 Surrey. Burnage High School, Manchester; Liverpool University, BSc., PhD. Lecturer, Liverpool University, 1990-1993. G. October 1995. ETC. 21 December 1995. Prop. Lyndsey Kushner QC. Sec. David Hernandez. Young Street Chambers, Manchester, 1995.

MANISTY, Henry QC (The Hon. Mr Justice Manisty)
Born 13 December 1808. Died 31 January 1890 aged 81. Durham Cathedral Grammar School; articled to Thorpe & Dickson, attorneys of Alnwick, Northumberland. Solicitor 1830. Practised for twelve years with Meggison, Pringle & Manisty of 3 King's (now Theobald) Rd, London. AAS. G. 20 April 1842. Call 23 April 1845; Bencher 1859; Treasurer 1861. 8 Serjeants Inn, 1848; Silk 1857. 9 King's Bench Walk, 1876. High Court Judge, Queen's Bench Division, 1876-1890. Kt. 1876. DNB. Times, 1 February 1890.

MANLEY, David Eric QC
Born 30 April 1956 Eccles. Cheadle Hulme School; Leeds University, LLB. I. July 1981. ETC. 1982. Prop. Christopher Rose QC. Sec. Roger Farley. Manchester Chambers; 460 Royal Exchange/ 40 King Street 1981. Assistant Recorder 1999. Recorder 2000. Silk 2003.

MANLEY, Hilary
Born 17 July 1966 Sheffield. Durham Johnson School; University College, London, LLB. G. 26 November 1996. ETC. December 1996. Prop. Peter Openshaw QC. Sec. Stuart Neale. Cobden House Chambers, 19 Quay Street, Manchester, 1996.

MANN, Sara Angela
Born 18 August 1971 Manchester. Bury Grammar School for Girls; Leeds Metropolitan University, LLB. M. November 1994. ETC. 20 December 1994. Prop. David Harris QC. Sec. Graham Wood. Same Liverpool Chambers at; 3rd floor, Peel House, Harrington Street, 1994-1998; 8th floor, India Buildings, Water Street, 12.1.1998. Member, Lord Chancellor's Domestic Violence Advisory Committee.

MANSFIELD, Gillian
BA (Warwick); LLM (Sheffield); CPE (Leeds). L. October 1994. Central Chambers, 89 Princess Street, Manchester, 2000. Company Lawyer, Phaidon Press, London N1, 2001.

MANSFIELD, Horatio
Born 1821. 5th son of John Mansfield of London. Trinity College, Cambridge, MA, 1845. AAS. I. 23 January 1847. Call 6 June 1853. 3 Pump Court, Temple, 1876-1887. Liverpool & Kirkdale Sessions. Not in 1888 Law List. Foster.

MANSFIELD, Hon. John William
Born 10 July 1857. 2nd son of William, Lord Sandhurst, GCB., GCSI. Wellington College; Trinity College, Cambridge, MA 1883. AAS. I. 31 December 1878. Call 26 January 1882. ETC. 6 February 1882. Prop. Russell QC. Sec. Segar. 5 Paper Buildings, 1884-1885; 2 Garden Court, 1886-1893; 1 Harcourt Buildings, 1894-1895; 2 Harcourt Buildings, 1896-1913. Room 203 Royal Courts of Justice, 1914-1922, Not in 1923 Law List. Foster.

MANSFIELD, Thomas Edward OBE
G. 3 July 1889. ETC. 14 July 1896. Prop. McCall QC. Sec. McKeand. Manchester Chambers; 4 St James's Square, 1890-1892; 23 King Street, 1897; 78 King Street, 1898-1911; 42 Spring Gardens, 1912-1914. Preston Chambers; 1 Chapel Walk, 1891-1897; Bank Chambers, 1898-1920. London Chambers; 15 Old Square; 2 New Square. Lancs. Chancery Court. OBE 1919.

MANSON, Keith
G. November 1964. 4th floor, Sunlight House, Quay Street, Manchester, 1976-1979. No chambers address 1980.

MANTELL, Charles (Barrie Knight) QC (The Rt. Hon. Lord Justice Mantell)

(DL)

Born 30 January 1937. Manchester Grammar School; Manchester University, LLM. Flying Officer, Royal Air Force, 1958-1961. G. May 1960; Bencher 1990. 3 King's Bench Walk, 1961. Pupilmaster T. Ian Payne. ETC. 1962. Circuit Junior, 1966. Manchester Chambers at; 40 Kennedy Street, 1962-1965; Ship Canal House, 1966-1973; 4th floor, Astley House, Quay Street, 1974-1977; 18 St John Street, 1978-1982. Recorder 1978-1982. Silk 1979. Judge, Supreme Court, Hong Kong, 1982-1985. Circuit Judge, 1985-1990. High Court Judge, Queens Bench Division, 1990-1997. Presiding Judge, Western Circuit, 1993-1996. Lord Justice of Appeal, 1 October 1997-23 March 2004. Kt. 1990. PC 1997. He presided over one of the most notorious trials of the century, that of Rosemary West in October 1995. She was convicted of murdering ten people. Her husband Fred, also charged, hanged himself in Winston Green Prison on New Years Day 1995. Kt. 1990. PC 1997. Judge of Appeal, Jersey and Guernsey, 2004. WW.

MANTELL, Sir John Iles
Born 1 December 1813. Eldest son of George Mantell, MD., of Faringdon, Berks. AAS. M. 1 November 1841. Call 18 June 1847. Queen's Advocate, Gambia, 1841-1847. Chief Justice, Gambia, 1847-1866. Kt., 9 August 1867. Stipendiary Magistrate for Division of Manchester & Borough of Salford, 1869-1879. Not in 1894 Law List.

MAQSOOD, Kalsoom
Born 6 October 1975, Blackburn. Sister of Zabeda Maqsood qv. Queen Park High School, Blackburn; Blackburn College; Nottingham Trent University, LLB, 1997. M. 8 October 1998. Research Officer, May 1999-August 2000. ETC. December 2000. Prop. Jonathan Foster QC. Sec. Nigel Poole. 18 St John Street, Manchester, September, 2000-2004. 3 Paper Buildings, 1 February 2004.

MAQSOOD, Zabeda Khartoon
Born 22 July 1974. Sister of Kalsoom Maqsood qv. LLB (Derby) G. 28 November 1996. ETC. 16 December 1997. Prop. Richard Henriques QC. Sec. Stephen Dodds. Pupilmaster, Paul Hart. 15 Winckley Square, Preston, September 1997.

MARCHINGTON, John Mellor
Born 9 April 1911 Stockport. Son of John & Nellie Marchington. Married to Margaret Helena Marchington of Kerridge, Cheshire. Manchester University, LLB. G. 13 June 1934. ETC. 27 February 1935. Prop. Lynskey KC. Sec. Jolly. 60 King Street, Manchester, 1936-1940. Enlisted 2 July 1940. Commissioned, Pilot Officer, RAFVR on 23 August 1941. Navigator of a Vickers Wellington of 27 Operational Training Unit which was lost at sea whilst en route to the Middle East on 9 January 1942. (32 years old). Runnymeade Memorial, Surrey. (Panel 70) at Cooper's Hill. 4 miles from Windsor on A308 to Egham. Information supplied by RAF, Personal Management Agency and Commonwealth War Graves Commission.

MARDER, Bernard Arthur QC (His Honour Judge Marder QC)
Born 25 September 1928. Bury Grammar School; Manchester University, LLB, 1951. G. July 1952. Pupilmaster, John Platts-Mills. London Chambers; 1 Harcourt Buildings, 1952-1953; 2 Pump Court, 1954-1956; 2 Paper Buildings, 1957-1960. 10 King's Bench Walk, 1961-1969; Gray's Inn Chambers, 1970-1980; 4-5 Gray's Inn Square, 1981-1983. Manchester Chambers; 60 King Street, 1955-1956; 36 St Ann Street, 1957-1969. Silk 1977. Recorder 1979-1983. Circuit Judge, 1983-1998. President, Lands Tribunal, 1993-1998. WW.

MARGOLIS, Morris
MA. L. 20 April 1921. ETC. 21 February 1923. Prop. Ashton KC. Sec. Jordan. 4 Paper Buildings, 1923; Farrars Building, 1924-1930; 6 Pump Court, 1931-1951. Advocate in HBM's Consular Courts in Egypt. Not in 1953 Law List.

MARKHAM, Andrea
Born 26 July 1971 Darwen, Lancs. Pleckgate High School, Blackburn; Cardiff University, LLB. G. 12 October 2000. ETC. 19 March 2002. Prop. David Steer QC. Sec. Deborah Lambert. Kenworthy's Chambers, 83 Bridge Street, Manchester, 1 October 2001.

MARKS, Richard Leon QC
Born 20 November 1953 Southport. Clifton College; Manchester University, LLB. G. July 1975. ETC. 1975. Pupilmaster, Helen Grindrod. Same Manchester Chambers at; Ship Canal House, King Street, 1975-1980; 2 Old Bank Street, 1981-1991; Peel Court Chambers, 45 Hardman Street, 1992. Assistant Recorder 1991. Recorder 1994. Silk 1999. President, Restricted Patients Panel, Mental Health Review Tribunal, 2000.

MARRIOTT, George Martin
Born 4 July 1952 Bramhall, 1st son of Roger Howard Marriott, engineer. King's School, Macclesfield; Hull University, LLB. AAS. M. 14 January 1974. Call 17 July 1975. Manchester Chambers; 67 Princess Street, 1977; Lawrence Buildings, 2 Mount Street, 1978-1981. Not in 1982 Bar Directory.

MARRS, Andrew Charles
Born 10 May 1965, Manchester. Birley High School; St Peter's Oxford, BA. I. November 1995. Pupilmaster, Cassidy. Kenworthy's Building, 83 Bridge Street, Manchester, 1995.

MARSDEN, Frederick John
Born 1845. Eldest son of Lt. Col. Frederick Carlton Marsden, CB. Rugby. Late 1st Royal East Middlesex Militia. AAS. I. 13 November 1865. Call 6 June 1868. ETC. 4 August 1868. Prop. Aspland QC. Sec. Baylis. No chambers address, 1876-1929. Private residence; Colne House, East Colne, Essex. Chief Magistrate, Calcutta. Not in 1930 Law List. Foster.

MARSH, Alfred
Born 1874. Only son of John Ranson Marsh of Wigton, analytical chemist. AAS. M. 10 December 1910. Call 17 November 1913. 11 King's Bench Walk, 1917-1934. No address, 1935-1953. Not in 1954 Law List.

MARSH, John
Born 23 June 1953 Bradford. Marple Hall Grammar School; Coventry University, BA. G, 14 July 1977. ETC. 23 May 1985. Prop. Brian Carter QC. Sec. Francis Coles. Pupilmaster, Victor Williamson. Manchester Chambers; 6th floor, Sunlight House, 1982; Central Street, 1982-1983; 121 Princess Street, 1983-1986; 3 Peter Street, 1986-1991; 3 Parsonage Gardens, 1991-1999; 5 John Dalton Street, 2000.

MARSHALL, Sir James CMG
Born 19 December 1829. Died 9 August 1889 aged 59. Exeter College, Oxford. AAS. L. 19 April 1865. Call 27 January 1868. ETC. 12 March 1868. Prop. Aspinall QC. Sec. Potter. He had a varied career as, curate, private tutor, teacher and Puisne Judge, later Chief Justice of the Gold Coast Colony. He retired in 1882 and was knighted, receiving CMG in 1887. DNB. Times, 14 August 1889.

MARSHALL, John
Born 14 May 1820. Eldest son of Thomas Harrison Marshall of Kingston-upon-Hull, shipowner. AAS. M. 25 April 1846. Call 23 November 1849. No chambers address, 1876-1890. Lancs. Chancery Court. Foster.

MARSHALL, Nicola Jane
M. October 1991. ETC 17 December 1992. Prop. Klevan QC. Sec. Webster. 16 Winckley Square, 1994. Stoke on Trent, 1997-1998. 40a Young Street, Manchester, 1999. No address, 2000-2001. Not in 2002 Bar Directory.

MARSHALL, Paul Robert
Born 19 February 1954. Manchester University, BEd. AAS. 24 October 1979. Call 23 November 1982. Manchester Chambers; 6th floor, Arkwright House, Parsonage Gardens, 1983-1986; 20 St Mary's Parsonage, 1987-1989; 3 Peter Street, 1990-1991; 18 Lloyd Street, 1992-1999; St John's Chambers, 2 St John Street, 2000.

MARSHALL, Thomas Frank
I. 29 June 1892. Liverpool Chambers; 8 Harrington Street, 1895-1908; 25 Lord Street, 1909-1914. Not in 1915 Law List.

MARTIN, Gerard James QC
Born 27 May 1955, Blackpool. St Joseph's College, Blackpool; Trinity Hall, Cambridge, MA. AAS. M. 4 January 1977. Harmsworth Scholar. Call 27 July 1978. ETC. 26 October 1978. Pupilmaster, Michael Shorrock. Same Liverpool Chambers at; 606 The Corn Exchange, Fenwick Street, 1978-1981; 1 Exchange Flags, Dale Street, 1982-1991; Exchange Chambers, Derby Square, 1992. Recorder & Silk, 2000.

MARTIN, John Vandeleur QC
Born 17 January 1948. Malvern College; Pembroke College, Cambridge, MA. L. July 1972; Bencher 1999. Circuit Junior, 1975. 14 Cook Street, Liverpool, 1974-1981; 3 New Square, 1982-1993; Wilberforce Chambers, 8 New Square, 1994. Silk 1991. Deputy High Court Judge, Chancery Division, 1993. WW.

MARTIN, Rachael Christina
BA (Sussex); LLM (Leics). I. November 1991. Manchester Chambers; 6th floor, Sunlight House, Quay Street, 1993-1994; 38 Young Street, 1995-1998. Admitted as a solicitor, 1998. Bobbetts Mackan, solicitors, Bristol, 2002.

MARTIN, Sir (Robert) Bruce QC
Born 2 November 1938. Shrewsbury School; Liverpool University, LLB 1959. AAS. M. 23 October 1956. Call February 1960. Liverpool Chambers; 14 Cook Street, 1961-1972; Peel House, Harrington Street, 1973-1986. Silk 1977. Recorder 1978-1986. Chairman, Bob Martin Co., since 1980. Vice Chairman, Mersey RHA, 1986-1988 (Member 1983-1988); Chairman, North West RHA, 1988-1994; Kt. 1992.Chairman, NHS Litigation Service, 1996-1999. WW.

MASON, Albert George Turner
Died September 1978. I. June 1950. Liverpool Chambers; 34 Castle Street, 1951-1955; Corn Exchange, Fenwick Street, 1956; 11 New Square, 1957; No address, 1958-1961; 17 North John Street, 1962-1964; No address, 1965-1968; 7 Rumford Street, 1969; 34 Castle Street, 1970-1972; Queen Avenue, 1973; 41 North John Street, 1974-1978; 14 Dale Street, 1978.

MASON, Alfred Victor
Born 1867. 2nd son of Thomas Mason of Colne, mill owner. Merton College, Oxford; AAS. M. 14 November 1890. Call 17 November 1893. ETC. 1 March 1894. Prop. Leese QC. Sec. Sharpe. 2 King's Bench Walk, 1895-1898; 3 Hare Court, 1899-1903; joined North Eastern Circuit with chambers at 23 Cheapside, Bradford. No address, 1941-1949. Not in 1950 Law List.

MASON, George
Born 1854. 3rd son of George Mason of Staffordshire. Jesus College, Cambridge, MA, 1881. AAS. I. 20 March 1877. Call 26 January 1880. ETC. 2 February 1880. Prop. Edwards QC. Sec. Collins. 13 South King Street, Manchester, 1881-1905. No address, 1906-1940. Not in 1941 Law List. Foster.

MASSEY, Stella Marie
BA (Oxon). M. February 1990. Manchester Chambers; 211, Deansgate, 1992-1996; Garden Court North Chambers, 1 Booth Street, 1997-1999; Central Chambers, 89 Princess Street, 2000.

MASSEY, Thomas
Born 18 November 1835. 3rd son of Richard Massey of Altrincham. Owen's College, Manchester. AAS. L. 11 November 1872. AAS. I. 10 June 1873. Call L. 7 June 1875. 56 Chancery Lane, 1876-1882; 12 Old Square, 1883-1895; 15 Old Square, 1897. No address, 1898-1924. Not in 1925 Law List. Foster.

MASSEY, Wayne Richard
BA. Leeds Chambers, 1987. No address, 1988-1993. Senior Crown Prosecutor, Stockport, 1994. Manchester Chambers; 211 Deansgate, 1995-1996; 3 The Parsonage, 1997-1999; 2001. Central Building, 2000.

MATES, (Thomas) Rory
Born 10 September 1963 Hanover, Germany. Stanbridge Earls; Metropolitan Police, 1982-1989. University of Kent at Canterbury, BA. M. October 1992. ETC. 21 December 1993. Prop. Nigel Gilmour QC. Sec. Peter Gregory. Liverpool Chambers; Peel House, Harrington Street, 1993-1998; 42 Castle Street, 1998-2002. Passed Californian Bar Examinations and has joined Brayton Purcell, Attorneys of San Francisco. Publication; Schofield's Election Law, 2nd edition.

MATHER, Alison Elisabeth
Born 8 October 1972, Wigan. St Peter's High School, Orrell; Lady Margaret Hall, Oxford, MA. L. 9 October 1997. ETC. 6 April 2000. Prop. Webster. Sec. Grennan. Kenworthy's Buildings, 83 Bridge Street, Manchester, January 2000.

MATHER, Harold
L. 17 November 1897. ETC. 16 February 1898. Prop. Pickford QC. Sec. Horridge. Liverpool Chambers; 8 Harrington Street, 1898-1900; 4 Harrington Street, 1901-1911; 9 Cook Street, 1912-1932. Lancs. Chancery Court. Not in 1933 Law List.

MATHIESON, Guy Alastair David
Born 2 November 1968 Edgeworth. Stepson of Rt. Hon. Lady Justice Smith DBE qv. Bolton School; University College, Swansea, BA. M. October 1993. ETC. 7 December 1993. Prop. Charles Bloom QC. Sec. John Philips. 28 St John Street, Manchester, September 1993. (now St Johns Buildings Chambers).

MATTAR, Frederick

I. 26 January 1933. ETC. 27 February 1935. Prop. Maxwell Fyfe QC. Sec. Unsworth. 3 Elm Court, 1935-1940; 4 Paper Buildings, 1941-1952; 2 Harcourt Buildings, 1953-1967. Not in 1968 Law List. Oxford Circuit, 1948.

MATTHEWS, Henry Lumley

Born 1853. 2nd son of Henry Matthews of Middlesex. AAS. M. 27 October 1870. Call 10 May 1876. 5 Essex Court, 1877, 1885; 3 Garden Court, 1878-1879; 4 Essex Court, 1880-1882; 3 Elm Court, 1883, 1886-1889. Equity draftsman & conveyancer. No address, 1890-1935. Not in 1936 Law List.

MATTINSON, Sir Miles Walker KC, MP.

Born 26 December 1854. Died 29 February 1944 aged 89. AAS. G. 18 April 1874; Bacon Scholar; 1st class studentship; certificate of honour; Call 28 January 1877; Bencher 1891. ETC. 23 February 1877. Prop. Edwards QC. Sec. Henry. 7 Crown Office Row, 1877-1878; 1 Cloisters, 1879-1885; 1 Garden Court, 1886-1940. No address, 1941-1944. MP (C) Liverpool, Walton, 1888-1892. Recorder of Blackburn, 1886-1922. Silk 1896. Kt. 1922. Publications; Law of Corrupt Practices at Elections; Selection of Precedents in Pleadings. WW.

MATTISON, Andrew

Mattison and Lynch. Funchal. February 2005.

Born 11 November 1941. Liverpool College; Liverpool University, LLB. G. November 1963. ETC. 1963. Pupilmaster, Monty Dovenor. Liverpool Chambers; 9 Rumford Street, 1963-1973; Fruit Exchange, Victoria Street, 1974-1991; Chavasse Court, 24 Lord Street, 1992-2001. Retired from practice December 2001.

MATUK, Helen Antoinette

Born 3 January 1967 Barnsley. Wakefield Girls' High School; Liverpool Polytechnic (now Liverpool John Moores University), LLB. G. July 1990. ETC. 1990. Prop. J J Rowe QC. Sec. Cynthia Pilling. 58 King Street Chambers, 51-53 South King Street, Manchester, 1994.

MAWDSLEY, David John

Born 20 September 1955, Liverpool. St Bonadventures, Liverpool; Liverpool John Moores University, LLB; University of East Anglia, BA (Modern History). G. November 1995. 6 Gray's Inn Road, 1997-1998. New Bailey Chambers, Liverpool, 1999.

MAWDSLEY, Matthew Edward

Born 2 November 1968 Manchester. Meole Brace, Shrewsbury; Manchester University, LLB. I. November 1991. ETC. February 1992. Prop. Richard Clegg QC. Sec. John Wishart. Manchester Chambers; Manchester House Chambers, 18-22 Bridge Street, 1991-1998; 38 Young Street, 1999-2001; 28 St John Street, 2001 (merged with 24a to form St John's Building on 23 September 2002).

MAX MULLER, John Heiberg

I. 19 November 1934. ETC. 9 July 1935. Prop. Lynskey KC. Sec. Karmel. Lamb Building, 1935-1938; 2 Harcourt Buildings, 1939-1941; 3 Paper Buildings, 1942-1946. Not in 1947 Law List.

MAXWELL, His Honour Alexander Hyslop

Born 10 May 1864, Liverpool. Died 7 March 1957 aged 92. Uppingham. Formerly a solicitor. AAS. M. 21 October 1886. Call 3 July 1889. ETC. 29 July 1889. Prop. Gully QC. Sec. Pickford. Circuit Junior, Winter 1890. Liverpool Chambers; Marldon Chambers, 30 North John Street, 1890-1895; Stephenson's Chambers, 25 Lord Street, 1896-1920. London Chambers; 2 Pump Court, 1904-1915; 2 Mitre Court Buildings 1916-1920. County Court Judge, Circuit 55, (Dorset, Hants., Somerset & Wilts), February 1920-1937. WW.

MAXWELL, Elaine (Mrs Goldman)
G. May 1955. Pupilmaster Bertram Benas. 14 Cook Street, Liverpool 1955-1968. Tribunal Chairman. Provided me with much useful information on her pupilmaster.

MAXWELL, Eric Frederick Mackenzie
I. 26 January 1910. ETC. 26 January 1911. Prop. Sanderson KC (for whom Ashton KC acted) Sec. Eustace Hills (for whom Brocklebank acted). Library Chambers, Temple, 1911-1924; Goldsmith Building & 27 Palace Chambers, Bridge Street, Westminster, 1925-1927; 3 Paper Buildings, 1928-1935; 4 Paper Buildings, 1936-1955; No address, 1956-1962; 2 King's Bench Walk (non practising), 1964-1970.

MAXWELL, John Joseph
Born 30 January 1950. St Francis Xaviers College, Liverpool; Liverpool Polytechnic (now Liverpool John Moores University) BA. I. July 1985. ETC. 22 May 1986. Prop. Michael Maguire QC. Sec. J V B Mockett. Liverpool Chambers; 2nd floor, Fruit Exchange, Victoria Street 1986-1988; 3rd floor, 46 Stanley Street 1988-1994. Manchester Chambers; Old Colony House, 6 South King Street, Manchester 1995-2001; Young Street Chambers, 2001.

MAXWELL, Michael Wyatt
Born 18 August 1915. I. November 1939. South Eastern Circuit. Pupilmasters, R C Vaughan & C L Henderson. 1 Garden Court, 1942-1945; Goldsmith Building, 1946-1951. Member of the Bar of Singapore & the Federation of Malaya, 1951-1964. ETC 1965. Liverpool Chambers; 17 North John Street, 1965-1970; 34 Castle Street, 1971-1972; Queen Avenue, Castle Street, 1973-1980. Retired from practice. Governor of two Liverpool schools.

MAXWELL, Walter
Born 1857. Youngest son of Lawrence Maxwell of Haslingden, Lancs. AAS. M. 11 January 1881. Call 17 November 1883. ETC. 28 January 1884. Prop. Collins QC. Sec. Nash. Manchester Chambers; 78 Cross Street, 1884-1891; 37 Brazennose Street, 1892-1897. Not in 1898 Law List.

MAYER, Sylvain KC
Born 9 August 1863. Died 13 September 1948 aged 85. University College School; University College, London, BA; Heidelberg University, PhD. AAS. M. 1 November 1884. Call 22 June 1887. Also, member, Grays. ETC. 7 August 1893. Prop. Shee QC. Sec. Mattinson. 1 Garden Court, 1887-1948. Silk 1913. Publications; Wrote "Papa's Honeymoon" (Criterion Theatre), 1890 & "A Gay Widower" (Vaudeville Theatre), 1892. Text books on Rating, Agricultural Holdings & Compensation; Reminiscences of a KC: Theatrical & Legal, 1924. WW.

MAYNARD-CONNOR, Giles
Born 6 August 1970 Doncaster. Queen Elizabeth Grammar School, Wakefield; Lancaster University (Central College), LLB. I. 24 November 1992. ETC. 1993. Prop. Anthony Elleray QC. Sec. Mark Cawson. Manchester Chambers; St James's Chambers, 68 Quay Street, 1992-2001; Exchange Chambers, 4 Ralli Courts, West Riverside, 15 March 2001.

MAZZAG, Anthony James
Born 18 July 1973, Essex. St Thomas Moore School, Westcliff, Essex; Sheffield University, MA. L. November 1996. ETC 1997. Prop. Shorrock QC. Sec. Christopher Melton. Peel Court Chambers, 45 Hardman Street, Manchester, 1997.

MEADOWCROFT, Stephen
Born 16 November 1945 Altrincham. North Cestrian Grammar School; G. November 1973. Manchester Chambers; Ship Canal House, King Street, 1973-1980; 2 Old Bank Street, 1981-1991; Peel Court Chambers, 45 Hardman Street, 1992.

MELLISH, Rt. Hon. Sir George
Born 19 December 1814. Died 15 June 1877 aged 62. Son of Edward Mellish, Dean of Hereford. Eton; University College, Oxford, MA., DCL; Hon Fellow 1872. Special pleader, 1840-1848. I. 17 June 1848; Bencher & Silk 1861; Reader 1875. Declined puisne judgeship. Lord Justice of Appeal, 1870-1877. PC 1870.

MELLOR, Frank Hamilton CBE., QC (His Honour Judge Hamilton CBE., QC).
Born 13 May 1854. Died 26 April 1925 aged 70. 10th son of Rt. Hon. Sir John Mellor. Brother of Sir James Mellor, Senior Master of the Supreme Court. Cheltenham College; Trinity College, Cambridge, BA, 1877; MA, 1889. AAS. L. 5 November 1877. AAS. I. 3 November 1880. Call 17 November 1880. ETC. 29 July 1882. Prop. Gully QC. Sec. McConnell. 2 Dr Johnson's Buildings, 1883; 3 Dr Johnson's Buildings, 1884-1898; 4 Paper Buildings, 1899-1911. Recorder of Preston, 1898-1921. Silk 1903. County Court Judge, Circuit 8, March 1911-1925. CBE 1918. Publications; Short & Mellor's Crown Office Practice. WW.

MELLOR, George Henry
Born 19 January 1853. 4th son of James Mellor of Liverpool, brewer. Lincoln College, Oxford, MA., BCL. AAS. L. 30 May 1874. Call 17 November 1877. ETC. 13 February 1879. Prop. Roscoe. Sec. J Williams. Equity draftsman & conveyancer. Lancs. Chancery Court. 89 Chancery Lane, 1878-1881; 2 Pump Court, 1882-1885. Liverpool Chambers; 18 Hunter Street, 1878; 11 South John Street, 1879-1880. No address, 1886-1909. Not in 1910 Law List.

MELSHEIMER (MELSOM), Rudolph Eyre
Born 1851. Only son of Rudolph Melsheimer of Blackheath, Kent. Trinity College, Cambridge, BA, 1872. AAS. I. 24 January 1871. Call 17 November 1874. ETC. 16 March 1875. Prop. Temple QC. Sec. Smyly. 7 Crown Office Row & 10 St James Square, Manchester, 1876; 2 Harcourt Buildings, 1877-1882; 2 Plowden Buildings, 1883-1894. Bombay, 1895-1919. Not in 1920 Law List. Publications; Editor of; Jervis, Office & Duties of a Coroner; of Atkinson, Office of Sheriff; The Law of Bills of Exchange; joint author of Law & Custom of the Stock Exchange. Foster.

MELTON, Christopher QC
Born 15 November 1958 Manchester. Manchester Grammar School; Bristol University, LLB. G. July 1982. ETC. December 1982. Prop. John Hugill QC. Sec. Nick Simmonds. Manchester Chambers; 2 Old Bank Street, 1982-1991; Peel Court Chambers, 45 Hardman Street, 1992-2001. Silk 2001. 25 Byrom Street, 2001. Counsel to the Shipman Inquiry. Deputy High Court Judge. WW.

MENARY, Andrew Gwyn QC
Born 29 March 1959, Enniskillen, Northern Ireland. Rodway High School, Bristol; Central London Polytechnic, BA. I. November 1982. 2 Garden Court, 1982-1983. Pupilmaster, Paul Randolf. ETC. 1983. Liverpool Chambers; Martins Buildings, Water Street, 1983-1999; 7 Harrington Street (merger with Corn Exchange), 6.9.1999. Recorder 2001. Silk 2003.

MERCER, David Paul
BA (Oxon). L. July 1980. Manchester Chambers; 43 King Street, 1981-1988; 5 John Dalton Street, 1989.

MERCER, Ian Stuart
Born 22 October 1976 Liverpool. Fairfield High School, Widnes; Officer in Royal Navy, 1996-1997. Liverpool John Moores University, LLB. L. 11 October 2001. ETC. 18 December 2001. Prop. David Steer QC. Sec. Philip Hall. Chavasse Court, 24 Lord Street, October 2001.

MERRIMAN, Rt Hon. Sir Frank Boyd QC, MP (First Baron Merriman of Knutsford)
Born 28 April 1880. Died 18 January 1962 aged 81. Winchester. I. 15 June 1904; Bencher 1927; Deputy Treasurer, 1949. ETC. 14 July 1904. Prop. Taylor KC. Sec. Maurice Hill. Pupilmaster, Gordon Hewart. Circuit Junior, Summer 1905. Manchester Chambers; 5 St James's Square, 1904-1911; 51 South King Street, 1912-1914 & 1918-1919. Served, 1914-1918 War; Deputy Assistant Adjutant General, 1917-1918; Depatches thrice & OBE 1918. Silk 1919. 6 Crown Office Row, 1919-1921; Farrars Building, 1922-1933. Recorder of Wigan, 1920-1928. MP (C) Manchester, Rusholme, 1924-1933. Solicitor General, 1928-1929 & 1932-1933. Kt. 1928. PC 1933. President, Probate, Divorce & Admiralty Division of the High Court of Justice, 1933-1962. Baron 1941. GCVO 1950. WW.

MERSEY, Viscount (See John Charles Bigham)

METCALF, Louise Karen
Born 23 June 1974, Hartlepool. High Tunstall Comprehensive School, Hartlepool; Hartlepool VI Form College; St Peter's College, Oxford, BA (Modern History). I. October 1997. Pupillage, 1 Crown Office Row, 1997-1998; pupilmasters, William Edis & David Hart. ETC. December 1998. Prop. Tim Holroyde QC. Sec. Christopher Cornwall. Exchange Chambers, Pearl Assurance House, Derby Square, Liverpool, 1998.

METCALFE, Herbert
Born 10 October 1887. Died 30 October 1940 aged 53. Son of James Metcalfe of Walton-le-Dale. Private education. Newspaper journalist. G. 24 June 1914. Lt., Lancs. Fusiliers & East Lancs. Regt., 1914-1918. 3 Elm Court, 1918; 4 Crown Office Row, 1919; Fountains Court, 1920-1929. Metropolitan Magistrate (Greenwich & Woolwich and at Old Street), 1 August 1929-1940.

METCALFE, Ian Michael
Born 5 September 1962, Penwortham, Preston. King Edward VII School, Lytham St Annes; Kings College, London, LLB. AAS. M. 24 January 1984. Call 26 November 1985. Pupillage; 1 Essex Court; pupilmasters, Nigel Rumfitt & Adrian Redgrave. ETC. 1987. Prop. David Poole QC. Sec. Howard Baisden. Same Manchester Chambers at; 67 Princess Street, 1986-1987; Hollins Chambers, 64a Bridge Street, 1987-1997; Cobden House Chambers, 19 Quay Street, 1997.

MEYER, Charles Julius
I. 17 November 1893. ETC. 16 March 1895. Prop. Bigham QC. Sec. Lawrence. Liverpool Chambers; 5 Cook Street, 1896-1908; 8 Harrington Street, 1909-1925. Equity draftsman & conveyancer. Not in 1926 Law List.

MICHOLLS, Sydney Philip
Born 1849. 2nd son of Henry Micholls of Manchester. New College, Oxford, BA, 1871. AAS. I. 22 November 1870. Call 26 January 1875. ETC. 16 March 1875. Prop. Temple QC. Sec. J Edge. 3 King's Bench Walk, 1877-1896. No address, 1897-1935. Not in 1936 Law List.

MILES, Nicola
Born 29 September 1976 Manchester. Knutsford High School; Leicester University, LLB. L. 14 October 1999. ETC. 16 December 1999. Prop. David Steer QC. Sec. Andrew Loveridge. 7 Harrington Street, Liverpool September, 1999.

MILLARD, Jonathan Neil
BSc (Aston). G. July 1984. 28 St John Street, Manchester, 1988-1989. Went into the Church. Now Rev. Jonathan Millard.

MILLER, Alexander (Sandy) Barrett
Born 1908. First son of Alexander Thomas Miller KC qv. Wadham College, Oxford. AAS. M. 14 January 1929. Call 8 June 1932. ETC. 1 February 1933. Prop. Goldie KC. Sec. Graham. Circuit Junior, Summer 1933. Lamb Building, 1933. 25 Castle Street, Liverpool, 1938-1955. No address, 1956-1963. Not in 1964 Law List.

MILLER, Alexander Thomas KC
Born 14 October 1875. Died 1 March 1942 aged 66. Eldest son of Alexander Allan Miller of Liverpool, solicitor. Father of Alexander Barrett Miller qv. Parkfield School, Liverpool; Brighton College; Liverpool University. Solicitor 1899. Lecturer, Liverpool University. AAS. M. 5 March 1908. Call 1 July 1908; Bencher 1927; Reader, Autumn 1938. 25 Lord Street, Liverpool, 1910-1919. Silk 1919. 2 Mitre Court Buildings, 1919-1921; Lamb Building, 1922-1942. WW.

MILLER, Alison Jane
Born 20 October 1975 Birkenhead. Wirral County Grammar School for Girls; Liverpool University, LLB. I. 14 October 1999. ETC. 16 December 1999. Prop. Andrew Edis QC. Sec. Nick Riddle. 14 Castle Street / Atlantic Chambers, Cook Street, Liverpool, September 1999.

MILLER, Robert Ormiston
BA (Oxon). I. July 1987. 14 Castle Street, Liverpool, 1988-1998. No address 1999. Not in 2000 Bar Directory.

MILLER, William
Born 8 December 1864 Wigton, Cumberland. Died 23 October 1945 aged 80. Rugby; Hertford College, Oxford, MA. Journalist and expert on Mediaeval & Modern Greek & Balkan History; FBA; FRHisS; Hon LLD (Athens). Numerous books on Greek & Balkan History. I. 28 January 1889. ETC. 21 February 1890. Prop. Gully QC. Sec. Dickinson. 5 Paper Buildings, 1891-1892; 2 Dr Johnson's Building, 1893-1896. No address, 1897-1940. Retired to South Africa. WW. DNB.

MILLERS, Harold Cuthbert Townley TD
Born 11 September 1903. Died 28 February 1968 aged 64. Wrekin; London University, BA. Preparatory schoolmaster, 1925-1931. G. 17 November 1931. ETC. 17 February 1932. Prop. Jackson KC. Sec. Butlin. 60 King Street, Manchester, 1932-1939. Lancashire Fusiliers (TA), 1936-1939; RA, 1939-1942; General Staff in Middle East, 1942-1945; Legal Advisor to BMA, Dodecanese, 1945. District Registrar, Manchester, 1946-1948. Registrar, Probate, Divorce & Admiralty Division of the Supreme Court, Somerset House, 1949-1968. WW.

MILLS, Frederick Hellewell
I. 28 January 1895. ETC. 14 March 1895. Prop. Pickford QC. Sec. Horridge. No address, 1895-1938. Not in 1935 Law List.

MILLS, John Saxon
I. 17 May 1905. ETC. 20 July 1905. Prop. Pickford KC. Sec. Sutton. 60 King Street, Manchester, 1907-1910. No address, 1911-1929. Not in 1930 Law List.

MILLS, (Reginald) Stuart
Born 2 February 1968. Liverpool Institute Grammar School for Boys; Liverpool John Moores University, LLB. Court Assistant/Court Clerk, Liverpool City Magistrates Court, 1985-1991. M. 13 October 1992. Fleet Street Chambers (now Furnival Chambers), 1991-1992. ETC. 20 December 1994. Prop. David Harris QC. Sec. John Leach. Liverpool Chambers; 24 Fenwick Street, 1993-1999; 14 Cook Street, 1999-2000; Oriel Chambers, 14 Water Street, October 2000.

MILLS, William Haslam
Born 20 September 1874. Died 22 June 1930 aged 55. Manchester Grammar School. G. 24 April 1907. ETC. 1 March 1909. Prop. Ashton KC. Sec. Rhodes. 2 Booth Street, Manchester 1911-1913. He was a journalist and writer employed by the Manchester Guardian, rising to Chief Reporter, 1914-1919. Director of Public Information, Ministry of Health, 1919-1920. He wrote the Centenary History of The Manchester Guardian in 1921 and a History of the Manchester Reform Club, the following year. Although he died in 1930, his name appears in the Law List until 1953 which shows that the final entry does not always indicate death.

MILNE, Alfred
Born 1819. 4th son of Oswald Milne of Prestwich Wood, Lancs. Trinity College, Cambridge, BA 1842. AAS. I. 7 May 1840. Call 6 June 1845. 4 Garden Court, 1848; St James's Square, Manchester, 1876-1900. Not in 1901 Law List.

MILNE, (Walter) Geoffrey DL
I. 2 May 1928. ETC 1928. Pupilmaster Philip M Oliver. Circuit Junior, Winter 1929. 26 King Street, Manchester, 1928-1933. Winner of Carlisle Cup for Golf, 1930 & 1931. He left the Bar in 1933 and became a farmer in Gloucestershire. He was a major in the Royal Glos. Hussars, 1939-1945. Deputy Lt., Glos., 1959. Died in 1997.

MILNE-REDHEAD, George Bertram
Born 1867. 3rd son of Richard Milne-Redhead of Springfield, Seedley, Manchester qv. Trinity College, Cambridge, MA. AAS. M. 26 March 1888. Call 29 June 1892. ETC. 4 March 1893. Prop. Addison QC. Sec. McKeand. Circuit Junior, Summer 1893 & Winter 1894. 3 Lincoln's Inn Fields, 1894; 3 Essex Court, 1895-1897. No address, 1898-1949. Not in 1950 Law List.

MILNE-REDHEAD, Richard
Born 1828. Only son of John Redhead of Manchester. Father of George Bertram Milne-Readhead qv. No chambers address, 1876-1910. FRGS., FLS., JP; Lancs. & West Riding, Yorks. Not in 1911 Law List. Foster.

MILWARD, Clement QC
Born 20 August 1821. Died 26 October 1890 aged 69. 3rd son of Rear Admiral Clement Milward of Somerset. AAS. M. 7 November 1843. Call 6 November 1846; Bencher 1865; Reader Autumn 1869; Treasurer 1879. 1 Paper Buildings, 1848; Silk 1865. 7 Fig Tree Court, 1876-1880. No address, 1881-1890. Foster.

MINTZ, Simon Harold
Born 15 March 1956 Birmingham. Harold Malley Grammar School; Newcastle-upon-Tyne University, BA. A solicitor in Liverpool & Manchester, 1983-1996. I. 1 December 1996. ETC. 1996. Prop. David Turner QC. Sec. Alan Sims. Chavasse Court, 24 Lord Street, Liverpool. 1996.

MISCAMPBELL, Norman Alexander QC, MP
Born 20 February 1925. St Edwards School, Oxford; Trinity College, Oxford. I. 1952; Bencher 1983. ETC. 12 June 1958. Prop. Goldie QC. Sec. Feeny. Circuit Junior, 1952. Same Liverpool Chambers at; 49 Castle Street. 1952-1966; 606 Corn Exchange. 1967-1982; 1 Exchange Flags, Dale Street. 1983-1997. Silk 1974. London Chambers, 1 Temple Gardens. Recorder 1977-1995. Member, Hoylake UDC, 1955-1961. Contested (C) Newton, 1955, 1959. MP (C) Blackpool North. 1962-1992. Member, Criminal Injuries Compensation Board. 1993-2000. WW.

MITCHELL, Robert Armstrong
Born 1869. Eldest son of William Charles Mitchell of Belfast, distiller. Trinity College, Dublin, LLB. AAS. M. 15 January 1890. Call 14 June 1893. ETC. 15 March 1894. Irish Bar E. 1899. No chambers address, 1895-1949. Not in 1950 Law List.

MITCHELL, Thomas Jarleth David
MA (Oxon). L. October 1995. ETC. 21 December 1995. Prop. Keith Goddard QC. Sec. Smith. Dean's Court Chambers, Manchester, 1995. Liverpool Chambers; Corn Exchange, Fenwick Street, March, 1997-1999; Martins Building, 1999. 11 King's Bench Walk, 2000.

MITCHELL, Thomas John
Born 1834. 2nd son of Alexander Mitchell of Aberdeen. AAS. I. 14 January 1861. Call 17 November 1863. No address, 1876-1934. Not in 1935 Law List. Foster

MITCHELL, William
Born 1848. 2nd son of William Mitchell, JP of Montrose, merchant & shipowner. AAS. M. 11 January 1879. Call 3 May 1882. ETC. 2 February 1883. Prop. Gully QC. Sec. McCall. 8 King's Bench Walk, 1886. 6 Pump Court, 1887-1889; 5 Essex Court, 1890; Lamb Building, 1891-1894; 1 Brick Court, 1895-1903; 1 Pump Court, 1905-1907. Not in 1908 Law List.

MOCATTA, Alan Abraham OBE., QC (The Hon. Mr Justice Mocatta)
Born 27 June 1907. Died 1 November 1990 aged 83. Clifton College; New College, Oxford, MA. I. 27 January 1930; Bencher 1960; Treasurer 1982. ETC. 17 February 1932. Prop. Hemmerde KC. Sec. Rhodes. 3 Essex Court, 1930-1939. Served War, 1939-1945; in field and rising to Lt. Col. In War Office. OBE 1944. 3 Essex Court, 1945-1961. Silk 1951. High Court Judge, Queen's Bench Division, 1961-1981. Kt. 1961. Member, Restrictive Practices Court, 1961-1981 (President, 1970-1981). President, Board of Elders, Spanish & Portuguese Jews Congregation, London, 1967-1982. Publications; Joint editor 14th-19th editions of Scrutton on Charterparties; Editor, 3rd edition, Rowlatt on Principal & Surety. WW.

MOCKETT, John Vere Brooke
G. February 1958. 4 Paper Buildings, 1958-1960; 3 Hare Court, 1961-1964; 3 King's Bench Walk, 1965-1967; 5 Essex Court, 1968; Office of DPP, 1969; Post Office Chambers, 26 Brown Street, Manchester, 1970-1971; Liverpool Chambers; 9 Rumford Street, 1972-1973; Queen Insurance Building, 13 Castle Street, 1974-1976; 41 North John Street, 1977-1978; 15 Victoria Street, 1979-1989; 46 Stanley Street, 1990-1996. Judge of Court of First Instance & Stipendiary Magistrate, Gibraltar, 1996-2001.

MOHYUDDIN, David Niaz
Born 18 September 1975, Lahore, Pakistan. Bolton School (Boys Division); Birmingham University, LLB. L. 14 October 1999. ETC. December 2000. Prop. Anthony Elleray QC. Sec. Maynard-Connor. Pupilmaster, Sterling. Manchester Chambers; St James's Chambers, 68 Quay Street, 2000-2001; Exchange Chambers; 4 Ralli Courts, West Riverside, 5 March 2001.

MOIR, John Lowndes
Born 1883. Physician and surgeon. AAS. M. 25 May 1932. Call 15 May 1935. ETC. 13 July 1938. Prop. Pritchard KC. Sec. Lloyd. No chambers address. Not in 1945 Law List.

MOLESWORTH, (George) Bagot (Gossett) Francis Richard Pigot
Born 23 January 1853. Eldest son of Francis Molesworth, Rector of St Mary's Church, Cambs. King's College, Cambridge, BA, 1875. Maths. Lecturer, 1875-1876. AAS. L. 2 May 1876. Call 25 June 1879. ETC. 2 August 1879. Prop. Herschell QC. Sec. Gully QC. 2 Plowden Buildings, 1881-1882. No address, 1883-1921. Not in 1922 Law List. Foster.

MOLYNEUX, Pauline Ann
LLB. G. June 1961. ETC 1961. 49 Castle Street, 1961-1965. British Council, Lima, Peru, 1966-1967. College of Law, 1972-1977. Not in 1978 Law List.

MONAGHAN, Mark Terence
Born 24 August 1964 Rochdale. Bolton School; Sheffield University, LLB. L. July 1987. ETC. 1988. Prop. Keith Goddard QC. Sec. John Broadley. Same Manchester Chambers; Hollins Chambers, 1988-1997; Cobden House Chambers, 19 Quay Street, 1998.

MONROE, Hubert Holmes QC
Born 2 July 1920. Died 5 June 1982 aged 61. Only son of Sir James Harvey Munroe KC, late Judge of the High Court, Lahore, India. Dragon School; Rugby; Corpus Christi College, Oxford, MA. Major, Royal Artillery, War of 1939-1945. AAS. M. 13 September 1945; Harmsworth Scholar; Call 26 January 1948; Bencher 1965. ETC. 4 March 1954. Prop. Brabin QC. Sec. Cantley. 2 Plowden Buildings, 1948-1953; 4 Pump Court, 1954-1971. Silk 1960. Special Commissioner of Income Tax, 1973-1982; Presiding Commissioner from 1977. Hon. Treasurer, Senate of the Inns of Court & Bar, 1975-1977. Hamlyn Lecturer, 1981 (Intolerable Inquisition? Reflections on the Law of Tax). WW.

MONTGOMERY, Arthur Hope
I. 17 November 1891. ETC. 7 March 1893. Prop. Gully QC. Sec. Bradbury. Manchester Chambers; 51 King Street, 1894-1897; 78 King Street, 1898-1948. Not in 1950 Law List.

MONTGOMERY, (Robert) Michael
Born 3 March 1941, Liverpool. Died 6 September 1998 aged 57. Son of Robert Zeeland Hollis Montgomery qv. Holt School, Liverpool; St Catharine's College, Cambridge, MA (German & Polish). BBC, 1962-1972; language supervisor in Polish Section; Deputy Head of Czech Service; Head of Brazilian Service; finally, in charge of the Central Book Unit in Bush House. I. July 1972. ETC 1972. Liverpool Chambers; 41 North John Street, 1973-1974; Fruit Exchange, Victoria Street, 1974-1988. Serious Fraud Office, 1988-1990. 3 Pump Court, 1990-1998. Standing Counsel to the Department of Trade & Industry Appeals Tribunals. Senior Adjudicator at the Immigration Appeals Court. Chairman, Social Security Tribunals. Times Obituary, 6 October 1998.

MONTGOMERY, Robert Zeeland Hollis
father of Michael Montgomery qv. Died 1989 aged c80. Served in Germany in War of 1939-1945. G. February 1952. Liverpool Chambers; the Temple, Dale Street, 1953-1956; 27 Dale Street, 1957-1976; Melbourne Buildings, North John Street, 1977-1988; Peel House, Harrington Street, 1989. Tenacious prosecutor. He had a dog called "Ricky." Judge Keith Lawton allowed "Ricky" to sit at Monty's feet in Court at Sessions House, Liverpool on the basis that the dog was likely to be less trouble than Monty.

MOODY, Norman Frederick
Formerly an Officer of Customs & Excise. I. February 1957. ETC. 1957. 60 King Street, Manchester, 1957-1970. Joined North Eastern Circuit in 1971 with Chambers at 38 Park Square, Leeds. Deputy Chairman, Traffic Commissioners, Yorkshire Area, 1977-1984. Not in 1999 Bar Directory.

MOON, Edward Robert Pacy MP
Born 1858. Died 11 September 1949. Eldest son of Robert Moon of Inner Temple, barrister. Winchester; New College, Oxford, MA. AAS. I. 2 July 1881. Call. 7 May 1884. ETC. 27 January 1885. Prop. Henn Collins QC. Sec. Synnott. 6 New Square, 1886-1895. Equity draftsman & conveyancer. MP (C) St Pancras, 1895-1906. Publication; Four Weeks as Acting Commandant at the Belgian Field Hospital, 1915. WW.

MOON, Sir Ernest Robert KCB., QC

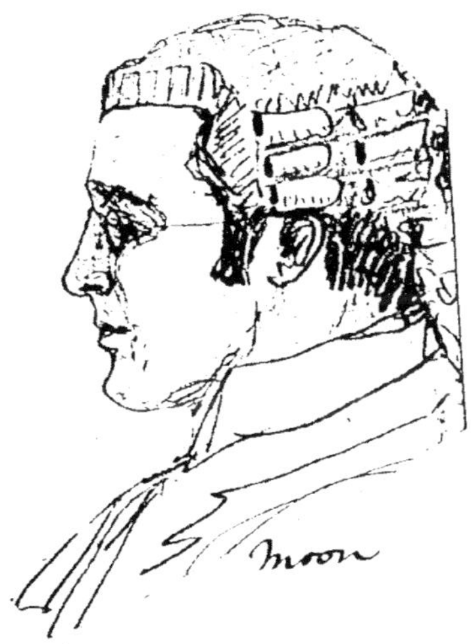

Born 21 June 1854. Died 31 May 1930 aged 75. 4th son of Sir Richard Moon, 1st Bt. Winchester; Trinity College, Cambridge, LLB, 1877. AAS. I. 19 March 1875. Call 18 November 1878; Bencher. ETC. 23 January 1880. Prop. Gully QC. Sec. Dickinson. 1 New Court, 1879; 2 Temple Gardens, 1880-1907. Silk 1902. Member of numerous Government boards & committees. Counsel to the Speaker of the House of Commons, 1908-1929. CB 1915. KCB 1919. WW. Foster.

MOORE, Andrew David
Born 23 February 1962. Godalming Grammar/6th Form College; Manchester University, BA., PhD. Solicitor, 1990-1996. I. November 1996. ETC. 1996. Prop. Martin Steiger QC. Sec. David Heaton. 18 St John Street, Manchester, 1996.

MOORE, Henry O'Hara
I. 6 June 1860. 5 Paper Buildings, 1876-1877. Liverpool Sessions & Liverpool Court of Passage. Not in 1878 Law List.

MOORE, Samuel
Born 1 December 1838. Eldest son of William Cameron Moore of Derbys. Trinity College, Cambridge, BA. AAS. L. 22 March 1879. Call 26 January 1882. 60 King Street, Manchester, 1883-1890; 2 Stone Buildings, 1891. Equity draftsman & conveyancer. Lancs. Chancery Court. Niger Territories, West Africa, 1892-1899. Returned to England 1900. No chambers address 1900-1920. Not in 1921 Law List.

MOORE, Stuart Archibald
Born September 1842. Died 29 June 1907 aged 64. 4th son of Barlow Brass Moore of South Lambeth, Surrey. Philological School, Marylebone Road. AAS. I. 24 January 1880. Call. 25 June 1884. ETC. 24 July 1885. Prop. Bigham QC. Sec. Henry. He must have left the Circuit because he was re-elected 9 July 1887. Prop. Littler QC. Sec. Page. 1 Serjeants Inn, 1885; 6 King's Bench Walk, 1887-1907. He is best known as a legal antiquary. His research and publications earned him a Times Obituary (6 July 1907) and an entry in DNB. Publications include; History of the Foreshore and claims relating thereto, 1888; Domesday Book for Northampton extended and translated, 1863. He was said to be one of the finest amateur seamen of his time; he commanded his own 80 ton fishing ketch, in which he carried the flag of the Vice-Commodore of the Royal Cruising Club all around Great Britain "with little regard for weather." DNB. Foster.

MOORE, Thomas
Born 1857. Only son of Edward Moore of Burnley. Jesus College, Cambridge, BA, 1880. AAS. I. 27 January 1879. Call 21 June 1882. ETC. 25 January 1884. Prop. Gully QC. Sec. Leese. No chambers address, 1885-1939. Not in 1940 Law List.

MOORE, William James
Born 1901. Eldest son of John Moore of Whitehaven. LLB (London); BSc (Liverpool). Schoolmaster in Rochdale. AAS. M. 29 October 1940. Call 7 July 1943. 26 King Street, Manchester, 1949-1954. No chambers address, 1955-1964. Not in 1965 Law List.

MORAN, Andrew Gerard QC.
Born 19 October 1953 Widnes. West Park Grammar School, St Helens; Britannia Royal Naval College, Dartmouth; Balliol College, Oxford, MA. Officer in Royal Navy, 1972-1976. G. November 1976. Bencher, Grays Inn 2005. ETC. 1977. Prop. Gerald Crowe QC. Sec. Alex Kennedy. Martins Building, Water Street, Liverpool, August 1976-April 1994. Assistant Recorder 1992. Silk 1994. Recorder 1995. 25 later 12 Byrom Street, Manchester, 1994, and at 22 Old Buildings. Acted in the Admiralty Court investigation into the loss of the MV Derbyshire. Assistant Deemster, Isle of Man. WW.

MORGAN, Edward Patrick
Born 12 October 1963, Liverpool. St Joseph's College, Upholland; University of Central Lancashire, LLB. FCIArb. Capital Taxation, 1985-1989. L. July 1989. ETC 1990. Pupilmaster, Andrew MacDonald. Liverpool Chambers; Fruit Exchange, Victoria Street, 1989-1992; Martins Building, 1992-1996. Manchester Chambers; Deans Court, 1995-2000; 18 St John Street, 2000. Tribunal Chairman, 2000. Member of Bar of Northern Ireland.

MORGAN, John Ambrose (His Honour John Morgan)
Born 22 September 1934. St Edward's College, Liverpool; Liverpool University, LLB, 1955. Solicitor 1958; Law Society, Local Government Prize. National Service, RAF, Hong Kong, 1958-1960. Local Government in Preston & Liverpool & private practice (J Frodsham & Sons, Prescot), 1960-1970. G. July 1970. ETC. 1970. Pupilmaster, Bert Andrew. Same Liverpool Chambers at; 14 Cook Street, 1970-1972; Peel House, Harrington Street, 1973-1990. Deputy Stipendiary Magistrate, 1982. Assistant Recorder 1983. Recorder 1988. Circuit Judge, Liverpool, 1990-2003. Liason Judge, North & South Sefton Magistrates. Chairman of Governors, St Edwards College, 1987-1995. Writer and broadcaster on Rugby Union football. President; Liverpool RFU, 1980-1982; Sefton Cricket Club; Bentley Operatic Society. After dinner speaker. Retirement tributes, Liverpool Law Courts, 6 June 2003. (Judge David Clarke QC /David Steer QC (Transcript in Circuit Records). WW.

MORGAN, Eric Wilfred DSC
Lt. Commander, Royal Navy. Colonial Magistrate. Translator of Russian epic poetry. MA (Oxon). L. January 1950. 2 Essex Court, 1950-1962; 8 King's Bench Walk, 1963-1967; 25 Bow Lane, Manchester, 1968-1975. Retired from Bar in 1976. Not in 2000 Bar Directory.

MORGAN, Lloyd John
Born 12 June 1965 Subiaco, Western Australia. Guilford Grammar School, WA; Curtin University; University of Western Australia; Northern Territory University, B.App.Sc (Surv. & Mapp.), MBA., LLB. Licenced Surveyor, WA. Barrister and Solicitor of the Supreme Court of WA & the High & Federal Court of Australia. M. March 1999. ETC. July 1999. Prop. Peter Birkett QC. Sec Andrew Sinker. Pupilmaster, Vincent Deane. Liverpool Chambers; Victoria Chambers, January 1999- October 1999; Oriel Chambers, 14 Water Street, October 1999- July 2001; 7 Harrington Street, July 2001.

MORGAN, Mervyn James Eversfield
MA (Oxon). I. 17 November 1931. ETC. 17 February 1932. Prop. Jackson. Sec. Gorman. Manchester Chambers; 4 Clarence Street, 1932-1934; 26 King Street, 1935-1936. Resident Magistrate, Kenya Colony, 1937-1941. Chief Magistrate, Palestine, 1942-1949. No address, 1950-1963. Not in 1964 Law List.

MORGAN, William Geraint Oliver QC., MP
Born 1 November 1920. Died 2 July 1995 aged 74. University College of Wales, Aberystwyth; Trinity Hall, Cambridge; London University, BA., LLB. Served War, 1939-1945; Suffolk Regt. & Royal Marines; Major. G. November 1947. Holt Scholar. ETC 1950. 1 Plowden Buildings, 1949. Liverpool Chambers; 34 Castle Street, 1950-1952; 9 Rumford Street, 1953-1957; 27 Dale Street, 1958-1961; 34 Castle Street, 1962-1973; Silk 1971. Queen Avenue; 1974-1983; 15 Victoria Street, 1984-1988. FCIArb. MP (C) Denbigh, October 1959-1983; Recorder 1972-1995. Chairman, Welsh Parliamentary Party, 1967. Member; Lord Chancellor's Committee on Recovery of Judgment Debts, 1965-1969; Investiture Committee of HRH The Prince of Wales, 1968-1969; Gorsedd of Bards of Royal National Eisteddfod of Wales, 1969. WW. Times Obituary, 6 July 1995.

MORIARTY, James
Born 1852. Eldest son of John Moriarty of Cork, solicitor. Stonyhurst College; Trinity College, Dublin. AAS. G. 1 November 1881. AAS. M. 8 August 1882. Call. 26 January 1884. ETC. 7 February 1884. Prop. Aspinall QC. Sec. Walton. 10 Orange Court, Liverpool, 1885-1895. No address, 1896-1899. Sydney, New South Wales, 1900-1938. Not in 1939 Law List.

MORLAND, Michael QC (The Hon. Mr Justice Morland)

(DL)

Born 16 July 1929. Eldest son of Edward Morland of Liverpool. Stowe; 2nd Lieutenant, Grenadier Guards, 1948-1949; served in Malaya; Christ Church, Oxford, MA (Jurisprudence). I. November 1953; Bencher 1979. ETC. 4 February 1954. Prop. Nelson QC. Sec. Nicklin. Circuit Junior, 1954. Liverpool Chambers; 27 Lord Street, 1953-1959; 10 Water Street, 1960-1970; 2nd floor, Oriel Chambers, Water Street, 1971-1972. Silk 1972. 12 King's Bench Walk, 1972-1989. Crown Court Recorder, 1972-1989. Member, Criminal Injuries Compensation Board, 1980-1989. High Court Judge, Queen's Bench Division, 1989-2004. Presiding Judge of the Northern Circuit, 1990-1995. Chairman of Committee of Inquiry into the death of Paul Brown which sat for 50 days in Wirral in 1980. Of those involved in the Inquiry, three became High Court Judges (Michael Morland, Heather Steel and Mark Hedley: Heather Steel and Mark Hedley having first been appointed Circuit Judges); seven went to the Circuit Bench (Simon Fawcus, Dick Hamilton, David Lynch, John Morgan, Peter Urquhart, Lyndsey Kushner and Keith Armitage (the last two having first taken Silk) and two are presently in Silk (Cherie Booth and David Aubrey). Michael was the trial judge in the very disturbing case of Thompson & Venables, two ten year old boys, who in 1993, were convicted of the murder of three year old James Bulger.

MORNINGTON, District Judge Marilyn Ann
Born 21 October 1954 Liverpool. Notre Dame, Woolton Hall, Liverpool; Sheffield University, LLB. AAS. M. 30 October 1974. Harmsworth & Blackstone Scholar; Call July 1976. ETC. December 1976. Pupilmaster, Eric Somerset Jones. Oriel Chambers, Water Street/ Covent Garden, Liverpool, 1976-1994. District Judge, Liverpool, 1994.

MORONEY, Mark
BA (Oxon). I. July 1969. 14 Cook Street, Liverpool, 1970-1971. Left the Circuit in 1971 to become an advocate of the Manx Bar.

MORRIS, Anthony Joseph
G. November 1986. Senior Crown Prosecutor, Rochdale, 1994-1997. Manchester Chambers; 3 The Parsonage, 1999; Central Chambers, 89 Princess Street, 2000.

MORRIS, Anthony Paul QC. (His Honour Judge Morris QC)
Born 6 March 1948. Manchester Grammar School; Keble College, Oxford, MA. G. July 1970; Bencher 2001. ETC. 1971. Prop. Patrick Russell QC. Sec. Kenneth Taylor. Same Manchester Chambers at; Ship Canal House, King Street, 1970-1980; 2 Old Bank Street, 1981-1991; Peel Court Chambers, 45 Hardman Street, 1992-2003. Assistant Recorder 1983. Recorder 1988. Silk 1991. Part time Chairman, Mental Health Review Tribunal, 2000-2003. Circuit Judge at the Central Criminal Court from 6 May 2003. WW. On several occasions between 1999 and 2001, Anthony cycled throughout France, Spain & Italy raising over £20,000 for charities.

MORRIS, Ben
Born 22 October 1959. Waterloo Grammar School, formerly a Merseyside Police Officer. Liverpool University, LLB. M. October 1996. ETC. 28 July 1998. Prop. Richard Henriques QC. Sec. Nadine Hope. Pupilmaster, Alison Gyn. Liverpool Chambers; Victoria Chambers; 19 Castle Street, 1998-1999; 25-27 Castle Street, 2000.

MORRIS, Graham Paul
Born 29 October 1952, Bridgewater, Somerset. Married to Helen Elizabeth Morris qv. Died September 1997 aged 44. Dunstable Grammar School; University College, London, LLB. G. July 1975. ETC. 1975. Pupilmaster, Ian Stanley. Martins Building, Water Street, Liverpool, 1977-1997. Assistant Recorder 1997. Tributes; Liverpool Law Courts, 17 September 1997 (Judge David Lynch/ Richard Henriques QC/ Robert Fordham QC/ Andrew Cross, solicitor); Memorial Schubert recital at Birkenhead School, 31 January 1998, (Tom Ryan/ David Galvani.) Transcripts in Circuit Records. Graham was an enthusiastic golfer, a member of Caldy Golf Club. To honour his memory, Martins Building Chambers presented to the Circuit an antique putter which, each year, goes to the runner up in the Carlisle Cup held at Formby Golf Club.

MORRIS, Helen Elizabeth
Widow of Graham Paul Morris qv. LLB (London) formerly a solicitor with Crown Prosecutions Service in Liverpool. G. 1996. ETC 1997. 25-27 Castle Street, Liverpool, 1996-1998. Helen is now back in a senior position with the CPS.

MORRIS, John William CBE., MC, KC (Baron Morris of Borth-y-Gest)
Born 11 September 1896. Son of Daniel Morris of Liverpool & Portmadoc. Died 9 June 1979 aged 82. Liverpool Institute; Served in Royal Welsh Fusiliers, 1916-1919 (2 years in France, Captain; MC). Trinity Hall, Cambridge, MA., LLB; Hon Fellow 1951; President Cambridge Union Society, 1919. Harvard Law School. I. 17 November 1921; Bencher 1943; Reader 1966; Treasurer 1967. ETC. 1 February 1922. Prop. Greaves Lord KC. Sec. Harold Smith. Farrar's Building, 1921-1945. Silk 1935. Judge of Appeal, Isle of Man, 1938-1945. He served on many Government Committees, Inquiries & Tribunals (CBE, 1945). High Court Judge, Queen's Bench Division, 1945-1951. Kt 1945. Lord Justice of Appeal, 1951-1960. PC. 1951. Law Lord, 1960-1975. Baron 1960. CH. 1975 (having served 30 years as a judge). WW.
It is said that when Lord Morris was sitting as a magistrate in North Wales, an advocate who had no idea who the chairman was, suggested that the bench should not worry too much about the law and leave it to the learned clerk.

MORRIS, June Victoria
Born 29 January 1961. Broadoak School; Manchester Metropolitan University, BA. L. October 1995. ETC. 21 December 1995. Prop. Michael Shorrock QC. Sec. Long. Peel Court Chambers. 45 Hardman Street, Manchester, 1995. Registered general nurse & midwife.

MORRIS, Owen Granville
Died December 1953 (Liverpool Daily Post, 10 December 1953). G. 27 June 1900. ETC. 9 August 1901. Prop. Hope KC. Sec. Greer. Liverpool Chambers; 8 Harrington Street, 1904-1906; 25 Lord Street, 1907-1929; 8 Cook Street, 1930-1941; 27 Dale Street, 1942-1949; 3 Cook Street, 1950-1953.

MORRIS, Patricia Barbara (later GROVER)
G. July 1952. 3 St James's Square, Manchester, 1955-1957. Legal Assistant rising to Assistant Solictor in Ministry of Housing & Local Government/Department of the Environment, 1961-1984.

MORRIS, Percy Copeland
LLB. I. 26 January 1887. ETC. 7 February 1887. Prop. Kennedy QC. Sec. Synott. 1 Garden Court, 1888-1911. Equity draftsman & conveyancer. No address, 1912-1927. Not in 1928 Law List.

MORRIS, His Honour Sir William (Gerard)
Born 20 June 1909. Died 13 January 1984 aged 74. Father of His Honour Judge William Morris qv. Bolton School; Gonville and Caius College, Cambridge. L. 26 January 1931. ETC. 18 February 1931. Prop. Jackson KC. Sec. Ormerod. Circuit Junior, Winter 1932. Manchester Chambers; 6 St Anne's Passage, 1931-1935; 43 King Street, 1936-1940. Squadron Leader, RAFVR, 1940-1945. 26 King Street, 1946-1961. Assistant Recorder, Salford, 1956-1961. Recorder of Liverpool, 1966-1967. Recorder of Manchester & Judge of Manchester Crown Court, 1967-1971. Circuit Judge & Honorary Recorder of Manchester, 1972-1977. Kt. 1972. WW.

MORRIS, William Patrick (His Honour Judge William Morris)
Son of His Honour Sir William Morris qv. L. July 1970. ETC. 2 November 1972. Prop. Patrick Russell QC. Sec. Charles Mantell. Manchester Chambers; Ship Canal House, King Street, 1972-1973; Astley House, Quay Street, 1974-1977; 18 St John Street, 1978-1995. Recorder 1988. Circuit Judge, 1995. Resident Judge, Bolton.

*** MORRITT, (Robert) Andrew QC (Rt. Hon. Lord Justice Morritt)**
Born 5 February 1938. Eton; Magdalene College, BA. 2nd Lt., Scots Guards, 1956-1958. L. February 1962; Bencher 1984. 7 Stone Buildings, 1962-1988. Silk 1977. High Court Judge, Chancery Division, 1988-1994. Kt. 1988, CVO 1989. Vice Chancellor of County Palatine of Lancaster, 1991-1994. Lord Justice of Appeal, 1994. PC 1994. Vice Chancellor of the Supreme Court, 2000. WW.

MORROW, Graham Eric QC
Born 14 June 1951, Liverpool. Liverpool College; Newcastle University, LLB. L. July 1974. Pupillage at 4 Essex Court; pupilmaster, Ian Hunter. ETC. November 1975. Prop. Michael Maguire QC. Sec. Michael Dingle. Liverpool Chambers; 2nd floor, Oriel Chambers, 14 Water Street, 1975-1982; chambers moved to; Refuge Assurance House, Derby Square, 1983-1996. Assistant Recorder 1990. Silk 1996. Exchange Chambers, Pearl Assurance House, 1996. Recorder 1997. WW.

MORT, Timothy James (His Honour Judge Mort)
Born 4 March 1950 Didsbury, Manchester. Clifton College, Bristol; Emmanuel College, Cambridge, MA. AAS. M. 14 October 1969. Call 20 July 1972. ETC. 2 November 1972. Prop. Patrick Russell QC. Sec. Gibb. Manchester Chambers; 601, Royal Exchange, 1972-1988; 8 King Street, 1989-1996. Recorder 1992. Circuit Judge, 13 May 1996. WW.

MORTON, David Michael
LLB. I. 25 November 1999. ETC. 14 December 1999. Prop. Peter Birkett QC. Sec. Roger Brown. Old Colony House, 6 South King Street, Manchester, 1999.

MOSS, Francis Wood Collins
I. 5 July 1905. ETC. 16 February 1906. Prop. Tobin KC. Sec. Leslie Scott. Alexandria, Egypt, 1908-1913. Not in 1914 Law List.

MOTTERSHEAD, Peter Michael Hall QC
Born 15 November 1926. Died 17 April 1985 aged 58. The King's School, Macclesfield. National Service, Border Regt., 1946-1948. Jesus College, Cambridge BA, 1951; MA 1954. I. November 1952. Admitted L. 1982. 4 Clarence Street, Manchester & 11 New Square, 1952-1985. Silk 1979. WW.

MOULDEN, Simon Peter
LLB (Leicester) ATT. I. October 1995. ETC. 21 December 1995. Prop. Roger Farley QC. Sec. O'Shea. Not practising at Bar.

MOULTON, Hon Hugh Lawrence Fletcher MC., MP
Born 1876. Died 4 January 1962. Only son of Baron Moulton of Bank, Lord of Appeal in Ordinary. Eton; King's College, Cambridge. AAS. M. 22 June 1896. Call 14 June 1899. ETC. 23 February 1903. Prop. McCall KC. Sec. Sanders. 11 King's Bench Walk, 1900-1915 & 1919-1940. Served in France & Belgium, 1915-1919, Major, MC. 1 KBW, 1941; 4 KBW, 1942-1956; 2 Paper Buildings, 1957-1962. MP (L) Salisbury, 1923-1924. Publications include; Life of Lord Moulton; Trial of Steinie Morrison; Powers & Duties of Education Authorities. WW.

MOUNSEY-HEYSHAM, George William
Born 3 April 1831. 2nd son of George Gil Mounsey of Cumberland, (assumed the additional surname of Heysham by Royal Licence in 1871) Trinity College, Cambridge, MA 1856. AAS. L. 19 April 1852. Call 30 April 1857. 40 Chancery Lane, 1876-1882. Equity draftsman & conveyancer. No address, 1883-1910. Not in 1911 Law List. Foster.

MOXON, Paul Bourchier
LLB. L. 17 November 1908. ETC. 9 July 1909. Prop. Taylor KC. Sec. Merriman. Manchester Chambers; 5 St James's Square, 1909-1912; Bank of England Chambers, Tib Lane, 1913-1921; 16 John Dalton Street, 1922-1924. No address, 1925-1928; Bank of England Chambers, 1929-1940. No address, 1941-1948. Not in 1949 Law List.

MUHAMMAD, Faqir
BA. G. November 1966. Member, Bar of Pakistan. Liverpool Chambers; 9 Rumford Street, 1969-1973; Fruit Exchange, Victoria Street, 1974-1976. No chambers address, 1977-1987. Fruit Exchange, 1988-1989. Not in 1990 Bar Directory.

MULCASTER, John Peter
Born 1818. Only son of John Mulcaster of Durham. AAS. M. 10 January 1840. Call 13 January 1843. Conveyancer based in Newcastle-upon-Tyne. JP., DL, Northumberland. Not in 1888 Law List.

MULHOLLAND, Helen Maureen
Born 28 March 1975 Manchester. Loreto Convent Grammar School; Birmingham University, BA. (Italian & French). M. 14 October 1999. ETC. 14 December 1999. Prop. Nicholas Braslavsky QC. Sec. Simon Hilton. Kings Chambers, 40 King Street, Manchester, September 2000.

MULHOLLAND, Michael
Born 4 July 1951, Stannington, Northumberland. St Mary's College, Middlesbrough; Keble College, Oxford, MA; Sidney Sussex College, Cambridge, Dip. Criminology. Lecturer, Leicester University, 1973-1975. G. November 1976. 11 King's Bench Walk, pupilmaster, Ian Davidson. Joined North Eastern Circuit in 1980 in Leeds Chambers. Northern Circuit, 1992. St James's Chambers, 68 Quay Street, Manchester, 1992.

MULHOLLAND, William QC (His Honour Judge Mulholland QC)
Born 19 January 1843. Died 21 August 1907 aged 64. Queen's College, Galway, MA; Royal University of Ireland. AAS. L. 9 May 1862. Irish Bar, Easter 1865. Call L. 7 June 1875; Bencher 1897. ETC. 17 August 1875. Prop. Russell QC. Sec. Greenhow. Liverpool Chambers; 4 Harrington Street, 1876-1880; Commerce Court, Lord Street, 1881-1894. Silk 1894. Goldsmith Building, 1895-1899. County Court Judge, Circuit 26 (Shropshire, Staffs, Warwicks.), October 1899-1907. W.W. Foster.

MULROONEY, Mark Terence Daniel
Born 29 June 1964, Liverpool. St Matthew's Infants & Junior Schools, Norris Green, Liverpool; St Edwards College, Liverpool; Kent University (Darwin College), BA (Law); Trinity Hall, Cambridge, M.Phil (Criminology). AAS. M. 30 July 1987. Call 28 July 1988. ETC. 1988. Pupilmaster, Henry Globe. Exchange Chambers, 1 Exchange Flags/ Derby Square, 1988.

MUNDY, Robert Geoffrey
Born 1943. Eldest son of Geoffrey Mundy of Wakefield, structural engineer. Birmingham University, LLB. AAS 23 November 1962. Call 22 November 1966. ETC. 1969. Same Manchester Chambers at; 3 St James's Square and 68 Quay Street, 1967-2000. Not in 2001 Bar Directory.

MUNFORD, Frederick
G. 20 June 1917. 3 St James's Square, Manchester, 1921-1928. No address, 1929-1953. Not in 1954 Law List.

MURDIN, Liam
Born 21 February 1973, Liverpool. Merchant Taylors' School; BA (Salford) L. 23 July 1998. 8 Fountains Court, Birmingham, September 1998-February 2000. Pupilmaster, Stephen Murray. ETC. December 2000. Prop. Tim King QC. Derby Square Chambers, Merchants Court, Liverpool February, 2000-2003; 18 St John Street, Manchester 2003.

MURRAY, Ashley Charles
Born 16 October 1951 Bury, Bury Grammar School; Birmingham University, LLB. M. July 1974. ETC. 1975. Prop. Eric Somerset Jones QC. Sec. John Stannard. Oriel Chambers, Liverpool, 1975. Assistant Recorder 1992. Recorder 1998.

MURRAY, Hon Dudley Oliphant
Born 20 November 1846. 2nd son of Alexander, 9th Lord Elibank. AAS. I. 15 April 1867. Call 26 January 1870. ETC. 4 August 1873. Prop. Williams. Sec. Welsby. 4 King's Bench Walk, 1876-1879; 5 KBW, 1880-1883; 4 Crown Office Row, 1884-1891. No address, 1892-1935. Not in 1936 Law List.

MURRAY, (John) Michael Andrew
Born 19 April 1952, Millom, Cumberland. Millom School; St Bees, Cumberland; Nottingham Trent, BA. AAS. M. 28 July 1978. Call. 27 November 1979. ETC. December 1979. Prop. Jack Price QC. Sec. Leslie Portnoy. Manchester Chambers; 60 King Street, 1979-1983; Crown Square Chambers, 1984-1993; 9 St John Street, 1994. Assistant Recorder 1999. Recorder 2000.

MURRAY, Richard Kennett
Born 29 July 1926, Miami, Florida. Eldest son of Charles Gilbert Murray of Winchester, businessman, nephew of Lord Donovan. Malvern College. Lt., Queen's Own Cameron Highlanders, September 1944-March 1948. University College, London, LLB. AAS. M. 3 June 1947. Call 22 June 1950. Work with Moral Rearmament in England & Germany 1950-1961. ETC. February 1961. Prop. Richard Bingham QC (for whom Winston Guthrie Jones QC acted). Sec. T H Pigot. Same Liverpool Chambers at; 14 Cook Street, 1961-1972; Peel House, Harrington Street, 1973-1989. Assistant Coroner (1979-1986)/Deputy Coroner, Liverpool, 1986-1999.

MUSSON, Thomas Meadows Barrow
Born 1891. Only son of Joseph Musson of Rainhill. BA (Cantab). AAS. M. 13 October 1922. Call 24 June 1925. 8 Harrington Street, 1931-1940. No address, 1941-1953. Not in 1954 Law List.

MUTH, Susanne
Born 1 July 1961 Bielefield, Minden, Germany. Herder Gymnasium (Grammar School) Minden; Lancaster University, LLB; Sheffield University, LLM (International & Commercial Law). Investment Banker in London, Cologne & Frankfurt. I. July 1998. ETC. October 1998. Pupilmaster, Peter Cowan. Oriel Chambers, 14 Water Street, Liverpool, September 1998-January 2000; Merchant Chambers, 1 North Parade, Parsonage Gardens, Manchester, January 2000. (merger with St Johns Buildings Chambers 2004).

MYBURGH, Philip Albert QC
Born 24 February 1841. Died 4 July 1892 aged 51. 5th son of Francois Gerard Myburgh of Cape of Good Hope, civil servant. South African College; London University, BA, 1860. AAS. I. 15 April 1858. Call 17 November 1862; Bencher 1886. 3 Paper Buildings, 1876-1892. Silk 1882. HM Standing Counsel in Supreme Courts of China & Japan. Admiralty Court practitioner. Foster.

MYER, Saul
MA., LLB. G. 28 January 1929. ETC. 15 February 1931. Prop. Laski KC. Sec. MacBeth. 5 Paper Buildings, 1930; 1 Harcourt Buildings, 1931-1940. No address, 1941-1945. 6 Pump Court, 1946; 1 Essex Court, 1947-1952; 1 Temple Gardens, 1953-1955. Not in 1956 Law List.

MYERS, Benjamin John
Born 19 March 1967 Stoke-on-Trent. Clayton High School; Leeds University, BA. Army Officer, 1989-1993. I. 14 October 1994. ETC. 13 December 1994. Prop. David Poole QC. Sec. Philip Andrews. Circuit Junior 1999. Young Street Chambers, 1994.

MYERS, James Frederick
MA., LLB. G. November 1950. Northern Circuit but no chambers address listed, 1950-1963. Joined North Eastern, 38 Park Square, Leeds, 1965-1987. Not in 1988 Bar Directory.

MYLONAS, Ioannis Socratous "John"
Born 1940. 2nd son of Socratis Mylonas of Amiandos, Cyprus, clerk. AAS. M. 6 September 1960. Call 19 July 1973. Liverpool Chambers; 41 North John Street, 1976-1978; 15 Victoria Street, 1979-1984. Not in 1985 Bar Directory.

N

NADIM, Ahmed
Born 7 March 1959 Pakistan. Ouldher School, Rochdale; Manchester University, BA. L. July 1982. ETC 1983. Prop. Benet Hytner QC. Sec. Leslie Portnoy. Manchester Chambers; Sunlight House, Quay Street, 1983-1994; Young Street Chambers, 1995. Recorder 2001.

NAHUM, Jack Messoud Eric di Victor QC.
Born 26 November 1906. Died 28 March 1959 aged 52. Twin brother of Baron the society photographer who died shortly before him. Clifton College, Merton College, Oxford, BA. I. 18 November 1929. ETC. 1930. Manchester Chambers; 4 Clarence Street, 1930-1934; 26 King Street, 1935-1939 & 1948-1953. Served War of 1939-1945; 7th Btn., the Cheshire Regt., 3.9.1939-February 1943, India & MEF; posted JAG Branch, Iraq 1943; DJA, MEF, Major, September 1944-August 1948. Silk 1953. 4 Brick Court 1953-1959.Defended Mrs Merrifield. See. Murder of the Blackpool Widow. Rupert Furneaux's Famous Criminal Cases Vol 1 p92-p117.WW.

NANCE, Francis James (His Honour Francis Nance)
Born 5 September 1915 South Africa. Died 4 June 1995 aged 79. Father of Francis Peter Nance qv. St Francis Xavier's College, Liverpool; Liverpool University, LLM, 1938. G. 17 November 1936. ETC. 27 January 1937. Prop. Sellers KC. Sec. Fred Pritchard. Pupilmasters, Fred Pritchard & Selwyn Lloyd. Liverpool Chambers; 25 Castle Street, 1936-1939. Served in Royal Corps of Signals, Captain, Normandy Invasion. NW Europe (despatches). 27 Lord Street, 1945-1946; 49 Castle Street, 1947-1965. 606 Corn Exchange, Fenwick Street, 1966 (Head of Chambers). Deputy Chairman, Lancs. Quarter Sessions, 1963-1971. Circuit Judge, formerly County Court Judge, 1966-1990. Tutor Judge, Judicial Studies Board. President, HM Council of Circuit Judges, 1984. Assistant Deemster, Isle of Man, 1990-1995. WW. Retirement Speeches, Liverpool Law Courts, 22 May 1990 (Judge Sir Sanderson Temple MBE.,QC / John Rowe QC/ Elizabeth Steel). Tributes, Liverpool Law Courts, 7 June 1995 (Judge Wickham/ Rodney Klevan QC.) Transcripts in Circuit Records. See; "The Last Two to Hang" by Elwyn Jones. Stein & Day, 1965. On the 13 August 1964. Peter Allen & Gwynne Evans were hanged having been convicted on clear evidence of the murder of John Alan West. They were the last two people to be hanged in Britain, Allen at Walton Prison and Evans at Strangeways. They were tried at Manchester Assizes before Ashworth J and a jury. Joseph Cantley QC prosecuted. Winston Guthrie Jones QC and Ifor Morris Jones appeared for Evans. Frank Nance and Dick Hamilton were for Allen.

NANCE, Francis Peter
Born 13 April 1947, Liverpool. Son of His Honour Francis Nance qv. St Francis Xavier's School, Liverpool. G. November 1970. ETC. 1971. Pupilmaster, Dick Hamilton. Same Liverpool Chambers; 606 The Corn Exchange, Fenwick Street, 1970-1981; 1 Exchange Flags, 1982-1991; Exchange Chambers, Pearl Assurance House, Derby Square, 1992.

NAQUI, (Syeda) Shazia Haider
Born 15 July 1975 Oldham. Altrincham Grammar School for Girls; London School of Economics, LLB. G. 1998. ETC. 1999. Prop. Keith Goddard QC. Sec. Susan Grocott. Queen's Chambers, 5 John Dalton Street, Manchester, November 1998.

NAPIER, Sir Walter John
Born 10 July 1857. Died 14 February 1945 aged 87. 2nd son of George Webster Napier of Alderley Edge. Rugby; Corpus Christi College, Oxford, MA., DCL. AAS. L. 18 July 1878. Studentship, Hilary 1881. Call 29 June 1881. ETC. 25 January 1883. Prop. Crompton QC. Sec. Scott. Manchester Chambers; 55 Cross Street, 1884-1887; 4 St James's Square, 1888-1889. Equity draftsman & conveyancer. Lancs. Chancery Court. Singapore, 1889. Attorney General, Straits Settlements, 1907-1909. Kt. 1909. Member, Surrey County Council, 1920-1925. Publication; Straits Settlements Law. WW. Foster.

NARAYAN, Hiranya Garbha 'Harry'
Born 23 November 1945, Guyana. Henry Thurnton Grammar School, London. L. Novenber 1970. Pupilmaster, Gavin Lightman. 9 Stone Building 1970-1977; 15 Old Buildings 1978-1980; 9 Stone Buildings 1981-1984. Manchester Chambers; 67 Princes Street 1984-1987; Hollins Chambers, 64a Bridge Street 1988-1997; Cobden House Chambers 1998. Recorder 1995. Adjudicator, 1998. Legal Assessor, GMC, PCC. 2002.

NASH, Thomas
L. 18 November 1872. ETC. 10 March 1873. Prop. Holker QC. Sec. Temple QC. 1 Dr Johnson's Building, 1876; 5 St James's Square, Manchester, 1877-1884. Salford & Manchester Sessions. Not in 1885 Law List.

NATHAN, Arthur Edward
L. 18 June 1890. ETC. 6 March 1893. Prop. Bigham QC. Sec. Yates. 2 Plowden Buildings, 1893-1896; 6 New Square, 1897-1923. No address, 1924-1949. Not in 1950 Law List.

NATION- DIXON, Kenneth Dixon Codrington
I. 24 April 1929. ETC. 18 February 1931. Prop. Lynskey KC. Sec. Sellers. 4 Temple Gardens, 1931-1932. No address, 1933-1953. Not in 1954 Law List.

NAWAZ, Mohammed
Born 22 October 1971 Lancashire. Thames Valley University, LLB; Queen's College, Cambridge, LLM. L. November 1995. ETC. 2 April 1996. Prop. Mukhtar Hussain QC. Sec. Philip Curran. Lincoln House Chambers, 1 Brazennose Street, Manchester, 1996.

NAYLOR, Douglas
I. May 1952. 60 King Street, Manchester, 1952-1956. No address, 1957-1963. Not in 1965 Law List.

NAYLOR, (Gordon) Keith TD (His Honour Judge Naylor TD)
Born 26 February 1933. Died 17 December 1990 (whilst attending the lawyers' service at Liverpool Cathedral) aged 57. Wallasey Grammar School; Liverpool University (Grotius Prize 1953, LLB 1955). National Service,

Cheshire Regiment 1955-1957, Command, 1956; served TA in same regiment, 1957-1970; Lt. Col., Liverpool University OTC 1975-1978 (Jubilee Medal); TA, Col., HQ, NW, District, 1979-1980. TD. 1973. G. November 1957. ETC. 1957. Pupilmaster, Glyn Burrell. Same Liverpool Chambers at; 49 Castle Street, 1957-1965; 606 The Corn Exchange, Fenwick Street, 1966-1981; 1 Exchange Flags, 1982-1990. Recorder, 1980-1985. Circuit Judge, Liverpool, 1985-1990. Obituaries; Liverpool Echo, 18.12.1990; Liverpool Daily Post, 20.12.1990. Tributes at Liverpool Law Courts, 19.12.1990 (Judge Ifor Morris Jones QC/ John Kay QC) Cuttings & transcript in Circuit Records. WW.

NAYLOR, Kevin Michael Thomas
Born 6 September 1961 Manchester. De La Salle Grammar School; Sheffield University, MB., Ch.B. MRCP., LLB., LLM (International & Commercial Law). Medical Practitioner, 1985-1992. L. October 1992. ETC. 7 December 1993. Prop. Brendan Hegarty QC. Sec. Jeffrey Terry. 8 King Street, Manchester 1993.

NAYLOR, Thomas Worthington
G. 19 November 1928, Certificate of Honour M. 1928. ETC. 9 July 1930. Prop. Jackson KC. Sec. Bailey. 3 Essex Court, 1930-1934. Not in 1935 List.

NEALE, Stuart
Born 10 March 1953 Glasgow. 1st son of Walter Bashford Neale of Sale, area sales manager. Married to Susan Neale (Morley) qv who is legal advisor to British Independent Motor Trade Association. Glasgow Academy; Christ College, Cambridge, MA. AAS. M. 28 October 1974. Call July 1976. ETC 1977. Prop. John Hugill QC. Sec. Michael Shorrock. Manchester Chambers; 67 Princess Street, 1977-1987; Hollins Chambers, 64a Bridge Street, 1987-1997; Cobden House Chambers, 19 Quay Street, 1997. Libel reader for local & national newspapers.

NEILL, William
Born 1859. Eldest son of Henry James Neill of Rockport, County Down. Trinity College, Cambridge, BA 1882. AAS. I. 8 November 1879. Call 18 April 1883. ETC. 27 January 1885. Prop. Bigham QC. Sec. Smyly. Circuit Junior, Summer 1885. 6 King's Bench Walk, 1885-1886; 1 Temple Gardens, 1887-1888; 2 Crown Office Row, 1889-1907; 2 Garden Court, 1908-1921. No address, 1922-1937. Not in 1938 Law List. Foster.

NEILL, William Alexander
Born 1834. Only son of Hugh Neill of Liverpool, FRAS. Trinity College, Cambridge, MA, 1858. AAS. I. 31 October 1853. Call 26 January 1857. No address, 1876-1896. Liverpool & Kirkdale Sessions. Not in 1897 Law List. Foster.

NEILSON, William
I. 17 November 1896. ETC. 19 February 1898. Prop. Pickford QC. Sec. Page. 6 Pump Court, 1902-1923. No chambers address, 1925-1949. Not in 1950 Law List.

NELSON, Edward Theophilus
Born 1874, Guyana. Died 1940 Hale, Cheshire aged 66. Son of Philip Nelson of Georgetown, Demerara. St Johns College, Oxford. AAS. L. 29 January 1902. Call 17 November 1904. The Circuit election records for the early 1900's are sketchy. I do not know when he was elected but he is shown in the Northern Circuit Bar Lists in the Law Lists from 1931. 78 King Street, Manchester, 1911-1940. Nelson was 35 years of age when he appeared for Cornelius Howard on committal proceedings at Duckingfield Magistrates Court in 1909. Howard was committed to Chester Assizes and tried by Pickford J and a jury on an allegation of murdering George Harry Storrs, a prominent Cheshire business man. Howard was acquitted. The following year Nelson defended at committal and at trial Mark Wilde who was charged with the same murder. He was also acquitted. Horridge J. presided. In "The Stabbing of George Harry Storrs", (Allison & Busby 1983). Jonathan Goodman says of Nelson;" The son of a builder ... an Oxford graduate, his name did nor appear in the Law List until 1909, perhaps because he was out of the country visiting his parents in Georgetown. The first West African had been called to the Bar in 1879 and there were a few Indian barristers. Nelson was one of the first, if not the first, West Indian to be allowed to wear a stuff gown in the English Courts." Goodman's researches indicate that Nelson was "clever, with a fiery temperament." I am grateful to Guy Holborn, Lincoln's Inn Librarian and the Trafford Local Studies Centre for the following: "A picture of Mr Nelson in his wig appears in the Stalybridge Reporter for 29 October 1910. For most of his life he lived in Hale. He was a much respected person and worked hard in local and civic affairs. He was a member of Hale Cricket Team and a photograph of the team of 1912 is held by the Studies Centre. In 1913 he was elected to Hale Urban District Council, winning his seat by a comfortable majority. He served as Chairman of the Council (1917) and Chairman of the Free Library (1920). The Hale Council Minutes for 5 August 1940 noted that a vote of condolence was carried in silence with all standing."

NELSON, Harry Ince QC
Born 29 May 1897. Died 1 August 1981 aged 84. Aldenham School. Lt., Royal Field Artillery, 1915-1919; served on Western Front (twice wounded). Pembroke, College, Oxford, BA., LLB. I. 26 January 1922; Bencher 1952. ETC. 1922. Circuit Junior, Summer 1923. Liverpool Chambers; 10 Cook Street, 1922-1941; 27 Dale Street, 1942-1945. Silk 1945. Goldsmith Buildings, 1945-1959. Judge; Salford Hundred Court, 1947-1948; Liverpool Court of Passage, 1948-1950. Recorder of Liverpool, 1950-1954. Commissioner of National Insurance, 1968-1969 (Deputy, 1959-1968) WW.

NELSON, Humphrey
Born 1856. Eldest son of Philip Nelson of Princes Road, Liverpool. AAS. M. 24 January 1887. Call 18 November 1889. ETC. 20 March 1890. Prop. Gully QC. Sec. Pickford. Liverpool Chambers; 8 Harrington Street, 1893-1908; 25 Lord Street, 1909-1915. Not in 1916 Law List.

NEVILLE, Ralph QC., MP (The Hon. Mr Justice Neville)
Born 13 September 1848. Died 13 October 1918 aged 70. Father of Ralph Neville OBE qv. Tonbridge School; Emmanuel College, Cambridge, MA 1874; Hon Fellow. AAS. L. 28 January 1869. Call 30 April 1872. Bencher. ETC. 1 August 1876. Prop. Russell QC. Sec. Gully. Liverpool Chambers; 11 Lord Street, 1877-1882; 25 Lord Street, 1883-1884. 7 New Square, 1877-1884; 16 Old Buildings, 1885-1888; 15 Old Buildings, 1889-1906. Silk 1888. MP (L) Liverpool Exchange, 1887-1895. High Court Judge, Queen's Bench Division, 1906-1918. Publications; Joint author, Railway & Canal Cases. WW.

NEVILLE, Ralph OBE
Born 1873. Only son of The Hon. Mr Justice Neville qv. LLM., (Cantab) AAS. M. 17 April 1896. Call 14 June 1899. ETC. 14 February 1901. Prop by his father. Sec. Squarey. Farrar's Building, 1903-1912; 5 Paper Buildings, 1913-1919; 2 Plowden Buildings, 1920-1923. Parliamentary draftsman. Not in 1924 Law List.

NEWELL, Simon Peter
Born 27 December 1950, Salford. St Joseph's College, Blackpool; University College, London, LLB. I. November 1973. ETC. 1975. Prop. George Carman QC. Sec. Anthony Jolly. Manchester Chambers; 36 St Ann Street, 1975-1980; 27 Byrom Street, 1981-1983; 26 Cross Street, 1984-1987; 83 Bridge Street, 1988-1990; 15 Winckley Square, Preston, 1990. Recorder 1999.

NEWMAN, Benjamin Hutchinson Jnr
Born 1873. Died 31 January 1954. Eldest son of Benjamin Hutchinson Newman of Larch Lea, Prenton Road East, Birkenhead, solicitor. Birkenhead School; Victoria University, Manchester, BA. AAS. M. 18 November 1895. Call 17 November 1898. ETC. 17 February 1899. Prop. Taylor QC. Sec. Pugh. Liverpool Chambers; 8 Harrington Street, 1899-1904; 8 Cook Street, 1905-1908; 25 Lord Street, 1909-1926; 5 Cook Street, 1931-1933. Associate, Northern Circuit, 1 Chapel Street, Preston, 1933-1944.

NEWMAN, Gerson
Died January 1975. Chairman, Liverpool & District Rent Tribunal, 1969-1975. I. 13 June 1934. ETC. 27 June 1934. Prop. Hemmerde QC. Sec. Howard Jones. Liverpool Chambers; 5 Cook Street, 1934-1939; 8 Cook Street, 1940-1941; 27 Dale Street, 1942-1948; 3 Cook Street, 1949-1958; 27 Dale Street, 1959-1975. He was an expert on the Law of Landlord and Tenant. I remember him in the early 60's. Whilst Gerson was waiting to get on County Court Judges would ask his view on other cases in the list.

NEWMAN, Henry Frederick
G. 17 November 1933. ETC. 27 June 1934. Prop. Lynskey KC. Sec. Sellers. Liverpool Chambers; 8 Harrington Street, 1934-1940; 14 Cook Street 1941-1946; 24 Dale Street 1947-1949. 4 Paper Buildings 1950-1951; 5 Paper Buildings, 1952; 2 Garden Court, 1953-1954; 1 Brick Court, 1955-1965. Legal Assistant rising to Assistant Solicitor, Foreign Compensation Commission, WC2, 1966-1980. Not in 1984 Bar Directory.

NEWTON, John David
Born 4 April 1921, Chesham, Bucks. Died 13 July 2000, Birkenhead aged 79. Father of Simon Newton qv. Berkhamsead School. Served in War of 1939-1945 in Royal Artillery and Indian Army (Major). University College, London LLB, 1947. AAS. M. 12 June 1944. Call 9 June 1948. Lecturer in Law, University College, Hull 1948-1951. Lecturer, then Senior Lecturer in Law, Liverpool University, 1951-1982. ETC 1951. Pupilmaster, Eric Griffiths. 20 North John Street, 1951-1985 (Head of Chambers on Joe Turner's retirement). Chancery Practitioner. Recorder, 1983-1992. Past President, Liverpool Athenaeum. Member, Institute of Conveyancers. Publications; Volumes on Rentcharges & Annuities in Halsbury's Laws of England (1982) & The Encyclopaedia of Forms & Precedents (1988). WW. Tributes at Liverpool Law Courts on 24 July 2000. (Judge David Clarke QC/ Judge David Gilliland QC/ Edward Bartley-Jones QC/ Simon Newton.

NEWTON, (John) Simon
Born 22 August 1945, Merthyr Tydfil. Son of John David Newton qv. Birkenhead School; University College, London, LLB. AAS. M. 10 January 1966. Call 16 July 1970. ETC. 1970. Pupilmaster, Robert Leech. Liverpool Chambers; 2nd floor, Oriel Chambers, 14 Water Street, 1970-1982; Derby Square Chambers, Merchants Court, 1983-2003 (Head of Chambers); Oriel Chambers, Water Street 2004. Deputy District Judge 1993-1999.

NEWTON, Lesley Anne (Her Honour Judge Newton)
Born 4 April 1955. Married to His Honour Judge Hernandez qv. Manchester University, LLB. AAS. M. 9 March 1976. Call 22 November 1977. 19 Baker Street, Middlesbrough, 1977-1979, North Eastern Circuit. ETC. 3 April 1979. Prop. Donald Hart QC. Sec. Ward. Manchester Chambers; 6th floor, Arkwright House, Parsonage Gardens, 1979-1994; 38 Young Street 1995-2001 (Head of Chambers 1997-2001). Assistant Recorder 1994. Recorder 1999. Circuit Judge, June 2001. WW.

NEWTON, Robert
Died January 1998. BA (Oxon). G. February 1958. Arden & Macaskie Scholar. Manchester Chambers; 4 Chapel Walks, 1960-1964; 601 Royal Exchange, 1965-1988; 8 King Street, 1989-1998.

NICHOL, Simon Bede
Born 11 December 1948 Hove, Sussex. De La Salle, Hove; UMIST, BSc. Dunderdale Wignall, 1982-1988. Crown Prosecutions Service, Manchester, 1988-1994. L. May 1994. ETC. 1994. Prop. Roger Farley QC. Sec. Howard Baisden. Same Manchester Chambers at; Hollins Chambers, 64a Bridge Street, 1994-1997; Cobden House Chambers, 19 Quay Street, 1998.

NICHOLLS, (Deborah) Jane
Born 29 August 1964 Middleton. Queen Mary School, Lytham; Keele University, BA. NCH Childrens' Home, November 1986-November 1987. Young & Lee, Solicitors, Birmingham, November 1987-Summer 1988. I. November 1989. ETC. 1990. Prop. Eric Somerset Jones QC. Sec. Anthony Edwards. Oriel Chambers, 14 Water Street, Liverpool, 1989.

NICHOLLS, Elizabeth Jane
Born 9 June 1960. Farnborough Hill School; Manchester University, BA (History). Dip. Law. I. July 1984. ETC. 1985. Prop. David Poole QC. Sec. David Allen. Manchester Chambers; Rational House, 64 Bridge Street, 1984-1995; Lincoln House Chambers, 1 Brazennose Street, 1996. Recorder 2002.

NICHOLLS, Reginald Hugh JP
G. 15 June 1904. No chambers address, 1934-1952. Not in 1953 Law List.

NICHOLSON, Amy Chantal
Born 8 November 1974 Birkenhead. Hills Road 6th Form College, Cambridge; Nottingham Trent University, LLB. L. November 1999. ETC. 12 December 2001. Prop. James Pickup QC. Sec. Denis Watson. Lincoln House Chambers, 1 Brazennose Street, Manchester, October 2001.

NICHOLSON, James Morton
I. 26 January 1887. ETC. 4 February 1888. Prop. Gully QC. Sec. Page. 11 King's Bench Walk, 1888-1889; 6 Crown Office Row, 1890-1906. No address, 1907-1935. Not in 1936 Law List.

NICHOLSON, Robert Herle
L. 17 November 1908. ETC. 4 July 1909. Prop. Landon KC. Sec. Pope. 22 Booth Street, Manchester, 1910-1924. 2 King's Bench Walk, 1925-1929; 2 Hare Court, 1930-1933. Not in 1934 Law List.

NICKLIN, His Honour Robert Shenstone
Born 1901. Died 4 January 1975. Son of P H S Nicklin of Blundellsands. Uppingham; University College, Oxford, MA. L. 24 June 1925. ETC. 15 July 1925. Prop. Greaves-Lord KC. Sec. Graham. Liverpool Chambers; 25 Lord Street, 1925-1930; 8 Harrington Street, 1931-1935; 34 Castle Street, 1936-1938; 27 Lord Street, 1939-1955 (Private, Intelligence Corps; Major, JAG's Dept.) Deputy Chairman, Quarter Sessions; Cumberland, 1953-1956; Nottingham, 1956-1957. County Court Judge, later Circuit Judge, 1955-1973 (Circuits 18 & 21). WW.

NICKSON, Percy
G. 28 June 1922. ETC. 12 July 1922. Prop. Greaves-Lord KC. Sec. Jalland. 60 King Street, Manchester, 1922-1928. No address, 1929-1930. Not in 1931 Law List.

NICOL, Donald Ninian
Born 8 October 1843. Died 27 July 1903 aged 59. Only surviving son of John Nicol of Ardmarnock, Argyll. Merchiston Castle School, Edinburgh; Glasgow University; Queen's College, Oxford, MA, 1872. AAS. M. 4 November 1865. Call. 26 January 1870. ETC. 19 August 1870. Prop. Manisty QC. Sec. J Edge. 7 Fig Tree Court, 1876-1880; 2 Harcourt Buildings, 1881-1903 (but did not practise). JP., DL (Argyllshire). MP (C) Argyllshire, 1895-1903. Not in 1904 Law List. WW.

NIELD, Basil Edward QC., MP (Sir Basil Nield CBE)

Born 7 May 1903. Died 4 December 1996 aged 93. Harrow School; Magdalen College, Oxford, MA. I. 6 May 1925; Bencher 1952; Reader 1976; Treasurer 1977. ETC. 13 June 1925. Prop. Jackson KC. Sec. Stephen Proctor (Whalley). Circuit Junior, Winter 1925. Liverpool Chambers; 25 Lord Street, 1925-1926; 8 Cook Street, 1927-1928; 5 Harrington Street, 1929-1941; 27 Dale Street, 1942-1945; Silk 1945. Served, 1939-1948 in Palestine, Persia, Iraq, Normandy, Low Countries, Rhine; Lt. Col., despatches, MBE (military). 1 Paper Buildings, 1945-1948; 2 Essex Court, 1949-1956. MP (C) Chester, 1940-1956. Chancellor, Diocese of Liverpool, 1948-1956. Recorder of Salford, 1948-1956. Recorder of Manchester and first judge of the Manchester Crown, 1956-1960. High Court Judge, Queen's Bench Division, 1960-1978. CBE 1956 Kt. 1957. WW.
He prosecuted Walter Rowland. See Celebrated Trials by Henry Cecil, David & Charles, 1975.
Publications; Farewell to the Assizes, Garnstone Press, 1972. He was the only High Court Judge to have sat in all 61 Assize Courts. Obituaries; Times, 9 December 1996; Guardian, 24 December 1996; Inner Temple Yearbook, 1997, Master David Clarke.

NIELD, Zoe Justine Kathryn
Born 28 October 1972 Manchester. The Manor School, Cheadle Hulme; Nottingham University, LLB. G. 8 October 1998. ETC. December 1998. Prop. Guy Gozem QC. Sec. Hugh Davies. Lincoln House Chambers, 1 Brazennose Street, Manchester, 1998-.

NILSON, Wendy Mary
Born 27 June 1956 Kampur, India. Married to Peter Grogan, solicitor. Hollies Convent School, Didsbury; Manchester University, LLB. G. 23 July 1998. ETC. 30 July 1998. Prop. Roger Farley QC. Sec. Roger Booth. Manchester Chambers; 6 South King Street, 1998-2001; Young Street Chambers, June 2001-. Formerly a solicitor with CPS.

NIMMO, Alexander
Born 1858. Elder son of Alexander Nimmo of Stirling. Trinity College, Cambridge, MA 1884. AAS. I. 12 November 1880. Call 17 November 1884. ETC. 31 July 1885. Prop. Kennedy QC. Sec. Mansfield. 5 Paper Buildings, 1886-1887. No address, 1888-1941. Not in 1942 Law List. Foster.

NIXON, Charles Jones
Born 1840. 3rd son of William Nixon of Liverpool. Wadham College, Oxford, BA, 1862. AAS. M. 30 October 1862. Call 9 June 1865. No address, 1876-1933. Liverpool Sessions & Liverpool Court of Passage. Not in 1934 Law List. Foster.

NOBLE, Andrew
Born 28 August 1960, Edinburgh. University of Manchester, LLB., Dip. QS., FRICS., FCIArb. Qualified Chartered Surveyor. L. 24 November 1992. Pupillage at Hardwicke Chambers, Lincoln's Inn. Pupilmaster, Ken Craig. Eldon Chambers, 30-32 Fleet Street E.C.4. & New Bailey Chambers, Preston. Merchant Chambers, Parsonage Gardens, Manchester 1996-, (now St Johns Building). Provincial Treasury Counsel 2001.

NOBLE, Arthur Edwin Randall
Born 27 March 1942. Son of Arthur Petrie Noble qv. Harrow; Trinity College, Dublin, BA. I. 25 July 1965. ETC. 1965. Prop. Richard Bingham QC. Sec. Tom Pigot. Liverpool Chambers; 14 Cook Street, 1965-1972; Peel House, Harrington Street, 1973-1998; Chavasse Court Chambers, 24 Lord Street, 1999. Assistant Recorder 1992. Recorder 1996. Member, Fisheries Board for Northern Ireland, 1968-1984.

NOBLE, Arthur Petrie
Died 17 July 1969. Father of Arthur Edwin Randall Noble qv. I. June 1939. ETC. 5 July 1939. Prop. Shawcross KC. Sec. Kennan. 34 Castle Street, Liverpool. He did not return to the Bar after the war and became a stockbroker in Chester. He also managed the family's salmon fishing business in Northern Ireland and was a member of the Fisheries Conservation Board.

NOBLE, Robert Emilius
I. 19 November 1894. ETC. 28 July 1905. Prop. Pickford KC. Sec. Taylor KC. 10 King's Bench Walk, 1905-1907. He joined the Midland Circuit in 1908 and thereafter practised from several London Chambers. Not in 1937 Law List.

NOLAN, Damian Francis
Born 25 February 1970, Liverpool. Brother of Dominic Nolan of Ropewalk Chambers, Nottingham. St Edwards College, Liverpool; Cardiff University, BSc(Econ). L.

October 199. Liverpool City Council, July 1994-September 1995. ETC. 1995. Prop. Stephen Riordan QC. Sec. David Owen. 25-27 Castle Street, Liverpool, 1995.

NORCROSS, Sarah Ann
LLB (London). G. October 1990. 28 St John Street, Manchester, 1992-1994. Not in 1995 Bar Directory.

NORMINGTON, Eric Arthur
LLB., BCL. G. 17 November 1927. ETC. 1927. 2 Booth Street, Manchester, 1930-1932. He the went into the Solicitors Department of the General Post Office rising to Senior Legal Assistant. Not in 1954 Law List.

NORRIS, George Henry
Born 1851. 2nd son of Thomas Norris of Stockport, merchant. AAS. L. 18 November 1880. Call. 3 May 1882. ETC. 29 January 1883. Prop. Crompton QC. Sec. Hopkinson. Manchester Chambers; 78 Cross Street, 1885-1890; 5 St James's Square, 1891-1918. Equity draftsman & conveyancer. Lancs. Chancery Court. No address, 1919-1928. Not in 1929 Law List.

NORTON, Richard Damian
Born 20 June 1969 Stockport. Married to Sally Harrison qv. Bishop Stortford College, Herts; Leeds University, LLB. L. November 1992. ETC. 17 December 1992. Prop. Anthony Rumbelow QC. Sec. Graham Platts. 28 St John Street, Manchester, 1992.

NOWELL, Denovan Godfrey
Born 13 September 1924 Wilmslow. Ryleys Preparatory School, Alderley Edge; Manchester Grammar School. Royal Air Force (Radar), 1943-1946. Dauntsey Scholar, Manchester University, LLB, 1949. G. January 1950; Lord Justice Holker Exhibitioner. ETC. 1950. Prop. William Gorman QC. Sec. Charles Norman Glidewell. Same Manchester Chambers; 28 Kennedy Street, 1950-1956; 25 Bow Lane, 1957-1976; 460 Royal Exchange, 1977-1983. Part time Lecturer, Manchester University. Member, Carlisle & Manchester Area Legal Aid Committees. Deputy Circuit Judge. Clerk to the General Commissioners of Taxes, 1966-1999. He appeared before the House of Lords in Beswick -v- Beswick and tells me that the following was read out at Mess after the decision at first instance:

There was an old coalman from Eccles
Who resolved to provide for his wife.
So he sold his goodwill, his lorry and scales
To his nephew - the light of his life.
His nephew agreed - though not by a deed
To pay his dear aunt a pension.
But later he found
That he was not bound
And therefore he changed his intention.
To pay money, you see
Seemed unnecessary
When the intended donee
Was not a party
To give to his widow he did not succeed
(As I said before, there was no deed).
A benefit to others did however ensue,
The others in question being Nowell and Fitzhugh. They
cared little for the widow
Still less for her mite
Luck to you Mrs Beswick –
We're all right!

NOWELL, Kate Louise
LLB (Cardiff). L. 10 October 1996. ETC. 16 December 1996. Prop. Philip Raynor QC. Sec. Simon Hilton. 40 King Street, Manchester, 1999.

NOWLAND, Lee Philip
Born 29 March 1974 Preston. All Hallows RC High School, Penwortham; Leicester University, LLB. Farleys, Solicitors, Blackburn, October 1996-October 1997. L. 22 May 1997. ETC. 16 December 1997. Prop. Keith Goddard QC. Sec. Longworth. Manchester Chambers; Old Colony House, 6 South King Street, October 1997-May 2001; 8 King Street, May 2001.

NUNAN, Manus
Born 26 March 1926, St Mary's College, Dublin: Trinity College, Dublin BA., LLB. Irish Bar; Kings Inns 1950. Colonial Legal Service, 1953; Crown Counsel, Nigeria, 1953-1962; Solicitor-General, Northern Nigeria, 1962-1964; Minister of Government, Northern Nigeria 1962; QC (Nigeria) 1962. G. June 1956. 21 Whitefriars, Chester (Wales & Chester Circuit), 1965-1966. Liverpool Chambers; 1st floor, Oriel Chambers, 14 Water Street, 1967-1981; 3rd floor, 27 Dale Street, 1982-1985. Recorder, 1978-1984. Moved to France and has lectured extensively throughout the English speaking world on Oscar Wilde, Dr Samuel Johnson, Talleyrand & Bernard Shaw. WW.

NUTTALL, Andrew Peter
Born 21 August 1954 Bolton. Bolton School; Wolverhampton University, LLB. L. November 1978. ETC. March 1979. Prop. Patrick Russell QC. Sec. Peter Crichton-Gold. Manchester Chambers; 9th floor, Sunlight House, Quay Street, 1979-1985; 6th floor, 1986-1990; Rational House/ Lincoln House Chambers, 1 Brazennose Street, 1990. Recorder 2003. Mountaineer, having climbed in Alaska, Alps & Himalayas. Recorder 2003.

NUTTALL, Ellis MP
Born 8 December 1890. Died 1 July 1951 aged 60. Eldest and only surviving son of Alfred Nuttall of Blackburn. Rugby; Trinity College, Oxford, MA. AAS. M. 13 April 1910. Call 27 January 1913. ETC. 18 February 1914. Prop. Hewart KC. Sec. Crawford. Elected as Circuit Junior, Winter 1914 but did not act as he joined HM Forces as soon as war was declared. RFA, 1914-1919 in Egypt, Gallipoli & France. 2 Harcourt Buildings, 1914 & 1919-1939. Served also in War of 1939-1945. MP (C) Birkenhead West, 1924-1929. WW.

NUTTALL, Harry Jnr
Born 1926. Only son of Harry Nuttall, Snr of Farnworth, Lancs. Trinity Hall, Cambridge, BA. AAS. M. 12 July 1950. Call 5 May 1953. ETC. 4 March 1954. Prop. Robertson Crichton QC. Sec. Perry. 78 King Street, Manchester, 1953-1957. Senior Legal Advisor, later, Assistant Solicitor, Department of Health & Social Security, 1958-1984. Not in 1985 Bar Directory.

NUTTALL, Thomas Kirkpatrick
L. 17 November 1890. ETC. 11 March 1891. Prop. Kennedy QC. Sec. Pickford. Liverpool Chambers; Stephenson's Chambers, Lord Street, 1891-1892; 2 Harrington Street, 1893-1896; 8 Harrington Street, 1897-1919 and at 6 New Court, 1914-1919. Not in 1920 Law List.

O

OAKES, Christopher Neil
Liverpool University, BSc (Eng). L. October 1996. Cobden House Chambers, 19 Quay Street, Manchester, 1996.

OAKES, Dawn Victoria
Durham University, BA. I. July 1981. Manchester Chambers; Lawrence Buildings, 2 Mount Street, 1984; 3 St James's Square, 1985. No address 1986-1988. Not in 1989 Bar Directory.

OAKES, Joseph Stewart
Born 7 January 1919. Royal Masonic School, Bushey; Stretford Grammar School; Manchester University, BA 1940 (Economics & Politics). Royal Signals, 1940-1948, Eighth Army, Captain. AAS. I. September 1945. Call November 1948. ETC. March 1949. Sec. Henry Burton. Same Manchester Chambers at 60 King Street, 1948-1960; 47 Peter Street, 1960-1970; Sunlight House, Quay Street, 1970-1983; 28 St John Street, 1983-1984. Head of Chambers. Pupils included Howard Bentham, Tony Gee & Bernard Lever. Sat as Chairman, Rent Assessment Committee; Deputy County Court Judge & Assistant Recorder at Blackburn; President, Mental Health Review Tribunals, 1971-1991. Sworn in as Crown Court Recorder at Liverpool by Mr Justice Mais on 11 November 1975. Sat until retirement from practice in 1984. WW.

O'BRIEN, Paul
Born 23 May 1948, Bradford; St Bede's Grammar School, Bradford; Manchester University, BA. G. November 1974. ETC. 1975. Prop. Christopher Rose QC. Sec. Rhys Davies. Same Manchester Chambers at; 4th floor Astley House, Quay Street, 1975-1977; 18 St John Street, 1978. Irish Bar 1990. Assistant Recorder 1996. Recorder 2000. Part time Immigration Appeal Adjudicator, 2001. Standing Counsel for Customs & Excise, 2002.

O'BRIEN, Sarah Anne Louise
Born 21 August 1974, Hull. Hull Grammar School. Banking; Lloyd's/TSB 1992-1994; NatWest 1994-1995; HSBC 1995-1997. Hull University, LLB. I. 23 July 1998. ETC. 2001. Prop. TimHolroyde QC. Sec. John McCarroll. Exchange Chambers, Pearl Assurance House, Derby Square, Liverpool, 2001.

O'BYRNE, Andrew John Martin
Born 24 May 1950, Dublin. St Joseph's College, Blackpool; Liverpool University, LLB. G. 4 July 1978. ETC. 26 October 1978. Prop. Donald Hart QC. Sec. Daniel Brennan. Same Manchester Chambers at; 2 Old Bank Street, 1978-1991; Peel Court Chambers, 45 Hardman Street, 1992.

O'BYRNE, James Stanislaus
Born 1886. Eldest son of J O'Byrne of Liverpool. Clerk in the Post Office when AAS. M. 19 November 1920. Call 19 November 1923. ETC. 25 June 1924. Prop. Greaves-Lord KC. Sec. Fraser Harrison. 25 Lord Street, Liverpool, 1924-1927. Manchester Chambers; 26 King Street, 1928-1935; 12 King Street, 1936; 6 St Ann's Passage, 1937-1940; 26 King Street, 1941-1943. Not in 1944 Law List.

O'DONOGHUE, His Honour Michael
Born 10 January 1929. Rhyl Grammar School; Liverpool University, LLB 1950. G. November 1951. National Service, Royal Air Force, Flying Officer, 1951-1953. ETC. 4 February 1954. Prop. Daniel Brabin QC. Sec. Melville Kennan. Pupilmasters, Melville Kennan & Joseph Turner. 20 North John Street, Liverpool, 1954-1982. Chancery Practitioner. Part time Law Lecturer,

Liverpool University, 1966-1982. Circuit Judge, 19 February 1982 – 30 March 1994. Part time Member, Lands Tribunal, 1990-1994. WW.

O'DONOHOE, Anthony Francis
Born 3 October 1958. De La Salle School; Liverpool University, LLB. AAS. M. 3 February 1982. Call. 28 July 1983. ETC. December 1983. Prop. Michael Maguire QC. Sec. John Leach. Liverpool Chambers; 10 James Street, 1984-1987; Fruit Exchange, Victoria Street, 1987-1991; Chavasse Court, 1992. Recorder 2002.

O'FEELY, Timothy O'Brien

4th son of Patrick O'Feely of Roscommon. LLD. AAS. G. 28 January 1858. Call. 26 January 1861. Liverpool Chambers 40 Castle Street, 1876-1888; 25 Lord Street, 1888-1902. No address, 1903-1912. Not in 1913 Law List.

OGDEN, Agnes Ruth
L. January 1950. ETC. 1950. 3 St James's Square, Manchester, 1950-1961. Did Land Registry work. Not in 1962 Law List.

O'HALLORAN, Jill
Born 20 September 1971, Leigh. St Mary's RC High School, Tyldesley, Manchester; University of Northumbria at Newcastle, LLB. G. 13 October 1994. King's Chambers, East Sussex, 1994-1995. Pupilmaster, Stephen Hall-Jones. Stephensons, Solicitors, Leigh, 1995-1997. ETC. 18 December 1997. Prop. Nigel Gilmour QC. Sec. Ashley Barnes. Liverpool Chambers; 24 Fenwick Street, 1998-2000; 14 Cook Street, 2000.

O'KEEFFE, Darren Philip De Voiels
Born 1 June 1961. St Mary's College, Crosby; New College, Oxford, MA. I. July 1984. ETC. 22 July 1986. Prop. Michael Maguire QC. Sec. Charles James. Liverpool Chambers; Derby Square Chambers, Merchants Court, 1986-2003; Oriel Chambers, 14 Water Street, Liverpool, 2004.

O'LEARY, Dean
Born 2 October 1965 Liverpool. Page Moss Comprehensive, Huyton; Royal Marines, 1985-1989. Liverpool John Moores University et al; LLM., MSc, BSc, Dip Law, Dip Arb. Dip IC Arb. Quantity Surveyor, 1994-1998; Senior Consultant, 1999-2001. L. 19 July 1999. ETC. 26 July 2001. Prop. Andrew Edis QC. Sec. David Flood. India Buildings Chambers, Water Street, Liverpoo,l 2001.

OLIPHANT-FERGUSON, George Henry Hewitt
Born 6 June 1817. Only son of George Henry Hewitt Oliphant. He assumed the additional name of Ferguson in 1861. Trinity College, Cambridge, BA, 1842. AAS. I. 20 April 1837. Call. 19 November 1843. No chambers address, 1876-1899. Publications; Law of Horses; Law of Church Ornaments & Utensils; Law of Pens & Prohibitions. JP. & DL., Cumberland. Foster.

OLIVER, Philip Milner CBE., MP
Born 1884 Manchester. Bowdon College; Manchester Grammar School; Corpus Christi College, Oxford, BA. L. 23 June 1909. ETC. 12 July 1909. Prop. Tobin KC. Sec. Acton. Circuit Junior, Summer 1910 and during the Great War. Manchester Chambers; 41 John Dalton Street, 1909-1928; 26 King Street, 1929-1948. MP (L) Manchester, Blackley, 1923-1924 & 1929-1931. OBE 1918. CBE 1920. No chambers address, 1949-1954. Not in 1955 Law List. Publications; Whatsoever Things; Genesis to Geneva. WW.

OLIVER, Stephen John Lindsay QC
Born 14 November 1938. Rugby School; Oriel College, Oxford, MA (Jurisprudence). National Service, 1957-1959; Royal Navy, Sub-Lt., (Submariner). AAS. M. 17 November 1960; Bencher 1987. ETC. 1964. 601 Royal Exchange/ 8 King Street, Manchester, 1964-1991. 4 Pump Court, 1964-1991. Assistant Boundary Commissioner, 1977. Silk 1980. Recorder, 1989-1991. Circuit Judge, 1991-1992. Presiding Special Commissioner, and President, VAT & Duties (formerly VAT) Tribunals 1992-. President, Financial Services & Markets Tribunal, 2001-. WW.

OLLERENSHAW, Frank
MA (Cantab). I. 17 November 1921. ETC. 4 March 1925. Prop. Eastham KC. Sec. Gorman. 3 Elm Court, 1922-1928; 60 King Street, Manchester, 1929-1932; 5 Pump Court, 1933-1963. Not in 1964 Law List.

OLSON, Ross Alexander
Born 18 June 1977, Nottingham. Bramcote Hills Comprehensive School, Nottingham; St John's College, Cambridge, MA. G. 14 October 1999. ETC. 14 December 1999. Prop. David Stockdale QC. Sec. Jonathan Grace. Dean's Court Chambers, 24 St John Street, Manchester, 1999-.

O'NEILL, Paul Gerard
LLB (Leeds). G. October 1994. Parsonage Chambers, 3 The Parsonage, Manchester 1997-1999. No address 2000. Not in Bar Directory 2001.

O'NEILL, Philip John
Born 27 August 1961, Hazel Grove. All Hallows Catholic High School, Macclesfield; Liverpool University, LLB. G. November 1983. Pupilmasters, David Radford & Nadine Radford. ETC. November 1984. Prop. William Waldron QC. Sec. Iain Goldrein. Liverpool Chambers; 5 & 48 Castle Street, 1984-1989; Corn Exchange (merger); 7 Harrington Street, 6.9.1999-. (merger with Martins Bank). Deputy District Judge 2000-.

OPENSHAW, (Charles) Peter (Lawford) QC (His Honour Judge Openshaw QC)

Born 21 December 1947. Son of late Judge William Harrison Openshaw qv; grandson of Sir James Openshaw OBE., JP qv; married to Caroline Swift QC qv. Harrow; St Catharine's College, Cambridge, MA. I. July 1970. ETC. 6 May 1971. Pupilmaster, Michael Lever. Circuit Junior, 1973. Same Manchester Chambers; Ship Canal House, 1971-1980; 2 Old Bank Street, 1981-1991; Peel House Chambers, 45 Hardman Street, 1992-1999. Assistant Recorder 1985. Silk & Recorder 1991. Senior Circuit Judge & Recorder of Preston, 1999-. DL., Lancs. 2000. Welcome Speeches at Preston Law Courts, 17 March 1999 (Judge Duckworth/ Richard Henriques QC. Transcript in Circuit records. WW.

OPENSHAW, Sir James OBE., JP

Born 13 April 1871. Died 1 January 1935 aged 63. Father of Judge William Openshaw qv and grandfather of Judge Peter Openshaw QC qv, elder son of Frederick Openshaw of Redvales, Bury and Hothersall Hall, Ribchester. Harrow; Trinity College, Cambridge. I. 17 June 1896. ETC. 15 July 1896. Prop. McCall QC. Sec. Byrne. Manchester Chambers; Duchy Chambers, Clarence Street, 1896-1908; 60 King Street, 1909-1912. On his father's death in 1912, he inherited the Hothersall Estate and retired from practice. Being too old for active service in the Great War, he took the post of Chairman of the Appeals Tribunal for recruitment applications. In 1917 he became Chairman of Preston Quarter Sessions, later being appointed Chairman of the County Quarter Sessions for Manchester (the Hundred of Salford) and Liverpool (the Hundred of West Derby) as well, all of which posts he held until his death. He was also active in many county and church affairs. He was Deputy Lieutenant of Lancashire; he was appointed OBE in 1920 and knighted in 1928. In 1906, he married Muriel Ellen, daughter of Rev. William James Melville, Rector of Ashton-in-Makerfield. His portrait hangs in Court Number One in The Sessions House, Preston. WW and information provided by Peter Openshaw.

OPENSHAW, William Harrison (His Honour Judge Openshaw)

Born 11 December 1912. Died 12 May 1981 aged 69. Son of Sir James Openshaw OBE qv, father of Judge Peter Openshaw QC qv. Harrow; St Catharine's College, Cambridge. I. 17 November 1936. ETC. 15 January 1937. Prop. William Gorman KC. Sec. Blackledge. Circuit Junior, Winter 1937. 60 King Street, 1937-1939 & 1945-1958. Served, 1939-1945 War in Western Desert and in Burma with Wingate's Chindits. He appeared as junior to Kenneth Burke for the defence of Walter Rowland- twice convicted of capital murder, In 1932 Rowland had been convicted of murdering his young daughter and was sentenced to death but the jury recommended him to mercy. He was reprieved and released in 1942. Four years later he was convicted of murdering a woman in Manchester. On this occasion sentence of death was carried out. See "The Trial of Walter Rowland" in the Celebrated Trials series (Henry Cecil, published by David & Charles in 1975). In 1957 he was appointed full time Deputy Chairman of Lancashire County Quarter Sessions; the following year, on the death of Arthur Jalland KC, he was appointed Chairman. The same year he became Recorder of Preston. He held both posts until the passing of the Courts Act 1971 when he was translated into a Circuit Judge and Honorary Recorder of Preston. He served as Deputy Lieutenant of Lancashire. In 1945 he married Elisabeth Joyce Emily Lawford, daughter of Capt. E D W Lawford DSO., OBE., RN. He died on 12 May 1981, being stabbed by a man whom he had many years before sent to Borstal. His portrait hangs beside that of his father in Court Number One in the Sessions House at Preston. He is also commemorated by the naming of Openshaw Place on which the new Combined Courts Building at Preston stands. Tributes; St George's Hall, Liverpool, 12 May 1981 (Mr Justice Peter Taylor/ Judge E S Temple MBE/ J M Collins QC); Sessions House, Preston, 20 May 1981. (Judge Kershaw/ Cecil Henriques) Transcripts in Circuit Records. WW and information supplied by Peter Openshaw.

OPPE, Albert Sanvil

I. 28 January 1895. ETC. 2 February 1899. Prop. Russell QC. Sec. Jordan. 7 New Square, 1900-1949; 20 Old Square, 1950-1953. Not in 1954 Law List.

ORFORD, Joseph Robinson

I. 18 June 1890. ETC. 30 July 1893. Prop. Yates QC. Sec. Sanderson. 2 Temple Gardens, 1892-1893; 2 Pump Court, 1894-1895. No address, 1896-1949. Not in 1950 Law List.

ORIOGUN, John

ETC. 21 December 1995. Prop. Brendan Hegarty QC. Sec. McDermott. Not in Bar Directory.

ORME, Richard Andrew

Born 18 July 1966 Warwicks. Cheltenham College; Universities; Leeds (BA) & Fudan, Peoples Republic of China. Samuel Montague, London 1989; Jardine Matheson, Hong Kong & Bangkok 1990. L. October 1993. ETC. 7 December 1993. Prop. Peter Openshaw QC. Pupilmaster, Wallace. Peel Court Chambers, 45 Hardman Street, Manchester, 1993.

ORMEROD, Rt. Hon. Sir Benjamin

Born 7 September 1890. Died 21 September 1974 aged 84. Elder son of John Aspden Ormerod JP of Blackburn. Queen Elizabeth's Grammar School, Blackburn; Manchester University. (Hon. LLD 1949).Solicitor, 1913. Captain, 4th Btn, East Lancs Regt September, 1914-January 1919. L. 2 July 1924; Bencher 1948. ETC. 15 July 1924. Prop. Greaves-Lord KC. Sec. Burgis. Manchester Chambers; 60 King Street, 1924-1930; 6 St Ann's Passage, 1931-1940. No address, 1941-1942; 43 King Street, 1943. County Court Judge, Circuit 14 and later 5, 1944-1948. High Court Judge, Probate, Divorce & Admiralty Division, 1948-1950; King's/Queen's Bench Division, 1950-1957. Lord Justice of Appeal, 1957-1963. Kt. 1948. PC 1957. WW.

ORR, John Wellesley

Born 11 September 1878, Urmston. Died 12 February 1956 aged 77. Only son of Arthur Wellesley Orr of Didsbury. Denstone; St John's College, Cambridge, BA. AAS. M. 13 November 1901. Call 15 June 1904. ETC. 20 July 1905. Prop. Shee KC. Sec. Fraser. 9 King's Bench Walk, 1904-1906; 3 Temple Gardens, 1907-1921; 4 Temple Gardens, 1922-1925; 1 Garden Court, 1926-1927. Stipendiary Magistrate for Manchester, 1927-1951. Member, Home Office Departmental Committee on Persistent Offenders, 1931. WW.

ORR, Julian Boyd
Born 9 May 1972. Married to Lindsay Sutton, solicitor. Caister Grammar School, Lincoln; Liverpool University, LLB. L. October 1995. ETC. 21 December 1995. Prop. Keith Goddard QC. Sec. Richard Hartley. Same Manchester Chambers; Hollins Chambers, 64a Bridge Street, 1997; Cobden House Chambers, 19 Quay Street, 1998.

ORR, Nicholas Guy
Born 2 October 1947, Cairo, Egypt. Wellington College; Bristol University, LLB. G. November 1970. ETC. 7 December 1972. Pupilmaster, Joseph Turner. Liverpool Chambers; 20 North John Street, 1972-1998; 14 Castle Street/Atlantic Chambers, Cook Street, 1998. Chancery Practitioner.

ORR, William Wyatt
Born 1847. Youngest son of William Orr of Armagh. Matric, Trinity College, Dublin. AAS. M. 7 November 1871. Call 28 June 1876. ETC. 23 March 1892. Prop. Ambrose QC. Sec. Fisher. 2 Essex Court, 1891-1911; 1 Cloisters, 1912-1916. Not in 1917 Law List. Foster.

ORRELL, John Edward
Born Bolton. Canon Slade Grammar School, Bolton. BA (Oxon). G. November 1957. 3 St James's Square, Manchester, 1960-1966. Left the Bar in 1966 to work for Crompton Parkinson, Leeds. Legal Advisor; B P Chemicals, SW1, 1981-1990; Sema Group Systems WC1, 1994-1995.

OSBORNE, Claire Elizabeth Ann
Born 23 November 1969 Enfield. Manchester University, BA. M. November 1994. ETC. 13 December 1994. Prop. Roger Farley QC. Sec. Nicholas Braslavsky. 40 King Street, Manchester, 1994-1997. Legal Advisor; Allied Dunbar Assurance PLC, Swindon, 1997-1998; Zurich Financial Services, 1999.

O'SHEA, John Anthony Andrew
Born 9 June 1961. Gunnersbury School, London; BA. AAS. M. 28 July 1982. Call 22 November 1983. ETC. 1985. Prop. Benet Hytner QC. Sec. J Ward. Manchester Chambers; 20 St Mary's Parsonage, 1985-1993; 58 King Street Chambers, 51-53 South King Street, 1994.

OSMAN, Robert Walter
Born 20 December 1947, Hatherop, Glos. Bishop Wordsworth, Salisbury; Leicester Polytechnic LLB. AAS. M. 9 February 1973. Call 18 July 1974 5 Essex Court/ 4 Brick Court 1975-1987. Pupilmaster, A Uziel-Hamilton. Carter Hodge, Solicitors, Southport 1987-1990. ETC. 1990. Prop. Keith Goddard QC. Sec. Shannon. Queen's Chambers, 5 John Dalton Street, Manchester 1990.

OSWALD, James Francis QC, MP
Born 21 November 1838 Limehouse, near London. Died 14 September 1908 aged 69. Stepney Grammar School; Islington Proprietary School; matriculated at St Edmund's Hall, Oxford. Solicitor 1861. AAS. M. 24 January 1867. Call 17 November 1869; Bencher 1893. ETC. 26 February 1870. Prop. Manisty QC. Sec. Gainsford Bruce. 10 Old Square, 1876-1883; 9 Stone Buildings, 1884-1886; 6 New Square, 1887-1904. No address, 1905-1908. Silk 1893. Member; General Council of the Bar, 1883-1897; Incorporated Council of Law Reporting, 1894-1897. MP (C) Oldham, 1895-1899. Publication; Contempt of Court textbook. WW.

OTTER-BARRY, William Whitmore
Born 6 March 1878. Died 2 September 1973 aged 95. Marlborough; Trinity College, Cambridge, BA. I. 18 November 1901. ETC. 17 February 1903. Prop. Taylor KC. Sec. G W Duncan. Circuit Junior, Autumn 1903 & Winter 1904. Lamb Building, 1903-1911; 2 Plowden Buildings, 1912. He then left the Bar and went into Insurance rising to General Manager and Director of Sun Insurance Office. JP & High Sheriff, Essex, 1946. Publications; Law relating to Fire Insurance, 1911, 3rd edition. WW.

OUGHTON, Richard Donald
Born 9 September 1955, Ipswich. Northgate Grammar School, Ipswich.; St Johns College, Cambridge, MA; University of Pennsylvania, LLM. L. July 1978. ETC. July 1980. Prop. Justin Price QC. Sec. Nicholas Riddle. Liverpool Chambers; 14 Cook Street, 1979-1985; 7 Queen Avenue, 1986-1992. Manchester Chambers; 72 Bridge Street, 1992-1997; Cobden House Chambers, 19 Quay Street, 1998. Publications; Author, 2nd & 3rd editions of Tyler's Family Provision; Assistant Editor, Fisher & Lightwood's Law of Mortgage, 10th edition & supplement.

OULTON, William Harold Stowe
Born 1 February 1869. Died 25 July 1941 aged 72. Leys School; Royal Institution, Liverpool; Christ's College, Cambridge, BA., LLB 1892, MA., LLM 1896. I. 26 April 1893. ETC. 20 July 1894. Prop. Pickford QC. Sec. Carver. Liverpool Chambers; Stephenson's Chambers, Lord Street, 1899-1908; 8 Harrington Street, 1909-1912; 13 Harrington Street, 1913-1924; 25 Lord Street, 1925. Revising Barrister. Assistant Recorder, Liverpool. Deputy Stipendiary, Liverpool. Metropolitan Magistrate, 1925-1940. WW.

OULTRAM, Jonathan Richard Gerard
LLB. M. 22 November 1988. Senior Crown Prosecutor; Inner London 1994; Bradford, 1997-2000. ETC. 6 April 2000. Prop. Jonathan Foster QC. Sec. Beverly Lunt. 51-53 South King Street, Manchester, 2000.

OVEREND, Charles William Pinkstone
Born 1848. Eldest son of Charles Corry Overend of Liverpool, merchant. Sidney Sussex College, Cambridge, BA 1870. AAS. L. 27 January 1868. Call 30 April 1873. ETC. 16 February 1873. Prop. Temple QC. Sec. Potter. 13 Harrington Street, Liverpool, 1880. London Chambers, 1881-1908. Not in 1909 Law List.

OWEN, David Meurig
Born 5 March 1959, Wirral. Helsby Grammar School; Keele University, BA (Law & American Studies). G. July 1981. ETC. 1984. Pupilmaster, G Locke. Liverpool Chambers; 2nd floor, Harrington Street, 1984-1994; 25-27 Castle Street, 1995.

OWEN, Rev. Eric Cyril Hammersley
Born 7 December 1946, Gresford. Grove Park Grammar School, Wrexham; Liverpool University, LLB. G. November 1969. ETC. 1969. Pupilmaster, A D Pappworth. 3rd floor, 27 Dale Street, Liverpool, 1969-1974. 21 Whitefriars, Chester (Wales & Chester Circuit), 1974-1990. 40 King Street, Manchester, 1990. Assistant Curate, Gresford, 1995. Publications; Editor, Graya Magazine; Consultant Editor; Litigation Practice; County Court Litigation.

OWEN, Fearnley Wells
I. 17 November 1892. ETC. 27 July 1893. Prop. Walton QC. Sec. Shaw. Circuit Junior, Winter 1895. 2 Harcourt Buildings, 1895-1897. Not in 1898 Law List.

OWEN, (Francis) David (His Honour Judge Owen)
Solicitor, October 1961-1966. G. July 1967. Same Liverpool Chambers at; 10 Water Street, 1967-1970; 2nd floor, 14 Water Street, 1970-1982; Refuge Assurance House, Derby Square, 1983-1991. Recorder 1988. Circuit Judge 1991.

OWEN, Gail Ann
Born 24 September 1958 London. Married to David Stuart Aubrey QC. qv. Hatfield Girls Grammar School; Lincoln Christ's Hospital; Liverpool University, LLB. G. November 1980. Dr. Johnson's Building, pupilmaster, Michael Brent. ETC. 1981. Same Liverpool Chambers at; Melbourne Buildings, 21 North John Street, 1981-1988; 3rd floor, Peel House, Harrington Street, 1989-1998; India Buildings, Water Street, 12.1.1998. Assistant Recorder 1999. Recorder 20.9.2000.

OWTRAM, Thomas Carey
I. 24 June 1925. ETC. 6 July 1927. Prop. Singleton KC. Sec. Longson. 78 King Street, Manchester, 1928-1932. Lancs. Chancery Court. No address, 1933-1953. Not in 1954 Law List.

P

PAGE, Ernest KC
Born 6 July 1848, Carlisle. Died 24 October 1930 aged 82. High School, Carlisle, Rossall. Solicitor, 1872-1875. AAS. I. 6 November 1875. Call 3 July 1878; Bencher 1909. ETC. 12 July 1878. Prop. Russell QC. Sec. Crompton. 3 Harcourt Buildings, 1879-1880; 1 King's Bench Walk, 1881-1930. Silk 1898. Recorder of Carlisle, 1904-1929. Honorary Freedom of Carlisle, 1926. WW.

PAGE, Richard
Born 1877. Eldest son of Richard Page of Knutsford, solicitor. Balliol College, Oxford. AAS. M. 17 June 1899. Call 17 November 1902. ETC. 5 February 1904. Prop. Pickford KC. Sec. Sutton. 78 King Street, Manchester, 1905-1910. Singapore, Straits Settlements, 1911-1937. 22a Raffles Place, Singapore, 1938-1955. Not in 1956 Law List.

PALEY, Mary Huscroft
G. July 1971. ETC 1973. Pupilmaster, Colin Cunningham. Liverpool Chambers 41 North John Street, 1973-1978; 15 Victoria Street, 1979-1985; 1st floor Fruit Exchange, Victoria Street, 1986. Retired from practice shortly after the death of her pupilmaster.

PALMER, Ernest George
L. 18 November 1901. ETC. 29 January 1902. Prop. Taylor KC. Sec. Hutchinson. 3 Harcourt Buildings, 1902-1934. No address, 1935-1961. Not in 1962 Law List.

PALMER, Sir (Herbert) Richmond KCMG., CBE
Born 20 April 1877. Died 22 May 1958 aged 81. Eldest son of Robert Palmer of Kirby Lonsdale, bank manager. Oundle; Trinity Hall, Cambridge, MA., LLB. AAS. M. 25 October 1899. Call 15 June 1910. Assistant Resident, Nigeria, 1904; Resident, Bornu Province, 1917. CMG 1922. CBE 1924. Lieut-Governor, Northern Provinces, Nigeria, 1925-1930. Governor & Commander in Chief; Gambia Colony, 1930-1933; Cyprus, 1933-1939. KCMG 1933. ETC. 1946. 10a Winckley Square, Preston & 3 Cook Street, Liverpool, 1947-1957. WW.

PALMER, Professor Norman Ernest
Born 16 August 1948. Palmer's Endowed School, Grays Thurrock; Magdalen College, Oxford, BA (Jurisprudence) 1969, BCL 1971, MA 1974. G. July 1973. Lecturer/Senior Lecturer in Law, Universities of Liverpool, Tasmania & Manchester, 1971-1981. 15 Victoria Street, Liverpool, 1982-1986. Joined the South Eastern Circuit with chambers in London. Professor of Law; Reading; Essex; Southampton & University College, London. Professor of the Law of Art & Cultural Property, UCL since 2001. Numerous publications commencing with the 5th edition of Crossley Vaines on Personal Property 1973 (with Ted Tyler qv) WW.

PANKHURST, Richard Marsden
Born 1835, Stoke on Trent. 2nd son of Henry Francis Pankhurst of Manchester. Died 1898. Manchester Grammar School; Owens College, Manchester; London University, BA 1856, LLD 1863. AAS. L. 18 November 1864. Call 11 June 1867. Manchester Chambers; 3 St James's Square, 1876-1884; 10 St James's Square, 1885-1898. 222-225 Strand WC2, 1885-1892; 5 New Square, 1893-1898. Equity draftsman & conveyancer.
Foster. Ingleby Kernaghan of Norbury, London is writing a biography of Richard Pankhurst and has kindly provided me with a synopsis which I have put in the Circuit Records. He was the husband of Emmeline and father of Christabel, Sylvia & Adela, the four women who founded the militant suffragette movement in 1903. He was instrumental in founding the Independent Labour Party along with his close friend Kier Hardy, the first Labour MP.

PAONESSA, Laura Alexandria
LLB (Manchester). M. October 1993. 5 John Dalton Street, Manchester, 1996-1997. No address 1998.

PAPPWORTH, Abram David ("Pappy")
BA., LLB. Lee & Powell Prizeman. G. 28 January 1935. ETC. 30 January 1935. Prop. Maxwell Fyfe KC. Sec. Basil Nield. Liverpool Chambers; 13 Harrington Street, 1935-1937; 8 Harrington Street, 1938-1940; 34 Castle Street, 1941-1954; 3 Cook Street, 1955-1958; The Temple, Dale Street, 1959-1969; 3rd floor, 27 Dale Street, 1970-1978. Deputy Circuit Judge. Not in 1979 Law List.

PARKER, Geoffrey
Born 31 October 1884, Preston. Died 11 April 1917 aged 32. Son of John Parker, solicitor & county coroner. King William College, Isle of Man. L. 27 June 1906. ETC. 4 August 1906. Prop. Langdon KC. Sec. Smitton. No chambers address recorded in Law Lists. Private D company, Artists' Rifles, 28 London Regt, 4 January 1916. Commissioned 2ndLt., 4th Btn, attached to 10 Btn, Loyal North Lancashire Regt, 26 June 1916. Killed in action, 11 April 1917 at Arras. Arras Memorial, Pas De Calais, France (Bay 7). Information supplied by the Public Records Office & Commonwealth War Graves Commission.

★ PARKER, Jonathan (Frederic) QC. (Rt. Hon. Lord Justice Parker)

(DL)

Born 8 December 1937. Son of Sir (Walter) Edmund Parker CBE. Winchester; Magdalene College, Cambridge, MA. I. July 1962; Bencher 1985. 11 Old Square, Lincoln's Inn, 1962-1991. Silk 1979. Recorder 1989-1991. Attorney General of Duchy of Lancaster, 1989-1991, High Court Judge, Chancery Division, 1991-2000. Kt 1991. Vice Chancellor, Co. Palatine of Lancaster, 1994-1998. Lord Justice of Appeal, 17 July 2000. WW.

PARKER, Robert Montgomery Birch
I. 19 November 1906. ETC. 17 July 1907. Prop. Sanderson KC. Sec. Scott. Goldsmith Building, 1908 & 1911-1914. No address, 1915-1953. Not in 1954 Law List.

PARKER, Steven Nigel
Born 4 December 1964 Glos., Monmouth School; Lanchester Polytechnic, LLB. G. November 1987. ETC. 1988. Prop. Michael Maguire QC. Sec. Iain Goldrein. Liverpool Chambers; Mason House, 48-50 Castle Street, 1987; merged with Corn Exchange, Fenwick Street, 1989-1999; 7 Harrington Street, 6.9.1999. (merger with Martins Bank). Deputy District Judge, 2001.

PARKIN, Jonathan
Born 3 June 1955. Clare College, Cambridge, MA. AAS. M. 6 July 1976. Call 21 November 1978. ETC. November 1979. Prop. Christopher Rose QC. Sec. Terence Rigby. Same Manchester Chambers at; 60 King Street, 1979-1983; Crown Square Chambers, 1 Deans Court, 1984-1993; 9 St John Street, 1994-2000. Assistant Recorder 1999. Recorder 2000. Full time Chairman, Employment Tribunals (Birmingham), February 2000.

PARKINSON, Frederick Beck
Born 6 May 1940. Manchester University, LLB. AAS. M. 10 July 1980. Call 23 July 1981. Manchester Chambers; 4th floor, Sunlight House, Quay Street, 1983-1984; Central Chambers, 1 Central Street, 1985-1987; 33 King Street West/ Old Colony House, 6 South King Street, 1995.

PARKINSON, William Harold
Born 21 January 1959. Highfield C of E Boys; University of Central Lancashire, LLB. Formerly a coal miner in Lancashire. L. October 1997. Pupilmaster, John Wishart. New Bailey Chambers, Liverpool 1997.

PARR, Cecil Francis JP
Born 2 August 1847. Died 13 January 1928 aged 80. 6th and youngest son of Thomas Parr of Grappenhall Heyes, Cheshire. Harrow; Exeter College, Oxford, BA. AAS. I. 28 January 1871. Call 17 November 1874. ETC. 27 January 1882. Prop. Gully QC. Sec. Bigham. 3 Pump Court, 1882; 1 Harcourt Buildings, 1883-1885. No address, 1887-1935. Although he died in 1928, his name appeared in the Law List until 1936. WW.

PARR, John Edward
Born 14 October 1961 Blackpool. Hutton Grammar School; Britannia Royal Naval College; Officer in Royal Navy, 1980-1994; Assistant Chief Naval Judge Advocate, 1990-1994; Lieut.-Commander. Reading University, LLB. AAS. M. 12 May 1988. Call 27 July 1989. ETC. 13 December 1994. Prop. Brendan Hegarty QC. Sec. Peter Main. 8 King Street, Manchester, 1994.

PARRY, Alison Jean
BA (Oxon). M. November 1986. ETC. 16 December 1986. 1st floor, Peel House, Harrington Street, Liverpool, 1987-1988. Not in 1989 Bar Directory.

PARRY, Christopher Philip
L. 12 October 1995. ETC. 15 April 2003. Prop. Richard Marks. Sec. Jeffrey Samuels. St Johns Buildings, 24a-28 St John Street, Manchester, 2003.

PARRY, Sir Edward Abbott (His Honour Sir Edward Parry)

Born 2 October 1863. Died 1 December 1943 aged 80. 2nd son of John Humffreys Parry, (1816-1880), Serjeant-at-Law. King's College School; Slade School of Art. AAS. M. 18 January 1882. Call 26 January 1885. 2 Middle Temple Lane, 1885; 2 Pump Court 1886; South Eastern Circuit, 1885-1886. ETC. 28 July 1886. Prop. Gully QC. Sec. Thompson. 41 John Dalton Street, Manchester, 1886-May 1894. County Court Judge, Manchester & Salford, May 1894 – 22 February 1911 when he transferred to Lambeth & West Kent County Courts, retiring on 19 May 1927. Kt. 1927. Numerous publications including; My Own Way 1932 (autobiography); What the Judge Saw; What the Judge Thought; Judgments in Vacation; Seven Lamps of Advocacy; The Persecution of Mary Stewart; many works of fiction; and plays, performed on the London stage. Pages 52-74 of Judgments in Vacation dealing with his time at Manchester County Court are conveniently reproduced in Sir Louis Blom Cooper's "The Language of the Law" Bodley Head 1965. On the 26 June 1898, at Manchester County Court he gave a judgment revoking the licence of a bailiff, whereupon the bailiff shot the judge twice in the head. He was seriously wounded but got back to work in the November. He said; " One of my worst misfortunes was that I had to grow a beard, and I looked like an anarchist." At page 45 of "Closed Chapters" Sir Gerald Hurst says this of Parry: The Vice-Chancellors were much less prominent in Manchester life than the County Court Judge, (Sir) Edward Parry, a man of great literary talent, an amusing after-dinner speaker, and a striking personality. His County Court was held at Quay Street in what was once Cobden's mansion (1836) and later the first site of Owens College. Parry was not deemed a great Judge by the Common Law Bar; but he had vision and humanity. He did well to brush aside the many technical difficulties which at that time beset awards of workmen's compensation, and he was always the poor litigant's friend. Unluckily he forgot Talleyrand's " *surtout point de zèle*", and his too frank dicta often failed to find acceptance in the Court of Appeal. He consoled himself by telling the story of the typical working man who emerged from the County Court in Quay Street saying of Parry that " he was a bloody fool but he did his best". His book, *My Own Story* (1932), ranks among the best legal autobiographies.

PARRY, Eryl Lloyd
MA (Oxon), L July 1966. ETC. July 1966. Liverpool Chambers; 9 Rumford Street, 1966-1973; Fruit Exchange,Victoria Street, 1974-1992. Chairman Industrial Tribunals 1992.

PARRY, John Idris
MA (Oxon), L. 26 January 1922. Liverpool Chambers; 25 Lord Street, 1927-1934; 8 Harrington Street, 1935-1938. No address, 1939-1946. Not in 1947 Law List.

PARRY-JONES, (John) Trevor
Born 25 September 1956, Bangor, North Wales. Fitzalan High School, Cardiff; University College of Wales, Aberystwyth, LLB. Solicitor, partner of Norton & Co., Liverpool, 1979-1991. G. February 1992. ETC. 1992. Pupilmaster, David Steer. Liverpool Chambers; Corn Exchange, Fenwick Street, 1991-1999; 7 Harrington Street, 6.9.1999. (merger with Martins Bank Chambers).

⋆ PARSONS, His Honour Albert KC
Born 1865. Died 7 April 1938. Father of Godfrey Valentine Hope Parsons qv. Bedford School; London University. M. June 1891. Joined Western and later North & South Wales Circuit. Goldsmith Building to 1917. Silk 1914. Recorder of Merthyr Tydfil, 1915-1917. County Court Judge, Circuit 7, (Lancs. & Cheshire) May 1917-1922; Circuit 54 (Bristol), 1922-1937. WW.

PARSONS, Godfrey Valentine Hope
Born 24 September 1894. Died 16 March 1948 aged 53. Son of His Honour Albert Parsons KC qv. Clifton College, Bristol. Captain & Adjutant, 15th Brigade, RHA, 29th Division, 1914-1918; Army of the Rhine 1918-1919. AAS. M. 14 November 1919. Call 10 May 1922. ETC. 20 June 1922. Prop. Singleton KC. Sec. Fraser Harrison. Liverpool Chambers; 5 Harrington Street, 1922; 25 Lord Street, 1923. In 1924 he joined South Wales and Chester Circuit, practising in Cardiff. He was Stipendiary Magistrate for Cardiff, 1946-1948. WW.

PARSONS, James
Born 1851. Only son of Rev. George Ludovig Parsons, late vicar of Kirkham, Lancs. New College, Oxford, BA 1872, MA. AAS. I. 8 January 1874. Call. 17 November 1876. ETC. 2 March 1877. Prop. Temple QC. Sec. Dickinson. Circuit Junior, Summer 1877. 3 Kings Bench Walk, 1877-1889. No address, 1890-1918. Not in 1919 Law List. Foster.

PARSONS, John Ramsay
Born 11 October 1853. Only son of John Parsons of East Grinstead, Sussex. St John's College, Oxford, MA. AAS. I. 8 January 1875. Call 7 May 1879. ETC. 7 February 1881. Prop. Temple QC. Sec. Cardwell. 8 King's Bench Walk, 1881; 1 Pump Court, 1882-1885; 1 Garden Court, 1886-1896. No address, 1897-1918. Not in 1919 Law List. Foster (records his name as James).

PART, Charles Thomas
Born 1848. Eldest son of Thomas Part of Astley Hall, Chorley. Trinity College, Cambridge, MA 1874. AAS. I. 27 January 1868. Call 6 June 1871. ETC. 28 July 1871. Prop. Holker QC. Sec. Edwards. Lamb Building 1876; 3 King's Bench Walk (North), 1877-1884; 12 King's Bench Walk (North), 1885-1900. No address, 1901-1926. Not in 1927 Law List. Foster.

PARTINGTON, Lisa Shirley
LLB. I. July 1989. ETC. December 1989. Prop. Charles Bloom QC. Sec. Charles Chruszcz. St John's Buildings, 24a-28 St John Street, Manchester, 1991.

PASS, Geoffrey James
Born 5 November 1950, Prestbury, Cheshire. Mosely Hall Grammar School, Cheadle; London School of Economics, LLB. AAS. M. 23 July 1973. Call 17 July 1975. Lecturer/Senior Lecturer, Manchester Metropolitan University, 1975-1990. ETC. 1991. Pupilmaster, Peter Winston Smith. 40 King Street, Manchester 1990.

PASSANT, Douglas Neville
LLB (London). L. November 1971. 4th floor, Sunlight House, Quay Street, Manchester, 1976-1977; 2 King's Bench Walk, 1978. No chambers address, 1979.

PATERSON, Frank David (His Honour Frank Paterson)

(RB)

Born 10 July 1918. Younger son of the late David Paterson and Dora Paterson. Married Barbara Mary Gillow, 1953. Calderstones Preparatory School and Quarry Bank High School, Liverpool; Liverpool University, LLB; Hon. LLD, 1993. G. November 1941. Warden, Unity Boys' Club, Liverpool, 1941; Assistant Warden, Florence Institute for Boys, Liverpool, 1943. ETC. July 1946. Prop. Basil Nield. Sec. Robertson Crichton. Pupilmasters, Harold Brown (Chancery) and Melville Kennan (Common Law). Liverpool Chambers; 20 Hackins Hey, 1946; 34 Castle Street, 1947-1968. (Head of Chambers). Chairman, Ministry of Pensions and National Insurance Tribunal, Liverpool, 1957. Assistant Deputy Coroner, Liverpool, 1960. Chairman, Mental Health Review Tribunal for South West Lancashire and Cheshire, 1963. (Subsequently President dealing with Restricted Patients). President, Liverpool Domestic Mission Society, 1953. Circuit Judge (formerly County Court Judge, Circuit 10), 1968-1993. Joint President, HM Council of Circuit Judges, 1987. Liason Judge, North and South Sefton (formerly Southport and Bootle) Magistrates. President, Merseyside Magistrates Association, 1978-1993. WW. Retirement Tributes at Liverpool Law Courts 8 July 1993 (Judge Wickham and William Waldron QC). Transcript in Circuit Records. Biographical sketch by Graeme Bryson in "Century of Liverpool Lawyers", Fagan, Bryson & Elston, Liverpool Law Society, 2002 in which Graeme Bryson says: "Frank became much in demand as an after dinner speaker. These were not off the cuff affairs but they were very carefully structured and brilliantly contrived, receiving rapturous applause." I have included the following extract from Frank's address, on the day of his retirement, to those assembled in the court of The Recorder of Liverpool. It is a fine example of his elegant humour: After referring to himself as being like a prisoner in the dock, he imagined his representative explaining that: The time was now approaching when few could remember the Judge when he was a practising barrister, if he ever had been, which some began to doubt. It was rumoured he was in his nineties. The administration, which at heart is a kindly body, allowed him to decline into a gentle old age. He was brought bundles of unwanted papers to file in the privacy of his room and permitted to do a little odd judicial job from time to time. It was appropriate therefore that his last usher should be one who spent his early working life with a building contractor. Like all persons associated with the odd jobs of the building trade in Liverpool he was Welsh concealing his true identity under the name of Jones. Whenever notification came of another appeal being allowed his usher would gently lead the Judge to the window of his Chambers. There usher and Judge would spend many happy hours surveying the roof tops of Liverpool noting the missing slates, the cracked chimney pots, the broken gutters. The usher would comfortingly explain that these simply symbolised the many odd jobs he had done, overruled by the storms of the Almighty to lie scattered before the public gaze like the transcripts of successful appeals on the Judge's desk. The usher would philosophically observe it was far worse to be overruled by Almighty God in heaven than by mere mortals in London.

PATERSON, James

3rd son of Alexander Paterson of Janefield Lauder. Berwickshire. AAS. M. 30 April 1847. Call 24 May 1850. Goldsmith Building, 1876-1894. Special pleader & parliamentary draftsman. Not in 1895 Law List. Foster.

PATTERSON, Frances Sylvia QC

Born 29 November 1954, Stockton-on-Tees. Queen's School, Chester; Leicester University, BA. AAS. M. 26 June 1975. Call November 1977. ETC. 3 April 1979. Pupilmaster, Philip Raynor. Same Manchester Chambers; 460 Royal Exchange, 1979-1987; 40 King Street, Manchester, 1988. Assistant Recorder 1997. Silk 1998. Recorder 2000. WW.

PAUL, Daniel John

Born 4 November 1964, Essex. Great Cornard Upper School, Suffolk; Open University, BA. M. October 1998. ETC. 1999. Prop. Eric Somerset Jones QC. Sec. Darren O'Keefe. Derby Square Chambers, Merchants Court, Liverpool, 1999-2003. Dean's Court Chambers, 24 St John Street, Manchester, 2003.

PAYN, Frederick William
I. 26 January 1899. ETC. 16 July 1901. Prop. Taylor QC. Sec. Aggs. 4 Temple Gardens, 1901-1902. No address, 1903-1949. Not in 1950 Law List.

PEACE, John
Born 1871. Elder son Henry Peace of Woodgreen, Wednesbury, Staffs., brassfounder & electrical engineer. Formerly a solicitor and residing at 10 Hamilton Road, New Brighton when AAS. M. 11 November 1918. Call 27 January 1919. 25 Lord Street, Liverpool, 1923-1924. Obituary notice in Liverpool Post and Mercury for 28 January 1925. He had been a farmer in Canada before qualifying as a solicitor. He served as a councillor for Wallasey and was the brother of Edwin Peace a former Mayor of Wallasey.

PEACOCK, Victoria Mary
Newcastle University, LLB. I. November 1981. 14 Winckley Square, Preston, 1984-1991. No address 1992-1993. Not in 1994 Bar Directory.

PEARCE, Richard William
Born 21 January 1963 Cheshire. Abbot Beyne School, Burton on Trent; Trinity College, Cambridge, BA. AAS. M. 1 November 1983. Call 25 July 1985. ETC. December 1985. Prop. John Hugill QC. Sec. Michael Shorrock. Same Manchester Chambers; 2 Old Bank Street, 1985-1991; Peel Court Chambers, 45 Hardman Street, 1992.

PEARSON, Charles Edmund
L. 4 May 1887. ETC. 1 August 1887. Prop. French QC. Sec. Walton. 2 Harcourt Buildings, 1889-1890. Special pleader, Liverpool & Kirkdale Sessions. No address, 1891-1940. Not in 1941 Law List.

PEARSON, Christopher John
BA. I. November 1980. Manchester Chambers; 9th & 6* floor, Sunlight House, Quay Street, 1984-1987; Central Buildings, 3 Peter Street, 1988-1991; 211 Deansgate, 1992. Not in 1993 Bar Directory.

PEARSON, Rebecca
Born 20 April 1973 Crewe. King's Grove County High School, Crewe; University of Stafford, LLB. G. 14 October 1999. ETC. 14 December 1999. Prop. J J Rowe QC. Sec. Michael Goldwater. Cobden House Chambers, 19 Quay Street, Manchester, September 1999.

PEARSON, Wendy
LLB (Lancs). L. November 1996. Queen's Chambers, 5 John Dalton Street, Manchester, 1999. No chambers address 2000.

⋆ PEEL, His Honour Robert OBE., KC
Born 3 February 1881. Died 28 April 1969 aged 88. Eldest son of William Peel of Knowlmere Manor, Clitheroe. Married Mary Beatrice, elder daughter of Sir Henry Worsley-Taylor KC. Winchester; New College, Oxford. L. June 1906. 4 New Square, 1910-1933. Silk 1930. Equity draftsman & conveyancer. Served European War, 1914-1919; 16th London Regt, Queen's Westminster Rifles; Deputy Judge Advocate-General, British Salonika Force and Army of the Black Sea, despatches, OBE 1917, Brevet Major. County Court Judge, Circuit 4 (North Lancs.), October 1933-1953. WW.

PEILE, Charles
Born 1837. 4th son of Thomas Williamson Peile DD., formerly Headmaster of Repton School and lately Vicar of St Paul's Church, Avenue Road, London. AAS. M. 8 January 1876 (having been a solicitor). Call 18 November 1878. ETC. 27 July 1879. Prop. Gully QC. Sec. Dickinson. 19 Old Buildings, 1881-1903. Equity draftsman & conveyancer. Lancs. Chancery Court. Foster.

PENK, George
MA. I. 4 June 1913. ETC. 28 January 1914. Prop. Tobin KC. Sec. Maxwell. Liverpool Chambers; 25 Lord Street, 1914-1934; 13 Harrington Street, 1935-1936; 10 Cook Street, 1937-1949; 3 Cook Street, 1950-1959. Not practising, 1960-1963. Not in 1964 Law List.

PENNIFER, Kelly
Born 5 May 1971 High Wycombe. Millfield School; King's College, London, LLB; La Sorbonne, Paris (Matrise en droit). M. 27 November 1994. Littleton Chambers, 3 King's Bench North, 1994-1995. Pupilmaster, Clive Freedman. ETC December 1996. Exchange Chambers, Pearl Assurance House, Derby Square, Liverpool, 20.11.1996.

PENNINGTON, Arthur Reginald
I. 17 November 1893. ETC. 1 March 1894. Prop. C A Russell. Sec. A G Sparrow. 18 Booth Street, Manchester, 1894-1900. Lagos; District Commissioner, 1901; Police Magistrate, 1902. Puisne Judge, Gold Coast, 1903-1908. Attorney General, Southern Nigeria, 1909-1914. KC (Nigeria), 1915. Puisne Judge, Nigeria, 1915-1923. Entry as KC, Nigeria, 1924-1949. Not in 1950 Law List.

PENNINGTON, James Dixon
Born 1857. 2nd son of William Pennington of Manchester, cashier. BA (London); BSc (Victoria). AAS. M. 10 May 1895. Call. 26 April 1899. ETC. 16 July 1903. Prop Taylor KC. Sec. Shawcross. No address, 1904-1933. Not in 1934 Law List.

*** PENRY-DAVEY, David (Herbert) QC (The Hon. Mr Justice Penry-Davey)**

(DL)

Born 16 May 1942. Hastings Grammar School; King's College, London, LLB; Fellow 1998. I. July 1965; Bencher 1993. South Eastern Circuit. 3 Temple Gardens, 1965-1973; 8 New Square, 1974-1992; 2-3 Gray's Inn, 1993-1997. Recorder 1986. Silk 1988. Leader, South Eastern Circuit, 1992-1995. Chairman, Bar Council, 1996. High Court Judge, Queen's Bench Division, 1997. Presiding Judge, Northern Circuit, 2000-2003. WW.

PEPPER, Theresa
Born 9 July 1950 Birmingham. Married to Rodney Lewton Halligan qv. Rye St Anthony School, Oxford. G. November 1973. ETC. December 1973. Prop. Michael Maguire QC. Sec. Norman Wootton. Same Liverpool Chambers; Fruit Exchange, Victoria Street, 1973-1991; Chavasse Court, 24 Lord Street, 1992. Head of Chambers. Assistant Recorder 1997. Recorder 2000.

PEREIRA, Bernard de Haan TD
G. 19 November 1923. ETC. 18 February 1925. Prop. Wingate-Saul KC. Sec. Lloyd-Jacob. 8 King's Bench Walk, 1925-1927; 2 Hare Court, 1928-1949. No address, 1950-1952. Assistant Judge Advocate General, 6 Spring Gardens SW1, 1953-1966. Not in 1967 Law List.

PEREZ, Edmund ("Eddie")
Born 9 December 1916 Guatamala. British Citizen. Victoria University, Manchester, LLB. G. 26 January 1938. ETC. 1 March 1939. Prop. Pritchard KC. Sec. Jalland. Pupilmasters, Harold Lightman & Arthur Jalland. Same Manchester Chambers; 40 Kennedy Street, 1939-1948. No address, 1949-1957. 25 Bow Lane, 1958-1976; 460 Royal Exchange, 1977-1989. Deputy President, Pensions Appeal Tribunals. Retired 1989.

PERRIN, Eugene Courtney
I. 26 January 1912. ETC.15 February 1912. Prop. Greer KC. Sec. Cuthbert Smith. 25 Lord Street, Liverpool, 1912-1923. No address, 1924-1953. Not in 1954 Law List.

PERRY, Amanda
LLB (Birmingham). L. November 1987. Manchester Chambers; 1st floor, 3 Peter Street, 1989-1991; 211 Deansgate, 1992. Fountain Chambers, 1 Watson Street, Middlesbrough, 1993.

PERRY, William Francis Nugent
L. 2 July 1930. ETC. 9 July 1930. Prop. Jackson KC. Sec. Gorman. Manchester Chambers; 60 King Street, 1930-1939. Clerk of Indictments & later Associate of the Northern Circuit based at 1 Chapel Street, Preston, 1940-1953. 78 King Street, 1954-1958; 60 King Street, 1959-1965. Not in 1966 Law List.

PERSHOUSE, Arthur Penrose
I. 12 June 1907; Certificate of Honour. ETC. 17 July 1907. Prop. Taylor KC. Sec. Maurice Hill. 2 King's Bench Walk, 1907-1912. No address, 1913-1919. Not in 1920 Law List.

PETCH, Arthur Logan
LLB. G. July 1943. ETC. 1945. Manchester Chambers; 60 King Street, 1945-1950; 40 Kennedy Street, 1951-1965; Ship Canal House, King Street, 1966-1975. Full Time Chairman, Industrial Tribunals, Manchester, 1976-1984. Mess held in Manchester on 19.7.1984 to mark his retirement.

PETERKIN, John Dysart MBE
Born 1916. Elder son of James Peterkin of Dunbarton, Schoolmaster. Major, HM Forces. Glasgow University, MA., LLB. AAS. M. 4 January 1946. Call 26 January 1949. 60 King Street, Manchester, 1950-1954. Federal Counsel, Malaya, 1955-1960. No professional address, 1961-1965. Deputy Chairman, Redditch UDC, 1970. Adjudicator, Immigration Appeals, 1971-1976; Chief Adjudicator, 1977-1978. Not in 1979 Bar Directory.

PETRIE, James Alexander
MA (Oxon). G. 8 June 1921. ETC. 31 January 1923. Prop. Merriman KC. Sec. Chorley. 2 King's Bench Walk, 1922-1923; 10 KBW, 1924-1933; 7 KBW, 1934-1966. Not practising, 1967-1978. Not in 1979 Law List.

PHELAN, Sarah
Born 29 June 1975, Liverpool. Daughter of Bernard Phelan, Liverpool solicitor. Upton Hall Convent School, Wirral; University of Leeds, (Trinity & All Saints College), BA (Psychology & Public Media) I. November 1999. Pupilmaster Jeffrey Clarke, London, ETC. April 2001. Prop. Keith Goddard QC. Sec. Tom Watson. Chavasse Court, 24 Lord Street, Liverpool, 21.3.2001.

PHELPS, Ernest James
I. 17 November 1892. ETC. 14 March 1894. Prop. Bigham QC. Sec. McConnell. 12 King's Bench Walk, 1895-1898. Irish Bar H. 1898. Silk (Ireland). No address, 1899-1943. Not in 1944 Law List.

PHILIPPS, Arthur Gaved
Born 1850. Only son of John Arthur Phillips of Kensington SW., civil engineer. AAS. M. 29 October 1888. Call 10 June 1891. ETC. 21 March 1893. Prop. Bigham QC. Sec. Pickford. 2 Garden Court, 1893-1895; 1 Garden Court, 1896-1910. Not in 1911 Law List.

PHILLIPS, Sir Herbert KCMG., OBE
Born 8 July 1878. Died 27 March 1957 aged 78. AAS. M. 23 October 1905. Call 24 June 1914. Career diplomat in China, 1898-1940. No chambers address. Consul at; Shanghai, 1913-1920; Foochow, 1921-1922; Newchang, 1922-1923; Harbin, 1923-1925; Inspector General of Consulates in Far East, 1926-1929; Consul-General; Canton, 1930-1936; Shanghai, 1937-1940. OBE 1918. CMG 1928. KCMG 1938. FRGS. WW.

PHILLIPS, John Andrew (His Honour Judge Phillips)
Born 26 May 1950. Fitzwilliam College, Cambridge. Member Fitzwilliam String Quartet, quartet in residence at York University, 1971-1974. G. July 1976. London pupillage. Pupilmaster, Timothy Nash. ETC 1977. Manchester Chambers; 12th floor, Sunlight House, Quay Street, 1977-1979; 28 St John Street, 1980-1998. Recorder 1993. Circuit Judge at Carlisle, 6 July 1998. Director of Studies, Judicial Studies Board. WW.

PHILLIPS, Paul Michael
Born 27 January 1961. BA (Cantab). AAS. M. 11 February 1981. Call 28 July 1983. Bridge Street Chambers, 72 Bridge Street, Manchester, 1986-1987. No address 1988. Not in 1989 Bar Directory.

PHILLIPS, Thomas Gerard
LLB (London). L. November 1979. Room 22, 3rd floor, 15 Victoria Street, Liverpool, 1980. Not in 1981 Bar Directory. Liverpool Prosecutions Book is indorsed "To Gibraltar 1.11.1984"

PHILP, David Hugh
Born 20 December 1947, Harrogate. Eldest son of Eric Henry Philp of Warrington, local government officer. Keble College, Oxford, BA. AAS. M. 30 July 1970. Call November 1972. Manchester Chambers; 25 Bow Lane, 1972-1974; Room 460, Royal Exchange, 1975-1976; 40 King Street, 1988-1989. Left Manchester for London to become a Company Legal Advisor.

PHILPOTTS, (Robert) John
Born 23 July 1955, Cheshire. Hereford Cathedral School; Liverpool University, BA., MPhil. Schoolmaster, 1977-1988. G. October 1990; Scarman Scholar. ETC. 1990. Pupilmaster, lain Goldrein. Corn Exchange, Fenwick Street, Liverpool, 1990-1992; 40 King Street, Chester (Wales & Chester Circuit), 1992-1999; Exchange Chambers, Pearl Assurance House, Derby Square, Liverpool, 1998. Member of Stewards' Enclosure at Henley Royal Regatta.

PHIPPS, John Christopher (His Honour Judge Phipps)
Born 29 August 1946 London. Liskeard Grammar School, Cornwall, Liverpool University, LLB. AAS. M. 20 September 1967. Call 16 July 1970. Same Liverpool Chambers; Oriel Chambers, 14 Water Street, 1971-1982; Refuge Assurance House, Derby Square, 1983-1996. Assistant Recorder 1989. Recorder 1993. Circuit Judge 24 June 1996. WW.

PHYTHIAN, Kenneth
Born 1920. Only son of Arthur Phythian of Greenfield, Oldham, confectioner. Captain in British Army. Queen's College, Cambridge, MA. AAS. M. 24 January 1946. Call 26 January 1948. ETC. 1948. 60 King Street, Manchester, 1948-1963. Not in 1964 Law List.

PICKAVANCE, Graham Michael
Born 29 September 1950, St Helens. St Francis Xavier School, Woolton, Liverpool; Liverpool University, LLB. G. November 1973. ETC. 1974. Pupilmaster, John Gore. Same Liverpool Chambers; Fruit Exchange, Victoria Street, 1973-1991; Chavasse Court, 24 Lord Street, 1991.

PICKAVANCE, Michael John
Born 17 November 1951 Liverpool. First son of W H J Pickavance of Southport, director of machine tool & engineering companies. Charterhouse; Liverpool University, LLB. AAS. M. 1 May 1972. Call 18 July 1974. ETC. November 1974. Pupilmaster, AD Papworth. Same Liverpool Chambers; 3rd floor, 27 Dale Street, 1974-1989; Corn Exchange, Fenwick Street, 1989-1999; 7 Harrington Street (merger with Martins Bank Chambers), 6.9.1999. Member, Royal Birkdale Golf Club. Joint Winner of Carlisle Cup in 1980 & 1995.

PICKERING, Joan Tremearne (Mrs Arthur)
Married to His Honour John Arthur DFC qv, sister of His Honour Richard Pickering qv, aunt of Andrew Pickering qv. Liverpool University, LLB. L. June 1949. ETC. 1949. Pupilmaster, Edward Youds. Liverpool Chambers; North House, 17 North John Street, 1949-1950; 3 Cook Street, 1951-1958; The Temple, Dale Street, 1959-1966; 606, The Corn Exchange, Fenwick Street, 1967-1976 (not in practice). Died 1995.

PICKERING, Percival Andrew QC
Born 1811. Died 7 August 1876. Son of Edward Rowland Pickering, London solicitor. Eton; Trinity College, Cambridge, BA 1832; St John's College, MA, 1835 (Fellow, 1833-1841). I. 4 May 1838; Bencher 1855; Reader 1869; Treasurer 1870. 2 Paper Buildings, 1848. Silk 1855. 6 King's Bench Walk, 1976. Recorder of Pontefract, 1853-1865. Judge of the Liverpool Court of Passage, 1867-1876. Queen's Attorney & Serjeant, Lancaster, 1868-1876. Foster.

PICKERING, (Richard) Andrew
Born 26 January 1963, West Kirby. Son of His Honour Richard Pickering qv, nephew of His Honour John Arthur DFC qv and of Joan Pickering (Mrs Arthur) qv. Kingsmead School; Birkenhead School; Magdalen College, Cambridge, BA (English Literature); MA. City University, Dip. Law. L. November 1987. London pupilmasters, Richard Methuen and Stephen Worthington. 12 King's Bench Walk, 1987-2001; 14 Castle Street/ Atlantic Chambers, Cook Street, 2001.

PICKERING, His Honour Richard Edward Ingham

(RB)

Born 16 August 1929. Father of (Richard) Andrew Pickering qv, brother of Joan Pickering (Mrs Arthur) qv, brother-in-law of His Honour John Arthur DFC qv. Birkenhead School; Magdalen College, Cambridge, MA. L. November 1953. ETC. November 1955. Prop. Daniel Brabin QC. Sec. Melville Kennan. Circuit Junior, 1960. Same Liverpool Chambers; 34 Castle Street, 1955-1972; 54 Castle Street, 1973-1981. Councillor, Hoylake UDC, 1961-1964. Mental Health Review Tribunals, 1967-2001 (Regional Chairman, 1979-1981). Legal Chairman, Ministry of Pensions and National Insurance Tribunal, 1967-1977. Part time Chairman, Liverpool Industrial Tribunal, 1977-1979. Recorder, 1977-1981. Circuit Judge, 1981-1998. Northern Circuit Representative, H M Council of Circuit Judges, 1984-1989. President, Clatterbridge Hospital League of Friends, 2001. Retirement Tributes at Liverpool Law Courts, 26 June 1998 (Judge David Clarke QC/ Richard Henriques QC). Transcript in Circuit Records. WW.

PICKFORD, William KC (Baron Sterndale)

Born 1 October 1848 Manchester. Died 17 August 1923 aged 74. Liverpool College, Exeter College, Oxford, BA, 1873; MA 1908; Hon Fellow 1916. I. 17 November 1874; Bencher 1902. ETC. 17 November 1875, Prop. Baylis. Sec. Tomlinson. Liverpool Chambers; 22 North John Street, 1875-1879; Commerce Chambers, Harrington Street, 1880-1888; 13 Harrington Street, 1889-1893. Silk 1893. 2 Mitre Court Buildings, 1897-1907. Recorder of Oldham, 1901-1904. Recorder of Liverpool, 1904-1907. High Court Judge, Queen's Bench Division, 1907. Lord Justice of Appeal, 1914. President, Probate, Divorce & Admiralty Division, 1918. Master of the Rolls, 1919-1923. Kt 1907. PC. 1914. WW. DNB. Biography, "A Perfect Judge" by Her Honour Jean Graham Hall & Douglas Martin (Barry Rose), 1999. As a junior his most notable cases were of murder by arsenical poisoning. The first in 1884 in which he was led for the defence by Henry Gordon Shee QC was the case of R- v- Flanagan and Higgins. Two sisters had poisoned the husband of Higgins after having taken out a substantial insurance policy on his life. Both sisters were executed. The second and more famous was in 1889 when he was led by Sir Charles Russell QC in the defence of Florence Maybrick who, despite evidence from a chemist that the husband was in the habit of taking "pick me up" tonics containing arsenic, was convicted of murdering her husband. She was sentenced to death, reprieved, and served 15 years imprisonment. There had been great disquiet at the verdict and it was generally felt that the conviction was against the weight of the evidence after an unfair summing up by a judge thought to have been very unwell. Petitions containing over half a million names were instrumental in the reprieve. One from the Northern Circuit Bar read; "Having paid great attention to the evidence in the case of Florence Maybrick, we humbly pray that you will recommend to Her Majesty to commute the death sentence and grant a reprieve on the ground that, such evidence, in view of the great conflict of medical testimony as to the cause of death, leaves so much doubt that it is expedient and unsafe to carry out an irrevocable sentence." In Silk, his work lay in the main part in Admiralty and Commercial cases. In 1905 he was leading counsel for Great Britain at the inquiry held in Paris into the attack by the Russian fleet upon Hull trawlers at the Dogger Bank. Further Reading; Trial of Mrs Maybrick. Edited by H B Irving. Notable British Trials. William Hodge & Co Ltd., 1912. Lady Poisoners (Flanagan & Higgins pages, 198-223) by David Parry. Bluecoat Press, Liverpool, 2001.

PICKUP, David Michael Walker

Born 21 January 1958. Geneva. Burnley Grammar School; Leeds University, LLB. I. 24 July 1984. ETC. 1984. Pupilmaster, Stephen Meadowcroft. Same Manchester Chambers; 2 Old Bank Street, 1984-1992; Peel Court Chambers, 45 Hardman Street, 1992. Publications; Trade Council Advertising & Free Movement Goods, 1985; Reverse Discrimination & Free Movement Workers, 1986; The Story of the Machine in Victorian England, 2001.

PICKUP, James Kenneth QC

Born 25 September 1952 Stalybridge. His father was a solicitor and Clerk to the Justices of Dukinfield, Hyde, Stalybridge & Mottram. Kings School, Macclesfield; Lincoln College, Oxford, MA., BCL. G. July 1976. ETC. 1976. Pupilmasters, J. Michael Lever & Helen Grindrod. Manchester Chambers; Ship Canal House, King Street/ 2 Old Bank Street, 1976-1985; Rational House, 64 Bridge Street / Lincoln House Chambers, 1 Brazennose Street, 1985. Assistant Recorder 1995. Recorder 1998. Silk 2000. First class rugby union with Oxford University & Sale, 1971-1972. First class cricket with Oxford University, 1972-1975. Minor Counties cricket with Cheshire, 1971-1985. Member; MCC; Cheshire CCC and Lancashire CCC. WW.

PIERPOINT, Katherine Anne

Born 23 June 1976, Cheshire. St Hilary's School, Alderley Edge; Nottingham Trent University, LLB. L. October 1998. ETC. December 1998. Pupilmaster, J Lasker. Circuit Junior, 2002. Lincoln House Chambers, 1 Brazennose Street, Manchester, 1998.

PIERPOINT, Robert MP

Born 8 June 1845. Died 22 January 1932 aged 86. Only son of Benjamin Pierpoint of Warrington. Eton; Christ Church, Oxford, MA, 1871. AAS. I. 10 June 1870. Call 7 June 1873. ETC. 14 August 1874. Prop. Greenhow. Sec. Shiell. 7 King's Bench Walk, 1876-1891. No address, 1892-1932. MP (C) Warrington, 1892-1906. WW. Foster.

PIGOT, His Honour Thomas Herbert QC
Born 19 May 1921. Died 10 September 1998 aged 77. Manchester Grammar School; Brasenose College, Oxford, BA 1941; MA 1946; BCL 1947. Commissioned Welch Regiment, 1942. Served N. Africa with Royal Lincs. Regt; wounded and taken prisoner 1943; released 1945. I. November 1947; Bencher 1985. 14 Cook Street, Liverpool until Silk in 1967 when he practised from 2 Pump Court. Member, Bar Council, 1970. Circuit Judge, 1972-1990 sitting at Liverpool and later at Reading. Common Serjeant in the City of London, 1984-1990. Deputy Senior Judge, Sovereign Base Area, Cyprus, 1971-1984 (Senior Judge, 1984-1990) WW. Times Obituary.

PILKINGTON, John Ormerod
Born 1854. Eldest son of William Ormerod Pilkington of Preston. Rugby; Trinity Hall, Cambridge, MA 1878. AAS. M. 26 January 1874. Call 17 November 1877. ETC. 20 March 1878. Prop. Higgin QC. Sec. Addison. Circuit Junior, 1878. 15 Lord Street, Liverpool. 3 Garden Court, 1879-1881; 8 Fig Tree Court, 1882; 11 King's Bench Walk, 1883-1891. No address, 1892-1935. Not in 1936 Law List. Capt. 1st Volunteer btn.
(late 11th Lancashire) 1881. Foster.

PILLING, Cynthia Dorothy
LLB. G. November 1959. Manchester Chambers; 2 Booth Street, 1960-1975; 13 Police Street, 1976-1979; 6th floor, Arkwright House, Parsonage Gardens, 1980-1986; 20 St Mary's Parsonage, 1987-1993.

PIRIE, His Honour David Anthony
L. February 1961. ETC. February 1962. Prop. Edward Wooll QC. Sec. David McNeill. Circuit Junior, 1963. 34/54 Castle Street, Liverpool, 1962-1987. Recorder 1981. Circuit Judge, 1987-12 June 2002. Retired aged 65.

PIXLEY, James Aikin

I. 4 May 1887. ETC. 28 July 1888. Prop. Aspland QC. Sec. Shee. Circuit Junior, Winter 1889. 8 Fig Tree Court, 1889; 3 Paper Buildings, 1890-1895. No address, 1896-1911. Not in 1912 Law List.

PLANT, Charles Alick
L. 17 November 1919. 44 Lune Street, Preston, 1922-1925. Not in 1926 Law List.

PLATT, Sir (Frank) Lindsey 2nd Bt
Born 16 January 1919. Died 11 February 1998 aged 79. Son of Sir Harry Platt a prominent orthapaedic surgeon who died in 1986 aged 100. Sir Harry established the first fracture clinic in Manchester Ancoats Hospital. Shortly after the Great War, he devised and pioneered techniques to treat shoulder conditions. Lindsey succeeded to the baronetcy on his father's death but refused to use the title. He was a member of the team prosecuting Nazi War criminals and later became a member of the Control Commission administering the British Occupied Zone of Germany. Sadly he collapsed and died chasing a thief near his home in Fallowfield. WW.

PLATTS, (Charles) Graham (Gregory) (His Honour Judge Platts)
Born 25 August 1956. Married to Hazel Carty qv. Cheadle Moseley Grammar School; Fitzwilliam College, Cambridge MA. G. July 1978. ETC. 3 April 1979. Prop. Donald Hart QC. Sec. F Brian Carter. Same Manchester Chambers; 12th floor, Sunlight House, Quay Street 1979-1981; 28 St John Street 1981. Assistant Recorder 1999. Recorder 2000. Circuit Judge 8 February 2005.

PLATTS, Robert
Born 10 May 1939 Manchester. Chadderton Grammar School; London University LLB; Bradford Management Centre, Bradford University MSc. A V Roe & Co 1955-1958. H M Customs & Excise 1958-1972. L. July 1973. ETC. April 1974. Prop. Patrick Russell QC. Sec. J V Williamson. Manchester Chambers; Post Office Chambers, 26 Brown Street 1973-1975; Booth Street 1976; 13 Police Street 1976-1978; Rational House Chambers, 64 Bridge Street 1978-1992; Lincoln House Chambers, 1 Brazennose Street 1992. Assistant Recorder 1990. Recorder 1994.

PLIMMER, Melanie Ann
Born 29 June 1972 Trinidad & Tobago. Bristol University LLB; London University LLM (Jurisprudence). G. March 1996. Member of Trinidad & Tobago Bar. 2nd floor, Waldorf House, Cooper Street, Manchester 1999.

POISSON, Rene
Born 30 April 1957, South Africa. Kings College, Wimbledon; Manchester University LLB. M. July 1979. ETC December 1979. Pupilmasters, Jack Price & Janet Smith. 60 King Street, Manchester 1979- 1980. Manchester Business School 1980-1982. JP Morgan & Co, 1982-. Managing Director & Senior Officer for corporate lending in Europe.

POLGLAISE, David Sutherland
Born 1 October 1969, Rolmford. Chasetown High School; Exeter College, Oxford MA. M. October 1993. Paralegal with Michael Halsall, solicitor January 1994-December 1995. ETC. 28 March 1996. Prop. Somerset Jones QC. Sec. Vincent Deane. Liverpool Chambers; Victoria Chambers at 25 Victoria Street/ 19 Castle Street January 1996-August 1999; 8th floor, India Buildings, Water Street August 1999.

POLLARD, Sir George Herbert MP
Born 20 October 1864. Died 27 August 1937 aged 72. Son of James Pollard of Southport. Oxford & Edinburgh Universities. Doctor of Medicine. I. 14 June 1893. ETC. 29 July 1893. Prop. Yates QC. Sec. W Hughes. 2 Brick Court, 1908-1909; 12 King's Bench Walk, 1910-1913. No address, 1914-1937. Member of Lancashire County Council. Mayor of Southport, 1886-1887. MP (L) Eccles, 1906-1918. Medical Officer and Member of the Medical Board, Ministry of Munitions. Kt. 1909. WW.

POLLARD, Ian Roy
Born 31 October 1931, Preston. Shebbear College, Beaworthy, N. Devon; Assoc, Cambourne School of Mines. G. November 1965. Pupilmaster, James Booth. 36 St Ann Street, Manchester, 1965-1972. Legal Advisor/Manager, Express Newspapers, 1972-1988 (Consultant 1989.)

PONTER, Ian Michael
Born 29 April 1968, Chatham, Kent. Married to Susan Harrison qv. Sir Joseph Williamson's Mathematical School for Boys, Kent; Keele University, BA (Law & Politics); Aberdeen University, LLM (environmental law). M. 14 October 1993. Pupilmasters, Toby Davy & David Lamming. 2-3 Gray's Inn Square, 1994-1999. ETC. 31 July 2001. Prop. Andrew Gilbart QC. Sec. John Barrett. 40 King Street, Manchester, 2000. Standing Counsel for Treasury Solicitor.

POOLE, David Anthony QC (The Hon. Mr Justice Poole)
Born 8 June 1938. 3rd son of William Poole, medical practitioner. Ampleforth; Jesus College, Oxford, MA; Hon Fellow 1997. UMIST (Dip. Tech Sc). AAS. M. 7 November 1962. Call 26 November 1968; Bencher 1992. ETC 1968. Prop. Leslie Rigg QC. Sec. Gerard Humphries. Same Manchester Chambers; 9 Albert Square, 1968-1972; Deans Court Chambers, 1 Deans Court, Crown Square, 1973-1984. Recorder 1983. Silk 1984. 1 Crown Office Row, 1984-1995. Chairman, Association of Lawyers for the Defence of the Unborn, 1985-1992. High Court Judge, Queen's Bench Division, 1995. Kt. 1995. WW.

POOLE, Nigel David
Born 10 November 1965, Shipley, West Yorkshire. Bradford Grammar School 1973-1983, (Head Boy); The Queen's College, Oxford, 1984-1987, BA. AAS. M. 21 September 1987. Call 21 November 1989. ETC. December 1989. Pupilmaster, Alastair Forrest. 18 St John Street, Manchester, 1989. Crown Counsel (Provincial Panel), 2000.

POPE, Samuel QC
Born 11 December 1826, Manchester. Died 22 July 1901 aged 74. Uncle of Samuel Pope qv. London University. AAS. M. 13 November 1855. Call 7 June 1858; Bencher 1870; Reader Lent 1877; Treasurer 1888. 3 King's Bench Walk, 1876-1893; 38 Parliament Street, Westminster, 1894-1901. Recorder of Bolton, 1869-1901. Contested (L); Stoke, 1859; Bolton, 1869. Silk 1869. Leader of the Parliamentary Bar. JP., DL; Merioneth. WW. DNB. Foster.

POPE, Samuel Jnr
Born 1868. Died 8 April 1935. Eldest son of William Rushton Pope of Scotch Plains, New Jersey, USA, merchant, nephew of Samuel Pope QC qv. Trinity College, Oxford, BA 1891. AAS. M. 4 November 1887. Call 26 January 1892. ETC. 8 March 1893. Prop. Gully QC. Sec. Parry. Manchester Chambers; 41 John Dalton Street, 1894-1897; 40 Kennedy Street, 1898-1919; 60 King Street, 1920-1921. Recorder of Burnley, 1915-1921. Metropolitan Magistrate, 1921-1935 (North London & Clerkenwell). Commissioner of Inquiry into Mining Disasters, including Whitehaven, 1910-1911. Commissioned by Home Secretary to enquire and report in the working conditions of women and children between 1907 and 1913. First Chairman of the Milk (Distributive) Trade Board for England & Wales, 1921-1922. WW.

PORTER, Sir Alexander
Born 27 February 1853. Died 11 October 1926 aged 73. Owens College, Manchester. AAS. M. 7 June 1902. Call 17 May 1905. ETC. 20 July 1905. Prop. Shee KC. Sec. Byrne. 60 King Street, Manchester, 1909-1926. City Councillor & JP for Manchester. Kt 1912. Lord Mayor of Manchester, 1916-1917. WW.

PORTER, David Leonard
Born 18 December 1957, Manchester. Son of Leonard James Porter qv. Xaverian College; Manchester University, LLB. L. July 1980. ETC. 1983. Pupilmaster, Bertram Maddocks. Manchester Chambers; 3 St James's Square, 1980-1984; St James's Chambers, 68 Quay Street, 1984.

PORTER, Leonard James
Born 1929. Father of David Porter qv. Manchester University. AAS. M. 14 November 1949. Call 1 July 1952. Prop. Daniel Brabin QC. Sec. Easton. 3 St James's Square & 68 Quay Street, Manchester, 1954-1986.

PORTNOY, Leslie Reuben
G. June 1961. ETC. 1961. Pupilmasters, Corcoran & Temple. Same Manchester Chambers; 60 King Street, 1961-1983; 1 Deans Court, 1984-1996; 9 St John Street, 1996-2000. Recorder, 1988-2000. Retired from Bar on 6 March 2000 and went to live in Israel.

POSTLETHWAITE, William Taylor
Born 1858. 2nd son of John Postlethwaite of Crewe, iron founder. Victoria University, Manchester. AAS. M. 23 November 1895. Call 22 June 1898. ETC. 18 July 1898. Prop. Byrne. Sec. Ferguson. 60 King Street, Manchester, 1899-1905. No address, 1906-1949. Not in 1950 Law List.

POTTER, John Charles
Born 1855. Eldest son of John Gerald Potter of Darwen, Lancs. Christ Church, Oxford, BA, 1878. AAS. I. 17 November 1874. Call 21 April 1880. ETC. 16 July 1881. Prop. Gully QC. Sec. Swift. 3 Dr Johnson's Buildings, 1882-1885. No address, 1886-1920. Not in 1921 Law List.

*** POTTER, Mark Howard QC (The Rt. Hon. Lord Justice Potter)**

(DL)

Born 27 August 1937. Perse School, Cambridge; Gonville & Caius College, Cambridge, BA 1960; MA 1963. G. November 1961; Bencher 1987. 2 Crown Office Row, 1962-1977; Fountains Court, 1978-1988. Silk 1980. Recorder 1986. High Court Judge, Queen's Bench Division (Commercial Court), 1988-1996. Presiding Judge, Northern Circuit, 1991-1994. Lord Justice of Appeal, 1996. President, Family Division 6 April 2005. WW.

POTTER, William QC

Born 1838. Died 5 December 1893. Only son of William Potter of Liverpool, merchant. Trinity College, Dublin, BA. 1859. AAS. I. 28 May 1858. Call 30 April 1861; Bencher 1881. 2 Paper Buildings, 1876-1882; 3 Crown Office Row, 1883; 5 Paper Buildings, 1884-1893. Silk 1880. Foster.

POTTS, Charles
I. 8 June 1921. ETC. 22 February 1922. Prop. Merriman KC. Sec. Clement Davies. 2 Mitre Court Buildings, 1922-1934. No address, 1935-1953. Not in 1954 Law List.

POTTS, Warren Nigel
BA. Formerly a solicitor. M. July 1995. ETC. 2 April 1996. Prop. Richard Henriques QC. Sec. Mark Lamberty. Pupilmaster, Nicholas Fewtrell. Queen's Chambers, 5 John Dalton Street, Manchester, 1996.

POVOAS, Simon John Spencer
Born 11 February 1971, Leicester. Married to Felicity Somerset Jones qv. City of Leicester School; University of Central England, Birmingham, LLB; Warwick University, MA (History of Art). L. October 1996. ETC. December 1996. Pupilmaster, Julie Forsyth. Circuit Junior, 1998. Chavasse Court, 24 Lord Street, Liverpool, 1996.

*** POWELL, John Joseph QC (His Honour Judge Powell QC)**
Born 3 September 1816. Died 15 September 1891 aged 75. Uncle of A J Powell QC. M. 28 May 1842. Call 16 April 1847; Bencher 1863; Reader Lent 1867; Treasurer 1875. 1 Church Yard Court. 1848. Silk 1863. Leader of the Oxford Circuit. MP for Gloucester 1862-1865. First Recorder of Wolverhampton 1864-1891. County Court Judge 1884-1891. Circuit 11 (Burnley, Colne & Nelson 1884-1886) and Circuit 47 (Kent & Surrey 1886-1891) Foster.

POWELL, Jonathan David
Born 21 March 1961 Kendal. Kendal Grammar School; King's College, London, LLB, 1983; LLM, 1987. I. November 1984. Solicitor, Stockport MBC, 1986-1987. Lecturer in Law, Durham University, 1980-1990. ETC. 12 December 2001. Prop. Peter Birkett QC. Pupilmaster, Robin Campbell. 116-118 Chancery Lane. FRGS., Legal Associate RTPI.

POWELL, Richard Albert Brakell
Born 21 July 1892. Died 19 April 1957 aged 64. Liverpool College (Governor); Hertford College, Oxford, BA. Admiralty & Ministry of Shipping, 1915-1919. I. 16 June 1920. Various London Chambers. Deputy County Court Judge. H M Treasury, 1940-1944. Freeman, City of London. Publication; with Sir R Burrows KC, 3rd edition of Odgers on the Common Law. WW.

POWER, Nigel John
Born 30 January 1968 Oswestry; married to Kate Symms qv. Fitzalan Comprehensive, Oswestry; Reading University, LLB. I. November 1992. ETC. 25 March 1993. Prop. Rodney Klevan QC. Sec. Anthony Barraclough. Same Liverpool Chambers; Peel House, Harrington Street, 1993-1994; 25-27 Castle Street, 1995.

POWIS, Lucy Elizabeth
Born 23 March 1970 Gloucester. The Archway School; Liverpool University, LLB. G. 13 October 1992. ETC. December 1992. Pupilmasters, Nicholas Braslavsky & David Manley. 40 King Street, Manchester, October 1992.

PRAED, Fitzpatrick William Bulkley
Born 23 June 1845. 3rd son of Bulkley John Mackworth Praed of Oulsden Hall, Suffolk. St John's College, Cambridge, BA 1871. AAS. I. 1 May 1876. Call 17 November 1879. ETC. 14 January 1885. Prop. Gully QC. Sec. J Lumb. 5 Crown Office Row, 1886-1889. No address, 1890-1935. Not in 1936 Law List. Foster.

PRATT, Patricia Mary
Born 27 September 1964 Liverpool. Helsby Grammar School; Liverpool University, LLB. L. October 1991. ETC. December 1991. Prop. David Harris QC. Sec. Ross Duggan. Same Liverpool Chambers; 3rd floor, Peel House, Harrington Street, November 1991-1997; 8th floor, India Buildings, Water Street, 1998.

PRATT, Richard James
Born 22 June 1956, Huyton, Liverpool. St Mary's College, Crosby; Lanchester Polytechnic, Coventry, BA. G. 24 July 1980. Pupilmasters, Dudley Bennett & Richard Mawrey of 2 Harcourt Buildings. ETC. December 1981. Prop. Justin Price QC. Sec. Iain Goldrein. Same Liverpool Chambers; 5 Castle Street, 1981-1987; 48 Castle Street, 1987-1989; merged with Corn Exchange, Fenwick Street, 1989-1999; merger with Martins Building to form 7 Harrington Street, 6.9.1999. Assistant Recorder 1997. Recorder 2000. Circuit Crier, 1990-1996.

PREST, Henry Edgar
Born 1844. 4th son of Rev. Charles Prest. AAS. I. 18 April 1865. Call 27 January 1868. ETC. 28 July 1871. Prop. Holker QC. Sec. Pope QC. Manchester Chambers; 61 Princess Street, 1876-1877; 4 St James's Square, 1878-1885. Not in 1886 Law List.

PRESTON, Charles James
Born 1818. Died 9 May 1896. 4th son of Richard Preston of Liverpool. Downing College, Cambridge, MA, 1849. AAS. I. 26 May 1837. L. 26 January 1843. 1 Mitre Court Building, 1848. Liverpool Sessions. Stipendiary Magistrate for Birkenhead, 18 May 1866-1896. JP, Cheshire. Foster.

PRESTON, Darren Samuel
Born 22 December 1968 Bolton. Married to Carolyn Bland qv. Liverpool University, LLB. G. October 1991. ETC. 1991. Prop. John Rowe QC. Sec. Richard Heap. Manchester Chanbers; Kenworthy's Buildings, 83 Bridge Street, 1991-1998; 51-53 South King Street, 1998.

PRESTON, Francis Montagu
Born 1862. 2nd son of Richard Montague Preston of Chester, solicitor. Trinity College, Cambridge, BA., LLB, 1883. AAS. I. 26 January 1881. Call 25 June 1884. ETC. 9 February 1885. Prop. Aspinall QC. Sec. Segar. Liverpool Chambers; Commerce Court, Lord Street, 1887-1890; 2 Harrington Street, 1900-1923. No address, 1924-1940. Not in 1941 Law List. Foster.

PRESTT, His Honour Arthur Miller QC

(HS)

Born 23 April 1925. Died 26 October 2002 aged 77. Bootham School, York; Trinity Hall Cambridge, MA. Served 13 Btn. Parachute Regiment in France, Belgium, India, Malaya, Java, 1944-1946. Major, Legal Staff & War Crimes Prosecutor, 1946-1947. AAS. M. 4 October 1943. Call 29 June 1949. ETC. 1950. Prop. William Gorman QC. Sec. Joseph Cantley. Same Manchester Chambers; 4 Chapel Walks, 1950-1964; 601 Royal Exchange, 1965-1970. Silk 1970. 2 Pump Court, 1971. Chairman, Mental Health Review Tribunal, 1963-1970. Deputy Chairman, Cumberland Quarter Sessions, 1966-1969 (Chairman, 1970-1971). Circuit Judge (formerly County Court Judge), 1971-1990. Hon. Recorder of Manchester & Senior Circuit Judge, Manchester, 1982-1990. Member; Scouts Association and Parachute Regiment Association. WW. Times Obituary, 20 December 2002; "In Brief" Obituary (Simon Fawcus), March 2003.

PRICE, (Arnold) Justin QC

Born 16 August 1919. Died 25 March 1987 aged 67. Only son of Sydney W Price, solicitor. St Christopher's School, Liverpool; Kingsmead School, Meols; Liverpool College; Liverpool University, Board of Legal Studies. Served War, 1939-1945; Royal Engineers TA and later 2nd Lt, Royal Military Police TA. AAS. M. 10 February 1949. Call 25 November 1952. Wales & Chester Circuit, 1950-1955. Resident Magistrate, Nyasaland, 1955; Magistrate N. Nigeria, 1957; Acting Chief Magistrate & Judge, High Court N. Nigeria, 1957-1960. Wales & Chester Circuit, 1960-1969. ETC. 1969. Liverpool Chambers; 7 Rumford Street, 1969; 34 Castle Street, 1970-1973; Queen Insurance Building/Queen Avenue, 1974-1983. Silk 1976. 2 Pump Court & Peel House, Harrington Street. WW.

PRICE, John Alan "Jack" QC

Born 11 September 1938 Stretford, Manchester. Stretford Grammar School; Manchester University, LLB. G. February 1961. ETC. March 1961. Pupilmaster, C T B Leigh. Manchester Chambers; 60 King Street, 1961-1980, (Head, 1978-1980); Silk 1980. 25 Byrom Street, 1980-1999; 12 Byrom Street, 1999. Deputy Circuit Judge 1974., Recorder June 1980. WW.

PRIESTLEY, Roderick Charles

Born 8 October 1971 Liverpool. Rugby School; Bristol University, BSc. G. November 1996. ETC. December 1996. Prop. Mukhtar Hussein QC. Sec. Peter Wright. Circuit Junior, 2000. Lincoln House Chambers, 1 Brazennose Street, Manchester, 1996.

PRINCE, John

G. May 1949. 60 King Street, 1950-1954. No address, 1955-1963. Not in 1964 Law List. Sandy Temple & Ivor Taylor have told me that Prince left the Bar to work for an oil company and that he was killed in a De Havilland Comet crash in South Africa.

PRIOR, Charles Robert Christopher

Born 19 May 1971 Bradford. Bradford Grammar School; Oriel College, Oxford, BA (Modern History), Dip Law (City). L. October 1995. ETC. 19 December 1995. Prop. Rodney Klevan QC. Sec Anthony Edis. 14 Castle Street/ Atlantic Chambers, Cook Street, Liverpool, 1995.

PRITCHARD, The Hon Sir Fred Eills

Born 23 June 1899. Died 10 August 1982 aged 83. Son of Fred Pritchard of Liverpool. Shrewsbury School; Liverpool University, LLM; (Hon LLD 1956). Commission, Royal Marine Artillery, 1917-1919. AAS. M. 18 August 1919. Call 25 April 1923; Bencher 1946; Reader Autumn 1957; Treasurer 1964; Master Emeritus, July 1980. Hon. Bencher G. 1965. ETC. 14 June 1923. Prop. Singleton KC. Sec. Gething. Liverpool Chambers; 25 Lord Street, 1923-1928; 3 Cook Street, 1929-1933; 25 Castle Street, 1934-1937. Silk 1937. 3 Brick Court, 1937 1939. Commission, Royal Artillery, 1939; Major, and Deputy Judge Advocate, 1939-1942; Lt-Col and Assistant Judge Advocate-General, 1942-1945. MBE 1942. Judge of the Salford Hundred Court of Record, 1944-1947. 1 Plowden Buildings, 1946-1947. High Court Judge, Queen's Bench Division, 1947-1953 (resigned). Director, Inns of Court School of Law, 1958-1968. Publications; The Common Calendar- a notebook on Criminal Law for Circuiteers; "Rigby"- a Memoir of Mr Justice Swift; with Glyn Blackledge, "Goldiana"- The Collected Sayings of Sir Noel Goldie KC., MP. WW.

PRITCHARD, Robert Albion
Born 1828. 7th son of William Pritchard of Doctors Commons, London. Lincoln College, Oxford, DCL. AAS. I. 23 January 1852. Call 30 April 1855. 6 Mitre Court Chambers, 1876; 3 Paper Buildings, 1877-1917. Registrar, later Senior Registrar, High Court of Justice, Probate Division. Law Reporter for Incorporated Council. Publications; Author, Digest of Divorce & Matrimonial Cases; Joint author, Digest of Law & Practice of High Court of Admiralty. Not in 1916 Law List. WW. Foster.

PRITCHARD, Rodney
Born 19 March 1941 Newton-le-Willows. Newton Grammar School; Bristol University, LLB. I. 23 June 1964. ETC. November 1964. Pupilmaster, Philip Hinchliffe. 60 King Street, Manchester, 1964-1978. Magistrate then Crown Counsel in Hong Kong, 1978-1984; Private Practice at Hong Kong Bar, 1984-1996. Kenworthy's Building, 83 Bridge Street, 1996-1999; New Bailey Chambers, Preston, 1999.

PRITCHARD, Sarah Jane
Born 10 August 1971 Coventry. Married to Jaime Hamilton qv. Finham Park Comprehensive School; Manchester University, LLB. G. October 1993. ETC. 7 December 1993. Prop. Roger Farley QC. Sec. Nicholas Braslavsky. 40 King Street, Manchester, 1993.

PRITCHETT, Stephen John
Born 20 December 1966 Ilkeston, Derbys. Ilkeston School; Liverpool University, LLB. L. July 1989. Hardwicke Scholar. ETC. 1990. Prop. David Turner QC. Sec. William George. 20 North John Street, Liverpool, 1990-1997; 40 King Street, Manchester, 1997.

PRITT, Denis Nowell QC., MP
Born 1887. Died 23 May 1972. 2nd son of Harry Walter Pritt of Preston, merchant. Winchester; London University, LLB. AAS. M. 1 May 1906. Certificate of Honour, E 1909. Call 17 November 1909; Bencher 1936; Reader Lent 1945; Master Emeritus 1958. 4 Essex Court, 1910-1913; 3 Essex Court, 1914-1920; 2 Harcourt Buildings, 1921-1923; 2 Pump Court, 1924-1941; 4 Paper Buildings, 1942-1946; 4 Essex Court, 1947-1952; Cloisters, 1953-1960. Silk 1927. MP (Soc) North Hammersmith, 1935-1950. Chairman; Howard League for Penal Reform; Bentham Committee for Poor Litigants. Professor of Law, University of Ghana. Numerous books on social and political matters and a 3 volume autobiography; "From Right to Left", 1965; "Brasshats & Bureaucrats", 1966; "The Defence Accuses", 1966. WW. DNB. After the "Reichstag" fire in 1933, Pritt and six other lawyers of various nationalities formed a commission of inquiry which concluded that the fire had been engineered for political reasons by the Nazi party. In 1952, he defended Jomo Kenyatta and other Africans on charges connected with Mau Mau terrorist activities in Kenya. James Comyn says: "It was said of Mr Justice Hilbery, who could at times be very awkward in court, that he once met that extraordinarily able man D N Pritt QC in Gray's Inn and admired his dog. " A lovely dog you have there, Pritt." "Yes Judge, but like all aristocratic looking creatures, very difficult." "Pritt", Hilbery J. used to say "is, I regret to say, a very common man."

PRIWES, Uriel Menahem
Born 1937. 1st son of Moshe Z Priwes of Tel-Aviv, Civil Servant & University Lecturer. Married to Atara Ben Tovim, Principal flautist with Royal Liverpool Philharmonic Orchestra (marr. dis). LLB, (London), B.Eng (McGill). Civil Engineer. Worked for London Transport Executive when AAS. M. 4 April 1963. Call 22 November 1966. ETC. 1966. Same Liverpool Chambers; 9 Rumford Street, 1966-1973; Fruit Exchange, Victoria Street, 1974-July 1975 when he went to practice law in Canada.

PROCTER, Henry Adam MP
Born 1883. Died 26 March 1955. Son of William Procter of Liverpool. Bethany College, West Virginia, USA; Universities of Melbourne & Edinburgh, MA., LLD. Served European War, 1916-1919; Retired 1922 with rank of Major. AAS. M. 10 October 1927. Call 17 November 1931. ETC. 5 July 1933. Prop. Lynskey KC. Sec. Gerrard. Goldsmith Building, 1937-1955. MP (U) Accrington, 1931-1945. Patented numerous inventions in connection with pulverised fuel. WW.

PROCTER, His Honour Sir William
Born 17 November 1871. Died 26 June 1951 aged 79. Solicitor in Liverpool 1899. G. 26 January 1905. Prop. Tobin KC. Sec. Greer. 25 Lord Street, Liverpool, 1905-1928. County Court Judge, Circuit 19, (Derby & Staffs), 1928-1930; Circuit 6, (Liverpool), 1931-1946. Kt, 1941. WW.

*** PROCTOR, His Honour Anthony James**
Born 18 September 1931. Mexborough Grammar School, Yorks.; St Catherine's College, Cambridge, MA., LLM. Flying Officer, Royal Air Force, 1953-1955. Articled to Sir Bernard Kenyon, County Hall, Wakefield, 1955-1958. Admitted Solicitor, 1958. Senior Prosecuting Solicitor, Sheffield Corporation, 1959-1964, Partner, Broomhead & Neals, solicitors, Sheffield, 1964-1974. District Registrar & County Court Registrar, Barrow-in-Furness, Lancaster &

Preston, 1974-1988. Recorder 1985-1988. President, Association of District & County Court Registrars, 1985-1986. Circuit Judge, 1988-2001. WW.

PROCTOR, Harry
BA., LLB. L. 26 January 1897. ETC. 2 February 1898. Prop. Carver QC. Sec. Mellor. 2 New Square, 1899-1903; 5 St James's Square, Manchester, 1904-1908. No address, 1909-1914. Not in 1915 Law List.

PROWSE, James Barrington
Born 19 October 1950 Horsham, Sussex. Cheadle Hulme School; Britannia Royal Naval College, Dartmouth; Lancashire Polytechnic, LLB. MBM, AMITD. I. July 1986. ETC. December 1986. Derby Square Chambers, Liverpool, 1987-2001. District Judge (Magistrates Court) 8 January 2001 (Deputy, 1995-2001).

PRUDHOE, Timothy Nixon
Born 27 October 1970 Nantwich. Sedbergh School; Manchester University, LLB. G. October 1994. ETC. 2 April 1996. Prop. Richard Henriques QC. Sec. Green. Queen's Chambers, 5 John Dalton Street, Manchester, 1996-2000.

PUGH, John Bishop
Born 12 June 1949, Liverpool. Birkenhead School; Liverpool University, LLB. L. July 1972. ETC. 20 March 1973. Prop. David McNeill QC. Sec. Eric Goldrein. Pupilmaster, Inge Bernstein. Liverpool Chambers; 54 Castle Street, 1973-1987; 14 Castle Street, 1987-1993; 3rd floor 14 Castle Street, 1993.

PUGH, John Hunter
Born 1848. Only son of John Pugh of Llansannan, Denbighs., Clerk in Holy Orders. Formerly a solicitor. AAS. 2 April 1883. Call 7 May 1884. ETC. 31 July 1885. Prop. Kennedy QC. Sec. Duncan. 4 Harrington Street, Liverpool, 1891-1901; 1 Plowden Building, 1902-1904; 2 Pump Court, 1905-1907. No address, 1908-1909. Not in 1910 Law List. Foster.

PUGH, Rowland Hill
I. 20 June 1917. No address, 1918-1953. Not in 1954 Law List.

PULLEY, William
L. 17 November 1852. Liverpool Chambers; Clarendon Rooms, South John Street, 1876-1878; Oxford Chambers, Lord Street, 1879-1882. Not in 1883 Law List.

PURCELL, Deidre Marie
Born 18 October 1964 Redbridge, Essex. La Sainte Union; Liverpool University, LLB. BBC Radio 4, 1986-1990. Global Gas PLC, 1991-1996. L. 23 November 2000. ETC. December 2000. Prop. Peter Birkett QC. Sec. Graham Wells. Liverpool Chambers; Derby Square Chambers 4 September 2000-2003. Bulk of chambers joined Oriel Chambers, 14 Water Street on 1 January 2004. 2nd beneficiary of an award from the Richard Isaacson Memorial Scholarship Fund.

PURCHASE, Henry George MP
Born 1873. Died 1945. Formerly departmental manager to wholesale manufacturers. LLD, (London). AAS. M. 8 November 1910. Call 4 June 1913. Liverpool Chambers; 13 Harrington Street, 1914-1917; 25 Lord Street, 1918-1921. 3 Paper Buildings, 1922-1932; 12 King's Bench Walk, 1933; 5 Crown Office Row, 1934-1939; 2 Paper Buildings, 1939-1945. MP (CL) Kennington Division of Lambeth, 1918-1922. Assistant Director, Ministry of Food, 1942-1943. Publications; Law Relating to Documents of Title to Goods. WW.

Q

QAZI, Jamaluddin
BA. L. November 1971. Manchester Chambers; 21 Spring Gardens 1973-1975. 4th floor, Sunlight House, Quay Street, 1976. Not in 1977 Bar Directory.

QUENBY, Richard Alan
BA. I. July 1985. St James's Chambers, 68 Quay Street, Manchester, 1989-1998. No address 1999.

QUINN, Amanda Jane
Born 24 October 1973, Wirral. Upton Hall Convent School; Liverpool John Moores University, LLB. with James Murray, Solicitors, 1999-2001. M. 11 October 2001. Pupilmaster, Diarmuid Flood. 14 Cook Street, Liverpool, 1 October 2001.

QURESHI, Khawar Mehmood
LLB., LLM (Cantab) M. October 1990. 1 Hare Court, 1995-2000; Serle Court, 6 New Square, Lincoln's Inn, 2000.

R

RABY, Percy
Born 1873. 4th son of William Raby of The Gables, Didsbury, iron merchant. Victoria University, Manchester, MA., LLB. AAS. M. 7 November 1893. Call 26 January 1897. ETC. 2 March 1897. Prop. Shee QC. Sec. Overend Evans, Manchester Chambers; 78 Cross Street, 1899-1908; 78 King Street, 1909-1911. No address, 1912-1928. Not in 1929 Law List. Equity draftsman & conveyancer.

RADCLIFFE, David Andrew
Born 13 June 1942, Glasgow. The Leys School; Aix Marseilles University; Fitzwilliam College, Cambridge, MA. I. July 1966. 14 Cook Street, Liverpool, 1966-1968, then joined South Eastern Circuit. 5 King's Bench Walk, 1969-1997; 18 Red Lion Court, EC4., 1998. Recorder 1987; Immigration Adjudicator, 1998; part time Special Adjudicator, 1998.

RADCLIFFE, John Percy
I. 12 May 1897. ETC. 22 February 1899. Prop. Taylor QC. Sec. Tobin. 41 Castle Street, Liverpool, 1903-1907. Lancs. Chancery Court. 8 The Close, Exeter, 1908-1925. Western Circuit. Not in 1926 Law List.

RADCLIFFE, Richard Duncan
Born 1845. Eldest son of Richard Radcliffe of Stoneycroft, West Derby, gent. Christ Church, Oxford, BA 1868. AAS. M. 28 January 1865. Call 18 November 1872. ETC. 28 March 1873. Prop. Torr QC. Sec. Hopwood., 3 Essex Court, 1876. No address, 1877-1935. Not in 1936 Law List. Foster.

RADFORD, Arthur
Born 1853. 2nd son of James Radford of Wrexham. Christ College, Cambridge LLM. AAS. I. 23 November 1872. Call 7 June 1875. ETC. 24 July 1876. Prop. Pope QC. Sec. Little. Law Association Rooms, 14 Cook Street, Liverpool, 1877-1895. Liverpool & Bolton Sessions. No address, 1896-1935. Not in 1936 Law List. Foster.

RADFORD, Ernest
Born 1853. 2nd son of Richard Radford of Manchester, Solicitor. Pembroke College, Cambridge, BA 1876. AAS. L. 17 November 1874. Call 18 November 1878. ETC. 6 March 1890. Prop. Ambrose QC. Sec. Ferguson. Manchester Chambers; 60 King Street, 1879-1889; 51 King Street, 1890-1897; 78 King Street, 1898-1926. Equity draftsman & conveyancer, Lancs. Chancery Court. Not in 1927 Law List. Foster.

RADLEY, Charles Poole
I. 26 January 1893. ETC. 20 March 1893. Prop. Walton QC. Sec. Tobin. 2 King's Bench Walk, 1895-1910. No address, 1911-1949. Not in 1950 Law List.

RAE, Charles Edward Leahart
Grandfather of James Robert Rae qv. I. 26 January 1909. ETC. 11 March 1909. Prop. Tobin KC. Sec. Leslie Scott. Circuit Junior, Winter 1910. No address, 1909-1915. Not in 1916 Law List.

RAE, James Robert
Born 2 June 1952, Rome. Grandson of Charles Edward Leahart Rae qv. Eton College; College of Law. I. July 1976. Pupilmasters, Maureen Campbell & Anthony Bridgden (Temple) ETC. 30 November 1978. Same Liverpool Chambers; 606 The Corn Exchange, 1978-1981; 1 Exchange Flags, 1982-1991; Exchange Chambers, Pearl Assurance House, Derby Square, 1992.

RAEBURN, Sir William Norman Bt, CBE., KC
Born 16 August 1877. Died 5 February 1947 aged 69. Eldest son of Sir William Hannay Raeburn, 1st Bt., of Glasgow, shipowner. Kelvinside Academy, Glasgow; Uppingham; Glasgow University, MA., LLB. AAS. M. 20 November 1900. Call 24 June 1903; Bencher 1927; Reader 1937. ETC. February 1905. Prop. Horridge KC. Sec. Kennedy. 5 Paper Buildings, 1905-1947. Silk 1919. CBE 1920. 2nd Bt., 1934. WW.

RAFFLES, Thomas Stamford
Born 18 September 1818. Eldest son of Rev. Thomas Raffles DD., of Liverpool. Glasgow University, BA 1838. AAS. I. 7 May 1836. Call 19 November 1841. 3 Hare Court, 1848. Judge of Salford Court of Record, 1859-1860. Stipendiary Magistrate for Borough of Liverpool, 1860-1891. Publications; Life of Rev. Dr. Raffles. Foster.

RAHMAN, Yaqub
Born 18 December 1965, East Dulwich, London. Northgate High School, Ipswich; Trinity College, Oxford, BA (Chemistry). Dip. Law. Waiter, Koh-I-Noor Tandoori Restaurant, Ipswich 1981-1988. Administrative Assistant, HM Customs & Excise, 1988-1989. Housing Benefits Officer, Oxford County Council, 1989. G. 15 October 1991. 2 Gray's Inn Square, 1991-1992. Pupilmaster Keith Knight. ETC. 1992. Pupilmaster, Charles Feeny. Liverpool Chambers; Peel House, Harrington Street, 1992-1999; Oriel Chambers, 14 Water Street, 1.3.1999. Junior Treasury Counsel, Common Law, Provincial Panel 2001. Double Blue (Basketball) 1987 & 1988.

RAIKES, His Honour Judge Francis William QC
Born 2 February 1842. Died 28 September 1906 aged 64. 2nd son of Henry Raikes, barrister & Registrar of Chester Diocesan Court, brother of the Rt. Hon. Henry Cecil Raikes MP. Shrewsbury School; Royal Academy, Gosport on Sea. Served three years in Merchant Navy followed by seven years in the Royal Navy as a Navigating Officer. Peterhouse, Cambridge, BA 1871; MA 1874; LLM 1876; LLD 1882. AAS. I. 20 November 1869. Call 18 November 1872. ETC. 25 February 1873. Prop. Kay QC. Sec. Ridley. 7 King's Bench Walk, 1876-1898. After 1876 a member of Northern & North Eastern Circuits. Admiralty Reporter for Law Times in Court of Appeal. Election Commissioner at Gloucester, 1880. County Court Judge, Circuit 16, (Ridings of Yorkshire), July 1898-1906. Publications; The New Practice (with Mr Justice Kennedy); Jurisdiction & Practice of County Courts in Admiralty (with Mr Kilburn). WW. Foster.

RAILTON, Ernest Henry
Born 3 May 1860. Elder son of Henry Railton of Snittlegarth, Carlisle. Rugby; Trinity College, Oxford, BA. AAS. I. 7 May 1881. Call 25 June 1884. ETC. 11 February 1886. Prop. Bigham QC. Sec. McCall. 1 Temple Gardens, 1886-1888; 6 Pump Court, 1889-1890; 7 Fig Tree Court, 1891-1900. No address, 1901-1933. Not in 1934 Law List. Foster.

RALEIGH, Hon Sir Thomas KCSI., KC
Born 2 December 1850 Edinburgh. Died 8 February 1920 aged 69. Balliol College, Oxford, BA 1875. All Souls College, Oxford; Fellow 1876; MA 1878; BCL 1890; DCL 1896. AAS. L. 24 January 1873. Call 13 June 1877. ETC. 2 August 1877. Prop. Herschell QC. Sec. Myburgh. 4 Brick Court, 1877-1881; 5 New Square, 1882-1889; 10 Old Square, 1905-1911. Reader in English Law at Oxford, 1884-1896. Contested; South Edinburgh, 1885; West Edinburgh, 1888. Registrar of the Privy Council, 1896-1899. Legal Member of the Viceroy's Council in India, 1899-1904. Vice-Chancellor, Calcutta University, 1900-1904. Member of the Council of India, 1909-1913. Publications; Elementary Politics, 1886; Outline of the Law of Property, 1889. CSI. 1902. KCSI. 1904. Silk 1908. WW. Foster.

RALSTON, William Ross
Born 31 October 1978 Aberdeen. Peterhead Academy; University of Northumbria at Newcastle, LLB. I. 12 October 2000. ETC. 2000. Prop. David Steer QC. Sec. Peter Davies. 7 Harrington Street, Liverpool, September 2000.

RAÑALES-COTOS, Tina
Born 15 April 1974 Bangor, N Wales. Ysgol Gyfun, Llangefhi, Anglesey; Leicester University, LLB (European Law); Brasenose College, Oxford, BCL. L. October 1999. Monckton Chambers, London, 1999-2000. Pupilmaster, Mark Harper. European Commission, Brussels, 2000-2001. ETC. March 2001. Prop. Michael Booth QC. Sec. Sarah Pritchard. Kings Chambers, 40 King Street, Manchester, March 2001.

RANKIN, Andrew QC
Born 3 August 1924. Father of William Peter Rankin qv. Royal High School, Edinburgh. Served War, 1939-1945, Sub-Lt., RNVR. Edinburgh University, BL 1946; Downing College, Cambridge, BA 1948. Lecturer in Law, Liverpool University, 1948-1952. G. May 1950. Lord Justice Holker Scholar. ETC. 1950. Pupilmaster, Robertson Crichton. 7 Rumford Street, Liverpool, 1950-1968. Silk 1968. 2 Hare Court, 1968-1983; 2 Serjeants Inn, 1984-1987; 218 Strand, 1988-1992; Queen Elizabeth Building, 1993-1996; 4 Field Court, 1997. Recorder, 1972-1997. University Blue; Edinburgh, 1943 & 1946; Cambridge, 1948. Publications; Levie's Law of Bankruptcy in Scotland. (4th edition). WW.

RANKIN, Ciaran Emmanuel
LLB. L. November 1988. Manchester Chambers; 20 St Mary's Parsonage, 1989-1993; 51-53 South King Street, 1994.

RANKIN, Rt. Hon. Sir George Claus
Born 12 August 1877. Died 8 April 1946 aged 68. George Watson's College; Edinburgh University; Trinity College, Cambridge; President of the Union. L. 26 January 1904; Bencher 1937. ETC. 17 February 1906. Prop. Pickford KC. Sec. Leslie Scott. 2 Mitre Court Buildings, 1906-1916. 2nd Lt., Royal Garrison Artillery, 1916; Lt, 1917. Puisne Judge, Calcutta, 1918-1926. Kt. 1925. Chief Justice, Calcutta, 1926-1934. PC 1935. Member, Judicial Committee of the Privy Council, 1935-1944. Hon. LLD, Edinburgh, 1937. Publications; Studies in Indian Law, 1946; editor of 11th edition of Mulla's Mahomedan Law, 1938. WW. DNB. He was probably the greatest judicial authority on Indian jurisprudence of his time. When he died Lord Maugham said of him " there has been no judge of my time who more greatly impressed me in a sphere he may be said to have made his own."

RANKIN, William Kerr

Born 18 July 1971 Worcester. Married to Rachel Hughes qv. Malvern College; Manchester University, LLB. G. October 1994. ETC. 20 December 1994. Prop. Nigel Gilmour QC. Sec. Christopher Alldis. Liverpool Chambers; ground floor, Peel House, Harrington Street, 1994-1999; Oriel Chambers, 14 Water Street, 1.3.1999.

RANKIN, William Peter

Born 21 July 1949. Son of Andrew Rankin QC qv. Wellington School, Bebington; Fitzwilliam College, Cambridge, MA. Dip HR (Strasbourg). Dip. ICEI (Amsterdam). G. November 1972. ETC 1972. Prop. Eric Somerset Jones QC. Sec. John Stannard. Pupilmasters, Scott Baker (Temple) & John Stannard. Liverpool Chambers; Oriel Chambers; 14 Water Street/ 5 Covent Garden, 1972.

RATHBONE, Herbert Reynolds

I. 28 January 1895. ETC. 18 March 1895. Prop. Walton QC. Sec. Carver. 15 Lord Street, Liverpool, 1895-1930. Not in 1931 Law List.

RATLEDGE, John

Born 8 August 1974, Preston. Adlington County Primary School; Bolton School; St John's College, Cambridge, BA., MPhil. Cambridge; Cricket Blue & Soccer Colour. L. 25 November 1999. ETC. 14 December 1999. Prop. Clement Goldstone QC. Sec. Graham Platts. 28 St John Street, Manchester, 2000.

RAWCLIFFE, (Anthony) Mark (Wilson)

Born 14 July 1972, Preston. Hutton Grammar School, Preston; Keble College, Oxford, BA (Modern History); Liverpool University, LLM. M. November 1996. ETC. December 1996. Pupilmaster, John Corless. 14 Castle Street/Atlantic Chambers, Cook Street, Liverpool, 1996.

RAWLINSON, Michael Edward

Born 2 June 1969, Littleborough, Lancs. St Bede's College, Manchester; Manchester University, LLB (Street Tort Prize). I. 26 November 1991 (Major Scholarship). ETC. December 1991. Prop. Charles Bloom QC. Sec. Charles Chruszcz. St John's Buildings, St John Street, Manchester, June 1991. Publications; The Criminal Injuries Compensation Scheme (Sweet & Maxwell Practitioner Series).

RAY, Frederick

Born 1866. 2nd son of William Ray of Whalley Range, Manchester, law stationer. Reporter when AAS. M. 26 April 1893. ETC. 26 February 1894. Prop Byrne. Sec. Kay. Manchester Chambers; 4 St James's Square, 1894-1901; 23 John Dalton Street, 1902-1936. Retired to West Didsbury, 1937-1944. Not in 1945 Law List.

RAYNER, Oscar Welwyn

I. 10 June 1891. ETC. 5 April 1892. Prop. Hopwood QC. Sec. Pickford. No address, 1892-1930. Not in 1931 Law List.

RAYNER, Sir Thomas Crossley

Born 19 April 1860, Manchester. Died 22 May 1914 aged 54. Only son of Thomas Rayner, MD., of Manchester. Owens College, Manchester. AAS. M. 12 June 1879. Call 3 May 1882. ETC. 15 July 1882. Prop. Gibbs QC. Sec. Elliot. 8 St James's Square, Manchester, 1882-1887. District Commissioner, Gold Coast Colony, 1887; Acting Queen's Advocate, 1890; Stipendiary Magistrate, Trinidad, 1891; Acting Puine Judge, 1891 & 1893; Acting Commissioner of Tobago, 1892; Chancellor of the Diocese of Trinidad, 1893; Puisne Judge of the Gold Coast Colony, 1894; Chief Justice of the Colony of Lagos, 1895-1902. Kt. 1899. KC & Attorney General (British Guiana), 1902; Chief Justice, British Guiana, 1912-1914. WW.

RAYNOR, Philip Ronald QC (His Honour Judge Raynor QC)

Born 20 January 1950. Roundhay School, Leeds; Christ's College, Cambridge (Scholar), MA. Lecturer in Law, Manchester University, 1971-1974. I. July 1973. ETC. Autumn 1973. Pupilmasters, George Spafford & Nigel MacLeod. Manchester Chambers; 25 Bow Lane, 1973-1976; 460 Royal Exchange, 1976-1987; 40 King Street, 1987-2001; Head of Chambers, 1996-2001. Recorder 1993. Silk 1994. Circuit Judge, May 2001. WW.

REA, Irene Leslie

BA (Belfast). ETC. 28 June 1979. Prop. Patrick Russell QC. Sec. A P Morris. 2 Old Bank Street, Manchester, 1979-1986; Door tenant, 1987-1994. Not in 1995 Bar Directory.

READ, Percy

Born 1862. 2nd son of John Read of Stockport. AAS. M. 15 November 1880. Call 25 June 1884. ETC. 22 July 1887. Prop. Hopwood QC. Sec. Wharton. No address, 1886-1910. Not in 1911 Law List. Foster.

READE, Kevin Majella
Born 3 September 1962, Liverpool. St Mary's College; Liverpool University, LLB. G. July 1983. ETC. December 1983. Pupilmaster, Robert Fordham. Circuit Junior, 1986. Liverpool Chambers; Martins Building, Water Street, 1983-1999; 7 Harrington Street (merger with Corn Exchange), 6.9.1999.

READING, First Marquess (See Rufus Isaacs)

REANEY, Janet Elizabeth
Born 26 January 1955, Whiston. Married to E Haygarth qv. St Hildas C of E High School, Liverpool; Downing College, Cambridge, MA. AAS. M. 4 February 1986. Call 23 July 1987. ETC. December 1987. Pupilmaster, Mark Hedley. Same Liverpool Chambers; 3rd floor, 27 Dale Street, 1987-1991; Corn Exchange, Fenwick Street, 1991-1999; 7 Harrington Street, (merger with Martins Building), 6.9.1999.

REARDEN, James Ambrose
G. 17 November 1922. 43 Castle Street, Liverpool, 1922-1926. No address, 1927-1953. Not in 1954 Law List. KC, Ireland.

REDFERN, Michael Howard QC

Born 30 November 1943, Burnley. Married to Her Honour Judge Eaglestone qv. Stretford Grammar School for Boys; Leeds University LLB. Teacher, 1966-1967; Lecturer, 1967-1968. I. July 1970; Bencher 2002. Pupilmaster, Denis Orde (North Eastern). ETC. 1970. Manchester Chambers; 47 Peter Street, 1970-1974; 12th floor, Sunlight House, Quay Street, 1975-1979; 28 St John Street (now St John's Building), 1980. Silk 1993. Recorder 1999. Chairman of the Royal Liverpool Childrens' Hospital Inquiry, (1999-2001) which found that for many years parents of children who had died at Alder Hey Hospital were not informed that organs had been removed and stored for research purposes. Circuit Leader 2005. WW.

REDMOND, Helen
Born 17 May 1976, Liverpool. St Bede's RC High School; Liverpool University, LLB., LLM. G. 14 October 1999. ETC. 14 December 1999. Prop. Ian Leeming QC. Sec. David Gilchrist. 9 St John Street, Manchester, 27.9.1999.

REDMOND, Peter William Dawson
LLM. G. February 1954. 9 Rumford Street, Liverpool, 1955-1957. No address, 1958-1963. Not in 1964 Law List.

REDMOND, Steven
BA. G. July 1975. ETC. 27 May 1982. Albert House, 192 Manor Street, Stoke-on-Trent (Midland & Oxford), 1978-1981. ETC. 27 May 1982. 9th & 6th floors, Sunlight House, Quay Street, Manchester, 1982-1988. 4 Fountain Court, Steelhouse Lane, Birmingham, 1989.

REDMOND, William Archer DSO
Born 1866. Died 17 April 1932. Only son of John Redmond, Chairman of the Irish Parliamentary Party. Clongowes; Trinity College, Dublin. Irish Bar, 1910. Served European War, 1914-1918; Captain in Irish Guards. MP Tyrone, 1910-1918. MP (N) Waterford, 1918-1922. G. 26 January 1921. ETC. 6 July 1921. Prop. Langdon KC. Sec. Pritt. Member, Dail Eireann for Waterford, 1923-1932. No chambers address. WW.

REECE, Francis Bertram CBE
Born 1888. Died 4 April 1971. Rossall; St John's College, Cambridge. I. 24 June 1914. ETC 1914. No address, 1914-1920. 3 Brick Court, 1921-1941 (Wales & Chester Circuit); 1 Garden Court, 1942-1943. Recorder of Birkenhead, 1935-1943. Metropolitan Magistrate, 1943-1961. (Tower Bridge, 1943-1948 & Bow Street, 1948-1961). CBE 1958. WW.

REED, Sir John (Seymour) Blake
Born 26 November 1882. Died 8 March 1966 aged 83. Manchester Grammar School; Jesus College, Oxford, MA; Hon. Fellow 1960. G. 12 June 1907. ETC. 21 February 1908. Prop. Tobin KC. Sec. Brocklehurst. Manchester Chambers; 5 St James's Square, 1908; 33 King Street, 1909-1914. Lt., RNVR, 1914-1918. 28 John Dalton Street, 1915-1918; 3 St James's Square, 1918-1919. Judge in Egyptian Native Courts, 1919-1924. OBE 1919. President, Land Court, Palestine, 1925. Judge in Mixed Court, Cairo, 1926-1932. Judge, Mixed Court of Appeal, Alexandria, 1932-1949. Kt 1950. Grand Officer, Order of the Nile. Publications; 25 Odes of Horace, 1942; More Odes of Horace, 1945. WW.

REED, John Foster
G. 7 June 1875. ETC. 13 March 1876. Prop. Edwards QC. Sec. Temple QC. 3 Pump Court, 1876-1882. No address, 1883. Not in 1884 Law List.

REEKERS, John William Austin
G. July 1971. 6 King's Bench Walk, 1980-1988. South Eastern Circuit. 2nd floor, Peel House, Harrington Street/ 25-27 Castle Street, Liverpool, 1989-1997. Not in Bar Directory 1998.

REES, Griffith Caradoc MP (His Honour Judge Rees)
Born 1868 Birkenhead. Died 20 September 1924. Liverpool Institute. Solicitor, 1895-1905. AAS. 2 October 1905. Call 17 November 1905. ETC. 16 February 1906. Prop. Shee KC. Sec. Riley. 3 Elm Court, 1906-1907; 2 Elm Court, 1908-1913; 5 Elm Court, 1916-1921. 8 Harrington Street, Liverpool, 1908-1915. MP (L) Carnarvon, 1915-1918. Parliamentary Secretary to Home Office, 1916-1917. County Court Judge, Circuit 29, (North Wales), December 1921-1924. WW.

REID, Linus
M. 1993. 18 St John Street, Manchester, 1996. Not in 1997 Bar Directory.

REID, Paul Campbell QC
Born 27 March 1949, Bramhall. Merchant Taylors' College, Crosby; Christ's College, Cambridge, MA (Engineering) G. July 1973. ETC. Autumn 1973. Pupilmaster, Cecil Henriques. Manchester Chambers; 2 Booth Street, 1973-1975; 13 Police Street, 1975-1978; Rational House, 64 Bridge Street, 1978-1993; Lincoln House Chambers, 1 Brazennose Street, 1993. Assistant Recorder 1989. Recorder 1993. Silk 2001. WW.

REISS, (Miss) Erna
L. 17 November 1925. ETC. 10 July 1930. Prop. Derbyshire KC. Sec. Spafford. Manchester Chambers; 3 St James's Square, 1935-1948; 7 Chapel Walks, 1949-1952. No address, 1953-1963. Not in 1964 Law List.

REYNOLDS, Basil John
MA (Cantab). G. November 1953. 3 St James's Square, Manchester, 1955-1956. No address, 1957-1963. Not in 1964 Law List.

REYNOLDS, Gary William
Born 9 June 1966, Birkenhead. Park High School; Portsmouth University, BSc. Quantity Surveyor, 1988-1996. Dip Law, (Staffs). L. November 1994. ETC. 1994. Prop. Jonathan Foster QC. Sec. A Dennett. Manchester Chambers; 18-22 Bridge Street, 1996-1998; 24a St John Street, 1998. (now St John's Building).

RHIND, Mark Alexander
Born 8 December 1966. Married to Rebecca Lloyd-Smith qv. Harrogate Grammar School; Manchester University, LLB. AAS. M. 9 March 1988. Call 21 November 1989. ETC 1989. Prop. JJ Rowe QC. Sec. Graham Campbell. Manchester Chambers; 211 Deansgate, 1991-1993; 38 King Street West, 1994-1995; 24a St John Street, 1991-2001; now at Peel Court Chambers, 45 Hardman Street.

RHODES, George KC
Born 1851. Died 23 September 1924. Father of His Honour Judge Harold Rhodes qv. Owens College, Manchester. Merchant in Manchester to 1889. Member, Manchester City Council, 1890-1892. G. 29 June 1892. Bencher 1909. ETC. 6 March 1893. Prop. Addison QC. Sec. Bradbury. Manchester Chambers; 78 Cross Street, 1893-1903; 78 King Street, 1904-1909 Silk 1909. 11 King's Bench Walk & 9 Bridge Street, Westminster, 1909-1924. Parliamentary committees. Recorder of Oldham, 1914-1924. JP, Cheshire & Lancs. Director of a colliery, rubber company & a mill. Publications; Manchester Municipal Code. WW.

RHODES, George Harold Lancashire TD
Born 29 February 1916. Son of Judge Harold Rhodes qv and grandson of George Rhodes KC qv. Shrewsbury School; The Queen's College, Oxford, MA 1941. Commissioned 52nd Field Regt. RA TA, 1938; War Service, BEF, 1940; Middle East 1942; Italy, 1943-1946; Major. TD 1946. G. November 1947. ETC. 1947. Circuit Junior, 1948. 43 King Street, Manchester, 1947-1953. Office of Judge Advocate General, 1953. Assistant Judge Advocate General, 1967. Chairman, Industrial Tribunals, Manchester, 1974. Regional Chairman; Manchester, 1985-1988; Liverpool, 1987-1988. WW.

RHODES, Harold (His Honour Judge Rhodes)
Born 1885. Died 17 October 1964. Son of George Rhodes KC qv. Father of George Harold Lancashire Rhodes qv. Bowdon College, Corpus Christie College, Oxford MA. I. 8 June 1910. ETC. 1 March 1911. Prop. Taylor KC. Sec. Burgis. 60 King Street, Manchester, 1911-1914. Served European War, 1914-1918; 29th Divisional Artillery, France, 1915-1918; Captain. 60 King

Street, 1918-1935; 43 King Street, 1936-1942. County Court Judge, Circuit 8, (Leigh & Manchester), 1942-1958. Deputy Chairman, Lancs. Quarter Sessions, 1942-1960. WW.

RHODES, Kenneth Thomas Lancashire
G. July 1952. 49 Castle Street, Liverpool, 1952-1960. No address, 1961-1963. Not in 1964 Law List.

RICE-JONES, His Honour Benjamin Rowland
Born 19 June 1888. Died 26 August 1978 aged 90. Temple Grove School; Clifton College; Christ's College, Cambridge, BA., LLB. I. 1 May 1912 (Certificate of Honour 1911). ETC. 14 June 1912. Prop. Taylor KC. Sec. Greaves Lord. 5 Harrington Street, Liverpool, 1912-1914. Served in HM Forces, 1914-1919; Inns of Court OTC. Royal Artillery (wounded at Ypres). Circuit Junior, Winter 1919. 5 Harrington Street, 1919-1928; 3 Cook Street, 1929-1945. Assistant Judge, Liverpool Court of Passage. County Court Judge, 1945-1960. (Circuit 12, Bradford, 1945-1952 & Circuit 56, Croydon, 1952-1960). WW.

RICHARDS, Lionel Henry
L. 26 January 1936. ETC. 1 July 1936. Prop. William Gorman KC. Sec. Smylie. 23 Old Square, 1936-1950. 78 King Street, Manchester, 1937-1940. No address, 1951-1963. Not in 1964 Law List.

RICHARDS, Roger Charnock
I. 22 April 1891. ETC. 28 July 1891. Prop. Leese QC. Sec. Ferguson. 5 Crown Office Row, 1892. 2 King's Bench Walk, 1893-1905. No address, 1906-1949. Not in 1950 Law List.

*** RICHARDS, His Honour Whitmore Lionel**
Born 12 September 1869. Died 21 November 1954 aged 85. Youngest son of Judge John Henry Richards, County Court Judge for County Mayo, Ireland. Rugby; Trinity College, Dublin, BA, 1891. L. 8 May 1895. 23 Old Square. Midland Circuit. County Court Judge, Circuit 7, (Birkenhead, Altrincham & Warrington), 1922-1942. WW.

RICHARDSON, Charles Garner
Born 25 June 1853. Only son of Charles Garner Richardson, of Hants., late 49th Regt. Trinity College, Cambridge, MA 1878. AAS. I. 17 July 1873. Call 28 June 1876. ETC. 11 July 1877. Prop. Ambrose QC. Sec. Crompton. 9 Old Square, 1877-1894. No address, 1895-1935. Not in 1936 Law List. WW.

RICHARDSON, Frank C
Born 1870. Died 31 July 1917. Marlborough; Christ Church, Oxford. I. 17 November 1891. ETC. 8 March 1893. Prop. Gully QC. Sec. McKeand. 1 Essex Court, 1893-1909. No address, 1910-1917. Between 1902 and 1911 he wrote 15 novels including King's Counsel; The Secret Kingdom & Love and Extras. WW.

RICHARDSON, Harold Slinsby Duncombe
Born 1844. Only son of Henry Marriott Richardson of Bolton, attorney & solicitor. AAS. M. 12 January 1863. Call 17 November 1865. No address, 1876-1884. Post Office Chambers, Hanley, Staffs., 1885-1899. Not in 1900 Law List.

RICHARDSON, Paul Brayshaw
Born 21 June 1948, Watford. Only son of Ronald Hugo Richardson, solicitor. Berkhamstead School; Trinity College, Cambridge, MA. AAS. M. 17 June 1969. Call 22 November 1972. ETC 1973. Prop. Patrick Russell QC. Sec. John Hugill. Same Manchester Chambers; Ship Canal House, King Street, 1973-1981; 2 Old Bank Street, 1982-1991; Peel Court Chambers, 45 Hardman Street, 1992-2002. Deputy District Judge (Magistrates), 1995-2002; District Judge, Doncaster Magistrates Court, 2002. WW.

RICHARDSON, Richard Taswell
Born 1853. Eldest son of Rev. Richard Richardson of Capenhurst. Marlborough; University College, Oxford, BA. AAS. I. 17 April 1875. Call 7 May 1879. ETC. 12 February 1880. Prop. Aspinall QC. Sec. Pickford. Liverpool Chambers; 10 Commerce Chambers, Lord Street, 1880-1882; 6 Cook Street, 1883; 13 Harrington Street, 1884-1895. No address, 1896-1935. Not in 1936 Law List. Foster.

RICHMOND, Thomas Henry
Eldest son of Thomas Ricmond of Sunny Brow, Kendal. Owens College, Manchester; London University, MA 1881; Christ Church, Oxford, MA., BCL 1884. AAS. G. 31 October 1882. Call. 17 June 1885. ETC. 20 July 1885. Prop. Gibbs QC. Sec. C A Russell. 2 Mitre Court, 1885; Commerce Chambers, 15 Lord Street, Liverpool, 1886. 5 Essex Court, 1887-1888. Not in 1889 Law List. Foster.

RICKARBY, William Edward
Liverpool University, LLB. G. July 1975. ETC 1975. Fruit Exchange, Victoria Street, Liverpool, 1975-1985. Crown Prosecutions Service, 1985-1995. 6 Fountain Court, Steelhouse Lane, Birmingham, 1996-, Midland & Oxford Circuit.

RIDDELL, David Andrew
MA (Cantab). M. October 1993. ETC. 7 December 1993. Manchester Chambers; Hollins Chambers, 64a Bridge Street, 1996-1997; Cobden House Chambers, 19 Quay Street, 1998.

RIDDLE, Nicholas Findlay
Born 21 May 1948 Bath. The King's School, Canterbury; Gonville and Caius College, Cambridge, MA. G. July 1970. ETC 1972. Prop. Eric Somerset Jones QC. Sec. E H Wells. Pupilmaster, Peter Rawson. Liverpool Chambers; 14 Cook Street, 1972-1985; 7 Queen Avenue, 1986-1996; 14 Castle Street, 1996-2003; Atlantic Chambers, Cook Street, 2003.

RIDEHALGH, Arthur
Born 10 April 1907. Died 7 September 1971 aged 64. Terra Nova Prep School, Birkdale; Sedbergh; Wadham College, Oxford, BA. G. 12 June 1929. ETC. June 1929. 2 Booth Street, Manchester, 1929-1935. Crown Attorney and Magistrate, St Kitts, Leeward Islands, 1935. Crown Counsel, Gold Coast, 1939; Solicitor General, Nigeria, 1946. Attorney General, Hong Kong, 1952. Retired from HM Overseas Service, 1962. KC, Nigeria, 1949; QC, Hong Kong, 1953. WW.

RIDING, Henry
Born 22 October 1958, Liverpool. Liverpool University, LLB. M. July 1981. ETC 1981. Pupilmaster, Michael Wolff. Liverpool Chambers; Melbourne Building, 21 North John Street, 1981-1988; 3rd floor, Peel House, Harrington Street, 1989-1993; Corn Exchange, Fenwick Street, 1994-1999; 7 Harrington Street (merger with Martins Building), 6.9.1999.

RIGBY, Esmond
G. 3 July 1935. ETC. 29 January 1936. Prop. Sellers KC. Sec. Shawcross. No address, 1936-1963. Not in Law List, 1964-1971. 9 Stone Buildings, 1972; 1 Stone Buildings, 1973; 41 North John Street, Liverpool, 1974. Not in 1975 Law List.

RIGBY, John Madeley
Born 1926. Only son of Richard Rigby of Wigan. Oriel College, Oxford, (MA), ATII. Gunner in Royal Artillery when AAS. M. 10 January 1945. Call. 27 November 1951. 78 King Street, Manchester, 1954-1958. No chambers address, 1959-1989. Not in 1990 Bar Directory.

RIGBY, Terence
Born 8 June 1948, Bolton. Married to C A Riley qv. Bolton School; Nottingham University, LLB 1969; Keble College, Oxford, BCL 1971. G. May 1971. Lord Justice Holker Scholar. ETC. 1971. Pupilmaster, Christopher Rose. Manchester Chambers; 60 King Street, 1971-1983; Crown Square Chambers, 1984-1993; 9 St John Street, 1994. Recorder 1997.

RIGG, (Harry Sibson) Leslie QC (His Honour Judge Rigg QC)
Born 8 November 1915. Died 11 June 1976 aged 60. Charterhouse; Lincoln College, Oxford. Manchester Regt; Staff Captain, 1939-1944. L. June 1944; Bencher 1966. ETC. 1946. Liverpool Chambers; 34 Castle Street, 1946-1949; 9 Rumford Street, 1950-1960. Silk 1960. 2 Paper Buildings, 1960-1970; 5 Essex Court, 1971-1972. Circuit Judge, 1972-1976. Recorder of Wigan, 1964-1971, Contested (C) Liverpool, Edge Hill, May 1955. WW.

RIGG, Herbert Addington KC
Born 7 March 1845. Died 7 March 1924 aged 79. Tonbridge School; Trinity College, Cambridge, BA 1868; MA 1871. AAS. I. 22 January 1866. Call 6 June 1871. ETC. 12 July 1871. Prop. Quain QC. Sec. Herschell. 4 Crown Office Row, 1876-1878; 9 King's Bench Walk, 1879-1908; 41 Parliament Street, 1903-1924, Parliamentary Draftsman. Silk 1906. JP., West Sussex. Deputy Chairman of Quarter Sessions for West Sussex. Alderman, West Sussex County Council. WW. Foster.

RIGG, Richard OBE., MP
Born 1877. Died 29 August 1942. Caius College, Cambridge, MA. I. 26 January 1899. Irish Bar M. 1902. 4 Brick Court, 1902-1908. No chambers address, 1909-1942. ETC. 3 July 1914. Prop. Tobin KC. Sec. Sharpe. Major, retd, 4th Border Regt. MP (R) North (Appleby) Division of Westmorland, 1900-1905. High Sheriff, Westmorland, 1909-1910. Mayor of the City of Westminster, 1939-1940. OBE 1918. TD. WW.

RILEY, Anthony
Born 12 December 1945 Liverpool. 3rd son of William Francis Riley of Liverpool, bus driver. Liverpool University, LLB. AAS. M. 2 November 1971. Call 19 July 1973. Liverpool Chambers; 27 Dale Street, 1975; State Insurance Building, 14 Dale Street, 1979. Not in 1980 Bar Directory.

RILEY, Christine Anne
Born 24 March 1951, Aldershot. Married to Terence Rigby qv. Bury Grammar School; Manchester University, LLB. G. July 1974. ETC. 1974. Pupilmaster, John

Hudson. Same Manchester Chambers; 60 King Street, 1974-1983; Crown Square Chambers, 1984-1993; 9 St John Street, 1994.

RILEY, (Henry) Lindon
LLB. Formerly a solicitor in St Helens. Rigby Swift's godfather. G. 17 November 1904. ETC. February 1905. Prop. William Pickford KC. Sec. Rigby Swift. Liverpool Chambers; Century Buildings, North John Street, 1906; 5 Harrington Street, 1907-1915. No chambers address, 1916-1918. Not in 1919 Law List.

RILEY, Richard
Born 1856. Eldest son of Henry Riley of Blackburn. Formerly a solicitor. AAS. M. 30 September 1898. Call. 26 January 1899. ETC. 2 February 1899. Prop. Shee QC. Sec. McKeand. No address, 1899-1903. Not in 1904 Law List.

RIMINGTON, George Arthur
Born 1857. Eldest son of Michael Rimington of Penrith. Queen's College, Oxford, BA. AAS. L. 26 January 1882. Call. 26 January 1885. ETC. 10 February 1886. Prop. Bigham QC. Sec. J A Hamilton. 8 Fig Tree Court, 1888-1892. No address, 1893-1931. Not in 1932 Law List.

RIMMER, Edward Johnson QC
Born 28 March 1883. Died 15 May 1962 aged 79. Bickerton House School, Birkdale; Liverpool University, BSc., MEng. Engineer. AMICE. L. 26 January 1912. ETC. 9 February 1912. Prop. Greer KC. Sec. Kennedy. Liverpool Chambers; 13 Harrington Street, 1912-1913; 25 Lord Street, 1914-1919. Goldsmith Building, 1920-1923; Farrars Building, 1924-1937; 3 Temple Gardens, 1938-1939; 2 Essex Court, 1940-1945; 11 Old Square, 1946-1959. Silk 1953. Parliamentary draftsman & committees. Publications; The Law Relating to the Architect, 1952. No Chambers address, 1960-1962. WW.

RIORDAN, Stephen Vaughan QC
Born 18 February 1950. St Albans. Wimbledon College; Liverpool University, LLB. I. July 1972. 3 Temple Gardens & 1 Paper Buildings. Pupilmasters, B M Cropper & F E Beezeley. ETC. December 1973. Sec. Justin Price. Same Liverpool Chambers; Queen Avenue, 1973-1983; 2nd floor, Peel House, Harrington Street, 1984-1994; 25-27 Castle Street, 1995-2004. (Head of Chambers, 1997) Assistant Recorder 1986. Recorder 1990. Silk 1992. WW.

RITCHIE, John
MA. I. 22 June 1887. ETC. 30 July 1890. Prop. Ambrose QC. Sec. Gully QC. 4 Harcourt Buildings, 1891-1949. Not in 1950 Law List.

RITTNER, George Hermann
I. 17 November 1902. ETC. 29 July 1903. Prop. Tobin KC. Sec. Otter Barry. 1 Hare Court, 1905-1922. No address, 1923-1949. Not in 1950 Law List.

ROBERTS, David Trevor
Born 1865. 2nd son of John Roberts of Abergele, merchant. Trinity College, Cambridge. AAS. M. 20 November 1886. Call 18 June 1890. ETC. 30 July 1890. Prop. Kennedy QC. Sec. Tobin. No address, 1891-1949. Not in 1950 Law List.

ROBERTS, Harold CVO
Born 3 March 1879. Died 29 June 1959 aged 80. 3rd son of James Haworth Roberts of Bury, cotton merchant. Rossall; Exeter College, Oxford, BA, 1901; MA, 1908. I. 11 June 1902. ETC. 16 July 1902. Prop. Shee KC. Sec. Graham. 78 King Street, Manchester, 1902-1925. Served European War, 1914-1918, Lt., RASC. Registrar, Lancs. Palatine Chancery Court, 1925-1951 at 4 Clarence Street, Manchester. Deputy Chancellor during vacations, 1947-1952. CVO 1951. JP., Lancs., 1933. WW.
In 1953 Roberts published privately "A Fragment from the unpublished reminiscences of an Old Man of Equity." A copy provided by Peter Openshaw is now in the Circuit Records. He begins "Arriving home in Southport from Oxford in 1901,1 proceeded without delay to set my course for the future. This I did by arranging to go at once as a pupil into the chambers of Jimmy Tweedale, the tiny and tubby Leader of the Lancashire Palatine Chancery Court with a big practice as an equity draftsman and a fairly good one in the Court of Chancery."

ROBERTS, John Houghton (His Honour Judge John Roberts)
Born 14 December 1947 Liverpool. Calday Grange Grammar School, West Kirby; Trinity Hall, Cambridge (Scholar), MA. AAS. M. 31 October 1967. Call 16 July 1970. ETC 1970. Prop. Michael Maguire QC. Sec. Roy Ward. Lecturer in Law, Liverpool University, 1969-1971. Same Liverpool Chambers; 2nd floor, Oriel Chambers, 14 Water Street, 1970-1982; Derby Square Chambers, Refuge Assurance House (later renamed Merchants Court), 1983-1993. Assistant Recorder 1983. Recorder 1988. Circuit Judge, 1993. Resident Judge, Bolton 1997-2001. Sitting at Liverpool, 2002. Captain, Heswall Golf Club, 2002. WW.

ROBERTS, Lisa
Born 2 February 1969, Manchester. Salendine Nook High School, Huddersfield; St Catherine's College, Oxford, BA (English). L. 14 October 1993. ETC. 7 December 1993. Prop. Mukhtar Hussain QC. Sec. James Gregory. Lincoln House Chambers, 1 Brazennose Street, September 1993.

ROBERTS, Mark
Born 31 May 1969 Leeds. Leeds Grammar School; University of East Anglia, LLB. Solicitor/partner, Hill, Dickinson. Solicitors, Liverpool, 1993-2001. G. 6 March 2001. ETC. 26 March 2002. Prop. David Steer QC. Sec. Peter Gregory. 7 Harrington Street, Liverpool, September 2001.

ROBERTS, Thomas
Born 1832. Eldest son of William Roberts of Manchester, gent. Special pleader & conveyancer. No address, 1876-1923. Not in 1924 Law List. Foster.

ROBERTS, Thomas Arthur
Born 1860. 4th son of Thomas Roberts of Kersal nr Manchester. Trinity College, Oxford, BA. AAS. I. 20 November 1875. Call 29 June 1881. ETC. 29 January 1883. Prop. West QC. Sec. Gouldthorpe. 2 Paper Buildings, 1886-1887; 11 King's Bench Walk, 1888-1889. No address, 1890-1940. Not in 1941 Law List. Publications; Principles of Equity. Foster

ROBERTS, Thomas Howes
Born 1846. Only son of Thomas Roberts of St Asaph. AAS. M. 19 January 1867. Call 17 November 1869. ETC. 23 March 1870. Prop. Leofric Temple QC. Sec. G Bruce. No address, 1876-1934. Not in 1935 Law List. Foster.

ROBERTS, Sir Thomas Lee
Born 8 August 1848, Stockport. Died 16 January 1924 aged 75. Eldest son of Thomas Roberts of Bolton, civil engineer & JP. Stockport Grammar School. Served articles with London Solicitors. AAS. I. 19 June 1876. Call. 25 June 1879. ETC. 19 July 1879. Prop. Hopwood QC. Sec. Williamson. Between 1879 and 1924 practised from 1, 3 & 5 Paper Buildings and from 6, 7 & 9 King's Bench Walk. Kt 1918. Foster & WW., in which he describes his chief enjoyment as "a well stocked library."

ROBERTSON, Alexander
Born 1840. Eldest son of James Robertson of Dundee. Edinburgh University, MA. AAS. L. 5 May 1868. Call 26 January 1871. ETC. 14 March 1872. Prop. Temple QC. Sec. C Foster. 2 Plowden Builings, 1876-1905; 3 Plowden Buildings, 1907-1909. No Chambers address 1910. Not in 1911 Law List. Parliamentary Committes. Member of the Faculty of Advocates, Scotland. Sheriff Substitute, Forfarshire. Foster.

ROBERTSON, Edmund QC, MP (Baron Lochee of Crowlie)
Born 28 October 1845 Scotland. Died 13 September 1911 aged 65. St Andrews University; Lincoln College, Oxford, BA 1870; Corpus Christi College, Oxford, MA 1874; Fellow 1870. Vinerian Scholar. Tancred Law Student. AAS. L. 16 June 1868. Call 17 November 1871. ETC. 14 March 1872. Prop. Hosack. Sec. Shiell. 5 Essex Court, 1877-1882; 4 Essex Court, 1883-1907. Silk 1895. MP (L) Dundee, 1885-1908. Civil Lord of the Admiralty, 1892-1895. Secretary to the Admiralty, 1905-1908. Publications; American Home Rule. WW. Foster.

ROBERTSON, George
I. 26 January 1926. ETC, 17 February 1926. Prop. Sandbach KC. Sec. Derbyshire. 6 St Anne's Passage, Manchester, 1926-1928. No address, 1929-1938. Not in 1939 Law List.

ROBERTSON, Helenus Macaulay
Born Aigburth, Liverpool 1 April 1881. Son of Sir Helenus and Lady Robertson. Eton; New College, Oxford. L. 5 July 1905. ETC. 1 August 1906. Prop. Pickford KC. Sec. Darby. 3 Temple Gardens, 1906-1914. Private, Inns of Court OTC, 6.8.1914; Discharged as Sgt upon appointment as Lt. in 3rd Btn, (Attd 2nd Btn.) Royal Welch Fusiliers on 12.1.1915; Promoted Captain; killed in action on 26 January 1916 at Cambrin, aged 34. Cemetery; Cambrin Churchyard Extension, Pas de Calais, France (Kl7). Information provided by Public Record Office & Commonwealth War Graves Commission.

ROBERTSON, (James) Graham
BSc (Microbiology). LLB. Scottish Bar, March 1983. G. February 1991. New Bailey Chambers, Preston, 1994.

ROBINOW, William
L. 17 November 1908. ETC. 26 February 1909. Prop. Langdon KC. Sec. Acton. No address, 1909-1953. Not in 1954 Law List.

ROBINS, Julian
Born 1836. 3rd son of George, Robins of London. AAS. I. 16 May 1857. Call 6 June 1860. Member of Northern & North Eastern Circuits, 1876-1908. 6 King's Bench Walk, 1886-1887; 4 Pump Court, 1888-1906. No address, 1907-1908. Not in 1909 Law List. Foster.

ROBINSON, Anne Louise
University of Keele, BA. L. 30.11.1978. ETC. 1978. Martins Building, Water Street, Liverpool, 1978-1984. Senior Crown Counsel, British Virgin Islands, 1987-1992. Attorney, San Diego, California, 1992-1995. Attorney & Barrister, British Virgin Islands, 1996.

ROBINSON, (Constance) Josephine (nee Slater)
Born 22 April 1939, Oldham. Hulme Grammar School for Girls; Liverpool University, LLB, 1960; UMIST, MSc, 1988. G. November 1962. Pupilmaster, F E Beazley (Temple). ETC. 1964. 36 St Ann Street, Manchester, 1964-1972. Part time Lecturer, Manchester Polytechnic, 1974-1980. Shared Lectureship, UMIST, 1980-1992. Deputy District Chairman, The Appeals Service, 1992. Non executive Director, East Cheshire NHS Trust, 1998-2005.

ROBINSON, Sir John Roland MP
BA., LLB. L. 29 April 1929. Certificate of Honour M 1928. ETC. 18 February 1931. Prop. Goldie KC. Sec. Rowson. Fountains Court, 1932-1936. No address, 1937-1963. Not in 1964 Law List. Not in WW. Member of Parliament. Kt 1954.

ROBINSON, Simon Robert
LLB. L. October 1991. ETC. 17 December 1992. Prop. Rodney Klevan QC. Sec. Webster. 16 Winckley Square, Preston, 1994; Manchester Chambers; 211 Deansgate, 1995; 1 Booth Street, 1996-1998; Waldorf House, Cooper Street, 1999. ACIArb.

ROBY, Arthur Godfrey KC
Born 1862. Died 15 April 1944. Son of Henry John Roby MP., LLD of Lancrigg, Grasmere. Manchester Grammar School; St John's College, Cambridge, BA 1884; MA 1903. I. 22 June 1887. ETC. 27 March 1890. Prop. Collins QC. Sec. Lazarus (Langdon). 1 & 5 St James's Square, Manchester, 1888-1919. Silk 1919. 1 New Square, 1919-1922. No address 1923-1944. WW.

ROCHE, Henry Philip
Born 1852. Eldest son of Henry Philip Roche, barrister. AAS. L. 30 December 1871. Call 17 November 1876. Registrar in Bankruptcy, 1881. Publications; Joint Author of the Law of Bankruptcy. No address, 1904-1920. Not in 1921 Law List.

RODDY, Maureen Bernadette (Her Honour Judge Roddy)
Born 13 October 1953 Manchester. Loreto College, Manchester; Queen Mary College, London, LLB., LLM. AAS. M. 5 October 1973. Call. July 1977. ETC. 1979. Prop. Bruce Martin QC. Sec. David Harris. Same Liverpool Chambers; Melbourne Building, 21 North John Street, 1979-1988; 3rd floor, Peel House, Harrington Street, 1989-1997; 8th floor, India Buildings, 12.1.1998-2001. Assistant Recorder 1992. Recorder 1997. Circuit Judge, Liverpool, 17.7.2001.

RODIKIS, Joanna
Born 7 November 1967, Nicosia, Cyprus. Came to this country as a refugee following the Turkish invasion of Cyprus in 1974. Father became a hotelier in Blackpool. Blackpool Collegiate; University of Central Lancashire, LLB. Marks & Spencer PLC, 1986-1989. M. 14 October 1993. ETC. December 1993. Prop. Rodney Klevan QC. Sec. Roger Baldwin. Pupilmaster Timothy White. Winckley Square, Preston, 1993-1994; Manchester Chambers; Old Colony House, 6 South King Street, 1994-2000; 24a St John Street (now St John's Building), October 2000.

ROGERS, Daniel James
Born 17 October 1973 Mancot, Flints. The King's School, Chester. Nottingham University, BA. I. 9 October 1997. ETC. 18 December 1997. Prop. Stephen Riordan QC. Sec. David Boulton. Pupilmaster, David Geey. Liverpool Chambers; Martins Building October, 1997-1999; 7 Harrington Street (merger with Corn Exchange), 6.9.1999.

ROGERS, David Geoffrey Fletcher
G. November 1953. ETC. 4 February 1954. Prop. Nelson QC. 7 King's Bench Walk & 24 Dale Street, Liverpool, 1954-1958. Left the Bar to become Legal Advisor to Monotype Corp Ltd in Surrey and later Dunlop Ltd SW1. Not in 1989 Bar Directory.

*** ROGERS, His Honour Graham**
Born 10 June 1907. Died 17 April 1973 aged 65. Repton School; King's College, Cambridge, BA 1929; MA 1936. I. 1930. Oxford Circuit. Served, War of 1939-1945 attaining rank of Colonel. Judge in charge of Control Commission Supreme Court, Germany, 1947; Chief Judge 1952; Recorder of Liverpool, 1954-1956. Metropolitan Magistrate, 1959-1961. Additional Judge, Central Criminal Court, 1964-1969. Circuit Judge and Judge of the Mayor's & City of London Court, 1972-1973. WW.

ROGERS, Jonathan
Born 21 June 1977 Campbelltown. Manchester University, LLB. M. 2000. ETC. 2000. Prop. David Turner QC. Sec. Simon Earlam. Exchange Chambers, Pearl Assurance House, Derby Square, Liverpool, 2000.

ROGERS, Murray Rowland Fletcher
Born 13 September 1899. Died 28 March 1991 aged 91. St Edward's School; RMC Sandhurst (2nd Lt., 8th Hussars, 1918-1921); Liverpool University, BA 1924. Schoolmaster to 1929. G. 18 November 1929. ETC. 29 January 1930. Liverpool Chambers; 45 Castle Street, 1930-1931; 43 Castle Street, 1932-1934; 5 Cook Street, 1935-1937. Magistrate, Nigeria, 1937-1942; Chief Magistrate, Palestine, 1942-1947; District Judge, Malaya, 1947-1949; President, Sessions Court, Malaya, 1949-1952; Judge of the Supreme Court, Sarawak, N Borneo & Brunei, 1952-1963. Member, Courts of Appeal for the Seychelles, St Helena & Falkland Islands Colony & Dependencies & The British Antartic Territory, 1965-1975. WW.

ROGERSON, Thomas Cooper
BCL. I. 26 January 1897. ETC. 27 July 1897. Prop. Hamilton QC. Sec. Langdon. 2 Dr Johnson's Building, 1897-1898; 3 Elm Court, 1899-1910. 16 John Dalton Street, Manchester, 1911-1924. 8 King's Bench Walk, 1921-1927; 2 Hare Court, 1928-1936. No address, 1937-1941. Not in 1942 Law List.

ROLLAND, Edward
Born 1840. Only son of John Rolland of Kirkcaldy, Fife. University of Edinburgh, MA. AAS. M. 17 November 1865. Call. 17 November 1868. ETC. 19 August 1870. Prop Holker QC. Sec. Littler. 3 Brick Court, 1876-1899. Not in 1900 Law List. Foster.

ROMAIN, Charan Margaret Helena
Leicester University, LLB. I. October 1991. Liverpool Chambers; Martins Building, Water Street, 1995-1999; 7 Harrington Street (merger with Corn Exchange), 6.9.1999-2000.

ROSCOE, Edward Stanley
Born 12 April 1849. Died 23 November 1932 aged 83. Radley College. AAS. L. 23 May 1868. Call 17 November 1871. ETC. 5 March 1872. Prop. Temple QC. Sec. Herschell QC. 1 Tanfield Chambers, 1976-1877; 4 Harcourt Buildings, 1878-1879; 1 King's Bench Walk, 1880-1904. Official Law Reporter in Admiralty Court, 1883. Assistant Admiralty Registrar, 1890. Admiralty Registrar, 1904. Registrar of the Prize Court, 1914. Assessor to the North Sea Inquiry, 1905. Publications; numerous on Admiralty & Historical matters including "Aspects of Dr Johnson", 1928 and "Rambles with a Fishing Rod." WW. Foster.

ROSE, Anthony Kenneth
Born 14 February 1953 Poole. University College, London, LLB., LLM. AAS. M. 25 July 1977. Call 21 November 1978. Pupilmaster, Ami Feder (Temple Gardens). ETC. October 1983. Same Liverpool Chambers; Fruit Exchange, Victoria Street, 1983-1991; Chavasse Court, 24 Lord Street, 1991.

ROSE, Christopher (Dudley Roger) QC. (The Rt. Hon. Lord Justice Rose)
Born 10 February 1937. Only son of Roger Rose, solicitor and Town Clerk. Morecambe Grammar School; Repton; Leeds University, LLB; Wadham College, Oxford (Eldon Scholar), BCL; Hon Fellow, 1993. Lecturer in Law, Wadham College, 1959-1960. Bigelow Teaching Fellow, University of Chicago, 1960-1961. AAS. M. 18 October 1957. Call 12 July 1960; Bencher 1983; Treasurer 2002. Harmsworth Scholar, 1961. ETC. 15 March 1962. Prop. Watson QC. Sec. E S Temple. 60 King Street, Manchester, 1962-1974. Silk 1974. 5 Essex Court, 1974-1985. Recorder 1978. Member, Senate of Inns of Court and Bar, 1983-1985. High Court Judge, Queen's Bench Division, 1985-1992. Kt. 1985. Presiding Judge, Northern Circuit, 1987-1990. Lord Justice of Appeal, 1992. PC 1992. Chairman, Criminal Justice Consultative Council, 1994-2000. Vice-President, Court of Appeal (Criminal Division), 1997. WW.

ROSE, Hubert Clarence
Born 1905. 3rd son of Henry Rose of Stockport, cashier and director of engineering company. When AAS. M. On 19 October 1943 he was Secretary of Amalgamated Licensed Retailers Society. Call 18 November 1946. 60 King Street, Manchester, 1948-1950. Not in 1951 Law List.

ROSE, Paul Bernard MP
Born 26 December 1935. Bury Grammar School; Manchester University, LLB. G. February 1958. ETC 1963. Pupilmaster, E S Temple. 60 King Street, Manchester, 1963-17.5.1971. Joined South Eastern Circuit. 10 Kings Bench Walk, 1971-1988. MP (Lab) Manchester, Blackley, 1964-1979. PPS to Minister of Transport, 1967-1968. H M Coroner, London Southern District, 1988. Publications include; Manchester Martyrs, 1970; Backbencher's Dilemma, 1981; Moonies Unmasked, 1981; (Jt) A History of the Fenian Movement in Great Britain, 1982. WW.

ROSEMARINE, Andrew

Born 26 October 1962, Hope, Greater Manchester. Manchester Grammar School; Wadham College, Oxford, MA., BCL; Brussels Institute (Lic. Spec. Dr. Eur). G. November 1989. London pupilage at Brick Court & 1 Essex Court. Former Head of Office, Frere Cholmeley Bischoff, Moscow. International Peace Process Advocate & Activist. ETC 2000. Prop. David Harris QC. Queen's Chambers, 5 John Dalton Street, Manchester, 2001.

ROSKILL, Sir Ashton Wentworth QC.

Born 1902. Died 23 June 1991. Eldest son of John Roskill KC qv. Brother of Eustace Wentworth Roskill, Law Lord, 1980-1986. Winchester; Exeter College, Oxford MA (Modern History); Hon Fellow 1989. I. 17 November 1925; Certificate of Honour 1925; Bencher 1958; Treasurer 1980; Hon Bencher. M. 1980. ETC. 6 July 1927. Prop. Wingate-Saul KC. Sec. Jalland. 2 Pump Court, 1925-1942; 3 Brick Court, 1942; 4 Brick Court, 1943-1952; Silk 1949. 3 Pump Court, 1953-1965; 8 King's Bench Walk, 1966-1991. War Office (Intelligence), 1940-1945. Chairman, Barristers Benevolent Association, 1968-1969. Chairman, Monopolies and Mergers Commission, 1965-1975. Kt. 1967. WW.

ROSKILL, John KC

Born 1860. Died 19 August 1940. Youngest son of Gustavius Roskill of Manchester. Father of Sir Ashton Wentworth Roskill QC qv and of Lord Roskill. Owen's College,Manchester; Corpus Christi, Oxford, BA 1883; MA 1886; BSc, Manchester. I. 26 January 1888. ETC. 5 February 1888. Prop. Addison QC. Sec. Goldthorp. 1 Paper Buildings, 1888-1933. Recorder of Burnley, 1907-1909. Judge of Salford Hundred Court of Record, 1909-1937. WW.

ROSS, Reginald James Blair (Hon. Mr Justice Ross)

Born 19 September 1871. 3rd son of Sir David Palmer Ross, CMC., Surgeon-General, British Guiana. Ipswich School; Gonville and Caius College, Cambridge, BA. I. 18 April 1894. ETC. 16 March 1895. Prop. Shee QC. Sec. W F K Taylor. 1 Harcourt Buildings, 1895-1908. District Commissioner, Lagos, 1908. Subsequently Police Magistrate and Solicitor General. Judge of the Supreme Court of Nigeria, 1915-1918. No address, 1919-1949. Not in 1950 Law List. WW. merely says "deceased." No date given.

ROSS, Sally-Ann

Born 21 January 1964, Stockport. Buxton Girls School; Keele University, BA (Law & Psychology). Articled Clerk, Cobbetts, solicitors, 1987-1989. G. October 1990. ETC. December 1990. Pupilmaster, Philip Cattan. 28 St John Street, Manchester, 1990.

ROSS-BROWN, James William KC

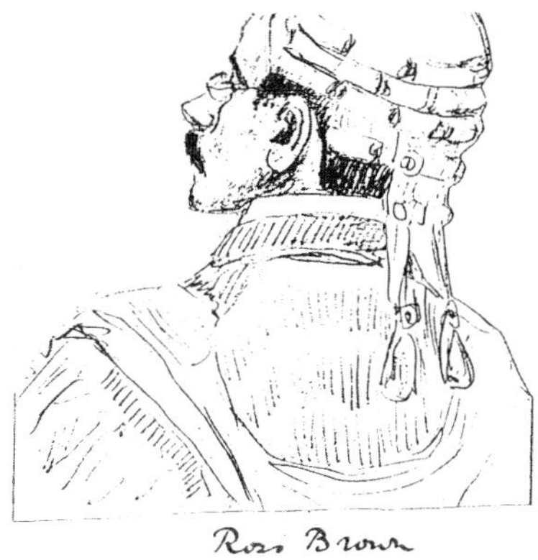

Born 29 September 1856, Douglas. Died 27 July 1938 aged 81. Son of James Brown, founder of Isle of Man Times. Began as a journalist; member of Daily Telegraph Parliamentary Staff. G. 25 April 1888: Bencher 1924. ETC. 6 March 1889. Prop. Gully QC. Sec. C A Russell. 3 Pump Court, 1888-1889. Liverpool Chambers; 12 Commerce Chambers, Lord Street, 1890-1892; Bristowe Chambers, 8 Harrington Street, 1893-1898; Stephenson's Chambers, Lord Street, 1899-1900; 8 Cook Street, 1901. 1 Plowden Buildings, 1902-1905; 2 Elm Court, 1906-1936; Palace Chambers, Bridge Street, Westminster, 1909-1912. No address, 1936-1938. Silk 1920. Member, Cheshire County Council. Editor of Local Government & Public Health sections of Chitty's Statutes. WW.

ROSTRON, Simpson

Born 24 April 1834. Only son of Laurence Rostron of Bowden. AAS. M. 21 January 1856. Call. 17 November 1858. 1 Hare Court, 1876-1906; 5 Crown Office Row, 1907. Not in 1908. Law List.

ROTCH, William Dixon

Born 1841. Only son of Thomas Rotch of Choisy, Guernsey. Exeter College, Oxford, BA 1862. AAS. I. 22 January 1862. Call. 17 November 1865. ETC. 21 March 1877. Prop. Russell QC. Sec. Potter. Liverpool Chambers; 4 Harrington Street, 1876-1883; 9 Cook Street, 1884-1908. 6 Crown Office Row, 1879-1901. Not in 1909 Law List.

ROTHERBY, Peter
Born 4 July 1972 Mirfield, WR Yorks. King James's School, Almondbury; Greenhead 6th Form College; University College, Oxford, BA. L. October 1994. ETC. 13 December 1994. Prop. Keith Goddard QC. Sec. Timothy Ryder. Queen's Chambers, 5 John Dalton Street, Manchester, 1994.

ROTHWELL, Sheila Margaret
LLB. I. November 1970. Ship Canal House, King Street, Manchester, 1970-1975. No address, 1976. Not in 1977 Law List.

ROTHWELL, Stephen John
Liverpool University, LLB. G. July 1977. ETC 1977. Pupilmaster Charles Bloom. Manchester Chambers; 12 floor, Sunlight House, Quay Street, 1977-1979; 28 St John Street, 1980-2000. Acting Stipendiary Magistrate. Died 25 August 2000 aged 46. Tributes, Manchester Law Courts 8 September 2000 (HH Judge Sir Rhys Davies QC/ Peter Birkett QC) Transcript in Circuit Records. Obituary, "In Brief" Issue 14. October 2000.

ROUSE, (Nigel) Philip
Born 5 April 1965, Salford. Hope High School, Salford. Manchester University, LLB. Formerly a solicitor, 1987-1992. G. 1 February 1993. ETC. 30 March 1993. Prop. Rodney Scholes QC. Sec. Christopher Elliott. Manchester Chambers; 6th floor, Sunlight House, 1.9.1993-1994; Young Street Chambers, 1995.

ROUSSACK, Jeremy Brian
Born 6 August 1959, Manchester. Manchester Grammar School; St John's College, Cambridge, MA., MB., B.Chir. FRCS.Ed; Dip Law (City). Qualified as a doctor in 1983. In practice for 12 years, finally specialising in heart and chest surgery. M. October 1996. London pupillage. ETC. December 1998. Prop. Michael Redfern QC. Sec. Roger Farley. 28 St John Street, Manchester (now St John's Building), 1998.

ROUTLEDGE, Rev. Canon (Kenneth) Graham
Born 21 September 1927. Died 18 May 1989 aged 61. Son of Edgar and Catherine Routledge, brother of the actress, Patricia Routledge, CBE. Birkenhead School. HM Forces, 1945-1948, RE & RAEC. Liverpool University, LLB 1951. AAS. M. 26 October 1949. Call. July 1952. Harmsworth Scholar. ETC. 1952. Pupilmasters, Andrew Rankin & Joseph Turner. Chancery Practitioner from 20 North John Street, Liverpool, 1952-1963. Tutor and Lecturer in Law, Liverpool University, 1952-1963. Member, Birkenhead Borough Council, 1960-1963. Left the Bar for the Church. Fitzwilliam College, Cambridge, BA (Theology), 1965; MA 1969. Curate, St George's Church, Stockport, 1966-1969. Lecturer in Law, Manchester University, 1966-1969. Corpus Christi College, Cambridge; Dean of Chapel, 1969-1977; Lecturer and Director of Studies in Law, 1972-1977; Fellow, 1969-1983. Canon Residentiary and Treasurer of Peterborough Cathedral, 1977-1982. Chancellor Diocese of; Ely, 1973; Peterborough, 1976; Lichfield, 1976. Canon Residentiary and Treasurer of St Paul's Cathedral, 1982-1989. WW.

ROUTLEDGE, Robert McKilliam
Born 1851. Died 12 August 1907. 6th son of William Routledge, manufacturer of Aberdeen. Aberdeen University. AAS. L. 2 November 1876. Call. 17 November 1879. ETC. 16 July 1881. Prop. Temple QC. Sec. Robertson. 12 King's Bench Walk, 1882-1884; 1 Elm Court, 1885-1891. Judge, Magistrate & Colonial Secretary, Falkland Islands, 1891. Stipendiary Justice, Trinidad, 1894-1901. Puisne Judge, Trinidad, 1901-1906. WW. Foster.

ROWE, Charles James
Born 1848. Eldest son of Charles Rowe of London. Trinity College, Cambridge, MA, 1874. AAS. I. 22 November 1869. Call 7 June 1873. ETC. 6 March 1874. Prop. Mellor. Sec. Williams QC. Circuit Junior, Summer 1874. 6 Crown Office Row, 1876-1877; 7 King's Bench Walk, 1878. 7 Crown Office Row, 1879-1882. No address, 1883-1901. Not in 1902 Law List.

ROWE, John Jermyn QC

Born 23 March 1936 Stockport. Eldest son of John Rowe of Stockport, bank manager. Son in law of His Honour Basil Gerrard. Qv. Manchester Grammar School; Brasenose College, Oxford, MA. AAS. M. 19 January 1957. Call 9 February 1960; Bencher 1985. ETC. 1960. Prop. Joseph Cantley QC. Sec. Kenneth Hollings. Circuit Junior, 1961; Hon. Secretary, 1970-1976 and Circuit Leader, 1988-1992. Manchester Chambers; 4 Chapel Walks, 1960-1964; 601 Royal Exchange, 1965-1982.

Recorder 1978. Silk 1982. 2 Pump Court, 1982-1988; 8 King Street, 1989-1999; 12 Byrom Street, 2000. Prosecuting Counsel to the Inland Revenue 1980-1982. Member, Parole Board, 1987-1990. Chairman of the Bar, 1993. Independent Reviewer for Parliament on the Prevention of Terrorism Act 1989 & Northern Ireland (Emergency Provisions) Act 1996. Member of the Bar of Ireland and Hon. Member of the Canadian Bar. Publications; Human Rights for Schools.

I append an extract from a foreword John wrote for the Bar Directory when he was Chairman of the Bar. "The Circuits of the Bar have endured for 800 years. It was in 1176 that Henry II sent out the Assize Judges on their journeys round the counties of England (Wales was included later). The Bar followed the Judges, and stayed in the towns where the Assizes were held. Today there are six Circuits. The North Eastern covers England east of the Pennines, and the Northern has the west; the Midland and Oxford has the great band of the middle of England from the Wash to the Welsh Borders; the Wales and Chester Circuit has the whole of Wales, from the sea to the marshes, together with the Cheshire plain; the South Eastern Circuit takes in the Home Counties, and Suffolk and Norfolk; the Western starts with Hampshire and goes out to the West Country. That is a somewhat rural description, but of course on each of the Circuits there are great cities and towns and conurbations where you will find a local Bar. One-third of the Bar practises in the provinces.

I have mentioned that in Plantagenet times the Bar followed the Judges; now they reside on Circuit. But they still dine together at the local hotel, at Bar Mess. On some Circuits this is a regular occurrence, as frequent as 25 times a year. At Mess, information is passed and views are exchanged. You hear of a particular decision on an award of damages, or a new point of law.

Undoubtedly the Mess tradition helps to maintain standards; a bond is formed between the members of the Circuit, and a collegiate attitude grows.

The Circuit system of the Bar is now as strong as it ever has been. I see it having a long life, certainly another 800 years, and I see it working as follows: finding new markets and adapting and educating itself; and then telling the clients about itself, preferably in several modern languages."

ROWLANDS, Gwynn Price

Born 18 January 1951 Bangor, brother of Rhys Price Rowlands, Recorder on the Wales & Chester Circuit. Friars School; Liverpool College; LSE; King's College; Manchester Business School. MA., LLB., MBA., Dip. Law. Admitted solicitor, 1976. I. May 1985. ETC 1985. Queen Elizabeth Building, 1985-1986; New Court, 1987-1989. 8 King Street, Manchester, 1989. Liverpool Chambers; 1st & ground floor, Peel House, Harrington Street, 1990-1998; 25-27 Castle Street, 1998. Part time Chairman, Industrial Tribunals, 1992.

ROWLEY, John James

Born 24 June 1964, Newcastle-under-Lyme. Son of District Judge John Rowley. Stonyhurst; Emmanuel College, Cambridge, MA (Classics). Dip. Law. L. July 1987; Hardwicke Scholar. ETC. December 1987. Prop. Charles Bloom QC. Sec. Michael Redfern. 28 St John Street, Manchester (now St John's Building), 1987. Regional Treasury Counsel, 2000. Recorder 2003.

ROWLEY, Karl John

Born 16 October 1969 England. Holden Lane High School; Oriel College, Oxford, MA., Dip Law. M. 13 November 1994. Regent Chambers, 29 Regent Road, Hanley, Stoke-on-Trent, 1994-1997. Midland Circuit. Pupilmaster, Peter Rank. ETC. 31 March 1998. Prop. L. Kushner QC. Sec. Lesley Newton. Young Street Chambers, Manchester, 1997.

ROWSON, Edmund KC

Died 18 December 1951. G. 16 April 1913. ETC. 15 June 1913. Prop. Greer KC. Sec. Riley. Liverpool Chambers; 5 Harrington Street, 1913-1928; 3 Cook Street, 1929-1931. Manchester Chambers; 4 Clarence Street, 1932-1934; 26 King Street, 1935-1947. Silk 1947. Farrar's Building, 1947; 1 Brick Court, 1948-1949; 1 Hare Court, 1950-1951. First Recorder of Blackpool, 1948-1951. Defended Connolly in Liverpool Cameo Murder case. WW, but very few details given.

ROXBOROUGH, Adam Benedict

Born 14 October 1964, Liverpool. St Edward's College, Liverpool; Manchester Metropolitan University, LLB. Formerly a solicitor. G. July 1998. ETC. December 1998. Prop. David Fish QC. Sec. Hugh McKee. Manchester Chambers; Manchester House Chambers, 1998-1999; 24a St John Street (now St John's Building), February 1999.

ROYDS, Edmund Albert Nuttall

Born 1845. 2nd son of Albert Hudson Royds of Worcester. Eton; Trinity College, Cambridge. Captain, 1st Royal Militia from 1872. AAS. M. 30 April 1868. Call 26 January 1871. ETC. 10 March 1871. Prop. Aspinall QC. Sec. L Temple. No address, 1876-1898. Not in 1899 Law List. Foster.

ROYDS, John Fletcher Twemlow
Born 1867. 2nd son of Charles Twemlow Royds of Heysham Rectory, Clerk in Holy Orders, MA., JP. Trinity College, Cambridge, BA. AAS. M. 19 November 1889. Call 29 June 1892. ETC. 22 March 1893. Prop. Bigham QC. Sec. C A Russell. 2 Brick Court, 1893-1898. 41 John Dalton Street, Manchester, 1899-1921. No address, 1922-1935. Not in 1936 Law List.

ROYLE, John Charles Fanshawe
L. 18 November 1912. ETC. 3 July 1913. Prop. Sanderson KC. Sec. Rankin. 2 Mitre Court Buildings, 1913-1921. No address, 1922-1953. Not in 1954 Law List.

RUAUX, Gillian Doreen (Her Honour Judge Ruaux)

(HS)

Born 25 March 1945. Bolton School; Manchester University, LLB., LLM. G. July 1968. ETC. 1968. Manchester Chambers; 9 Albert Square, 1968-1972; Dean's Court Chambers, 1 Dean's Court, Crown Square, 1973-1993. Recorder 1990. Circuit Judge, Bolton, 1993. WW.

RUBIN, Anthony John Meek
Born 1 November 1934 Manchester. Manchester Grammar School; Bristol University. G. May 1960. ETC. 1960. Pupilmaster, William Morris. Circuit Junior, 1962. 26 King Street, Manchester, 1960-1963. Member of the Bar of Israel. In public & private practice in Israel, 1963-1976. 68 Quay Street, Manchester 1976 to retirement in 2000.

RUCK, Mary Ida
Born 22 March 1968, Swindon. Married to Timothy Storrie qv. Malmesbury Comprehensive School; Cardiff University, BA; King's College, London, MA. Davies Arnold Cooper, solicitors, 1990-1992. G. October 1993. South Eastern Circuit, 1993. 10 King's Bench Walk, 1993-1999. Pupilmaster, John Evan Jones. ETC. 1999. Prop. Anthony Russell QC. Sec. Christopher Melton. Peel Court Chambers, 45 Hardman Street, Manchester, 1999. Publications; Editor, Fatal Accidents section of Butterworth's Personal Injury Service.

*** RUDLAND, Martin William (His Honour Judge Rudland)**
Born 13 March 1955, Sheffield. Rowlinson School, Sheffield; Sheffield University, LLB. M. July 1977; Harmsworth Scholar, 1977. North Eastern Circuit, 1978. Pupilmaster, Peter Charlesworth. Leeds Chambers; 10 Park Square (formerly, 37 Park Square), 1977-2001; 6 Park Square, May 2001-July 2002. Assistant Recorder, 1992; Recorder, 1996. Circuit Judge, 2002.

RULE, Jonathan Daniel
Born 7 January 1969, Sutton Coldfield. Lichfield Friary Grange Comprehensive; University College, Oxford, BA. G. November 1993. ETC. 13 December 1994. Prop. Anthony Elleray QC. Sec. Robert Sterling. Manchester Chambers; St James's Chambers, 68 Quay Street, 1993-1997; Merchant Chambers, 1 North Parade, Parsonage Gardens, 1997. Merger with St Johns Buildings Chambers, 2004. Member, Stockport Borough Council.

RUMBELOW, (Arthur) Anthony QC (His Honour Judge Rumbelow QC)
Born 9 September 1943 Salford. Salford Grammar School; Queens' College, Cambridge, BA (Squire Scholar). AAS. M. 31 January 1964; Harmsworth Exhibitioner & Astbury Scholar; Call 18 July 1967. ETC. November 1967. Prop. Godfrey Heilpern QC. Sec. Ivor Taylor. Manchester Chambers; 47 Peter Street, 1967-1974; 12th floor, Sunlight House, Quay Street, 1975-1979; 28 St John Street, 1980-2002. Recorder 1986. Chairman, Medical Appeals Tribunal, 1988-2002. Silk 1990. Legal Member, Mental Health Review Tribunals, 2001. Circuit Judge, 24 June 2002. Member, Rochdale MBC, 1982-1984. WW.

RUSCOE, Janet Caroline
Born, Manchester. Sale Girls Grammar School; University of Northumbria, LLB; Manchester University, LLM. L. October 1995. New Walk Chambers, 27 New Walk, Leicester, 1996-1999; Midland Circuit, December 1996. Pupilmaster, Sean McGovern. ETC. 1999. Kenworthy's Chambers, 83 Bridge Street, Manchester, May 1999.

RUSHTON, Edward
Born 1820. Eldest son of Edward Rushton, barrister of Inner Temple. Jesus College, Cambridge, BA 1846. AAS. I. 30 October 1843. Call 8 June 1849. 1 Mitre Court Building, 1876-1900. Not in 1901 Law List. Foster.

RUSHTON, Thomas Edward.
Born 1879. Eldest son of James Thomas Rushton of Blackpool, auctioneer, valuer and fire loss assessor. AAS. M. 8 January 1900. Call 17 November 1902. ETC. 20 July 1905. Prop. Shee KC. Sec. Roe Rycroft. No address, 1905-1908. 78 King Street, Manchester, 1909-1910. No address, 1911-1953. Not in 1954 Law List.

RUSHTON, William Lowes
youngest son of Edward Rushton of Liverpool, barrister. AAS. G. 28 January 1861. Call 26 January 1865. 2 Plowden Buildings, 1876-1882. No address, 1883-1909. Not in 1910 Law List. Foster.

RUSHWORTH, Herbert
Born 1849. Eldest son of Edmund Rushworth of St Marylebone NW., surveyor. AAS. M. 24 January 1876. Call M. 18 November 1878. ETC. 27 January 1879. Prop. Temple QC. Sec. Collins. 1 Pump Court, 1878-1882; Lamb Building, 1883; 4 Brick Court, 1884-1900. Equity draftsman & conveyancer. Not in 1901 Law List. Foster.

RUSSELL, Anthony Patrick QC (His Honour Judge Russell QC)
Born 11 April 1951, Bebington. Nephew of Rt. Hon. Sir Patrick Russell qv. King's School, Chester; Pembroke College, Oxford, BA 1973; MA 1977. AAS. M. 17 September 1971. Call 18 July 1974. ETC. 1974. Prop. Patrick Russell QC. Sec. Michael Lever. Circuit Junior, 1977. Same Manchester Chambers; Ship Canal House, King Street, 1974-1980; 2 Old Bank Street, 1981-1991; Peel Court Chambers, 45 Hardman Street, 1992-2004. Assistant Recorder 1989. Member, Bar Council, 1987-1994. Standing Counsel for the Inland Revenue, 1993-1996. Recorder, 1993. Editor, "In Brief", the Northern Circuit Newsletter, 1997-2004. Silk 1999. Circuit Judge, Preston, 27 July 2004. WW.

RUSSELL, His Honour Judge The Hon. Arthur
Born 19 February 1861. Died 22 November 1907 aged 46. Eldest son of Lord Russell of Killowen qv. Beaumont College, Old Windsor; Oriel College, Oxford, MA (BA 1886). I. 17 November 1886. ETC. 24 January 1887. Prop. Gully QC. Sec. Collins QC. Pupilmaster, J Gorell Barnes. 3 Brick Court, 1888; 2 Paper Buildings, 1889-1894; 5 Paper Buildings, 1895-1900. Special pleader & admiralty courts. Counsel in the Parnell Commission. Secretary to the Lord Chief Justice (his father), 1894-1900. Editor, Times Law Reports, 1890-1900. County Court Judge, Circuit 45, (Berkshire & Surrey), October 1900-1907. WW.

RUSSELL, Sir Charles QC., MP (Baron Russell of Killowen)
Born 10 November 1832 Newry, Co. Down. Died 10 August 1900 aged 67. St Vincent's College, Castlenock. Admitted solicitor, 1854 practising in Londonderry & Belfast. Trinity College, Dublin. L. 26 January 1859; Bencher 1872; Treasurer 1893. ETC. 1859. 3 Brick Court, 1876-1883; 10 New Court, Carey Street, 1884-1894. MP (L) Dundalk, 1880-1885; South Hackney, 1885-1894; Attorney General, 1886 & 1892-1894. Lord of Appeal in Ordinary, 1894. Lord Chief Justice of England, 1894. GCMG, 1893. PC. WW. DNB. Further Reading; Biography by R Barry O'Brien, 1901. He was a vigorous advocate of Home Rule. He defended C S Parnell before the Commission in 1888 and Mrs Maybrick on a charge of poisoning her husband in 1889. He tried the Jameson Raiders in 1896. His entry in DNB records him as a man of great ability but an aggressive advocate. He was at his best exposing the fraudulent witness. "He felt the indignation and contempt which he poured on such a witness...... His extraordinary power when addressing a jury was owing not so much to any oratorical display as to the authority which he could always exercise over those he sought to influence. Spellbound under his vigorous and often passionate reasoning, their verdict was often due to the merits not of the litigant but of his counsel." He did well from the beginning usually in the Liverpool Court of Passage. His fee books show that in his third year he made over £300 and the next year £1000. In "Seven Lamps of Advocacy" Judge Parry says: "Charles Russell had a continuous spate of energy. Many of us can remember him, tireless and active himself, bustling into the robing room at St George's Hall, Liverpool, and finding several members of the Junior Bar standing around the fire. "Why are you loafing about here?", he asked, "Why don't you do something?" "We have nothing to do," said the Junior Bar. "Why don't you go to the races?" he rejoined. "Do something!"

RUSSELL, Charles Alfred QC
Born 12 April 1855. Died 21 June 1926 aged 71. 2nd son of His Honour Judge John Archibald Russell QC qv. University College School; University College, London, BA., LLB. AAS. G. 30 October 1875. Holt Scholar; 1st class studentship, 1877. Call 3 July 1878; Bencher 1894. ETC. 10 July 1878. Prop. Temple QC. Sec. Crompton. 2 Harcourt Buildings, 1878-1926. Silk 1896.

RUSSELL, John Archibald QC (His Honour Judge Russell QC)
Born 25 November 1816. Died 18 November 1899 aged 82. Father of Charles Alfred Russell QC qv. Glasgow Grammar School; Glasgow High School; Edinburgh University, BA, 1835; Glasgow University, LLB, 1851. AAS. G. 2 November 1838. Call 17 November 1841; Bencher 1868; Treasurer, 1874. 1 Child's Place, Temple, 1848. JP., Lancs. Professor of English Law, University College, London, 1850-1869; Life Governor. Silk 1868. Examiner to Inns of Court. Solicitor General, County Palatine of Durham, 1862-1869. Recorder of Bolton, 1869-1890. County Court Judge, Circuit 8, (Manchester), 1869-1890. Publications; Treatise on Mercantile Agency; Editor, Chitty on; Contracts; Bills of Exchange; and Best on Evidence. WW. Foster.

RUSSELL, Peter John
BA., LLM (London). I. July 1975. ETC. 3 April 1979. Prop. Patrick Russell QC. Sec. Hodgson. Manchester Chambers; 43 King Street, 1980-1988; 5 John Dalton Street, 1989-1993. No address 1994. Not in 1995 Bar Directory.

RUSSELL, (Thomas) Patrick QC (Rt. Hon. Sir Patrick Russell)

(RB)

Born 30 July 1926 Urmston, Manchester. Died 28 October 2002 aged 76. Urmston Grammar School; Manchester University, LLB; Hon. LLD 1988. Intelligence Corps & RASC, 1945-1948. AAS. M. 13 April 1945. Call 29 January 1949; Bencher 1978. ETC. February 1947. Prop. William Gorman KC. Sec Arthur E Jalland. Manchester Chambers; 40 Kennedy Street, 1949-

Dinner to mark Lord Justice Russel's retirement, Manchester 7 December 1996.

1965; Ship Canal House, King Street, 1966-1971; Prosecuting Counsel to Post Office, 1961-1970. Assistant Recorder of Bolton 1963-1970. Recorder of Barrow in Furness, 1970-1971. Silk 1971. 5 Essex Court, 1971-1980. Crown Court Recorder, 1972-1980. Leader of the Northern Circuit, 1978-1980. Member of Senate, Inns of Court and the Bar, 1978-1980. High Court Judge, Queen's Bench Division, 1980-1986. Kt. 1980. Presiding Judge of the Northern Circuit, 1983-1987. Lord Justice of Appeal, 1987-1996. PC 1987. Judge of the Court of Appeal, Gibraltar, 1998-1999. President, Lancashire CCC, 1999-2000. WW. Obituaries; Daily Telegraph, 2.11.2002; Times, 7.11.2002. "In Brief" March 2003 (Anthony Russell QC) Tributes at Liverpool Law Courts, 30 October 2002 (The Lord Chief Justice (Lord Woolf), Mr Justice Leveson and David Steer QC. Transcript in Circuit Records. Memorial Services; St Ann's Church, Manchester, 11 January 2003. Temple Church, 26 March 2003. The following extract is from the Daily Telegraph: "As a barrister Russell always went straight to the heart of the case, he was a highly persuasive and deadly cross examiner. Adept at getting on the wave length of both juries and judges, he was particularly strong in criminal trials, where his knowledge of the law was deemed second to none He was later an outstanding judge. His summings-up were remarkable for their succinctness; he was notable for expressing complicated ideas clearly and for delivering word perfect ex tempore judgments." Lord Justice Rose said of him: "His outstanding qualities were his loyalty to his family, friends, the North and the Circuit, unimpeachable integrity in his private and professional life, and a self deprecating sense of humour. Behind a sometimes curmudgeonly exterior he was the gentlest and the kindest of men."

RUSSELL, Thomas Taylor
I. 10 May 1922. Pupilmaster, John Brown Sandbach. Manchester Chambers; St Anne's Passage, 1927-1929; 60 King Street, 1930-1936. Chief Police Magistrate, Fiji, 1937-1940; Crown Counsel & Assistant Legal Advisor, Malaya, 1941-1947; Puisne Judge, Malaya, 1948-1954. No address, 1955-1963. Not in 1964 Law List.

RUSSELL, Walter
G. 6 June 1894. ETC. 14 March 1895. Prop. Pickford QC. Sec. Steel. 4 Paper Buildings, 1895-1899. 25 Lord Street, 1900-1908. No address, 1909-1931. Not in 1932 Law List.

RUSSELL, William CB
Born 7 April 1868. Died 9 December 1931 aged 63. Craigmont House, Edinburgh; MA., BCL (Oxon). I. 14 June 1893. ETC. 13 February 1894. Prop. Gully QC. Sec. Page. 1 King's Bench Walk, 1894-1921. Parliamentary draftsman & committees. Secretary to Royal Commission on Coal Supplies, 1901-1905. Member, Departmental Committee on Railway Amalgamations, 1910-1911. Served in Ministry of Munitions & other Government Departments, 1916-1919. Member, Geological Survey Board, 1920-1923. CB 1905. WW.

RUTHERFORD, Arthur
Born 1866. 5th son of William Rutherford of Great Crosby and brother of John Rutherford qv. Brasenose College, Oxford, BA. AAS. M. 18 November 1887. Call 18 June 1890. ETC. 6 August 1890. Prop. Kennedy QC. Sec. W F Taylor. No address, 1891-1896. Wason Chambers, 4 Harrington Street, Liverpool, 1897-1908. No address, 1909-1931. Not in 1932 Law List.

RUTHERFORD, John
Born 1861. 3rd son of William Rutherford of Great Crosby and brother of Arthur Rutherford qv. London University, LLB. AAS. M. 20 April 1880. Call 26 January 1884. ETC. 14 February 1884. Prop. Gully QC. Sec. Kennedy. Wason Chambers, 4 Harrington Street, Liverpool, 1886-1928. No address, 1929-1931. Not in 1932 Law List. Pupilmaster of Bertram Benas. Foster.

RUTLEDGE, Sir (John) Guy QC
Born 18 March 1872. Died 15 February 1930 aged 57. Queen's College, Galway; Royal University, Dublin, MA, 1894. I. 30 June 1897. ETC. 19 February 1898. Prop. Pickford QC. Sec. Horridge. Stephenson's Chambers, 25 Lord Street, Liverpool, 1899-1908. 8 King's Bench Walk, 1908. Secretary, Burma Legislative Council, 1908. Government Advocate, 1908-1919. Judge, Chief Court, Lower Burma, 1919 & 1921-1922. Judge of High Court of Burma, 1922; Chief Justice, 1925-1930. Silk 1921. Kt. 1926. WW.

RYAN, Nicholas Joseph
Born 23 August 1957, Liverpool. Woolton College; Liverpool Bluecoat; University of London, Dept of Slavonic & East European Studies, BA (History); Dip. Law (Westminster University). Civil Service, 1980-1982. G. July 1984. Pupilmasters; 3 Temple Gardens, (Sam Wiggs) & 7 Stone Buildings (J Bishop) ETC. 12 December 1985. Prop. John Kay QC. Sec. J V B Mockett. Liverpool Chambers; 2nd floor, Fruit Exchange, Victoria Street, 1985-1989; 46 Stanley Street, 1990-1994; 14 Castle Street/ Atlantic Chambers, Cook Street, 1994.

RYAN, Thomas Patrick Francis
Keele University, BA. G. July 1979. ETC. 21 May 1981. Same Liverpool Chambers; 2nd floor, Oriel Chambers, 14 Water Street, 1981-1982; Derby Square Chambers, 1983-1998. Chairman, Employment Tribunals, 1998. Recorder 2000.

RYCROFT, Frederick William Roe
Born 1854. Formerly a Manchester solicitor. Father of George Jessel Rycroft qv. AAS. M.10 March 1893. Call 26 March 1893. ETC. 2 August 1893. Prop. Gates QC. Sec. Maurice Hill. Manchester Chambers; 4 St James's Square, 1894-1897; 62 King Street, 1898-1904; 8 St James's Square, 1905-1908; 26 King Street, 1909-1924. Deputy Coroner. Salford. Not in 1925 Law List.

RYCROFT, George Jessel
Born 1883.elder son of Frederick William Roe Rycroft qv. AAS. M. 9 November 1901. Call 15 June 1904. ETC. 15 July 1904. Prop. Shee KC. Sec. Byrne. Manchester Chambers; No address, 1904-1908; 36 King Street, 1909-1921; 26 King Street, 1922-1940. Manchester City Coroner, London Road, Manchester, 1941-1963. Not in 1964 Law List.

RYDER, Ernest Nigel TD., QC (The Hon. Mr Justice Ryder)

Born 9 December 1957, Bolton. Bolton School; Peterhouse, Cambridge, MA. Merchant Bankers, Grindley Brandt & Co, 1979-1980. G. July 1981. ETC. 1981. Prop. Richard Clegg QC. Sec. Christopher Tetlow. Pupilmasters, Julian Hall & Christopher Tetlow. Manchester Chambers; 601 Royal Exchange / 8 King Street, 1981-1999; Deans Court Chambers, 24 St John Street, 1999. Assistant Recorder, 1997. Silk 1997. Recorder, 2001-2004. Deputy High Court Judge 2001-2004. Counsel, North Wales Tribunal of Inquiry, 1996-1999. Assistant Boundary Commissioner, 1999-2004. Command, Duke of Lancaster's Own Yeomanry, 1982; Squadron Leader, 1990. Squadron Leader, Royal Mercian and Lancastrian Yeomanry, 1992. TD, 1996. High Court Judge, Family Division, 2004. Kt. 2004. Family liason Judge, Northern Circuit, 2005. WW.

RYDER, Timothy Robert
Born 16 August 1954 Bolton. Stowe School; Corpus Christi, Cambridge MA. AAS. M. 19 January 1976. Call 28 July 1977. ETC 1977. Prop. Christopher Rose QC. Sec. John Lord. Circuit Junior, 1979. Manchester Chambers; 43 King Street, 1977-1989; Queen's Chambers, 5 John Dalton Street 1989. Assistant Recorder 1998. Recorder 2000.

RYLAND, Ernest Charles
L. 8 May 1895. ETC. 31 July 1895. Prop. Mullholland QC. Sec. Sharpe. 9 Cook Street, Liverpool, 1898-1934. Lancs. Chancery Court. Not in 1935 Law List.

RYLANDS, John Paul
Born 10 March 1846. AAS. M. 30 January 1882. Call 26 January 1885. ETC. 17 February 1886. Prop. Crompton QC. Sec. Welsby. Liverpool Chambers; 25 Lord Street, 1886-1887; 8 Harrington Street, 1888-1908. No Address, 1909-1923. Not in 1924 Law List. Publications include; The Holcroft Family; Visitations of Cheshire; Visitations of Dorset and Lancashire & Cheshire Funeral Certificates. Foster.

RYLANDS, (Margaret) Elizabeth
Born 4 June 1951 Hazel Grove, Stockport. Mount Carmel School, Cheshire; Bristol University, LLB. AAS. M. 4 March 1971. Call 27 November 1973. Irish Bar 1991. ETC. 1974. Pupilmaster, Richard Clegg. Same Manchester Chambers; 601 Royal Exchange, 1974-1988; 8 King Street, 1989. Assistant Recorder 1998. Recorder 2000.

RYLANDS, Sir (William) Peter Bt.
Born 23 October 1868. Died 22 October 1948 aged 79. Charterhouse; Trinity College, Cambridge. I. 6 June 1894. ETC. 14 March 1895. Prop. Hopwood QC. Sec. Henry. New Court, 1895-1898. No address, 1899-1948. President; Iron, Steel & Wire Manufacturers Association; Federation of British Industries; High Sheriff, Cheshire, 1935-1936. WW.

S

SABREY, Karim Samir
Born 9 March 1968 Cairo, Egypt. University of Central Lancashire, BA. I. November 1992. ETC. December 1992. Prop. John Burke QC. Sec. John Wishart. Manchester Chambers; Manchester House Chambers, 18-22 Bridge Street, 1992-1999; 8 King Street, 1999.

★ SACHS, The Hon Sir Michael (Alexander Geddes)

(RB)

Born 8 April 1932 Glasgow. Died 25 September 2003 aged 71. Sedbergh; Manchester University, LLB. National Service, 1957-1959. Admitted as a solicitor, 1957. Partner in Slater Heelis & Co of 71 Princess Street, Manchester, 1962-1984. President, Manchester Law Society, 1978-1979. Council, Law Society, 1979-1984 (Chairman, Standing Committee on Criminal Law, 1982-1984). Deputy Circuit Judge, 1977-1980. Recorder, 1980-1984. Circuit Judge, 1984-1993. (sitting exclusively on crime initially in Liverpool and later in Manchester). Michael's speciality was the long multi-handed drugs trial or gangland killing over which he exercised great control. He is particularly remembered for presiding over the 16 week trial of Kevin Taylor and others who were acquitted of charges of conspiracy to defraud and the 5 month trial in 1993 of 11 men who were convicted of riot at Strangeways prison. High Court Judge, Queen's Bench Division 1993-2003. The first solicitor to be appointed to the High Court. Kt. 1993. Hon. LLD, Manchester 1994. KSS 1980. Obituary, Times, 1 October 2003. Tributes at Liverpool Law Courts, 2 October 2003 (Judge Henry Globe QC/ David Steer QC) Transcript in Circuit Records.
Michael had a dry wit. When asked why he had been chosen as the first solicitor High Court Judge, he replied: "It was certainly not for my youthful good looks." Recently in Liverpool in a dreary criminal case he was asked by a Silk at 11.30am whether it would be a convenient moment for a coffee break. "Never touch the stuff" said Michael, "It keeps me awake." Michael was a first rate gurner. Once, after making a number of submissions without merit, Counsel rose again. Michael pulled a face. "Is your Lordship unwell?" enquired Counsel. "No," said Michael, "but I have a feeling I'm about to be."

SADIQ, Tariq Mahmood
Born 10 November 1968. Nottingham. Manvers Pierpont School, Nottingham; University of Kent at Canterbury, BA. G. November 1993. ETC. 1998. Prop. Charles Garside QC. Sec. Jonathan Parker. 9 St John Street, Manchester, 1993. Attorney General's; Provincial Panel, 2000.; Prosecution Panel B List, 2002.

SAFFER, Soloman
Born 1880. 4th son of Nathan Saffer of Leeds, manufacturer. AAS. M. 26 October 1907. Call 8 June 1910. ETC. 25 February 1911. Prop. Langdon KC. Sec. Gibbons.7 Kennedy Street, Manchester, 1912-1914. No address, 1915-1953. Not in 1954.

SAMPSON, Edward Joseph
I. 11 June 1902. Manchester Chambers; 40 Kennedy Street, 1904; 78 King Street, 1905-1908; 16 John Dalton Street, 1909-1910. No address, 1911-1953. Not in 1954 Law List.

SAMSON, William Leopold
Born 1882. Eldest son of Charles Leopold Samson of 31 Booth Street, Manchester, solicitor. Magdalen College, Oxford. AAS. M. 27 May 1902. Call 24 April 1907. ETC. 15 February 1908. Prop. C A Russell KC. Sec. Crawford. 3 Paper Buildings, 1909-1914. No address, 1915-1923. Not in 1924 Law List.

SAMUELL, Charles Simpson
Born 1824. 2nd son of Simpson Samuell of Liverpool. AAS. I. 28 May 1859. Call 30 April 1862. 53 North John Street, 1876-1901. No address, 1902-1911. Not in 1912 Law List.

SAMUELS, Harry OBE
Born 1894. 2nd son of Morris Samuels of Liverpool, jeweller. MA (Oxon). Secretary of "Zionist Organisation" when AAS. M. 12 October 1920. Call 26 January 1923. North Eastern Circuit. 5 Essex Court, 1924; 8 Old Square, 1925-1931. ETC. 17 July 1931. Prop. Lynskey KC. Sec. Sellers. 10 Cook Street, Liverpool, 1932-1937. 11 King's Bench Walk, 1938-1940; 1 King's Bench Walk, 1941; 4 King's Bench Walk, 1942-1946; 1 Essex Court, 1947-1948; 4 Paper Buildings, 1949-1951; 5 Paper Buildings, 1952-1976. Not in 1977 Law List.

SAMUELS, Jeffrey Keith
Born 9 July 1965, Manchester. Stockport Grammar School; Leeds University, LLB. AAS. M. 2 June 1987. Call 28 July 1988. ETC. 1988. Pupilmaster, Susan Klonin. Manchester Chambers; 33 King Street West, 1988-1994; Manchester House Chambers, 1994-1995; 28 St John Street, (now St John's Buildings), 1995.

SAMUELS, John Gordon
G. January 1950. ETC. 1950. Pupilmaster, Melville Kennan. 34 Castle Street, Liverpool, 1950-1953. Crown Counsel, Tanganyika Territory, 1954-1959. No address, 1960-1963. Not in 1964 Law List.

SAMUELSON, James
Born 20 January 1829. Son of Samuel Henry Samuelson of Kingston upon Hull, merchant. AAS. M. 18 April 1867. Call 26 January 1870. ETC. 26 March 1870. Prop. J J Aston QC. Sec. R G Williams. No chambers address, 1876-1935. Not in 1936 Law List. Founder and sometime editor of the Popular Science Review and the Quarterly Journal of Science. Publications; Roumania, Past & Present; History of Drink. Foster.

SANDARS, Edmund Thomas
I. 17 November 1898. ETC. 9 August 1901. Prop. Russell QC. Sec. Shaw. 3 Dr Johnson Buildings, 1902; 1 Temple Gardens, 1903-1907; 5 Paper Buildings, 1908-1910; 3 Hare Court, 1911-1928. No address, 1929-1942. Not in 1943 Law List.

SANDBACH, Francis John Vaudrey
son of John Brown Sandbach KC qv. G. 19 November 1923. ETC. 20 February 1924. Prop. Wingate-Saul KC. Sec. Jordan. Circuit Junior, Summer 1924 & Attorney General of Circuit. Manchester Chambers; 6 St Ann's Passage, 1924-1935; 43 King Street, 1936-1940; 60 King Street, 1941-1957. Not in 1958 Law List.

SANDBACH, Frederic Keal
G. 15 June 1904. ETC. 3 February 1906. Prop. Tobin KC. Sec. Grant. No address, 1907. Not in 1908 Law List.

SANDBACH, Henry
I. 22 June 1887. ETC. 28 July 1888. Prop. Gibbs QC. Sec. Shee. 12 King's Bench Walk, 1891-1893; 1 Harcourt Buildings, 1894-1895. No address, 1896-1940. Not in 1941 Law List.

SANDBACH, John Brown KC

Born 1 January 1878. Died 27 August 1951 aged 73. Father of Francis John Vaudrey Sandbach qv. Leys School; King's College, Cambridge. I. 11 June 1902. ETC. 5 February 1903. Prop. Shee KC. Sec. Gibbons. St Ann's Passage, Manchester, 1903-1925. Silk 1925. 6 Pump Court, 1926. Metropolitan Magistrate, 16.3.1926-4.10.1947 (South Western, 1926-1928; Lambeth, 1928-1924; Marlborough Street, 1934-1947). Publications; Law of the Motor Car; This Old Wig (Autobiography). WW.

SANDBACH, Samuel Henry
Born 1846. Eldest son of Samuel Sandbach of Handley, Cheshire. Eton; University College, Oxford, MA, 1873. AAS. I. 15 April 1867. Call 27 January 1873. ETC. 28 March 1873. Prop. Hosak. Sec. McConnell. No address, 1877-1935. Not in 1936 Law List. Foster.

SANDBERG, Samuel Louis Graham
Born 9 December 1851 Yorkshire. Died 2 March 1905 aged 53. Son of Paul Louis Sandberg, missionary and vicar of St John's Church, Birkenhead who spoke thirteen languages. Samuel's mother Maria spoke only seven. Liverpool College, 1861-1863; Enfield School, Birkenhead, 1863-1867; Trinity College, Dublin, BA. AAS. I. 9 June 1871. Call 30 April 1874. ETC. 28 March 1876. Prop. Hopwood QC. Sec. Bremner. No chambers address. He did little work at the Bar. He went into the Church and later to India. His entry in DNB is due to his eminence as a Tibetan Scholar. He wrote; "A Manual of Colloquial Tibetan" and compiled "A Tibetan-English Dictionary." DNB. Foster.

SANDER, Andrew Thomas
Born 26 November 1947 Farnborough, Kent. St Mary's Grammar School, Sidcup; Liverpool University, LLB. Lecturer in Law, Liverpool University, 1970-1971. AAS. M. 16 February 1968. Call 24 November 1970. ETC. 1972. Prop. Michael Maguire QC. Sec. Eric Somerset Jones. Same Liverpool Chambers; Oriel Chambers/ Covent Garden/ 14 Water Street, Liverpool, 1972. (Head of Chambers). Assistant Recorder 1988. Recorder 1991.

SANDERS, Gregory John Michael
BA (Oxon). I. July 1967. ETC 1968. Manchester Chambers; Albert Square, 1968-1969; 26 Brown Street, 1970. Temporary Legal Assistant, Inland Revenue, Somerset House, 1971-1972. No address, 1973-1974. Not in 1975 Law List.

SANDERS, (James) Damian
Born 16 March 1966 St Asaph. Denbigh High School; Huddersfield University, LLB. AAS. M. 24 July 1987. Call 22 November 1988. ETC. November 1989. Prop. David Clarke QC. Sec. John Mockett. Liverpool Chambers; Fruit Exchange, Victoria Street, 1989-1990; 46 Stanley Street, 1990-1994; 3rd floor, Peel House, Harrington Street, 1994-1998; India Buildings, Water Street, 1998.

SANDERSON, Rt Hon. Sir Lancelot QC, MP
Born 24 October 1963. Died 9 March 1944 aged 80. Elstree School, Harrow; Trinity College, Cambridge, BA., LLB 1885; MA 1895. I. 26 January 1886; Bencher 1912. ETC. 31 July 1886. Prop. Bigham QC. Sec. Segar. Circuit Junior, Winter 1887. 1 Garden Court, 1886-1887; 2 Garden Court, 1888-1892; 2 Mitre Court Buildings, 1893-1903; 2 Pump Court, 1904-1906; 2 Mitre Court Buildings, 1908-1915. Recorder of Wigan, 1901-1915. Silk 1903. MP (U) Appleby Division of Westmorland, 1910-1915. Vice Chancellor, Calcutta University, 1915. Chief Justice, Bengal, 1915-1926. Kt 1915. Member, Judicial Committee of the Privy Council, 1926-1944. PC 1926. Chairman of Quarter Sessions; Lancashire, 1926.; Westmorland, 1927. WW.

SANDIFORD, David Charles
Born 24 December 1970 Bolton. Bolton School, Boys Division; St Edmund Hall, Oxford, BA. G. October 1995. ETC. 21 December 1995. Prop. Keith Armitage QC. Sec. Eccles. 8 King Street, Manchester, 1995. Cricket Blue, 1991; Vincent's Club; MCC, Playing Member.

SASSE, Toby William
Born 1 November 1965 York. Married to Leona Harrison qv. Ampleforth College; Exeter University, LLB. Royal Navy, 1984. AAS. M. 19 November 1986. Call 28 July 1988. ETC. 1988. Prop. Donald Hart QC. Sec. Jonathan Foster. 18 St. John Street, Manchester, 1988.

SASTRY, Bob Ajay Dwarakanath
Exeter University, LLB. I. 10 October 1996. ETC. 30 July 1998. Prop. Roger Farley QC. Sec. Russell. Manchester Chambers; 2nd floor, Greggs Building, 1 Booth Street, 1999; Central Chambers, 89 Princess Street, 2000.

SAUNDERS, Vincent Albert
Born 18 November 1925. Died 22 June 1999 aged 73. LLB (London). L. June 1961. ETC February 1962. Same Liverpool Chambers; North House, 17 North John Street, 1962-1971; Martins Building, Water Street, 1972-1984; (Head of Chambers). Deputy Circuit Judge. Member, North West Area Legal Aid Appeals Committee. Legal Member, Mental Health Review Tribunal to 1997. Tributes, Liverpool Law Courts, 29 June 1999 (Judge David Lynch). Transcript in Circuit Records.

SAUVAIN, Stephen John QC
Born 3 June 1949, King's Lynn. King Edward VII Grammar School. King's Lynn; Sidney Sussex College, Cambridge, MA., LLB. Lecturer in Law, Manchester University, 1971-1978. L. July 1977. ETC. 1977. Pupilmaster, Harold Singer. Same Manchester Chambers; 460 Royal Exchange, 1977-1987; King's Chambers, 40 King Street, 1987. Silk 1995. Assistant Boundary Commissioner, 2000. Publications; Highway Law 1988, 2nd edition, 1997; editor, Encyclopaedia of Highway Law and Practice. WW.

SAVILL, Mark Ashley
Born 17 May 1969, Eastbourne, married to Rachel Shenton qv. Eton; Durham University (St Hild & St Bede), BA. I. November 1993. ETC. 13 December 1993. Prop. Keith Goddard QC. Sec. John Duncan. Circuit; Junior, Winter 1996; Secretary, 2003. General Council of the Bar, 1998. Pupillage at Fenners Chambers, Cambridge, 1993-1994. Dean's Court Chambers Crown Square/ 24 St John Street, Manchester, 1994.

SAWYER, John Frederick
Born 4 April 1955 Oxford. Abingdon School (Royce's); Warwick University, LLB., MBDVI. I. November 1978. Magistrates Clerk, 1977-1986. Crown Prosecution Service, Senior Prosecutor, 1986-1996. ETC. 1998. Prop. Eric Somerset Jones QC. Sec. Norman Wright. Oriel Chambers, 14 Water Street, Liverpool, March 1997. Deputy District Judge (Magistrates Courts), November 2000.

SCALLY, Josephine Theresa Sarah
Manchester University, BA. L. February 1984. Manchester Chambers; Conavon Court, 13 Blackfriars Street, 1984-1989; Manchester House Chambers, 18-22 Bridge Street, 1990-1996. Not in 1997 Bar Directory.

SCANLAN, Thomas MP
Born 1873. Died 9 January 1930. Son of Mathew Scanlan of Drumscliff, Co. Sligo. Catholic College, Sligo; St Andrew's University (University College). MP (N) North Sligo, 1909-1918. G. 26 January 1912. ETC. 20 February 1914. Prop. Hemmerde KC. Sec. Rees. 3 Brick Court, 1916-1924. Metropolitan Magistrate (Westminster, South Western & Lambeth), 1924-1927. 3 Plowden Buildings, 1928; 5 Pump Court, 1929-1930. WW.

SCARLETT, His Honour James Harvey Anglin

(UPA)

Born 27 January 1924. Nephew of Walter Lyon Blease qv. Shrewsbury School; Christ Church, Oxford, MA. Lieutenant, Royal Artillery, 1943-1947. I. November 1950. ETC. 7 February 1952. Prop. Harry Nelson KC. Sec. Lyon Blease. Circuit Junior, 1960. Pupilmasters, The Hon. Thomas Gabriel Roche (Temple) & Joseph Davies. Goldsmith Buildings, 1950-1954. Malayan Civil Service, 1955-1958. Same Liverpool Chambers; 27 Lord Street/10 Water Street/ 2nd floor, Oriel Chambers, 14 Water Street, 1959-1974. Recorder, 1972-1974. Circuit Judge, Canterbury & environs, 1974-1989. WW.

SCARR, John Geoffrey Rearnley

Born 12 July 1910. Died 11 November 1982 aged 72. King's School, Ely; Trinity College, Cambridge, MA., LLB. L 28 January 1935. ETC. 13 July 1938. Prop. Lynskey QC. Sec. Graham. Preston Chambers; 1 Chapel Street, 1936-1939. Major, Far East & War Office, 1939-1945. 38 Fishergate, 1945-1953. Colonial Service; Resident Magistrate & Coroner, N. Rhodesia, 1953; Chief Judicial Commissioner, Western Pacific High Commission Territories, 1959; Judge, Supreme Court, Nassau & Bahamas, 1961-1965. Publications; Law & Practice of Land Registration in N. Rhodesia; N. Rhodesian Law Reports, 1949-1954. WW.

SCARTH, Anita Mary

Born 19 September 1949, Stratford-upon-Avon. Married to Paul Stockton qv (marr. diss.), only daughter of Lancelot Brian Scarth, Detective Superintendent of Police. Keele University. AAS. M. 17 January 1972. Call 18 July 1974. 7 Fountain Court, Steelhouse Lane, Birmingham, 1975-1976. 21 North John Street, Liverpool, 1977-1981.

SCHOLES, Harry Allan

G. January 1947. Manchester Chambers; 60 King Street, 1948-1955; 36 St Ann Street, 1956-1963. Not in 1964 Law List.

SCHOLES, Michael Howard

Born 23 February 1951, Liverpool. Quarry Bank Grammar School; Liverpool University, LLB. Solicitor 1974-1994. I. July 1995. ETC. September 1995. Prop. David Harris QC. Sec. Ray Herman. Same Liverpool Chambers; 3rd floor, Peel House, Harrington Street, 1995-1998; India Buildings, Water Street, 1998.

SCHOLES, Rodney James QC

Born 26 September 1945, Manchester. Wade Deacon Grammar School, Widnes; St Catherine's College, Oxford (Scholar), BA., BCL. L. July 1968; Hardwick & Mansfield Scholar; Bencher 1997. ETC. July 1968. Prop. Godfrey Heilpern QC. Sec. Benet Hytner. Manchester Chambers; 47 Peter Street/12th floor, Sunlight House/ 28 St John Street, 1968-1987. Assistant Recorder 1982. Recorder 1986. Silk 1987. 25 later 12 Byrom Street, 1987.

SCHUSTER, Sir Claud GCB., CVO., QC (First Baron Schuster of Cerne)

Born 22 August 1869. Died 28 June 1956 aged 96. Winchester College; New College, Oxford. I. 28 January 1895; Bencher 1925; Treasurer 1947. ETC. 14 March 1895. Prop. Bigham QC. Sec. Hamilton. Circuit Junior, Summer 1895. Various Government Departments and finally Clerk to the Court in Chancery and Permanent Secretary to the Lord Chancellor, 1915-1944. He was a keen mountaineer and skier- the first man to be president both of the Ski Club of Great Britain and of the Alpine Club. As Treasurer of Inner Temple in 1947, he played a major role in planning the reconstruction of the Inn after the bombing during the war. Publications; Peaks & Pleasant Pastures, 1911; Men, Women & Mountains: Days in the Alps and Pyrenees, 1931; Sweet Enemy, 1934; Postscript to Adventure. Biography; "Yes, Lord Chancellor; A Biography of Lord Schuster-Permanent Secretary to 10 Lord Chancellors." Her Honour Jean Graham Hall. Barry Rose Law Publishers Ltd., 2003. Kt. 1913. CVO 1918. Silk 1919. KCB 1920. GCB 1927. Baron 1944. Sheriff of Dorset, 1941. WW. DNB,

SCHWABE, Sir Walter (George Salis) KC

Born 3 March 1872. Died 21 April 1931 aged 59. Son of Major-General George Salis Schwabe, CB. Marlborough; Trinity College, Oxford, BA (Law). I. 26 January 1897. ETC. 27 July 1898. Prop. Pickford QC. Sec. Isaacs. 2 Paper Buildings, 1897; 1 Garden Court, 1898-1906; 2 Garden Court, 1907-1913; Silk 1913. 7 King's Bench Walk, 1914-1921.(Captain, 19 Btn., City of London Volunteer Regt during First World War). Chief Justice of the Madras High Court, 1921-1924. Kt. 1922. Publications; (Jt) Schwabe & Branson's Law of the Stock Exchange; Effect of War on Stock Exchange. WW.

SCHWANN, Frederick Holland
LLB. I. 28 April 1899. ETC. 27 January 1901. Prop. Pickford QC. Sec. Sanderson. 2 Stone Building & Crown Office Row, 1903; 3 New Court, 1904; 2 New Court, 1905-1913; 11 Old Square, 1914-1916. Not in 1917 Law List.

SCORAH, Christopher James
Born 1 August 1968. BA (Oxon). AAS. M. 1 November 1989. 8 King Street, Manchester, 1993.

SCOTT, Ernest Leopold
Born 1879. Only son of Henry Scott of Fulham, Middlesex, foreman tailor. MA (Cantab). Lecturer and tutor in mathematics. AAS. M. 11 October 1924. Call 19 November 1928. ETC. 18 February 1931. Prop. Jackson KC. Sec. Hinchliffe. 3 Middle Temple Lane, 1931-1944. Not in 1945 Law List.

SCOTT, Sir John KCMG
Born 4 June 1841, Wigan. Died 1 March 1904 aged 62. Son of Edward Scott of Wigan, solicitor, father of Rt. Hon. Sir Leslie Scott qv and of John Willoughby Scott qv. Bruce Castle School, Tottenham; Pembroke College, Oxford, BA 1865, MA 1868; Hon Fellow 1898. AAS. I. 29 April 1862. Call 17 November 1865. 2 Brick Court, 1876. Judge, later Vice President, International Court of Appeal in Egypt, 1874-1882. Puisne Judge, Bombay, 1882-1890. Judicial Advisor to the Khedive of Egypt, 1890-1898. KCMG 1894. Freedom of the Borough of Wigan, 1894. Deputy Judge Advocate-General of the Army, 1898-1904. Publications; Bills of Exchange, 1869. WW. DNB.

SCOTT, John Alexander
Born 1846. Only son of Alexander John Scott, professor at Owen's College, Manchester. Balliol College, Oxford, BA. AAS. I. 17 January 1868. Call 17 November 1871. ETC. 31 July 1872. Prop. Herschell QC. Sec. Edwards. 6 Crown Office Row, 1876-1890. 41 John Dalton Street, Manchester, 1890-1893. Not in 1894 Law List.

SCOTT, John Willoughby DSO
Born 25 January 1879. Son of Sir John Scott KCMG qv and brother of Rt. Hon. Sir Leslie Scott qv. I. 26 January 1911. ETC. 7 February 1912. Prop. Leslie Scott KC. Sec. Beazley. Goldsmith Building, 1912-1914. Commissioned Lieutenant in Royal Garrison Artillery. Later Lieut-Colonel, 8 Somerset Light Infantry. Killed in action 23 April 1917 at Cabaret Rouge aged 38 years. DSO 1.1.1917 and mentioned in despatches three times. Cemetery; Cabaret Rouge British Cemetery, Souchez, Pas de Calais, France. Grave Reference XV.G.ll. Information from the Public Records Office & Commonwealth Graves Commission.

SCOTT, Leslie Frederic KC, MP (The Rt. Hon. Sir Leslie Scott)
Born 29 October 1869 Hornsey. Died 19 May 1950 aged 80. Eldest son of Sir John Scott KCMG qv and brother of John Willoughby Scott qv. Rugby; New College, Oxford, BA 1892; MA 1895; Fellow 1939. I. 6 June 1894; Bencher. ETC. 20 July 1894. Prop. Walton QC. Sec. Maurice Hill. Admitted M. 17 March 1906. Liverpool Chambers; Commerce Court B, 11 Lord Street, 1896-1899; 10 Cook Street, 1900-1906. Goldsmith Building, 1907-1935. Silk 1909. MP (C) Liverpool Exchange, 1910-1929. Solicitor General, 1922. Kt 1922. Lord Justice of Appeal, 1935-1948. PC. 1927. Publications; The Effect of War on Contracts, 1914; (with Bertram Benas) The New Law of Property Acts 1925. WW. DNB.

SCOTT, Matthew James Alexander
I. 28 November 1996. ETC. 18 December 1997. Prop. Edward Bartley-Jones QC. Sec. Cadwallader. Not in 1999 Bar Directory.

SCOTT, Peter Cunningham
Born 1 February 1941 Keighley, Yorks. Eedest son of Leslie Thomas Scott of Heysham, group consultant anaesthetist. Tonbridge School. M. July 1971. 60 King Street, Manchester, 1971-1974. Not in 1975 Law List.

*** SCOTT, Richard Rashleigh Folliott QC (Baron Scott of Foscote)**
Born 2 October 1934. Michaelhouse College, Natal; University of Cape Town, BA; Trinity College, Cambridge, BA., LLB; (Rugby Blue). I. November 1959; Bencher 1981. 11 Old Square, 1959-1983. Silk 1975. Chairman of the Bar, 1982-1983. Vice-Chancellor, Duchy & County Palatine of Lancaster, 1987-1991 (Attorney General, 1980-1983). High Court Judge, Chancery Division, 1983-1991. Kt. 1983. Lord Justice of Appeal, 1991-1994; PC 1991. Vice Chancellor, Supreme Court, 1994-2000. Head of Civil Justice, 1995-2000. Lord of Appeal in Ordinary, 2000. Baron 2000. WW.

SCULLY, His Honour James Aloysius
Born 13 February 1856 Tipperary. Died 5 February 1929 aged 74. 3rd surviving son of James Scully of Dublin, High Sheriff of County Tipperary. Stonyhurst College; London University, BA. AAS. M. 14 January 1876. Call. 27 January 1879. ETC. 20 February 1888. Prop. Gully QC. Sec. Synnott. 1 Pump Court, 1876-1896; 15 Old Square, 1897-1903. Liverpool Chambers; 8 Harrington Street, 1893-1894; 5 Cook Street, 1895-1896. Lancs. Chancery Court. County Court Judge (Southern Counties and later West London, Marylebone & Clerkenwell), 1903-1928. WW.

SEANOR, James Richard
BA (London); LLB (Manchester). G. 11 May 1892. ETC. 26 February 1894. Prop. Yates QC. Sec. Byrne. Manchester Chambers; 26 Brazennose Street, 1903-1921; 43 Derby Street, 1922-1927. Not in 1928 Law List.

SEARLE, Barrie
Born 2 July 1953, Southport. King George V School, Southport; Liverpool University, LLB. AAS. 2 March 1972. Call 17 July 1976. ETC. March 1976. Pupilmaster, David Hodson. Same Manchester Chambers; 3 St James's Square, 1975-1984; St James's Chambers, 68 Quay Street, 1985. Assistant Recorder 1999. Recorder 2000. Legal Assessor, General Medical Council, 2002.

SEATON, James Stuart
Born 1862. Died 19 February 1929. Only son of William Seaton of Manchester. Pembroke College, Oxford, BA. AAS. M. 15 November 1884. Call 22 June 1887. ETC. 1 August 1887. Prop. French QC. Sec. Walton. York Chambers, Brazennose Street, Manchester, 1889-1895. Professor of Law, Owens College (Manchester University), 1896-1920. WW.

SECHIARI, Helen Louise
LLB. L. November 1991. Manchester House Chambers, 18-22 Bridge Street, Manchester, 1994-2000.

SEDDON, Reuben Cowburn
BA. L. 28 June 1933. ETC. 10 July 1935. Prop. Gorman KC. Sec. Walmsley. Manchester Chambers; 78 King Street, 1934-1958; 196 Deansgate, 1959-1960. Not in 1961.

SEDGWICK, Anthony William
Born 1933. Only son of Ernest Sedgwick of Manchester, clerk. Brasenose College, Oxford. AAS. M. May 1952. Call 8 February 1955. 36 St Ann Street, Manchester, 1957-1959. Solicitor General, Bermuda, 1964-1972. Hong Kong & Bermuda Bars, 1976. 1 Harcourt Buildings, 1977-1984. Not in 1985 Bar Directory.

SEED, Stephen Nicholas
Born 7 January 1969 Warrington. Rossall School; Manchester Polytechnic, LLB. G. October 1991. ETC. 17 December 1992. Prop. Rodney Klevan QC. Sec. Martin Littler. Pupilmaster, Barry Gilbert. Kenworthy's Buildings, 83 Bridge Street, Manchester, 1992-1995. Liverpool Chambers; Martins Building, Water Street, 1995-1999; 7 Harrington Street (merger with Corn Exchange), 6.9.1999.

SEGAR, George Xavier

Born 1838. Died 17 February 1901. Son of HH Judge Robert Segar QC, 1801-1861,(Recorder of Wigan), father of Robert Stanislaus Segar qv. Stonyhurst College; London University, BA, 1859. AAS. I. 9 November 1859. I. 11 June 1862. Law Association Rooms, 13 Harrington Street, Liverpool, 1876-1901. Recorder of Oldham, 1899-1901. WW.

SEGAR, Robert Stanislaus
Born 1879. Eldest son of George Xavier Segar qv. University College, Victoria University. AAS. M. 11 November 1899. Call 24 June 1903. ETC. 5 August 1903. Prop. Pickford KC. Sec. Butler. Liverpool Chambers; 10 Cook Street, 1903-1913; 43 Castle Street, 1936-1937. 2 The Cloisters, 1914. No address, 1915-1935 & 1938-1953. Not in 1954 Law List.

SELBY, First Viscount (See William Court Gully)

SELBY, Second Viscount (See James William Herschell Gully)

SELLARS, Michael John
Born 18 July 1957, Singapore. Married to Wendy Lloyd qv; brother in law of Heather Lloyd qv and Nick Kennedy qv. Wrekin College; University College, Durham, BA. I. July 1980. ETC. December 1980. Pupilmaster, Donald Forster. Same Liverpool Chambers; 54 Castle Street, 1980-1986; 14 Castle Street, 1987-2003; Atlantic Chambers, Cook Street, 2003-.

SELLERS, Alan Mitchell
Born 27 December 1960 Stranraer, Scotland. Fulwood School; Lancaster University (Grizedale College), LLB. Trainee solicitor, Central Lancs. Development Corporation, 1984-1985. Roscoes, solicitors, 1985-1991. G. July 1991. ETC. December 1991. Prop. Nigel Gilmour QC. Sec. Bryan Joynes. Pupilmaster, William Rankin. Liverpool Chambers; Oriel Chambers, 5 Covent Garden, 1991-1996; ground floor, Peel House, Harrington Street, 1996-1998; 2nd floor, 42 Castle Street, 1998-.

SELLERS, Frederick Aked MC., KC (The Rt. Hon Sir Frederic Sellers)

Born 14 January 1893. Died 20 March 1979 aged 86. Silcoates School; Liverpool University, BA., LLB; Hon LLD, 1956. Captain, King's (Liverpool) Regt, 13 Btn, 1914-1918. MC 1916; two Bars, 1918. G. 14 May 1919; Bencher, 1938; Treasurer, 1952. 5 Crown Office Row 1920-1921. 10 Cook Street, Liverpool, 1922-1935. Silk 1935. 2 Harcourt Buildings, 1935-1941; Goldsmith Building, 1942-1946. Recorder of Bolton, 1938-1946. High Court Judge, Queens Bench Division, 1946-1957. Kt 1946. Lord Justice of Appeal, 1957-1968. PC 1957. Trial Judge in R -v- Walter Rowlands (1946) Celebrated Trials (Henry Cecil). David & Charles. He also tried Stanley Setty (See " A Century of Liverpool Lawyers" Fagan, Bryson & Elston. Liverpool Law Society, 2002). Tributes; St George's Hall, Liverpool (Caulfield J / Judge E Sanderson Temple QC). Memorial Service, 18 May 1979, Gray's Inn Chapel (Lord Denning). Both transcripts in Circuit Records. WW.

SELLERS, Graham
Born 3 March 1967 Kingston-upon-Hull. Bilton High School; Staffordshire University, LLB; Hughes Hall, Cambridge, LLM. AAS. M. 2 September 1988. Call 16 October 1990. ETC 1992. Prop. John Kay QC. Sec. William George. Liverpool Chambers; 20 North John Street, 1991-1997; 14 Castle Street/ Atlantic Chambers, Cook Street, 1997-.

SELLERS, His Honour Norman William Malin "Norrie"

Born 29 August 1919. Died 28 December 1993 aged 74. Son of Rt. Hon. Sir Frederic Sellers qv. Merchant Taylors' School, Crosby; Silcoates School, Wakefield; Hertford College, Oxford, MA. Officer, RNVR, 1940-1965 (despatches, HMS Nelson, 1942). Lt-Commander, 1953, comd., HMS Mersey. G. November 1947. ETC 1948. Circuit Junior, Summer 1948. Liverpool Chambers; 49 Castle Street, 1948-1958; 14 Cook Street, 1959-1972; ground floor, Peel House, Harrington, 1973-1974. Recorder 1972. Circuit Judge, Preston, 1974-1990. WW.

SELLERS, William
Born 1859. Eldest son of William Sellers, surgeon. MD when AAS. M. 3 November 1897. Call 27 June 1900. ETC. 4 February 1901. Prop. Shee QC. Sec. Langdon (Lazarus). Manchester Chambers; 40 Kennedy Street, 1901-1904; 78 King Street, 1905-1918. Not 1919 Law List.

SEN, Sheila Ruth
LLB (London); Manchester University, (MJur). I. July 1974. Manchester Chambers; 4th floor, Astley House, Quay Street, 1977; 18 St John Street, 1978-1988. No address, 1989-1994. Not in 1995 Bar Directory.

SENIOR, Mark
Born 29 September 1967, Liverpool. St Edwards College, Liverpool. Lancaster University, LLB 1989; Liverpool University, MA (English) 1999. Solicitor; Morecroft, Urquhart, 1993-1998; Louis Berkson & Globe, 1998-2002. G. July 2002. ETC. December 2002. Prop. Timothy King QC. Sec. Ross Duggan. India Buildings, Water Street, Liverpool, June 2002.

SEPHTON, Craig Gardner QC
Born 7 December 1957, Umtali, Southern Rhodesia. Ecclesbourne School, Duffield, Derbys.; Lincoln College, Oxford MA., BCL. AAS. M. 23 October 1978. Call 23 July 1981. ETC. December 1982. Prop. Keith Goddard QC. Sec. Raymond Machell. Deans Court Chambers; Crown Square/ 24 St John Street, Manchester, 1984. Silk 2001. Recorder 2002. WW.

SERLE, Thomas
L. 26 January 1859. West Riding of Yorkshire Sessions, 1876-1880. Not in 1881 Law List.

SETON-KARR, Sir Henry MP
Born 5 February 1853, India. Died 29 May 1914 aged 61. Harrow; Corpus Christi College, Cambridge, BA 1876, MA. AAS. L. 31 March 1874. Call 25 June 1879. ETC. 11 July 1879. Prop. Myburgh. Sec. Dickinson. 2 Pump Court, 1882-1885. No chambers address, 1886-1914. MP (C) St Helens, 1885-1906. Publications; The Call to Arms, 1900-1901; My Sporting Holidays, 1904. Kt. & CMG., 1902. WW.

SETTLE, Alfred George Towers
Born 1883. Only son of John Towers Settle of Barrow in Furness, doctor. AAS. M. 2 May 1905. Call 1 July 1908. ETC. 15 June 1909. Prop. Tobin KC. Sec. Sharpe. 1 Pump Court, 1910-1921. No address, 1922-1953. Not in 1954 Law List.

SHAFI, Mohammed Imran
Born 2 July 1972 Rochdale. Greenhill High School; University of East London, LLB; University of Liverpool, LLM. L. November 1996. ETC. December 1996. Prop. Keith Goddard QC. Sec. Richard Heap. Kenworthy's Chambers, 83 Bridge Street, Manchester, May 1998.

SHAFIQ, Tahir
G. February 1986. St James's Chambers, 68 Quay Street, Manchester, 1987-1988. Mohinda & Co., solicitors, 1989. Not in 1990 Bar Directory.

SHAND, His Honour Sir Charles Lister

Born 2 December 1846 Liverpool. Died 4 April 1925 aged 78. Harrow; Trinity College, Oxford, BA, 1868, MA, 1871. AAS. I. 1 May 1866. Call 10 June 1870. ETC. 10 March 1871. Prop. Holker QC. Sec. Mellor. Circuit Junior, Summer 1871. 12 King's Bench Walk, 1876. Liverpool Chambers; 13 Harrington Street, 1877-1886; 25 Lord Street, 1887-1889. County Court Judge, Circuit 6, (Liverpool), April 1889-1921. WW.

SHANNON, (Thomas) Eric
Born 10 January 1947, Bolton. 2nd son of Thomas Eric Shannon, company secretary. Thornleigh Salesian College, Bolton; St Catherine's College, Oxford, BA (Mathematics). Teacher. IBM, 1970-1972. AAS. M. 31 July 1972. Call 26 November 1974. ETC. 1974. Prop. T P Russell QC. Sec. H Day. Manchester Chambers; 43 King Street, 1974-1988; Queen's Chambers, 5 John Dalton Street, 1989. Attorney, California.

SHARE, ALAN
G. February 1957. 25 Bow Lane, Manchester, 1958-1960. No address 1961-1963. Not in 1964 Law List

SHARPE, Joseph
Born 1859. Died 5 July 1930. Liverpool College; New College, Oxford, BA 1883; MA. AAS. M. 28 October 1880. Call 19 May 1886. ETC. 19 January 1887. Prop. Gibbs QC. Sec. Shee. 1 The Cloisters, 1887-1889; 6 Pump Court, 1890-1911; 1 Tanfield Court, 1912-1916; 3 Plowden Buildings, 1917-1922. Stipendiary Magistrate, West Ham, 1922-1925. Metropolitan Magistrate, Thames Court, Stepney, 31.1.1925-1930. WW. In "This Old Wig" another Metropolitan Magistrate, J G Sandbach KC. qv., says this of Sharpe: "The last of the real Circuiteers who regularly went the whole circuit was Joseph Sharpe. A big, powerful man, he was of pure yeoman stock. His family had farmed their own land for more than five hundred years in that corner of the extreme north of Lancashire which runs into Cumberland and Westmorland, north of Barrow. He was a bachelor and had rooms in Bury Street, but his true home was the country. He knew the name of every wild flower and where it grew, every bird and where it built, every breed of sheep, and was familiar with the local history of the north-west of England and all its antiquities. Thomas Hardy might have done justice to him. He had a brief or two in each circuit town-probably just about enough to pay his expenses. At Appleby and Carlisle he spent the weekends taking enormous walks into his beloved country. And yet, in spite of these simple tastes, he was a gourmet and loved entertaining. He had a theory that the correct procedure was not to say 'What shall we drink with dinner tonight', but to choose your wine first and build your dinner round your wine; there was no rationing in those spacious days."

SHARPE, Malcolm David
Born 6 July 1966, Liverpool. St Edward's College, Liverpool; Sheffield University, LLB. Queen's University, Belfast, LLM. L. July 1989. ETC. December 1990. Prop. Brian Leveson QC. Sec. Andrew Edis. 14 Castle Street/ Atlantic Chambers, Cook Street, Liverpool, 15.10.1990. Part time Lecturer in Child Care at Liverpool University.

SHARPLES, John
ETC. 17 December 1992. No other information.

SHAW, Arthur Barnsley
I. 17 November 1886. ETC. 29 July 1889. Prop. Henn Collins QC. Sec. Pixley. 2 Pump Court, 1890-1892; 2 Harcourt Buildings, 1893-1901; 9 King's Bench Walk, 1902-1911. Not in 1912 Law List.

SHAW, Frank
I. 26 January 1906. ETC. 2 February 1906. Prop. Tobin KC. Sec. Maxwell. Liverpool Chambers; 10 Cook Street, 1909-1915; 25 Lord Street, 1916-1923. No address, 1924-1953. Not in 1954 Law List.

SHAW, Nicola Jane Duckworth
Born 8 May 1965 Penistone, West Yorkshire. King Edward VI School, Morpeth, Northumberland; Leeds University, BA. L. 13 October 1992. ETC. 15 December 1992. Prop. Robert Fordham QC. Sec. Andrew Menary. Liverpool Chambers; Martins Building, Water Street, September 1992-1999; 7 Harrington Street (merger with Corn Exchange), 6.9.1999-2001; Broad Chare Chambers, Newcastle upon Tyne, November 2001. North Eastern Circuit. 7.

SHAWCROSS, Rt. Hon. Sir Hartley William Shawcross QC., MP (Baron Shawcross of Friston)

Born 4 February 1902 Giessen, Germany. Died 10 July 2003 aged 101. Dulwich College. Certificate of Honour E. 1925. G. 6 May 1925; Bencher 1939. London pupilage; pupilmaster Henry St. John Field. ETC. 1927. Liverpool Chambers; 5 Harrington Street, 1927-1933; 43 Castle Street, 1933-1934. 1 Hare Court, 1934-1939. Silk 1939. Goldsmith Buildings, 1939; 5 Paper Buildings, 1940-1952; 1 Harcourt Buildings, 1953-1958 when he retired from the Bar. Senior Law Lecturer, Liverpool University, 1927-1934; Hon., LLM. Regional Commissioner, North Western Region, 1942-1945. Recorder of Salford, 1941-1945. MP (Lab) St Helens, 1945-1958. Attorney General, 1945-1951. Chief UK Prosecutor at the trials of the Nazi War Criminals at Nuremberg. President of the Board of Trade, 1951. Recorder of Kinston upon Thames, 1946-1961. After retiring from the Bar and from politics in 1958, he went into the City becoming a Director of Shell; EMI; Rank,Hovis,McDougall; BSA; Hawker Siddley; Times Newspapers; the Observer and Morgan Guarantee Trust. He also served on numerous government and public boards and commissions. Kt. 1945. PC 1946. Baron 1959. GBE 1974. WW. Obituaries; Times 15 July 2003; Daily Telegraph 11 July 2003. Autobiography; "Life Sentence" Constable, 1995.

Lord Shawcross was involved in many notable cases including: Appearing for the mine owners at the Inquiry into the disaster at Gresford Colliery in 1934 when 265 miners perished.

In 1936 he was led by J C Jackson KC against Norman Birkett KC in the trial of Dr Buck Ruxton who was convicted of murdering his wife and was executed. (See Notable British Trials).

In 1945, in his first case as Attorney General he prosecuted William Joyce ("Lord Haw Haw") for high treason. Joyce had throughout the war broadcast propaganda from Germany intended to demoralize the British public. Although Joyce was an American citizen, he held a British passport. It was held by the House of Lords that this meant he owed allegiance to the Crown. He was executed. (See Notable British Trials) In 1945 he also prosecuted Dr Alan Nunn May, sentenced to 10 years penal servitude for passing atomic bomb secrets to the Russians.

In 1949 he prosecuted John George Haigh for murdering Mrs Durand-Deacon and then disposing of her body in a tank of sulphuric acid. Another "Notable British Trial."

In 1950 he prosecuted Klaus Fuchs for doing precisely what Dr May had done. Fuchs received 18 years.

Without doubt the highlight of his career was his contribution to the conviction of Goering, Hess, Ribbentrop, Keitel and others at Nuremberg. It is right to acknowledge the immense contribution of Maxwell Fyfe, Elwyn Jones, Griffith-Jones and others throughout the whole of the trial but Shawcross's opening and closing submissions (with almost a year between each) were masterful and instrumental in achieving convictions.

Rodney Klevan QC, Lord Shawcross QC and Lord Justice Russell. Adelphi Hotel, Liverpool 1992.

Many will remember the Mess at the Liverpool Adelphi Hotel to mark his 90th birthday and that he held his huge audience spellbound with a delightful half hour speech without the benefit of a note.

SHAWCROSS, William Henry
Born 1858. 2nd son of John Thomas Shawcross of Southport, Congregational Minister. AAS. M. 24 January 1891. Call 17 November 1893. ETC. 26 February 1894. Prop. Kay. Sec. Byrne. Manchester Chambers; 4 St James's Square, 1895-1908; 5 St. James's Square, 1909-1921; 30 John Dalton Street, 1922-1934. Not in 1935 Law List.

SHEE, Henry Gordon QC

Born 1 April 1847 London. Died 13 February 1909 aged 61. 2nd son of The Hon. Mr Justice Shee. Ushaw College; Christ Church, Oxford. AAS. I. 29 April 1867. Call 30 April 1870; Bencher 1899. ETC. 23 August 1870. Prop. Manisty QC. Sec. Leofric Temple. Commerce Chambers, 13 Lord Street, Liverpool, 1876-1879; 1 Harcourt Buildings, 1880-1887; 12 King's Bench Walk, 1888-1892; Silk 1892. 1 Harcourt Buildings, 1893-1909. Recorder of Burnley, 1893-1907. Judge, Salford Hundred Court of Record, 1893-1909. Recorder of Liverpool, 1907-1909. Contested Whitehaven (L), 1886 & 1891. WW.

SHEFFIELD, Baron (See Rt. Hon Edward Lyulph Stanley)

SHEFFIELD, Lord (See Hon Sir Arthur Lyulph Stanley)

SHEIL, James
Born 2 July 1829. Died 12 December 1908 aged 79. Eldest son of late James Sheil QC (Ireland). Trinity College, Dublin, BA 1848. AAS. G. 6 May 1848. Call 7 June 1852; Bencher 1884; Treasurer 1890. 7 Crown Office Row, 1876-1879. Revising Barrister, Northern Circuit. Metropolitan Magistrate, 1879-1904. (Hammersmith and Wandsworth, 1879-1886; Southwark, 1886-1890; Westminster, 1890-1904). WW. Foster.

SHELBOURNE, Sir Philip
Born 15 June 1924. Died 15 April 1993 aged 68. Radley College; Corpus Christi College, Oxford, MA; Harvard Law School. I. November 1950; Hon. Bencher 1984. ETC. 4 March 1954. Prop. Brabin QC. Sec. Cantley. 2 Plowden Buildings, 1951-1953; 4 Pump Court, 1954-1962. (taxation specialist). Partner, N M Rothschild & Sons, 1962-1970. Chm., Drayton Gp & Dayton Group, 1973-1974. Chm & Chief Executive; Samuel Montague & Co., 1974-1980; BNOC., 1980-1982. Chm., Britoil, 1982- 1988. Member, SIB., 1987-1988. Chm., Henry Ansbacher Holdings, 1988-1991. Deputy Chairman, Panel on Take-overs and Mergers, 1987-1991. WW.

SHELLEY-THOMPSON, Albert James
Born 1874. Son of Charles Thompson of Birkenhead, Minister of Religion. AAS. M. 21 October 1910. Call 4 June 1913. ETC. 3 July 1913. Prop. Rigby Swift KC. Sec. Riley. 14 Harrington Street, Liverpool, 1913-1915. No address, 1916-1924. Not in 1925 Law List.

SHELTON-AGAR, Charles Wedderburn Shelton
BA (Cantab). G. July 1965. Manchester Chambers; 9 Albert Square, 1965-1972; 1 Deans Court, Crown Square, 1973-1991; Lloyds House Chambers, Lloyd Street, 1992-1994.

SHENTON, Rachel Claire
Born 9 April 1971 Cheshire. Married to Mark Savill qv. Altrincham Girls Grammar School; University of Central Lancashire, (External London LLB). M. November 1993. Crown Prosecution Service, 1993-1995. Wales & Chester Circuit, 1995-2000. ETC. 27 July 2000. Prop. Peter Birkett QC. Sec. Jennifer Caldwell. 18 St John Street, Manchester, 2000.

SHEPHERD, Joanne Elizabeth
Born 28 January 1969, Lancaster. University College of North Wales, Bangor; University of Huddersfield, BA (History). I. 14 October 1993. Pupilllage at 1 Dr. Johnson Building. Pupilmaster, Clifford Mailer. St Albans Chambers, 1993-1999. ETC. 8 July 2003. Prop. Keith Goddard QC. Sec. Keith Thomas. New Bailey Chambers, Preston, July 1999.

SHEPHERD-CROSS, Cecil Herbert Shepherd
I. 15 June 1904. ETC. February 1905. Prop. Horridge KC. Sec. Byrne. 60 King Street, Manchester, 1905-1908. No address, 1909-1953. Not in 1954 Law List.

SHERIDAN, Paul Adrian
Born 3 May 1954, Prestwich, Manchester. Cousin of District Judge Jackson (Wigan County Court). De La Salle College, Salford; Queen's College, Belfast, LLB.

Member of Northern Ireland Bar, 20.9.1977; pupilmaster, Mervin Morrow. L. November 1984. ETC. 17 December 1985. Prop. Richard Henriques QC. Sec. John Wishart. Manchester Chambers; 1 Central Street, 1985-1987; 12 Blackfriars Street, 1988-1989; Manchester House Chambers, 18-22 Bridge Street, 1990-1999; Peel Court Chambers, 45 Hardman Street, 20.7.1999.

SHERMAN, Susan Elizabeth
Born 21 September 1968 Liverpool. Stanley High School, Southport; University of Central Lancashire, LLB. Lehman Bros International, London, 1991-1993. M. November 1993. ETC. 21 December 1993. Prop. Stephen Riordan QC. Sec. John McDermott. Chavasse Court, 24 Lord Street, Liverpool, 1993.

SHIELL, Anthony George
Born 1842. Eldest son of John Sheill of Dundee, JP. St Peter's College, Cambridge, LLB, 1866. AAS. M. 7 November 1864. Call 11 June 1867. ETC. 28 March 1868. Prop. Temple QC. Sec. Heath. 4 Garden Court, 1876; 3 Temple Gardens, l877. Calcutta, India, 1878-1880. 3 Temple Gardens, 1881. No address, 1882-1919. Not in 1920 Law List. Foster.

SHOLICAR, Ann
Born 28 June 1966 Liverpool. Liverpool Girls College; Archbishop Blanch School; LCD/ Court Service (Liverpool Law Courts), January 1984-October 2000. Liverpool John Moores University, LLB. L. 22 November 2000. ETC. 14 December 2000. Prop. Andrew Edis QC. Sec. Malcolm Sharpe. Pupilmasters, Malcolm Sharpe & Ruth Howe. Liverpool Chambers; 14 Castle Street, 1 November 2000-8 June 2001; Derby Square Chambers, Merchants Court, 18 June 2001- 31 December 2003 when chambers closed and the majority joined Oriel Chambers, 14 Water Street.

SHORROCK, James Godby
Born 10 December 1910. Died 23 May 1987 aged 76. Father of (John) Michael Shorrock QC qv. Clifton; Hertford College, Oxford, BA. I. 26 January 1934. ETC. 28 February 1934. Prop. Lynskey KC. Sec. Gerrard. Manchester Chambers; 3 St James's Square, 1934-1939. Served War of 1939-1945; Major, RA (TA) and Judge Advocate Generals Department. 4 Chapel Walks, 1945-1964; 601 Royal Exchange, 1965-1972. Deputy Chairman, Westmorland Quarter Sessions, 1955-1971. Legal Member, Mental Health Review Tribunal, 1960-1963. Recorder of Barrow in Furness, 1963-1971. WW.

SHORROCK, (John) Michael QC
Born 25 May 1943, Gatley, Cheshire. Son of James Godby Shorrock qv. Clifton College, Bristol; Pembroke College, Cambridge, MA. I. 1966; Bencher 1995. ETC. 1966. Prop. Godfrey Heilpern QC. Sec. Patrick Russell. Circuit Junior, Winter 1968. Circuit Secretary, 1981-1985. Same Manchester Chambers; Ship Canal House, King Street, 1966-1976; Old Bank Street, 1976-1992; Peel Court Chambers, 45 Hardman Street, 1992. Recorder 1982. Silk 1988. Criminal Injuries Compensation Board, 1995-2000. Criminal Injuries Appeal Panel, 1996. Governor, William Hulme's Grammar School, 1999. WW.

SHORT, Anna Louise
Born 19 January 1974 Huddersfield. Shelley High School, Huddersfield; Trinity Hall, Cambridge, BA. G. November 1997.Barnard Inn Chambers, 20-23 Holborn EC1; pupilmaster, Timothy Bowles. ETC. 2000. Prop. Gerard McDermott QC. Sec. David Eccles. 8 King Street, Manchester, 2000.

SHUTT, Herbert Cecil
Born September 1888. I. 4 June 1913. ETC. 2 February 1914. Prop. Sanderson KC. Sec. Miller. Home address; Halewood House, Gateacre, Liverpool. Private, Inns of Court OTC, 29 October 1914. Lieutenant, 3rd Btn (attached to 1st Btn) Royal Scots Fusiliers, 22 August 1916. Killed in action 13 November 1916, aged 28 at Thiepval. Thiepval Memorial, Somme, France (Pier and Face 3 c) Information provided by Public Records Office and Commonwealth War Graves Commission.

SICHEL, Walter Sydney
Born 22 February 1855. Died 7 August 1933 aged 78. Harrow; Balliol College, Oxford, MA (BA, 1877). AAS. L. 12 November 1875. Call 17 November 1879. ETC. 18 July 1883. Prop. Gully QC. Sec. French. 2 Dr Johnson's Buildings, 1884-1891. No address, 1892-1933. Historical biographer (Lives of Bolingbroke; Disraeli and Lady Hamilton). WW.

SIDDALL, Nicholas Michael
Born 30 January 1975 Scarborough. Scalby School, Scarborough; Downing College, Cambridge, BA. M. 9 October 1997. ETC. 16 December 1997. Prop. Roger Farley QC. Sec. Braslavsky. 40 King Street, Manchester, 1997.

SIDEBOTTOM, Herbert
Born 21 December 1872 Manchester. Died 19 March 1940. Roehampton aged 67. Manchester Grammar School; Balliol College, Oxford. I. 26 January 1912. ETC. 28 February 1912. Prop. W F K Taylor KC. Sec. Gordon Hewart. 2 Harcourt Buildings, 1912-1921. 78 King Street, Manchester, 1922-1932. He never practiced at The Bar. He was a journalist on the staff of the Manchester Guardian for 22 years and later with the Daily Chronicle. He contributed to the Sunday Times (Scrutator) & to the Daily Sketch (Candidus). Publications; England & Palestine, 1918; Pillars of the State, 1921; Great Britain & Palestine, 1937. WW. DNB.

SIDEBOTTOM, Samuel Richards
I. 17 November 1921. ETC. 22 February 1922. Prop. Langdon KC. Sec. Thorpe. 2 Harcourt Buildings, 1923-1924; 3 Brick Court, 1925-1930; 2 Garden Court, 1931-1933; 2 Paper Buildings, 1934-1936. Not in 1937 Law List.

SIDGREAVES, Sir Thomas
Born 3 January 1831. Died September 1889 aged 58. 2nd son of George Sidgreaves of Preston. Stonyhurst; London University, BA. AAS. I. 24 January 1854. Call 6 June 1857. Chief Justice, Straits Settlements, 1871. Kt. 28 January 1874. Foster.

SILVERBECK, Rachel Naomi
Born 2 April 1972, Liverpool. Niece of His Honour Judge Henry Globe QC qv. King David School, Liverpool; Newcastle University, BA. M. October 1996. ETC. 1996. Prop. Henry Globe QC. Sec. Richard Isaacson. Exchange Chambers, Pearl Assurance House, Derby Square, Liverpool, 1996.

SIM, Archibald Coysgarne
Born 14 October 1855. 3rd son of Alexander Sim of Harrow Weald Park, Middlesex. New College, Oxford, BA 1877. AAS. I. 23 March 1876. Call 25 June 1879. ETC. 9 February 1880. Prop. Russell QC. Sec. Bigham. Circuit Junior, Summer 1880. 8 King's Bench Walk, 1880; Goldsmiths Buildings, 1881; 77 Chancery Lane, 1882-1884; 21 Old Square, 1885-1895. No address, 1895-1918. Not in 1919 Law List.

SIMMONDS, Alexandra Margot Rachel
Born 11 March 1976, Bolton. Daughter of Nicholas Simmonds qv and Suzanne Gerrard qv. Bolton School (Girls' Division); Birmingham University, LLB. G. 8 October 1998. ETC. December 1998. Prop. Michael Shorrock QC. Sec. Richard Pearce. Peel Court Chambers, 45 Hardman Street, Manchester, September 1998.

SIMMONDS, Nicholas Harold
Born 27 November 1945 Barrow. Married to Suzanne Gerrard qv, father of Alexandra Simmonds qv. Barrow Grammar School; Manchester University, LLB. G. July 1969. ETC. 1969. Pupilmaster, Kenneth Taylor. Same Manchester Chambers; Ship Canal House, King Street, 1969-1980; 2 Old Bank Street, 1981-1991; Peel Court Chambers, 45 Hardman Street, 1991. Assistant Recorder, 1983. Promising career not realised due to ill health.

SIMMS, Alan John Gordon
Born 3 April 1954 Liverpool. Liverpool Collegiate School. External London; MA., LLB. L. November 1976. ETC. June 1980. Prop. Michael Maguire. Sec. Andrew Mattison. Same Liverpool Chambers; Fruit Exchange, Victoria Street, 1980-1991; Chavasse Court, 24 Lord Street, 1991. Part time Lecturer, Liverpool John Moores University. External Examiner (Universities) in Forensic Sciences. Legal Member, Mental Health Review Tribunal, 1994.

SIMON, Sir John S.L., MP
Born 9 December 1818, Montego Bay, Jamaica. Died 24 June 1897 aged 78. Son of Isaac Simon, merchant and landed proprietor of the same place. Public schools in Jamaica; private schools in Liverpool; University College, London, LLB, 1841. AAS. M. 29 October 1839. Call 4 November 1842. 3 Brick Court, 1848, Liverpool Sessions; 1 Dr Johnson's Buildings, 1877-1885. Serjeant-at-Law, 15 April 1864; patent of precedence, next after Thomas Kingdom Kingdom QC, January 1868. MP (L) for Dewsbury, 1868-1888. Kt. 1886. A founder of the Anglo Jewish Association. WW. DNB.
He was the second member of the Jewish faith to be called to the Bar. The first was Sir Francis Henry Goldsmid. In April 1858 he successfully defended Simon Bernard from the accusation of complicity with Orsini in the attempt to assassinate Napoleon III.

SIMONS, Richard Graham
Born 1 May 1965, Stoke-on-Trent. Married to Samantha Birtles qv. Alsager School; Coventry University, LLB. G. February 1991. ETC. April 1991. Prop. David Poole QC. Sec. Andrew Nuttal. Manchester Chambers; Rational House, 64 Bridge Street, 1991-1995; Lincoln House Chambers, 1 Brazennose Street, 1995.

SIMPSON, Alexander William TD
Born 20 June 1929. Elder son of William Adamson Simpson of Bamber Bridge, Preston, medical practitioner. Jesus College, Cambridge, MA. AAS. M. 16 May 1950. Call 6 July 1954. ETC. 1954. Prop. Alex Carmel QC (for Neville Laski QC). Sec. R C Seddon. Manchester Chambers; 78 King Street, 1954-1958; 196 Deansgate, 1959-1986, then Vice President (England & Wales) VAT & Duties Tribunals.

SIMPSON, Alexandra Katherine
Born 12 February 1952 Coventry. LLB. L. November 1989. Manchester Chambers; 38 King Street West, 1992-1995; 24a St John Street (now St John's Buildings), 1996.

SIMPSON, Edgar Hope
L. 30 June 1897. ETC. 23 February 1900. Prop. Pickford KC. Sec. Carver QC. 2 Harrington Street, 1900-1902. Lancs. Chancery Court. Not in 1903 Law List.

SIMPSON, Paul Richard
Born 12 November 1958 Whiston. Brother of Gaynor Simpson, barrister & Graeme Simpson, solicitor. Liverpool Bluecoat School; Liverpool University, LLB. L. November 1980. ETC. 1982. Prop. Michael Maguire QC. Sec. John Leach. Pupillage at 5 Essex Court (Patrick O'Connor) & 3 Temple Gardens (Duncan Pratt). Liverpool Chambers; Scottish Life House, 10 James Street, 1982-1989; 24 Fenwick Street, 1990-1999; 2nd floor, 14 Cook Street, 2000. New Bailey Chambers, Liverpool, 2004.

SIMPSON, Raquel
Born 13 March 1968, Lytham-St-Annes. Rossall School; London School of Economics, LLB. I. October 1990. Pupilmaster, Paul Garlick. Legal Officer, Inland Revenue Solicitors Office, Somerset House. WC2, 1992-1994. ETC. 2 April 1996. Prop. Richard Henriques QC. Sec. Paul Dockery. 18 St John Street, Manchester, 1996.

SINCLAIR, John Alexander
Born 1868. Only son of John Sinclair of Liverpool, doctor of medicine. AAS. M. 14 November 1887. Call 26 January 1892. ETC. 18 March 1893. Prop. Walton QC. Sec. Morris. 5 Essex Courto 1893; Lamb Building, 1894-1899; 4 Brick Court, 1900-1909. Not in 1910 Law List.

SINCLAIR, Robert Charles
L. January 1951. ETC. 7 February 1952. Prop. Edward Wooll QC. Sec. Fairclough. Liverpool Chambers; 34 Castle Street, 1952-1955; Corn Exchange, Fenwick Street, 1956-1957. 2 Pump Court, 1958. No address, 1959-1967. Not in 1968 Law List.

SINGER, Andrew Michael
Born 22 July 1967. Son of His Honour Harold Singer qv. Bury Grammar School; Fitzwilliam College, Cambridge, MA. G. November 1990. Atkin Building, Temple, 1990-1991. ETC. December 1991. Pupilmaster David Manley. King's Building, 40 King Street, Manchester, October 1991. Legal Assessor, General Medical Council, 2002.

SINGER, His Honour Harold Samuel

Born 17 July 1935. Father of Andrew Singer qv. Salford Grammar School; Fitzwilliam House, Cambridge, MA. G. July 1957. ETC. February 1958. Pupilmasters, George Spafford & Iain Glidewell. Same Manchester Chambers; 25 Bow Lane, 1958-1976; 460 Royal Exchange, 1977-1984. Recorder, 1981-1984. Circuit Judge, Manchester, 1984-2003. Tributes; Manchester, Crown Square, 5 September 2003. (Judge David Maddison/ David Steer QC). Transcript in Circuit Records. WW.

SINGH, Anthony Bharat
Born 9 March 1979 Salford. Bolton School, Boys' Division; Sheffield University, LLB. G. 11 October 2001. ETC. 12 December 2001. Prop. Stephen Grime QC. Sec. T Smith. Deans Court Chambers, 24 St John Street, Manchester, 18.9.2001.

SINGH-HAYER, Bansa
Born 18 November 1963 Bloxwich, West Midlands. Lancashire University, LLB. G. 12 November 1988. Legal Consultant, Professional Legal Advisory Service, Leeds, 1989-1990. ETC. 1991. Prop. John Burke QC. Sec. Beverly Lunt. Manchester Chambers; 20 St Mary's Parsonage, 1990-1993; 58 King Street Chambers, 51-53 South King Street, 1994.

SINGLETON, John Edward KC., MP (Rt. Hon. Lord Justice Singleton)
Born 18 January 1885 St Michael's on Wyre, Lancashire. Died 6 January 1957, Pateley Bridge, Yorkshire aged 71. Royal Grammar School, Lancaster; Pembroke College, Cambridge, MA., LLB; Hon Fellow, 1938. I. 19 November 1906; Bencher 1929; Treasurer 1952. ETC. 20 February 1907. Prop. Sanderson KC. Sec. Riley. Liverpool Chambers; 5 Harrington Street, 1917-1912; Stephenson's Chambers, 25 Lord Street, 1913-1914 & 1918-1919. Captain in RFA, serving in Belgium & France, 1914-1918 (mentioned in despatches). 5 Harrington Street, 1920-1922. Silk 1922. 6 Crown Office Row, 1922-1929; 4 Paper Building, 1930-1934. MP (C) Lancaster, 1922-1923. Recorder of Preston, 1928-1934. Judge of Appeal, Isle of Man, 1928-1933; High Court Judge, Queen's Bench Division, 1934-1948. Kt. 1948. Lord Justice of Appeal, 1948-1957. PC 1948. Hon. LLD, Liverpool University, 1949. WW. DNB.
Lord Hodson says: "He was a man of stout Lancastrian common sense, ready to apply the law, if possible, in the simplest manner, without recourse to subtlety, and anxious at all times to do justice. He was not concerned to extend the law or to be remembered for the grace of his judgments but rather to perform that which he had to do as a just and workmanlike professional."
His book 'Conduct at the Bar' (1933) set out his views on how a barrister should behave and is required reading even now for every entrant to the profession. His most notable trials as a judge were:
1 Dr Buck Ruxton for the murder of his wife and their housemaid in 1936. J C Jackson KC led Maxwell Fyfe KC and Hartley Shawcross for the Crown. Norman Birkett KC led Philip Kershaw for the Defendant. It was an extremely complicated trial which took 11 days at Manchester Assizes. A full account is in Notable British Trials. 1937. William Hodge & Co Ltd., and in Montgomery Hyde's "Norman Birkett" Hamish Hamilton, 1964.
2 The trial of Peter Barnes & others for the IRA Coventry Explosion of 1939. Notable British Trials, Vol. 77. Letitia Fairfield, William Hodge & Co Ltd.

SINGLETON, Sarah Louise
Born 9 March 1962 London. Rodean; Lancaster Girls' School; Hertford College, Oxford, BA (Jurisprudence). AAS. M. 25 January 1982. Call July 1983. ETC. March 1984. Prop. Brian Carter QC. Sec. Rodney Scholes. Circuit Junior, Winter 1988. (First woman Junior). 28 St John Street, Manchester, 1984. Assistant Recorder, 1999. Recorder, 2000.

SINGTON, Alan John Campbell
I. 17 November 1909. No address, 1910-1953. Not in 1954 Law List.

SINGTON, Alfred
Born 1852. 2nd son of Adolphus Sington of Manchester, merchant. AAS. I. 11 January 1873. Call 17 November 1875. ETC. 13 March 1876. Prop. Higgin QC. Sec. Smyly. Manchester Chambers; 8 St James's Square, 1876-1880; 9 St James's Square, 1881-1887; 4 Harcourt Buildings, 1888-1907. Not in 1909 Law List. Foster.

SINGTON, Edward Claude
I. 16 June 1920. ETC. 9 July 1920. Prop. Wingate-Saul KC. Sec. Leigh. Manchester Chambers; 10 St James's Square, 1921-1924; 44 King Street, 1925-1928; Bank of England Chambers, Tib Lane, 1929-1941. No address, 1942-1953. Not in 1954 Law List.

SINKER, Andrew Tennant
Born 8 July 1968 Hitchin, Herts. Oundle School, Northants; Leeds University, LLB. L. October 1991. ETC. 20 December 1994. Prop. Timothy King QC. Sec. Vincent Deane. 3 Hare Court, 1991-1993; 3 Temple Gardens, 1993-1994. Liverpool Chambers; Victoria Chambers, 19 Castle Street, 1994-1999; New Bailey Chambers, Liverpool, 1999.

SINNETT, Peter Anthony
Born 3 April 1960 Liverpool. St Francis Xavier's College, Liverpool; Liverpool University, 1978-1981, LLB; Pembroke College, Cambridge, 1981-1982; LLM. M. 22 November 1983 (withdrew 23.4.1991 but re-admitted in 2001 when rules on joint qualifications were relaxed). ETC. 1984. Prop. Eric Somerset Jones QC. Sec. Andrew Sander. Oriel Chambers, 14 Water Street, Liverpool, 1983-1991. Partner, Berman's, Solicitors, Liverpool 1991.

SKINNER, John Edwin Hilary
Born 11 January 1839, London. Died November 1894 in Algiers aged 55. Elder son of Allen Maclean Skinner QC. London University. AAS. L. 11 January 1859. Call 27 January 1862. 3 Dr Johnsons Buildings, 1876-1894. War correspondent of the Daily News covering Franco German War and wars in Denmark & Egypt. Assistant Judicial Commissioner, Cyprus, 1881. DNB. Foster.

SLACK, His Honour George Granville
Born 11 July 1906. Accrington Grammar School; London University, BA (History), 1926; LLB, 1929; LLM, 1932. G. 12 June 1929. ETC. 18 February 1931. Prop. Eastham KC. Sec. Lustgarten. 3 Elm Court, 1931-1940; 1 Essex Court,

1941-1943. RAFVR, 1943-1946. 3 Essex Court, 1946-1957; Queen Elizabeth Building, 1958-1966. County Court, later Circuit Judge, 1966-1981. WW.

SLACK, Kevin John
Born 27 July 1975 Sheffield. King Ecgbert Comprehensive, Sheffield, 1986-1991; King Edward VII Comprehensive School, Sheffield, 1991-1993; Emmanuel College, Cambridge, MA (Law) (Rowe & Maw Scholar; Rodwell Prize & Vaughan Bevan Prize (twice)); G. 9 October 1997 (Prince of Wales Scholarship). ETC. 18 December 1997. Prop. David Turner QC. Sec. Christopher Cornwall. Exchange Chambers, Pearl Assurance House, Derby Square, Liverpool, 1997.

SLAGG, John Parker
I. 26 January 1893. ETC. 4 March 1893. Prop. Addison QC. Sec. Byrne. No address, 1893-1949. Not in 1950 Law List.

SLATER, Constance Josephine (Mrs Robinson)
LLB (Liverpool); MSc (UMIST). G. November 1962. 36 St Ann Street, Manchester 1965-1974. Not in practice, 1975-1992. Part time Chairman, Social Security Appeals Tribunals, 1993. Not in 1994 Bar Directory.

SLATER, Cyril
L. 8 May 1895. ETC. 2 March 1922. Prop Mayer QC. Sec. Slater. 19 Old Square, 1907-1909. No address, 1910-1949. Not in 1950 Law List.

SLATER, Iain James
Born 1 July 1960 Kincardine. Penwortham County Secondary School; Lancashire Polytechnic, LLB. Preston Borough Council, 1980-1990. L. 15 October 1991. ETC. 17 December 1992. Prop. Rodney Scholes. Sec. Nigel Beeson. Winckley Court Chambers, Preston, 1992-1994; Victoria Chambers, 19 Castle Street, Liverpool, 1995-1999.

SLATER, John Albert
Born 20 November 1840. 4th son of John Slater of Bolton JP. AAS. L. 3 May 1873. Call 26 January 1876. ETC. 2 March 1877. Prop. Ambrose QC. Sec. J B Edge. 18 South King Street, Manchester, 1880-1904. Not in 1905 Law List.

SLATER, John James Gregson
L. 8 May 1895. ETC. 5 March 1897. Prop. Leese QC. Sec. McKeand. Manchester Chambers; 20 Kennedy Street, 1897; 34 Kennedy Street, 1898-1905; 60 King Street, 1906-1912; 21 Birley Street, Blackpool, 1913-1920; 18 Tib Lane, 1921-1928. No address, 1929-1932. Not in 1933 Law List.

SLATER, John Herbert
Born 10 April 1854. Elder son of Edwin Slater of Bristol. Formerly a solicitor. AAS. M. 5 June 1882. Call 6 June 1883. ETC. 18 July 1886. Prop. Addison QC. Sec. Byrne. 3 Plowden Buildings, 1884-1894. No chambers address, 1895-1921. Not in 1922 Law List. Foster.

SLATER, John Sisson
MA., LLD., FRAS, JP. I. 13 June 1888. ETC. 27 July 1888. Prop. Aspland QC. Sec. McNab. 1 Essex Court, 1889; 1 Garden Court, 1890-1908; 2 Elm Court, 1909-1913. 156a Palace Chambers, Bridge Street, Westminster, 1908-1915. Parliamentary draftsman & committees. Also had chambers at 5 Harrington Street, Liverpool. No address, 1916-1917. Not in 1918 Law List.

SLINGER, His Honour Judge Edward
Born 2 February 1938. Accrington Grammar School; Balliol College, Oxford, BA, 1958. Articled to his uncle Edwin Slinger of Sharples, Son & Slinger, Accrington, October 1958-1961. Admitted as a solicitor, October 1961. Ramsbottom & Co., 1961-1995 (partner from 1964). Deputy Registrar, 1982-1988. President, Blackburn Incorporated Law Association, 1986. Assistant Recorder, 1988. Recorder, 1992. Circuit Judge, Preston, 1995. Member, Immigration Appeal Tribunal, 1997. Lancashire County Cricket Club; Captain 2nd XI 1967-1975; Vice Chairman, 1985-1998; Trustee, 1978-1996; Vice President, 2000. Deputy Chairman, Discipline Committee, Test & County Cricket Board (now English Cricket Board), 1990. WW.

SMART, David Wedderburn
L. 29 June 1938. Liverpool Chambers; 9 Cook Street, 1939-1946; 20 Hackins Hey, 1947-1958. No address, 1959-1963. 88 Kingsway WC2, 1964-1976. Not in 1977 Law List.

SMELT, Sidney
Born 1848. 2nd son of Thomas Smelt of Manchester, merchant. St John's College, Cambridge. AAS. I. 21 May 1872. Call 13 June 1877. No address, 1877-1903. Not in 1904 Law List. Foster.

SMITH, Adrian Charles (His Honour Judge Adrian Smith)
Born 25 November 1950. Father of Sophie Smith qv. Blackpool Grammar School; Queen Mary College, University of London, LLB. L. July 1973. ETC. November 1973. Prop. Ted Wells. Sec. Donald Forster. 54/ 14 Castle Street, Liverpool, 1973-1996. Recorder, 1994. Circuit Judge, Manchester, 16 December 1996. Legal Member, Restricted Panel, NW Mental Health Review Tribunal, 2002. WW.

SMITH, Alice Josephine Clifford

I. 29 June 1927. No address, 1928-1961. Not in 1962 Law List.

SMITH, Andrew William

Manchester University LLB. L. October 1996. 24a St John Street, Manchester, 1999.

SMITH, Francis Digby Edward

Born 1908. 1st son of Edward Goldwin Smith of Birkenhead, estate agent. AAS. M. 6 February 1929. Call 8 June 1932. ETC. 15 June 1932. Prop. Goldie KC. Sec. Fyfe. Liverpool Chambers; 5 Harrington Street, 1935-1941; 27 Dale Street, 1942-1949. No address, 1950-1963. Not in 1964 Law List.

SMITH, Frederick

Born 1845. Died 9 December 1888 aged 43. Father of Frederick Edwin Smith qv & of Harold Smith qv, eldest son of Thomas Smith of Birkenhead, gent. Liverpool Institute High School. Left school at 16 and joined the army, serving in India (North West Frontier), 1861-1866. Worked in family estate agents business, 1866-1883. King's College, London. AAS. M. 26 January 1884. Call 7 July 1886. London pupillage in the chambers of F A Inderwick KC. ETC. 31 July 1886. Prop. Bigham QC. Sec. Segar. Mayor of Birkenhead 1888 but died one month after his election. Liverpool Chambers but no chambers address is recorded.

SMITH, Frederic Cuthbert

17 November 1891. ETC. 5 April 1892. Prop. Bigham QC. Sec. Tobin. Liverpool Chambers; 8 Harrington Street, 1892-1902; 8 Cook Street, 1903-1908; 8 Harrington Street, 1909-1912. 2 Mitre Court, 1907; 1 Garden Court, 1908-1912. Not in 1913 Law List.

SMITH, Rt. Hon. Sir Frederick Edwin Smith KC., MP (The First Earl of Birkenhead)

Born 12 July 1872, 32 Pilgrim Street, Bikenhead. Died 30 September 1930 aged 58. Son of Frederick Smith qv and brother of Sir Harold Smith qv. Birkenhead School; Wadham College, Oxford, MA; President, Oxford Union Society, 1893; Vinerian Law Scholar, 1895; Fellow & Lecturer, Merton College, Oxford, 1896. G. 14 June 1899; Bencher 1908; Treasurer 1916. ETC. 16 February 1900. Prop. Taylor QC. Sec. Leslie Scott. Liverpool Chambers; 14 Cook Street, 1900-1902; 25 Lord Street, 1903-1908. Silk 1908. 4 Elm Court, 1908-1919. MP (U) Liverpool, Walton, 1906-1918; Liverpool, West Derby, 1918-1919. Served, European War, 1914; on active service with Indian Corps in France (despatches); Major, King's Own Oxfordshire Hussars. Solicitor General, 1915. Attorney General (with Cabinet Seat), 1915-1919. Lord Chancellor, 1919-1922. Secretary for India, 1924-1928. Director, ICI and of Tate & Lyle, 1928-1930; Chairman, Greater London and Counties Trust, 1929-1930. High Steward, Oxford University, 1922; Rector, Aberdeen University, 1926. PC 1911. Kt 1915. Baronet, 1918. Baron 1919, Viscount (Furneux) 1921. Earl 1921. GCSI. 1928. Publications are numerous and include: Fourteen English Judges, 1926; Famous Trials of History 1926; Law, Life & Letters, 1927; More Famous Trials,

1928; The Speeches of Lord Birkenhead, 1929. Biographies; "Lord Birkenhead" by "Ephesian" (Bechhofer Roberts), Mills & Boon, 1926. "Our Lord Birkenhead; an Oxford Appreciation", Ivor Thomas, Putnam, 1930. "Smith of Birkenhead" H A Taylor, Stanley Paul, 1931. "The Earl of Birkenhead" by his son, 2 vols, 1933 & 1935, Thornton, Butterworth. This was revised and re-issued in one volume by Eyre & Spottiswood in 1959. "The Lives of the Lord Chancellors 1885-1940" by Professor R F V Heuston. Pages 353-402. Clarendon Press, Oxford, 1964. "F E Smith; First Earl of Birkenhead" by John Campbell, Jonathan Cape, 1983. "The Glittering Prizes" by William Camp, MacGibbon & Kee, 1960. A Century of Liverpool Lawyers, pages 56-68. Noel Fagan. Liverpool Law Society, 2002. WW. DNB. In the DNB entry Lord Schuster says that "his sharp tongue, his aggressive demeanour and the cynical attitude which at times he at times assumed made many enemies and not only among his political foes." George Dangerfield in his "The Strange Death of Liberal England" said "Many people loved him, most distrusted him, some despised him, and he despised almost everybody" but then went on to comment, "he was without question the most fascinating creature of his times."''There can be no doubt but that he was a man of great intellect and ability who achieved much in a short life span. The following very brief outline of some of his achievements should whet the appetite for John Campbell's book or that of Professor Heuston which are my favourites and used copies are still readily available:

1. In 1903 he was junior to Alfred Tobin KC in the prosecution at St George's Hall, Liverpool of three members of the crew of the SS Veronica for the murder of the Captain and six members of the crew. They were tried solely on the charge of murdering the Captain. All three were convicted after a jury retirement of 15 minutes and were shortly afterwards executed. See Notable British Trials volume 76 "The Veronica Trial" Keeton & Cameron (William Hodge & Co Ltd, 1953).
2. In 1910 he successfully defended Ethel le Neve who was the mistress of Dr Crippen. She was charged with being an accessory after the fact to Crippen's murder of his wife. See Notable British Trials; The Trial of Hawley Harvey Crippen, edited by Filson Young, 1920.
3. In 1916 as Attorney General he prosecuted the Irish patriot, Sir Roger Casement for treason in travelling to Germany to recruit Irish prisoners of war to fight with the Germans for Irish freedom. Casement was convicted and executed. The full story is told in Notable British Trials "The Trial of Sir Roger Casement" H. Montgomery Hyde, 1960. What is of particular interest to today's lawyer is that it was not thought inappropriate that the Attorney General, who conducted the prosecution, should be the person to give or, in this case, refuse the fiat necessary to enable an appeal to go to the House of Lords.
4. Lord Birkenhead together with Lloyd George, Austen Chamberlain and Birkenhead's great friend, Winston Churchill were instrumental, with Arthur Griffith and Michael Collins on the Irish side, in arranging the Irish Treaty leading to the Free State Constitution in 1922.
5. King George V expressed reservations to Lloyd George on F E's suitability as Lord Chancellor, "not feeling sure that Sir Frederick has established such a reputation in men's minds as to ensure that the country will welcome him to the second highest position which can be occupied by a subject of the Crown." The press were less restrained saying that the appointment "laughable", "frivolous" and "carrying a joke too far." He proved them all wrong. He was an excellent Judge. Lord Schuster says: "He soon acquired great authority among his legal colleagues. The time had come when he could bring into play the learning he had acquired as a teacher and practitioner. His demeanour as a judge was dignified and impressive. He kept the Court together. His judgments were composed with great care and after close consultation with colleagues. In style they were vigorous and often witty He was entirely free from political bias in his appointment of judges. He recommended the appointment of six High Court judges, one of whom became a Law Lord and two went to the Court of Appeal. He appointed ten judges to the County Court Bench." Professor Heuston agrees. He says: "As Lord Chancellor, Birkenhead takes a very high place in the list of holders of that office. From the very start he devoted his great talents to excelling in all three of the aspects of the work of Lord Chancellor, in Cabinet, as head of the judicial system and as Speaker of the House of Lords. Any fears that he might have behaved in a frivolous or light-weight fashion were quickly dispelled His judgments show a remarkable width of learning and scholarly research set forth in a vigorous and lively prose style." Lord Dunedin writing of Lord Birkenhead in 1930 said : "I do not believe that that the judgments of any judge taken as a whole would show a higher degree of excellence than his."

SMITH, Sir Harold KC., MP

Born 18 April 1876. Died 10 September 1924 aged 48. Son of Frederick Smith qv; brother of F E Smith qv. Birkenhead School. He then went into the cotton industry and later into the family firm of surveyors and valuers in Liverpool & Birkenhead until 1908 when he began to read for the Bar. G. 26 January 1911; Bencher 1920. ETC. 13 February 1911. Prop. Alfred Tobin KC. Sec. Miller. Liverpool Chambers; 25 Lord Street, 1911-1912; 8 Harrington Street, 1913-1923. 4 Elm Court, 1911-1924. Birkenhead Councillor, 1904-1907. MP (C) Warrington, 1910-1922; Liverpool Wavertree, 1922-1924. Hon. Lt., RNVR. Secretary to Official Press Bureau during First World War. Counsel to Ministry of Agriculture & Fisheries and Office of Works, 1921. Kt. 1921. Recorder of Blackburn, 1922-1924. Silk 1923. John Campbell in "F E Smith: First Earl of Birkenhead" says: "Harold was a fluent and forceful speaker in the same caustic style (as his brother); a much better organizer, and an even better all round games player (He played rugby for Birkenhead Park and was a fine golfer and tennis player). He inherited from his father an exceptional talent as an amateur actor. Beerbohm Tree who saw him in a Birkenhead Dramatic Society production of "Trilby", urged him to turn professional. One of Harold's plays "The March Hare" had a short run at the Ambassador Theatre in 1913." WW.

SMITH, Harry

MA., LLB., PhD. G. November 1957. ETC. 1957. Pupilmaster, Edward Youds. North House, 17 North John Street, Liverpool, 1957-1961. 60 King Street, Manchester, 1964-1966. Faculty of Law, Monash University, Clayton, Victoria, Australia, 1967-1970. Department of Legal Studies, Birmingham Polytechnic, 1971-1978. Assistant Director, Wolverhampton Polytechnic, 1979-1986. No business address, 1987-2001.

SMITH, Henry

Born 1831. Eldest son of Richard Smith of Urswick, Lancs. Eton; Clare College, Cambridge, MA 1856. Late captain, 7th Royal Lancs. Militia. AAS. I. 19 April 1852. Call 30 April 1856. Shown as living in Egremont, Cheshire and later Ulverston. No chambers address, 1876-1896. Not in 1897 Law List.

SMITH, Henry Everard

I. 17 November 1905. ETC. 23 July 1907. Prop. Taylor KC. Sec. Crawford. 3 Essex Court, 1908-1941. No address, 1942-1953. Not in 1954 Law List.

SMITH, (Herbert) Stephenson

I. 17 November 1886. ETC. 24 January 1887. Prop. Addison QC. Sec. McKeand. 4 St James's Square, Manchester, 1888-1894. No address, 1895-1899. Not in 1900 Law List.

SMITH, Janet (Hilary) QC (The Rt. Hon. Lady Justice Smith DBE)

(DL)

Born 29 November 1940. Bolton School. L. 1972; Bencher 1992. ETC. 2 November 1972. Prop. Godfrey Heilpern QC. Sec. Christopher Rose. Manchester Chambers; 60 King Street, 1972-1983. Crown Square Chambers, 1 Deans Court, 1984-1986. Silk 1986. 5 Essex Court and later 25 Byrom Street, Manchester. Recorder 1988. Member, Criminal Injuries Compensation Board, 1988-1992. High Court Judge, Queen's Bench Division, 1992-2002. Employment Appeal Tribunal, 1994-2002. Presiding Judge, North Eastern Circuit, 1995-1998. Chairman, Security Vetting Appeals Panel, 2000-2002. Chairman, Civil Committee, Judicial Studies Board, 2000-2002. Chairman, Shipman Inquiry 2001-2005. Lady Justice of Appeal, November 2002. DBE 1992. PC 2002. WW.

Harold Shipman was a GP who practiced in Todmorden and later in Hyde. He was convicted, on the 31 January 2000, of murdering fifteen of his women patients, between 1995 and 1998, by administering lethal doses of diamorphine. After a trial at Preston Crown Court which lasted 57 days and which was prosecuted by Richard Henriques QC, the trial judge, Mr. Justice Thayne Forbes, when sentencing Shipman to 15 life terms, said that he intended to recommend to the Home Secretary "that life means life and that you spend the remainder of your days in prison." A public inquiry was announced to commence in 2001 to be chaired by Dame Janet. The first report of the Inquiry was published in July 2002. It ran to 2000 pages. Dame Janet said Shipman began to murder his patients shortly after he entered practice in Todmorden in 1975, and over a 23 year period he had murdered 215 of his patients with "a real suspicion that he could have claimed another 45 victims." The Inquiry continues in order "to devise improved systems so as to ensure that such a terrible betrayal of trust by a family doctor can never happen again." Shipman committed suicide by hanging himself in his cell at Wakefield Prison on 13 January 2004.

SMITH, Jason
Born 16 May 1965 Liverpool. Liverpool Collegiate; Liverpool University. AAS. M. 3 July 1987. Call 27 July 1989. ETC. December 1989. Prop R J D Livesey QC. Sec. Neville Biddle. Liverpool Chambers; 1st floor, Peel House, Harrington Street 1989-1998; 25-27 Castle Street 1998.

SMITH, Jeffrey Frank Gilbert
Born 1930. Only son of Frank Smith of St Annes-on-Sea, chartered accountant. Manchester University. AAS. M. 29 September 1947. Call 5 February 1952. 26 King Street, Manchester, 1955-1963. Not in 1964 Law List.

SMITH, Jonathan Michael
Born 2 October 1967 Wolverhampton. Liverpool Polytechnic, LLB. G. October 1991. Manchester Chambers; 72 Bridge Street, 1991-1997; Cobden House Chambers, 1998.

SMITH, Joseph James
Born 1840. Eldest son of James Smith of Heywood. London University, BA. AAS. I. 1 May 1869. Call 6 June 1872. ETC. 6 August 1872. Prop. Pope QC. Sec. Ambrose. 60 King Street, Manchester, 1876-1895. No address, 1896-1935. Not in 1936 Law List. Foster.

SMITH, Kenneth Edgar Johnson
G. November 1955. Liverpool Chambers; 3 Cook Street, 1956-1958; 3rd floor, 27 Dale Street, 1959-1973. Not practising, 1974-1982. Not in 1983 Bar Directory.

SMITH, Lorna Marie
M. 9 October 1997. ETC. 14 December 1999. Prop. L. Kushner QC. Sec. Yvonne Coppel. 24a St John Street, Manchester, 1999.

SMITH, His Honour Mark Barnet
Born 11 February 1917. Died 15 September 1994 aged 77. Freehold Council School, Oldham; Manchester Grammar School; Sidney Sussex College, Cambridge, MA (Natural Sciences). Assistant Examiner in HM Patent Office, 1939. Served, 1940-1946, Staff Sergeant, RA. Returned to Patent Office as Examiner. AAS. M. 2 March 1942. Call 17 November 1948. ETC. 1949. 6 Pump Court, 1949-1972. Also a member of Ghana Bar. Temporary Recorder of Folkestone, 1971. Crown Court Recorder, 1972. Circuit Judge 1972-1987. WW.

SMITH, Mark William
Nottingham University, LLB. G. March 1997. Kenworthy's Building, 83 Bridge Street, Manchester, 1999.

SMITH, Matthew James
Born 13 May 1969, St Helens. St Aelred's RC High School; Trinity Hall, Cambridge BA. L. October 1991. ETC. 1992. Pupilmaster Nicholas Braslavsky. Kings Chambers, 40 King Street, Manchester 1992.

SMITH, Matthew Hall
Born 29 May 1974, Southport. Son of His Honour Judge Peter Smith qv. Merchant Taylors', Crosby; King George V Sixth Form College, Southport; St Edmund Hall, Oxford, BA. M. 11 March 1999. ETC. 23 March 1999. Prop. Philip Raynor QC. Sec. Lesley Anderson. Pupilmasters, Lesley Anderson & Stephen Pritchett. King's Chambers, 40 King Street, Manchester, 1999. In practice as Matthew Hall.

SMITH, Michael Joseph
Born 25 May 1966, Leigh, Lancs. St Mary's High School, Astley; Christ Church, Oxford, MA., BCL. L. July 1989. ETC. December 1989. Prop. Rhys Davies QC. Sec. Christopher Tetlow. Pupilmasters, Tetlow & McDermott. 8 King Street, Manchester, 1989.

SMITH, Percival Frere
I. 17 November 1902. Advocate of Supreme Court of South Africa, Johannesburg, Transvaal, 1910-1918. 12 King's Bench Walk, 1919-1928. Goldsmith Building, 1929-1959; 1 Essex Court, 1960-1963. Not in 1964 Law List.

SMITH, Peter Geoghegan
Born 2 October 1929, Sydney, New South Wales. Father of (Warwick) Timothy (Creswell) Smith qv. Bradford Grammar School; Brasenose College, Oxfordf MA., BCL. AAS. M. 8 November 1951. Call 6 July 1954. ETC. 1955. Prop. Daniel Brabin QC. Sec. Gordon Clover. 1 Paper Buildings, 1955. Same Liverpool Chambers; 47 Castle Street, 1956-1965; 606 The Corn Exchange, Fenwick Street, 1966-1981; Exchange Flags, 1982-1991; Exchange Chambers, Pearl Assurance House, Derby Square, 1992 until retirement in 1999. Assistant Recorder/ Deputy Circuit Judge.

SMITH, Peter Richard
Born 1960 Lancashire. St Joseph's School. ICI, Laboratory Chemist, 1978-1981. Lancaster University, LLB. I. November 1988. ETC. 1989. Prop. Rodney Scholes QC. Sec. John McNeil. Manchester Chambers; 38 King Street West, 1989-1995; 24a St John Street (now St John's Buildings), 1995-

SMITH, Peter William (His Honour Judge Peter Smith)
Born 31 December 1945, Orrell, Lancs. Father of Matthew Hall Smith qv. Arnold School, Blackpool; Downing College, Cambridge, MA. AAS. M. 27 September 1967. Call 25 November 1969. ETC. 1969. Pupilmaster, Keith Lawton. Same Liverpool Chambers; North House, 17 North John Street, 1969-1971; Martins Building, Water Street, 1972-1994.(practised as William Smith). Deputy Judge Advocate, 1983-1984. Recorder, 1991-1994. Mental Health Review Tribunal, 1993. Circuit Judge, Preston, 1994. WW.

SMITH, Peter Winston QC (The Hon. Mr Justice Peter Smith)

(DL)

Born 1 May 1952 Taiping, Malaysia. Bridlington Grammar School; Selwyn College, Cambridge, BA, 1974; MA, 1976. L. July 1975; Bencher 2000. ETC. 3 April 1979. Prop. Christopher Rose QC. Sec. Roger Farley. Pupilmasters, E L G Tyler, Joseph Turner, Roger Farley. Lecturer, Manchester University, 1977-1983. Same Manchester Chambers; 460 Royal Exchange, 1979-1987; 40 King Street, 1988-2000. Silk 1992. Assistant Recorder, 1994. Deputy High Court Judge, Chancery Division, 1996. Recorder, 1997. High Court Judge, Chancery Division, 2002. Kt. 2002. Member, Panel of Chairmen, Competition Appeal Tribunal, 2004. WW.

SMITH, Rachel Catherine
Born 20 April 1966 London. Parkstone Grammar School, Poole; Leeds University, BA. L. 16 October 1990. ETC. December 1990. Prop. John Hugill QC. Sec. Bernard Wallwork. Peel Court Chambers, 45 Hardman Street, Manchester, 1990.

SMITH, Richard
Born 1843. Eldest son of John Smith of Kynsal Lodge, Audlem, Cheshire. Balliol College, Oxford, BA, 1871. AAS. M. 12 January 1881. Call 17 November 1883. ETC. 26 January 1884. Prop. Addison QC. Sec. J W Hamilton. 41 John Dalton Street, Manchester, 1884-1895. No address, 1896-1904. Not in 1905 Law List. Foster.

SMITH, Robert
L. October 1995. New Bailey Chambers, Preston, 1999; Mercury Chambers, Leeds, 2000.

SMITH, Samuel Harold MC., OBE
Born 1888. Died 31 August 1971. Leys School, Cambridge; Caius College, Cambridge, LLB, 1911. I. 16 April 1913. ETC. 18 February 1914. Prop. Hewart KC. Sec. Sandbach. 1 King's Bench Walk, 1914. Served War of 1914-1918. (MC & French Croix de Guerre, 1917; despatches twice); Major, 5th Btn., Cheshire Regt. 2 Temple Gardens, 1918-1923; 11 King's Bench Walk, 1924-1934; 5 Paper Buildings, 1935-1940; Goldsmith Building, 1941-1950. Lt. Col, Deputy Director, Army Welfare Services, 1940-1944. OBE, 1943. Director, Legal Division, Allied Commission for Austria, 1947-1948. 3 Hare Court, 1951-1963. Chairman, Bucks. Quarter Sessions, 1955. WW.

SMITH, Sidney
Born 1919. Only son of Sydney Smith of Stockport. Manchester University, MA. AAS. M. 4 September 1946. Call 26 January 1948. ETC. 1948. Manchester Chambers; lb Cooper Street, 1950-1953; 24 Brazennose Street, 1954-1958. No address, 1959-1963. Not in 1964 Law List.

SMITH, Sophie Louise Elizabeth
Born 26 April 1977, Liverpool. Daughter of His Honour Judge Adrian Smith qv. Huyton College School for Girls; Merchant Taylors' School for Girls; Liverpool University,

LLB. L. 14 October 1999. ETC. 14 December 1999. Prop. Andrew Edis QC. Sec. Stuart Driver. Circuit Junior, 2001. 14 Castle Street/ Atlantic Chambers, Cook Street, Liverpool, 1999.

SMITH, Stephen Vernon
LLB (London). I. 1 November 1969. ETC. 1969. Pupilmaster, Gerald Crowe. Martins Building, Water Street, Liverpool, 1971-1984. Practised as Stephen Vernon. Left to join the CPS rising to HM Deputy Chief Inspector of the Crown Prosecution Service based in York. Since 2004, Branch Prosecuting Solicitor for Wirral.

SMITH, (Warwick) Timothy (Creswell)
Born 16 June 1959, Liverpool. Son of Peter G Smith qv. Birkenhead School; Trinity College, Cambridge, MA. AAS. M. 11 January 1980. Call 29 July 1982. Pupilmasters, Julian Cooke (3 Essex Court) and Christopher Cochrane (8 New Square). ETC. 23 May 1985. Deans Court Chambers, Crown Square/ 24 St John Street, Manchester, 1985. Assistant Recorder, 1999. Recorder, 2000. FCIArb. Mediator (Academy of Experts). Legal Assessor, General Medical Council, 2002-.

SMITH, William Richard Trevor
L. 28 January 1924. ETC. 25 June 1924. Prop. Singleton KC. Sec. Glover. No address, 1925-1927. Not in 1928 Law List.

SMITH, William Walter
Born 1854. Only son of William Smith of Prestwich, Lancs. Trinity College, Cambridge, BA, 1876. AAS. I. 11 January 1875. Call 17 November 1877. ETC. 25 March 1878. Prop. Higgin QC. Sec. Edwards QC. 5 Hare Court, 1878-1879; 2 Mitre Court Buildings, 1880-1883; 54 John Dalton Street, Manchester, 1884-1993; 168 Palace Chambers, Bridge Street, Westminster, 1885-1893. Not in 1894 Law List. Foster.

SMITH-CARINGTON, Neville Woodford MP
Born 1878. Died 7 October 1933. Harrow; Exeter College, Oxford, MA., BCL. I. 24 June 1903. ETC. 15 July 1903. Prop. Alfred Tobin KC. Sec. Graham. 78 King Street, Manchester. 1906-1933. Equity draftsman & conveyancer but did not practise. MP (C) Rutland & Stamford, 1923-1933. President, Shire Horse Society, 1931. WW.

SMITH-HUGHES, Jack OBE
Born 27 November 1918. Died 1994 aged 75. The Leys, Cambridge; Worcester College, Oxford, MA. Served War of 1939-1945. Lt., RASC in Crete. He was captured by the Germans after the Battle of Crete in 1941. He escaped to Cairo, joined the Special Operations Executive and in October 1941 slipped back into Crete. For 3 months he arranged air drops and saw to the evacuation of the remaining Allied troops. He later directed operations from Cairo, having been promoted to Major, and returned to the island in 1943 and in 1944 to assess the situation. His exploits are mentioned in "The Cretan Runner" by George Psychoundakis (translated by Patrick Leigh Fermor), published by Efstathiadis Group SA., in 1993. For his role in Crete Smith-Hughes was appointed OBE and Chevalier of the Royal Order of George I with crossed swords by Greece. I. June 1947. Army Legal Services, 1950-1958. In practice in London. ETC. 1964. 9 Rumford Street, Liverpool, 1964-1972. In 1972 after the death of his wife, he moved to practise law in Tortola in the British Virgin Islands where he served as Chief Magistrate & Acting Attorney General. Publications; Unfair Comment on Some Victorian Trials; Six Ventures in Villainy; Eight Studies in Justice; Nine Verdicts on Violence. (all published by Cassells). Obituary, Daily Telegraph, 15 March 1994.

SMITTON, Frederic Harrison
L. 17 November 1902. ETC. 22 January 1903. Prop. Horridge KC. Sec Tobin. Circuit Junior, Spring & Summer, 1903. 8 King's Bench Walk, 1904-1910; 2 Plowden Buildings, 1911-1927. Not in 1928 Law List.

SMYLIE, Robert Romily
Irish Bar, 1900. G. 1 May 1912. Manchester Chambers; 78 King Street, 1923-1941; 26 King Street, 1942-1949. No address, 1950-1963. Not in 1964 Law List.

SMYLY, His Honour William Cecil KC
Born 2 January 1840 Dublin. Died 4 March 1921 aged 81. 3rd & youngest son of John George Smyly QC., DL of Dublin. Harrow; Trinity College, Cambridge LLB, 1863. Captain, Cambridge University Boat Club, 1862-1863; Captain, First Trinity Boat Club, 1861-1862. AAS. I. 29 May 1861. Call 26 January 1865. 4 St James's Square, Manchester, 1876-1879; 5 King's Bench Walk, 1879-1880; 3 Temple Gardens, 1881-1895. Silk 1891. County Court Judge, 1895-1915, (Circuit 19, Derbys., 1895-1902) and (Circuit 40, Bow & Shoreditch, 1902-1915). WW.

SMYTH, John Rodney
BA (Cantab). I. July 1975. 2nd floor, Oriel Chambers, Water Street, Liverpool, 1977-1978. No address, 1979-1980. Not in 1981 Bar Directory.

SNARR, Matthew
Manchester University, LLB. I. 2001. ETC. 12 December 2001. Prop. Charles Garside QC. Sec. Charles Kennedy. 9 St John Street, Manchester, 2001.

SNEADE, William Buckley
G. February 1952. ETC. 14 February 1952, Prop. Wooll QC. Sec. Nance. 49 Castle Street, Liverpool, 1952-1956. No chambers address, 1957-1963. General Post Office, St Martins-le-Grand, EC1, 1964-1966. Not in 1967 Law List.

SNELL, John
LLB. I. July 1973. 6 Princess Street, Manchester, 1977. 24 Millstone Lane, 1978-1986 (Midland & Oxford Circuit); 19 Colegate, Norwich & 5 Pump Court, 1987-1990 (South Eastern Circuit); 24 Millstone Lane, Leicester, 1990-1991 (Midland & Oxford); 27 New Walk, Leicester, 1992.

SNOW, Thomas
Born 1837. Eldest son of Thomas Frotson Snow of Bristol. Exeter College, Oxford, MA. AAS. I. 17 April 1861. Call 17 November 1865. Liverpool Chambers; Wason Chambers, Harrington Street, 1877-1883; Equity Chambers, 9 Cook Street, 1884-1892; 13 Old Square, 1893-1894; 3 King's Bench Walk, 1894-1915. Not in 1916 Law List. Equity draftsman & conveyancer. Publications; (joint editor); A Treatise on the Chancery Practice of the County Palatine of Lancaster. Foster.

SNOWDEN, Martine Jayne
Born 9 November 1976 Salisbury. Archbishop Blanche School, Liverpool; Liverpool University, LLB. L. 12 October 2000. ETC. December 2000. Prop. David Turner QC. Sec. Simon Berkson. Exchange Chambers, Pearl Assurance House, Derby Square, Liverpool, 2000.

SOMERSET JONES, Eric QC
Born 1926. Died 11 November 2002. Father of Felicity Somerset Jones qv. Birkenhead Institute; Royal Air Force, 1944-1947; Pilot Instructor, Ceylon. Lincoln College, Oxford, MA. AAS. M. 6 October 1948. Call 23 May 1952. ETC. 1952. Prop. Robertson Crichton QC. Sec. Ralph Rodman Gardner. Circuit Attorney General. Liverpool Chambers; 7 Rumford Street, 1952-1966; Oriel Chambers, 14 Water Street, 1967-1978 (Head of Chambers). Silk 1978. Goldsmith Buildings, 1978-2000. (Head of Chambers). Lord Chancellor's County Court Rules Committee, 1975-1978. General Council of the Bar, 1990-1994. Mess in Manchester in 2000 to mark the retirements of Eric and of Michael Maguire QC. Tributes, Liverpool Law Courts, 14 November 2002 (Judge David Clarke QC/ David Steer QC). Transcript in Circuit Records. WW.

SOMERSET JONES, Felicity
Born 10 April 1970, Wirral. Daughter of Eric Somerset Jones QC qv, married to Simon Povoas qv. The Queen's School, Chester; Liverpool University, BA (English Language & Literature). City University, London, Dip Law. M. 13 October 1994. ETC. 20 December 1994. Prop. Eric Somerset Jones QC. Sec. Peter Cowan. Circuit Junior, 1997-1998. Oriel Chambers/ 5 Covent Garden/ 14 Water Street, Liverpool, 1994.

SOMERVILLE, John James
BA., BL. G. 26 January 1926. Liverpool Chambers; 9 Cook Street, 1932-1934; 8 Cook Street, 1935-1940; 3 Cook Street, 1941-1957; Oriel Chambers, 14 Water Street, 1958-1970. Also Preston Chambers. Lancs. Chancery Court. Not in 1971 Law List.

SOMERVILLE, Thomas Clinton
Born 22 December 1952 Istanbul. Tonbridge School; Bristol University, BA. AAS. M. 19 July 1976. Call 26 July 1979. Irish Bar, 1983-1989; Law Library, Dublin. ETC. 1989. Liverpool Chambers; 1st & ground floors, Peel House, Harrington Street, 1998-1999; Oriel Chambers, 14 Water Street, 1.3.1999.

SOWLER, Thomas
I. 17 November 1890. ETC. 27 February 1891. Prop. Ambrose QC. Sec. J W Hamilton. No address, 1892-1899. Not in 1900 Law List.

SPAFFORD, Christopher Howsin
Born 1887. Eldest son of Howsin Spafford of Buxton, merchant, father of George Christopher Howsin Spafford qv. AAS. I. 22 January 1907. Call 8 June 1910. ETC. 1 March 1911. Prop. Langdon KC. Sec. Hewart. Acting Circuit Junior, 1914-1918. Circuit Junior, Summer 1919. Manchester Chambers; 60 King Street, 1914-1921; 3 St James's Square, 1922-1948. No address 1949. Not in 1950 Law List.

SPAFFORD, George Christopher Howsin
Born 1 September 1921. Son of Christopher Howsin Spafford qv. Rugby. Served, RA, 1939-1946 (Captain). Brasenose College, Oxford, MA., BCL. Hon LLM, Manchester, 1992. University of Wales College of Cardiff, LLM, 1994. AAS. M. 1 January 1940. Call 26 January 1948. ETC. 1948. Same Manchester Chambers; 28 Kennedy Street, 1948-1956; 25 Bow Lane, 1957-1976; 460 Royal Exchange, 1977-1988. Recorder, 1975-1988. Chancellor of the Diocese of Manchester, 1976-1996. WW.

SPARROW, Arthur Goldsmith
Born 1858. Eldest son of Christopher Sparrow of Manchester, merchant. St John's College, Cambridge, BA, 1880. AAS. L. 27 April 1880. Call 26 January 1884. ETC. 18 July 1884. Prop & Sec. not recorded. 4 St James's Square, Manchester, 1889-1893; 7 Crown Office Row, 1894-1899; 2 Cooper Street, Manchester, 1898. No address, 1900-1904. 12 King's Bench Walk, 1905-1909. No address, 1910-1940. Not in 1941 Law List. Foster.

SPARROW, David Gordon
MA (Oxon). L. July 1972. ETC. 13 February 1973. Sec. Dwyer. 67 Princess Street, Manchester, 1973-1982 and in Hong Kong. 1 Gray's Inn Square, 1986-1988. Not in 1989 Bar Directory.

SPARROW, Judge Gerald
Cambridge University (President of the Union and of the Law Society) and Inner Temple. Joined Neville Laski's chambers at 3 St James's Square. Manchester in 1925. In 1930 he was appointed a Judge of the International Court in Bangkok. He was a prisoner of the Japanese from 1941-1945. He set up in private practice until he returned to England in 1954 writing for a living. He wrote about 40 books, many of which concerned lawyers, criminals and the courts including:- The Great; Judges; Conspirators; Spies; Traitors and Defenders.

SPARROW, John Walter Gerald
I. 16 June 1926. ETC. 7 July 1926. Prop. Jackson KC. Sec. Laski. Circuit Junior, Winter 1927. 3 St James's Square, Manchester, 1926-1932. No address, 1933-1953. Not in 1954 Law List.

SPARROW, William John

Born 1851. Eldest son of John Stephen Sparrow of Puddington Hall, Cheshire, JP. The Oratory, Edgbaston; London University, BA, 1875, LLB 1878. AAS. L. 19 March 1875. Call 15 May 1878. ETC. 2 August 1878. Prop. Aspinall QC. Sec. Walton. Liverpool Chambers; 6 Cook Street, 1878-1883; 13 Harrington Street, 1884-1914. Not in 1915 Law List. Foster.

SPEAR, Sarah Vanessa
Born 29 December 1972 Manchester. Stockport Grammar School; St Hilda's College, Oxford, MA (Carr Prizewinner). I. 9 October 1997 (Major Scholarship) ETC. 16 December 1997. Prop. Clement Goldstone QC. Sec. John Jones. 28 St John Street, Manchester, 1997. (now St Johns Buildings Chambers).

SPEARING, Rachel
Born 7 September 1973 Wirral. Highfield; Calday Grange Grammar School, West Kirby; Liverpool University, LLB. Davies, Wallis, Foyster, Solicitors, Liverpool, 1998-1999.1. 8 October 1999. ETC. December 2000. Prop. David Steer QC. Sec. Peter Gregory. 7 Harrington Street, Liverpool, 2000-2002.

SPEDDING, John Anthony
I. 19 June 1901. ETC. 29 January 1902. Prop. Pickford QC. Sec. Sanderson. 10 King's Bench Walk, 1902-1914. No address, 1915-1940. Not in 1941 Law List.

SPENCE, Thomas
Eldest son of Charles Spence of Manchester, merchant. AAS. M. 4 November 1850. Call 17 November 1858. No address, 1876-1897. Not in 1898 Law List. Special pleader & conveyancer. Brazilian Jurisconsult. Publication; Author; Manual for Bar Students.

SPENCER, Hannah Katya
Born 1970. Jesus College, Oxford, BA (Jurisprudence). I. February 1993. 5 Pump Court, 1993-1996. Manchester Chambers; 9 St John Street, April 1996-1999; Deans Court Chambers, 24 St John Street, 2000.

SPINKS, Frederic Lowten SL., MP
Born 27 December 1816. Died 27 December 1899 aged 83. Youngest son of John Spinks of the Inner Temple. King's College, London; Magdalene College, Cambridge, MA, 1843. AAS. I. 3 May 1839. Call 5 May 1843. 3 Paper Buildings, 1848. Salford Sessions. Serjeant-at-Law, 27 May 1862 (The Last Serjeant at the English Bar). MP (C) Oldham, 1874-1880. JP., DL; Kent. WW. Foster.

SPINKS, Thomas QC
Born 26 September 1819. Died 14 January 1899 aged 79. Son of William Spinks of London. Merchant Taylors School, Walworth, London; St John's College, Oxford, BCL, 1845; DCL, 1849. Advocate, Doctors Commons, 1849; Librarian, 1860; Treasurer, 1866 & 1868. Law Reporter, 1853-1855. I. 17 November, 1858: Bencher 1867; Reader 1883. Silk 1866. 3 Paper Buildings, 1876-1880. Registrar, York District Probate Registry, 1880-1886.

SPROAT, Francis Edward Weston
MA., BCL. I. 6 May 1925. ETC. 24 June 1925. Prop. Singleton KC. Sec. Kenyon. 3 Essex Court, 1925-1928; 1 Temple Gardens, 1929-1940. No address, 1941-1963. Not in 1964 Law List.

SQUAREY, Tucker Fulton

Born 9 October 1852. Eldest son of Andrew Tucker Squarey of Bebington, near Birkenhead, solicitor. Pembroke College, Oxford. AAS. M. 3 June 1874. Call 17 November 1877. ETC. 3 April 1878. Prop. Gully QC. Sec. Collins. Liverpool Chambers; 8a Lord Street, 1878-1884; 15 Lord Street, 1885-1892; Stephenson's Chambers, 25 Lord Street, 1893-1897. 2 Garden Court / 38-39 Parliament Street, Westminster, 1895-1913. Parliamentary draftsman. Palace Chambers, 9 Bridge Street, Westminster, 1913-1924. Not in 1925 Law List. Foster.

STABLES, Christopher Hilton
Born 24 April 1964 Liverpool. Liverpool Bluecoat School; Liverpool University, LLB. G. 16 October 1990. ETC. 1990. Prop. John Kay QC. Sec. David Turner. Exchange Chambers, Pearl Assurance House, Derby Square, 1992-. Fellow, Royal Geographical Society. Alpine mountaineer.

STADDEN, Jodie
G. 10 October 1996. ETC. 16 December 1997. Prop. Peter Winston Smith QC. Sec. Paul Chaisty. 40 King Street, Manchester, 1997-1998. Not in 1999 Bar Directory.

STAFFURTH, Henry
Born 1846. 3rd son of William Staffurth. Emmanuel College, Cambridge, LLM. AAS. L. 7 November 1868. Call 26 January 1872. ETC. 5 August 1881. Prop. Gully QC. Sec. French. Manchester Chambers; 5 St James's Square, 1883-1888; 9 St James's Square, 1889-1894; 77 King Street, 1895-1911. Not in 1912 Law List. Foster.

STALKER, Monica
Manchester University, LLB. G. July 1967. Manchester Chambers; 43 King Street, 1968-1988; 5 John Dalton Street, 1989-1999. No address 2000-.

STAMMERS, Joseph
2nd son of Joseph Stammers of Essex. AAS. G. 20 February 1828. Call 1 May 1833. 4 King's Bench Walk, 1848. No chambers address, 1876-1885. Not in 1886 Law List. Foster.

*** STANGER, His Honour Henry Yorke KC**
Born 11 November 1849. Died 19 April 1929 aged 79. Lincoln College, Oxford, BA. AAS. L. 10 June 1871. Call 6 June 1874. 3 Cobden Chambers, Pelham Street, Nottingham (Midland Circuit). Silk 1895. MP (L) North Kensington, 1906-1910. Recorder of Nottingham, 1909-1911. County Court Judge, 1910-1922. (Circuit 7, Lancashire & Cheshire, 1910-1914; living at Penhard Rd, Victoria Rd, New Brighton) and (Circuit 54, Bristol & Somerset, 1914-1922). WW.

STANLEY, Hon. Sir Arthur Lyulph MP (5th Baron Sheffield of Roscommon and 5th Baron Stanley of Alderley)
Born 14 September 1875. Died 22 August 1931 aged 55. Only son of Edward Lyulph Stanley (4th Baron Sheffield) qv. Eton; Balliol College, Oxford, MA. Captain, Anglesey RE Militia, Boer War, 1899-1901. I. 27 January 1902. ETC. 7 July 1903. Prop. Pickford KC. Sec. Maurice Hill. 4 Harcourt Buildings, 1903-1906 No Chambers address, 1907-1931. MP for Eddisbury Division of Cheshire, 1906-1910. Parliamentary Private Secretary to Postmaster General, 1906-1910. High Sheriff of Anglesey, 1913. Governor of Victoria, 1914-1919. KCMG 1914. Burke's Peerage.

STANLEY, Rt. Hon Edward Lyulph MP (4th Baron Sheffield of Roscommon in the Peerage of Ireland and 4th Baron Stanley of Alderley in the Peerage of the United Kingdom)
Born 16 May 1839, London. Died 18 March 1925 Alderley Park aged 85. Father of 5th Baron Sheffield qv. Eton; Balliol College, Oxford, MA; Fellow, 1862-1869. AAS. I. 22 April 1861. Call 17 November 1865. 1 Paper Buildings, 1876-1901. MP (L) Oldham, 1880-1885. He was a pioneer in the field of education and the housing of the poor. He sat on many government and local authority boards and committees. PC 1910. Publications; Our National Education, 1899. WW. DNB, Burke's Peerage.

STANLEY, Henry
G. 18 November 1901. ETC. 4 February 1902. Prop. Pickford KC. Sec. Byrne. 60 King Street, Manchester, 1902. No address, 1903-1907; Preston Chambers; County Chambers 1908; 38 Fishergate, 1909-1911; 12 Guildhall Street, 1912-1917; 23 Chapel Walks, 1918-1932; 6 St Wilfred Street, 1933-1934. Not in 1939 Law List.

STANLEY, Ian James
Died 9 September 1983 aged 43. Liverpool University, LLB. L. February 1964. Pupilmaster, John Edward Jones. Liverpool Chambers; North House, 17 North John Street, 1964-1971; Martins Building, Water Street, 1972-1977; Melbourne Building, 21 North John Street, 1978-1983. Tributes; St George's Hall, Liverpool, 13 September 1983 (Judge E S Temple QC/ Michael Maguire QC). Transcript in Circuit Records.

STANLEY, Rt. Hon. Oliver Frederic George
Born 4 May 1896. Died 10 December 1950 aged 54. Son of the 17th Earl of Derby. Eton; Major, RFA; served European War, 1914-1918 (MC., 1917; Croix de Guerre; despatches). G. 17 November 1919. ETC. 1920. Circuit Junior, Summer 1920. 4 Brick Court, 1922-1934. No chambers address thereafter. MP (C);Westmorland, 1924-1945; Bristol West, 1945-1950. Minister of Transport, 1933-1934. Minister of Labour, 1934-1935; President of the Board of Education, 1935-1937; President of the Board of Trade, 1937-1940; Secretary of State for War, 1940. Secretary of State for the Colonies, 1942-1945. PC 1934. WW.

STANNARD, John Anthony (His Honour Judge Stannard)

(RB)

Born 30 September 1931. Died 12 February 1992 aged 60. Quarry Bank High School, Liverpool; Trinity College, Cambridge (Major Scholar) MA. L. February 1956; (Chomley Scholar, 1953; Cassels Scholar, 1954). ETC. 1956. Same Liverpool Chambers; 7 Rumford Street, 1956-1966; Oriel Chambers, 14 Water Street, 1967-1983 (Head of Chambers). Recorder, 1980-1983. Circuit Judge, Liverpool, 1983-1992. Northern Circuit; Official Referee Business from 1984; Commercial Judge from 1990. WW. Tributes: Liverpool Law Courts, 13 February 1992 (Judge Wickham QC/ John Kay QC) Transcript in Circuit Records.

STANSBY, (Hilary) Alexandra
Born 9 December 1951 Kent. Blackheath High School, London; Girton College, Cambridge, MA. Formerly archeologist/prehistoric osteologist at British Museum, 1973-1984. AAS. M. 25 February 1983. Call 26 November 1985. ETC. 1985. Prop. Donald Hart QC. Sec. Frank Burns. Manchester Chambers; 26 Cross Street, 1985-1987; Kenworthy's Buildings, 83 Bridge Street, 1988-1999; Young Street Chambers, 2000.

STANSFIELD, His Honour James Warden
Born 7 April 1906. Died 30 September 1991 aged 85. King's School, Maclesfield; Sidney Sussex College, Cambridge. I. 12 June 1929. 3 St James's Square, Manchester, 1933-1939 & 1945-1963. Served, 1939-1945 War; Royal Air Force, Middle East, and Staff of Judge Advocate General; formerly RAFVR, Squadron Leader. Chairman: Manchester Licensing Planning Committee, 1955-1963; Mental Health Review Tribunal, 1962; Warrington Licensed Premises Committee, 1970. Circuit Judge, (formerly County Court Judge), 1963-1978, Circuits, 14, 4 & 9. WW.

STANSFIELD, John Oliver
MA (Oxon). G. July 1952. 34 Castle Street, Liverpool, 1953-1962. 2 Booth Street, Manchester, 1962-1963. Legal Assistant rising to Assistant Solicitor in Ministry of Agriculture, Fisheries, Food & Forestry Commission, 1964-1991. No address, 1992-1999. Not in Bar Directory 2000.

STARFORTH, Michael John CBE
G. June 1947. 60 King Street, Manchester, 1950-1953. Uganda; Crown Counsel, 1954-1959; Senior Crown Counsel, 1960-1963; Solicitor General, 1964. Senior Legal Assistant Parliamentary Counsel to HM Treasury, 1965-1971. Not in 1972 Law List. CBE. 1966.

STATHAM, Richard Jervis
I. 12 May 1897. ETC. 31 July 1897. Prop. Shee QC. Sec. Horridge. No address, 1898-1900. 8 Harrington Street, Liverpool, 1901-1902. Not in 1903 Law List.

STAUNTON, William John Paul
Born 18 May 1962 Belfast. St Patrick's College, Knock, Belfast; St Catherine's College, Cambridge, MA. AAS. M. 2 July 1984. Call 4 February 1986. ETC 1986. 6 King's Bench Walk, 1986-1987. Manchester Chambers; 3 St James's Square, 1988-1989; 20 St Mary's Parsonage, 1990-1993; 58 King Street Chambers, 51-53 South King Street, 1994.

*** STEAVENSON, His Honour David Fenwick**
Born 10 September 1844. Died 12 March 1920 aged 75. King William's College, Trinity Hall, Cambridge BA., LLB. Rowed in Cambridge University Eight 1864, 1865, 1866. AAS. I. 12 January 1864. Call 17 November 1866. North Eastern Circuit. 11 King's Bench Walk 1883-1888; 12 King's Bench Walk 1889-1891. County Court Judge, Circuit 3 (Cumberland & Westmorland) October 1891-1912. WW. Foster.

STEEL, Allan Gibson KC

Born 24 September 1858. Died 15 June 1914 aged 55. Son of Joseph Steel, JP of Liverpool. Marlborough; Trinity College, Cambridge, BA 1881. AAS. I. 7 November 1879. Call 17 November 1883. ETC. 14 February 1884. Prop. Temple QC. Sec. Kennedy. 2 King's Bench Walk, 1883-1884. Stephenson's Chambers, 25 Lord Street, Liverpool, 1885-1901. Silk 1901. 3 Dr Johnson's Building, 1901-1914. Recorder of Oldham, 1904-1914. I am grateful to Sir Michael Morland who alerted me to Steel's remarkable cricketing exploits. Steel came from a cricketing family, being the sixth of seven brothers, four of whom at one time or another played in the Lancashire County Cricket team. He played for Cambridge from 1878-1881, captaining the side in 1880. In 1878 the team played eight matches and won all, including one against the Australians. That year Steel was the greatest all rounder of the team averaging 37, and his bowling took 75 wickets in 282 overs at an average of 9 runs per wicket. In the whole season he headed the All England bowling averages taking 164 wickets at an average of 9 runs per wicket. It was difficult combining cricket with a very large commercial practice but he performed well whenever he found the time to play. In 1884 he scored 145 for England against a very strong Australian side. In 1902 he was president of MCC. Alfred Cochrane writing in DNB said "His career as a cricketer was comparatively short, but for a season or two his all round ability made him second only to W G Grace as a match winning force." He had two sons both of whom were killed in the War of 1914-1918. WW. DNB. Obituary in Wisden's Cricketers Almanac, 1915. Further Reading:- Wisden Anthology; 1864-1900 (p. 327-328); 1900-1914 (p. 414-417).

STEEL, (Anne) Heather (The Hon Mrs Justice Steel DBE)

(DL)

Born 3 July 1940, Cheshire. Daughter of His Honour Edward Steel qv, sister of Her Honour Judge Elizabeth Steel qv. Howell's School, Denbigh; Liverpool University, LLB. G. November 1963; Bencher 1993. ETC. 1963. Pupilmaster, Tom Pigot. Same Liverpool Chambers; 14 Cook Street, 1963-1974; Ground floor, Peel House, Harrington Street, 1973-1986. Recorder 1984-1986. Prosecuting Counsel to DHSS on circuit, 1984-1986. Circuit Judge, 1986-1993. (Resident Judge, Preston, 1992-1993). Member, Criminal Committee, Judicial Studies Board, 1992-1995. President, Merseyside Medico Legal Society, 1992-1994, High Court Judge, Queen's Bench Division, 1993-2001. Law Faculty Assoc, Liverpool University, 1994. Member, Council of Rossall School, 1990. Member, Guild of Freemen, City of London, 1996. Freeman, City of London, 1993. Liveryman, Pattenmakers' Co., 1993 (Upper Warden, 2002-March 2003). Judge of Appeal, Jersey & Guernsey 2004.I have placed in the Circuit Records the following transcripts: Tributes at Preston Law Courts on 30 July 1993 (Judge Lockett / Richard Henriques QC) Welcome at Reading Law Courts on 6 October 1993 (John Rowe QC / Anna Worrall QC) Retirement Tributes for Heather Steel & Ann Ebsworth at Liverpool Law Courts on 31 July 2001 (Mr Justice Sachs / Judge David Clarke QC / Henry Globe QC). Judge of Appeal, Jersey & Guernsey, 2004. WW.

STEEL, His Honour Edward

Born 9 May 1906 Warrington. Died 15 January 1976 aged 69. Father of: The Hon Mrs Justice Heather Steel qv and Her Honour Judge Elizabeth Steel qv. Boteler Grammar School, Warrington; Hutton Grammar School, Preston; Liverpool University, LLB. Articled to his father Thomas Steel. Admitted as a solicitor, November 1928. G. 9 June 1937. ETC. 23 June 1937. Prop. Lynskey KC. Sec. Birley. Liverpool Chambers; 43 Castle Street, 1937-1939. Active Service in Western Desert, 1939-1942; Lt. Colonel, Judge Advocate-General's Department. Judge Advocate, in trial of War Criminals in Germany & Gestapo in Norway, 1942-1945. 34 Castle Street, 1945-1946; 24 Dale Street, 1947-1952. Assistant Recorder, Liverpool City Quarter Sessions, 1948-1956. 14 Cook Street, 1953-1958. Chancellor; Diocese of Liverpool, 1957-1976; Manchester, 1971-1976. Circuit Judge, (formerly County Court Judge), January 1958-1976. (Circuit 12, Yorkshire, 1958; Circuit 10, Oldham, 1958-1961; Circuit 5, Salford, 1961; Circuit 8, Manchester, 1961-1971. Deputy Chairman, Lancashire County Quarter Sessions, 1959-1971. Chairman, Cheshire County Quarter Sessions, 1961-1971. JP. Cheshire, 1958. WW.

STEEL, Elizabeth Mary DL (Her Honour Judge Steel DL)

Born 28 November 1936. Daughter of His Honour Edward Steel qv; sister of Dame Heather Steel DBE. qv. Howells School, Denbigh; Liverpool University, LLB. Articled, 1955-1958 to Douglas Kewish (later District Registrar & Head of

County Courts Branch of Lord Chancellor's Department) of H G C Day & Co of Castle Street, Liverpool; articles transferred to Joseph Roberts of Percy Hughes & Roberts of Birkenhead, 1958-1960. Admitted as a solicitor, 1960, remaining with P H & R until 1967. John A Behn Twyford & Co, 1967-1980 (Partner, 1969-1980); Partner, Cuff Roberts & Co, 1980-1991. Race Relations Board, 1970-1978. President, Liverpool Law Society, 1989-1990. Recorder, 1989. Chairman, Steering Committee, Hillsborough Solicitors Group, 1989-1991. DL., Merseyside, 1991. Circuit Judge, 5 November 1991. Governor, Liverpool John Moores University, 2001. President, Athenaeum, Liverpool, 2002-2003. WW.

STEELE, Oswald Innes

Born 1841. Only son of Alexander Steele of Kent. Exeter College, Oxford, BA, 1864; MA. AAS. I. 18 January 1865. Call 27 January 1868. ETC. 5 August 1868. Prop. Manisty QC. Sec. G Bruce. 2 Essex Court, 1876-1880; 5 Essex Court, 1881-1882; 2 Tanfield Court, 1883-1885. No address, 1886-1893. Not in 1894 Law List. Foster.

STEER, David QC

(TM)

Born 15 June 1951 St Helens. Rainford High School; Manchester Polytechnic, BA (Law). AAS. M. 8 October 1971. Call 26 November 1974; Bencher 2001. ETC. 1974. Prop. Gerald Crowe QC. Sec. A D Pappworth. Same Liverpool Chambers; 3rd floor, 27 Dale Street, 1974-1989; Corn Exchange, Fenwick Street, 1989-1999 (Head of Chambers); 7 Harrington Street, (merger with Martins Building), 6.9.1999. (Head of Chambers). Assistant Recorder, 1987. Recorder, 1991. Silk 1993. Member, Bar Council, 1995-1997. Leader of the Northern Circuit, 2002-2004. WW.

STEIGER, Martin Thomas TD., QC (His Honour Judge Steiger TD., QC)

Lancaster Royal Grammar School; Nottingham University, LLB. I. November 1969. ETC. 1969. Manchester Chambers; 60 King Street, 1969-1973; 4th floor, Astley House, Quay Street, 1974-1977; 18 St John Street, 1978-2001. Recorder 1989. Silk 1994. Circuit Judge, July 2001.

STEIN, Leonard Jacques OBE

Born 12 December 1887 London. Died 23 April 1973, London, aged 85. St Paul's School; Balliol College, Oxford. President of the Oxford Union, 1910. I. 1 May 1912. ETC. 3 July 1913. Proposer & seconder not recorded. 1 Temple Gardens, 1912-1914. Staff Captain, serving in France & Egypt, 1914-1918. Palestine Military Administration, 1918-1920. 3 Paper Buildings, 1920-1932; 2 Pump Court, 1933-1941; 4 Brick Court, 1942-1952; 3 Pump Court, 1953-1963. Political Secretary, World Zionist Organisation, 1920-1929. Honorary Legal Advisor, Jewish Agency for Palestine, 1929-1939. President: Anglo Jewish Association, 1939-1949; Jewish Historical Society of England, 1964-1965. OBE 1953. Publications; Zionism, 1925; Syria, 1926; The Balfour Declaration, 1961; Weizmann and England, 1965; (joint editor) Letters & Papers of Chaim Weitzmann, Vol 1, 1968. He was editor of the Jewish Chronicle for 36 years. WW. DNB. Further Reading:- "The Making of Manchester Jewry" by Bill Williams, 1976.

STEIN, Walter Harold Arthur Oscar Alois

BA (Cantab). G. 20 June 1928. ETC. 19 February 1929. Prop. Hemmerde KC. Sec. Baucher. Liverpool Chambers; 15 Lord Street, 1929; 21 Harrington Street, 1930-1938. Not in 1939 Law List.

STEINTHAL, Alfred Ernest

Born 5 May 1858. Eldest son of Rev. S Steinthal of Manchester. Owen's College, Manchester; Trinity College, Cambridge, MA, Fellow 1884; London University, MA 1881. AAS. L. 25 March 1880. Call 26 January 1884. Prop. Aspland QC. Sec. Byrne. 78 King Street, Manchester, 1886-1895. Assistant Registrar, Lancs. Chancery Court, Manchester, 1896-1921; Registrar, 1922-1929. Not in 1930 Law List. Foster.

STEMP, Leslie Fawcett MBE

Born 1893. Eldest son of George Walter Stemp of Croydon, corn merchant. London University, BA., LLB. AAS. M. 10 November 1919. Call 26 January 1921. ETC. 31 January 1923. Prop. Merriman KC. Sec. Blackwell. 1 Brick Court, 1922; Farrar's Building, 1923-1940. No address, 1941-1949. Legal Officer to the Gas Council, 1950-1959. MBE 1951. No business address, 1960-1963. Not in 1964 Law List.

STENHAM, Bernard Basil

BA., LLB (Cantab). I. 17 November 1914. ETC. 7 July 1920. Prop. Wingate-Saul KC. Sec. Lustgarten. Eight sets of chambers in London, between 1914 and 1967, finally at 12 King's Bench Walk. Not in 1968 Law List.

STEPHEN, Sir Herbert. 2nd Bt.
Born 25 June 1857. Died 23 October 1932 aged 75. Eldest son of Sir James Fitzjames Stephen, 1st Bt. and High Court Judge. Rugby; Trinity College, Cambridge. LLM, 1882. AAS. I. 8 November 1878. Call 29 June 1881. Pupilmaster, John Gorell Barnes. 4 Paper Buildings, 1881-1889. Clerk of Assize for the Northern Circuit, 1889-1927. ETC. 1 February 1906 by special resolution of Grand Court at Manchester. Publications; Law Relating to Malicious Prosecutions; Prisoners on Oath; (jointly), A Digest of the Law of Criminal Procedure in Indictable Offences, 1883. WW. Foster.

STEPHENS, Thomas Smithson
L. 26 January 1904. ETC. 7 February 1906. Prop. Tobin KC. Sec. Radford. 78 King Street, Manchester, 1909-1942. No address, 1943-1953. Not in 1954 Law List.

STEPHENSON, Anthony Mark
Born 28 September 1959. Glenburn School; University of Central Lancashire, LLB. G. 27 November 1997. ETC. December 1998. Prop. David Harris QC. Sec. Nigel Beeson. Liverpool Chambers; 24 Fenwick Street/ 14 Cook Street, 1998-2000; Oriel Chambers, 14 Water Street, 16 September 2000.

STEPHENSON, Cookson
Born 1833. Only son of William Stephenson of Holmfirth, Yorks. Trinity College, Cambridge, MA 1859. AAS. L. 25 April 1854. Call 17 November 1859. No address, 1876-1893. West Riding of Yorkshire Sessions. Not in 1894 Law List. Foster.

STERLING, Robert Alan
Born 1 June 1948, Manchester. Brother of Valerie Sterling at Leeds Bar. Manchester Grammar School; Corpus Christi College, Cambridge, MA. G. July 1970. ETC. 1975. Pupilmaster, Leonard Porter. Manchester Chambers; 3 St James's Square, 1970-1984; 68 Quay Street, 1984.

STERNDALE, Baron (See William Pickford)

STEVENSON-COPPIN, Noel Guilbert
G. 2 July 1924. ETC. 28 January 1925. Prop. Jackson KC. Sec. Hooper. No address, 1924-1951. 3 Hare Court, 1952-1957. Not in 1957 Law List.

STEWART, Archibald Hepburne
Born 1862. 2nd son of Alan Duncan Stewart of Perthshire, civil engineer. AAS. M. 27 April 1882. Call 17 June 1885. ETC. 16 July 1888. Prop. Henn Collins QC. Sec. Aitken. 2 Pump Court, 1885-1895. No address, 1896-1940. Not in 1941 Law List.

STEWART, Hans Hamill
Born 1853. Youngest son of John Thomas Hamill Stewart of County Down formerly of Cheltenham. Trinity College, Dublin, BA. AAS. I. 21 April 1875. Call 26 April 1880. ETC. 16 July 1881. Prop. Gully QC. Sec. Crompton. 3 Dr Johnson's Building, 1882-1884; 5 Pump Court, 1885; 4 Raymond Building, 1886; 2 Middle Temple Lane, 1887-1889. No address, 1890-1891. Not in 1892 Law List. Foster.

STEWART, Sir Mark John MacTaggart Bt., MP
Born 12 October 1834, East Lothian. Died 26 September 1923 aged 88. Winchester College; Christ Church, Oxford, MA 1860. AAS. I. 17 November 1856. Call 27 January 1862. No chambers address, 1876-1923. Special pleader, Cumberland, Westmorland & Liverpool Sessions. Hon. Col. 1st Admin. Brigade, Ayr & Galloway Artillery Volunteers. MP (C) Wigtown Burghs, 1874-1880. Stewartry of Kirkudbright, 1885-1906 & 1910. Breeder of Ayrshire cattle on 18,000 acres. DL., JP. Bt., 1892. WW. Foster.

STEWART, Stephen Paul QC (His Honour Judge Stewart QC)

(DL)

Born 9 October 1953 Manchester. Stand Grammar School, Whitefield, Manchester; St Peter's College, Oxford, MA; half blue for badminton. M. 17 July 1975 (Harmsworth Major Exhibition, 1973; Harmsworth Scholar, 1975) ETC. December 1975. Prop. Ivor Taylor QC. Sec. Anthony Rumbelow. Same Manchester Chambers; 12th floor, Sunlight House, Quay Street, 1975-1979; 28 St John Street, 1979-1996. Assistant Recorder, 1995. Silk 1996. 25 Byrom Street, 1996-1999; Recorder 1999. 12 Byrom Street, 2000-2003. Deputy Judge, Technology & Construction Court, 2000-2003. Senior Circuit Judge and Designated Civil Judge for Merseyside, 21 July 2003. WW.

STEWART, William John

Born 1849. Died 31 August 1908. Only son of William Goldfinch Stewart of Liverpool, assistant collector of customs. Liverpool College; Exeter College, Oxford, BA,

1872. AAS. I. 18 November 1869. Call 13 June 1877. ETC. 26 July 1877. Prop. Gully QC. Sec. Myburgh. 30 North John Street, Liverpool, 1877-1891. Stipendiary Magistrate for Liverpool, 16 February 1891-1908. WW. Foster.

STEWART-BROWN, Egerton
MA. I. 14 June 1893. ETC. 2 August 1893. Prop. Pickford QC. Sec. A H Maxwell. Liverpool Chambers; 13 Harrington Street, 1893-1906; 8 Cook Street, 1907-1938. Not in 1939 Law List.

STEWART-JONES, Thorold Arthur
I. 26 April 1899. ETC. July 1900. Prop. Ferguson QC. Sec. Maurice Hill. 2 King's Bench Walk, 1901-1902; 3 Paper Buildings, 1903-1911. No address, 1912-1927. Not in 1928 Law List.

STEWART-SMITH, Sir Dudley KC, MP
Born 3 February 1857. Died 9 May 1919 aged 62. University College, London; London University, LLB. Solicitor, 1879. M. 26 January 1886; Bencher 1911; ad eundem L 8 November 1900. Chairman, Lancaster Quarter Sessions (Salford Hundred). Silk 1902. MP (L) Kendal, 1906-1910. JP; Westmorland; Lancashire and Cheshire. Vice-Chancellor, County Palatine of Lancaster, 1912-1919. Publications; Law of Winding Up and Reconstruction of Joint-Stock Companies. Kt. 1917. WW.

*** STEYN, Johan QC (Baron Steyn of Swafield)**
Born 15 August 1932. Jan van Riebeek School, Cape Town, South Africa; University of Stellenbosch, BA., LLB; University College, Oxford, MA; Hon Fellow 1995. South African Bar, 1958-1973; Senior Counsel, Supreme Court of South Africa. L. February 1973; Bencher 1985. 4 Essex Court, 1973-1985. Silk 1979. High Court Judge, Queen's Bench Division, 1985-1991. Kt 1985. Presiding Judge, Northern Circuit, 1989-1991. Lord Justice of Appeal, 1992-1995. PC 1992. Lord of Appeal in Ordinary, 1995. Baron 1995. WW.

STOCKDALE, David Andrew QC
Born 9 May 1951, Bolton Abbey, North Yorkshire. Giggleswick School (Governor 1982.; Chairman 1997.); Pembroke College, Oxford, MA. AAS. M. 13 March 1973. College of Law, 1973-1975. Call 17 July 1975; Bencher 2003. ETC. 1976. Sec. Keith Goddard. Circuit Junior, Spring 1978. Pupilmasters, Michael Tillett, 39 Essex Street, June- December 1975; Keith Goddard, January-June 1976. Deans Court Chambers, Crown Square/ 24 St John Street, Manchester, 1976. Assistant Recorder 1990. Recorder 1993. Silk 1995. WW.

STOCKLEY, Ruth Angela
Born 6 September 1964 Wigan. Upholland Grammar School; Nottingham University, LLB. L. July 1988. ETC. 1989. Prop. John Hoggett QC. Sec. Stephen Sauvain. Kings Chambers, 40 King Street, Manchester, July 1988. Assistant Editor of Sweet & Maxwells, Encyclopaedia of Highway Law & Practice. President, Manchester Law Library.

STOCKTON, Fay
LLB. L. July 1976. Manchester Chambers; 4 Clarence Street, 1978-1983; 72 Bridge Street, 1984-1987; 40 King Street, 1988-1991; 1 Essex Court 1992-1996; 1 Essex Court & 28 St John Street, Manchester 1997. No address 1998.

STOCKTON, (John) Paul
Born 4 October 1948, Birmingham. Only son of Arthur Clifford Stockton, clerk. Married to Anita Scarth qv. (marr. diss.). BA (Oxon); Cornell University, USA. AAS. M. 20 July 1972. Call November 1974. ETC. 1975. Same Liverpool Chambers; 27 Dale Street, 1975-1976; Melbourne Buildings, 21 North John Street, 1977-1981. Joined Lord Chancellor's Department in 1981 and has held the following posts:- Principal Private Secretary to the Lord Chancellor (Lord Mackay); Deputy Registrar of Criminal Appeals; Deputy Circuit Administrator, South Eastern Circuit; Director of Tribunal Operations, Court Service; Head of LCD Criminal Justice Division.

STOCKWELL. Matthew Charles
Born 21 December 1975 Liverpool. Liverpool College; Liverpool John Moores University, LLB; Trinity College, Dublin, LLM. G. 8 October 1998. ETC. 16 December 1999. Prop. Andrew Edis QC. Sec. Simon Holder. India Buildings, Water Street, Liverpool, October 2000.

*** STONE, Sir (John) Leonard OBE., QC**
Born 6 November 1896. Died 3 January 1978 aged 81. Father of Richard Frederick Stone QC. qv. Malvern College. Served European War, 1914-1918; Comm., Worcester Regt, October 1914; Gallipoli, Army of the Black Sea, Control Officer, Eskishehir, 1919-1920; Inter Allied Commission of Inquiry, Turco-Greek War, 1921 (despatches thrice). G. 26 January 1923; Bencher 1942; Treasurer 1956. L. 1931. 3 Stone Buildings, 1923-1933; 4 New Square, 1934-1943. Chief Justice of the High Court, Bombay, 1943-1947. OBE & Kt., 1943. Vice-Chancellor, County Palatine of Lancaster, 1948-1963. WW.

STONE, Richard Frederick QC
Born 11 March 1928. Son of Sir (John) Leonard Stone OBE., QC., qv. Lakefield College School, Canada; Rugby; Trinity Hall, Cambridge, MA. Lt., Worcester Regt., 1946-1948. G. November 1952; Bencher 1974; Treasurer, 1992. Admiralty pupillage with J B Hewson (Temple). ETC. 1953. Sec. Jeffreys Collinson. Circuit Junior, Summer 1955. Liverpool Chambers; 27 Lord Street, 1953-1959; 10 Water Street, 1960-1967. Queen Elizabeth Building, 1958-1996. Silk 1968. 4 Field Court, 1997. Member of Panel of Lloyds Arbitrators in Salvage Cases, 1968-1999. Panel of Wreck Commissioners, 1968-1998. WW.

STOREY, Robert Holme
Died 15 January 1956. Son of Sir Thomas Storey. Fettes College, Edinburgh; Clare College, Cambridge, MA 1895. I. 17 November 1896. ETC. 25 January 1898. Prop. Pickford QC. Sec. Sanderson. 2 Mitre Court Buildings, 1897. No Chambers address, 1898-1956. Denbighshire; JP., 1904; County Councillor, 1907. Herefordshire; JP., 1920; High Sheriff, 1938. WW.

STORRIE, Timothy James
Born 26 August 1967 Bury. Married to Mary Ruck qv. Loreto College, Manchester; Mansfield College, Oxford, BA; Dip. Law (Staffs). Freelance journalist/sub editor. M. October 1993. ETC. 7 December 1993. Prop. Roger Farley QC. Sec. Longworth. Manchester Chambers; Old Colony House, 6 South King Street, 1993-2000; Lincoln House Chambers, 1 Brazennose Street, 2000. Editor, Cassell's English Usage, London, 1991.

STOUT, Roger Charles
Born 19 March 1948, Manchester. Bury Grammar School; Exeter University, BA (Politics). G. November 1976. ETC. 1977. Pupilmaster, John Burke. 18 St John Street, Manchester, 1977.

STRATHCARRON, First Baron (See (James) Ian MacPherson)

STRETTELL, Kathleen Marjorie
G. 11 May 1927. ETC. 14 June 1928. Prop. Jackson KC. Sec. Sellers. No address, 1928-1953. Not in 1954 Law List.

STRINGER, Rosemary
MA (History). Trade journalist/editor for 2 years. Postgraduate Diploma in Law. M. 25 July 2002; Harmsworth Scholar. ETC. 17 December 2002. Prop. Michael Redfern QC. Sec. Philip Grundy. St John's Buildings, 24a-28 St John Street, Manchester, 2002.

STUART, Douglas Cecil Rees
I. 10 May 1911. ETC. 28 February 1912. Prop. Taylor KC. Sec. Gordon Hewart. Palatine Buildings, Norfolk Street, Manchester, 1912-1913. 2 Harcourt Buildings, 1914-1919; 1 Brick Court, 1920-1921. No address, 1922-1953. Not in 1954 Law List.

STUART, (Douglas) Mark
Born 17 March 1961, Burnley. Queen Elizabeth Grammar School, Blackburn; Newcastle University, BA. G. November 1985. Pupilmaster, John Evans, London. ETC. 1987. 14/15 Winckley Square, Preston, 1986.

STUART, Francis David
BA (London) G. July 1973. 20 North John Street, Liverpool, 1977-1983. No address 1984. All Saints Vicarage, Oldham, 1985-1990. Not in 1991 Bar Directory.

*** STURGESS, His Honour Hugh (Murray) KC**
Born 26 August 1863. Died 12 October 1952 aged 89. Winchester; Keble College, Oxford, BA 1864. L. 28 January 1889; Bencher 1926; Treasurer 1945. 2 Temple Gardens, 1911-1912. Silk 1912. London & Oxford Circuit. County Court Judge, 1913-1928, (Circuit 4, Preston, 1913-1921; Circuit 37, West London, 1921-1928). WW.

STUTTART, Arthur Rupert Davies
Born 16 July 1943 Accrington. Accrington Grammar School; Christ Church, Oxford, MA. President, Oxford University Law Society. AAS. M. 12 March 1965; Harmsworth Scholar. Call 7 February 1967. ETC. March 1969. Prop. David MacNeil QC. Sec. Philip Hinchliffe. Manchester Chanbers; 60 King Street, 1967-1979; 3 St James's Square, 1979-1994; Manchester House Chambers, 1994-1998; Queen's Chambers, 5 John Dalton Street, 1998. Deputy Stipendiary Magistrate, Merseyside, 1988-1993. Publications; An English Law Notebook; The Wonderful Discoverie of Witchcraft in Lancashire (Editor).

SUGDEN, Frank Edward
Born 1890. Son of William Arthur Sugden of Oldham, commission agent. AAS. M. 29 September 1916. Call 27 January 1919. 1 Temple Gardens, 1922; 3 Paper Buildings, 1923; 2 Elm Court, 1924-1925; 3 Plowden Buildings, 1926-1941; 3 Middle Temple Lane, 1942-1960. No chambers address, 1961-1977. Not in 1978 Law List.

SUGDEN, Sir Wilfrid Hart MP
Born Bolton. Died 27 April 1960. Waterloo School; London University. G. 26 January 1928. ETC. 19 February 1929. Prop. Goldie KC. Sec. Leigh. M. 17 April 1930. 1 New Court, 1929-1931; 1 Brick Court, 1932-

1934; 2 Dr Johnson's Buildings, 1935-1944; 1 Essex Court, 1945-1952; 2 Harcourt Buildings, 1953-1957. No address, 1958-1960. Member, Oldham Town Council, 1912-1918. MP (U) Royton, 1918-1923; The Harlepools, 1924-1929; Leyton West, 1931-1935. PPS to the last Chief Secretary for Ireland, 1921-1922. Kt., 1922. WW.

SULLIVAN, Alexander Martin MP
Born 1830. Died 1884. (Father of Serjeant Sullivan 1871-1959, "The Last Serjeant). Irish Bar, 1876. I. 23 November 1877. ETC. 8 February 1879. Prop. Russell QC. Sec. Temple. 3 Dr Johnson's Buildings, 1878-1884.

SUMMERFIELD, Donald
Born 1908. Son of Stephen Summerfield of Manchester, railway representative (commercial). Manchester University, MA. AAS. M. 28 June 1935. Call 17 November 1938. ETC. 1 March 1939. Prop. William Gorman KC. Sec. Lustgarten. Manchester Chambers; 48 King Street, 1940; 28 Kennedy Street, 1948-1956; 25 Bow Lane, 1957-1960. HM Coroner for Manchester, 1961-1978. Not in 1979 Law List.

SUMMERFIELD, Woolf
MA., BCL (Oxon); LLB (London). Yarborough Anderson Scholar, 1921. I. 10 May 1922. ETC. 26 February 1936. Prop. Lynskey KC. Sec. Burton. 2 Pump Court, 1929-1932; 4 Crown Office Row, 1933-1940; 5 King's Bench Walk, 1941-1950; 2 Hare Court, 1951-1963. Not in 1964 Law List.

SUMMERS, Walter
I. 25 April 1888. ETC. 16 July 1888. Prop. Aspland QC. Sec. Walton. 12 King's Bench Walk, 1890; 6 Crown Office Row, 1891-1900. No address 1901-1940. Not in 1941 Law List.

SUMNER, Viscount (See John Andrew Hamilton)

SUMNER, David Moorcroft
Born 28 July 1938, Great Harwood, Lancs. Brother is solicitor/partner in J Budd & Co of Blackpool. Rossall School. National Service with King's Regiment in Germany, 1955-1957. L. May 1963. ETC. 1963. Pupilmaster, Cecil Q Henriques. Manchester Chambers; 2 Booth Street, 1963-1970; 13 Police Street, 1970-1978; Rational House, 64 Bridge Street, 1978-1992; Lincoln House Chambers, 1 Brazennose Street, 1992 until retirement in July 2002. Recorder 1982-2002. Special Adjudicator (Immigration) 1998.

SURRIDGE, Charles Ernest North
L. 14 May 1924. ETC. 15 July 1924. Prop. Atkinson KC. Sec. Abbott. No address, 1925-1953. Not in 1954 Law List.

SURRIDGE, Charles William West
I. 11 June 1902. ETC. 5 February 1903. Prop. Taylor KC. Sec. Acton. 41 John Dalton Street, Manchester, 1904-1924. No address, 1925-1937. Not in 1938 Law List.

SURTEES, John Oliver
Born 20 May 1823. 4th son of William Villiers Surtees of Regents Park. Charterhouse. AAS. M. 13 January 1846. Call 12 January 1849. Salford Sessions but no address, 1881-1906. Not in 1907 Law List. Foster.

SUTTON, Edmund
Born 9 April 1844. Only son of Isaac Sutton of Congleton, Cheshire. Trinity College, Oxford, BA. 1865. AAS. I. 16 April 1868. Call 7 June 1869. ETC. 4 August 1869. Prop. Manisty QC. Sec. Shield. 1 Elm Court, 1876-1878; 11 King's Bench Walk, 1879-1882. Manchester Chambers; Dalton Chambers, John Dalton Street, 1879-1889; 3 Clarence Street, 1890-1903; Bank of England Chambers, Tib Lane, 1904-1918. No address, 1919-1922. Not in 1923 Law List. Foster.
Robert Jackson in "The Chief", his biography of Gordon Hewart refers to Sutton at p. 36-37. He describes a Law Lord referring to him as the greatest living authority on the English Common Law. "He never took Silk but his fees "were as large as any Silk could command." In Hewart's time, Sutton refused to go into court without one or two juniors. He was one of the most unusual men at the Bar. "He was tall and gaunt and habitually wore an old frock coat, so that he looked like Little Nell's grandfather."

SUTTON, Keith Andrew
Born 4 January 1963. Southend High School; Leicester Polytechnic, LLB. Employed in banking & telecommunications. G. November 1988. ETC. Summer 1989. Prop. John Rowe QC. Sec. Iain Goldrein. Circuit Junior, 1991. Liverpool Chambers; Corn Exchange, Fenwick Street, 1989-1999; 7 Harrington Street, 6.9.1999-. (merger with Martins Building).

SUTTON, Ruth Deborah
Born 17 March 1971 Manchester. Edgbaston High School, Birmingham; Manchester University, LLB. M. November 1994. ETC. July 1995. Prop. Keith Goddard QC. Sec. Yvonne Coppel. St John's Buildings, 24a-28 St John Street, Manchester, April 1995-2001. Door tenant 2002, proposing to move to Australia.

SWALLOW, Luther James
L. 28 June 1911. ETC. 25 July 1911. Prop. Taylor KC. Sec. Wingate-Saul. 60 King Street, Manchester, 1912-1917. Not in 1918 Law List.

SWEENEY, Linda Mary
Born 29 November 1960, Bolton. Mount St Joseph Grammar School, Bolton; Manchester University, LLB. Bolton Metro., 1988-1992; Salford City Council, 1992-94; Flint & Holmes, Solicitors, 1995-1999. M. 25 November 1999. ETC. 14 December 1999. Prop. Lindsay Kushner QC. Sec.Yvonne Coppel. 24a St John's Street, Manchester (now St John's Buildings, 1999.

SWIFT, Caroline Jane QC
Born 30 May 1955, Morecambe. Married to His Honour Judge Peter Openshaw QC., DL. Lancaster Girls Grammar School; University of Durham (St Aidan's College), BA; President, Durham Union Society 1975. I. November 1977; Bencher 1997. ETC. 1978. Prop. Benet Hytner QC. Sec. Jack Price. Manchester Chambers; 60 King Street/ 1 Dean's Court, 1978-1993; 25 later 12 Byrom Street, 1993. And at 22 Old Buildings. Assistant Recorder 1992. Silk 1993. Recorder 1995. Deputy High Court Judge, 2000. Leading Counsel to the Shipman Inquiry, 2000. Publications; (jointly), Ribchester, 100 years in photographs, 1994; Ribchester, a Millennium Record, 2001. WW.

*** SWIFT, David Rowland (His Honour Judge Swift)**
Born 21 April 1946. Kingsmead School, Hoylake; Ruthin School; Liverpool College of Commerce. Articled Clerk with Percy Hughes & Roberts, Solicitors of Birkenhead, 1964-1969. Admitted as a solicitor, 1 January 1970. Partner with the same firm, 1970-1997. Recorder 1993. President, Liverpool Law Society, 1995-1996. Circuit Judge, 31 January 1997. Northern Circuit Representative, HM Council of Circuit Judges, 2003. FRSA. Publications; Proceedings before the Solicitors' Disciplinary Tribunal, 1996. WW.

SWIFT, Herbert Henry

Born 27 April 1836. Only son of John Swift of London. Trinity College, Cambridge MA, 1865. AAS. I. 28 April 1865. Call 27 January 1868. ETC. 9 March 1868. Prop. Holker QC. Sec. Charles Russell. Circuit Junior, Summer 1868. 5 Brick Court, 1876-1881; 8 Fig Tree Court, 1882-1888; 12 King's Bench Walk, 1889-1897. No chambers address, 1898-1913. Not in 1914 Law List. Foster.

SWIFT, Rigby Philip Watson KC, MP (The Hon Mr Justice Swift)

Born 7 June 1874 St Helens. Died 19 October 1937 aged 63. Eighth child of Thomas Swift of St Helens, barrister qv. Parkfield School, Liverpool. London University External, LLB. L. 26 June 1895: Bencher 1916. Admitted M. 14 December 1910. ETC. 30 July 1895. Prop. Pickford QC. Sec. Ross Brown. Liverpool Chambers; Bristowe Chambers, 8 Harrington Street, 1895-1903; Stephenson's Chambers, 25 Lord Street, 1904-1910. 1 Garden Court, 1911-1920. MP (C) St Helens, 1910-1918. Recorder of Wigan, 1915-1920. High Court Judge, Queens Bench Division, 1920-1937. Kt. 1920. Hon. LLD, Liverpool, 1930. WW. DNB (John Singleton qv). Biography; The Life of Mr Justice Swift by E S Fay, 1939; A Century of Liverpool Lawyers by Fagan, Bryson & Elston, Liverpool Law Society, 2002; Foul Bills & Dagger Money (Chapter 16) His Honour Dick Hamilton. In November 1910 Swift represented the mine owners at the Inquiry into the disaster at the Whitehaven colliery when an explosion and fire in the workings under the sea caused the death of 132 miners. In 1920 Lord Birkenhead appointed Swift and His Honour Judge Acton to the King's Bench Division of The High Court, thereby raising the numbers from 15 to 17. (There are presently 72). Swift became the youngest High Court Judge at 46 and Acton was the first County Court Judge to go to the High Court. Swift tried many notable cases. They included:

1. The trial of 19 members of the IRA for treason-felony in 1921 having set 40 incendiary fires in Manchester including the destruction of the Manchester City football stands.
2. The Trial of Frederick Nodder (Notable British Trials, volume 72 Winifred Duke, 1950). Nodder murdered a young girl in 1937. The child had not then been found and Nodder was convicted of abduction and sentenced by

Swift in March to the maximum of seven years. The girl's body was found three months later. Nodder was convicted of murder before Mr Justice MacNaughton and later executed.

One of the pleasures in compiling this Directory has been corresponding with people who have a keen interest in circuit history. On such is His Honour Edgar Fay QC now in his 96th year. A former Official Referee of the Supreme Court, he wrote Swift's biography in 1939, the year of my birth. He has kindly sent me many photographs, scrap books (compiled by Archibald Evans who was Swift's clerk) and counsels notebooks which Swift used when appearing at Liverpool County Court. I have placed them all in the Circuit Records. He also told me of his happy memories of the Northern Circuit. He first went to St George's Hall in 1933 as marshal to Mr Justice Hawke who tried a Liverpool solicitor, Stephenson and others for conspiracy falsely to move and maintain pleas, (claiming damages for road traffic accidents which had not happened.) The trial lasted 28 days, then the longest ever trial in Liverpool. (I have the newspaper clippings). He returned to Liverpool two years later as marshal to Mr Justice Singleton and finally in 1971 he came to us, in his own right, as a Commissioner of Assize.

SWIFT, Thomas

Born 1832. Died 26 September 1899 aged 67. Father of the Hon. Mr Justice Swift qv. A solicitor in St Helens; admitted 1862. AAS. L 31 October 1881. Call 17 November 1882. ETC. 25 January 1883. Prop. Addison QC. Sec. Leresche. Liverpool Chambers; 10 Orange Court, 1883-1889; 12 Commerce Chambers, Lord Street, 1890-1892; Bristowe Chambers, 8 Harrington Street, 1893-1899.

SWIFT, Steven Geoffrey

Born 6 May 1967 Winchester. Married to Anya Horwood qv. Cowley High School, St Helens; Lancaster University, LLB. I. November 1991. Prop. John Kay QC. Sec. Ruth Howe. 46 Stanley Street, 1991-1995; ground floor, Peel House, Harrington Street, 1995-1998; India Buildings, Water Street, March 1998.

★ SYCAMORE, Phillip (His Honour Judge Sycamore)

Born 9 March 1951. Lancaster Royal Grammar School; Holborn College of Law (External, LLB (London)). Solicitor, 1975. Partner, Lonsdales, Solicitors, 1980-2001. Assistant Recorder 1994. Recorder 1999. President of the Law Society, 1997-1998. Circuit Judge, 2001. Liason Judge, Mental Health Review Tribunal, 2001. WW.

SYLVESTER, Mio Paul

Born 7 August 1955 London. King's College School, Wimbledon; Downing College, Cambridge, MA., LLB. AAS. M. 18 October 1978. Call 24 July 1980. New York Bar, 1981. Manchester Chambers; 2 Old Bank Street, 1986-1991; 40a Young Street, 1999. London Chambers; 3 Temple Gardens, 1992-1999; 11 King's Bench Walk, 2000.

SYMMS, Kathryn Ann

Born 4 November 1967. Married to Nigel Power qv. Ecclesbourne School, Derby; Emmanuel College, Cambridge, MA. G. October 1990. ETC. December 1991. Prop. Rodney Klevan QC. Sec. Stuart Baker. 3 Raymond Building, 1990-1991. Liverpool Chambers; Martins Building, Water Street, 1991-1999; 7 Harrington Street, (merger with Corn Exchange), 6.9.1999.

SYMONDS, William

I. 26 January 1898. ETC. 2 February 1898. Prop. Pickford QC. Sec. Sutton. Manchester Chambers; 77 King Street, 1899-1903. Shanghai/Hankow, China, 1904-1913. 78 King Street, 1914-1920; Bank of England Chambers, Tib Lane, 1921-1930. Not in 1931 Law List.

SYNNOTT, Nicholas Joseph

Born 1856. Died 13 August 1920. Stonyhurst College; University of London, BA, 1877. AAS. M. 15 November 1876. Call 25 June 1879. ETC. 12 July 1880. Prop. Russell QC. Sec. Smelt. 1 Dr. Johnson's Buildings, 1881-1883; 1 Pump Court, 1884-1885; 1 Garden Court, 1886-1912. No address, 1913-1920. High Sheriff, County Kildare, 1906. Governor of the Bank of Ireland and Director of Great Southern & Western Railway. Member, Royal Commission on Income Tax, 1919. WW.

SZLUMPER, William Weeks

From a family of railway engineers. M.Ins.CE. L. 12 June 1907. South Wales & Chester Circuit, 1907-1911. ETC. 23 February 1911. Prop. Forbes Lankester KC. Sec. Raeburn. 17 Victoria Street, Westminster, parliamentary draftsman & committees, 1912-1934. No chambers address, 1935-1939. Not in 1940 Law List.

T

TAFT, Christopher Heiton
Born 27 September 1974, Burnley. St Wilfrid's C of E High School, Blackburn; Clitheroe Royal Grammar School; Manchester University, LLB. M. October 1997. Pupilmaster, Barrie Searle. St James's Chambers, 68 Quay Street, Manchester, 1997.

TAHOURDIN, Charles John
Born 1841. Eldest son of Charles Tahourdin of Westminster, solicitor, brother of Graham Tahourdin qv. Lincoln College, Oxford, BA, 1863. AAS. L. 23 November 1863. Call 26 January 1867. 61 Carey Street, W.C., 1881-1889; No address, 1890-1892; 1 Mitre Court, 1893-1896. No address, 1897-1914. Not in 1915 Law List. Equity & parliamentary draftsman & conveyancer. Foster.

TAHOURDIN, Graham
Born 1854. 7th son of Charles Tahourdin of Westminster, solicitor, brother of Charles John Tahourdin qv. St John's College, Oxford, BA. 1877. AAS. I. 13 November 1875. Call 26 January 1880. ETC. 12 July 1880. Prop. Russell QC. Sec. Aspinall QC. 3 Harcourt Buildings, 1882-1884; 1 Mitre Court Buildings, 1885-1894. Manchester & Salford Sessions. No address, 1895-1927. Not in 1928 Law List. Foster.

TAIT, Campbell
Born 30 January 1956 Edinburgh. Died January 2004 aged 47. Acklam Hall; Queen Mary College, London, LLB. M. November 1979. ETC. December 1979. Prop. Benet Hytner QC. Sec. Philip Clegg. Same Manchester Chambers; Rational House, 64 Bridge Street, 1979-1995; Lincoln House Chambers, 1 Brazennose Street, 1996-2004. Recorder 2000. Tributes; Manchester Law Courts, January 2004 (Judge David Maddison/David Steer QC).

TALBOT, Dennis
Born 5 January 1945, Bolton. Altrincham Grammar School; ACMA. In industry and business as finance director, management consultant and company chairman, 1969-1985. G. July 1985. ETC. 1986. Pupilmaster, Iain Goldrein. Mason House, 48-50 Castle Street/Corn Exchange, Liverpool 1985-1994; 40 King Street, Chester, 1994-1997; Exchange Chambers, Liverpool, 1994.

TALBOT, Edward
L. 26 January 1888. ETC. 12 March 1890. Prop. Addison QC. Sec. Sutton. Manchester Chambers; 4 St James's Square, 1891-1892; 37 Brown Street, 1893-1936. Lancs. Chancery Court. Not in 1937 Law List.

TALBOT, (Richard) Kevin (Kent)
Born 27 November 1947 Liverpool. Married to Alexandra King qv. Wrekin College, Wellington, Shropshire; Liverpool John Moores/ University College, London, LLB. I. July 1970. ETC. 1970. Prop. Tom Pigot QC. Sec. John Gore; Liverpool Chambers; Fruit Exchange, Victoria Street (pupilage), 1970-1971; Martins Building, Water Street, 1971-1985. Deans Court Chambers, Manchester, 1985. Assistant Recorder 1989. Recorder 1993.

TANKEL, Ruth Shoshana (nee Hyman)
Born 7 February 1961 London. Hasmonean Grammar School/ Carmel College; Manchester University, LLB. AAS. M. 14 April 1983. Call 26 July 1990. ETC. 1991. Pupilmasters, Lesley Newton and Barrie Searle. CPS, trainee pupil, September 1990-February 1991. Manchester Chambers; Sunlight House, 1990-1991; St James's Chambers, 68 Quay Street, March 1991.

TARSH, Edith Vera
Married to Jack Tarsh qv. L. July 1930. No address, 1930-1950. Liverpool Chambers; 34 Castle Street, 1951; 24 Dale Street, 1952-1956; 27 Dale Street, 1957-1958. No address, 1959-1961. Not in 1962 Law List.

TARSH, Jack
Born 1904. Died September 1956 aged 52. Married to Edith Tarsh qv. Medical doctor. L. July 1946. ETC 1946. Liverpool Chambers; 34 Castle Street, 1947-1951; 24 Dale Street, 1952-1956. Chairman, Bootle National Insurance Tribunal.

TATTERSALL, Geoffrey Frank QC
Born 22 September 1947 Ashton-under-Lyne. Manchester Grammar School; Christ Church, Oxford, MA. L. July 1970; Tancred studentship in Common Law; Bencher 1997. ETC. December 1970. Pupilmasters, Andrew Gibb and Desmond Franks. Member of the Bar of New South Wales 1992 (Senior Counsel 1995). Manchester Chambers; 601 Royal Exchange/ 8 King Street, 1970-1992. Recorder 1989. Silk 1992. 25 Byrom Street, now 12 Byrom Street, 1992. Member, General Synod 1995. Judge, Court of Appeal, Isle of Man, 1997. Diocesan Chancellor: Carlisle, 2003; Manchester, 2004. WW.

TAYLEUR, Charles William
Born 1837. Eldest son of William Houlbrooke Tayleur of Torquay. Trinity College, Cambridge. AAS. L. 28 May 1861. Call 6 June 1864. No address, 1876-1933. Not in 1934 Law List. Foster.

TAYLOR, Charles
I. 26 January 1891. ETC. 29 July 1891. Prop. Gully QC. Sec. Hughes. 2 Dr Johnson's Buildings, 1892-1895; 11 New Square, 1896-1902; 23 Old Square, 1903-1913. No chambers address, 1914-1949. Not in 1950 Law List.

TAYLOR, David Christopher
Born 12 September 1975, Cheshire. St Ambrose College; HMC Grammar School for Boys; Liverpool John Moores University, LLB. L. 8 October 1998. Solicitors' offices in Chester & Manchester, August 1998-January 2001. ETC. March 2001. Prop. David Turner QC. Sec. Simon Holder. Circuit Junior, 2002-2003. India Buildings, Water Street, Liverpool, January 2001.

TAYLOR, Francis Willis
Born 1847. Eldest son of Francis Taylor of Manchester, merchant. University College, Oxford, MA. AAS. I. 14 November 1868. Call 6 June 1872. ETC. 27 March 1876. Prop. Hopwood QC. Sec. Kinghorn. Commerce Chambers, Lord Street, Liverpool, 1876-1880. Registrar, Liverpool District of Lancs. Chancery Court, 9 Cook Street, Liverpool, 1880-1914. No address, 1915-1925. Not in 1926 Law List. Foster.

TAYLOR, Helga June
G. November 1952. Liverpool Chambers; 24 Dale Street, 1952-1955; 36 Dale Street, 1956-1960; 9 Rumford Street, 1961-1973; Fruit Exchange, Victoria Street, 1974-1984. Ceased practice, 1985. Door tenant, Chavasse Court.

*** TAYLOR, His Honour Judge Henry Gawan**
Born 16 December 1855. Died 9 December 1928 aged 72. Trinity Hall, Cambridge, BA; London University, LLB. L. 17 November 1882. North Eastern Circuit based in Newcastle -upon-Tyne, 1882-1912. County Court Judge, Circuit 3, (Lancashire & Cumberland), 1912-1928. WW. Foster.

TAYLOR, Herbert
Born 1909. Elder and surviving son of John Fielding Taylor of Oldham. B.Com., FCII. Insurance official when AAS. M. 28 April 1939. Call 17 November 1942. c/o Royal Insurance Co Ltd, 1 North John Street, Liverpool, 1942-1964. Not in 1965 Law List.

TAYLOR, Jean
G. 23 July 1998. ETC. 6 April 2000. Prop. Jonathan Foster QC. Sec. Beverly Lunt. Kingsgate Chambers, 9-21 Princess Street, Manchester, 2000.

TAYLOR, John Francis
Born 1855. 3rd son of John Taylor of Sligo. Trinity College, Dublin. AAS. M. 5 June 1880. Readmitted 24 November 1888. Call 18 June 1890. Irish Bar, 1882. ETC. 31 March 1892. Prop. McCall QC. Sec. Mulholland. No address, 1891-1897. 1 Dr Johnson's Building, 1898-1902. Not in 1903 Law List.

TAYLOR, Jonathan Ford
Born 12 June 1968 Blackpool. Cousin of Elaine Kellett-Bowman, barrister & MEP. Arnolds School, Blackpool, 1973-1986; Reading University, LLB. M. November 1991. ETC. December 1991. Prop. David Harris QC. Sec. Judith Daley. Circuit Junior, 1995. Same Liverpool Chambers; 3rd floor, Peel House, Harrington Street, September 1991-1997; India Buildings, Water Street, 12.1.1998.

TAYLOR, Julian Richard
Born 14 October 1962 Manchester. Winchester College; Bristol University, LLB. AAS. M. 15 January 1985. Call 24 July 1986. ETC. 1986. Prop. Benet Hytner QC. Sec. Peter Openshaw. Same Manchester Chambers; 2 Old Bank Street, 1986-1991; Peel Court Chambers, 45 Hardman Street, 1992.

TAYLOR, Julie
Born 24 April 1964, Blackpool. Married to John Taylor, solicitor. Fleetwood Grammar School. Solicitors' clerk with; Ingham Clegg & Crowther, 1980-1985 and John Budd & Co, 1985-1991. Lancashire Polytechnic, LLB. I. November 1992. ETC. 17 December 1992. Prop. Keith Goddard QC. Sec. Simon Newell. 15 Winckley Square, Preston, 1992.

TAYLOR, Kenneth John (His Honour Judge Kenneth Taylor)
Born 29 March 1929. Died 20 June 1995 aged 66. William Hulme's Grammar School, Manchester; Manchester University, LLB. AAS. M. 8 January 1948. Call 26 January 1951. ETC. 1951. Pupilmaster, John Addleshaw. Manchester Chambers; 3 St James's Square, 1951-1966; Ship Canal House, King Street, 1967-1973; 4th floor Astley House, Quay Street, 1974-1977 (Head of Chambers). Recorder 1972. Circuit Judge, 1977-1995. Resident Judge, Stoke-on-Trent. Obituaries; Times, June 1995; Birmingham Post, 21 June 1995; The Sentinel, 20 June 1995. Tributes at Stafford Law Courts, 20 June 1995 (Judge Allardice/ Mr Elsom) Transcript in Circuit Records. WW.

TAYLOR, Margaret Sylvia (nee Parry)
G. November 1954. Oriel Chambers, 14 Water Street, Liverpool, 1967-1968. Legal Assistant rising to Senior Legal Assistant at the Board of Trade, 1969-1974. Not in 1975 Law List.

TAYLOR, (Michael) Paul
Born 24 October 1957 Orrell. St John Rigby Grammar School; Leeds University, LLB. G. November 1985. Crown Prosecution Service, 1986-1991. ETC. 1991. Prop. Anthony Gee QC. Sec. Clement Goldstone. 28 St John Street, Manchester, 1991-2002. Exchange Chambers, 2002.

TAYLOR, His Honour (Ralph) Ivor QC
Born 26 October 1927. Stand Grammar School, Whitfield. Royal Air Force, 1945. Manchester University. G. January 1951. ETC early 1951. Pupilmasters, Henry Burton & Godfrey Heilpern. Manchester Chambers; 60 King Street, 1951-1960; 47 Peter Street, 1961-1973. Standing Counsel to Inland Revenue, Northern Circuit, 1969-1973. Recorder 1972-1976. Silk 1973. 5 Essex Court, 1973-1976. Circuit Judge, 1976-1994. Sat as a deputy to 1999. President, Manchester & District Medico Legal Society, 1974-1975. Governor, Royal Manchester Childrens' Hospital and Member, Management Committee, Salford Hospital, 1967-1970. WW.

TAYLOR, Roger Nicholas
BA (Oxon). I. July 1973. 2 Booth Street, Manchester, 1975-1976. No chambers address, 1977-1983. Not in 1984 Law List.

TAYLOR, Samuel QC
Born 8 March 1821. Died 26 November 1896 aged 75. 2nd son of Thomas Taylor of Manchester. Rugby; Brasenose College, Oxford, BA 1843, MA 1846. AAS. I. 22 November 1842. 1 Elm Court, 1848. 4 St James's Square, Manchester, 1876-1890. No address, 1891-1896. Deputy Recorder of Manchester, 1874-1896.

TAYLOR, Samuel junior
Born 4 July 1859. Eldest son of late Samuel Taylor of Eccleston Hall, Lancs. Trinity College, Cambridge, BA 1882. Late Lt., 3rd Btn, South Lancs. Regt. AAS. I. 11 October 1880. Call 7 May 1884. ETC. 17 July 1884. Prop. Smyly. Sec. Henry. 13 King's Bench Walk, 1885; 3 Dr Johnson's Buildings, 1886-1892. No address, 1893-1935. Not in 1936 Law List. Foster.

TAYLOR, Stephen James
Born 1844. Eldest son of William Taylor of Hazlehead, Yorks. AAS. L. 19 May 1866. Call 30 April 1869. ETC. 17 July 1869. Prop. Holker QC. Sec. Crompton. 33 Westgate Street, Newcastle-on-Tyne, 1876-1895. Conveyancer. No address, 1896-1920. Not in 1921 Law List. Foster.

TAYLOR, William
G. 13 May 1908. ETC. 1 March 1909. Prop. Landon KC. Sec. Cunliffe. Manchester Chambers; 22 Booth Street, 1909-1910; 78 King Street, 1911-1954. No address, 1955-1962. Not in 1963 Law List.

TAYLOR, Sir William Francis Kyffin GBE., KC., DL. (Rt. Hon. Baron Maenan of Ellesmere)

Singleton J, Lord Mayor Alderman Lancashire, Shawcross, Lord Maenan, Fraser Harrison, Scott LJ, Morris J, Sellers J. Adelphi Hotel, 17 July 1948.

Born 9 July 1854 Liverpool. Died 22 September 1951 aged 97. Eldest son of Ven. William Francis Taylor, DD., formerly Vicar of St Chrysostom, Everton and Archdeacon of Liverpool. Liverpool College; Exeter College, Oxford, BA. AAS. I. 29 January 1875. Call 7 May 1879; Bencher 1905; Treasurer 1926; Master of the Garden, 1927. ETC. 31 July 1879. Prop. Hopwood QC. Sec. William Rann Kennedy. Liverpool Chambers; 7 Commerce Chambers, Lord Street, 1879-1889; Bristowe Chambers, 8 Harrington Street, 1889-1892; 13 Harrington Street, 1893-1895. Silk 1895. London Chambers; 1 Pump Court, 1885-1889; 1 Garden Court, 1889-1892; 2 Mitre Court Buildings, 1893-1894; 1 Harcourt Buildings, 1895-1897; 4 Harcourt Buildings, 1898-1941; 3 Hare Court, 1942-1945; 2 Dr Johnson's Buildings, 1946-1951. Recorder of Bolton, 1901-1903. Judge of Appeal, Isle of Man, 1918-1921. Presiding

Judge, Liverpool Court of Passage, 1903-1948. Chairman, Shropshire Quarter Sessions, 1927-1947. Railway and Canal Commissioner, 1930. Publications; (Joint author), the Law Affecting the Contract of Affreightment, KBE, 1918, GBE, 1929. DL & JP, Shropshire. WW.

I have in the Circuit Records: A record of the speeches given on 22 March 1930 by the Rt. Hon. Gordon, Baron Hewart of Bury (Lord Chief Justice) and Lord Maenan at a dinner to mark Lord Maenan attaining 50 years membership of the Circuit. A record of the speeches of Lord Justice Scott and Sir Hartley Shawcross at a dinner given by past and present practitioners of the Liverpool Court of Passage, at the Adelphi Hotel, Liverpool on 17 July 1948.

I often heard it said of Lord Maenan by local solicitors and managing clerks that the Court of Appeal reversed him once only but the House of Lords quickly corrected that error. Whether or not it is true, it indicates the regard in which he was held by the Liverpool practitioners. According to the 1997 edition of the Guinness Book of Records, Lord Maenan holds the record of the greatest age at which a British Judge has sat; 93 years and 9 months. His memory was preserved by his Inn when in 1957 Francis Taylor Building in the Temple was completed. In "Political Adventure", Lord Kilmuir writes:

> One reason why the standard was high in Liverpool was the existence of the Court of Passage, This is a Court with unlimited jurisdiction in amount, but with a geographical limit of the City and Port of Liverpool. Charles Russell, the first Lord Russell of Killowen,had come down and practised in the Court, although he was not a local, and those I have mentioned as my predecessors and contemporaries at the Bar had been trained in it. We had the immense advantage in my generation of being trained by Sir Francis Kyffin-Taylor. By one of those accidents of judicial patronage he failed to become a High Court Judge. I heard F E Smith say afterwards in his own way, 'The only mistake I made as Lord Chancellor was not appointing Taylor a judge, but I made the not unnatural error of thinking he was too old.' Horridge had been made a judge after his sensational defeat of Balfour in the General Election of 1906. Taylor had missed his turn and F. E. had failed to put things right. But what a wonderful judge he was! No slipshod argument, no careless word, no irrelevant cross-examination got away without either a word from him which we all feared, not so much because it was a reprimand but because we loved him so much, or else the arching of his mouth, which was quite enough to pull someone back into the proper line of the case.

In "Life Sentence", Lord Shawcross spoke in similar glowing terms:

> My first case in Liverpool was an affair before Mr Registrar Cripps of the Court of Passage. This was a local but historical court with unlimited civil jurisdiction, and much civil litigation went there rather than to the High Court. It was presided over by perhaps the most distinguished judge I have known, Sir Francis Kyffin Taylor, who later became Lord Maenan. He was a gentleman of the old school and a great lawyer, and he taught me all I know of the art and responsibility of advocacy.

TEHRANI, Christopher

LLB. I. November 1990. Manchester Chambers; 211 Deansgate, 1993-1994; 38 King Street West, 1995. 2nd floor, 8 King's Bench Walk, 1996.

TELFER-SMOLLETT, Charles Edward Drummond

Father of Major-General Alexander Telfer-Smollett, Lieut-Governor of Guernsey. I. 26 January 1887. Commerce Chambers, Lord Street, Liverpool, 1892-1896. No address, 1897-1940. Lieut.Col., 1903. Not in 1941 Law List.

TEMKIN, David Jeremy

Born 5 September 1972, Liverpool. Brother-in-law of Ian Harris qv. King David High School, Liverpool; St Catherine's College, Oxford, BA. Secondary school history teacher, 1995-1997. I. 27 July 2000. ETC. December 2000. Prop. Michael Shorrock QC. Sec. Andrew Long. Circuit Junior, 2003. Peel Court Chambers, 45 Hardman Street, Manchester, 2000. The Times Newspaper/Thompson Holidays' Young Travel Writer of the Year, 2000. Drummer in Jazz/Dance Band.

TEMKIN, Sefton David

G. July 1952. 78 King Street, Manchester, 1956-1959. 5 New Square, 1953-1968. No address, 1969-1971. Not in 1972 Law List.

TEMPLE, Eleanor Louise

Born 5 November 1976 Keighley. Guiseley School; St John's College, University of Durham, LLB. I. July 2000. ETC. December 2000. Prop. Peter Winston Smith QC. Sec. Lesley Anderson. Pupilmasters, Stephen Pritchett and Lesley Anderson. King's Chambers, 40 King Street, Manchester, October 2000.

TEMPLE, Ernest Sanderson MBE., QC (His Honour Sir Sanderson Temple MBE., QC)

(RB)

Born 23 May 1921 Westmorland. Died 7 August 1999 aged 78. Son of Ernest Temple, senior partner of Temple & Bargh, solicitors of Kendal. Father of Simon Temple qv. Kendal School; Queen's College, Oxford, MA. Served in the Border Regiment in India and Burma rising to Lieutenant-Colonel (despatches, 1945 and MBE, 1946). G. January 1943. ETC. 1946. Pupilmaster, Edmund Rowson. Manchester Chambers; 26 King Street, 1946-1961; 60 King Street, 1962-1977 (Head of Chambers). Deputy Recorder of Salford, 1962-1965. Member, Bar Council, 1965. Deputy Chairman, Agricultural Land Tribunal (Northern), 1966-1969. Deputy Chairman, Westmorland Quarter Sessions, 1967-1969 (Chairman, 1969-1971). Silk 1969. Crown Court Recorder, 1972-1977. Circuit Judge, 1977-1991. Honorary Recorder of Kendal, 1972-1991; Liverpool, 1978-1991; Lancaster, 1987-1999. First Honorary Citizen of Kendal, 24 March 1992.

Chairman: Arnside/Silverdale Landscape Trust, 1987-1999; North West Area Point to Point Association, 1987-1999. President, British Harness Racing Club, 1991-1999. Joint Master, Vale of Lune Hunt, 1963-1985. Hon. FICW. Kt. 1988. Retirement Tributes at Liverpool Law Courts, 20 December 1991 (Judge Paterson / J J Rowe QC). WW.

Obituaries; Liverpool Daily Post, 10 August 1999; Daily Telegraph, 12 August 1999; Times, 28 August 1999; "In Brief" Issue 11, October 1999 (Judge David Lynch). Tributes; Preston Law Courts, 9 August 1999 (Judge Openshaw QC / Roderick Carus QC); Liverpool Law Courts, 10 August 1999 (Judge David Clarke QC/ William Waldron QC).

I have dedicated this Directory to Sandy. I first saw him in action in a jury trial in St George' Hall in 1969. He had just taken silk. He held the jury in a spell using elegant words and phrases of a bygone age. We were fortunate in Liverpool to have him as our Recorder for 14 years and we got to know him very well. If a man had to go to prison then to prison he would go but Sandy would try to avoid that course if at all possible. In this regard he saw himself as a disciple of Charles Henry Hopwood QC, the Recorder of Liverpool, 1886-1904, dubbed "Hopwood the Good" by the Humanitarian League for his compassionate approach to sentencing. I have spoken of Sandy's mastery of the English language. Here is an extract from his summing up on 23 March 1980 in a case of affray at the Beresford Arms public house in Liverpool 8. Having reminded the jury of a remark made earlier by Cunningham, who defended, that the officer in charge of the case was then engaged in diving on the German Grand Fleet in Scapa Flow Sandy continued his summing up thus:

"99 years ago, amongst ships of the Royal Navy which bombarded Alexandria, was HMS Condor. She was commanded by Charles William de la Poer Beresford. 3 years later he went to the relief of General Gordon up the Nile. He entered Parliament, and continued to serve in the Royal Navy until 1911. He remained a member of Parliament until 1916, by which time he had become an Admiral and was created Baron Beresford of Melammeh and Curraghmae, in the County of Wexford, from which his ancestors had come. His father was Earl of Waterford. Liverpool University conferred upon him an honorary Doctorate of Laws and some brewery has, I assume, honoured and perpetuated his name and memory by calling one of their houses in Liverpool by the name and presumably the sign of the "Beresford Arms." It stands at the present time in the road which also bears the Admiral's distinguished family name. He died in 1919, and no doubt it would disturb His Lordship's eternal rest were he to know that the house which bears his proud name is today, as the evidence shows, apparently frequently dubbed by its patrons 'The Nut House.'

There are many stories of Sandy. At the tributes in Liverpool on 10 August 1999, Bill Waldron QC reminded us of two:

Sandy settled a divorce petition which included the following allegation: "The Respondent absconded from matrimonial cohabitation and has not returned thereto." Came the inevitable request for further and better particulars of the precise manner of the absconding. Reply from Sandy, "Initially as a pedestrian and thereafter as a fare paying passenger on a Ribble omnibus."

Sandy often umpired coach and four driving competitions. He once sat behind HRH Prince Philip to assess his driving skills. On a difficult part of the course, the coach overturned spilling out all occupants. Prince Philip came to Sandy profuse in his apologies. "Don't worry, Sir", said Sandy. "I imagine your family's good for the damages."

James Fowler has reminded us of Sandy's skill in divorce proceedings in asking the leading question which gave the appearance of not being leading e.g. "Madam, please tell His Honour what it was your husband poured over your head out of the teapot."

He was a man of Westmorland whose roots were firmly in the North. Indeed on taking Silk in 1969, he broke tradition by insisting on remaining in his chambers in Manchester. He was heavily involved in countryside matters. I have his learned paper asserting public rights of way across Morecambe Bay. He wrote it in 1992 when Lancashire County Council questioned such rights.

Sandy had a great love for the Circuit and a feel for its history which he demonstrated on important public occasions such as the last sitting of Westmorland Quarter Sessions at the Town Hall, Kendal on 30 December 1971 when he said:

"My Lord Lieutenant, High Sheriff, Mr Ward QC., Ladies and Gentlemen. It is an ancient tradition and privilege that Chairmen of County Quarter Sessions sit with their hats on. It is a tradition and privilege which by operation of law in less than thirty hours time will become incapable of future further observance. It is therefore not inappropriate that that tradition should here be recognized and exercised, certainly for the last time in Westmorland and it may well be for the last time in England."

The Chairman donned a bowler hat and treated of those famous Circuiteers who had graced the County. "This Sessions lies on the Northern Circuit; that, if I may say so, is an undoubted advantage in itself. Throughout its long history, this Quarter Sessions has been well served by Counsel. To all who have carried their bag on the Northern Circuit, I, on behalf of the Magistracy of this County, express our gratitude. What a host they were, what a talented host they were. Think of them; Boswell, who was Recorder of Carlisle; Macaulay, who was to write "The Lays"; Park, who was later to become Baron Park and then Lord Wensleydale, Supreme Master of the Common Law; Scarlett who was to become Abinger; Brougham, who came here and when he left Kendal was cheered as he went on his way to defend a Queen's honour against a charge of adultery, and about his vigorous defence of Her you may read in that epic, written by another Westmerian, Roger Fulford's "Trial of Queen Caroline."

Think of Herschell and Frederick Smith (both Lord Chancellors). Merriman came here, later and for so long to be President of the Probate, Divorce & Admiralty Division.

More recently, David Patrick Maxwell Fyfe later to sit on the Woolsack; Hartley Shawcross, to be Attorney General; and even more recently, Fenton Atkinson later to be Lord Justice of Appeal; and Daniel Brabin, High Court Judge. I look back with pleasure to have been opposed in those benches not more than 14 years ago by John Widgery, who was later to become and now is Lord Chief Justice of England. All those this little Court, peripatetic between here and Appleby, it has heard and known them all."

(DL)

After he retired Sandy never lost his interest in the Circuit. He regularly attended Mess even when his health was failing. He would telephone me in the Judges' Dining Room at Liverpool at least once each week with what he called "intelligence" of long retired Circuiteers. We would have a leisurely lunch at Yealand Hall and then travel throughout Cumbria and North Lancashire debriefing Circuit ancients. Sandy was very proud that his son Simon had prospered on Circuit and that his pupil Christopher Rose had been appointed Lord Justice of Appeal and Vice President of the Court of Appeal, Criminal Division.

On 9 April 2000 I was privileged to represent the Circuit at Tabley House, near Knutsford at the running of the Sandy Temple Invitation, a two mile flat race to mark Sandy's contribution as North West Area, Point to Point, Chairman. Sandy's sister, Mrs Jennifer Harrison, presented the prizes to the winning owner and rider.

Sandy was no mean performer on horseback having won the Bar point to point in 1954, 1970 & 1971. He hit the national headlines in December 1994 when he purchased a "zonkey", a cross between a zebra and donkey and trained it to pull a trap through the lanes at Yealand Redmayne. A photograph of him being led in after his 1954 winning ride hangs in the Bar robing room in Liverpool. A portrait in oils of Sandy, commissioned by Liverpool Bench and Bar in 1988 on the occasion of his knighthood, spends six months with the Judges and six months with the Bar. In his twenty two years as Chairman of Quarter Sessions and Recorder of Liverpool Sandy paid many tributes to those Circuiteers who had "gone to join the great majority." I include him in the words he often used:

"We do not forget, and he never forgot, that he was a member of the Northern Circuit, thus he was one of us and we have lost one of ours."

TEMPLE, Leofric QC
Born 1819. Died 6 March 1891. 4th son of Christopher Temple QC of Hall Place, Surrey, Master of the Bench, brother of Christopher Temple, puisne judge, Ceylon. AAS. L. 22 November 1837. Call 4 May 1843; Bencher 1872. 1 Essex Court, 1848. 1 Tanfield Chambers, 1876-1878; 1 King's Bench Walk, 1879-1888. No address, 1889-1891. Deputy Recorder of Liverpool, 1879-1891. Recorder of Carlisle, 1880-1891. Publications; joint editor of Chitty, Precedents of Pleadings; Report of Criminal Appeal Cases, 1848-1851. Foster.

TEMPLE, Simon Ernest William
Born 6 September 1950, Halton, Lancaster. Son of His Honour Sir Sanderson Temple MBE., QC. Qv. and grandson of Ernest Temple, solicitor. St Bees School, Cumbria; Keele University, BA (Law & French). G. July 1977. Pupilmaster, Robert Johnson, 2nd floor, Queen Elizabeth Building. ETC. 1978. Pupilmasters, Arthur Stuttard & Jack Price. Same Manchester Chambers; 60 King Street/ Crown Square/ 9 St John Street, 1978.

TERRY, (Robert) Jeffrey
Born 10 September 1952, Stockport. William Hulme's Grammar School, Manchester; King's College, London, LLB; City University, LLM (Business Law). FCIArb, 1996., FSALS., CEOR Accredited Mediator, 1997. L. July 1976. Legal Advisor, Citizens Advice Bureau, 1976-1978. Pupilmaster, Colin Manning. 1 Garden Court, 1978-1989. 8 King Street, Manchester, 1989.

TETLOW, Christopher Bruce (His Honour Judge Tetlow)
Born 27 February 1943, Hale. Stowe School; Magdalene College, Cambridge, MA. AAS. M. 10 November 1965. Call May 1969. ETC. 1970. Pupilmaster, Martin Collins. Manchester Chambers; 601 Royal Exchange, 1970-1988; 8 King Street, 1989-1992. Recorder 1990. Circuit Judge 1992. WW.

THEEMAN, Frederick Walter
LLB (London). G. 25 April 1923. ETC. 11 July 1924. Prop. Atkinson KC. Sec. Clifton. 11 King's Bench Walk, 1924-1925; 2 Elm Court, 1926-1937. Resident Magistrate; Jamaica, 1937; Tanganyika Territory, 1938-1953. No address, 1954-1963. Not in 1964 Law List.

THIN, Harry Maxwell
Born 1866. 2nd son of James Thin of Brixton Rd, London. AAS. M. 11 January 1892. Call 23 April 1902. ETC. 5 July 1902. Prop. Page KC. Sec. William Russell. 5 Essex Court, 1903-1909; 4 Elm Court, 1910-1941. No address, 1942-1953. Not in 1954 Law List.

THOKA, Michael
Born 1 September 1960. City of London Polytechnic, BA. AAS. M. 13 September 1982. Call 22 November 1983. Member of Bar of Trinidad & Tobago. 2 Temple Gardens, 1992. Chavasse Court, 1993-1995. Sedan House, Stanley Place, Chester, 1996-1998. 18 Lloyds House, Lloyd Street, Manchester, 1999. Not in 2000 Bar Directory.

THOMAS, Alfred Patten (His Honour Judge Thomas)

Born 1860, Liverpool. Died 30 March 1931. 2nd son of William Thomas of Liverpool, accountant. Liverpool College. Merchants clerk, 1877-1884. University College, London, BA 1884; LLB 1886; LLD 1888. AAS. M. 15 November 1883. Call 7 July 1886. ETC. 31 July 1886. Prop. Bigham QC. Sec. Pickford. Liverpool Chambers; 13 Harrington Street, 1887-1895; 8 Harrington Street, 1896-1907. Professor of Commercial Law, Liverpool University, 1903-1907. Hon, Professor of International Law, Liverpool University. County Court Judge, Circuit 6, (Liverpool), March 1907-1931. WW.

THOMAS, Arthur Chilton

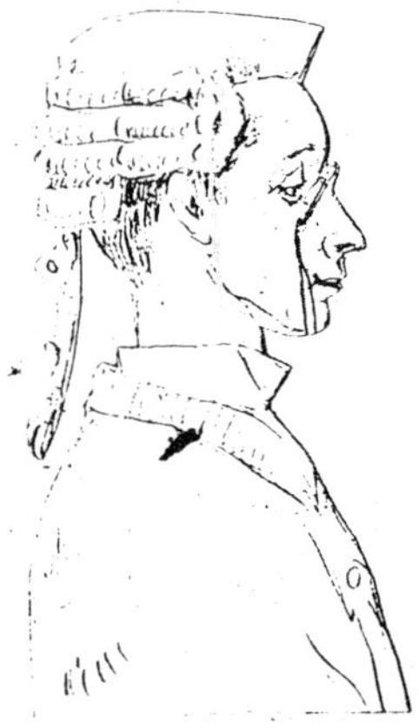

I. 7 July 1886. ETC. 4 August 1887. Prop. French QC. Sec. Walton. Liverpool Chambers; Marldon Chambers, 30 North John Street, 1889-1893; 7 Cook Street, 1894-1906. Not in 1907 Law List.

THOMAS, Brinley Whynford
LLB (London). G. November 1970. 43 King Street, Manchester 1972-1973. Not in 1974 Law List.

THOMAS, Clare Rachel
Born 27 May 1976, Blackburn. Daughter of Keith Thomas qv. Westholme School, Blackburn; Hull University, LLB. I. 8 October 1998. ETC. 1998. Prop. Keith Goddard QC. Sec. Keith Thomas. Pupilmaster, Pat Bailey. New Bailey Chambers, Preston, September 1998. Member; Pegasus Club; Equine Lawyers Association.

THOMAS, Ernest Chester
Born 26 October 1850 Birkenhead. Died 5 February 1892 aged 41. Eldest son of John Thomas of Merlock Hall, Ashton under Lyne. Manchester Grammar School; Trinity College, Oxford, BA, 1875. AAS. G. 7 May 1874. Call 29 June 1881. ETC. 18 July 1881. Prop. Crompton QC. Sec. Collins. 2 South Square, 1882; 13 South Square, 1883; 3 Harcourt Buildings, 1884-1890. No address, 1891-1892. Publications; Leading Cases in Constitutional Law, 1876; Leading Statutes Summarised for the Use of Students. He is best known as a librarian and bibliographer. His main claim to fame is his 1888 edition of "The Philobiblon of Richard de Bury, Treasurer and Chancellor of Edward III." He acted as honorary secretary of the Library Association for 12 years. DNB. Foster.

THOMAS, Gareth
Born 25 September Bangor. Rock Ferry High School; University College Wales at Aberystwyth, LLB. ACII. G. July 1977. ETC. 22 July 1986. Prop. Somerset Jones QC. Sec. Andrew Sander. Oriel Chambers, 5 Covent Garden/ 14 Water Street, Liverpool, 1986-1999. Arden Chambers, 27 John Street, WC1, 2000.

THOMAS, John William
Born 1887. Eldest son Richard Thomas of Manchester. Manchester University BSc. Electrical engineer. AAS. M. 20 November 1924. Call June 1927. 60 King Street, Manchester, 1930-1958. No address, 1959-1963. Not in 1964 Law List.

THOMAS, Keith Sinclair
Born 29 May 1946, Norwich. Father of Clare Rachel Thomas qv. King Edward VII School, Lytham; Merton College, Oxford, MA. G. July 1969. ETC. February 1970. Prop. Bingham QC. Sec. Anthony Jolly. Manchester Chambers; 36 St Ann Street, 1970-1980; 27 Byrom Street; Queen's Chambers, Manchester & Preston. New Bailey Chambers, Preston, 1998. Lecturer in Animal Welfare Law. Advisor to British Harness Racing Club (Chairman of Appeal). Member, Pegasus Club.

THOMAS, (Philip) Andrew
Liverpool University, LLB. G. November 1970. ETC. 1970. Pupilmaster, A D Pappworth. 3rd floor, 27 Dale Street, Liverpool, 1973-1978. Admitted as a solicitor, December 1981. Moved to Barnstable and later South Moulton. Died circa. 1989.

THOMPSON, George Rodie
Born 1846. 3rd son of Henry Thompson of Thingwall, near Liverpool. Trinity College, Cambridge, BA, 1870. AAS. I. 19 November 1868. Call. 26 January 1872. ETC. 11 March 1872. Prop. Pope QC. Sec. R G Williams. 6 Crown Office Row, 1876-1891. No address, 1892-1915. Not in 1916 Law List.

THOMPSON, Henry Bates
L. 17 November 1911. ETC. 30 January 1913. Prop. Rigby Swift KC. Sec. Riley. 5 Harrington Street, Liverpool, 1914-1915. No address, 1916-1919. Gresham Chambers, Wolverhampton. Oxford Circuit, 1920-1924. No address, 1925-1953. Not in 1954 Law List.

THOMPSON, Sir (Henry Francis) Herbert, 2nd Bt.
Born 2 April 1859. Died 26 May 1944 aged 85. Only son of Sir Henry Thompson MD., FRCS. Marlborough; Trinity College, Cambridge, BA, 1881. AAS. I. 18 November 1878. Call 26 January 1882. ETC. 25 January 1884. Prop. Gully

QC. Sec. Mellor. 12 King's Bench Walk, 1884-1887. No address, 1888-1940. Not in 1941 Law List. FBA, 1933, Hon, DLitt (Oxon); Fellow, University College, London. 2nd Bt., 1889. He took up, aged 40, his real life work, Egyptology and at the time of his death he was regarded as being among the first three or four Coptic scholars of his day. One of his many achievements was his editing, in 1924 of the earliest known papyrus manuscript of St John's Gospel which had been discovered in Egypt by J L Starkey. WW. DNB. Foster.

THOMPSON, James
Born 1858. 2nd son of James Thompson of Blackburn, cotton manufacturer. AAS. M. 31 January 1888. Call 29 June 1892. ETC. 8 March 1893. Prop. Addison QC. Sec. Parry. 4 Paper Buildings, 1893-1897. Not in 1898 Law List.

THOMPSON, James Gilbert
I. 26 January 1909. ETC. 1909. 25 Lord Street, Liverpool, 1914-1923. No address, 1924-1953. Not in 1954 Law List.

THOMPSON, John QC (The Hon. Mr Justice Thompson)
Born 16 December 1907 Glasgow. Died 11 July 1995 aged 87. Bellahouston Academy; Glasgow University, MA; Oriel College, Oxford, MA. AAS. M. 3 May 1929. Call 26 January 1933; Bencher 1961; Reader, Lent 1971; Treasurer 1978. ETC. 15 March 1933. Prop. Gorman KC. Sec. Cairns. 3 King's Bench Walk, 1933-1939; Farrars Building, 1940-1952. 1 Temple Gardens, 1953-1961. Vice-Chairman, Bar Council, 1960-1961. High Court Judge, Queen's Bench Division, 1961-1982. Kt. 1961. Publications; (ed with H R Rogers) Redgrave's Factories, Truck and Shops Acts. WW.

THOMPSON, John Bruce
I. 27 January 1930. No address, 1935-1963. Not in 1964 Law List.

THOMPSON, Jonathan Richard
Born 23 July 1967 Manchester. Manchester Grammar School; St John's College, Cambridge, MA (Law); Clare College, Cambridge, LLM (International Law). I. 16 October 1990. ETC. December 1990. Prop. J J Rowe QC. Sec. Tim Mort. 8 King Street, Manchester, 1990.

THOMPSON, Patrick Miles
Born 22 August 1968 Liverpool. St Edwards College, Liverpool; Manchester University, LLB. G. October 1990. ETC. November 1990. Prop. Keith Goddard QC. Sec. Monica Stalker. Queen's Chambers, 5 John Dalton Street, Manchester, 1990.

THOMPSON, Ruth Elizabeth Sophia
I. 27 January 1930. ETC. 1930. 5 Crown Office Row, 1930-1932 & 1938; 2 Paper Buildings, 1939-1941. No address, 1942-1963. Not in 1964 Law List.

THOMPSON, His Honour Thomas Perronet Edward
Born 4 May 1813. Died 25 August 1904 aged 91. Son of General Thomas Perronet Thompson MP. Beverley Grammar School; Queen's College, Cambridge, BA, 1835; MA, 1838. AAS. L. 20 April 1835. Call 22 November 1838. 21 Old Square, 1848. Recorder of Scarborough, January-March 1872. County Court Judge, Circuit 6, April 1872-1889. JP, Lancashire. Foster.

THOMPSON, William
Born 1852. 3rd son of late Alderman Thompson of Burnley, spinner and manufacturer. AAS. M. 26 January 1896. Call 17 November 1898. ETC. 23 February 1900. Prop. Shee QC. Sec. Shawcross. Manchester Chambers; 40 Kennedy Street, 1901-1908; 78 King Street, 1909-1930. No address, 1931-1938. Not in 1939 Law List.

THOMPSON, William Briggs
I. 29 June 1892. ETC. 13 February 1895. Prop. Shee QC. Sec. Sharpe. 4 Paper Buildings, 1896-1899; 2 Temple Gardens, 1900-1912; 4 Harcourt Buildings, 1913-1941. No chambers address, 1942-1962. Not in 1963 Law List.

THOMSON, Vanessa Elizabeth
Born Ashton under Lyne. Hulme Grammar School for Girls, Oldham; Liverpool University, LLB. L. 8 October 1998. ETC. 17 December 1998. Prop. Peter Birkett QC. Sec. Richard Heap. Pupilmaster, Deborah Lambert. Kenworthy's Chambers, 83 Bridge Street, Manchester, 1998.

THORESBY, Frederick
I. 17 November 1911. 2 Elm Court, 1918-1921. No address, 1922-1953. Not in 1954 Law List.

THORNBER, John Barker
I. 26 January 1876. York Assizes. Liverpool & Kirkdale Sessions. Not in 1877 Law List.

THORNE, Zöe Amanda
Born 18 July 1976, Chester. Darland High School, Rossett; Liverpool John Moores University, LLB. Storrar, Cowdry, Solicitors, Chester, June 1998-October 1999. L. 22 July 1999. ETC. 13 April 2000. Prop. David Turner QC. Sec. Paul Simpson. Pupilmaster Nigel Beeson. 14 Cook Street, Liverpool, October 1999.

THORPE, John Henry OBE., KC., MP.
Born 7 August 1887. Died 31 October 1944 aged 57. Father of (John) Jeremy Thorpe PC., MP., former Leader of the Liberal Party. Leatherhead; Trinity College, Oxford, BA 1909. I. 26 January 1911; Bencher 1941. ETC. 1 March 1911. Prop. Langdon KC. Sec. Hewart. Circuit Junior, Winter 1912. Served European War, 1914-1918; Captain 7th Btn., Manchester Regt (despatches, OBE). Legal Advisor to Military Government, Cologne, 1919. MP (U) Manchester, Rusholme, 1919-1923. 6 Crown Office Row, 1919-1921; Farrars Building, 1922-1927 & 1940-1944; 4 New Court, 1928-1939. Silk 1935. Recorder of Blackburn, 1925-1944. Deputy Chairman, Middlesex Quarter Sessions, 1941-1944. WW.

THRELFALL, Thomas
Born 31 December 1842. Died 3 February 1907 aged 64. Son of John Mayor Threlfall of Liverpool and Salford, brewer. AAS. I. 9 November 1865. Call 17 November 1868. ETC. 8 March 1869. Prop. Jones QC. Sec. Pickering QC. 3 Tanfield Close, 1876-1889; 1 Temple Gardens, 1890-1891; 2 Paper Buildings, 1892-1898. No address, 1899-1907. Chairman; Management Committee, Royal Academy of Music; Associated Board of Royal Academy of Music and Royal College of Music for local examinations; Threlfall's Brewery. WW.

THURLOW, Henry Frederick
I. 6 June 1866. 5 Brick Court, 1876-1878. Not in 1879 Law List.

THURSBY, Sir John (Omerod Scarlett) 2nd Bt.
Born 27 April 1861. Died 26 December 1920 aged 59. Eton; Trinity College, Cambridge, BA. L. 17 November 1891. ETC. 16 February 1906. Prop. Sanderson KC. Sec. Wingate Saul. No address, 1906-1920. High Sheriff, Lancashire, 1905. President; British Chess Federation; Burnley Chamber of Commerce. Steward, Jockey Club. DL., JP., 2nd Bt., 1887. WW.

TIDSWELL, Richard Thomas
Born March 1830. 3rd and youngest son of Thomas Earnshaw Tidswell of Withington. Worcester College, Oxford, MA. AAS. I. 19 January 1854. Call 26 January 1857. 5 Harrington Street, Liverpool, 1876-1881. 1 Brick Court, 1876-1881 & 1891-1894. 8 Fig Tree Court, 1882-1888; 11 Old Square 1890; No address, 1895-1903. Not in 1904 Law List. Additional revising barrister, 1868. Deputy County Court Judge, 1876-1877. Publications; Innkeepers' Legal Guide; (Joint author) Divorce Law & Practice. Foster.

TIMMIS, Thomas Sutton
Father of Captain Shirley Sutton Timmins, High Sheriff of Buckinghamshire, 1941-1942. L. 26 January 1891. ETC. 29 July 1891. Prop. French QC. Sec. Fort. 2 Paper Buildings, 1892-1930. No address, 1931-1933. Not in 1934 Law List.

TINDALL, Paul Robert
Born 17 February 1975. Nottingham University, BA; Bristol University, LLM. G. 14 October 1999. ETC. 14 December 1999. Prop. David Berkley QC. Sec. Stephen Pritchett. Pupilmasters, Lesley Anderson & Stephen Pritchett. Manchester Chambers; 40 King Street, September 1999-May 2001; St James Chambers, June 2001.

TIPPING, Joseph Henry Atherton
MA., LLM. L. 28 January 1889. ETC. 8 March 1890. Prop. Ambrose QC. Sec. Scott. 48 King Street, Manchester, 1892-1909. No address, 1910-1940. Not in 1941 Law List.

TITCHMARSH, Katherine Elizabeth
Born 11 April 1976 Liverpool. Birkenhead High School GPDST; Sheffield University, LLB. L. 26 November 1998. ETC. December 1998. Prop. David Harris QC. Sec. Louis Browne. 8th floor, India Buildings, Water Street, Liverpool, 2000.

TOAL, David John
Born 12 September 1965 Manchester. St Bede's College, Manchester; Urmston Grammar School for Boys; Liverpool Polytechnic (now Liverpool John Moores University), LLB. G. February 1990. ETC. 1990. Prop. David Poole QC. Sec. Paul McDonald. Manchester Chambers; 33 King Street West, 1991-1994; Old Colony House, 6 South King Street, 1995-2000; Peel Court Chambers, 45 Hardman Street, 2000.

TOBIN, His Honour Sir Alfred Aspinall KC

Born 26 December 1855. Died 30 November 1939 aged 83. 3rd son of James Asinall Tobin of Eastham House, Cheshire, merchant. Rugby School; University College,

Oxford, BA 1878. AAS. M. 8 May 1876. Call 9 June 1880; Bencher 1912; Reader, Lent 1923; Treasurer 1930. ETC. 27 July 1880. Prop. Gully QC. Sec. Kennedy. Circuit Junior, Winter 1881. Stephenson's Chambers, 15 Lord Street, Liverpool, 1880-1903. Silk 1903. 8 King's Bench Walk, 1903-1910; 2 Plowden Buildings, 1911-1915. MP (U) Preston, 1910-1915. Recorder of Salford, 1904-1915. County Court Judge, 1915-1935; Hereford & Shropshire, 1915 1919; Westminster, 1919-1935. Kt., 1919. He defended Crippen in 1910. See Notable British Trials; The Trial of Hawley Harvey Crippen edited by Filson Young, William Hodge & Co Ltd, 1920. WW.

TODD, David Cargill
I. 17 November 1933. ETC. 30 January 1934. Prop. Singleton KC. Sec. Ashworth. Circuit Junior, Summer 1934. Goldsmith Building, 1934-1940. No address, 1941-1963. Not in 1964 Law List.

TOMLINSON, Frederic Philip
I. 17 November 1871. ETC. 6 March 1873. Prop. Aspinall QC. Sec. Kemplay QC. Circuit Junior, Summer 1873. 4 Harcourt Buildings, 1876-1879; 1 Temple Gardens, 1880-1883. Not in 1884 Law List.

TOMLINSON, Sir Thomas Symonds
Born 2 November 1877. Died 18 April 1965 aged 87. Marlborough; Trinity College, Cambridge. I. 28 January 1901. ETC. 29 January 1902. Prop. Shee KC. Sec. Mellor. 4 Paper Buildings, 1902-1907. Zanzibar; Town Magistrate, 1907; Assistant Judge, 1911; Judge, 1919; Chief Justice, 1925-1928. Kt. 1925. JP. Lancashire. WW.

TOMLINSON, Sir William Edward Murray First Bt., MP.
Born 4 August 1838, Heysham. Died 17 December 1912 aged 74. Westminster; Christ Church, Oxford, MA. AAS. I. 30 March 1860. Call 26 January 1865; Bencher. ETC. 5 August 1868. Prop. Manisty QC. Sec. Jones QC. 4 Old Buildings, 1876-1878; 6 Old Buildings, 1879; 12 Old Buildings, 1880-1910; 7 Stone Buildings, 1911-1912. Law Reporter in Vice Chancellor Malins Court. Retired major; 1st vol. Btn., Loyal North Lancashire Regt and Hon Col. MP (C) Preston, 1882-1906. First Bt., 1902. VD., DL., FRGS., JP, Lancashire. WW.

TORR, John Berry QC
Born November 1817. Died 9 March 1878 aged 60. 5th son of Rev. John Torr of Devon. Father of James Fenning Torr of Middle Temple. Bideford Grammar School; studied medicine in London & Paris. AAS. M. 18 January 1847. Call 3 May 1850; Bencher 1874. 1 Essex Court, 1876-1878. Silk 1872. Recorder of Hastings. Editor and part owner of Salopian Journal & Court Gazette.

TOWNEND, His Honour John Philip
Born 20 June 1935. St Joseph's College, Blackpool; Manchester University, LLB. National Service, 1957-1958. G. June 1959. Law Lecturer, Gibson & Weldon, 1960-1965. Assistant Legal Advisor, Pilkington Bros., 1966-1968. Legal Advisor, Honeywell Ltd & G Dew Ltd., 1968-1970. ETC. 1970. Prop. Benet Hytner QC. Sec. George Carman. Manchester Chambers; 47 Peter Street, 1970-1974; 12th floor, Sunlight House, Quay Street, 1975-1979; 28 St John Street, 1980-1987. Recorder, 1985-1987. Circuit Judge, 1987-2001. WW.

TOWNLEY, Frank
Born 3 May 1924. Died 8 March 1982 aged 57. Chorley Grammar School; Wigan Mining & Technical College. Wigan Coal Corporation, 1940-1942. Royal Navy, 1943-1946. King's College, London, LLB, 1949. G. January 1950. ETC. 1951. No chambers address recorded. Customs & Excise, 1952-1977 (Legal Assistant rising to Principal Assistant Solicitor) WW.

TRACY FORSTER, Jane Elizabeth
Born 17 August 1953, Liverpool. Bellerive School, Liverpool; Liverpool University, LLB. I. July 1975. ETC. 1975. Ground floor, Peel House, Harrington Street, Liverpool, 1975-1986. 13 King's Bench Walk, & 32 Beaumont Street, Oxford, 1987. Midland & Oxford Circuit.

TRAVERS, Daniel Grant
Born 24 June 1976, Chester. The King's School, Chester; Leeds Metropolitan University, LLB. L. 14 October 1999. ETC. 16 December 1999. Prop. Henry Globe QC. Sec. Gordon Cole. Exchange Chambers, Pearl Assurance House, Derby Square, Liverpool, September 1999.

TRAVERS, David
Born 19 March 1957. University College, London, LLB., LLM. AKC. AAS. M. 23 January 1978. Call 23 July 1981. Manchester Chambers; 26 Cross Street, 1983-1987; Kenworthy's Buildings, 83 Bridge Street, 1988. 3 Fountains Court, Steelhouse Lane, Birmingham, 1989. Midland & Oxford Circuit.

TREBLE, Paul Joseph
Born 27 September 1963 Herts. Sponne School, Towcester; Sheffield University, BSc. Geology Researcher, 1985-1988. Marketing, 1988-1992. L. November 1994. ETC. 13 December 1994. Prop. Roger Farley QC. Sec. Beverly Lunt. Kingsgate Chambers, 51-53 South King Street, Manchester, 1994.

TREVELYAN, Walter Blackett
Born 17 March 1821. 2nd and eldest surviving son of Raleigh Trevelyan of Nether Witton, Northumberland. Gonville & Caius College, Cambridge, BA, 1844. AAS. L. 18 November 1844. Admitted M. 10 April 1858. Call. M. 30 April 1858; Bencher 3 November 1882: Reader, Lent 1892. 9 King's Bench Walk, 1876-1891; 1 Hare Court, 1892-1894. Not in 1895 Law List. Foster.

TRIGGER, Ian James Campbell (His Honour Judge Trigger)
Born 16 November 1943. Ruthin School; University College Wales, Aberystwyth, LLB; Downing College, Cambridge MA., LLM. Lecturer in Law, UWIST 1967-1970. I. November 1970. ETC 1970. Oriel Chambers, 5 Covent Gardens/ 14 Water Street, Liverpool, 1970-1993. Recorder 1990-1993. Circuit Judge, 1993. President, Mental Health Review Tribunal, 1995. Chairman, Immigration Appeal Tribunal, 1999. WW.

TRIPPIER, Lady Ruth
Born 9 August 1955. Married to Sir David (Austin) Trippier. The Hulme Grammar School for Girls; Manchester University, LLB. Mediator, Academy of Experts. G. July 1978. ETC. 3 April 1979. Prop. George Carman QC. Sec. Stephen Grime. Dean's Court Chambers, Cumberland House/ 24 St John Street, Manchester, 1978.

TRISTRAM, Thomas Henry QC
Born 25 September 1825. Died 8 March 1912 aged 86. Durham School; Lincoln College, Oxford, BCL, 1850; DCL 1854. Admitted I and called to the Bar of Doctors' Commons, 2 November 1855. 1 King's Bench Walk, 1876-1883; 12 King's Bench Walk, 1884-1912. Chancellor of the Dioceses of London, Hereford, Ripon, Wakefield and Chichester. Commissary General of the Diocese and City of Canterbury. Silk 1881. Publications; Treatise on the Contentious Probate Practice in the High Court of Justice. WW.

TROTMAN, Timothy Oliver
Born 30 April 1960, Nottingham. Nottingham High School; St John's College, Cambridge, MA. AAS. M. 17 June 1981. Call 28 July 1983. ETC. 1984. Pupilmaster, Raymond Machell. Dean's Court Chambers, Cumberland House/ 24 St John Street, Manchester, 1983.

TROTTER, Henry John MP
Born 1836. 2nd son of William Trotter of Bishop Auckland, Co. Durham. Oriel College, Oxford, MA 1863. FSA. Lately a Lieutenant, 2nd West Yorkshire Yeoman Cavalry. JP., DL., County Durham. 2 Harcourt Buildings, 1876-1888. Not in 1889 Law List. Foster.

TROTTER, His Honour Richard Stanley

Born 29 June 1903. Died 17 January 1974 aged 70. Shrewsbury School; Magdalen College, Oxford, BA, 1925. I. 26 January 1926. ETC. 16 June 1926. Prop. Singleton KC. Sec. Lynskey. Liverpool Chambers; 3 Cook Street, 1929-1930; 43 Castle Street, 1932-1941; 34 Castle Street, 1942-1946; 24 Dale Street, 1947-1958; 27 Dale Street, 1954-1961. Circuit Judge (formerly County Court Judge) at Liverpool, 1961-1973. WW.

TUCKER, Nicholas James
Born 23 February 1970 Portsmouth. Clare College, Cambridge, BA. I. October 1993. ETC 1993. Lincoln House Chambers, 1 Brazennose Street, Manchester, 1996-1999. 17 Carlton Crescent, Southampton, 2000.

TUCKER, Paul Geoffrey
Born 6 March 1967 Scarborough. Raincliffe Comprehensive/ Scarborough 6th Form College; Selwyn College, Cambridge, MA. G. November 1990. ETC. December 1990. Prop. Janet Smith QC. Sec. Nick Braslavsky. Pupilmasters, Philip Raynor & Nick Braslavsky. King's Chambers, 40 King Street, Manchester, 1990-.

TUNSTILL, Harry Knowles
Born 1858. Eldest son of Joseph Tunstill of Burnley. Trinity College, Oxford, MA. AAS. I. 6 November 1880. I. 17 November 1883. ETC. 25 January 1884. Prop. Smyly. Sec. Shee. 6 King's Bench Walk, 1884-1886; Goldsmith Building, 1887-1893; 3 Dr Johnson's Buildings, 1894-1896; 1 King's Bench Walk, 1897; 3 Dr Johnson's Building, 1898-1913. No address, 1914-1940. Not in 1941 Law List.

TURNER, Charles William I.
I. 30 April 1870. ETC. 1 August 1873. Prop. Herschell QC. Sec. Roscoe. 3 Harcourt Buildings, 1876-1880. Not in 1881 Law List.

TURNER, David Andrew QC
Born 6 March 1947, Southport. Nephew of Joseph Turner qv. King George V School, Southport; Queen's College, Cambridge, MA., LLM. G. February 1971; Bencher 2001. ETC. Easter 1971. Prop. David McNeill QC. Sec. Joseph Turner. Same Liverpool Chambers; 606 The Corn Exchange, 1971-1981; Exchange Chambers at; 1 Exchange Flags, 1982-1991; and at Pearl Assurance House, Derby Square, 1992-. Assistant Recorder 1987. Recorder 1990-. Silk 1991. Leading Counsel for the defence of Thompson ,one of two eleven year olds, charged with the murder of the child James Bulger. Cambridge Footlights, 1967-1969. Founder member of 'Prestons' the Northern Circuit Band which gives its services for charitable causes.

TURNER, Frederick Bancroft
Born 1889. Died 20 August 1966. 2nd son of Robert Turner of Manchester, solicitor. Manchester University, BA., LLB. AAS. M. 22 November 1911. Call 12 June 1918. ETC 1920. Circuit Junior, Winter 1920. Manchester Chambers; 60 King Street, 1920-1935; 43 King Street, 1936-1938. Stipendiary Magistrate, Salford, 1938-1951. WW.

TURNER, Harold Pilkington
Born 1868. Only son of David Turner of Bamford, merchant. Manchester University. AAS. M. 18 November 1892. Call 26 June 1895. ETC. July 1895. Prop. Ambrose QC. Sec. Sutton. 60 King Street, Manchester, 1896-1908. No address, 1909-1949. Not in 1950 Law List.

TURNER, Joseph
Born 1911. Died November 1986 aged 75. Wigan Grammar School; Liverpool University, LLM. Articles with Arthur Smith and Broadie Smith of Wigan. Admitted as a solicitor. Lecturer, London School of Economics. Served in Royal Air Force, 1941-1945. Joe's pupil, Bill George, tells me that Joe distinguished himself by being mentioned in despatches and by never being issued with a sidearm. Apparently he was issued with a "deficiency chit" which he placed in his holster for production when threatened. Joe defended at court martial a man who had been sending home in packages a complete dispatch riders motor bike. He was caught trying to smuggle out the sidecar. He was acquitted. G. May 1946. Lecturer, later Queen Victoria Professor of Law and Dean of the Law Faculty at Liverpool University retiring from teaching in the mid 50's to concentrate on his practice at the Liverpool Chancery Bar. He was a pupil of Edward Ackroyd at 15 Union Court later moving to 20 North John Street where in due course he was Head of Chambers and the foremost chancery practitioner in Liverpool. I recall instructing him in the early 1960's to obtain an injuction to prevent "Lulu and the Luvvers" from appearing at a restaurant in the basement of the Royal Liver Building as it was thought that wild music would cause young people to lose control and damage the premises. In 1962 Joe was persuaded to undertake for six years the post of part time Professor of Property Law at Manchester University. Joe retired from practice and teaching in 1977. He had sat as a Deputy High Court Judge. His pupils included Graham Routledge, Judges; Michael O'Donoghue, David Gilliland QC and William George; his nephew David Turner QC and Mr. Justice Peter Smith.

TURNER, Mark George QC
Born 27 August 1959 Kendal. Holme Park School; Sedbergh School; Queen's College, Oxford, BA. G. July 1981. Bencher Grays Inn 2004. ETC. 1982. Prop. Keith Goddard QC. Sec. Raymond Machell. Dean's Court Chambers at; Crown Square and at 24 St John Street, Manchester, 1981. Treasurer, Grays Inn Circuit Committee, 1996. Assistant Recorder 1998. Silk 1998. Recorder 2000. Publications; Occupational Rhinitis, 1998; Occupational Asthma, 1998. WW.

*** TURNER, His Honour Judge Richard Whitbourn**
Born 2 November 1867. Died 20 November 1932 aged 65. Merchant Taylors' School; Trinity Hall Cambridge, BA. M. 26 January 1891. 1 Brick Court (South Eastern Circuit). Acting Secretary to Lord Reading, Lord Chief Justice, 1915-1919. County Court Judge, Circuit 11, (Burnley, Nelson & Colne), October 1919-1923; Circuit 18, (Nottingham), 1923-1928; Circuit 34, (Middlesex & Uxbridge), 1928-1932. Athletic Blue; won 100 yards & 440 yards (Oxford v Cambridge) 1889. WW. Foster.

TWEEDALE, James Arthur
Born 1861. 3rd son of James Frederick Tweedale of Oldham, solicitor. Trinity College, Cambridge, BA., LLB, 1884. AAS. I. 2 July 1881. Call 26 June 1884. ETC. 27 January 1885. Prop. Henn Collins QC. Sec. J M Yates. Manchester Chambers; 4 St James's Square, 1886-1895; 78 King Street, 1896-1913. Lancs. Chancery Court. Not in 1914 Law List. Foster.

TWEEDSMUIR, First Baron (See John Buchan)

TYLER, Edward Lawson Griffin
MA (Oxon). L. July 1962. Cholmeley Scholar. Liverpool Chambers; 20 North John Street, 1962-1964; 14 Cook Street, 1965-1976 when he emigrated to Australia. Publications; Editor, Fisher & Lightfoot, Law of Mortgages; joint editor of Crossley Vaines on Personal Propery and of Tyler on Family Provision.

TYLER, Paula Margot
Born 1961. University College, London BSc. Solicitor, 1989-1997. M. 27 November 1997. ETC. 16 December 1997. Prop. Lindsey Kushner QC. Sec. Lesley Newton. Young Street Chambers, Manchester 1997.

TYNDALE, Geoffrey Clifford QC
Born 19 February 1887. Died 6 May 1966 aged 79. Epsom College; Keble College, Oxford, BA (History) 1909: MA 1932; LLB (London). I. 27 January 1913. ETC. 29 January 1914; Bencher 1950. Prop. Greer QC. Sec. Davies. 5 Pump Court, 1914-1915; 1 Dr Johnson's Building, 1917-1920; 5 Pump Court, 1921-1966. Silk 1943. WW.

TYRELL, Richard Mark Lawrence
Born 15 November 1953 Middlesbrough. Acklam Hall Grammar School, Middlesbrough; Sheffield University, LLB. Solicitor, 1978, CPS, 1979-1987. Legal Department ICI, 1987-1992. Partner, Hammond Suddards, 1992-1993. G. November 1993. ETC. 21 December 1993. 28 St John Street, Manchester November 1993. (now St Johns Buildings Chambers). Part time Chairman, Employment Tribunals, July 2001.

TYTHCOTT, Elisabeth Claire
Born 5 July 1966 Norwich. Hewett School; University of Huddersfield, LLB (Business Law). I. November 1989. Chesham Amalgamations & Investments Ltd., September 1989-April 1991. ETC. December 1991. Prop. Rodney Klevan QC. Sec. James Bonney. 18 St John Street, Manchester, May 1991.

U

UFF, David Charles
Born 15 September 1958 Great Yarmouth. Haslingden Grammar School; Brunel University, LLB. G. July 1981. ETC. 1981. Prop. Keith Goddard QC. Sec. Barry Woodward. Manchester Chambers; 67 Princess Street, which moved to Hollins Chambers, 64a Bridge Street which merged and moved to Cobden House Chambers, Quay Street, 1981-February 2001; Merchant Chambers, 1 North Parade, Parsonage Gardens February 2001-2004; (merger with St Johns Buildings Chambers, 2004.)

ULLSWATER, First Viscount (See James William Lowther)

UNSWORTH, Sir Edgar (Ignatius Godfrey) CMG
Born 18 April 1906. Stonyhurst College; Manchester University, LLB. G. 14 May 1930. ETC. 9 July 1930. Prop. Derbyshire KC. Sec. Jolly. 3 St James's Square, Manchester, 1930-1937. Crown Counsel: Nigeria, 1937; Northern Rhodesia, 1942; Solicitor General: N. Rhodesia, 1946; Federation of Malaya, 1949. Attorney General: N. Rhodesia, 1951-1956; Nigeria, 1956-1960. Federal Justice, Supreme Court, Nigeria, 1960-1962. Chief Justice: Nyasaland, 1962-1964; Gibraltar, 1965-1976. Justice of Appeal, Gibraltar, 1976-1981. Publications; Laws of Northern Rhodesia (revised edition), 1949. Q.C (N Rhodesia), 1951. CMG. 1954. Kt. 1963. WW.

UNSWORTH, Ian Stephen
Born 7 December 1966, Billinge. Married to Michelle Unsworth, solicitor. Ashton Grammar School; three years in commerce. Huddersfield University, LLB. L. 13 October 1992. Wales & Chester Circuit, October 1993. Pupilmaster, Thomas Teague. 40 King Street, Chester, September 1992-December 1999. ETC. December 2000. Prop. Tim Holroyde QC. Sec. James Rae. Exchange Chambers, Pearl Assurance House, Derby Square, Liverpool, December 1999.

UNWIN, Reginald
I. 27 January 1902. ETC. 25 July 1902. Prop. Shee KC. Sec. Evans. 40 King Street, Manchester, 1902-1913. No address, 1914-1944. Not in 1945 Law List.

URQUHART, His Honour Peter William Gordon

(TM)

Born 18 March 1934. Liverpool College; Peterhouse, Cambridge, MA., LLB. Admitted as a solicitor, October 1960 having been articled to J Stuart Crook who was also the Wallasey coroner. Lovell, White & King, Serjeants' Inn, 1960-1962; Bremner Sons & Corlett, Liverpool, 1962-1984; Urquhart, Knight & Broughton, Liverpool, 1984-1992. Member: Lord Chancellor's Legal Aid Advisory Committee, 1974-1980: Equal Opportunities Commission, 1977-1982. Recorder, 1990-1992. Circuit Judge, 21 July 1992-12 July 2001. Retirement tributes at Liverpool Law Courts, 12 July 2001 (Judge David Clarke QC/ Edward Bartley-Jones QC/ E Goldsmith) Transcript in Circuit Records. WW.

USHER, Neil Morris
Born 23 March 1964. Derby Grammar, Bury; Hull University, BA. National Youth Officer, Labour Party, 1988-1991. M. October 1993. ETC. 1993. Prop. Roger Farley QC. Sec. Patrick Cassidy. Manchester Chambers; Kenworthy's Buildings, 83 Bridge Street, October 1993-October 1998; Lincoln House Chambers, 1 Brazennose Street, October 1998.

V

VAINES, James Crossley
LLM. G June 1942. Liverpool Chambers; 3 Cook Street, 1946-1958; The Temple, Dale Street, 1959-1969; 606 The Corn Exchange, 1970-1976. Lecturer in Law, Liverpool University. Publications; Personal Property. Not in 1977 Law List.

VALENTINE, Justin
Born 31 July 1966, Bristol. King Edward VI High School, Stafford; University of Swansea, BSc(Econ); Bristol University, MSc. Dip Law. Research Assistant, University of Kent at Canterbury, 1995-1997. M. October 1999. Pupillage in Temple; pupilmasters, Richard Roberts (Lamb Building) and Joe Smouha (Essex Court Chambers). ETC. December 2000. Prop. Peter Birkett QC. Sec. John Lambert. Manchester Chambers; Old Colony House, October, 2000-July 2001; Derby Square Chambers, Merchants Court, July 2001-2003; 6 South King Street, Manchester, 2003.

VARDON, Richard Stanhope
Birmingham University, LLB. G. November 1985. ETC. 17 December 1985. Prop. John Burke QC. Sec. Jonathan Geake. 18 St John Street, Manchester, 1985.

VAUGHAN, Francis Martin
I. 26 January 1927. ETC. 30 January 1929. Prop. Singleton KC. Sec. Nelson. 4 Elm Court, 1929-1937; 2 Harcourt Buildings, 1939-1940. No address, 1941-1953. Not in 1954 Law List.

VAUGHAN, Simon Peter
LLB (Nottingham); LLM (London). G. November 1989. Manchester Chambers; Manchester House Chambers, 18-22 Bridge Street, 1994-2000; 8 King Street, 2001.

VAUGHAN-DAVIES, Geoffrey
MA (Cantab). I. June 1953. Manchester Chambers; 28 Kennedy Street, 1953-1956; 25 Bow Lane, 1959-1970. Deputy Assistant Registrar of Criminal Appeals, 1971-1978. Assistant Director (Legal Division), later, Assistant Solicitor, Office of Fair Trading, Chancery Lane, EC4., 1979-1990. No professional address, 1991.

VERDIN, Sir Richard Bertram OBE
Born 1912. Died 16 August 1978. Harrow; Magdalen College, Oxford. Served with Cheshire Yeomanry, 1931-1954; Lt. Col., 1952; TD. I. June 1938. ETC. 1 February 1939. Prop. Pritchard KC. Sec. Selwyn Lloyd. Liverpool Chambers; 27 Lord Street, 1939-1946; 49 Castle Street, 1947-1958. Liason Officer, Ministry of Agriculture, Fisheries & Food, 1958-1971. Chairman, County Agricultural Executive Committee. President, Landowners Country Association, 1959-1961. Deputy Chairman, Meat & Livestock Commission, 1967-1973. OBE 1954. DL., JP. Kt. 1962. Publications; History of the Cheshire (Earl of Chester's) Yeomanry, 1971. WW.

VERNON, Stephen (See Stephen Vernon Smith)

VICKERS, Guy Julian Courtney
Born 10 February 1964, Newcastle upon Tyne. Malvern College, Corpus Christi, Oxford, BA. AAS. M. 15 December 1983. Call 25 November 1986. ETC. November 1987. Pupilmasters, Charles Machin and Richard Anelay. 1 King's Bench Walk, 1986-1987. Lecturer, Manchester University, 1987-1989. Manchester Chambers; Bridge Street Chambers, 72 Bridge Street, 1987-1989; 28 St John Street, 1989-2002; Exchange Chambers, 2002.

*** VINCENT, Robin Anthony CBE**

(DL)

Born 27 February 1944. King's School Worcester. Clerk, Worcester Quarter Sessions, 1962-1970. Thereafter posts with Worcester: Justices; Crown and County Courts. Principal Chief Clerk, Manchester Crown Court, 1982-1986. Head of Division, Lord Chancellor's Department, 1986-1989. Personnel Management, 1991-1993;. Judicial Appointments, 1993. Circuit Administrator, Northern Circuit, 1993-2001. Honorary Member of Circuit, 2001. Since his retirement in 2001, Robin has been putting his great experience to good use by helping the United Nations to set up courts overseas. A keen and able cricketer. WW.

VITTIC, Nick
LLB (Sussex). I. February 1992. ETC. 17 December 1992. Prop. Rodney Scholes QC. Sec. Paul Chambers. 38 King Street West, 1992-1993. Not in 1994 Bar Directory.

VOLLENWEIDER, Amiot Marcus Ellerton
Born 15 February 1976 Liverpool. Shrewsbury School; Birmingham University, BSc (Psychology); Manchester Metropolitan University, Dip. Law. G. 12 October 2000. ETC. December 2000. Prop. Peter Birkett QC. Sec. Anthony O'Donohoe. Chavasse Court, 24 Lord Street, Liverpool, 2000.

VOS, Andrew Mitchell
MA (Cantab). G. July 1978. ETC. 26 October 1978. Manchester Chambers; Lawrence Building, 2 Mount Street, 1981-1984; 3 St James's Square, 1985-1989. Legal Advisor, IBM, 1990-1994. UK Group Advisor, Sema Group UK Ltd, 1998-2000; Senior Negotiation Executive, Global Service, IBM 2001; Senior Consultant, Grosvenor Consultancy Services, 2002.

VOS, His Honour Geoffrey Michael
Born 18 February 1927. St Joseph's College, Blackpool; Gonville & Caius College, Cambridge, MA., LLB. G. June 1950. ETC. 1950. Pupilmaster, Cecil Henriques. Manchester Chambers; 2 Booth Street, 1950-1975; 13 Police Street, 1976-1978. Recorder, 1976-1978. Circuit Judge (North East) 1978-1994. WW.

VOS, Philip KC
Born 1891. Died 6 January 1948. Owen's School; London School of Economics; Caius College, Cambridge, BA, 1913; Scholar and Research Student in Economics, 1909-1914. Served European War; Lt., Norfolk Reg't (Croix de Guerre avec palme); Assistant Director of Priority, War Office, 1917-1918. I. 8 June 1921. ETC. 14 June 1921. Prop. Oulton. Sec. Rice Jones.7 King's Bench Walk, 1921-1928; 5 Paper Buildings, 1929; 2 Dr Johnson's Building, 1930-1932; 4 Crown Office Row, 1933-1940; 2 Hare Court, 1941-1948. Silk 1937. Publications; The Necessity for Capitalism, 1929; The Betrayal of the Nation, 1931. WW.

VYVYAN, R. Henry S.
I. 30 April 1858. 12 King's Bench Walk, 1877-1881. Not in 1882 Law List.

W

WACHTEL, David Michael Peter
L. July 1975. Liverpool Chambers; Queen Insurance Building "D", Queen Avenue, 13 Castle Street, 1978-1979; Queen Avenue, 16 Castle Street, 1980. Not in 1981 Bar Directory.

WADDINGTON, David Charles QC., MP (Baron Waddington of Read in the County of Lancashire)
Born 2 August 1929. Sedbergh; Hertford College, Oxford, BA; Hon Fellow 1998. G. June 1951; Bencher 1985. 2nd. Lt., Royal Lancers, 1951-1953. 3 St James's Square, Manchester, 1954-1971. Silk 1971. 2 Pump Court, 1971-1992. MP (C); Nelson & Colne, 1968-1974; Clitheroe 1979-1983; Ribble Valley, 1983-1990. Minister of State, Home Office, 1983-1987. PC. 1987. Home

Secretary, 1989-1990. Baron 1990. Lord Privy Seal & Leader of the House of Lords, 1990-1992. DL., Lancs., 1991. Governor & Commander in Chief of Bermuda, 1992-1997. GCVO, 1994. WW.

WAINWRIGHT, William
Born 1853. 2nd surviving son of Richard Wainwright of Liverpool. AAS. M. 10 January 1885. Call 17 November 1887. ETC. 24 February 1888. Prop. Kennedy QC. Sec. Stewart. No address, 1890-1940. Not in 1941 Law List.

WAITE, William Thomas
G. 10 May 1876. 7 Crown Office Row, 1877-1878; 1 Cloisters, 1879; 89 Chancery Lane, 1880; 77 Chancery Lane, 1881-1882; 3 Essex Court, 1883. Not in 1884 Law List.

WALDRON, William Francis
Born 27 October 1957 Liverpool. Son of William Henry Waldron QC. qv. St Edward's College, Liverpool. University College of Wales, Cardiff, LLB. C.B.C. Independent Radio Company, Cardiff, 1980-1985. G. November 1986. ETC. 16 December 1986. Prop. William Waldron QC. Sec. Denis Clark. Circuit Junior, Summer 1989. Circuit Secretary. Exchange Chambers; 1 Exchange Flags/ Pearl Assurance House, Derby Square 1986. Assistant Recorder, 1999. Recorder, 2000.
Licensed to fly aeroplanes and plays the guitar.

WALDRON, William Henry QC
Born 11 March 1927 at 43 Lambeth Rd, Liverpool 4. Father of William Francis Waldron qv. St Francis Xaviers College, Liverpool. Royal Air Force, 1945-1948. Articled Clerk, 1948-1953. Solicitor in Liverpool, June 1953-1969. Sydney Haworth, 41 North John Street, 1953-1955; Swancott, Morgan, Hannaford & Taggart of the same address, 1956-1962; Herbert J Davies, Berthen & Munro, 36 Dale Street, 1963-1969. G. February 1970. ETC. February 1970. Sec. Robert Leech. 2nd floor, 14 Water Street, Liverpool, 1970-1982. Silk 1982. Goldsmith Building, 1982-1986. Exchange Chambers; 1 Exchange Flags/ Pearl Assurance House, Liverpool, 1986-2003. Contested (Lab) Liverpool Garston in 1966 and halved the Conservative majority. Assistant Recorder 1978. Recorder 1981-1997 (aged 70). Hon. Fellow, Liverpool John Moores University, 2003. Bill retired on a high note. In June 2003, he persuaded the Court of Appeal on the Liverpool Cameo Murder reference that despite the fact that his client Connolly had pleaded guilty in 1950 to robbery rather than risk being hanged for murder (as happened to his co-accused Kelly) the conviction should be quashed. Statements made by crucial prosecution witnesses, which proved conclusively that those witnesses had lied on important issues, had not been disclosed to the defence.

WALKER, James George
I. July 1886. ETC. 24 January 1887. Prop. Kennedy QC. Sec. Shee. 4 Harcourt Buildings, 1888-1892. No address, 1893-1923. Not in 1924 Law List.

WALKER, Jane
Born 21 May 1965, Oldham. Failsworth School; Balliol College, Oxford, MA. AAS. M. 18 February 1986. Call 23 July 1987. ETC 1988. Pupilmaster, Leslie Hull. Crown Square Chambers, 1 Deans Court, 1987-1993; 9 St John Street, 1994-1999; 28 St John Street, April 1999. (now St Johns Buildings Chambers). Lecturer, Bar Vocational Course, Manchester Metropolitan University, 1999-2000.

WALKER, John Ewart
I. 11 June 1902. ETC. 5 February 1903. Prop. Pickford KC. Sec. Frank Dodd. 1 Paper Buildings, 1937-1940; New Court, 1941-1956. No address, 1957-1962. Not in 1963 Law List.

WALKER, Margaret Jean
LLB (Exeter). I. July 1965. Manchester Chambers; 2 Booth Street 1973-1974; 13 Police Street 1976-1977. Not in 1978 Law List.

WALKER, Thomas
1. 25 April 1888. ETC. 16 July 1888. Prop. Henn Collins QC. Sec. C A Russell. York Chambers, Brazennose Street, Manchester, 1889-1893. Not in 1894 Law List.

WALL, Jacqueline Francoise
Born 26 September 1964, Ormskirk. Married to Peter Murphy, solicitor. Merchant Taylors' School for Girls; Lancaster University, LLB. G. July 1986. ETC. 16 December 1986. Pupilmaster, Inge Bernstein. Liverpool Chambers; 14 Castle Street, 1986-1996; 3rd floor, Peel House, Harrington Street, 1996-1998; chambers moved to India Buildings, Water Street, 12.1.1998.

★ WALL, Nicholas (Peter Rathbone) QC. (Rt. Hon. Lord Justice Wall)

(DL)

Born 14 March 1945. Dulwich College; Trinity College, Cambridge, MA; President, Cambridge Union Society, 1967. G. 1969; Bencher 1993. Silk 1988. Assistant Recorder, 1988. Recorder, 1990. High Court Judge, Family Division, 1993-2004. Kt. 1993. Liason Judge, Northern Circuit, 1996-2001. Honorary Member of Circuit, 2001. Judge of the Employment Appeal Tribunal, 2001-2004. Lord Justice of Appeal 12.1.2004. PC. 2004. Book collector, binder & restorer. WW.

WALLACE, Adrian Robert
Born 20 January 1958 Winchester. Trinity Hall, Cambridge, BA. M. July 1979. ETC./ December 1979. Same Manchester Chambers; 2 Old Bank Street, 1979-1991; Peel Court Chambers, 45 Hardman Street, 1992.

WALLACE, George Williamson CB
Born 1862. Died 28 November 1952. Fettes College, Edinburgh; Corpus Christi College, Oxford. I. 3 July 1889. ETC. 20 March 1890. Prop. Barnes QC. Sec. Fort. 6 King's Bench Walk, 1891-1941. Charity Commission, 1893-1932; Assistant Commissioner, 1893; Commissioner, 1921; Chief Commissioner for England & Wales, 1924-1932. CB. 1929. WW.

WALLIS, Hon. John Edward
Born 1821. Eldest son of Edward Wallis of London, father of John Edward Power Wallis qv. AAS. I. 9 December 1841. Call 29 January 1847. 5 Paper Buildings, 1876-1879. Consular Service; Consul at Port Said, 1879-1882. Judge of the International Court of First Instance, Port Said and later Judge in the Mixed Tribunals at Alexandria, 1883-1887. Not in 1888 Law List.

WALLIS, Rt. Hon. Sir John Edward Power
Born 1 November 1861. Died 8 June 1946 aged 84. Eldest son of John Edward Wallis qv. Downside College, Bath; London University, MA. AAS. M. 11 January 1883. Call 26 January 1886. ETC. 1 August 1887. Prop. French QC. Sec. Walton. 1 Garden Court, 1888-1891; 2 Mitre Court Buildings, 1892-1895; 1 Harcourt Buildings, 1896-1900. Reader in Constitutional Law at Inns of Court, 1892-1897. Madras: Advocate-General, 1900-1907; Puisne Judge, 1907-1914; Vice-Chancellor, University, 1908-1916; Chief Justice, 1914-1921. Member of Judicial Committee of the Privy Council, 1926-1946. Publications; edited vols. 4-8 of State Trials for State Trials Committee. Kt. 1912, PC. 1926.

WALLWORK, Bernard Graham Frank
Born 9 March 1953, Farnworth, Bolton. Only son of Frank Wallwork, dental surgeon. Canon Slade Grammar School, Bolton; Pembroke College, Oxford, MA. AAS. M. 10 March 1975. Call 23 November 1976. ETC. 1977. Prop. Michael Lever QC. Sec. Donald Hart. Manchester Chambers; Pupillage, 18 St John Street, March 1977-Summer 1998; Ship Canal House, King Street/ 2 Old Bank Street, 1978-1992; 28 St John Street, 1992. (now St Johns Buildings Chambers). Assistant Recorder 1997. Recorder 2000.

WALMESLEY, Oswald
L. 28 January 1889. ETC. 20 March 1890. Prop. Gully QC. Sec. Walton. 2 Stone Buildings, 1891-1910. Not in 1911 Law List.

WALMESLEY, His Honour Allan QC.
Born 22 July 1889. Died 25 September 1963 aged 74. Son of George Doxon Walmesley of Darwen, Lancs. Blackburn Grammar School; Sedbergh. Solicitor (Cliffords Inn prize), 1910. L. 26 January 1923 (Certificate of Honour). London University, LLB, 1923. ETC. 1923. 78 King Street, Manchester, 1923-1948. Silk 1948. County Court Judge, 1948-1962. (Circuit 5, 1948-1953; Circuit 4, 1954-1962) WW.

WALMISLEY, Lisa Catherine
Newcastle University, LLB. M. 27 July 2000. ETC. 18 December 2001. Prop. Edward Bartley Jones QC. Sec. Kelly Pennifer. Pupilmaster, John McCarroll. Exchange Chambers, Pearl Assurance House, Derby Square, Liverpool, 2000.

WALMSLEY, Air Commodore John Banks CBE., DFC., QC.
Born 9 October 1896. Died 28 October 1976 aged 80. Shrewsbury School; Sandhurst. Pilot in RFC & RAF in European War 1914-1918; DFC. 1918; Greek Military Cross. G. 17 November 1924. ETC. 28 January 1925. Prop. Singleton KC. Sec. Hodgson. 5 Harrington Street, Liverpool 1924-1933. Office of Judge Advocate-General 1933-1948. (Middle East, 1936-1940). CBE, 1946. Director of Legal Services, Air Ministry 1948-1957. Silk 1955. WW.

WALMSLEY, Robert Benjamin
Born 1860. Eldest son of George William Walmsley of Church. Lancs. Trinity College, Cambridge, BA, 1881. AAS. I. 10 January 1882. I. 17 November 1884. ETC. 30 January 1885. Prop. Ambrose QC. Sec. French. 5 Paper Buildings, 1884-1885; Goldsmith Buildings, 1886-1894. No address, 1895-1940. Not in 1941 Law List. Foster.

WALSH, Leslie
Born 6 May 1903. Died 4 January 1986 aged 82. Son of Rt. Hon. Stephen Walsh MP. Wigan Grammar School; Victoria University, Manchester, LLB; St John's College, Oxford BCL. G. 29 June 1927. ETC. 1927. Manchester Chambers; 6 St Ann's Passage, 1927-1931; 60 King Street, 1932-1935; 43 King Street, 1936-1951. Royal Air Force, 1940-1945. Stipendiary Magistrate; Salford, 1951-1974; Greater Manchester, 1974-1975. Hon. MA, Salford, 1976. WW.

WALSH, Martin
Born 7 January 1955. St Bede's College, Manchester; University of Manchester, LLB; College of Law, Chester. Solicitor, 1979-1990; partner, Cyril Morris Arkwright of Bolton, 1980-1990. G. November 1990. ETC. December 1990. Prop. Michael Shorrock QC. Sec. Bernard Lever. Peel Court Chambers, 45 Hardman Street, Manchester, 1990-. Recorder, 2000-.

WALTER, Arthur James KC
Born 25 February 1862. Died 9 April 1919 aged 57. Son of James Walker of West Dulwich, solicitor. Dulwich College (Governor); London University, LLB. I. 17 November 1885; Bencher 1914. ETC. 20 July 1887. Prop. Henn Collins QC. Sec. Neill. 1 Pump Court, 1887-1888; 3 Crown Office Row, 1889-1908; Silk 1906; 5 Fig Tree Court, 1909-1919. Specialist in patent trade mark and technical litigation. A founder member of the Automobile Club. WW.

WALTER, Hubert Conrad
MA., LLB (Cantab). G. May 1952. ETC. 1953. 4 Clarence Street, Manchester, 1953-1954. 7 Gray's Inn Square, 1955; 11 New Square, 1956-1964; 2 South Square, 1965-1968; 2 Gray's Inn Square, 1969-1970. Not in 1971 Law List.

WALTON, Joseph QC (The Hon. Mr Justice Walton)

Born 25 September 1845, Liverpool. Died 12 August 1910aged 64. Eldest son of Joseph Walton of Fazakerley, Lancs, father of Philip Walton qv. St Francis Xaviers College, Salisbury Street, Liverpool; Stonyhurst; London University, BA (mental & moral science), 1865. AAS. L. 20 November 1865. Call 16 November 1868; Bencher 1896. ETC. 29 March 1869. Prop. Jones QC. Sec. C Russell. Liverpool Chambers; 6 Cook Street, 1878-1883; 13 Harrington Street, 1884-1885. 1 Garden Court, 1886-1901. Counsel to the Jockey Club. Silk 1892. Commercial & shipping cases. Recorder of Wigan, 1895-1901. Chairman, Bar Council, 1899. High Court Judge, Queen's Bench Division, 1901-1910. Kt. 1901. President, Medico-Legal Society, 1905. Yachtsman and frequent winner at the Oxford and Aldeburgh regattas. Publications; Practice and Procedure at the Court of Common Pleas at Lancaster, 1870. He was one of the editors of the "White Book" for 1884 & 1885. WW. DNB. Obituary, Times, 15 August 1910.

WALTON, Philip
son of Mr Justice Walton qv. L. 19 November 19 November 1906. ETC. 25 February 1907. Prop. Pickford KC. Sec. Rutledge. Liverpool Chambers; 25 Lord Street, 1907; 13 Harrington Street, 1908-1910; 15 Lord Street, 1911. 1 Brick Court, 1912. Singapore, 1912-1914. Gunner, Singapore Volunteer Artillery. Died 18 February 1915. Buried, Kranji War Cemetery, Singapore. Grave Reference 37.G.24. The cemetery in 22 kilometres north of Singapore on the north side of Singapore Island overlooking the Straits of Johore. Information supplied by the Commonwealth War Graves Commission.

WANNOP, Arthur Edward
Born 1849. 2nd son of Rev. William Wannop of Burscough, Lancs. Brasenose College, Oxford, MA., BCL 1872. AAS. I. 8 November 1869. Call 26 January 1876. ETC. 31 July 1886. Prop. Henn Collins QC. Sec. Lumb. Law Court Chambers, Chancery Lane WC., 1877-1878. Liverpool Chambers; North Crescent Chambers, 3 Lord Street, 1879; Wason's Building, 4 Harrington Street, 1880-1883; Equity Chambers, 9 Cook Street, 1884-1902. No address, 1903-1935. Not in 1936 Law List.

WARD, Andrew
Born 25 August 1977, Salford. Son of Monica Stalker qv and District Judge (Magistrates Court) Peter Ward. St Bede's College, Manchester; Jesus College, Oxford, BA., BCL. M. 27 July 2000. ETC. December 2000. Prop. Keith Armitage QC. Sec. Digby Jess. 8 King Street, Manchester, October 2000.

WARD, John
MA (Oxon). L. April 1948. ETC. 1948. Manchester Chambers; 4 Clarence Street, 1953-1954; 78 King Street, 1955-1958; 2 Booth Street, 1959-1975; 13 Police Street, 1976-1979; 6th floor, Arkwright House, Parsonage Gardens, 1980-1983; 20 St Mary's Parsonage, 1984-1991. Preston Chambers; 1 Chapel Street, 1948-1951; 10a Winckley Square, 1953-1957. No chambers address, 1992. Died August 1999.

WARD, His Honour Roy Livingstone QC
Born 31 August 1925. Died 24 June 2003 aged 77. 4th son of David Livingstone Ward of Preston, Presbyterian Minister, married, 1972, Barbara Anne Brockbank qv (marr. diss.). Taunton School; Served, RAF, 1943-1947 (commnd., 1945). Pembroke College, Cambridge, BA. AAS. M. 4 November 1947. Call 3 May 1950. ETC. 1950. Liverpool Chambers; 27 Lord Street, 1950-1959; 10 Water Street, 1960-1969; 2nd floor, Oriel Chambers, 14 Water Street, 1970-1972. Silk 1972. Goldsmith Building, 1972-1979. Recorder, 1972-1979. Circuit Judge (Worcs.), 1979-1994. WW.

WARD, Rt. Hon. William Dudley MP
Born 1877. Died 11 November 1946. Eton; Trinity College, Cambridge. (rowed three years in Cambridge eight). I. 15 June 1904. ETC. February 1905. Prop. Tobin KC. Sec. F E Smith. 1 Hare Court, 1905-1906; 4 Elm Court, 1907-1910. No chambers address, 1911-1946. MP (Co. L.), Southampton, 1906-1922. Treasurer of His Majesty's Household, 1901-1912; Vice-Chamberlain, 1917-1922. PC. 1922. WW.

WARE, William Augustine Hibbert
Born 1869. Only son of Titus Hibbert Ware of Bowden, Cheshire, barrister. University of London. AAS. M. 3 November 1891. Call 6 June 1894. ETC. 13 July 1894. Prop. Addison QC. Sec. McKeand. 60 King Street, Manchester, 1906-1908. Not in 1909 Law List.

WARNE, Peter Laurence
I. 1 November 1993. Hollis Whiteman Chambers, London, 1993-April 2002. ETC. 20 July 2002. Prop. James Pickup QC. Lincoln House Chambers, 1 Brazennose Street, Manchester, 2002.

WARNOCK, (Alastair) Robert (Lyon) (His Honour Judge Warnock)
Born 23 July 1953, Birkenhead. Sedbergh; University of East Anglia, BA (Economics & History). L. November 1977. ETC. 30 November 1978. Pupilmaster, Anne Downey. Circuit Junior, 1980. Liverpool Chambers; 54 Castle Street/ 14 Castle Street/ Atlantic Chambers, Cook Street, 1977-2003. Assistant Recorder 1995. Recorder 1999. Circuit Judge, 2003.

WARNOCK, Ceri Ailsa
Born 8 May 1970, Sale, Cheshire. Sale Girls' Grammar School; St Bede's College; University of Wales (Cardiff), LLB. G. October 1993. ETC. September 1994. Prop. Charles Bloom QC. Sec. Lesley Newton. Young Street Chambers, Manchester, 1993.

WARR, Henry Denny

Born 1843. Eldest son of George Winter Warr of 52 Upper Parliament Street, Liverpool, curate of St Saviours Church, Liverpool. Trinity Hall, Cambridge, MA, 1870. AAS. M. 2 November 1865. Call. 26 January 1871. ETC. 23 March 1871. Prop. Pickering QC. Sec. McConnell. 2 Paper Buildings, 1876-1894; 5 Paper Buildings, 1895-1899. No address, 1900-1921. Not in 1922 Law List. Common Law Lecturer to the Law Society, 1881-1882. Secretary to the City Liveries' Companies Commission. Foster.

WARREN, Henry Hatchell
I. 26 January 1877. ETC. 2 March 1877. Prop. Pope QC. Sec. Crompton. 2 Tanfield Court, 1877-1878; 1 Dr Johnson's Buildings, 1879-1880. Not in 1881 Law List.

WASON, Rt. Hon Eugene MP
Born 26 January 1846. Died 19 April 1927 aged 81. Son of Rigby Wason MP, Ipswich, father of Rigby Wason qv. Rugby; Wadham College, Oxford, BA, 1868; MA, 1870. AAS. M. 10 November 1865. Call 10 June 1870. ETC. 4 August 1870. Prop. Aspinall QC. Sec. Hosack. Disbarred in 1872 to enable him to become a solicitor in 1876. Struck off the Rolls so that he could be re-admitted to M. on 15 January 1886. 1 Garden Court, 1886-1891. No chambers address, 1886-1927. MP (L); South Ayrshire, 1885-1886, 1892-1895; Clackmannan & Kinross, 1899-1918. PC. 1907. DL., JP, Ayrshire. WW.

WASON, Rigby
Born 1873. Eldest son of Rt. Hon Eugene Wason qv. AAS. M. 28 February 1898. Call 11 June 1902. ETC. 1 July 1902. Prop. McCall KC. Sec. Tobin. 8 King's Bench Walk, 1903-1904. No address, 1906-1953. Not in 1954 Law List.

WATERHOUSE, Edward Kenneth
eldest son of Edward Waterhouse of Birkenhead, wharfinger. FCII. AAS. 7 December 1935. Call 17 November 1938. 1 North John Street, Liverpool (Offices of Royal Insurance Co Ltd), 1939-1952. No address, 1953. Not in 1954 Law List.

WATKINS, Peter William
MA., BCL. L. February 1952. Manchester Chambers; 4 Clarence Street, 1952-1982; Bridge Street Chambers, 72 Bridge Street, 1984-1997; Cobden House Chambers, 19 Quay Street, 1998-1999. Not in 2000 Bar Directory.

WATSON, Barbara Joan (Her Honour Judge Watson)
Born 13 October 1950. Nelson Grammar School; Southampton University, LLB, 1972. G. July 1973. ETC. 1973. Manchester Chambers; 36 St Ann Street, 1973-1975; 27 Byrom Street, 1981-1983. 14 later, 15 Winckley Square, Preston, 1983-2000. Lecturer in Law, Manchester Polytechnic, 1973-1980. Recorder, 1997-2000. Circuit Judge, Preston 20.12.2000. Honorary Recorder of Burnley 2004. WW.

WATSON, David Sidney
Born 11 December 1939 March, Cambridgeshire. King's School, Peterborough; Bristol University, LLB. G. July 1963. ETC. 1963. Prop. Edward Wooll QC. Sec. Henry Lachs. Liverpool Chambers; 27 Dale Street, 1963-1971. Solicitor, June 1972-1999; with Silverbeck & Co., Liverpool and with Lynskey & Dunning, Kirkby. Returned to the Bar in October 1999 at India Buildings Chambers, Water Street, Liverpool. Deputy District Judge, 1993.

WATSON, David William
15 August 1967, Durham. Married to Rachael Banks qv. Local schools in Chester-le-Street; Brunel University, LLB. AAS. M. 22 January 1988. Call 16 October 1990. 3 Temple Gardens (3rd floor), 1991-1997, pupilmaster, N Wilcox. ETC. 18 December 1997. Prop. Andrew Edis QC. Sec. Adrian Lyon. 14 Castle Street/ Atlantic Chambers, Cook Street, Liverpool, 1997.

WATSON, Dennis
Born 7 June 1963, Crosby. Brother in law of Richard Hunt qv. Uppingham; Leeds Polytechnic, BA (Law). I. July 1985. ETC. 12 December 1985. Prop. R J D Livesey QC. Sec. Heather Steel. Circuit Junior, 1988. Ground floor, Peel House, Harrington Street, Liverpool and now Lincoln House Chambers, 1 Brazennose Street, Manchester. Member, Northern Circuit Executive Committee. Recorder 2003.

WATSON, Joseph Stanley MBE., QC.
Born 13 September 1910. Died 30 March 1991 aged 80. Rossall School; Jesus College, Cambridge, MA. I. 17 November 1933; Bencher 1961. ETC. 20 January 1934. Prop. Goldie KC. Sec. Pritchard. Liverpool Chambers; 25 Castle Street, 1933-1939. War of 1939-1945; Major; received the surrender of Rhodes from General Wagener in 1945; Greek War Cross; MBE, 1946. 27 Lord Street, 1945-1946; 49 Castle Street, 1947-1955. Silk 1955. 1 Temple Gardens, 1955-1957; 4 Paper Buildings, 1958-1965. Recorder of Blackpool, 1961-1965. Social Security (formerly National Insurance) Commissioner, 1965-1985. WW.

WATSON, Sharon
Born 6 October 1965, Co. Durham. Ian Rumsey Comprehensive; University of East Anglia, BA (English Literature). M. November 1994. Pupilmaster, Colin Challinger. New Bailey Chambers, Preston.

WATSON, Thomas

Born 1830. Eldest son of Thomas Watson of St Helens, merchant. Glasgow University; London University, BA. AAS. L. 6 November 1857. Call 6 June 1861. 4 St James's Square, Manchester, 1876-1893. Not in 1894 Law List. Foster.

WATSON, Tom Bradley
Born 22 February 1966 Ormskirk. Liverpool College; University College North Wales at Bangor, BA; Keele University, MA; Dip. Law. I. October 1990. ETC. December 1990. Prop. Michael Maguire QC. Sec. Theresa Pepper. Same Liverpool Chambers; 2nd floor, Fruit Exchange, Victoria Street, October 1990-April 1991; Chavasse Court, 24 Lord Street, 1991.

WATSON, William Coleman
Born 1845. Eldest son of William Watson of Dublin. Trinity College, Dublin, BA, 1866. AAS. L. 20 November 1865. Call 26 January 1870. ETC. 11 March 1870. Prop. Quain QC. Sec. Charles Russell. Circuit Junior, Summer 1870. 3 Brick Court, 1876-1882. No address, 1883-1918. Not in 1919 Law List. Foster.

WAUD, Brian Wilkes
Born 4 June 1837. 2nd son of Edward Waud of Leeds. University College, Oxford, 1860. AAS. I. 21 November 1859. I. 17 November 1862. No address, 1876-1890. Not in 1891 Law List. Foster.

WAYNE, Robert Sewallis
Born 1840. 4th son of Rev. William Henry Wayne of Wenlock, Salop. Trinity College, Cambridge, MA, 1867. AAS. I. 14 November 1865. Call 17 November 1868. ETC. 10 March 1871. Prop. Pope QC. Sec. Crompton. 3 (North) King's Bench Walk, 1876. No address, 1877-1934. Not in 1935 Law List. JP, Merionethshire. Foster.

WEARING, James Williamson
Born 1864. Eldest son of Stephen Wright of Lancaster. London University. AAS. M. 15 December 1885. Call 19 November 1888. ETC. 16 July 1889. Prop. Gully QC. Sec. Sanderson. No address, 1890-1940. Not in 1941 Law List.

WEATHERALL, Julia
Brunel University, LLB. I. July 1985. Manchester Chambers; 43 King Street, 1987-1988; 5 John Dalton Street, 1989-1994. 4 Camden Place, Preston, 1995. Cleveland Chambers, 63-65 Borough Road, Middlesbrough, 1996-1999. Cathedral Chambers, Dean Street, Newcastle upon Tyne, 2000.

WEBBER, George Julius
Born 1899. 1st son of Joseph Webber of Higher Broughton, Manchester, merchant. London University, LLB; London University, LLM., LLD. AAS. M. 13 October 1919. Certificate of Honour; Studentship. Call 26 January 1922. ETC. 2 March 1922. Prop. Ashton KC. Sec. T B Leigh. Manchester Chambers; 40 South King Street, 1922-1932; 78 King Street, 1933-1934. 2 Garden Court, 1935-1936; 2 Harcourt Buildings, 1937-1941; 4 Paper Buildings, 1942-1944; 6 Pump Court, 1945-1975. Not in 1976 Law List. Publications; The Effect of War on Contracts, Solicitors' Law Stationery Society, August 1945.

WEBSTER, Alistair Stevenson QC
Born 28 April 1953 Rochdale. Son of His Honour Ian Stevenson Webster qv. Hulme Grammar School, Oldham; Brasenose College, Oxford, BA (Jurisprudence). AAS. M. 28 October 1974. Call July 1976. Bencher 2004. ETC. 1976. Prop. Patrick Russell QC. Sec. Richard Henriques. Manchester Chambers; 13 Police Street, 1976-1977; Rational House, 64 Bridge Street, 1979-1995; Lincoln House Chambers, 1 Brazennose Street, 1996. Honorary Secretary, Northern Circuit, 1988-1993. Assistant Recorder 1992. Silk 1995. Member, Bar Council, 1995-1996. Recorder 1996. WW.

WEBSTER, His Honour Ian Stevenson
Born 20 March 1925. Died 9 March 2000 aged 76. Father of Alistair Stevenson Webster QC. qv. Rochdale Grammar School; Manchester University. Sub. Lieut. (A) RNVR, 1944. AAS. M. 28 February 1946. Call 17 November 1948. ETC. Spring 1949. Prop. William Gorman KC. Sec. S R Baker. Manchester Chambers; 2 Booth Street, 1949-1975; 13 Police Street, 1976. Assistant Recorder of Oldham, 1970; of Salford, 1971. Crown Court Recorder, 1972-1976 & 1981. Chairman, Industrial Tribunals, Manchester, 1976-1981. Circuit Judge, Burnley, 1981-1995. Resident Judge, Burnley, 1985-1995 & Honorary Recorder, 1991-1995. Liason Judge for Benches of Burnley, Reedley, Accrington, Rochdale, Middleton and Heywood. WW.

WEBSTER, Leonard
Born 23 March 1946 Sheffield. Educated in Liverpool. Huddersfield University, BA. Formerly an officer in the Army Legal Corps. L. July 1984. ETC. 1991. Manchester Chambers; Hollins Chambers, 64a Bridge Street, 1991-1997; Cobden House Chambers, 19 Quay Street, 1998-2001; 24a St John Street, 2001. (now St John's Buildings after merger with 28 St John's Buildings on 23.9.2002.)

WEBSTER, Robert Grant MP
Born 1845. Died 14 January 1925. Only son of R Webster of Montrose. Radley; Trinity College, Cambridge, LLB. AAS. I. 16 November 1866. Call. 17 November 1869. ETC. 23 February 1871. Prop. Holker QC. Sec. Herschell. Practised from several addresses in the Temple. MP (C) St Pancras, E, 1886-1899. Publications; Shoulder to Shoulder, 1873; The Trade of the World, 1880; Law Relating to Canals; Japan, from the Old to the New, 1905; The Awakening of an Empire, 1917. WW. Foster.

WEDDERSPOON, Rachel Leone
Born 30 November 1969 Reading. Dartford Grammar School; Manchester University, LLB. M. October 1993. ETC. 7 December 1993. Prop. Ian Leeming QC. Sec. John Dowse. 9 St John Street, Manchester, 1993.

WEITZMAN, David QC., MP
Born 18 June 1898. Died 6 May 1987 aged 88. Hutcheson's Grammar School, Glasgow; Manchester Central School. Private, 3rd Btn, Manchester Regiment, 1916. Manchester University, BA. History, 1921. G. 17 November 1922. ETC. 11 June 1924. Prop. Eastham KC. Sec. Leigh. 3 Paper Buildings, 1924-1940; 2 Paper Buildings, 1941-1948; 10 King's Bench Walk, 1949-1976; Devereux Chambers, 1977-1985. MP (Lab): Stoke Newington, 1945-1950; Hackney North & Stoke Newington, 1950-1979. WW.

WELFORD. Alfred William Baker
L. 22 June 1898. ETC. 20 February 1900. Prop. Pickford KC. Sec. Horridge. Lamb Building, 1902-1912; 1 Tanfield Court, 1913-1915; 1 Paper Buildings, 1916-1941. Not in 1942 Law List.

WELLS, Edmund Holland TD
Born 6 September 1926. Died 14 July 1974 aged 47. Eldest son of Eric Wright Wells, chartered accountant, father of Graham Holland Wells qv. Preston Grammar School; Brasenose College, Oxford, BA., BCL. AAS. M. 16 September 1946. Call 26 January 1951. ETC. 6 March 1952. Prop. Edward Wooll QC. Sec. Backhouse. Liverpool Chambers; 20 Hackins Hey, 1952-1964; 14 Cook Street, 1965-1974. Lancs. Chancery Court.

WELLS, Graham Holland
Born 28 May 1959, Birkenhead. Son of Edmund Holland Wells qv. Shrewsbury School; Brasenose College, Oxford, MA. AAS. M. 11 March 1981. Call 29 July 1982. Pupilmaster, Andrew Jordan (London). ETC. 1983. Prop. William Waldron QC. Sec. F David Owen. Refuge Assurance House/ Merchants Court, Derby Square, Liverpool, 1983-31.12.2003 when chambers closed and those remaining joined Oriel Chambers, 14 Water Street, Liverpool.

WELSBY, Charles

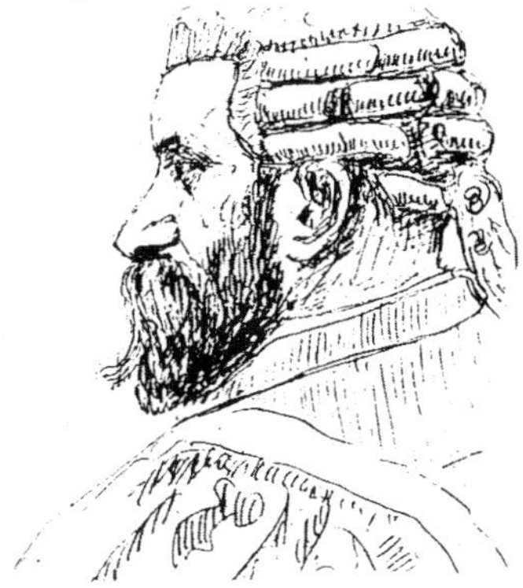

Born 1846. Eldest son of Thomas Welsby of Chester. St John's College, Cambridge, BA, 1869. AAS. I. 13 June 1867. Call 26 January 1871. ETC. 14 March 1872. Prop. L. Temple QC. Sec. Bruce. 4 Harcourt Buildings, 1876-1879; 2 Mitre Court Buildings, 1880-1885. 15 Stephenson's Chambers, 25 Lord Street, Liverpool, 1883-1891. Not in 1892 Law List. Foster.

WELSON, James Beavan
LLM. G. 4 June 1913. 114 Chancery Lane WC., 1913-1919; 54-55 and later 61-62 Coleman Street, EC2, 1920-1929; 1 North John Street, Liverpool (the offices of Royal Insurance Co Ltd), 1930- 1944; ETC. 1944. Bank Chambers, 3 Cook Street, 1944-1950. Retired to Birkenhead, 1950-1963. Not in 1964 Law List.

WERTHEIMER, John
Born 27 November 1860. Eldest son of Charles John Wertheimer of London. London University. AAS. M. 3 November 1879. Call 21 June 1882. ETC. 24 July 1883. Prop. Hopwood QC. Sec. Costelloe. 5 New Court, Carey Street, 1886-1887. Not in 1888 Law List. Foster.

WEST, Henry Wyndham QC., MP
Born 7 November 1823. Died 25 November 1893 aged 70. Eldest son of Martin John West, barrister. Eton; Christ Church, Oxford, BA, 1845. AAS. L. 5 May 1845. AAS. I. 27 March 1848. Call I. 5 May 1848; Bencher 1868. 10 King's Bench Walk, 1876-1893. Recorder of: Scarborough, 1857-1868; Manchester, 1865-1893. Attorney General for the Duchy of Lancaster, 1861-1893. Silk 1868. Judge of Salford Hundred Court of Record, 1868-1893. MP, Ipswich, 1868-1874 & 1883-1886. Foster.

WESTBROOK, Simon Nicholas
LLB., FCIArb. I. July 1973. Member of Hong Kong Bar. 43 King Street, Manchester, 1973-1980. In practice in Hong Kong, 1981.

WHALLEY, Philip Guy Rothay CBE
Born 6 April 1901 Liverpool. Died 1 March 1950 aged 49. Aldenham School; Gonville & Caius College, Cambridge, MA., LLB (Cantab). L. 28 January 1924; Tancred Scholar. ETC. 30 January 1924. Prop. Greaves-Lord KC. Sec. Chappell. Circuit Junior, Winter 1924. 10 Cook Street, Liverpool, 1925-1929. Joined Lewis's Ltd, 1929. Ministry of Food, 1940-1945; Deputy Secretary. Member, Council of Industrial Design, 1944. Vice-President, Royal Society of Arts, 1949. Joint Managing Director of Lewis's Ltd and Associated Companies. CBE, 1945. WW.

WHARTON, Charles Henry Marriott
Born 1851. Younger son of George Frederick Wharton of Manchester, attorney at law. AAS. 23 January 1872. Call 17 November 1874. ETC. 16 March 1875. Prop, Leofric Temple QC. Sec. Baylis. Manchester Chambers; Cross Street Chambers, 1876-1908; 7 St James's Square, 1909-1921. 16 John Dalton Street, 1922-1924. No address, 1925-1927. Not in 1928 Law List. Publications; The Whole Law Relating to Innkeepers. Foster.

WHEATLEY, Geraint Rhys
St Edmund Hall, Oxford, BA (Law). G. 2001. ETC. 12 December 2001. Prop. Peter Winston Smith QC. Sec. Mark Harper. King's Chambers, 40 King Street, Manchester, 2001.

WHEELDON, Sarah Helen Elizabeth
Born 14 March 1966 Ashton-under-Lyne. Withington Girls School; St Andrew's University, MA. Dip Law. G. 16 October 1990. ETC. December 1991. Prop. Rodney Scholes QC. Sec. Barrie Searle. St James's Chambers, 68 Quay Street, Manchester, 1990.

WHEELER, His Honour Thomas Whittenbury QC
Born 28 April 1839. Son of Serjeant Thomas Wheeler, LLD., County Court Judge. Westminster School; Trinity Hall, Cambridge, BA, 1863; MA, 1878. AAS. I. 26 April 1861. Call 26 January 1865; Bencher 1894. 4 Crown Office Row, 1876-1894; 1 King's Bench Walk, 1895-1902; 11 King's Bench Walk, 1903-1905. Silk 1886. Publications; Law of Dilapidation, 1887; Betterment; The Good Old Times, 1888; Contracts Implied by Law, 1897. County Court Judge, Circuit 35, (Norfolk, Suffolk & Cambs.), 1905-1918. WW. Foster.

WHEELHOUSE, Sir William St James QC., MP.
Born 1821. Died 8 March 1886. Eldest son of James Wheelhouse of Yorkshire. AAS. G. 15 November 1839; Call 1 May 1844; Bencher 1877; Treasurer 1882. MP, Leeds, 1868-1880. Silk 1877. Member, Council of Legal Education. Kt. 1882. 10 King's Bench Walk, 1876-1881; 2 Crown Office Row, 1882-1886. Publications; Law of Elections. Foster.

WHELAN, Geoff
Born 22 April 1971 Salford. St Bede's School, Manchester. G. March 1996. Kenworthy's Chambers, 83 Bridge Street, Manchester, 1996.

WHINCUP, Michael Hynes
Born 1930. Younger son of Harry Hynes Whincup of Wallasey, secondary school teacher. Liverpool University, LLM. AAS. M. 20 January 1950. Call 24 November 1953. ETC. 4 February 1954. Prop. Goldie QC. Sec. Rigg. 9 Rumford Street, Liverpool, 1954-1963. Not in 1964 Law List.

WHITE, Alfred Cromwell
Born 1848. Youngest son of James White of Brighton. Christ Church, Oxford, BA, 1871. AAS. M. 23 November 1868. Call 30 April 1875. ETC. 22 July 1875. Prop. Herschell QC. Sec. Crompton. 3 Harcourt Buildings, 1876-1897. Not in 1898 Law List. Foster.

WHITE, Sir Charles Arnold
Born 17 September 1858. Died 6 September 1931 aged 72. Only son of Thomas White of Bowden, Cheshire. New College, Oxford, BA, 1881. AAS. I. 7 May 1879. Call 17 November 1883. ETC. 31 July 1885. Prop. Gully QC. Sec. Higgins. 3 Temple Gardens, 1885-1893; 4 Temple Gardens, 1894-1898. Madras: Advocate-General, 1898; Chief Justice, 1899-1914. Kt. 1900. Member of the Council of the Secretary of State for India, 1915-1922. Publications; Joint editor: Wilson's Judicature Acts; Annual County Court Practice. WW. Foster.

WHITE, Patrick Herbert
Born 1857. 2nd son of Rev. Verner Moore White of London. St Peter's College, Cambridge, 1879. AAS. I. 9 April 1879. Call 17 November 1882. ETC. 3 August 1883. Prop. Myburg QC. Sec. Russell. 5 King's Bench Walk, 1884-1924. No address, 1925-1934. Not in 1935 Law List. Foster.

WHITE, Rachel Dorothy
Born 2 June 1975, Manchester University, BA., Dip. Law. M. November 2000. Pupilmaster, Patrick Cassidy. Kenworthy's Chambers, 83 Bridge Street, Manchester, 2000.

WHITE, Timothy Gordon
Born 16 April 1956 Rochdale. Kirkham Grammar School; Liverpool John Moores University, BA. AAS. M. 18 July 1977. Call. 27 July 1978. ETC. February 1979, Prop. Patrick Russell QC. Sec. Anthony Jolly. Manchester Chambers; 36 St Ann Street, 1979-1980; 27 Byrom Street, 1981-1983. 14 later 15 Winckley Square, Preston, 1984.

WHITEHALL, Richard Langdale
Born 1 April 1974 Newcastle-upon-Tyne. Royal Grammar School, Newcastle-upon-Tyne; Cardiff University, LLB (Law & French), LLM. L. 23 July 1998. ETC. December 1998. Prop. Peith Goddard QC. Sec. Timothy Smith. Dean's Court Chambers, 24 St John Street, Manchester, 7.9.1998.

WHITEHEAD, James Graham
G. 29 April 1931. ETC. 2 July 1931. Prop. Neville Laski KC. Sec. Emlyn Jones. 4 Clarence Street, 1931-1963. Not in 1964 Law List.

WHITEHURST, Ian John
Born 11 November 1971 Stoke-on-Trent. Haywood High School; Hull University, LLB. I. 24 November 1994. ETC. 16 December 1999. Prop. Nigel Gilmour QC. Sec. Peter Goodbody. New Bailey Chambers, Preston, 1997-1999. Liverpool Chambers; Oriel Chambers, 14 Water Street, September 1999-2002; 7 Harrington Street, 2002.

WHITELEY, Ronald Ernest
I. 12 June 1907. ETC. 6 March 1908. Prop. Tobin KC. Sec. Rigby Swift. 5 Harrington Street, Liverpool, 1909-1926. No address, 1927-1953. Not in 1954 Law List.

WHITELEY, Sir Norman Henry Pownall MC
Born 29 June 1883 Manchester. Died 12 April 1957 aged 73. Emmanuel College, Cambridge, BA. I. 18 November 1907. ETC. 24 February 1908. Prop. Langdon KC. Sec. Acton. 41 John Dalton Street, Manchester, 1908-1921. Entered army as a private, 7th Manchester Regt in August 1914, Served in Egypt, Gallipoli, Palestine & Arabia. Demobilizes as Major (MC., Croix de Guerre, Order of the Crown of Italy). Deputy Public Prosecutor: Penang, 1921; Singapore, 1922. Puisne Judge, Straits Settlements and Judge, Federated Malay States, 1929-1937. Acting Chief Justice: Straits Settlements, 1936; Federated Malay States, 1937. Chief Justice, Uganda, 1937-1947. Kt. 1941. Chairman, Uganda Cotton Industry, 1948. WW.

WHITTAKER, Abraham Longdale
I. 19 November 1894. ETC. 1 August 1895. Prop. Bigham QC. Sec. J A Hamilton. London Chambers; 4 Temple Gardens, 1895-1908; and eventually 5 King's Bench Walk, 1921-1936. No address, 1937-1949. Not in 1950 Law List.

WHITTAKER, Oldham
I. 22 April 1891. ETC. 18 July 1892. Prop. Gully QC. Sec. Cottingham. Circuit Junior, Winter 1893. 2 Harcourt Buildings, 1893; 3 King's Bench Walk, 1894-1900; 1 Harcourt Buildings, 1901-1910; 2 Harcourt Buildings, 1911-1913. No address, 1914-1930. Not in 1931 Law List.

WHITTINGHAM, Timothy Septimus
LLB. G. May 1969. ETC. 8 July 1969. Prop. Hinchliffe QC. Sec. Hardy. 3 St James's Square, Manchester, 1969-1984; St James's Chambers, 68 Quay Street, Manchester, 1985. Emigrated to Australia, 1985.

WHITTY, Walter Devereux
Born 1836. 3rd son of Michael James Whitty of Liverpool, journalist. AAS. I. 20 November 1863. Call 18 November 1867. ETC. 28 March 1868. Prop. Baylis. Sec. Foard. 1 Pump Court, 1876-1879. No address, 1880-1894. Not in 1895 Law List. Foster.

WHITTY, Walter Patrick
BA (London). I. 19 November 1888. Equity Chambers, 9 Cook Street, Liverpool, 1889-1944. Equity draftsman & conveyancer. Lancs. Chancery Court. Not in 1945 Law List.

WHITWORTH, Frank QC
MA (Cantab), G & I., 26 January 1934. ETC. 27 February 1935. Prop. Fyfe KC. Sec. Stenham. 11 King's Bench Walk, 1935-1940. No address, 1941-1945. Goldsmith Building, 1946-1972; 13 King's Bench Walk, 1973-1988. South Eastern Circuit from 1948. Not in 1989 Law List. Silk 1965. Recorder 1972. Judge, Court of Appeal, Channel Islands.

WHITWORTH, John Haworth MC., DSO.
Born 26 September 1879 Alderley Edge. Son of John & Marian Whitworth and husband of Ida Mary of Bowden. Wadham College, Oxford. Certificate of Honour H. 1903. I. 26 January 1904. ETC. 3 February 1906. Prop. Tobin KC. Sec. Maberly. 77 King Street, Manchester, 1906-1914. Lancs. Chancery Court. Commissioned as Captain, Manchester Regt 1914; Promoted Major. Mentioned in despatches. Died of wounds at Rouen, 31 March 1918 aged 38. Cemetery, St Sever Cemetery, Rouen. Grave Ref, officers B. 5. 10. The cemetery is about 3 kms south of Rouen. Information supplied by Commonwealth War Graves Commission. In his memoirs, "Closed Chapters' Sir Gerald Hurst KC says, "In my own generation my rivals included J H Whitworth, a man of character and a fine soldier, a Liberal candidate for Knutsford who died of wounds in France in 1918."

WHYATT, Michael George
Born 11 March 1963 Stockport. New Mills School; Manchester Polytechnic, LLB. G. February 1992. ETC. 1992. Pupilmaster, John Appleton. 15 Winckley Square, Preston, 1992. Fell Runner (Second in English Championships, 1989/1990. Builds and flies aeroplanes.

WHYTE, Anne Lynne
Born 19 June 1969 Germany. Luckley Oakfield, Wokingham, Berks; Worcester College, Oxford, BA (Modern History). City University, Dip Law. L. February 1993. Pupilage at 1 Crown Office Row. ETC. 23 March 1994. 14 Castle Street/ Atlantic Chambers, Cook Street, Liverpool, 1994. Member, Merseyside Legal Services Commission Review Panel.

WICKHAM, His Honour William Rayley

(DL)

Born 22 September 1926. Sedbergh School. Served in 1939-1945 War; Army, 1944-December 1947. Brasenose College, Oxford, MA., BCL. I. January 1951. London pupilage. Pupilmasters; F Bower Alcock and J S Bass. Aden: Magistrate, 1953; Chief Magistrate, 1958; Acting Chief Justice, 1959. Tanganyika: Crown Counsel, 1959; Asst. to Law Officers, 1961-1963. ETC. 1963. Pupilmaster, Michael Maguire. Same Liverpool Chambers; 10 Water Street, 1963-1969; 2nd floor, Oriel Chambers, 14 Water Street, 1970-1975. Crown Court Recorder, 1972-1975. Circuit Judge, 1975-1997. Senior Circuit Judge and Honorary Recorder of Liverpool, 1992-1997. Retirement Tributes at Liverpool Law Courts, 30 April 1997 (Mr Justice Kay/ Richard Henriques QC. Transcript in Circuit Records. WW.

WIGGLESWORTH, Raymond QC
Born 24 December 1947, Lytham St Annes. Andsell County School; Manchester University, LLB. G. July 1974. ETC. 1974. Prop. Patrick Russell QC. Sec. Kenneth Taylor. Manchester Chambers; 4th floor, Astley House, 1974-1976; 18 St John Street, 1976. Assistant Recorder 1988. Recorder 1990. Standing Counsel to H M Customs & Excise, 1995-1999. Silk 1999. WW.

WIGODER, Basil Thomas QC (Baron Wigoder of Cheetham in the City of Manchester)
Born 12 February 1921. Died 12 August 2004, aged 83. Manchester Grammar School; Oriel College, Oxford, MA. G. November 1946; Bencher 1972; Treasurer 1989. ETC. 1947. 1 Dr Johnson's Buildings, 1948-1967; 3 Temple Gardens, 1968-1990. He joined South Eastern Circuit, 1949. Recorder, 1972-1984. Silk 1966. Liberal politician and Chief Whip in House of Lords, 1977-1984. Baron, 1974. WW. Times Obituary 2 September 2004.

WIHL, Oscar Morris
BA., LLB. L. 14 June 1893. ETC. 23 February 1894. Prop. Gully QC. Sec. Aitken. Manchester Chambers; 24 Kennedy Street, 1894-1896; 32 Kennedy Street, 1896-1902. No address, 1903-1925. Living in Colwyn Bay, 1926-1949. Not in 1950 Law List.

WILBRAHAM, Donald Fortescue
L. 22 April 1891. ETC. 14 July 1892. Manchester Chambers; 9 St James's Square, 1893; 77 King Street, 1894-1896. Registrar of Supreme Court, Freetown, Sierra Leone, 1897-1908; Attorney General, Sierra Leone, 1909-1915. Not in 1916 Law List.

WILBRAHAM, Henry
L. 8 May 1851. Registrar, Lancs. Chancery Court, Manchester District, 1857-1883. Not in 1884 Law List.

WILDING, Thomas Samuel
Certificate of Honour T. 1913. I. 4 June 1913. ETC. 18 February 1914. Prop. Tobin KC. Sec. Barne. Goldsmith Buildings, 1918-1919; 3 Essex Court, 1920. Not in 1921 Law List.

WILKINS, John Edwards
FRGS. Born 1827. 2nd son of John North Wilkins of Bourton on the Water, Glos. AAS. I. 15 January 1848. Call 26 January 1854. ETC. 14 March 1870. Prop. Leofric Temple QC. Sec. G Bruce. 4 Paper Buildings, 1876-1889. Not in 1890 Law List. Consul-General at Chicago, USA, 1857. Foster.

WILKINSON, Benjamin Gregory
Born 1846. Youngest son of William Wilkinson of Tadcaster, Yorks. Wesleyan Minister when AAS. M. 20 January 1883, Call 17 November 1885. ETC. 2 February 1899. Prop. Shee QC. Sec. McKeand. 37 Park Square, Leeds, 1891-1893. Manchester Chambers; 4 St James's Square, 1894-1899; 7 Brazennose Street, 1900-1906. No address, 1907-1930. Not in 1931 Law List.

WILKINSON, Henry Spencer
Born 1 May 1853 Manchester. Died 31 January 1937 aged 83. Owens College, Manchester; Merton College, Oxford, MA. Fellow of All Souls College, Oxford. AAS. L. 28 January 1876. Call 9 June 1880. ETC. 12 July 1880. Prop. Temple QC. Sec. Hopkinson. Duchy Chambers, Clarence Street, Manchester, 1881-1888. On Staff of Manchester Guardian, 1882-1892; of Morning Post, 1895-1914. Chichele Professor of Military History, 1909-1923. Has written many books and essays on military affairs. His "Brain of an Army" and "The French Army before Napoleon." were regarded as authoritative and influential. His opinion was sought by many senior military men. WW. DNB.

*** WILKINSON, Kenneth Henry Pinder (His Honour Judge Wilkinson)**
Born 5 August 1939. Wigan Grammar School; Manchester University, LLB. Admitted as a solicitor, 1965. In private practice, 1965-1980. District Judge, Liverpool 1980-1996. Assistant Recorder 1990. Recorder 1993. Circuit Judge 1996. Designated Family Judge, Merseyside, December 2002. Member; Matrimonial Cases Rules Committee, 1978-1980; County Court Rules Committee, 1988-1992. WW.

WILKINSON, Oliver Nicholas
BA (Cantab). G. July 1962. Pupilmaster, Gerard Humphreys. Manchester Chambers; 9 Albert Square, 1963-1972; Deans Court Chambers, Crown Square, 1973-1985.

WILKINSON, Rowland
only son of John Wilkinson of York. AAS. G. 3 November 1862. Call 9 June 1865. ETC. 4 August 1868. Prop. Holker QC. Sec. H Hills. North Crescent Chambers, 3 Lord Street, Liverpool, 1879-1886; 3 Mitre Court, 1887; 12 King's Bench Walk, 1888; 4 Brick Court, 1889-1892. No address, 1893-1934. Not in 1935 Law List.

WILLEMS, Marc Paul Bernard Alfred
Born 6 May 1966 Manchester. Married to Julia Cheetham qv. St Bede's College, Manchester; Nottingham University, BA (Law). L. 27 November 1990. ETC. 1991. Prop. Anthony Gee QC. Sec. David Berkley. Manchester Chambers; Hollins House Chambers, 64a Bridge Street, 1990-1997; Cobden House Chambers, 19 Quay Street, 1997.

WILLIAMS, Andrew Arthur
Born 2 November 1971 Liverpool. Liverpool Blue Coat School; Birmingham University, LLB. G. October 1994. ETC. 1995. Prop. William Waldron QC. Sec. William George. Liverpool Chambers; 20 North John Street, March 1995-August 1997; 14 Castle Street/ Atlantic Chambers, Cook Street, August 1997. University Land Law Lecturer.

WILLIAMS, Brian David
Born 14 May 1958. Moseley Hall School; Manchester University, LLB. I. July 1986. ETC. 1986. Prop. Rhys Davies QC. Sec. Martin Steiger. 18 St John Street, Manchester, 1987.

WILLIAMS, Brian Herbert
BA (Cantab). G. January 1949. ETC. 1949. 14 Cook Street, Liverpool, 1950-1963. Not in 1964 Law list.

WILLIAMS, David Henry
Born 16 March 1946 Denbigh. Denbigh Grammar; Lancaster, Cartmel, LLB. Solicitor, 1975-1990. G. February 1990. ETC. April 1990. Prop. David Harris QC. Sec. Bryn Holloway. Liverpool Chambers; 3rd floor, Peel House, Harrington Street, February 1990-August 1995; Chavasse Court, 24 Lord Street 1995. Recorder 2000.

WILLIAMS, Doiran George
Born 27 June 1926. Hereford Cathedral School; Colwyn Bay Grammar School; Liverpool College; John F Hughes School, Utica, New York, Served in Infantry, 1944-1947. G. November 1952. Pupilmaster, Edward Youds. Liverpool Chambers; North House, 17 North John Street, 1953-1955; 36 Dale Street, 1956-1958. Office of Director of Public Prosecutions, 1959-1986; Principal Assistant Director, 1982-1986. Chairman, Medical Appeals Tribunals, 1987-1998. Ordained deacon, 1993; priest 1994. WW.

WILLIAMS, Eric
I. 17 November 1931. ETC. 17 February 1932. Prop. Lynskey KC. Sec. Rhodes. No address, 1937-1963. Not in 1964 Law List.

WILLIAMS, Francis Joseph
BA. I. November 1984. 1st floor, 121 Princess Street, Manchester, 1986-1987. No chambers address, 1988.

WILLIAMS, Frederick
L. 17 November 1855. 1 Tanfield Court, Temple, 1876. Not in 1877 Law List.

WILLIAMS, Graham Ellis
formerly a solicitor with Hill Dickinson, Liverpool. M. 25 July 2002. ETC. 19 December 2002. Prop. Timothy King QC. Sec. Simon Newton. Liverpool Chambers; Derby Square Chambers, Merchants Court, 2002-2003; when chambers closed he moved to Oriel Chambers, 14 Water Street 1.1.2004.

WILLIAMS, James
Born 1851. Died 3 November 1911. Liverpool College; Lincoln College, Oxford, MA; DCL, 1878; Fellow. All Souls Reader in Roman Law in the University of Oxford. Hon. LLD, Yale. AAS. L. 27 January 1872. Call 17 November 1875. ETC. 13 March 1876. Prop. L. Temple. Sec. Crompton. Circuit Junior, Summer 1876. 5 Essex Court, 1876-1880; 1 New Square, 1881-1886; 11 Old Square, 1887-1890; 2 Pump Court, 1891-1897; New Court, 1898-1911. Publications include; Schoolmaster and the Law, 1890; Wills & Succession, 1890; Law of Education, 1892; Institutes of Justinian, 1893; Dante as a Jurist, 1906. WW.

WILLIAMS, (John) Glyn
Born 30 May 1958, Manchester. Manchester High School of Art & Music; Manchester University, BA (Philosophy). I. 11 November 1981. ETC. 23 May 1985. Prop. Ian Leeming QC. Sec. Richard Johnson. Pupilmaster, Derek Mallard. Manchester Chambers; 196 Deansgate, 1981-1989; 18 St John Street, 1989-1998; 15 Winckley Square, Preston, 1999-2000; 8 King Street, Manchester, 2001.

WILLIAMS, John Herbert
Born 1857. Eldest son of John Herbert Williams, barrister. Trinity College, Cambridge, LLB, 1880; LLM. AAS. M. 8 November 1878. Call. 29 June 1881. ETC. 16 July 1881. Prop. Pope QC. Sec. Collins. Circuit Junior, Winter 1882. 3 Dr Johnson's Buildings, 1882-1917. Not in 1918 Law List. North Wales & Chester Circuit from 1885. Foster.

WILLIAMS, John Leighton
BA. G. July 1978. ETC. 28 June 1979. Prop. Christopher Rose QC. Sec. Woodward. 67 Princess Street, Manchester, 1979-1981. Not in 1982 Law List.

WILLIAMS, Lewis

Born 1840. Died 14 January 1899 (See Liverpool Prosecutions Book). Eldest son of William Williams of Everton, Lancs. St John's College, Cambridge, BA, 1861. AAS. I. 2 May 1861. Call 26 January 1864. 1 Brick Court, 1876. 5 Harrington Street, 1877-1885; 1 Brick Court, 1886-1891. No address, 1892-1895; 1 Brick Court, 1896-1899.

WILLIAMS, Mary Lewis OBE
Cheltenham Ladies College; Lady Margaret Hall, Oxford. I. 27 January 1936. ETC. 13 February 1936. Prop. William Gorman KC. Sec. Leo Gradwell. Pupilmaster, Harry Nelson. Liverpool Chambers; 10 Cook Street, 1936-1940. No address, 1941-1945. 3 Cook Stree,t 1946-1956. On 28 August 1956 appointed Assistant Clerk of Assize and Deputy Clerk of The Crown, St George's Hall, Liverpool. In 1972 appointed Courts Administrator, Liverpool. Not in 1974 Law List. OBE upon retirement.

WILLIAMS, Roland P
G. 19 June 1901. ETC. 12 August 1901. Prop. Commins. Sec. Thomas. 2 Essex Court, 1902-1906; 1 Elm Court, 1907. Menai Bridge, North Wales, 1908-1949. Not in 1950 Law List.

WILLIAMS, Sarah Victoria McMorran
Born 16 February 1971 Chester. Abbey Gate College, Cheshire; Bristol University, BA (History); College of Law, Chester, Dip. Law. I. November 1995. ETC. 21 December 1995. Prop. Rodney Klevan QC. Sec. Paul O'Brien. 18 St John Street, Manchester, 1995.

WILLIAMS, Thomas Hitchon
Born 1922. Only son of Thomas Williams of Stalybridge, Cheshire, general practitioner. BA (Cantab). AAS. M. 5 November 1940. Call 9 June 1948. 26 King Street, Manchester, 1949-1954. 1 Harcourt Buildings, 1955. No chambers address, 1956-1963. Not in 1964 Law List.

WILLIAMS, Victor Owen
Born 1897. Only son of Thomas Williams of Oxton, Cheshire. AAS. M. 9 July 1920. Call 26 January 1922. 6 Crown Office Row, 1922-1933; 3 Paper Buildings, 1934-1969. The Rectory Farm, Taplow, Bucks., 1970-1973. Not in 1974 Law List.

WILLIAMS, Walter Vere Vaughan
Born 1840. 5th son of Rt. Hon. Sir Edward Vaughan Williams. Christ College, Oxford. AAS. L. 21 January 1863. AAS. I. 15 January 1868. Call I. 27 January 1868. ETC. 13 August 1868. Prop. Manisty QC. Sec. Bacon. 7 King's Bench Walk, 1876-1889. Not in 1890 Law List. Publications; Law & Practice in Bankruptcy; (Joint) Williams' Law of Executors. Foster.

WILLIAMS, Zillah Elizabeth
Liverpool University, LLB. L. 9 0ctober 1997. ETC. 19 December 2002. Prop. Timothy King QC. Sec. Ray Herman. India Buildings, Water Street, Liverpool, 2002.

WILLIAMSON, Alfred John
Born 1848. Only son of William Williamson of Heaton Norris, Stockport. St John's College, Cambridge, BA 1873. AAS. I. 22 April 1873. Call 25 April 1877. ETC. 11 July 1877. Prop. Hopwood QC. Sec. Nash. No address, 1877-1935. Not in 1936 Law List. Foster.

WILLIAMSON, (John) Victor
I. July 1963. ETC. 1963. Manchester Chambers; 43 King Street, 1963-1967; Northern Assurance Building, Albert Square, Manchester, 1968-1969; Post Office Chambers, 26 Brown Street, 1970-1976; 4th floor Sunlight House, Quay Street, 1977-1985; 1 Central Street, 1984-1985; 33 King Street West, 1988-1993. Not in 1994 Bar Directory.

WILLIAMSON, Patrick Lawrence Victor
Keele University, BSc. I. November 1989. Manchester Chambers; 33 King Street West, 1992-1994; Old Colony House, 6 South King Street, 1995.

WILLINK, Rt. Hon. Sir Henry Urmston MC., QC
Born 7 March 1894, Liverpool. Died 1 January 1973 aged 78. Son of William Edward Willink, architect. Eton; Trinity College, Cambridge, MA., DCL (Lambeth). Royal Field Artillery, 1914-1919; Acting Major; MC, Croix de Guerre avec palme, despatches. I. November 1920; Bencher 1942. ETC. 15 June 1921. Prop. Miller KC. Sec. Goldie. Pupilmaster, W A Jowitt. 1 Brick Court, 1921-1925; 3 Essex Court, 1926-1948. Silk 1935. Special Commissioner for London Region, 1940-1943. MP (Nat. C) Croydon North, 1940-1948. Minister of Health, 1943-1945. PC. 1943. Chancellor of the Dioceses of Norwich, St Edmundsbury & Ipswich, 1948-1955. High Bailiff of Westminster, 1942-1967. Chairman, Royal Commission on Betting, 1949; Police, 1960. Hon. LLD, Liverpool. In 1948 he gave up politics and the law to become Master of Magdelene College, Cambridge (1948-1966). He was so well regarded as to be permitted to hold the post for two years beyond normal retiring age. Hon. Fellow, 1966-1973. Vice Chancellor of the University of Cambridge, 1953-1955. Dean of the Arches, Master of Faculties, Vicar General of the Province of Canterbury and Auditor of the Chancery Court of York, 1955-1970. First Bt. 1957. WW. DNB.

WILLITTS, Timothy Leonard
Born 12 August 1966 Stockport. Broadway Comprehensive, Cheadle; Birmingham University, LLB. G. November 1989. ETC. November 1989. Prop. Richard Clegg QC. Sec. Stuart Neale. Manchester Chambers; Hollins Chambers, 64a Bridge Street, 1990-1997 which became Cobden House Chambers, 19 Quay Street, 1997.

WILLMER, Henry Gordon OBE., KC. (The Rt. Hon. Lord Justice Willmer)
Born 11 August 1899. Died 17 May 1983 aged 83. Son of A J Willmer of Birkenhead. Birkenhead School; Corpus Christi College, Oxford, BA, 1922; MA, 1950. I. 17 November 1924; Bencher 1946; Treasurer 1969. ETC. 28 January 1925. Prop. Greaves-Lord KC. Sec. Hodgson. 3 Temple Gardens, 1924-1925; 4 King's Bench Walk, 1926-1940. Admiralty practitioner. Silk 1939. Royal Artillery, TA, 1925-1938. TD. Coast Artillery, 1940-1943. Col. with Allied Military Government, Italy, 1943-1945. OBE, 1945. High Court Judge, Probate, Divorce and Admiralty Division, 1945-1958. Kt. 1945. Lord Justice of Appeal, 1958-1969. PC. 1958. Trustee, Thalidomide Childrens' Trust, 1973-1981. Chairman, Marine Board investigating the loss of Amoco Cadiz, 1978-1980. Hon. LLD, Liverpool, 1966. After retirement Sir Gordon Willmer sat occasionally in the Court of Appeal. I did my first Court of Appeal case before him and Lord Justices Megaw and Orr, thirty five years ago. He was very kind to a nervous novice from the north and I have not forgotten that. WW.

WILLS, Janice Marie
Born, Liverpool. Notre Dame High School for Girls, Woolton, Liverpool; Liverpool John Moores University, LLB. Liverpool City Council, 1980-1987. G. October 1991. ETC. 1993. Prop. Roger Farley QC. Sec. Maurice Greene. Manchester Chambers; Kenworthy's Buildings, 83 Bridge Street, 1991-1998; St James's Chambers, 68 Quay Street, 1998-2000; Young Street Chambers at: 38 Young Street, 2000-2004; and at 76 Quay Street, 2004. Publications; Tolleys Insurance Law and Practice.

WILSON, Andrew Brocket
I. 4 May 1887. Bristowe Chambers, 8 Harrington Street, Liverpool, 1889-1908. Lancs. Chancery Court. No address, 1909-1915. Not in 1916 Law List.

WILSON, Catherine Mary
BA (Oxon). L. July 1988. 8 King Street, Manchester, 1990-1992. Not in 1993 Bar Directory.

WILSON, Christopher Mounsey
I. 17 November 1886. ETC. 14 January 1887. Prop. Littler QC. Sec. Page. 4 Harcourt Buildings, 1888-1889. No address, 1890-1892. 6 Crown Office Row, 1893-1903. Not in 1904 Law List.

WILSON, James Bargrave Wyborn
L. 17 November 1885. ETC. 30 January 1886. Prop. Ambrose QC. Sec. Ferguson. 13 King's Bench Walk, 1887-1888; 1 Elm Court, 1889-1896. No address, 1897-1928. Not in 1929 Law List.

WILSON, John Barker
Born 13 July 1944, Lydney, Glos. Lancaster Royal Grammar School; Britannia Royal Naval College, Dartmouth. Local Government Officer, 1963-1978. In business, 1978-1987. Lancaster University (Fylde College), LLB. I. July 1988. ETC. 1989. Pupilmasters, N F Riddle and J Steel. Manchester Chambers; 3 Peter Street, 1989-1991; 211 Deansgate, 1991-1992; 38 King Street West, later 24a St John Street and now St John's Buildings March, 1993.

WILSON, John James
Born 11 February 1854. 2nd son of James Wilson of Eccles, Lancs. AAS. M. 7 January 1873. Call 26 January 1876. ETC. 13 March 1876. Prop. Higgins QC. Sec. Torr QC. 3 Plowden Buildings, 1877-1882; 6 Crown Office Row, 1883-1888. No address, 1889-1935. Not in 1936 Law List.

WILSON, Marion Janet
LLB (Lanc.). M. October 1991. Manchester House Chambers, 18-22 Bridge Street, Manchester, 1994-1998. 5 Fountain Court, Steelhouse Lane, Birmingham, 1999.

WILSON, Pamela
LLB(London). I. November 1976. Fruit Exchange Buildings. Victoria Street, Liverpool, 1979-1985. No chambers address, 1986-1988. Not in 1989 Bar Directory.

WILSON, Richard Bethell
L. 1 July 1908. ETC. 25 February 1911. Prop. Mellor KC. Sec. Acton. 60 King Street, Manchester, 1911-1921. No address, 1922-1953. Not in 1954 Law List.

WILSON, Stephen
I. 28 June 1911. ETC. 7 July 1911. Prop. Taylor KC. Sec. Kennedy. Liverpool Chambers; 13 Harrington Street, 1911-1913; 25 Lord Street, 1914-1923. No address, 1924-1953. Not in 1954 Law List.

WILSON, Sir (William) Courthope (Townshend) KC
Born 1865. Eldest son of Richard Duff Wilson of Liverpool. Birkenhead School; Liverpool Institute High School. G. 9 May 1900: Bencher 1920; Treasurer 1932. ETC. 20 February 1902. Prop. Horridge KC. Sec. Keogh. Liverpool Chambers; 4 Harrington Street, 1901; 5 Harrington Street, 1902-1919. Silk 1919. 6 New Court, 1919-1921; 15 Old Square, 1922-1937. Vice-Chancellor of the County Palatine of Lancaster, 1925-1936. 1 Percy Street, Liverpool 8, 1937-1940. WW.

WILSON-BARNES, Lucy Emma
Born 23 May 1966 Manchester. Manchester High School for Girls; Warwick University, BA. I. July 1989. ETC. 1989. Prop. Rhys Davies QC. Sec. Anthony Elleray. St James's Chambers, 68 Quay Street, Manchester, 1989. Junior Counsel for the Crown (Provincial Panel), 2000.

WIMPFHEIMER, Maximilian (Maxwell Wimpole from 1922)
I. 24 June 1903. ETC. February 1905. Prop. Horridge KC. Sec. Ross Brown. 2 Elm Court, 1906-1910; 1 Garden Court, 1911-1921. No address, 1922-1953. Not in 1954 Law List.

WINGATE-SAUL, Bazil Sylvester (His Honour Judge Wingate-Saul)
Born 15 June 1906. Died 4 October 1975 aged 69. Son of Sir Ernest Wingate Saul KC qv. and uncle of Giles Wingate Wingate-Saul QC qv. Rugby; St John's College, Oxford. I. 26 January 1928: Bencher 1958. ETC not recorded but it is noted that he was Circuit Junior in

Winter 1928. Manchester Chambers; 3 St James's Square, 1928-1929; 60 King Street, 1930-1939. Royal Berkshire Regt in War of 1939-1945. 3 (South) King's Bench Walk, 1946-1949; 6 King's Bench Walk, 1950-1952; 3 Temple Gardens, 1953-1959. Junior Counsel to; Ministry of Agriculture & Fisheries and Food; Forestry Commission; and Commissioners of Crown Lands, 1949-1959. Recorder of Oldham, 1950-1959. County Court Judge, 1959-1975; Circuit 56, (Kent & Surrey). He was junior counsel for the Crown in R-v-Rowland (1946). Celebrated Trials, Henry Cecil, published by David & Charles in 1975.

WINGATE-SAUL, Sir Ernest Wingate KC
Born 25 March 1873. Died 13 December 1944 aged 71. Eldest son of William Wingate Wingate Saul, father of His Honour Judge Wingate-Saul qv, grandfather of Giles Wingate Wingate-Saul QC qv. Rugby; Christ Church, Oxford, BA, 1895; MA, 1898. I. 12 May 1897. ETC. 27 July 1897. Prop. Shee QC. Sec. Overend Evans. Manchester Chambers; 40 King Street, 1897-1898; Duchy Chambers, Clarence Street, 1899-1908; 60 King Street, 1909-1919. Silk 1919. 8 King's Bench Walk, 1919-1927; 2 Hare Court, 1928. No address, 1929-1944. Recorder of Preston and Judge and Assessor of Borough Court of Pleas, 1921-1928. Judge of Appeal in the Isle of Man, 1925-1928. Umpire: under the Unemployment Insurance Act, 1928-1944; and under the Reinstatement in Civil Employment Act, 1944. WW.

WINGATE-SAUL, Giles Wingate QC.
Born 9 March 1945, Hartford, Cheshire. Grandson of Sir Ernest Wingate Wingate-Saul KC qv and nephew of His Honour Judge Wingate-Saul qv. Winchester College; Southampton University, LLB. Schoolmaster, Eton College, 1964. I. November 1967. ETC. November 1967; Bencher 1993. Prop. Derek Hodgson QC. Sec. Martin Collins. Manchester Chambers; 601 Royal Exchange, 1967-1983. Silk 1983. 5 Essex Court, 1983-1989. 12 Byrom Street later 25 Byrom Street, Manchester, 1989. Recorder 1984. Deputy High Court Judge, 1991. Deputy Judge of the Technology & Construction Court.

WINSTANLEY, Hubert
L. 26 January 1877. 21 Harrington Street, Liverpool, 1877-1883. Registrar, Lancs. Chancery Court, Manchester District, 1884-1924. No address, 1925-1936 save for private address in Knutsford. Not in 1937 Law List.

WINSTANLEY, James Winckworth
Born 1817. 3rd son of John Strange Winstanley of London. King's College, London. AAS. L. 21 May 1834. Call 11 June 1839. 26 Chancery Lane, 1848. Equity draftsman & conveyancer. Registrar, Lancs. Chancery Court, Liverpool District, 1853-1880. No address, 1881-1891. Not in 1892 Law List. Foster.

WISHART, John Duckworth Scott
Born 15 April 1942, Accrington. Queen Elizabeth Grammar School, Accrington. HNC in Mechanical & Production Engineering. Qualified engineer. Ashton Brothers & Co, Textile Manufacturers, 1960-1969; Daimler-Benz AG, Stuttgart, 1969-1972; Civilian Instructor, US Armed Forces in Germany, 1972-1973. G. 18 July 1974. ETC. 1976. Prop. Douglas Brown QC. Sec. Lindsey Platt. Pupilmaster, John Victor Williamson. Manchester Chambers; Post Office Chambers, 26 Brown Street, 1976; 4th floor, Sunlight House, Quay Street, 1977-1983; Conavon Chambers, 12 Blackfriars Street, 1984-1989; Manchester House Chambers, 18-22 Bridge Street, 1990-1999 (Founder & Head of Chambers); 28 St John Street October 1999-31.12. 2001. In practice from home, June 2002.

WITT, George
G. 28 April 1915. No address, 1916-1921. Not in 1922 Law List.

WITHINGTON, Neil Robert
Born 6 September 1956 Manchester. William Hulme's Grammar School, Manchester; Brasenose College, Oxford, MA., BCL. AAS. M. 18 January 1978. Call 23 July 1981. ETC. 1981. Prop. Benet Hytner QC. Sec. Rodney Scholes. 28 St John Street, Manchester, September 1981-July 1986. ICI, Legal Department: Pharmaceuticals Division, 1986-1990; at Millbank, London, 1990-1993. BAT Industries: Senior Lawyer, 1993-1995; Assistant General Counsel & Head of Product Litigation, 1996-1998; Deputy General Counsel, 1998. Sessional Lecturer, Osgoode Hall Law School, Toronto, 1979-1980. Visiting Professor, University of Oklahoma Law School, 1980.

WOLFF, Michael Emanuel

(DC)

Born 8 October 1940 Nakuru, Kenya. Prince of Wales School, Nairobi; Liverpool University, LLB. G. 29 June 1964. ETC. November 1964. Prop. Winston Guthrie Jones QC. Sec. Henry Lachs. Same Liverpool Chambers at; 27 Dale Street, 1964-1976; Melbourne Buildings, 21 North John Street, 1977-1988; 3rd floor, Peel House, Harrington Street, 1989-1998; India Buildings, Water Street, 12.1.1998. Deputy Circuit Judge, 1979-1985. Recorder, 1985-1998.

WOLSTENHOLME, Alan James
Born 10 April 1966 Bury. Leeds University, LLB. L. July 1989. Manchester Chambers; Rational House, 64 Bridge Street, 1994-1995; Lincoln House Chambers, 1 Brazennose Street, 1996-2000; 24a St John Street, 2000. (now St Johns Buildings).

WOOD, Agnes Ruth
Manchester University, LLB. L. January 1950. No address, 1950-1961. 3 St James's Square, Manchester, 1962-1978. Not in 1979 Law List.

WOOD, Alan Holden
I. 3 July 1935. ETC. 10 July 1935. Prop. Lynskey KC. Sec. Gerrard. 3 St James's Square, Manchester, 1935-1940. No address, 1940-1949. 1 Hare Court, 1949. No address, 1950-1961. Not in 1962 Law List.

WOOD, Daniel James
Born 12 November 1972 Liverpool. Bluecoat School, Liverpool; BSc, MSc., Liverpool; LLB, Leeds. L. 27 July 2000. Cobleys, solicitors, Liverpool, 2000-2001. ETC. 26 July 2001. Prop. Iain Goldrein QC. Sec. Nigel Beeson. 14 Cook Street, Liverpool, April 2001. New Bailey Chambers, Liverpool, 2004.

WOOD, Frederick
Born 1849. 2nd surviving son of James Wood of Monument House, Wigan. Formerly a solicitor of Southport when AAS. M. 1 November 1887. Call 19 November 1890. ETC. 20 March 1890. Prop. Gully QC. Sec. McConnell. Various chambers addresses in London between 1891 and 1909 and finally at 2 Essex Court, 1906-1909. No address, 1910-1940. Not in 1941 Law List.

WOOD, Graham Nash QC
Born 21 May 1957, Liverpool. Brother of David Wood, partner in Davies, Wallis & Foyster, solicitors. Liverpool College; Leeds University, LLB. AAS. M. 19 April 1978. Call 26 July 1979. ETC. December 1979. Prop. Michael Maguire QC. Sec. Ian Stanley. Liverpool Chambers; Melbourne Buildings, 21 North John Street, 1979-1988; 3rd floor, Peel House, Harrington Street, 1989-1998; India Buildings, Water Street, 12.1.1998-2002. Silk 2002. Exchange Chambers, Pearl Assurance House, Derby Square, 2002. Legal Aid Area Committee Member, 1994-2001. Assistant Recorder 1996. Recorder 2000. Deputy Chancellor, Diocese of Liverpool, 2002. Lay Reader, Church of England. Publications; Bingham's Negligence Cases, revised edition, 1994; 4th edition, 2002. WW.

WOOD, Ian Robert
Born 29 July 1967 Berwick-on-Tweed. Manchester University, BA (Law & Accountancy). AAS. M. 13 February 1989. Call 16 October 1990. 8 King Street, Manchester, 1992.

WOOD, John
G. 3 July 1935. ETC. 26 February 1936. Prop. William Gorman KC. Sec. Atkinson. Circuit Junior, Winter 1936. Died in road traffic accident in 1936. 3 St James's Square, Manchester, 1935-1936. The 'Old Northern Circuit Cup' for which the Northern & North Eastern Circuits have competed at golf each year since 1936 is inscribed "In memory of John Wood. Junior of the Northern Circuit, October-December 1936."

WOOD, Sir John Crossley
LLB., LLM (Manchester). G. June 1950. Manchester Chambers; 43 King Street, 1955-1988; 5 John Dalton Street, 1989. Chairman; Industrial & Mental Health Tribunals. Member, Judicial Studies Tribunals Committee.

WOOD, Michael John
Born 7 June 1944 Sheffield. Sheffield University, BA (Modern Languages), LLB; Bradford University, Management Centre, DiplA (Marketing & International Trade). Senior Manager & Management Consultant for ten years. L. November 1989. Exchange Chambers, Pearl Assurance House, Derby Square, Liverpool, October 1990.

WOOD, Percy
Born 17 February 1932 Bolton. Bolton School (1943-1950). Army; 9th Lancers, 1951-1953; TA, (Duke of Lancaster's Own Yeomanry), 1953-1957. Trinity College, Cambridge, BA, 1956; MA, 1960. Teacher, 1957-1961. AAS. G. February 1955. Call 7 February 1961. ETC. 1961. Prop. Joseph Cantley QC. Sec. J W Stansfield. Same Manchester Chambers; 3 St James's Square, 1961-1984; St James's Chambers, 68 Quay Street, 1984. Between 1970 and 1996 has held the Circuit office of Cryer, Solicitor General and Attorney General. Deputy Circuit Judge/Assistant Recorder, 1978-1986. Percy has provided me with a splendid discretion statement which covers two sides of A4 detailing the Petitioner's sexual exploits with thirty different women in places as far apart as West Indies, Malta, Singapore, Hong Kong, Mombassa, Ceylon, Aden, Naples, Sicily and Nuneaton. It concludes with the immortal compulsory words, "save as aforesaid, I have not committed adultery."

WOOD, Ralph (His Honour Judge Wood)
Born 26 April 1921. Died 4 November 1986 aged 65. Wilmslow Preparatory School; King's School, Macclesfield; Served war of 1939-1945; Commissioned, Somerset Light Infantry in England, India & Manipur, 1941-1946. Exeter College, Oxford. G. November 1948. ETC. 1949. 60 King Street, Manchester, 1949-1972. Deputy Chairman, Lancashire Quarter Sessions, 1970-1971. Circuit Judge, 1972-1986. WW.

WOODARD, Mortimer Neville
Born 1840. Son of the Rev. Nathaniel Woodard of Henfield, Sussex. Late of the 88th Regt. AAS. M. 28 October 1865. Call 6 June 1868. ETC. 11 August 1868. Prop. Jones QC. Sec. Manisty QC. Circuit Junior, Spring 1869. 32 South King Street, Manchester, 1876. 4 Garden Court, 1876-1883; 4 Brick Court, 1884-1888. Not in 1889 Law List. Foster.

WOODBURNE, George Burgess Lancaster
Born 29 May 1855. Only son of George Woodburne of Salford. Owens College, Manchester BA; Queen's College, Oxford, BA, 1878; MA. AAS. L. 11 January 1878. Call 17 November 1880. ETC. 24 January 1881. Prop. Hopwood QC. Sec. Sutton. 6 Stone Building, 1881-1883. Manchester Chambers; 41 John Dalton Street, 1884-1891; 18 South King Street, 1892-1902. Not in 1903 Law List. Foster.

WOODHALL, Gary
Born 11 January 1975 Hartlepool. Billingham Campus School; Trinity College, Cambridge, BA (Law) (Double First). G. 9 October 1997. ETC. December 1997. Prop. Rod Carus QC. Sec. Nicholas Clarke. 9 St John Street, Manchester, 1998.

WOODHOUSE, John Sidney Lister VRD
MA (Cantab). G. June 1949. 60 King Street, Manchester, 1949-1953. Left the Bar to join Associated Octel Company Ltd of Ellesmere Port & London; Assistant Company Secretary.

WOODHOUSE, Samuel Henry
Born 2 March 1848. Eldest son of Samuel Woodhouse of Norley Hall, Cheshire, JP. Eton; University College, Oxford, BA, 1871. AAS. L. 13 November 1872. Call 7 June 1875. ETC. 13 July 1875. Prop. Herschell QC. Sec. Mellor. Circuit Junior, Spring 1876. 22 North John Street, Liverpool, 1876-1879. Retired in 1879. No address, 1979-1935. Not in 1936 Law List.

WOODS, Lynn
Born 1938. Only daughter of Herbert Woods of Bolton, tool room superintendent at De Havilland. St Anne's College, Oxford, MA. AAS. M. 12 March 1959. Call 9 February 1965. ETC. 15 June 1965. Manchester Chambers; 60 King Street, 1965-1983; Crown Square Chambers. 1 Dean's Court, 1984-1993; 9 St John Street, 1994-1995. No address, 1996.

WOODS, Rachael Helen
Born 5 October 1969 Lincoln. Kesteven & Grantham Girls' School; Manchester Polytechnic, LLB. G. 13 October 1992. ETC. 16 December 1996. Prop. Roger Farley QC. Sec. Paul Sheridan. Manchester House Chambers, 18-22 Bridge Street, Manchester, September 1997-July 1999. Crown Prosecution Service, 1999-2000. Queen's Chambers, 5 John Dalton Street, 2000.

WOODWARD, Alison Jane
Born 23 February 1970, Sheffield. Daughter of His Honour Judge Woodward qv and sister of Joanne Woodward qv. Cheadle Hulme Grammar School; Sheffield University, LLB. G. October 1992. Prop. Rodney Klevan QC. Sec. Michael Goldwater. Manchester Chambers; Hollins Chambers; 64a Bridge Street, 1992-1997 which became Cobden House Chambers, 19 Quay Street, 1998-2001; Dean's Court Chambers, 24 St John Street, 2001.

WOODWARD, Barry (His Honour Judge Woodward)
father of Joanne and Alison Woodward qv. Sheffield University, LLM. Teacher, 1961-1970. G. November 1970. Manchester Chambers; Post Office Chambers, 26 Brown Street, 1970-1971; 67 Princess Street, 1972-1984. Chairman, Industrial Tribunals, Manchester Region, 1984-1990. Assistant Recorder, 1985. Recorder, 1988. Circuit Judge, Manchester, 5.12.1990. Resident Judge, Minshull Street, Manchester, 2002. Temporary Additional Judge of Employment Appeals Tribunal, 2002. WW.

WOODWARD, Edward Gilbert
Born 11 June 1900. Died 11 March 1950 aged 49. Only son of Edward Robert Woodward of 3 Plowden Buildings, barrister. Shrewsbury School; Balliol College, Oxford, MA., BCL. TA, 1922-1939. AAS. M. 18 June 1920. Call 19 November 1923. ETC. 25 February 1925. Prop. Wingate-Saul KC. Sec. F J V Sandbach. 8 King's Bench Walk, 1924-1927; 2 Hare Court, 1928-1948. Metropolitan Magistrate, Bow Street, 1948-1950. Publications; Archbold's Poor Law, 16th edition, 1930; books on road traffic law. WW.

WOODWARD, Joanne Claire
Born 25 December 1966, Sheffield. Daughter of His Honour Judge Woodward qv and sister of Alison Woodward qv. Manchester Warehousemans & Clerks, Cheadle Hulme; Manchester Metropolitan University, LLB. G. November 1989. ETC. 1989. Prop. David Poole QC. Sec. John Broadley. Manchester Chambers; Hollins Chambers, 64a Bridge Street, 1989-1997 which became Cobden House Chambers, 19 Quay Street, 1998.

WOODWARD, John Edward
Born, Blackburn. Lawrence House School, Giggleswick. Lorry driver, 1976-1978. Preston Polytechnic, 1980-1983, LLB. L. November 1984. ETC. 1986. Prop. Michael Maguire QC. Sec. Gordon Bellis. 3rd floor, 27 Dale Street, 1986-1990; Kenworthy's Buildings, 83 Bridge Street, Manchester, 1990-1992; 15 Winckley Square, Preston, 1993-.

WOOLFENDEN, Ivan Peter
Born 1962 Liverpool. Royal Grammar School, High Wycombe; Jesus College, Oxford, BA. M. July 1985. ETC. 1986. Prop. Brian Leveson QC. Sec. Sean Duncan. 14 Castle Street/ Atlantic Chambers, Cook Street, Liverpool, 1986. Publications; Chapter on Vibration White Finger in 2nd edition of Industrial Disease Litigation, Sweet & Maxwell.

WOOLL, Edward OBE., QC.
Born 31 March 1878 Liverpool. Died 20 May 1970 aged 92. Eldest son of Rev. C W Wooll, Vicar of Ditton, Lancs. Liverpool College; New College, Oxford. I. 26 January 1903. ETC. 19 February 1903. Prop. A G Steel KC. Sec. F E Smith. Liverpool Chambers; 10 Cook Street, 1903; Stephenson's Chambers, 25 Lord Street, 1904-1920; 24 North John Street, 1920; 26 North John Street, 1921-1928; 1 King's Bench Walk, 1929-1934; 1 Hare Court, 1935-1939; 34 Castle Street, Liverpool, 1940-1943; Goldsmith Building, 1944-1954; 1 Hare Court, 1955-1965; retired from 2 Pump Court in October 1965. Cheshire Yeomanry, 1914-1927; Captain; Cavalry Corps, H Q. BEF, 1916-1919; despatches, twice, OBE. Contested (C): St Helens, 1922; Hull, Central, 1923. Recorder of Carlisle, 1929-1963. Silk 1949. In the days before elected Leaders, as the senior silk, he was Leader of the Northern Circuit. Plays: Libel, 1934; Moral Gestures, 1937; The Last Will, 1964. Unpublished plays: The Lady Helen Hautbois; The Breach. Novels: There is a Tide, The Lodestar, Libel, The Nettle. Layman's Guide to Libel. Libel was his most successful work. Alec Guinness made his first appearance on the professional stage in a non speaking part as a junior barrister in Libel. It was directed by Leon M Lion at the Playhouse Theatre in London in 1934. Anthony Asquith directed the film of Libel in 1959, starring Dirk Bogarde and Olivia de Havilland. I take from Dick Hamilton's "Foul Bills & Dagger Money" the best known story of Wooll:
"When, (in 1918), Armistice came it was Wooll's duty to accept the keys of the surrendered city of Cologne from its then Mayor, Konrad Adenauer. After the Nazis came to power, Wooll made one of those gestures typical of him. He visited Germany, and had to complete a questionnaire which asked whether he had visited Germany before, and if so, in what capacity. "Yes", wrote Wooll to the first question – "as Conqueror", to the second one. The Nazis cannot have been amused." WW.
See 'A Century of Liverpool Lawyers' pages 101-104 (William Lister).

WOOLLAM, John Victor MP
Born 14 August 1927. Liverpool University. I. November 1952. 24 Dale Street, 1953-1955. No address, 1956-1963. Not in 1964 Law List. Contested (C) Scotland Division of Liverpool, 1950. MP (C) Liverpool, West Derby, 1954-1964. Parliamentary Private Secretary to the Minister of Labour, 1960-1962. WW.

WOOLLEY, (Edward) Timothy (Starbuck)
Born 1943. 2nd son of Edward James Starbuck Woolley of Derby, consultant physician. Epsom College, Surrey. AAS. M. 2 October 1964. Call 18 July 1968. Pupilmaster, Roy McAulay (Midland & Oxford Circuit). ETC. 1969.

North House, 17 North John Street, Liverpool, 1969-1973. Hong Kong: Legal Aid Officer, 1973-1977; Senior Legal Aid Officer, 1977-1979; Assistant Principal Legal Aid Officer, 1979-1984; Assistant Director of Legal Aid, 1984-1985; Master, High Court, 1985-1997; Secondment, Chief Registrar, Supreme Court, Brunei, 1987-1989; Registrar, Court of Final Appeal, Hong Kong (replacing the Privy Council on 1.7.1999), 1997-2004 when he retired to Australia.

WOOSEY, Elizabeth Jane
Born 2 March 1969, Whiston. Tower College, Rainhill, 1973-1985; St Edward's College, Liverpool, 1985-1987; Liverpool University, LLB. L. 29 July 1993. Pupilmaster, Peter Moss. 3 Temple Gardens, 1992-1993; 1 Dr Johnson's Building, 1993-1994. VAT Advisor, Price Waterhouse, London Bridge, 1994-1997. ETC. 28 July 1998. Prop. Richard Henriques QC. Sec. Nadine Hope. Victoria Chambers, 19 Castle Street, Liverpool, 1997-1999. 5 John Dalton Street, Manchester, 1999. Grade 8 pianist.

WOOTTON, Norman Godfrey
Born 10 April 1926. Died 27 March 2000 aged 73. The Grammar School, Crewe; Liverpool University, LLB. G. 1951. ETC. 1951. Liverpool Chambers; 34 Castle Street, 1951-1955; Corn Exchange, Brunswick Street, 1956-1957; 9 Rumford Street, 1958-1973; Fruit Exchange, Victoria Street, 1974-1976. Recorder, 1972-1996. Stipendiary Magistrate for Merseyside, 1976-1994. WW.

WORRALL, Anna Maureen QC
Born 16 September 1938, Bramhall. Eldest daughter of T B Worrall of Hazel Grove, accountant. Married to G H G Williams QC (Midland & Oxford Circuit). Hillcrest School, Bramhall; Loreto College, Llandudno; Manchester University, LLB. AAS. M. 8 November 1956. Call 24 November 1959; Bencher 1996. ETC. November 1959. Pupilmaster, Basil Gerrard. 4 Chapel Walks, Manchester, 1959-1963; 2 Harcourt Buildings, 1970-1973; Cloisters, Pump Court, 1973-2000; Lamb Building, 2000. Lecturer in Law, Holborn College of Law, 1964-1969. Director, Inner London Education Authority Educational Television Service, 1969-1971. Recorder 1987. Silk 1989. President, Mental Health Review Tribunals, 1995. WW.

WORRALL, Shirley Vera Frances
LLB. G. November 1987. 8 King Street Chambers, Manchester, 1990-2002. Not in 2003 Bar Directory.

WORSLEY-TAYLOR, Sir Henry Wilson QC., MP., First Bt.
Born 25 July 1847. Died 27 June 1924 aged 76. Only son of James Worsley of Accrington. He assumed the name and arms of Taylor in 1881 in accordance with the will of his cousin, Miss Pilling-Taylor. Harrow; Exeter College, Oxford, BA, 1870. AAS. I. 15 November 1867. Call 1 May 1871; Bencher 1894; Reader, Lent 1906. ETC. 27 February 1872. Prop. Charles Russell QC. Sec. Mellor. Goldsmith Building and Preston Sessions, 1871-1882. Parliamentary Bar from Palace Chambers, 9 Bridge Street, Westminster, 1882-1901. Silk 1891. Moreton Hall, Whalley, Lancs., 1902-1924. Chairman, Lancashire Quarter Sessions at Preston, 1893-1917. Recorder of Preston, 1894-1898. MP (C) Blackpool, 1900-1906. JP., DL., First Bt. 1917. WW.

WORTHINGTON, John Morton CVO
Born 16 July 1883. Died 5 June 1956 aged 72. Son of J H Worthington of Fulwood. Preston Grammar School. Solicitor, 1905. L. 26 January 1921. ETC. 15 June 1921. Prop. Greaves-Lord KC. Sec. Singleton. Winckley Street, Preston, 1921-1926. Equity draftsman & conveyancer. Registrar, Lancs. Chancery Court, Preston District, 1926-1955. CVO. 1954. JP., Lancs., 1933. WW.

WORTHINGTON, Michael Law
Born 7 May 1915, Prestbury. Son of Walter and Muriel Worthington and husband of Heather Frances Worthington. Oxford University Air Squadron, 1933-1936. L. 9 June 1937. ETC. 6 July 1937. Prop. William Gorman QC. Sec. Alan Walmsley. 78 King Street, Manchester 1937-1939. Lancs. Chancery Court. Commissioned as a Pilot Offficer, RAFVR, 30.11.1939. Promoted to Flying Officer, 30.11.1940. Pilot of an Armstrong Whitworth Whitley of 502 Squadron which was lost near BallyKelly on 7 December 1940. He was 25 years of age. Buried, "old ground", south east of church at St Peter's, Prestbury. Information supplied by RAF Personnel Management Agency and Commonwealth War Graves Commission.

WORTLEY, Ben Atkinson CMG., OBE., QC.
Born 16 November 1907. Died 9 June 1989 aged 81. LLD (Manchester); LLM (Leeds). G. April 1947; Hon Bencher 1989. Manchester Chambers; 4 Chapel Walks, 1947-1964; 601 Royal Exchange, 1965-1975. Professor of Jurisprudence and International Law at Manchester University, 1946-1975, then Emeritus. Numerous publications include: Jurisprudence, 1967; part editor, Dicey's Conflict of Laws, 1949; Law of the Common Market, 1974. OBE. 1946, Silk 1969, CMG. 1978. WW.

WORTLEY, Hon Francis Dudley Montagu Stuart
Born 23 July 1829. Father of Major-General Edward Stuart Wortley and Lieut-General Sir Richard Stuart Wortley. AAS. I. 2 May 1851. Call 1 May 1854. No address, 1876-1893. Not in 1894 Law List.

WRENN, Helen Margaret
Born 26 November 1965 Worcester. Married to Andrew Carney qv. Droitwich High School; Leeds University, BA (English/History). Postgraduate Tutor, University of Aristotle, 1988-1990. (Greek Speaker) Self employed, 1990-1993. I. November 1994. 17 Bedford Row, 1994-1995; pupilmaster, John Critchley. ETC. 19 December 1995. Prop. Robert Fordham QC. Sec. Stephen Knapp. Liverpool Chambers; Martins Building, Water Street, 1994-1999; 7 Harrington Street 6.9.1999. (merger with Corn Exchange).

WRIGHT, Alastair David
Born 15 August 1967, Oldham. Brother of Peter Wright QC. qv. Hulme Grammar School, Oldham; Mansfield College, Oxford, MA., Dip. Law. L. October 1991. ETC. November 1991. Prop. A A Rumbelow QC. Sec. Stephen Stewart. 28 St John Street, Manchester, 1991. (now St Johns Buildings Chambers).

WRIGHT, Charles Francis
Born 1 October 1852. 2nd son of James Wright of Edinburgh. Brasenose College, Oxford, BA, 1876, BCL, 1879. AAS. I. 17 November 1873. Call 17 November 1877. ETC. 21 January 1879. Prop. Leofric Temple QC. Sec. Cardwell. Circuit Junior, Summer 1879. 8 King's Bench Walk, 1880; 6 Pump Court, 1881-1885. No address, 1886-1911. Not in 1912 Law List. Foster.

WRIGHT, David William
Liverpool University, LLB. G. November 1986. 196 Deansgate, Manchester, 1986-1989. Not in 1990-1993 Bar Directories. Law Department, Royal Bank of Scotland, Deansgate, Manchester, 1994. Not in 1995 Bar Directory.

WRIGHT, Eric Blackwood
Born 1 May 1860 Middleton, Tyas, Yorks. Died 10 April 1940 aged 79. Eldest son of Rev. Charles Henry Wright, DD., of St Mary's, Antrim. Trinity College, Dublin, BA, 1882; LLB, 1884; LLD, 1905. AAS. M. 16 November 1882. Call 17 June 1885. 1 Garden Court, 1891-1892; 3 Dr Johnson's Building, 1893 (Midland & Oxford Circuit). ETC. 6 March 1893. Prop. McCall QC. Sec. Parry. 13 Harrington Street, Liverpool, 1893-1894; "B" Commerce Court, Liverpool, 1895-1902. 5 Fig Tree Court, 1903; 2 Brick Court, 1904. Seychelles Islands: Chief Justice, 1905-1909; Administrator, 1907. Stipendiary Justice, Trinidad, 1912-1923. Judge of the Supreme Court of Trinidad & Tobago, 1914-1920. Legal Advisor to the Ministry of Munitions, French Section, 1920; Fellow of Royal Empire Society. Publications; Law of Principal & Agent, 1894; 2nd edition, 1902; The Law of Negligence, 1898. WW.

WRIGHT, Gerard Henry QC
Born 23 July 1929. Stonyhurst College. Served Army, 1947-1949, rank T, Captain. Lincoln College, Oxford, BA., BCL. G. February 1954. (Arden & Barstow Scholar). ETC. 4 March 1954. Prop. Robertson Crichton QC. Sec. Leslie Rigg. Liverpool Chambers; 9 Rumford Street, 1954-1957; 27 Dale Street, 1958-1973. Silk 1973. 13 King's Bench Walk, 1973-1980; Melbourne Buildings, 21 North John Street, 1981-1988; 3rd floor, Peel House, Harrington Street, 1989-1994; 25-27 Castle Street, 1995-1999. KHS. 1974; KCHS. 1979; KCSHS. 1992, Auxilaire de l'Hospitalite de Notre Dame de Lourdes, 1982, Titulaire, 1985. Publications; (with others) Test Tube Babies – a Christian View, 1984. WW.

WRIGHT, Hugh, junior
Born 1868. 2nd son of Hugh Wright of Attiory, Wigtownshire. Edinburgh University, MA. AAS. M. 13 January 1888. Call 17 November 1890. ETC. 15 July 1891. Prop. McCall QC. Sec. Green. 4 Middle Temple Lane, 1891-1893. No address, 1894-1949. Not in 1950 Law List.

WRIGHT, Norman Alfred
Born 20 January 1951 London. Married to District Judge Susan Wright, Liverpool. Bradford Grammar School; Liverpool University, LLB. G. 26 November 1974. ETC. December 1974. Prop. Michael Maguire QC. Sec. Eric Somerset Jones. Same Liverpool Chambers; Oriel Chambers, 5 Covent Garden/ 14 Water Street, Liverpool, July 1974. Assistant Recorder 1993. Recorder 1999.

WRIGHT, Peter Duncan QC
Born 2 November 1957 Oldham. Brother of Alistair Wright qv. Chadderton Grammar School for Boys; Hull University, LLB. I. July 1981. ETC. December 1981. Prop. Jack Price QC. Sec. Paul Reid. Manchester Chambers; Rational House, 64 Bridge Street, 1981-1995, which became Lincoln House Chambers, 1 Brazennose Street, 1995. Silk 1999. Recorder 2001. WW.

WRIGHT, Richard Thomas
Born 2 June 1846. Eldest son of Rev. John Wright of Bury, Dissenting Minister. Owen's College, Manchester; Christ College, Cambridge, MA (late fellow & tutor). AAS. L. 12 November 1867. Call 10 June 1870. ETC. 10

March 1871. Prop. Higgin QC. Sec. Hopwood. 3 Dr Johnson's Building, 1881-1887. No address, 1888-1931. Not in 1932 Law List. Foster.

WRIGHT, Sir Robert Samuel (The Hon. Mr Justice Wright)
Born 20 January 1839. Died 13 August 1904 aged 65. Eldest son of Rev. Henry Edward Wright, Rector of Litton, Somerset. King's School, Bruton, Somerset; Balliol College, Oxford, BA, 1862; BCL, 1863; MA, 1864; Fellow, 1861-1880; Hon. Fellow, 1892. AAS, I. 20 November 1861. Call 9 June 1865; Bencher 1891. ETC. 30 March 1872. Prop. Butt QC. Sec. Stanley. 1 Paper Buildings, 1876-1891. Junior Counsel to the Treasury, 1883. High Court Judge, Queen's Bench Division, 1890-1904. Publications; Golden Treasury of Ancient Greek Poetry, 1882; Possession in the Common Law (with Sir Frederick Pollock), 1888. WW. DNB.

WRIGHT, Sidney
Born 1859. 2nd son of Henry Wright of Hampton Court, Middlesex. AAS. I. 16 May 1878. Call 11 May 1881. ETC. 24 July 1883. Prop. Crompton QC. Sec. Sutton. 2 Paper Buildings, 1886-1894; 5 Paper Buildings, 1895-1896; 11 King' Bench Walk, 1897-1902. No address, 1903. Not in 1904 Law List.

WRIGHT, Yasmin Tajdin
Born 17 September 1964. Fitzalan High School, Cardiff; Manchester Metropolitan University, LLB. I. November 1990. ETC. 1991. Pupilmaster, Roger Brown. 33 King Street West, Manchester, 1990-1991; New Bailey Chambers, Preston, 1993.

WRIGLEY, Frank Thomas
L 25 April 1888. ETC. 27 July 1888. Prop. Henn Collins QC. Sec. Henry. 4 Paper Buildings, 1890-1892. No address, 1893-1940. Not in 1941 Law List.

Y

YATE-LEE, His Honour Judge Lawford
Born 17 June 1838 London. Died 17 May 1901 aged 62. Eldest son of John Yate-Lee of Bebington, Cheshire, barrister. Royal Institute, Liverpool; Emmanuel College, Cambridge, BA, 1860; MA, 1863. L. 17 November 1864. 61 Carey Street, WC., 1876. Equity draftsman & conveyancer. Lancs. Chancery Court. County Court Judge, Circuit 9, (Stockport, Ashton-u-Lyne and Stalybridge, May 1896-1901. Publications; Law & Practice of Bankruptcy and Imprisonment for Debt. JP, Worcs. WW.

YATES, John
L. 27 January 1890. ETC. 11 March 1891. Prop. French QC. Sec. Pickford. 13 Harrington Street, Liverpool, 1890-1902. No address, 1903-1938. Not in 1939 Law List.

YATES, John Lowndes
Born 1855. 2nd son of William Lowndes Yates of Congleton, barrister. Trinity Hall, Cambridge. AAS. M. 1 May 1874. Call 13 June 1877. ETC. 18 July 1878. Prop. Gully QC. Sec. Aspland. 6 Crown Office Row, 1879-1881; 1 Dr. Johnson's Building, 1882-1885; 6 Crown Office Row, 1886. No address,1887-1889. Not in 1890 Law List. Foster.

YATES, Joseph Maghull QC.
Born 19 June 1844. Died 17 April 1916 aged 71. Son of His Honour Joseph St. John Yates qv. Westminster School; Trinity College, Cambridge, BA, 1867. AAS. I. 27 April 1866. Call 26 January 1869. ETC. 3 August 1869. Prop. Hosack. Sec. Baistow. 9 St James's Square, Manchester, 1876-1889; 4 St James's Square, 1890-1893. Silk 1893. 1 Kings Bench Walk, 1893-1894. Recorder of Salford, 1889-1904. Chairman of Quarter Sessions, Salford Hundred, and Stipendiary Magistrate, Manchester Division of Lancashire, 1894-1916. WW. Foster.

YATES, Joseph Mervyn St. John
L. 6 May 1903. ETC. 16 July 1903. Prop. Pickford KC. Sec. Acton. Bank of England Chambers, Tib Lane, Manchester, 1903-1921. No address, 1922-1925. Judge, Kingston, Jamaica, 1926. Circuit Judge, Ashanti, 1927-1930. Puisne Judge, Gold Coast, 1931-1939. No address, 1940-1953. Not in 1954 Law List.

YATES, Joseph St. John (His Honour Judge Yates)
Born 16 October 1808. Died 2 March 1887 aged 78. Grandson of Mr Justice Yates, eldest son of Joseph Yates of Peel Hall, Lancs., barrister, father of Joseph Maghull Yates QC. qv. Charterhouse; Christ Church, Oxford. County Court Judge, Circuit 9, 1847-1882. JP, Lancs, Cheshire & Derbys. Previously Judge of Small Debts Court of Glossop and commissioner of bankruptcy in the Manchester list. Deputy Steward of the Manor and Forest of Macclesfield. Foster.

YATES, William Flood
Born 1832. Only son of William Yates of Irwell House, Lancs. University College, Durham, MA. AAS. I. 19 January 1857. Call 17 November 1859. No address, 1876-1901. Not in 1902 Law List.

YERBURGH, Robert Armstrong MP
Born 17 January 1853, Died 18 December 1916 aged 63. Rossall; Harrow; University College, Oxford, BA, 1877. AAS, 26 September 1877. Call 9 June 1880. ETC. 12 July 1880. Prop. Higgin QC. Sec. Temple QC. 4 Harcourt Buildings, 1882-1889. No address, 1890-1916. Not in 1917 Law List. Late Major, 2nd Volunteer Btn., Cheshire Regt. President, Navy League. MP (C) Chester, 1886-1906. WW.

YERBURGH-BONSEY, Harold Robert OBE
Born 1878. 4th son of Rev. William Bonsey of Lancaster, AAS. M. 6 May 1898. Call 11 June 1902. ETC. 11 July 1902. Prop. Horridge KC. Sec. Sanderson. 4 Elm Court, 1902-1906. No chambers address, 1907-1932. Not in 1933 Law List.

YIP, Amanda Louise
Born 23 April 1969, Liverpool. Daughter of The Rt. Hon. Lord Justice Kay qv. Merchant Taylors' School for Girls, Crosby; Emmanuel College, Cambridge, MA. G. October 1991. Inns of Court, Certificate of Honour. Macaskie Award. ETC. December 1991. Prop. John Kay QC. Sec. Tim Holroyde. Exchange Chambers, Pearl Assurance House, Derby Square, Liverpool, 1991.

YOUDE, Barrie Michael Fergus
Born 26 January 1943, Birkenhead. Grandson of William Fergus Youde, partner of Walker, Smith & Way, solicitors of Chester. Liverpool College; Licensed Liverpool Pilot, 1966-1988. Liverpool Polytechnic, (now Liverpool John Moores University), LLB 1989. I. November 1990. ETC. 1991. Prop. John Rowe QC. Sec. John Mockett. 46 Stanley Street, Liverpool, 1991-1994. Now a solicitor with Bullivant Jones of Liverpool. Publications; 'Beyond the Bar – A Light History of the Liverpool Pilot Service' (1994).

YOUDS, Edward Ernest (His Honour Edward Youds)
Born 21 November 1910. Died August 2003 Liverpool, aged 92. Birkenhead School; Magdalene College, Cambridge, BA., LLB. G. 24 June 1936. ETC. 1936. Pupilmaster, James Fraser Harrison. Liverpool Chambers; 3 Cook Street, 1936-1951; North House, 17 North John Street, 1952-1966. Served, 1940-1945; France & Germany; dispatches, 1945. Deputy Chairman, Lancs. Quarter Sessions, 1961-1966. County Court Judge, Liverpool, 1966-1969. Puisne Judge, High Court of Uganda, 1969-1972. Circuit Judge, Bedford, 1972-1985. Retired to the Isle of Man. WW.

YOUNG, Keith Rymer
BA., LLB (Cantab). G. 17 November 1920. ETC. 1920. Circuit Junior, Summer 1922. Liverpool Chambers; 5 Harrington Street, 1921-1922; 25 Lord Street, 1923-1927; 15 Union Court, 1928-1933; 3 Cook Street, 1934-1940. District Probate Registrar, Liverpool, 1941-1963. Not in 1964 Law List.

YOUNG, Simon
Queen's College, Cambridge, MA. I. 1998. 4 Paper Buildings, 1998-2002. 8 King Street Chambers, Manchester, 2002. Contributing Editor of Professional Negligence Liability, 2000.

YOUNG, William Eaton
Born 7 February 1848. Queen's College, Oxford, BA., BCL. AAS. I. 12 April 1872. Call 26 January 1875. ETC. 16 March 1876. Prop. Edwards QC. Sec. Tomlinson. 9 St James's Square, Manchester, 1876-1878. No address, 1879-1933. Not in 1934 Law List. Foster.

YOUNGER, George Robert
BA., BCL. G. 25 April 1923. ETC. 18 February 1925. Prop. Jackson KC. Sec. Jordan. Circuit Junior, Summer 1926. 2 Mitre Court, 1924-1929; 3 Stone Buildings, 1930-1939; 17 Old Buildings, 1940-1948. No address, 1949-1963. Not in 1964 Law List.

Z

ZALIN, Jonathan Sydney
LLB (London) G. July 1973. Liverpool Chambers; Queen's Avenue, Castle Street, 1977-1983; 2nd floor, Peel House, Harrington Street, 1984-1987. Left the Bar in 1987 to work for a local solicitor. He died shortly afterwards.

ZEITLYN, Elsley
Born 1878. 3rd son of Bernard de Beer Zeitlyn, Chief Rabbi of Paris. Jesus College, Oxford. AAS. M. 3 December 1902. Call 9 May 1906. ETC. 28 February 1907. Prop. Rufus Isaacs KC. Sec. F E Smith. 4 Elm Court, 1907-1909; 1 Elm Court, 1910-1929; 3 Essex Court, 1930-1936; 2 Crown Office Row, 1937-1941. No address, 1942-1953. Not in 1954 Law List.

*** ZENTAR, Rémy Paul**
Born 10 November 1946 Manchester. Denstone College, Manchester; Manchester University, LLB., LLM., PhD. Senior Lecturer, Manchester Polytechnic (now Manchester Metropolitan University), 1972-1977. G. 24 July 1997. ETC. 16 December 1997. Prop. Lyndsey

Kushner QC. Sec. Yvonne Coppel. 24a St John Street Manchester (now St John's Buildings), September 1997. Publications; Practitioners Guide to Family Law Act 1996, Part IV; Practitioners Guide to Child Law, 1987.; both with monthly updating letters.

ZIGMOND, Joseph (His Honour Judge Zigmond)
MRCS(Eng)., LRCP (London). G. November 1946. Manchester Chambers; 60 King Street, 1947-1960; 47 Peter Street, 1961-1967. Circuit Judge (formerly County Court Judge), 1967-1981. Not in 1982 Bar Directory. Not in WW.

ZOLLNER, Roland
Born 1 May 1954 Liverpool. Liverpool College; Liverpool Polytecnic (now Liverpool John Moores University), BA. AAS. M. 3 February 1975. Call July 1978. Liverpool Chambers; 15 Victoria Street, 1978-1983; 10 James Street, 1984-1985. Crown Prosecutions Service, February 1985. Senior Crown Prosecutor, Bootle & Crosby.

RECENT ELECTIONS TO THE CIRCUIT

ARMSTRONG, Michael Stephen
Born Belfast. Wallace High School, Lisburn; Manchester University LLB. I. 10 October 2002. ETC. 19 December 2002. Prop. Timothy King QC. Sec. Simon Dawes. Liverpool Chambers; Derby Square, Merchants Court September 2002-December 2003; Atlantic Chambers, January 2004.

ASHWORTH, Jenny Francis
Born 10 May 1979 Halifax. The Crossley Heath Grammar School, Halifax; BA (Accounting & Law). L. 10 October 2002. Lord Denning Scholarship 2002. ETC. 17 December 2002. Prop. Keith Goddard QC. Sec. Michael Hayton. Deans Court Chambers, 24 St John Street, Manchester 2002.

ASLETT, Pepin
Born 14 June 1974 Whiston. Akeley Wood School, Bucks; University of Buckinghamshire LLB. L. 26 November 1996. Northampton Chambers 1996-1999. Attorney, Bermuda 1999-2002. ETC. 9 December 2003. Prop. David Berkley QC. Sec. David Uff. Merchant Chambers, Manchester 2003.

ATHERTON, Charlotte Bess
Born 16 April 1980 Scarborough. Pocklington School; Sheffield University LLB. G. 24 July 2003. ETC. 18 December 2003. Prop. William Waldron QC. Sec. William F Waldron. Exchange Chambers, Pearl Assurance House, Derby Square, Liverpool, 15 September 2003.

BARTON, Hugh Barton
Born 9 October 1963. Latymer Upper School; Exeter University BA. M. November 1989. Pupilmasters; Jonathan Ferris (13 Kings Bench Walk 1989-1994) and Penny Barrett (Doughty Street 1994-2002). ETC. 8 July 2003. Prop. Alistair Webster. Sec. Suzanne Goddard. Lincoln House Chambers, Manchester 2002.

BERRY, Karl Derek
Born 6 February 1976, Whalley, Wilpshire. Bolton School (Boys' Division); Kings College, London, BA. M. 25 November 1999. ETC. 15 April 2003. Prop. John Jones QC. Sec. Sara Dodd. Kingsgate Chambers, 9-21 Princess Street, Manchester 2003. Formerly associate advocate in the Isle of Man.

BILSLAND, Alisan
Born 24 September Newcastle-upon-Tyne. King Edward VI Grammar School, Chelmsford; Durham University (Collingwood College) BA. L. 23 November 2000. ETC. 9 December 2003. Prop. Ian Leeming QC. Sec. James Hurd. Pupilmaster Michael Mulholland. St James's Chambers, 68 Quay Street, Manchester October 2001-.

BIRKETT, Alice Emily
Born 6 January 1979 London. Maidstone Girls' Grammar School; University of Newcastle-upon-Tyne BA. L. 10 October 2002. ETC. 19 December 2002. Prop. Timothy King QC. Sec. Tim Holloway. Liverpool Chambers; Derby Square Chambers, Merchants Court September 2002-December 2003; Oriel Chambers, 14 Water Street January 2004.

BLEWITT, Jennifer
Born 16 September 1978 Newcastle. Central Newcastle High School (GPDST); University of Northumbria LLB. M. 26 July 2001. Office of the Treasury Solicitor, London October 2001- February 2002. ETC. 17 December 2002. Prop. Michael Shorrock QC. Sec. Jeremy Grout-Smith. Peel Court Chambers, 45 Hardman Street, Manchester 1 October 2002.

BRANDON, Louise Ann
Born 28 November 1979 Chorley, Lancs. Leyland St Mary's RC., GM. High School; University of Manchester BA (Government & Law). M. 24 July 2003. ETC. 9 December 2003. Prop. Alan Conrad QC. Sec. Jamie Hamilton. 9 St John Street, Manchester September 2003.

BURNS, Judith Linda
Born 21 May 1978 Manchester. Upton Hall Convent School, Wirral; Sheffield University LLB. M. 11 March 2001. 4 Kings Bench Walk, April 2001-April 2002 (pupillage). ETC. July 2002. Prop. Timothy King QC. Sec. Graham Wells. Derby Square Chambers, Merchants Court, April 2002-December 2003; Oriel Chambers, 14 Water Street, January 2004.

CLINE, Robert James
Born 28 August 1979 Manchester. Manchester Grammar School; Jesus College, Cambridge, 1998-2001, BA (Law). G. 10 October 2002. Legal Advisor, Trafford Magistrates Court, August 2002-July 2003. ETC. 18 December 2003. Prop. John Benson QC. Sec. Malcolm Sharpe. Altantic Chambers, Cook Street, Liverpool, September 2003.

CHESTER, Mark James
L. 28 November 2002. ETC. 19 December 2002. Prop. John Benson QC. Sec. Ivan Woolfenden. Atlantic Chambers, Cook Street, Liverpool.

COFFELL, John Edward
Born 8 January 1972 Durham. Durham School; Christ Church, Oxford MA. Post Graduate Certificate in Education (Cambridge). Classics Teacher, Glenalmond

College 1997-2000. M. 26 July 2001. ETC. 17 December 2002. Prop. Peter Birkett QC. Sec. Richard Varden. 18 St John Street, Manchester September 2002.

CONNOLLY, Stephen James
Born 20 June 1967. St Thomas More High School, Preston; Newman College, Preston; University of Buckingham LLB. Partner, Halliwell Landau, solicitors, 1994-2003. L. 27 November 2003. ETC. 9 December 2003. Prop. Mark Cawson QC. Sec. Neil Cadwallader. Exchange Chambers, 7 Ralli Courts, West Riverside, Manchester 2003.

CRAINE, Michael Alexander
Born 26 February 1964. L. 1999. ETC. 8 July 2003. Prop. Keith Goddard QC. Sec. Keith Thomas. Pupilmaster, Patricia Bailey. New Bailey Chambers, Preston.

DAGNALL, Jane Mary
Born 30 July 1964 Bury, Lancs. Wolgarston High School, Penkridge, Staffs; City of Birmingham Polytechnic LLB. I. 1 November 1987. Court Clerk, Oldham Magistrates, 1987-1988; Senior Crown Prosecutor, Greater Manchester, 1998-2003. ETC. 9 December 2003. Prop. Anthony Gee QC. Sec. Philip Cattan. St John's Buildings, 24a-28 St John Street, Manchester, 1 September 2004.

DAWSON, Richard Jon Foster
Born 11 September 1977 Keighley, West Yorks. The Crossley Heath School, Halifax; Sheffield University, BSc (Environmental Geology); Manchester Metropolitan University, Post Graduate Diploma in Law, Diploma in Legal Practice. Praxis Partners, solicitors, Leeds, August 2001-February 2002. M. 11 October 2001. ETC. July 2002. Prop. Roger Farley QC. Sec. Mark Ford. Young Street Chambers, February 2002.

DEL PRIORE, Assunta Maria Louisa
Born 29 August 1966 Glasgow. Bellahouston Academy, Glasgow; Edinburgh University, MA. Curator of Photography & Fine Art, Royal Naval Museum, Portsmouth, 1994-1996. M. 8 September 1998. Verulam Chambers, 1998-1999; Mitre House Chambers 1999-2001. Pupilmasters; Sailesh Mehta and Francis Gilbert. Mace & Jones, solicitors, 2001-2002. ETC. 15 April 2003. Prop. Roger Farley QC. Sec. Hilary Manley. Cobden House Chambers, 19 Quay Street, Manchester 2002.

DICKINSON, Russell
Born 11 October 1976 Solihull. Solihull School; University of Durham (Hatfield College) BA. Corporate Finance Graduate with Hawkpoint Partners. Investment Banking in London, 1998-1999. L. 25 July 2002. ETC. 17 December 2002. Prop. Gerard McDermott QC. Sec. Michael Smith. 8 King Street Chambers, Manchester 2002.

DONALDSON, Sarah Ruth
Born 15 December 1976 Cambridge. Altwood C of E Comprehensive School; St Anne's & Wolfson Colleges, Oxford, BA., MPhil. Administrative Assistant 2001. I. 24 July 2003. ETC. 9 December 2003. Prop. Jonathan Foster QC. Sec. T W Sasse. 18 St John Street, Manchester 29 September 2003.

ELLIS, Sarah Louise
Born 3 July 1975 Slough. Upton Grammar School, Slough; Reading University, BA (Politics & International Relations). L. 22 July 1999. ETC. July 2002. Prop. Timothy King QC. Sec. David Brunnen. Liverpool Chambers; Derby Square Chambers, Merchants Court April 2002-December 2003; Oriel Chambers, 14 Water Street January 2004.

ESCORIZA, Natalia
Born 11 October 1973 Barcelona. McAuley School; Aston University BSc; Edinburgh University, MSc; College of Law, Postgraduate Diploma in Law. M. 28 November 2002. Southernham Chambers, 33 Southernham East, Exeter, October 2002- September 2003. Pupilmaster, Christopher Naish. ETC. 9 December 2003. Prop. Keith Goddard QC. Sec. Beverly Lunt. Kingsgate Chambers, 9-21 Princess Street. Manchester, October 2003.

FARLEY, David Dunbar
Born 17 July 1977, Blackburn. Son of Roger Farley QC qv. Queen Elizabeth's Grammar School, Blackburn; Lancaster University (St Martin's College), BA. Sporting Life 1998-2000. M. 11 October 2001. ETC. 17 December 2002. Prop. by his father. Sec. Ahmed Nadim. Young Street Chambers, 76 Quay Street, 2 September 2002.

FITZPATRICK, Denise
Born 17 December 1977 Stockport. Bramhall High School, Stockport; Mount Carmel School (VI Form), Alderley Edge. Lancaster University, LLB. M. 27 July 2000. Bournemouth Magistrates Court, 2000-2001; Preston Magistrates Court, 2001-2002. ETC. 17 December 2002. Prop. Roger Farley QC. Sec. Richard Heap. Pupilmaster, Mark Smith. Kenworthy's Chambers, 83 Bridge Street, Manchester 2002.

FORD, Andrew James
Born 29 September 1973, Ormskirk. West Park School, St Helens; Sheffield University, BA. M. 9 October 1977; Harmsworth Scholar 1996-1997. Goldsmith's Chambers, Temple, September 1997-December 2001. Pupilmaster, John Burrow. ETC. 19 December 2002. Prop. David Steer QC. Sec. Richard Pratt. 7 Harrington Street, Liverpool, January 2002.

FRIEND, Mark Owen
Born 12 January 1979 Newcastle-upon-Tyne. St Cuthbert's High School, Newcastle; Leeds Metropolitan University, LLB. L. 14 March 2002. ETC. 18 March 2004. Prop. David Steer QC. Sec. Michael Blakey. Young Street Chambers, 76 Quay Street, Manchester 2 February 2004.

GEE, Caroline Louise
Born 26 January 1979 St Mary's Hospital, Manchester. Daughter of His Honour Judge Anthony Gee QC, qv. Cheadle Hulme School; University of Leeds, LLB (Law with European Law). G. 27 July 2003. ETC. 9 December 2003. Prop. by her father. Sec. Paul Taylor. Exchange Chambers, Manchester & Liverpool 1 March 2004.

GEORGE, Mark McHallam
Born 10 July 1952 London. St Benedict's, Ealing, 1959-1970; St John's College, Cambridge, BA (Anglo-Saxon, Norse & Celtic Studies). I. 1 November 1976. Two Garden Court, London, 1997. Pupilmaster, Audrey Sander; Garden Court North Chambers, Manchester, July 2000. ETC. July 2002. Prop. James Pickup QC.

GIANOTA, Caterina
Born 6 June 1962, Bromborough. Bellerive Girls' Grammar School; Aberdeen University, BSc (Physics with Theoretical Physics). L. 10 October 2002. ETC. 10 April 2003. Prop. John Benson QC. Sec. Gerald Baxter. 25-27 Castle Street, Liverpool, October 2002.

GILBART, Thomas Christie
Born 13 August 1980, Manchester. Son of His Honour Judge Gilbart QC qv. Manchester Grammar School; University College, London LLB. M. 27 November 2003. ETC. 9 December 2003. Prop. by his father. Sec. Alaric Bassano. 9 St John Street, Manchester, 22 September 2003.

GLEESON, Michael
Born 17 November 1972. Glamorgan University BA. G. 16 November 1998. ETC. 18 March 2004. Prop. Roger Farley QC. Sec. Michael Knowles. Cobden House Chambers, 19 Quay Street, Manchester 2004.

GRANT, Chudi Paul
Born 13 January 1960. High School of Art, Cheetham; Manchester Metropolitan University (North Trafford College) LLB. L. 28 November 2002. ETC. 8 July 2003. Prop. Anthony Gee QC. Sec. Richard Heap. Pupilmaster, Mark Smith. Kenworthy's Chambers, 83 Bridge Street, Manchester, April 2003.

GRAY, John Kevin
Born 14 January 1978 Whiston. St Edward's College, Liverpool; Liverpool University, LLB; Manchester University, MA. L. 11 October 2001. Legal Executive Officer, H M Customs & Excise 2002-2003. ETC. 18 December 2003. Prop. John McDermott QC. Sec. Yaqub Rahman. Oriel Chambers, 14 Water Street, Liverpool, 2003.

GREGG, Rebecca Mary
Born 22 January 1977 Liverpool. Formby High School; King George V Sixth Form College; Nottingham Trent University LLB. L. 13 March 2003. ETC. 18 March 2004. Prop. Roger Farley QC. Sec. Carolyn Johnson. Pupilmaster Paula Fallows. Cobden House Chambers, 19 Quay Street, Manchester 2003.

HAMMOND, Fayaz Benjamin
G. 14 October 1999. ETC. 9 December 2003. Prop. David Allan QC. Sec. James Hurd. Pupilmaster, Barrie Searle. St James's Chambers, 68 Quay Street, Manchester.

HATFIELD, Sally Anne
Born 3 May 1964 Portsmouth. Portsmouth High School; Lincoln College, Oxford BA. I. 1 November 1988. Doughty Street Chambers, 1990. Pupilmaster, Stephen Irwin. ETC. 9 December 2003. Prop. Howard Bentham QC. Sec. Richard Pearce. Peel Court Chambers, 45 Hardman Street, Manchester, 2003.

HAWKS, James Philip
Born 5 August 1961. Austin Friars School, Carlisle; Keble College, Oxford, MA; University of Toronto, MA; Heythrop College, University of London, MTh. Formerly a solicitor. G 27 November 2003. ETC. 23 March 2004. Prop. David Steer QC. Sec. Neville Biddle. 25-27 Castle Street, Liverpool, 2003.

HERTZOG, Frances Dawn
Born Stockport. Mount Carmel Convent School, Alderley Edge. Liverpool University, LLB. G. 27 November 2001. Leigh, Day & Co., solicitors, 3 December 2001-15 June 2003. ETC. 18 December 2003. Prop. John McDermott QC. Sec. Gerald Baxter. 25-27 Castle Street, Liverpool, 30 June 2003.

HEYWORTH, Victoria Sophie Dorothea
Born 12 October 1978 Manchester. Cheadle Hulme School; Leeds University, 1997-2001, LLB (Law & French). G. 24 July 2003. ETC. 9 December 2003. Prop. Stephen Grime QC. Sec. Richard Whitehall. Pupilmaster, Peter Burns. Deans Court Chambers, Manchester, 6 October 2003.

HILL, Claire Louise
Born 6 June 1980 Sheffield. Humberston Comprehensive; Manchester University, LLB (English Law & French Law). L. 24 July 2003. ETC. 9 December 2003. Prop. Ian Leeming QC. Sec. James Hurd. St James's Chambers, 68 Quay Street, Manchester, 29 September 2003.

HILLAS, Samantha
Born 16 May 1972 Bradford. Bradford Grammar School; Hull University, LLB. I. 10 October 1996. With solicitors; Lees Lloyd Whitley, 1997-2001; Jackson & Canter, 2001; Percy Hughes & Roberts, 2001-2003. ETC. 18 December 2003. Prop. Timothy King QC. Sec. Simon Newton. Liverpool Chambers; Derby Square Chambers, Merchants Court, February- December 2003; Atlantic Chambers, Cook Street, December 2003.

HIRST, Rebecca Elizabeth
Born 19 January 1977 Leeds. Leeds Girls' High School; Lancaster University (Cartmel College), LLB. G. 15 November 1999. Lamb Building. ETC. 17 December 2002. Prop. Roger Farley QC. Sec. Michael Goldwater. Cobden House Chambers, 19 Quay Street, Manchester 2002.

HOLLAND, Samantha Jane
Born 20 October 1971 Beckenham, Kent. Tunbridge Wells Girls' Grammar School; University of Aberdeen, MA (Philosophy); University of Iowa, MA., PhD; Sheffield Hallam University Postgraduate Diploma in Law. University Lecturer; Aberdeen, 1993; Iowa, 1994-1996 & 1999; Sheffield Hallam, 1996-1999 & 2000-2001. M. 25 July 2002. ETC. 19 December 2002. Prop. David Turner QC. Sec. Tanya Griffiths. Pupilmasters, Tanya Griffith & Louis Browne. Exchange Chambers, Liverpool & Manchester, October 2002.

HOWE, Andrew Peter
Born 7 September 1979 Birkenhead. Calday Grange Grammar School, West Kirby; University of Lancaster, LLB. L. 28 November 2002. ETC. 19 December 2002. Prop. Timothy King QC. Sec. Suzanne Evans. Oriel Chambers, 14 Water Street, Liverpool, September 2002. Circuit Junior, 2004.

HUGHES, Kathryn Sally
Born 5 May 1974 Liverpool. Archbishop Blanch School, Liverpool; Sheffield University BA (Law). Goodmans, solicitors, 2000-2003. I. March 2003. ETC. 17 July 2003. Prop. David Turner QC. Sec. Theresa Pepper. Chavasse Court Chambers, 24 Lord Street, Liverpool, 2003.

HUNTER, John Zuccolotto
L. 28 November 2002. ETC. 17 December 2002. Prop. Andrew Gilbart QC. Sec. Paul Tucker. Kings Chambers, 40 King Street, Manchester.

JONES, Gareth Edward
Born 8 December 1978 Dundee, Scotland. Uplands Community College, Wadhurst, East Sussex; Aberystwyth University LLB (Law with Spanish). M. 10 October 2002. ETC. 17 December 2002. Prop. Alistair Webster QC. Sec. Joe Boyd. Lincoln House Chambers, 1 Brazennose Street, Manchester, 2002.

JONES, Katie Laura
Born 11 February 1980 Shrewsbury. Shrewsbury High School; Birmingham University LLB. G. 9 October 2003. ETC. 9 December 2003. Prop. Michael Shorrock QC. Sec. David Pickup. Peel Court Chambers, 45 Hardman Street, Manchester, 2003.

KARIM, Sheikh Mohammed Samiul
Born 9 September 1978 Mansfield, Notts. Nottingham Boys' High School, King's College, London, LLB., LLM., Postgraduate Diploma in Law. G. 28 November 2002. ETC. 19 December 2002. Prop. Timothy King QC. Sec. David Polglase. Pupilmaster, Simon Holder. India Buildings, Water Street, Liverpool, 2002.

KAJUE, Soria Keziah
LLB. M. October 2001. ETC. July 2002. Young Street Chambers, Manchester.

LANCASTER, Roger
Born 4 February 1951 Biddulph. Biddulph Grammar School; Leicester University, LLB. Solicitor with Halliwell, Landau, 1982-2002 (Senior Partner 1995-2000). M. 28 November 2002. ETC. 9 December 2003. Prop. Andrew Gilbart QC. Sec. M Carter. Kings Chambers, 40 King Street, Manchester, December 2002.

LANGLEY, Sarah Elizabeth
Born 30 March 1979 Liverpool. Archbishop Blanch C of E School; University of Wales, Aberystwyth, LLB. L. 22 November 2001. ETC. 18 December 2003. Prop. David Steer QC. Sec. Andrew Loveridge. 7 Harrington Street, Liverpool, 14 July 2003.

LAWRENCE, Benjamin Richard
Born 19 August 1981 Nottingham. Denes High School, Lowestoft, Suffolk. Manchester University LLB. Olliers, solicitors, 2002-2003. L. 13 March 2003. ETC. 9 December 2003. Prop. Anthony Gee QC. Sec. Keith Harrison. St Johns Buildings, 24a-28 St John Street, Manchester, 1 September 2003.

LAWSON-ROGERS, Stuart QC
Born 23 March 1946, Wembley, Middlesex. Son of George Henry Roland Rogers CBE., MP. and Mary Lawson. Buckingham College, Harrow; London School of Economics, LLB. G. July 1969. Lamb Building, 1969-1990. Pupilmaster, John Newey; 23 Essex Street, 1990-2003 (currently door tenant). ETC. 18 December 2003. Prop. David Steer QC. Sec. Richard Pratt. 7 Harrington Street, Liverpool, August 2003. Assistant Recorder 1987. Recorder 1989. Silk 1994. Assistant Commissioner, Parliamentary & Local Government Boundary Commns., 1988-, Legal Assessor, GMC and GDC, 1988. Standing Counsel (Crime, SE Circuit) to HM Customs & Excise 1989-1994. DTI Inspector (Insider Dealing) 1989. Department of Transport Inspector, Merchant Shipping Act 1988, 1989-1990. Director Watford AFC Ltd 1990-1996. WW.

LEE, Sarah-Jane
Born 13 October 1979, Billinge. St Mary's RC High School and Sixth Form College; Staffordshire University, LLB. L. November 2002. Clerk with Ricksons, solicitors, 2002-2003. ETC. 9 December 2003. Prop. Andrew Gilbart QC. Sec. Michael Whyatt. 15 Winckley Square, Preston, 15 September 2003.

LEENE, Sharon Anabel
Born 8 May 1974, Lucknow, India. St Damian's RC High School & Xaverian Sixth Form College, Manchester; Leeds University, LLB (English Law & French Law). G. October 1996. 187 Fleet Street, 1996-2003 (now associate member). Pupilmaster, Stephen Walsh. ETC. 9 December 2003. Prop. Howard Bentham QC. Sec. Andrew Long. Peel Court Chambers, 45 Hardman Street, Manchester, 2003.

McCLOSKEY, Louise
Born 3 December 1979. The Belvedere School GDST, Liverpool; Liverpool John Moores University, LLB. G. 10 October 2002. ETC. 17 July 2003. Prop. David Turner QC. Sec. Ian Harris. Exchange Chambers, Pearl Assurance House, Derby Square, Liverpool, 30 June 2003.

McKINLAY, Kirsty Elizabeth
Born 7 June 1977, Whalley, Lancs. Clitheroe Royal Grammar School; University of Newcastle-upon-Tyne, LLB. L. 8 March 2001. Employed pupilage with Hammonds, solicitors, Leeds, December 2001-December 2003. Pupilmaster Patrick Walker (North Eastern Circuit). ETC. 18 March 2004. Prop. David Steer QC. Sec, David Hernandez. Young Street Chambers, 76 Quay Street, Manchester, January 2004.

MCMURTRIE, Christopher Jonathan
Born 9 March 1980, Nuneaton. Lymm High School; University of Leicester, LLB; University of Keele, LLM. G. 24 July 2003. ETC. 9 December 2003. Prop. Andrew Gilbart QC. Sec. Christine Riley. Pupilmasters, Christine Riley and Gillian Irving. 9 St John Street, Manchester, 22 September 2003.

MAGUIRE, Clodagh Mary
Born Manchester. Stockport Grammar School; Salford University BSc, 2000. I. 27 November 2003. ETC. 9 December 2003. Prop. Keith Goddard QC. Sec. Bansa Singh Hayer. Kingsgate Chambers, 9-21 Princess Street, Manchester 2003.

MAYOH, Michelle
Born 13 February 1978 Chester. Ellesmere Port Catholic High School; Liverpool John Moores University, LLB. L. 29 July 2003. ETC. 18 December 2003. Prop. David Turner QC. Sec. David Casement. Exchange Chambers, Pearl Assurance House, Derby Square, Liverpool, 2003.

MENSAH, Lorraine Sonia Louise
Born 13 November 1973 Liverpool. Halewood Community Comprehensive School; Liverpool University LLB. G. 9 October 1997. With Jackson & Canter, solicitors, Liverpool, October 1997-July 2002. ETC. 19 December 2002. Prp. Graham Wood QC. Sec. David Flood. India Buildings, Water Street, Liverpool 2002.

MENZIES, Jennifer Mary
Born 17 April 1946 Liverpool. Wirral Grammar School; Lymm Grammar School; Liverpool John Moores University, LLB. Between 1964 and 2002 various employments as medico-legal secretary, purser/chief steward and accounts clerk. M. 10 October 2002. Prop. Timothy King QC. Sec. Stephen Bedford. Pupilmaster, Michael Kennedy. India Buildings, Water Street, Liverpool, 2002.

MIDDLETON, Christopher Michael
Born 8 May 1979 Belfast. Methodist College, Belfast; Nottingham University LLB. I. 10 October 2002. ETC. 19 December 2002. Prop. Timothy King QC. Sec. John Gruffyd. Oriel Chambers, 14 Water Street, Liverpool 2002.

MULDERIGG, Joseph Paul
L. 28 November 2002. ETC. 9 December 2003. Prop. Ian Leeming QC., Sec. James Hurd. Pupilmaster, Michael Mulholland. St James's Chambers, 68 Quay Street, Manchester.

NUTTER, Julian
Born 7 July 1957 Liverpool. Sir John Deane's Grammar School, Northwich, Liverpool University LLB. G. November 1979. 4 Kings Bench Walk, 1982-1984 (pupilmaster, Nicholas Freeman); 5 Paper Buildings, 1984-1990; 1 Crown Office Row, 1990-1992; 1 Dr Johnson's Buildings 1992-1993; 3 Athol Street, Douglas, Isle of Man, 1994-2002; 7 Harrington Street, Liverpool 2002. ETC. 18 December 2003. Prop. David Steer QC. Sec. Richard Pratt.

O'CALLAGHAN, Mark
Born 1 February 1978 Liverpool. The Blue Coat School, Liverpool; Oriel College, Oxford, MA. I. 11 October 2001. ETC. 15 April 2003. Prop. Gerard McDermott QC. Sec. Simon Vaughan. 8 King Street Chambers, Manchester 2003.

PARRY, Philip Christopher
Born 23 June 1973, Salford. Sheffield University LLB. L. 12 October 1995. With Russell & Russell, solicitors, Bolton 1996-2000 and DLA, solicitors, 2000-2003, ETC. 15 April 2003. Prop. Richard Marks QC. Sec. Jeffrey Samuels. St John's Buildings, 24a-28 St John Street, Manchester 2003.

PILLING, David Jonathan
M. 18 October 1999. ETC. 17 December 2002. Prop. Michael Redfern QC. Sec. Christopher Limb. Young Street Chambers, 76 Quay Street, Manchester.

POJUR, David Elliot
Born 1 May 1979 Manchester. King David School, Manchester; Manchester University, LLB. M. 21 November 2001. ETC. 15 April 2003. Prop. Roger Farley QC. Sec. Beverly Lunt. Pupilmaster, John Cartwright. Kingsgate Chambers, 9-21 Princess Street, Manchester, 2002.

POOLE, Alexander David
Born 3 June 1977 Manchester. Son of The Hon. Mr Justice Poole qv. Manchester Grammar School; Edinburgh University MA. I. 10 October 2002. Prop. Keith Goddard QC. Sec. Nicholas Grimshaw. Deans Court Chambers, Manchester 2002.

PRITCHARD, Cecilia Mary
Born Billinge, Wigan. Daughter of Rodney Pritchard qv. and Dorothy Pritchard, solicitor. Repton Preparatory School, Derbyshire, 1985-1988; Queen Margaret's School, Yorkshire, 1988-1993; Oxford Brookes University LLB. M. 23 July 1998. ETC. 15 April 2003. Prop. Roger Farley QC. Sec. Jeremy Dable. New Bailey Chambers, Preston & Liverpool.

PROBERT, Sarah Kate Elizabeth
Born 10 July 1977. Greenhead College, Huddersfield; Keele University, LLB. M. November 2000. ETC. 9 December 2003. Prop. Jonathan Foster QC. Sec. Paul Hart. 15 Winckley Square, Preston March 2003.

QUIGLEY, Louise Kirsten
Born 18 August 1980 Edinburgh. St David's High School; Manchester University BA (Law & Government). I. 27 November 2003. ETC. 9 December 2003. Prop. David Berkley QC. Sec. David Uff. Merchants Chambers, North Parade, Parsonage Gardens, Manchester October 2003.

REID, Martin Joseph
Born 11 October 1980 Liverpool. St Francis Xavier's College, Liverpool; Brasenose College, Oxford, BA (Law). I. 27 November 2003. ETC. 18 December 2003. Prop. David Steer QC. Sec. Richard Pratt. 7 Harrington Street, Liverpool, 15 September 2003.

RIGBY, Timothy James
Born 7 October 1979. Son of Terence Rigby qv. and Christine Riley qv. St Edwards School, Oxford; University of Kent, LLB. G. 27 November 2003. ETC. 18 March 2004. Prop. Gerard McDermott QC. Sec. Timothy Hodgson. 8 King Street Chambers, Manchester, 2003.

ROWAN, Gregg Nicholas
Born 16 September 1977 Rochdale. Our Lady's RC High School, Lancaster; Kings College, London, LLB; Keble College, Oxford, BCL., MPhil; Pantheon-Sorbonne, LLM. L. 9 October 2003. ETC. 9 December 2003. Prop. Andrew Gilbart QC. Sec. Andrew Grantham. Pupilmaster, Mark Harper. Kings Chambers, 40 King Street, Manchester, October 2003.

RYAN, Patrick Terence
Born 29 March 1981 Birkenhead. Son of Thomas Patrick Francis Ryan qv. Douai School; Manchester University, BA. I. 9 October 2003. ETC. 9 December 2003. Prop. Anthony Gee QC. Sec. Richard Heap. Kenworthy's Chambers, 83 Bridge Street, Manchester, 1 September 2003.

SAMUEL, Adam Gareth
I. 24 July 2003. ETC. 9 December 2003. Prop. Anthony Gee QC. Sec. James Rowley. St Johns Buildings, 24a-28 St John Street, Manchester.

SANTAMERA, Louise Alexandria
Born 4 January 1963 Liverpool. Sacred Heart RC School for Girls; Liverpool University, BA (Latin American Studies); Manchester Metropolitan University, Postgraduate Diploma in Law. Jackson & Canter, Solicitors, Liverpool 2000-2001. G. 10 October 2002. ETC. 10 April 2003. Prop. Margaret de Haas QC. Sec. Ashley Barnes. Pupilmaster, Nigel Beeson. 14 Cook Street, Liverpool, August 2002. New Bailey Chambers, Liverpool, 2004.

SAVAGE, Jonathan Howard
Born Salford. The Heys, Prestwich; Manchester Metropolitan University, LLB. Crown Prosecutions Service, 2 April 1991-19 September 2003. G. 9 October 2003. ETC. 9 December 2003. Prop. Alan Conrad QC. Sec. Michael Murray. 9 St John Street, Manchester, 22 September 2003.

SAYERS, Lynne
Born 17 May 1964. Wallasey. Weatherhead High School; Liverpool John Moores University, LLB. L. 10 October 2002. ETC. 17 December 2002. Prop. Keith Goddard QC. Sec. Leonard Webster. Pupilmaster, Steven Wild. Central Chambers, 89 Princess Street, Manchester, 2002.

SEARLE, Jason Ario Xavier
Born 22 May 1968 Withington. Parrswood High School; University of East London, LLB. Trooper, 21 SAS (Artist's Rifles) VR Regiment (Reserve), 1988-1991. M. 14 October 1993. North Manchester Law Centre, 1993-1994. Weightman Vizards, solicitors, 41 Spring Gardens, Manchester, 2001-2003. ETC. 9 December 2003. Prop. David Berkley QC. Sec. Stefan Brochwiez-Lewinski. Merchants Chambers, North Parade, Parsonage Gardens, Manchester, 2003.

SHARPE, Martin Laurence
Born 28 April 1962. Wheatley Park School, Oxon; Manchester University, LLB; Liverpool University MA. M. November 1989. 1 Pump Court, 1989-1998. Pupilmaster, Paul Higham; Tudor Street, London, 1998-2000; Garden Court North Chambers, Manchester, 2000. ETC. 8 July 2003. Prop. Keith Goddard QC. Sec. Mark George.

SHIELDS, Joshua Adam
Born 5 March 1975. Royal Grammar School, Newcastle-upon-Tyne; Trinity Hall, Cambridge, BA. M. March 2000. ETC. 8 July 2003. Prop. Edward Bartley Jones QC. Sec. Christopher Cooke. Exchange Chambers, Manchester & Liverpool.

SIGEE, Peter Howard
Born 2 February 1972 Manchester. Manchester Grammar School; Birmingham University, LLB; Manchester Metropolitan University, MA. Solicitor, 1997-2002. M. 28 December 2002. ETC. 14 March 2003. Prop. John Benson QC. Sec. Ivan Woolfenden. Exempted from pupilage. Atlantic Chambers, Cook Street, Liverpool, 1 January 2003.

SIMKIN, Ian James
Born 22 November 1969, Stoke-on-Trent. Newcastle High School (Boys); Manchester Polytechnic BA (Economics), Diploma in Law. I. 1 February 1995. 7 Stone Buildings September 1995-April 1996. Pupilmaster John Cooper. ETC. July 2002. Prop. Roger Farley QC. Sec. David Hernandez. Young Street Chambers, Manchester.

SKEATE, Ian Robert
L. November 2002. ETC. 9 December 2003. Prop. Anthony Gee QC. Sec. Graham Platts. St Johns Buildings, Manchester.

SMITH, Michael David
Born 13 April 1979 Withington, Manchester. Altrincham Grammar School; Sheffield University, LLB. Tuckers, solicitors, August 2001-February 2002. L. 11 October 2001. ETC. July 2002. Prop. Roger Farley QC. Sec. Marc Willems. Cobden House Chambers, 19 Quay Street, Manchester 2002.

SORABJI, John Robert
Born 19 June 1972 Stockport. Stockport School; Bramhall High School; The Queen's College, Oxford, 1991-1994, MA; Manchester University, 1995-1996. MPhil; University College, London, 2001-2002, LLM. I. 11 October 2001. ETC. 17 December 2002. Prop. Gerard McDermott QC. Sec. Stephen Davies. 8 King Street Chambers, Manchester, 2003. Judicial Assistant to Lord Justice Dyson, January 2004-July 2004.

STEWARD, Claire Marion
Born 11 November 1978 Manchester. Sale Grammar School; Manchester University BA (Modern History & Economics). L. 28 November 2002. ETC. 17 December 2002. Prop. Nicholas Braslavsky QC. Sec. Lucy Powis. Pupilmasters, Lucy Powis & Sarah Pritchard. Kings Chambers, 40 King Street, Manchester & 5 Park Square East, Leeds, 1 October 2002.

STEWARD, Mark David
Born 17 December 1968 Manchester. Parrswood School, Didsbury; Bournemouth University, BA (Law). Solicitor with Maxwell Entwistle & Byrne, 1996-2002. I. 28 November 2002. ETC. 19 December 2002. Prop. David Turner QC. Sec. Theresa Pepper. Chavasse Court, Lord Street, Liverpool, October 2002.

STRINGER, Rosemary Charlotte
Born 17 May 1974 Benfleet, Essex. The Coopers' Company & Coburn School, Upminster; Lancaster University BA., MA; City University, Postgraduate Diploma in Law. Trade Journalist 1998-2000. M. 25 July 2002. ETC. 17 December 2002. Prop. Michael Redfern QC. Sec. Philip Grundy. St Johns Buildings, 24a-28 St John Street, Manchester, 4 September 2002.

SWAIN, Jaqueline Susan
Born 17 August 1976. Wigan. Standish High School; Winstanley College; Leicester University, LLB. L. 8 October 1998. 2 New Street, Chambers, Leicester, 1998-1999. Pupilmaster, Paul Spencer. Court Clerk, Trafford Magistrates Court, 1999-2002. Neil Miller & Co, solicitors, 2002-2003. ETC. 18 December 2003. Prop. David Steer QC. Sec. Richard Pratt. Pupilmaster, Peter Gregory. 7 Harrington Street, Liverpool October 2003.

TAFT, Christopher Heiton
Born 27 September 1974. Manchester University, LLB. M. October 1997. ETC. 9 December 2003. Prop. Ian Leeming QC. Sec. James Hurd. Pupilmaster, Barrie Searle. St James's Chambers, 68 Quay Street, Manchester.

TAYLOR, Alexander
Born 16 June 1979 Blackpool. King Edward VII School, Lytham; Bristol University & Universite de Potiers, Euro LLB. L. 27 November 2003. ETC. 9 December 2003. Prop. Stephen Grime QC. Sec. Timothy Edge. Deans Court Chambers, 24 St John Street, Manchester, 10 September 2003.

TAYLOR, Christian
Born 22 March 1977. Bramhall High School; St Edmunds, Cambridge, BA., Postgraduate Diploma in Law. L. 24 July 2003. ETC. 18 December 2003. Prop. David Turner QC. Sec. Simon Earlham. Exchange Chambers, Derby Square, Liverpool, October 2003.

THOMAS, Dawn Marie
Born 12 November 1967. LLB., LLM. L. 11 October 2001. ETC. 8 July 2003. Prop. Anthony Gee QC. Sec. Richard Heap. Kenworthy's Chambers, 83 Bridge Street, Manchester 1 May 2002.

TRAYNOR, David Andrew
St Mary's College, Crosby; The Queen's College, Oxford, BA (Jurisprudence). L. 10 October 2002. ETC. 17 December 2002. Prop. David Steer QC. Sec. Katherine Johnson. 15 Winckley Square, Preston, 15 September 2002.

TYLER, William John
Born 30 November 1978 Manchester. Manchester Grammar; Birmingham University, BA (Geography), CPE, BVC. Charles Schwab, Europe, 2000-2001. I. 9 October 2003. ETC. 9 December 2003. Prop. Keith Goddard QC. Sec. Mark Savill. Puilmasters, Mark Saville & Glenn Campbell. Deans Court Chambers, 24 St John Street, Manchester, September 2003.

VICARY, Joanna Claire
Born 19 December 1980 Exeter. The Mount School, York; Merton College, Oxford, BA (Jurisprudence). M. 24 July 2003. ETC. 9 December 2003. Prop. Ian Leeming QC. Sec. David Gilchrist. 9 St John Street, Manchester 21 September 2003.

WARNE, Peter Lawrence
I. 1 November 1993. Lincon House Chambers, Manchester.

WHATLEY, Paul Donald
L. 11 October 2002. ETC. 17 December 2002. Prop. Roger Farley QC. Sec. Richard Oughton. Codben House Chambers, 19 Quay Street, Manchester,

WILLIAMS, Graham Ellis
Born 4 July 1968, Ormskirk. Brother of Rob Williams (partner Weightman Vizards), married to Judith Williams (Legal Dept. West Lancs. District Council). Ormskirk Grammar School; Essex University LLB. Solicitor, September 1992. Whittle Robinson, 1990-1993; Hill Dickinson, 1993-2002 (partner, 1997-2002). M. 25 July 2002. ETC. 19 December 2002. Prop. Timothy King QC. Sec. Simon Newton. Pupilmasters, James Byrne & Simon Newton. Derby Square Chambers, Merchants Court, Liverpool 12 September 2002-31 December 2003; Oriel Chambers, 14 Water Street, Liverpool, 1 January 2004.

WILLIAMS, Zillah Elizabeth
Born 18 November 1972, Liverpool. Merchant Taylors' Girls' School, Crosby; Liverpool University LLB (English Law & German Law). L. 9 October 1997. Mitre Court Chambers, Temple, October 1997-May 2001. Pupilmaster, Bartholomew V. O'Toole; 5 Kings Bench Walk, May 2001-October 2002. ETC. 19 December 2002. Prop. Timothy King QC. Sec. Ray Herman. India Buildings, Water Street, Liverpool, October 2002.

WRIGHT, Paul Andrew
Born 9 January 1978 Liverpool. The John Hanson School, Andover, Hanys; Manchester Metropolitan University BA (Criminology). I. 9 October 2003. ETC. 18 December 2003. Prop. John McDermott QC. Sec. Michael Bagley. Pupilmaster, Heather Lloyd. Chavasse Court Chambers, 24 Lord Street, Liverpool 2003.

STOP PRESS

Elections to Circuit in July 2004

LIVERPOOL
15 July 2004.

★ NICOLA JANE DAVIES
M. 27 July 1978. Prop. David Steer QC. Sec. Brian Cummings.

LEAH ANNE DILLON
L. 26 July 2003. Prop. David Steer QC. Sec. Trevor Parry Jones. 7 Harrington Street, Liverpool.

JUSTIN MCVITIE
I. 23 November 1995. Prop John McDermott QC. Sec. Tom Watson. Chavasse Court, Lord Street, Liverpool.

MANCHESTER
27 July 2004.

SARAH JANE BOOTH
G. 25 November 1999. Prop. Howard Bentham QC. Sec. Roger Green. Queen's Chambers, 5 John Dalton Street, Manchester.

RICHARD HENRY ENGLISH
L. 24 July 2002. Prop. Alistair Webster QC. Sec. Bernadette Baxter. Lincoln House Chambers, Manchester.

GIVEN LADI HENSHAW
M. 18 November 2000. Prop. David Steer QC. Sec. Jaime Hamilton. Pupilmaster Tonia Grace. Central Chambers, Manchester.

CHRISTOPHER MARSHALL JACKSON
M. November 2002. Prop. Keith Goddard QC. Sec. Christopher Limb. Young Street Chambers, Manchester.

PATRICK CHARLES SLEVIN
M. 9 October 2003. Prop. Keith Goddard QC. Sec. Beverly Lunt. Kingsgate Chambers, Manchester.

★ **Nicola Davies** is with Merseyside Crown Prosecutions Service. She is the first 'employed' barrister to be elected to the Circuit.

Manchester. 7 December 2004
Robert Akers
Sophie Allan
Rehana Begum
Laura Bell
Anna Louise Bentley
Kate Louise Bramall
Martin Budworth
Jonathan Butters
Simon William Edward Charles
Timothy Richard Connolly
Philip John De Berry
Ian Denham
Nicholas Mark Flanagan
Francesca Maria Assunta Gardner
Abigail Rachel Hudson
Natasha Jane Leach
Sarah Michelle Lewis
Susan Ann Lewis
Meghann Rose McTague
Peter Marcus
Benjamin Francis Joseph Morris
Paul Murphy
Daniel Northall
Anna Louise Patterson
Sally Julliet Penni
Bradley Russell Pomfret
William James Poole
Segey Prokofiev
Craig Ralph
Sarah Katrina Reid
Aksha Shahid
Sarah Elizabeth Alexandra Sutherland
Phillippa Waddell
Adam Watkins

Liverpool. 16 December 2004
Rebecca Ackerley
Catherine Elizabeth Bartlett
Oliver James Alexander Cook
Donald Fraser
Peta Margaret Harrison
Stephen McNally
Catherine Louise Rimmer
Kirsty Elisabeth Robinson
David Tinkler
Kathleen Sarah Upton
Alexander David Watson

When I was called in 1968, there were 252 names on the Northern Circuit Bar List. There are now over 1000. In 1968 only 19 were women (7.5%). Of the 161 elected between July 2002 and December 2004, there were 72 women (44.7%).

(TM)

Queen Elisabeth II Law Courts, Liverpool, 16 December 2004, 'Farewells'.

Christopher & Peter Lynch in Chambers.

Sources and Suggested Further Reading

The Law List from 1876.

Waterlow's Directory of Solicitors and Barristers.

Bar Directory.

Hazell's Guide and Holborn Law Society Bar List.

Haver's Companion to the Bar.

Who's Who from 1897.

Dictionary of National Biography.

Men at the Bar, Joseph Foster, 1885.

Dictionary of Legal Biography, 1845-1945. A B Schofield, Barry Rose, 1998.

Biographical Dictionary of the Common Law. A W B Simpson, Butterworths, 1984.

Sources of Biographical Information on Past Lawyers. Guy Holborn, British and Irish Association of Librarians, 1999.

Middle Temple Admission Registers, Butterworths.

Middle Temple Bench Books, Middle Temple.

Lincoln's Inn Black Books, Vols 5 and 6.

Judges of England, 1066-1870, Edward Foss, John Murray, 1870.

The Judges of England 1272-1990 and Law Officers and Kings Counsel, both by Sir John Sainty and published by the Selden Society.

The Victorian Chancellors, Vol 2, J B Atlay, Little, Brown & Co, 1908.

The Independence of the Judiciary, Robert Stephens, Oxford University Press, 1993.

The Lives of the Lord Chancellors, R F V Heuston, Vol 1, 1885-1940. Vol 2, 1940-1970, Oxford University Press, 1964 and 1987.

Yes, Lord Chancellor, A Biography of Lord Schuster, Jean Graham Hall and Douglas F Martin, Barry Rose, 2003.

A Perfect Judge, A Biography of Lord Sterndale, Jean Graham Hall and Douglas F Martin, Barry Rose, 1999.

Life Sentence, The Memoirs of Hartley Shawcross, Constable & Co, 1995.

Selwyn Lloyd, D R Thorpe, Jonathan Cape, 1989.

Mr Speaker, Sir, Selwyn Lloyd, Jonathan Cape, 1976.

Political Adventure: The Memoirs of the Earl of Kilmuir, Weidenfeld & Nicolson, 1964.

The Chief: Biography of Gordon Hewart, Robert Jackson, Harrap, 1959.

Farewell to the Assizes: The Sixty One Towns, Sir Basil Nield, Garnstone Press, 1972.

Rufus Isaacs: First Marquess of Reading, by his son, Vol 1, 1860-1914. Vol 2, 1914-1935, Hutchinson, 1942 and 1945.

Lord Reading, C J C Street, Frederick Stokes & Co, New York, 1928.

Lord Reading, H Montgomery Hyde, Heineman, 1967.

Lord Reading and his Cases, Derek Walker-Smith, Chapman and Hall, 1934.

Lord Reading, Denis Judd, Weidenfeld & Nicolson, 1982.

Frederick Edwin, Earl of Birkenhead by his son, two volumes, Thornton Butterworth, 1933 and 1935. In 1965, the Second Earl wrote an updated, one-volume edition which was published by Eyre and Spottiswoode.

F E Smith: First Earl of Birkenhead, John Campbell, Jonathan Cape, 1983.

Famous Trials of History, Lord Birkenhead, Hutchinson & Co, 1926.

His Honour Sir Edward Parry: My Own Way: An Autobiography, Cassell & Co, 1932;

What the Judge Thought, T, Fisher Unwin Ltd, 1922;

What the Judge Saw, Smith, Elder & Co, 1912.

Brief Life, Harold Jager, Henry Young & Sons Ltd, Liverpool, 1934.

Judah P. Benjamin, The Jewish Confederate, Eli N Evans, Free Press, New York, 1988.

Judah P. Benjamin, Confederate Statesman, Robert Douthat Meade, Oxford University Press, New York, 1943.

According to the Evidence, Gerald Abrahams, Cassell, 1958.

Jack Smith-Hughes, all published by Cassells:

Unfair Comment.

Six Ventures in Villainy.

Eight Studies in Justice.

Nine Verdicts on Violence.

The Life of Lord Russell of Killowen, R Barry O'Brien, Smith, Elder & Co, 1901.

John Gorell Bames: First Lord Gorell by J E G de Montmorency, John Murray, 1920.

The Life of Mr Justice Swift, E S Fay, Methuen, 1939.

No Ordinary Man: A Life of George Carman, Dominic Carman, Hodder & Stoughton, 2002.

Edgar Lustgarten:

The Judges and the Judged, Odhams Press, 1961.

The Murder and the Trial, Odhams Press, 1960.

Dick Hamilton:

Foul Bills & Dagger Money, Cassells, 1979.

All Jangle and Riot, Professional Books, 1986.

This Old Wig, J B Sandbach KC, Hutchinsons.

From The Loom to the Lawyer's Gown: Life of Mark Knowles, Barrister, S W Partridge & Co, 1885.

The Cameo Murders, Barry Shorthall, The Bluecoat Press, 1999.

The Stabbing of George Harry Storrs, Jonathan Goodman, Allison & Busby, 1983.

Autobiography of D N Pritt, three volumes, Lawrence & Wishart, 1965-1966.

Top Brass and No Brass, Sir Ralph Kilner Brown, Book Guild, 1991.

Closed Chapters, Sir Gerald Hurst KC, Manchester University Press, 1942.

Judge Gerald Sparrow: Lawyer at Large and many books on criminal topics mainly published by John Long in the 1960s and 1970s.

Tales from a Palm Court, Ronnie Knox-Mawer, Souvenir Press, 1986.

As Far As I Remember, Michael Kerr, Hart Publishing, 2002.

The Last Two To Hang (Allen and Evans), Elwyn Jones, Stein & Day, New York, 1965.

A Century of Liverpool Lawyers, Fagan, Bryson and Elston, The Bluecoat Press, Liverpool, for Liverpool Law Society, 2002.

The Trial of Walter Rowland, Henry Cecil, David & Charles, 1975.

The Wallace Case, John Rowland, Carroll & Nicholson, 1949.

The Killing of Julia Wallace, Jonathan Goodman, Charles Scribner's Sons, New York, 1969, foreword by Edgar Lustgarten.

Notable British Trials published by William Hodge & Co Ltd:

The Veronica Trial, G W Keeton and John Cameron, 1952.

Buck Ruxton, R H Blundell and G Haswell Wilson, 1937.

Florence Maybrick, H B Irving, 1912.

The Trials of Brian Donald Hulme, Ivan Butler, David & Charles, 1976.

'Goldiana': A selection from the figures of speech of Sir Noel Goldie KC, MP.